A Handbook to Literature

fifth edition

C. Hugh Holman
Late of the University of North Carolina, Chapel Hill

William Harmon
University of North Carolina, Chapel Hill

Based on the Original Edition
by William Flint Thrall and Addison Hibbard

Macmillan Publishing Company
New York

Collier Macmillan Publishers
London

Macmillan Publishing Company
866 Third Avenue, New York, N.Y. 10022
Collier Macmillan Canada, Inc.

Library of Congress Cataloging-in-Publication Data
Holman, C. Hugh (Clarence Hugh).
A handbook to literature.
"Based on the original edition by William Flint Thrall
and Addison Hibbard."
Includes index.
1. Literature—Dictionaries. 2. English literature—
Outlines, syllabi, etc. 3. American literature—Outlines,
syllabi, etc. I. Harmon, William.
II. Thrall, William Flint. Handbook to
literature. III. Title.
PN41.H6   1986   803   85-24133
ISBN 0-02-553430-0

Macmillan books are available at special discounts for bulk purchases
for sales promotions, premiums, fund-raising, or educational use.
For details, contact:

Special Sales Director
Macmillan Publishing Company
866 Third Avenue
New York, N.Y. 10022

10   9   8

Printed in the United States of America

Preface
to the Fifth Edition

Fifteen hundred chances to put in my two cents' worth have amounted to a good deal more than thirty dollars' worth of enjoyment. In preparing the newest edition of this *Handbook*, I have experienced two pleasures to which many are tempted but few are treated: amending a classic and improving a friend.

It has been my privilege, first, to tamper with the *Handbook* in the hope of making it handier. The first edition came out in 1936, and both William Flint Thrall and Addison Hibbard died during the 1940s, long before I could have a chance to meet them. They share the distinction of having inaugurated a *Handbook* that for fifty years has served many thousands of readers as an aid in the understanding and enjoyment of reading and as a stimulus to further reading; and the Thrall-Hibbard *Handbook* has achieved for many the stature and familiarity of a classic in its own right.

It has been my privilege, second, to try to make improvements in a friend. We seldom do such a thing with our friends, because we like them as they are, as we like ourselves, warts and all. But a reference work, which is obliged to remain a satellite orbiting an ever-changing body of material, can become a friend that is nothing but warts or—to shift the figure from the Cromwellian to the Johnsonian mode—a horse that is nothing but pasterns; and we have to supplement and revise.

Another pleasure, in fact, has come in the very witnessing of change in a world of new thresholds and new anatomies. O how the mighty have fallen, yes, but O how—at the same time—the humble have risen. Meek irony began, back in 1936, as a lowly figure, then inherited the earth and became *the* trope for a while, and now, as far as I can tell, survives chiefly in the cramped lexicon of sports announcers. Even meeker onomatopoeia—a figure so low that it may not belong to speech at all, being just raw noise—is now enjoying a vogue and may reap its reward in heaven. The world has turned upside down several times since 1936—which was before *Finnegans Wake, Four Quartets, Paterson, The Pisan Cantos, A Streetcar Named Desire, The Well Wrought Urn, Anatomy of Criticism, Gravity's Rainbow,* and much else—and a handbook has to keep up. (A fourth pleasure: As I think of what I have done, revising a book that was first written by people I never knew and was published fifty years ago, before I was born, I think of another revision to be undertaken fifty years hence, after I am gone, by somebody not yet born whom I shall never know. To her or him or them, I say, "Look into your heart and rewrite! That's what I did, and that's what I'm sure Thrall, Hibbard, and Holman did before me.")

C. Hugh Holman, who was my close friend for many years, prepared revised editions that appeared in 1960, 1972, and 1980. Adding a lot and subtracting a little, I have left hardly a paragraph unchanged, but I think I have kept faith with Hugh's style.

He and Thrall were here at Chapel Hill for all of their teaching careers, and Hibbard spent many good years here before moving to Northwestern. Although I was not around to witness the publication of the first edition, I did get to Chapel Hill in time, fifteen years ago, to know three of the scholars—

Richmond Bond, Dougald MacMillan, and Robert Sharpe—whose help Thrall and Hibbard had acknowledged in 1936 and who were still on hand to give me help in the 1970s. Chapel Hill is like that, and this *Handbook* is, among other things, testimony to a spirit of cooperation that has animated this English Department for many decades.

I want to do some acknowledging of my own, although I can never hope to mention all who have helped so generously. Professors Seymour Chatman (Berkeley), Susan Wolfson (Rutgers), Robert Collier (Northern Kentucky), Charles Berger (Yale), and M. J. M. Ezell (Texas A&M) furnished criticism, information, and encouragement. Diana Francoeur has been an ideal editor. My children, Sally and Will, have helped with the index considerably more than filial obligation requires, and I daresay that my son knows more about Allardyce Nicoll than any other eleven-year-old on earth. This, finally, is the place to say that the errors are mine. All right: the errors are mine—and Thrall's, Hibbard's, and Holman's. I like to think of the four of us as a small phalanx of readers and teachers who have done our collective best in a continuing effort to be stimulating and helpful, so much so that we are willing to risk some small errors in the service of a large benefit to other readers.

WILLIAM HARMON

To the User
of This Handbook

The *Handbook* proper is an alphabetical listing of words and phrases pertaining to the study of English and American literature. The listings concentrate on definition, explanation, and illustration, with no attempt to be exhaustive or complete. As with the first edition, the fifth edition provides selected references for the more important, difficult, or controversial entries.

There are cross references at the proper places in the listing. The essential information on a given term appears in its alphabetical place. In the body of an article, a term used in a sense that is defined elsewhere in the *Handbook* is printed in SMALL CAPITALS. The term being defined and sometimes its synonyms and derivatives are printed in *italics*. If other articles in the *Handbook* seem helpful, the statement "See AN APPROPRIATE ARTICLE" is made at the end of the entry. For example, the entry on **Complication** includes the terms PLOT, RESOLUTION, DRAMATIC STRUCTURE, RISING ACTION, ACT, and TRAGEDY, all of which are defined in the *Handbook;* each therefore appears in SMALL CAPITALS that indicate that entries thereon may be consulted if one of them is not clear. Furthermore, the entry concludes with the statement "See DRAMATIC STRUCTURE, ACT," which means that these entries may help with the understanding of *complication*. The word *complication* itself is italicized since it is the term being defined.

This edition includes a new feature, the Index of Proper Names, which attempts to list names of all actual persons mentioned in the body of the *Handbook* proper. The Index gives the title (or short title) of the articles in which the person is mentioned.

Contents

A

Abbey Theatre: Associated with the drama of The IRISH LITERARY REVIVIAL, the *Abbey Theatre* was an outgrowth of an earlier group, the Irish Literary Theatre, founded by W. B. Yeats and Lady Gregory in 1899, which became the Irish National Theatre Society in 1902. In 1904 the company moved to the *Abbey Theatre* in Dublin. It endured, producing PLAYS with a markedly national emphasis, until the theater burned in 1951. W. B. Yeats was director of the *Abbey Theatre* until his death in 1939. Among the major playwrights of the company were Yeats, Lady Gregory, J. M. Synge, Sean O'Casey, James Stephens, and Lord Dunsany. See CELTIC RENAISSANCE.

Abecedarius: An ACROSTIC, the initial letters of whose successive lines (STROPHES or STANZAS) form the alphabet. Strictly speaking, each word in a line should begin with the same letter, although this difficult task is seldom attempted. See ACROSTIC.

Abridgment: A shortened version of a work, but one that attempts to preserve essential elements ^ee ABSTRACT, EPITOME, SYNOPSIS, PRÉCIS.

Absolute: A term applied to anything totally independent of influences, limitations, controls, or modifiers. In grammar, it refers to a word, such as "unique," which cannot be compared or qualified, or to a phrase that is free of the customary syntactical relationships to other parts of the sentence. In CRITICISM, it implies inviolable standards by which a work of art should be measured. An absolutist CRITIC holds that there are fundamental and immutable values that determine moral and aesthetic worth.

Abstract: A severe ABRIDGMENT that summarizes the principal ideas or arguments advanced in a much longer work. *Abstracts* of scholarly articles and dissertations are widely produced today. In reference to language, the term *abstract* is opposed to CONCRETE; it indicates words or statements that separate attributes from their physical or material embodiments. When art is being referred to, the term means nonrepresentational or nonobjective. See ABSTRACT POETRY.

Abstract Poetry: A term used by Dame Edith Sitwell to describe POETRY analogous in its use of sounds to abstract painting in its use of colors and shapes. In abstract painting, the meaning results from the arrangement of colors and shapes without the representation of objects; in *abstract poetry*, words are chosen not for their customary meanings but for the effect produced by tonal qualities, RHYMES, and RHYTHMS, thus frequently sacrificing sense to aural effects. See ABSTRACT.

Absurd: A term applied in contemporary literature and criticism to the sense that human beings are cut off from their original religious and metaphysical roots and live in meaningless isolation in an alien universe. Although the literature of the *absurd* employs many of the devices of EXPRESSIONISM and

1

SURREALISM, its philosophical base is a form of EXISTENTIALISM that views human beings as moving from the nothingness from which they came to the nothingness in which they will end through an existence marked by anguish and absurdity. They live in a world where there is no way to establish a significant relationship between themselves and their environment. Albert Camus' *The Myth of Sisyphus* is one of the central expressions of this philosophy. Extreme forms of illogic, inconsistency, and nightmarish FANTASY mark the literature expressing this concept. The idea of the *absurd* has been powerfully expressed in DRAMA (see ABSURD, THEATER OF THE) and in the NOVEL, where Joseph Heller, Thomas Pynchon, Günter Grass, and Kurt Vonnegut, Jr. have practiced it with distinction. See ABSURD, THEATER OF THE, ANTI-HERO, ANTI-NOVEL.

[References: Arnold P. Hinchliffe, *The Absurd*, 1969; Wolodymyr T. Zyla, ed., *From Surrealism to the Absurd* (1970).]

Absurd, Theater of the: A kind of DRAMA that presents a view of the absurdity of the human condition by the abandoning of usual or rational devices and by the use of nonrealistic form. It expounds an existential ideology and views its task as essentially metaphysical. Conceived in perplexity and spiritual anguish, the *theater of the absurd* portrays not a series of connected incidents telling a story but a pattern of images presenting people as bewildered beings in an incomprehensible universe. The first true example of the *theater of the absurd* was Eugène Ionesco's *The Bald Soprano* (1950). The term was invented by the American CRITIC Martin Esslin. The most widely acclaimed PLAY of the school is Samuel Beckett's *Wating for Godot* (1953). Other playwrights in the school, which flourished in Europe and America in the 1950s and 1960s, include Jean Genêt, Arthur Adamov, Edward Albee, Arthur Kopit, and Harold Pinter. See ABSURD; BLACK HUMOR.

[Reference: Martin Esslin, *The Theatre of the Absurd*, 3rd ed. (1980).]

Academic Drama: Plays written and performed in schools and colleges in the ELIZABETHAN AGE. See SCHOOL PLAYS.

Academies: Associations of persons brought together for the advancement of culture and learning within their special fields of interest. The term is derived from "the olive grove of Academe" where Plato taught at Athens. One general purpose of the literary *academies* has been, to quote the expressed purpose of *l'Académie française* (originated *ca.* 1629), "to labor with all care and diligence to give certain rules to our language and to render it pure, eloquent, and capable of treating the arts and sciences." A secondary objective has often been that of immortalizing great writers, though the success with which great writers have been recognized by such organizations is relatively small. In addition to the French Academy and the Royal Society of London for Improving Natural Knowledge, the following are important: The Royal Academy of Arts founded in 1768 (England); the *Real Academia Española* founded in 1713 (Spain); and the AMERICAN ACADEMY OF ARTS AND LETTERS founded in 1904. More like the original academy of Plato was the famous "Platonic Academy" led by Marsilio Ficino at Florence in the late fifteenth century, which disseminated the doctrines of Neo-Platonism.

Acatalectic: Metrically complete; applied to a LINE that carries out fully the basic metrical pattern of the POEM. See CATALEXIS.

Accent: In traditional English METRICS, the emphasis given a syllable in articulation. Perhaps no aspect of PROSODY has been the subject of greater disagreement than that dealing with *accent;* it is considered to be a matter of force, of timbre, of duration, of loudness, of pitch, and of various combinations of these. Customarily, however, it is used to describe some aspect of emphasis, as opposed to duration or QUANTITY. A distinction is sometimes made between *accent* as the normal emphasis on a syllable and STRESS as the emphasis required by the METER.

In VERSIFICATION *accent* usually implies contrast; that is, a patterned succession of opposites, in this case, accented and unaccented syllables. In traditional terminology ICTUS is the name applied to the STRESS itself, ARSIS the name applied to the stressed syllable, and THESIS the name applied to the unstressed syllable. It should be noted, however, that the Greek usage, predating this Latin usage, applied THESIS to the stressed and ARSIS to the unstressed syllables.

There are three basic types of *accent* in English: WORD ACCENT, or the normal placement of STRESS on the syllables of a word; RHETORICAL ACCENT, in which the placement of STRESS is determined by the meaning of the sentence; and METRICAL ACCENT, in which the placement of STRESS is determined by the metrical pattern of the line. If the METRICAL ACCENT does violence to the WORD ACCENT, the resulting alteration in pronunciation is called WRENCHED ACCENT, a phenomenon common in the FOLK BALLAD. See QUANTITY, METRICS, SCANSION, STRESS.

[Reference: R. M. Alden, *An Introduction to Poetry* (1909).]

Accentual-Syllabic Verse: VERSE dependent for the establishment of its RHYTHM both on the number of syllables to the LINE and on the pattern of accented and unaccented syllables. The basic METERS in English POETRY are *accentual-syllabic.* See METER, FOOT.

Accismus: A form of IRONY, a pretended refusal that is insincere or hypocritical. Caesar's refusal of the crown, as it is reported by Casca in Shakespeare's *Julius Caesar* (I, ii), is an example of *accismus,* as is Richard's disavowal of his kingly qualities in Shakespeare's *Richard III* (III, vii).

Acephalous: "Headless"; see HEADLESS LINE.

Acronym: A word formed by combining the initial letters or syllables of a series of words to form a name, as "radar," from "*ra*dio *d*etecting *a*nd *r*anging." An *acronym* is a type of ACROSTIC.

Acrostic: A composition, usually VERSE, arranged in such a way that it spells words, phrases, or sentences when certain letters are selected according to an orderly sequence. It was used by early Greek and Latin writers as well as by the monks of the Middle Ages. Though creditable verse has appeared in this form, *acrostics* are likely to be tricks of versifying. An *acrostic* in which the initial letters form the word is called a *true acrostic;* one in which the final letters form the word is called a TELESTICH. An example of a true *acrostic-telestich* presented through a RIDDLE follows: 1. By Apollo was my first made. 2. A shoemaker's tool. 3. An Italian patriot. 4. A tropical fruit. Answer: *Lamb* and *Elia:*

1. L		yr	E
2. A		w	L
3. M		azzin	I
4. B		anan	A

An acrostic in which the middle letters form the word is called a MESOSTICH; one in which the first letter of the first LINE, the second letter of the second line, the third letter of the third line, etc., form the word is called a *cross acrostic*, of which Poe's "A Valentine" is an example. An *acrostic* in which the initial letters form the alphabet is called an ABECEDARIUS.

Act: A major division of a DRAMA. The major parts of the Greek PLAYS were distinguished by the appearance of the CHORUS, and they generally fell, as Aristotle implies, into five parts. The Latin tragedies of Seneca were divided into five *acts;* and when English dramatists in the ELIZABETHAN AGE began using *act* divisions, they followed their Roman models, as did other modern European dramatists. In varying degrees the five-*act* structure corresponded to the five main divisions of dramatic action: EXPOSITION, COMPLICATION, CLIMAX, FALLING ACTION, and CATASTROPHE. Freytag wrote of the *"act* of introduction," the *"act* of the ascent," the *"act* of the climax," the *"act* of the descent," and the *"act* of the catastrophe"; but such a correspondence, especially in Elizabethan plays, is by no means always apparent. The five-*act* structure was followed until the late nineteenth century when, under the influence of Ibsen, the fourth and fifth *acts* were combined. In the twentieth century, the standard form for serious drama has been three *acts,* for MUSICAL COMEDY and COMIC OPERA usually two; but great variation is used, with serious plays frequently divided into EPISODES or SCENES, without *act*-division. Late in the nineteenth century a shorter form, the ONE-ACT PLAY, developed. See DRAMATIC STRUCTURE, FREYTAG'S PYRAMID.

Action: In any work of FICTION, the series of events that constitute the PLOT, what the characters say, do, think, or in some cases fail to do. In the crudest sense, the *action* of a PLAY, a SHORT STORY, a NARRATIVE POEM, or a NOVEL is the answer to the question "What happened?" See PLOT.

Adage: A PROVERB or wise saying made familiar by long use. Examples: "No bees, no honey" (Erasmus, *Adagia*); "A stitch in time saves nine." See PROVERB.

Adaptation: The rewriting of a work from its original form to fit it for another medium; also the new form of such a rewritten work. A NOVEL may be "adapted" for the stage or motion pictures or television; a PLAY may be rewritten as a novel; the new form of such a modification is called an *"adaptation."* The term implies an attempt to retain the characters, actions, and as much as possible of the language and tone of the original; *adaptation* thus differs significantly from the reworking of a SOURCE.

Adonic Verse: In Greek and Latin PROSODY, the METER that consists of a DACTYL and a SPONDEE, as $\_\ \cup\ \cup\ |\_\_$, or TROCHEE, as $\_\ \cup\ \cup\ |\_\ \cup$, probably so called after the Adonia, the festival of Adonis.

Adventure Story (or **Film**):   A STORY in which ACTION—always exterior, usually physical, and frequently violent—is the predominant material, stressed above CHARACTERIZATION, MOTIVATION, or THEME. SUSPENSE is engendered by the question, "What will happen next?" rather than "Why?" or "To whom?" In a broader sense, as Henry James insisted in "The Art of Fiction," everything in FICTION can be thought of as an adventure; he said, "It is an adventure—an immense one—for me to write this little article." In FILM CRITICISM a recognizable subgenre of the *adventure film* is the outdoor-*adventure film,* of which the WESTERN is the most popular form.

Adversarius: The CHARACTER in a FORMAL SATIRE who is addressed by the PERSONA of the SATIRE and who functions to elicit and to shape that speaker's remarks or comments. Arbuthnot is *adversarius* to Pope in "The Epistle to Dr. Arbuthnot." Such a character serves to create a dramatic situation within which he or she may speak or play a role similar to that of a STRAIGHT MAN in a MINSTREL SHOW.

Aesthetic Distance: A term used to describe the effect produced when an emotion or an experience, whether autobiographical or not, is so objectified by the proper use of FORM that it can be understood as being independent of the immediate experience of its maker. The term is also used to describe the reader's or audience's awareness that art and reality are separate. In this sense it is sometimes called "psychic distance." It is closely related to T. S. Eliot's OBJECTIVE CORRELATIVE. See OBJECTIVITY.

Aestheticism: A late nineteenth-century literary movement that rested on the credo of "ART FOR ART'S SAKE." Its roots reached back to Theophile Gautier's preface to *Mademoiselle de Maupin* (1835), which claimed that art has no utility, Poe's theory of "the POEM *per se*" and his rejection of the "heresy of the didactic," Baudelaire's *Les Fleurs du Mal,* and Mallarmé. Its origins had a close kinship to the reverence for beauty of the Pre-Raphaelites. Its dominant figures were Oscar Wilde, who insisted on the separation of art and morality, and Wilde's master, Walter Pater. The English PARNASSIANS—Ernest Dowson, Lionel Johnson, Andrew Lang, and Edmund Gosse—were a part of the movement but were primarily concerned with questions of form rather than sharp separations of art from moral issues. Tennyson angrily paraphrased "ART FOR ART'S SAKE" as meaning:

> The filthiest of all paintings painted well
> Is mightier than the purest painted ill!

Aesthetics: The study or philosophy of the beautiful in nature, art, and literature. It has both a philosophical dimension—What is art? What is beauty? What is the relationship of the beautiful to other values?—and a psychological dimension—What is the source of aesthetic enjoyment? How is beauty perceived and recognized? From what impulse do art and beauty arise? The aesthetic study of literature concentrates its attention on the sense of the beautiful rather than on moral, social, or practical considerations. When pursued with great vigor, it leads to "ART FOR ART'S SAKE" and AESTHETICISM.

Aet., Aetat.: Abbreviations for the Latin phrase *aetatis suae,* of his or her age. The term is used to designate the year of a person's life at which an event occurred, a picture was made, or a work composed. A picture of Henry David Thoreau bearing the legend *"aet.* 35," would be one made during Thoreau's thirty-fifth year, that is, when he was thirty-four years old.

Affective Fallacy: A term used in contemporary criticism to describe the error of judging a work of art in terms of its results, especially its emotional effect. It was introduced by W. K. Wimsatt, Jr., and M. C. Beardsley (see *The Verbal Icon,* by Wimsatt) to describe the "confusion between the poem and its result (what it *is* and what it *does*)." It is a converse error to the INTENTIONAL FALLACY. Notable examples of the *affective fallacy* are Aristotle's CATHARSIS and Longinus' "transport."
[Reference: W. K. Wimsatt, *The Verbal Icon* (1954).]

Affective Stylistics: A study, promoted by the practical and theoretical criticism of Stanley Fish, that recognizes the essential impossibility of isolating an ideal text or work that is not "always already" the product of a prior act of reading and interpretation by the original writer or some subsequent editor. Since no ideal text can be found, the reader is forced to rely on affective responses that can be traced or related to stylistic elements. Such responses need not be vitiated by hopeless relativism, inescapable subjectivity, or whimsical impressionism that add up to the vagaries of "irresponsible response." Rather, such relativism and irresponsible subjectivism are countered by the concept that an "ideal reader" possesses common or public information that permits the understanding of all pertinent frames of literary and historical references as well as the aesthetic or linguistic conventions that govern and shape the text. This information is shared and respected by so-called interpretive communities.
[Reference: Stanley Fish, *Self-Consuming Artifacts: The Experience of Seventeenth-Century Literature* (1972).]

Afro-American Literature: Frequently called BLACK LITERATURE, both terms refer to writings by American Negroes. The formal study of such writing, long a neglected area of American literary scholarship, is increasingly important in America. This heightened interest in the work of Americans of African ancestry has come about for two primary reasons: the growing recognition in the last half century of black people as a significant part of American culture and the development during the same period of a body of Negro writing of impressive scope and quality.

For all practical purposes, *Afro-American Literature* began in the eighteenth century with the poetry of two Negro slaves, Jupiter Hammon and Phillis Wheatley. The first half of the nineteenth century saw further efforts by slave poets, among them George Moses Horton, but it was particularly marked by a flood of autobiographical records of the slaves' terrible experiences, known as SLAVE NARRATIVES, of which the most famous is that by Frederick Douglass. There was also a flood of polemical pamphlets and fiery sermons by Negroes, and in 1853 William Wells Brown, an escaped slave, published the first novel by an American Negro, *Clotel, or, the President's Daughter.* As the century closed, Charles W. Chesnutt began publishing the novels that established him as an important literary figure.

In the twentieth century a host of skillful Negro writers have produced work of high quality in almost every field. There have been poets such as Paul Laurence Dunbar, James Weldon Johnson, Langston Hughes, Arna Bontemps, Countee Cullen, Gwendolyn Brooks (who was in 1949 the first American Negro to receive the PULTIZER PRIZE), Michael Harper, Nikki Giovanni, Don L. Lee, Ethridge Knight, and Clarence Major. The century has been particularly rich in Negro novelists, including such writers as W. E. B. DuBois, Walter White, Jean Toomer, Claude McKay, Zora Neale Hurston, Ann Petry, Richard Wright, Ralph Ellison, James Baldwin, and Ishmael Reed. There have been a number of Black playwrights, among them Hall Johnson, Wallace Thurman, Langston Hughes, Lorraine Hansberry, Ossie Davis, and Imamu Baraka.

These Amerian Negroes, by writing with passion and conviction of the place they and their race have occupied and endured in a predominantly white society, have broadened the range, enriched the sympathy, and deepened the quality of American literary expression. Their contributions, notable most obviously for their power, are major forces changing the earlier American literary monolith of the white middle class.

[References: Houston A. Baker, Jr., *Black Literature in America* (1971); Henry-Louis Gates, Jr., ed., *Black Literature and Literary Theory* (1984); Darwin Turner, ed., *Black Literature: Essays* (1969); William D. Washington, ed., *Black Literature: An Anthology of Outstanding Black Writers* (1972).]

Age of Johnson in English Literature: The interval between 1750 and 1798 was a markedly transitional age in English literature. The NEOCLASSICISM that dominated the first half of the century was yielding in many ways to the impulse toward ROMANTICISM, although the period was still predominantly neoclassical. The NOVEL, which had come into being in the decades before 1750, continued to flourish, with sentimental attitudes and GOTHIC horrors becoming a significant part of its content. Little was accomplished in DRAMA, except for the creation of "laughing" COMEDY by Sheridan and Goldsmith in reaction against SENTIMENTAL COMEDY. The chief POETS were Burns, Gray, Cowper, Johnson, and Crabbe—a list that indicates how thoroughly the pendulum was swinging away from Pope and Dryden. Yet it was Dr. Samuel Johnson, poet, lexicographer, essayist, novelist, journalist, and neoclassic critic, who was the major literary figure, and his friend Boswell's biography of him (1791) was the greatest work of the age, challenged for such an honor, perhaps, only by Gibbon's monumental history, *The Decline and Fall of the Roman Empire* (1776). An interest in the past, particularly in the Middle Ages, in the primitive, and in the literature of the folk was developing and was feeding with increasing strength the growing tide of ROMANTICISM. In recent criticism and literary history it is often called the AGE OF SENSIBILITY, emphasizing the emergence of new attitudes and the development of SENSIBILITY as a major literary expression. See NEOCLASSIC PERIOD, AGE OF SENSIBILITY, SENSIBILITY.

Age of Reason: A term often applied to the NEOCLASSIC PERIOD in English literature and sometimes to the REVOLUTIONARY AND EARLY NATIONAL PERIOD IN AMERICAN LITERATURE, because these periods emphasized self-knowledge, self-control, rationalism, discipline, and the rule of law, order, and decorum in public and private life and in art. See NEOCLASSIC PERIOD, REVOLUTIONARY AND EARLY NATIONAL PERIOD IN AMERICAN LITERATURE.

Age of the Romantic Movement in England, 1798–1832: Although a major Romantic POET, Robert Burns, had died in 1796, William Blake's *Songs of Innocence* had appeared in 1789, and adumbrations of ROMANTICISM had been apparent in English writing throughout much of the eighteenth century, the publication of *Lyrical Ballads* by Wordsworth and Coleridge in 1798 is often regarded as marking the beginning of a period of more than three decades in which ROMANTICISM triumphed in British letters, a period that is often said to have ended in 1832, with the death of Sir Walter Scott. During these thirty-four years, the poetic careers of Wordsworth, Coleridge, Byron, Shelley, and Keats flowered; Scott created the HISTORICAL NOVEL and made it a force in international literature; Wordsworth and Coleridge articulated a revolutionary theory of Romantic POETRY; Jane Austen wrote her NOVELS OF MANNERS; Mary Shelley uncannily combined the GOTHIC NOVEL and SCIENCE FICTION, along with philosophic vision; and Lamb, DeQuincey, and Hazlitt raised the PERSONAL ESSAY to a high level of accomplishment. ROMANTICISM did not die with Sir Walter Scott, but the decade of the thirties saw it begin a process of modification as a result of the varied forces of the Victorian world that played upon it. See ROMANTICISM, ROMANTIC PERIOD IN ENGLISH LITERATURE, and *Outline of Literary History*.

Age of Sensibility: A name frequently applied by contemporary critics and literary historians, such as W. J. Bate, Harold Bloom, and Northrop Frye, to the last half of the eighteenth century in England, the time called by older historians and critics the AGE OF JOHNSON. The use of the term *Age of Sensibility* results from seeing the interval between 1750 and 1798 as a seedfield for emerging ROMANTIC qualities in literature, such as PRIMITIVISM, SENSIBILITY, and the originality of the individual talent. The older term, AGE OF JOHNSON, tends to emphasize the strong continuing NEOCLASSIC qualities in the literature of the time. See AGE OF JOHNSON, NEOCLASSIC PERIOD, AGE OF THE ROMANTIC MOVEMENT, ROMANTIC PERIOD IN ENGLISH LITERATURE.

Agon: Literally a contest of any kind. In Greek TRAGEDY it was a prolonged dispute, often a formal debate in which the CHORUS divided and took sides with the disputants. In the OLD COMEDY in Greece this debate, called epirrhematic *agon*, involved an elaborate and stylized series of exchanges between the CHORUS and the debaters, and addresses to the audience. In discussions of PLOT, it has come to mean simply "conflict." The CHARACTERS in a work of FICTION are designated in terms of their relationship to this conflict; PROTAGONIST, ANTAGONIST, DEUTERAGONIST, and so on.

Agrarians: Literally people living close to the land, in an agricultural society, or espousing the merits of such a society, as the Physiocrats did. In this sense most espousers of pastoral traditions are *agrarians*. Thomas Jefferson was a noted early American *agrarian*. In current literary history and criticism, however, the term is usually applied to a group of Southern American writers who published in Nashville, Tennessee, between 1922 and 1925, *The Fugitive*, a LITTLE MAGAZINE of POETRY and some CRITICISM championing agrarian REGIONALISM but attacking "the old high-caste Brahmins of the Old South." Most of its contributors were associated with Vanderbilt University; among them were John Crowe Ransom, Allen Tate, Donald Davidson, Robert Penn Warren, and Merrill Moore. In the 1930s they championed an agrarian economy as opposed to that of industrial capitalism and issued a collective manifesto, *I'll Take My Stand.* They were active in the publication between 1933 and 1937 of *The American Review,* a socioeconomic magazine that also analyzed contemporary literature. They found an effective literary organ in *The Southern Review* (1935–1942) under the editorship of Cleanth Brooks and Robert Penn Warren. In addition to their poetry and novels, the *Agrarians* have been prominent among the founders of the NEW CRITICISM.

Agroikos: A CHARACTER added by Northrop Frye to the traditional three STOCK CHARACTERS of Greek OLD COMEDY. The usual *agroikos* is a rustic who is easily deceived, a form of the country bumpkin. See OLD COMEDY, STOCK CHARACTERS.

Alazon: The braggart in Greek COMEDY. He takes many forms: the quack doctor, the religious fanatic, the swaggering soldier, the pedantic scholar—anyone who is pretentious through his sense of self-importance and who is held up to ridicule because of it. From Plautus' *Miles Gloriosus* he enters English literature where he is a STOCK CHARACTER in ELIZABETHAN DRAMA. He has been widely used in other literary forms, particularly the NOVEL. James Fenimore Cooper's Dr. Obed Battius, in *The Prairie,* is a good example of a later mutation of this character. See MILES GLORIOSUS.

Alba: A Provençal lament over the parting of lovers at the break of day, the name coming from the Provençal word for "dawn." It has no fixed metrical form, but each STANZA usually ends with *"alba."* The medieval *albas* were inspired in large part by Ovid. With the TROUBADOURS the *albas* grew to a distinct literary form. On occasion they were religious, being addressed to the Virgin. See AUBADE.

Alcaics: VERSES written according to the manner of the ODES of Alcaeus, usually a four-stanza POEM, each STANZA composed of four lines, the first two being HENDECASYLLABIC, the third being nine syllables, and the fourth DECASYLLABIC. Since the CLASSICAL pattern is based on quantitative DACTYLS and TROCHEES, exact English *Alcaics* are practically impossible. The most notable English attempt is in Tennyson's "Milton," which begins:

$$\text{O} \mid \text{mighty-} \mid \text{mouth'd in} \mid \text{ventor of} \mid \text{harmon} \mid \text{ies,}$$

$$\text{O} \mid \text{skill'd to} \mid \text{sing of} \mid \text{Time or E} \mid \text{ternit} \mid \text{y,}$$

$$\text{God-} \mid \text{gifted} \mid \text{organ-} \mid \text{voice of} \mid \text{England,}$$

$$\text{Milton, a} \mid \text{name to re} \mid \text{sound for} \mid \text{ages.}$$

Alexandrianism: The spirit prevailing in the literary and scientific work of Hellenistic writers flourishing in Alexandria for about three centuries after 325 B.C. The literature is distinguished by originality, novelty, learning, and devotion to ancestral models. The academic studies are distinguished by bibliophilia, attention to detail, the establishment and collection of canons, and thoroughgoing editing and annotating. The greatest names associated with *Alexandrianism* are those of Callimachus, Philetas, Theocritus, and Lycophron.

Alexandrine: A VERSE with six IAMBIC feet (IAMBIC HEXAMETER). The form, that of HEROIC VERSE in France, received its name possibly from the fact that it was much used in Old French romances of the twelfth and thirteenth centuries describing the adventures of Alexander the Great, or possibly from the name of Alexandre Paris, a French poet who used this METER. Its appearance in English has been credited to Wyatt and Surrey. Perhaps the most conspicuous instance of its successful use in English is by Spenser, who, in his SPENSERIAN STANZA, after eight PENTAMETER lines employed a HEXAMETER line (*Alexandrine*) in the ninth. Both the line and its occasional bad effect are described in Pope's COUPLET:

> A needless Alexandrine ends the song,
> That, like a wounded snake, drags its slow length along.

Some *Alexandrines,* far from needless, are used to avoid the monotony and patness of PENTAMETER in certain STANZAS, such as RHYME ROYAL (see Wordsworth's "Resolution and Independence") and the SONNET (see Keats's "On Sitting Down to Read *King Lear* Once Again" and Longfellow's "Mezzo Cammin").

Alienation Effect: This term—which translates the German *Verfremdungseffekt*—was put forward by the playwright Berthold Brecht as a desirable quality of theater, by means of which the AUDIENCE is kept at a distance such that unthinking emotional and personal involvement is inhibited while political messages are delivered. The *alienation effect* can be achieved by any device that departs from representational REALISM and fidelity to everyday experience: masks, alien setting, disturbances of time sequence, rupturing of the FOURTH WALL. The *alienation effect* in some ways resembles the "defamiliarization" of the RUSSIAN FORMALISTS and the general notion of AESTHETIC DISTANCE.

Allegory: A form of extended METAPHOR in which objects, persons, and actions in a NARRATIVE, either in PROSE or VERSE, are equated with meanings that lie outside the NARRATIVE itself. Thus, it represents one thing in the guise of another—an abstraction in that of a concrete IMAGE. By a process of double signification, the order of words represents actions and characters, and they, in turn, represent ideas. *Allegory* often clarifies this process by giving patently meaningful names to persons and places. The characters are usually PERSONIFICATIONS of abstract qualities, the action and the setting representative of the relationships among these abstractions. *Allegory* attempts to evoke a dual interest, one in the events, characters, and setting presented, and the other in the ideas they are intended to convey or the significance they bear. The characters, events, and setting may be historical, fictitious, or fabulous; the test is that these materials be so employed that they represent meanings independent of the action in the surface story. Such meaning may be religious, moral, political, personal, or satiric. Thus, Spenser's *The Faerie*

Queene is on one level a chivalric ROMANCE, but it embodies moral, religious, social, and political meanings. Bunyan's *Pilgrim's Progress* describes the efforts of a Christian to achieve a godly life by triumphing over inner obstacles to his faith, these obstacles being represented by outward objects such as the Slough of Despond and Vanity Fair.

It is important but by no means always easy to distinguish between *allegory* and SYMBOLISM, which attempts to suggest other levels of meaning without making a structure of ideas the controlling influence in the work, as it is in *allegory.* The traditional distinction between "symbol" and *allegory* is put forth by Coleridge, whose *Statesman's Manual* argues that "an allegory is but a translation of abstract notions into picture-language," while "a Symbol always partakes of the Reality which it makes intelligible."

Among the kinds of *allegory,* in addition to those suggested above, are PARABLE, FABLE, APOLOGUE, EXEMPLUM, and BEAST EPIC. See also ANAGOGE, FOUR SENSES OF INTERPRETATION.

[References: H. Berger, Jr., *The Allegorical Temper* (1957); Angus Fletcher, *Allegory: The Theory of a Symbolic Mode* (1964); Edwin Honig, *Dark Conceit: The Making of Allegory* (1959); C. S. Lewis, *The Allegory of Love* (1936); Rosemund Tuve, *Allegorical Imagery* (1966).]

Alliteration: The repetition of initial identical consonant sounds or any vowel sounds in successive or closely associated syllables, especially stressed syllables. A good example of consonantal *alliteration* is Coleridge's lines:

> The fair breeze blew, the white foam flew,
> The furrow followed free.

Vowel *alliteration* is shown in the sentence: "Apt alliteration's artful aid is often an occasional ornament in prose." *Alliteration* of sounds within words appears in Tennyson's lines:

> The *m*oan of doves in i*mm*emorial elms,
> And *m*ur*m*uring of innu*m*erable bees.

Several different patterns of *alliteration* can be seen in one of Housman's STANZAS:

> These, in the day when heaven was falling,
> The hour when earth's foundations fled,
> Followed their mercenary calling
> And took their wages and are dead.

One pattern connects the initial consonants of "day," "dead," and the stressed middle syllable of "foundations." Another connects "falling," "fled," "followed," and "foundations," in the last of which the alliterated syllable is relatively unstressed. Yet another pattern, somewhat harder to hear and see, connects the initial vowels in "hour" and "earth's."

OLD ENGLISH VERSIFICATION rested in large measure on *alliteration,* as did much Middle English POETRY. In modern VERSE, *alliteration* has usually been a secondary ornament, although POETS as unlike as Whitman, Swinburne, Pound, Eliot, and Auden have made extensive and skillful use of it.

Alliterative Romance: A METRICAL ROMANCE written in ALLITERATIVE VERSE, especially one produced during the revival of interest in alliterative POETRY in the fourteenth century, e.g., *William of Palerne* (unrhymed long lines similar to the ALLITERATIVE VERSE of the OLD ENGLISH PERIOD), *Sir Gawain and the Green Knight* (in stanzas of varying numbers of long lines followed by five short rhymed lines), and the "alliterative" *Morte Arthure.* See MEDIEVAL ROMANCE.

Alliterative Verse: A term applied to VERSE forms, usually Germanic or Celtic in origin, in which the metrical structure is based on some pattern of repetition of initial sounds within the lines. The most common form in English is Old English poetry and Middle English forms between the twelfth and fourteenth centuries. See OLD ENGLISH VERSIFICATION, MIDDLE ENGLISH PERIOD.
    [Reference: R. M. Alden, *English Verse* (1903).]

Alloeostropha: Milton's term for the variable division of the choric odes in *Samson Agonistes* into what he called irregular "stanzas or pauses."

Allonym: The name of an actual person other than the author that is signed by the author to a work. The term is also applied to the work so signed. Compare with PSEUDONYM, which is a fictitious name assumed by the author. A recent writer on economics, George J. W. Goodman, has adopted "Adam Smith" as his *allonym,* presumably in homage to the eighteenth-century Scottish economist of that name (1723–1790).

Allusion: A FIGURE OF SPEECH that makes brief reference to a historical or literary figure, event, or object. Biblical *allusions* are frequent in English literature, such as Shakespeare's "A Daniel come to judgment," in *The Merchant of Venice.* Strictly speaking, *allusion* is always indirect. It seeks, by tapping the knowledge and memory of the reader, to secure a resonant emotional effect from the associations already existing in the reader's mind. When, for example, Melville names a ship the *Pequod* in *Moby-Dick,* the reader with a knowledge of New England history will suspect the vessel to be fated for extinction. The effectiveness of *allusion* depends on a body of knowledge shared by writer and reader. Complex literary *allusion* is characteristic of much modern writing, and discovering the meaning and value of the *allusions* is frequently essential to understanding the work. A good example is T. S. Eliot's *The Waste Land* and the author's notes to that POEM. James Joyce employed *allusions* of all kinds, many obscure and very complex. Although usage has never been precise, *allusion* ought to be distinguished carefully from outright quotation, obvious ECHO, and direct or annotated reference.
    [Reference: John Hollander, *The Figure of Echo: A Mode of Allusion in Milton and After* (1981).]

Almanac: In medieval times an *almanac* was a permanent table showing the movements of the heavenly bodies, from which calculations for any year could be made. Later, *almanacs* or calendars for short spans of years and, finally, for single years were prepared. A further step came with the inclusion of useful information, especially for farmers. This use of the *almanac* as a storehouse of general information led ultimately to such modern works as the annual *World Almanac,* a compendium of historical and statistical data not limited to the single year. As early as the sixteenth century, forecasts, first of the weather and later of such events as plagues and wars, were important features of *almanacs.*

The *almanac* figures but slightly in literature. Spenser's *Shepheardes Calender* (1579) takes its title from a French "Kalendar of Shepards" and consists of twelve POEMS, under the titles of the twelve months, with some attention paid to the seasonal implications. By the latter part of the seventeenth century, *almanacs* contained efforts at humor, consisting usually of coarse jokes. This feature was elaborated somewhat later, with some refinement such as MAXIMS and pithy sayings, as in Franklin's *Poor Richard's Almanac* (1732–1758), itself partly inspired by the English comic *almanac, Poor Robin.* In Germany in the eighteenth and nineteenth centuries, *almanacs* included printed POETRY of a high order. The Davy Crockett *almanacs,* issued in America between 1835 and 1856, recorded many frontier TALL TALES based mainly on oral tradition and helped to preserve a significant aspect of American culture.

Altar Poem: Another term for a CARMEN FIGURATUM, a POEM in which the LINES are so arranged that they form a design on the page, taking the shape of the subject of the POEM, frequently an altar or a cross. See CARMEN FIGURATUM.

Ambages: A form of CIRCUMLOCUTION in which the truth is spoken in a way that tends to deceive or mislead. The RIDDLE:

> Brothers and sisters have I none,
> But this man's father is my father's son,

is an example in which the relationship of "this man" to the speaker (i.e., son to father) is concealed in an accurate statement.

Ambiguity: The expression of an idea in language that gives more than one meaning and leaves uncertainty as to the intended significance of the statement. The chief causes of unintentional *ambiguity* are undue brevity and compression, "cloudy" reference of pronoun, faulty or inverted sequence, and the use of a word with two or more meanings. A writer who aims to be clear should avoid ambiguous wording such as "the days before us" or "He helped the lady across the street." Attempts to combine causation and negation often produce unwanted ambiguity, as in "He was not in the hospital because he was sick."

However, in literature of the highest order may be found another aspect of *ambiguity,* which results from the capacity of language to function on levels other than that of DENOTATION. In literature, words demonstrate an astounding capacity for suggesting two or more equally suitable senses in a given context, for conveying a core meaning and accompanying it with overtones of great richness and complexity, and for operating with two or more meanings at the same time. One attribute of the finest poets is their ability to tap what I. A. Richards has called the "resourcefulness of language" and to supercharge words with great pressures of meaning. The kind of *ambiguity* that results from this capacity of words to stimulate simultaneously several different streams of thought, all of which make sense, is a characteristic of the richness and concentration that make great POETRY. Since modern English lacks the inflections that distinguish nominative nouns from those in oblique cases, syntactic *ambiguity* arises in clauses that depart from the usual subject-verb-object arrangement. The line "And all the air a solemn stillness holds" (Gray's "Elegy Written in a Country Churchyard") is wonderfully ambiguous: all the air holds a stillness, and a stillness holds all the air. In a grammatically animated passage in Tennyson's "Lucretius," two figures follow each other in hallucinatory *ambiguity:* "And here an Oread . . . a satyr, a satyr, see, / Follows" in a show of "Twy-natured" syntactic doubleness. A handful of English words— "still," "fast," "certain," "primate," "phenomenon," "let," "doubt,"—can have meanings that are not only different but virtually antithetical. *Ambiguity* at this extreme pitch has been exploited in POEMS by T. S. Eliot and Robert Frost. Early in this century, Sigmund Freud, inspired by the now-discredited speculations of the linguist Karl Abel, suggested that the language of dreams made use of what he and Abel called "the antithetical sense of primal words." Even a simple matter like the versatility of the *s* suffix in modern English (plural noun, singular possessive noun, third-person singular present-tense verb) can furnish a species of *ambiguity,* as in such titles as Joyce's *Finnegans Wake* and Richard Wilbur's *The Beautiful Changes.*

William Empson, in *Seven Types of Ambiguity* (1930), extended the meaning of the term to include these aspects of language. Although there have been those who feel that another word besides *ambiguity* should be used for these characteristics of language functioning with artistic complexity (among those suggested have been MULTIPLE MEANINGS and PLURISIGNATION), Empson's "seven types" of linguistic complexity "which adds some nuance to the direct statement of prose" have proved to be effective tools for the examination of literature. These "types of *ambiguity*" are (1) details of language that are effective in several ways at once; (2) alternative meanings that are ultimately resolved into the one meaning intended by the author; (3) two seemingly unconnected meanings that are given in one word; (4) alternative meanings that act together to clarify a complicated state of mind in the author; (5) a simile that refers imperfectly to two incompatible things and by this "fortunate confusion" shows the author discovering the idea as he or she writes; (6) a statement that is so contradictory or irrelevant that readers are made to invent their own interpretations; and (7) a statement so fundamentally contradictory that it reveals a basic division in the author's mind.

Ambiguity is thus a literary tool of great usefulness in suggesting various orders and ranges of meanings and enriching by holding out multiple possibilities. Its uses range from simple double meanings for words, through such devices as the alternative choices that Hawthorne uses in *The Scarlet Letter,* to symbols with heavy freights of meanings. See AMPHIBOLOGY.

[Reference: William Empson, *Seven Types of Ambiguity,* 2nd ed. (1947).]

Ambivalence: The existence of mutually conflicting feelings or attitudes. The term is often used to describe the contradictory attitudes an author takes toward characters or societies and also to describe a confusion of attitude or response called forth by a work. The opening of Keats's "On Sitting Down To Read *King Lear* Once Again"—"O golden-tongued Romance, with serene lute! / Fair-plumèd Syren, Queen of far-away!"—furnishes a number of examples of *ambivalence*, especially in the complicated mixture of feelings as the poet bids "Adieu" to the dangerously attractive muse. "Golden-tongued" suggests "wonderfully melodious" but also "deceptive"; "serene" suggests "peaceful" but also "falsely placid"; "fair-plumèd" suggests both "attractive" and "showy and shallow"; "Syren" embraces both "attractive" and "dangerously seductive"; "far-away" suggests "enchanted realms" but also "escapist imaginations"—and all of these ambivalences are underscored by the way the accent shifts within a single consonantal frame in "serene" and "Syren."

American Academy of Arts and Letters: An organization brought into being in 1904 to recognize distinguished accomplishment in literature, art, or music. The American Social Science Association in 1898, realizing the need for a society devoted entirely to the interests of letters and the fine arts, organized the National Institute of Arts and Letters with membership limited to 250. Six years later a smaller society composed of the fifty most distinguished members of the Institute was organized as the *American Academy of Arts and Letters.* Only members of the Institute may be elected to the Academy. The seven first elected to membership were: William Dean Howells, Augustus Saint-Gaudens, Edmund Clarence Stedman, John LaFarge, Samuel Langhorne Clemens, John Hay, and Edward MacDowell. Annually the National Institute awards its gold medal for distinguished work in literature and the arts; every five years it confers the William Dean Howells medal for the best American fiction.

American Indian Literature: The writings and oral traditions of the aboriginal tribes of America. Originally transmitted almost entirely by word of mouth, the literature was at first such as could easily be memorized: the rituals of annual festivals, tribal traditions, narrative accounts of gods and heroes. Since much of this literature grew up about the rhythmic accents of the ceremonial drum, it took on a regularity of metric pattern that gave it the quality of POETRY. Another part, perhaps less associated with ceremonials, was more simply natural in its recounting of events and took the form of PROSE. A characteristic quality of these languages is the building of many ideas into one term. ("Hither-whiteness-comes-walking" being, according to Mary Austin, the Algonquin parallel for "dawn.") Most of this literature known to us today is confined to a few types: the EPIC, the FOLKTALE, the DRAMA, ritualistic and ceremonial exercises, and NARRATIVES of adventure. In recent years there has been a substantial revival of interest in this literature, and concurrently the term "Native American" has come into use.

[References: Thomas E. Sanders and Walter W. Peek, *Literature of the American Indian* (1973); Alan R. Velie, ed., *American Indian Literature: An Anthology* (1979).]

American Language: A term used to designate certain idioms and forms peculiar to English speech in America. These differences arise in several ways: some forms originate in America independently of English speech ("gerrymander" is an example); some expressions that were once native to England have been brought here and have lived after they had died out in England ("fall" for "autumn"); and certain English forms have taken on modified meanings in America (as we use "store" for "shop"). Besides these matters of vocabulary,

H. L. Mencken points out six respects in which American expression differs from English: syntax, intonation, slang, idiom, grammar, and pronunciation.

Although for years the sensitiveness of Americans made many of them deny the existence of anything like an *American language,* its existence has been recognized and its nature applauded for over a half century. As a unique language of American literary art, it is impressively present in the work of writers like Mark Twain, Ring Lardner, Ernest Hemingway, and J. D. Salinger.

[References: Sir William Craigie and J. R. Hulbert, eds., *A Dictionary of American English on Historical Principles* (1938–44); G. P. Krapp, *The English Language in America* (1925); Hans Kurath and Raven I. McDavid, eds., *Linguistic Atlas of the United States and Canada* (1939–continuing); Albert W. Marckwardt, *American English* (1958); M. M. Mathews, ed., *A Dictionary of Americanisms* (1951); H. L. Mencken, *The American Language,* with *Supplements* (1919–48); Thomas Pyles, *Words and Ways of American English* (1952).]

American Literature, Periods of: Any division of the literary history of a nation is an arbitrary oversimplification. In the case of America, where the national record long predates the development of a self-sufficient literature, the problem is complicated further by the fact that most divisions into early periods are based on political and social history and most divisions into later periods on the dominance of literary types or movements. Almost all historians of *American literature* have made their own systems of period division. In this Handbook *American literature* is treated in a chronological pattern set against the dominant English movements in the *Outline of Literary History,* and the characteristics of its own periods are treated in the following articles:

> COLONIAL PERIOD, 1607–1765
> REVOLUTIONARY AND EARLY NATIONAL PERIOD, 1765–1830
> ROMANTIC PERIOD, 1830–1865
> REALISTIC PERIOD, 1865–1900
> NATURALISTIC AND SYMBOLISTIC PERIOD, 1900–1930
> MODERN PERIOD, 1930–1960
> CONTEMPORARY PERIOD, 1960–

If read in sequence, these articles will give a brief history of American writing by periods.

Amoebean Verses: Pastoral VERSES in matched STROPHES or STANZAS spoken by two speakers alternately. CLASSICAL examples are found in Theocritus and Virgil; Sidney's "Ye Goatherd Gods" (*Arcadia*) is an *amoebean* double SESTINA.

Amphibology (or **Amphiboly**): A term applied to statements capable of two different meanings, a kind of AMBIGUITY. In literature, *amphibology* is usually intentional when it occurs. The witches' prophecies in *Macbeth* and Fedallah's deceptive assurances to Captain Ahab in *Moby-Dick* are well-known examples.

Amphibrach: A metrical FOOT consisting of three syllables, the first and last unaccented, the second accented. An example is *ar range ment.*

Amphigory or **Amphigouri:** VERSE that sounds well but contains little or no sense or meaning; either NONSENSE VERSE, like Edward Lear's, or nonsensical

PARODY, like Swinburne's self-mockery in "Nephelidia," which begins: "From the depth of the dreamy decline of the dawn through a notable nimbus of nebulous noonshine," or more general PARODY, such as,

> Moon milk and soft curds of milky way
> Mingle in the intricacies of my equation,
> O Calculus in calculable!

Amphimacer: A metrical FOOT consisting of three syllables, the first and last accented, the second unaccented. An example is *nev er more.*

Amphisbaenic Rhyme: Named for the monster in Greek FABLE that has a head at each end and can go in either direction, the term is used to describe backward RHYME—that is, two rhyme words the second of which inverts the order of the first, as "step" and "pets." While *amphisbaenic* is a nicely INKHORN term, it is not really very accurate. A better word may be "boustrophedonic," which means "moving alternately left to right and right to left" and applies to certain ancient methods of writing. Edmund Wilson explored the effects of this sort of RHYME in some of his VERSE, not all of it light; and Wilson's experiments subsequently bore fruit in the work of his friend Vladimir Nabokov.

Amplification: A FIGURE OF SPEECH in which bare expressions, likely to be ignored, misunderstood, or underestimated because of bluntness, are emphasized through restatement with additional detail. The device is used in music, oratory, and POETRY quite commonly. The chief danger of *amplification* is that prolix writers will so elaborate a statement as to rob it of even its original force.

Ana: Miscellaneous sayings, ANECDOTES, gossip, and scraps of information about a particular person, place, or event; or a book that records such sayings and anecdotes. Englishmen in the seventeenth century were much devoted to this type of writing, *The Table Talk of John Selden* (1689) being typical. The term also exists as a suffix, as in Goldsmith*ana*, where it denotes a collection of information about Goldsmith.

Anachronism: Assignment of something to a time when it was not in existence. Shakespeare is guilty of sundry *anachronisms* such as Hector's learned reference to Aristotle in *Troilus and Cressida.* The *anachronism*, however, is usually a greater sin to the realist than to the romanticist. Humorists sometimes use *anachronisms* as comic devices. Mark Twain's *A Connecticut Yankee in King Arthur's Court* rests on a sustained, satiric *anachronism.*

Anacoluthon: The failure, accidental or deliberate, to complete a sentence according to the structural plan on which it was started. It may be a mistake, as in a sentence that loses its way: "The police arrested the man whom they thought was an escaped convict"—in which "whom" begins as a potential object, as its case-ending requires, but becomes the subject of a subordinate clause. In literary practice, however, the device can work as a powerful index of anxiety or disturbed coherence. Something of this sort occurs in the opening lines of Tennyson's "Ulysses":

> It little profits that an idle king,
> By this still hearth, among these barren crags,
> Match'd with an aged wife, I mete and dole
> Unequal laws unto a savage race . . . .

Here "an idle king" promises to function as the subject of a noun clause but turns out to be merely in apposition with the true subject, "I." The end of Yeats's "The Second Coming" begins as a statement but abruptly turns into a question:

> The darkness drops again; but now I know
> That twenty centuries of stony sleep
> Were vexed to nightmare by a rocking cradle,
> And what rough beast, its hour come round at last,
> Slouches towards Bethlehem to be born?

Anacreontic Poetry: VERSE in the mood and manner of the LYRICS of the Greek POET Anacreon; that is, POEMS characterized by an erotic, amatory, or Bacchanalian spirit. The characterstic *Anacreontic* LINE consists of a PYR-RHIC foot, two TROCHEES, and a SPONDEE, for which the nearest regular English counterpart would be trochaic tetrameter. Whatever the rhythm, *Anacreontic* verses in English tend to be tetrameter, such as the tune called "Anacreon in Heaven," which was appropriated as the setting of Francis Scott Key's POEM, "The Star-Spangled Banner." The best-known overtly *Anacreontic* poems in English are by Abraham Cowley and Thomas Moore.

Anacrusis: A term denoting one or more extra unaccented syllables at the beginning of a VERSE before the regular RHYTHM of the line makes its appearance. Literally an upward or back beat. The third LINE of the following STANZA by Shelley is an example:

> What thou art we know not;
> What is most like thee?
> *From* rainbow clouds there flow not
> Drops so bright to see
> As from thy presence showers a rain of melody.

Anadiplosis: A kind of REPETITION in which the last word or phrase of one sentence or LINE is repeated at the beginning of the next. These lines from Bartholomew Griffin's *Fidessa* illustrate the term:

> For I have loved long, I crave reward
> Reward me not unkindly: think on kindness,
> Kindness becommeth those of high regard
> Regard with clemency a poor man's blindness.

Anagnorisis: In DRAMA, the DISCOVERY or RECOGNITION that leads to the PERIPETY or REVERSAL.

Anagoge (or Anagogy): In Biblical and allegorical interpretation, the mystical or spiritual meaning. For example, when certain passages in Virgil were interpreted in the Middle Ages as foretelling the coming of Christ, they were being given anagogical interpretations. It is the highest of the FOUR SENSES OF INTERPRETATION, the others being the literal, the allegorical, and the moral. Thus, Jerusalem is literally a city, allegorically the Church, morally the believing soul, and anagogically the heavenly City of God. These levels of meaning are regularly applied to Dante's *Divine Comedy.*

Anagram: A word or phrase made by transposing the letters of another, as "cask" is an *anagram* of "sack." *Anagrams* have usually been employed simply as a trifling exercise of ingenuity, but writers sometimes use them to conceal proper names or to veil messages. It is said, too, that some of the astronomers of the seventeenth century used *anagrams* to conceal certain of their discoveries until it was convenient to announce their findings. *Anagrams* have been used frequently as a means of coining PSEUDONYMS, as "Calvinus" became "Alcuinus," and "Bryan Waller Procter" became "Barry Cornwall, poet"; "Arouet, l.j." *(le jeune)*, *u* being a variant of *v* and *j* a variant of *i*, is said to have been the basis of the name "Voltaire." *Erewhon* (nowhere) is an instance of an *anagram* as a book title. Some *anagrams* that seem frivolous contain hints of deeper seriousness, as in Edmund Wilson's rearrangement of Ezra Pound's name into "azure pond" or Vladimir Nabokov's creation of the sinister "Vivian Darkbloom" from the letters of his own name. The modern American poet A. R. Ammons uses a number of serious *anagrams* in his work ("scared sacred" and "cold clod clam calm," for example). Another contemporary, Robert Morgan, has written a serious POEM called "Spore Prose" that consists entirely of pairs of *anagrams* associated with a mountain graveyard ("slate tales," "stone notes," and "hated death," for example). A variety of the *anagram,* the PALINDROME, is an arrangement of letters that give the same meaning whether read forward or backward, and is illustrated in the remark by which Adam is alleged to have introduced himself to his wife: "Madam, I'm Adam." It may be noted that the celebrated "Et tu, Brute?" in Shakespeare's *Julius Caesar* is nearly a PALINDROME.

Analecta (Analects): Literary gleanings, fragments, or passages from the writings of an author or authors; also the title for a collection of choice extracts, for example, *Analects of Confucius.*

Analepsis: In the terminology of Robert Graves's *The White Goddess,* a type of vision or trance in which something from the past or the unconscious mind is restored to vivid life in the present of conscious mind. Generally, *analepsis* means any recovery or restoration; a POEM by W. H. Auden includes the witty phrase "analeptic swig."

Analogism versus Anomalism: A philosophical debate, traceable to classical antiquity and continuing today, that has to do with the question of the genesis and operation of some such cultural institution as language. Is language analogous to a world or a mind; or is language an anomalous structure with no positive connection to structures outside itself? Certain lineaments of this debate can be seen in the radical difference between NOMINALISM and REALISM and in the disagreement among modern linguists as to whether or not language is "motivated."

Analogue: Something that is analogous to or like another given thing. An *analogue* may mean a cognate, or a word in one language corresponding with one in another, as the English "mother'" is an *analogue* of the Latin *mater*. In literary history two versions of the same story may be called *analogues*, especially if no direct relationship can be established. Thus, the story of the pound of flesh in *Gesta Romanorum* may be called an *analogue* of the similar PLOT in *The Merchant of Venice*.

Analogy: A comparison of two things, alike in certain aspects; particularly a method used in EXPOSITION and DESCRIPTION by which something unfamiliar is explained or described by comparing it to something more familiar. In ARGUMENTATION and logic, *analogy* is frequently used to justify contentions. *Analogy* is widely used in POETRY and other forms of imaginative writing; a SIMILE is an expressed *analogy*, a METAPHOR an implied one. See SIMILE, METAPHOR.

Analysis: A method by which a thing is separated into parts, and those parts are given rigorous, logical, detailed scrutiny, resulting in a consistent and relatively complete account of the elements of the thing and the principles of their organization. See ANALYTICAL CRITICISM.

Analytic Editing: A term used in filmmaking and FILM CRITICISM for a special process by which a director and an editor of a film so select the details in a scene that an emphatic meaning is imposed on the viewer; thus *analytic editing* refers to a director's fundamental approach to cinematic expression. The details selected and the amount of attention given to each become the "language" of the scene. Alfred Hitchcock is often considered the greatest practitioner of *analytic editing*.

Analytical Criticism: A term applied to CRITICISM that views the work of art as an autonomous whole and believes that its meaning, nature, and significance can be discovered by applying rigorous and logical systems of analysis to its several parts and their organization. The work of the New Critics is often called *analytical criticism*. See ANALYSIS; CRITICISM, TYPES OF; THE NEW CRITICISM.

Anapest: A metrical FOOT consisting of three syllables, with two unaccented syllables followed by an accented one (˘ ˘ ∕). The following lines from Shelley's *The Cloud* are anapestic:

> ˘ ˘ ∕   ˘   ˘ ∕   ˘ ˘ ∕   ˘   ˘ ∕
> Like a child from the womb, like a ghost from the tomb,
>
> ˘ ˘ ∕ ˘ ˘ ∕   ˘ ˘ ∕
> I arise and unbuild it again.

Anaphone (or Anaphony): The acoustic counterpart of the ANAGRAM. In an *anaphone*, the sounds composing one word or phrase are rearranged to make another word or phrase. In Laura (Riding) Jackons's line "Thus is a universe very soon," it can be heard (though not seen) that the sounds of "very soon" are nearly the same as those of "universe." Some *anaphones* are ANAGRAMS, and vice versa, but such equivalence is not always the case; "ocean" and "canoe" are perfect anagrams but do not sound much alike.

Anaphora: One of the devices of REPETITION, in which the same expression (word or words) is repeated at the beginning of two or more LINES, clauses, or sentences. It is one of the most obvious of the devices used in the POETRY of Walt Whitman, as these opening lines from one of his POEMS show:

> As I ebb'd with the ocean of life,
> As I wended the shores I know,
> As I walk'd where the ripples continually wash you Paumanok.

The Old Testament is clearly one source and example of this practice.

Anastrophe: Inversion of the usual, normal, or logical order of the parts of a sentence. *Anastrophe* is deliberate rather than accidental and is used to secure RHYTHM or to gain emphasis or EUPHONY. Anything in language capable of assuming a usual order can be inverted. *Anastrophe* can apply to the usual order of adjectives in English, so that Arnold's "melancholy, long, withdrawing roar," Eliot's "one-night cheap hotels," and Yeats's "terrified vague fingers" all depart from the customary sequence (presumably "long, withdrawing melancholy roar," "cheap one-night hotels," and "vague terrified fingers"). Other common patterns of *anastrophe* affect the adjective-noun succession (inverted in many places in POETRY, such as Poe's "midnight dreary") and the standard subject-verb-object order of syntax. For example, the prodigious opening STROPHE of Whitman's "Out of the Cradle Endlessly Rocking" is a single sentence twenty-two lines long marked by extreme INVERSION: twenty substantial lines of adverbial and adjectival matter (showing much ANAPHORA), then the main subject, "I," then some protracted adjectival matter, then the object, "a reminiscence," and, finally, after some two hundred preliminary words, the main verb, "sing."

Anathema: A formal and solemn denunciation or imprecation, particularly as pronounced by the Greek or Roman Catholic Church against an individual, an institution, or a doctrine. The form conventionally reads: *Si quis dixerit,* etc., *anathema sit,* "If any one should say (so and so) let him be anathema." One of its most notable appearances in English literature is in Sterne's *Tristram Shandy* (III, xi).

Anatomy: Used as early as Aristotle in the sense of logical dissection or ANALYSIS, this term, which meant "dissection" in a medical sense, came into common use in England late in the sixteenth century in the meaning explained by Robert Burton in his *Anatomy of Melancholy* (1621): "What it is, with all the kinds, causes, symptoms, prognostickes, and severall cures of it." There are several pieces in English literature preceding Burton in which the medical sense of *anatomy* is still less evident, such as Thomas Nash's *Anatomy of Absurdity,* and John Lyly's *Euphues, the Anatomy of Wit.* The *anatomies* anticipated to some degree the characteristics of the ESSAY and philosophical and scientific treatises of the seventeenth century. The term is also used in Northrop Frye's *Anatomy of Criticism* to designate the kind of NARRATIVE PROSE work organized around ideas and dealing with intellectual themes and attitudes by piling up masses of erudition around the THEME, after the manner of MENIPPEAN SATIRE. Sterne's *Tristram Shandy* is an example, as are the whaling chapters in Melville's *Moby-Dick.*

[Reference: Northrop Frye, *Anatomy of Criticism* (1957).]

Ancients and Moderns, Quarrel of the: The controversy that took place in France and England in the late seventeenth and early eighteenth centuries over the relative merits of classical and contemporary thinkers, writers, and artists. Some of the forces that stimulated the dispute were the RENAISSANCE, which produced a reverence for classical writers; the growth of the new science in the seventeenth century; and the doctrine of progress.

In France the dispute centered on the vigorous advocacy of the moderns by Charles Perrault, Fontenelle, Thomas Corneille, and others. They were opposed by Boileau, Racine, La Fontaine, La Bruyère, and others. Perrault in *Parallèles des anciens et des modernes* (1688–1697) and Fontenelle in *Digression sur les anciens et les modernes* (1688) held that in art and POETRY the moderns show superior taste and greater polish of form when compared with the ancients.

In England the BATTLE OF THE BOOKS began with the publication of Sir William Temple's *An Essay upon the Ancient and Modern Learning* (1690). Temple rejected the doctrine of progress, criticized the Royal Society, upheld the claims of the ancients, and denied that they were inferior to the moderns. He was answered in 1694 by William Wotton in *Reflections upon Ancient and Modern Learning,* in which he gave the palm to the moderns in most branches of learning. The scientific as opposed to the literary aspects of the quarrel were particularly stressed in England, the English moderns generally being willing to admit the superiority of the ancients in such fields as POETRY, oratory, and art.

An episode arose over the *Letters of Phalaris,* which Temple listed as a praiseworthy ancient work. Charles Boyle presently republished these letters and attacked Dr. Richard Bentley for an alleged slight. When Wotton published a second edition of his essay (1697), Bentley included in it an appendix that not only criticized Boyle's edition but presented evidence, later elaborated in his famous *Dissertation* (1699), for believing that the Phalaris letters were spurious. Bentley employed the methods of the new science in the field of classical literature itself, and his study went far toward initiating modern historical scholarship. Jonathan Swift, in the "digressions" ᴜᶜ the *Tale of a Tub* (written *ca.* 1696) and in his famous *Battle of the Books* (written *ca.* 1697, pub. 1704)— the most important literary document produced by the controversy in England—undertook the defense of his patron Temple, though Swift's SATIRE is not altogether one-sided.

[References: A. E. Burlingame, *The Battle of the Books* (1920); J. B. Bury, *The Idea of Progress* (1920).]

Anecdote: A short NARRATIVE detailing particulars of an interesting EPISODE or event. In careful usage the term most frequently refers to a narrated incident in the life of an important person and should lay claim to an element of truth. Though *anecdotes* are often used as the basis for short stories, an *anecdote* differs from a SHORT STORY in that it lacks complicated PLOT and relates a single EPISODE. At one time the term connoted secret and private details of a person's career given forth in the spirit of gossip, though now it is used generally to cover any brief NARRATIVE. Anecdotic literature has a long heritage extending from ancient times and comprising books as different as the *Deipnosophistae* of Athenaeus, the *Lives* of Plutarch, the *Anecdotes* of Percy, and the *Anecdota* of Procopius.

[References: Donald Hall, ed., *The Oxford Book of American Literary Anecdotes* (1981); James Sutherland, ed., *The Oxford Book of Literary Anecdotes* (1975).]

Anglo-Catholic Revival: A movement in the second third of the nineteenth century in England, centered primarily at Oxford University. The revival moved from reform of the Established Church to espousal of the Catholic Church. See OXFORD MOVEMENT.

Anglo-French: The French language as it was used in England from 1100–1350. See ANGLO-NORMAN (LANGUAGE).

Anglo-Irish Literature: Literature produced in English by Irish writers, especially those living in Ireland. It is usually actuated by a conscious effort to utilize Celtic materials, often employing a style flavored by Irish idioms, called "Hibernian English" or "Anglo-Irish." See CELTIC RENAISSANCE.

Anglo-Latin (LITERATURE):   A term applied to the learned literature produced in Latin by English writers or others dwelling in England during the MIDDLE ENGLISH PERIOD. It is largely in PROSE and includes CHRONICLES, serious treatises on theology, philosophy, law, history, and science, though SATIRE (like Walter Map's *De Nugis Curialium*) and LIGHT VERSE (like the GOLIARDIC SONGS) were also written, as well as HYMNS, prayers, and religious PLAYS. See ANGLO-NORMAN PERIOD and MIDDLE ENGLISH PERIOD.
[Reference: W. H. Schofield, *English Literature from the Norman Conquest to Chaucer* (1906).]

Anglo-Norman (Language):   The term *Anglo-Norman* (also ANGLO-FRENCH) is applied to the French language as it was used in England in the period following the Norman Conquest (*ca.* 1100–1350) and also to the literature written in *Anglo-Norman*. The relations of France and England were so close that it is difficult to be certain in all cases whether a given writer or work of this period is to be classed as *Anglo-Norman* or merely as French. Although the terms *Anglo-Norman* and ANGLO-FRENCH are commonly used interchangeably, some writers restrict ANGLO-FRENCH to French that shows the definite influence of English idioms. *Anglo-Norman*, often restricted to the early period of Norman times (1066 and immediately following), sometimes denotes pieces written in England by persons of Norman descent using the Norman dialect of French. A third term, *Franco-Norman*, is also used in this sense. See ANGLO-NORMAN PERIOD.

Anglo-Norman Period: The period in English literature between 1100 and 1350, so-called because of the dominance of Norman-French culture, art, and language. The period is also often called the Early MIDDLE ENGLISH PERIOD and is frequently dated from the triumph of William the Conqueror at the Battle of Hastings in 1066, although it was early in the twelfth century before the impact of Norman culture was marked on the English or before the Norman conquerors began to think of themselves as inhabitants of the British Isles.
    In Europe this was the age of the great crusades and the period of the

dominance of French literature. In England, under Henry I, Stephen, and the Plantagenet Kings Henry II, Richard the Lion-Hearted, and John, the conquered Saxon natives and the Norman lords were establishing the working pattern of government that reached its epitomizing statement in the *Magna Charta* of 1215. Throughout the period the characteristics that are usually associated with England were developing. Feudalism was established. Parliament came into being, with a movement toward definite limits on the power of the monarchy. Oxford and Cambridge rose as strong universities. The Old English language, the tongue of conquered slaves for a period after the Conquest, not only survived in the period but blended with the French dialect of the Norman victors. Gradually it emerged as the language of England, a fact that King John's successor, Henry III, recognized when in 1258 he used English as well as French in a proclamation. By 1300 English was becoming again the language of the upper classes and was beginning to displace French in schools and legal pleadings. Henry III was succeeded in 1272 by the first of the three Edwards, who ruled England for more than a hundred years (until 1377).

Latin was the language used for learned works, French for courtly literature, and English chiefly for popular works—religious PLAYS, METRICAL ROMANCES, and popular BALLADS. On the continent Dante, the *Chanson de Roland,* and Boccaccio flourished. In England and France the body of legend and artful invention that gave England its national hero, Arthur, was coming into being in French, Latin, and English through the work of writers like Chrétien de Troyes, Wace, Geoffrey of Monmouth, Walter Map, and Layamon. (See ARTHURIAN LEGEND.)

Writings in native English were few. The last entry in the *Anglo-Saxon Chronicles* was made at Peterborough in 1154. About 1170 a long didactic poem in FOURTEENERS, the *Poema Morale,* appeared. Early in the twelfth century English METRICAL ROMANCES using English themes began to appear, the first being *King Horn,* and flourished throughout the period. The DRAMA made its first major forward leaps in this period. The first recorded MIRACLE PLAY in England, *The Play of St. Catherine,* was performed at Dunstable about 1100. By 1300 the MYSTERY PLAYS were moving outside the churches and into the hands of the town guilds. The establishment of the Feast of Corpus Christi in 1311 led to the great extension of the CYCLIC DRAMAS and to the use of movable stages or PAGEANTS. The Chester CYCLE was composed around 1328.

Native English poetry, both in the older alliterative tradition and in the newer French forms, continued to develop. About 1250 came "The Owl and the Nightingale," the most famous English DÉBAT poem; about the same time LYRIC VERSE was getting under way with poems like "The Cuckoo Song" ("Summer is i-cumen in"). About 1300 came the heavily didactic *Cursor Mundi,* and around 1340 the popular *The Pricke of Conscience,* describing the misery of earth and glory of heaven and often ascribed to Richard Rolle of Hampole.

But, significant as these works are in the developing strength of native English writing, the period between 1100 and 1350 is predominantly the age of the Latin CHRONICLE and of the glories of French and ANGLO-NORMAN writings. Throughout the period, but particularly in the twelfth century, a veritable cultural renaissance was expressing itself in England primarily through imaginative literature written in ANGLO-NORMAN. In general, it follows the lines of the contemporary literature of France and embraces RO-MANCES, TALES, historical works, political POEMS and SATIRES, LEGENDS, and SAINTS' LIVES, didactic works, LYRICS and DÉBATS, as well as religious DRAMA. The rich culture of the court of Henry II proved a fertile field for these works, and the problem of deciding which shall be classed as ANGLO-NORMAN and which as French defies solution today. By 1350, however, the French qualities of grace, harmony, humor, and chivalric idealism, together with the many characteristic French LYRIC forms, worldly subjects, and syllabic METERS, had been absorbed into the mainstream of English writing; and, in FOLK BALLAD, in CYCLE PLAY, in both ALLITERATIVE VERSE and accentual POEM, England was ready for a new flowering of native literary art. See *Outline of Literary History,* under "Anglo-Norman Period."

Anglo-Saxon: A Teutonic tribal group resident in England in post-Roman times. In the fifth and sixth centuries, the Angles and Saxons from the neighborhood of what is now known as Schleswig-Holstein, together with the Jutes, invaded and conquered Britain. From the Angles came the name *England* (Angle-land). After Alfred (ninth century), king of the West Saxons, conquered the Danish-English people of the Anglian territory, the official name for his subjects was, in Latin, *Angli et Saxones,* (the English themselves were inclined to use the term *Engle* and call their language *Englisc*). In later times the term *Anglo-Saxons* came to be used to distinguish the residents of England from the Saxons still resident in Europe proper. The term is now broadly used to designate the English peoples whether resident in England, America, or the various possessions; and an even broader and looser usage persists in the mildly calumniatory word "Anglo" and the easy ACRONYM "WASP" (*W*hite *A*nglo-*S*axon *P*rotestant), which is indifferently applied to persons with no particular claim to being either *Anglo-Saxon* or Protestant. See OLD ENGLISH PERIOD, ENGLISH LANGUAGE.

Anglo-Saxon Versification: A term referring to the principles of accentual-alliterative VERSE written by ANGLO-SAXON authors in England between the seventh and the twelfth centuries. See the definition of the more widely used term OLD ENGLISH VERSIFICATION.

Angry Young Men: A group of British playwrights and novelists in the 1950s and 1960s who demonstrated a particular bitterness in their attacks on outmoded social and political values, particularly those resulting from bourgeois attitudes. The phrase comes from the title of Leslie Paul's AUTOBIOGRAPHY, *The Angry Young Man* (1951). The archetypal example of an *Angry Young Man* is the PROTAGONIST of John Osborne's PLAY *Look Back in Anger* (1957). Other examples are such NOVELS as Kingsley Amis's *Lucky Jim* (1954), John Braine's *Room at the Top* (1957), and Alan Sillitoe's *Loneliness of the Long Distance Runner* (1960). A possible American counterpart, in THEME if not in CHARACTER and ACTION, is Joseph Heller's *Something Happened* (1975). The PROTAGONISTS of these NOVELS and PLAYS are examples of the ANTI-HERO.

Angst: A term used in EXISTENTIAL CRITICISM to describe both the individual and the collective anxiety-neurosis of the period following the Second World

War. This feeling of anxiety, dread, or anguish is notably present in the works of writers like Jean-Paul Sartre and Albert Camus. See EXISTENTIALISM.

Animal Epic: A medieval literary form consisting of linked stories dealing with animal characters. See the extended definition under the more common term BEAST EPIC.

Animism: The belief that animals and inanimate objects can possess souls. In certain forms of primitive religion and art and in some literary conventions, natural objects are invested with human characteristics. Trees, bodies of water, and suchlike objects are given human personalities and even superhuman counterparts, such as dryads and nymphs.

Annals: Narratives of historical events recorded year by year. Such records in Rome in Cicero's time were known as *annales maximi* because they were kept by the pontifex maximus. ANGLO-SAXON monks in the seventh century developed another sort of *annals* by recording in ecclesiastical calendars after given dates important events of the year. This practice developed into such records as the *Anglo-Saxon Chronicles.* Both *annals* (as in Ireland) and CHRONICLES (as in England) were frequently written long after the events recorded had taken place, the dating being sometimes more or less speculative, especially when efforts were being made to "synchronize" events in secular and in Biblical or ecclesiastical history. The term *annals* in modern times is used rather loosely for historical NARRATIVE not necessarily recorded by years and for digests and records of deliberative bodies and of scientific and artistic organizations, such as *Annals of Congress, Annals of Music, Annals of Mathematics.* Although *annals* and CHRONICLES are often used interchangeably, *annals* technically implies a greater emphasis upon the succession of events from year to year. When used in a figurative sense, the term implies events of great moment, as in Gray's reference to "The short and simple annals of the poor," and Carlyle's statement that "happy are the people whose annals are blank." See CHRONICLE.

Annotation: The addition of explanatory notes to a text by the author or an editor to explain, translate, cite sources, give bibliographical data, comment, GLOSS, or PARAPHRASE. A VARIORUM EDITION represents the ultimate in *annotation.* An *annotated* BIBLIOGRAPHY, in addition to the standard bibliographical data, includes comments on the works listed.

Annuals: Books appearing in successive numbers at intervals of one year and usually reviewing the events of the year within specified fields of interest, as college *annuals.* The term is sometimes applied also to such COMPENDIUMS as the *World Almanac,* embracing historical data and miscellaneous statistics covering a long range of years.

In nineteenth-century England and America the term was used to designate yearly compilations of TALES, POEMS, and ESSAYS, illustrated with plates and handsomely bound, issued in the fall of the year for sale around Christmas as GIFT-BOOKS. Successful in England between 1822 and 1856, they were equally popular in America. They are significant in American literary history because they were the best market in the first half of the nineteenth century for short FICTION, and several works by the likes of Hawthorne, Poe, and Simms first appeared in them. They bore descriptive and sentimental titles, such as *The Gift, Friendship's Offering, The Odd-Fellow's Offering,* and *The Token.*

Antagonist: The character in FICTION or DRAMA who stands directly opposed to the PROTAGONIST. A rival or opponent of the PROTAGONIST. See AGON, PROTAGONIST.

Anthem: In its specific and restricted sense, an *anthem* is an arrangement of words from the BIBLE, usually from the PSALMS, planned for church worship. Originally the music for an *anthem* was arranged for responsive singing. In its common and popular use, an *anthem* is any SONG of praise, rejoicing, or reverence. These emotions, when related to a country, find expression in national *anthems;* when in praise of a deity, in religious *anthems.* See ANTIPHON.

Anthology: Literally "a gathering of flowers," the term designates a collection of writing, either PROSE or POETRY, usually by various authors. Although *anthologies* are made by many different principles of selection and to serve a wide variety of purposes, one of their important uses is the introduction of contemporary, little-known writers to the public. The *Anthology,* perhaps the most famous of all such collections, is a gathering of some 4,500 short Greek POEMS composed between 490 B.C. and A.D. 1000. The BIBLE is sometimes considered an *anthology* and so is the Koran. A number of *anthologies* have been important in English literary history, among them *Tottel's Miscellany* (1559), which published the chief works of Wyatt and Surrey; *England's Helicon* (1602), which published works of Sidney and Spenser; Percy's *Reliques of Ancient English Poetry* (1765); Palgrave's *Golden Treasury* (1861), a collection of standard works of English POETS; and the various *Oxford Books.*

Anthropomorphism: The ascription to animals or inanimate objects of human forms, emotions, or characteristics. In most mythologies the gods are described as having human form and attributes. In a sense *anthropomorphism* is a frequently unconscious way of DESCRIPTION by ANALOGY. Whereas *anthropomorphism* is the conceptual presentation of some nonhuman entity in human form, PERSONIFICATION is the much more limited rhetorical presentation of some nonhuman entity in figuratively human form or with figuratively human qualities. To represent Zeus as an "all-father" with human qualities and features is *anthropomorphism;* to represent time as "Father Time" carrying a scythe and an hourglass is PERSONIFICATION.

Antibacchius: A metrical FOOT of three syllables, the first two of which are stressed and the third unstressed, if the verse is accentual. If the VERSE is QUANTITATIVE, the first two are long and the third short. An example is:

Climb down the / high mountains.

Anticlimax: The arrangement of descriptive or NARRATIVE details such that the lesser, the trivial, or the ludicrous appears at the point where something greater and more serious is expected. The term is customarily used to describe a stylistic effect resulting from a sudden or gradual decrease in interest or importance in the items of a series. *Anticlimax* is both a weakness and a strength in writing; when effectively and intentionally used, it greatly increases emphasis through its humorous effect; when unintentionally employed, its result is bathetic (see BATHOS). An example of its deliberate use, heightened by ANAPHORA, is found in Pope's *Rape of the Lock:*

> Not youthful kings in battle seiz'd alive,
> Not scornful virgins who their charms survive,
> Not ardent lovers robb'd of all their bliss,
> Not ancient ladies when refus'd a kiss,
> Not tyrants fierce that unrepenting die,
> Not Cynthia when her manteau's pinn'd awry,
> E'er felt such rage, resentment, and despair,
> As thou, sad virgin! for thy ravish'd hair.

Unintentional *anticlimax* may be illustrated by this sentence (if it *is* unintentional): "The duty of a sailor in the navy is to protect his country and to peel potatoes."

Anti-Hero: The PROTAGONIST of a modern PLAY or NOVEL who has the converse of most of the traditional attributes of the HERO. This HERO is graceless, inept, sometimes stupid, sometimes dishonest. The first clear example may be Charles Lumley, in John Wain's *Hurry On Down* (1953), although certainly the concept of a PROTAGONIST without heroic qualities is as old as the PICARESQUE NOVEL. Jim Dixon, in Kingsley Amis's novel *Lucky Jim* (1954), Jimmy Porter, in John Osborne's play *Look Back in Anger* (1956), and Yossarian, in Joseph Heller's novel *Catch-22* (1961), are all excellent examples.

Anti-Intellectualism: A philosophic doctrine that, assigning reason or intellect a subordinate place, questions or denies the ability of the intellect to comprehend the true nature of things. PRAGMATISM, POSITIVISM, and Bergsonism are all systems that represent a basic *anti-intellectualism*. So, too, do some of the aesthetic systems of the present deny to the intellect a significant place in the creation of a work of art. Anything that celebrates feeling over thought, intuition over logic, action over contemplation, results over means, experience over tradition, and license over discipline tends toward *anti-intellectualism*. Obviously the twentieth century is a period in which *anti-intellectualism* has been powerful, both as a consciously held philosophical position and in the form of the common person's contempt for those who live largely through the application of intellectual judgments to the world.

Antimasque: A GROTESQUE, usually humorous dance interspersed among the beautiful and serious actions and dances of a MASQUE. Often performed by professional actors and dancers, it served as a foil to the MASQUE proper, performed by courtly amateurs. The development and possibly the origin of the *antimasque* are due to Ben Jonson. See MASQUE.

Antimeria: A species of ENALLAGE, using one part of speech for another, as in "But me no buts." "But," a conjunction, is used here as first a verb and then a noun. Shakespeare used *antimeria* often, as in "His complexion is perfect gallows" (*The Tempest*, I, i) and "The thunder would not peace at my bidding" (*King Lear*, IV, vi). Another practitioner of conspicuous *antimeria*, Gerard Manley Hopkins, used the nouns "self" and "justice" as verbs, and the verb "achieve" as a noun (in the phrase "The achieve of, the mastery of the thing").

Antimetabole: The REPETITION of words in successive clauses in reverse grammatical order. *Antimetabole* is a FIGURE OF SPEECH much like CHIASMUS, which is a form of REPETITION using reverse grammatical order but not the same words. Moliere's sentence, "One should eat to live, not live to eat" and President J. F. Kennedy's "Ask not what your country can do for you but what you can do for your country" are examples of *antimetabole*. See CHIASMUS.

Anti-Novel: A contemporary form of FICTION produced by writers convinced that the literal phenomenon of experience, not abstracted, internalized, or "anthropomorphized" through METAPHOR, is the proper subject matter of the novelist interested in representing reality without imposed interpretations. The *anti-novel* experiments with fragmentation and dislocation on the assumption that the reader will be able to reconstruct reality from these disordered and unevaluated pieces of direct experience. The *anti-novel* is essentially a French form. The best known of the anti-novelists is Alain Robbe-Grillet, who believes that the external world is objective and must be described without social or moral superstructures. He eschews all metaphorical language and employs a neutral, flat STYLE. The refusal to allow order into their fictional world leads the anti-novelists to positions similar to some of those of a modern group to whom they seem opposed, the antirealists. The most complete example of the *anti-novel* is probably Robbe-Grillet's *Le Voyeur;* other important writers in the school include Nathalie Sarraute, Michel Butor, and Claude Simon.

Antiphon: The VERSE or VERSES of a PSALM, traditional passage, or portion of the liturgy, chanted or sung by alternating choirs during Divine Office in the Roman Catholic Church. DRAMA grew from additions to antiphonal chants in the liturgy. Originally *antiphon* and ANTHEM were synonymous.

Antiphrasis: IRONY, the satirical or humorous use of a word or phrase to convey an idea exactly opposite to its real significance. Thus, in Shakespeare's *Julius Caesar*, Antony ironically refers to Caesar's murderers as "honourable men."

Antiquarianism: The study of the past through available relics, usually literary or artistic. The antiquarian impulse is associated with history, FOLKLORE, social customs, patriotism, religion, and other interests, and has existed in all nations, even in their primitive periods. The medieval CHRONICLES and SAINTS' LIVES reflect it, as does such a specific movement as the revival of native English ALLITERATIVE VERSE in the fourteenth century.

 Antiquarianism as an organized effort in England, however, is associated with the sixteenth and later centuries. In 1533 Henry VIII appointed John Leland the "King's Antiquary" and sent him throughout England to examine and collect old documents. Leland's notes were used by later writers like Holinshed and formed the basis for the Society of Antiquaries (1572–1605), of which Sir Walter Ralegh, John Donne, and other literary men were members. Much RENAISSANCE literature, such as the CHRONICLES, HISTORY-PLAYS, TOPOGRAPHICAL POEMS (like Drayton's *Polyolbium*), and patriotic EPICS (like Spenser's *The Faerie Queene*), reflects the antiquarian movement. William Camden was one of the greatest of Elizabethan antiquarians. In the seventeenth century Fuller's *Worthies,* John Aubrey's *Lives,* Sir Thomas Browne's *Vulgar Errors,* and the books of Anthony à Wood (historian of Oxford University) were antiquarian in spirit. In the eighteenth century *antiquarianism* was largely motivated by the interest in primitive peoples, and resulted in Bishop Percy's *Reliques of Ancient English Poetry* (a collection of old BALLADS), Walpole's *Castle of Otranto,* the CELTIC REVIVAL, and the LITERARY FORGERIES of Chatterton and Macpherson and formed an important phase of the ROMANTIC MOVEMENT. The GOTHIC NOVELS and the METRICAL ROMANCES and HISTORICAL NOVELS of Scott reflect it, as, in their way, do the NOVELS of the Brontë sisters.

[Reference: H. R. Steeves, *Learned Societies and English Literary History* (1913).]

Antirealistic Novel: The contemporary NOVEL of FANTASY, illogicality, and absurdity. The *antirealistic novel* is a fictional counterpart of the THEATER OF THE ABSURD and other modern movements that are extreme manipulations, and often the elimination, of expected and customary forms. Thus, the writer of the *antirealistic novel* abandons many of the expected elements of realistic FICTION, such as coherent PLOT, SETTING, MOTIVATION, CHARACTERIZATION, cause and effect, and even syntax and logic on occasion. The first-generation *antirealists* included James Joyce, Kafka, and the French SURREALISTS. They produced vivid dramatizations of subconscious experience, as in the Nighttown sequence and Molly Bloom's monologue in *Ulysses,* and in Kafka's *The Castle.* The second generation included writers like Djuna Barnes (*Nightwood*), Malcolm Lowry (*Under the Volcano*), Nathanael West (*The Day of the Locust*), and Henry Miller. The major *antirealists* at present are Samuel Beckett, Jorge Luis Borges, John Hawkes, Joseph Heller, and Donald Barthelme. They are producing works that dispose of PLOT and reduce people to minimal selves in vivid states of anxiety, such as Beckett's *Molloy;* VIGNETTES presenting a fully imagined new order of reality radically different from ours, such as Borges' brief tales; works that distort real experience in the manner of dreams, such as Hawkes' nightmare NOVELS, *The Cannibal* and *The Lime Twig;* and portrayals of an insane kind of order, such as Heller's *Catch-22* and Thomas Pynchon's *The Crying of Lot 49.* The *antirealistic novel* is not merely a rejection of the traditional methods of REALISM, it is also a profound expression of a distrust of reason in the world, a means of expressing the author's sense of the ABSURD. See ABSURD, SURREALISM.

Antispast: In PROSODY a FOOT consisting of four syllables, with the ACCENTS falling on the two middle syllables, or a VERSE pattern in which an IAMBIC foot is followed by a TROCHAIC FOOT, as in beyond going.

Antistrophe: One of the three stanzaic forms of the Greek choral ODE, the others being STROPHE and EPODE. It is identical in METER with the STROPHE, which precedes it. As the chorus sang the STROPHE, they moved from right to left; while singing the *antistrophe,* they retraced these steps exactly, moving back to the original position. (See ODE.) In RHETORIC *antistrophe* is the reciprocal conversion of the same words in succeeding phrases or clauses, as T. S. Eliot's "The desert in the garden the garden in the desert."

Antithesis: A FIGURE OF SPEECH characterized by strongly contrasting words, clauses, sentences, or ideas, as in "Man proposes, God disposes." *Antithesis* is a balancing of one term against another for emphasis. Although an attractive device when used skillfully, *antithesis* can become a vice with writers who make a mannerism of it, as the minor neoclassic POETS often did. The second LINE of the following COUPLET by Pope is an example of *antithesis:*

> The hungry judges soon the sentence sign,
> And wretches hang that jury-men may dine.

True antithetical structure demands that there be not only an opposition of idea, but that the opposition in different parts be manifested through similar grammatical structure—the noun "wretches" being opposed by the noun "jury-men" and the verb "hang" by the verb "dine" in the preceding example. In the celebrated portrait of the foppish "Sporus" in Pope's "Epistle to Dr. Arbuthnot," excessive *antithesis* itself becomes a ground for indictment and an explicit term of acid malediction:

> His wit all seesaw between *that* and *this,*
> Now high, now low, now master up, now miss,
> And he himself one vile antithesis.

Antonomasia: A FIGURE OF SPEECH in which a proper name is substituted for a general idea that it represents, as in "Some mute inglorious Milton here may rest," where "Milton" is used for "poet." *Antonomasia* also is used to describe the substitution of an EPITHET for a proper name, as in using "The Iron Duke" to stand for Wellington, or "The Prince of Peace" for Christ. It is a form of PERIPHRASIS.

Aphaeresis: The omission of an initial, unstressed syllable—usually a vowel— at the beginning of a word, as in "'mid" for "amid," or "'neath" for "beneath."

Aphorism: A concise statement of a principle or precept given in pointed words. The term was first used by Hippocrates, whose *Aphorisms* were tersely worded medical precepts, synthesized from experience. It was later applied to statements of general principle briefly given in a variety of practical fields, such as law, politics, and art. The opening sentence of Hippocrates' *Aphorisms* is a justly famous example: "Life is short, art is long, opportunity fleeting, experimenting dangerous, reasoning difficult." The term *aphorism* usually implies specific authorship and compact, telling expression.

[References: W. H. Auden and Louis Kronenberger, eds., *The Faber Book of Aphorisms* (1964); John Gross, ed., *The Oxford Book of Aphorisms* (1983).]

Apocalyptic: A term applied to literature that predicts the ultimate destiny, usually destruction, of the world, often through a kind of SYMBOLISM that is obscure, strange, or difficult. *Apocalyptic* writing has also the character of imminent catastrophe, is likely to be grandiose or unrestrained and wild, and often suggests a terrible final judgment. The term is taken from the Apocalypse, the final book of the New Testament, commonly called the Revelation of St. John, a work which describes through complex SYMBOLISM the ultimate end of the world. *Apocalyptic* writing, prophesying the end of the world, was common in Jewish and Christian writing between 200 B.C. and A.D. 150. The "prophetic books" of the poet William Blake are considered *apocalyptic,* as is some of the poetry of William Butler Yeats. American fiction is frequently said to have an *apocalyptic* tradition, which includes the work of Charles Brockden Brown, Edgar Allan Poe, Nathaniel Hawthorne, and William Faulkner.

Apocopated Rhyme: RHYME in which the final stressed syllable of a word ending in that stressed syllable is rhymed with the stressed syllable of a word ending in a stressed syllable followed by an unstressed syllable (see MASCULINE RHYME and FEMININE RHYME). A convention sometimes used in modern PO-ETRY, it was also a feature of the BALLAD, as in these LINES:

> Fly around, my pretty little Miss,
> Fly around, I say,
> Fly around, my pretty little Miss,
> You'll drive me almost crazy.

The rhymes here consist of *say* and *cra.* The feminine ending of *crazy* makes this *apocopated rhyme.*

Apocope: The omission of one or more letters or syllables from the end of a word, as "even" for "evening" or "bod" for "body." Now and then, it should be noted, an apostrophe at the end of a written word will suggest that *apocope* has taken place when, in fact, something different has occurred. The change from "the other" to "t'other" and that from "going" to "goin'" are not, strictly speaking, *apocope* but rather the substitution of one phoneme for another: /t/ for /ð/ in the former, /n/ for /ŋ/ in the latter.

Apocrypha: *Apocrypha* commonly means "spurious" or "doubtful," because "apocrypha," which originally meant hidden or secret things, became the term used to denote Biblical books not regarded as inspired, and hence excluded from the sacred CANON. Saint Jerome (A.D. 331–420) is said to be the first writer to apply the term to the uncanonical books now known as the *Apocrypha.* Apocryphal books connected with both the Old and the New Testaments circulated in great numbers in the early Middle Ages. Almost all literary types found in the BIBLE are represented by apocryphal compositions. Examples of Old Testament Apocrypha include: the Book of Enoch (vision), Life of Adam and Eve (LEGEND), the Wisdom of Solomon (WISDOM LITERATURE), the Testament of Abraham (TESTAMENT), and the Psalter of Solomon (HYMNS). New Testament types include: Acts of Matthew (apostolic "acts"), Third Epistle to the Corinthians (EPISTLE), Apocalypse of Peter (vision), and Gospel of Peter (gospel). These books abound in miracles, accounts of the boyhood of Jesus, reported wise sayings of sacred character, and martyrdoms. The influence of apocryphal literature, blended with authentic Biblical influence, was exerted on such medieval literary types as saints' LEGENDS, visions, sermons, and even ROMANCES. Certain books accepted by the medieval church but rejected by Protestants became apocryphal in the sixteenth century, such as Ecclesiasticus, Baruch, and Maccabees, though they were often printed in Protestant Bibles as useful for edification but not authoritative in determining doctrine.

In a non-Biblical sense, *apocrypha* is applied to writings that have been attributed to authors but have not been generally accepted into the canon of their works. Thus, there are Chaucer *apocrypha* and Shakespeare *apocrypha.*

Apolelymenon: Milton's term for the MONOSTROPHIC design of such CHO-RUSES as those in his *Samson Agonistes.*

Apollonian (or, earlier, **Apollinian**): A term used, along with DIONYSIAN, by Friedrich Nietzsche, in *The Birth of Tragedy,* to designate contrasting elements in Greek TRAGEDY. Apollo, the god of youth and light, stood for reason, culture, and moral rectitude. Dionysus, the god of wine, stood for the irrational and undisciplined. These contrasting terms connote much the same thing as CLASSI-CISM and ROMANTICISM, and are very similar to Matthew Arnold's HELLENISM and HEBRAISM, to Schopenhauer's *The World as Will and Idea,* and to Schiller's antinomy of the naïve and the sentimental. When used in a phrase such as "*Apollonian* criticism," the intent is to emphasize form, technique, enlighten-ment, and the role of reason in works of art.

Apologue: A fictitious NARRATIVE about animals or inanimate objects, which, by acting like human beings, reflect human weaknesses and follies. A more bookish term for FABLE. See FABLE.

Apology: Two special uses of the word may be noted. It often appears in literature, especially in literary titles, in its older sense of "defense," as in Stevenson's *Apology for Idlers* and Sidney's *Apologie for Poetrie.* The Latin form is also used in this sense, as in Cardinal Newman's *Apologia pro Vita Sua.* No admission of wrong doing or expression of regret is involved. *Apology* is also an old spelling for APOLOGUE, a FABLE.

Apophasis: A rhetorical FIGURE in which one makes an assertion while seem-ing or pretending to suppress or deny it. "Were I not aware of your high reputation for honesty, I should say that I believe you connived at the fraud yourself."

Apophrades: In the ancient Greek calendar, unlucky or unclean days that fell towards the end of a month; the last two days of the Flower Festival in the month of Anthesterion were thought to be a gloomy and forbidden time when the dead visited their old houses. Recently the term has been appropri-ated in Harold Bloom's CRITICISM as the name of a "revisionary ratio" in which a dead precursor returns.

[Reference: Harold Bloom, *A Map of Misreading* (1975).]

Apophthegm: See APOTHEGM.

Aporia: A difficulty, impasse, or point of doubt and indecision. Used to describe a species of irony in which a speaker expresses uncertainty but really intends none, as in this sentence: "I don't know what scares me more—your stupidity or your dishonesty." *Aporia* has also been used by recent critics to indicate a point of "undecidability" in a text, which indicates the site at which the text most obviously dismantles or deconstructs itself.

Aposiopesis: The intentional failure to complete a sentence. As a FIGURE OF SPEECH, the form may be used to convey extreme exasperation or to imply a threat, as, "If you do that, why, I'll————." *Aposiopesis* differs from ANACOLUTHON in that the latter completes a sentence in irregular structural arrangement; the former leaves the sentence incomplete. Instances are graphically furnished by a fragmentary passage near the end of Eliot's "The Hollow Men":

> For Thine is
> Life is
> For Thine is the

and in the climactic 28th stanza of Hopkins's "The Wreck of the Deutschland":

> But how shall I . . . make me room there:
> Reach me a . . . Fancy, come faster—
> Strike you the sight of it? look at it loom there,
> Thing that she . . . there then!

Apostrophe: A FIGURE OF SPEECH in which someone (usually, but not always absent), some abstract quality, or a nonexistent personage is directly addressed as though present. Characteristic instances of *apostrophe* are found in invocations:

> And chiefly, Thou, O Spirit, that dost prefer
> Before all temples the upright heart and pure,
> Instruct me, for Thou know'st.

Or an address to God, as in Emily Dickinson's:

> Papa Above!
> Regard a Mouse.

Early in Shakespeare's *Julius Caesar,* Cassius, who is actually talking to Brutus, exclaims, "Age, thou art sham'd! / Rome, thou hast lost the breed of noble bloods!" The form is frequently used in patriotic oratory, the speaker addressing some glorious leader of the past and invoking his or her aid in the present, as in Wordsworth's lines:

> Milton! thou shouldst be living at this hour:
> England hath need of thee. . . .

Since *apostrophe* is chiefly associated with deep emotional expression, the form is readily adopted by humorists for purposes of PARODY and SATIRE.

Apothegm: An unusually terse, pithy, witty saying, even more concise and pointed than an APHORISM. One of the best known, attributed by Francis Bacon to Queen Elizabeth I, is "Hope is a good breakfast, but it is a bad supper."

Apposition: The placing in immediately succeeding order of two or more coordinate elements, one of which is an explanation, qualification, or modification of the first. Customarily but not always, the element in apposition comes second. Compare "My uncle, a man of honor, took no advantage of his opponent's mistake" and "A man of honor, my uncle took no advantage of his opponent's mistake." The former is the normal order, but the latter is also possible. Walt Whitman's long catalogs, as in section 33 of "Song of Myself," represent extended *apposition.*

Apprenticeship Novel: A NOVEL that recounts the youth and young adulthood of a sensitive PROTAGONIST who is attempting to learn the nature of the world, discover its meaning and pattern, and acquire a philosophy of life and "the art of living." Goethe's *Wilhelm Meister* is the archetypal *apprenticeship novel;* noted examples in English are Samuel Butler's *The Way of All Flesh,* James Joyce's *A Portrait of the Artist as a Young Man,* Somerset Maugham's *Of Human Bondage,* and Thomas Wolfe's *Look Homeward, Angel.* The *apprenticeship novel* is now usually called a BILDUNGSROMAN. It is also sometimes called an ENTWICKLUNGSROMAN, or "novel of development," or an ERZIE-HUNGSROMAN, or "novel of education." When an *apprenticeship novel* deals with the development of an artist or writer, it is called a KÜNSTLERROMAN.

A Priori Judgment: Deductive reasoning, based on a hypothesis or theory rather than experiment or experience. In *a priori judgments,* conclusions are reached by reasoning from assumed principles that are considered to be self-evident because they are universal and necessary. In the philosophy of Kant, for example, the term is applied to anything that is considered as antecedently necessary to make experience in general intelligible. The term, when used in literary CRITICISM, is usually pejorative, implying arbitrary judgments based on preconceived postulates. See AXIOM.

Apron Stage: The *apron* is the portion of a stage that extends in front of the PROSCENIUM arch. If all or most of the stage is in front of any devices that could give it a frame, the STAGE is called an *apron stage.* The Elizabethan stage, which was a raised platform surrounded on three sides by the audience, is the outstanding example in the history of the British theater.

Ara: A lengthy and formal CURSE, IMPRECATION, ANATHEMA, or MALEDICTION. Psalm 109 is a classic example.

Arabesque: A style of decorative design favored by the Moors as a means of giving play to their aesthetic creativity without violating the Mohammedan prohibition against reproducing natural forms. It employs intricate patterns of interlaced lines from stylized flowers, foliage, fruits, and animal outlines in geometrical or calligraphic designs. The term was used in German ROMANTIC CRITICISM and FICTION to describe a fictional creation that, as defined by Sir Walter Scott in his ESSAY "On the Supernatural in Fictional Composition" (1827), "resembles the arabesque in painting, in which is introduced the most strange and complicated monsters . . . and . . . other creatures of the romantic imagination." Edgar Allan Poe probably got the term from Scott's essay, where it is used as a rough SYNONYM for GROTESQUE. Poe applied the term to his stories in which the material was selected for its strangeness and its appeal to the sense of wonder. He distinguished between the GROTESQUE, which had an element of horror, and the *arabesque,* which had an element of wonder, in his *Tales of the Grotesque and Arabesque* (1840).

Arcadian: Arcadia, a picturesque plateau region in Greece, the reputed home of pastoral poetry, was portrayed by pastoral POETS as an ideal land of rural peace and contentment. *Arcadian* thus suggests rural withdrawal and simple happiness and is applied to any person or place that possesses idealized rural simplicity such as that exhibited by the shepherds in conventional pastoral POETRY. It is synonymous with BUCOLIC or PASTORAL. Sir Philip Sidney, following Italian precedent, uses *Arcadia* as the title of his famous PASTORAL ROMANCE. See ECLOGUE, PASTORAL, IDYLL.

Archaism: Obsolete phrasing, IDIOM, syntax, or spelling. Used intentionally, an archaic STYLE can be useful in recreating the atmosphere of the past, as in Spenser's *The Faerie Queene* and Keats's "The Eve of St. Agnes." Unless carefully controlled, however, *archaisms* result in an artificial and affected STYLE so absurd as to defeat the purpose of the writer.

Archetype: A term brought into literary criticism from the psychology of Carl Jung, who holds that behind each indivdual's "unconscious"—the blocked-off residue of the past—lies the "collective unsconscious" of the human race— the blocked-off memory of our racial past, even of our prehuman experiences. This unconscious racial memory makes powerfully effective for us a group of "primordial images" shaped by the repeated experience of our ancestors and expressed in MYTHS, religions, dreams, fantasies, and literature. T. S. Eliot says, "The pre-logical mentality persists in civilized man, but becomes available only to or through the poet." The "primordial image" that taps this "pre-logical mentality" is called the *archetype.*

The literary CRITIC applies the term to an IMAGE, a descriptive detail, a PLOT pattern, or a CHARACTER type that occurs frequently in literature, MYTH, religion, or FOLKLORE and is, therefore, believed to evoke profound emotions because it touches the unconscious memory and thus calls into play illogical but strong responses. The archetypal critic studies the POEM, PLAY, or NOVEL in terms of the IMAGES or patterns it has in common with other poems, plays, or novels, and thus by extension as a portion of the total human experience. In this sense the *archetype* is, as Northrop Frye defines it, "a symbol, usually an image, which recurs often enough in literature to be recognizable as an element of one's literary experience as a whole."

In earlier senses, the term refers to the original model or pattern from which something develops. In this sense it is a near SYNONYM of PROTOTYPE. It is also used to refer to a no-longer-extant manuscript from which others were copied.

[References: Maud Bodkin, *Archetypal Patterns in Poetry* (1934); Bettina Knapp, *A Jungian Approach to Literature* (1984).]

Architectonics: A critical term that expresses collectively those structural qualities of proportion, UNITY, EMPHASIS, and scale that make a piece of writing proceed logically and smoothly from beginning to end with no wasted effort, no faulty omissions. The requirements of *architectonics,* a term borrowed from architecture, are felt to have been fulfilled when a piece of literature impresses a reader in the same way as a building, carefully planned and constructed, impresses a spectator. Currently the term is used to describe the successful achieving of organic UNITY, of "the companionship of the whole," in which the parts are not only perfectly articulated but combined into an integrated whole, so that the work has meaning not through its parts but through its totality.

Archive: The repository for historical documents or public records; also the documents and records stored there. Since the eighteenth century, *archive* has been used metaphorically as the title for academic, historical, and scientific PERIODICALS.

Arena Stage: A stage on which the actors, surrounded by the audience, make exits and entrances through the aisles. Sometimes, especially in England, the stage is against a wall, with the audience on three sides. The *arena stage* is often called THEATER IN THE ROUND. It differs from the traditional APRON STAGE, which extends in front of any framing devices.

Areopagus: The "hill of Ares," the seat of the highest judicial court in ancient Athens. By association the name has come to represent any court of final authority. In this sense Milton used the term in his *Areopagitica,* addressed to the British parliament on the question of censorship and the licensing of books.

"The Areopagus" is the name of what some literary historians believe was a sort of literary club existing in London shortly before 1580, supposed to be analogous with the *Pléiade* group in France. Whether there was a formal club or not is doubtful, but certain writers, including Gabriel Harvey, Sir Philip Sidney, Edmund Spenser, and Sir Edward Dyer, engaged in a "movement" to reform English VERSIFICATION on the principles of classical PROSODY. In their best work, however, Sidney and Spenser abandoned these experiments in CLASSICAL measures in favor of Italian, French, and native English forms.

Argument: A PROSE statement summarizing the plot or stating the meaning of a long POEM or occasionally of a PLAY. The best known English examples are Milton's *Arguments* to each of the books of *Paradise Lost.* The term is sometimes used by the New Critics to describe the THESIS of a poem.

Argumentation: One of the four chief "forms of discourse," the others being EXPOSITION, NARRATION, and DESCRIPTION. Its purpose is to convince by establishing the truth or falsity of a proposition.

Arianism: A Christian heresy expounded by Arius, a priest in Alexandria, in the fourth century. Airus believed that God is ultimately single, unknowable, and alone; that Christ was created by God and is not, therefore, equal to him; and that in the incarnation Christ assumed a body but not a human soul and was, therefore, neither fully human nor divine. *Arianism* was condemned by the First Council of Nicaea (325); but, in the confusion of beliefs and allegiances that followed, the Arians for a time triumphed. By 379, however, *Arianism* was outlawed in the Roman Empire. *Arianism* has remained a doctrinal interpretation that has from time to time proved attractive. Milton is accused of tending toward it in his interpretation of the relationship of God and Christ in *Paradise Lost,* although he has also been vigorously—and usually effectively—defended against the charge.

Aristotelian Criticism: Literally, criticism by Aristotle, as in the *Poetics,* or CRITICISM that follows the method of analysis used by Aristotle in the *Poetics,* although the exact nature of the Aristotelian method has been a subject of much debate (see CRITICISM.). In present-day critical parlance, however, the term *Aristotelian criticism* is frequently used in contrast to the term PLATONIC CRITICISM, particularly by the New Critics. In this sense, the term implies a judicial, logical, formal criticism that is centered in the work rather than in its historical, moral, or religious context and that finds its values either within the work itself or inseparably linked to the work; the term is roughly synonymous with *intrinsic.* Aristotle's chief contribution is a closely reasoned ARGUMENT in favor of a complex relation—cause and effect, means and end, form and matter—among six qualitative parts or elements of the literary art, particularly as they figure in tragic DRAMA: PLOT (*mythos*), CHARACTER (*ethos*), thought and feeling (*dianoia*), DICTION (*lexis*), sound (*melos*), and SPECTACLE (*opsis*). In an artful arrangement, these elements combine to arouse and release certain emotions, which are said to be "purged" by the experience of poetry. Among Aristotle's other contributions are such terms and concepts as the TRAGIC FLAW (HAMARTIA) and purgation (CATHARSIS). See CRITICISM, TYPES OF: PLATONIC CRITICISM; AUTOTELIC; THE CHICAGO CRITICS.

[References: R. S. Crane, *Critics and Criticism* (1952); Leon Golden, tr., *Aristotle's Poetics,* with commentary by O. B. Hardison, Jr. (1968); Elder Olson, ed., *Aristotle's Poetics and English Literature* (1965).]

Arminianism: An anti-Calvinistic theology, founded by Jacobus Arminius (Jacob Harmensen) in Holland in the early seventeenth century. It opposes the Calvinistic doctrines of election, reprobation, and absolute predestination, asserting that the human will can forfeit divine grace after receiving it. It was a strong element in the theological arguments in England and America in the seventeenth and eighteenth centuries. In America, Jonathan Edwards was its most powerful attacker. See CALVINISM.

Arsis: In METRICS the term is usually applied today to a stressed syllable. In Greek usage, however, *arsis* was the name of the unstressed syllable. See ACCENT, THESIS.

Art Ballad: A term occasionally used to distinguish the modern or literary BALLAD of known authorship from the early BALLADS of unknown authorship. Some successful *art ballads* are "La Belle Dame sans Merci" by Keats, "Rosabelle" by Scott, and "Sister Helen" by Dante Gabrielle Rossetti. Possibly the most famous POEM imitating the BALLAD manner is *The Rime of the Ancient Mariner* by Coleridge.

Art Epic: A term sometimes employed to distinguish such an EPIC as Milton's *Paradise Lost* or Virgil's *Aeneid* from so-called FOLK EPICS such as *Beowulf,* the *Nibelungenlied,* and the *Iliad* and *Odyssey.* The *art epic* is supposed to be more sophisticated, more highly idealized, and more consciously moral in purpose than the FOLK EPIC, which it imitates. The author takes greater liberties with the popular materials being treated and expects less credulity. The events narrated are in a more remote past. The present-day tendency to discredit the theories of EPIC origins advanced by the romantic critics of the eighteenth century is breaking down the distinction between the two kinds, the FOLK EPICS now being viewed as the work of single POETS who worked according to traditional artistic technique. See EPIC.

"Art for Art's Sake":   The doctrine, corresponding to the French "l'art pour l'art," that art is its own excuse for being, that its values are aesthetic and not moral, political, or social. *"Art for Art's Sake"* was the basic position of AESTHETICISM. See AESTHETICS, AESTHETICISM.

Art Lyric: The *art lyric* is characterized by a minuteness of subject, great delicacy of touch, much care in phrasing, artificiality of sentiment, and formality. Avoiding passionate outbursts, the *art lyric* harks back to the kinds of subject matter that Horace and Petrarch wrote about—the tilt of a lady's eyebrow, the glow of a cheek, the gleam of lips. With Herrick, Lovelace, Jonson, and Herbert, RENAISSANCE English writers polished and perfected their SONGS to gemlike brightness; with Shelley and Keats the *art lyric* began to carry ABSTRACT ideas. The *art lyric* differs from other LYRICS in the degree to which the poet's self-conscious struggle for perfection of form dominates the spontaneity of feeling. Certain French FORMS, such as the TRIOLET, the BALLADE, the RONDEAU, and the RONDEL, are examples of this highly self-conscious manner of writing.

Arthurian Legend: Probably the LEGEND of Arthur grew out of the deeds of some historical person. He was probably not a king, and it is very doubtful that his name was Arthur. He was presumably a Welsh or Roman military leader of the Celts in Wales against the Germanic invaders who overran Britain in the fifth century. The deeds of this Welsh hero gradually grew into a vast body of romantic story that provided a glorious past for the Britons to look back upon. When Arthur developed into an important king, he yielded his position as a personal hero to a group of great knights who surrounded him. These knights of the Round Table came to represent all that was best in the age of chivalry, and the stories of their deeds make up the most popular group ("Matter of Britain") of the great CYCLES of MEDIEVAL ROMANCE.

There is no mention of Arthur in contemporary accounts of the Germanic invasion, but a Roman citizen named Gildas who lived in Wales mentions in his *De Excidio et Conquestu Britanniae* (written between 500 and 550) the Battle of Mt. Badon, with which later accounts connect Arthur and a valiant Roman leader of a Welsh rally, named Ambrosius Aurelianus. About 800, Nennius, a Welsh chronicler, in his *Historia Britonum* uses the name Arthur in referring to a leader against the Saxons. About a century later an addition to Nennius's history called *Mirabilia* gives further evidences of Arthur's development as a hero, including an allusion to a boar hunt of Arthur's that is detailed in the later Welsh story of Kilhwch and Olwen (in the *Mabinogion*). There are other references to Arthur in the ANNALS of the tenth and eleventh centuries, and William of Malmesbury in his *Gesta Regum Anglorum* (1125) treats Arthur as a historical figure and identifies him with the Arthur whom the Welsh "rave wildly about" in their "idle tales." A typical British Celt at this time believed that Arthur was not really dead but would return.

About 1136 Geoffrey of Monmouth, in his *Historia Regum Britanniae*, professedly based on an old Welsh book, added a wealth of matter to the Arthurian legend—how much of it he invented cannot now be determined— such as the stories of Arthur's supernatural birth, his weird "passing" to Avalon to be healed of his wounds, and the abduction of Guinevere by Modred. Geoffrey probably was attempting to create for the Norman kings in England a glorious historical background. He traces the history of the Britons from Brut, a descendant of Aeneas, to Arthur. Soon after Geoffrey, additions to the story were made by the French poet Wace in his *Roman de Brut*, and a little later appear the famous ROMANCES of Chrétien de Troyes, in Old French, in which Arthurian themes are given their first highly literary treatment. About 1205 the English poet Layamon added some details in his *Brut*. By this time Arthurian legend had taken its place as one of the great THEMES of MEDIEVAL ROMANCE.

The popularity of Arthurian tradition reached its CLIMAX in medieval English literature in Malory's *Le Morte Darthur* (printed 1485), a book destined to transmit Arthurian stories to many later English writers, notably Tennyson. Spenser used an Arthurian background for his romantic EPIC *The Faerie Queene* (1590), and Milton contemplated a national EPIC on Arthur. Interest in Arthur decreased in the eighteenth century, but Arthurian topics were particularly popular in the nineteenth century, the best known treatment appearing in Tennyson's *Idylls of the King.* Tennyson's version and E. A. Robinson's *Merlin*, *Lancelot*, and *Tristram* show how different generations have modified the Arthurian stories to make them express contemporary modes of thought and individual artistic ends. Arthurian themes received powerful and sympathetic musical treatment in an opera by Dryden with music by Purcell, *King Arthur*, and in some of Richard Wagner's operas. The burlesquing treatment of chivalry in Mark Twain's *A Connecticut Yankee in King Arthur's Court* is in contrast to the usual romantic idealization, as is T. H. White's tetralogy of novels published under the collective title, *The Once and Future King*, which attests to the continuing strength of the *Arthurian legend* and was the basis of an enormously popular musical drama, *Camelot*. See MEDIEVAL ROMANCE, CHRONICLE.

[References: J. D. Bruce, *The Evolution of Arthurian Romance* (1923); E. K. Chambers, *Arthur of Britain* (1927); Roger Sherman Loomis, ed., *Arthurian Literature in the Middle Ages: A Collaborative History* (1959); M. W. MacCallum, *Tennyson's Idylls of the King and Arthurian Story* (1894); G. H. Maynadier, *The Arthur of the English Poets* (1935); James W. Spisak and William Matthews, eds., *Caxton's Malory: A New Edition of Sir Thomas Malory's Le Morte Darthur* (1984); Beverly Taylor and Elisabeth Brewer, *The Return of King Arthur* (1983); Eugène Vinaver, *The Works of Sir Thomas Malory* (1954).]

Article: A PROSE composition, usually comparatively brief and always nonfiction, that deals with a single topic. Longer than a NOTE but shorter than a MONOGRAPH, an *article* is customarily a direct, expository, or descriptive factual statement. Although it is a type of FORMAL ESSAY, it usually has less dignity and weight and is frequently considered to be journalistic as opposed to belletristic. It usually appears in newspapers, MAGAZINES, JOURNALS, ENCYCLOPEDIAS, handbooks, and textbooks. See ESSAY.

Artificial Comdey: A term sometimes used (as by Lamb) for COMEDY reflecting an artificial society, like the COMEDY OF MANNERS.

Artificiality: A term used to characterize a work that is consciously and deliberately mannered, affected, elaborate, conventional, studied, or self-conscious. There is little question that Lyly's STYLE is artificial and that Burns's is not; about writers like Donne, Hemingway, and Durrell, however, debate can and does continue.

Aside: A dramatic CONVENTION by which an ACTOR directly addresses the audience but is not supposed to be heard by the other actors on the stage. In RENAISSANCE DRAMA the device was widely used to allow the inner feelings of the CHARACTER to be made known to the audience, as witnessed by the fact that Hamlet's very first line is an *aside.* In the nineteenth century the CONVENTION was used for melodramatic and comic effect. Eugene O'Neill's *Strange Interlude* (1928) was a serious, successful, and extended application of the *aside* to the modern theater. By a custom of the theater, the speaker of an *aside* is assumed to be telling the truth. See SOLILOQUY.

Assonance: Similar vowel sounds in stressed syllables that end with different consonant sounds. *Assonance* differs from RHYME in that RHYME is a similarity of vowel and consonant. "Lake" and "fake" demonstrate RHYME; "lake" and "fate" *assonance.*

    Assonance is a common substitution for END RHYME in the popular BALLAD, as in these lines from "The Twa Corbies":

> —In behint yon auld fail dyke,
> I wot there lies a new-slain Knight.

Such substitution of *assonance* for END RHYME is found more frequently in modern POETRY than in that of earlier times, but, even so, it has never been a common device. Examples are Yeats's *assonance* RHYME of "love" and "enough" and Pound's of "produced" and "abused."

    As an enriching ornament within the line, *assonance* is of great use to the POET. Poe and Swinburne used it extensively for musical effect. Gerard Manley Hopkins introduced modern poets to its wide use. The skill with which Dylan Thomas manipulates *assonance* is one of his high achievements. Note its complex employment in the first stanza of Thomas's "Ballad of the Long-Legged Bait":

> The bows glided down, and the coast
> Blackened with birds took a last look

> At his thrashing hair and whale-blue eye;
> The trodden town rang its cobbles for luck.

Assonance is involved in "bows" (pronounced "boughs") and "down"; "blackened," "last," "thrashing," "hair," "whale," and "rang"; "took" and "look"; and "trodden" and "cobbles." (Note the pattern of ALLITERATION in this STANZA and that the rhyming of "look" with "luck" is an example of CONSONANCE.) See RHYME.

Asyndeton: A condensed form of expression in which elements customarily joined by conjunctions are presented in series without the conjunctions. The most famous example is probably Caesar's *"Veni, vidi, vici"* (I came, I saw, I conquered). Almost equally well known to Americans is Lincoln's ". . . government of the people, by the people, for the people. . . ." Normally, as in both these examples, the omitted conjunction is of the "coordinating" sort. *Asyndeton* affects "subordinating" conjunctions only in such cases as the substitution of "a man I know" for "a man whom I know."

Atmosphere: The prevailing TONE or MOOD of a literary work, particularly— but not exclusively—when that MOOD is established in part by SETTING or landscape. It is, however, not simply SETTING but rather an emotional aura that helps to establish the reader's expectations and attitudes. Examples are the somber mood established by the DESCRIPTION of the prison door in the opening chapter of Hawthorne's *The Scarlet Letter*, the brooding sense of fatality engendered by the description of Egdon Heath at the beginning of Hardy's *The Return of the Native*, the sense of "something rotten in the state of Denmark" established by the scene on the battlements at the opening of *Hamlet*, or the opening STANZA of Poe's "The Raven."

Attic: Writing characterized by a clear, simple, polished, and witty STYLE. Attica, today a province of Greece, was formerly one of the ancient Greek states, with Athens as its capital city. Attica rose to such fame for its culture and art that it survives in *Attic*, which denotes grace and culture and the classic in art. Joseph Addison is a favorite example of an English author who may be said to have written *Attic* PROSE.

Attic Salt: *Salt* in this sense means WIT. *Attic salt* is writing distinguished by its classic refinement, its intellectual sharpness, and its elegant but stinging WIT. See ATTIC.

Aubade: A LYRIC about dawn or a morning SERENADE, a SONG of lovers parting at dawn. A French form originally, it differs from the Provençal ALBA in usually being joyous, whereas the ALBA is a lament. Shakespeare's "Hark! Hark! the Lark" and Browning's "The Year's at the Spring" are good English examples. See ALBA.

Aube: A morning SONG by a lady in a COURTLY LOVE triangle, expressing regret that the approach of dawn heralds the parting of the lovers. The *aube* was a highly conventionalized LYRIC sung by the Provençal TROUBADOURS. See ALBA, AUBADE.

Augustan: Specifically refers to the age of the Emperor Augustus of Rome (ruled 27 B.C. to A.D. 14). But, since the time of Augustus was notable for the perfection of letters and learning, the term has, by analogy, been applied to other epochs in world history when literary culture was high. As Virgil and Horace made the *Augustan* Age of Rome, so Addison and Steele, Swift, and Pope are said to have made the *Augustan* Age of English letters. In a narrow sense the term *English Augustan Age* applies only to the reign of Queen Anne (1702–1714); in a broader sense it is sometimes given the dates of Pope—1688–1744. The writers of the age were self-consciously *"Augustan,"* aware of the parallels of their writing to Latin literature, given to comparing London to Rome and, in the case of Pope, addressing George II satirically as "Augustus." See NEOCLASSIC PERIOD and the *Outline of Literary History,* where the period 1700–1750 is designated the "Augustan Age."

[References: J. E. Butt, *The Augustan Age,* 2nd ed. (1962); Ian P. Watt, *The Augustan Age* (1968).]

Augustinianism: The doctrines of St. Augustine of Hippo (354–430), author of *Confessions,* the first extended, honest self-analysis, and of the monumental *De Civitate Dei* (*The City of God*), as well as a vast amount of other writing. He strongly defended the orthodox view of God and human beings against the heresies of Pelagius, who held that there is no original sin, that the human will is absolutely free, and that the grace of God is universal but not indispensable. In opposing PELAGIANISM, St. Augustine exalted the glory of God, stressed original sin, and asserted the necessity of divine grace. His is essentially the view that, in the RENAISSANCE, became known as CALVINISM. See CALVINISM.

Auteur Theory: A term, drawn from the French *politiques des auteurs,* used in FILM CRITICISM, where it is applied to a critical method by which a FILM is viewed as the product of its "auteur" or director, and is judged by the quality of its expression of the director's personality or world view. One of the principal FILM THEORIES, *auteur theory* is more likely to relate a film to others by the same director than it is to consider the particular film as an example of its GENRE or as a reflection of its capacity to record and reveal reality.

Autobiography: The story of a person's life as written by that person. Although a common loose use of the term includes under autobiographical writings MEMOIRS, DIARIES, JOURNALS, and LETTERS, distinctions among these forms need to be made. DIARIES, JOURNALS, and LETTERS are not extended, organized NARRATIVES prepared for the public eye; *autobiographies* and MEMOIRS are. But, whereas MEMOIRS deal at least in part with public events and noted personages other than the author, an *autobiography* is a connected NARRATIVE of the author's life, with some stress on introspection. Notable great *autobiographies*—and works that tend to clarify the distinction made above—are St. Augustine's *Confessions,* Benvenuto Cellini's *Autobiography,* Franklin's *Autobiography,* Coleridge's *Biographia Literaria,* and Adams's *The Education of Henry Adams.* Simulated *autobiography* is a device often used in the NOVEL as in Defoe's *Moll Flanders,* and NOVELS can on occasion be *autobiography* in the guise of FICTION, as in those of Thomas Wolfe and in James Joyce's *A Portrait of the Artist as a Young Man.* See BIOGRAPHY.

[Reference: James Olney, ed., *Autobiography: Essays Theoretical and Critical* (1980).]

Autotelic: A term applied to a work that is nondidactic; that is, one whose end, purpose, or intention is within itself and not dependent on the achievement of objectives outside the work. The term is used by the New Critics to indicate a POEM that speaks its own truth in its own terms rather than referring for its value to some external truth. See BELIEF, THE PROBLEM OF.

Avant-Garde: A military METAPHOR drawn from the French (vanguard, or van of an army) and applied to new writing that shows striking (and usually self-conscious) innovations in STYLE, FORM, and subject matter. The military origin of the term is appropriate, for in every age the *avant-garde* (by whatever name it is known) makes a frontal and often an organized attack on the established FORMS and literary traditions of its time. See ANTI-NOVEL, ANTIREALISTIC NOVEL, SURREALISM.

Awakening, The Great: A phrase applied to a great revival of emotional religion in America which took place about 1735–1750, the movement being at its height about 1740–1745 under the leadership of Jonathan Edwards. It arose as an effort to reform religion and morals. Religion, under the "Puritan hierarchy" led by the Mathers, had become rather formal and cold, and the clergy somewhat arrogant. The revival meetings began as early as 1720 in New Jersey. In 1734 Edwards held its first great revival at Northampton, Massachusetts. In 1738 the famous English evangelist George Whitefield began his meetings in Georgia and in 1739–1740 made a spectacular evangelistic tour of the colonies, reaching New England in 1740. Whitefield's meetings were marked by great emotional manifestations, such as trances, shoutings, tearing of garments, faintings. In 1740–1742 Edwards conducted a long "revival" at Northampton, preached in other cities, and published many sermons, including *Sinners in the Hands of an Angry God.* The conservatives, or "Old Lights," representing the stricter Calvinists, led by the faculties of Harvard and Yale, protested against the emotional excesses of the movement; they were answered by Edwards in his *Treatise on the Religious Affections* (1746). Yet Edwards himself opposed the more extreme exhibitions of emotionalism, and by 1750 a reaction against the movement was underway. See CALVINISM, DEISM, PURITANISM.

Axiom: A MAXIM or APHORISM whose truth is held to be self-evident. In logic an *axiom* is a premise accepted as true without the need of demonstration and is used in building an argument. See A PRIORI JUDGMENT, MAXIM.

B

Bacchius (or **Bacchic**): In METRICS, a three-syllable FOOT usually defined quantitatively as a short followed by two longs or qualitatively as a weak followed by two strongs. Applicable mostly to writing in classical antiquity and to Latin more than to Greek, the *Bacchius* has not been transferred usefully to the PROSODY of VERSE in English; nor has the reverse, called "antibacchius" or "palimbacchius." For some reason, George Saintsbury (*Historical Manual of English Prosody*) reversed the usual definitions of "bacchius" and "antibacchius," but neither term matters enough for anyone to have noticed or minded.

Background: A term borrowed from painting, where it signifies those parts of the painting against which the principal objects are portrayed. In literature the term is rather loosely used to specify either the SETTING of a piece of writing or the TRADITION and POINT OF VIEW from which an author presents his or her ideas. Thus, one might speak either (1) of the Russian *background* (SETTING) of *Anna Karenina* or (2) of the *background* of education, philosophy, and convictions from which Tolstoy wrote the NOVEL.

Baconian Theory: This theory—that the PLAYS of William Shakespeare were written by Francis Bacon—grew out of an eighteenth-century English suggestion that Shakespeare, an unschooled countryman, could not have written the PLAYS attributed to him. In the nineteenth century the idea that the PLAYS were by Bacon developed in England and America, with the American Delia Bacon being a particularly influential advocate of *Baconian* authorship. Other persons than Bacon have been suggested as authors of the plays, among them the Earl of Oxford, Sir Walter Ralegh, and Christopher Marlowe (who, according to this theory, was not murdered in 1593). The evidence for any of these theories is fragmentary and inconclusive at best and, at its worst, absurd; and our steadily growing scholarly knowledge of Shakespeare and his world increasingly discredits these theories without silencing their advocates.

Bad Quartos: A. W. Pollard's term for certain notably corrupt, garbled, and nearly incoherent early EDITIONS of Shakespeare's PLAYS, in particular the first quartos of *Romeo and Juliet, King Henry the Fifth, Hamlet,* and *The Merry Wives of Windsor.* There has been a good deal of conjecture as to the source of these *Bad Quartos,* and some scholars have suggested the inclusion of other texts (for example, the "pied bull" 1608 EDITION of *King Lear*) in the category.

[References: Oscar James Campbell, ed., *The Reader's Encyclopedia of Shakespeare* (1966); A. W. Pollard, *Shakespeare Folios and Quartos* (1909).]

Bagatelle: In general, a trifle; in art, a work explicitly identified or labelled as a trifle (although some, such as Beethoven's musical *bagatelles,* are hardly trivial).

Balance: In RHETORIC *balance* is used to characterize a structure in which parts of the whole—as words, phrases, or clauses in a sentence—are set off against each other so as to emphasize a CONTRAST in MEANING. Macaulay's sentence, "The memory of other authors is kept alive by their works; but the memory of Johnson keeps many of his works alive," is an example. *Balance* applies also to the placement of a pause or CAESURA in the syllabic middle of a LINE of VERSE. In lines with an even number of feet and of syllables, a balancing caesura has the effect of stability, as in Marvell's "We would sit down, and think which way . . ." and Hardy's "And consummation comes, and jars two hemispheres." Such a caesura after a stressed syllable is called "masculine" and differs markedly from the effect of *balance* that creates a "feminine" caesura in the middle of a ten-syllable line, with a much less stable result, as in Enobarbus's lines in *Antony and Cleopatra:* "The barge she sat in, like a burnish'd throne, / Burnt on the water. The poop was beaten gold. . . ." As a critical term *balance* is often used to characterize nicety of proportion among the various elements of a given piece of writing. A story, for example, wherein SETTING, CHARACTERIZATION, and PLOT are carefully planned, with no element securing undue emphasis, might be said to have fine *balance.*

Ballad: A FORM of VERSE to be sung or recited and characterized by its presentation of a dramatic or exciting EPISODE in simple NARRATIVE form. F. B. Gummere describes the *ballad* as "a POEM meant for singing, quite impersonal in material, probably connected in its origins with the communal dance, but submitted to a process of oral tradition among people who are free from literary influences and fairly homogeneous in character." Though the *ballad* is a form still much written, the so-called popular *ballad* in most literatures belongs to the early periods before written literature was highly developed. Traditional or "popular" *ballads* still appear, however, in isolated sections and among illiterate and semiliterate peoples. In America the folk of the southern Appalachian mountains have maintained a *ballad* tradition, as have the cowboys of the western plains and people associated with labor and protest movements, particularly those marked by violence. In Australia the "bush" *ballad* is still vigorous and popular. In the West Indies the "Calypso" singers produce something close to the *ballad* with their impromptu SONGS. Debate continues as to whether the *ballad* originates with an individual composer or as a group or communal activity. Whatever the origin, the FOLK BALLAD is, in almost every country, one of the earliest forms of literature.

Certain common characteristics of these early *ballads* should be noted: the supernatural is likely to play an important part in events, physical courage and love are frequent themes, the incidents are usually such as happen to common people (as opposed to the nobility) and often have to do with domestic episodes, slight attention is paid to CHARACTERIZATION or DESCRIPTION, transitions are abrupt, ACTION is largely developed through DIALOGUE, tragic situations are presented with the utmost simplicity, INCREMENTAL REPETITION is common, a single EPISODE of a highly dramatic nature is presented, and often the *ballad* is brought to a close with some sort of summary STANZA. The greatest impetus to the study of *ballad* literature was given by the publication in 1765 of Bishop Percy's *Reliques of Ancient English Poetry.* The standard modern collection still is *The English and Scottish Popular Ballads* (1882–1898) edited by Francis James Child.

The tradition of composing story-songs about current events and personages has been common for a long time. Hardly an event of national interest escapes being made the subject of a so-called *ballad*. Casey Jones, the railroad engineer; Floyd Collins, the cave explorer; the astronauts–all have been the subjects of *ballads*. Popular songs, particularly those engendered by the youthful protest movements, have revived the *ballad* form; for example, "Hang Down Your Head, Tom Dooley," or the *ballads* of Bob Dylan or Joan Baez. Strictly speaking, however, these are not *ballads* in the traditional sense; that form probably belongs to a period in the history of Western civilization which is past. See ART BALLAD, BALLAD STANZA, BROADSIDE BALLAD, FOLK BALLAD.

[References: Bertrand H. Bronson, *The Ballad as Song* (1969); D. C. Fowler, *A Literary History of the Popular Ballad* (1968); G. H. Gerould, *The Ballad of Tradition* (1932).]

Ballad-Opera: A sort of BURLESQUE opera that flourished on the English stage for several years following the appearance of John Gay's *The Beggar's Opera* (1728), still the best known example. Modeled on Italian OPERA, which is burlesqued, it told its story in SONGS set to old tunes and appropriated various elements from FARCE and COMEDY. See OPERA, COMIC OPERA.

Ballad Stanza: Ths stanzaic FORM of the popular or FOLK BALLAD. Usually it consists of four lines, rhyming *abcb,* with the first and third lines carrying four accented syllables and the second and fourth carrying three. There is variation in the number of unstressed syllables. The RHYME is often approximate, with ASSONANCE and CONSONANCE frequently appearing. A REFRAIN is not uncommon. The last STANZA of "Sir Patrick Spens" illustrates both the alternation of TETRAMETER and TRIMETER and the substitution of ASSONANCE for RHYME:

> Half o'er, half o'er to Aberdour
> It's fifty fadom deep,
> And there lies guid Sir Patrick Spens
> Wi' the Scots lords at his feet.

Ballade: One of the most popular of the artificial French VERSE forms. The *ballade* should not, however, be confused with the BALLAD. The *ballade* form has been rather liberally interpreted. Early usage most frequently demanded three STANZAS and an ENVOY, though the number of lines per STANZA and of syllables per line varied. Typical earmarks of the *ballade* have been: (1) the REFRAIN (uniform as to wording) carrying the MOTIF of the POEM and recurring regularly at the end of each STANZA and of the ENVOY; (2) the ENVOY, by nature a peroration of climactic importance and likely to be addressed to a high member of the court or to the poet's patron; and (3) the use of only three (or at the most four) RHYMES in the entire POEM, occurring at the same position in each STANZA and with no rhyme-word repeated except in the REFRAIN. Stanzas of varied length have been used in the *ballade,* but the commonest is eight lines rhyming *ababbcbc,* with *bcbc* for the ENVOY. A good example of early use of English *ballade* form is Chaucer's "Balade de bon conseyl." One of the best-known modern *ballades* is Dante Gabrielle Rossetti's rendering in English of François Villon's "Ballade of Dead Ladies."

Banality: A quality used to describe statements that lack effectiveness and seem tasteless or offensive because they express what has been too often thought by too many in METAPHORS and CLICHÉS so conventional that they lose the ability to communicate. *Banal* is perhaps best defined by citing some of its common synonyms: hackneyed, commonplace, stale, STEREOTYPED, trite. See CLICHÉ.

Barbarism: A mistake in the form of a word, or a word that results from such a mistake. Strictly speaking, a *barbarism* results from the violation of an accepted rule of derivation or inflection, as *hern* for *hers, goodest* for *best, clomb* for *climbed.* Originally it referred to the mixing of foreign words and phrases in Latin or Greek. See SOLECISM.

Bard: In modern use, simply a "poet." Historically the term refers to POETS who recited VERSES glorifying the deeds of HEROES and leaders, to the accompaniment of a musical instrument such as the harp. *Bard* technically refers to the early POETS of the Celts, as TROUVÈRE refers to those of Normandy, SKALD to those of Scandinavia, and TROUBADOUR to those of Provence. See WELSH LITERATURE.

Baroque: A term of uncertain origin applied first to the architectural style that succeeded the classic style of the RENAISSANCE and flourished, in varied forms in different parts of Europe, from the late sixteenth century until well into the eighteenth century. The *baroque* is a blending of PICTURESQUE elements (the unexpected, the wild, the fantastic, the accidental) with the more ordered, formal style of the "high RENAISSANCE." The *baroque* stressed movement, energy, and realistic treatment. Although the *baroque* is bold and startling, even fantastic, its "discords and suspensions" are consciously and logically employed. The change to the *baroque* was a radical effort to adapt the traditional modes and forms of expression to the users of a self-conscious modernism. In its efforts to avoid the effects of repose, tranquillity, and complacency, it sought to startle by the use of the unusual and unexpected. This led sometimes to grotesqueness, obscurity, asymmetry, and contortion. The term in its older or "popular" sense implied the highly fantastic, the whimsical, the bizarre, the DECADENT.

The realization that the *baroque* arose naturally from existing conditions and is a serious and sincere STYLE, resting upon a sober intellectual basis and designed to express the newer attitudes of its period, has had the effect not only of causing the *baroque* to be regarded with more sympathy and seriousness than formerly but also of extending the use of the term to literature as well as to painting and sculpture. Students of literature may encounter the term (in its older English sense) applied unfavorably to a writer's literary STYLE; or they may read of the *baroque* period or "Age of *Baroque*" (late sixteenth, seventeenth, and early eighteenth centuries); or they may find it applied descriptively and respectfully to certain stylistic features of the *baroque* period. Thus, the broken rhythms of Donne's VERSE and the verbal subtleties of the English METAPHYSICAL poets have been called *baroque* elements. Richard Crashaw is said to have expressed the *baroque* spirit in his POETRY.

"*Baroque* Age" is often used to designate the period between 1580 and 1680 in the literature of Western Europe, between the decline of the RENAISSANCE and the rise of the ENLIGHTENMENT. See ROCOCO, CONCEIT, METAPHYSICAL POETRY.

[References: Imbrie Buffum, *Studies in the Baroque from Montaigne to Rotrou* (1957); Lowry Nelson, *Baroque Lyric Poetry* (1961); Murray Roston, *Milton and the Baroque* (1980); Harold B. Segel, *The Baroque Poem* (1974).]

Basic English: A simplified English for non-English-speaking peoples, consisting of a vocabulary of 850 words, of which 600 are nouns, 150 adjectives, and 100 "operators" (verbs, adverbs, prepositions, and conjunctions). It was set up by C. K. Ogden, acting on a suggestion in the works of Jeremy Bentham. In America its strongest advocate was I. A. Richards. The New Testament and certain of Plato's works were "translated" into *Basic English.* At one time, before the Second World War, the movement enjoyed a measure of publicity and popularity. Ezra Pound, in a letter to Ogden, offered, not entirely in jest, to try to compose a "Canto" in *Basic English.* (He never did so.) Now, however, the movement seems defunct.

Bathos: The effect resulting from the unsuccessful effort to achieve dignity, PATHOS, elevation, or sublimity of STYLE; an unintentional ANTICLIMAX, dropping from the sublime to the ridiculous. The term gained currency from Pope's use of it in a "Martinus Scriblerus" paper, which ironically defended the commonplace effects of the English POETASTERS on the ground that depth (*bathos*) was a literary virtue of the moderns, as contrasted with the height (*hypsos*) of the ancients. An example of *bathos* given by Pope is:

> Advance the fringed curtains of thy eyes,
> And tell me who comes yonder.

Here the author (Temple) fails because of the (unintentional) ANTICLIMAX resulting from the effort to treat poetically a commonplace idea. The PATHETIC FALLACY is sometimes responsible for a "bathetic" effect. If a NOVEL, PLAY, or FILM tries to make readers or spectators weep and succeeds only in making them laugh, the result is *bathos.*

Battle of the Books, The: A quarrel between adherents of classical and of modern writing in the late seventeenth and early eighteenth centuries. See ANCIENTS AND MODERNS, QUARREL OF THE.

Beast Epic: A medieval literary FORM consisting of a series of linked stories grouped around animal characters and often presenting satirical comment on the contemporary life of church or court by means of human qualities attributed to beast characters. Some scholars believe that the stories were developed from popular tradition and were later given literary form by monastic scholars and TROUVÈRES who molded the material at hand; others find the origin in the writing of Latin scholastics. The oldest example known seems to be that of Paulus Diaconus, a cleric at the court of Charlemagne, who wrote about 782–86. Whether the form first developed in Germany or France is a question of scholarly debate, though there is no doubt that in the twelfth and thirteenth centuries the *beast epics* were very popular in northern France, western Germany, and Flanders. The various forms of the *beast epic* have one EPISODE generally treated as the nucleus for the story, such as the healing of the sick lion by the fox's prescription that he wrap himself in the wolf's skin. Some of the other animals common to the form, besides Reynard the Fox, the lion, and the wolf, are the cock (Chanticleer), the cat, the hare, the camel, the ant, the bear, the badger, and the stag. The best known of the *beast epics*—and the most influential—is the *Roman de Renard*, a poem of 30,000 lines comprising twenty-seven sets or "branches" of stories.

Beast Fable: A short TALE in which the principal actors are animals. See FABLE, BEAST EPIC.

Beat Generation: A group of American POETS and novelists of the 1950s and 1960s in romantic rebellion against the culture and value systems of America. They expressed their revolt through literary works of loose STRUCTURE and slang DICTION. To prevailing "establishment" values, they opposed an anti-intellectual freedom, often associated with religious ecstasy, visionary states, or the effect of drugs. The group's ideology included some measure of PRIMITIVISM, ORIENTALISM, experimentation, eccentricity, and reliance on inspiration from modern jazz (bebop especially) and from such earlier visionaries as Blake and Whitman. Among the leading members of the loose group were the POETS Allen Ginsberg, Gregory Corso, and Lawrence Ferlinghetti, and the novelists Jack Kerouac and William Burroughs.
 [Reference: Bruce Cook, *The Beat Generation* (1971).]

Beginning Rhyme: RHYME that occurs in the first syllable or syllables of VERSES. It is so rare that few examples can be found among serious literature, but the beginning of W. S. Merwin's "Noah's Raven" will serve as an illustration:

> Why should I have returned?
> My knowledge would not fit into theirs.
> I found untouched the desert of the unknown . . . .

Belief, Problem of: The question of the degree to which the aesthetic value of a literary work is necessarily or properly affected by the acceptability to a reader of its doctrine or philosophic or religious assumptions. Although the question is certainly as old as Plato, it has assumed an unusual relevance in present-day CRITICISM because the traditional answer—that doctrinal acceptability is one of the necessary conditions for aesthetic value—has been brought into serious question by a group of critics, notably those usually designated New Critics. See AUTOTELIC.

Belles-Lettres: Literature, more especially that body of writing, comprising DRAMA, POETRY, FICTION, CRITICISM, and ESSAYS, that lives because of inherent imaginative and artistic rather than scientific, philosophical, or intellectual qualities. Lewis Carroll's *Alice in Wonderland,* for example, belongs definitely to the province of *belles-lettres,* while the mathematical works of the same man, Charles Lutwidge Dodgson, do not. Now sometimes used to characterize light or artificial writing.

Benthamism: The philosophy of Jeremy Bentham. It holds that the ultimate goal of all individuals should be to achieve the greatest happiness for the greatest number. See UTILITARIANISM.

Bestiary: A type of literature, popular during the medieval period, in which the habits of beasts, birds, and reptiles were made the text for allegorical and mystical Christian teachings. These *bestiaries* often ascribed human attributes to animals and were designed to moralize and to expound church doctrine. The natural history employed is fabulous rather than scientific and has helped to make popular in literature such abnormalities as the phoenix, the siren, and the unicorn. Many qualities that literature familiarly attributes to animals come from the *bestiaries*. The development of the type, first attributed to Physiologus, a Greek sermonizer of about A.D. 150, was rapidly taken over by Christian preachers and homilists throughout Europe. The *bestiary* in one form or another has appeared in various world literatures: ANGLO-SAXON, Arabic, Armenian, English, Ethiopian, French, German, Icelandic, Provençal, and Spanish. Kenneth Rexroth's "A Bestiary" is a good modern instance of the form, with its parts arranged according to the alphabet and its LINES disposed syllabically, as in the entry for "Lion":

> The lion is called the king
> Of beasts. Nowadays there are
> Almost as many lions
> In cages as out of them.
> If offered a crown, refuse.

Bibelot: Literally any small curio or artistic trinket, the term is used to designate an unusually small book, sometimes called a "miniature edition."

Bible: Derived from a Greek term meaning "little books," *Bible* is now applied to the collection of writings known as the Holy Scriptures, the sacred writings of the Christian religion. Of the two chief parts, the Old Testament consists of the sacred writings of the ancient Hebrews, and the New Testament of writings of the early Christian period. The Jewish Scriptures include three collections—The Law, The Prophets, and Writings—written in ancient Hebrew at various dates in the pre-Christian era. The New Testament books were written in the Greek DIALECT employed in Mediterranean countries about the time of Christ. An important Greek form of the Hebrew *Bible* is the Septuagint, dating from the Alexandrian period (third century B.C.). Latin versions were made in very early times, of both the Old and New Testament books, including many of the APOCRYPHA. The most important Latin version, translated by St. Jerome about A.D. 400, is known as the VULGATE. This Latin translation was the *Bible* of the Middle Ages. See next three topics and DEAD SEA SCROLLS.

Bible as Literature: The high literary value of many parts of the BIBLE has been almost universally recognized. Many English authors, including Milton, Wordsworth, Scott, and Carlyle, have paid tribute to Biblical literature, Coleridge even rating the style of Isaiah and the Epistle to the Hebrews as far superior to that of Homer, Virgil, or Milton. The literary qualities of the BIBLE are accounted for partly by the THEMES treated, partly by the character of the Hebrew language, and partly by the literary skill exhibited by Biblical writers and translators. The THEMES of Biblical literature are among the greatest that literature can treat: God, humanity, the physical universe, and their interrelations. Such problems as morality, relationship of human beings to the unseen world, and ultimate human destinies are treated with an intensity and vigor seldom matched in world literature. The character of the Hebrew language, abounding in words and phrases of CONCRETE, sensuous appeal and lacking the store of ABSTRACT words characteristic of the Greek, imparted an emotional and imaginative richness to Hebrew writings of a sort that lends itself readily to translation (the idea of pride, for example, is expressed by "puffed up"). The BIBLE is partly in PROSE and partly in VERSE, the principles of Hebrew VERSE being ACCENT and PARALLELISM rather than METER. The literary types found in the BIBLE have been variously classified. A few examples may be given: the SHORT STORY, Ruth, Jonah, Esther; biographical NARRATIVE, the story of Abraham in Genesis; love LYRIC, Song of Solomon; the battle ODE, the SONG of Deborah (Judges 5); EPIGRAM, in Proverbs and elsewhere; devotional LYRIC, PSALMS; dramatic philosophical POEM, Job; ELEGY, LAMENT of David for Saul and Jonathan (2 Samuel 1:19–27); LETTERS, the EPISTLES of Paul.

[References: C. A. Dinsmore, *The English Bible as Literature* (1931); J. H. Gardiner, *The Bible as English Literature* (1906); R. G. Moulton, *The Literary Study of the Bible* (1895); I. F. Wood and E. Grant, *The Bible as Literature* (1914).]

Bible, English Translations of: From Caedmon (seventh century) to Wycliffe (fourteenth century) there were TRANSLATIONS and PARAPHRASES in OLD ENGLISH and in MIDDLE ENGLISH of various parts of the BIBLE, all based on the Latin VULGATE. The parts most frequently translated were the Gospels, the PSALMS, and the Pentateuch. The Caedmonian poetic PARAPHRASES (seventh century) are extant, but Bede's PROSE translation of a portion of the Gospel of St. John (seventh century) is not. From the ninth century come GLOSSES of the Book of PSALMS and PROSE translations by King Alfred. The West Saxon Gospels and the GLOSSES in the Lindisfarne Gospels date from the tenth century, while Aelfric's incomplete translations of the Old Testament date from the late tenth and early eleventh centuries. The subordinate position occupied by the English language for some time after the eleventh century perhaps accounts for the lack of translations in MIDDLE ENGLISH times until the fourteenth century, when there was renewed activity in preparing English versions and commentaries, notably by Richard Rolle of Hampole. In about 1382 came the first edition of the Wycliffe Bible, largely the work of Wycliffe himself. A revision of this work, chiefly the work of John Purvey, 1388, though interdicted by the church from 1408 to 1534, circulated freely in manuscript form for the next 150 years.

Printed English BIBLES first appeared in the sixteenth century, products of the new learning of the HUMANISTS and the zeal of the Protestant Reformation. They were mainly based on Greek and Hebrew manuscripts, or recent translations of such manuscripts. Some important English translations are: (1) William Tyndale–the New Testament (1525–26), the Pentateuch (1530), Jonah (1531). Tyndale is credited with the creation of much of the picturesque phraseology that characterizes later English translations. (2) Miles Coverdale, first complete printed English Bible (1535), based on Tyndale and a Swiss-German translation. (3) "Matthew's" Bible (1537), probably done by John Rogers, based on Tyndale and Coverdale, important as a source for later translations. (4) Taverner's Bible (1539), based on "Matthew's" Bible, but revealing a tendency to greater use of native English words. (5) The Great Bible (1539), sometimes called Cranmer's Bible, because Cranmer sponsored it and wrote a preface for the second edition (1540)—a very large volume designed to be chained to its position in the churches for the use of the public. Coverdale superintended its preparation. It is based largely on "Matthew's" Bible. (6) The Geneva Bible (1560), the joint work of English Protestant exiles in Geneva, including Coverdale and William Whittington, who had published in 1557 in Geneva an English New Testament, which was the first version in English divided into the familiar chapters and verses. It became the great Bible of the PURITANS and ran through sixty editions between 1560 and 1611. (7) Bishops' Bible (1568), prepared by eight bishops and others and issued to combat the Calvinistic, antiepiscopal tendencies of the Geneva Bible. (8) The Rheims-Douai Bible (1582), a Catholic translation based on the VULGATE, issued to counteract the Puritan Geneva Bible and the Episcopal Bishops' Bible. The Old Testament section was not actually printed till 1609.

By far the most important and influential of English Bibles is the "Authorized" or King James Version (1611). It is a revision of the Bishops' Bible and was sponsored by King James I. The translators, about fifty of the leading Biblical scholars of the time, including PURITANS, made use of Greek and Hebrew texts. This version is the most widely read English Bible, and it exerted a profound influence on the literature of the English and American peoples through subsequent centuries.

The Revised Version (1885) and the standard American edition of the Revised Version (1901), the joint work of English and American scholars, were modern versions that aimed chiefly at scholarly accuracy.

A group of American Biblical scholars produced in 1946 an extensive revision of the King James Version of the New Testament, bringing to bear the wealth of textual discovery and scholarship that we now have, and in 1952 they added the Old Testament. This translation, known as the Revised Standard Version, although generally considered inferior to the King James Version from a literary point of view, has attained wide usage because of its accuracy and clarity. A number of renderings into contemporary and idiomatic English have been made in this century of the whole or parts of the Bible. Notable among them are the translations into American idiom by James Moffatt and by Edgar Goodspeed and the translations into British idiom by J. B. Phillips and by Father Ronald Knox. Close PARAPHRASES in the current idiom, often using contemporary slang, such as the *Good News Bible,* are popular today, and there are several such versions.

The most important recent translation is *The New English Bible,* prepared by a joint committee of the Protestant Churches of the British Isles, who were joined by observers representing the Roman Catholic Church. This version is a totally new translation, utilizing all known manuscripts, including recent discoveries such as the DEAD SEA SCROLLS. It aims at—and generally achieves—accuracy, clarity, and graceful dignity. *The New Testament* appeared in 1961, *The Old Testament* and the APOCRYPHA in 1970.

Another new version that seems certain to have wide use and a long life is *The New American Bible,* translated by the Catholic Biblical Association of America. This completely new translation began to be published in parts in 1952, at which time it was known as the Confraternity version. The entire

Bible, with the earlier translations revised, was published as *The New American Bible* in 1970. The aim of the translators was to make as exact a version as possible, resting on modern textual scholarship and resisting modification for the sake of literary quality.

[References: John Brown, *The History of the English Bible* (1912); Frederick Harrison, *The Bible in Britain* (1949); C. S. Lewis, *The Literary Impact of the Authorised Version* (1950); A. W. Pollard, ed., *Records of the English Bible* (1911).]

Bible, Influence on Literature: The influence of the BIBLE upon English literature is so subtly pervasive that it can merely be suggested, not closely traced. Much of its influence has been indirect—through its effect on language and on the mental and moral interests of the English and American people. The English Bibles of the sixteenth century brought the common people a new world by the revival of ancient Hebrew literature. The picturesque imagery and phraseology enriched the lives of the people and profoundly affected not only their conduct but their language and literary tastes.

Great authors commonly show a familiarity with the BIBLE, and few great English and American writers of recent centuries can be read with satisfaction by one ignorant of Biblical literature. The Authorized Version of the BIBLE has affected subsequent English literature in the use of Scriptural themes (Milton's *Paradise Lost,* Bunyan's *Pilgrim's Progress,* Byron's *Cain*); scriptural phraseology, allusions, or modified quotations (as "selling birthright" for a "mess of pottage"); and incorporation, conscious or unconscious, of Biblical phraseology into common speech ("highways and hedges," "thorn in the flesh," "a soft answer"). The BIBLE is thought to have been highly influential in substituting pure English words for Latin words (Tyndale's vocabulary is 97 percent English, that of the Authorized Version, 93 percent). The style of many writers has been directly affected by study of the BIBLE, as has Bunyan's, Smart's, Lincoln's, and Hemingway's. Whitman's prosodic methods as well as his vocabulary demonstrate a great debt to the Hebrew POETS and prophets. Novelists of twentieth-century America are increasingly turning to the BIBLE for THEMES and PLOTS, such as Hemingway's *The Sun Also Rises* and Steinbeck's *East of Eden;* or for what Theodore Ziolkowski has called "fictional transfigurations of Jesus," such as Faulkner's *Light in August* and *A Fable,* Steinbeck's *The Grapes of Wrath,* and Fitzgerald's *The Last Tycoon.*

[Reference: Northrop Frye, *The Great Code: The Bible and Literature* (1982).]

Bibliography: Used in several senses. The term may be applied to a SUBJECT BIBLIOGRAPHY; this is a list of books or other printed (or manuscript) material on any chosen topic. A subject *bibliography* may aim at comprehensiveness, even completeness; or it may be a selective list of only such works as are most important, or most easily available, or most closely related to a book or article to which it may be attached. *Bibliographies* following a serious ESSAY, for example, may be merely a list of sources used by the writer of the ESSAY, or they may be meant to point out to the reader sources of additional information on the subject. In a related use, the word designates a list of works of a particular country, author, or printer ("national" and "trade" *bibliography*). *Bibliographies* of these kinds are sometimes called

ENUMERATIVE BIBLIOGRAPHIES. The process of making such lists either by students or by professional bibliographers is also referred to as *bibliography*.

In an analytical sense, as it is used by book collectors, bibliophiles, and textual scholars, *bibliography* means the history of book production, the history of writing, printing, binding, illustrating, and publishing. It involves a consideration of all the details of transmitting a text into book form. *Bibliography* in this sense is used by scholars in TEXTUAL CRITICISM—the employing of bibliographical evidence to help settle such questions as the veracity of a text, the order of publication, and the relative value of different editions of a book; whether certain parts of a book were intended to be a part of it originally or were added afterwards; whether a later edition was printed from an earlier; and other such problems, which often have an important literary bearing. This sort of bibliographical work has been much stressed in the twentieth century, especially by members of the London Bibliographical Society, one striking result being the discovery of the forged dates on certain QUARTOS of Shakespeare's PLAYS, actually printed in 1619 but assigned earlier dates on the title pages. (See TEXTUAL CRITICISM.)

Another use of the term *bibliography* is to denote the methods of work of student and author: reading, research, taking of notes, compilation of *bibliography*, preparation of manuscript for the press, publication, etc. These last two uses of the word are of special interest to advanced students who take university courses in *bibliography*.

"A *bibliography* of *bibliographies*" is a list of lists of works dealing with a given subject or subjects. An "annotated *bibliography*" is one in which some or all of the items listed are followed by brief description or critical comment.

[References: Fredson T. Bowers, *Bibliography and Textual Criticism* (1964), and *Principles of Bibliographical Description* (1949); A. Esdaile, *Manual of Bibliography*, 5th ed. (1981); Philip Gaskell, *A New Introduction to Bibliography* (1972); R. B. McKerrow, *An Introduction to Bibliography for Literary Students* (1927); H. B. Van Hoesen and F. K. Walter, *Bibliography* (1928).]

Bildungsroman: A NOVEL that deals with the development of a young person, usually from adolescence to maturity; it is frequently autobiographical. Dickens's *Great Expectations* and Samuel Butler's *The Way of All Flesh* are standard examples. *Bildungsroman* and APPRENTICESHIP NOVEL are virtually synonymous, both being derived from Goethe's *Wilhelm Meister's Apprenticeship*, but *Bildungsroman* is currently the more fashionable. See APPRENTICESHIP NOVEL.

[Reference: Randolph P. Shaffner, *The Apprenticeship Novel* (1984).]

Billingsgate: Coarse, foul, vulgar, violent, abusive language. The term is derived from the fact that the fishmongers in *Billingsgate* fish market in London achieved distinction for the scurrility of their language.

Biographical Fallacy: The interpretation of a work of art through too heavy a reliance on aspects of the maker's life as the basis for understanding. The more common term is GENETIC FALLACY.

Biography: A written account of a person's life, a life history. *Biography* derives its impetus from the commemorative instinct, the didactic or moralizing instinct, and, perhaps most important of all, the instinct of curiosity. LETTERS, MEMOIRS, DIARIES, JOURNALS, and AUTOBIOGRAPHIES, though they spring from these same desires, must be distinguished from *biography* proper. MEMOIRS, DIARIES, JOURNALS, and AUTOBIOGRAPHIES are closely related to each other in that each is recollection written down by the subject of the work. LETTERS are likely to be colored by various prejudices and purposes. The writer may or may not have been spontaneous in his or her correspondence. The editor may or may not be completely honest in the editing of the letters. Nearer the *biography* than any of these forms—and yet not an exact parallel—is the "life and times" book. In this kind of writing the author is concerned with two points: the life of the central figure and the period in which this figure lived. The writer may do a very fascinating book, interesting as well as instructive, but pure *biography,* in the more modern sense, does not look two ways; it centers its whole attention on the character and career of its subject.

In England the word *biography,* as a term denoting a form of writing, first came into use with Dryden, who, in 1683, defined it as "the history of particular men's lives." Today the term carries with it certain definite demands. It must be a history, but an accurate history; one that paints not only one aspect of the person but all important aspects. It must be the life of a "particular" person focused clearly on that person with more casual reference to the background of the social and political institutions of the subject's time. It must present the facts accurately and must make some effort to interpret these facts in such a way as to present character and habits of mind. It must emphasize personality, and this personality must be the central thesis of the book. If the biographer looks at the times, it must be only with the purpose of presenting a well-constructed and unified impression of the personality of the subject; if the biographer introduces LETTERS and ANECDOTES (as he or she surely will), it will be only such as reflect this central conception of personality. *Biography* today, then, may be defined as the accurate presentation of the life history from birth to death of an individual, along with an honest effort to interpret the life so as to offer a unified impression of the character, mind, and personality of the subject.

Just how this modern attitude differs from past conceptions may best be appreciated after a brief survey of the history of the *biography* as a literary type. English *biography* begins perhaps with the ancient runic inscriptions that celebrated the lives of heroes and recorded the exploits of deceased and legendary warriors. It is an element in such early ANGLO-SAXON verse as *Beowulf* and the *Widsith* fragment. And in these early manifestations we find what was, probably, the first conception of *biography*—the commemorative instinct, the "cenotaph-urge." These accounts were written to glorify.

This desire to commemorate greatness was, later on, united with a second purpose—the encouragement of morality. This purpose accounts for HAGIOGRAPHY, records of saints. Great men and women were commemorated for their virtue, their vices being conveniently overlooked. The lives of the saints occupied the attention of scholars in the monasteries. One list of early English historical material reports 1,277 writings, almost all of which were devoted to the glorification of one or another Irish or British saint. Even Bede (who died in 735) was little more than a hagiographer. It was not until Bishop

Asser wrote his *Life of Alfred the Great* (893) that anything closely resembling *biography* appears.

With Monk Eadmer of the twelfth century, English *biography* reached another milestone. Eadmer, in his *Vita Anselmi,* somehow managed to humanize his subject beyond the capability of former biographers. Introducing LETTERS into his NARRATIVE and reporting ANECDOTES and conversation, he wrote what may be the first pure *biography* in England. The fourteenth- and fifteenth-century *biography* gradually became somewhat less serious, less commemorative, and less didactic.

In the middle of the sixteenth century William Roper (1496–1578), More's son-in-law, wrote what is now most often referred to as the first English *biography,* his *Life of Sir Thomas More,* and George Cavendish (1500–1561) wrote his *Life of Wolsey.* With these two books, English *biography* had arrived as a recognized form of literature. The didactic purpose and the commemorative spirit were still present, but both books made a greater effort to avoid prejudice than previous writers had made. Both books resorted to EPISODE, ANECDOTE, and fairly vivid DIALOGUE. Both books devoted their space to the life of one person, the *Wolsey* beginning with the birth of the subject and ending with the death. Both books made an avowed declaration to follow the truth.

The seventeenth century was, in general, a time of brevities. The character sketch, the ANA, flourished. The CHARACTER was the contemporary enthusiasm. John Aubrey wrote his frank, gossipy *Minutes for Lives* as brief estimates of his contemporaries. Thomas Fuller wrote his *Worthies.* DIARIES, LETTERS, and MEMOIRS were plentiful—for example, the *Memoirs of Lady Fanshawe* and the *Memoirs of Colonel Hutchinson.* The first worthwhile AUTOBIOGRAPHY, perhaps, is that of Lord Herbert. But were it not for Izaak Walton's *Lives* (1640–1678), the century would be largely lacking in *biography.* Walton has been considered the first English professional biographer because he attempted the form deliberately and sustained it over a long period. Opposed to Walton and his biographical manner was Thomas Sprat, whose *Life of Cowley* appeared in 1668. It is to him that the Victorian demand for "decency" in *biography* seems largely due, for Sprat wrote a life that was a cold and dignified thing, formal and proper, emasculated and virtuous. "The tradition of 'discreet' biography," writes one critic, "owes its wretched origin to him."

If *biography* almost stood still during the seventeenth century, the eighteenth saw it march forward to the greatest accomplishment it has enjoyed. Boswell's *Life of Johnson* stands, probably for all time, at the head of any list of *biographies.* Two lesser luminaries were Roger North and William Mason—North (*Lives of the Norths*), who insisted that PANEGYRIC be avoided and wrote brightly and colloquially, and Mason (*Life and Writings of Gray*), who carried further the use of letters and largely left his reader to deduce the character of his subject by simply furnishing a wide range of illustrative material. Dr. Johnson himself dignified *biography* by developing a philosophy for the writing of the form and by his insistence that to a real biographer truth was much more important than respect for a dead man or his relatives. In his *Lives of the Poets* he himself practiced his doctrines. The writing of the supreme English *biography* was, however, reserved for Johnson's biographer—James Boswell. What is important is the new twist that Boswell gave to biographic method. He used most of the methods developed by earlier writers, but he wrought of them a new combination. Humor of a sort was here, as well as a great wealth of petty detail from which readers might make their own deductions; here, too, were the ANECDOTE and ANA of the seventeenth century; and here were intimacy and personal comment. To Boswell was given the privilege of making *biography* actual, real, convincing. In the work of Boswell, *biography* painted a living, breathing human being.

The Boswell tradition was in a fair way of being accepted when Victorianism, with its studiousness, its two-volume "life and letters" *biography*, its "authorized" biographies more or less controlled by relatives of the hero, blurred the picture. True enough, in the nineteenth century, there had been Tom Moore's *Life of Sheridan* and *Letters and Journals of Lord Byron*, as well as Lockhart's *Life of Scott*. But on the whole the freedom that Boswell had brought to this writing was restricted and confined by the Victorians. Religious orthodoxy, piety, and moral judgments were in the saddle. Tennyson spoke for the epoch when he thundered, "What business has the public to know about Byron's wildnesses? He has given them fine work and they ought to be satisfied."

The growing scientific attitude had become operative on *biography* by the early years of the twentieth century, and it brought with it not only a rejection of the polite reticence of the Victorian biographer but also a direct attack on the admiration of famous people. Lytton Strachey, in *Eminent Victorians* (1918) and *Queen Victoria* (1921), wrote lives that were brief, ironic, artistically shaped, and (his critics declare) too often inaccurate. Coupled with Strachey's method have been the assumptions of psychologists, particularly those of Freud, and our century has seen a host of biographical studies that are virtually attempts to read the hidden emotional life and even the unconscious experiences and motives of the subject. Van Wyck Brooks's studies of Mark Twain and of Henry James as the products of frustration are particularly significant for the American literary student, although Gamaliel Bradford's "psychographs" may have more enduring value as *biography*. Philip Guedalla in England and Richard Ellmann in America have made the twentieth century not only a period in which *biography* has been popular and widely read and written but also one in which at its best it has achieved high distinction. Literary *biography* has excelled, for some reason, in the portrayal of FICTION writers. To Ellmann's *biography* of James Joyce on the roll of honor, one could add Carlos Baker's life of Hemingway, Joseph Blotner's of Faulkner, and Matthew J. Bruccoli's of Fitzgerald.

[References: Waldo H. Dunn, *English Biography* (1916); Leon Edel, *Literary Biography* (1959); Mark Longaker, *English Biography in the Eighteenth Century* (1931); Harold Nicolson, *Development of English Biography* (1928); E. H. O'Neill, *A History of American Biography* (1961); D. A. Stauffer, *English Biography Before 1700* (1930).]

Black Humor: The use of the morbid and THE ABSURD for darkly comic purposes in modern FICTION and DRAMA. The term refers as much to the TONE of anger and bitterness as it does to the grotesque and morbid situations, which often deal with suffering, anxiety, and death. *Black humor* is a substantial element in the ANTI-NOVEL and the THEATER OF THE ABSURD. Joseph Heller's *Catch-22* is an almost archetypal example. Other novelists working in the tradition of *black humor* include Günter Grass, Mordecai Richler, Thomas

Pynchon, and Kurt Vonnegut. Successful playwrights using *black humor* include Edward Albee, Harold Pinter, and Eugene Ionesco, who called it "tragic farce."

[Reference: Max F. Schulz, *Black Humor Fiction in the Sixties* (1973).]

Black Letter: A heavy typeface with angular outlines and thick, ornamental serifs. Also called "Gothic," "church text," and "Old English," it was widely used in early printing. The term implies an early work, as in *"black letter book,"* where the kind of type indicates the age of the work.

Black Literature: A term for literary materials produced by Black authors. See AFRO-AMERICAN LITERATURE.

Black Mountain School: A label applied to certain writers —Charles Olson, Robert Creeley, and Robert Duncan among them—associated with Black Mountain College, an experimental school in North Carolina. They published the *Black Mountain Review,* which was highly influential in the PROJECTIVE VERSE movement. The school itself was a bold experiment in aesthetic education, which included architecture and the graphic arts as well as literature; in its idealism and spirit, the school resembled the BROOK FARM enterprise. Members of the group, including Josef Albers and Jonathan Williams, went on to other and different callings, but the energy of the *Black Mountain School* continues to make itself felt long after the institution as such has gone out of business. The sense of community and adventure persisted in the work of the members and in that of associated artists, such as Denise Levertov and Fielding Dawson, who had only a limited connection with the school itself. See PROJECTIVE VERSE.

[Reference: Martin Duberman, *Black Mountain: An Exploration in Community* (1972).]

Blank Verse: Unrhymed IAMBIC PENTAMETER. This form, generally accepted as that best adapted to dramatic VERSE in English, is commonly used for long POEMS whether dramatic, philosophic, or narrative. The freedom gained through lack of RHYME is offset by the demands for variety, which may be obtained by the skillful POET through a number of means: the shifting of the CAESURA, or pause, from place to place within the line; the shifting of the STRESS among syllables; the use of the RUN-ON LINE, which permits thought-grouping in large or small blocks (verse "paragraphs"); variation in tonal qualities by changing the level of DICTION from passage to passage; and, finally, the adaptation of the form to reflect differences in the speech of characters and in emotional expression.

Blank verse appears to have first found general favor in England as a medium for dramatic expression, but with Milton it was turned to EPIC use and since then has been employed in the writing of IDYLLS and LYRICS. The distinction of the first use of *blank verse* in English, though the claims are not quite clear, is usually given to Surrey, who used it in his translation of parts of the *Aeneid* (before 1547). The earliest dramatic use of *blank verse* in English was in Sackville and Norton's *Gorboduc,* 1561; the earliest use in DIDACTIC POETRY was in Gascoigne's *Steel Glass,* 1576; but it was only with Marlowe (prior to 1593) that the form first reached the hands of a master capable of using its range of possibilities and passing it on for Shakespeare and Milton to develop. After suffering something of an eclipse during the eighteenth century, *blank verse* enjoyed a new robustness in the work of Wordsworth, Tennyson, and Browning during the nineteenth century. (Some of the SONGS in Tennyson's *The Princess*—"Tears, Idle Tears," "O Swallow, Swallow," and "Now Sleeps the Crimson Petal"—belong to that extremely rare and engaging category, the *blank verse* LYRIC.) In the twentieth century memorable *blank verse* has been written by Yeats, Pound, Eliot, Frost, and— with particular distinction and dignity—Stevens.

[References: R. M. Alden, *An Introduction to Poetry* (1909); J. A. Symonds, *Blank Verse* (1895).]

Blason: Generally, a rationally ordered POEM of praise or blame, proceeding detail by detail. Specifically, in the form called *blason du corps feminin,* an ENCOMIUM for a beloved, beautiful woman. A contemporary example has been produced by O. B. Hardison. (The poem is "Ptolemy's Journal" in the volume *Pro Musica Antiqua*—1977.)

Bleed: A term used in printing to describe the trimming of the edges of a sheet or a page in such a way that some of the type or illustration is cut off. If an illustration is so printed that it comes to the very edge of the page, leaving no margin, it is said that the illustration *"bleeds off."* A page so printed or trimmed is called a *"bleed* page."

Block Books: Books printed from engraved blocks of wood, a practice followed in Flanders and Germany early in the fifteenth century. The printing was on only one side of the sheet, and, in being bound together to make a book, the sheets were often glued together to form pages printed on both sides.

Bloomsbury Group: A group of writers and thinkers, many of whom lived in Bloomsbury, a residential district near central London. These writers, of whom Virginia Woolf was the unofficial leader, began meeting early in the twentieth century and became a powerful force in British literary and intellectual life in the 1920s and 1930s. Their philosophy was derived from G. E. Moore's *Principia Ethica,* which asserts that "the pleasures of human intercourse and the enjoyment of beautiful objects" are the rational ends of social progress. Among the members of this informal and highly sophisticated group were John Maynard Keynes, Lytton Strachey, Clive Bell, Roger Fry, E. M. Forster, Duncan Grant, and David Garnett.

[References: Quentin Bell, *Bloomsbury* (1969); Leon Edel, *Bloomsbury: A House of Lions* (1979).]

Blues: An AFRO-AMERICAN FOLK SONG developed by the Negroes of the southern United States. A *blues* is characteristically short (three-line STANZA), melancholy in TONE, marked by frequent REPETITION, and sung slowly in a minor mode. Probably each *blues* was originally the composition of one person, but so readily are *blues* appropriated and changed that in practice they are a branch of FOLK LITERATURE. The class three-line *blues* STANZA is much like a HEROIC COUPLET with the first LINE repeated and, frequently, with a conspicuous CAESURA after the second foot of each line:

> Gonna lay my head right on the railroad track,
> Gonna lay my head right on the railroad track,
> 'Cause my baby, she won't take me back.

Some of Pope's lines can be made into admirable *blues* LYRICS:

> A heap of dust alone remains of thee,
> A heap of dust alone remains of thee,
> 'Tis all thou art, and all the proud shall be!

Having begun in the lively environment of AFRO-AMERICAN SONG, the *blues* have now grown in scope beyond the orbits implied by both "Afro-American" and "song," so that Jack Kerouac could call a book of POEMS *Mexico City Blues: 242 Choruses.*

[References: Imamu Amiri Baraka, *Blues People: Negro Music in White America* (1963); S. B. Charters, *The Roots of the Blues* (1981); W. C. Handy, *Blues: An Anthology* (1926).]

Bluestockings: A term applied to women of pronounced intellectual interests. It gained currency after 1750 as a result of its application (for reasons not now easy to establish beyond dispute) to a group of women of literary and intellectual tastes who held in London assemblies or "conversations" to which "literary and ingenious men" were invited. It was the English equivalent of the French *salon.* There was no formal organization, and the personnel of the group changed from time to time, so that no exhaustive "membership" list can be given. Among the *bluestockings* were Mrs. Elizabeth Montagu (the "Queen of the Blues"), Hannah More, Fanny Burney, and Mrs. Hester Chapone. Horace Walpole was one of the male "members," and Dr. Samuel Johnson, Edmund Burke, and David Garrick were at times frequent visitors. The group's activities were directed toward encouraging an interest in literature, fostering the recognition of literary genius (see PRIMITIVSM), and hence helping to remove the odium that had attached to earlier "learned ladies." It has been used as a term of opprobrium to describe pretentiously intellectual and pedantic women.

[References: Walter Sidney Scott, *The Bluestocking Ladies* (1947); C. B. Tinker, *The Salon and English Letters* (1915).]

Blurb: A term applied in the book trade to the hyperbolically encomiastic descriptive matter printed on the jackets of new books, usually extravagant in its claims. The term was invented by Gelett Burgess before the First World War.

Boasting Poem: A POEM or section of a poem in which characters boast of their mighty exploits; frequently found in oral literatures and in works such as BALLADS and EPICS. In the BIBLE David is said to have slain his ten thousands; in English perhaps the clearest examples appear in *Beowulf,* in passages such as Unferth's boast and Beowulf's account of his slaying of Grendel. An American FOLK SONG called the "The Tin Angel Brag" is a recent example:

> I was born about ten thousand years ago,
> There ain't nothin' in the world that I don't know

> I saw Peter, Paul, and Moses playin' ring
> around the roses,
> And I'll whup the guy what says it isn't so.
>
> Queen Elizabeth she fell in love with me,
> We was married in Milwaukee secretly,
> But I got tired of sugar and went off with
> General Hooker
> And was fightin' skeeters down in Tennessee.

Bob and Wheel: Terms invented during the nineteenth century to describe a phenomenon peculiar to the revival of ALLITERATIVE verse in the later MIDDLE ENGLISH PERIOD: after several unrhymed alliterative LINES, the POEM (most often a MEDIEVAL ROMANCE) shifts into a set of rhymed lines, the first, or *"bob,"* very short and the remainder, or *"wheel,"* typically a short-lined rhymed QUATRAIN.

Bombast: Originally, any sort of ornamental but unnecessary padding; PLEO-NASM. Now mostly limited to ranting, insincere and extravagant language, and exaggerated grandiloquence. Elizabethan TRAGEDY, especially early SENE-CAN plays, contains much bombastic style, marked by extravagant IMAGERY. A good example comes from *Hamlet:*

> Roasted in wrath and fire,
> And thus o'er-sized with coagulate gore,
> With eyes like carbuncles, the hellish Pyrrhus
> Old grandsire Priam seeks.

Bon Mot: A witty REPARTEE or statement. A clever saying. Sometimes abbreviated to "mot."

Book Sizes: To understand some of the terms used in describing *book sizes,* such as QUATRO and OCTAVO, it is helpful to visualize a sheet of paper, "foolscap" size, 17 inches by 13½ inches.

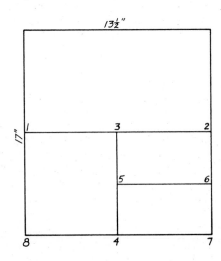

When this sheet is folded along 1–2, 3–4, and 5–6, the resulting folds mark off the sizes of pages. Thus 1–2–7–8 represents one of two leaves cut from the original foolscap and is, therefore, a FOLIO (Latin for *leaf*) sheet or page; 2–3–4–7 represents one-fourth of the original sheet and, therefore, gives us a QUARTO page; 2–3–5–6 constitutes one-eighth of the original and gives us an OCTAVO page. A *book size,* then, is determined by the number of book leaves cut from a single large sheet. To determine the number of pages cut from the original sheet, count the number of pages to a SIGNATURE; this may often be done by noting the occurrence of the SIGNATURE marks (themselves sometimes called SIGNATURES) that appear at regular intervals at the foot of a page. These symbols, usually numerals or letters, may be found regularly in early printed books and sometimes in those recently printed. They indicate the beginning of new SIGNATURES. The number of leaves (not pages) in a single SIGNATURE shows the number of leaves cut from the original sheet and is, therefore, the indication of the book size. When there are two leaves to the SIGNATURE, the book is a FOLIO; when there are four leaves, it is a QUARTO; and so on. The following table shows the principle as it manifests itself in the more frequently used book sizes:

No. of Folds	No. of Leaves	Pages to Signature	Name
1	2	4	FOLIO
2	4	8	QUARTO (4to)
3	8	16	OCTAVO (8vo)
	12	24	DUODECIMO (12mo)
4	16	32	sixteenmo (16mo)
5	32	64	thirty-twomo (32mo)
6	64	128	sixty-fourmo (64mo)

This would all be very simple, but for the fact that in modern printing there is a variety of sizes of original stock. In addition to the "foolscap 8vo" in the example, we may have Post 8vo, Demy 8vo, Crown 8vo, Royal 8vo, etc., the terms Demy, Crown, and the others referring to varying sizes of original sheets that, in turn, give varying sizes of pages. So complicated has the whole question become that expert bibliographers urge more attention to the position of the watermark on the page (a guide to book measurements too complicated to discuss here) and even then frequently give up the question in despair. Publishers and librarians arbitrarily use 12mo, OCTAVO, etc., for books of certain sizes regardless of the number of pages to the signature.

Bourgeois Drama: A nearly obsolete term applied to PLAYS that show the life of the common folk and the middle class rather than that of the courtly or the rich. Such widely differing kinds of plays as Heywood's *Interludes, Gammer Gurton's Needle,* Dekker's *Shoemaker's Holiday* (REALISTIC COMEDY,) and Lillo's *The London Merchant* (domestic tragedy) are embraced in the term, which in a broad sense refers to the development of middle-class subject matter.

Bourgeois Literature: Literature produced primarily to appeal to the middle-class reader. Compare BOURGEOIS DRAMA, wherein *bourgeois* does not denote the class of readers but the social sphere of the subject and action.

Bourgeois Tragedy: PLAYS with somber and often pathetic PLOTS dealing with the life of middle-class PROTAGONISTS. The term, synonymous with DOMESTIC TRAGEDY, embraces plays as different as O'Neill's *Beyond the Horizon,* Lillo's *The London Merchant,* and Arthur Miller's *The Death of a Salesman.* See DOMESTIC TRAGEDY.

Bouts-rimés: A kind of literary game in which players are given lists of rhyming words and are expected to write impromptu VERSES with the RHYMES in the order given. The game has been popular in France since the seventeenth century; it was a popular pastime of the BLUESTOCKINGS in England; and clubs devoted to it sprang up in Scotland in the nineteenth century.

Bowdlerize: To expurgate a piece of writing by omitting material considered offensive or indecorous. *Bowdlerize* derives from Thomas Bowdler, an English physician, who published (in 1818) an expurgated edition of Shakespeare.

Box Set: A stage set that realistically represents a room with a ceiling and three walls, the FOURTH WALL being imagined as existing between the audience and the actors.

Brachycatalectic: A VERSE that lacks two syllables, normally unstressed. If what is lacking amounts to a PYRRHIC, then a whole FOOT is omitted. Usually, however, what is omitted is the unstressed part of an ANAPEST or DACTYL, as in Yeats's LINE "Hearts with one purpose alone" (in a generally anapestic environment).

Braggadocio: A vain, pretentious, noisy, and boasting braggart who is actually a craven coward. Although the name comes from such a character in Spenser's *The Faerie Queene,* the *braggadocio* is really a STOCK CHARACTER with a long history stretching back to Greek and Roman COMEDY. See MILES GLORIOSUS, ALAZON.

Brahmins: Members of the highest caste among the Hindus. The name is applied to the highly cultivated and socially exclusive families of New England, particularly in the nineteenth century. In his novel *Elsie Venner,* Oliver Wendell Holmes uses the term to characterize "the harmless, inoffensive, untitled aristocracy," particularly of Boston and its environs, which became "a caste by the repetition of the same influences generation after generation." The term is customarily used derisively. John P. Marquand's character George Apley in *The Late George Apley* is a typical *Brahmin* of relatively late vintage.

Breton Lay: The term refers both to the relatively brief FORM of the medieval French ROMANCES, professed to have been sung by Breton minstrels on Celtic themes, and to the English medieval POEMS written in imitation of such French works. See BRETON ROMANCE and LAY.

Breton Romance: A medieval French METRICAL ROMANCE, emphasizing love as the central force in the PLOT. *Breton romances* drew on the traditions of COURTLY LOVE and frequently dealt with LEGENDS such as the Tristan and Iseult stories or the Arthurian materials. "The Franklin's Tale," in Chaucer's *Canterbury Tales,* is a short FORM of the *Breton romance* called the BRETON LAY.

Breve: The name of the symbol (⌣) used to indicate a short syllable in the SCANSION of QUANTITATIVE VERSE and an unstressed syllable in ACCENTUAL-SYLLABIC VERSE.

Breviary: A collection of lessons, calendars, and outlines for services to aid Roman Catholic priests in reciting the Divine Office for each day and in discharging other churchly responsibilities. The *Breviary* contains the Church calendar, Psalter, collects and lessons, collects for the Saints' Days, hours of the Virgin, and burial services, but not the communion service of Mass.

Brief: A condensed statement, a résumé, of the main arguments or ideas presented in a speech or piece of writing. In legal practice, a formal summary of laws and authorities bearing on the main points of a case; in church history, a papal letter less formal than a bull.

British Library (earlier, **British Museum**): Of importance to students of literature since it houses probably the most important library in the world, the collection, founded in 1753 through a bequest from Sir Hans Sloane, now embraces over 6,000,000 printed volumes, 10,000 INCUNABULA, and 75,000 manuscripts. It is located in Great Russell Street, in Bloomsbury, London. The *British Library* is particularly wealthy in its collection of manuscripts including, besides the famous Harleian and Cottonian MSS., a series of documents from the third century to the present. Particularly noteworthy are its collections comprising English historical CHRONICLES, ANGLO-SAXON materials, charters, Arthurian romances, the Burney Collection of CLASSICAL manuscripts, Greek papyri, the genealogical records of English families, and Irish, French, and Italian manuscripts. From time to time it has been given by bequest special libraries such as Archbishop Cranmer's Collection, the Thomas Collection, the C. M. Cracherode Collection, and the Sir Joseph Banks Collection. Other important features are its assortment of items from American, Chinese and Oriental, Hebrew, and Slavonic literatures. According to the British copyright law, the *Library* receives copies of every publication seeking copyright protection. The result is an astonishing grouping together in one place of the learning and literatures of the world.

Broadside Ballad: Soon after the development of printing in England, BALLADS were prepared for circulation on FOLIO sheets, printed on one side only, two pages to the sheet, and two columns to the page. Because of their manner of publication, these were called *broadsides*. These BALLADS ranged from reproductions of old popular BALLADS of literary distinction to semi-illiterate screeds with little poetic quality. These *broadsides* had great variety of subject matter: accidents, dying speeches of criminals, miraculous events, religious and political harangues. Many were satirical, with unscrupulous personal invective. In the sixteenth century, the heyday of their popularity, they served, as one critic states, as a "people's YELLOW JOURNAL."
  [References: William Chappell and J. W. Ebsworth, eds., *The Roxburghe Ballads,* 9 v. (1871–99); H. E. Rollins, ed., *The Pack of Autolycus* (1927, reprinted 1969), and *A Pepysian Garland* (1922, reprinted 1971).]

Brochure: Originally a small work or PAMPHLET with its pages stitched or wired, not bound; now any relatively brief work regardless of type of binding.

Broken Rhyme: The breaking of a word at the end of a LINE for the sake of a RHYME. The novelty and disruption of this rare device have limited its use largely to various sorts of comic VERSE, including SATIRE and DOGGEREL. Instances of such use turn up in Donne's Satires III and IV:

> Gracchus loves all as one, and thinks that so
> As women do in divers countries go
> In divers habits, yet are still one kind,
> So doth, so is religion; and this blind-
> ness too much light breeds. . . .

>   [I]t pleased my destiny
> (Guilty of my sin of going), to think me
> As prone to all ill, and of good as forget-
> ful, as proud, as lustful, and as much in debt. . . .

E. E. Cummings indulged in a great deal of *broken rhyme* and went so far as to use two broken words to achieve CONSONANCE in a rhyme-slot (the "vac" of "vacuum" and the "democ" of "democracy"). More recently, the songwriter Arlo Guthrie has this *broken rhyme* in a LYRIC: "I don't want to die, / I just want to ride my motorcy- / cle." In the nineteenth century Gerard Manley Hopkins bodily explored the use of *broken rhyme* in a wholly serious POEM, "The Windhover," the first LINE of which contains a striking example:

> I caught this morning's minion, king-
>   dom of daylight's dauphin, dapple-dawn-drawn Falcon, in his
>   riding
> Of the rolling level underneath him steady air, and striding
> High there, how he rung upon the rein of a wimpling wing.

See also FUSED RHYME.

Brook Farm: A UTOPIAN experiment in communal living, sponsored by the Transcendental Club of Boston. The farm, located at West Roxbury, Massachusetts, then nine miles from Boston, was taken over in 1841 by a joint stock company, headed by George Ripley and called, in full, "The Brook Farm Institute of Agriculture and Education." The basic reasons for the scheme were efforts to provide for the residents opportunity for cultural pursuits and leisure at little cost, the farm being supposed, through the rotation of labor of the members, to support the residents who, in most of their time, were to be free to attend lectures, read, write, and converse. The project was influenced by the doctrines of François Fourier and Robert Owen. While many transcendentalists were interested in the enterprise, it was not the outgrowth of a general activity on their part. Hawthorne was there for a short period (see *The Blithedale Romance*) as were other prominent leaders, but such personages as Emerson, Alcott, and Thoreau never actively took part. Dissension among the members, the discovery that the soil was inadequately fertile, and the burning of a new and uninsured central "phalanstery" (the name for a dwelling at such a community) were some of the reasons that in 1846 brought about the end of the project. See TRANSCENDENTALISM.

[References: Edith Roelker Curtis, *A Season in Utopia: The Story of Brook Farm* (1961); Edwin James Sceery, *Transcendentalism: A Story of Brook Farm* (1940); Lindsay Swift, *Brook Farm* (1906, reprinted 1961).]

Bucolic: A term used for PASTORAL writing that deals with rural life in a manner rather formal and fanciful. The plural *bucolics* refers collectively to the PASTORAL literature of such writers as Theocritus and Virgil. In the present loose usage the expression connotes simply POETRY with a rustic background—as in W. H. Auden's mixed sequence called *Bucolics*—and is not necessarily restricted to VERSE with the conventional PASTORAL elements. See PASTORAL.

Buffoon: A comic character—akin to the CLOWN, fool, and jester—given to raillery, boasting, and indecency.

Burden: A CHORUS or REFRAIN.

Burlesque: A form of COMEDY characterized by ridiculous exaggeration. This distortion is secured in a variety of ways: the sublime may be made absurd; honest emotions may be turned to SENTIMENTALITY; a serious subject may be treated frivolously or a frivolous subject seriously. The essential quality that makes for *burlesque* is the discrepancy between subject matter and STYLE. That is, a STYLE ordinarily dignified may be used for nonsensical matter, or a STYLE very nonsensical may be used to ridicule a weighty subject. *Burlesque*, as a form of art, manifests itself in sculpture, painting, and even architecture, as well as in literature. It has an ancient lineage in world literature: an author of uncertain identity used it in the *Battle of the Frogs and Mice* to TRAVESTY Homer. Aristophanes made *burlesque* popular, and in France, under Louis XIV, nothing was sacred to the satirist. Chaucer in *Sir Thopas* burlesqued MEDIEVAL ROMANCE as did Cervantes in *Don Quixote*. One of the best known uses of *burlesque* in DRAMA is Gay's *The Beggar's Opera*. In recent use the term—already broad—has been broadened still further to include stage entertainments consistings of SONGS, skits, and dances, usually raucous. A distinction between *burlesque* and PARODY is often made, in which *burlesque* is a TRAVESTY of a literary FORM and PARODY a TRAVESTY of a particular work. It has been suggested that PARODY works by keeping a targeted style constant while lowering the subject, *burlesque* or TRAVESTY by keeping a targeted subject constant while lowering the style. Since "travesty" is connected to "transvestite," the procedure may be expected to change the clothing, so to speak, or the style of a normally dignified subject. See TRAVESTY, PARODY.
[References: Richmond P. Bond, *English Burlesque Poetry, 1700–1750* (1932); V. C. Clinton-Baddeley, *The Burlesque Tradition in the English Theatre after 1660* (1952); Peter Hobley Davison, *Popular Appeal in English Drama to 1850* (1982); John D. Jump, *Burlesque* (1972); George Kitchin, *A Survey of Burlesque and Parody in English* (1931).]

Burletta: Term used in the late eighteenth century for a variety of musical dramatic forms, somewhat like the BALLAD-OPERA, the EXTRAVAGANZA, and the PANTOMINE. One of its sponsors (George Colman, the younger) asserted that the proper use of the word was for "a DRAMA in RHYME, entirely musical—

a short comick piece consisting of recitative and singing, wholly accompanied, more or less, by the orchestra." The form persisted into the nineteenth century, when Henry Mayhew was one of the practitioners.

Burns Stanza: A variant form of the TAIL-RHYME STANZA, named for Robert Burns who used it frequently. It consists of six lines rhyming *aaabab* with TETRAMETER in the *a*-lines and DIMETER or TRIMETER in the *b*-lines. The following STANZA from Burns's "Lines to John Lapraik" illustrates the *Burns stanza:*

> Your critic-folk may cock their nose
> And say, "How can you e'er propose,
> You wha ken hardly verse frae prose,
>   To mak a sang?"
> But, by your leave, my learned foes,
>   Ye're may be wrang.

Buskin: A boot, thick-soled and reaching halfway to the knee, worn by Greek tragedians with the purpose of increasing their stature, even as comedians wore SOCKS for the opposite purpose. By association *buskin* has come to mean TRAGEDY. Milton used "the buskin'd stage" and "Jonson's learned SOCK" to characterize TRAGEDY and COMEDY respectively. The Greek for *buskin*, CO-THURNUS, is used both for *buskin* and for the dignified tragic spirit.

C

Cabal: An English word derived from the French *cabale* ("cabala") and given added impact by a false or popular etymology construing it as an ACRONYM formed from the first letters of the names of Charles II's unpopular ministry, Clifford, Ashley, Buckingham, Arlington, and Lauderdale; hence an ACROSTIC.

Cacophony: The opposite of EUPHONY; a harsh, unpleasant combination of sounds or tones. Though most specifically a term used in the CRITICISM of POETRY, the word is also employed to indicate any disagreeable sound effect in other forms of writing. *Cacophony* may be an unconscious flaw in the poet's music, or it may be used consciously for effect, as Browning and Hardy often used it. *Cacophony* is an intractable term because the classification of a given sound or combination as harsh tends to be relative and subjective. Words with harsh meanings will sound harsh whether or not they possess any acoustic features that are correspondingly harsh. Even so, it is difficult to imagine anyone's regarding such a monstrosity as "sphygmomanometer" as anything but cacophonous. See EUPHONY.

Cadence: In one sense the sound pattern that precedes a marked pause or the end of a sentence, making it interrogatory, hortatory, pleading, or such. In another sense it is the RHYTHM established in the sequence of stressed and unstressed syllables in a phrasal unit. In a third and broader sense it is the rhythmical movement of VERSE or PROSE when it is read aloud, the modulation produced by the rise and fall of the voice, the RHYTHM that sounds the "inner tune" of a sentence or a VERSE. *Cadence* is customarily used to refer to a larger and looser group of syllables than the formal, metrical movement of regular ACCENTUAL-SYLLABIC VERSE. Modern POETS, such as Pound and William Carlos Williams, urge the substitution of *cadence* for the conventional prosodic devices, following the ground-breaking example of Whitman. See FREE VERSE.

Caesura (or Cesura): A pause or break in a LINE of VERSE. Originally, in CLASSICAL literature, the *caesura* characteristically divided a FOOT between two words. Usually the *caesura* has been placed near the middle of a VERSE. Some POETS, however, have sought diversity of rhythmical effect by placing the *caesura* anywhere from near the beginning of a line to near the end. Examples of variously placed *caesuras* are shown in these lines by Marvell.

> Had we but world enough, || and time
> This coyness, lady, || were no crime.
> We would sit down, || and think which way
> To walk, || and pass our long love's day.
> Thou by the Indian Ganges' side
> Shouldst rubies find; || I by the tide
> Of Humber would complain. || I would
> Love you ten years before the flood,
> And you should, if you please, || refuse
> Till the conversion of the Jews.

Viewed in another sense, the *caesura* is an instrument of prose RHYTHM that cuts across and, by varying, modifies the regularity of accentual VERSE. The interplay of PROSE sense and VERSE demand can be observed in the preceding selection. Metricists who follow closely the classical distinctions use *caesura* to indicate a pause within a FOOT and DIERESIS to indicate a pause that coincides with the end of the FOOT. This distinction is seldom made in English METRICS, where *caesura* is employed as the generic term. Strict constructionists have also insisted that the *caesura* ought to be the single principal pause in a given line; but, just as some lines have no *caesura*, others may have two or more. If the *caesura* comes after an unstressed syllable, as in

> To err is human, ‖ to forgive, divine.

it is called a *feminine caesura*.

Calendar: Any of various systems for demarcating the segments of time, as days, weeks, months, and years; or a table that lists such arbitrary divisions. The term is occasionally used in literature when some temporal structure is given a work, as in Spenser's *Shepheardes Calendar,* which consists of twelve POEMS entitled for the twelve months. See ALMANAC.

Calligraphy: The art of beautiful writing in the sense of penmanship. In literature the significance of the term springs from the development of the art during the Middle Ages when the monks gave much attention to copying ancient manuscripts.

Calvinism: The great religious conflict of medieval times was between AUGUSTINIANISM, which exalted the glory of God at the expense of dignity of human beings (stressing original sin and the necessity of divine grace), and PELAGIANISM, which asserted the original innocence of human beings and their ability to develop moral and spiritual power through their own efforts. ARMINIANISM was a compromise between these positions, insisting upon the part both God and human beings must play in human redemption. *Calvinism* was a RENAISSANCE representative of the Augustinian point of view.

Some understanding of the teachings of *Calvinism*—the charter of which is John Calvin's famous *Institutes of the Christian Religion* (1536)—is important to the student of literature. The essential doctrines of the system are frequently summed up in the famous Five Points: (1) total depravity, the natural inability of human beings to exercise free will, since they inherited corruption from Adam's fall; (2) unconditional election, which manifests itself through God's election of those to be saved, despite their inability to perform saving works; (3) prevenient and irresistible grace, made available in advance but only to the elect; (4) the perseverance of saints, the predetermined elect inevitably persevering in the path of holiness; and (5) limited atonement, human corruption being partially atoned for by Christ, this atonement being provided the elect through the Holy Spirit, giving them the power to attempt to obey God's will as it is revealed in the BIBLE.

This system developed both zeal and intolerance on the part of the elect. It fostered education, however, which in early New England was regarded as a religious duty, and thereby profoundly affected the development of

American culture. To this attitude of the Calvinistic PURITANS may be traced much of the inspiration for such things as the founding of many colleges and universities, the creation of a system of public schools, and the great activity of early printing presses in America—as well as the development of religious sects. Historically, especially in Europe, it is probable that the political effects of *Calvinism* have encouraged freedom and popular government. According to the theories of certain early modern historians and sociologists (for example, Max Weber), the "Protestant ethic," specifically in the form of *Calvinism*, generated an emphasis on industry and frugality, which in turn generated the conditions that made modern capitalism possible.

In New England the COVENANT THEOLOGY early softened and modified *Calvinism*, but the term PURITAN in America usually refers, at least in a philosophical sense, to a belief in the doctrines of *Calvinism*. See AUGUSTINIAN-ISM, ARIANISM, ARMINIANISM, COVENANT THEOLOGY, PELAGIANISM.

[References: G. P. Fisher, *History of Christian Doctrine* (1896); John Thomas McNeill, *The History and Character of Calvinism* (1954); William Shurr, *Rappaccini's Children: American Writers in a Calvinist World* (1981); Page Smith, *As a City upon a Hill* (1966); R. H. Tawney, *Religion and the Rise of Capitalism* (1926); Max Weber, *The Protestant Ethic and the Spirit of Capitalism* (tr. 1930).]

Calypso: A type of music originated in the West Indies, particularly Trinidad. It is a BALLAD-like improvisation in African RHYTHMS. The singers, who compose as they sing, frequently deal with current topics, often in a satiric manner. The pinnacle of *calypso* invention came in a contest in 1937 on the assigned topic of the fate of Edward VIII; the winning improvisation concluded, "You can't abdicate and eat it too."

Camera Eye Narration: A kind of storytelling, resembling the "Camera Eye" sections of John Dos Passos' *U.S.A.* (1936), in which the writing gives the appearance or impression of being thoroughly objective, realistic, and anatomical.

Canon: In its simplest sense, a standard of judgment; a criterion. *Canon* is applied to the authorized or accepted list of books belonging in the Christian BIBLE by virtue of having been declared to be divinely inspired. APOCRYPHAL books are uncanonical. A similar use of the term is illustrated in the phrase "the Saints' *Canon*," the list of saints actually authorized or "canonized" by the Church. The term is often extended to mean the accepted list of books of any author, such as Shakespeare. Thus, *Macbeth* belongs without doubt in the *canon* of Shakespeare's work, while *Sir John Oldcastle*, though printed as Shakespeare's soon after his death, is not canonical, because the evidence of Shakespeare's authorship is unconvincing.

Canso: A Provençal love SONG, usually in STANZAS, sung by the TROU-BADOURS. Compare with the variant form CANZO, which is peculiar to northern France.

Cant: Insincere, specious language calculated to give the impression of seriousness or religious fervor. In critical writing the term is used to signify the language and phraseology characteristic of a profession or art, as "the peda-gogue's *cant*," "the artist's *cant*." In this sense of a special language, the term indicates any technical or special vocabulary or dialect, as "thieves' *cant*," "beggars' *cant*." More loosely still, the word signifies any insincere, superficial display of language, planned to convey an impression of piety and conviction but devoid of genuine emotion of feeling; that is, language used chiefly for display or effect. See JARGON.

Canticle: Originally, a prose chant or hymn taken verbatim from a Biblical text; later applied to any CHANT, such as St. Francis's "Cantico del Sole," and, in modern usage, to any POEM, such as Edith Sitwell's "Canticle of the Rose," with its explicit genesis in the rhythms and symbols of historical religion, and a popular song by Paul Simon called "Canticle." *Canticle* is also used to translate the Italian *cantica* (plural *cantiche*), which indicates a grouping of CANTOS, as in Dante's *Divine Comedy* (the *Inferno*, for example, is one of the three *cantiche* or *canticles* of the poem).

Canto: A section or division of a long POEM. Derived from the Latin *cantus* (SONG), the word originally signified a section of a NARRATIVE POEM of such length as to be sung by a minstrel in one singing. The books of Spenser's *The Faerie Queene* and Byron's *Childe Harold's Pilgrimage* are divided into *cantos*. Early in this century, Ezra Pound published pieces at first called "can-tos of a poem of some length" and eventually called that POEM simply *The Cantos*.

Canzo: A love SONG, sung by the TROUVÈRES of northern France. Compare with CANSO.

Canzone: A lyrical POEM, a SONG or BALLAD. In several ways similar to the MADRIGAL, the *canzone* is a short POEM consisting of equal STANZAS and an ENVOY of fewer lines than the STANZA. It is impossible to be specific about the VERSE FORM since different writers have wrought wide variations in struc-ture. The number of lines per STANZA ranges from seven to twenty, and the ENVOY from three to ten. Petrarch's *canzoni* usually consisted of five or six STANZAS and the ENVOY. In general it may be said that the *canzone* resembles the CHANT ROYAL, though its conventions are less fixed. The *canzone* is thought to have originated in Provence during the Middle Ages, and Giraud de Borneil is credited with having first evolved the pattern, which has proved very popular in Italy. Others than Petrarch who have written *canzoni* are Dante, Tasso, Leopardi, Chiabrera, and Marchetti. Frequent subjects used were love, nature, and a wide range of emotional reactions to life, particularly if sad. The term and the aspects of the medieval FORM it designated are used by contemporary poets on occasion for POEMS of considerable complexity.

Caricature: Writing that exaggerates certain individual qualities of a person and produces a BURLESQUE, ridiculous effect. *Caricature* more frequently is associated with drawing than with writing, since the related literary terms—SATIRE, BURLESQUE, and PARODY—are more commonly used. *Caricature*, un-like the highest SATIRE, is likely to treat merely personal qualities; although, like SATIRE, it also lends itself to the ridicule of political, religious, and social foibles. A work of FICTION, history, or BIOGRAPHY that traffics in excessive distortion of exaggeration may be dismissed as a *caricature.*

[Reference: T. Wright, *History of Caricature and Grotesque in Literature and Art* (1865).]

Carmen Figuratum: A FIGURE POEM, a POEM so written that the form of the printed words suggests the subject matter; the device is not common in English and is sometimes considered a form of false WIT. Examples are Herbert's "Easter Wings," the humorous "long and sad tail of the Mouse," in *Alice in Wonderland,* Dylan Thomas's "Vision and Prayer," and all of the poems in a book called *Types of Shape* by John Hollander. Since any piece of writing looks like something and has a graphic, visual aspect, any kind of writing may partake of figuration, as when Keats uses capitals to draw attention to the "M" of mountains and the "V" of valleys, when Cummings writes about the "mOon," or (a specimen unearthed by W. K. Wimsatt) a magazine piece points to the answerable style of "bOsOm." Figuration of one sort or another has also been used by A. R. Ammons (particularly in keyboard games included in *The Snow Poems*) and Albert Goldbarth. The term *Calligramme* is also applied to FIGURE, POEMS, after Guillaume Apollinaire's collection entitled *Calligrammes* (1918).

Carol (*Carole*): In medieval France a *carole* was a dance. The term later was applied to the accompanying SONG. The leader sang the STANZAS, the other dancers singing the REFRAIN. The *carole* became very popular and in the twelfth and thirteenth centuries, spreading through other European countries, was instrumental in extending the influence of the French LYRIC. Later, *carol* came to mean any joyous SONG, then a HYMN of religious joy, and finally a Christmas HYMN in particular. Some *carols,* such as "Joseph was an old man," were definitely popular, belonging to the culture of the folk, while later ones, such as Charles Wesley's "Hark, the Herald Angels Sing," are the product of a rather more sophisticated literary effort. The Christmas HYMN is called a *noël* in France.

[References: Douglas Brice, *The Folk-Carol of England* (1967); Percy Dearmer et al., eds., *The Oxford Book of Carols* (1928); R. L. Greene, ed., *The Early English Carols* (1935); E. B. Reed, ed., *Christmas Carols Printed in the Sixteenth Century* (1932); Erik Routhey, *The English Carol* (1958).]

Caroline: Applied in general to the age of Charles I of England (1625–1642) and in particular to the spirit of the court of Charles. Thus, *Caroline* might cover all the literature of the time, both Cavalier and PURITAN, or it might be used more specifically for writings by the royalist group, such as the CAVALIER LYRICISTS. *Caroline* literature was in some senses a carry-over from the ELIZABETHAN and JACOBEAN periods. Melancholy not only characterized the work of the METAPHYSICAL POETS but permeated the writings of both the conflicting groups, PURITAN and Cavalier. Drama was decadent; ROMANTICISM was in decline; CLASSICISM was advancing; the scientific spirit was growing in spite of the absorption of the people in violent religious controversies. It was in *Caroline* times that the PURITAN migration to America was heaviest. The *Caroline* Age was the last segment of the RENAISSANCE in England, if the COMMONWEALTH is considered an interregnum between the

RENAISSANCE and the NEOCLASSIC PERIOD. See RENAISSANCE for a sketch of the literature; see BAROQUE, JACOBEAN, CAVALIER LYRICISTS; see also "Caroline Age" in the *Outline of Literary History.*

Carpe Diem: "Seize the day." The phrase was used by Horace and has come to be applied generally to literature, especially to LYRIC POEMS, which exemplify the spirit of "Let us eat and drink, for tomorrow we shall die." The THEME was very common in sixteenth- and seventeenth-century English love POETRY; lover-poets continually were exhorting their mistresses to yield to love while they still had their youth and beauty, as in Robert Herrick's famous

> Gather ye rosebuds while ye may,
> Old Time is still a-flying;
> And this same flower that smiles today,
> Tomorrow will be dying.

Perhaps justly the most famous English example is Andrew Marvell's "To His Coy Mistress." Persisting into modern times and gaining in depth and subtlety, the theme figures in Henry James's *The Ambassadors* and "The Beast in the Jungle" and—as is almost too obvious to need pointing out—in Saul Bellow's *Seize the Day.*

Catalexis: Incompleteness of the last FOOT of a LINE; truncation by omission of one or two final syllables; the opposite of ANACRUSIS. *Catalexis* secures variety of metrical effects. The term ACATALECTIC is used to designate particular lines where *catalexis* is *not* employed. Such a pedantic double negative seems a needlessly fanciful way of saying that verse is not abnormal. Indeed, if a piece is generally regular, there is no use in saying that all the lines are ACATALECTIC. The term is best reserved for lines that are alternately *catalectic* and ACATALECTIC, as in Poe's description of the rhythm and meter of "The Raven": "The former is trochaic—the latter is octameter acatalectic, alternating with heptameter catalectic repeated in the refrain of the fifth verse, and terminating with tetrameter catalectic." (To Poe's credit, the next sentence begins, "Less pedantically. . . .") In the following lines by Thomas Hood, written in DACTYLIC DIMETER, the second and fourth are *catalectic* because the second FOOT of each lacks the two unaccented syllables that would normally complete the DACTYL. The first and third lines, in which the unaccented syllables are *not* cut off and which therefore are metrically complete, are ACATALECTIC.

> One more unfortunate,
> Weary of breath,
> Rashly importunate,
> Gone to her death!

Catalexis is also applied to the truncation of an initial unstressed syllable; the resulting line is called HEADLESS. *Catalexis* of two syllables, as in the lines by Hood, is sometimes called BRACHYCATALEXIS.

Catalog: A list of people, things, or attributes. *Catalogs,* sometimes extended to great length, are characteristic of much primitive literature and of much that is not so primitive as well. The EPIC uses the *catalog* of HEROES, of ships, of armor, and such. The BIBLE has many *catalogs*, the most notable example being the genealogy of Jesus in Matthew, chapter I. In the RENAISSANCE, one of the conventions of the SONNET and the LYRIC was the *catalog* of the physical charms of the beloved. (See BLASON.) In modern POETRY the *catalog* has been used by Walt Whitman, William Carlos Williams, Ezra Pound, A. R. Ammons, and Gary Snyder. For an impressively extended *catalog*, see Whitman's *Song of Myself*, section 15.

Catastasis: In DRAMA, the heightening; the third of the four parts into which the ancients divided a PLAY. See DRAMATIC STRUCTURE. In RHETORIC it is the narrative part of the introduction of a speech.

Catastrophe: The conclusion of a PLAY, particularly a TRAGEDY; the last of the four parts into which the ancients divided a play. It is the final stage in the FALLING ACTION, ending the dramatic CONFLICT, winding up the PLOT, and consisting of the actions that result from the CLIMAX. Since it is used mostly in connection with a TRAGEDY and involves the death of the HERO, it is sometimes used by extension to designate an unhappy ending (or event) in nondramatic FICTION and even in life. In the strict sense of DRAMATIC STRUCTURE, however, every DRAMA has a *catastrophe;* see the line in *King Lear:* "Pat, he comes, like the catastrophe of the old comedy." Today, however, DÉNOUEMENT is more commonly used than *catastrophe* in this sense. See DRAMATIC STRUCTURE, DÉNOUEMENT.

Catch: In music a ROUND for at least three voices, in which each singer begins a line or a phrase behind the preceding one. The *catch* was a popular musical form in the seventeenth and eighteenth centuries and still occurs predominantly in children's songs. It is now usually called a ROUND. In METRICS the term *catch*, applied to an extra unstressed syllable at the beginning of a line that would normally begin with a stressed syllable, is a form of ANACRUSIS. *Catch* was also applied in the seventeenth and eighteenth centuries to the intermingling of strong and weak voices in SONGS wherein the strong voices furnish a bawdy twist. Jonathan Swift wrote such VERSES.

Catchword: A word so often repeated that it is identified with a person or object. In printing, *catchword* has two meanings. The current usage of the term is as the name for a word printed at the top of a column or a page to indicate the first or last word on that page (normally, as in the boldface *catchwords* in this book, the first entry on even-numbered pages and the last on the odd-numbered). At the bottom of each page, under the last word or segment on the last line, early printers customarily printed the first word of the next page. This word was called a *catchword*.

Catharsis: In the *Poetics* Aristotle, in defining TRAGEDY, sees its objective as being "through pity and fear effecting the proper purgation [*catharsis*] of these emotions," but he fails to explain what he means by "proper purgation." In his time it had both a medical and a religious signification. In medical terms *catharsis* referred to the discharge from the body of the excess of elements produced by a state of sickness and thus the return to bodily health.

Viewed in this sense, *catharsis* is the process by which an unhealthy emotional state produced by an imbalance of feelings is corrected and emotional health restored. An AMBIGUITY in the wording of the Greek original makes it possible that what is purged is not the emotions but the complications of the PLOT. In religious terms, as expressed several places by Plato, *catharsis* is the process by which the soul collects its elements, brings itself together from all parts of the body, and can exist "alone by itself, freed from the body as from fetters."

Whatever Aristotle means thereby, *catharsis* remains one of the great unsettled issues in CRITICISM. That it implies a beneficial cathartic effect produced by witnessing a tragic ACTION is clear; how it is produced is what is in question. Some believe that the spectators of a TRAGEDY, by vicarious participation, learn through the fate of the tragic HERO, that fear and pity are destructive and thereby learn to avoid them in their own lives (this interpretation is clearly didactic). Others believe that the spectator, being human and thus subject to disturbing emotions of fear and pity, has this emotional imbalance rectified and these internal agitations stilled by having an opportunity vicariously to expend fear and pity on the tragic HERO. Still others see the tragic HERO as a scapegoat on which the excessive emotions of the spectator can be placed, leaving the spectator at the end calm, "all passion spent." R. B. Sharpe, in *Irony in the Drama*, suggests that before the conclusion of a TRAGEDY the HERO comes to represent to the spectator "what Jung calls a symbol and Frazer a scapegoat—that is, a human figure upon whom we are able to load our emotions, from our loftiest to our lowest, our hopes, and our sins, through such a deep and complete emotional identification that he can carry them away with him into heaven or the wilderness and so free us of the burden and the tension of keeping them for ourselves. This empathic identification is . . . catharsis." Critics have been playing variations on these interpretations ever since Aristotle, and the provocative concept of *catharsis*, although useful and instructive, is certain to remain unclear.

[Reference: Alice Lotvin Birney, *Satiric Catharsis in Shakespeare* (1973).]

Cauda: Another name for the "tail" or short LINE found in certain VERSE-forms. See TAIL-RHYME ROMANCE and TAIL-RHYME STANZA.

Caudate Sonnet: An Italian FORM, rarely adopted into English, in which a standard fourteen-line SONNET is augmented by the addition of other LINES, including "tails." Milton's "On the New Forcers of Conscience under the Long Parliament" is a clear example; Hopkins's "That Nature Is a Heraclitean Fire and of the Comfort of the Resurrection" probably qualifies.

Causerie: An INFORMAL ESSAY, usually on a literary topic, and frequently in a series. The term is applied to such ESSAYS because of their similarity to *Causeries du lundi* by Charles Augustin Sainte-Beuve. In the strictest sense it probably should be limited to the kind of combined biographical and critical treatments for which Sainte-Beuve was noted. Edmund Wilson wrote literary ESSAYS that might be called *causeries*.

Cavalier Lyric: A POEM characteristic of the CAVALIER LYRICISTS; light-hearted in tone; graceful, melodious, and polished in manner; artfully showing Latin classical influences; sometimes licentious and cynical or epigrammatic and witty. At times it breathed the careless BRAGGADOCIO of the military swashbuckler, at times the aristocratic ease of the peaceable courtier. Many of the poems were OCCASIONAL, as Suckling's charming if DOGGEREL-like "Ballad upon a Wedding" or Lovelace's pensive "To Althea from Prison." The THEMES were love, war, chivalry, and loyalty to the king. The term *Cavalier Lyric* is also applied to a later POEM that illustrates the spirit of the times of the CAVALIER LYRICISTS, such as Browning's "Cavalier Tunes" ("Marching Along," "Give a Rouse," and "Boot and Saddle").

Cavalier Lyricists: The followers of Charles I (1625–1649) were called Cavaliers, as opposed to the supporters of Parliament, who were called ROUNDHEADS. The *Cavalier Lyricists*, a group of the former who composed light-hearted POEMS, included Thomas Carew, Richard Lovelace, and Sir John Suckling. These were soldiers and courtiers first and authors of CAVALIER LYRICS only incidentally. Robert Herrick, although he was a country parson and not a courtier, is often classed with the *Cavalier Lyricists* because many of his poems included in *Hesperides* are in the vein of the Cavaliers. See CAVALIER LYRIC.

   [References: Thomas Clayton, *Cavalier Poets* (1978); Carl Holliday, *The Cavalier Poets* (1911, reprinted 1974); Robin Skelton, ed., *The Cavalier Poets* (1970).]

Celtic Literature: Literature produced by a people speaking any of the Celtic DIALECTS. Linguistically, the Celts are divided into two main groups. The "Brythonic" Celts include the Ancient Britons, the Welsh, the Cornish (Cornwall), and the Bretons (Brittany); while the Goidelic (Gaelic) Celts include the Irish, the Manx (Isle of Man), and the Scottish Gaels. At one time the Celts, an important branch of the Indo-European family, dominated Central and Western Europe. The Continental Celts (including the Bretons) have left no literature. The Celts of Great Britain and Ireland, however, have produced much literature of interest to students of English and American literature. See IRISH LITERATURE, WELSH LITERATURE, SCOTTISH LITERATURE, CELTIC RENAISSANCE.

Celtic Renaissance (or Celtic Revival or Irish Renaissance): A general term for a movement aimed at the preservation of the Gaelic language (the GAELIC MOVEMENT), the reconstruction of early Celtic history and literature, and the stimulation of a new literature authentically Celtic (especially Irish) in spirit. From early in the nineteenth century there had been a growing interest in Celtic antiquities, and much work was done in the collection, study, printing, and translation of manuscripts embodying the history and literature of ancient Ireland. There also developed the practice of collecting and printing folktales preserved in oral tradition. In the 1890s came the GAELIC MOVEMENT, which stressed the use of the Gaelic language. More fruitful was the contemporaneous Anglo-Irish movement, which stimulated the production of a new literature in English (or "Anglo-Irish") by Irish writers on Irish THEMES and in the Irish spirit. Standish O'Grady's imaginative treatment of Irish history (1880) provided impetus to the movement, and THEMES drawn from ancient Irish tradition were exploited in VERSE and DRAMA. Fortunately, genuinely talented writers were at hand to further the project, such as W. B. Yeats, George W. Russell ("A.E."), George Moore, J. M. Synge, and (later) James Stephens, Lord

Dunsany, and Sean O'Casey. From the beginning Lady Gregory was an enthusiastic worker—as collector, popularizer, essayist, and playwright. A striking phase of the *Celtic Renaissance* was its DRAMA. In 1899, under the leadership of Yeats, Moore, Edward Martyn, Lady Gregory, and others, the Irish Literary Theater was founded in Dublin. For it, Yeats and Martyn wrote some PLAYS employing Irish folk-materials. Later Yeats joined another group more devoted to the exploitation of native elements, The Irish National Theatre Society, to which he attracted J. M. Synge, the most gifted playwright of the movement, whose *Playboy of the Western World* (1907) and *Deirdre of the Sorrows* (1910) attracted wide recognition. This group worked in the famed ABBEY THEATRE. Later exemplars of dramatic activity were Lord Dunsany and Sean O'Casey. Still later, Brendan Behan (1923–1964), who could write poems in the Irish Gaelic language, excelled in DRAMA, JOURNALISM, travel writing, FICTION, and AUTOBIOGRAPHY.

[References: Ernest Boyd, *Ireland's Literary Renaissance* (1916, reprinted 1968); Douglas Hyde, *Literary History of Ireland* (1900, reprinted 1967).]

Celtic Revival: A term sometimes used for the GAELIC MOVEMENT, the CELTIC RENAISSANCE, or the IRISH LITERARY MOVEMENT, as well as for the eighteenth-century movement described next.

Celtic Revival, The (Eighteenth Century): A literary movement that, in the last half of the eighteenth century, stressed the use of the historical, literary, and mythological traditions of the ancient Celts, particularly the Welsh. Through confusion, Norse mythology was included. *The Celtic Revival* was a part of the ROMANTIC MOVEMENT, in that it stressed the primitive, the remote, the strange, and the mysterious; and it aided the revolt against pseudo-classicism by substituting a new mythology for classical MYTHS and figures. Specifically it was characterized by an intense interest in the druids and early Welsh BARDS, numerous TRANSLATIONS and IMITATIONS of early Celtic POETRY appearing in the wake of the discovery of some genuine examples of early Welsh VERSE. The most influential and gifted POET in the group was Thomas Gray, whose "The Bard" (1757) and "The Progress of Poesy" (1757) reflect early phases of the movement. The most spectacular figure in the group of "Celticists" was James Macpherson, whose long POEMS, *Fingal* (1762) and *Temora* (1763)—chiefly his own invention but partly English renderings of genuine Gaelic pieces preserved in the Scottish Highlands—he published as TRANSLATIONS of the poems of a great Celtic poet of primitive times, Ossian. Both Gray's and Macpherson's work influenced a host of minor poets, who were especially numerous and active in the last two decades of the century. There was also a considerable reflection of the movement in the DRAMA, for example, Home's *The Fatal Discovery* (acted 1769).

[Reference: E. D. Snyder, *The Celtic Revival in English Literature* (1923, reprinted 1965).]

Center for Editions of American Authors (CEAA): A committee of scholars representing the American Literature Section of the Modern Language Association of America for the production of definitive EDITIONS of nineteenth-century American authors. It has now been replaced by the CENTER FOR SCHOLARLY EDITIONS. The *CEAA*, as it was commonly called, established editorial procedures, oversaw the work of editors, and approved texts for publication. It enunciated rigorous and highly sophisticated principles for textual editing; after verification that these principles has been meticulously followed in the preparation of a volume, it awarded the volume the right to display the *Center's* seal of approval. Among the authors having editions sponsored by the *CEAA* are Washington Irving, Charles Brockden Brown, Stephen Crane, Emerson, Howells, William James, Mark Twain, Melville, Simms, Thoreau, and Whitman.

Center for Scholarly Editions (CSE): The broad functions of the *Center for Scholarly Editions* are the same as those of the CENTER FOR EDITIONS OF AMERICAN AUTHORS, which it replaced in 1976 on the expiration of the CEAA grants from the National Endowment for the Humanities. Like the CEAA, the *CSE* is administered by a committee of the Modern Language Association. However, it places no restrictions on the content of the EDITIONS with which it concerns itself, any kind of work or document from any nation and in any language being eligible for aid by the *Center*. Its goal is to serve as a clearing-house for information about scholarly editing, to offer advice and consultation to editors of scholarly projects, and to award its emblem to volumes that are found to merit it. See CENTER FOR EDITIONS OF AMERICAN AUTHORS.

Cento: A literary patchwork, usually in VERSE, made up of scraps from one or many authors. An example is a fifth-century life of Christ by the Empress Eudoxia, which is in VERSE with every line drawn from Homer.

Chain Rhyme: Uncommon in English, this device incorporates elements of ECHO and IDENTICAL RHYME so that the sound of the last syllable of one LINE recurs as the sound of the first syllable of the next but with a change of meaning. *Chain rhyme* would occur, say, if a line ending "weight" were succeeded by one beginning "wait." Hopkins's "The Leaden Echo and the Golden Echo" furnishes an instance wherein the Leaden Echo's last word is "despair" and the Golden Echo's first word is "Spare!" There is a contemporary example by Fred Chappell.

Chain Verse: POETRY in which the STANZAS are linked through some pattern of REPETITION. The last LINE of one STANZA may be the first of the next, producing a linked group of STANZAS that may be considered a *chain*. The SESTINA may be considered a sort of *chain* with links formed by the repetition of words, phrases, or lines in a predetermined pattern. In Samuel Daniel's *Delia* the last line of one SONNET may be the first line of the next, but the pattern is inconsistent. The linkage may also be secured by the repetition of RHYME. The VILLANELLE, a nineteen-line POEM in TERCETS followed by a QUATRAIN and having only two RHYMES and frequent repetition of lines, is a complex example of *chain verse*.

Chanson: A SONG. Originally composed of two-line STANZAS of equal length (COUPLETS), each STANZA ending in a REFRAIN, the *chanson* is now more broadly interpreted to include almost any simple POEM intended to be sung.

Chanson de geste: A "SONG of great deeds." A term applied to the early French EPIC. The earliest and best existing example, the *Chanson de Roland,* dates from *ca.* 1100. The early *chansons de geste* are written in ten-syllable LINES marked by ASSONANCE and grouped in STROPHES of varying length. CYCLES developed, such as that of Charlemagne (*geste du roi*); that of William of Orange, which reflects the efforts of Christian heroes against the invading Saracens; and that dealing with the strife among the rebellious Northern barons. The stories generally reflect chivalric ideals with little use of love as the THEME. The FORM flourished for several centuries, a total of about eighty examples being extant. These EPIC tales supplied material ("Matter of France") for MEDIEVAL ROMANCE, including English ROMANCES. See MEDIEVAL ROMANCE.

[References: W. P. Ker, *Epic and Romance* (1908, reprinted 1957); George Saintsbury, *The Flourishing of Romance* (1897).]

Chant: Loosely used to mean a SONG, but more particularly the term signifies the intoning of words to a monotonous musical measure of few notes. The words of the *chants* in the English Church are drawn from such Biblical sources as the PSALMS. CADENCE is an important element, and usually one note (the "reciting note") is used for a series of successive words or syllables. DIRGES are often chanted. REPETITION of a few varying musical phrases is a characteristic, and the intonation of the voice plays an important role. *Chants* are generally considered less melodious than SONGS. In some *chants,* the words come from a PROSE text.

Chant Royal: One of the most complex FRENCH verse FORMS. The tradition for this VERSE form demands a dignified, heroic subject such as can best be expressed in rich DICTION and courtly formalities of speech. The *chant royal* consists of sixty lines arranged in five STANZAS of eleven LINES each and an ENVOY of five LINES, the ENVOY ordinarily starting with an INVOCATION in the manner of the BALLADE. The usual RHYME SCHEME is *ababccddedE* for the STANZA and *ddedE* (as in the last five lines of the STANZA) for the ENVOY. The preceding capital *E* indicates the recurrence of a complete line as a REFRAIN at the end of each STANZA and at the close of the ENVOY. All STANZAS must follow the same pattern, and no RHYME word may appear twice, except in the ENVOY. Thus, the POET must accomplish the difficult feat of producing sixty lines on only five RHYME sounds. The *chant royal* was popular in France in the fourteenth century, when it was extensively used by Eustace Deschamps, Charles d'Orleans, and Jean Marot. Until the late 1970s, it looked as though the *chant royal* was so difficult that it had to be restricted to a few cases of mannered LIGHT VERSE. That misconception was corrected when the first POEM in the first issue of *Poetry* magazine edited by John Frederick Nims was Robert Morgan's "Chant Royal," which nobly satisfies all of the topical and formal requirements.

Chantey (Shanty): A sailors' SONG marked by strong RHYTHM and, in the days of sail, used to accompany certain forms of repetitive hard labor (such as weighing anchor) performed by seamen working in a group. The leader of the singing was referred to as the "chantey man," his responsibility being to sing a line or two introductory to a REFRAIN joined in by the whole group.

Chapbook: A small book or PAMPHLET, usually a single SIGNATURE of sixteen or thirty-two pages, poorly printed and crudely illustrated, which was sold to the common people in England and America through the eighteenth century by peddlers or "chapmen." *Chapbooks* dealt with all sorts of topics and incidents: travel tales, murder cases, prodigies, strange occurrences, witchcraft, BIOGRAPHIES, religious LEGENDS and tracts, stories of all sorts. The term has been revived in this century as the name for miscellaneous small books and PAMPHLETS.

Character: A complicated term that includes the idea of the moral constitution of the human personality (Aristotle's sense of *ethos*), the presence of moral uprightness, and the simpler notion of the presence of creatures in art that seem to be human beings of one sort or another; *character* is also a term applied to a literary form that flourished in England and France in the seventeenth and eighteenth centuries. It is a brief descriptive SKETCH of a personage who typifies some definite quality. The person is described not as an individualized personality but as an example of some vice or virtue or type, such as a busybody, a glutton, a fop, a bumpkin, a garrulous old man, a happy milkmaid, etc. Similar treatments of institutions and inanimate things, such as "the *character* of a coffee house*," also employed the term, and late in the seventeenth century, by a natural extension of the tradition, *character* was applied to longer compositions, sometimes historical, as Viscount Halifax's *Character of Charles II.* The vogue of *character*-writing followed the publication in 1592 of a Latin translation of Theophrastus, an ancient Greek writer of similar sketches. Though the *character* may have influenced Ben Jonson in his treatment of HUMOURS in COMEDY, the first English writer to cultivate the form as such was Bishop Joseph Hall in his *Characters of Virtues and Vices* (1608). Two of his successors were Sir Thomas Overbury (1614) and John Earle (1628). Later, under the influence of the French writer La Bruyère, *characters* became more individualized and were combined with the ESSAY, as in the PERIODICAL ESSAYS of Addison and Steele. Subjects of *characters* were given fanciful proper names, often Latin or Greek, such as "Croesus." See ESSAY.

[Reference: E. N. S. Thompson, *Literary Bypaths of the Renaissance* (1924).]

Characterization: In the LYRIC, the ESSAY, and the AUTOBIOGRAPHY, the author reveals aspects of his or her own CHARACTER; in the BIOGRAPHY and the HISTORY, the author presents the characters of actual persons; and in FICTION (the DRAMA, the NOVEL, the SHORT STORY, and the NARRATIVE POEM), the author reveals the characters of imaginary persons. The creation of these imaginary persons so that they exist for the reader as lifelike is called *characterization*. The ability to characterize is a primary attribute of a good writer.

There are three fundamental methods of *characterization* in FICTION: (1) the explicit presentation by the author of the character through direct EXPOSTION, either in an introductory block or more often piecemeal throughout the work, illustrated by action; (2) the presentation of the character in action, with little or no explicit comment by the author, in the expectation that the reader will be able to deduce the attributes of the actor from the actions; and (3) the representation from within a CHARACTER, without comment on the character by the author, of the impact of actions and emotions on the character's inner self, with the expectation that the reader will come to a clear understanding of the attributes of the character.

It is difficult to distinguish among these methods of *characterization* without discussing them in terms of narrative POINT OF VIEW. Usually the explicit method results when the story is told by a first-person NARRATOR, such as Dickens's David Copperfield or Sterne's Tristram Shandy, or by an OMNISCIENT AUTHOR, such as Fielding in *Tom Jones* or Thackeray in *Vanity Fair*. The success of the explicit method of *characterization* rests at least in part on the nature of the NARRATOR. The presentation of characters through actions is essentially the dramatic method. It is the traditional way of establishing character in the DRAMA; so much so, in fact, that only by changing some of the DRAMATIC CONVENTIONS, as in the use of a CHORUS, or EXPRESSIONISM, or in PLAYS like O'Neill's *Strange Interlude,* can other methods of *characterization* be used in the theater. We know Hamlet through what he says and does; the riddle of what Shakespeare intended his true character to be is forever unanswerable. The NOVEL and the SHORT STORY in this century have frequently adopted the dramatic technique by making objective presentations of characters in action without authorial comment, to such an extent that the SELF-EFFACING AUTHOR has become a commonplace. Writers of the REALISTIC NOVEL, such as Bennett, Galsworthy, and Howells, usually employ this method of character presentation. The presentation of the impact of external events and emotions on the PROTAGONIST'S inward self begins with the novels of Henry James, whose *The Ambassadors* is an excellent example, and continues into the IMPRESSIONIST NOVEL and the STREAM OF CONSCIOUSNESS NOVEL where, through INTERIOR MONOLOGUES, the subconscious or unconscious mind of the character is presented, as in Joyce's *Ulysses* or Faulkner's *The Sound and the Fury.*

But, regardless of the method by which a CHARACTER is presented, the author may concentrate on a dominant trait to the exclusion of other aspects of personality, or the author may attempt to present a fully rounded creation. If the presentation of a single dominant trait is carried to an extreme, not a believable character but a CARICATURE will result. If this method is handled with skill, it can produce striking and interesting two-dimensional characters that lack depth. Mr. Micawber in *David Copperfield* comes close to being such a two-dimensional character through the emphasis that Dickens puts upon a very small group of characteristics. Sometimes such characters are given descriptive names, such as Mr. Hammerdown, the auctioneer in *Vanity Fair.* On the other hand, the author may present so convincing a congeries of personality traits that a complex rather than a simple character emerges; such a CHARACTER is three-dimensional or, in E. M. Forster's term, "ROUND." As a rule, the major characters in a FICTION need such three-dimensional treatment, while minor characters are often handled two-dimensionally. It seems likely that, to be fully convincing, a character ought to involve some deep division, contradiction, or PARADOX. The fascination of Richardson's Clarissa Harlowe, for example, lies partly in her "divided mind" that involves a dialectical tension between impulses so virtuous as to seem angelic and normal erotic impulses. Shaw's Saint Joan combines nearly irreconcilable components of two antithetical types: the *ingénue* and the MILES GLORIOSUS. Sometimes just a title, such as *Lord Jim,* can reflect such a contradiction or anomaly. (F. Scott Fitzgerald observed that a writer who sets out to create an individual may create a type at the same time, but one who sets out to create a type will create nothing.) Some human creatures portrayed in literature are hardly distinct characters at all but mere properties or furnishings; on the other hand, some nonhuman entities, such as animals, machines, houses, and cities, may function fully as characters. Rome has such a role in Shakespeare's so-called Roman Tragedies, as do the City of London in Eliot's *The Waste Land* and various great rivers in Mark Twain's *Huckleberry Finn* and Conrad's *Heart of Darkness*.

Furthermore, a character may be either STATIC or DYNAMIC. A STATIC CHARACTER is one who changes little if at all. Things happen *to* such a character without things happening *within*. The pattern of action reveals the character rather than showing the character changing in response to the actions. Sometimes a STATIC CHARACTER gives the appearance of changing simply because our picture of the character is revealed bit by bit; this is true of Uncle Toby in *Tristram Shandy*, who does not change, although our view of him steadily changes. A DYNAMIC CHARACTER, on the other hand, is one who is modified by actions and experiences, and one objective of the work in which the character appears is to reveal the consequences of these actions. Most great DRAMAS and NOVELS have DYNAMIC CHARACTERS as PROTAGONISTS. SHORT STORES are more likely to reveal STATIC CHARACTERS through action than to show changes in DYNAMIC CHARACTERS resulting from actions.

Ultimately every successful character represents a fusion of the universal and the particular and becomes an example of the CONCRETE UNIVERSAL. It is in this dramatic particularization of the typical and universal that one of the essences of *characterization* is to be found. Our minds may delight in abstractions and ideas, but it is our emotions that ultimately give the aesthetic response, and they respond to the personal, the particular, the CONCRETE. This is why a NOVEL speaks to us more durably than an ALLEGORY, why Hamlet has an authority forever lacking in the "Indecisive Man" in a seventeenth-century CHARACTER. See POINT OF VIEW, NOVEL, SHORT STORY, DRAMA, PLOT, CONCRETE UNIVERSAL.

[References: E. M. Forster, *Aspects of the Novel* (1927); W. J. Harvey, *Character and the Novel* (1965); Edwin Muir, *The Structure of the Novel* (1928, reprinted 1963).]

Charm: A primordial formulaic utterance—related to the SPELL, the CURSE, and the RIDDLE—designed to have magical influence in the conduct of life. It may involve a request for good luck or the "apotropaic" desire to ward off evil; it may be motivated by something as mundane as the need to find lost objects or win a contest. The etymological relation between *charm* and the Latin *carmen* ("song," "poem"), like the relation between "grammar" and "glamor," registers the antiquity and persistence of the connections between speech and magic. See CURSE; RIDDLE; SPELL.

Chartism: A nineteenth-century English political movement, the object of which was to win more social recognition and improved material conditions for the lower classes. The Chartists advocated universal suffrage, vote by ballot, annual parliaments, and other reforms. This agenda is given in the *People's Charter* (1838). Carlyle's *Chartism* (1839) is an attack on the movement. The chartist agitation is favorably reflected in some of Kingsley's NOVELS. See IN-DUSTRIAL REVOLUTION.

[References: Asa Briggs, ed., *Chartist Studies* (1959); David J. V. Jones, *Chartism and the Chartists* (1975); J. T. Ward, *Chartism* (1973).]

Chaucerian Stanza: A seven-line IAMBIC PENTAMETER STANZA, rhyming *a-babbcc,* it is also called the *Chaucerian seven-line stanza* and the *Troilus stanza.* See RHYME ROYAL.

Chiaroscuro: Contrasting light and shade. Originally applied to painting, the term is used in the CRITICISM of various literary FORMS involving the contrast of light and darkness, as in much of Hawthorne's and Nabokov's FICTION and in Faulkner's *Light in August.*

Chiasmus: A type of BALANCE in which the second part is balanced against the first but with the parts reversed, as in Coleridge's LINE, "Flowers are lovely, love is flowerlike," or Pope's "Works without show, and without pomp presides." In general, any elements subject to arrangement can take on this chiastic or mirror-image design (x-shaped, like the Greek letter *chi*). Such phrases as "Firestone snow-tire" and "moonstruck mushroom" display phonemic *chiasmus.* Keats's line "Out went the taper as she hurried in" comprises two clauses with syntactic *chiasmus:* adverb, verb, subject; subject, verb, adverb—with a nice play between "out" and "in." *Chiasmus* is sometimes combined with *ellipsis,* as in these passages from Pope and Hardy:

> And has not Colley still his lord and whore?
> His butchers Henley? his freemasons Moore?
> ·
> I left no calling for this idle trade,
> No duty broke, no father disobeyed.
> ·

> The land's sharp features seemed to be
>   The Century's corpse outleant,
> His crypt the cloudy canopy,
>   The wind his death-lament.

Chicago Critics: A group of literary CRITICS, associated with the University of Chicago, who in 1952 published *Critics and Criticism;* also used to mean the followers of such a group. The *Chicago Critics* have theories about the history of CRITICISM and about the PRACTICAL CRITICISM of literary texts. As historians, they are pluralists, who attempt to value critical systems in terms of their assumptions about literature and their contributions to our understanding of literature. As critics, they are Neo-Aristotelian, being concerned with the PRACTICAL CRITICISM of individual works of literature, emphasizing the principles that govern their construction and tending to see literary texts in broadly defined generic classifications. Among the *Chicago Critics* are Ronald S. Crane, Elder Olson, Richard McKeon, Wayne Booth, Norman Maclean, W. Rea Keast, and Austin M. Wright. See CRITICISM, TYPES OF.
  [Reference: R. S. Crane, *Critics and Criticism* (1952).]

Chivalric Romance: MEDIEVAL ROMANCE reflecting the customs and ideals of CHIVALRY. See MEDIEVAL ROMANCE, ARTHURIAN LEGEND, COURTLY LOVE, CHIVALRY IN ENGLISH LITERATURE.

Chivalry in English Literature: The system of manners and morals known as *chivalry,* a product of the feudal system of the Middle Ages, was presented in MEDIEVAL ROMANCE in a highly idealized form amounting almost to a religious faith for the upper classes, and it has furnished colorful subject matter for much later literature. The medieval knight, seen in the light of literary idealization (as a matter of fact, the typical medieval knight had many unlovely characteristics), has been portrayed not only by the many writers of MEDIEVAL ROMANCE, but by later POETS like Chaucer, with his "parfit, gentle knight" and Spenser, who fills *The Faerie Queene* with a procession of courteous and heroic Guyons, Scudamores, and Calidores. Knights whose high oaths bind them to fidelity to God and king, truth to their lady-loves, and ready service for all damsels in distress or other victims of unjust tyrants, cruel giants, or fiendish monsters, have become commonplaces of romantic literature.

Chivalric knights figure importantly in such HISTORICAL NOVELS as Scott's *Ivanhoe* and find lofty, sympathetic treatment in Tennyson's *Idylls of the King*. King Arthur, speaking in Tennyson's *Guinevere*, expresses well the ideals of chivalric knighthood:

> I made them lay their hands in mine and swear
> To reverence the King, as if he were
> Their conscience, and their conscience as their King,
> To break the heathen and uphold the Christ,
> To ride abroad redressing human wrongs,
> To speak no slander, no, nor listen to it,
> To honor his own word as if his God's,
> To lead sweet lives in purest chastity,
> To love one maiden only, cleave to her,
> And worship her by years of noble deeds,
> Until they won her.

A more faithful picture may be found in the pages of Malory's *Le Morte Darthur*, where the glamour of knighthood, with all the effort to idealize Lancelot and Arthur and find in the "good old days" a perfect pattern for later times, is not allowed to obscure some of the less pleasing actualities of medieval knighthood. So glorious a thing as *chivalry* has not, of course, gone unnoticed by the satirists. The early seventeenth century produced not only the immortal *Don Quixote* in Spain but Beaumont and Fletcher's dramatic BURLESQUE *The Knight of the Burning Pestle* in England, while modern America has brought forth the broadly comic *A Connecticut Yankee in King Arthur's Court* (Mark Twain) as well as the more subtly mocking *Galahad* (John Erskine) and "Childe Roland, etc." (Elder Olson). See ARTHURIAN LEGEND.

[References: Larry D. Benson and John Leyerle, eds., *Chivalric Literature* (1980); Diane Bornstein, *Mirrors of Courtesy* (1975); Lee C. Ramsey, *Chivalric Romances: Popular Literature in Medieval England* (1983); W. H. Schofield, *Chivalry in English Literature* (1912).]

Choliambus: The most important variety of SCAZON because it has to do with the IAMBIC RHYTHM that is the most important in English. There are subtle refinements in the use of this device by the ancients; in English all that matters is that the last FOOT in a prevalently IAMBIC line is not an IAMB, ANAPEST, AMPHIBRACH, or SPONDEE, but a TROCHEE or DACTYL. In the commonest form, the fifth foot of a LINE that is basically IAMBIC PENTAMETER is supplanted by a TROCHEE. Such double frustration of the ear's expectation can be deeply unsettling. There are instances in Tennyson's "Lucretius" ("Strikes through the wood, sets all the tops quivering") and Stevens's "Sunday Morning" ("Elations when the forest blooms; gusty"). Among Eliot's POEMS, *choliambus* occurs in both the last line of "Gerontion" ("Thoughts of a dry brain in a dry season") and the first of *The Waste Land* ("April is the cruellest month, breeding"). *Choliambus* differs radically from the common "FEMI-NINE" line-ending, which means that the final IAMB is replaced by an AMPHI-BRACH (or is simply augmented by one or more unaccented syllables). See SCAZON.

Choral Character: A CHARACTER in a PLAY or a NOVEL who stands aside from the ACTION and comments on it or speaks about it as a communal voice. See CHORUS.

Choriambus: In METRICS a FOOT in which two accented syllables flank two unaccented syllables: $´ ˘ ˘ ´$. This FOOT is sometimes used in a VERSE form called *choriambics*, in which the LINE consists of a TROCHEE, three *choriambics*, and an IAMBUS. Swinburne used the form, as did Rupert Brooke, whose line: "I have | tend ed and loved | year up on year, | I in the sol | i tude" illustrates the *choriambic* line.

Chorus: In ancient Greece, the groups of dancers and singers who partici-pated in religious festivals and dramatic performances. Also the SONGS sung by the *chorus*. At first the choral songs made up the bulk of the PLAY, the spoken MONOLOGUE and DIALOGUE being interpolated. Later, however, the *chorus* became subordinate, offering inter-act comments. Finally, it became a mere LYRIC used to take up the time between ACTS. In ELIZABETHAN DRAMA the role of the *chorus* was often taken by a single actor, who recited PROLOGUE and EPILOGUE and gave inter-act comments that linked the ACTS and foresha-dowed coming events. So in Sackville and Norton's *Gorboduc*, the "first" Eng-lish TRAGEDY, the *chorus* consists of a few STANZAS accompanied by a DUMB show that foreshadows the coming ACTION. In Kyd's *Spanish Tragedy* the part of the *chorus* is played by a ghost and the figure Revenge. Shakespeare sometimes employed the *chorus,* as in *Pericles,* where the old POET Gower, accompanied by a DUMB SHOW, provides PROLOGUE and inter-act comment, and in *King Henry the Fifth,* where the *chorus* comments on the ACTION, explains change of SCENE, and (in a thoroughly traditional CONVENTION of choric behavior) begs for the indulgence of the spectators. Sometimes, within the PLAY proper, one of the characters, like the Fool in *King Lear,* is said to play a *"chorus*-like" role when he comments on the action.

Although no longer common, the *chorus* is still used occasionally by the modern playwright, notably T. S. Eliot in *Murder in the Cathedral.* Sometimes a *chorus*-character—one whose role in the DRAMA is to comment on the AC-TION—is used; such a CHARACTER is Seth Beckwith in O'Neill's *Mourning Becomes Electra.* Novelists, too, have used the *chorus,* sometimes as a group of characters who comment on ACTION, sometimes as a single CHARACTER. Both Scott and Hardy used *choruses* of rustics. The group of goodwives in the first SCENE of Hawthorne's *The Scarlet Letter* serves the function of a *chorus.* The CONFIDANTE of the Henry James novel is a *chorus*-character.

In music, a *chorus* may be a composition in at least four parts written for a larger group of singers, and the term is also applied to the singers of such choral compositions. It is also applied to a REFRAIN repeated after each STANZA of a POEM or a SONG.

Chrestomathy: A collection of choice passages to be used in the study of a language or a literature and, thus, a kind of ANTHOLOGY. When the term is used today, it may signify a volume of selected passages or stories by a single author; *chrestomathy* was used in this sense by H. L. Mencken, whose adoption of a word so pretentious must have been at least partly in jest.

Christianity, Established in England: There were Christians in Roman Britain as early as the third century, and probably there was an organized church as early as A.D. 314, when the bishops of London and York are said to have attended a church council in Gaul. After the lapse into barbarism that followed the Germanic invasions of the fifth century, *Christianity* was reintroduced directly from Rome by St. Augustine, who landed in Kent in A.D. 597. (This was not St. Augustine of Hippo, who died early in the fifth century.) It flourished in southeastern England under Ethelbert, spread northward, and gained a foothold in Northumbria under Edwin (d. 633), who had married a Kentish princess. Another group of missionaries soon came into Northumbria from the celebrated Celtic monastery of Iona, an island off the west coast of Scotland. Iona had been established in A.D. 563 by St. Columba, a missionary from Ireland, where a form of *Christianity* reflecting the monastic ideals of Bishop Martin of Tours (flourished *ca.* 385) had been introduced from Gaul in the fourth or early fifth century. The Celtic and Roman churches differed in certain doctrines and customs (such as the date for Easter, the form of baptism, and style of tonsure for priests). The resulting disputes were settled in favor of the Roman party at the Synod of Whitby in 664.

The establishment of *Christianity* in England profoundly affected literature, since the Church was for centuries the chief sponsor of learning. The pagan literature that survived from early Germanic times passed through the medium of Christian authors and copyists, who gave a Christian coloring to the writings that they did not wholly reject. For centuries most writings owed both their inspiration and direction to a Christian spirit. The Christianization of the great body of Arthurian romances in the thirteenth century is an outstanding example of the dominance of *Christianity* over medieval literary activity.

Chronicle: A name of certain forms of historical writing. *Chronicles* differ from ANNALS in their concern with larger aspects of history. Though there were PROTOTYPES in Hebrew, Greek, Latin, and French, the comprehensive medieval *chronicles* in English and their RENAISSANCE successors matter most to the student of ENGLISH LITERATURE. The *Anglo-Saxon Chronicle,* begun under King Alfred late in the ninth century and carried on by various writers in a number of monasteries, has been called the "first great book in English PROSE." The record begins with 60 B.C. and closes with 1154 ("Peterborough" version). Alfred and his helpers revised older minor *chronicles* and records and wrote firsthand accounts of their own times. The work as a whole is a sort of historical miscellany, sometimes sketchy in detail and detached in attitude, at other times lively, partisan, and detailed. An important Old English POEM preserved through its inclusion in the *Anglo-Saxon Chronicle* is the spirited *Battle of Brunanburh*. A famous Latin PROSE *chronicle* is Geoffrey of Monmouth's *History of the Kings of Britain* (*ca.* 1136), which records not only legendary British history but also romantic accounts of King Arthur. The earliest important VERSE *chronicle* in Middle English is Layamon's *Brut* (*ca.* 1205), based on Wace's French poetic version of Geoffrey. A long POEM composed in an imaginative and often dramatic vein, it exhibits a picturesque STYLE sometimes reminiscent of Old English POETRY.

Later Middle English *chronicles* include those of Robert of Gloucester (late thirteenth century), Robert Manning of Brunne (1338), Andrew of Wyntoun (*Original Chronicle of Scotland,* early fifteenth century), John Hardyng (late fifteenth century), and John Capgrave (fifteenth century). With the rise of the Tudor dynasty came a wave of patriotism, one result of which was the production in the sixteenth century of many *chronicles*—some in Latin PROSE, some in English VERSE; some mere abstracts, some very voluminous; some new compositions, some retellings of older ones. Some of the more important *chronicles* of Elizabeth's time, besides the famous *Mirror for Magistrates,* are Richard Grafton's (1563), John Stowe's (1565, 1580, 1592), and Ralph Holinshed's (1578). Not only are portions of this mass of *chronicle*-writing themselves of genuine literary value, full of ANECDOTE and DESCRIPTION, but some of them were important as SOURCES for Shakespeare and other dramatists. See CHRONICLE PLAY.

Chronicle Play: A type of DRAMA flourishing in the latter part of Elizabeth's reign, which drew its English historical materials from the sixteenth-century CHRONICLES, such as Holinshed's, and stressed the patriotism of the times. It enjoyed increasing popularity with the outburst of nationalistic feeling following the defeat of the Spanish Armada (1588) and served as a medium for teaching English history to the uneducated. The STRUCTURE of the earlier *chronicle plays* was very loose, UNITY consisting mainly in the inclusion of the events of a single king's reign. The number of CHARACTERS was large. The PLAYS featured pageantry (coronations, funerals) and other spectacular elements, such as battles on the stage. The serious ACTION was often relieved by comic scenes or subplots, as in Shakespeare's famous "Falstaff plays" (*King Henry the Fourth,* 1, 2; *King Henry the Fifth*). The tendency to merge with ROMANTIC COMEDIES appeared as early as Greene's *James IV* (*ca.* 1590); in Shakespeare's *Cymbeline* (*ca.* 1610) the CHRONICLE material is completely subordinated to the demands of ROMANTIC COMEDY. The relation of the *chronicle play* to TRAGEDY is likewise important. Shakespeare's *Richard III* (*ca.* 1593) exemplifies the tendency of the *chronicle play* to develop into TRAGEDY OF CHARACTER, a movement that culminates in such plays as *King Lear* (1605) and *Macbeth* (1606). The term HISTORY PLAY is sometimes applied to a restricted group of *chronicle plays* like Shakespeare's *King Henry the Fifth,* which are unified but are neither COMEDY nor TRAGEDY. The earliest true *chronicle play* is perhaps *The Famous Victories of Henry V* (*ca.* 1586). Peele's *Edward I* (1590–91) and Marlowe's *Edward II* (1592) are among the best pre-Shakespearean *chronicle plays.*

[References: Irving Ribner, *The English History Play in the Age of Shakespeare* (1957); F. E. Schelling, *The English Chronicle Play* (1902).]

Chronological Primitivism: The belief that the lives and actions of human beings were generally better at an earlier stage of history than at present. See PRIMITIVISM.

Ciceronian Style: A highly ornamental STYLE, modeled after Cicero, the Roman orator, who was noted for his prose RHYTHMS, his cadenced periodic sentences, and his use of BALANCE and ANTITHESIS. The *Ciceronian style* is particularly rich in its use of FIGURES OF SPEECH. It was very popular with the writers of the English RENAISSANCE (see PURIST), and Samuel Johnson in the eighteenth century and Thomas Babington Macaulay in the nineteenth are outstanding practitioners of *Ciceronian style.* It should be compared with the SENECAN STYLE.

"Ciceronians": A group of Latin stylists in the RENAISSANCE who would not use any word that could not be found in Cicero's writings. See PURIST.

Cinéma Vérité: A method of filmmaking that relies on portable equipment and small camera crews. It has been used primarily in making documentary films because the camera can go almost anywhere and capture unstaged ACTION, even when the filmmaker is involved in the ACTION, too. The method has been effectively used for regular FILMS also. Since a measure of selection, perspective, judgment, and editing cannot be avoided, the "verity" of *cinéma vérité* is relative and metaphoric.

Cinquain: Originally applied to a medieval five-line STANZA of varying METER and RHYME SCHEME, *cinquain* is now often used for any five-line STANZA. More precisely, however, it is applied to the five-line STANZA used by Adelaide Crapsey, consisting of five unrhymed LINES of, respectively, two, four, six, eight, and two syllables.

Circumlocution: Roundabout DICTION, in which many words are used where a few would have served. It is a form of PERIPHRASIS.

Classic (noun): In the singular, *classic* is usually applied to a piece of literature that by common consent has achieved a recognized superior status in literary history; also an author of similar standing. Thus, *Paradise Lost* is a *classic* in English literature. Given the connection with "class," a *classic* may be strictly considered as the defining member of a class of whatever sort. Anything may be a classic: a shirt, a batting stance, an utterance. General Sherman's celebrated telegram to the 1868 Republican Convention—"If nominated I will not run, if elected I will not serve"—is a *classic* of brevity, as well as the *classic* statement of a politician refusing an offer or overture, so that we still speak of a "Sherman-like" statement. The plural is used in the same sense, as in the phrase "the study of English *classics*"; it is also used collectively to designate the literary productions of Greece and Rome during the period called "*classical* antiquity."

Classic, Classical (adjectives): Used in senses parallel with those given under CLASSIC (noun); hence, of recognized excellence or belonging to established tradition, as a *classical* piece of music or "a *classic* pronouncement"; used specifically to designate the literature or culture of Greece and Rome or later literature that partakes of its qualities. *"Classical* literature" may mean Greek and Roman literature, or literature that has gained a lasting recognition, or literature that exhibits the qualities of CLASSICISM. The adjective has acquired a bewildering array of meanings. In scientific parlance, *"classical* mechanics" means physics before the acceptance of quantum mechanics and theories of relativity. Pathologists speak of *"classic* symptoms" and lawyers of *"classic* cases." When a sporting tournament can be called a "first annual Virginia Slims *classic,"* the concept has lost most of its meaning and life.

Classical Tragedy: This term may refer to the TRAGEDY of the ancient Greeks and Romans, as Sophocles' *Antigone;* or to tragedies with Greek or Roman subjects, as Shakespeare's *Coriolanus;* or to modern tragedies modeled on Greek or Roman TRAGEDY or written under the influence of the critical doctrines of CLASSICISM. The earliest extant English TRAGEDY, Sackville and Norton's *Gorboduc* (acted 1562), is sometimes called *classical* because it is written in the manner of the SENECAN TRAGEDIES. Ben Jonson's tragedies *Catiline* and *Sejanus* not only are based on Roman themes but are *classical* in their conscious effort to apply most of the "rules" of tragic composition derived from Aristotle and Horace. In spite of the fragmentariness of Aristotle and the occasional disorder of Horace, the rules derived from them favor unity, sobriety, order, wholeness, and balance. In the Restoration period John Dryden, under the influence of the French *classical tragedies* of Racine, advocated CLASSICAL rules and applied them in part to his *All for Love,* which contrasts with Shakespeare's romantic treatment of the same story in *Antony and Cleopatra.* Joseph Addison's *Cato* has been referred to as "the triumph of *classical tragedy."* See CLASSICISM, TRAGEDY, SENECAN TRAGEDY, UNITIES, ROMANTIC TRAGEDY, NEOCLASSIC PERIOD.

Classicism: As a critical term, a body of doctrine thought to be derived from or to reflect the qualities of ancient Greek and Roman culture, particularly in literature, philosophy, art, or CRITICISM. *Classicism* stands for certain definite ideas and attitudes, mainly drawn from the critical utterances of the Greeks and Romans or developed through an imitation of ancient art and literature. These include restraint; restricted scope; dominance of reason; sense of FORM; UNITY of design and aim; clarity; simplicity; BALANCE; attention to structure and logical organization; chasteness in STYLE; severity of outline; moderation; self-control; intellectualism; DECORUM; respect for tradition; IMITATION; conservatism; maturity; and good sense.

The Greeks were notable for their clarity of thought that found articulation in lucid designs and that placed a premium on communication *among* people rather than self-expression *by* a person. UNITY was a dominating idea in the minds of the Greeks, and they characteristically constructed buildings around central ideas, expending great effort in making the structures symmetrical, logical, balanced, harmonious, and shapely. They had a marked sense of appropriateness or DECORUM and in structure, STYLE, and subject worked with what was fitting and dignified. Restraint of the passions, emphasis upon the common or general attributes of people and states, and a dispassionate objectivity made them the natural foes of enthusiasm, of uniquely personal states and emotions of peevish idiosyncrasy, and of excessive subjectivity. Although not all Greek or Roman writers displayed all these characteristics, some combination of such qualities is what is usually implied by *classicism*.

In English literature *classicism* has been an important force, often an issue since RENAISSANCE times. The humanists became conscious advocates of CLASSICAL doctrine, and even such an essentially romantic artist as Spenser fell strongly under its influence, not only drawing freely upon CLASSICAL materials but definitely espousing CLASSICAL doctrines and endeavoring to imitate such CLASSICAL masters as Virgil and Homer. Sir Philip Sidney, though he wrote PASTORAL ROMANCES, speaks mainly as a classicist in his critical essay, *The Defence of Poesie*. Ben Jonson stands as the stoutest RENAISSANCE advocate of *classicism*, both in dramatic CRITICISM and in his influence upon English POETRY. Milton has been said to show a perfect balance of ROMANTICISM and *classicism*. The CLASSICAL attitude, largely under French inspiration, triumphed in the RESTORATION and AUGUSTAN AGES, and John Dryden, Joseph Addison, and Alexander Pope, together with Samuel Johnson of the next generation, stand as exemplars of the CLASSICAL (or NEOCLASSIC) spirit in literature and CRITICISM. Though nineteenth-century literature was largely romantic (or in its later phases realistic), the vitality of the CLASSICAL attitude is shown by the critical writings of such thinkers as Cardinal Newman, Matthew Arnold, and Walter Pater. In the twentieth century there has been a strong revival of CLASSICAL attitudes in the literary practice and the critical principles of writers like T. E. Hulme, Wyndham Lewis, T. S. Eliot, and Ezra Pound, and a good deal of the most distinguished POETRY and CRITICISM today is redolent of *classicism*. The austere sentiment for order that animated the CRITICISM of Irving Babbitt and Paul Elmer More in the first third of this century persisted in the "reactionary" thought of Allen Tate and still endures in the CRITICISM of Hugh Kenner, Guy Davenport, and others. See HUMANISM, NEOCLASSICISM, CLASSICAL, ROMANTICISM, REALISM, NEW CRITICISM.

[References: Irving Babbitt, *The New Laokoön* (1910); W. J. Bate, *From Classic to Romantic* (1961); W. J. Courthope, *Life in Poetry, Law in Taste* (1901); Sherard Vines, *The Course of English Classicism* (1930).]

Clerihew: A form of LIGHT VERSE invented by and named for Edmund Clerihew Bentley (1875–1956), who also wrote DETECTIVE fiction. In its proper form, the *clerihew* concerns an actual person, whose name makes up the first line of a QUATRAIN with a strict *aabb* RHYME SCHEME and no regularity of RHYTHM or METER. Bentley himself wrote dozens, and some of the best recent examples are the work of W. H. Auden. Here are two contemporary *clerihews*:

> Cesare Borgia
> Would probably have preferred the way things were
> . done in Georgia
> Before the Emancipation
> Proclamation.

> Henry James
> Came up with some pretty ridiculous names,
> E.g., "Caspar Good-
> wood."

Cliché: From the French word for a stereotype plate; a block for printing. Hence, any expression so often used that its freshness and clarity have worn off is called a *cliché*, a stereotyped form. A *cliché* probably begins as an arrestingly colorful expression, possibly in a literary work, but heedless repetition soon dulls the original brightness. Since the user pays no mind to the real meaning of the words, *cliché* DICTION often devolves into MIXED METAPHOR: "The new policy is just the tip of the iceberg, but it has already bred verbal pyrotechnics that throw a wet blanket over the in-depth brainstorming of seminal issues."

Climax: In RHETORIC a term used to indicate a rising order of importance in the ideas expressed. Such an arrangement is called climactic, and the item of greatest importance is called the *climax*. Earlier, the term meant such an arrangement of succeeding clauses that the last important word in one is repeated as the first important word in the next, each succeeding clause rising in intensity or importance.

In large compositions—the ESSAY, the SHORT STORY, the DRAMA, or the NOVEL—the *climax* is the point of highest interest, whereat the reader makes the greatest emotional response. In DRAMATIC STRUCTURE *climax* designates the turning point in the ACTION, the CRISIS at which the RISING ACTION reverses and becomes the FALLING ACTION. In Freytag's five-part view of DRAMATIC STRUCTURE, the *climax* is the third part or third ACT. Both narrative FICTION and DRAMA have tended to move the *climax*, in the sense of turning action and of highest response as well, nearer the end of the work and thus have produced structures less orderly than those that follow FREYTAG'S PYRAMID. In speaking of DRAMATIC STRUCTURE, *climax* is synonymous with CRISIS. However, CRISIS is used exclusively in the sense of STRUCTURE, whereas *climax* is used as a synonym for CRISIS *and* as a description of the intensity of interest in the reader or spectator. In this latter sense *climax* sometimes occurs at points other than the CRISIS. See CRISIS, DRAMATIC STRUCTURE.

Clinamen: A TROPE, meaning a "swerving away," latterly adopted in Harold Bloom's CRITICISM to describe the inaugural gesture of a typical "strong" post-Enlightenment LYRIC.

Cloak and Dagger: A type of NOVEL or a PLAY that deals with espionage or intrigue. The NOVELS of John Buchan, Ian Fleming, and Helen MacInnes can properly be so designated; the espionage NOVELS of Graham Greene and John Le Carré perhaps cannot, since they lack the requisite romantic aura. Compare with CLOAK AND SWORD.

Cloak and Sword: The term comes from the Spanish *comedia de capa y espada*, a dramatic type of which the ingredients were gallant cavaliers, lovely ladies, elegance, adventure, and intrigue. In English it refers to swashbuckling PLAYS or NOVELS characterized by much ACTION and presenting gallant heroes (often occupied in some attractive but outlawed activity, such as piracy, gambling, or theft) in love with fair ladies, with glamorous color thrown over all. SETTINGS and CHARACTERS are often, although not necessarily, Mediterranean; the manners are courtly and gracious; the PLOTS are full of intrigue and twists and turns, with plenty of surprises and narrow escapes. The PLAYS of Lope de Vega, Dumas' *The Three Musketeers*, Rafael Sabatini's *Scaramouche*, and immense numbers of popular movies, television programs, and best-selling

NOVELS are examples (as well as testimony to the continuing appeal of the type). *Cloak and sword* ROMANCES were very popular in America between 1890 and 1915.

Closed Couplet: Two successive LINES rhyming *aa* and containing a grammatically complete, independent statement. It is "closed" in the sense that its meaning is complete within the two lines and does not depend on what precedes or follows for its grammatical structure or thought. Almost all instances in English are IAMBIC TETRAMETER or PENTAMETER, as in these *closed couplets* by Blake and Pope:

> A dog starved at his Master's Gate
> Predicts the ruin of the State

> Avoid extremes, and shun the fault of such
> Who still are please'd too little or too much.

Closet Drama: A PLAY (usually in VERSE) designed to be read rather than acted. Notable examples are Seneca's TRAGEDIES, Milton's *Samson Agonistes*, Shelley's *The Cenci*, Browning's *Pippa Passes*, and the ONE-ACT PLAYS that W. D. Howells wrote for the *Atlantic Monthly*. Giving the term a broader meaning, some writers include in it such dramatic POEMS as Swinburne's *Atalanta in Calydon* and other products of the effort to write a literary DRAMA by imitating the style of an earlier age, such as Greek DRAMA. Such poetic DRAMAS as Tennyson's *Becket* and Browning's *Strafford* are sometimes called *closet dramas* because, though meant to be acted, they are more successful as literature than as acted DRAMA. In England the nineteenth century was noted for the production of *closet drama*, perhaps because the actual stage was so monopolized by BURLESQUE, MELODRAMA, OPERETTA, and such light forms that serious writers were stimulated either to attempt worthier DRAMAS for the contemporary stage or at least to preserve the TRADITION of literary DRAMA by imitating earlier masterpieces. Charles Lamb declared that all of Shakespeare's tragedies ought to be regarded as *closet dramas* because they were inevitably debased in production. See DRAMATIC POETRY, POETIC DRAMA, PASTICHE.

[References: T. H. Dickinson, *The Contemporary Drama of England* (1917); Brander Matthews, *A Study of the Drama* (1910).]

Clown: A comic CHARACTER originally with a marked rustic quality, much like the hick, bumpkin, or yokel. The nameless "Clown" in *Othello,* is merely a servant who makes jokes, mostly lewd PUNS. Later, in performances that call for a high degree of skill, such as the circus and the rodeo, the *clown* emerged as a character whose ineptitude parodies the virtuosity of the central personages. Nowadays *clowns* are associated with a certain outlandish style of costume and makeup.

Cock-and-Bull Story: A long, rambling, somewhat vague and unlikely STORY, a meandering TALL TALE. The term is very old, probably of folk origin. In *The Anatomy of Melancholy*, Robert Burton writes those whose "whole delight is . . . to talk of a cock and bull over a pot." *Tristram Shandy* ends with

Parson Yorick's statement that it has all been a *cock-and-bull story*. Nowadays, the suggestion of rambling has been taken over by the "shaggy dog" story, and the *cock-and-bull story*, because of the connotation of "bull," has come to mean an account that is bogus or hypocritical.

Cockney School: A derogatory title applied by *Blackwood's Magazine* to a group of nineteenth-century writers including Hazlitt, Leigh Hunt, Keats, and Shelley, because of their alleged poor taste in such matters as DICTION and RHYME. The offending RHYMES included *name–time* and *vista–sister,* which, the suggestion was, could rhyme only to a cockney ear. One sentence from the denunciation in *Blackwood's Magazine* will illustrate the whole spirit of the attack: "They [the "cockney" writers] are by far the vilest vermin that ever dared to creep upon the hem of the majestic garment of the English muse." The attack reflected the Tory belief that those of "low" breeding would inevitably embrace cockney politics and produce cockney VERSE. The famous attack on Keats (August, 1818) associates his "bad" VERSE with his radical political friends and his "lowly" beginnings as an apothecary's apprentice.

Coda: A conclusion of a work. The *coda* usually restates or summarizes or integrates the preceding THEMES or movements. The term is also applied to a tailpiece added to a CAUDATE SONNET.

Code: Generally, an assigned or established meaning for some arbitrary SYMBOL, such as the conventional *codes,* official or unofficial, by which a simple red light means "stop," "the port (left) side of a ship," or "prostitution." More formally, in LINGUISTICS, a "prearranged set of rules for converting messages from one sign system into another" (Hartmann and Stork). According to a model proposed by Roman Jakobson, the *code* or general verbal language is one of six components of an act of communication (the other five being the speaker or originator, the addressee, the message, the contact, and the environment of reference). Roland Barthes' *S/Z* offers a set of *codes* involved in the disentanglement of a literary text: the "proairetic" (for PLOT sequences), the "hermeneutic" (for interpreting and solving mysteries), the "semic" (for STEREOTYPES of CHARACTER and conduct), and the "referential" (for culturally shaped information). It is common for a developed *code* to provide its users with a paradigm of units (such as a vocabulary) along with syntactical rules for their arrangement. *Codes* are sometimes distinguished from ciphers, which are used to transform a text or a signal into a state intelligible only to those possessing the "key" to the decipherment or decryption.
    [References: Roland Barthes, *S/Z* (tr. 1975); Jonathan Culler, *Roland Barthes* (1983); R. R. K. Hartmann and F. C. Stork, eds., *Dictionary of Language and Linguistics* (1972).]

Codex: A manuscript BOOK, particularly of Biblical or CLASSICAL writing. There are over 1200 Biblical manuscripts (dating from the fourth to the sixteenth century) that exist as *codices.* Originally manuscripts were written on rolls of papyrus or parchment, but as early as the first century manuscripts were being assembled into book form or *codices.*

Coherence: A principle demanding that the parts of any composition be so arranged that the meaning of the whole may be immediately clear and intelligible. Words, phrases, clauses, within the sentence; and sentences, paragraphs, and chapters in larger pieces of writing are the units that, by their progressive and logical arrangement, make for *coherence* or, contrariwise, by illogical arrangement, result in incoherence. Literature has no need, however, of unilateral *coherence* in all its particulars. Occasional incoherence—or even unsuitable *coherence*—may perfectly register uncertainty, anxiety, terror, confusion, illness, or other common states.

Coincidence: The coinciding of events so that the movement of a PLOT is determined or significantly altered without a sense of necessity or causal relationship among the events. If two CHARACTERS by accident happen to be in the same place with results that are important to one or both, it is called *coincidence.* In CLASSICAL TRAGEDY such occurrences were considered the working out of Fate, and the same concept of human lives being drastically affected by seemingly accidental events is used in NOVELS and DRAMAS that are deterministic, such as Thomas Hardy's NOVELS and Eugene O'Neill's DRAMAS. In COMEDY and particularly in FARCE, *coincidence* is very common. It is also used widely today in the THEATER OF THE ABSURD, the ANTI-NOVEL, and the ANTIREALISTIC NOVEL, where the occurrence of fortuitous conjunctions of CHARACTERS with grave consequences reflects the "motiveless malignity" of a hostile or indifferent universe. Since any element in literature is a contrivance, the work can seem either arbitrary or governed by necessity. The devices of RHYTHM, foreshadowing, and artful arrangement make what may seem improbable (such as COINCIDENCE) probable and can make the probable seem inevitable by the confluence of acoustic, grammatical, and thematic rhythms.

Coined Words: Words consciously and arbitrarily manufactured, as opposed to those entering the language as a result of some more usual process of language development. Many words that were originally *coined words* (such as *telephone, airplane,* and *Kodak*) have become accepted terms. Constantly occurring examples of such words are those coined by commercial firms on the lookout for catchiness and enduring appeal; some of these are more or less arbitrary (such as "Kodak"), others are formed on some principle of imitation or combination (such as the words ending in "co," which stands for "company," as in Nabisco," "Texaco," "Sunoco"). Some *coinages*—such as "zipper" and "cellophane"—lose their proprietary lineaments and take their place in the language at large. At the moment, "Xerox" seems to be on the way of becoming "xerox." The coining of words is a rare and strange practice, but it can be entertaining (as in "palimony") and it has an honored place in literature. Swift, Horace Walpole, Poe, and Lewis Carroll indulged in coining; "BLURB" began as a happy coinage; James Joyce did so much coining that *Finnegans Wake* can be viewed as a one-man mint. See ACRONYM.

Collaboration: The working together of two or more people. Beaumont and Fletcher are a famous instance of *collaboration* in English literature. Despite the premium placed on individual effort in the arts, the importance of *collaboration* cannot be denied; there are instances of *collaboration* of one or another degree between Wordsworth and Coleridge, Conrad and Ford, Pound and Eliot, Fitzgerald and Hemingway. In a somewhat larger sense, any literary work can be considered a *collaboration* involving the writer and several others: forebears, friends, relatives, stenographers, printers, editors, publishers, performers, readers, and critics.

Collage: In the pictorial arts the technique by which materials not usually associated with one another, such as newspaper clippings, labels, cloth, wood, bottle tops, or theater tickets, are assembled and pasted together on a single surface. By analogy, *collage* is applied in literature to works incorporating quotations, ALLUSIONS, foreign expressions, and nonverbal elements. James Joyce, T. S. Eliot, and Ezra Pound use the device extensively, as do writers of the ANTI-NOVEL. The closing section of Eliot's *The Waste Land* is an example of the use of *collage*. See PASTICHE and MONTAGE, from which it should be distinguished.

Collate: To compare in detail two or more texts, versions, STATES, EDITIONS, IMPRESSIONS, or printings in order to determine and record the points of agreement and disagreement; also to verify the order of the sheets or SIGNATURES of a book before binding.

Collective Unconscious: A term from Jungian psychology, used in archetypal CRITICISM to refer to inherited ideas or concepts that persist as a so-called racial memory in each individual's unconscious mind and thus produce on the unconscious level attitudes and responses over which the individual has no control. See ARCHETYPE, JUNGIAN CRITICISM, MYTH.
[Reference: C. G. Jung, *The Collective Unconscious in Literature* (tr. 1967).]

Colloquialism: An expression used in informal conversation but not accepted universally in formal speech or writing. A *colloquialism* lies between the upper level of dignified, formal, academic, or "literary" language and the lower level of slang. It may differ from more formal language in pronunciation, grammar, vocabulary, syntax, IMAGERY, or CONNOTATION. As in the case of SLANG, a colloquial expression eventually may be accepted as "standard" usage. The rejection of *colloquialism* from formal writing is a matter less of snobbery than of practicality: the resources of writing are really not very well designed for the answerable representation of the graces peculiar to living speech, so that an effort to be familiar—as in the use of contractions and variants like "gal" instead of "girl"—may look more like a case of uneasy strain. Even so, the sensitive employment of *colloquialism* can ventilate a text most refreshingly. For all his reputation for stuffiness and elaboration, Henry James was a master of *colloquialism*, including the use of SLANG, contractions, and lively conversational rhythms. See SLANG, PROVINCIALISM, DIALECTS.

Colloquy (or **Colloquium**): A conversation or DIALOGUE, especially one in the nature of a formal discussion or a conference; used in this sense occasionally in literary titles, as Erasmus's *Colloquies*. See DIALOGUE.

Colonial Period in American Literature, 1607–1765: From the founding of the colony at Jamestown, which began the *Colonial Period* in America, until the Stamp Act in 1765 finally forced the colonists to see themselves as separate from their motherland, the writing produced in America was generally utilitarian, polemical, or religious. Three major figures emerged in this period: Edward Taylor, whose religious METAPHYSICAL POETRY, written at the close of the seventeenth century and the beginning of the eighteenth, did not see publication until 1937; Jonathan Edwards, whose religious and philosophical treatises have not been surpassed by an American; and Benjamin Franklin, whose Addisonian rephrasings of the teachings of the ENLIGHTENMENT are the stylistic epitome of the period.

That BELLES-LETTRES should not have flourished is hardly surprising. Whether PURITANS of the North or ROYALISTS of the South, the colonists were uniformly engaged throughout the period in possessing the land, cultivating it, making it safe and fruitful. Wilderness, Indians, and disease were common foes that demanded the strict attention of the early colonists. Wealth, government, progress, and political rights absorbed the attention of the Americans of the later *Colonial Period.*

The seventeenth century was the age of travel and personal records, DIARIES, historical and descriptive accounts, sermons, and a little VERSE—largely instructive, like Wigglesworth's *The Day of Doom,* or religious, like the *Bay Psalm Book* and the numerous funeral ELEGIES. Only Anne Bradstreet, "The Tenth Muse Lately Sprung Up in America," raised a poetic voice to be joined by that of Taylor.

In the eighteenth century the dangers of early colonization were over, but the colonial attitude persisted. Religious controversy was prevalent. Newspapers and ALMANACS flourished. Jonathan Edwards both in the pulpit and in his writing demonstrated his greatness as a thinker and a teacher. Benjamin Franklin created what was perhaps the first fully realized and widely popular American fictional character in Richard Saunders of *Poor Richard's Almanac.* William Byrd wrote with Cavalier grace and urbanity about life in Virginia and North Carolina. But little important VERSE and no native DRAMA emerged. As the period in which Americans had thought and acted like colonials drew to a close in the 1760s, a vast amount of writing had been done in America, some of it of a high quality, but very little that did not self-consciously take English authors as models and even less that could merit the term *belletristic.* See the section on "Colonial Period in American Literature," in *Outline of Literary History.*

Colophon: A publisher's symbol or device formerly placed at the end of a book but now more generally used on the title page or elsewhere near the beginning. The function of *colophons* is to identify the publisher. *Colophons* at different times and with different publishers have incorporated one or more of these items: title and author of book, the printer, the date and place of manufacture. The earliest known use of *colophons* was in the fifteenth century, when they were likely to be complete paragraphs wherein the author addressed the reader in a spirit of reverence—now that the reader had finished reading the author's work. Sir Thomas Malory, for example, closes *Le Morte Darthur* with the statement that it "was ended in the ix yere of the reygne of Kyng Edward the fourth" and asks that his readers "praye for me whyle I am on lyue that God sende me good delyuerance, and when I am deed I praye you all praye for my soule." The term is also applied to any device, including the words "The End" or "Finis," that marks the conclusion of a printed work.

Column: One of two or more vertical sections of printed material that lie side by side on a page. In a more literary sense, a feature ARTICLE that appears periodically in a newspaper or a MAGAZINE and is written by a single author. It may be comic, literary, religious, recreational, instructive, polemical, or gossipy. Although a *column* can be serious and solemn, as Walter Lippmann's were, it is the closest modern approximation to the eighteenth-century periodical ESSAY. During the first half of the twentieth century, the syndicated *column* enjoyed great popularity and was a powerful creator and creature of taste and fashion. Two of the best-known American columnists—and exemplars of the use of initials in bylines—were Bert Leston Taylor ("B. L. T.") and Franklin P. Adams ("F. P. A.").

Comedy: In medieval times the word *comedy* was applied to nondramatic literary works marked by a happy ending and a less exalted STYLE than that in TRAGEDY. Dante's *Divine Comedy*, for example, was named a *comedy* by its author because of its "prosperous, pleasant, and desirable" conclusion and because it was written not in Latin but in the vernacular "in which women and children speak."

Compared with TRAGEDY, *comedy* is a lighter form of DRAMA that aims primarily to amuse and that ends happily. It differs from FARCE and BURLESQUE by having a more sustained PLOT, weightier and subtler DIALOGUE, more lifelike CHARACTERS, and less boisterous behavior. The borderline, however, between *comedy* and other dramatic forms cannot be sharply defined, as there is much overlapping of technique, and different "kinds" are frequently combined. Even the difference between *comedy* and TRAGEDY tends to disappear in their more idealistic forms. HIGH COMEDY and LOW COMEDY may be further apart than are TRAGEDY and some serious *comedy*. Psychologists have shown the close relation between laughter and tears; and *comedy* and TRAGEDY alike sprang, both in ancient Greece and in medieval Europe, from diverging treatments of ceremonial performances. Typically, both *comedy* and TRAGEDY begin with some disturbance of equilibrium and end with some establishment or restoration of order.

Since *comedy* strives to provoke smiles and laughter, both WIT and HUMOR are utilized. In general, the comic effect arises from a recognition of some incongruity of speech, ACTION, or CHARACTER. The incongruity may be verbal, as with a play on words; or bodily, as when stilts are used; or satirical, as when the effect depends on the beholder's ability to perceive the discrepancy between fact and pretense exhibited by a braggart. The range of appeal here is wide, varying from the crudest effects of obscene LOW COMEDY to the subtlest and most idealistic reactions aroused by some HIGH COMEDY.

Viewed in another sense, *comedy* may be considered to deal with people in their human state, restrained and often made ridiculous by their limitations, faults, bodily functions, and animal nature. In contrast, TRAGEDY may be considered to deal with people in their ideal or godlike state. *Comedy* has always regarded human beings more realistically than TRAGEDY and drawn its laughter or SATIRE from the spectacle of individual or collective human weakness or failure; hence its tendency to contrast appearance and reality, to deflate pretense, and to mock excess. The judgment made by *comedy* is almost always critical.

English *comedy* developed from native dramatic forms growing out of the RELIGIOUS DRAMA, the MORALITY PLAYS and INTERLUDES, and possible folk games and PLAYS and the performances of wandering entertainers, such as dancers and jugglers. In the RENAISSANCE the rediscovery of Latin *comedy* and the effort to apply the rules of classical CRITICISM to DRAMA profoundly affected English *comedy*. Foreign influences also have at times been important, as the French influence on Restoration *comedy* or the Italian on Jacobean PASTORAL DRAMA. The more ambitious *comedy* of the earlier Elizabethans was ROMANTIC, while the *comedy* of the seventeenth century, both Jacobean and Restoration, was prevailingly REALISTIC (though the Fletcherian TRAGI-COMEDY flourished early in the century). SENTIMENTAL COMEDY was dominant in the eighteenth century but was opposed late in the period by a revival of the realistic COMEDY OF MANNERS. In the early nineteenth century such light forms as BURLESQUE and OPERETTA were popular, serious *comedy* again appearing late in the century. Some of the more prominent authors of English theatrical *comedy* are: John Lyly, Robert Greene, George Peele, William Shakespeare, Ben Jonson, George Chapman, Thomas Middleton, Thomas Heywood, John Fletcher, Philip Massinger (Elizabethans and Jacobeans); Sir George Etheredge, William Congreve, and Thomas Shadwell (Restoration); Richard Steele, Richard B. Sheridan, Oliver Goldsmith (eighteenth century); T. W. Robertson (mid-nineteenth century); H. A. Jones, Oscar Wilde, A. W. Pinero, G. B. Shaw, J. M. Barrie, Philip Barry, S. N. Behrman, Neil Simon, and Woody Allen (late nineteenth and twentieth centuries).

The nomenclature employed in describing different kinds of *comedy* being somewhat confused, it is impossible in this handbook to include all the terms. An effort has been made to include the most important, however. See HIGH COMEDY, LOW COMEDY, REALISTIC COMEDY, ROMANTIC COMEDY, COURT COMEDY, TRAGICOMEDY, SENTIMENTAL COMEDY, COMEDY OF MANNERS, COMEDY OF MORALS, INTERLUDE, TRAGEDY, DRAMA, WIT AND HUMOR.

[References: Lane Cooper, *An Aristotelian Theory of Comedy* (1922); Bonamy Dobrée, *Restoration Comedy, 1660–1720* (1924); Allardyce Nicoll, *The Theory of Drama* (1931); Wylie Sypher, ed., *Comedy* (including George Meredith's *An Essay on Comedy* and Henri Bergson's *Laughter* (1956); A. H. Thorndike, *English Comedy* (1929).]

Comedy of Humours: A term applied to the special type of REALISTIC COMEDY that was developed in the closing years of the sixteenth century by Ben Jonson and George Chapman and that derives its comic interest largely from the exhibition of CHARACTERS whose conduct is controlled by some one characteristic or whim or HUMOUR. Some single psychophysiological HUMOUR or exaggerated trait of character gave the important figures in the ACTION a definite bias of disposition and supplied the chief motive for their actions. Thus, in Jonson's *Every Man in His Humour* (acted 1598), which made this type of PLAY popular, all the words and acts of Kitely are controlled by an overpowering suspicion that his wife is unfaithful; George Downright, a country squire, must be "frank" above all things; the country gull in town determines his every decision by his desire to "catch on" to the manners of the city gallant. In his "Induction" to *Every Man out of His Humour* (1599) Jonson explains his character-formula thus:

> Some one peculiar quality
> Doth so possess a man, that it doth draw
> All his affects, his spirits, and his powers,
> In their confluctions, all to run one way.

The *comedy of humours* owes something to earlier vernacular COMEDY but more to a desire to imitate the classical COMEDY of Plautus and Terence and to combat the vogue of ROMANTIC COMEDY. Its satiric purpose and realistic method are emphasized and lead later into more serious character studies, as in Jonson's *The Alchemist.* It affected Shakespeare's art to some degree—the "humourous" man appearing now and again in his plays (Leontes in *The Winter's Tale* is a good example)—and most of Shakespeare's tragic heroes are such because they allow some one trait of character (such as jealousy or fastidiousness) to be overdeveloped and thus to upset the balance necessary to a poised, well-rounded personality. The *comedy of humors* was closely related to the contemporary COMEDY OF MANNERS and exerted an important influence upon the COMEDY of the Restoration Period. See COMEDY OF MANNERS.

Comedy of Intrigue: A COMEDY in which the manipulation of the ACTION by one or more CHARACTERS to their own ends is of more importance than the CHARACTERS themselves are. Another name for COMEDY OF SITUATION.

Comedy of Manners: A term most commonly used to designate the REALISTIC, often satirical, COMEDY of the Restoration, as practiced by Congreve and others. It is also used for the revival, in modified form, of this COMEDY a hundred years later by Goldsmith and Sheridan, as well as for another revival late in the nineteenth century. Likewise, the REALISTIC COMEDY of Elizabethan and Jacobean times is sometimes called *comedy of manners.* In the stricter sense of the term, the type is concerned with the manners and conventions of an artificial, highly sophisticated society. The stylized fashions, manners, and outlook of this social group dominate the surface and determine the pace and tone of this sort of COMEDY. CHARACTERS are more likely to be types than individualized personalities. PLOT, though often involving a clever handling of situation and intrigue, is less important than ATMOSPHERE, DIALOGUE, and SATIRE. The DIALOGUE is witty and finished, sometimes brilliant. The appeal is intellectual but not imaginative or idealistic. SATIRE is directed in the main against the follies and deficiencies of typical characters, such as fops, would-be wits, jealous husbands, coxcombs, and others who fail somehow to conform to the conventional attitudes and manners of elegant society. This SATIRE is directed against the aberrations of social behavior rather than of human conduct in its larger aspects. A distinguishing characteristic of the *comedy of manners* is its emphasis on an illicit love duel, involving at least one pair of witty and often amoral lovers. This prevalence of the immoral "love game" is explained partly by the manners of the time and social groups concerned and partly by the special satirical purpose of the comedy itself. In its SATIRE, REALISM, and employment of "humours" the *comedy of manners* was indebted to Elizabethan and Jacobean COMEDY. It owed something, of course, to the French *comedy of manners* as practiced by Molière.

The reaction against the questionable morality of the PLAYS and a growing sentimentalism brought about the downfall of this type of COMEDY near the close of the seventeenth century, and it was largely supplanted through most of the eighteenth century by SENTIMENTAL COMEDY. Purged of its objectionable features, however, the *comedy of manners* was revived by Goldsmith and Sheridan late in the eighteenth century and in a somewhat new and brighter garb by Oscar Wilde late in the nineteenth century. The *comedy of manners* has been popular in the twentieth century in the works of playwrights like Noel Coward, Somerset Maugham, and Philip Barry.

A few typical *comedies of manners* are: Wycherley, *The Plain Dealer* (1674); Etheredge, *The Man of Mode* (1676); Congreve, *The Way of the World* (1700); Goldsmith, *She Stoops to Conquer* (1773); Sheridan, *The Rivals* (1775) and *The School for Scandal* (1777); Wilde, *The Importance of Being Earnest* (1895); Maugham, *The Circle* (1921); Coward, *Private Lives* (1931); and Barry, *The Philadelphia Story* (1939). For a couple of decades, roughly from 1930 to 1950, adaptations of the *comedy of manners* constituted a popular film genre. See HIGH COMEDY, REALISTIC COMEDY, COMEDY OF HUMOURS.

[References: David L. Hirst, *Comedy of Manners* (1979); Kenneth Muir, *The Comedy of Manners* (1970); Allardyce Nicoll, *A History of Restoration Drama,* 2nd ed. (1928); John Palmer, *The Comedy of Manners* (1913, reprinted 1962).]

Comedy of Morals: A term applied to COMEDY that uses ridicule to correct abuses, hence a form of dramatic SATIRE, aimed at the moral state of a people or a special class of people. Molière's *Tartuffe* (1664) is often considered a *comedy of morals.*

Comedy of Situation: A COMEDY concentrating chiefly on ingenuity of PLOT rather than on CHARACTER interest; COMEDY OF INTRIGUE. Background is less important than ridiculous and incongruous situations, a heaping up of mistakes, PLOTS within plots, disguises, mistaken identity, unexpected meetings, close calls. A capital example is Shakespeare's *The Comedy of Errors,* a play in which the possibilities for confusion are multiplied by the use of twin brothers who have twins as servants. In each case the twins look so much alike that at times they doubt their own identity. A COMEDY of this sort sometimes approaches FARCE. Ben Jonson's *Epicoene* and Middleton's *A Trick to Catch the Old One* are later Elizabethan *comedies of situation* or intrigue. A modern example is Shaw's *You Never Can Tell.* The phrase *comedy of situation* is sometimes used also to refer merely to an incident, such as Falstaff's description of his fight with the robbers in Shakespeare's *King Henry the Fourth,* Part I. See FARCE-COMEDY.

Comic Opera: An OPERETTA, or comedy OPERA, stressing SPECTACLE and music but employing spoken DIALOGUE. An early example is Sheridan's *The Duenna* (1775). The best-known *comic operas* are those of Gilbert and Sullivan, such as *The Mikado,* produced in London, chiefly at the Savoy (constructed for the purpose) in the 1870s and 1880s. See BALLAD-OPERA.

Comic Relief: A humorous SCENE, INCIDENT, or speech in the course of a serious FICTION or DRAMA. Such comic intrusions are usually introduced to provide relief from emotional intensity and, by contrast, to heighten the seriousness of the story. The original sense, related to "elevate," implies any sort of contrast, as that between high and low or raised and flat in a so-called relief map. The later sense of "easing" may not always apply to *comic relief*, since it can have the nearly immediate effect of deepening tragic pain with scarcely a moment's relaxation. When properly employed, it can enrich and deepen the tragic implications of the ACTION. Notable examples are the drunken porter scene in *Macbeth* (see De Quincey's essay, "On the Knocking at the Gate in Macbeth"), the gravedigger scene in *Hamlet*, and Mercutio's personality in *Romeo and Juliet*. Although not a portion of Aristotle's formula for a TRAGEDY, *comic relief* has been almost universally employed by English playwrights.

Comitatus: The Latin name for the band of military adherents and dependents around a king, hero, or other leader, to whom they are bound by mutual ties of fidelity and allegiance. Originally a group of warriors, the *comitatus* was transformed, in the late Middle Ages, into a more general court of supporters. The concept of fellowship and the dedication to revenge make the *comitatus* an important element in early Germanic culture and its literature, including *Beowulf*.

Commedia Dell'arte: Improvised COMEDY; a form of Italian LOW COMEDY dating from very early times, in which the actors, who usually performed conventional or STOCK parts, such as the "pantaloon" (Venetian merchant), improvised their DIALOGUE, though a PLOT or SCENARIO was provided. A "harlequin" interrupted the ACTION at times with low buffoonery. A parallel or later form of the *commedia dell'arte* was the masked COMEDY, in which conventional figures (usually in masks) spoke particular dialects (as the Pulcinella, the rogue from Naples). There is some evidence that the *commedia dell'arte* colored English LOW COMEDY from early times, but its chief influence on the English stage came in the eighteenth century in connection with the development of such SPECTACLE forms as the PANTOMIME. The *commedia dell'arte* also influenced the theatrical practice of Shakespeare and Molière.

Common Measure: A STANZA form, also called COMMON METER, defined next.

Common Meter: A STANZA of four LINES, the first and third being IAMBIC TETRAMETER (eight syllables, ⌣´,⌣´,⌣´,⌣´) and the second and fourth IAMBIC TRIMETER (six syllables, ⌣´,⌣´,⌣´), rhymed *abab* or *abcb*. Isaac Watts wrote many such QUATRAINS:

> There is a land of pure delight
>   Where saints immortal reign;
> Infinite day excludes the night,
>   And pleasures banish pain.

It is distinguished from the BALLAD STANZA principally by its metrical regularity. Often called COMMON MEASURE, it is designated in hymnals by the abbreviation *C.M.* Although exceptions on both sides abound, the most usual RHYME SCHEME for the BALLAD type of QUATRAIN is *abcb*, and that of *common meter* is *abab*.

Commonplace Book: A classified collection of quotations or ARGUMENTS prepared for reference purposes. Thus, a reader interested in moral philosophy might collect thoughts and quotations under such heads as truth, virtue, or friendship. *Commonplace books* were utilized by authors of ESSAYS, theological ARGUMENTS, and other serious treatises. The *Commonplace Book* of John Milton is still in existence. The term is also sometimes applied to private collections of favorite pieces of literature such as the poetical MISCELLANIES of Elizabethan times. It is in this sense that W. H. Auden's *A Certain World* is a *commonplace book*. R. W. Stallman's *The Critic's Notebook* is an excellent *commonplace book* of the NEW CRITICISM.

Commonwealth (or Puritan) Interregnum: The period between the execution of Charles I in 1649 and the restoration of the monarchy under Charles II in 1660, during which England was ruled by Parliament under the control of the PURITAN leader Oliver Cromwell, whose death in 1658 marked the beginning of the end of the Commonwealth. John Milton was Latin Secretary in the Commonwealth government. Although the theaters were closed in 1642, dramatic performances continued more or less openly, but the only significant new DRAMA was D'Avenant's *The Siege of Rhodes* (1656), a spectacle PLAY heralding the HEROIC DRAMA soon to come in the RESTORATION. It was an age of major PROSE works: Milton's political PAMPHLETS, Hobbes's *Leviathan* (1651), Jeremy Taylor's *Holy Dying* and *Holy Living* (1650, 1651), Walton's *The Compleat Angler* (1653), and works by Sir Thomas Browne and Thomas Fuller. The age delighted in translations of the contemporary French prose ROMANCES, and in 1654 Roger Boyle published *Parthenissa*, a precursor of the NOVEL. In POETRY Vaughan, Waller, Cowley, D'Avenant, and Marvell flourished; the metaphysical strain continued; and two attempts at the EPIC were made, D'Avenant's *Gondibert* (1650) and Cowley's *Davideis* (1656), but both are incomplete. By the end of the *Commonwealth Interregnum*, John Dryden's poetic career was under way. He and Marvell, both of whose best works were to come later, shared with Milton the honor of being the best POETS of a troubled time, although they wrote little poetry during it. According to some accounts, the Protectorate is limited to a period between 1653 and 1659 inside the limits of the *Commonwealth Interregnum*.

Companion Poems: POEMS by the same author designed to complement each other. Each of the POEMS is complete by itself, but each is enriched and broadened in feeling or meaning when viewed with its *companion poem*. Milton wrote complementary *companion poems*, not only in the obvious set-piece pairing of "L'Allegro" and "Il Penseroso" but also in the much larger orbit of *Paradise Lost* and *Paradise Regained*. Robert Browning was fond of *companion poems* and may be said to have specialized therein: "Johannes Agricola in Meditation" and "Porphyria's Lover" are *companion poems*, as are "The Italian in England" and "The Englishman in Italy," "Home-Thoughts, from Abroad" and "Home-Thoughts, from the Sea," "Meeting at Night" and "Parting at Morning," "Fra Lippo Lippi" and "Andrea del Sarto," "Love in a Life" and "Life in a Love," "Before" and "After," "One Way of Love" and "Another Way of Love," "Natural Magic" and "Magical Nature," and "The Cardinal and the Dog" and "The Pope and the Net." The POEMS constituting Eliot's *Four Quartets*, with their matching titles and general structural parallels and resemblances, qualify as *companion poems*.

Comparative Literature: The study of literatures of different languages, nations, and periods with a view to examining and analyzing their relationships.
In the Middle Ages the literatures of Western Europe were generally considered to be parts of a unified whole, mostly because they were frequently
written in a common language, Latin. In the nineteenth century, concurrently
with the beginnings of the comparative study of religion and mythology, various European scholars began to develop theories and methods for the comparative study of the literatures of different languages and nationalities. Among
these scholars were Villemain, Ampère, Baldensperger, Sainte-Beuve, Taine,
Brunetière, and Brandes. Several different approaches to the examination of
comparative literatures have developed: the study of popular forms, such as
LEGENDS, MYTHS, and EPICS; the study of literary GENRES and FORMS—what
Brunetière called the *évolution des genres;* the study of sources, particularly
those that different literatures have in common; the study of mutual influences
among authors and movements; and the study of aesthetic and CRITICAL THEO-
RIES and methods. *Comparative literature* is now a major field of literary
study.

[References: Robert J. Clements, *Comparative Literature as Academic Discipline* (1978); Henry Gifford, *Comparative Literature* (1969); Ulrich Werner
Weisstein, *Comparative Literature and Literary Theory* (tr. 1973).]

Compendium: A brief condensation of a longer work or of a whole field of
knowledge. A *compendium* is a systematic presentation of essentials. It differs
from an ABRIDGMENT in that it does not attempt to present the general characteristics of the work or works from which its data are drawn. Indeed, it most
often is used to present a concise and well-organized summary of data on a
specific subject drawn from many sources, no single one of which is imitated
in tone or organization.

Compensation: In METRICS a means of making up for omissions in a line; a
form of SUBSTITUTION. Such omissions are usually unstressed syllables; the
customary means of compensating for their absence is the pause, which has
the effect of a *rest* in music, as Tennyson's lines illustrate:

> Break, break, break
> On thy cold grey stones, O Sea!

These lines have three stressed syllables each and metrically they are approximately equivalent, despite there being only three syllables in the first but
seven in the second. The pronounced pauses following each word of the first
LINE compensate for the unstressed syllables that have been omitted. This
phenomenon, which may seem sophisticated, can be seen at work in lines as
simple as "One, two, / Buckle your shoe." See SUBSTITUTION.

Complaint: A LYRIC poem, common in the Middle Ages and the RENAIS-
SANCE, in which the POET (1) laments the unresponsiveness of his mistress,
as in Surrey's "A Complaint by Night of the Lover Not Beloved"; (2) bemoans
his unhappy lot and seeks to remedy it, as in "The Complaint of Chaucer to

his Empty Purse"; or (3) regrets the sorry state of the world, as in Spenser's *Complaints.* In a *complaint,* which usually takes the form of a MONOLOGUE, the POET commonly explains his sad mood, describes the causes of it, discusses possible remedies, or appeals to some lady or divinity for help from his distress. Ezra Pound's Canto XXXVI is a studied "compleynt," and Samuel Beckett, in some youthful POEMS, revived the Provençal *complaint* form called *Enueg* for some poems of his own. The BLUES may be seen as a modern version or counterpart of the *complaint.*

Complication: That part of a PLOT in which the entanglement caused by the CONFLICT of opposing forces is developed. It is the tying of the knot to be untied in the RESOLUTION. In the five-part idea of DRAMATIC STRUCTURE, it is synonymous with RISING ACTION. The second ACT of a five-act TRAGEDY has been called "the act of *complication.*" See DRAMATIC STRUCTURE, ACT.

Composition in Depth: A term in FILM CRITICISM THAT describes a method by which everything in the field of vision of the camera, from immediate foreground to deep background, is kept in focus. This method is in contrast to ANALYTIC EDITING and to MONTAGE, in that the camera remains in a relatively fixed position and the ACTION unfolds before it. *Composition in depth* is often called DEEP FOCUS. An early and distinguished example is Orson Welles's *Citizen Kane.* See ANALYTIC EDITING, MONTAGE.

Comstockery: Overzealous, prudish monitoring and censorship of the arts because of their supposed immorality. The term is derived from Anthony Comstock (1844–1915), an American reformer.

Concatenation: A name sometimes applied to CHAIN VERSE.

Conceit: Originally the term, almost synonymous with "idea," "concept," or "conception," implied something conceived in the mind. Its later application to a type of poetic METAPHOR retains the original sense, in that *conceit* implies ingenuity whether applied to the Petrarchan conventions of the ELIZABETHAN PERIOD or the elaborate and witty extended analogies of the writers of META-PHYSICAL VERSE.

The term designates an ingenious and fanciful notion or conception, usually expressed through an elaborate ANALOGY and pointing to a striking parallel between ostensibly dissimilar things. A *conceit* may be a brief METAPHOR, but it also may form the framework of an entire POEM. In English there are two basic kinds of *conceit:* the PETRARCHAN CONCEIT, most often found in love POEMS and SONNETS, in which the subject is compared extensively and elaborately to some object, such as a rose, a ship, a garden; and the METAPHYS-ICAL CONCEIT, in which complex, startling, paradoxical, and highly intellectual analogies abound. Modern *conceits* turn up in protracted ANALOGIES, such as those in Pound's "Portrait d'une Femme" ("Your mind and you are our Sargasso Sea") and Frost's single-sentence sonnet that begins, "She is as in a field a silken tent."

In the eighteenth and nineteenth centuries the term took on a derogatory sense, the *conceit* being considered strained, arbitrary, affected, and false. Samuel Johnson was particularly devastating on the METAPHYSICAL CONCEIT.

Today the term is more nearly neutral, being used to describe the unhappy overreaches of POETS as well as their striking and effective comparisons. In contemporary VERSE the *conceit* is again a respected vehicle for the expression of witty perceptions and telling ANALOGIES. In the past century the *conceit* has figured less in British POETRY than in the work of a number of Americans, such as Pound and Frost, mentioned previously, as well as Dickinson, Eliot, Ransom, and Allen Tate. It is rare in *prose,* but instances have been identified in the Jacobean sermons of John Donne and Lancelot Andrewes. See META-PHYSICAL CONCEIT, PETRARCHAN CONCEIT, CONTROLLING IMAGE, METAPHYS-ICAL VERSE, BAROQUE, GONGORISM, MARINISM.

[References: Lu Emily Pearson, *Elizabethan Love Conventions* (1933); K. K. Ruthven, *The Conceit* (1969); F. E. Schelling, *English Literature During the Lifetime of Shakespeare* (1910).]

Concordance: An alphabetical index of most or all of the words in a text or in the works of an author. Today *concordances* are usually produced by computers.

Concrete Poetry: POETRY that exploits the graphic, visual aspect of writing; a specialized application of what Aristotle called *opsis* ("spectacle") and Pound "phanopoeia." A *concrete poem* is one that is also a work of graphic art; the painter Paul Klee produced some early examples. The contemporary American ANAGRAM "Seascape" shows the way in which such poetry can take advantage of the visible shapes of letters and words to make a picture:

oceanoceanocean

oceancanoeocean

oceanoceanocean

[References: Mary Ellen Solt, *Concrete Poetry: A World View* (1969); Emmett Williams, ed., *An Anthology of Concrete Poetry* (1967).]

Concrete Universal: A critical term used to designate the idea that a work of art expresses the universal through the concrete and the particular. The quarrel between the universal and the particular in literature is at least as old as Aristotle, who located POETRY between the universals of philosophy and the particulars of history. The writers in periods of CLASSICISM and NEO-CLASSICISM tend to stress the universal; those in periods of ROMANTICISM and REALISM the particular. Yet, if literature is "knowledge brought to the heart," it must talk ultimately of universals but express them dramatically in CONCRETE TERMS in particular instances. See UNIVERSALITY, ARCHETYPE, ALLEGORY.

[Reference: W. K. Wimsatt, *The Verbal Icon* (1954).]

Condensation: A shortened form of a longer work but one that attempts to retain its salient characteristics, including STYLE. *Condensation* is very much like ABRIDGMENT in basic meaning; however, it is usually applied to a shortened version of a work of FICTION, whereas the application of ABRIDGMENT is broader.

Confession: A form of AUTOBIOGRAPHY that deals with customarily hidden or highly private matters. The *confession* usually has a theoretical or intellectual emphasis in which religion, politics, art, or some such ideological interest is important. One distinctive aspect of the *confession* is the way in which it gives an intellectualized account of intensely personal and introverted experiences. It is what the author has learned about such matters that makes his or her inner life a fitting subject for a book. St. Augustine established the form with his *Confessions* in the fifth century. Sir Thomas Browne's *Religio Medici* and John Bunyan's *Grace Abounding* were seventeenth-century English *confessions*. Jean-Jacques Rousseau gave it a modern form and popularity with his *Confessions* in the eighteenth century. Thomas De Quincey's *Confessions of an English Opium Eater* and Alfred de Musset's *Confessions d'un enfant du siècle* are nineteenth-century examples. Elements of *confession* turn up in Eliot's *Four Quartets,* Pound's *Pisan Cantos,* and later, at a pitch that approaches amiable CARICATURE, in Norman Mailer's *Armies of the Night.* In a somewhat narrower sense, the privileged credibility of the so-called deathbed *confession* informs Browning's "The Bishop Orders His Tomb at Saint Praxed's Church."

The term *confession* is often applied to fictional works that place an emphasis on the introspective view of a CHARACTER in the process of developing attitudes toward life, religion, or art. In this sense the APPRENTICESHIP NOVEL, the BILDUNGSROMAN, and the KÜNSTLERROMAN are all *confessions.*

Confessional Poetry: A term applied to the work of a group of contemporary POETS whose POETRY features a public and sometimes painful display of private, personal matters. In *confessional poetry* the POET often seems to address the audience directly, without the intervention of a PERSONA. Notable examples of such POETS are Allen Ginsberg, Sylvia Plath, Anne Sexton, Robert Lowell, and John Berryman.

[Reference: Robert S. Philips, *The Confessional Poets* (1973).]

Confidant (feminine, **Confidante**): A CHARACTER in a NOVEL or a DRAMA who takes little part in the ACTION but is a close friend to the PROTAGONIST and who receives the confidences and intimate thoughts of the PROTAGONIST. The use of the *confidant* enables a dramatist to reveal the thoughts and intentions of the PROTAGONIST without the use of ASIDES or SOLILOQUIES or the POINT OF VIEW of an OMNISCIENT AUTHOR. Well-known *confidants* are Horatio in *Hamlet,* Dr. Watson in the Sherlock Holmes stories, and Maria Gostrey in James's *The Ambassadors.* James referred to Maria Gostrey and similar *confidantes* as FICELLES, who function primarily as a means of allowing central characters to comment on their own experience. See CHORUS, FICELLE.

Conflict: The struggle that grows out of the interplay of the two opposing forces in a PLOT. *Conflict* provides interest, suspense, and tension. At least one of the opposing forces is usually a person, or, if an animal or an inanimate object, is treated as though it were a person. This person, usually the PROTAGONIST, may be involved in *conflicts* of four different kinds: (1) a struggle against nature, as in Jack London's "To Build a Fire"; (2) a struggle against another person, usually the ANTAGONIST, as in Stevenson's *Treasure Island* and most MELODRAMA; (3) a struggle against society, as in the novels of Dickens and George Eliot; or (4) a struggle for mastery by two elements within the person, as in the RESTORATION HEROIC DRAMA or in *Macbeth.* A fifth possible kind of *conflict* is often cited, the struggle against Fate or destiny; however, except where the gods themselves actively appear, such a struggle is realized though the action of one or more of the four basic *conflicts*. Seldom do we find a simple, single *conflict* in a PLOT, but rather a complex one partaking of two or even all of the preceding elements. For example, the basic *conflict* in *Hamlet* may be interpreted as a struggle within Hamlet himself, but it is certainly also a struggle against his uncle as ANTAGONIST and, if the Freudian interpretations of motive are accepted, even a struggle against nature and destiny. Dreiser's *Sister Carrie* records a girl's struggle against society, as represented by the city, and yet it is a struggle against her animal nature and even partly with herself. Even so seemingly simple a story as London's "To Build a Fire," in which the PROTAGONIST battles the cold unsuccessfully, is also the record of an inner *conflict. Conflict* not only implies the struggle of a PROTAGONIST against someone or something, it also implies the existence of some MOTIVATION for the *conflict* or some goal to be achieved thereby. *Conflict* is the raw material out of which PLOT is constructed. In the terminology associated with Greek DRAMA, the *conflict*, in the form of an extended debate, was called the AGON. Our terms PROTAGONIST and ANTAGONIST are derived from the roles these CHARACTERS play in the *conflict*. See PLOT, MOTIVATION, PROTAGONIST, ANTAGONIST, DRAMATIC STRUCTURE.

Connecticut Wits: A group of eighteenth-century American POETS associated with Hartford, Connecticut, and often called the HARTFORD WITS, under which heading they are discussed. Much later, the term was applied rather derisively to such poets as Richard Wilbur and James Merrill who lived awhile in Connecticut and dealt in wit of some sort.

Connotation: The emotional implications that words may carry, as distinguished from their denotative meanings. *Connotations* may be (1) private and personal, the result of individual experience, (2) group (national, linguistic, racial), or (3) general or universal, held by all or most people. *Connotation* depends on usage in a particular linguistic community and climate. A purely private and personal *connotation* cannot be communicated; the *connotation* must be shared to be intelligible to others. See DENOTATION.

Consonance: The use at the ends of VERSES of words in which the final consonants in the stressed syllables agree but the vowels that precede them differ, as "add-read," "bill-ball," and "born-burn." In view of the vagaries attending the ways in which vowels are pronounced and spelled, most so-called EYE RHYMES (such as "word" and "lord," or "blood," "food," and "good") are instances of *consonance*, as are the hymnals' rhymes between "river" and "ever" or "heaven" and "given." Shelley seems uncommonly fond of *consonance*, as in several terminations in "Ode to the West Wind" ("even," "Heaven," "striven"; "tone," "one"; "fierce," "universe"; "Wind," "behind"). Emily Dickinson was another devotee, and in her RIDDLE poem beginning "I like to see it lap the Miles" all of the rhyming positions are superseded by *consonance* ("up" "step"; "peer," "pare"; "while," "hill"; and "Star," "door"). *Consonance* is also sometimes called HALF RHYME and SLANT RHYME. See ASSONANCE.

Conte: The French word for TALE, *conte* is used in several and sometimes conflicting senses. In its original sense it referred to a short TALE of adventure.

It came in the nineteenth century, particularly in France, to be used for SHORT STORIES of tightly constructed PLOT and great concision, such as those by Maupassant. In this sense it designates a work shorter and more concise than a NOUVELLE. However, in England the term is sometimes used for a work longer than a SHORT STORY and shorter than a NOVEL. This usage is flatly contradictory to the modern French usage. In most cases the reader must consider both the nation and the period to which *conte* is assigned to determine whether it refers to a TALE of marvelous adventures, a tightly knit SHORT STORY, or a NOVELLA.

Contextualism: Although *contextualism* may simply refer to the relation of a work of verbal art to its various contexts, such as social, cultural, or biographical environments, it is today applied in a narrower sense to CRITICISM for which the verbal structure of a literary work is the autonomous context that generates self-referential meanings. *Contextualism* in this sense sees the work, independent of all forms of external discourse, as providing its own self-sufficient structure. *Contextualism* thus is similar to the NEW CRITICISM, in that it regards a work of literary art as totally untranslatable, its meaning a function of its literal verbal configuration. The system builds on that of I. A. Richards. Among its advocates are Cleanth Brooks, Eliseo Vivas, and Murray Krieger.

Contrapuntal: The adjectival form of *counterpoint,* a musical term. It is derived from the Latin phrase *punctus contra punctum,* meaning point against point. In music the term refers to compositions in which there is a combination of parts or voices, each independently significant and rendered simultaneously or in close sequence with others to form a complex but coherent texture. By analogy *contrapuntal* is applied to literary works in which elements are played against each other by being presented simultaneously or in very close sequence, often creating the effect of MONTAGE or in film of ANALYTIC EDITING. In *Vanity Fair,* for example, the fortunes of Amelia and Becky are in *contrapuntal* relation to each other, one improving as the other deteriorates. An interesting experiment in *contrapuntal* construction of a NOVEL is Aldous Huxley's *Point Counter Point.*

Contrast: A device by which one element is thrown into opposition to another for the sake of emphasis or clarity. The effect of the device is to make both contrasted ideas clearer than either would have been if described by itself. The principle of *contrast,* however, serves other purposes than definition or clarity. Skillfully used, *contrast* may become, like colors to the painter or chords to the musician, a means of arousing deep emotions.

Controlling Image: An IMAGE or METAPHOR that runs throughout and determines the form or nature of a literary work. Frost's sonnet "The Silken Tent" involves the *controlling image* that the title indicates; the *controlling image* of the following POEM by Edward Taylor is the making of cloth:

> Make me, O Lord, thy Spinning Wheele compleat;
> Thy Holy Worde my Distaff make for mee.
> Make mine Affections thy Swift Flyers neate,
> And make my Soule thy holy Spoole to bee.

My Conversation make to be thy Reele,
And reele the yarn thereon spun of thy Wheele.

Make me thy Loome then, knit therein this Twine:
And make thy Holy Spirit, Lord, winde quills:
Then weave the Web thyselfe. The yarn is fine.
Thine Ordinances make my Fulling Mills.
Then dy the same in Heavenly Colours Choice,
All pinkt with Varnish't Flowers of Paradise.

Then cloath therewith mine Understanding, Will,
Affections, Judgment, Conscience, Memory;
My Words and Actions, that their shine may fill
My wayes with glory and thee glorify.
Then mine apparell shall display before yee
That I am Cloathed in Holy robes for glory.

See FUNDAMENTAL IMAGE, CONCEIT, METAPHYSICAL CONCEIT, IMAGE.

Convention: A literary *convention* is any device, STYLE, or subject that has become a recognized means of literary expression, an accepted element in technique. The use of ALLITERATIVE VERSE among the ANGLO-SAXONS and of the HEROIC COUPLET in the time of Dryden or Pope are *conventions* in this sense. The personified virtues of the MORALITY PLAYS, the braggart soldier of the Elizabethan stage, and the fainting heroine of sentimental FICTION are examples of conventional STOCK CHARACTERS. Features that become *conventions* usually arise from original freshness of appeal, acquire a comfortable familiarity, and eventually, through excessive or unskillful use, become distasteful and fall into disuse. Sometimes, however, discarded *conventions* can come back to life, as when the French POET Villon successfully revived the BALLADE. Poetic IMAGERY tends to become conventional, as when a CODE of EPITHETS, adjectives, METAPHORS, and SIMILES came to be regarded by the Augustans as "poetic." Every medium of literary expression has its necessary *conventions,* that is, its accepted techniques for expressing its materials. The DRAMA has such *conventions* as the SOLILOQUY, in which a CHARACTER speaks his or her thoughts but is not overheard by others on the stage, and the invisible FOURTH WALL through which the audience watches the action on a BOX SET. The NOVEL and the SHORT STORY employ the *convention* that ACTION recorded in the past tense is assumed to be unresolved at the time of reading. There are also *conventions* of subject matter; today, for example, frank treatment of sex has become so conventional as to be almost obligatory in FICTION. Although *conventions* can be trite and even painful when overdone, it should be recognized that they are also essential to communication. See TRADITION, STOCK CHARACTERS, MOTIF, DRAMATIC CONVENTIONS.
[Reference: J. L. Lowes, *Convention and Revolt in Poetry* (1919).]

Conversation Piece (or Conversation Poem): Some of Horace's works are called *sermones,* which does not mean "sermon" in the modern homiletic sense but rather "discourse" or "conversation" with an addressee and some element of serious SATIRE. Although rather relaxed and informal, the *conversation poem* develops only among cultivated writers in periods of marked refinement. Coleridge, who omitted SATIRE, perfected the form in such personal works as "The Eolian Harp," "This Lime-Tree Bower My Prison," and "Frost at Midnight." The typical example represents only one side of a conversation, which may be with an interlocutor who is absent or asleep. The FORM is not strictly defined, but most are in BLANK VERSE. Among modern writers, Robert Frost and W. H. Auden, openly imitating Horace, have produced *conversation poems* with more bite but less intensity than Coleridge's. See also DRAMATIC MONOLOGUE.

Copy: Material, either in manuscript or printed form, that is to be set in type or duplicated by some other printing process. The term is used in the singular without an article, as "When can you supply *copy* for the printer?" *Copy* that has been set and that bears printers' and editors' markings is called "foul."

Copy Text: That particular text of a work used by a textual scholar as the basic text against which to compare various EDITIONS, IMPRESSIONS, and ISSUES in an effort to arrive at the closest possible approximation of the author's original intent. If the author's manuscript exists, it is usually used as the *copy text;* if no manuscript exists, the first printed EDITION set directly from the author's manuscript is usually the *copy text,* although works that have undergone major revision by the author between EDITIONS present complex problems.

Copyright: The exclusive legal right to publish or reproduce for sale works of literature and art. A *copyright* is designed to protect an author, artist, or publisher from having others make and sell copies of works without permission. Books, articles, PLAYS, musical compositions, pictures, films, recordings, and other forms of art can be protected by *copyright.* A *copyright* protects the unique form or mode of expression; subject matter and ideas cannot be copyrighted. Secondary rights—the right to serialize, to adapt unique content to another medium, such as stage, motion picture, or television, to store on computer tape, to reproduce by various processes—are highly complex and present complicated problems.

The right to reproduce works is protected for the author or publisher in the United States by a Copyright Act, passed in 1976, which became effective on January 1, 1978. This Act gives *copyright* protection for the life of the author plus fifty years. It extends the *copyright* protection for existing published works to seventy-five years. Such rights had been protected by an Act of 1909, which had given protection for twenty-eight years, renewable once, making a maximum protection of fifty-six years. In England the Copyright Act of 1911 protects a work for the author's life plus fifty years. The International Copyright Convention of 1891 is an agreement dealing with international aspects of *copyright* protection, but it is generally considered inadequate.

Coronach: A SONG of lamentation; a funeral DIRGE. A Gaelic word reflecting a custom in Ireland (where KEENING is the common term) and in the Scottish Highlands. The word means a "wailing together," and a typical *coronach* was sung by women. In one of his NOVELS Sir Walter Scott says, "Their wives and daughters came, clapping their hands, and crying the coronach, and shrieking." In *The Lady of the Lake* (stanza xvi of canto III) appears a *coronach* of Scott's composition:

> He is gone on the mountain,
> He is lost to the forest,
> Like a summer-dried fountain,
> When our need was the sorest. . . .

Corpus Christi Plays: Medieval religious PLAYS based on the BIBLE and performed by town guilds on movable wagons, or PAGEANTS, as a part of the procession on Corpus Christi day (the first Thursday after Trinity Sunday). See MYSTERY PLAYS.

Correlative Verses: Verses that take the form of abbreviated sentences having a linear correlative relationship. An example is Milton's lines from *Paradise Lost:*

> Air, water, earth
> By fowl, fish, beast, was flown, was swum, was walked.

These lines constitute three correlative sentences: "Air by fowl was flown. Water by fish was swum. Earth by beast was walked." Another example is these lines from the *Greek Anthology:*

> You [wine] are boldness, youth, strength, wealth, country
> To the shy, the old, the weak, the poor, the foreign.

These lines constitute five correlative statements, beginning: "You, wine, are boldness to the shy, youth to the old," and so on. *Correlative verses* were frequent in CLASSICAL Greek and Latin POETRY and in medieval and Renaissance writing. They can become bewildering. Ophelia's great lament on Hamlet's ostensible madness ("Oh, what a noble mind is here o'erthrouwn!") continues with a conspicuously disturbed *correlative* line: "The courtier's, soldier's, scholar's, eye, tongue, sword . . . quite, quite down!"

Cothurnus: The BUSKIN, a thick-soled, laced boot worn by actors in Greek TRAGEDY. See BUSKIN.

Counterplayers: The CHARACTERS in a DRAMA who plot against the HERO or heroine, e.g., Claudius, Polonius, Laertes, and their associates in *Hamlet.* See ANTAGONIST.

Counterplot: A secondary PLOT that contrasts with the principal PLOT of the work; a SUBPLOT.

Counterpoint Rhythm: A term used by Gerard Manley Hopkins to describe the superimposing of a different RHYTHM on one already established. According to Hopkins we hear the new RHYTHM but still remember the old, so that two RHYTHMS run concurrently in our minds. Milton was, Hopkins asserted, the great master of *counterpoint rhythm,* and the choruses of *Samson Agonistes* were excellent examples of it. The following chorus LINES, which follow speeches in regular IAMBIC PENTAMETER, are examples (the mind is hearing the PENTAMETER behind them):

> Just are the ways of God,
> And justifiable to Men;
> Unless there be who think not God at all.

It should be noted, however, that Karl Shapiro feels that such a CHORUS in *Samson Agonistes* "flows by the count of ear and no more scans . . . than Hebrew." Certainly *counterpoint rhythm* is sufficiently subjective to defy precise analysis. Hopkins applied the term to conspicuous instances of rhythmic substitution, as in his line "Generations have trod, have trod, have trod," in which the first word furnishes two TROCHEES in counterpoint to the IAMBS that the prevailing RHYTHM leads the ear to anticipate.

Coup de Théâtre: A surprising and usually unmotivated stroke in a DRAMA that produces a sensational effect; by extension, any piece of claptrap or anything designed solely for effect.

Couplet: Two lines of VERSE with similar END-RHYMES. Formally, the *couplet* is a two-line STANZA with both grammatical structure and idea complete within itself, but the form has gone through numerous adaptations, the most famous being HEROIC VERSE. In French literature *couplet* is sometimes used in the sense of STANZA. It is customary but not essential that the length of each LINE be the same. *Couplets* are usually written in OCTOSYLLABIC and DECASYLLABIC lines. Shakespeare always ends his SONNETS with a *couplet,* and often he will use a *couplet* to signal the end of a SCENE that is otherwise in PROSE or BLANK VERSE, as at the end of act II of *Hamlet:*

> I'll have grounds
> More relative than this. The play's the thing
> Wherein I'll catch the conscience of the King.

See CLOSED COUPLET, HEROIC VERSE.

Court Comedy: COMEDY written to be performed at the royal court. *Love's Labour's Lost* is a *court comedy* belonging to Shakespeare's early period. Some years before Shakespeare came to London, the Elizabethan *court comedy* had been developed to a high degree of effectiveness by John Lyly in such plays as *Endimion* and *Alexander and Campaspe*. Characteristics include: artificial PLOT; little ACTION; much use of mythology; pageantry; elaborate costuming and scenery; prominence of music, especially SONGS; lightness of TONE; numerous and often balanced CHARACTERS (arranged in contrasting pairs); artificial STRUCTURE; STYLE marked by WIT, grace, verbal cleverness, quaint IMAGERY; PUNS; prose DIALOGUE; witty and saucy pages; eccentric CHARACTERS such as braggarts, witches, and alchemists; much farcical ACTION; and allegorical meanings sometimes embodied in the CHARACTERS and ACTION. Though some of these traits of the Lylian *court comedy* dropped out later, *court comedy* in the seventeenth century retained many of them and was operatic in tone and spectacular in presentation. See MASQUE.

Courtesy Books: A class of books that, flourishing in late RENAISSANCE times, dealt with the training of the "courtly" person. Often in DIALOGUE form, the *courtesy book* discussed such questions as the qualities of a gentleman or court lady, the etiquette of COURTLY LOVE, the education of the future courtier or prince, and the duties of a state counsellor. The *courtesy book* originated in Italy, the most famous example being Castiglione's *Il Cortegiano,* "The Courtier" (1528), which exerted great influence on English writers, especially after its translation into English by Sir Thomas Hoby in 1561. The earliest English *courtesy book* is Sir Thomas Elyot's *Book Named the Governour* (1531).

Somewhat similar to the *courtesy books,* but not to be confused with them, were the numerous ETIQUETTE BOOKS written not to explain the character of the noble or royal person but to deal with the problems of conduct confronting the well-bred citizen as well as the "gentleman." One of the best is *Galateo* by the Italian Della Casa. Early English examples of this type are *The Babees Book* and *The Boke of Curtasye* (1450).

Many books of the seventeenth century carried on the tradition: Henry Peacham's *Compleat Gentleman,* 1622 (courtly); Richard Brathwait's *The English Gentleman,* 1630 (PURITAN); and Francis Osborne's *Advice to a Son,* 1658 (a precursor of Lord Chesterfield's *Letters*). By extension, *courtesy book* can be applied to a POEM like Spenser's *The Faerie Queene,* since one of its objects is to portray the moral virtues. A similar extension has applied the term to Franklin's *Autobiography,* which was written to instruct Franklin's son in the ways of the world.

Courtly Love: A philosophy of love and a code of lovemaking that flourished in chivalric times, first in France and later in other countries, especially in England. The exact origins of the system cannot be traced, but fashions set by the Provençal TROUBADOURS and ideas drawn from the Orient and especially from Ovid were probably the chief sources. The conditions of feudal society and the veneration of the Virgin Mary, both of which tended to give a new dignity and independence to women, also affected it. The method of debate or SOLILOQUY by which *courtly love* finds expression in literature was probably indebted to scholastic philosophy.

According to the system, falling in love is accompanied by great emotional disturbances; the lover, bewildered, helpless, and tortured by mental and physical pain, exhibits certain "symptoms," such as pallor, trembling, loss of appetite, sleeplessness, sighing, and weeping. He agonizes over his condition and indulges in endless self-questioning and reflections on the nature of love and his own wretched state. His condition improves when he is accepted, and he is inspired by his love to great deeds. He and his lady pledge each other to secrecy, and they must remain faithful in spite of all obstacles. Andreas Capellanus late in the twelfth century wrote a treatise that summarized prevailing notions of *courtly love* through imaginary conversations and through his thirty-one "rules." According to the strictest code, true love was held to be impossible in the married state. Hence, some authorities distinguish between true *courtly love* as it is illustrated in the story of Lancelot and Guinevere in Chrétien's "The Knight of the Cart," and Ovidian love. Basically, *courtly love* was illicit and sensual, but a sort of Platonic idealism soon appeared and is found in the usual literary presentation.

Courtly love ideas abound in medieval ROMANCE and are perhaps not unconnected with the Petrarchan and Platonic love doctrines found in Elizabethan SONNET SEQUENCES. The system of *courtly love* largely controls the behavior of the CHARACTERS in Chaucer's *Troilus and Criseyde*. C. S. Lewis made a detailed study of *courtly love* in *The Allegory of Love*. See COURTS OF LOVE.

[References: Sarah F. Barrow, *Medieval Society Romances* (1924); T. P. Cross and W. A. Nitze, *Lancelot and Guenevere: A Study of the Origins of Courtly Love* (1930); W. G. Dodd, *Courtly Love in Gower and Chaucer* (1913, reprinted 1959); C. S. Lewis, *The Allegory of Love* (1936); H. O. Taylor, *The Medieval Mind*, 2 vol. (1914, reprinted 1959).]

"Courtly Makers": Sometimes applied to any court POET, *"courtly makers"* more accurately refers to court POETS of the reign of Henry VIII who introduced the "new poetry" from Italy and France into England. *"Maker"* was used in the sixteenth century, in both Scotland and England, for POET. The work was imitative and experimental, based on FORMS and fashions developed by the Italians. The *"courtly makers"* were most successful in poetic translations or paraphrases and in SONGS. Henry VIII himself was credited with the authorship of words and music of several graceful SONGS. The introduction of the SONNET into English is due to the efforts of the two most important POETS of the group, Sir Thomas Wyatt and the Earl of Surrey. BLANK VERSE was introduced by Surrey. Other *"courtly makers"* were William Cornish, Lord Vaux, Lord Rochford (George Boleyn), Sir Anthony St. Leger, Lord Morley (Henry Parker), Sir Francis Bryan, Sir Thomas Chaloner, John Heywood, Robert Fairfax, and Robert Cooper. Most of the work of these men has perished, for their ideas of "gentlemanly" conduct did not encourage them to publish, POETRY being cultivated as an incidental grace. Manuscript collections were made for private libraries, however; such a collection, now known as *Tottel's Miscellany*, published in 1557, exerted a powerful influence on Elizabethan POETRY. The chief importance of the *"courtly makers"* lies in the pioneer character of their work, for their efforts were brought to flowering by succeeding poetic generations.

Courts of Love: Tribunals for settling questions involved in the system of COURTLY LOVE. The judge, a court lady or Venus herself, would hear debate on such questions as: "Can a lover love two ladies at once?" "Are lovers or married couples more affectionate?" Though it was once believed that such courts were actually held in high society in chivalric times, modern scholarship is inclined to regard the *courts of love* as primarily a literary CONVENTION. The term *court of love* is also sometimes extended to include allegorical and processional PAGEANTS such as the Masque of Cupid passage in Spenser's *The Faerie Queene* (book III, cantos xi–xii). The phrase is sometimes used loosely as a synonym for COURTLY LOVE.

Covenant Theology: A seventeenth-century modification of the doctrines of CALVINISM, particularly important in New England. *For divine decrees as a basis for election*, it substitutes the idea of a contractual relationship between God and the human race. *Covenant theology* held that God promised Adam and his posterity eternal life in exchange for absolute obedience. When Adam broke this covenant, he incurred punishment as a legal responsibility for himself and his posterity. However, God made another covenant with Abraham, promising human beings the ability to struggle toward perfection. During THE GREAT AWAKENING Jonathan Edwards attacked the *Covenant theology* and urged a return to CALVINISM. See CALVINISM; AWAKENING, THE GREAT.

Cowleyan Ode: A form of the IRREGULAR ODE used by Abraham Cowley in the seventeenth century. See ODE, IRREGULAR ODE.

Crisis: In a FICTION or a DRAMA the point at which the opposing forces that create the CONFLICT interlock in the decisive ACTION on which the PLOT will turn. *Crisis* is applied to the EPISODE or INCIDENT wherein the situation of the PROTAGONIST is certain either to improve or worsen. Since *crisis* is essentially a structural element of PLOT rather than an index of the emotional response that an event may produce in a reader or spectator, as CLIMAX is, the *crisis* and the CLIMAX do not always occur together. See CLIMAX, PLOT, CONFLICT, DRAMATIC STRUCTURE.

Critic: One who estimates and passes judgment on the value and quality of literary or artistic works. The term is used for a great variety of persons ranging from the writers of brief REVIEWS and notices in the popular press to expounders of the aesthetic principles that define the nature and function of art. A *critic* may employ many different types of CRITICISM and support many different theories of art. According to an old-fashioned distinction, CRITICS publish their findings in REVIEWS, scholars theirs in JOURNALS. See CRITICISM and CRITICISM, TYPES OF.

Critical Realism: A term applied to realistic FICTION in the late nineteenth and early twentieth centuries, particularly in America. The MUCKRAKERS belong to the school of *critical realism.* Vernon L. Parrington gave the term currency in his posthumously published (1930) third volume of *Main Currents in American Thought,* which he called *The Beginnings of Critical Realism in America,* where he uses the term to refer to the tendency of writers and intellectuals in the period between 1875 and 1920 to apply the methods of realistic FICTION to the CRITICISM of society and the examination of social issues. It ought to be emphasized that the REALISM in such *critical realism* is not purely realistic, in a simple sense, but is another CONVENTION of language and literature; like so-called *cinéma vérité,* it is inescapably implicated in the choices and techniques of craft; a mirror more than a window, it is really no more or less "real" than any other kind of FICTION.

Criticism: The ANALYSIS, study, and evaluation of individual works of art, as well as the formulation of general methodological or aesthetic principles for the examination of such works. From the earliest days of literary history, *criticism* has been a major aspect of literary theory and practice. In recent times, literary CRITICISM has come to have less to do with judgments of value or importance and more to do with descriptive analysis.

M. H. Abrams, in *The Mirror and the Lamp,* has pointed out that all critical theories, whatever their language, discriminate four elements in "the total situation of a work of art," and he discriminates among both the kinds of *criticism* and the history of critical theory and practice in terms of the dominance of one of these elements. They are: (1) the *work,* that is, the thing made by the maker, the POEM produced by the POET, the artifact created by the artificer; (2) the *artist,* the maker, the POET, the artificer; (3) the *universe,* that is, the NATURE that is imitated, if art is viewed as IMITATION, the materials of the real world or the world of ideal entities out of which the work may be thought to take its subject; and (4) the *audience,* the readers, spectators, or listeners to whom the work is addressed. To view art basically in terms of the universe, in terms of what is imitated, is to follow the MIMETIC THEORY. To view art basically in terms of its effect on the audience is to use the PRAG-MATIC THEORY. To view art basically in terms of the *artist,* that is, as expressive of the maker, is to employ the EXPRESSIVE THEORY. And to view art basically in its own terms, seeing the *work* as a self-contained entity, is to exemplify the OBJECTIVE THEORY. (It ought to be noted that these categories are them-selves the material of critical debate, and some schools of thought assert that the artwork is not a finite product but rather an indefinite process. For others, the work *per se* simply has no existence; the so-called work has to be something perceived—and partly created or completed—by the active HERMENEUTIC participation of many audiences. Still others deny that independent texts or works exist in any mode of being that permits discussion; all that exists is a network of complex relations among texts. For others, the production of art is not a creative act of invention but an impersonal catalytic assembling of conventional elements. Besides, few terms are more vexatiously nebulous than MIMETIC, PRAGMATIC, EXPRESSIVE, and OBJECTIVE.)

Even so, a backward glance over the history of criticism in the light of Abrams' formulations is revealing. The MIMETIC THEORY is characteristic of the classical age, with Aristotle as its great expounder. Horace, however, intro-duced the idea of instruction with pleasure—*utile et dulce*—and the effect on the audience was central to his view of art. From Horace through most of the eighteenth century, the PRAGMATIC THEORY was dominant, although the NEOCLASSIC critics revived a serious interest in IMITATION. Indeed, as Abrams asserts, "the pragmatic view, broadly conceived, has been the principal aesthetic attitude of the Western world." At the same time, it is true that *criticism* through the eighteenth century was securely confident of the imita-tive nature of art. With the beginnings of ROMANTICISM came the EXPRESSIVE THEORY, in a sense the most characteristic of the ROMANTIC attitudes. When Wordsworth calls POETRY "the spontaneous overflow of powerful feeling," the *artist*—construed as a person of extraordinary feeling, emotion, and sensi-bility—has moved to the center. Now the poet's IMAGINATION is a new force in the world and a source of unique knowledge, and expression is the true function of art. Beginning in the nineteenth century and becoming dominant in the twentieth has been the notion of the "poem *per se* . . . written solely for the poem's sake," as Poe expressed it. Here FORM and STRUCTURE, patterns of IMAGERY and SYMBOLS, become the center of the critic's concern, for the *work* of art is viewed as a separate cosmos. However, increasing interest in psychology has kept the contemporary CRITIC also aware of the fact that the *audience* functions in the work of art, and views of the MYTH current today tend to bring the *artist* back to a central position and at the same time to value in terms of the *audience* the truth the artist speaks through his or her ARCHETYPAL patterns and IMAGES from the racial unconsciousness. These views of *criticism* will help us chart its history.

The first important critical treatise, the *Poetics* of Aristotle (fourth century B.C.), has proved to be the most influential. This Greek philosopher defined POETRY as an idealized representation of human action, and TRAGEDY as a serious, dramatic representation or IMITATION of some magnitude, arousing pity and fear wherewith to accomplish a CATHARSIS of such emotions; tragedies ought to have UNITY and completeness of PLOT, with beginning, middle, and end. The *Poetics* also treats the element of CHARACTER in TRAGEDY and the relation of TRAGEDY to EPIC. Aristotle's treatise on the Homeric EPIC has not survived. The great attention given by the ancients to RHETORIC is also important critically, though developed largely because of the interest in oratory. The great influence of the *Poetics* began in the RENAISSANCE.

Another important Greek document is the treatise of Longinus, *On the Sublime* (date uncertain, perhaps third century after Christ). Very different from the *Poetics* of Aristotle in content and spirit, this work acclaims sublimity, height, and IMAGINATION in a STYLE that is itself enthusiastic and eloquent. Longinus finds the sources of the SUBLIME in great conceptions, noble passions, and elevated DICTION.

The foremost Latin CRITIC was Horace, whose *Art of Poetry* (known variously as *Ars Poetica, De Arte Poetica,* and *Epistle to the Pisos*), written as an informal EPISTLE in VERSE, has exercised considerable influence. It discusses types of POETRY and of CHARACTER, stresses the importance of Greek models, emphasizes the importance of DECORUM, and advises the POET to write for both entertainment and instruction. Many of Horace's phrases have entered the language of *criticism,* such as *ut pictura poesis,* "poetry, like painting"; *limae labor,* "the labor of the file" (i.e., revision); *aut prodesse aut delectare,* "either to profit or to please"; *purpureus pannus,* "purple patch"; and *in medias res,* "in the midst of things." The influence of Horace's *criticism* was especially great in England in the sixteenth and seventeenth centuries. Quintilian's *Institutes of Oratory* is, after Horace's epistle, perhaps the most important Latin critical treatise. Other ancient CRITICS include Plato, Dionysius of Halicarnassus, Plutarch, and Lucian among the Greeks; and Cicero, the Senecas, Petronius, and Macrobius among the Latin writers. The art of RHETORIC constituted an integral part of this literary *criticism.*

In the Middle Ages most *criticism* dealt with Latin VERSIFICATION, RHETORIC, and grammar. The ecclesiastical theologians who dominated intellectual life regarded literature as a servant of theology and philosophy, so that interest in imaginative literature as such declined. CLASSICAL literature was little known, and there was not much contemporary literature of a sort to arouse critical interest. The rhetoricians dealt in detail with technical matters of vital interest to the creative writer: FIGURATIVE LANGUAGE; organization; beginnings; endings; development (amplification, condensation); and STYLE—especially the adaptation of STYLE to type of composition. The influence of such teachings on the early work of Chaucer has been shown in detail.

The teachings of St. Augustine (d. 430) contributed to the distrust of literature on moral and religious grounds, a distrust that persisted through the Middle Ages into modern times. His attack on imaginative writing produced replies that anticipate later critical attitudes and arguments, including the arguments that the literary and the moral points of view should not be confused and that the ancients should be followed. Isidore of Seville (sixth and seventh centuries) listed the types and kinds of literature (based on Biblical FORMS).

At the end of the medieval period a great CRITIC appeared in the Italian POET Dante, whose *De Vulgari Eloquentia* (early fourteenth century) discusses the problems of vernacular literature and reflects CLASSICAL ideas on DECORUM, IMITATION, and the nature of the POET. He discusses DICTION, sentence structure, STYLE, VERSIFICATION, and DIALECTS. Petrarch and Boccaccio, Italian writers of the fourteenth century, produced critical works that belong in part to the medieval period and in part to the RENAISSANCE, which they helped to usher in. Boccaccio's defense of POETRY in Books XIV and XV of his *Genealogia Deorum Gentilium* is particularly important to students of later *criticism.*

The RENAISSANCE reacted against the theological interpretation of POETRY, which it attempted to justify as an independent art, along lines suggested by humanistic ideals. In Italy, Vida, Robortelli, Daniello, Minturno, Giraldi Cinthio, J. C. Scaliger, Castelvetro, and others were concerned with such topics as: POETRY as a form of philosophy and an imitation of life; the doctrine of VERISIMILITUDE; pleasurable instruction as the object of POETRY; the theory of DRAMA, especially TRAGEDY—the tragic HERO and the UNITIES were much debated; and the theory of the EPIC poem. The causes for the growth of CLASSICISM have been assigned to HUMANISM, Aristotelianism, and RATIONALISM—with PLATONISM, medievalism, and nationalism acting as ROMANTIC forces. These tendencies toward CLASSICISM actuated Italian *criticism* of the sixteenth century and French *criticism* of the seventeenth. The first French critical works were rhetorical and metrical, the most important being Sibilet's *Art of Poetry* (1548); but the first highly significant French *criticism* centered on the *Pléiade,* a group interested in refining the French language and literature by imitations of the CLASSICS, Ronsard being its most famous writer and Du Bellay being the author of its manifesto, his epochal *Defence and Illustration of the French Language* (1549). Among the prominent seventeenth-century French CRITICS were Malherbe, who reacted strongly against the *Pléiade;* Chapelain; Corneille; Saint-Évremond; d'Aubignac; Rapin; Le Bossu; and Boileau, whose influence was especially powerful. These writers illustrate the course of French *criticism* in the direction of CLASSICISM, a rational crystallizing of poetic theory, and a codification of the principles of literary STRUCTURE.

In RENAISSANCE England the earliest critical utterances concerned RHETORIC and DICTION, as in the "prefaces" of the printer Caxton (late fifteenth century) and the RHETORICS of Leonard Cox (*ca.* 1530) and Thomas Wilson (1553). As early as Sir Thomas Elyot's *Book Named the Governour* (1531), the claims of English as a vehicle for literature were being urged against the extreme humanist opposition to the vernacular as crude and transitory. The development of a native literature stimulated discussions of how best to build up the English vocabulary; the extreme humanists and INKHORNISTS, who favored the adoption of heavy Latin and Greek words, were opposed by those who stressed a native lexicon (see PURISTS). Much attention was given to DECORUM and IMITATION. The first technical treatise on English VERSIFICATION was Gascoigne's *Certain Notes of Instruction* (1575). VERSE devices already developed in English, including RHYME, were perfected in the face of a critical sentiment for such CLASSICAL FORMS as the unrhymed HEXAMETER. Practice ran ahead of theory in this matter, as may be seen by comparing the creative practice of Sidney and Campion with their critical condemnation of RHYME. Campion's essay, *Observations in the Art of English Poesie* (1602), was effectively answered by Samuel Daniel's *A Defence of Rime.* Similarly, Shakespearean ROMANTIC TRAGEDY developed in spite of the prevailing critical insistence on the UNITIES.

A lively critical issue centered on the defense of literature in the face of the Puritan attack based on moral grounds, a movement aimed at the DRAMA in particular, as in Stephen Gosson's *The School of Abuse* (1579). Many of these critical questions were treated in Sidney's *Defence of Poesie* (pub. 1595), the most significant piece of *criticism* of the period. Sidney stressed the vatic function of the POET, exalted POETRY above philosophy and history, answered the objections to poetic art, examined the types of POETRY, and assigned praise and blame among the writers of the preceding generation on the basis of their conformity to CLASSICAL principles as expressed by the Italian CRITICS. Important critical ideas came from Francis Bacon (*Advancement of Learning,* 1605) and Ben Jonson in *Timber: or Discoveries.* Jonson, a man of vast learning and uncommon common sense, shows a definite tendency toward the NEOCLASSICISM that was to become the center of English *criticism* for more than a century.

The next master CRITIC was John Dryden, with his numerous prefaces and ESSAYS, the best known being the *Essay of Dramatick Poesie* (1668). This treatise, written in DIALOGUE form, fairly presents the claims of "ANCIENTS AND MODERNS," of French and English dramatists; RHYME, TRAGICOMEDY, and the UNITIES receive consideration; the influence of Corneille is apparent; and much PRACTICAL CRITICISM and dramatic expression keep the ESSAY from being entirely theoretical. In his *Preface to the Fables* (1700) Dryden gives a noteworthy estimate of the genius of Chaucer. Other critics of the RESTORATION AGE include Sir Robert Howard, Thomas Rymer, the Earls of Mulgrave and Roscommon, and Sir William Temple. The foreign influence was predominantly French.

Alexander Pope was not merely the leading POET of his generation but also its most significant CRITIC with the prefaces to his translation of Homer, his edition of Shakespeare, and his *Essay on Criticism* (1711)—one of the best pieces of VERSE CRITICISM in the language. Here Pope set forth the NEOCLASSIC principles of following NATURE and the ancients, outlined the causes of bad *criticism,* described the good CRITIC, and concluded with a short history of *criticism.* Joseph Addison's critical papers in the *Spectator* (1711–1712) on TRAGEDY, WIT, BALLADS, *Paradise Lost,* and the pleasures of the IMAGINATION were designed for a popular audience, but they influenced formal *criticism* and aesthetic theory. The NEOCLASSICAL CRITICS in general devoted themselves to such topics as reason, correctness, WIT, TASTE, GENRES, rules, IMITATION, the CLASSICS, the function of the IMAGINATION, the status of emotion, and the dangers of enthusiasm. As the sway of authority weakened, the historical point of view gained in acceptance; TEXTUAL CRITICISM became more scientific. Samuel Johnson was the major defender of the older order; his large body of *criticism* is in his PERIODICAL ESSAYS, the preface to his edition of Shakespeare, and his *Lives of the Poets.*

Joseph Warton (*Essay on the Genius and Writings of Pope,* 1756, 1782) refused Pope the highest rank among POETS because of insufficient emotion and IMAGINATION; Thomas Warton (*Observations on The Faerie Queene of Spenser,* 1754) emphasized the emotional quality of the POET; Young (*Conjectures on Original Composition,* 1759) spoke in favor of independence and against the IMITATION of other writers; Hurd (*Letters on Chivalry and Romance*, 1762) justified GOTHIC manners and design, Spenser's POETRY, and the Italian POETS, and attacked some of the main tenets of the AUGUSTANS. The ROMANTIC impulse was growing. Other eighteenth-century CRITICS included John Dennis, Henry Fielding, Edmund Burke, Oliver Goldsmith, Lord Kames, Hugh Blair, and Sir Joshua Reynolds.

The volume of POEMS by Wordsworth and Coleridge titled *Lyrical Ballads* (1798) is frequently cited as formally ushering in the Romantic movement. For the second edition (1800) Wordsworth wrote a preface that acted as a manifesto for the new school and set forth his own critical creed. His object was to "choose incidents and situations from common life," to write in the "language really used by men." Wordsworth was reacting to what he considered the artificial poetic practice of the preceding era; he condemned the use of PERSONIFICATION and "POETIC DICTION." There could be "no essential difference between the language of prose and metrical composition." Wordsworth defined the POET as a "man speaking to men" and POETRY as "the spontaneous overflow of powerful feelings," which originates in emotion "recollected in tranquillity."

Coleridge was a great critic. In the *Biographia Literaria* (1817) he explained the division of labor in the *Lyrical Ballads:* his own endeavors "should be directed to persons and characters supernatural, or at least romantic; yet so as to transfer from our inward nature a human interest and a semblance of truth sufficient to procure for these shadows of imagination that willing suspension of disbelief for the moment, which constitutes poetic faith"; while Wordsworth was "to propose to himself as his object, to give the charm of novelty to things of every day, and to excite a feeling analogous to the supernatural, by awakening the mind's attention to the . . . loveliness and the wonders of the world before us." Coleridge disagreed with Wordsworth's statements about the principles of METER and POETIC DICTION: genuinely rustic life is not favorable to the formation of intelligible DICTION; POETRY is essentially ideal and generic; the language of Milton is as much that of real life as is that of the cottager; art strives to give pleasure through beauty. Coleridge's discussion of the IMAGINATION and the FANCY has had wide influence. English ROMANTICISM found some sources in the philosophy, AESTHETICS, and literature of German ROMANTICISM.

Other critics of importance in the first half of the nineteenth century were Lamb, Hazlitt, and Leigh Hunt. Lamb's *criticism* was charming and enthusiastic but eccentric, capricious, and unorganized; saturated with good TASTE and great originality, it stimulated the appreciation of earlier English literature. Hazlitt is remarkable for many happy phrases, sound judgment, and an infectious spirit. Hunt is a most catholic and readable CRITIC. The POET Shelley's *Defence of Poetry* (1821) is an impassioned *apologia* reminiscent of RENAISSANCE treatises. Other critics of this period are: Blake, Newman, Carlyle, De Quincey, Landor, Hallam, and Macaulay. The Whig *Edinburgh Review* (edited by Francis Jeffrey) and the Tory *Quarterly Review* (edited by William Gifford) voiced fundamentally conservative opinions and dominated periodical *criticism*.

Matthew Arnold, the leading English CRITIC of the second half of the nineteenth century, thought of POETRY as a "criticism of life" and of *criticism* itself as the effort to "know the best that is known and thought in the world and by in its turn making this known, to create a current of true and fresh ideas." FORM, order, and measure constituted the CLASSICAL qualities that Arnold admired. Seeking to judge literature by high standards, he used specimens (or TOUCHSTONES) of great POETRY as well as his own sensitive TASTE in forming judgments. (However, not all of Arnold's specimens are uniformly appropriate.) "The grand style," he said, "arises in poetry, when a noble nature, poetically gifted, treats with simplicity or with severity a serious subject." The greatness of a POET "lies in his powerful and beautiful application of ideas to life." Three of his better known critical ESSAYS are *The Function of Criticism* (1865), *The Study of Poetry* (1888), and *On Translating Homer* (1861).

In the later nineteenth century ROMANTICISM remained strong, but REALISM and IMPRESSIONISM were gaining ground. The expansion of natural science helped the progress of realistic and naturalistic *criticism* (see NATURALISM), which reacted against both CLASSICISM and ROMANTICISM. HISTORICAL CRITICISM, the attempt to understand a work in the light of "race, momentum, and *milieu,*" in process of development for at least two centuries, at last crystallized in the writings of the Frenchmen Saint-Beuve and Taine. IMPRESSIONISM, growing out of ROMANTICISM, obtained an eloquent advocate in Walter Pater. Victorian CRITICS discussed such topics as the function of art and literature, the role of morality, the place of the IMAGINATION, the problems of STYLE, the province of the NOVEL, and the theory of the comic. As *criticism* tended away from the application of standards toward the use of impressionistic methods, German influence yielded ground to the French. Significant contributions were made by Thackeray on the English humorists; John Stuart Mill on the nature of POETRY; Walter Bagehot on pure, ornate, and GROTESQUE art in POETRY; Pater on STYLE and on HEDONISM in art; George Meredith on the comic spirit; Leslie Stephen on the eighteenth century; and Swinburne on the Elizabethan and Jacobean dramatists.

Criticism in America, besides reflecting, sometimes tardily, European attitudes, has been concerned with questions peculiar to a literature growing out of a transplanted culture. To what extent is American literature derivative and imitative? How can American literature develop a purely American spirit? What is this spirit? What is the effect of Puritan ethics on American literature? How has the frontier affected it?

Early nineteenth-century *criticism,* as evidenced by the earlier numbers of the *North American Review* (estab. 1815), was conservative and NEOCLASSIC. Pope and the Scottish school reigned. Later, the ROMANTIC attitude triumphed, and Byron, Scott, Wordsworth, and eventually Shelley, Keats, Coleridge, Carlyle, and Tennyson were exalted. The earlier writer-CRITICS were in the main ROMANTIC: Poe, Lowell, and Emerson. Poe, however, stressed workmanship, technique, STRUCTURE, reason, and the divorce of art and morality. He enunciated independent theories of the LYRIC and the SHORT STORY. Emerson believed art should serve moral ends; asserted that all American literature was derivative but should not be; and assumed the ROMANTIC attitude toward NATURE and individualism. Lowell is first impressionistic and ROMANTIC, at times professedly realistic, and eventually CLASSICAL and ethical after his revolt against SENTIMENTALISM.

After the Civil War a strong critical movement toward REALISM found two powerful exponents, William Dean Howells and Henry James. Interested almost exclusively in FICTION, they advanced a theory that the fidelity of the *work* to the *universe,* defined in a materialistic or psychological-social sense, was the object of art. REALISM was defined by Howells as "nothing more and nothing less than the truthful treatment of material." Yet there were aspects of the PRAGMATIC THEORY here, for he saw a moral obligation resting on the *artist* in terms of the *effects* of the works on the *audience.* At the close of the century, under the influence of the French, particularly Zola, a group of American novelists proposed a theory that was frankly MIMETIC; this is the application of scientific method, even of quasi-scientific law, to enhance the seriousness and increase the depth of the portraying of the actual by the artist. The theory is NATURALISM, and Frank Norris was its most vocal expounder as the century ended. However, Henry James, in critical ESSAYS already written and in the prefaces that he prepared for the collected edition of his NOVELS in the first decade of the twentieth century, was to make the most significant formulation of critical principles about FICTION that an American has produced. James and Poe emerge from nineteenth-century America as the most powerful and original American CRITICS of that age. Although he conspicuously lacked James's wit, urbanity, common sense, and good manners, Poe was undeniably a prodigious genius whose example foreshadowed James's fastidious craftsmanship, attention to detail, and devotion to logic and symmetry. Poe has also been credited with inventing or improving the SHORT STORY, SCIENCE FICTION, DETECTIVE FICTION, the symbolist POEM, the NEW CRITICISM, and a potently iconoclastic style of critical combat later to be adopted by Mencken, Pound, and Eliot. Whatever may be the just apportionment of credit, Poe and James together created a vivid and practical critical spirit that suffused the thought and practice of their contemporaries (as in Mark Twain's hilarious bill of complaint against "Fenimore Cooper's Literary Offenses") and all of their important successors.

In England and America the first decade of the twentieth century saw a continuation of the concern with REALISM and NATURALISM, but little serious critical examination of them. IMPRESSIONISM and "appreciation," led in England by Walter Pater and his followers and in America by James Huneker, ruled the day. In the second decade a group of Americans, under the leadership of Van Wyck Brooks, attacked the cultural failures of America and began the search for a "usable past," a search which was to occupy men like Randolph Bourne, Lewis Mumford, and Bernard De Voto down to the 1950s and which saw in 1927–1930 in Vernon L. Parrington's *Main Currents in American Thought* one of the major documents in critical scholarship. At the same time, in England two young Americans, Ezra Pound and T. S. Eliot, were learning with T. E. Hulme to distrust ROMANTIC EXPRESSIONISM and to turn to formalism and objectivity. Whatever their ideology, Pound and Eliot, especially between 1920 and 1935, eloquently synthesized the most vital thought of their seniors (particularly James, F. H. Bradley, Henri Bergson, Irving Babbitt, and Paul Elmer More) and espoused the cause of their most influential contemporaries (particularly James Joyce, Wyndham Lewis, W. C. Williams, Marianne Moore, and Ford Madox Ford). In the 1920s the impact of the new psychologies was deeply felt in England, particularly in the work of I. A. Richards whose reaction against IMPRESSIONISM expressed itself in efforts to make an exact science of the examination of how literature produced psychological states in its reader. He was followed by Herbert Read and William Empson. In

America, Freudian psychology was applied to literary problems by a variety of CRITICS, but the strong movement was the NEW HUMANISM, which, under the leadership of Babbitt and More, formulated a critical position resting on the traditional moral and critical standards of the humanists.

In the 1930s, as a partial aftermath of the financial collapse, came a wave of critics espousing Marxist and near-Marxist ideas—a specialized form of PRAGMATIC THEORY—in both England and America. The major English Marxist was Christopher Caudwell. While no Americans approached him in excellence, critics like Granville Hicks and V. F. Calverton urged the reading of literature in the light of radical social views. During the 1930s in America, reacting both against the New Humanists and the Marxist CRITICS came a group, drawn largely from the AGRARIANS, who vigorously embraced an OBJECTIVE THEORY of art. Led by John Crowe Ransom, who gave them a name and something resembling a credo in his book *The New Criticism,* these essentially conservative and antiromantic writers—Allen Tate, Robert Penn Warren, Donald Davidson, Yvor Winters, and later Cleanth Brooks—started from the position of T. S. Eliot and Ezra Pound and quickly formed themselves into a powerful force in the formal *criticism* of literature. At the same time a similar group, though much less organized, was practicing a stringent and aesthetically centered *criticism* in England, among them Eliot himself, F. R. Leavis, and Cyril Connolly. In both England and America, the theories of Carl Jung about the racial unconscious (see ARCHETYPE) have received vigorous expression by writers like Maud Bodkin in England and Francis Fergusson in America. At about the same time, during the 1930s, Edmund Wilson emerged as a CRITIC of eclectic taste, catholic learning, and trenchant style. Gertrude Stein delivered her *Lectures in America* that established her as a critical personage of rare insight, scope, and force. R. G. Collingwood, with an intellectual pedigree traceable to John Ruskin and William Morris in England and Benedetto Croce in Italy, combined the EXPRESSIVE and PRAGMATIC approaches in a brilliant one-man application of critical procedures that located art as a psychosomatic transaction in persons who live by an interlocking series of perceptions, intuitions, and expressions. Centered in Chicago and often called the CHICAGO CRITICS, a group of neo-Aristotelians led by Ronald Crane, Richard McKeon, Norman Maclean, and Elder Olson, have formulated a kind of formal *criticism* based on Aristotle's principles. From this group have come Wayne Booth's *The Rhetoric of Fiction,* a major critical effort to come to grips with FICTION, and the critical studies of Austin M. Wright who, like Crane and Booth, has concentrated on FICTION.

The method of Husserl, commonly known as PHENOMENOLOGY, has become a widely used method for CRITICS who lean toward EXISTENTIALISM, such as J. Hillis Miller and Paul Brodtkorb. The liveliest recent critical concept, however, is STRUCTURALISM, a method of analysis inspired by structural LINGUISTICS and structural anthropology. In the pioneering linguistic science of the Swiss Ferdinand de Saussure (1857–1913), language is treated as a system of signifying and signified elements that are related arbitrarily, without "motivation" or causal association. In this complex network of relations, meaning is generated by binary distinctions with no extrinsic reference or positive terms. The -*s* suffix in English, for example, has no particular meaning except as a convenient means of distinguishing contrasted forms: singular and plural nouns, plural and singular verbs, as well as nominative and possessive nouns. The

-*s* that makes a singular noun plural makes a plural verb singular in the third person and present tense. Such a system of analysis, refined by many complications, was subsequently applied to signs not strictly linguistic, such as patterns of kinship and the logic of myth, by the French anthropologist Claude Lévi-Strauss. In time, certain thinkers were able to extend the structuralist manner to psychoanalysis (Jacques Lacan), to fashion (Roland Barthes), and to anything, including an artwork, that can be considered as having a structure like that of a Saussurean language. The CHARACTER of Jay Gatsby in Fitzgerald's NOVEL, say, is not defined as a function of Fitzgerald's personality or American history or any oral dictum (such as "Crime does not pay") but rather as an entity determined and animated by a web of essentially binary relations: Jay Gatsby and James Gatz, Gatsby and Tom, Gatsby and Daisy, Gatsby and Myrtle, Gatsby and Wilson, Gatsby and Carraway, and so on, all adding up to a massive self-standing structure radiant with dramatic meanings potentiated by the linkage between extreme charisma and extreme bureaucracy.

Such scrutiny of structure has been succeeded by "deconstructionist criticism"—exemplified by the markedly creative Jacques Derrida—in which ever more presuppositions of truth and reference come into question. DECONSTRUCTION begins at a point where the work or text seems to differ from itself and so to undo, dismantle, or deconstruct its own premises. Gatsby, say, as the title of the NOVEL invites the reader to ask, is both great and not great, at one and the same time, and this contradiction or APORIA calls into question the hierarchical presupposition implied in the binary contrast of "great" and "small." It has become the habit of DECONSTRUCTION to deconstruct everything, including itself, but always—and in an increasing number of disciplines beyond literature and literary theory—in the interest of questioning previously unquestioned postulates of order. The hierarchies in question are such pairs as nature–culture, presence–absence, man–woman, and work–play, with the first term in each pair understood as the privileged one. As a spirit, outlook, or general approach to thinking—and in spite of charges of negativism and nihilism—DECONSTRUCTION in most of its various modes has been abundantly productive of new readings.

The twentieth century has been called an age of *criticism;* and in the richness and complexity of its systems, the rigor of its application, and the enthusiasm of its espousal of the cause of the literary arts, it can wear that title with honor. See CRITICISM, TYPES OF.

[References: M. H. Abrams, *The Mirror and the Lamp* (1953); Walter J. Bate, ed., *Criticism: The Major Texts* (1948); M. C. Beardsley, *Aesthetics from Classical Greece to the Present* (1966); A. Bosker, *Literary Criticism in the Age of Johnson* (1930, reprinted 1970); E. B. Burgum, *The New Criticism* (1930); S. H. Butcher, *Aristotle's Theory of Poetry and Fine Art* (1895, reprinted 1951); R. S. Crane, *Critical and Historical Principles of Literary History* (1967); Jonathan Culler, *Structuralist Poetics* (1975); David Daiches, *Critical Approaches to Literature* (1956); J. F. D'Alton, *Roman Literary Theory and Criticism* (1931); G. E. De Mille, *Literary Criticism in America* (1931); W. H. Durham, ed., *Critical Essays of the Eighteenth Century, 1700–1725* (1915, reprinted 1961); Terry Eagleton, *Literary Theory: An Introduction* (1983); Norman Foerster, *American Criticism* (1928, reprinted 1962), and (ed.) *American Critical Essays XIX and XX Centuries* (1930); Northrop Frye, *Anatomy of Criticism* (1957); Ann Jefferson and David Robey, eds., *Modern Literary*

Theory: A Comparative Introduction (1983); George Saintsbury, *A History of Criticism,* 3 vols. (1908, reprinted 1949); G. Gregory Smith, ed., *Elizabethan Critical Essays* (1904, reprinted 1950); J. H. Smith and E. W. Parks, eds., *The Great Critics,* 3rd ed. (1951); J. E. Spingarn, *History of Literary Criticism in the Renaissance,* 2nd ed. (1908, reprinted 1963), and (ed.) *Critical Essays of the Seventeenth Century,* 3 vols. (1908–09); René Wellek, *A History of Modern Criticism,* 4 vols. (1955–65); René Wellek and Austin Warren, *Theory of Literature,* 2nd ed. (1956); W. K. Wimsatt and Cleanth Brooks, *Literary Criticism: A Short History* (1957).]

Criticism, Types of: *Criticism* is a term that has been applied since the seventeenth century to the description, justification, ANALYSIS, or judgment of works of art. There are many ways in which *criticism* may be classified. Some of the more common classifications are given here, as supplementary to M. H. Abrams's discrimination among the major critical theories as MIMETIC, PRAGMATIC, EXPRESSIVE, and OBJECTIVE (see CRITICISM). One common dichotomy for *criticism* is ARISTOTELIAN VS. PLATONIC. In this sense ARISTOTELIAN implies a judicial, logical, formal *criticism* that tends to find the values of a work either within the work itself or inseparably linked to the work; and PLATONIC implies a moralistic, utilitarian view of art, where the values of a work reside in the usefulness of art for ulterior purposes. Such a view of PLATONIC CRITICISM is narrow and in part inaccurate, but those who hold it point to the exclusion of the POET from Plato's Republic. Essentially what is meant by the ARISTOTELIAN-PLATONIC dichotomy is an intrinsic-extrinsic separation.

A separation between *relativistic* and *absolutist criticism* is also often made, with the *relativistic* CRITIC employing any or all systems that will aid in elucidating a work of art, whereas the *absolutist* CRITIC holds that there is one proper procedure or set of principles and no others should be applied to the critical task. The *relativistic* position may be aligned with philosophies called *dualism* or *pluralism* (the latter embraced by R. S. Crane), as the *absolutist* position matches the philosophy known as *monism* (of which Crane accused Cleanth Brooks).

There is also an obvious division between THEORETICAL CRITICISM, which attempts to arrive at general principles and to formulate inclusive aesthetic and critical tenets, and PRACTICAL CRITICISM (sometimes called "applied" criticism), which concentrates on particular works.

Criticism may also be classified according to its purpose. The principal purposes that CRITICS have had are: (1) to justify or explain one's own work (Dryden, Wordsworth, Henry James); (2) to defend imaginative art in a world that finds its value questionable (Sidney, Shelley, the NEW CRITICISM); (3) to prescribe rules for writers and to legislate taste for the audience (Pope, Boileau, the Marxists); (4) to interpret works to readers who might otherwise fail to understand or appreciate them (Edmund Wilson, Matthew Arnold); (5) to judge works by clearly defined standards of evaluation (Samuel Johnson, T. S. Eliot); (6) to discover and to apply the principles that describe the foundations of good art (Addison Coleridge, R. G. Collingwood, I. A. Richards).

Criticism is also often divided into the following types in literary and critical histories: (1) IMPRESSIONISTIC, which emphasizes how the work of art affects the CRITIC; (2) HISTORICAL, which examines the work against its historical surroundings and the facts of its author's life and times; (3) TEXTUAL, which attempts by all scholarly means to reconstruct the original manuscript or textual version of the work; (4) FORMAL, which examines the work in terms of the characteristics of the type or GENRE to which it belongs; (5) JUDICIAL, which judges the work by a definable set of standards; (6) ANALYTICAL, which attempts to get at the nature of the work as an object in itself through the detailed ANALYSIS of its parts and their organization; (7) MORAL, which evaluates the work in relation to human life; (8) MYTHIC, which explores the nature and significance of the ARCHETYPES and archetypal patterns in the work; (9) STRUC-TURAL, which studies literature as a quasi-linguistic structure whose meanings are made possible through codes or systems of CONVENTION; and (10) PHENO-MENOLOGICAL, which makes an existential (see EXISTENTIALISM) analysis of the worlds created in the consciousness by the language of art. Many other adjectives attach themselves to criticism: idealistic, academic, philological (meaning some emphasis on historical linguistics), technical (meaning, for litera-ture, concentration on DICTION, grammar, PROSODY, and graphic effects), es-tablishmentarian, and so forth.

These widely differing classification systems for *criticism* are not mutually exclusive, and there are certainly others. These will serve, however, to indicate that critics have employed a great variety of strategies in getting at art and communicating what they find there.

Critique: A critical examination of a work of art, usually literary, with a view to determining its nature and assessing its value according to some established standards. A *critique* is rather more serious and judicious than a REVIEW.

Cross-alliteration: ALLITERATION of two separate consonants or clusters ar-ranged as *xyxy* or *xyyx*, in PROSE or VERSE. Examples are Browning's LINE "Which *C*laus of Inns*br*uck *ca*st in *br*onze for me" ("My Last Duchess") and Henry James's phrase "the *sh*adow of a *ch*ange and the *ch*ill of a *sh*ock" ("The Beast in the Jungle"). See CYNGHANEDD.

Cross-cutting: A term used in FILM CRITICISM to describe repeated move-ments within a connected sequence from one location or subject to another. It is used to suggest simultaneous or parallel actions. First used extensively by D. W. Griffith in 1915 in *Birth of a Nation, cross-cutting* is a staple method for suspense and "chase" films.

Crossed Rhyme: A term applied to COUPLETS, usually HEXAMETER or longer, in which the words preceding the CAESURA rhyme, as in Swinburne's lines:

> Thou has conquered, O pale Galilean; the world has grown grey
>   from thy breath;
> We have drunken of things Lethean, and fed on the fullness of
>   death.

Such a COUPLET tends to break into four short LINES rhyming *abab*. The term is also sometimes applied to QUATRAINS with an *abab* RHYME pattern. See also LEONINE.

Crown of Sonnets: Seven SONNETS interlinked by having the last LINE of the first form the first line of the second, the last line of the second form the first line of the third, and so forth, with the last line of the last SONNET repeating the first line of the first. Donne's "La Corona" is an example.

Cruelty, Theater of: A concept of DRAMA, originated in the 1930s by Antonin Artaud, in which the theater becomes a ceremonial act of magic purgation. Artaud meant by the term a theater that could demonstrate human beings' inescapable enslavement to things and to circumstance. He hoped to raise (or return) the theater to a level of religious ceremony. In so doing he subordinated words to ACTION, gesture, and sound in an effort to overwhelm the spectator and liberate instinctual preoccupations with crime, cruelty, and eroticism. It is called the *theater of the cruel* because it utilizes all means of shock to make the spectator aware of—and even participate in—the fundamental cruelty of life. Artaud delivered several manifestoes and projected plays based on Bluebeard and the Marquis de Sade, but he did not complete them. His theories, however, and the *theater of cruelty* appear importantly in the work of several contemporary playwrights, among them Peter Brook, Jean-Louis Barrault, Roger Blin, and Jean Genet. The most widely successful example of the *theater of cruelty* is Peter Weiss's *The Persecution and Assassination of Jean-Paul Marat as Performed by Inmates of the Asylum of Charenton under the Direction of the Marquis de Sade,* commonly known as *Marat/Sade.* See ABSURD, THEATER OF THE.

Cryptarithm: A sophisticated puzzle in which letters of the alphabet are assigned a numerical value such that a spelled-out formula (normally addition) is true of both the words and the numbers. A specialized form is the "zero-sum game":

$$
\begin{array}{ll}
\text{ZERO} & 2391 \\
\text{ZERO} = & 2391 \\
\underline{\text{ZERO}} & \underline{2391} \\
\text{NONE} & 7173
\end{array}
$$

This was a trivial pastime of negligible literary interest until the American POET George Starbuck used it in a serious POEM. Two other examples:

$$
\begin{array}{ll}
\text{NIHIL} & \text{ZILCH} \\
\underline{\text{NIHIL}} & \underline{\text{ZILCH}} \\
\text{ZILCH} & \text{NIL} \\
& \underline{\text{NIL}} \\
& \text{NAUGHT}
\end{array}
$$

Cubist Poetry: POETRY that attempts to do in VERSE what the cubist painters do on canvas; that is, take the elements of an experience, fragment them (creating what Picasso calls "destructions"), and then so rearrange them that a meaningful new synthesis is made (Picasso's "sum of destructions"). Some of the writings of Gertrude Stein, E. E. Cummings, Kenneth Rexroth, and John Ashbery could be classified as *cubist,* especially if the conventional sequential arrangement of words and other elements is superseded by something like a simultaneous graphic display.

Cultural Primitivism: The belief that NATURE (construed as what exists undisturbed by human artifice) is preferable and fundamentally better than any aspect of human culture (any area of human activity in which people have modified or ordered NATURE). This belief distrusts artifice, logic, social and political organizations, rules, and CONVENTIONS. See PRIMITIVISM, CHRONO-LOGICAL PRIMITIVISM.

Curse: An INVOCATION that calls on a supernatural being to visit evil on someone. In this sense it is a MALEDICTION; or, if a formal and solemn IMPRECA-TION, an ANATHEMA. The term *curse* is also used for the effects that result from the INVOCATION of great evil, as in "the curse of the Pyncheons," in Hawthorne's *The House of the Seven Gables,* in which the *curse* put on the Pyncheon family by Matthew Maule darkens the history of succeeding generations. See ANATHEMA, IMPRECATION, MALEDICTION, ARA.

Curtain: A piece of heavy material that screens the STAGE from the audience and by being raised or opened and lowered or closed marks the beginning and end of an ACT or a SCENE. The *curtain* in this sense came into use in the early seventeenth century along with the development of the PROSCENIUM ARCH. By metonymic extension, *curtain* is used for a LINE, speech, or situation at the end of an ACT or SCENE, just before the *curtain* falls. The endings of portions of a DRAMA are sometimes called *curtains,* as in the expression "quick *curtain*" for a sudden conclusion to a SCENE, or "strong *curtain*" for a dramatically powerful conclusion, or "*curtain* speech" for the final speech of an ACT or a PLAY. The term "*curtain* speech" also applies to a talk given in front of the *curtain* after the conclusion of a performance.

Curtain Raiser: A short PLAY—either one-act or a SKIT—presented before the principal dramatic production on a program. By analogy, the term is applied to anything preliminary.

Curtal Sonnet: A term used by Gerard Manley Hopkins for a SONNET that has been curtailed or shortened. The challenge, according to Hopkins, was to shorten the OCTAVE to a SESTET while preserving the numerical ratio of the first subdivision to the second. Since 8:6::6:4.5, Hopkins's *curtal sonnet* is divided into parts consisting of six LINES and four and a half lines. The OCTAVE is shortened to a SESTET and rhymes *abcabc.* The SESTET is shortened to a QUATRAIN and rhymes either *dbcd* or *dcbd.* A half-line rhyming *c* ends the POEM. Hopkins' "Pied Beauty" is a famous example of a *curtal sonnet.*

Cut: In FILM CRITICISM, a switch from one IMAGE to another. The *cut* is the most common transitional device in filmmaking. The noun form *cut* is also applied to an uninterrupted sequence. As a verb, *cut* describes the act of terminating a SCENE or an IMAGE preparatory to presenting another. See CROSS-CUTTING.

Cycle: A term, originally meaning "circle," applied to a collection of POEMS or ROMANCES centering on some outstanding event or CHARACTER. Cyclic NARRATIVES are commonly accumulations of TRADITION given literary form by a succession of authors rather than by a single writer. "Cyclic" was first applied to a series of EPIC poems intended to supplement Homer's account of the Trojan War and written by a group of late Greek POETS known as the Cyclic Poets. Other examples of cyclic NARRATIVE are the Charlemagne EPICS and Arthurian ROMANCES, such as the "Cycle of Lancelot." The MEDIEVAL religious DRAMA presents a cyclic treatment of Biblical THEMES.

Cyclic Drama: The great CYCLES of MEDIEVAL religious DRAMA. See MYSTERY PLAY.

Cynghanedd: Originally a medieval Welsh term covering a wide and sophisticated range of VERSE devices, the term was revived in the late nineteenth century by Gerard Manley Hopkins to refer to various harmonious patterns of interlaced multiple ALLITERATION (see CROSS-ALLITERATION). Simpler sorts of alliteration are linear and unilateral—as in the common American lunch-counter order "A *c*up of *c*offee and a *p*iece of *p*ie" or Keats's deliberately archaistic line "A shielded scutcheon *bl*ushed with *bl*ood of *q*ueens and *k*ings." Interlacing alliteration, however, in such patterns as *xyyx* and *xyxy* (much the commonest), produces a quadratically ornate effect, such as sometimes occurs in vernacular phrases ("*t*emp*e*st in a *t*eap*o*t," "*p*artridge in a *p*ear *tr*ee) and the Biblical collocation of *s*words-*p*loughshares and *s*pears-*p*runing-hooks. There is conspicuous and complex *cynghanedd* in Macbeth's description of life as a "tale / Told by an idiot, *f*ull of *s*ound and *f*ury, / *S*igni*f*ying nothing" and in Wordsworth's noble tribute to Milton: ". . . and yet thy *h*eart / The *l*ow*l*iest *d*uties on *h*erself *d*id *l*ay." As noted, instances of *cynghanedd* turn up in the vernacular and in PROSE (as in the phrase "*t*oothp*a*ste and *t*oilet *p*aper" in Thomas Heggen's *Mister Roberts* and Faulkner's vivid evocation of a hog's gait as a "*t*winkling *p*urp*o*seful *p*orcine *t*rot"), but the most distinguished, varied, and engaging employment remains that in almost all of Hopkins's mature POEMS. The most salient such use is in the sonnet beginning "As *k*ingfishers *c*atch *f*ire, *dr*agon*f*lies *dr*aw *fl*ame" and the end of "God's Grandeur":

> Because the Holy Ghost over the bent
> World *br*oods with *w*arm *br*east and with ah! *br*ight *w*ings.

Cynicism: Doubt of the generally accepted standards or of the innate goodness of human action. In literature the term characterizes writers or movements distinguished by dissatisfaction. Originally the expression came into being with a group of ancient Greek philosophers, led by Antisthenes and including such others as Diogenes and Crates. The major tenets of the cynics were belief in the moral responsibility of individuals for their own acts and the dominance of the will in its right to control human action. Reason, mind, will, and individualism were, then, of greater importance than the social or political conduct so likely to be worshiped by the multitude. This exaltation of the individual over society makes most unthinking people contemptuous of the cynical attitude. Any highly individualistic writer, scornful of accepted social standards and ideals, is, for this reason, called cynical. Almost every literature has had its schools of cynics. *Cynicism* is not necessarily a weakness or a vice, and the cynics have done much for civilization. Samuel Butler's *Way of All Flesh* and W. Somerset Maugham's *Of Human Bondage* are examples of the cynical NOVEL. The THEATER OF THE ABSURD, the THEATER OF CRUELTY, and many ANTIREALISTIC NOVELS of today reflect *cynicism* of one sort or another.

D

Dactyl: A FOOT consisting of one accented syllable followed by two unaccented, as in the word *mannikin.* See METER and VERSIFICATION.

Dadaism: A movement in Europe during and just after the First World War, which attempted to suppress the logical relationship between idea and statement, argued for absolute freedom, held meetings at bars and in theaters, and delivered itself of numerous nonsensical and seminonsensical manifestoes. It was founded in Zurich in 1916 by Tristan Tzara (who then went to Paris) with the ostensibly destructive intent of perverting and demolishing the tenets of art, philosophy, and logic and replacing them with conscious madness as a protest against the insanity of the war. Similar movements sprang up in Germany, Holland, Italy, Russia, and Spain. About 1924 the movement developed into SURREALISM. In certain respects it seems to have been a forerunner of the ANTIREALISTIC NOVEL and the THEATER OF THE ABSURD.
    [References: C. W. E. Bigsby, *Dada and Surrealism* (1972); Mary Ann Caws, *The Poetry of Dada and Surrealism* (1970); Alan Young, *Dada and After: Extremist Modernism and English Literature* (1981).]

Dandyism: A literary STYLE used by the English and French DECADENT writers of the last quarter of the nineteenth century. The term is derived from *dandy,* a word descriptive of one who gives exaggeratedly fastidious attention to dress and appearance. *Dandyism* as a literary STYLE is marked by excessively refined emotion and PRECIOSITY of language. One or another species of *dandyism* has been associated with the life or work of Byron, Poe, Wilde, Wallace Stevens, and James Merrill, as well as a long succession of French writers from Baudelaire to the present. A somewhat more subtle and profound ideology than superficial emphasis on the sartorial may suggest, thoroughgoing *dandyism* reflects a preference for culture over nature, city over country, manner over matter, surface over substance, and art over life.

Dark Ages: The medieval period. Use of the term is vigorously objected to by most modern students of the Middle Ages, since it reflects the now-discredited view that the period was characterized by intellectual darkness—an idea that arose from lack of information about medieval life. The period, as a matter of fact, was characterized by intellectual, artistic, and even scientific activity that led to high cultural attainments. Most present-day writers, therefore, avoid using *"Dark Ages."* Some who do use it restrict it to the earlier part of the Middle Ages (fifth to eleventh centuries).
    [Reference: W. P. Ker, *The Dark Ages* (1904, reprinted 1979).]

Dead Metaphor: A FIGURE OF SPEECH used so long that it is now taken in its denotative sense only, without the conscious comparison or ANALOGY to a physical object it once conveyed. For example, in the sentence "The keystone of his system is the belief in an omnipotent God," "keystone"—literally an actual stone in an arch—functions as a *dead metaphor.* Many of our ABSTRACT

131

TERMS are *dead metaphors.* Their presence prompted Emerson to call language "fossil poetry." By historical association that may devolve into sentimentality or superstition, an age-old etymologizing habit tries to trace every abstraction to some primordial physical entity. Most Latinate abstractions seem to be *dead metaphors,* as in the connection between "inspiration" and a Latin verb meaning "to breathe into."

Dead Sea Scrolls: Documents written between the first century B.C. and about A.D. 50 and discovered in 1947 and later in caves near the Dead Sea, on the border of Jordan and Israel. The principal finds were in caves on or near the site of the Qumran community, a group who lived an ascetic religious life much like the Essenes. The scrolls, stored in jars, contain portions of every book of the BIBLE except Esther; these manuscripts, almost a thousand years older than any previously known versions of the Bible, have been of paramount interest and concern to students of the Bible. Also found at Qumran were original books of the Qumran sect and groups of devotional POEMS. To those concerned in any way with the Biblical texts, the discovery of the *Dead Sea Scrolls* has been an event of incalculable importance.

Débat: A type of literary composition, usually in VERSE, highly popular in the Middle Ages, in which two persons or objects, frequently allegorical, debate some specific topic and then refer it to a judge. The *débat* may reflect the influence of the "pastoral contest" in Theocritus and Virgil. It was particularly popular in France, where the subjects ranged over most human interests, such as theology, morality, politics, COURTLY LOVE, and social questions. In England the *débat* tended to be religious and moralistic. The best English example is *The Owl and the Nightingale (ca.* 12th century), interpretation of which has caused much scholarly debate.

Decadence: A term denoting the decline, or degeneration, or deterioration that commonly marks the end of a great period. *Decadent* qualities include self-consciousness, a restless curiosity, an oversubtilizing refinement, confusion of GENRES, and often moral perversity. The term, however, is relative and does not always suggest the same qualities to the same writers, and no two periods of *decadence* can be alike. In English drama the period following Shakespeare was marked by such *decadent* qualities as a relaxing of critical standards, a breaking down of types (COMEDY and TRAGEDY merging), a lowered moral tone, sensationalism, overemphasis on some single interest (like PLOT-construction or "prettiness" of STYLE), a decreased seriousness of purpose, and a loss of poetic power. The "silver age" of Latin literature (reign of Trajan), including such writers as Tacitus, Juvenal and Martial (satirists), Lucan, and the Plinys, is called *decadent* in relation to the preceding "golden age" of Augustus made illustrious by Virgil, Horace, Ovid, and Livy. In the last half of the nineteenth and the early years of the twentieth centuries, *decadence* found a special expression in the work of a group known as the DECADENTS. Nowadays the term is used to describe a period or a work of art in which a deteriorating purpose or loss of adequate subject matter is combined with an increasing skill and even hypertrophied virtuosity of technique to produce an exaggerated sensationalism. Some feel that many contemporary art forms, particularly NOVELS and FILMS, are *decadent,* but some such term has been invoked for centuries by conservative CRITICS when confronted with any novelty or departure from petrified norms. Some art is indeed genuinely *decadent* and pernicious, but art called *decadent* (including the POETRY of Wordsworth and Eliot) is likely to become in time the least *decadent* sort of orthodoxy.

Decadents: A group of late nineteenth- and early twentieth-century writers, principally in France but also in England and America, who held that art was superior to nature and that the finest beauty was that of dying or decaying things. In both their lives and their art, they attacked the accepted moral and social standards of their time. In France the group included Verlaine, Rimbaud, Baudelaire, Huysmans, and Villiers de l'Isle-Adam. In England the *decadents* included Oscar Wilde, Ernest Dowson, Aubrey Beardsley, and Frank Harris. In America the sentiment is best represented by Edgar Saltus, although there are *decadent* qualities in Stephen Crane. See DANDYISM.

De Casibus: Latin, "on the falls." John Lydgate translated Boccaccio's *De Casibus Virorum Illustrium* as *Falls of Princes* (1494). In 1974, when a friend suggested the writing of a *de casibus* poem on the resignation of the President of the United States, a POET commented, "De casibus ain't what dey used to be."

Decasyllabic: A LINE composed of ten syllables. IAMBIC PENTAMETER and TROCHAIC PENTAMETER create *decasyllabic* lines.

Deconstruction: A widespread philosophical and critical movement that owes its name and recent energy to the precepts and examples of Jacques Derrida, whose works have been available in English translation since the 1960s. Precursors of the movement include Ernst Cassirer (especially his distinctions between the concept of the thing and the concept of relation, set forth as early as 1910); modern phenomenological philosophers (Husserl and Heidegger foremost among them); Ferdinand de Saussure and his scientific LINGUISTICS based on closed systems of arbitrarily connected signifiers and signifieds with no absolute or substantial reference and no positive extrinsic terms); a number of Nietzschean revisionists, chiefly in France; Kenneth Burke, with his "logological" emphasis on a rhetoric of relations over a logic of substances; and the example of many artists in many fields, particularly James Joyce in *Finnegans Wake*.

   Perhaps the most important doctrine leading to *deconstruction* is Saussure's conclusion that "in language there are only differences. Even more important: a difference generally implies positive terms between which the difference is set up; but in language there are only differences *without positive terms.*" As the "linguistic model" is extended to describe other systems, the concept of thing, substance, event, and absolute recedes, to be superseded by the concept of relation, ratio, construct, and relativity, all covered by Derrida's stimulating coinage "DIFFÉRANCE," which includes difference, differing, deferring, and deferral. Once one realizes that what seems to be an event is really a construct of a quasi-linguistic system, then one is in a position to undo the construct or to recognize that the construct, by its very nature, has already undone, dismantled, or deconstructed itself—with far-reaching implications for thought of every sort. *Deconstruction* affords a perspective from which any number of modern movements can be seen as parts of a generalized shift from a logocentric metaphysic of presence to a new recognition of the play of differences among relations. There is something deconstructive about what Darwin did to the biological hierarchies of present-past and human-animal; what Freud did to the psychological hierarchies of adult-child, reason-dream, conscious-unconscious, and several others; what Schönberg did to the sentiments of the diatonic scale, which privileged the tonic and dominant over other notes in a scale; what Picasso (who called his art "a sum of destructions") did to hierarchies of perspective and orientation in painting; and much else. One recent effect of *deconstruction* has been the undoing of the old order creation-criticism, so that a number of academic CRITICS, including Harold Bloom and Geoffrey Hartman, have been producing critical texts that are, in effect if not in explicit form, PROSE POEMS.

[References: Jonathan Culler, *On Deconstruction* (1982), and *Structuralist Poetics* (1975); Paul de Man, *Allegories of Reading* (1979), and *Blindness and Insight* (1971); Jacques Derrida, *Of Grammatology* (tr. 1976), and *Writing and Difference* (tr. 1978); Judith Fetterley, *The Resisting Reader: A Feminist Approach to American Fiction* (1978); Barbara Johnson, *The Critical Difference* (1980); Christopher Norris, *Deconstruction, Theory and Practice* (1982); Michael Ryan, *Marxism and Deconstruction* (1982).]

Decorum: A critical term loosely describing what is proper to a CHARACTER, subject, or SETTING in a work. According to classical standards, the UNITY and harmony of a composition could be maintained by the observance of DRAMATIC PROPRIETY. The STYLE should be appropriate to the speaker, the occasion, and the subject matter. So RENAISSANCE authors were careful to have kings speak in a "high" STYLE (such as majestic BLANK VERSE), old men in a "grave" STYLE, clowns in PROSE, and shepherds in a "rustic" STYLE. Puttenham (1589) cites as an example of the lack of DECORUM the case of the English translator of Virgil who said that Aeneas was fain to "trudge" out of Troy (a beggar might "trudge," but not a great hero). Beginning in the RENAISSANCE the type to which a CHARACTER belonged was regarded as an important determinant of his or her qualities; age, rank, and status were often held as fundamental in CHARACTERIZATION. But on the use of *decorum in* the *Iliad* Pope said: "The speeches are to be considered as they flow from the characters, being perfect or defective as they agree or disagree with the manners of those who utter them. As there is more variety of characters in the *Iliad,* so there is of speeches, than in any other poem," and "Homer is in nothing more excellent than in that distinction of characters which he maintains through his whole poem. What Andromache here says can be spoken properly by none but Andromache." *Decorum* has often considered the controlling critical idea of Horace's poetic doctrine and of the NEOCLASSIC Age in England.

Deep Focus: In FILM CRITICISM a method by which objects both near and far away are simultaneously in focus. It is widely used in realistic filmmaking. A common synonym is COMPOSITION IN DEPTH.

Deep Image: IMAGES from the subconscious, dreams, hallucinations, or fantasies are called *deep images* by certain POETS aand CRITICS, among them Robert

Bly. The deep, underground, or subterranean IMAGE, as the terms may suggest, argues with IMAGIST fervor for the image in general as the central motivation in a POEM and for a specific sort of image in particular: not merely an ornament or conceit but a figure conforming to Freud's notion that dream-language puts image and quantity in the place of idea and quality. Any palpable image can take on "deep" characteristics, depending on the setting and situation, but it seems likely that the unconscious deals in elemental tokens, such as the explicit images presented in Bly's "When the Dumb Speak":

> Then the images appear:
> Images of death,
> Images of the body shaken in the grave,
> And the graves filled with seawater;
> Fires in the sea,
> The ships smoldering like bodies,
> Images of wasted life. . . .

Definition: A brief EXPOSITION of a term designed to explain its meaning. The simplest logical or formal *definitions* consist of two elements: (1) the general class (*genus*) to which the object belongs and (2) the specific ways (*differentiae*) in which the object differs from others in the same class. For instance, in the first sentence of this entry "brief exposition" furnishes the class to which *definition* belongs and "designed to explain its meaning" shows the way in which *definition* differs from other expositions. For the sake of efficiency, it is best to locate an object in a relatively small class: one would ordinarily define "ant" as a kind of insect, say, and not merely as a kind of creature or entity. To define a receiver as "something that receives" is to waste time in *definition* by synonymic or circular *definition*. Likewise, reciprocating identifications do little toward proper defining or explaining. Consider: "A typhoon is a hurricane in the eastern hemisphere, and a hurricane is a typhoon in the western hemisphere." It is possible, however, to provide a reasonably effective definition simply by giving an apt example, summary, or paraphrase. Rarely are single-sentence *definitions* satisfactory in themselves. But these principles of a *definition* act as guides in forming longer expositions in which both the second and third elements of the *definition* may be extended almost indefinitely.

It is important to remember that a *definition* is a statement about the meaning of an expression—a word, phrase, or sentence. In the strictest sense the full statement, "A radio is an instrument for transmitting and receiving wireless messages," is the *definition:* it asserts that the term "radio" has the same meaning as the element following "is." There are, therefore, many different proper *definitions* of any term.

Definitive Edition: An EDITION of a work assumed to have final or permanent authority. It is sometimes a final text or revision, which the author wishes to be considered the accepted version, such as the 1891–1892 edition of *Leaves of Grass,* of which Whitman said, "As there are now several editions of L. of G., different texts and different dates, I wish to say that I prefer and recommend this present one, complete, for future printing. . . ." The term is also applied to editions determined by scrupulous application of rigorous principles of textual editing, such as those produced under the aegis of the CENTER FOR SCHOLARLY EDITIONS of the Modern Language Association of America.

Deism: The religion of those who believe in a God who rules the world by established laws but not in the divinity of Christ or the inspiration of the BIBLE; "natural" religion, based on reason and a study of NATURE as opposed to "revealed" religion. The scientific movement, which grew out of the new knowledge generated by the discoveries and theories of Columbus, Copernicus, Galileo, Francis Bacon, and later the members of the Royal Society, furthered the development of a rationalistic ideology that more and more tended to rely on reason instead of revelation in the consideration of the relation of human beings to God and the universe. *Deism*, a product of this general point of view, also absorbed something from the theological movements of ARIANISM (opposition to the doctrine of the Trinity) and ARMINIANISM (which stressed moral conduct as a sign of religion and opposed the doctrine of election; see CALVINISM). The prevalent notion that the deists believed in an "absentee" God, who, having created the world and set in motion machinery for its operation, took no further interest, is not applicable to all eighteenth-century deists, some of whom even believed in God's pardoning of the sins of the repentant.

The following statements encapsulate the beliefs of the English deists: (1) The BIBLE is not the inspired word of God; it is good so far as it reflects "natural" religion and bad so far as it contains "additions" made by superstitious or designing persons. (2) Certain Christian theological doctrines are the product of superstition or the invention of priests and must be rejected; for example, the deity of Christ, the doctrine of the Trinity, and the theory of the atonement for sins. (3) God is perfect, is the creator and governor of the universe, and works not capriciously but through unchangeable laws (hence "miracles" are to be rejected as impossible). (4) Human beings are free agents, whose minds work as they themselves choose; even God cannot control their thoughts. (5) Since human beings are rational creatures like God, they are capable of understanding the laws of the universe; and as God is perfect, so can human beings become perfect through the process of education. They may learn of God through a study of NATURE, which shows design and must therefore be an expression of God. (6) Practical religion for the individual consists in achieving virtue through the rational guidance of conduct (as exemplified in the scheme for developing certain moral virtues recorded by Franklin in his *Autobiography*).

[References: Ernst Cassirer, *The Philosophy of the Enlightenment*, tr. 1951; James Collins, *God in Modern Philosophy*, 1959; H. E. Cushman, *Beginner's History of Philosophy*, vol. 2, 1920; G. P. Fisher, *History of Christian Doctrine*, 1896, reprinted 1978; John Orr, *English Deism: Its Roots and Its Fruits*, 1934; J. H. Randall, *The Making of the Modern Mind*, 1926, reprinted 1976; Leslie Stephen, *History of English Thought in the Eighteenth Century*, 3rd ed., 2 vols. 1902, reprinted 1962; N. L. Torrey, *Voltaire and the English Deists*, 1930).]

Demotic Style: A term applied by Northrop Frye to a STYLE shaped by the DICTION, RHYTHMS, syntax, and associations of ordinary speech. It is differentiated from the HIERATIC STYLE, which uses various CONVENTIONS and ornaments to create a consciously elevated literary expression.

Denotation: The specific, exact meaning of a word, independent of its emotional coloration or associations. See CONNOTATION.

Dénouement: The final unraveling of the PLOT in DRAMA of FICTION; the solution of the mystery; the explanation or outcome. *Dénouement* implies an ingenious untying of the knot of an intrigue, involving not only a satisfactory outcome of the main situation but an explanation of all the secrets and misunderstandings connected with the plot COMPLICATION. In DRAMA *dénouement* may be applied to both TRAGEDY and COMEDY, though the common term for a tragic *dénouement* is CATASTROPHE. The final scene of Shakespeare's *Cymbeline* is a striking example of how clever and involved a dramatic *dénouement* may be: exposure of villain, clearing up of mistaken identities and disguises, reuniting of father and children, and reuniting of husband and wife. By some writers *dénouement* is used as a synonym for FALLING ACTION. See also CATASTROPHE, DRAMATIC STRUCTURE, SHORT STORY.

Description: One of the four chief types of composition (see ARGUMENTATION, EXPOSITION, and NARRATION) that has as its purpose the picturing of a scene or setting. Though sometimes used apart for its own sake (as in Poe's *Landor's Cottage*), it more often is subordinated to one of the other types of writing; especially to NARRATION, with which it most frequently goes hand in hand. Descriptive writing is most successful when its details are carefully selected according to some purpose and to a definite POINT OF VIEW, when its IMAGES are concrete and clear, and when it makes discreet use of words of color, sound, and motion.

Detective Story: A NOVEL or SHORT STORY in which a crime, usually a murder—the identity of the perpetrator unknown—is solved by a detective through a logical assembling and interpretation of palpable evidence, known as clues. This definition is the accepted one for the true *detective story*, although in practice much variation occurs. If the variations are too great, however—such as the absence of the detective, a knowledge from the beginning of the identity of the criminal, or the absence of reasoning from clues—the story falls into the looser category of MYSTERY STORY. The specific form *detective story* had its origin in "The Murders in the Rue Morgue" by Edgar Allan Poe (1841). In this and other tales, "The Purloined Letter," "The Mystery of Marie Rogêt," and "Thou Art the Man," Poe is said to have established every one of the basic CONVENTIONS of the *detective story*. The form has been remarkably popular in England and America as light entertainment for the intellectual. Generally, American *detective stories* have had greater sensationalism and action than the English, which have usually placed a premium on tightness of PLOT and grace of STYLE. The greatest of *detective story* writers was Sir Arthur Conan Doyle, whose Sherlock Holmes stories seem to have established a character, a room, a habit, a few gestures, and a group of phrases in the enduring heritage of English-speaking readers. "S. S. Van Dine" (Willard Huntington Wright) carried ingenious plotting to a very high level in America in the 1920s in his Philo Vance stories, a course in which he was ably followed by the authors of the Ellery Queen NOVELS. The introduction of brutal REALISM coupled with a poetic and highly idiomatic STYLE in the *detective stories* of Dashiell Hammett in the 1930s has resulted in distinguished work by Raymond

Chandler and Ross MacDonald. In England the ingenuity of Agatha Christie and John Dickson Carr (also "Carter Dickson"), the skill and grace of Dorothy Sayers, and the urbanity of the New Zealander Ngaio Marsh made significant contributions to the form. The distinguished English POET C. Day Lewis, under the pen name "Nicholas Blake," wrote an entertaining series of *detective* novels with a HERO whose style and manner were supposedly based on those of Day Lewis's friend, W. H. Auden. The Americans who write as "Emma Lathen" and "Amanda Cross" are producing distinguished *detective stories* in the tradition of the NOVEL OF MANNERS. All of these practitioners have made it a point of honor to observe the fundamental rule of the *detective story* (and the rule that most clearly distinguishes it from the MYSTERY STORY): that the clues contributing to a logical solution be fairly presented to the reader at the same time that the detective receives them and that the detective deduce the answer from a logical reading of these clues. See MYSTERY STORY.

[References: Jacques Barzun and W. H. Taylor, *A Catalogue of Crime* (1971); Julian Symons, *Mortal Consequences: A History from the Detective Story to the Crime Novel* (1972).]

Determinism: The belief that all apparent acts of the will are actually the result of causes that determine them. When used as a term to describe a doctrine in a literary work, *determinism* has a wide range of philosophical possibilities, and the possible determining forces are many. In CLASSICAL literature it may be fate or necessity. In writing produced by Christians of Calvinistic leanings it may be the predestined will of God (see CALVINISM). In naturalistic literature it may be the action of scientific law (see NATURALISM). In Marxist writing, it may be the inevitable operation of economic forces (see MARXISM). In the orthodox Freudian scheme of *determinism*, every detail of daily life, including such seemingly negligible matters as slips of the tongue and pen, is the traceable result of latent psychic mechanisms, so that casual forgetting becomes an episode of suppression or repression, and ostensibly random choices are far from random. In all these cases CHARACTERS illustrate *determinism* because their actions are controlled from without rather than being the products of free will. One function of many literary devices, such as rhythmic REPETITION and RHYME, is to introduce new dimensions of determination and *determinism* in arrays otherwise governed only by whim, guesswork, serendipity, or mere possibility.

Deus ex Machina: The employment of some unexpected and improbable incident in a STORY or PLAY to make things turn out right. In the ancient Greek theater, when gods appeared, they were lowered to the STAGE from the "machine" or stage structure above. Such abrupt but timely appearance of a god, when used to extricate mortal characters from a situation so perplexing that the solution seemed beyond mortal powers, was referred to in Latin as the *deus ex machina* ("god from the machine"). The term now characterizes any device whereby an author solves a difficult situation by a forced invention. A villain may fail to kill a HERO because he has forgotten to load his revolver. A long-lost brother, given up for dead, suddenly appears on the scene provided with a fortune he has won in foreign parts, just in time to save the family from disgrace or a sister from an unwelcome marriage. Reliance on the *deus ex machina* is commonly recognized as evidence of deficient skill in PLOT-making or an uncritical willingness to disregard the probabilities. Though it is sometimes employed by good authors, it is found most frequently in MELO-DRAMA. See PLOT, COUP DE THÉÂTRE.

Deuteragonist: The ACTOR taking the part second in importance to the PRO-TAGONIST in a Greek DRAMA. Historically Aeschylus added a second actor to the traditional religious ceremonials, thus making DRAMA possible; this second actor was called the *deuteragonist.* By analogy, the term is sometimes applied to a CHARACTER who serves as a FOIL to the leading character.

Devil's Advocate: One who, at the examination of the claims of a person to canonization, argues the claim of Satan to the soul by marshalling all the person's sins and all other evidence against sainthood. The term has come to be applied to anyone who presents an unpopular or apparently erroneous side in order to bring out the whole truth, or who opposes a case with which he or she does not really disagree in order to test or strengthen its validity.

Dial, The: A PERIODICAL published in Boston from 1840 to 1844 as the organ of the New England transcendentalists. Margaret Fuller was its first editor (1840–42) and Emerson the second (1842–44). Among the most famous contributors were Alcott, Emerson, Margaret Fuller, Lowell, Thoreau, and Jones Very.

In 1860 another organ of TRANSCENDENTALISM named *The Dial* appeared briefly in Cincinnati, edited by Moncure Conway and with contributions by Emerson, Alcott, and Howells. From 1880 to 1929, a distinguished literary periodical was published under the name *The Dial,* first in Chicago and after 1916 in New York. Until 1916 it was a conservative literary REVIEW. From 1916 to 1920, under the editorship of Conrad Aiken, Randolph Bourne, and Van Wyck Brooks, it was a radical JOURNAL of opinion and CRITICISM, publishing writers like Dewey, Veblen, Laski, and Beard. After 1920 it became the most distinguished literary monthly in America, noted for its reproductions of modern graphic art and for its advocacy of modern movements. It published such writers as Thomas Mann, T. S. Eliot, and James Stephens. Marianne Moore was editor from 1926 until publication ceased in 1929.

Dialectic: In the broadest sense, simply the art of ARGUMENTATION or debate, but the term is customarily used in one of its more restricted senses. In CLASSI-CAL literature it refers to the tradition of continuing debate or discussion of eternally unresolved issues, such as "beauty versus truth" or "the individual versus the state." Plato's *Dialogues* are supreme examples of this kind of *dialectic.* In philosophy *dialectic* is applied to a systematic ANALYSIS of a problem or idea. The most frequent system is that of Hegel, a modification of which Marx employed, in which the material at issue is analyzed in terms of THESIS, ANTITHESIS, and synthesis (see HEGELIANISM). In CRITICISM the term is often applied to the ideas, logic, or reasoning that gives STRUCTURE to certain works, such as Aldous Huxley's *Point Counter Point* or Sartre's NOVELS. W. B. Yeats exploited the *dialectic* structure inherent in the RHYME scheme of OTTAVA RIMA (*ababab cc*) to create a number of potently dramatic POEMS, such as "Among School Children," in which the driving energy is generated by dialectical oppositions (walking and dancing, youth and age, man and woman, sacred and secular, labor and play, Plato and Aristotle, past and present, nature and culture) and resolutions. Similarly, T. S. Eliot's *Four Quartets* draw their forcible drama from oppositions and resolutions involving time and eternity, action and suffering, purgatory and paradise.

Dialects: When the speech of two groups or of two persons representing two groups both speaking the same "language" exhibits very marked differences, the groups or persons are said to speak different *dialects*. (A personal version of a language is sometimes called an "idiolect.") If the differences are very slight, they may be said to represent "subdialects" rather than *dialects*. If the differences are so great that the two groups or persons cannot understand each other, especially if they come from separate political units or countries, they are said to speak different languages. Yet the gradations are so subtle that no scientific method has been devised for distinguishing between a language and a *dialect*. The chief cause of the development of *dialects* is isolation or separation because of lack of easy communication. Natural barriers such as mountain ranges and social barriers caused by hostility tend to keep groups from frequent contact with each other, with the resultant development of habitual differences in speech habits, leading toward the formation of *dialects* or even languages. Likewise among neighboring groups, the *dialect* of one group commonly becomes dominant, as did West Saxon in early England.

When the Teutonic tribes came to England from the Continent in the fifth century, they spoke separate *dialects* of West Germanic. In Old English times (fifth to eleventh centuries) there were four main *dialects:* (1) Northumbrian (north of the Humber River) and (2) Mercian (between the Thames and the Humber), both being branches or subdialects of the original Anglian *dialect;* (3) the Kentish (southeastern England), based on the language of the Jutes, and (4) the Saxon (southern England). The early literature produced in the Northern districts (seventh to ninth centuries) is preserved chiefly in normalized Southern (West Saxon) versions from the tenth and eleventh centuries. In Middle English times the old *dialects* appear under different names and with new subdialects. Northumbrian is called Northern; Saxon and Kentish are called Southern; the Northern English spoken in Scotland becomes Lowland Scottish; Mercian becomes Midland and is broken into two main subdialects, West Midland and East Midland. The latter was destined to become the immediate parent of modern English. Middle English literature, therefore, exists in a variety of *dialects,* more or less clearly differentiated. Layamon's *Brut* and *The Owl and the Nightingale,* for example, are in the Southern dialect; *Cursor Mundi* and *Sir Tristrem* are in Northern; the *Ormulum* is early Midland, while *Havelok the Dane, Piers Plowman,* and the POETRY of Chaucer are in later Midland. The Middle English *dialects* differed in vocabulary, sounds, and inflections, so that Northerners and Southerners had difficulty in understanding each other. A few examples of the differences may be given: In Northern, "they sing" would be "they singes"; in Midland, "they singen"; in Southern, "they singeth." Northern "kirk" is Southern "church." The present participle in Northern ended in *-ande;* in Southern in *-inde* or *-inge;* in Midland, in *-ende* or *-inge.* Though the literary language in modern times has been standardized, it must not be supposed that *dialects* no longer exist, especially in oral speech. Skeat lists nine modern *dialects* in Scotland; in

England proper he finds three groups of Northern, ten groups of Midland, five groups of Eastern, two groups of Western, and ten groups of Southern.

American *dialects* are less marked than English *dialects*, although some dialectal differences are easily discernible. However, only in areas where a local *patois*, such as Cajun in Louisiana or Gullah on the South Carolina coast, is spoken do Americans have serious difficulty in understanding one another. Three broad dialectal areas are generally recognized in the United States, although their speeches are sometimes given differing names. These areas are: New England and eastern New York, the speech of which is usually called "Eastern"; the area south of Pennsylvania and the Ohio River, extending westward beyond the Mississippi River into Texas, the speech of which is usually called "Southern"; and the broad area that extends from New Jersey on the Atlantic coast, through Pennsylvania and western New York into the middle west and the southwest and then over all the Pacific Coast, an area that comprises more than three-fourths of the American population; the speech of this area is usually called "General American" and sometimes "Western." Modern methods of transportation and mass communication are steadily leveling American speech and eradicating dialectal differences. At one time a great number of conventionalized subdialects were recognized and exploited in LO- CAL COLOR writings; most of these have today merged into the speech patterns of "General American." As a result of the work on the *Linguistic Atlas of the United States* (see AMERICAN LANGUAGE), much more accurate records of remaining regional and local differences of speech were made, although at the time when they were being lost. Dialectal differences in America are matters of vocabulary, grammar, and pronunciation.

Dialogue: Conversation of two or more people. Most common in FICTION, particularly in DRAMAS, NOVELS, and SHORT STORIES, *dialogue* is sometimes used in general expository and philosophical writing. An analysis of *dialogue* as employed by great writers shows that it embodies certain values: (1) It advances the ACTION in a definite way and is not used as mere ornamentation. (2) It is consistent with the character of the speakers. It varies in TONE and expression according to the nationalities, DIALECTS, occupations, and social levels of the speakers. (3) It gives the *impression* of naturalness without being an actual, *verbatim* record of what may have been said, since FICTION is concerned with "the semblance of reality," not with reality itself. (4) It presents the interplay of ideas and personalities among the people conversing; it sets forth a conversational give and take—not simply a series of remarks of alternating speakers. (5) It varies in DICTION, RHYTHM, phrasing, sentence length, and such, according to the various speakers participating. The best writers of *dialogue* know that rarely do two or more people of exactly the same cultural and personal background meet and converse, and the *dialogue* they write notes these differences. (6) It serves, at the hands of some writers, to give relief from passages essentially serious or expository.

It should be noted, however, that in the Elizabethan DRAMA the CONVEN-TION of using BLANK VERSE and high RHETORIC for noble or elevated CHARAC-TERS and PROSE for underlings and comic characters modifies these rules, as did the doctrine of DECORUM in the seventeenth and eighteenth centuries. Furthermore, PLAYS of WIT, such as those by Oscar Wilde, and plays of idea, such as those by G. B. Shaw, unhesitatingly take liberties with the idea of appropriateness to station and CHARACTER in *dialogue*. In a VERSE drama the *dialogue* is in a form of measured language unlike that ever actually spoken by any living person, but audiences through the centuries have become inured to this CONVENTION, as outlandishly unrealistic as it may sometimes seem.

The *dialogue* is also a specialized literary composition in which two or more CHARACTERS debate or reason about an idea or a proposition. There are many notable examples in the world's literature, the best known being the *Dialogues* of Plato. Others include Lucian's *Dialogues of the Dead,* Dryden's *Essay of Dramatick Poesie,* Landor's *Imaginary Conversations,* and scattered modern examples by Paul Valéry, T. S. Eliot, Elder Olson, and Hugh Kenner.

Diary: A day-by-day CHRONICLE of events, a JOURNAL. Usually a personal and more or less intimate record of events and thoughts kept by an individual. Not avowedly intended for publication—though it is difficult to insist on this point since many diarists have certainly kept a possible audience in mind—most *diaries*, when published, have appeared posthumously. The most famous *diary* in English is that of Samuel Pepys, which details events between January 1, 1660, and May 29, 1669. Other important English *diaries* are those of John Evelyn, Bulstrode Whitelock, George Fox, Jonathan Swift, John Wesley, Fanny Burney, Virginia Woolf, and Evelyn Waugh. Noted American diarists include Samuel Sewall, Sarah K. Knight, and William Byrd. Anais Nin's prodigious *diary,* edited in seven substantial volumes covering the period from 1931 to 1974, combines gossip and philosophy in a richly detailed record of encounters with interesting personages, including Henry Miller and Gore Vidal, all over Europe and America. As a conscious literary device, as in Lockwood's "outer" narrative in *Wuthering Heights,* the *diary* furnishes a resilient format and the engaging illusion of privileged access to confidential materials. The *diary* has, in late years, become a conscious literary form used by travelers, statesmen, and politicians as a convenient method of presenting the run of daily events in which they have had a hand. See AUTOBIOGRAPHY, BIOGRAPHY.

[References: Arthur Ponsonby, *English Diaries* (1923), and *More English Diaries* (1927).]

Diatribe: Writing or discourse characterized by bitter INVECTIVE or abusive argument; a harangue. Originally it was a treatment in DIALOGUE of a limited philosophical proposition in a simple, lively, conversational tone. Popular with the Stoic and Cynic philosophers, it became noted for the abusiveness that led to its present-day meaning.

Dibrach: A term applied in Greek and Latin PROSODY to a FOOT consisting of two short or unstressed syllables. It is another name for the PYRRHIC.

Diction: The use of words in oral or written discourse, now ordinarily divided into vocabulary (words and other small units considered one by one in terms of plain or fancy, current or archaic, Germanic or Latinate, native or foreign, and so forth) and syntax (the order or arrangement of words considered as formal patterns construable as simple or complex, ordinary or extraordinary, loose or periodic, complete or fragmentary, and so forth). Some analysts speak of "level" of vocabulary and "texture" of syntax. The two constituents of *diction* permit independent classification, so that many of Robert Frost's lines (such as "Something there is that doesn't love a wall" and "Whose woods these are I think I know") display simultaneously a marked simplicity of vocabulary but a marked oddness of syntax. Certain sorts of *diction* can become an author's typical habit and distinctive stylistic signature, as in the combination of question and elliptical absolute found in many of W. B. Yeats's most celebrated passages (such as "And what rough beast, its hour come round at last . . ." and "What youthful mother, a shape upon her lap . . .").

There are at least four levels of *diction:* formal, informal, colloquial, and SLANG. Formal refers to the level of usage common in serious books and lofty discourse; informal refers to the level of usage found in the relaxed but polite and cultivated conversation; colloquial refers to everyday usage and may include terms and constructions accepted in that group but not universally acceptable; and SLANG refers to a group of newly COINED WORDS that are not yet a part of formal usage.

It should be noted that the accepted *diction* of one age is often unacceptable to another. See POETIC DICTION.

Dictionaries: At different times during their five hundred years of development, English *dictionaries* have emphasized different elements and have passed through an evolution as great as any of our literary forms or tools. In their modern form *dictionaries* arrange their words alphabetically, give explanations of the meanings, the derivations, the pronunciations, illustrative quotations, along with IDIOMS, SYNONYMS, and antonyms. Sometimes, however, the "dictionary" is restricted to word-lists of special significance, such as *dictionaries* of law or medicine.

English LEXICOGRAPHY began with attempts to define Latin words by giving English equivalents. The *Promptorium Parvulorum* (1440) of Galfridus Grammaticus, a Dominican monk of Norfolk, printed by Pynson in 1499 was an early example. Which publication deserves to be called the first English *dictionary* is difficult to say because the evolution was so gradual that the conception of what constituted a good word-book differed from year to year. Vizetelly gives credit to Richard Huloet's *Abecedarium* (1552) as the first *dictionary;* some believe that the first person to succeed in defining all words in good usage in English was Nathaniel Bailey, whose major work was not published until 1721; *The Dictionary of Syr T. Eliot, Knyght* (1538) appears to have been the first work to establish the term *"dictionary."*

The early word-books started off listing simply the "hard words" that people might not be expected to know; the classification was sometimes alphabetical, sometimes by subject matter. Later lexicographers regarded themselves as guardians of national speech and listed only those words dignified enough to be of "good usage"; the function of these compilers was to standardize and stabilize the national language. Illustrative of this point of view were the collections of such scholarly academies as those of Italy and France; and, indeed, Dr. Samuel Johnson, an academy in himself, first held and later abandoned this same sort of ideal. Archbishop Trench, a British scholar, declared roundly in 1857 that a proper *dictionary* was really an "inventory of language" including colloquial uses as well as literary uses, and Trench's insistence on the philological attitude for the lexicographer probably did much to develop the modern word-book "on historical principles."

Some of the titles important in the evolution of the *dictionary* are:

John Florio (1598), *A Worlde of Wordes.*

Robert Cawdrey (1604) (who used English words only), *A Table Alphabeticall Contyning and Teaching the True Writing and Understanding of Hard Usuall English Wordes.*

Randle Cotgrave (1611), *A Bundle of Words.*

John Bullokar (1616), *An English Expositor.*

Henry Cockeram (1623), *The English Dictionarie* (in which "idiote" was defined as "an unlearned asse").

Thomas Blount (1656), *Glossographia.*

Edward Phillips, (1658), *A New World in Words.*

Nathaniel Bailey (1721), *Universal Etymological English Dictionary.*

Samuel Johnson (1755), *Dictionary of the English Language* (in which 50,000 words were explained. The most ambitious volume published up to that time. The personal element injected into definitions gives us such famous explanations as that for *oats:* "a grain which in England is generally given to horses, but in Scotland supports the people," and, further, that *Whig* was "the name of a faction" while *Tory* signified "one who adhered to the antient constitution of the state and the apostolical hierarchy of the Church of England, opposed to a Whig").

Thomas Sheridan (1780), *Complete Dictionary of the English Language* (which gave special emphasis to pronunciation).

Samuel Johnson (1798?) *A School Dictionary.* The first American *dictionary.* This Johnson was not related to the earlier Dr. Samuel. This first American *dictionary* simplified some of the English spellings and began the use of phonetic marks as aids to pronunciation.

Noah Webster (1828), *American Dictionary;* the most famous name in American lexicography.

Joseph Emerson Worcester (1846), *Universal and Critical Dictionary of the English Language.*

In 1884 the great work *A New English Dictionary on Historical Principles* was begun in England. Edited by James A. H. Murray, Henry Bradley, and W. A. Craigie, this dictionary is more commonly called the *New English Dictionary* or the *Oxford English Dictionary,* and it is often referred to as the *OED* or *O.E.D.* It was completed in 1928 and augmented by a supplementary thirteenth volume in 1933. Beginning forty years later, additional supplements, projected for four large volumes, were issued to correct errors and bring the work up to date. A standard feature of *Notes and Queries* for more than a century now has been the offering of suggestions for earlier citations and variant meanings, so that use of the *OED* now calls for consulting the main dictionary, one or two supplements, and *Notes and Queries.* The earlier volumes, largely covering the first part of the alphabet, tend to be more subject to error than do the later. Despite these difficulties, the *OED* is easily the greatest of all English *dictionaries* in the fullness of its illustrative examples and in its elaborate analysis of the meanings and etymologies. The citations are drawn from English writings ranging in date from the earliest writings to the contemporary. It is particularly valuable for its dated quotations of actual sentences showing the meanings of a word at various periods. It contains a total of more than 500,000 words. The chief American dictionary, based on current usage, is the third edition of *Webster's New International Dictionary*. See LEXICOGRAPHY.

Didactic Novel: Although the term is often applied to any NOVEL plainly designed to teach a moral lesson, such as the Horatio Alger books, it is properly used as a SYNONYM for the EDUCATION NOVEL, an eighteenth-century form presenting an ideal education for some young person. See EDUCATION NOVEL.

Didactic Poetry: POETRY that is intended primarily to teach a lesson. The distinction between *didactic poetry* and nondidactic poetry is difficult to make and always involves a subjective judgment of the author's purpose. For example, Bryant's "To a Waterfowl" is obviously concerned with an ethical or religious idea; yet it is not generally considered *didactic*, perhaps because most readers sense that the idea of a protective Providence is dramatically appropriate to the physical and emotional situation—that the POET is communicating his feeling about the idea rather than communicating the idea itself. On the other hand, Pope's *Essay on Criticism* is an emphatic instance of *didactic poetry*. See DIDACTICISM.

Didacticism: Instructiveness in a literary work, one of the purposes of which appears to be to give guidance, particularly in moral, ethical, or religious matters. Since all literary art exists in order to communicate something—an idea, a teaching, a precept, an emotion, an attitude, a fact, an autobiographical incident, a sensation—the ultimate question of *didacticism* in a literary work appears to be one of the author's actual or ostensible purpose. If, of Horace's dual functions of the artist, instruction is selected as the primary goal, the artist is didactic in intent, or we may say that the purpose of the work is didactic. Another way of stating the problem is to say that if the thing to be communicated takes precedence as an act of communication over the artistic qualities of the FORM through which it is communicated, the work is didactic. Viewed in still another way, a work is didactic if it would have as its ultimate effect a meaning or a result outside itself. In a sense those who divide CRITICISM into PLATONIC and ARISTOTELIAN are dividing the purposes of literary art into didactic and nondidactic. From this definition it is obvious that *didacticism* is an acceptable aspect of literature, at least up to a certain point, despite the fact that the term usually carries a derogatory meaning in CRITICISM. The principle in *didactic* art is basically that the subject, TONE, and FORM are determined and shaped by considerations, temporary and local, that lie beyond or outside the precinct of art proper. The projected lesson may be simply intellectual, as in such mnemonic rhymes as "*I* before *e* / Except after *c*" and "Thirty days hath September . . ." or simultaneously intellectual and moral, as in the NURSERY RHYME "One, two, / Buckle your shoe . . ." wherein the odd-numbered LINES teach counting and the even-numbered inculcate tidiness ("shut the door, "pick up sticks," "lay them straight," and so forth). Allegorical and SATIRIC POETRY, such as Dante's *Comedy* and Pope's

The Dunciad, certainly have some intellectual and moral didactic dimensions. A sophisticated POEM like Frost's "Provide, Provide" may seem didactic in its use of several devices (memorable RHYME, REPETITION, EXEMPLUM, imperative mood, APHORISM, and so forth), but the final shape and purpose of the poem is the expression of literary CHARACTER in a thoroughly artistic and nondidactic way. Sententious characters in a mimetic work may be developed by didactic means, such as the outsized fabric of fatherly advice delivered by Polonius in *Hamlet.* In this remarkable twenty-five-line speech, the point is not whether "Neither a borrower or a lender be," say, is intellectually true, morally good, or philosophically wise, but whether it advances our understanding of Polonius's CHARACTER. Apart from the truth or wisdom of what the MAXIMS may urge, the speech is inconsistent, long-winded, *cliché*-ridden, and inappropriate to the situation (Polonius has come to make Laertes hurry up). The speech shows Polonius to be forgetful, foolish, hypocritical, and touchingly solicitous as a father. The objection to *didacticism* results from a feeling that, if carried too far or borne too self-righteously, it will subvert the object of literature to lesser and ignoble purposes.

Among those who make didactic demands of literature today are the practitioners of MORAL CRITICISM, the Marxists, those who measure literature by sociological standards, and those who insist that literature be "relevant." The most bitter foes of *didacticism* are probably the New Critics, who do not declare POETRY to be meaningless but who declare its significant meaning to be intrinsic. See AUTOTELIC; BELIEF, THE PROBLEM OF; ARISTOTELIAN CRITICISM; PLATONIC CRITICISM; NEW CRITICISM; CRITICISM, TYPES OF; CRITICISM; PARAPHRASE, HERESY OF; PROPAGANDA NOVEL.

Diegesis: A statement, description, or narration without explanation, conclusion, or judgment; an obsolescent theological term recently resurrected by critical theorists.
[Reference: Roland Barthes, *The Responsibility of Forms* (tr. 1985).]

Dieresis: A term in METRICS to designate the situation where the pause in a LINE of VERSE falls at the end of a FOOT; now usually called CAESURA. See CAESURA.

Différance: A virtually untranslatable French NEOLOGISM introduced by Jacques Derrida to combine various DENOTATIONS and CONNOTATIONS of *difference, differing, deferring,* and *deferral*—with particular reference to Ferdinand de Saussure's celebrated concept that "in language there are only differences *without positive terms.*" For the *signifier* and the *signified* to exist and operate, it is inescapably necessary for them to differ between themselves; if they did not differ, they would not be related except by a species of identity or redundancy, neither of which would permit signification. Since they must differ, there is, and always has been, a space or gap between them that constitutes a trace of absence such that any construct has already begun to dismantle or deconstruct itself. Derrida has explained *différance* as "a structure and a movement that cannot be conceived on the basis of the opposition presence/absence. *Différance* is the systematic play of differences, of traces of differences, of the spacing by which elements relate to one another. This spacing is the production, simultaneously active and passive (the *a* of *différance* indicates this indecision as regards activity and passivity, that which cannot yet be governed and organized by that opposition), of intervals without which the 'full' terms could not signify, could not function."

[Reference: Jonathan Culler, *On Deconstruction* (1982).]

Difficulty: Formerly considered an incidental feature of certain sophisticated pieces of writing, especially a good deal of POETRY and PROSE in the seventeenth century, and now regarded as a general feature of all reading to an extent. Like AMBIGUITY and OBSCURITY, *difficulty* contributes to suspense and even to surprise. Conceivably, some difficulty of access may create involvement and engagement on the reader's part.

Digest: A systematic arrangement of condensed materials on some specific subject, so that it summarizes the information on that subject. By extension, *digest* is often applied to a JOURNAL that publishes CONDENSATIONS or ABRIDGMENTS of material previously published elsewhere, such as *The Reader's Digest*.

Digression: The insertion of material often not closely related to the subject in a given work. In a well-knit PLOT, a *digression* violates UNITY. In the FAMILIAR ESSAY it is a standard device, and it was sometimes used in the EPIC. The device was particularly popular in seventeenth- and eighteenth-century English writing, notable examples being the *digressions* in Swift's *Tale of a Tub* and Sterne's "Digression on Digressions" in *Tristram Shandy*. If a *digression* is lengthy and formal, it is sometimes called an EXCURSUS. Nowadays, in such works as Thomas Pynchon's NOVELS, the protracted comic *digression* has become virtually as important and extensive as the main body of the work itself.

Dilettante: One who follows an art for the sake of delight rather than as a serious profession. In literature, as with the other arts, the term has taken on a derogatory meaning, however, and is usually employed to indicate one who talks about books and writers from hearsay and careless reading, perhaps of REVIEWS, as opposed to the student who makes a careful and critical study of literature. Originally a *dilettante* meant an amateur; now it usually means a dabbler.

Dime Novel: A cheaply printed, paperbound TALE of adventure or detection, originally selling for about ten cents; an American equivalent of the British PENNY DREADFUL. They were SHORT NOVELS, dealing with the American Revolution, the Civil War, the frontier, lurid crime and spectacular detection, and sometimes exemplary actions for moral instruction of the young. The first *dime novel* was *Malaeska: The Indian Wife of the White Hunter* by Anne Stephens, published by the firm of Beadle and Adams in 1860. It sold over 300,000 copies in one year. During the Civil War *dime novels* were popular with the troops, and afterwards they continued to be popular until the 1890s, when boys' stories, such as the Frank Merriwell and the Rover Boys series, and the PULP MAGAZINES began to replace them. At the height of their popularity, they were written—or at least ostensibly written—by men like Ned Buntline, Colonel Prentiss Ingraham, and W. F. "Buffalo Bill" Cody about their own adventures. The two most popular series were the "Deadwood Dick" stories of the frontier by Edward L. Wheeler and the "Nick Carter" detective stories by various writers. The firm of Street and Smith published more than a thousand Nick Carter *dime novels*. Present-day counterparts are some of the cheaper and more sensational "paperback originals." One of the popular series of these paperbacks today is, significantly, the Nick Carter books. See PENNY DREADFUL.

[References: Albert Johannsen, *The House of Beadle and Adams and Its Dime and Nickel Novels*, 3 vols. (1962); Edmund Pearson, *Dime Novels* (1929).]

Dimeter: A LINE of VERSE consisting of two FEET. See SCANSION.

Diminishing Age in English Literature, 1940–1965: The coming of the Second World War in 1939 marked a profound change in all aspects of British life. A beleaguered nation struggling desperately for survival devoted most of its energies for six years to defeating its military enemies. Then, with many of its finest young people dead, its major cities in shambles, and its economy greatly weakened, it had to spend another decade reestablishing itself. Certain ceremonial and traditional events, such as the coronation of Elizabeth II in 1952, seemed to have as much beneficial influence as public events did in the reassertion of the sense of nation and tradition. Also, during the cold war, the defection of intelligence officer Philby and others to the Russians and the discovery that he had been a "double agent" had a depressing symbolic value for the English. Greatly weakened foreign influence and major internal economic and political problems made England during this quarter-century a "diminished thing."

Perhaps the most challenging experimental writer of the period was Samuel Beckett, in both the NOVEL and DRAMA. As a satirist and social commentator, George Orwell wrote brilliantly in such novels as *1984* and in ESSAYS. Joyce Cary continued the realistic tradition in FICTION, as Graham Greene produced philosophical novels in the TRADITION of Conrad. Lawrence Durrell, C. P. Snow, and Anthony Powell embarked on long, ambitious series of novels. Stephen Spender and W. H. Auden continued as the leading poetic voices to be joined by the Welsh POET Dylan Thomas during his brief, intense career. Sir John Betjeman, Louis MacNeice, and Philip Larkin were important POETS of the time. Christopher Fry joined T. S. Eliot in an effort to revive VERSE DRAMA. Sean O'Casey continued the strength of the Irish theater, and John Osborne initiated the DRAMA of the "ANGRY YOUNG MEN." F. R. Leavis was the most respected critical voice and *Encounter* the best critical JOURNAL. It was a time of literary effort and respectable activity, but it clearly lacked the dominating literary voices needed to make a good age. Significantly, toward the end of this period, the greatest aesthetic energy showed in films, television, and the popular songs of the Rolling Stones and the Beatles.

Dionysian: A term used by Friedrich Nietzsche to designate the spirit in Greek TRAGEDY associated with Dionysus, the god of wine. It refers to states of the ecstatic, orgiastic, or irrational. Nietzsche associates it with lunar-nocturnal creative and imaginative power and contrasts it with the critical and rational qualities represented by the solar-diurnal APOLLONIAN. See APOLLONIAN.

Dipody (or **Dipodic Verse**): In CLASSICAL PROSODY, a MEASURE consisting of two metrical feet, usually slightly different. The METER of DIALOGUE in

Greek TRAGEDY is three *dipodies,* or twelve syllables, in this case IAMBIC. Much VERSE in NURSERY RHYMES and BALLADS is *dipodic.* In these cases the term refers to succeeding feet with strong STRESS in one and a weaker STRESS in the other, such feet functioning as a metrical unit, a MEASURE, as in this LINE from Eliot's *The Waste Land:*

> And a clatter and a chatter from within

which looks like HEADLESS iambic VERSE with uneven STRESS but is actually *dipodic verse. Dipodic verse* lends itself easily to SYNCOPATION.

Direct Camera: A style of objective, essentially nonnarrative, nonstaged film-making used in producing documentary FILMS since the early 1960s. Like CINEMA VÉRITÉ, it uses light, highly mobile equipment.

Dirge: A wailing SONG sung at a funeral or in commemoration of death. A short LYRIC of lamentation. See CORONACH, ELEGY, MONODY, PASTORAL ELEGY, THRENODY.

Discordia Concors: A term used by Samuel Johnson to describe unfavorably "a combination of dissimilar images or discovery of occult resemblances in things apparently unlike" in METAPHYSICAL POETRY. He derived the term by inverting Horace's phrase *concordia discors,* "harmony in discord." See METAPHYSICAL POETRY.

Discovery: In a TRAGEDY the revelation of a fact previously unknown, knowledge of which now results in the turning of the ACTION. See DRAMATIC STRUCTURE.

Disguisings: In medieval times (and in some places into the twentieth century) a species of game or SPECTACLE with a procession of masked figures. *Disguisings* were usually of a popular or folk character. See MASQUE.

Disinterestedness: An ideal quality of objectivity and impartiality unpolluted by illegitimate self-interest or by conflict of interest. The term—as promoted by Kant, Keats, Hazlitt, and Arnold—ought to be distinguished scrupulously from "uninterestedness," with which it is often confounded. To be uninterested is not to care; to be disinterested is to care but on an impartial basis with no self-interest.

Dissertation: A formal EXPOSITION written to clarify some scholarly problem. *Dissertation* is sometimes used interchangeably with THESIS, but the usual practice, at least in American academic circles, is to reserve *dissertation* for the more elaborate projects written "in partial fulfillment of the requirements for the doctor's degree" and to limit the use of THESIS to smaller enterprises submitted for the bachelor's or master's degree. Of course these words as employed in academic circles belong to the CANT of college language since both THESIS and *dissertation* are commonly used off college campuses simply to signify careful, thoughtful discussions, in writing or speech, on almost any serious problem. In literature the term has been used lightly, as in Lamb's

"A Dissertation on Roast Pig" and formally as in Bolingbroke's *Dissertation on Parties* or in Newton's *dissertations;* here the term implies learned formality.

Dissociation of Sensibility: A term given wide currency by T. S. Eliot (in his ESSAY of 1921, "The Metaphysical Poets") to describe a disjunction of thought and feeling in the writers of the seventeenth and later centuries. Earlier writers, and particularly John Donne, had had "direct sensuous apprehension of thought." To them a thought was an experience and thus affected their sensibility. For these writers, mind and feeling functioned together and thus they possessed "a mechanism of sensibility which could devour any kind of experience." In the seventeenth century, says Eliot, a *dissociation of sensibility* set in, fostered by Milton and Dryden, who performed a part of the total poetic function so well that the rest of it appeared not to exist and, in their imitators, did not exist. In the eighteenth and nineteenth centuries, as language grew in refinement and subtlety, feeling tended to become cruder. The result was POETS who thought but neither felt their thoughts nor fused thought and feeling in their POETRY or, in other words, POETS who suffered from a *dissociation of sensibility.* Eliot seems to have drawn the idea of *dissociation* from his study of French thinkers, particularly Remy de Gourmont and Lucien Lévy-Bruhl. The latter considered primitive people to be "pre-logical" creatures with no sense of a difference between past and present, life and death, nature and culture, self and other, so that the acquisition of civilization and logical thought represents a surrender of a "participatory" mentality and, in effect, a *dissociation of sensibility.* This *dissociation,* however, takes place some millennia earlier than the seventeenth century that Eliot located as the setting of the *dissociation* that engaged his attention and provoked his attack. Critics since Eliot's original formulation of his diagnosis have found him to be vague and historically inaccurate—there being plenty of dissociated sensibilities before the seventeenth century and plenty of marvelously unified sensibilities afterwards, including Byron's and Eliot's—but the general emphasis on the harmony of thought and feeling is well-taken and certainly useful in the study of Donne, Marvell, and others.

Dissonance: Harsh and inharmonious sounds, a marked breaking of the music of a VERSE of POETRY, which may be intentional, as it often is in Browning and Hardy, but when unintentional is a flaw. The term is also sometimes applied to RHYMES that fail by a slight margin to be perfect because of variations in vowel sounds too slight to earn them the name of ASSONANCE; a form of HALF RHYME or SLANT RHYME.

Distance: The degree of dispassionateness with which reader or audience can view the people, places, and events in a literary work; or the degree of disinterest that the author displays toward his or her CHARACTERS and ACTIONS. *Distance* is a noun; its use as a verb is a BARBARISM but has found some currency in such phrases as "distancing device." See AESTHETIC DISTANCE, DISINTERESTEDNESS, ALIENATION EFFECT.

Distich: A COUPLET. Any two consecutive LINES in similar FORM. An EPIGRAM or MAXIM completely expressed in couplet form, as in Pope's COUPLET:

> Hope springs eternal in the human breast;
> Man never is, but always to be, blest.

See STITCH.

Distributed Stress: A term used for a situation in METRICS wherein each of two syllables takes, or shares, the STRESS. Also called HOVERING STRESS or RESOLVED STRESS. The following lines from Walt Whitman's "Tears" show *distributed stress* in "swift steps" and "night storm":

O storm, embodied, rising, careering with swift steps a long the beach!

O wild and dismal night storm, with wind—O belching and desperate!

See HOVERING STRESS.

Dithyramb: Literary expression characterized by wild, excited, passionate language. Its LYRIC power relates it most nearly to VERSE though its unordered sequence and development, its seemingly improvised quality, often give it the form of PROSE. Dithyrambic VERSE, as it is usually called, was probably meant originally to be accompanied by music and was historically associated with Greek ceremonial worship of Dionysus. It formed the model for the choral element in Greek VERSE, later developing into the finer quality we know in Greek TRAGEDY. Rather rare in English, dithyrambic VERSE is most closely related to the ODE; it finds its best expression in Dryden's *Alexander's Feast.* By extension the term is applied to any wild CHANT or SONG or to PROSE that is particularly extravagant in its CADENCES and IMAGES.

Ditty: A SONG, a REFRAIN. The term is used for any short, simple, popular melody. The term is also used, in the sense of THEME, to refer to any short, apt saying or idea running through a composition.

Divine Afflatus: A phrase used to mean poetic inspiration, particularly the exalted state immediately preceding creative composition, when the POET is felt to be receiving inspiration directly from a divine source. The doctrine of divine inspiration for poets was advocated by Plato. Although the phrase and doctrine have been used in a serious and sincere sense by such a POET as Shelley, the term is often used now contemptuously to imply a pretentious overvaluation in a POET or a bombastic spirit in an orator, whose fervid STYLE or manner is not justified by the actual uninspired substance of the POEM or ORATION.

Doctrinaire: An adjective applied to one whose attitude is controlled by pre-conception and who disregards other points of view as well as practical considerations. This view is likely to be theoretical, dogmatic, narrow, and one-sided, as compared with practical and broad-minded. CRITICISM like Dr. Samuel

Johnson's may be *doctrinaire* because it is controlled by a limited code of critical doctrines. Literature itself may be called *doctrinaire* when written, like some of Carlyle's books, to demonstrate such a doctrine as "hero-worship" or the "gospel of work"; or like a NOVEL of William Godwin's, to preach a social doctrine. Politically, the word was applied to the constitutional royalists in France after 1815. See DIDACTICISM.

Documentary Novel: A form of FICTION in which there is an elaborate piling up of factual data, frequently including materials such as newspaper articles, popular SONGS, legal reports, and trial transcripts. The term was used by F. O. Matthiessen to characterize the massive amount of factual detail used in the NOVELS of Theodore Dreiser. *Documentary novels* are usually written by naturalistic novelists such as Émile Zola, Dreiser, John Dos Passos, and James T. Farrell. After the Second World War, the tradition was carried on by Norman Mailer.

Doggerel: Rude composition in VERSE. Any poorly executed attempt at PO-ETRY. Characteristic of *doggerel* verse are monotony of RHYME and RHYTHM, cheap sentiment and trivial, trite subject matter. Some *doggerel* does, however, because of certain humorous and BURLESQUE qualities, become amusing and earn a place on one of the lower shelves of literature. Doctor Johnson's parody of Percy's "Hermit of Warkworth" is an example:

> As with my hat upon my head
> I walk'd along the Strand,
> I there did meet another man
> With his hat in his hand.

See also HUDIBRASTIC VERSE, SKELTONIC VERSE.

Dolce Stil Nuovo: The "sweet new style" (called so in Dante's Purgatory) that flourished among LYRIC POETS in certain Romance languages during the thirteenth century with a premium on lucidity and complex musicality. This style, which contributed to Dante's adoption of the Tuscan vernacular and TERZA RIMA for his *Comedy*, was the chief precursor and exemplar of modern RHYMED VERSE in Indo-European languages.

Domestic Tragedy: TRAGEDY dealing with the domestic life of commonplace people. The English stage at various periods has produced tragedies based on the lives not of high-ranking historical personages (see TRAGEDY) but of everyday contemporary folk. Running contrary to the prevailing critical conceptions of the proper sphere of TRAGEDY, *domestic tragedy* was long in winning critical recognition. In Elizabethan times were produced such powerful *domestic tragedies* as the anonymous *Arden of Feversham* (late sixteenth century), Thomas Heywood's *A Woman Killed with Kindness* (acted 1603), and the anonymous *Yorkshire Tragedy* (1608). This early Elizabethan *domestic tragedy* specialized in murder stories taken from contemporary bourgeois life. Although the characters are far from commonplace, it is possible to consider Shakespeare's *Othello* as something of a *domestic tragedy*. In the eighteenth century *domestic tragedy* reappeared, tinged this time with the SENTIMENTAL-ISM of the age, as in George Lillo's *The London Merchant* (1731) and EDWARD MOORE'S *The Gamester* (1753), in which the tragic HERO is a gambler who, falsely accused of murder, takes poison and dies just after hearing that a large amount of money has been left to him. The eighteenth-century *domestic trag-edy* was crowded out by other forms, though the idea was taken over by foreign playwrights and later in the nineteenth century reintroduced from abroad, especially under the influence of Ibsen, since whose time the old con-ception of TRAGEDY as possible only with HEROES of high rank has given way to PLAYS that present fate at work among the ordinary. John Masefield's *Tragedy of Nan* (1909) may be noted as an early twentieth-century example of the form. O'Neill's *Desire Under the Elms*, Miller's *The Death of a Salesman* and *All My Sons*, and Williams's *Cat on a Hot Tin Roof* are all examples of *domestic tragedy*.

[References: Ernest Bernbaum, *The Drama of Sensibility*. (1915); Allar-dyce Nicoll, *British Drama* (1925, reprinted 1978), and *A History of Early Eighteenth-Century Drama* (1925); Robert M. Smith, ed., *Types of Domestic Tragedy* (1928); A. H. Thorndike, *Tragedy* (1908, reprinted 1965).]

Donnée: Literally, the given—that is, the element or elements of a literary work on which the author exercises skill and IMAGINATION in making the finished work. The term, introduced by Henry James, is based on an ANALOGY to a problem in geometry in which certain data are given, out of which the solver of the problem works out the meaning or solution. A frequent phrase of James's in his prefaces about the *donnée*—"something might be made of that"—is illuminating. The *donnée* can be SETTING, CHARACTERS, situation, even theme or idea. In any case, it is the raw material with which the artist starts in making a work of art. That London, say, is a city of a certain size and sort is a *donnée* of much literature, and it would be fatuous to make it into a humble hamlet or to suppose it an arctic or equatorial environment, except in SCIENCE FICTION. William Faulkner uses the homely metaphor of the lumber in the carpenter's shop for the same idea as *donnée*.

Doric: The *Doric* DIALECT in ancient Greece was thought of as unrefined, and *Doric* architecture was marked by simplicity and strength rather than complexity and beauty of detail. So a rustic of "broad" DIALECT may be referred to as *Doric*, and such simple idyllic pieces as Tennyson's *Dora* or Wordsworth's *Michael* may be said to exhibit *Doric* qualities. It is often applied to PASTORALS. Perhaps the best single synonym is "simple." See ATTIC, with which *Doric* was and is in conscious contrast.

Double Dactyls: A form of LIGHT VERSE consisting of two STANZAS, each having four LINES of two DACTYLS. It was promoted by Anthony Hecht and John Hollander in the collection *Jiggery-Pokery*. The rules for the FORM are complex. The first line must be a jingle, such as "Jiggery-pokery." The second line must be a name. The last lines of each STANZA must RHYME, and the second STANZA must have one line that is a single word. The most dazzling example of diplodactylic virtuosity is George Starbuck's "Monarch of the Sea," in which the required name is *four* DACTYLS ("Admiral Samuel/Eliot Morison") and the second STANZA contains *two* successive one-word lines ("Historiog-raphy's/Disciplinarian").

Double Entendre: A statement that is deliberately ambiguous, one of whose possible meanings is risqué or suggestive of some impropriety. In *Romeo and Juliet,* Mercutio executes a notable *double entendre* when he tells the Nurse (who has asked about the time of day), " 'Tis no less, I tell ye; for the bawdy hand of the dial is now upon the prick of noon." The *entendre* is *double* here because a dial does have a "hand" and the circumference is marked with "pricks"; by adding "bawdy" to his statement, Mercutio explicitly doubles the meanings of "hand" and "prick" and brings out the still-current vulgar sense of the latter. Later in the same scene, Mercutio sings a SONG that involves PUNS on "hair," "hare," "hoar," and "whore"; these are not *double entendres.* A *pun* is understood to mean a play on different words that happen to sound alike; a *double entendre* has to do with a single word that happens to have more than one meaning. Both PUN and *double entendre* differ from AMBIGUITY, which refers to a multiplicity of meanings, all of which may be decent. AMBIGUITY may lead to some confusion—as in "He helped the old man across the street"—and even to undecidable contradiction—as in "He is not in the hospital because he is sick."

Double entendre is not good French—the proper French phrase for "double meaning" is *double entente*—but it has been used since Dryden as an English term applied to ambiguities in which one of the meanings is indecent. It should not be italicized in normal usage.

Double Rhyme: FEMININE RHYME; that is, RHYME in which the similar stressed syllables are followed by identical unstressed syllables. "Stream" and "beam" are RHYMES; "streaming" and "beaming" are *double rhymes.* "Double" is a misnomer, since in either case the RHYME is a single phenomenon involving stressed syllables. Genuine doubleness of RHYME, as between "wild-wood" and "childhood," is called "compound" RHYME by some prosodists.

Drama: Aristotle called *drama* "imitated human action." But since his meaning of IMITATION is in doubt, this phrase is not as simple or clear as it seems. Professor J. M. Manly saw three necessary elements in *drama:* (1) a STORY (2) told in ACTION (3) by ACTORS who impersonate the CHARACTERS of the STORY. This admits such forms as PANTOMIME, but many believe that spoken DIALOGUE must be present.

Drama arose from religious ceremonial. Greek COMEDY developed from those phases of the DIONYSIAN rites that dealt with the theme of fertility. Greek TRAGEDY came from the DIONYSIAN rites dealing with life and death; and MEDIEVAL DRAMA arose out of rites commemorating the birth and the resurrection of Christ. These three origins seem independent of one another. The word COMEDY is based on a word meaning "revel," and early Greek COMEDY preserved in the actors' costumes evidences of the ancient phallic ceremonies. Comedy developed away from this primitive display of sex interest in the direction of greater DECORUM and seriousness, though the OLD COMEDY was gross in character. SATIRE became an element of COMEDY as early as the sixth century B.C. Menander (342–291 B.C.) is a representative of the NEW COMEDY—a more conventionalized form that was imitated by the great Roman writers of COMEDY, Plautus and Terence, through whose plays CLASSICAL COMEDY was transmitted to the Elizabethan dramatists.

The word TRAGEDY seems to mean a "goat-song" and may reflect

DIONYSIAN death and resurrection ceremonies in which the goat was the sacrificial animal. The Dithyrambic CHANT used in these festivals, perhaps the starting point of TRAGEDY, developed into the ceremonial SONG. The SONG then became a primitive duologue between a leader and a CHORUS, developed NARRATIVE elements, and reached a stage in which it told some STORY. Two leaders appeared instead of one, and the CHORUS receded somewhat into the background. The great Greek authors of TRAGEDIES were Aeschylus (525–456 B.C.), Sophocles (496–406 B.C.), and Euripides (480–406 B.C.). Modeled on these were the Latin CLOSET DRAMAS of Seneca (4? B.C.–A.D. 65), which exercised a profound influence on RENAISSANCE TRAGEDY (see SENECAN TRAGEDY).

The decline of Rome witnessed the disappearance of acted CLASSICAL DRAMA. The MIME survived for a uncertain period and perhaps aided in preserving the tradition of acting through wandering entertainers (see JONGLEUR, MINSTREL). Likewise, dramatic ceremonies and customs, some of them perhaps related to the ancient DIONYSIAN rites themselves, played an uncertain part in keeping alive in medieval times a sort of substratum of dramatic consciousness. Scholars are virtually agreed, however, that the great institution of MEDIEVAL DRAMA in Western Europe, leading as it did to modern *drama*, was a new form that developed around the ninth century from the ritual of the Christian Church (see MEDIEVAL DRAMA). The dramatic forms resulting from this development, MYSTERY or CYCLIC PLAYS, MIRACLE PLAYS, MORALITIES, flourishing especially in the fourteenth and fifteenth centuries, lived on into the RENAISSANCE.

The new interests of the RENAISSANCE included TRANSLATIONS and IMITATIONS of CLASSICAL DRAMA, partly through the medium of SCHOOL PLAYS, partly through the work of university-trained professionals engaged in supplying *dramas* for the public stage, the court, or such institutions as the INNS OF COURT, and partly through the influence of CLASSICAL dramatic CRITICISM, much of which reached England through Italian scholars. Thus, a revived knowledge of ancient *drama* united with the native dramatic traditions developed from medieval forms and techniques to produce in the later years of the sixteenth century the prodigiously robust phenomenon known as ELIZABETHAN DRAMA, with its patriotic CHRONICLE PLAYS, TRAGEDIES OF BLOOD, COURT COMEDIES, ROMANTIC COMEDIES, PASTORAL PLAYS, satirical PLAYS, and realistic presentations of London life. These *dramas* were written by a group of gifted, versatile dramatists, led by Shakespeare. English *drama* demonstrated DECADENT tendencies in JACOBEAN and CAROLINE times, and in 1642 the PURITANS officially closed the theaters.

The efforts of Ben Jonson in Elizabethan times to insist on the observance of CLASSICAL rules bore late fruit when in RESTORATION times, under the added influence of French *drama* and theory, English *drama* was officially revived under court auspices. NEOCLASSIC tendencies held sway. The HEROIC PLAY and the new COMEDY OF MANNERS flourished, followed in the eighteenth century first by SENTIMENTAL COMEDY and DOMESTIC TRAGEDIES and in the latter part of the century by a chastened COMEDY OF MANNERS under Goldsmith and Sheridan.

MELODRAMA and SPECTACLE reigned through the early nineteenth century, efforts to produce an *actable* literary *drama* proving futile. The later nineteenth century witnessed an important revival of serious *drama*, with a tendency, however, away from the established traditions of poetic TRAGEDY and COMEDY in favor of shorter PLAYS stressing ideas or problems and depending much on DIALOGUE.

In America theatrical performances occurred early in the eighteenth century in Boston, New York, and Charleston, South Carolina, though no *drama* was written by an American until about the middle of the century, when important groups of professional ACTORS also appeared. The imitative early *drama* was dependent on English originals or models. The Revolutionary War produced some political PLAYS. The first native TRAGEDY was Thomas Godfrey's *Prince of Parthia* (acted in 1767), and the first COMEDY professionally produced was Royall Tyler's *The Contrast (1787)*. The early nineteenth century witnessed a growing interest in the theater, William Dunlap and John Howard Payne ("Home, Sweet Home") being prolific playwrights. Increased use was made of American THEMES. In the middle of the century George Henry Boker produced notable ROMANTIC TRAGEDIES in VERSE, and literary *drama* received some attention. American dramatic art advanced in the period following the Civil War with such writers as Bronson Howard, though it was restricted greatly by commercial theatrical management. The early twentieth century produced several dramatists of note (William Vaughn Moody, Percy MacKaye, Josephine Peabody) and witnessed the growth of the LITTLE THEATER MOVEMENT.

There has been a healthy rebirth of dramatic interest and experimentation in the twentieth century both in Great Britain and in the United States. In the Irish Theatre, under the leadership of people like Lady Gregory and Douglas Hyde, a vital *drama* has emerged, with original and powerful PLAYS from the likes of W. B. Yeats, J. M. Synge, Padraic Column, and Sean O'Casey (see CELTIC RENAISSANCE). In England the influence of Ibsen (also important on the Irish playwrights) made itself strongly felt in the PROBLEM PLAYS and DOMESTIC TRAGEDIES of Henry Arthur Jones and Arthur Wing Pinero, in the witty and highly intellectual *drama* of G. B. Shaw, and in the realism of W. S. Houghton and John Galsworthy. Somerset Maugham, Noel Coward, and James Barrie were active producers of COMEDY; John Masefield gave expression to the tragic vision in a long series of PLAYS. T. S. Eliot and Christopher Fry revived and enriched VERSE *drama*. Also important is John Osborne, the leader of England's "ANGRY YOUNG MEN" (*Look Back in Anger*), and the absurdist playwrights Harold Pinter and Tom Stoppard.

The twentieth century saw the development of a serious American *drama*. Early in the century REALISM, which had had its first important American dramatic representation in J. A. Herne's *Margaret Fleming* in 1890, was followed, sometimes afar off, by MacKaye and Moody. But it remained for the craftsmanship, experimentation, and imagination of Eugene O'Neill to give a truly American expression to the tragic view of experience. Thornton Wilder, Philip Barry, Lillian Hellman, Sidney Howard, Robert Sherwood, Tennessee Williams, Arthur Miller, and Edward Albee have given America a serious *drama* for the first time in its history. Barry, S. N. Behrman, George Kaufman, John van Druten, Neil Simon, and Woody Allen have practiced the comic craft with skill. Maxwell Anderson revived the VERSE play successfully, and Rodgers and Hammerstein gave the MUSICAL COMEDY unexpected depth and beauty in *Oklahoma!* and other "musicals." Later, beginning in the 1970s, Stephen Sondheim continued this enrichment, deepening and dignifying musical theatre.

Details of dramatic history are given throughout the *Outline of Literary History.* See also COMEDY, CONFLICT, CHARACTERIZATION, DRAMATIC STRUCTURE, PLOT, and TRAGEDY.

[References: William Archer, *The Old Drama and the New* (1923); Blanch M. Baker, *Dramatic Bibliography* (1933); C. F. Tucker Brooke, *The Tudor Drama* (1911, reprinted 1964); E. K. Chambers, *The Elizabethan Stage,* 4 vols. (1923), and *The Medieval Stage,* 2 vols. (1903); B. H. Clark, *European Theories of the Drama* (1929, reprinted 1965), and *A Study of Modern Drama,* rev. ed. (1938); T. H. Dickinson, *Outline of Contemporary* Drama (1927, reprinted 1969); Walter P. Eaton, *The Drama in English* (1930); John Gassner and Edward Quinn, eds., *The Reader's Encyclopedia of World Drama* (1969); Richard Gilman, *The Making of Modern Drama* (1974); H. D. F. Kitto, *Form and Meaning in Drama* (1956); Brander Matthews, *The Development of the Drama* (1903, reprinted 1923), and *Study of the Drama* (1910); Allardyce Nicoll, *British Drama* (1925, reprinted 1978), *The Theory of Drama* (1931), and *World Drama* (1950, reprinted 1976); A. H. Quinn, *History of the American Drama,* 3 vols. (1927, reprinted 1980); F. E. Schelling, *Elizabethan Drama,* 2 vols. (1908, reprinted 1959); A. W. Ward, *A History of English Dramatic Literature,* 2nd ed., 3 vols. (1899); Karl Young, *The Drama of the Medieval Church,* 2 vols. (1933, reprinted 1951).]

Dramatic Conventions: Although the DRAMA is, as Aristotle asserted, an IMITATION of life, the stage and the printed page present physical difficulties for the making of such IMITATIONS. The various devices that have been employed as substitutions for reality in the DRAMA and that the audience must accept as real although it knows them to be false are called *dramatic conventions.* One approaching a DRAMA must, in the first place, accept the fact of impersonation or representation. The actors on the stage must be taken as the persons of the STORY (though this acceptance by no means precludes a degree of detachment sufficient to enable the spectator to appraise the art of the actor). The stage must be regarded as the actual SCENE or geographical SETTING of the ACTION. The intervals between ACTS or SCENES must be expanded or contracted imaginatively to conform to the needs of the story. Moreover, one must accept special CONVENTIONS, not inherent in DRAMA as such but no less integral because of their traditional use, such as the SOLILOQUY, the ASIDES, the fact that ordinary people are made spontaneously to speak in highly poetic language and that actors speak louder than would be natural, pitching their voices to reach the most distant auditor rather than the persons in the group on the stage. Similarly one must be prepared at times to accept costuming that is conventional or symbolic rather than realistic. By CONVENTION almost too obvious to mention, stage characters speak in our own language, even though everyone recognizes that the Romans in *Julius Caesar* could never have spoken Elizabethan English.

In the ELIZABETHAN THEATER the spectator had to picture the platform imaginatively as in a number of different places; in the modern theater the spectator must accept the idea of the invisible FOURTH WALL through which he or she views interior actions. All means of getting inside the minds of CHARACTERS—and they are many—are CONVENTIONS (even if only within the single PLAY; see O'Neill's *Strange Interlude*) that are successful exactly to the extent that the audience is willing to believe them. Even the CURTAIN that opens and closes the DRAMA is in its way as pure a CONVENTION as the CHORUS of a Greek TRAGEDY. See CONVENTION.

Dramatic Irony: The words or acts of a CHARACTER in a PLAY may carry a meaning unperceived by the character but understood by the audience. Usually the character's own interests are involved in a way he or she cannot understand. The IRONY resides in the contrast between the meaning intended by the speaker and the different significance seen by others. The term is occasionally applied also to nondramatic NARRATIVE and is sometimes extended to include any situation (such as mistaken identity) in which some of the actors on the stage or some of the characters in a story are "blind" to facts known to the spectator or reader. So understood, *dramatic irony* is responsible for much of the interest in FICTION and DRAMA because the reader or spectator enjoys being in on the secret. For an example see TRAGIC IRONY.
[Reference: Germain Dempster, *Dramatic Irony in Chaucer* (1932, reprinted 1959).]

Dramatic Monologue: A POEM that reveals "a soul in action" through the speech of one CHARACTER in a dramatic situation. The CHARACTER is speaking to an identifiable but silent listener at a dramatic moment in the speaker's life. The circumstances surrounding the conversation, one side of which we "hear" as the *dramatic monologue,* are made clear by implication in the POEM, and a deep insight into the character of the speaker may result. Although quite an old form, the *dramatic monologue* was brought to a very high level by Robert Browning, who is often credited with its creation (although scores of speeches in Dante's *Comedy* and especially in the *Inferno* amount to posthumous *dramatic monologues*). Tennyson used the FORM on occasion, and contemporary POETS have found it congenial, as witness the work of Robert Frost, Allen Tate, and T. S. Eliot. It ought to be noted that the name *dramatic monologue* was not used by the nineteenth-century masters of the form and, furthermore, that there are importance differences among the *dramatic monologue* (best exemplified by Browning's "My Last Duchess"), the SOLILOQUY (Browning's "Soliloquy of the Spanish Cloister"), and the EPISTLE (Browning's "Cleon" and "An Epistle"), although all three involve a single sustained utterance, typically by a CHARACTER about whom the reader knows something beforehand. Most of the successful POEMS of this category are spoken not by newly created three-dimensional figures but by historical people (such as Fra Lippo Lippi and Lucretius), characters from MYTH, LEGEND, or literature (such as a duke, a bishop, and a *gerontion,* or "little old man"). Some early twentieth-century POEMS by Eliot and Conrad Aiken seem to belong among *dramatic monologues,* but in some cases (Eliot's "The Love Song of J. Alfred Prufrock" and "Gerontion," for example) the utterance is not patently delivered in a charged dramatic situation to a readily identifiable interlocutor, so that the poems may be related less to the fully formed *dramatic monologue* than to the INTERIOR MONOLOGUE or some type of MEDITATIVE POETRY. See SOLILOQUY, EPISTLE, INTERIOR MONOLOGUE, MEDITATIVE POETRY.
[Reference: Alan Sinfield, *Dramatic Monologue* (1977).]

Dramatic Poetry: A term that, logically, should be restricted to POETRY employing dramatic FORM or some element of dramatic technique. The DRAMATIC

MONOLOGUE is an example. The dramatic quality may result from the use of DIALOGUE, MONOLOGUE, vigorous DICTION, BLANK VERSE, or the stressing of tense situation and emotional CONFLICT. Because of the presence of dramatic elements in the POEMS to be included in the volume *Bells and Pomegranates, No. III* (1842), Browning used the phrase "Dramatic Lyrics" as a subtitle. However, the phrase *dramatic poetry* is indefinite enough to include compositions that, like Shakespeare's *The Tempest,* may be more properly classed as POETIC DRAMA, or that, like Browning's *Pippa Passes,* are more commonly called CLOSET DRAMAS. But the question quickly becomes otiose; as one of the speakers in Eliot's "A Dialogue on Dramatic Poetry" asks, ". . . What great poetry is not dramatic? . . . Who is more dramatic than Homer or Dante?"

Dramatic Propriety: The principle that a statement or an ACTION within any dramatic situation is to be judged not in terms of its correspondence to standards external to the dramatic situation but in terms of its appropriateness to the specific context within which it occurs. Cleanth Brooks argues, for example, that the statement "Beauty is truth, truth beauty" in Keats's "Ode on a Grecian Urn" is a dramatic statement appropriate to the urn that may utter it and has, therefore, "precisely the same status" as "Ripeness is all" in *King Lear.* We properly ask not whether it is an abstract truth but whether it is in character for the speaker and proper to the dramatic context. Many of the New Critics argue that every POEM implies a speaker and is, therefore, a little DRAMA. For them the principle of *dramatic propriety* takes on cardinal importance.

Dramatic Structure: The ancients compared the PLOT OF A DRAMA to the tying and untying of a knot. The principle of dramatic CONFLICT, though not mentioned as such in Aristotle's definition of DRAMA, is implied in this figure. The technical STRUCTURE of a serious PLAY is determined by the necessities of developing this dramatic CONFLICT. Thus, a well-built TRAGEDY will commonly show the following divisions, each representing a phase of the dramatic CONFLICT: introduction, RISING ACTION, CLIMAX or CRISIS (turning point), FALLING ACTION, and CATASTROPHE. The relation of these parts is sometimes represented graphically by the figure of a pyramid, called FREYTAG'S PYRAMID, the rising slope suggesting the RISING ACTION or tying of the knot, the falling slope the FALLING ACTION or resolution, the apex representing the CLIMAX.

The *introduction* (or EXPOSITION) creates the tone, gives the SETTING, introduces some of the CHARACTERS, and supplies other facts necessary to the understanding of the PLAY, such as events in the story supposed to have taken place before the part of the ACTION included in the PLAY, since a PLAY, like an EPIC, is likely to plunge IN MEDIAS RES, "into the midst of things." In *Hamlet,* the bleak midnight scene on the castle platform, with the appearance of the ghost, sets the keynote of the TRAGEDY, while the conversation of the watchers, especially the words of Horatio, supply antecedent facts, such as the quarrel between the dead King Hamlet and the King of Norway. The ancients called this part the PROTASIS.

The RISING ACTION (or COMPLICATION) is set in motion by the EXCITING FORCE (in *Hamlet* the ghost's revelation to Hamlet of the murder) and continues through successive stages of CONFLICT between the HERO and the COUNTERPLAYERS up to the CLIMAX or turning point (in *Hamlet* the hesitating failure of the HERO to kill Claudius at prayer). The ancients called this part the EPITASIS.

The downward or FALLING ACTION stresses the activity of the forces opposing the HERO and, while some suspense must be maintained, the trend of the ACTION must lead logically to the disaster with which the TRAGEDY is to close. The FALLING ACTION, called by the ancients the CATASTASIS, is often set in movement by a single event called the tragic force, closely related to the CLIMAX and bearing the same relation to the FALLING ACTION as the EXCITING FORCE does to the RISING ACTION. In *Macbeth* the tragic force is the escape of Fleance after the murder of Banquo. In *Hamlet* it is the "blind" stabbing of Polonius, which sends Hamlet away from the court just as he appears about to succeed in his plans. The latter part of the FALLING ACTION is sometimes marked by an event that delays the CATASTROPHE and seems to offer a way of escape for the HERO (the apparent reconciliation of Hamlet and Laertes). This is called the "moment of final suspense" and aids in maintaining interest. The FALLING ACTION, usually shorter than the RISING ACTION, is often attended by some lowering of interest (as in the case of the long conversation between Malcolm and MacDuff in *Macbeth*), since new forces must be introduced and an apparently inevitable end made to seem temporarily uncertain. RELIEF SCENES are often resorted to in the FALLING ACTION, partly to mark time, partly to provide emotional relaxation for the audience. The famous scene of the gravediggers in *Hamlet* is an example of how a RELIEF SCENE may be justified through its inherent dramatic interest and through its relation to the serious action (see COMIC RELIEF).

The CATASTROPHE, marking the tragic fall, usually the death, of the HERO (and often of his opponents as well) comes as an unavoidable outgrowth of the action. It satisfies not so much by a gratification of the emotional sympathies of the spectator as by its logical conformity and by a final presentation of the nobility of the succumbing HERO. A "glimpse of restored order" often follows the CATASTROPHE proper in a Shakespearean TRAGEDY, as when Hamlet gives his dying vote to Fortinbras as the new king.

This five-part *dramatic structure* Freytag believed to be reflected in a five-act structure for TRAGEDY. However, the imposing of a rigorous five-act structure on Elizabethan tragedy is questionable, since relatively few PLAYS fall readily into the pattern of an ACT OF EXPOSITION, an ACT OF RISING ACTION, an ACT OF CLIMAX, an ACT OF FALLING ACTION, and an ACT OF CATASTROPHE. It should be noted too that this structure based on the analogy of the tying and untying of a knot is applicable to COMEDY, the NOVEL, and the SHORT STORY, with the adjustment of the use of the broader term DÉNOUEMENT for CATASTROPHE in works that are not tragic, despite the synonymy of CATASTROPHE and DÉNOUEMENT. (See ACT, CATASTROPHE, and DÉNOUEMENT.)

During the nineteenth century conventional structure gave way to a newer technique. First, COMEDY, under the influence of French bourgeois COMEDY, the "well-made play" of Eugéne Scribe and others, developed a set of technical CONVENTIONS all its own; and as a result of the movement led by Ibsen, serious DRAMA cast off the restrictions of five-act TRAGEDY and freed itself from conventional formality. By the end of the century the traditional five-act structure was to be found only in poetic or consciously archaic TRAGEDY, of which the connection with the stage was artificial and generally unsuccessful. However, the fundamental elements of *dramatic structure* given here remained demonstrably present, though in modified form, in these newer types of PLAYS. If at first glance it seems that Ibsen opens one of his DOMESTIC TRAGEDIES at or just before the tragic force, the EXPOSITION, the EXCITING FORCE, and the RISING ACTION that brought about the situation with which he opens are still present and are communicated to the audience by implication and FLASHBACK. The fundamental *dramatic structure* seems timeless and impervious to basic change. See TRAGEDY, CONFLICT, ACT, CATASTROPHE, CLIMAX, CRISIS, PLOT.

[References: William Archer, *Play-Making* (1912, reprinted 1960); G. P. Baker, *Dramatic Technique* (1919, reprinted 1971); G. Freytag, *The Technique of the Drama* (1863, tr. reprinted 1968).]

Dramatis Personae: The CHARACTERS in a DRAMA, a NOVEL, or a POEM. The term is also applied to a listing of the characters in the program of a PLAY, at the beginning of the printed version of a play, or sometimes at the beginning of a NOVEL. Such a list often contains brief characterizations of the persons of the work and notations about their relationships. By extension, the term *dramatis personae* is sometimes applied to the participants in any event.

Dramatism: A system for analyzing literature developed by Kenneth Burke. It assumes that literature is a form of ACTION—"Somebody is always doing something to somebody else." Burke sees literature as fundamentally related in structure to the sentence patterns of Indo-European languages: that is, subject ("somebody") verb ("is doing") object ("something") indirect object ("to somebody else"). Hence, Burke names his major works on literary analysis a "grammar" and a "rhetoric." His system can be applied to all literary GENRES. Any literary work contains, he asserts, five elements, which he uses in special senses: ACT (what happened?), SCENE (where?), agent (who did it?), agency (how?) and purpose (why?). Simple though such a scheme seems when so outlined, it becomes extremely complex in Burke's hands, for he combines, in finding the answers, most systems of human knowledge.

Drame: A form of PLAY between TRAGEDY and COMEDY developed by the French in the eighteenth century and later introduced into England, where it is often called a *"drama."* It is a serious play, of which the modern PROBLEM PLAY is an example.

Drawing Room Comedy: A form of the COMEDY OF MANNERS that deals with high society. It is called a *drawing room comedy* because it is usually a WELL-MADE PLAY with its actions centered indoors, often literally in a drawing room. See COMEDY OF MANNERS.

Dream Allegory (or Vision): The dream was a conventional narrative frame that was widely used in the Middle Ages and is still employed on occasion. The NARRATOR falls asleep and while sleeping dreams a dream that is the actual STORY told in the dream frame. In the Middle Ages the device was used for ALLEGORY. Among the major *dream allegories* are: *The Romance of the Rose*, Dante's *Comedy*, Chaucer's *The Book of the Duchess* and *The*

House of Fame, The Pearl, and *The Vision of Piers Plowman.* The *dream allegory* forms the narrative frame for Bunyan's *Pilgrim's Progress,* Keats's *The Fall of Hyperion,* and (by adaptation to something like SCIENCE FICTION) Edward Bellamy's *Looking Backward.* See ALLEGORY, FRAME-STORY.

Droll: A short dramatic piece (also known as "drollery" or "droll humor") cultivated on the COMMONWEALTH stage in England as a substitute for full-length or serious PLAYS that were not permitted by the government. A *droll* was likely to be a "short, racy, comic" SCENE selected from some popular PLAY (as a Launcelot Gobbo scene from *The Merchant of Venice*) and completed by dancing somewhat in the manner of the earlier JIG.

[Reference: Leslie Hotson, *The Commonwealth and Restoration Stage* (1928, reprinted 1962).]

Dumb Show: A pantomimic performance used as part of a PLAY. The term is applied particularly to such specimens of silent acting as appeared in Elizabethan DRAMA. The *dumb show* provided a spectacular element and was often accompanied by music. Sometimes it employed allegorical figures like those in the MORALITY PLAY and the MASQUE. Sometimes it foreshadowed coming events in the ACTION or provided comment like that of the CHORUS. Sometimes it appeared as PROLOGUE or between ACTS, and sometimes it was an integral part of the ACTION, being performed by the CHARACTERS of the PLAY proper. Whatever its origin, it seems to have appeared first in the third quarter of the sixteenth century in the Senecan plays (see SENECAN TRAGEDY). It continued in use well into the seventeenth century. More than fifty extant Elizabethan plays contain *dumb shows.* That in Shakespeare's *Hamlet* (act III, scene ii) is unusual in that it is preliminary to a show that is itself a "play within a play." Other well-known Elizabethan plays containing *dumb shows* are Sackville and Norton's *Gorboduc* (1562), Robert Greene's *James the Fourth* (1591), John Marston's *Malcontent* (1604), John Webster's *Duchess of Malfi* (1614), and Thomas Middleton's *The Changeling* (1623). See DISGUISINGS, MASQUE, PAGEANT, PANTOMIME.

[References: J. W. Cunliffe, *Early English Classical Tragedies* (1912); Dieter Mehl, *The Elizabethan Dumb Show* (tr. 1966).]

Duodecimo: A BOOK SIZE, designating a book whose SIGNATURES result from sheets folded to twelve leaves or twenty-four pages. Its abbreviation is 12 mo. See BOOK SIZES.

Duologue: A SCENE or a short PLAY with only two ACTORS; a dramatic performance limited to two speakers.

Duple Meter: In METRICS a line consisting of two syllables.

Dynamic Character: A CHARACTER in a FICTION or DRAMA who develops or changes as a result of the ACTIONS of the PLOT. See CHARACTERIZATION.

Dystopia: Literally "bad place." The term is applied to accounts of imaginary worlds, usually in the future, in which present tendencies are carried out to their intensely unpleasant culminations. George Orwell's *1984* and Aldous Huxley's *Brave New World* are notable examples. See UTOPIA.

E

Early Tudor Age, 1500–1557: During the early years of the sixteenth century, the ideals of the RENAISSANCE were rapidly replacing those of the Middle Ages. The REFORMATION of the English church and the revival of learning known as HUMANISM modified English life and thought substantially. In literature it was a time of experimentation and of extensive formal borrowings from French and Italian writings. Wyatt and Surrey imported the Italian SONNET, TERZA RIMA, and OTTAVA RIMA, and Surrey first used BLANK VERSE, while Barclay and Skelton continued the older satiric tradition. Sir Thomas Elyot and Sir Thomas More were the major PROSE writers, and the translators and the chroniclers were adding to English knowledge and to English prose STYLE alike. The late MEDIEVAL DRAMA was still dominant, with the MYSTERY PLAYS, MORALITIES, and INTERLUDES in great vogue, although SCHOOL PLAYS were beginning to introduce new elements into the DRAMA, notably in *Ralph Roister Doister*, the first "regular" English COMEDY. Perhaps the most important single book, from a literary point of view, was *Tottel's Miscellany* (1557), a collection of the "new poetry" that paved the way for Elizabethan POETS. See RENAISSANCE and *Outline of Literary History.*

Early Victorian Age, 1832–1870: This period was a time of the gradual lessening of the romantic impulse and the steady growth of REALISM in English letters. Even if the romantic impulse remained powerful, the enactment or realization of it suffered a falling off, and many critics have come to regard this period as one of heightened or even pathological ROMANTICISM of spirit. It bears to ROMANTICISM much the same relation that the AGE OF JOHNSON bears to the NEOCLASSIC PERIOD—it is an age in which the seeds of the new movement were being sown, but one that was still predominantly of the old. In POETRY, the voices of the major romantics had been stilled by death, except for that of Wordsworth, and a new poetry more keenly aware of social issues and more marked by doubts and uncertainties resulting from the pains of the INDUSTRIAL REVOLUTION and the advances in scientific thought appeared. The chief writers of this POETRY were Tennyson, Browning, Arnold, and the young Swinburne. In the NOVEL Dickens, Thackeray, the Brontë sisters, and Trollope flourished. In the ESSAY Carlyle, Newman, Ruskin, Arnold, and De Quincey did outstanding work. See VICTORIAN PERIOD IN ENGLISH LITERATURE, VICTORIAN, and *Outline of Literary History.*

Echo: A complex, subtle, and multifarious acoustic phenomenon involving a faint but perceptible REPETITION inside a work ("aged thrush" *echoes* "ancient pulse" in both sound and meaning in Hardy's "The Darkling Thrush") or between works (the "low damp ground" in Eliot's *The Waste Land* may *echo* the "old camp ground" of the sentimental tenting song).
[Reference: John Hollander, *The Figure of Echo: A Mode of Allusion in Milton and After*, 1981.]

Echo Verse: A LINE or more often a POEM in which the closing syllables of one line are repeated, as by an echo, in the following line—and usually making up that line—with a different meaning and thus forming a reply or a comment. Barnaby Barnes's lines,

> Echo! What shall I do to my Nymph when I go to behold her?
>   Hold her!

form an example. Much later and a good deal more seriously, Gerard Manley Hopkins exploited the device in "The Leaden Echo and the Golden Echo." The device is as old as the *Greek Anthology*. It flourished in the sixteenth and seventeenth centuries, most often as a device in PASTORAL POETRY and DRAMA.

Eclogue: Literally, *eclogue* in Greek meant "selection" and was applied to various kinds of POEMS. From its application to Virgil's PASTORAL poems, however, *eclogue* came to have its present restricted meaning of a formal PASTORAL poem following the traditional technique derived from the IDYLLS of Theocritus (third century B.C.). Conventional *eclogue* types include: (1) the singing match: two shepherds have a singing contest on a wager or for a prize, a third shepherd acting as judge; (2) the rustic DIALOGUE: two "rude swains" engage in banter, perhaps over a mistress, perhaps over their flocks; (3) the DIRGE or LAMENT for a dead shepherd (see PASTORAL ELEGY); (4) the love-LAY: a shepherd may sing a SONG of courtship or a shepherd or shepherdess may complain of disappointment in love; (5) the EULOGY. In RENAISSANCE times, following Mantuan's Latin *eclogues* (fifteenth century), the *eclogue* was used for veiled SATIRE, particularly SATIRE against the corruptions of the "pastors" of the clergy, against political factions, and against those responsible for the neglect of POETRY. The earliest and most famous collection of conventional *eclogues* in English literature is Spenser's *The Shepheardes Calender* (1579), made up of one *eclogue* for each month. By the eighteenth century a distinction was made between *eclogue* and PASTORAL, the term *eclogue* being used to describe the FORM and PASTORAL the content. Hence, *eclogue* came to mean a DRAMATIC POEM, with little ACTION or CHARACTERIZATION, in which sentiments are expressed in DIALOGUE or SOLILOQUY, and *eclogues* laid in towns became possible. *The Age of Anxiety,* by the twentieth-century POET W. H. Auden, is subtitled *A Baroque Eclogue.* See PASTORAL.

Edinburgh Review: A quarterly JOURNAL of CRITICISM founded in 1802 by Francis Jeffrey, Sydney Smith, and Henry Brougham. The founders determined on a vigorous, outspoken policy, which not only made a successful publication (10,000 circulation after ten years) but also stirred up the whole English-reading world. Among the contributors to the *Review* were some of the most brilliant writers of the time, including the editors themselves and such worthies as Walter Scott, Henry Hallam, and Francis Horner. The motto of the publication—*Judex damnatur, cum nocens absolvitur,* "the judge is condemned when the guilty man is acquitted"—indicates clearly the rigorous policy of the founders, who were predominantly Whig in attitude. After seven years of being browbeaten, the Tories started a rival journal, the QUARTERLY REVIEW (1809). The two publications rode literary and political prejudices hard and enlivened British CRITICISM.

One of the abhorrences of the *Edinburgh Review* was the "lakers" (LAKE

School of writers), particularly Southey and Wordsworth. An article by Henry Brougham called "Hours of Idleness" (reviewing an early volume by Byron) provoked Byron's famous satire, *English Bards and Scotch Reviewers.* Later contributors included Macaulay, Carlyle, Hazlitt, and Arnold. The *Edinburgh Review* ceased publication in 1929.

Editing: The preparation of manuscript for the compositor and printer. The term is also applied to the establishment of texts and to the preparation of annotated EDITIONS. (See BIBLIOGRAPHY.) In filmmaking, *editing* is the establishment of the sequence or STRUCTURE of a FILM by selecting and splicing together into a final form the various shots of a FILM. *Editing* joins shots into SCENES and provides transitions among them.

Edition: The entire number of bound copies of a book printed at any time or times from a single typesetting or from plates or other modes of reproduction made from a single typesetting. The copies made from one continuous operation at one time are called a PRINTING or an IMPRESSION. Thus, there may be several PRINTINGS or IMPRESSIONS in an *edition.* As applied to old books, however, *edition* and IMPRESSION are practically synonymous, because of the practice of "distributing" type (taking it apart) after a printing. The term ISSUE is applied to a distinct set of copies of an *edition* that are distinguishable from other copies of that *edition* by variations in printed matter. *Edition* is also applied to a set of copies differing in some way other than in printed matter from others of the same text, as "the illustrated *edition,*" "the ten-volume *edition,*" or a special form of an author's work, as "the centennial *edition* of Emerson," or an especially edited work, as "Merritt Hughes's *edition* of *Paradise Lost.*" In describing books the terms *edition,* PRINTING, IMPRESSION, and ISSUE need to be used carefully.
 [References: Philip Gaskell, *A New Introduction to Bibliography* (1972); R. B. McKerrow, *An Introduction to Bibliography for Literary Students* (1927).]

Editorial: A short expository or argumentative ESSAY used in newspapers or MAGAZINES. The purpose of the *editorial* is usually to discuss current events, and the subjects treated may range from matters of purely local importance to international affairs. The usual *editorial* form falls naturally into three divisions: a statement of the event or situation to be discussed, a clarification of this situation through elaboration of the points concerned, and an expression of the opinion of the editor or editorial office.

Education Novel: A FORM of the NOVEL developed in the late eighteenth century, presenting in fictional form a plan for the education of a young person into a desirable citizen and a morally and intellectually self-reliant individual. Among its significant forerunners were the Elizabethan COURTESY BOOKS. Rousseau's *Emile* (1762) was the model for most *education novels.* The form was immensely popular in England in the last third of the eighteenth century, examples being Henry Brooke's *Fool of Quality,* Thomas Day's *Sanford and Merton,* Elizabeth Inchbald's *Simple Story,* and Maria Edgeworth's serialized *Parent's Assistant.* The *education novel* was also attractive to American novelists between 1790 and 1820, notably the Reverend Enos Hitchcock. In one sense the *education novel* is a forerunner of the APPRENTICESHIP NOVEL or BILDUNGSROMAN, but these are broader in scope, deeper in CHARACTERIZA-TION, and more interested in the development of a philosophy of life. The term ERZIEHUNGSROMAN, literally "novel of education," is also more like the APPRENTICESHIP NOVEL than the *education novel* in its eighteenth-century sense.

Edwardian Age: The period in English literature between the death of Victoria in 1901 and the beginning of the First World War in 1914, so-called after King Edward VII, who ruled from 1901 to 1910. It was a period marked by a strong reaction in thought, conduct, and art to the stiff propriety and conservatism of the Victorian Age. The typical attitude of the Edwardians was critical and questioning. There was a growing distrust of authority in religion, morality, and art, a basic doubt of the conventional "virtues," and a deep-felt need to examine critically existing institutions. These attitudes expressed themselves in literature that was brilliant and elegant, although not always deep or enduring.

The CELTIC RENAISSANCE in Ireland awakened the dramatic talents of Lady Gregory, Douglas Hyde, Lennox Robinson, J. M. Synge, and W. B. Yeats; the intellectual DRAMA of G. B. Shaw continued the Ibsen influence; James Barrie and Lord Dunsany kept romance and whimsy alive on the stage. In England John Galsworthy was producing social PLAYS, such as *The Silver Box, Strife,* and *Justice.*

In POETRY it was an age of endings and beginnings. Victorianism lingered on in the VERSES of the LAUREATE, Alfred Austin (succeeded in 1913 by Robert Bridges), and in the work of Noyes and Kipling. W. B. Yeats flourished; Masefield's first volumes appeared; and Hardy's ambitious *The Dynasts* made its appearance.

But it was predominantly an age of PROSE. REALISM and NATURALISM advanced steadily. In the NOVELS of Arnold Bennett were detailed pictures of the grim commonplace; in those of Galsworthy the beginnings of the SAGA of the middle classes. H. G. Wells launched his novelistic CRITICISMS of society; Kipling recorded the march of empire; Ford Madox Ford began to flourish in CRITICISM, journalism, and FICTION. But the greatest writers of PROSE in the British Isles in the *Edwardian Age* were James Joyce, whose *Dubliners* appeared in 1914, and Joseph Conrad, who published distinguished work, including *Youth* and *Nostromo.* Other works of distinction or promise included Butler's *The Way of All Flesh,* Hudson's *Green Mansions,* Stephens's *Crock of Gold,* and Barrie's *The Admirable Crichton.*

English writing was moving away from its older orientations: in the *Edwardian Age* the best dramatist was an Irishman, Shaw; the best POET an Irishman, Yeats; the best novelist an expatriated Pole, Conrad; and the figure with greatest promise for the future an Irishman, Joyce.

[References: Samuel Hynes, *Edwardian Occasions* (1972), and *The Edwardian Turn of Mind* (1968).]

Effect: Totality of impression or emotional impact on the reader. "The tale of *effect*" was a term used to describe GOTHIC and horror stories of the type published in *Blackwood's Magazine* in the first half of the nineteenth century. Poe considered the primary objective of the SHORT STORY to be the achieving of a unified *effect*. The *effect* striven for may be one of horror, mystery, beauty, or whatever the writer's mood dictates, but once the *effect* is decided, everything in the story—PLOT, CHARACTERIZATION, SETTING—must work toward this controlling purpose. One of the paragraphs in Poe's CRITICISM of Hawthorne's *Twice-Told Tales* stands out as the best explanation of this principle:

> A skillful literary artist has constructed a tale. If wise, he has not fashioned his thought to accommodate his incidents; but having conceived, with deliberate care, a certain unique or single *effect* to be wrought out, he then invents such incidents—he then combines such events as may best aid him in establishing his preconceived *effect*. If his very initial sentence tend not to the outbringing of this *effect*, then he has failed in his first step. In the whole composition there should be no word written, of which the tendency, direct or indirect, is not to the one preëstablished design. And by such means, with such care and skill, a picture is at length painted which leaves in the mind of him who contemplates it with a kindred art, a sense of the fullest satisfaction.

To study *effect* is to put less emphasis on an author's supposed intention, and it is altogether possible for literature to produce *effects* not intended or even contemplated by the author. See AFFECTIVE FALLACY, INTENTIONAL FALLACY.

Eiron: A basic comic CHARACTER in Greek DRAMA. The *eiron* is a swindler, a trickster, a hypocrite, or a picaresque rogue. He pretends to ignorance in order to hide his knowledge and to trick others. He is the opposite of the ALAZON, who pretends to more knowledge than he has. The term is sometimes applied to figures in TRAGEDY who deceive through feigned ignorance; Hamlet is an example. IRONY—saying the opposite of what is meant—is the characteristic rhetorical device of the *eiron* (from whom it gets its name). See ALAZON.

Eisteddfod: A Welsh festival of POETRY and SONG, dating back many centuries. Now annual and more or less official, the *eisteddfod* has been important in maintaining communication among writers and preserving traditions and standards.

Elaboration: A rhetorical method for developing a THEME or picture in such a way as to give the reader a completed impression. This may be done in various ways, such as: REPETITION of the statement or idea, a change of words and phrases, or supplying of additional details. Over*elaboration*, however, immediately becomes a fault, since it results in diffuseness, wordiness, and stupidity. *Elaboration* is also used as a critical term characterizing a literary, rhetorical STYLE that is ornate. See AMPLIFICATION.

Electra Complex: In psychoanalysis, an obsessive attachment of a daughter to her father and, thus, the female counterpart of the OEDIPUS COMPLEX. The term is often used in CRITICISM of a psychological bent to describe PLOT situations. It gets its name from Electra, in Greek mythology and DRAMA, a daughter of Agamemnon and Clytemnestra, who with her brother Orestes avenged the death of their father, Agamemnon, by killing their mother and her lover, Aegisthus. See OEDIPUS COMPLEX.

Elegiac: In classical PROSODY, a METER used in the DISTICH employed for lamenting or commemorating the dead; it consists of a VERSE of DACTYLIC HEXAMETER followed by one of PENTAMETER. The ancient POETS used *elegiacs* not only for THRENODIES but also for SONGS of war and love. The *elegiac* meter has been popular in Germany but rarely used in England and America, except by Longfellow and Edmund Wilson. Coleridge's translation of Schiller's DISTICH will serve as an example:

> In the hexameter rises the fountain's silvery column,
> In the pentameter aye falling in melody back.

In English CRITICISM, *elegiac* is used as an adjective to describe POETRY expressing sorrow or lamentation (as in *elegiac* strains) or belonging to or partaking of an ELEGY.

Elegiac Stanza: The IAMBIC PENTAMETER QUATRAIN, rhyming *abab*. The *elegiac stanza* takes its name from Thomas Gray's "Elegy Written in a Country Churchyard," which is composed in such stanzas. Although such a QUATRAIN, rhyming *abab* and called the HEROIC QUATRAIN, was a STANZA of long standing before Gray used it, in the last half of the eighteenth and the nineteenth centuries it was usually employed, after Gray's example, in writing VERSES expressing sorrow or lamentation.

Elegy: A sustained and formal POEM setting forth the poet's meditations on death or another solemn THEME. The meditation often is occasioned by the death of a particular person, but it may be a generalized observation or the expression of a solemn MOOD. A classical FORM, common to both Latin and Greek literatures, the *elegy* originally signified almost any type of serious, subjective meditation on the part of the POET, whether this reflective element concerned death, love, or war, or merely the presentation of information. In CLASSIC writing the *elegy* was more distinguishable by its use of ELEGIAC METER than by its subject matter. The Elizabethans used the term for love POEMS, particularly COMPLAINTS. Up through the end of the seventeenth century, *elegy* could mean both a love POEM and a poem of mourning. Thereafter, the poem of mourning became virtually the only meaning of *elegy*. Notable English *elegies* include the OLD ENGLISH POEM "The Wanderer," *The Pearl,* Chaucer's *Book of the Duchess,* Donne's "Elegies," Gray's "Elegy Written in a Country Churchyard," Tennyson's "In Memoriam," and Whitman's "When Lilacs Last in the Dooryard Bloom'd." These poems indicate the variety of method, MOOD, and subject encompassed by the term *elegy*. A specialized form of *elegy*, popular with English poets, is the PASTORAL ELEGY of which Milton's "Lycidas" is an outstanding example. See PASTORAL ELEGY, DIRGE, MONODY.
  [References: J. C. Bailey, *English Elegies* (1900, reprinted 1976); C. M. Gayley and B. P. Kurtz, *Methods and Materials of Literary Criticism* (1920).]

Elements: In ancient and medieval cosmologies, the fundamental constituents, or *elements,* of the universe were earth, air, fire, and water. Each was considered to have certain basic characteristics: earth was cold and dry; air was hot and moist; fire was hot and dry; and water was cold and moist. The

HUMOURS of the body were closely allied to the four *elements*. The term *elements* is also applied to the bread and wine in the Eucharist. See HUMOURS.

Elision: The omission of part of a word for ease of pronunciation, for EU- PHONY, or for rhythmic effect. *Elision* is most often accomplished by the omission of a final vowel preceding an initial vowel, as "th'orient" for "the orient," but it also occurs between syllables of a single word, as "ne'er" for "never."

Elizabethan Age: The name given to the segment of the RENAISSANCE during the reign of Elizabeth I (1558–1603). The term is sometimes extended to in- clude the JACOBEAN PERIOD (1603–1625). An age of great nationalistic expan- sion, commercial growth, and religious controversy, it saw the development of English DRAMA to its highest level, a great outburst of LYRIC song, and a new interest in CRITICISM. Sidney, Spenser, Marlowe, and Shakespeare flour- ished; and Bacon, Jonson, and Donne first stepped forward. It has justly been called the "Golden Age of English Literature." For details of its literary history, see "Elizabethan Age" in *Outline of Literary History;* for a sketch of its litera- ture see RENAISSANCE.

Elizabethan Drama: This phrase is commonly used for the body of RENAIS- SANCE English DRAMA produced in the century preceding the closing of the theaters in 1642, although it is sometimes employed in a narrower sense to designate the DRAMA of the later years of Elizabeth's reign and the few years following it. Thus, Shakespeare is an Elizabethan dramatist, although more than one third of his active career lies in the reign of James I. Modern English DRAMA not only came into being in the ELIZABETHAN AGE but developed so rapidly and brilliantly that the Elizabethan era is the golden age of English DRAMA.

Lack of adequate records makes it impossible to trace the steps by which *Elizabethan drama* developed, though the chief elements contributing to it can be listed. From MEDIEVAL DRAMA came the TRADITION of acting and certain CONVENTIONS approved by the populace, including some buffoonery. From the MORALITY PLAYS and the INTERLUDES came comic elements. With this medieval heritage was combined the classical TRADITION of DRAMA, partly drawn from a study of the Roman dramatists, Seneca (TRAGEDY) and Plautus and Terence (COMEDY), and partly from humanistic CRITICISM based on Aris- totle. This CLASSICAL influence appeared first in the SCHOOL PLAYS. Later it affected the DRAMA written under the auspices of the royal court and of the INNS OF COURT. Eventually it influenced the PLAYS of the university-trained playwrights connected with the public stage. The modern theater arose with *Elizabethan drama* (see PUBLIC THEATERS, PRIVATE THEATERS). For types of *Elizabethan drama* and names of dramatists see *Outline of Literary History* and TRAGEDY, ROMANTIC TRAGEDY, CLASSICAL TRAGEDY, TRAGEDY OF BLOOD, COMEDY, COMEDY OF HUMOURS, COURT COMEDY, REALISTIC COMEDY, CHRONI- CLE PLAY, and MASQUE.

[References: C. F. Tucker Brooke, *The Tudor Drama* (1911, reprinted 1964); E. K. Chambers, *The Elizabethan Stage*, 4 vols. (1923); T. S. Eliot, *Essays on Elizabethan Drama* (1956); F. E. Schelling, *Elizabethan Drama*, 2 vols. (1908, reprinted 1959).]

Elizabethan Literature: Literature produced in England during the ELIZA-
BETHAN AGE; that is, 1558–1602, although the meaning is often extended to
include the JACOBEAN PERIOD and is sometimes given as wide a scope as
1550–1660. See ELIZABETHAN AGE.

Elizabethan Miscellanies: Poetical ANTHOLOGIES compiled in the ELIZA-
BETHAN AGE. See MISCELLANIES, POETICAL.

Elizabethan Theaters: Public and private playhouses that developed and
flourished in the ELIZABETHAN AGE. See PUBLIC THEATERS, PRIVATE THE-
ATERS.

Ellipsis, or ellipse: A FIGURE OF SPEECH characterized by the omission of
one or more words that, while essential to the grammatic structure of the
sentence, are easily supplied by the reader. The effect of *ellipsis* is rhetorical;
it makes for EMPHASIS of statement. The device often traps the unwary user
into difficulties, since carelessness will result in impossible constructions. The
safe rule is to be sure that the words to be supplied occur in the proper
grammatic form not too remote from the place the *ellipsis* occurs. In the
following quotation from Thomas Hardy's "The Darkling Thrush," the first
clause contains the "seemed to be" that is omitted by *ellipsis* in the second
and third:

> The land's sharp features seemed to be
> The century's corpse outleant,
> His crypt the cloudy canopy,
> The wind his death-lament.

(Note that the INVERSION in the middle clause complicates the effect of the
ellipsis.)

Emblem Books: An "emblem" consisted of a motto expressing some moral
idea and accompanied by a picture and a short POEM illustrating the idea.
The POEM was always short—SONNETS, EPIGRAMS, MADRIGALS, and various
STANZA forms being employed. The picture (originally itself the "emblem")
was symbolic. A collection of emblems was known as an *emblem book.* Emblems and *emblem books,* which owed their popularity partly to the newly
developed art of engraving, were very popular in all Western European languages in the fifteenth, sixteenth, and seventeenth centuries. Examples of
emblems are: the motto *Divesque miserque,* "both rich and poor," illustrated
by a picture of King Midas sitting at a table where everything was gold and
by a verse or "posie" explaining how Midas, though rich, could not eat his
gold; *Parler peu et venir au poinct,* "speak little and come to the point,"
illustrated by a QUATRAIN and a picture of a man shooting at a target with
a crossbow. Several of Spenser's POEMS, such as *The Shepheardes Calender*
and *Muitopotmos,* show the influence of emblems. Shakespeare seems to have
made much use of emblem literature, as in the casket SCENE in *The Merchant
of Venice.* Francis Quarles is the author of an interesting seventeenth-century
emblem book.
   [References: Henry Green, *Shakespeare and the Emblem Writers* (1870);
E. N. S. Thompson, *Literary Bypaths of the Renaissance* (1924).]

Emendation: A change made in a literary text by an editor for removing error or supplying a supposed correct reading that has been obscured or lost through textual inaccuracy or tampering. Probably the most celebrated *emendation* is Lewis Theobald's change of "a table of greens fields" (*King Henry the Fifth,* II, iii) to "a' babbled of green fields."

Empathy: The act of identifying ourselves with an object and participating in its physical and emotional sensations, even to the point of making our own physical responses, as, standing before a statue of a discus thrower, we flex our muscles to hurl the discus. *Empathy* may be extended to an inanimate object, an animal, or a person. It may be active, in that it results in the creative process, or it may be passive, in that it results from reading and appreciation. It is to be contrasted with "sympathy" through which we have a fellow-feeling for someone, for *empathy* implies an "involuntary projection of ourselves" into something or someone else. Some modern CRITICS see in *empathy* the key to the nature and meaning of art. The term is a translation of Hermann Lotze's word *Einfühlung*—"feeling into"—and it entered our critical vocabulary in this century.

Emphasis: A principle of RHETORIC dictating that important elements be given important positions and adequate development whether in the sentence, the paragraph, or the whole composition. The more important positions are, naturally, at the beginning and end. But *emphasis* may also be secured (1) by REPETITION of important ideas; (2) by the development of important ideas through supplying plenty of specific detail; (3) by the allotment of more space to the more important phases of the composition; (4) by the contrast of one element with another, since such contrast focuses the reader's attention on the point in question; (5) by careful selection of details so chosen that subjects related to the main idea are included and all irrelevant material excluded; (6) by climactic arrangement; and (7) by mechanical devices such as capitalization, italics, symbols, and different colors of ink.

Empiricism: In philosophy the drawing of rules of practice not from theory but from experience. Hence, an empirical method is sometimes equivalent to an "experimental" method or scientific knowledge. In medicine, however, an "empiric" usually means a quack. The empirical method, in the sense of the experimental, is important in literary theories of NATURALISM.

Enallage: The intentional substitution of one grammatical form for another, as past for present tense, singular for plural, noun for verb. It is a very common figure, as in "toe the line" or "boot the ball." A famous example is Shakespeare's "But me no buts" (*Richard II*). The POETRY of Gerard Manley Hopkins furnishes many kinetic instances: preposition for conjunction, adverb for preposition, objective for nominative, and—particularly—verb for noun ("the achieve of, the mastery of the thing") and vice versa ("the just man justices").

Enchiridion: A handbook or manual; a VADE MECUM.

Enclosed Rhyme: A term applied to the RHYME pattern of the *In Memoriam* STANZA: *abba.*

Encomium: In Greek literature a POEM or speech in praise of a living person, object, or event, but not a god, delivered before a special audience. Originally a choral HYMN in celebration of a HERO at the conclusion of the Olympic games, then a EULOGY of the host at a banquet, and finally any EULOGY, the *encomium* was apparently first used by Simonides of Ceos and later by Pindar. Encomiastic VERSE, often in the form of the ODE, has been written by many English POETS, including Milton, Dryden, Gray, Wordsworth, and Auden.

Encyclopedia (or **Encyclopaedia**):   An inclusive COMPENDIUM of information. The term comes from the Greek words for "circle" and "instruction." The original "circle of instruction" embraced THE SEVEN LIBERAL ARTS. The word was first used in English in Sir Thomas Elyot's *The Boke of the Governour* (1531). There are three major types of *encyclopedias:* comprehensive, taking all knowledge for their province, such as the *Encyclopaedia Britannica* (first edition in 1771); those universal in scope but limited in coverage, such as the *Columbia Encyclopedia;* and those limited to special subjects or interests, such as the *Encyclopaedia of the Social Sciences* or the *Catholic Encyclopaedia.*

End Rhyme: RHYME that occurs at the ends of LINES in a POEM. The most common kind of RHYME in English POETRY. See RHYME.

End-stopped Lines: Lines of VERSE in which both the grammatical structure and the sense reach completion at the end of the LINE. The absence of ENJAM-BEMENT, or RUN-ON LINES. As in Pope's

> All are but parts of one stupendous whole,
> Whose body Nature is, and God the soul.

English Language: The *English language* developed from the West Germanic dialects spoken by the Angles, Saxons, and other Teutonic tribes who participated in the invasion and occupation of England in the fifth and sixth centuries, a movement that resulted in the obliteration of the earlier Celtic and Roman cultures in the island. The word *English* applied to the language reflects the fact that Anglo-Saxon literature first flourished in the North and was written in the Anglian DIALECTS (hence *Englisc,* "English") spoken in Northumbria and Mercia. Later, under King Alfred, the West Saxon region became the cultural center. The word *Englisc* was still employed as its name, however, and the earlier Anglian literature was copied in the West Saxon dialect, now commonly referred to as OLD ENGLISH, or "Anglo-Saxon." As a language West Saxon was very different from modern English. It had grammatical gender, declensions, conjugations, tense-forms, and case-endings. The word "stone," for example, had six forms (singular: *stān, stānes, stāne;* plural: *stānas, stāna, stānum*) representing five cases (nominative, genitive, dative, accusative, instrumental). Pronouns and verbs likewise possessed inflectional systems. In addition, the four great DIALECTS of the OLD ENGLISH PERIOD (Northumbrian, Mercian, West Saxon, Kentish) differed among themselves in grammar, pronunciation, and vocabulary. The first writing was in RUNES, which were displaced later by the Roman alphabet used by the Christian missionaries. Specimens of OLD ENGLISH have survived from as early as the eighth century, but most of the existing manuscripts are in West Saxon of the tenth and eleventh centuries. Though a few Latin and fewer Celtic words were added to the vocabulary in OLD ENGLISH times, most of the words were Germanic, consisting of words used by the Angles and Saxons, augmented by the introduction of Danish and Norse words as the result of later invasions.

The changes that have made modern English look like a different language from OLD ENGLISH come from the operation of certain tendencies in language development, such as the progressive simplification of the grammar; and the accidents of history, such as the NORMAN CONQUEST and the growth of London as a cultural center. The greatest change took place in the earlier part of the period known as MIDDLE ENGLISH (*ca.* 1100–*ca.* 1500) or a little earlier. The leveling of inflections and other simplifying forces, already under way in late OLD ENGLISH times, were accelerated by the results of the NORMAN CONQUEST, which dethroned English as the literary language, in favor of the French of the newcomers (see ANGLO-FRENCH and ANGLO-NORMAN). Left to the everyday use of the native population, English changed rapidly in the direction of modern English. By late MIDDLE ENGLISH times (fourteenth century) the process of simplification had gone so far that in Chaucer's time almost all the old inflections were either lost or weakened to a final -*e,* often unpronounced. The introduction of French words in the MIDDLE ENGLISH period enriched the English vocabulary. In the fourteenth and fifteenth centuries a significant step toward the development of a standardized, uniform language came with the new prominence given the London DIALECT (largely East Midland), which thus became the basis for modern English. This development arose chiefly from the growing importance of London commercially and politically, the influence of the writings of Chaucer and his followers, the adoption of English instead of French in the courts and schools (fourteenth century), and the employment of this DIALECT by Caxton, the first English printer (late fifteenth century).

Modern English (*ca.* 1500 on) has been marked by an enormous expansion in vocabulary, the new words being drawn from many sources, chiefly Latin and French. Since French is itself based on Latin, English has acquired many doublets, such as "strict" and "strait," permitting further developments in shades of meaning. Other such pairs are "fragile" and "frail" and "regal" and "royal." An examination of a DICTIONARY will show the vast preponderance of foreign words over native English words, though the latter include the more frequently used words of everyday intercourse, such as "man," "wife," "child," "go," "hold," "day," "bed," "sorrow," "hand." The stylistic effect of English PROSE writing is greatly affected by the nature of the vocabulary used, particularly as between native English words and those derived from Latin, either directly or through French. The native words in general give an effect of simplicity and strength, while the Latin or Romance words impart smoothness and make possible fine distinctions in meaning. Germanic words generally consist of a few long and varied syllables, Latinate words of many short and uniform syllables; compare the valences of "happiness" and "felicity" or "sisterhood" and "sorority." Modern English has also drawn freely on many other sources for new words. Greek, for example, has been turned to for scientific terms, new words being formed from Greek root-meanings and affixes. In grammar the simplification has been retarded in modern times by such conservative forces as grammars, DICTIONARIES, printers, and school-teachers. Likewise, spelling and pronounciation have become fixed in some-what chaotic and archaic forms by the influence of the same standardizing tendencies, as well as the mass media.

Today only a quarter of the words in common usage in English are of OLD ENGLISH derivation, yet those that determine the nature of the lan-guage—articles, pronouns, and connecting words—are of OLD ENGLISH origin. What inflectional endings remain for pronouns, adjectives, and adverbs are OLD ENGLISH, as are our verb forms. We have retained the Germanic word order, the Germanic tendency to associate ACCENT and loudness and to stress the first syllable of nouns. We have borrowed three-fourths of our words but have always fitted them into an English frame. The result is that English remains basically a Germanic tongue, which perpetually renews itself at the fountain of the world's languages. See OLD ENGLISH, MIDDLE ENGLISH, AN-GLO-NORMAN, DIALECTS, AMERICAN ENGLISH.

[References: A. C. Baugh, *A History of the English Language*, 2nd ed. (1963); O. F. Emerson, *History of the English Language* (1895); J. B. Greenough and G. L. Kittredge, *Words and Their Ways in English Speech* (1901); Otto Jespersen, *Growth and Structure of the English Language* (1905, reprinted 1971); G. H. McKnight, *Modern English in the Making* (1928); Thomas Pyles and John Algeo, *The Origins and Development of the English Language* (1982); B. M. H. Strang, *A History of English* (1971).]

English Literature, Periods of: The division of a nation's literary history into periods offers a convenient method for studying authors and movements. Hence, most literary histories and anthologies are arranged by periods. In the case of English literature, there are almost as many arrangements as there are books on the subject. This lack of uniformity arises chiefly from two facts. In the first place, periods merge into one another because the supplanting of one literary attitude by another is a gradual process. Thus, the earlier roman-ticists are contemporary with the later neoclassicists, just as the neoclassical attitude existed in the very heyday of Elizabethan ROMANTICISM. Dates given in any scheme of literary periods, therefore, must be regarded as approximate and suggestive only, even when they reflect some definite fact, as 1660 (the Restoration of the Stuarts) and 1798 (the publication of *Lyrical Ballads*). In the second place, the names of periods may be chosen on very different princi-ples. One plan is to name a period for its greatest or its most representative author: Age of Chaucer, Age of Spenser, etc. Another is to coin a descriptive adjective from the name of the ruler: Elizabethan Period, Jacobean Period, Victorian Period. Or pure chronology or names of centuries may be preferred: Fifteenth-Century Literature, Eighteenth-Century Literature, etc. Or descrip-tive titles designed to indicate prevailing attitudes or dominant fashions or "schools" of literature may be used: NEOCLASSICISM, ROMANTICISM, AGE OF REASON. Logically, some single principle should control in any given scheme, but such consistency is seldom found. The table that follows gives the scheme used in this book.

Historical sketches of the periods listed in this table are given in the Hand-book, and briefer descriptions of the subdivisions of periods (here called uni-formly *ages*) are also given in the *Handbook*. The *Outline of Literary History* follows this table and gives details of general and literary history.

PERIODS OF ENGLISH LITERATURE

428–1100 Old English Period
1100–1350 Anglo-Norman Period
1350–1500 Middle English Period
1500–1660 Renaissance Period
    1500–1557 Early Tudor Age
    1558–1603 Elizabethan Age
    1603–1625 Jacobean Age
    1625–1649 Caroline Age
    1649–1660 Commonwealth Interregnum
1660–1798 Neoclassic Period
    1660–1700 Restoration Age
    1700–1750 Augustan Age
    1750–1798 Age of Johnson
1798–1870 Romantic Period
    1798–1832 Age of the Romantic Movement
    1832–1870 Early Victorian Age
1870–1914 Realistic Period
    1870–1901 Late Victorian Age
    1901–1914 Edwardian Age
1914–1965 Modern or Modernist Period
1965– Post-Modernist or Contemporary Period

English Sonnet: The name applied to a form of the SONNET consisting of three QUATRAINS followed by a COUPLET, rhyming *abab cdcd efef gg*. It is often called the SHAKESPEAREAN SONNET. See SONNET.

Enjambement: The continuation of the sense and grammatical construction of a VERSE or COUPLET on to the next VERSE or COUPLET. *Enjambement* occurs in RUN-ON LINES and offers contrast to END-STOPPED LINES. The first and second LINES from Milton given below, carried over to the second and third for completion, are illustrations of *enjambement:*

> Or if Sion hill
> Delight thee more, and Siloa's brook, that flow'd
> Fast by the oracle of God.

Enlightenment: A philosophical movement of the eighteenth century, particularly in France but effectively over much of Europe and America. *The Enlightenment* celebrated reason, the scientific method, and human beings' ability to perfect themselves and their society. It was the outgrowth of a number of seventeenth-century intellectual attainments and currents: the discoveries of Sir Isaac Newton, the RATIONALISM of Descartes and Pierre Bayle, and the EMPIRICISM of Francis Bacon and John Locke. The major champions of its beliefs were the *philosophes,* who made a critical examination of previously accepted institutions and beliefs from the viewpoint of reason and with a confident faith in natural laws and universal order. The *philosophes* agreed on faith in human rationality and the existence of discoverable and universally valid principles governing human beings, nature, and society. They opposed intolerance, restraint, spiritual authority, and revealed religion. They were deists (see DEISM) and political theorists who considered the state a proper instrument of progress. *The Encyclopedie* of Denis Diderot epitomized the doctrines of the *Enlightenment.* Among the leading French figures in the *Enlightenment* were Montesquieu, Voltaire, Buffon, Turgot, and the *Physiocrats.* In England Addison, Steele, Swift, Pope, Edward Gibbon, Hume, Adam Smith, and Jeremy Bentham responded to elements of *Enlightenment* thought; as did Moses Mendelssohn, Lessing, Herder, and Kant in Germany. In America Benjamin Franklin, Tom Paine, and Thomas Jefferson were profoundly influenced by the principles of the *Enlightenment.* The *Enlightenment* was the intellectual ferment out of which the French Revolution came, and it gave philosophical shape to the American Revolution and the two basic documents of the United States, the Declaration of Independence and the Constitution. See AGE OF JOHNSON, AGE OF REASON, and DEISM.

Enthymeme: A SYLLOGISM informally stated and omitting one of the two premises—either the major or the minor. The omitted premise is to be understood. Example: "Children should be seen and not heard. Be quiet, John." Here the obvious minor premise—that John is a child—is left to the ingenuity of the reader.

Entr' acte: An entertainment, often musical, in the interlude between the ACTS of a PLAY.

Entwicklungsroman: In German CRITICISM a term designating a type of BILDUNGSROMAN in which major emphasis is placed on the development of the principal CHARACTER. In English and American CRITICISM the minute differences in such terms as *Entwicklungsroman* and ERZIEHUNGSROMAN are infrequently encountered. See BILDUNGSROMAN and APPRENTICESHIP NOVEL.

Enumerative Bibliography: A listing of works of a particular country, author, printer, or type, or on a particular subject. See BIBLIOGRAPHY.

Envelope: A device in POETRY in which a LINE or group of lines encloses a body of VERSE, giving a sense of structure and completeness. Sometimes a complete STANZA may be repeated to form an *envelope,* as in Keats's "The Mermaid Tavern." Whitman frequently used the device as an organizational principle. The *In Memoriam* STANZA is often called an *envelope* STANZA because the RHYMES of the first and last lines enclose the middle lines, as in:

> We have but faith: we cannot know,
>> For knowledge is of things we see;
>> And yet we trust it comes from thee,
> A beam in darkness: let it grow.

Envoy (envoi): A conventionalized STANZA appearing at the close of certain kinds of POEMS; particularly associated with the French BALLADE form. The *envoy* (1) is usually addressed to a prince, a judge, a patron, or other person of importance; (2) repeats the REFRAIN line used throughout the BALLADE; (3) consists normally of four LINES (though not necessarily so limited); (4) usually employs the *bcbc* RHYME scheme. An *envoy* comes as a shorter STANZA at the end of the CHANT ROYAL and the SESTINA. At times, the *envoy* serves merely as a conventional summary and conclusion; at other times, however, as in the FREE-VERSE *"Envoi"* that closes Ezra Pound's *Hugh Selwyn Mauberley,* an *envoy* functions as a "sending" or "dispatching" POEM. This usage tallies with the common diplomatic meaning of *envoy,* "one who is sent." An earlier English form of the plural, *invoyes,* meant "a list of things sent" and became the modern "invoice," which has been used in contemporary POETRY for a certain kind of POEM that is a "sending" and, by a punning analogy with INSCAPE and INSTRESS, contains an inner voice. See BALLADE.

Epanalepsis: The REPETITION at the end of a clause of a word or phrase that occurred at its beginning, as in Shakespeare's LINES from *King John* (II, i):

> Blood hath bought blood, and blows have answer'd blows:
> Strength match'd with strength, and power confronted power.

The device is used extensively by Milton and Whitman.

Epanaphora: The REPETITION of words or phrases at the beginning of LINES or sentences; commonly called ANAPHORA. See ANAPHORA.

Epanodos: The REPETITION of the same word or phrase at the beginning and middle or at the middle and end of a sentence, as in *Ezekiel,* 35:6—"I will prepare thee unto blood, and blood shall pursue thee: sith thou hast not hated blood, even blood shall pursue thee." The term is also used for the reiteration of two or more things so as to make distinctions among them, as in "Mary and Elizabeth both spoke; Mary quietly but Elizabeth in harsh and angry tones." *Epanados* is sometimes applied to the progressive REPETITION of words or phrases, such as these in Touchstone's speech in *As You Like It* (III, ii): "Why, if thou never wast at court, thou never saw'st good manners; if thou never saw'st good manners, then thy manners must be wicked; and wickedness is sin, and sin is damnation. Thou art in a parlous state, shepherd." *Epanodos* is also applied to the return to the main subject after a DIGRESSION.

Epic: A long narrative POEM in elevated STYLE presenting CHARACTERS of high position in adventures forming an organic whole through their relation to a central heroic figure and through their development of EPISODES important to the history of a nation or race. According to one theory, the first *epics* took shape from the scattered work of various unknown POETS, and through gradual accretion these EPISODES were molded into an ordered sequence. This theory has largely given way to the belief that, although the materials of the *epic* may have developed in this way, the *epic* POEM itself is the product of a single genius who gives it STRUCTURE and expression. *Epics* without certain authorship are called FOLK EPICS, whether the scholar believes in a folk or a single-authorship theory of origins.

   Both FOLK and ART EPICS share a group of common characteristics: (1)

the HERO is a figure of imposing stature, of national or international importance, and of great historical or legendary significance; (2) the SETTING is vast, covering great nations, the world, or the universe; (3) the ACTION consists of deeds of great valor or requiring superhuman courage; (4) supernatural forces—gods, angels, and demons—interest themselves in the ACTION and intervene from time to time; (5) a STYLE of sustained elevation and grand simplicity is used; and (6) the *epic* POET recounts the deeds of the HEROES with a measure of objectivity. To these general characteristics (some of which are omitted from particular *epics*) should be added a list of common devices or CONVENTIONS employed by most *epic* POETS: the POET opens by stating the THEME, invokes a MUSE, and opens the narrative IN MEDIAS RES—in the middle of things—giving the necessary EXPOSITION later; the poet includes CATALOGS of warriors, ships, armies; the poet gives extended formal speeches by the main CHARACTERS; and the poet makes frequent use of the EPIC SIMILE.

A few of the more important FOLK EPICS are: Homer's the *Iliad* and the *Odyssey*, the Old English *Beowulf*, the East Indian *Mahabharata*, the Spanish *Cid*, the Finnish *Kalevala*, the French *Song of Roland*, and the German *Nibelungenlied*. Some of the best-known ART EPICS are: Virgil's *Aeneid*, Dante's *Divine Comedy* (although it lacks many of the distinctive characteristics of the *epic*), Tasso's *Jerusalem Delivered*, Milton's *Paradise Lost*. American POETS in the late eighteenth and early nineteenth centuries struggled to produce a good *epic* POEM on the American adventure, but without success. Longfellow's *Hiawatha* is an attempt at an Indian *epic*. Whitman's *Leaves of Grass*, considered as the AUTOBIOGRAPHY of a generic American, is sometimes called an American *epic*, as are Stephen Vincent Benét's *John Brown's Body*, Ezra Pound's *Cantos*, and Hart Crane's *The Bridge*.

In the Middle Ages there was a great mass of literature verging on the *epic* in form and purpose though not answering strictly to the conventional EPIC FORMULA. These POEMS are variously referred to as *epic* and as ROMANCE. Spenser's *The Faerie Queene* is the supreme example.

[References: John Clark, *A History of Epic Poetry* (1900); W. M. Dixon, *English Epic and Heroic Poetry* (1912); C. M. Gayley and B. P. Kurtz, *Methods and Materials of Literary Criticism* (1920); W. P. Ker, *Epic and Romance* (1896, reprinted 1957); Paul Merchant, *The Epic* (1971); E. M. W. Tillyard, *The English Epic and Its Background* (1954); Anthony C. Yu, ed., *Parnassus Revisited: Modern Critical Essays on the Epic Tradition* (1973).]

Epic Formula: The CONVENTIONS of STRUCTURE employed by most EPIC poets, such as the statement of THEME, the INVOCATION to the MUSE, beginning IN MEDIAS RES, CATALOGS of warriors, extended formal speeches, and similar structural devices. See EPIC.

Epic Question: The request or question addressed to the MUSE at the beginning of an EPIC poem; the answer constitutes the NARRATIVE of the work.

Epic Simile: An elaborated comparison. The *epic simile* differs from an ordinary SIMILE in being more involved and ornate, in a conscious imitation of the Homeric manner. The secondary object or VEHICLE is developed into an independent aesthetic object, an IMAGE that for the moment upstages the primary object or TENOR with which it is compared. The following *epic simile* is from *Paradise Lost:*

> Angel Forms, who lay entranced
> Thick as autumnal leaves that strow the brooks
> In Vallombrosa, where the Etrurian shades
> High over-arched embower; or scattered sedge
> Afloat, when the fierce winds Orion armed
> Hath vexed the Red-Sea coast, whose waves o'erthrew
> Busiris and his Memphian chivalry,
> While with perfidious hatred they pursued
> The sojourners of Goshen, who beheld
> From the safe shore their floating carcasses
> And broken chariot-wheels.

Such a protracted comparison seems, on the one hand, to lead away from the presence of the TENOR or subject, while at the same time making a vivid argument about the multitude of "Angel Forms" now rhetorically reduced in dignity to mere vegetation helplessly acted on by a more powerful force. The *epic simile* is also called the HOMERIC SIMILE.

Epicurean: A philosophical position similar to that of the Greek Epicurus, who saw philosophy as the art of making life happy, with pleasure the highest goal of human beings, and pain and emotional disturbance the greatest evils. But Epicurus was not a simple hedonist (see HEDONISM); for him pleasure came not primarily from sensual delights but from serenity. Thus, intellectual processes were, he held, superior to bodily pleasures. He rejected the belief in an afterlife and the influence of the gods in human affairs, strongly asserted human freedom, and accepted the atomic theory of Democritus. In his social code Epicurus emphasized honesty, prudence, and justice, but chiefly as means through which one encounters the least trouble from society. The *Epicurean*, therefore, seeks not wine, women, and song but serenity of spirit. The term *Epicurean* is often but erroneously considered synonymous with hedonistic.

Epideictic Poetry: POETRY written for special occasions, primarily for the pleasure and edification of its audience. Aristotle divided RHETORIC into deliberative (to persuade), forensic (to condemn or praise actions), and *epideictic* (to demonstrate in ceremonial praise). CLASSICAL poetry grew increasingly *epideictic*, particularly in its decadent period. Common types of *epideictic poetry* are the ENCOMIUM, the EPITHALAMIUM, and the PROTHALAMIUM.

Epigone: A less distinguished follower or imitator of a work, an author, or a literary movement. The term comes from the Epigonoi, who were the sons of the Seven against Thebes and who imitated their fathers by themselves unsuccessfully attacking Thebes. Thus "Thyrsis," by Matthew Arnold, might be called an *epigone* of the great English PASTORAL ELEGY tradition, or the HISTORICAL NOVELS of G. P. R. James might be called *epigones* of Sir Walter Scott's Waverley Novels.

Epigram: Any pithy, pointed, concise saying. An *epigram* is often antithetical, as "Man proposes but God disposes," or La Rochefoucauld's "Only those deserving of scorn are apprehensive of it." This use of the word is derived from certain qualities of a type of POEM known as an *epigram*. Originally (in ancient Greece) an *epigram* meant an inscription, especially an EPITAPH. Then it came to mean a short POEM summing up what is to be made permanently memorable, as though it were such an inscription. Hence, the *epigram* was characterized by compression, pointedness, clarity, BALANCE, and polish. Examples of the ancient *epigram* may be found in the *Greek Anthology* and in the work of the Roman POET Martial (A.D. 40–104), whose work supplied models for Ben Jonson, the greatest writer of *epigrams* in English. Martial had used the *epigram* for various THEMES and purposes: EULOGY, friendship, compliment, EPITAPHS, philosophic reflection, JEUX D'ESPRIT, and SATIRE. Although numerous *epigrams* were written by sixteenth-century English writers, notably John Heywood, they did not conform closely to the CLASSICAL type, reflecting various forms of medieval HUMOR and SATIRE. With the revolt against Elizabethan ROMANTICISM just before 1600, the classical *epigram* was cultivated, chiefly as a VEHICLE for SATIRE. Many collections were published between 1596 and 1616, including a famous one of Sir John Harington (1615). Jonson wrote not only satirical *epigrams* but EPISTLES, VERSES of compliment, EPITAPHS, and reflective VERSES. An *epigram* of this period was typically a short POEM consisting of two parts, an introduction stating the occasion or setting the TONE, and a conclusion sharply and tersely giving the main point. In the eighteenth century the spirit though not the FORM of the *epigram* continued. Many of Pope's COUPLETS are *epigrams* when separated from their context. Coleridge, too, indulged in the *epigram* on occasion, but Walter Savage Landor was its greatest and most persistent user after Jonson. In the twentieth century a number of POETS kept up the TRADITION of *epigrams* telling and witty: Robert Frost, Howard Nemerov, Richard Wilbur, X. J. Kennedy, J. V. Cunningham, Jonathan Williams, and John Hollander.

An *epigram* is related to, but distinguished from, an APHORISM. An APHORISM, usually in PROSE, states a general truth or principle in some memorable form; an EPIGRAM, usually in VERSE, wittily makes a particular point in a polished, satirical, paradoxical way.

[Reference: T. K. Whipple, *Martial and the English Epigram* (1925).]

Epigraph: An inscription on stone or on a statue or a coin. In literature an *epigraph* is a quotation on the title page of a book, or a motto heading a chapter or section of a work.

Epilogue: A concluding statement; an appendix to a composition. Sometimes used in the sense of a PERORATION to a speech but more generally applied to the final remarks of an ACTOR addressed to the audience at the close of the PLAY. An *epilogue* is opposed to a PROLOGUE, a speech used to introduce the play. Puck, in *A Midsummer Night's Dream,* recites an *epilogue* that is characteristic of RENAISSANCE plays in that it bespeaks the goodwill of the audience and courteous treatment by critics. As the use of *epilogues* became more general, POETS of reputation were often paid to contribute *epilogues* to PLAYS much as PREFACES written by prominent authors are now sometimes paid for by publishers. *Epilogues* were a part of major dramatic efforts in the late seventeenth and eighteenth centuries, disappearing from common use about the middle of the nineteenth. They are now rarely employed.

Epiphany: Literally a manifestation or showing-forth, usually of some divine being. The Christian festival of *Epiphany* commemorates the manifestation of Christ to the Gentiles in the form of the Magi. It is celebrated on "Twelfth Night," January 6. *Epiphany* has been given wide currency as a critical term by James Joyce, who used it to designate an event in which the essential nature of something—a person, a situation, an object—was suddenly perceived. It is thus an intuitive grasp of reality achieved in a quick flash of recognition in which something, usually simple and commonplace, is seen in a new light, and, as Joyce says, "its soul, its whatness leaps to us from the vestment of its appearance." This sudden insight is the *epiphany*. But the term is also used for a literary composition that presents such *epiphanies,* so that we say that the stories that make up Joyce's *Dubliners* are *epiphanies.*

Episode: An incident presented as one continuous action. Though having a UNITY within itself, the *episode* in any composition is usually accompanied by other *episodes* woven together to create a SHORT STORY, DRAMA, or NOVEL. Originally, in Greek DRAMA, an *episode* referred to that part of a TRAGEDY presented between two CHORUSES. More narrowly, the term is sometimes used to characterize an incident injected into a piece of FICTION simply to illuminate CHARACTER or to create background when it bears no definite relation to the PLOT and in no way advances the ACTION.

Episodic Structure: A term applied to writing that consists of little more than a series of incidents. Simple NARRATIVE as opposed to NARRATIVE with PLOT. In this type of writing the *episodes* succeed each other, with no particularly logical arrangement (except perhaps that of chronology) or COMPLICATION. Travel books naturally fall into *episodic structure.* The term is applied also to long narratives that may contain complicated PLOTS, like the Italian ROMANTIC EPIC, if the ACTION is made leisurely by the use of numerous *episodes* employed to develop CHARACTER or PLOT. The METRICAL ROMANCE and the PICARESQUE NOVEL are said to have *episodic structure,* since the events that occur in them have little causal relationship and are together because they happened in chronological order to a single CHARACTER. As a rule, a work with *episodic structure* has little or no central PLOT.

Epistle: Theoretically an *epistle* is any LETTER, but in practice the term is limited to formal compositions written to a distant individual or group. The most familiar use of the term, of course, is to characterize certain books of the New Testament. The *epistle* differs from the common LETTER in that it is a conscious literary form rather than a spontaneous, chatty, private composition. Ordinarily the *epistle* is associated with scriptural writing of the past, but this is by no means a necessary restriction since the term may be used to indicate formal LETTERS having to do with public matters and with philosophy as well as with religious problems. It is regularly applied to the formal LETTERS of dedication that appear in books. Pope used it to describe formal LETTERS in VERSE.

Epistolary Novel: A NOVEL in which the NARRATIVE is carried forward by LETTERS written by one or more of the CHARACTERS. It has the merit of giving the author an opportunity to present the feelings and reactions of CHARACTERS without the intrusion of the author; it further gives a sense of immediacy, since the LETTERS are usually written in the thick of the ACTION. The *epistolary novel* also enables the author to present multiple POINTS OF VIEW on the same event through the use of several correspondents. It is also a device for creating VERISIMILITUDE, the author merely serving as "editor" for the correspondence. Obvious disadvantages are the fact that the correspondents in an *epistolary novel* become incredible and indefatigable scribblers under the most surprising circumstances and the fact that the enforced objectivity of the "editor" shuts the author off from comment on the ACTIONS of the CHARACTERS.

Samuel Richardson's *Pamela* (1740) is frequently considered the first English *epistolary novel*, although the use of LETTERS to tell stories and to give racy gossip and sage instruction goes back in England at least as far as Nicholas Breton's *A Poste with a Packet of Mad Letters* (1602) and includes such other precursors as Aphra Behn's *Love Letters Between a Nobleman and His Sister* (1682). Richardson's *Clarissa Harlowe* (1748) is certainly the greatest, as it is the most extended, of *epistolary novels*. The FORM was popular in the eighteenth century, particularly for the SENTIMENTAL NOVEL. Other notable examples are Smollett's *Humphry Clinker* (1771) and Fanny Burney's *Evelina* (1778). The epistolary method has not often been successfully used in the nineteenth and twentieth centuries, although the use of LETTERS within NOVELS has been common. J. P. Marquand's *The Late George Apley* and John O'Hara's *Pal Joey* are modern instances of epistolary FICTION. See NOVEL.

[References: Godfrey Frank Singer, *The Epistolary Novel*, 1963; Natascha Würzbach, ed., *The Novel in Letters*, (1969).]

Epistrophe: A rhetorical term applied to the REPETITION of the closing word or phrase at the end of several clauses, sentences, or VERSES, as in Sidney's "And all the night he did nothing but weep Philoclea, sigh Philoclea, and cry out Philoclea" (*The New Arcadia*).

Epitaph: An inscription used to mark burial places. Commemorative VERSES or LINES appearing on tombs or written as if intended for such use. Since the days of early Egyptian records, *epitaphs* have had a long and interesting history, and, while they have changed as to purpose and form, they show less development than most literary types. The information usually incorporated in such memorials includes the name of the deceased, the dates of birth and death, age, profession (if a dignified one), together with some pious motto or INVOCATION. Many prominent writers—notably Jonson, Milton, and Pope—have left *epitaphs* they wrote in tribute to the dead. Early *epitaphs* were usually serious and dignified—since they appeared chiefly on the tombs of the great—but more recently they have, either consciously or unconsciously, taken on humorous qualities. One of the most famous inscriptions is that marking Shakespeare's burial place:

> Good frend, for Jesus sake forbeare
> To digg the dust enclosed here;
> Bleste be ye man yᵗ spares thes stones,
> And curst be he yᵗ moves my bones,—

But this is as much a CURSE as an *epitaph*. "O rare Ben Jonson"—which may be a serious PUN on *orare* (pray for)—and "*Exit* Burbage" are two examples of effective *epitaphs*. A famous French inscription is from Père Lachaise in Paris:

> Ci-gît ma femme: ah! que c'est bien
> Pour son repos, et pour le mien!

The *epitaph* "On the Countess Dowager of Pembroke," once attributed to Ben Jonson but now credited to William Browne, deserves quotation:

> Underneath this sable hearse
> Lies the subject of all verse:
> Sidney's sister, Pembroke's mother.
> Death, ere thou hast slain another,
> Fair and learned and good as she,
> Time shall throw a dart at thee.

Epitasis: A term used by the ancients to designate the RISING ACTION of a DRAMA. See DRAMATIC STRUCTURE.

Epithalamium (Epithalamion): A bridal SONG; a song or POEM written to celebrate a wedding. Many ancient POETS (the Greek Pindar, Sappho, and Theocritus and the Roman Catullus) as well as modern poets (the French Ronsard and the English Spenser) have cultivated the FORM. Perhaps Spenser's *Epithalamion* (1595), written to celebrate his own marriage, is the finest of the English marriage hymns. The successive STANZAS in this POEM treat such topics as: invocation to the MUSES to help praise his bride; awakening of the bride by music; decking of the bridal path with flowers; adorning of the bride by nymphs; assembling of the guests; description of the physical and spiritual beauty of the bride; the bride at the altar; the marriage feast; welcoming the night; asking the blessing of Diana and Juno and the stars. Any number of later works, from Coleridge's *Rime of the Ancient Mariner* to Salinger's "Raise High the Roof Beam, Carpenters," exploit various engaging features of the TRADITION of the *epithalamium*.

Epithet: Strictly, an adjective or adjective phrase used to point out a characteristic of a person or thing, as Goldsmith's "noisy mansions" (for schoolhouses), but sometimes applied to a noun or noun phrase used for a similar purpose, as Shakespeare's "the trumpet of the dawn" (for the cock). Many considerations enter into the success of an *epithet*, such as its aptness (indeed, *epithet* is actually used sometimes rather loosely to mean any apt phrase), its freshness, its pictorial quality, its connotative value (what it suggests rather than says), and its musical value. Memorable *epithets* are often figurative, as Keats's "snarling trumpets" and Milton's "laboring clouds."

The so-called HOMERIC EPITHET, often a compound adjective, as "all-seeing" Jove, "swift-footed" Achilles, "blue-eyed" Athena, "rosy-fingered" dawn, depends on aptness combined with familiarity rather than on freshness or variety. It is almost a formulaic part of a name. Since *epithets* often play a prominent part in the name-calling that characterizes INVECTIVE or personal SATIRE, some persons have the mistaken notion that an *epithet* is always uncomplimentary. A TRANSFERRED EPITHET is an adjective used to limit grammatically a noun that it does not logically modify, though the relation is so close that the meaning is left clear, as Shakespeare's "dusty death," or Milton's "blind mouths." The same device turns up in such common terms as "foreign policy" and "abnormal psychology": the policy itself is not foreign but rather domestic—one state's policy with respect to foreign states; the psychology itself is not abnormal but rather normal—the psychological study of abnormality.

Epitome: A summary or ABRIDGMENT. A condensed statement of the content of a book. A "miniature representation" of a subject. Thus, Magna Charta has been called the *epitome* of the rights of English people, and Ruskin referred to St. Mark's as an *epitome* of the changes of Venetian architecture through a period of nine centuries.

Epode: One of the three STANZA forms employed in the PINDARIC ODE. The others are STROPHE and ANTISTROPHE. See ODE.

Eponym: The name of a person so commonly associated with some widely recognized attribute that the name comes to stand for the attribute, as Helen for beauty, Croesus for wealth, Machiavelli for duplicity, or Caesar for dictator. *Eponym* also means the name of some historical or legendary personage, such as Hellen, Romulus, Israel, or Bolívar, whose name has been bestowed on a place or people (Hellas, Rome, Israel, Bolivia). Some *eponyms* are clearly traceable, such as those of Constantinople and Leningrad; others, such as the HERO called Dardanus in the prehistory of the Dardans, are more obscure. Sometimes names that become applied to general entities—such as *bloomers* and *boycott*—are also called *eponyms*.

Epyllion: A NARRATIVE POEM usually presenting an EPISODE from the heroic past and resembling an EPIC in THEME, TONE, and method but much briefer and more limited in scope. Matthew Arnold's *Sohrab and Rustum* and Tennyson's *Idylls of the King* are *epyllions*.

Equivalence: In METRICS, a kind of SUBSTITUTION, in which a FOOT equal to the one expected but different from it is used in a VERSE. In QUANTITATIVE VERSE, one long syllable was considered the *equivalent* of two short syllables, and thus a SPONDEE (two long syllables) could be substituted for an ANAPEST (two shorts and a long). See SUBSTITUTION, COMPENSATION.

Equivocation: The use of a word in two distinct meanings, possibly with the intention to deceive. See EQUIVOQUE.

Equivoque: A kind of PUN in which a word or phrase is so used that it has two different but appropriate meanings. If the *equivoque* is used with the intention to deceive, the result is EQUIVOCATION, as in "Nothing is too good for him," which sounds like a compliment and is intended as a condemnation.

Erastianism: The doctrine that the civil authority has dominance over the church in all matters. It is attributed to Thomas Erastus, a sixteenth-century Swiss theologian, who insisted that the civil authority and not the church should act in all punitive measures but did not intend to give the state authority in ecclesiastical matters, although the doctrine named for him came to mean such dominance. *Erastianism* became an issue in England during the OXFORD MOVEMENT controversies. The Public Worship Act of 1874 attempted to "put down Ritualism" as it had developed under the OXFORD MOVEMENT. The Act was vigorously and successfully resisted by Pusey and his followers as an instance of *Erastianism*.

Erotic Literature: A type of writing characterized by treatment of sexual love in more or less explicit detail. Although the inclusive term "the literature of love" includes the *erotic*, writings customarily labeled "love story" or "love poetry" usually avoid the specific sexual details ordinarily associated with *erotic literature*. On the other hand, *erotic literature* need not include PORNOGRA-PHY, which employs sexual material as an end in itself. In *erotic literature* the sexual element is made a portion of the aesthetic, thematic, or moral aspect of the work; that is, it exists as a contributing part to some other objective than titillation or sexual arousal. Erotic elements may be used aesthetically, as in Ovid's *Ars amatoria* or Spenser's *Epithalamion;* thematically, as in Indian scriptures or D. H. Lawrence's *Lady Chatterley's Lover;* or metaphorically, as in the Biblical "Song of Songs." In the medieval FABLIAUX erotic materials were put to comic use, sometimes with great skill, as in Chaucer's "Miller's Tale." In writers as dissimilar as Baudelaire, Walt Whitman, and William Faulkner, sexual materials are used as controlling METAPHORS to state and underscore THEMES. Love and its sexual expression are among the permanent central issues of literature, and they are present to some degree in most of the world's great writing.

    [References: H. H. Hyde, *A History of Pornography* (1964); Gershon Legman, *The Horn Book* (1964).]

Erziehungsroman: The NOVEL of upbringing or education. Strictly speaking, *Erziehungsroman* and BILDUNGSROMAN are synonymous, but in customary usage BILDUNGSROMAN is the more generic term, including the *Erziehungsroman, the* ENTWICKLUNGSROMAN, and the KÜNSTLERROMAN. These fine distinctions, except for KÜNSTLERROMAN, tend to be lost, in English and American CRITICISM.

Escape Literature: Writing whose clear intention is to amuse and beguile its readers by offering them a strange world or exciting adventures or puzzling mysteries. It aims at no higher purpose than amusement. Adventure stories, DETECTIVE STORIES, TALES of FANTASY, and many humorous stories are frankly *escape literature,* and they exist for no other purpose than to translate readers for a time from the care-ridden actual world to an entrancing world of the imagination. Longfellow, in "The Day is Done," defined the effect of *escape literature* well:

> Come, read to me some poem,
>   Some simple and heartfelt lay,
> That shall soothe this restless feeling,
>   And banish the thoughts of day.
>   . . . . .

And the night shall be filled with music.
And the cares that infest the day
Shall fold their tents, like the Arabs,
And as silently steal away.

Esemplastic: A term applied by Samuel Taylor Coleridge to the quality in the IMAGINATION that enables it to shape disparate things into a unified whole. The word means "molding into a unity."

Esperanto: An artificial speech constructed from roots common to the chief European languages and designed for universal use. *Esperanto* was devised by Dr. L. L. Zamenhof, a Russian, and took its name from Zamenhof's PSEUD-ONYM, "Dr. Esperanto," used in signing his first pamphlet on the subject in 1887. The grammar is so simple as to be clear after a few minutes' study, the spelling is strictly phonetic, the language is euphonious and adaptable, and pronunciation is easy since the ACCENT always falls on the penult. However, *Esperanto* gives little promise today of becoming a universal tongue.

Essay: A moderately brief PROSE discussion of a restricted topic. Because of the wide application of the term, no satisfactory definition can be arrived at; nor can a wholly acceptable "classification" of *essay* types be made. Among the terms that have been used in attempting classifications of the *essay* are: moralizing, critical, character, anecdotal, letter, narrative, aphoristic, descriptive, reflective, biographical, historical, periodical, didactic, editorial, whimsical, psychological, outdoor, nature, comical, and personal. Such a list is incomplete; obviously, classifying the *essay* has eluded human skill. A basic and very useful division can, however, be made: FORMAL and INFORMAL. The INFORMAL ESSAY, sometimes called the "true" *essay*, includes moderately brief aphoristic *essays* like Bacon's, PERIODICAL ESSAYS like Addison's, and PERSONAL ESSAYS like Lamb's. Qualities that make an *essay* INFORMAL include: the personal element (self-revelation, individual tastes and experiences, confidential manner), humor, graceful STYLE, rambling STRUCTURE, unconventionality or novelty of THEME, freshness of FORM, freedom from stiffness and affectation, incomplete or tentative treatment of topic. Qualities of the FORMAL ESSAY include: seriousness of purpose, dignity, logical organization, length. The term may include both short discussions, expository or argumentative (such as the serious magazine ARTICLE) and longer treatises (such as the chapters in Carlyle's *Heroes and Hero-Worship*). However, a sharp distinction between even FORMAL and INFORMAL ESSAYS cannot be maintained at all times. In the following sketch the INFORMAL ESSAY will be given chief consideration, since it falls better into the realm of literature.

When the French philosopher Montaigne retired from active life, he collected pithy sayings—MAXIMS, APHORISMS, ADAGES, APOTHEGMS, PROVERBS—along with ANECDOTES and quotations from his readings in the CLASSICS. A collection of such wise sayings upon a single topic was known in France as a *leçon morale*. Montaigne developed the habit of recording also the results of a searching self-analysis and became attracted by the idea that he was himself representative of human beings in general. He published his first collection of such writings in two volumes in 1580 under the title *Essais*—the first use of the word for short PROSE discussions. The word means "attempts," and by its use Montaigne meant to indicate that his discussions were tentative compared with ordinary philosophical writings. By adding the personal element to the aphoristic *leçon morale,* Montaigne created the modern *essay.* "Myself," he said, "am the groundwork of my book." The new edition, which included the third volume (1588), gave even greater emphasis to the personal element. Mainly philosophical and ethical, the *essays* cover a wide range of topics, such as "Of Idleness," "Of Liars," "Of Ready and Slow Speech," "Of Smells and Odors," "Of Cannibals," "Of Sleeping," "Upon Some Verses of Virgil."

When Francis Bacon published in 1597 his first collection of aphoristic *essays,* he borrowed his title, *Essays,* from Montaigne's book—and became the first English "essayist." The ten *essays* initially published were short and consisted chiefly of a collection of MAXIMS on a given subject. The book was very popular, and enlarged editions were issued in 1612 and 1625. The later *essays* are longer, more personal, and developed by a wealth of illustration, quotation, and FIGURES OF SPEECH. Bacon's STYLE achieved a compactness, clarity, imaginative richness, phrasal power, and sentence rhythm that have made his *essays* a part of the world's literature. The "aphoristic" quality of his STYLE is seen in such typical quotations as these: "The errors of young men are the ruin of business," and "He that hath a wife and children hath given hostages to fortune." Bacon's *essays* are highly practical and utilitarian. Like the Renaissance COURTESY BOOKS, they had for their chief purpose the giving of useful advice to those who wished to get on in practical life, especially as men of affairs.

After Bacon the seventeenth century contributed little to the development of the INFORMAL ESSAY. Owen Felltham's *Resolves* (1620) shows the application of Bacon's method to religious topics. Sir William Cornwallis's *Essays* (1600, 1610, 1616) reflects the method of Montaigne. Better essayists appeared after the RESTORATION. Sir William Temple, the statesman, and Abraham Cowley, the POET, wrote PERSONAL ESSAYS while living in retirement, Cowley's being particularly happy efforts. Though the INFORMAL ESSAY, strictly defined, received little attention in this century, there was much PROSE writing closely related to the INFORMAL and FORMAL ESSAY. The chapters of Sir Thomas Browne's *Religio Medici* (1642) in their STYLE as well as their tendency toward self-revelation and moralizing suggest the INFORMAL ESSAY. So do the miscellaneous sketches in Ben Jonson's *Timber, or Discoveries Made upon Men and Matter* (1640). Dryden's *Essay of Dramatick Poesie* (1668) is an example of a critical *essay* in conventional DIALOGUE form. The numerous PREFACES and books on literary CRITICISM from the late sixteenth and early seventeenth centuries are also forerunners of the later critical *essay.* Milton's *Areopagitica,* in form an argumentative address, is a masterly example of a FORMAL ESSAY. Related to *essay* writing are such long PROSE treatises as Robert Burton's *Anatomy of Melancholy* (1621), Locke's *Essay Concerning Human Understanding* (1690), and Izaak Walton's *Compleat Angler* (1653). The LETTER or formal EPISTLE as a vehicle for writing much like the INFORMAL ESSAY appeared in James Howell's *Epistolae Ho–Elianae: Familiar Letters* (1650). The seventeenth century also saw the development in English of the CHARACTER, a brief sketch of a quality or personality type. It became popular and exerted an appreciable influence on the PERIODICAL ESSAY of the eighteenth century, partly, to be sure, through the work of a French writer of

CHARACTERS, La Bruyère, who had combined the CHARACTER with the *essay*. The EPIGRAM, as written by Ben Jonson, in its depiction of moral and social types, sometimes became a sort of counterpart of the CHARACTER and may have influenced *essay* writers.

The second great step in the history of the INFORMAL ESSAY came in the early years of the eighteenth century with the creation by Steele and Addison of the PERIODICAL ESSAY, a new form that achieved great popularity and attracted some of the best writers of the time. In 1691 had appeared Dunton's *Athenian Gazette*, a new type of PERIODICAL, small in format and designed to entertain as well as instruct. A feature of Daniel Defoe's *A Weekly Review of Affairs in France* (1704) had been a department called "Advice from the Scandalous Club," gossipy in character. From this germ Richard Steele developed the new *essay* in his *Tatler* (1709–1711). The purpose of the papers was "to recommend truth, innocence, honor, virtue, as the chief ornaments of life." Joseph Addison soon joined Steele, and the two later launched the informal daily *spectator* (1711–1712; 1714). The new *essay* was affected not only by its periodical form, which prescribed the length, but by the general spirit of the times. RENAISSANCE individualism was giving way to a centering of interest in society, and the moral reaction from the excesses of the RESTORATION AGE made timely the effort of the essayists to reform the manners of the age, refine its tastes, and provide topics for discussion at the popular coffee houses of London.

As compared with earlier *essays*, the PERIODIAL ESSAY is briefer, less aphoristic, less intimate and introspective, less individualistic, less "learned," and more informal in STYLE and TONE, making more use of HUMOR and SATIRE and embracing a wider range of topics. The appeal is to the middle classes as well as to the cultivated few, but the city reader seems always to have been in the authors' minds. Addison referred to two types of *Spectator* papers: "serious essays" on such well-worn topics as death, marriage, education, and friendship; and "occasional papers," dealing with the "folly, extravagance, and caprice of the present age." The latter class especially aided in fixing as a tradition of the INFORMAL ESSAY that delightful informality, whimsicality, HUMOR, and grace that appear in scores of *essays* on such topics as women's fashions, dueling, witchcraft, coffee houses, and family portraits. The type developed much machinery such as fictitious characters, clubs, and imaginary correspondents.

The popularity of the FORM led to many imitations, such as the *Guardian*, the *Female Tatler*, and the *Whisperer*, and men like Swift, Pope, and Berkeley contributed *essays* to some of them. Fielding incorporated *essays* in *Tom Jones*. Later in the century Dr. Samuel Johnson (in the *Rambler*, 1750–1752, and the *Idler* papers, 1758–1760), Lord Chesterfield, Horace Walpole, and Oliver Goldsmith appeared as accomplished informal essayists. Goldsmith's *Letters from a Citizen of the World* (1760–1761) are noted examples of the form. After Goldsmith the *essay* declined as a literary form.

A revival of interest in the writing of both FORMAL and INFORMAL ESSAYS accompanied the ROMANTIC MOVEMENT. The informal type responded to the impulses of the time. The production of the PERSONAL ESSAY was stimulated by the development of a new type of periodical: *Blackwood's Magazine* (1817) and the *London Magazine* (1820), which provided a market for the *essays* of Lamb, Hazlitt, Hunt, De Quincey, and others. Lamb's *Essay of Elia* (begun in 1820) exhibited an intimate STYLE, an autobiographical interest, a light and easy HUMOR and sentiment, an urbanity and unerring literary TASTE. Even the novelists took up *essay* writing (Dickens, *Sketches by Boz*, 1836; Thackeray, *Roundabout Papers*, (1860–1863). Freed from the space restrictions of the *Tatler* type and encouraged by a reading public eager for "original" work, these writers modified the Addisonian *essay* by making it more personal, longer, and more varied in THEME and by freeing it from the stereotyped features of the earlier form. Late in the century a successor to Lamb appeared in Robert Louis Stevenson, for whose whimsical humor, nimble imagination, and buoyant STYLE, the PERSONAL ESSAY formed an ideal medium (*Virginibus Puerisque*, 1881; *Memories and Portraits*, 1887). Later writers of the INFORMAL ESSAY in England are A. C. Benson, G. K. Chesterton, E. V. Lucas, George Orwell, Malcolm Muggeridge, and Laurie Lee.

The FORMAL ESSAY of the early nineteenth century was largely the result of the appearance of the critical magazine, especially the *Edinburgh Review* (1802), the *Quarterly Review* (1809), and the *Westminster Review* (1824). Book reviews in the form of long critical *essays* were written by Francis Jeffrey, T. B. Macaulay, Thomas De Quincey, Sir Walter Scott, Thomas Carlyle, and later by George Eliot, Matthew Arnold, and many others. The manner of the FORMAL ESSAY appears also in the works of many other PROSE writers of the century. The separate chapters in the books of such writers as Thomas Carlyle, John Ruskin, Walter Pater, Charles Kingsley, Leslie Stephen, Walter Bagehot, T. H. Huxley, Matthew Arnold, and Cardinal Newman are essaylike treatments of phases of the historical, biographical, scientific, educational, religious, and ethical topics concerned.

Though there is some reflection of *essay* literature in such early American writers as Cotton Mather, Jonathan Edwards, Benjamin Franklin, Thomas Jefferson, Alexander Hamilton, and such "itinerant" Americans as Tom Paine and J. H. St. John de Crèvecoeur, the first really great literary essayist in America is Washington Irving, whose *Sketch-Book* (1820) contains *essays* of the Addisonian type. Some of H. D. Thoreau's works (e.g., *Walden*) exhibited characteristics of the INFORMAL ESSAY, and Oliver Wendell Holmes in *The Autocrat of the Breakfast Table* (1857) was a successful writer of informal, humorous *essays*. Ralph Waldo Emerson, reminiscent of Bacon in his aphoristic style, fired with transcendental idealism, became the best known of all American essayists. James Russell Lowell (*Among My Books*, 1870, 1876) is another notable writer of *essays*, as is Edgar Allan Poe, who produced important critical *essays*. Later able essayists, formal or informal, include G. W. Curtis, C. D. Warner, W. D. Howells, Mark Twain, and John Burroughs. More recent names are those of Henry Van Dyke, Paul Elmer More, William Beebe, Christopher Morley, James Thurber, E. B. White, and Gore Vidal.

The FORMAL ESSAY, instead of crystallizing into a set literary type, has tended to become diversified in form, spirit, and length, according to the THEME and serious purpose of its author. At one extreme it is represented by the brief, serious magazine ARTICLE and at the other by scientific or philosophical treatises, which are books rather than *essays*. The technique of the FORMAL ESSAY is now practically identical with that of all factual or theoretical PROSE writing in which literary effect is secondary to serious purpose. Its tradition has doubtless tended to add clarity to English prose STYLE by its insistence on unity, STRUCTURE, and perspicacity.

The INFORMAL ESSAY, on the other hand, beginning in aphoristic and moralistic writing, modified by the injection of the personal element, broadened and lightened by a free treatment of human manners, controlled somewhat in STYLE and length by the limitations of periodical publication, has developed into a recognizable literary GENRE, the first purpose of which is to entertain, in a manner sprightly, light, novel, or humorous. As such, the form has aided in giving something of a Gallic grace to other forms of PROSE composition, notably letterwriting. But valuable though its contributions to prose writing have been and respected as it is today as a literary GENRE, the INFORMAL ESSAY has had few skillful or serious practitioners in the twentieth century. After the Second World War, the frontier between FICTION and journalism became a robust environment for essayists such as James Baldwin, John Hersey, Norman Mailer, William F. Buckley, Jr., John McPhee, Roy G. Blount, Jr., and Tom Wolfe.

[References: R. M. Alden, ed., *Essays, English and American*, rev. ed. (1927); W. F. Bryan and R. S. Crane, *The English Familiar Essay* (1916); Walter Graham, *English Literary Periodicals* (1930); Robert Scholes and Carl H. Klaus, *Elements of the Essay* (1969); Hugh Walker, *English Essays and Essayists* (1915, reprinted 1923).]

Establishing Shot: In filmmaking and FILM CRITICISM, the opening shot of a sequence, usually with a substantial distance between the camera and the SCENE, so that the CHARACTERS and ACTIONS are visibly placed in their physical context. It is usually followed by the camera's moving in closer for later shots. It is for the filmmaker somewhat like the PANORAMIC METHOD for the FICTION writer.

Ethos: In RHETORIC the character or quality of the speaker or writer as reflected in speech or writing; the character or set of emotions that a speaker or writer enacts in order to affect an audience. Aristotle divided the persuasive elements of a speech into the means or devices of RHETORIC and the persuasive value of the speaker's (and, by extension, the writer's) character. The *ethos* of a speech or a piece of writing may also be considered the image of its maker that it projects as a whole or total discourse. For Aristotle the personal image of a persuasive speaker or writer should be that of a person of intelligence, rectitude, and goodwill. Quintilian distinguished between PATHOS, which he used for violent emotions, and *ethos*, which he used for the calmer emotions that tend to be continuous. In RENAISSANCE CRITICISM, *ethos* was often used simply as a description of CHARACTER. In Aristotle's *Poetics, ethos* (moral character) ranks after *mythos* (PLOT) among the qualitative parts of a literary work.

Etiquette Books (Renaissance): Books of instruction in manners, conduct, and the art of governing for young princes and noblemen. See COURTESY BOOKS.

Eulogy: A formal, dignified speech or writing, highly praising a person or a thing. See ENCOMIUM.

Euphemism: A FIGURE OF SPEECH in which indirectness replaces directness of statement, usually in an effort to avoid offensive bluntness in some subject involving delicacy or taboo. To say "at liberty" instead of "out of work," "senior citizens" instead of "old people," "in the family way" instead of "pregnant," "antisemite" instead of "Jew-hater," and "pass away" instead of "die" is to practice *euphemism* of one sort or another. It is possible for *euphemism* to signal false delicacy, insincerity, sentimentality, or excessive modesty; *euphemism* may also mean a decent respect for the feelings of others. There can also be a measure of IRONY in *euphemism,* as when a NOVEL about desertion in wartime is called *A Farewell to Arms.*

Euphony: A quality of STYLE marked by pleasing combinations of sounds. Opposite of CACOPHONY, which is the subjective impression of unpleasantness of sound. It has been difficult to establish that sounds as such can be either pleasing or unpleasing in isolation from meaning: it is conceivable that "South Dakota" or "free refills" may impress certain partisans as beautiful sounds. In some cases, the relative difficulty of certain articulations in a given language may constitute CACOPHONY, while relative ease makes for *euphony;* but these responses remain relative and subjective. Some hearers find *euphony* even in "Schenectady" and "sphygmomanometer."

Euphuism: An affected STYLE of speech and writing that flourished late in the sixteenth century in England, especially in court circles. It took its name from *Euphues* (1578, 1580) by John Lyly. The chief characteristics of *euphuism* are: balanced construction, often antithetical and combined with ALLITERA-TION: excessive use of the RHETORICAL QUESTION; and a heaping up of SIMILES, illustrations, and examples, especially those drawn from mythology and "unnatural natural history" about the fabulous habits and qualities of animals and plants. Following are some typical passages from *Euphues:* "Be sober but not too sullen; be valiant but not too venturous"; "For as the finest ruby staineth the color of the rest that be in place, or as the sun dimmeth the moon, so this gallant girl more fair than fortunate and yet more fortunate than faithful," etc.; "Do we not commonly see that in painted pots is hidden the deadliest poison? that in the greenest grass is the greatest serpent? in the clearest water the ugliest toad?"; "Being incensed against the one as most pernicious and enflamed with the other as most precious."

Lyly did not invent *euphuism;* rather he combined and popularized elements that others had developed. Important forerunners of Lyly in England were Lord Berners, in his translation of Froissart's *Chronicle* (1523, 1525); Sir Thomas North's translation (1557) of *The Dial of Princes* by Guevara (whose Spanish itself was highly colored); and George Pettie in his *A Petite Palace of Pettie his Pleasure* (1576). One of Pettie's sentences, for example, reads: "Nay, there was never bloody tiger that did so terribly tear the little lamb, as this tyrant did furiously fare with the fair Philomela."

The chief vogue of *euphuism* was in the 1580s, though it was employed much later. The court ladies cultivated it for social conversation, and such writers as Robert Greene and Thomas Lodge used it in their NOVELS (as *Menaphon* and *Rosalynde*). Sir Philip Sidney reacted against it and was followed by many others. Shakespeare both employed it and ridiculed it in *Love's Labour's Lost.* In a justly famous scene between Falstaff and Prince Hal, Shakespeare mocks the euphuistic style (*Henry IV, Part One, II, iv*).

Though the extravagance and artificiality of *euphuism* make it seem ludicrous to a modern reader, it actually played a powerful and beneficial role in the development of English PROSE. It established the idea that PROSE (formerly heavy and Latinized) might be written with IMAGINATION and FANCY, while its emphasis on short clauses and sentences and on balanced construction aided in imparting clarity. These virtues of clearness, lightness, and pleasant ornamentation remained as a permanent contribution after a better TASTE had eliminated the vices of extravagant artificiality.

[References: R. W. Bond, ed., *The Complete Works of John Lyly*, Vol. 1 (1902); W. L. Rushton, *Shakespeare's Euphuism* (1871).]

Exciting Force: In a DRAMA the force that starts the CONFLICT of opposing interests and sets in motion the RISING ACTION of the PLAY. Example: the witches' prophecy to Macbeth, which stirs him to schemes for making himself king. See DRAMATIC STRUCTURE.

Excursus: A formal, lengthy DIGRESSION. See DIGRESSION.

Exegesis: An explanation and interpretation of a difficult text. It is usually applied to the detailed study of the BIBLE. When used in reference to a literary text, it usually implies a close ANALYSIS and is equivalent to explication. See EXPLICATION DE TEXTE.

Exemplum (Exempla): A moralized TALE. Just as modern preachers often make use of "illustrations," so medieval preachers made extensive use of TALES, ANECDOTES, and INCIDENTS, both historical and legendary, to point morals or illustrate doctrines. Often highly artificial and to a modern reader incredible, these "examples" seem to have appealed very strongly to medieval congregations because of their concreteness and narrative and human interest, as well as their moral implications. Collections of *exempla,* classified according to subject, were prepared for the use of preachers. An important book of the sort was Jacques de Vitry's *Exempla* (early thirteenth century). At times sermons degenerated into mere series of ANECDOTES, sometimes even humorous in character. Dante in thirteenth-century Italy and Wycliffe in fourteenth-century England protested against this tendency, and Wycliffe as an element in his reform program omitted *exempla* from his own sermons.

The influence of *exempla* and example-books on medieval literature was great, as may be illustrated from several of Chaucer's POEMS. The *Nun's Priest's Tale,* for example, itself cast into sermon form, uses *exempla,* as when Chanticleer tells Pertelot ANECDOTES to prove that dreams have a meaning. The *Pardoner's Tale* is itself an *exemplum* to show how Avarice leads to an evil end.

[Reference: A. J. Mosher, *The Exemplum in the Early Religious and Didactic Literature of England* (1911).]

Existential Criticism: A comtemporary school of CRITICISM, led by Jean-Paul Sartre, that questions the legitimacy of the traditional critical questions and examines a literary work in terms of the ways in which it explores the *existential* questions and in terms of its *existential* impact on the reader. See EXISTENTIALISM.

Existentialism: A term applied to a group of attitudes current in philosophical, religious, and artistic thought during and after the Second World War, which emphasizes existence rather than essence and sees the inadequacy of the human reason to explain the enigma of the universe as the basic philosophical question. The term is so broadly and loosely used that an exact definition is not possible. In its modern expression it had its beginning in the writings of the nineteenth-century Danish theologian, Søren Kierkegaard. The German philosopher Martin Heidegger is important in its formulation, and the French novelist-philosopher Jean-Paul Sartre has done most to give it its present form and popularity. *Existentialism* has found art and literature to be unusually effective methods of expression; in the NOVELS of Franz Kafka, Dostoyevski, Camus, and Simone de Beauvoir, and in the PLAYS and NOVELS of Sartre and Samuel Beckett, and the PLAYS of Eugène Ionesco, it has found its most persuasive media.

Basically the existentialist assumes that existence precedes essence, that the significant fact is that we and things in general exist, but that these things have no meaning for us except as we can create meaning through acting upon them. Sartre claims that the fundamental truth of *existentialism* is in Descartes' formula, "I think; therefore, I exist." The existential philosophy is concerned with the personal "commitment" of this unique existing individual in the "human situation." It attempts to codify the irrational aspect of human nature, to objectify nonbeing or nothingness and see it as a universal source of fear, to distrust concepts, and to emphasize experiential concreteness. The existentialist's point of departure is human beings' immediate awareness of their situation. A part of this is a sense of meaninglessness in the outer world; this meaninglessness produces in them a discomfort, an anxiety, a loneliness in the face of human limitations and a desire to invest experience with meaning by acting upon the world, although efforts to act in a meaningless, "absurd" world lead to anguish, greater loneliness, and despair. Human beings are totally free but also wholly responsible for what they make of themselves. This freedom and responsibility are the sources for their most intense anxiety. Such a philosophical attitude can result in nihilism and hopelessness, as, indeed, it has with many of the literary existentialists. Patently, however, purely nihilistic art is a practical impossibility, any creative act constituting a gesture of at least some small affirmation.

The existential view can assert the possibility of improvement. Most pessimistic systems find the source of their despair in the fixed imperfection of human nature or of the human context; the existentialist, however, denies all absolute principles and holds that human nature is fixed only in that we have agreed to recognize certain human attributes; it is, therefore, subject to change if human beings can agree on other attributes or even to change by a single person if the person acts authentically in contradiction to the accepted principles. Hence, for the existentialist, the possibilities of altering human nature and society are unlimited, but, at the same time, human beings can hope for aid in making such alterations only from within themselves.

In contradistinction to this essentially atheistic *existentialism*, there has also developed a sizable body of Christian existential thought, represented by Karl Jaspers, Jacques Maritain, Nicolas Berdyaev, Martin Buber, Paul Tillich, and others.

[References: Hazel E. Barnes, *The Literature of Possibility* (1959); Arturo Fallico, *Art and Existentialism* (1962); Walter Odajnyk, *Marxism and Existentialism* (1965).]

Exordium: In CLASSIC RHETORIC the first of the seven parts of an ORATION (see ORATION). By extension, *exordium* is now applied to the introductory portion of a composition or a discourse. Edgar Allan Poe, for example, opens his section of critical notices in *Graham's Magazine* for January, 1842, with an *"Exordium"* in which he sets forth his critical principles.

Expatriate: A term applied to those who leave their native lands and reside elsewhere. A number of American writers have been *expatriates.* Among them are Henry James and T. S. Eliot, who became British subjects; Ezra Pound, Henry Miller, James Jones, Richard Wright, and James Baldwin. The most celebrated American group of *expatriates* were those who lived in Paris following the First World War, including Gertrude Stein, Ernest Hemingway, Malcolm Cowley, and Louis Bromfield. Other noted *expatriates* are the Polish writer Joseph Conrad, who lived much of his mature life in England, and the Irish writer James Joyce, who lived for a long time on the Continent.

Expletive: An interjection to lend emphasis to a sentence or, in VERSE especially, the use of a superfluous word (some form of the verb "to do," for example) to make for RHYTHM. Profanity is, of course, another form of *expletive* use. Careless speech is full of superfluous words that are *expletive* in nature. A common colloquial *expletive* is "you know" added frequently to a statement, as "I went home, you know, at ten o'clock."

Explication de texte: A method, which originated in the teaching of literature in France, involving the painstaking ANALYSIS of the meanings, relationships, and AMBIGUITIES of the words, IMAGES, and small units that make up a literary work. It is one of the tools of the New Critics and certain later scholars, such as Hugh Kenner. See ANALYTICAL CRITICISM, AMBIGUITY, NEW CRITICISM, EXEGESIS.

Exposition: One of the four chief types of composition, the others being ARGUMENTATION, DESCRIPTION, and NARRATION. Its purpose is to explain something. *Exposition* may exist apart from the other types of composition, but frequently two or more of the types are blended, DESCRIPTION aiding *exposition,* ARGUMENT being supported by *exposition,* NARRATION reinforcing by example an *exposition.* The following are some of the methods used in *exposition* (they may be used singly or in various combinations): identification, DEFINITION, classification, illustration, comparison, and ANALYSIS.

In DRAMATIC STRUCTURE the *exposition* is the introductory material, which creates the TONE, gives the SETTING, introduces the CHARACTERS, and supplies other facts necessary to an understanding of the PLAY. See DRAMATIC STRUCTURE.

Expressionism: A movement affecting painting, the DRAMA, the NOVEL, and POETRY, which followed and went beyond IMPRESSIONISM in its efforts to "objectify inner experience." Fundamentally it means the willing yielding up of the REALISTIC and NATURALISTIC methods, of VERISIMILITUDE, in order to use external objects in art not as representational but as transmitters of the internal impressions and moods of a CHARACTER or of the artist. In painting, for instance, "childhood" might be shown not through a conventional representational picture of children at play or at school but by seemingly unarticulated and exaggerated physical details that suggest "childhood" or convey the impression that the artist has of the concept "child."

As an organized literary movement *expressionism* was strongest in the theater in the 1920s, and its entry into other literary forms was probably through the stage. *Expressionism* had its origin in the German theater in the early years of the century. It was a response to several different forces: the growing size and mechanism of society, with its tendency to depress the value of the arts, made artists seek new ways of making art forms valuable instruments for human beings; at the same time depth psychologists, notably Freud, laid bare the phantasms in the depths of the human mind and offered artists a challenge to record them accurately; meanwhile MARXISM had instructed even non-Marxist artists that the individual was being lost in a mass society; to these pressures came the example of the DRAMAS of Strindberg, whose PLAYS *The Dance of Death* (1901) and *A Dream Play* (1902) employ extensive nonrealistic devices. The German dramatists Wedekind, Georg Kaiser, and Ernst Toller and the Czech dramatist Karel Capek (the author of the nightmarish FANTASY of the future, *R. U. R.*) were the major figures in the European expressionistic drama, which flourished in the 1920s. It was marked by unreal atmosphere, a nightmarish quality of ACTION, distortion and oversimplification, the de-emphasis of the individual (CHARACTERS were likely to be called the "Father" or the "Bank Clerk"), antirealistic stage SETTINGS, and staccato, telegraphic DIALOGUE. The expressionistic DRAMA was strongly influential on Pirandello and Lorca. For American students it is most important in its impact on Eugene O'Neill, whose *Emperor Jones* attempts to project by symbolic scenes and sound effects the racial memories of a modern Negro. Elmer Rice's *The Adding Machine,* which uses moving stages and other nonrealistic devices to express the mechanical world seen by one cog in it named Mr. Zero, is an almost equally noted example. Elements of *expressionism* can be seen in the PLAYS of Thornton Wilder, Arthur Miller, and Tennessee Williams.

In the NOVEL the presentation of the objective outer world as it expresses itself in the impressions or moods of a CHARACTER is a device widely used. The most famous extended example is Joyce's *Finnegans Wake,* although the expressionistic intent and method are often apparent in works using the STREAM OF CONSCIOUSNESS technique, as witness the "Circe" episode in Joyce's *Ulysses.* Probably the most complete transfer of the quality of expressionistic DRAMA to the NOVEL, however, is to be found in the works of Franz Kafka. The ANTIREALISTIC NOVEL is also a GENRE in the expressionistic tradition. It is possible to include certain more recent novelists, such as Kurt Vonnegut, Jr., and Thomas Pynchon, in the expressionistic tradition.

The revolt against REALISM, the distortion of the objects of the outer world, and the violent dislocation of time sequence and spatial logic in an effort accurately but not representationally to show the world as it appears to a troubled mind can be found in modern POETRY, particularly that of T. S. Eliot, whose *The Waste Land* is the poetic CLASSIC of the movement. See IMPRESSIONISM, REALISM.

[Reference: Ulrich Eerner Weisstein, ed. *Expressionism as an International Literary Phenomenon* (1973).]

Expressive Theory of Criticism: A term, used by M. H. Abrams, that designates a theory that holds the object of the artist to be the expression of the artist's emotions, impressions, or beliefs; an essential doctrine of the ROMANTIC critics. See CRITICISM.

Extravaganza: A fantastic, extravagant, or irregular composition. It is most commonly applied to dramatic compositions such as those of J. R. Planché, the creator of the dramatic *extravaganza*. Planché himself defined it as a "whimsical treatment of a poetical subject as distinguished from the broad caricature of a tragedy or serious opera, which was correctly described as burlesque." The subject was often a FAIRY TALE. The presentation was elaborate and included dancing and music. An example is Planché's *Sleeping Beauty* (acted 1840). A later use of *extravaganza*, still current, is to designate any extraordinarily spectacular theatrical production. *Extravaganza* is also applied to fantastic musical compositions, especially musical CARICATURES. In literature the term is occasionally used to characterize such rollicking or unrestrained work as Butler's *Hudibras,* a CARICATURE of the English PURITANS.

Eye Dialect: The phonetic misspelling of a word to suggest DIALECT, even though the common pronunciation of the word is what the speaker said. In the sentence "Ah cain't kum raht naow," "kum" is an *eye dialect* spelling. The other words in the sentence are all pronounced by the speaker in nonstandard ways; "kum" could have been spelled "come" with the same resulting sound. *Eye dialect* is often used for comic effect and is sometimes called comic misspelling.

Eye Rhyme: RHYME that appears correct from the spelling but is not so from the pronunciation, as "watch" and "match" or "love" and "move." Both these examples, displaying the notorious vagaries of vowels in English spelling, are actually cases of CONSONANCE. Other *eye rhymes*—"imply" and "simply," "Venus" and "menus," "laughter" and "daughter"—scarcely qualify as any sort of rhyme at all, even so-called HALF RHYME or SLANT RHYME. Ezra Pound's *Hugh Selwyn Mauberley* wittily exploits a thematically significant *eye rhyme* between "mistress" and "distress," in which the only proper RHYMES exist between the stressed syllable of one word with the unstressed of the other.

F

Fable: A brief TALE, either in PROSE or VERSE, told to point a moral. The CHARACTERS are most frequently animals, but people and inanimate objects are sometimes the central figures. *Fables* have to do with supernatural or unusual incidents and often have their origin in FOLKLORE sources. By far the most famous *fables* are those accredited to Aesop, a Greek slave living about 600 B.C.; but almost equally popular are those of La Fontaine, a Frenchman writing in the seventeenth century, because of their distinctive HUMOR and WIT, their wisdom and sprightly SATIRE. Other important fabulists are Gay (England), Lessing (Germany), and Krylov (Russia). A *fable* in which the characters are animals is called a BEAST FABLE, a FORM that has been popular in almost every period of literary history, usually as a satiric device to point out human follies. The BEAST FABLE continues to be vigorous in such diverse works as Kipling's *Jungle Books* and *Just So Stories,* Joel Chandler Harris's Uncle Remus stories, and George Orwell's *Animal Farm.* Many CRITICS, particularly in the NEOCLASSIC PERIOD, have used *fable* as a term for the PLOT of a FICTION or a DRAMA. See BEAST EPIC, BESTIARY, ALLEGORY.

Fabliau (*Fabliaux*): A humorous TALE popular in medieval French literature. The *fabliaux* gained wide diffusion largely through the popularity of the JONGLEUR, who spread them throughout France. The conventional VERSE FORM of the *fabliau* was the eight-syllable LINE. *Fabliaux* were stories of various types, but one point was uppermost—their humorous, SLY SATIRE on human beings. These stories, which were often bawdy, dealt familiarly with the clergy, ridiculed womanhood, and were pitched in a key that made them readily and boisterously understandable to the uneducated. The form was also present in English literature of the MIDDLE ENGLISH PERIOD, Chaucer especially leaving examples of *fabliaux,* in the tales of the Miller, Reeve, Friar, Summoner, Merchant, Shipman, and Manciple. Although *fabliaux* often had ostensible "morals" appended to them, they lack the serious intention of the FABLE, and they differ from the FABLE too in always having human beings as CHARACTERS and in always maintaining a realistic TONE and manner.

Fairy Tale: A STORY relating mysterious pranks and adventures of supernatural spirits who manifested themselves in the form of diminutive human beings. These spirits possessed certain qualities that are constantly drawn on for TALES of their adventures: supernatural wisdom and foresight, a mischievous temperament, the power to regulate the affairs of human beings for good or evil, the capacity to change themselves into any shape at any time. *Fairy tales* as such—though they had existed in varying forms before—became popular toward the close of the seventeenth century. Almost every nation has its own fairy literature, though the FOLKLORE element embodied in *fairy tales* prompts the growth of related TALES among different nations. Some of the great source-collections are the *Contes de ma Mère l'Oye* of Perrault (French) and those of the Grimm brothers in German and of Keightley and Croker in English. Hans Christian Andersen, of Denmark, is probably the most famous writer of original *fairy tales.* English writers of original *fairy tales* include Ruskin, Kingsley, Wilde, and Kipling.

Falling Action: The second "half" or RESOLUTION of a dramatic PLOT. It follows the CLIMAX, beginning often with a tragic force, exhibits the failing fortunes of the HERO (in TRAGEDY) and the successful efforts of the COUNTER-PLAYERS, and culminates in the CATASTROPHE. See DRAMATIC STRUCTURE.

Falling Rhythm: In METRICS a FOOT in which the first syllable is accented, as in a TROCHEE or a DACTYL. Coleridge's VERSES on the poetic feet illustrate it:

> Trochee is in falling double,
> Dactyl is falling, like—Tripoli.

Familiar Essay: The more personal, intimate type of INFORMAL ESSAY. It deals lightly, often humorously, with personal experiences, opinions, and preju-dices, stressing especially the unusual or novel in attitude and having to do with the varied aspects of everyday life. Goldsmith, Lamb, and Stevenson were particularly successful in the form. See ESSAY.

Fancy: In English literature *fancy* and IMAGINATION were SYNONYMS until the nineteenth century, although John Dryden had assigned a comprehensive role to IMAGINATION and had limited *fancy* to language and variations of a thought and Joshua Reynolds had associated IMAGINATION with genius and *fancy* with TASTE. The term *fancy* is now used almost exclusively in the Coleridgean opposition of IMAGINATION and *fancy,* in which *fancy* is "me-chanic," "logical," "the aggregative and associative power," "a mode of Mem-ory emancipated from the order of time and space." IMAGINATION is, on the other hand, "organic" and "creative." For Coleridge *fancy* is a distinct faculty, dependent for its materials on the primary IMAGINATION and confined to manipulating, combining, and arranging phenomenal materials but incapable of the creation of materials. *Fancy* is, therefore, the lesser faculty by far. See IMAGINATION.

Fantastic Poets: A term applied by Milton to the school of metaphysical POETS (see METAPHYSICAL POETRY).

Fantasy: Though sometimes used as an equivalent of FANCY and even of IMAGINATION (see IMAGINATION and FANCY), *fantasy* is usually employed to designate a conscious breaking free from reality. The term is applied to a work that takes place in a nonexistent and unreal world, such as fairyland, or concerns incredible and unreal CHARACTERS, as in Maeterlinck's *The Blue Bird,* or employs physical and scientific principles not yet discovered or con-trary to present experience, as in some SCIENCE FICTION and UTOPIAN fiction. *Fantasy* may be employed merely for the whimsical delight of author or reader, or it may be the means used by the author for serious comment on reality. The most sustained examples of *fantasy,* combining both intentions, in recent literature are the novels of James Branch Cabell laid in the mythical kingdom of Poictesme. The Brontë children created a *fantasy* world called Gondal, which they equipped with a geography, history, and even newspapers. Austin Tappan Wright's *Islandia* is an enormous fictional record of an imaginary world. J. R. R. Tolkien's three NOVELS with the collective title *The Lord of the Rings* are currently proving the still strong appeal of *fantasy.*
[Reference: Lin Carter, *Imaginary Worlds* (1973).]

Farce: The word developed from Late Latin *farsus,* connected with a verb meaning "to stuff." Thus, an expansion or amplification in the church liturgy was called a *farse.* Later, in France, *farce* meant any sort of extemporaneous addition in a PLAY, especially comic jokes or gags, the clownish actors speaking "more than was set down" for them. In the late seventeenth century *farce* was used in England to mean any short humorous PLAY, as distinguished from regular five-act COMEDY. The development in these plays of certain elements of LOW COMEDY is responsible for the usual modern meaning of *farce:* a dramatic piece intended to excite laughter and depending less on PLOT and CHAR-ACTER than on exaggerated, improbable situations, the HUMOR arising from gross incongruities, coarse WIT, or horseplay. *Farce* merges into COMEDY, and the same PLAY (e.g., Shakespeare's *The Taming of the Shrew*) may be called by some a *farce,* by others a COMEDY. James Townley's *High Life Below Stairs* (1759), with the production of which Garrick was connected, has been termed the "best farce" of the eighteenth century. In the American theater, Brandon Thomas's *Charley's Aunt* (1892), dealing with the extravagant events resulting from a female impersonation, is the best-known American *farce,* although *farce* is the stock-in-trade of motion-picture and television comedians. See FARCE-COMEDY.

Farce-Comedy: A term sometimes applied to comedies that rely for their interest chiefly on farcical devices (see FARCE, LOW COMEDY) but that contain some truly comic elements elevating them above most FARCE. Shakespeare's *The Taming of the Shrew* and *The Merry Wives of Windsor* are called *farce-comedies* by some. One writer distinguishes between the *farce-comedy* of Aristophanes (loose STRUCTURE, variety of appeal, operatic quality) and that of Plautus (careful STRUCTURE, intricate INTRIGUE, broad HUMOR). More recently, *farce-comedy* has been detected in Oscar Wilde's PLAYS— especially *The Importance of Being Earnest*—and in many subsequent presentations, such as movies with W. C. Fields, the Marx Brothers, Woody Allen, and Richard Pryor, as well as such television productions as "The Honeymooners."
[Reference: R. M. Smith, ed., *Types of Farce-Comedy* (1982).]

Fatalism: The theory that certain future events must occur regardless of our present actions or choices. Strictly speaking, *fatalism* removes ethical concerns from human actions, for fate indifferently assigns each person to the predetermined course of events. The Greeks held to the idea of the allotment, by the Moirai, to each individual at birth of a certain quantity of misfortune that he or she must endure. The Romans saw their gods, the Parcae, spinning human destiny. In Islamic belief everything is ruled by an inexorable fate, called Kismet. It is important to distinguish between fate and chance. If fate is conceived to be operative, any event, however independent of the actions or merits of an individual, is the result of an impersonal force predetermining it and everything else that happens. If chance is believed to be operative, the event is accidental rather than part of a design, the working of COINCIDENCE rather than of fate. Although *fatalism* often coincides with a belief in PREDESTINATION, as in CALVINISM or Islamic belief, it does not necessarily entail the existence of a purposive agent through whose de cree the necessary events occur; it merely asserts that these necessary events are inevitable.

Fates, The: The Greeks and Romans believed that *the Fates* controlled the birth, life, and death of all human beings. The Romans called them the Parcae, the Greeks the Moirai. They were three sisters who controlled the thread of life. Clotho held the distaff; Lachesis spun the thread; and Atropos cut the thread to end life. See FATALISM.

Federalist Age in American Literature: The period between the formation of the national government and the "Second Revolution" of Jacksonian Democracy. It is called the *Federalist Age* because of the dominance of the Federalist Party. The period extends from 1790 to 1830. Internationally, the age saw the emergence of the United States as a world force through the War of 1812. Internally it was an "Era of Good Feeling," with the sectional and social issues that were later to plague the nation just beginning to be felt. It was an age of rapid literary development. In 1790 the United States could boast of few distinguished writers of any kind and almost none of belletristic excellence; at its close America was clearly ready for the artistic burgeoning that marked the period from 1830 to the Civil War. POETRY moved from the imitative NEOCLASSICISM of Barlow and Dwight, through the limited ROMANTICISM of Freneau, to the first notable American achievements in VERSE in the work of Bryant. The NOVEL, first practiced in America in 1789, saw good work by Charles Brockden Brown and H. H. Brackenridge and the establishment of a distinctively American ROMANCE with the Leatherstocking Tales of James Fenimore Cooper. Irving in his burlesque *Knickerbocker's History of New York* and in his ESSAYS and TALES found an international audience. The *North American Review,* founded in 1815, was a thriving quarterly. In the decade 1800–1810, Hawthorne, Simms, Whittier, Longfellow, Poe, and Holmes were born; and 1819 was an *annus mirabilis,* being the birth year of Lowell, Melville, and Whitman. By 1830 the NEOCLASSIC, restrained, aristocratic Federalist that America had been had given way to a romantic, exuberant, democratic young giant that was flexing its muscles and was beginning effectively to express itself in art as well as action. See *Outline of Literary History* and REVOLUTIONARY AND EARLY NATIONAL PERIOD IN AMERICAN LITERATURE.

Feminine Ending: An extra-metrical syllable, bearing no STRESS, added to the end of a LINE in IAMBIC or ANAPESTIC METER. This variation gives a sense of movement and an irregularity to the METER, which make for grace and lightness. The FORM is perhaps most commonly used in BLANK VERSE. The second of these lines by Shakespeare is an illustration:

> O! I could play the woman with mine eyes
> And braggart with my tongue. But gently heav*ens*,
> Cut short all intermission.

Feminine Rhyme: A RHYME in which the rhyming stressed syllables are followed by an undifferentiated identical unstressed syllable, as *waken* and *forsaken.* It is also called DOUBLE RHYME. In Chaucer, the *feminine rhyme* was very common because of the frequent recurrence of the final -*e* in Middle English. The phenomenon may be random, in which case *feminine rhymes* will almost always be in the minority, or there may be some patterned arrangement. In the latter case—as in Shakespeare's "Oh Mistress Mine," Longfellow's "Snowflakes," and Browning's "Soliloquy of the Spanish Cloister"—the normal tendency is for *feminine rhymes* to precede MASCULINE. The opposite effect, MASCULINE before *feminine rhymes,* as in E. A. Robinson's "Miniver Cheevy," seems syncopated, ironic, and even unsettling.

Feminism: In literature and CRITICISM, a general position, not necessarily confined to women, having to do with the advocacy and encouragement of equal rights and opportunities for women—politically, socially, psychologically, personally, and aesthetically. The movement is old, but the modern flourishing of *feminism* has taken place since the Second World War and has been traced by some to the publication of Simone de Beauvoir's *The Second Sex* in 1949. Subsequent changes in awareness led to the establishment of women's studies as a subject of JOURNALS, programs, and curricula; and the end of the 1960s and beginning of the 1970s witnessed the appearance of many books devoted to the problem: Robin Morgan, ed., *Sisterhood Is Powerful* (1970); Vivian Gornick and Barbara K. Moran, eds., *Woman in a Sexist Society* (1971); Theodore and Betty Roszak, eds., *Masculine/Feminine: Readings in Sexual Mythology and the Liberation of Women* (1969); Miriam Schneir, ed., *Feminism: The Essential Documents* (1972); Mary Daly, *The Church and the Second Sex* (1968) and *Beyond God the Father* (1973); Germaine Greer, *The Female Eunuch* (1971); Kate Millett, *Sexual Politics* (1971); and many others. Sandra M. Gilbert and Susan Gubar's *The Madwoman in the Attic* (1979) and Elaine Showalter's *A Literature of Their Own* (1977) contributed much to the development of a distinctively Anglo-American "gynocritical" *feminism.* In 1985 Gilbert and Gubar produced the epochal 2457-page *Norton Anthology of Literature by Women: The Tradition in English.* The *Classroom Guide* for that volume sets forth a valuable list of "crucial strategies" that contribute to the evolution of curricula in women's studies and also constitute an agenda for further work: critique, recovery, reconceptualization, and reassessment.

[Reference: Sandra M. Gilbert and Susan Gubar, eds., *The Norton Anthology of Literature by Women: The Tradition in English* (accompanied by separately published *Classroom Guide*) (1985).]

Festschrift (plural, **Festschriften**): From the German words for celebration and writing. A volume of miscellaneous learned ESSAYS by several hands, written by the students, colleagues, or admirers of a distinguished scholar and presented on some special occasion, such as retirement or seventieth birthday.

Feudalism: The system of social and political organization that prevailed in Western Europe during a large part of the medieval period. It developed from the anarchy that followed the fall of Charlemagne's empire in the ninth century. In feudal theory every landholder was merely the tenant of some greater landlord. Thus, the barons or powerful prelates were the tenants of the king; the lesser lords, knights, and churchmen were tenants of the barons and prelates; while the serfs and "villeins" were tenants of the lesser nobles. In practice—as the whole system was based on force—the relations were more complicated: even kings sometimes owed allegiance to a great churchman or baron. Furthermore, there were interlocking fealties, by which one lord might owe allegiance to two kings, so that his allegiance to one might be set aside if that one attacked the other. As rent, the various groups paid to their immediate superiors "service," which might consist of visible property or of military aid. Socially, there were two sharply defined classes: the workers (villeins or free renters; serfs or bondmen); and the "prayers and fighters" (knights, upper clergy, lords). *Feudalism* broke down in the fifteenth century. The ideals of chivalry (see CHIVALRY IN ENGLISH LITERATURE) grew partly out of *feudalism* and powerfully affected the character of much medieval and even RENAISSANCE literature, notably the ROMANCES and ROMANTIC EPICS. The feudal social order is pictured in Chaucer's *Canterbury Tales,* and its evils are set forth in the *Vision of Piers Plowman* (fourteenth century).

Ficelle: Literally the strings by means of which puppets are controlled. The term is used by Henry James as a substitute for CONFIDANTE, a means by which a SELF-EFFACING AUTHOR conveys necessary information to the reader. See CONFIDANT.

Fiction: NARRATIVE writing drawn from the IMAGINATION of the author rather than from history or fact. The term is most frequently associated with NOVELS and SHORT STORIES, though DRAMA and NARRATIVE POETRY are also FORMS of *fiction;* and FABLES, PARABLES, FAIRY TALES, and FOLKLORE contain fictional elements. Sometimes authors weave fictional episodes about historical characters, epochs, and settings and thus make "historical *fiction.*" Sometimes authors use imaginative elaborations of incidents and qualities of a real person in a BIOGRAPHY, resulting in a type of writing popular in recent years, the "fictional BIOGRAPHY." Sometimes the actual events of the author's life are presented under the guise of imaginative creations, resulting in "autobiographical *fiction.*" Sometimes actual persons and events are presented under the guise of *fiction,* resulting in the ROMAN À CLEF. The chief function of *fiction* is to entertain, to be "interesting" in Henry James's phrase; but it often serves also to instruct, to edify, to persuade, or to arouse. It is one of the major devices by which human beings communicate their visions of the nature of reality in concrete terms.

Since *fiction* is a subject matter rather than a type of literature, one interested in any of the particular forms that *fiction* assumes should turn to the articles on specific types, such as NOVEL, SHORT STORY, DRAMA, NARRATIVE POEM, FABLE, for details of the history and STRUCTURE of these types. *"Fiction"* is now often used to describe any literary construction or "making"—any of the ways in which writing seeks to impose order on the flux of thought or experience, as in "the poetics of fiction." See also FORMALISM (RUSSIAN), NARRATOLOGY.

[References: Wayne Booth, *The Rhetoric of Fiction* (1961); Northrop Frye, *Anatomy of Criticism* (1957); Frank Kermode, *The Sense of an Ending* (1967); Sheldon Sacks, *Fiction and the Shape of Belief* (1964); Robert Scholes and Robert Kellogg, *The Nature of Narrative* (1966); Mark Spilka, ed., *Towards a Poetics of Fiction* (1977).]

Figurative Language: Intentional departure from the normal order, construction, or meaning of words in order to gain strength and freshness of expression, to create a pictorial effect, to describe by ANALOGY, or to discover and illustrate similarities in otherwise dissimilar things. *Figurative language* is writing that embodies one or more of the various FIGURES OF SPEECH, the most common of which are: ANTITHESIS, APOSTROPHE, CLIMAX, HYPERBOLE, IRONY, META-PHOR, METONYMY, PERSONIFICATION, REPETITION, SIMILE, SYNECDOCHE. These figures are often divided into two classes: TROPES, literally meaning "turns," in which the words in the figure undergo a decided change in meaning, and RHETORICAL FIGURES in which the words retain their literal meaning but their rhetorical pattern is changed. An APOSTROPHE, for example, is a RHETORICAL FIGURE, and a METAPHOR is a TROPE. See IMAGERY METAPHOR, TROPE, FIGURES OF SPEECH.

Figure Poem: A POEM written so that the shape of its printed words suggests, or is appropriate to, its subject matter. See CARMEN FIGURATUM.

Figures of Speech: The various uses of language that depart from customary construction, order, or singificance in order to achieve special effects or mean-ings. *Figures of speech* are of two major kinds: rhetorical figures, which are departures from customary or standard uses of language to achieve special effects without a change in the radical meaning of the words; and TROPES, in which basic changes in the meaning of words occur. *"Figures of speech"* is a term sometimes used as synonymous with rhetorical figures, and "figures of thought" as synonymous with TROPES; but *figures of speech* and figures of thought in this distinction have undergone so many changes and direct reversals of meaning from the CLASSICAL rhetoricians to the present that their use in this way almost always results in confusion. It is therefore best to use *figures of speech* as the generic term and to use rhetorical figures and TROPES as the subgenera. It is possible to distinguish figures of thought, *figures of speech,* and figures of sound. In Cassius' LINE early in Shakespeare's *Julius Caesar*—"Rome thou hast lost the breed of noble bloods"—we see all three sorts of figure. The APOSTROPHE "Rome" (Cassius is really talking to Brutus) is one of the RHETORICAL FIGURES. The SYNECDOCHE "blood" (using one common part of the organism conventionally to represent human quality in the abstract) is a TROPE. The PENTAMETER, the IAMBIC RHYTHM, and the complex REPETITION of certain sounds (*b* and *l* in particular) are emphatic figures of sound.

*Filidh (*plural, *fili*):* Early Irish professional POETS. See IRISH LITERATURE.

Film: Literally a sheet or roll of transparent material coated with a light-sensitive emulsion for making photographs or moving pictures. By extension, a motion picture made or preserved on such material is itself called a *film.* The term is applied to an individual motion picture, to motion pictures as an art form, as in FILM CRITICISM, and to the industry engaged in making motion pictures. In American FILM CRITICISM *film* has largely replaced the term "cinema," which was once widely used.

Film Criticism: The ANALYSIS and evaluation of specific FILMS by applying to them various standards, theories, and aesthetic beliefs, such as AUTEUR THEORY and FORMATIVE THEORY. The serious and sophisticated ANALYSIS of FILM is a relatively young but very vigorous form of contemporary CRITI-CISM.

Film Theory: The branch of FILM CRITICISM concerned with general or abstract principles governing FILM as an artistic medium. It can be called the AESTHETICS of FILM.

Fin de Siècle: "End of the century," a phrase often applied to the last ten years of the nineteenth century. The 1890s were a transitional period, one in which writers and artists were consciously abandoning old ideas and conventions and attempting to discover and set up new techniques and artistic objectives. One writer (Holbrook Jackson) has noted three main characteristics of the decade in art and literature: DECADENCE, exemplified in Oscar Wilde and Aubrey Beardsley; REALISM or "sense of fact," represented by Gissing, Shaw, and George Moore, with their reaction against the sentimental; and radical or revolutionary social aspirations, marked by numerous new "movements" (including the "new woman," who dared ride a bicycle and seek political suffrage) and by a general sense of emancipation from the traditional social and moral order. When the term *fin de siècle* is used about a literary work, it usually is in the sense of DECADENCE or PRECIOSITY. See EDWARDIAN AGE.

Final Suspense, Moment of: A term used to indicate the ray of hope sometimes appearing just before the CATASTROPHE of a TRAGEDY. Thus, Macbeth's continued faith that he cannot be hurt by any man born of woman keeps the reader or spectator in some suspense as to the apparently inevitable tragic ending. See DRAMATIC STRUCTURE.

Fixed Poetic Forms: A name sometimes given to definitely prescribed patterns of VERSE and STANZA. Although FORMS like the SONNET, the SPENSERIAN STANZA, and RHYME ROYAL are "fixed" forms in this general sense, the term usually refers to a specific group of stanzaic patterns that originated in France. See FRENCH FORMS.

Flashback: A device by which the writer of a FICTION, a DRAMA, or a FILM presents SCENES or INCIDENTS that occurred prior to the opening SCENE of the work. It is a method of presenting EXPOSITION dramatically. Various devices may be used, among them recollections of the CHARACTERS, narration by the characters, dream sequences, and reveries. Notable examples in the theater occur in Elmer Rice's *Dream Girl* and Arthur Miller's *Death of a Salesman.* Maugham used the *flashback* skillfully and effectively in *Cakes and Ale,* and it is employed consistently in the novels of John P. Marquand. Commonly enough, as in John O'Hara's NOVEL *Ten North Frederick* and the FILM version thereof, a work may begin with a funeral or other such terminal event and then go back into the past to show what passed before, so that a large part of the work is technically one protracted *flashback.* See EXPOSITION.

Flat Character: A term used by E. M. Forster to describe a CHARACTER constructed around a single idea or quality, like the HUMOURS CHARACTERS of the seventeenth-century stage. A *flat character* never surprises the reader, is immediately recognizable, and can usually be represented by a single sentence, as "I never will desert Mr. Micawber," which, Forster asserts, *is* Mrs. Micawber and is *all* she is. The term usually is employed in contrast to ROUND CHARACTER. See CHARACTERIZATION and ROUND CHARACTER.

Fleshly School of Poetry, The: A critical ESSAY in the *Contemporary Review*, October, 1871, signed "Thomas Maitland," a PSEUDONYM for Robert W. Buchanan. The CRITIC took to task Swinburne, Morris, and Rossetti, though most of the article is couched as a review of Rossetti's POEMS and Rossetti himself draws most of the fire. Buchanan accused the three of being in league to praise each other's work and refers to them as the "Mutual Admiration School." The following passage makes clear the general tone of Buchanan's criticism:

> The fleshly gentlemen have bound themselves by solemn league and covenant to extol fleshliness as the distinct and supreme end of poetic and pictorial art, to aver that poetic expression is greater than poetic thought, and by inference that the body is greater than the soul, and sound superior to sense; and that the poet, properly to develop his poetic faculty, must be an intellectual hermaphrodite. . . .

Rossetti replied with "The Stealthy School of Criticism," published in *The Athenaeum* (December 16, 1871).

Flyting: An extended and vigorous verbal exchange. In OLD ENGLISH POETRY it was a boasting match between warriors before combat. Similar boasting matches are found in Greek, Arabic, Celtic, Italian, and Provençal literature. It is typical of the CYCLES of Charlemagne. However, it has been from the sixteenth century to the present a marked characteristic of Scottish writing, where it is an exchange of personal abuse or ridicule in VERSE between two CHARACTERS in a POEM or between two POETS. In a *flyting* the poets attack each other in scurrilous VERSE, filled with vigorous and vulgar invective and profanity. *The Flyting of Dunbar and Kennedie* is an example from sixteenth-century Scotland.

Foil: A *foil* is literally a "leaf" or sheet of bright metal placed under a piece of jewelry to increase its brilliance. In literature, by extension, the term is applied to any person or sometimes an object that through strong contrast underscores or enhances the distinctive characteristics of another. Thus, Laertes, Fortinbras, and even the Players—all of whom are willing and able to take action with less reason than Hamlet has—serve as *foils* to Hamlet. Usually in soliloquies, Hamlet explicitly recognizes that the *foils'* readiness to act accentuates his own delays.

Folio: A standard-size sheet of paper folded in half. The term is also used to describe a volume made up of *folio* sheets—that is, whose SIGNATURES result from sheets folded to two leaves or four pages. It is the largest regular BOOK SIZE. Shakespeare's PLAYS were first assembled in a *folio* edition in 1623, and the term *folio* is used to designate any of the early collections of Shakespeare's works. Hence, it takes on a special meaning, referring in this case to content rather than BOOK SIZE. The word is also used by editors and printers to refer to page numbers.

Folk Ballad: An anonymous BALLAD transmitted by oral tradition and usually existing in many variant forms. In America *folk ballad* is often associated with the FOLK SONGS of the people of the Appalachian mountains, of the cowboys of the western plains, and of the labor movement. The term is frequently, though inappropriately, used today by popular singers to designate a kind of contemporary SONG, usually accompanied by a guitar, that simulates *folk ballads.* See BALLAD and FOLK SONG.

Folk Drama: In its stricter and older sense, as usually employed by folklorists, the term means dramatic activities of the folk—the unsophisticated treatment of folk THEMES by the folk themselves, particularly activities connected with popular festivals and religious rites (for the development of ancient Greek DRAMA from such forms, see DRAMA). Medieval *folk drama* took such forms as the sword dance, the St. George PLAY, and the mummers' play. The MEDIEVAL religious DRAMA, though based on scriptural materials and a religion with a fully developed theology, is by some regarded as a form of *folk drama,* and the "folk" CHARACTER of such twentieth-century plays as Marc Connelly's *Green Pastures* is commonly recognized. The religious DRAMA of the Middle Ages (see MEDIEVAL DRAMA), however, is usually treated as a special FORM, not as *folk drama.*

Another sense in which *folk drama* is being employed, especially in America, includes PLAYS that, while written by sophisticated and consciously artistic playwrights, reflect the customs, language, attitudes, and environmental difficulties of the folk. These PLAYS are commonly performed, not by the folk themselves, but by amateur or professional actors. They tend to be realistic, close to the soil, and sympathetically human. The plays of J. M. Synge, Lady Gregory, and other authors of the CELTIC RENAISSANCE and the American plays by Paul Green and others published in the several volumes of *Carolina Folk-Plays* are examples. The latter reflect especially the life of the Negro and the Southern "mountain folk."

[Reference: E. K. Chambers, *The English Folk-Play* (1933).]

Folk Epic: An EPIC by an unknown author or authors or of doubtful attribution or assumed to be the product of communal composition. See EPIC, ART EPIC.

Folklore: A term first used by W. J. Thoms in the middle of the nineteenth century as a substitute for "popular antiquities." The existence of varied conceptions of the term makes definition difficult. The one adopted by the Folklore Society of London about 1890 is: "The comparison and identification of the survivals of archaic beliefs, customs, and traditions in modern ages." Alexander H. Krappe, in *The Science of Folk-lore* (1930) affirms that *folklore* "limits itself to a study of the unrecorded traditions of the people as they appear in popular fiction, custom and belief, magic and ritual," and he regards it as the function of *folklore* to reconstruct the "spiritual history" of the human race from a study of the ways and sayings of the folk as contrasted with sophisticated thinkers and writers. Although concerned primarily with the psychology of early peoples or with that of the less cultured classes of society, some of the forms of *folklore* (for example, superstitions and proverbial sayings) belong also to the life of modern peoples, literate as well as illiterate, and may therefore be transmitted by written record as well as by word of mouth. *Folklore* includes MYTHS, LEGENDS, STORIES, RIDDLES, PROVERBS, NURSERY RHYMES, charms, spells, omens, beliefs of all sorts, popular BALLADS, cowboy SONGS, plant lore, animal lore, and customs dealing with birth, initiation, courtship, marriage, death, and work and amusements. The relations of *folklore* to sophisticated literature are important but not always easy to trace. A FOLKTALE may be retold by an author writing for a highly cultivated audience and later in a changed form again be taken over by the folk. Folk customs are associated with the development of dramatic activity because of the custom of performing PLAYS at folk festivals.

Literature is full of elements taken over from *folklore*, and some knowledge of the formulas and CONVENTIONS of *folklore* can aid the understanding of great literature. The acceptance of the rather childish love-test in *King Lear* may rest on the fact that the MOTIF was an already familiar one in *folklore*. The effects of such works as Coleridge's *Christabel* or Keats's *Eve of St. Agnes* depend on the recognition of popular beliefs, while some familiarity with fairy lore is necessary if one is to appreciate fully the quality of James Stephens's *The Crock of Gold*. The MEDIEVAL ROMANCE *Sir Gawain and the Green Knight*, written for a cultivated audience, centers on the folk formula of the challenging of a mortal by a supernatural being to a beheading contest: the binding force of the covenant between Gawain and the Green Knight is explained by primitive attitudes rather than by rational rules of conduct. Shakespeare's *Hamlet* is a retelling of an old, popular tale of the "exile-and-return" FORMULA and may have its origins, as Francis Fergusson has suggested, in a series of religious rituals.

The study of *folklore* in America, particularly that of the cowboy, the mountaineer, and the Negro, has received increasing attention in the twentieth century.

[References: Jan Harold Brunvand, *The Story of American Folklore: An Introduction* (1968); Richard M. Dorson, ed., *Folklore and Folklife: An Introduction* (1972), and *Handbook of American Folklore* (1983); Sir James G. Frazer, *The Golden Bough*, 3rd ed., 9 vols. (1913, reprinted 1980); G. L. Gomme, *Handbook of Folklore* (1890, reprinted 1967); E. S. Hartland, *The Science of Fairy Tales* (1890); A. H. Krappe, *Science of Folklore* (1930, reprinted 1974); J. A. Macculloch, *The Childhood of Fiction* (1905).]

Folk Song: A SONG of unknown authorship preserved and transmitted by oral tradition. It is generally believed to be the expression of a whole singing community. *Folk songs* are very old and appear in all cultures, although they flourish best in illiterate communities. Today there is a self-conscious effort by popular singers and composers to simulate the effects of *folk songs* in their BALLADS and protest SONGS. See BALLAD and FOLK BALLAD.

Folktale: A short NARRATIVE handed down through oral tradition, with various tellers and groups modifying it, so that it becomes a STORY of cumulative authorship. Most *folktales* eventually move from oral tradition to written form. Noted collections of such *tales* from oral tradition have been made, among them Jakob and Wilhelm Grimm's collection of *Märchen*, which resulted from their interviews with German peasants who retold stories handed down in their families over generations. *The Thousand and One Nights, or Arabian Nights' Entertainments* derives from Persian and Egyptian *folktales*. In

America a famous example is Joel Chandler Harris's Uncle Remus stories, a collection of transplanted African *folktales* told by plantation slaves. The frontier has been an active source for American *folktales* dealing with characters such as Paul Bunyan, Johnny Appleseed, John Henry, and Mike Fink. The content of *folktales* ranges from MYTH through LEGENDS, FABLES, TALL TALES, ghost stories, and humorous ANECDOTES to FAIRY TALES. On occasion a CHARACTER or a STORY that had a clear literary origin by various means becomes folk property and functions as a *folktale*. Rip Van Winkle, created by Washington Irving, and Uncle Tom, from Harriet Beecher Stowe's *Uncle Tom's Cabin*, are examples.

[References: Richard M. Dorson, *America in Legend* (1974); Stith Thompson, *The Folktale* (1946).]

Foot: In PROSODY the unit of RHYTHM in a VERSE, whether QUANTITATIVE or ACCENTUAL-SYLLABIC. The concept of *foot* and the names by which the various *feet* are known in English PROSODY are borrowings from CLASSICAL PROSODY, which has only QUANTITATIVE VERSE. The result has been substantial confusion. Most English prosodists consider the fundamental character of regular English VERSE (as opposed to OLD ENGLISH VERSE or experimental VERSE) to be a RHYTHM consisting of units of accented and unaccented syllables, arranged in various patterns, called *feet*. The LINE of VERSE usually consists of definite numbers of specific *feet*. The most common English *feet* are:

> IAMB: ˘ ´, as in "re‍túrn"
>
> TROCHEE: ´ ˘, as in "dóuble"
>
> ANAPEST: ˘ ˘ ´, as in "contravéne"
>
> DACTYL: ´ ˘ ˘, as in "mérrily"
>
> SPONDEE: ´ ´, as in "fóotbáll"

The PYRRHIC: ˘ ˘, as in "the sea|son of|mists," is usually included, although a few prosodists deny it a place in English VERSE, believing that an accented syllable must always be present in a *foot*. In any event, it is virtually inconceivable that a whole POEM could be written in the *pyrrhic rhythm*, if, indeed, it be a *rhythm* at all.

Other *feet* than these are sometimes used in English VERSE, most of them being of CLASSICAL origin and occurring sporadically in English and frequently appearing to result from, or at least to be describable as, SUBSTITUTION when they do occur. Among them are:

> AMPHIBRACH: ˘ ´ ˘, as in "arrángement"
>
> AMPHIMACHER: ´ ˘ ´, as in "áltitúde"
>
> ANTIBACCHIUS: ´ ´ ˘, as in "hígh móuntain"

BACCHIUS: ⌣ ⁄⁄, as in "aboveboard"

CHORIAMBUS: ⁄ ⌣ ⌣ ⁄, as in "year upon year"

PAEON: ⁄ ⌣ ⌣ ⌣, as in "vegetable," although the accent may occupy any one of the four possible positions in a PAEON.

See METER, SCANSION.

Foregrounding: The effect, in any art, of giving emphatic but unaccustomed prominence to something. A *line* of *verse* ordinarily foregrounds a regular *rhythm* in language not found in speech or *prose*. Once a *verse* idiom becomes established, the prevailing rhythm recedes into the "background" so that a different rhythm will be foregrounded. In Hopkins's line "Generations have trod, have trod, have trod," the double *trochee* "generations" is foregrounded against the surrounding background of *iambs*. The management of *foregrounding* is one of the most powerful devices available to the artist.

Foreshadowing: The arrangement and presentation of events and information in a FICTION or a DRAMA in such a way that later events in the work are prepared for. *Foreshadowing* can result from the establishment of a MOOD or ATMOSPHERE, as in Hardy's *The Return of the Native* or the first ACT of *Hamlet*. It can result from an event that adumbrates the later ACTION, as does the SCENE with the witches at the beginning of *Macbeth*. It can result from the appearance of physical objects or facts, as the clues do in a DETECTIVE STORY, or from the revelation of a fundamental and decisive character trait, as in the opening chapter of Edith Wharton's *The House of Mirth*. In all cases, the purpose of *foreshadowing* is to prepare the reader or viewer for ACTION to come.

Foreword: A short, introductory statement that explains some aspect of the work to follow and puts the reader in a proper relation to it. *Foreword* is virtually synonymous with PREFACE or INTRODUCTION, except that a *foreword* is often by a person other than the author of the main work, whereas a PREFACE or INTRODUCTION is usually by the author.

Forgeries, Literary: Plagiarists offer as their own what someone else has written. Literary forgers offer as the genuine writing of another what they have themselves composed. Their motive may be to supply authority for some religious or political doctrine or scheme, or it may be to cater to some prevailing literary demand (as when spurious BALLADS were composed in the eighteenth century in response to the romantic interest in old BALLADS), or it may be, as Bacon would say, "for the love of the lie itself." *Literary forgeries* seem to be numerous in all countries and in all ages. A book of nearly 300 pages by J. A. Farrer gives accounts of many famous *literary forgeries,* yet, as Andrew Lang says, several additional volumes would be needed to make the account of known forgeries complete. It is possible here to call attention to but a few cases.

The Greek statesman Solon inserted forged VERSES in the revered *Iliad* to further his political purposes. A forged "diary" of a supposed soldier in the Trojan War, Dares the Phrygian, actually composed by some Roman about the fourth century after Christ, had the effect of turning the sympathy of European peoples from the Greeks to the Trojans and of supplying an account of the war that for over a thousand years was accepted as more "authentic" than Homer's. In addition it supplied the kernel for what developed into one of the most famous love stories of all time, that of Troilus and Cressida. A famous Italian scholar, Carlo Sigonio, about 1582 composed what pretended to be the lost *Consolatio* of Cicero. The imitation was so clever and the genuineness of the document so effectively argued by Sigonio himself that, although there was always some doubt, it was not till 200 years later that the facts were discovered.

In English literary history an example is afforded by Thomas Chatterton (1752–1770), the "boy poet," who wrote faked POEMS and PROSE pieces supposed to have been written by a fifteenth-century priest. Chatterton was only twelve years old when he began his forgeries, but his imitation of medieval English was so clever and his actual poetic gifts were so great that his efforts attracted wide attention before his suicide at the age of eighteen. About the same time came another famous case of an effort to supply the current romantic interest in the medieval and the primitive with supposedly ancient pieces of literature, James Macpherson's "Ossianic" poems (1760–1765). Macpherson seems to have made some use of genuine Celtic tradition but in the main to have composed himself the epic *Fingal,* which he claimed had been written in the third century by Ossian, son of Fingal. Macpherson's public was sharply divided between those who accepted this "discovery" as geniune and those who, like Doctor Johnson, denounced it as an imposture. The episode is referred to as the OSSIANIC CONTROVERSY.

Just as it is not easy for editors and publishers to detect all plagiarized writing presented to them, so it is difficult for them to avoid being exploited by literary forgers, who sometimes mix the authentic and the spurious so cleverly that not only the editors and publishers, but the general public and professional CRITICS, are deceived. And this is as true of the twentieth century as of the eighteenth. The most celebrated recent case is Clifford Irving's spurious AUTOBIOGRAPHY of Howard Hughes that fooled (for a while) a number of readers, magazines, and publishers. See PLAGIARISM.

Another kind of *literary forgery* results from the manufacture of spurious EDITIONS of works. The works themselves are authentic—they were actually written by the authors to whom they are ascribed—but the editions are not authentic. Such *forgery* is directed toward the bibliophile rather than the literary scholar, although such EDITIONS produce bibliographical difficulties. Thomas Wise, for example, created a number of bogus first EDITIONS of nineteenth-century English works.

[References: Denis Dutton, ed., *The Forger's Art* (1983); J. A. Farrer, *Literary Forgeries* (1907); Wilfred Partington, *Forging Ahead* (1939, rev. ed. 1946).]

Form: A term used in CRITICISM to designate the organization of the elementary parts of a work of art in relation to its total EFFECT. VERSE *form* refers to the organization of rhythmic units in a LINE. STANZA *form* refers to the organization of the VERSES. The *form* of the IMAGES refers to the interrelationships among the IMAGES in a work. The *form* of the ideas refers to the organization or structure of thought in the work.

In a common division, CRITICS distinguish between *form* and content, *form* being the pattern or STRUCTURE or organization that is employed to give expression to the content. A similar distinction is often made between "conventional" *form* and organic *form*. This is the difference between what Coleridge called "mechanic" *form* and *form* that "is innate; it shapes, as it develops, itself from within, and the fullness of its development is one and the same with the perfection of its outward form." Another way of expressing this difference is to think of "conventional" *form* as representing an ideal pattern or shape that precedes the content and meaning of the work and of organic *form* as representing a pattern or shape that develops as it is because of the content and meaning of the work. "Conventional" *form* presupposes certain characteristics of organization or pattern that must be present in the work and that are used as tests for the ultimate merit of the work as art— the chief one usually being UNITY. Organic *form* asserts that each POEM has, as Herbert Read has said, "its own inherent laws, originating with its very invention and fusing in one vital unity both structure and content."

Form is also used to designate the common attributes that distinguish one GENRE from another. In this sense *form* becomes an abstract term describing not one work but the commonly held qualities of many. This abstract *form* in NEOCLASSIC periods tends to become a legislative device, a congeries of "rules" to be followed. See STRUCTURE, GENRE.

Formal Criticism: CRITICISM that examines a work of art in terms of the characteristics of the type or GENRE to which it belongs. See CRITICISM, TYPES OF; FORM.

Formal Essay: A serious, dignified, logically organized ESSAY, written to inform or persuade. See ESSAY.

Formal Satire: One of the two broad, major categories of SATIRE; the other is INDIRECT SATIRE. In *formal* (or direct) *satire*, the PERSONA speaks in the first person either directly to the reader or to the ADVERSARIUS in the SATIRE. See ADVERSARIUS, SATIRE.

Formalism or Formalist Criticism: A term sometimes applied to any CRITIC or CRITICISM that seems to emphasize the FORM of the artwork, with "form" variously construed to mean generic form, type, verbal form, grammatical and syntactical form, rhetorical form, or VERSE form (STANZA, RHYME, METER, etc.) It is applied to NEW CRITICS, CHICAGO CRITICS, and students of PROSODY, such as Paul Fussell (in view of his *Theory of Prosody in Eighteenth-Century England* and *Poetic Meter and Poetic Form*). In most cases the name is applied to the species of study that this *Handbook* categorizes as the OBJECTIVE THEORY OF ART. One can usefully distinguish "containing form" from "shaping form" (as does Northrop Frye in *Anatomy of Criticism*, 1957), but, beyond that, the whole FORM-formal-FORMALISM family is beset by problems of reference. With a clearly tangible object of culture, such as a cup, we can use Aristotle's echelon of four "causes"—final, formal, material, and efficient—and say that the size and shape are the formal cause, which some efficient cause (a cupmaker, say) imposes on some material cause (such as wood or clay) to serve some final cause, such as holding liquids. With artworks, however, it is difficult to specify what the FORM is, since PLOT may be the form that contains the CHARACTERS, the characters the form that contains the thoughts and feelings, the thoughts and feelings the form that shapes the DICTION, the diction the form that shapes the acoustic effects, and so on.

Formalism (Russian): A lively and important multidisciplinary school of thinkers and artists who flourished around 1920. Influenced by Husserlian PHENOMONOLOGY and Saussurean LINGUISTICS, Russian Formalists emphasized FORM over content, "device" over message, and strangeness over familiarity. Everyday language being sentenced to fall into banality and automatic flatness, it is the function of literary language by its unusual "literariness" to break up predictable patterns—of sound, grammar, PLOT—by means of conspicuous "defamiliarization" (*ostranenie*) that restores freshness and vitality to language. The most important members of the school—who resisted being called a school and even being classified as Formalists—were Viktor Šklovskij, Roman Jakobson, Boris Èjchenbaum, Lev Jakubinskij, Vladimir Propp, Boris Tomaševskij, Jurij Tynjanov, Grigorij Vinokur, and Viktor Žirmunskij.

[References: Victor Erlich, *Russian Formalism: History—Doctrine*, 3rd ed. (1969); Frederic Jameson, *The Prison-House of Language: A Critical Account of Structuralism and Russian Formalism* (1972); Peter Steiner, *Russian Formalism: A Metapoetics* (1984).]

Format: The physical makeup of a book, MAGAZINE, or newspaper, including such matters as page size, typeface, margins, paper, and binding. *Format* has been extended in meaning to include the general structure or plan of a wide variety of things and activities; one may speak, for example, of the *format* of a debate.

Formative Theory: A form of FILM CRITICISM that, looking on the actual world as the raw material with which the creative IMAGINATION works, places its emphasis on how various FILM techniques are employed to manipulate that material, using it not as statement in itself but as a means by which statements are made. It is broadly but not exclusively related to EXPRESSIONISM in DRAMA.

Formula: A hackneyed sequence of events characteristic of some popular forms of writing. "Low budget" motion pictures with similar PLOTS are said to follow a *formula*. In television dramatic series *formula* is almost always present and easily recognizable. Many DETECTIVE STORIES and WESTERN STORIES are written to *formula*, in that the same ingredients show up in much the same relationships in their PLOTS. The number of PLOTS is limited, however, and the implicit criticism of triteness in the term *formula* is probably as much a condemnation of inartistic execution as it is of stereotyped PLOT.

Foul Copy: Manuscript that has already been used for typesetting by a printer. It bears printer's marks, editor's queries, and frequently spike holes, ink stains, and fingerprints (and occasionally authors' execrations against editors).

Foul Proof: Marked printer's proof from which corrections have been made. See FOUL COPY.

Four Ages: A scheme of great antiquity, dividing history into a line or cycle of ages, conventionally associated with gold, silver, brass, and iron. The scheme appears in Hindu and Roman cosmologies, in Giambattista Vico's fourfold vision of the world (more or less preserved in the structure of Joyce's *Finnegans Wake*), in a wittily rearranged order (iron, gold, silver, brass) in Thomas Love Peacock's "The Four Ages of Poetry," and in Northrop Frye's *Anatomy of Criticism* (in the form of a cycle of MYTH, ROMANCE, MIMESIS, IRONY).

Four Senses of Interpretation: The levels frequently used in interpreting scriptural and allegorical materials; they are the literal, the allegorical, the moral or tropological, and the spiritual or anagogical. See ANAGOGE.

"Fourteeners":   A VERSE FORM consisting of fourteen syllables arranged in IAMBIC feet. The commonest employment of the measure is in COUPLETS of IAMBIC HEPTAMETER. George Chapman in the 1590s translated the *Iliad* in this METER, but in recent years the FORM has fallen into disuse.

Fourth Wall: The invisible wall of a room through which the audience witnesses the ACTION occurring on a stage imagined as a room with four walls and a ceiling, the *fourth wall* being presented as just behind the CURTAIN. One of the most striking uses of the *fourth wall* was in a SCENE of William Gillette's PLAY *Sherlock Holmes,* when Holmes, sealed in a room, taps the walls and continues tapping the *fourth wall* while the sound effects of the tapping continue without interruption. See BOX SET.

Framework-Story: A STORY inside a narrative setting or *framework,* a STORY within a STORY. This is a CONVENTION frequently used in CLASSICAL and modern writing. Perhaps the best-known examples are found in the *Arabian Nights,* the *Decameron,* and the *Canterbury Tales.* Chaucer, for example, introduced in his Prologue a group of people making a pilgrimage. We are told something about each of his CHARACTERS, how they meet at the Tabard Inn, and how they proceed on their journey. This general setting may be thought of as the *framework;* the stories that the various pilgrims tell along the way are stories within the general *framework,* or *framework-stories.* The extent to which the *framework* becomes an actual PLOT within which other PLOTS are inserted varies greatly. In the *Decameron* the tellers of the tales assemble and talk, and there is no PLOT in the *framework.* In the *Canterbury Tales* there is a PLOT in the *framework,* although a very limited one. In a work like *Moby-Dick,* in which the NARRATOR participates in an ACTION within which the story of Ahab's quest for the whale occurs, both *framework* and *framework-story* are inextricably mixed. *Frankenstein* is a frame-tale, since the STORY of Victor Frankenstein and his monster-creature is included in Robert Walton's account of his northward explorations, related in letters to his sister. What most readers think of as the real story of *Wuthering Heights* is the account of Heathcliff, but that is included inside the first-person account of the "outer" NARRATOR, Lockwood. A half-century later, Joseph Conrad was fond of a similar form of framing, which led in some cases to three or four degrees of quotation as the nameless narrator tells what a story-telling character (Marlow, say) tells about what other characters say, and so forth. The *framework* was particularly popular around the turn of the twentieth century with such writers as Kipling, in "The Man Who Would Be King"; Joel Chandler Harris, in the Uncle Remus stories; Mark Twain, in "Jim Baker's Blue Jay Yarn"; and Henry James, in *The Turn of the Screw,* in which the STORY does not return to the frame situation at the end, with the result that the unclosed frame leaves unanswered questions.

Franco-Norman: A term applied to material written in England shortly after the Norman Conquest by Normans or persons of Norman descent using the Norman DIALECT of French. See ANGLO-NORMAN (LANGUAGE).

Free Verse: POETRY based on the irregular rhythmic CADENCE of the recurrence, with variations, of phrases, images, and syntactical patterns rather than the conventional use of METER. RHYME may or may not be present in *free verse,* but when it is, it is used with great freedom. In conventional VERSE the unit is the FOOT, or the LINE; in *free verse* the units are larger, sometimes being paragraphs or STROPHES. If the *free verse* unit is the line, as it is in Whitman, the line is usually determined by qualities of RHYTHM and thought rather than FEET or syllabic count.

   Such use of CADENCE as a basis for POETRY is very old. The poetry of the BIBLE, particularly in the King James Version, which attempts to approximate the Hebrew CADENCES, rests on cadence and PARALLELISM. The *Psalms* and The *Song of Solomon* are noted examples of *free verse.* Milton sometimes substituted rhythmically constructed VERSE paragraphs for metrically regular LINES, notably in the CHORUSES of *Samson Agonistes,* as this example shows:

> But patience is more oft the exercise
> Of Saints, the trial of thir fortitude,
> Making them each his own Deliver,
> And Victor over all
> That tyranny or fortune can inflict.

Walt Whitman's *Leaves of Grass* was a major experiment in cadenced rather than metrical VERSIFICATION. The following lines are typical:

> All truths wait in all things,
> They neither hasten their own delivery nor resist it,
> They do not need the obstetric forceps of the surgeon.

Matthew Arnold sometimes used *free verse,* notably in "Dover Beach." But it was the French POETS of the late nineteenth century—Rimbaud, Laforgue, and others—who, in their revolt against the tyranny of strict French VERSIFICATION, established the VERS LIBRE movement, from which the name *free verse* comes.

   In the twentieth century *free verse* has had widespread usage by most POETS, of whom Rilke, St.-John Perse, T. S. Eliot, Ezra Pound, Wallace Stevens, and William Carlos Williams are representative. Such a list indicates the great variety of subject matter, effect, and TONE that is possible in *free verse* and shows that it is much less a rebellion against traditional English METRICS than a modification and extension of the resources of our language. Eliot, as quoted by Pound, once remarked that "no *vers* is *libre* for the man who wants to do a good job," meaning, probably, that language or any other form of conduct is inescapably so governed by rules and CONVENTIONS that any sense of "freedom" has to be illusory.

[References: Laurence Binyon, *Tradition and Reaction in Modern Poetry* (1926, reprinted 1970); Charles O. Hartman, *Free Verse* (1980); Graham Hough, *Free Verse* (1958); Amy Lowell, *Tendencies in Modern American Poetry* (1917); J. L. Lowes, *Convention and Revolt in Poetry* (1919); Walter Sutton, *American Free Verse* (1973).]

French Forms: (Sometimes referred to as the FIXED POETIC FORMS.) A name given to certain definitely prescribed VERSE patterns that originated in France largely during the time of the TROUBADOURS. The more usual *French forms* are: BALLADE, CHANT ROYAL, RONDEAU, RONDEL, SESTINA, TRIOLET, and VILLANELLE. These are all explained in their proper places in this *Handbook*.

[References: Helen Louise Cohen, *Lyric Forms from France* (1922); Clive Scott, *French Verse-Art* (1980).]

Freudianism: The psychological doctrines advanced by Sigmund Freud and his disciples. In Freud's system the great source of psychic energy is in the unconscious, which influences every action but through forces and means not subject to recall or understanding by normal processes. The mind has three major areas of activity: the id, which is in the unconscious and is a reservoir of instinctual impulses, working always for the gratification of its instincts (primarily sexual) through the pleasure principle; the superego, which is an internal censor bringing social pressures—reality—to bear on the id; and the ego, which is the part of the id that is modified by contact with the social world. The ego, which is consciousness, must always mediate among the demands of social pressure or reality, the libidinal demands for satisfaction arising from the id, and the claims of the superego. A mature ego conforms to the reality principle, i.e., the denial of immediate pleasure to avoid painful consequences or to make gratification possible later. Furthermore, the ego has various defense mechanisms, in addition to repression and sublimation, with which to protect itself against the demands of the id. In a rare expression of optimism, Freud once said, "Where id was, ego shall be."

Although Freud himself was most interested in the pathological aspects of psychoanalysis, the schema of the human mind that he unfolded has had incalculable influence on almost all literary forms and practically all writers in the twentieth century. The emphasis on the unconscious with its hidden springs of motivation, the drama of the eternal conflict of id, ego, and superego, and the PLOT situations inherent in relationships such as those in the OEDIPUS COMPLEX—all have been grist for the mills of the creative mind as well as instruments for the critical faculty. Biographers have tried to unlock the mysteries of creative personalities, as Marie Bonaparte did in *The Life and Works of Edgar Allan Poe*. CRITICS have seen character relationships in literary works in new lights, as Ernest Jones did in *Hamlet and Oedipus*. Imaginative overviews of literary history colored by psychoanalytical assumptions have been taken, as Leslie Fiedler did in *Love and Death in the American Novel*. Freud and his disciples, whether understood or misunderstood, used properly or improperly, have proved a fructifying force in contemporary literature.

[Reference: F. J. Hoffman, *Freudianism and the Literary Mind*, 2nd ed. (1957).]

Freytag's Pyramid: A diagrammatic outline of the STRUCTURE of a five-ACT TRAGEDY, given by Gustav Freytag in *Technik des Dramas* (1863):

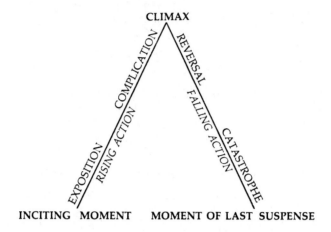

This pyramid has been widely accepted as a means of getting at the PLOT STRUCTURE of many kinds of FICTION in addition to DRAMA. See appropriate entries for the terms on the pyramid, PLOT, and DRAMATIC STRUCTURE.

[Reference: G. Freytag, *The Technique of the Drama* (1863, tr., reprinted 1968).]

Frontier Literature: In America, writing about the frontier and frontier life. Up to 1890, when all the free lands had generally been claimed, one aspect of American history was the steady westward movement of the frontier. Cooper, for example, could write of the frontier as being in New York State; Brackenridge in *Modern Chivalry* saw the wilds of Pennsylvania as the outer edge of cultivation; Simms in his border romances could see Georgia and Alabama as untamed wildernesses. It has been observed that Horace Greeley, when he enjoined young men to "go west," was probably thinking about Pittsburgh. Mark Twain in *Roughing It* could picture a primitive West. The extent to which this westward-moving frontier colored and shaped American thought and life and the extent to which its passing marked a sharp turn in the character of the American experience are matters of debate among historians and literary scholars. But, whatever one may think of Frederick Turner's much-praised and often-attacked thesis that the frontier has been the dominant influence in American history, there is little question that it has consistently found literary expression in a robust, humorous, often crude body of SONGS, TALES, and books that have been marked by a realistic view of life, sanguine contemplation of violence, and immense gusto. Much of the writing of this frontier was subliterary, confined to oral tradition and to newspapers, but it kept constantly alive in America a hearty HUMOR and a healthy REALISM, even in the face of the GENTEEL TRADITION. Important writers in the frontier tradition have been T. B. Thorpe, Timothy Flint, Augustus Baldwin Longstreet, Joseph Glover Baldwin, Artemus Ward, Caroline Kirkland, Joseph Kirkland, Bret Harte, Mark Twain, and Hamlin Garland. Whether the ultimate effect of the frontier on writers growing up in it was good or bad was a question that precipitated one of the most bitter critical controversies in American literary history, that between Van Wyck Brooks and Bernard De Voto over Brooks's thesis that the frontier was one of the stifling and frustrating influences that bridled Mark Twain's genius. Some of Larry McMurty's NOVELS—*Leaving Cheyenne; Horseman, Pass By; The Last Picture Show*—qualify as the contemporary counterpart of *frontier literature.*

[References: William Humphrey, *Ah, Wilderness!: The Frontier in American Literature* (1977); Howard Mumford Jones, *The Frontier in American Fiction* (1956); Annette Kolodny, *The Land Before Her* (1984).]

Fu: A technical term used in the Briggsian school of alfresco FILM CRITICISM; appropriated from the Chinese "kung fu," the Briggsian application of *fu* means mindless violence. The term seldom appears alone; instead, it is used as a suffix appended to the instrument or perpetrator of the violence, as in "firehose *fu*," "chainsaw *fu*," or "bimbo *fu.*"

Fugitives, The: A group of POETS and CRITICS associated with Vanderbilt University in Nashville, Tennessee, who in the 1920s published the MAGAZINE *The Fugitive.* They later came to be known as the *Fugitive*–Agrarians. See AGRARIANS.

Funambulism: Literally tightrope walking. The term has been used to describe the sense of precariousness and danger apparent in some modern writing; hence, it is a way of expressing anxiety. Behind it is the idea that, in an age of uncertainties, the writer and the intellectual must always be an acrobat, engaging in difficult balancing acts between extremes.

Fundamental Image: A central or controlling figure around which a work is organized. When the controlling figure is a METAPHOR, it is called a CONTROLLING IMAGE, a device often used in METAPHYSICAL VERSE. *Fundamental image* is used to designate the simpler, nonmetaphorical use of some important aspect or feature of an object being described or discussed. This reduction of the complex whole to one main feature or unifying principle simplifies and focuses the description in such a way as to make for clearness. The famous description of the battle of Waterloo, in which Victor Hugo employed the outline of the letter *A* as illustrative of the position of the various armies, is a notable example of the clarifying value of the *fundamental image.* A more recent example is the passage in T. S. Eliot's "Burnt Norton" beginning "Here is a place of disaffection," which seems general and even rather vague until one associates the TONE and details with the Gloucester Road underground station. See CONTROLLING IMAGE.

Fused Rhyme: A curious phenomenon, scarcely found anywhere in English outside a few POEMS by Gerard Manley Hopkins, in which a *rhyme* sound is begun but suspended at the end of a LINE and is not completed until the beginning of the next. Here are three instances from Hopkins's "The Wreck of the Deutschland":

> leeward . . . drew her / Dead . . . endured.

> rest of them . . . unconfessed of
>   them . . . breast of the / Maiden

> door / Drowned . . . Reward . . . Lord.

Fustian: A coarse, thick, short-napped cotton cloth, usually dyed some dark color to resemble velveteen. By extension, it is used as a derogatory term for overblown, pretentious, empty speech or writing. Thomas Heywood, in *Faire Maid of the Exchange* (II, iii), speaks of "Some scurvy quaint collection of *fustian* phrases, and uplandish words."

G

Gaelic Movement: A movement that began late in the nineteenth century, especially as embodied in the Gaelic League, founded by Douglas Hyde in 1893, which aimed at the preservation of the Gaelic language. Celtic speech had been gradually giving way to English since the seventeenth century and had not been permitted in the new schools established in the middle of the nineteenth century. The *Gaelic Movement* attempted to foster the production of a new native IRISH LITERATURE in Gaelic. Hyde himself wrote PLAYS in Gaelic. Though the movement attracted wide attention and some controversy, it has not been notably successful in stopping the advance of English as a spoken language in Ireland; and, on the literary side, it has been overshadowed by the IRISH LITERARY MOVEMENT, which encouraged the use of English in creating a new IRISH LITERATURE exploiting Irish materials. See CELTIC RENAISSANCE.

Gallicism: A word, phrase, or idiom characteristic of the French language, or a custom or turn of thought suggestive of the French people. The term is applied to any borrowing from the French, especially one in which the borrower stops short of using the French word correctly and without disguise. Although *Gallicisms* have obviously enriched and enlivened the language, they often become forms of affectation. Words like "morale" and "mystique," which look and sound French, have acquired senses in English that are different and even remote from their French meaning. The French sense of psychological *moment* (meaning "momentum") wandered into English as a "moment" of time (expanded by Ezra Pound into a title, "The Psychological Hour"). The almost meaningless word "rationale," which is Latin and strictly ought to be pronounced as four syllables (two *trochees*), has become a three-syllable AMPHIMACER as though it were French; it is not. The use of this latter pronunciation of "rationale" meaning nothing more than "reason" is one sort of *Gallicism*.

Gasconade: Since the natives of Gascony (in France) were considered inveterate boasters, *gasconade* came to mean bravado or boastful talk. Vainglorious FICTION may be called *gasconade*.

Gathering: A group of leaves in a book cut from a single printer's sheet after it has been folded. A FOLIO makes a *gathering* of two leaves or four pages, a QUARTO one of four leaves or eight pages (see BOOK SIZES). A *gathering* is often called a SIGNATURE, from the marking placed on its first page. Modern printers use *gathering* to mean the process by which SIGNATURES or *gatherings* are assembled to make a book; they rarely use it in the sense of SIGNATURE. See SIGNATURE.

Generative Metrics: A theory of METRICS employing the methods of transformational-generative LINGUISTICS. This theory sees a number of positions in a LINE rather than a number of FEET. The line "When I consider how my light is spent" is said to have ten positions rather than five IAMBIC FEET.

The STRESSES on positions are those that result from the assignment of STRESS in transformational-generative linguistics rather than how the line is read aloud, if the two differ. STRESS maximum—that is STRESS relatively greater than that in positions on either side of it—normally does not fall on a weak position. In the IAMBIC line the odd positions are usually considered weak and the even ones strong. However, certain phrasal STRESS situations—in transformational-generative linguistics—can result in STRESS maximum falling on odd positions. So far, *generative metrics* has been applied primarily to IAMBIC lines in an attempt to do for "metricality" what transformational-generative LINGUISTICS does for "grammaticality." Its use thus far has largely been by linguists rather than literary students.

[Reference: Morris Halle and S. J. Keyser, *English Stress* (1971).]

Geneva School of Criticism: A group of literary CRITICS, including Georges Poulet, Marcel Raymond, Albert Béguin, and J. Hillis Miller, who see a literary work as a series of existential expressions of the author's individual consciousness. Although they vary in method and emphasis—Poulet, for example, seeing the author's consciousness displayed in temporal and spatial coordinates and Miller in the expression of an immanent reality—the group is consistent in placing the highest value on individual consciousness and in seeing literature as the expression of that consciousness revealed in the act of reading. See also PHENOMENOLOGY.

Genre: Used in literary CRITICISM to designate the distinct types or categories into which literary works are grouped according to FORM or technique or, sometimes, subject matter. The term comes from French, in which it means "KIND" or "type." In its customary application it is used loosely, since the varieties of literary "kinds" and the principles on which they are made are numerous. The traditional *genres* include TRAGEDY, COMEDY, EPIC, LYRIC, and PASTORAL. Today a division of literature into *genres* would also include NOVEL, SHORT STORY, ESSAY, and, perhaps, TELEVISION PLAY and motion picture SCENARIO. The difficulty resulting from the loose use of the term is easily illustrated: NOVEL designates a *genre*, but so does PICARESQUE NOVEL; LYRIC designates a *genre*, but so does SONNET, as do both ELEGY and PASTORAL ELEGY.

Genre classification implies that there are groups of formal or technical characteristics existing among works of the same generic "kind" regardless of time or place of composition, author, or subject matter; and that these characteristics, when they define a particular group of works, are of basic significance in talking about literary art. Prior to the ROMANTIC AGE in England, there was a tendency to assume that literary "kinds" had an ideal existence and obeyed "laws of kind," these laws being criteria by which works could be judged. In the ROMANTIC AGE, *genre* distinctions were often looked upon merely as restatements of CONVENTIONS and were suspect. Today CRITICS frequently regard *genre* distinctions as useful descriptive devices but rather arbitrary ones. See FORM, KIND.

In painting the term *genre* is applied to works that depict ordinary, everyday life in realistic terms. By extension, the term is sometimes used in literary CRITICISM to designate a POEM that deals with commonplace or homely situations in subdued tones. By this usage, Whittier's "Snow-Bound" is sometimes called "a *genre* study."

[Reference: Rosalie L. Colie, *Genre-Theory in the Renaissance* (ed. Barbara Lewalski) (1973).]

Genre Criticism: That type of CRITICISM dedicated to defining and distinguishing GENRES and tracing their histories and interactions. It is particularly useful in understanding how a work came to be at a given time and why some problematical works have been ignored or misunderstood on account of some confusion of their category. *Moby-Dick,* say, which is classifiable as an ANATOMY, cannot be understood or enjoyed if it is approached as a NOVEL of adventure or education. See CHICAGO CRITICS; STRUCTURALISM.

A term also applied to the method of FILM CRITICISM that analyzes and evaluates a FILM in terms of the particular GENRE to which it belongs, such as WESTERN, detective, gangster, or romantic COMEDY. The GENRE FILM critic usually employs one of two distinct approaches. In the first the GENRE is seen as an original pattern or model for a kind of statement or ACTION, as an ARCHETYPE. In the second the GENRE is seen as employing a group of CONVENTIONS whose uses in a particular FILM are evaluated. *Genre criticism* is the most widely—and often unconsciously—used critical method for analyzing FILM.

[Reference: Northrop Frye, *Anatomy of Criticism* (1957).]

Genteel Comedy: A term employed by Addison to characterize such early eighteenth-century COMEDY as Cibber's *The Careless Husband.* This COMEDY was a sort of continuation of the Restoration COMEDY OF MANNERS, adapted to the polite, genteel manners of the age of Anne. Compared with Restoration COMEDY, the moral TONE was higher, the motives of the CHARACTERS more artificial, the WIT less brilliant, and the general ATMOSPHERE sentimentalized.

Genteel Tradition: A tradition of correctness and conventionality in American writing in the latter part of the nineteenth and the early part of the twentieth centuries. It was largely, although not exclusively, associated with New England. Both REALISM and NATURALISM were in differing ways reactions against the *genteel tradition.* Among its leading figures were R. H. Stoddard, Bayard Taylor, E. C. Stedman, T. B. Aldrich, and E. R. Sill. See BRAHMINS.

[Reference: George Santayana, *The Genteel Tradition* (ed. Douglas L. Wilson) (1967).]

Georgian: Used with reference to two distinct periods in English literary history. In the first it pertains to the reigns of the four Georges (1714–1830). The Romantic POETS from Wordsworth to Keats have been called *"Georgians"* in this sense. A group of minor POETS including Thomas Lovell Beddoes, W. M. Praed, and Thomas Hood are sometimes styled the "second *Georgian* school," as opposed to the earlier group. They are looked on as representing a transition from the Romantic to the Victorian poets. From 1912 to 1922 there appeared five anthologies of modern VERSE entitled *Georgian Poetry, Georgian* here referring to the reign of George V (1910–1936). These volumes, according to their editor, E. H. Marsh, reflect a belief that English POETRY was "once again putting on new strength and beauty" and beginning a new *"Georgian"* period. W. W. Gibson, Rupert Brooke, John Masefield, and Walter de la Mare are representative of the poets included. The term is also applied to the GEORGIAN AGE, the period between the beginning of the First World War and the beginning of the Second.

Georgian Age in English Literature, 1914–1940: The *Georgian Age in English Literature* begins with the First World War and extends into the Second World War. It is named for George V, although he reigned from 1910 to 1936. The beginning of the First World War effected a fundamental change in English life and thought, a true start of a new age, marked by a long and bitter struggle for national survival, by a flowering of talent and experiment in the 1920s, and by the harshness of the Great Depression in the 1930s. In 1940 England had become once more an embattled fortress, destined to suffer six years of harsh attack and the destruction of much of its finest talent.

It was a rich period for the NOVEL. The Edwardians Galsworthy, Wells, Bennett, and Conrad continued to do fine work, and in the 1920s an experimental FICTION was triumphantly developed by Dorothy Richardson, Virginia Woolf, and James Joyce. In the 1930s Aldous Huxley, Evelyn Waugh, and Graham Greene joined Maugham and Lawrence in producing FICTION that constituted a serious commentary on social and moral values. The theater was marked by the social DRAMA of Galsworthy, Jones, and Pinero, and the PLAYS of ideas of Shaw. Maugham and Coward practiced the COMEDY OF MANNERS with distinction. Throughout the *Georgian Age* Yeats was a major poetic voice, as was T. S. Eliot, whose *The Waste Land* was the most important single poetic publication. The publication of the POETRY of Gerard Manley Hopkins posthumously in 1918 added significantly to the new poetry. T. E. Hulme, Wyndham Lewis, I. A. Richards, T. S. Eliot, Herbert Read, and William Empson created an informed, basically anti-Romantic, analytical CRITICISM. MODERNISM found its doctrines and its voice and did much of its best work during the *Georgian Age.*

It was a time of national troubles, of major war, of deep depression, and of declining empire, yet the literary expression of the age was vital, fresh, and profoundly experimental. By the coming of the Second World War, the chief literary figures were turning inward, but they still showed little of the diminishment that was to come.

Georgic: A POEM about farming activities and the practical aspects of rustic life; so called from Virgil's *Georgics.*

Gest: An old word occasionally found in English, especially in literary titles from the medieval period, meaning a TALE of war or adventure, as the *Gest Historiale of the Destruction of Troy* (fourteenth century). The word is probably borrowed from the more common word in Old French, *geste,* as in the CHANSON DE GESTE. The corresponding Latin word appears in a somewhat similar sense in the title of the famous collection of STORIES written in Latin about 1250, the *Gesta Romanorum,* "deeds of the Romans."

Gestalt: A configuration of physical, biological, or psychological phenomena so constructed and interrelated that the whole possesses properties not derivable from its parts or their simple sum. As Herbert Read has suggested, such a theory is congenial to Coleridge's view of a work of art. The term comes from *Gestalt* psychology. Some literary CRITICS, among them Herbert J.

Muller, see in it a concept that allows concrete experience to precede logical analysis. Leonard Meyer has systematically applied *Gestalt* principles to the study of music, which, given its emphasis on purely formal and physical qualities, seems amenable to this kind of analysis. The *Gestalt* CRITIC sees all the elements of any work of art or literature as being variables with values that depend on their position in the "configuration" and on its total effect. A variable element like rain, say, seems more or less neutral until it becomes part of some *Gestalt*—physical and symbolic—and means one thing (positive) in Eliot's *The Waste Land* and quite another thing (negative) in Hemingway's *A Farewell to Arms.*

Ghazal, or **Ghasel:**   A flexible LYRIC form, usually in a small number of COUPLETS with or without RHYME, first employed in various Middle Eastern literatures (Persian and Arabic) and later enjoying a vogue among German ROMANTICISTS (F. Schlegel and Goethe) and just recently among contemporary American POETS.

Ghostwriter: One who does journalistic writing to be published under the name of another. Business people, artists, athletes—in fact almost anyone who is much in the public eye but who is also either unskilled or uninterested in writing—often allow their names to be attached to articles and stories relating to their special fields and written by journalists employed for the purpose. *Ghostwriting* is more frequently used in the preparation of newspaper and MAGAZINE ARTICLES than in the writing of books, although it is by no means unknown in book publishing.

Gift Books: Miscellaneous collections of literary materials—SHORT STORIES, ESSAYS, POETRY—published annually in book form for purchase as gifts. They were popular in England and America in the nineteenth century. Their value in American literary history has been great. See ANNUALS.

Gleeman: A musical entertainer among the ANGLO-SAXONS. *Gleemen* were usually traveling professionals who recited POETRY (especially STORIES) composed by others, though some of them were original POETS. They were sometimes attached to kings' courts but occupied a less dignified and permanent position than the SCOP. In the main, the SCOP composed and the *gleeman* sang or recited the SCOPS'S compositions, to the accompaniment of the harp or other instrument. Some writers, however, both medieval and modern, use the term loosely for any kind of medieval composer or reciter.

Gloss: An explanation. A difficult word in a text might be explained by a marginal or interlinear word or phrase, usually in a more familiar language. Thus, Greek manuscripts were *glossed* by Latin copyists who gave the readers the Latin word or phrase equivalent to the difficult one in Greek. Similar bilingual *glosses* were inserted in medieval manuscripts by scribes who would explain Latin words by native, vernacular words. Some of the earliest examples of written Irish, for example, are found in the margins and between the lines of Latin manuscripts written in the early Middle Ages. Extended explanatory and interpretative comment on medieval scriptural texts were called *glosses.* They have been used extensively in interpreting medieval literature in recent years. Later the word came to have a still broader use in "E. K.'s" *"Gloss"* to Spenser's *The Shepheardes Calender* (1579), which undertakes not only to explain the author's purpose and to comment on the degree of his success, but also to supply "notes" explaining difficult words and phrases and giving miscellaneous "learned" comments. The marginal *gloss* that Coleridge supplied in 1817 for his early *Rime of the Ancient Mariner* is more than a summary of the STORY; it amounts to a different version of the story, with Coleridge using the form both self-consciously and ironically. Among modern writers, Paul Valéry and James Joyce made occasional use of marginal *glosses,* as has James Dickey in one POEM.

The word is sometimes used in a derogatory sense, as when to *"gloss"* a passage means to misinterpret it and "to *gloss* over" is used in the sense of "explain away" or excuse. "Glossaries" developed from the habit of collecting *glosses* into lists.

Gnomic: Aphoristic, moralistic, sententious, from *gnome,* a pithy Greek POEM that expressed a general truth wittily. The "*Gnomic* Poets" of ancient Greece (sixth century B.C.) arranged their wise sayings in a series of MAXIMS; hence, the term *gnomic* was applied to all POETRY that dealt in a sententious way with ethical questions, such as the "wisdom" poetry of the BIBLE, the Latin *sententiae,* the Saemundian *Edda,* and the gnomic VERSES in Old English. Although more properly applied to a STYLE of POETRY, as to some of the verse of Francis Quarles, the prose style of Bacon's early ESSAYS is also called *gnomic* when marked by the use of APHORISMS.

[Reference: Blanche C. Williams, ed., *Gnomic Poetry in Anglo-Saxon* (1914).]

Gnosticism: The beliefs and practices of various cults in late pre-Christian and early Christian times. The *Gnostics* claimed that human beings had an immediate knowledge of spiritual truth that was available to them through faith alone. The *Gnostics* claimed mystic and esoteric religious insights, placed great emphasis on transcendent human knowledge, and believed that all matter is evil. They incorporated some Christian beliefs into their system. The *Gnostics* believed that the world is ruled by evil archons, one of whom was the Jehovah of the Old Testament, who held the spirit of humanity captive. Jesus Christ was interpreted as a special power (an aeon) sent from the heavens to restore to human beings the lost knowledge of their divine nature and powers. There were many cults of *Gnostics* incorporating elements of many religions in this syncretic movement, which later merged with MANICHAEISM. *Gnosticism* was the great heresy against which many of the early formal doctrinal statements of the church were formulated.

The terms *Gnosticism* and *gnostic* are used metaphorically today to describe beliefs and attitudes that assign to human beings unlimited powers of mind and knowledge to human beings and the capability of attaining their own salvation unaided.

Goliardic Verse: Lilting Latin VERSE, usually satiric, composed by university students and wandering scholars in Germany, France, and England in the twelfth and thirteenth centuries. *Goliardic verse* celebrated wine, women, and song; was often licentious; and was marked by irreverent attacks on church and clergy. Its dominant theme was CARPE DIEM. Its name comes from a legendary bishop and "archpoet," Golias. Another of the *Goliardic* POETS was Walter Map, to whom more verses have been attributed than he could possibly have written.

Gongorism: A highly affected STYLE taking its name from Luis de Góngora y Argote, a Spanish POET (1561–1627), whose writings exhibited to a high degree the various qualities characteristic of the stylistic extravagances of the time, such as the introduction of new words (NEOLOGISMS), innovations in grammar, BOMBAST, PUNS, PARADOXES, CONCEITS, and obscurity. It reflects both cultism (affected language) and conceptism (strained figures, obscure references). It has some of the qualities of EUPHUISM. See MARINISM, CONCEIT.

[References: E. K. Kane, *Gongorism and the Golden Age* (1928); Michael Woods, *The Poet and the Natural World in the Age of Gongora* (1978).]

Gothic: Though the Goths were a single Germanic tribe of ancient and early medieval times, the meaning of *Gothic* was broadened to signify Teutonic or Germanic and, later, "medieval" in general. In architecture, *Gothic,* though it may mean any style not CLASSIC, is more specifically applied to the style that succeeded the Romanesque in Western Europe, flourishing from the twelfth to the sixteenth centuries. It is marked by the pointed arch and vault, a tendency to vertical effects (suggesting aspiration), stained windows (mystery), slender spires, flying buttresses, intricate traceries, and especially by wealth and variety of detail and flexibility of spirit. Applied to literature, the term was used by the eighteenth-century NEOCLASSICISTS as synonymous with "barbaric" to indicate anything that offended their CLASSIC tastes. Addison said that in both architecture and literature those who were unable to achieve the CLASSIC graces of simplicity, dignity, and UNITY resorted to the use of foreign ornaments, "all the extravagances of an irregular fancy." The romanticists of the next generation, however, looked with favor upon the *Gothic;* to them it suggested whatever was medieval, natural, primitive, wild, free, authentic, romantic. Indeed, they praised such writers as Shakespeare and Spenser because of their *Gothic* elements—variety, richness, mystery, aspiration. Later vigorous celebrators of the *Gothic* were John Ruskin, Walter Pater, and Henry Adams. See GOTHIC NOVEL.

[References: Linda Bayer-Berenbaum, *The Gothic Imagination: Expansion in Gothic Literature and Art* (1981); Bertrand Evans, *Gothic Drama from Walpole to Shelley* (1947); G. R. Thompson, ed., *The Gothic Imagination: Essays in Dark Romanticism* (1974).]

Gothic Novel: A FORM of NOVEL in which magic, mystery, and chivalry are the chief characteristics. Horrors abound: one may expect a suit of armor suddenly to come to life, while ghosts, clanking chains, and charnel houses impart an uncanny atmosphere of terror. Although anticipations of the *Gothic novel* appear in Smollett (especially in *Ferdinand Count Fathom,* 1753), Horace Walpole was the real originator, his famous *Castle of Otranto* (1764) being the first. Its setting is a medieval castle (hence the term "Gothic") with long underground passages, trap doors, dark stairways, and mysterious rooms whose doors slam unexpectedly. William Beckford's *Vathek, an Arabian Tale* (1786) added the element of Oriental luxury and magnificence to the species. Mrs.

Anne Radcliffe's five romances (1789–1797), especially *The Mysteries of Udol-pho,* added to the popularity of the form. Her emphasis on SETTING and STORY rather than on CHARACTER delineation became conventional, as did the types of characters she employed. Succeeding writers who produced Gothic RO-MANCES include: Matthew ("Monk") Lewis, William Godwin, and Mary Woll-stonecraft Shelley, whose *Frankenstein* is a striking performance in the tradi-tion. The FORM spread to practically every European literature, being especially popular in Germany. In America the type was cultivated early by Charles Brockden Brown. The *Gothic novels* not only are of interest in them-selves but have exerted a significant influence on other forms. This influence made itself felt in the POETRY of the ROMANTIC PERIOD, as in Coleridge's *Christabel* and *Kubla Khan,* Wordsworth's *Guilt and Sorrow,* Byron's *Giaour,* and Keats's *Eve of St. Agnes.* Some of the ROMANCES were dramatized, and some DRAMAS not based on romances, like Byron's *Manfred* and Morton's *Speed the Plough,* have *Gothic* elements. The NOVELS of Scott, Charlotte Brontë, and others, as well as the mystery and horror type of SHORT STORY exploited by Poe and his successors, contain materials and devices traceable to the *Gothic novel.* The term is today often applied to works, such as Daphne du Maurier's *Rebecca,* that lack the GOTHIC setting or the medieval ATMO-SPHERE but that attempt to create the same ATMOSPHERE of brooding and unknown terror as the true *Gothic novel.* It is also applied to a host of currently popular TALES of "damsels in distress" in strange and terrifying locales—a type ridiculed as early as Jane Austen's *Northanger Abbey.* In our time the great Danish writer "Isak Dinesen" (PSEUDONYM of Karen Christence Dinesen, Baroness Blixen-Finecke) has used "Gothic" in titles to indicate simultaneously a literal SETTING in northern Europe and a fantastic spirit combining horror, crime, ROMANCE, and REALISM.

[References: Brendan Hennessy, *The Gothic Novel* (1978); Montague Sum-mers, *The Gothic Quest: A History of the Gothic Novel* (1938); Ann B. Tracy, *The Gothic Novel, 1790–1830* (1981).]

Götterdämmerung: A German word literally meaning "the twilight of the gods." It is the title of the last of Richard Wagner's music DRAMAS in *The Ring of the Nibelung.* In English the word is used to describe a massive collapse and destruction with great violence and disorder. It has certain affini-ties to APOCALYPTIC writing dealing with grandiose, unrestrained, and wild catastrophe.

Graces, The: In Greek MYTH, the three sister goddesses who confer grace, beauty, charm, and joy on human beings and NATURE. They are Aglaia (spendor or elevation), Euphrosyne (mirth), and Thalia (abundance).

Grand Style, The: A concept traceable back as far as CLASSICAL antiquity (Longius) and coming forward to theorists of the eighteenth and nineteenth centuries (Edmund Burke and Matthew Arnold), involving a host of lofty ele-ments: nobility of CHARACTER, SUBLIMITY of conception, dignified simplicity or severity of utterance, elevation of sentiment, and grandeur of scope.

"Graveyard School": A phrase used to designate a group of eighteenth-cen-tury POETS who wrote long POEMS on death and immortality. The "graveyard"

POETRY was related to early stages of the English romantic movement. The graveyard poets tried to get the atmosphere of "pleasing gloom" by realistic efforts to call up not only the horrors of death but the very "odor of the charnel house." An early exemplar or forerunner of the school was Thomas Parnell, whose "Night-Piece on Death" (1722) not only anticipates some of the sentiment of Gray's famous "Elegy Written in a Country Churchyard" (1751)—the most famous POEM produced by the group—but whose "long palls, drawn hearses, cover'd steeds, and plumes of black" show an approach to the phraseology of Robert Blair's "The Grave" (1743), one of the most typical POEMS of the movement, and of the "Night-Thoughts" (1745) of Edward Young, an influential writer of melancholy VERSE. These last two writers, says W. L. Phelps, reflect "the joy of gloom, the fondness for bathing one's temples in the dank night air and the musical delight of the screech owl's shriek." While the *Graveyard School* was philosophically contemplating immortality, the lasting effect of their POETRY, with the exception of a few pieces such as Gray's "Elegy," has been one element in the GOTHIC aspect of ROMANTICISM. In America the poetry of the *Graveyard School* was reflected in Philip Freneau's "The House of Night" (1779) and most notably in William Cullen Bryant's famous "Thanatopsis" (1817).

[Reference: Amy L. Reed, *The Background of Gray's Elegy: A Study in the Taste for Melancholy Poetry, 1700–1751* (1924, reprinted 1962).]

Great Awakening, The: A famed religious revival in America between 1735 and 1750. See AWAKENING, THE GREAT.

Great Chain of Being: The belief that everything in the created universe partakes of a hierarchical system, extending upward from inanimate matter, to things that have life but do not reason, to the rational human being, whom Pope called "a creature in a middle state," to angels, and finally to God. Each thing in nature occupies its proper place in this *great chain of being*. The idea of the universe as a hierarchical system is very old; it found expression in Plato's *Timaeus* and *The Republic;* but the figure of the *chain* is probably from Milton's LINES" . . . hanging in a golden chain / This pendent world." The concept of the *great chain of being* was powerful and widespread in the seventeenth and eighteenth centuries. Pope gave it clear expression in his *Essay on Man:*

> Vast chain of being! which from God began,
> Natures aethereal, human, angel, man,
> Beast, bird, fish, insect, what no eye can see,
> No glass can reach; from Infinite to thee,
> From thee to nothing.—On superior pow'rs
> Were we to press, inferior might on ours;
> Or in the whole creation leave a void,
> Where, one step broken, the great scale's destroy'd:
> From Nature's chain whatever link you strike,
> Tenth, or ten thousandth, breaks the chain alike.

A more optimistic concept of upward progression through the *great chain of being* was expressed by Emerson in his COUPLET:

Striving to be man, the worm
Mounts through all the spires of form.

[Reference: A. O. Lovejoy, *The Great Chain of Being: A Study in the History of an Idea*, 1936, reprinted 1964.]

Grotesque: A term applied to a decorative art in sculpture, painting, and architecture, characterized by fantastic representations of human and animal forms often combined into formal distortions of the natural to the point of comic absurdity, ridiculous ugliness, or ludicrous CARICATURE. It was so named after the ancient paintings and decorations found in the underground chambers (*grotte*) of Roman ruins. By extension, *grotesque* is applied to anything having the qualities of *grotesque* art: bizarre, incongruous, ugly, unnatural, fantastic, abnormal. Poe called one of his collections *Tales of the Grotesque and Arabesque* (1840), suggesting a fairly precise distinction between the spirits of Christian northern Europe and Muslim western Asia.

In the twentieth century *grotesque* has come to have special literary meanings. CRITICS use "the *grotesque*" to refer to special types of writing, to kinds of fictional CHARACTERS, and to subject matters. The interest in the *grotesque* is usually considered an outgrowth of contemporary interest in the irrational, distrust of any cosmic order, and frustration at our lot in the universe. In this sense, *grotesque* is the merging of the comic and tragic, resulting from our loss of faith in the moral universe essential to TRAGEDY and in a rational social order essential to COMEDY. Where nineteenth-century CRITICS like Walter Bagehot saw the *grotesque* as a deplorable variation from the normal, Thomas Mann sees it as the "most genuine style" for the modern world and the "only guise in which the sublime may appear" now. Flannery O'Connor seems to mean the same thing when she calls the *grotesque* character "man forced to meet the extremes of his own nature."

Although German writers have practiced the *grotesque* with distinction, notably Thomas Mann and Günter Grass, William Van O'Connor seems to have been correct when he called the *grotesque* an American GENRE. Sherwood Anderson called his *Winesburg, Ohio* "The Book of the Grotesque," and defined a *grotesque* CHARACTER as a person who "took one of the [many] truths to himself, called it his truth, and tried to live by it." Such a person, Anderson asserted, "became a grotesque and the truth he embraced a falsehood." But the *grotesque* can have other origins and objectives than the psychological. Whenever in modern FICTION characters appear who are either physically or spiritually deformed and perform actions that are clearly intended by the author to be abnormal, the work can be called *grotesque*. It may be used for allegorical statement, as Flannery O'Connor uses it in her NOVELS and SHORT STORIES. It may exist for comic purposes, as it does in the work of Eudora Welty. It may be the expression of a deep moral seriousness, as it is in the NOVELS and SHORT STORIES of William Faulkner. It may make a comment on human beings as animals, in works like Frank Norris's *McTeague* and *Vandover and the Brute*. It may be used for SATIRE, as Nathanael West uses it in his NOVELS. It may be a basis for social commentary, as it is in the works of Erskine Caldwell. Clearly, the *grotesque* is a mode of writing compatible with the spirit of this century and amenable to many kinds of uses.

[References: Arthur Clayborough, *The Grotesque in English Literature* (1965); Willard Farnham, *The Shakespearean Grotesque* (1971); Geoffrey Galt Harpham, *On the Grotesque* (1982); W. J. Kayser, *The Grotesque in Art and Literature* (tr. 1968); Neil Rhodes, *Elizabethan Grotesque* (1980); Philip Thomson, *The Grotesque* (1972).]

Grub Street: Because struggling hacks lived in Grub Street in London (now Milton Street), the phrase *Grub Street,* since the eighteenth century, has meant either the "tribe" of poor writers living there or the qualities that characterized such authors. *Grub Street* POETS were bitterly attacked by Pope, and *Grub Street* has been used contemptuously by Doctor Johnson, Byron, and others to suggest "literary trash."

Grundy, Mrs.: A CHARACTER from Thomas Morton's play *Speed the Plough,* who does not actually appear in the PLAY but of whose judgments everyone in the play is very much afraid. The question "What will *Mrs. Grundy* say?" points to her symbolic value as a strict upholder of social conventions and an intolerant advocate of pointless propriety.

H

Hagiography: The lives of the saints, particularly those devoted to the glorification of one or another Irish or British saint. Hence, by extension, a BIOGRAPHY that praises the virtues of its subject. Continuing certain habits of biography derived from CLASSICAL antiquity (Plutarch and Suetonius) and the New Testament—as well as legal requirements of evidence for formal canonization—*hagiography* developed a set of CONVENTIONS (such as miracles and martyrdom) that continued to influence literature, and especially DRAMA, as recently as Shaw's *Saint Joan,* Gertrude Stein's *Four Saints in Three Acts,* Eliot's *Murder in the Cathedral,* and, it can be argued, J. D. Salinger's STORIES about Seymour Glass.

Haiku: A form of Japanese POETRY that states in three LINES of five, seven, and five syllables a clear picture designed to arouse a distinct emotion and suggest a specific spiritual insight. Unlike *senryu,* which is also in seventeen syllables but has a lighter mood, *haiku* poetry is deeply serious and also profoundly conventional. Every season, element, bird, flower, insect, and so forth comes equipped with a large set of associations that the *haiku* exploits, often with astonishing originality. Approximations of the spirit of *haiku* have been found in many Western writers—Wordsworth, Thoreau, Pound, Bly, Snyder—usually in short POEMS but also in short passages of PROSE; and attempts have been made to produce translations of original *haiku* (the best by R. H. Blyth and the Greek master George Seferis), but the spirit as well as the FORM tend to get lost. For one thing, the Japanese syllable is an uncommonly short and uniform entity, typically consisting of one simple consonant followed by one simple vowel (as in "sayonara") with no marked STRESS on any syllable. Since an English syllable can contain as many as seven or eight separate sounds (as in "strengths" and "traipsed"), seventeen English syllables will probably cover significantly more time than seventeen Japanese syllables, so that someone who writes seventeen English syllables under the impression that they constitute a *haiku* is almost certainly wrong. A closer formal approximation in English would be eleven syllables arranged in a symmetrical pattern of three, five, three. (The Japanese are not fussy about the seventeen: some *haiku* run somewhat longer, and nobody objects.)
[Reference: R. H. Blyth, *A History of Haiku,* 2 vols. (1963–64).]

Half Rhyme: Imperfect RHYME, the result usually of CONSONANCE, but occasionally of ASSONANCE. See RHYME, SLANT RHYME, ASSONANCE, CONSONANCE.

Hamartia: The error, frailty, mistaken judgment, or misstep through which the fortunes of the HERO of a TRAGEDY are reversed. Aristotle asserts that the PROTAGONIST of a TRAGEDY should be a person "who is not eminently good or just, yet whose misfortune is brought about by some error or frailty." This error or frailty is not necessarily a flaw in character, although *hamartia* is often inaccurately called the tragic flaw. Aristotle sees a movement from happiness to misery as essential to TRAGEDY, and he says, "It is their characters that give men their quality, but their doings that make them happy or the opposite." Hence, *hamartia* can be an unwitting, even a necessary, misstep in "doing" rather than an error in character. *Hamartia* may be the result of bad judgment, bad character, ignorance, inherited weakness, accident, or any of many other possible causes. It must, however, express itself through a definite ACTION or the failure to perform a definite ACTION. In Aristotle *hamartia* is an element of the PLOT. See TRAGEDY.

Hapax Legomenon: Literally, from the Greek "something said only once." A word or grammatical FORM that occurs only once, either because of genuine uniqueness or because all other occurrences have been lost. Several instances turn up in CLASSICAL and medieval texts, and there are some *hapax legomena* in Shakespeare, Swift, and T. S. Eliot. The "Moby" in *Moby-Dick* seems to be something of a *hapax legomenon,* as may be the "wuthering" in *Wuthering Heights.*

Harangue: A speech designed to arouse strong emotions and delivered to a crowd in a vehement and declamatory manner. Antony's speech to the Roman populace over Caesar's body, in Shakespeare's *Julius Caesar,* is a well-known example. Today the term is often applied to any form of rabble-rousing address.

Harlem Renaissance: The first major, self-conscious literary movement of American black writers, although there had been much black writing in America earlier. Immediately after the First World War, as a result of a massive black migration to Northern cities, a group of young, talented black writers congregated in Harlem, a predominantly black section of New York City, and made it the cultural and intellectual capital of black America. Harlem became for blacks and sophisticated whites alike a center for primitive and folk culture and beauty, linked to the seductive beat of African jazz rhythms. Carl Van Vechten, a white writer, celebrated Harlem as *Nigger Heaven* in an appreciative NOVEL of that name. The artistic and literary of New York considered a visit to the Cotton Club, where Duke Ellington played his jazz, a necessary journey. DuBose Heyward and Julia Peterkin, southern novelists, gave in *Porgy* and *Scarlet Sister Mary* immensely popular pictures of primitive blacks; however, the motive force of the *Harlem Renaissance* was not this fashionable position among intellectual whites but the accumulation in Harlem of an impressively articulate group of writers who created the true power of the *Renaissance.* They were Langston Hughes, POET, novelist, and playwright; Jean Toomer, author of the distinguished collection of POETRY and poetic PROSE, *Cane;* the poets Countee Cullen and Claude McKay; the novelists Eric Waldron and Zora Neale Hurston; and the poet and novelist Arna Bontemps, who was to become the historian of the movement. The *Harlem Renaissance* was the first intellectual and artistic movement that brought black America emphatically to the attention of the entire nation. The defining event of the *Harlem Renaissance* was the publication in 1925 of an ANTHOLOGY of current black writing, *The New Negro: An Interpretation,* edited with a prophetic introduction by Alain Locke. The "New Negro," whom Locke announced and whose work he presented, found in the conditions of life, character, and experience of the black people a common and beautiful aspect of American life, and one that the "New Negro" celebrated with energy and passion.

[References: Arna Bontemps, ed., *The Harlem Renaissance Remembered* (1972); Nathan Irvin Huggins, *Harlem Renaissance* (1971); Margaret Perry, *The Harlem Renaissance* (1982).]

Harlequinade: A PLAY in which a "harlequin" or buffoon stars. See COMMEDIA DELL' ARTE, PANTOMIME.

Hartford Wits: A group of Connecticut writers, many of whom were graduates of Yale, active about the period of the American Revolution. The three most prominent were Joel Barlow, Timothy Dwight, and John Trumbull; some others in the group were Richard Alsop, Theodore Dwight, and Lemuel Hopkins. Conservative in politics and philosophy, these men were, as well, conservative in their literary models, following Addison and Pope, the two literary gods of their century. Some of their best-known works are Trumbull's *M'Fingal*, Timothy Dwight's *Conquest of Canaan* (an epic POEM of eleven books mingling Christian and Revolutionary history), and Barlow's *Columbiad,* planned as another American EPIC, a ten-book recitation of the glories of the future America as revealed to Columbus in prison. They are also known as the CONNECTICUT WITS.

Head Rhyme: ALLITERATION; REPETITION of the same sound at the beginning of two or more words or syllables. See ALLITERATION.

Headless Line: A LINE of VERSE from which an unstressed syllable has been dropped at the beginning. See CATALEXIS.

Hebraism: The attitude that subordinates all other ideals to those of conduct, obedience, and ethical purpose. It is opposed to the Hellenistic conception of life that subordinates everything to the intellectual. The two terms, *Hebraism* and HELLENISM, have each taken on a special and limited significance—neither of which is fully fair to the genius of the two peoples—as the result of critical discussion centering on the question of conduct and wisdom in living. In modern literature the most notable discussion of the two conflicting ideals is found in Matthew Arnold's *Culture and Anarchy:*

> We may regard this energy driving at practice, this paramount sense of the obligation of duty, self-control, and work, this earnestness in going manfully with the best light we have, as one force. And we may regard the intelligence driving at those ideas which are, after all, the basis of right practice, the ardent sense for all the new and changing combinations of them which man's development brings with it, the indomitable impulse to know and adjust them perfectly, as another force. . . . And to give these forces names from the two races of men who have supplied the most signal and splendid manifestations of them, we may call them respectively the forces of Hebraism and Hellenism. . . . The governing idea of Hellenism is *spontaneity of consciousness:* that of Hebraism, *strictness of conscience.*

Hedge Club: An informal group of Transcendentalists living in or near Boston, headed by Frederick Henry Hedge. See TRANSCENDENTAL CLUB.

Hedonism: A philosophical doctrine that pleasure is the chief good of human beings. It takes two forms; in one, following the doctrines of the Cyrenaic school of philosophy, founded by Aristippus in the fifth century B.C., the chief good is held to be the gratification of the sensual instincts. In the other, following Epicurus, the absence of pain rather than the gratification of pleasurable impulses is held to be the source of happiness. Today *hedonism* is generally associated with sensual gratification; its motto might be "Eat, drink, and be merry, for tomorrow we may die" (see CARPE DIEM), and it is held to be in contrast to the teachings of Epicurus. See EPICUREAN.

Hegelianism: The philosophical system devised by G. W. F. Hegel in the early nineteenth century. Its basic assumption is that what is real is rational, so that a logical relation exists among all things. Anything less than a totality of rational relationships represents distortions of reality. History is the process by which reason realizes itself in human affairs. DIALECTIC reasoning is a process by which all things pass through ascending stages, moving from THESIS to ANTITHESIS to synthesis, the synthesis then becoming a new thesis. Such DIALECTIC reasoning is the method by which human beings can understand history and the development of consciousness and freedom. Hegel's ideas were powerfully influential on many British and American writers in the nineteenth century. As modified by Karl Marx, they continue to exert great influence in human thought.

Hellenism: The Greek spirit, which manifests itself in the celebration of the intellect and of beauty. See HEBRAISM.

Hemistich: A half-LINE of VERSE. See -STICH.

Hendecasyllabic Verse: A VERSE of eleven syllables, frequent in Greek and Latin POETRY and a standard LINE in Italian poetry. The FORM was originated by Catullus. Its English users have been few, the chief among them being Tennyson.

Hendiadys: A FIGURE OF SPEECH in which an idea is expressed by giving two components as though they were independent and connecting them with a coordinating conjunction rather than subordinating one part to the other. "Try and do better" instead of "Try to do better" is an example. The *hendiadys* was common in Greek and Latin writing and continues to turn up in modern languages in certain cases in which "and" or some other coordinating conjunction joins words (like "Sturm und Drang," "sound and fury," "fun and games") not exactly on the same level. A similar sort of "SLEIGHT OF 'AND'" yields Dylan Thomas's phrase "five and country senses." Arguably, Gray's ". . . and leaves the world to darkness and to me" constitutes a *hendiadys*.

Heptameter: A LINE of VERSE consisting of seven FEET. See SCANSION.

Heptastich: A seven-LINE STANZA. See STANZA.

Heresy of Paraphrase, The: When Robert Frost remarked that POETRY is what is lost in translation, he was suggesting much the same point that modern CRITICS make when they call PARAPHRASE heretical. A work of art means what it means in the terms in which it delivers that meaning, so that paraphrase, summary, ABRIDGMENT, expansion, or TRANSLATION is bound to miss the point, usually by understating the complexity and misconstruing the uniqueness of the original statement.

[Reference: Cleanth Brooks, *The Well Wrought Urn* (1947).]

Hermeneutic Circle: The notion that a reader cannot understand any part of a text until the whole is understood, while the whole cannot be understood until all the parts are understood. Presumably, one reads piecemeal, provisionally modifying the sense of the whole as one accrues experience of the parts, and one accrues experience of the parts—including the understanding that they *are* parts—in accordance with the ever-changing experience of the whole that the parts have been constituting. You cannot interpret what a given part of *King Lear* means, let us say, until you know what the totality of the PLAY means; and you cannot know what the totality means until you know what the parts mean. W. Wolfgang Holdheim has extended such a philosophy of literary reading to include "the insight that human perception and understanding always proceed from foreknowledge of a (however dimly apprehended) totality that is gradually modified and clarified in a mutual approximation of the one and the multitude, the comprehensive and the subordinate, the whole and its parts."

[Reference: W. Wolfgang Holdheim, *The Hermeneutic Mode* (1984).]

Hermeneutics: A term once limited to the interpretation of religious texts, particularly the allegorical, but lately enjoying a new life as a SYNONYM for "theory of interpretation"—including the theory that a work of art considered *as* a work of art cannot (according to T. S. Eliot) be interpreted, because there is nothing to interpret. Since the time when Eliot's dismissal was possible—and in spite of it—*hermeneutics* has become an important part of literary theory, with a background in modern LINGUISTICS and philosophy; nowadays, *hermeneutics* refers to the theory of perception and understanding, along with the premises, procedures, methods, and limitations of what is generally meant by "interpretation."

[References: E. D. Hirsch, *Validity in Interpretation* (1967); W. Wolfgang Holdheim, *The Hermeneutic Mode* (1984); R. E. Palmer, *Hermeneutics* (1969).]

Hermeticism: A rather mysterious body of mystical and occult doctrine, even extending to alchemy and spiritualism, that has been important to a number of modern artists whose interests transcend the mechanical representation of an actual, secular, "real" world.

Hero or Heroine: The central CHARACTER (masculine or feminine) in a work of FICTION or a DRAMA. The terms are applied to the characters who are the focus of the readers' or the spectators' interest, often without reference to the superiority of the moral qualities of one character over another. Used as a technical term in describing a work of FICTION, *hero* (or *heroine*) refers to a relationship of character to ACTION; therefore, the less loaded term PRO-TAGONIST is probably preferable. See PLOT, STRUCTURE, PROTAGONIST.

Heroic Couplet: IAMBIC PENTAMETER lines rhymed in pairs. The favorite METER of Chaucer—*The Legend of Good Women* is an instance—this VERSE form did not come into its greatest popularity, however, until the middle of the seventeenth century (with Waller and Denham), after which time it was long the dominant mode for the POETIC DRAMA. The distinction of having made first use of the *heroic couplet* in dramatic composition is variously given to Orrery's *Henry V*, in which it was used throughout, and Etheredge's *The Comical Revenge,* in which it was employed for most passages of dramatic action. Both of these PLAYS date from 1664. D'Avenant had as early as 1656 made some use of the *heroic couplet* in his *Siege of Rhodes.* The FORM became best known with Dryden, who used it in such PLAYS as *Tyrannick Love, The Conquest of Granada,* and *Aureng-Zebe.* With Pope the *heroic couplet* became so important and fixed a form—for various purposes—that its influence dominated English VERSE for many years, until the romanticists dispelled the tradition in their demand for a new freedom. An example of the *heroic couplet* from Pope is:

> But when to mischief mortals bend their will,
>
> How soon they find fit instruments of ill!

In the NEOCLASSIC PERIOD, the *heroic couplet* was usually made up of a rhymed pair of END-STOPPED LINES, the *couplet* forming a short STANZA. The use of marked CAESURAS and a highly symmetrical grammatical structure made the *heroic couplet* a form well adapted to epigrammatic expression and to balanced sentences marked by symmetry and ANTITHESIS. The inherent symmetry and DECORUM of the *heroic couplet* make it an answerable medium for (1) the EXPOSITION of ideas of order and (2) the showing-up of rogues and hypocrites who embody disorder and discrepancy. In the ROMANTIC AGE, poets like Keats, in *Endymion,* retained rhymed pairs of IAMBIC PENTAMETER lines but abandoned the other restrictions of the *heroic couplet,* although Byron used and defended Pope's sort of *couplet.*

Heroic Drama: A type of TRAGEDY and TRAGI-COMEDY that developed in England during the RESTORATION. It was characterized by excessive SPECTA-CLE, violent emotional conflicts in the main CHARACTERS, extravagant bombastic DIALOGUE, and EPIC personages as chief CHARACTERS. The heroic PLAY usually had its SETTING in a distant land such as Mexico, Morocco, or India. Its HERO is constantly torn between his passion for some lady (more than likely a captive princess or the daughter of his greatest enemy) and his honor or duty to his country. If he is able to satisfy the demands of both love and duty, the play ends happily for HERO and HEROINE and unhappily for the VILLAIN and villainess. The HEROINE is always a paragon of virtue and honor, often torn between her loyalty to her VILLAIN-father and her love for the HERO. The VILLAIN is usually a tyrant and usurper with an overweening passion for power or else with a base love for some beautiful and virtuous lady. The villainess is the dark, violently passionate rival of the HEROINE. The hero's rival in love is sometimes the VILLAIN and sometimes the hero's best friend. All are unreal, all speak in HYPERBOLE, all rant and rage. Since the HEROIC COUPLET developed at the same time as the *heroic drama,* the writers of heroic plays commonly, though not always, wrote in HEROIC COUPLETS. The ACTION of the PLAY was grand, often revolving around the conquest of some empire. The scenery used in producing the heroic play was elaborate.

The influences that combined to produce the *heroic drama* were the romantic PLAYS of the Jacobeans, especially those of Beaumont and Fletcher; the development of OPERA in England; and the French court romances by Scudéry and La Calprenède, some of which were brought to England by the court of Charles II. Though elements of the heroic play appear in Davenant's *Siege of Rhodes* (1656), the Earl of Orrery perhaps wrote the first full-fledged *heroic drama, The General* (1664). Dryden, however, is the greatest exponent of the type, his *Conquest of Granada* typifying all that is best and worst in the species. Elkanah Settle, Nahum Tate, Nathaniel Lee, Sir Robert Howard, John Crowne, and Thomas Otway are others who cultivated the *heroic drama.* Although the faults of the type were recognized early, the most brilliant attack being *The Rehearsal* (1671), a satirical PLAY by George Villiers, Duke of Buckingham, and others, *heroic drama* flourished until about 1680, and its extravagances affected eighteenth-century TRAGEDY.

[References: L. N. Chase, *The English Heroic Play* (1903); Allardyce Nicoll, *A History of Restoration Drama, 1660–1700,* 2nd ed. (1928); B. J. Pendlebury, *Dryden's Heroic Plays* (1923, reprinted 1967).]

Heroic Line: IAMBIC PENTAMETER is called the *heroic line* in English POETRY because it is often used in EPIC or heroic poetry. In CLASSICAL literature the *heroic line* was the DACTYLIC HEXAMETER; in French literature it was the ALEXANDRINE. During the seventeenth century in England the term *heroic line* was applied to the IAMBIC PENTAMETER COUPLET because of its extensive use in HEROIC DRAMA.

Heroic Quatrain: Four LINES of IAMBIC PENTAMETER (or, much more rarely, TETRAMETER) rhyming *abab,* a component of the Shakespearean SONNET, used as a STANZA by Dryden and others, but brought to such perfection in Gray's "Elegy Written in a Country Churchyard" that no employment remained for it afterwards except in a rather grim TRAVESTY in the third part of T. S. Eliot's *The Waste Land.*

Heroic Stanza: A name sometimes applied to the HEROIC QUATRAIN.

Heroic Verse: POETRY composed of IAMBIC PENTAMETER lines and rhymed in LINE-pairs. Also called HEROIC COUPLETS. See HEROIC LINE.

Heteromerous Rhyme: A fairly rare species of multiple RHYME (also called "mosaic") in which, typically, one word is forced into a RHYME with two or more words. Being somewhat strained and exotic, most rhymes of this sort tend to be outlandish and comic, as in Byron's *Don Juan:*

> But—Oh! ye lords of ladies intellectual,
> Inform us truly, have they not hen-pecked you all?

Some serious uses have been made of *heteromerous rhyme,* notably by Browning, Yeats, and Eliot. Gerard Manley Hopkins once courageously rhymed "I am and" with "diamond."

Hexameter: A LINE of six metrical FEET. As a CLASSICAL verse FORM in Latin or Greek POETRY, in which languages the *hexameter* was the conventional medium for EPIC and DIDACTIC POETRY, the term was definitely restricted to a set pattern: six feet, the first four of which were DACTYLS or SPONDEES, the fifth almost always a DACTYL (though sometimes a SPONDEE, in which case the VERSE is called spondaic), the sixth a SPONDEE or TROCHEE. True *hexameters* of the CLASSICAL sort are scarce in English POETRY because of the supposed rarity of SPONDEES in our language. However, poets writing in English, notably Longfellow in *Evangeline,* have variously modified the CLASSICAL form to adapt it to the exigencies of our language and have left us *hexameters* much less strictly patterned than the CLASSICAL. See ALEXANDRINE, ELEGIACS.

Hexastich: Any STANZA of six LINES. See STANZA.

Hiatus: A pause or break between two vowel sounds not separated by a consonant. It is the opposite of ELISION, which prompts the sliding over of one of the vowels, whereas a *hiatus* occurs only in a break between two words when the final vowel of the first and the initial vowel of the second are each carefully enunciated. In logic *hiatus* signifies the omission of one of the logical steps in the process of reasoning.

Hieratic Style: Literally *priestly* or appropriate to the priestly class, *hieratic* was applied to a STYLE of ancient Egyptian writing that was highly conventional. It is used by Northrop Frye to designate a self-consciously formal and elaborate STYLE, in contrast to the DEMOTIC STYLE, or STYLE of ordinary speech. See DEMOTIC STYLE.

Hieronymy: The idea of sacred names and naming, more recently applied to any special name (or "proper" noun) for persons, places, gods, days, months, and so forth. According to one eccentric critical dogma, POETRY is distinguished by the foregrounded presence of *hieronymy* and its antithetical complement, ONOMATOPOEIA.

High Comedy: Pure or serious COMEDY, as contrasted with LOW COMEDY. *High comedy* rests on an appeal to the intellect and arouses "thoughtful" laughter by exhibiting the inconsistencies and incongruities of human nature and by displaying the follies of social manners. The purpose is not consciously didactic or ethical, though serious purpose is often implicit in the SATIRE that is frequently present in *high comedy.* Thoughtful amusement is aimed at. Emotion, especially SENTIMENTALITY, is avoided. If a man makes himself ridiculous by his vanity or ineffective by his stupid conduct or blind adherence to tradition, *high comedy* laughs at him. An ability to perceive promptly the incongruity exhibited is demanded of the audience, so that *high comedy* may seem to be written for the few. As George Meredith suggests in his ESSAY on *The Idea of Comedy,* care must be taken that the laughter provoked be not derisive but intellectual. An exhibition of poverty, for example, since it ridicules our unfortunate nature instead of our conventional life, is not truly comic. "But when poverty becomes ridiculous" by attempting "to make its rags conceal the bareness in a forlorn effort at decency," or foolishly tries to rival the ostentation of the rich, it becomes a fit THEME for comic presentation. Although *high comedy* actually offers plenty of superficial laughter that the average playgoer or reader can enjoy, its higher enjoyment demands a certain intellectual acumen, poise, and philosophic detachment. "Life is a comedy to him who thinks." But the term *high comedy* is used in various senses. In NEOCLASSIC times a criterion was its appeal to and reflection of the "higher" social class and it observance of DECORUM, as illustrated in Etheredge and Congreve. In a broader sense it is applied to some of Shakespeare's PLAYS, such as *As You Like It,* and to modern comedies of G. B. Shaw. See COMEDY, COMEDY OF MANNERS, COMEDY OF HUMOURS, REALISTIC COMEDY, COMEDY OF MORALS.

Higher Criticism: A term applied to certain aspects of the intensive study of Biblical texts in the nineteenth century. The *higher criticism* seeks to determine the authorship, date, place of origin, circumstances of composition, author's purpose and intended meaning, and the historical credibility of the various books of the BIBLE. It is called the *higher criticism* in contrast to the much less common term "lower criticism," which refers to the establishment of the text itself. The *higher criticism* is important in literary study not only for its method but also for its impact on the religious thought of the nineteenth and twentieth centuries.

[Reference: William Robertson Smith, *The Old Testament in the Jewish Church* (1881).]

Historical Criticism: CRITICISM that describes and evaluates a work in terms of the social, cultural, and historical context in which it was produced and published and the facts of its author's life. The historical CRITIC attempts to re-create through some historical process the meaning and the values of the work for its own time; the critic's objective is not to elucidate the meaning of the work for the present so much as it is to lead the reader in the present into a responsive awareness of the meaning the work had for its own age. The issues defined as the concern of the HIGHER CRITICISM are all matters of concern for the historical critic as well. See CRITICISM, TYPES OF; and HIGHER CRITICISM.

Historical Fiction: FICTION whose setting is in some earlier time than that in which it is written. Arguably, *historical fiction* can be any in which the temporal SETTING is of paramount importance, so that a contemporary work, set in "the present" can be *historical,* and so can a work of SCIENCE FICTION, set in the future. See HISTORICAL NOVEL.

Historical Novel: A NOVEL that reconstructs a personage, a series of events, a movement, or the spirit of a past age and pays the debt of serious scholarship to the facts of the age being re-created. The CLASSIC formula for the *historical novel,* as evolved by Scott and given expression in his numerous prefaces and introductions to the Waverly Novels, calls for an age when two cultures are in conflict, one dying and the other being born; into this cultural conflict, fictional personages are introduced who participate in actual historical events and move among actual personages from history; these fictional CHARACTERS undergo and give expression to the impact of the historical events on people living through them, with the result that a picture of a bygone age is given in personal and immediate terms. *Ivanhoe,* with its disinherited Saxon HERO in a Norman would, is a striking example. *Historical novels* that take this task seriously have been called NOVELS OF MANNERS laid in the past.

The extent to which actual historical events of some magnitude must be present, the extent to which actual historic personages must be actors in the STORY, the time that must have elapsed between the events of the STORY and its writing are among the questions to which both historical novelists and CRITICS of the FORM have given varying answers. There has been little dispute, however, over the responsibility of the historical novelist to give a truthful picture of an age or over the fact that the *historical novel* is often centered in a social context. Two tendencies to depart from the "FORMULA" should be noted: one is "the costume romance," in which history is exploited as a background for a series of adventurous or sexual exploits; the other is the "novel of the character" laid in the past, in which the setting and the age are of secondary importance to the representation of a group of characters; *The Scarlet Letter* is a classic example of the latter.

Although writers have combined FICTION and history since time began and although literary historians have found adumbrations of the *historical novel* in many forms and works, it required the development of a serious view of history before a serious *historical novel* could develop. This view came in the eighteenth century, and various writers began seriously to attempt works that would correspond to the ideals of the *historical novel,* but it remained for Sir Walter Scott in *Waverley* in 1814 to establish the form. Among his noted successors have been Thackeray, Alexander Dumas, Victor Hugo, Tolstoi, James Fenimore Cooper, Bulwer-Lytton, Charles Reade, Hervey Allen, and Kenneth Roberts. More recently, *historical novels* have been attempted by Robert Graves, Gore Vidal, John Barth, Erica Jong, and Norman Mailer. See NOVEL.

[References: H. Butterfield, *The Historical Novel* (1924); G. Lukács, *The Historical Novel* (tr. 1965); Brander Matthews, *The Historical Novel and Other Essays* (1901); Nicholas Rance, *The Historical Novel and Popular Politics in Nineteenth-Century England* (1975).]

Historicism: A sophisticated and relatively recent series of concepts about works of literature and their relationships to the social and cultural contexts within which they were produced. Although HISTORICAL CRITICISM and scholarly pursuits such as literary history are frequently elements in it, the primary concern of *historicism* is methodological and systematic. It strives to establish relationships among the historical context in which the work was produced, the work as an imaginative artifact, the impact of the work on the social and cultural elements of its own world, and the significance of the work for the reader in a later and different world.

There are four broad concepts of *historicism*. The metaphysical or ideal concept, following Hegel, interprets the work in terms of a transcendental continuity of historical process. The naturalistic or positivistic concept sees the work as a sociological key to contemporary social meanings and values, as did St.-Beuve and Taine. The nationalistic sees the work as an expression of political and folk ideals framed by national boundaries, as do workers in the field of American Studies. The fourth and most frequent form of *historicism* is aesthetic. For it the work has unique value as a created artifact, shaped to some important degree by the forces of its time, but in its uniqueness also helping to shape its time; having a meaning appropriate to its own world and age and understandable fully only in terms of its own world and age, yet having a significance for our world and time, a significance that is a function of all these elements. Roy Harvey Pearce and William Morris practice aesthetic *historicism* with distinction. There are many views on these issues, but all of them are concerned with the complex problems resulting from a work's being a discrete and timeless aesthetic object that, to be understood fully, must be seen also as a product of historical forces.

History Play: Strictly speaking, any DRAMA whose time setting is in some period earlier than that in which it is written. It is most widely used, however, as a SYNONYM for CHRONICLE PLAY.

Holograph: A document or manuscript completely handwritten by the author. *Holographs* of important literary works not only have very high value for the bibliophile and the collector but are frequently of inestimable worth in determining something of the author's intention.

Holy Grail: The cup from which Christ is said to have drunk at the Last Supper and which was used to catch his blood at the Crucifixion. It became the center of a tradition of Christian MYSTICISM and eventually was linked with Arthurian ROMANCE as an object of search on the part of Arthur's knights. The *grail* as it appears in early Arthurian literature (Chrétien's *Perceval*) is perhaps of pagan origin, some sort of magic object not now to be traced with assurance. In the POEMS of Robert de Boron (*ca.* 1200) it appears as a mystic symbol and is connected with Christian tradition (having been brought to England by Joseph of Arimathea). In the Vulgate Romances (see VULGATE), two great CYCLES are devoted to the *grail,* the first or "History" dealing with the Joseph tradition, the second or "Quest" dealing with the search for it by Arthurian knights. Perceval, the first HERO of the quest, because he was not a pure knight, and Lancelot, because he was disqualified by his love for Guinevere, gave place to Galahad, the wholly pure knight, conceived as Lancelot's son and Perceval's kinsman. The pious quest for the *grail,* no less than the sinful love of Lancelot and Guinevere, helped bring about the eventual downfall of the Round Table fellowship. See ARTHURIAN LEGEND.
    [References: Robert Jaffray, *King Arthur and the Holy Grail* (1928); A. E. Waite, *The Holy Grail: The Galahad Quest in the Arthurian Literature* (1961).]

Homeric: Indicative of or resembling the work of the Greek EPIC POET Homer (*ca.* 8th century B.C.), author of the *Iliad* and the *Odyssey;* hence possessing grandeur and imposing magnitude, having heroic dimensions. *Homeric* events, for example, are large, world-shaking, and of great importance.

Homeric Epithet: An adjectival phrase so often repeated in connection with a person or thing that it almost becomes a part of the name, as "swift-footed Achilles." See EPITHET.

Homeric Simile: An EPIC SIMILE, an unusually elaborate comparison, extending over a number of LINES of VERSE, in which the second of the objects being compared is described at great length. It is considered characteristic of the EPIC style. See EPIC SIMILE.

Homily: A form of oral religious instruction given by an ordained minister with a church congregation as audience. The *homily* is sometimes distinguished from the sermon in that the sermon usually is on a THEME drawn from a scriptural text and a *homily* usually gives practical moral counsel rather than discussion of doctrine. The distinction is by no means rigorously maintained. OLD ENGLISH literature contains *homilies* by Aelfric and Wulfstan.

Homoeoteleuton: Sameness or similarity of endings of consecutive words or words near each other, often considered unsettling or graceless but sometimes unavoidable, as in adjacent adverbs ("relatively easily"), verbal forms ("emerging meaning becoming fashionable"), accidental sameness of affixes ("truly holy family"), or, rarely, echoic names (Lyndon Johnson, Dudley Bradley, Albert Talbert, Jason Mason). Since most instances of *homoeoteleuton* have to do with unstressed syllables, it can usually be distinguished from proper RHYME.

Homostrophic: Consisting of structurally identical STROPHES; hence, made up of STANZAS of the same pattern. A HORATIAN ODE is *homostrophic.* See HORATIAN ODE.

Horatian Ode: Horace applied the term *ode* to comparatively informal POEMS written in a single stanzaic form, in contrast to the STROPHE, ANTISTROPHE, and EPODE of the PINDARIC ODE. The term *Horatian ode* is, therefore, often applied to such poems. Notable examples are Marvell's "Horatian Ode upon Cromwell's Return from Ireland," and Keats's "Ode on a Grecian Urn." See ODE.

Horatian Satire: SATIRE in which the satiric voice is indulgent, tolerant, amused, and witty. The speaker holds up to gentle ridicule the absurdities and follies of human beings, aiming at producing in the reader not the anger of a Juvenal (see JUVENALIAN SATIRE) but a wry smile. Much of Pope's SATIRE is Horatian, as is that common to the COMEDY OF MANNERS or NOVELS like those of John P. Marquand.

Hornbook: A kind of primer common in England from the sixteenth to the eighteenth centuries. On a sheet of vellum or paper were printed the alphabet, combinations of consonants and vowels commonly used in making up syllables, the Lord's Prayer, and a list of Roman numerals. The sheet was mounted on wood and covered (for protection) by transparent horn (hence, *hornbook*). Its most famous use in literature is in *The Gull's Hornbook* by Thomas Dekker, an amusing and satirical "primer" of instructions for the young innocent of early seventeenth-century London. The *hornbook* here supplies a framework for a social SATIRE.

Hovering Stress or Accent: A term designating the metrical effect that results from two adjacent syllables sharing the ICTUS, so that the STRESS appears to hover over both syllables. It is also called DISTRIBUTED STRESS and RESOLVED STRESS. It appears often in the work of Gerard Manley Hopkins and is sometimes considered a metrical device used by Whitman. See DISTRIBUTED STRESS for an example.

Hubris or **Hybris:** Overweening pride or insolence that results in the misfortune of the PROTAGONIST of a TRAGEDY. It is the particular form of tragic flaw that results from excessive pride, ambition, and overconfidence. *Hubris* leads the PROTAGONIST to break a moral law, attempt vainly to transcend normal human limitations, or ignore a divine warning with calamitous results. The excessive ambition of Macbeth is a standard example of *hubris* in English DRAMA. See TRAGEDY.

Hudibrastic Verse: The OCTOSYLLABIC COUPLET as adapted by Samuel Butler in his MOCK HEROIC POEM, *Hudibras.* In this long POEM, published in three parts between 1663 and 1678, Butler satirized the PURITANS of England. *Hudibras* was conspicuous for its HUMOR, its BURLESQUE elements, its MOCK EPIC form, and its wealth of satiric EPIGRAM. The METER is IAMBIC TETRAMETER in rhyming COUPLETS. It is filled with outrageous RHYMES that are often double and even triple. The term is used today to characterize VERSE following Butler's general manner and particularly his shocking RHYMES. Here is a typical passage, which concerns astrologers:

> They'll find in the physiognomies
> O' the planets all men's destinies;
> Like him that took the doctor's bill
> And swallowed it instead o' the pill;
> Cast the nativity o' the question,
> And from positions to be guessed on,
> As sure as if they knew the moment
> Of native's birth, tell what will come on't.

Humanism: Broadly, this term suggests any attitude that tends to exalt the human element or stress the importance of human interests, as opposed to the supernatural, divine elements—or as opposed to the grosser, animal elements. So a student of human affairs may be called a *humanist,* and the study of human beings as human beings, i.e., of the human race rather than of individual human beings, has been called *humanism.* In a more specific sense, *humanism* suggests a devotion to those studies supposed to promote human culture most effectively—in particular, those dealing with the life, thought, language, and literature of ancient Greece and Rome. In literary history the most important use of the term is to designate the revival of CLASSICAL CULTURE that accompanied the RENAISSANCE. The RENAISSANCE humanists found in the CLASSICS a justification to exalt human nature and build a new and highly idealistic gospel of progress upon it. Also they found it necessary to break sharply with medieval attitudes that had subordinated one aspect of human nature by exalting the supernatural and divine. The RENAISSANCE humanists agreed with the ancients in asserting the dignity of human beings and the importance of the present life, as against those medieval thinkers who considered the present life useful chiefly as a preparation for a future life.

RENAISSANCE *humanism* developed in the fourteenth and fifteenth centuries in Italy and was marked by a passion for rediscovering and studying ancient literature. It spread to other Continental countries and finally to England, where efforts to develop humanistic activities culminated successfully late in the fifteenth century with the introduction of the study of Greek at Oxford (see OXFORD REFORMERS). Early humanists—in particular the so-called Christian Humanists—in England applied themselves to mastering the Greek and Latin languages and to applying their new methods to theology, statecraft, education, CRITICISM, and literature. Unlike some Continental humanists, the English group, though they reacted against medieval asceticism and SCHOLASTICISM and attacked abuses in the Church, retained their faith in Christianity. Indeed, they believed that the best of classical culture could be fused with Christianity—a fact that accounts for seemingly incongruous mixtures of paganism and Christianity in much RENAISSANCE literature, notably the POETRY of Spenser and Milton. The efforts of such men as Dean John Colet and Erasmus to reform church conditions and theology through education and an appeal to reason were checked by the success of the more radical Lutheran movement. The "modern" character of this *humanism* may be indicated by recalling a few of its political and educational doctrines: political institutions are of human, not divine, origin and exist for human good, the monarch's "duties" being of greater concern than his "rights"; war is unchristian and inhumane and should be resorted to only when approved by the people themselves; the highest human happiness can come only through the virtuous life, which in turn can best be achieved through the control of reason, buttressed by education; women should be educated; nature should be employed as an educational tool; physical education is of the utmost importance; schoolmasters should be learned and gentle.

A later phase of humanistic activity was its interest in literary CRITICISM, through which it affected powerfully the practice of RENAISSANCE authors. The validity of critical ideas drawn from Aristotle and Horace was asserted, and the production of a vernacular literature that imitated the CLASSICS was advocated. Though this led to some unsuccessful efforts to restrict the English vocabulary and to repress native VERSE FORMS in favor of classical words and FORMS, in general humanistic CRITICISM exerted a wholesome effect on literature by lending it dignity (as in the EPIC and TRAGEDY) and grace (as in the Jonsonian LYRIC) and by stressing restraint and FORM. Its influence was especially great in the DRAMA, where it aided in establishing unified STRUCTURE. The texture of RENAISSANCE literature, too, was greatly enriched by the familiarity with the incidents, CHARACTERS, motives, and IMAGERY of classical mythology, history, and literature. Sidney's *Defence of Poesie* is generally taken as the first major document in English CRITICISM, and the establishment of the classical attitude (see CLASSICISM) through the influence of Jonson and (later) Dryden and Pope and others was itself a fruit of RENAISSANCE *humanism*. A tracing of the effects of *humanism* on the literature of the seventeenth and eighteenth centuries would largely coincide with the history of CLASSICISM and NEOCLASSICISM. One of the phases of the reaction against ROMANTICISM in the nineteenth century was a revival of *humanism*, as exemplified in Matthew Arnold. More recently, certain public figures (called "pulpit bullies" by detractors) have taken to using "secular humanism" as a label for any ideology not meeting their standards of spiritual correctness. See HUMANISM, THE NEW.

[References: Frederick B. Artz, *Renaissance Humanism, 1300–1550* (1966); Douglas Bush, *The Renaissance and English Humanism* (1939).]

Humanism, The New: A philosophical-critical movement called *The New Humanism* took place in America between 1910 and 1930, inspired in large part by the humanist position of Matthew Arnold. Its leaders were Irving Babbitt, Paul Elmer More, Norman Foerster, and Robert Shafer. *The New Humanism* was in large part a reaction against certain forms of REALISM and particularly of NATURALISM, which the New Humanists believed overstressed the animal elements in human nature. The movement was a protest against the philosophies and psychologies of "our professedly scientific time." No complete codification of the tenets of the New Humanists can be made, but the following summary, based on Foerster's *American Criticism,* suggests their general attitudes: *The New Humanism* assumes (1) that assumptions are unavoidable, (2) that the essential quality of experience is not natural but ethical, (3) that there is a sharp dualism between human beings and nature, and (4) that human will is free.

This reaction against the tenets of an age of science and artistic self-expression, however, failed to achieve a large following outside academic circles. The popular CRITIC Stuart Sherman was active in it for a while, and the POET-CRITIC T. S. Eliot, who had been Babbitt's student and remained a friend of both Babbitt and More, was an interested observer. After 1930 it fell before attacks by two enemies, the sociological critics and the advocates of the NEW CRITICISM (Allen Tate most articulately), a movement that effectively raised the New Humanists' standard of the validity of the art object in an age of science and yet one that began partially as a reaction against the strict morality and the intolerance of the contemporary in art, which *New Humanism* had often displayed. See NEW CRITICISM, CRITICISM.

[References: Irving Babbitt, *Rousseau and Romanticism* (1919, reprinted 1947); Norman Foerster, *Toward Standards* (1930, reprinted 1966), and (ed.) *Humanism and America* (1930); L. J. A. Mercier, *American Humanism and the New Age* (1948), and *The Challenge of Humanism* (1933); R. Shafer, *Paul Elmer More and American Criticism* (1935).]

Humor: A term used in English since the early eighteenth century to denote one of the two major types of writing (*humor* and WIT) whose purpose is the evoking of some kind of laughter. It is derived from the physiological theory of HUMOURS, and it was used to designate a peculiar disposition that led to a person's readily perceiving the ridiculous, the ludicrous, and the comical and effectively giving expression to this perception. In the eighteenth century it was used to name a comical mode that was sympathetic, tolerant, and warmly aware of the depths of human nature, as opposed to the intellectual, satiric, intolerant quality associated with WIT. However, it is impossible to discuss *humor* separately from WIT, and the reader is referred to the article on WIT and HUMOR.

Humours (or Humors):   In the old theory of physiology the four chief liquids of the human body—blood, phlegm, yellow bile, and black bile—were known as *humours.* They were closely allied with the four ELEMENTS. Thus blood, like *air,* was hot and moist; yellow bile, like *fire,* was hot and dry; phlegm, like *water,* was cold and moist; black bile, like *earth,* was cold and dry. Both physical diseases and mental and moral dispositions ("temperaments") were caused by the condition of the *humours*. Disease resulted from the dominance of some element within a single *humour* or from a lack of balance or proportion among the *humours* themselves. The *humours* gave off vapors that ascended to the brain. An individual's personal characteristics, physical, mental, and moral, were explained by his or her "temperament" or the state of the person's *humours*. The perfect temperament resulted when no one *humour* dominated. The sanguine person had a dominance of blood, was beneficent, joyful, amorous. The choleric person was easily angered, impatient, obstinate, vengeful. The phlegmatic person was dull, pale, cowardly. The melancholic person was gluttonous, backward, unenterprising, thoughtful, sentimental, affected. A disordered state of the *humours* produced more exaggerated characteristics. These facts explain how the word *humour* in Elizabethan times came to mean "disposition," then "mood," or "characteristic peculiarity," later specialized to "folly," or "affectation." By 1600 it was common to use *humour* as a means of classifying CHARACTERS. The influence on ELIZABETHAN literature of the doctrines based on *humours* was very great, and familiarity with them is an aid in understanding such characters as Horatio, Hamlet, and Jacques in Shakespeare. Many passages often taken as figurative may have had a literal meaning to the Elizabethans, as "my liver melts." See COMEDY OF HUMOURS, ELEMENTS.

Hymn: A LYRIC POEM expressing religious emotion and generally intended to be sung by a CHORUS. Church and theological doctrine, pious feeling, and religious aspiration characterize the ideas of these LYRICS, though originally the term referred to almost any SONG of praise, whether of gods or famous people. The early Greek and Latin Christian churches developed many famous *hymn* writers, and the importance of *hymns* during the Dark and Middle Ages can hardly be exaggerated, since they gave the great mass of people a new VERSE FORM as well as a means of emotional expression. The twelfth and thirteenth centuries saw the greatest development of Latin *hymns* (*Dies Irae*, etc.). The wide use of *hymns* helped to destroy certain literary CONVENTIONS of the past and exerted an important influence on the VERSIFICATION of English and German POETRY as well as that of the Romance languages. Some famous *hymn* writers of England are Charles and John Wesley, Isaac Watts, John Newton, Cowper, Keble, Toplady, and Newman; of America, Whittier, Holmes, Longfellow, P. P. Bliss, and Phillips Brooks. See ANTHEM, TROPE.
[Reference: J. B. Reeves, *The Hymn as Literature* (1924).]

Hymnal Stanza: A four-LINE STANZA most often in IAMBIC TETRAMETER and TRIMETER, rhyming either *abcb* or *abab*. Often called COMMON MEASURE.

Hypallage: A FIGURE OF SPEECH in which an EPITHET is moved from the proximate to the less proximate of a group of nouns, as when Virgil writes of "the trumpet's Tuscan blare" when the normal order would be "the Tuscan trumpet's blare."

Hyperbaton: A FIGURE OF SPEECH in which the normal sentence order is transposed or rearranged in a major way, usually for rhetorical or poetic effect. These LINES from Book II of Milton's *Paradise Lost* illustrate *hyperbaton:*

> Which when *Beëlzebub* perceiv'd, than whom
> *Satan* except, none higher sat, with grave
> Aspect he rose . . .

Hyperbole: A FIGURE OF SPEECH in which conscious exaggeration is used without the intent of literal persuasion. It may be used to heighten effect, or it may be used to produce comic effect. Macbeth is using *hyperbole* in the following LINES:

> No; this my hand will rather
> The multitudinous seas incarnadine,
> Making the green one red.

Hypercatalectic or **Hypermetrical:** A LINE OF POETRY with an extra syllable at its end. Many of Chaucer's lines are *hypercatalectic* when the terminal -*e*'s at the ends of lines are pronounced, such as these:

> Short was his gowne, with sleeves long and wyde.
> Wel koude he sitte on hors and faire ryde.

Hypotaxis: An arrangement of clauses, phrases, or words in dependent or subordinate relationships indicative of the relationships among the thoughts that these elements represent. The phrase *hypotactic style* refers to a kind of writing that uses subordination to reflect the logical, causal, temporal, or spatial relations among things discussed. Occasionally, *hypotaxis* refers to the use of a subordinate clause in a place where one might normally expect a coordinate. Instead of the coordination of " 'Twas the night before Christmas, and all through the house . . ." for example, Clement Moore actually wrote ". . . when all through the house." In any event, PARATAXIS is a feature of ordinary speaking—especially the naive, simple, rustic, or juvenile—and *hypotaxis* of writing. See PARATAXIS.

Hysteron Proteron: A FIGURE OF SPEECH in which what should logically come last comes first. Dogberry's speech in *Much Ado About Nothing* is an example: "Masters, it is proved already that you are little better than false knaves, and it will go near to be thought so shortly."

I

Iamb (Iambus): A metrical FOOT consisting of an unaccented syllable and an accented (⌣ ´). The most common metrical measure in English VERSE. A LINE from Marlowe will serve as an illustration:

$$\overset{\smile}{\text{Come}} \ \overset{\prime}{\text{live}} \ | \ \overset{\smile}{\text{with}} \ \overset{\prime}{\text{me}} \ | \ \overset{\smile}{\text{and}} \ \overset{\prime}{\text{be}} \ | \ \overset{\smile}{\text{my}} \ \overset{\prime}{\text{love}}$$

Icon: In the Eastern Churches, a stylized representation of a sacred personage. In modern critical usage, *icon* has come to mean a SIGN that goes beyond the mere arbitrary or conventional system of reference—in which there is no necessary resemblance between the sign and that which is referred to (the signified)—and somehow resembles, in form or shape or nature, that which it signifies. "Cuckoo"—to take a low-level example—refers to the sound made by a certain bird and also to the bird itself; while "cuckoo" does not equal the sound, it does bear a measure of acoustic resemblance and so can be called an *"icon"* and not just an arbitrary sign. At a higher level of "iconicity" than the simple resemblance between two sounds, the SIGN "cuckoo" refers to the source or maker of the sound and not just the sound itself; this process is a kind of METONYMY, by which the bird's call is made to stand for the bird itself. At more sophisticated levels of representation and presentation, a verbal or aesthetic *icon* both says and shows what it means: it states a case and also embodies or enacts the case.

[References: Jonathan Culler, *Structuralist Poetics* (1975); C. W. Morris, *Signs, Language, and Behavior* (1946); W. K. Wimsatt, *The Verbal Icon* (1954).]

Ictus: In VERSIFICATION, the ACCENT or STRESS that falls on a syllable; *ictus* does not refer to the stressed syllable but to the STRESS itself. See ACCENT.

Identical Rhyme: A phenomenon, also called *rime riche*, in which a syllable both begins and ends in the same way as a rhyming syllable, without being the same word. If two LINES end with "rain" (as in Eliot's "Gerontion"), that is simple REPETITION. If, however, "rain" occurs in a rhyming position with "rein" or "reign," that is *identical rhyme;* but "rain" (noun) and "rain" (verb) are not, since they are forms of the same basic word. One of John Peale Bishop's SONNETS is composed entirely of *identical rhymes.* That is virtually unique in English, but such patterns are relatively common in French, which relies on *identical rhymes* much more than English does. One of Mallarme's sonnets has these rhyming words: *temps, s'extenue, nue* (noun), *tends, meditants, avenue, nue* (adjective), *contents, sure, morsure, amant, touffe, diamant, etouffe.* This quatrain by Emily Dickinson shows both simple REPETITION and *identical rhyme:*

> All men for Honor hardest work
> But are not known to earn—
> Paid after they have ceased to work
> In Infamy or Urn—

See RHYME.

Idiom: A use of words, a grammatic construction peculiar to a given language, or an expression that cannot be translated literally into a second language. "To carry out" may be taken as an example. Literally it means, of course, to carry something out (of a room perhaps), but idiomatically it means to see that something is done, as "to carry out a command." *Idioms* in a language usually arise from a peculiarity that is syntactical or structural—as in a common but untranslatable phrase like "How do you do?"—or from the obscuring of a meaning in a METAPHOR (as in the preceding example). The adjectives "brief" and "short" mean much the same, but their adverbial forms, by a twist of *idiom,* are different; compare "I'll be there shortly" and "I'll be there briefly."

Idyll (or Idyl): Not so much a definite poetic GENRE (like the SONNET, for instance) as a descriptive term applied to one or another of the poetic GENRES that are short and possess marked descriptive, NARRATIVE, and PASTORAL qualities. In this popular sense, Whittier's "Maud Muller" might be called an *idyll.* PASTORAL and descriptive elements are usually the first requisites of the *idyll,* although the PASTORAL element is usually presented in a conscious literary manner. The point of view of the *idyll* is that of a civilized and artificial society glancing from a drawing-room window over green meadows and gamboling sheep, or of the weekend farm viewed through a picture window. Historically the term goes back to the *idylls* of Theocritus, who wrote short pieces depicting the simple, rustic life in Sicily to please the civilized Alexandrians. It has also been applied to long descriptive and NARRATIVE POEMS, particularly Tennyson's *Idylls of the King.* See PASTORAL, EPYLLION.

Image: Originally a sculptured, cast, or modeled representation of a person; even in its most sophisticated critical usage, this fundamental meaning is still present, in that an *image* is a literal and concrete representation of a sensory experience or of an object that can be known by one or more of the senses. It functions, as I. A. Richards has pointed out, by representing a sensation through the process of being a "relict" of an already known sensation. The *image* is one of the distinctive elements of the "language of art," the means by which experience in its richness and emotional complexity is communicated, as opposed to the simplifying and conceptualizing processes of science and philosophy. The *image* is, therefore, a portion of the essence of the meaning of the literary work, never a mere decoration.

Images may be either "tied" or "free," a "tied" *image* being one so employed that its meaning and associational value are the same or nearly the same for all readers; and a "free" *image* being one not so fixed by context that its possible meanings or associational values are limited; it is, therefore, capable of having various meanings or values for various people.

Images may also be either literal or figurative, a literal *image* being one that involves no necessary change or extension in the obvious meaning of the words, one in which the words call up a sensory representation of the literal object or sensation; and a figurative *image* being one that involves a "turn" on the literal meaning of the words. An example of a collection of literal *images* may be seen in Coleridge's "Kubla Khan":

> In Xanadu did Kubla Khan
> A stately pleasure-dome decree:

> Where Alph, the sacred river, ran
> Through caverns measureless to man
> Down to a sunless sea.

These *images* apparently represent a literal scene. The literal *image* is one of the basic properties of prose FICTION, as witness such different writers as Joseph Conrad and Ernest Hemingway, whose works are noted for the evocative power of their literal *images*. The opening lines of this Wordsworth sonnet show both kinds of *images*, literal and figurative:

> It is a beauteous evening, calm and free;
> The holy time is quiet as a Nun
> Breathless with adoration; the broad sun
> Is sinking down in its tranquillity.

The two middle lines are highly figurative, whereas the first and fourth lines are broadly literal, although there are figurative "turns" present by implication in "free" and "tranquillity."

The qualities usually found in *images* are particularity, concreteness, and an appeal to sensuous experience or memory—an appeal that seems to work best through specifically visual *images*. See IMAGERY, SYMBOL, METAPHOR, FIGURATIVE LANGUAGE.

[Reference: Don Cameron Allen, *Image and Meaning: Metaphoric Traditions in Renaissance Poetry,* 2nd ed. (1968).]

Imagery: A term used widely in contemporary CRITICISM, *imagery* has a great variety of meanings. In its literal sense it means the collection of IMAGES within a literary work or a unit of a literary work. In a broader and different sense it is synonymous with TROPE or FIGURE OF SPEECH. Here the TROPE designates a special usage of words in which there is a change in their basic meanings. There are four major types of TROPES: IMAGES, which, in the strictest sense, are literal and sensory and properly should not be called TROPES at all; SYMBOLS, which combine a literal and sensuous quality with an abstract or suggestive aspect; SIMILE, which describes by explicit ANALOGY; and META-PHOR, which describes by implied ANALOGY. Not only do these four types of TROPES define the meaning of *imagery*, they also suggest the ranges of possible application that are to be found in the term.

Many contemporary CRITICS are concerned over the "structure of IM-AGES," "the IMAGE-clusters," "IMAGE patterns," and "thematic *imagery.*" Such patterns of *imagery*, often without the conscious knowledge of author or reader, are sometimes taken to be keys to a "deeper" meaning of a literary work or pointers to the unconscious motivations of its author. A few critics tend to see the "IMAGE pattern" as indeed being the basic meaning of the work and a sounder key to its values and interpretation than the explicit statements of the author or the more obvious events of PLOT or ACTION. One of the notable contributions of the New Critics has been their awareness of the importance of the relationships among IMAGES to the nature and meaning of LYRIC POETRY. Such patterning is important in FICTION, as well, contrasting IMAGES of light and dark being among the most conspicuous.

A study of the *imagery* of a literary work may center itself on the physical world that is presented through the language of the work; on the rhetorical patterns and devices by which the TROPES in the work are achieved; on the psychological state producing the work and providing its special and often hidden meaning; on the ways in which the pattern of its IMAGES reinforces (or on occasion contradicts) the ostensible meaning of discursive statement, PLOT, and ACTION in the work; or on how the IMAGES strike responsively on resonant points in the racial unconscious, producing the emotive power of ARCHETYPES and MYTH. See IMAGE, METAPHOR, FIGURATIVE LANGUAGE, NEW CRITICISM, ALLEGORY.

Imagination: The theories of POETRY advanced by the romantic critics of the early nineteenth century (Wordsworth, Coleridge, and others) led to many efforts to distinguish between *imagination* and FANCY, which had formerly been virtually synonymous. The word *imagination* had passed through three stages of meaning in England. In RENAISSANCE times it was opposed to reason and regarded as the means by which poetical and religious conceptions could be attained and appreciated. Thus, Bacon cited it as one of the three faculties of the rational soul: "history has reference to the memory, POETRY to the *imagination*, and philosophy to the reason"; and Shakespeare says the POET is "*of imagination* all compact." In the NEOCLASSIC PERIOD it was the faculty by which IMAGES were called up, especially visual IMAGES (see Addison's *The Pleasures of the Imagination*), and was related to the process by which "IMITATION of nature" takes place. Because of its tendency to transcend the testimony of the senses, the poet who might draw on *imagination* must subject it to the check of reason, which should determine its form of presentation. Later in the eighteenth century the *imagination,* opposed to reason, was conceived as so vivid an imaging process that it affected the passions and formed "a world of beauty of its own," a poetical illusion that served not to affect conduct but to produce immediate pleasure.

The romantic critics conceived the *imagination* as a blending and unifying of the powers of the mind that enabled the POET to see inner relationships, such as the identity of truth and beauty. So Wordsworth says that poets:

> Have each his own peculiar faculty,
> Heaven's gift, a sense that fits him to perceive
> Objects unseen before . . .
> An insight that in some sort he possesses, . . .
> Proceeding from a source of untaught things.

This conception of *imagination* necessitated a distinction between it and FANCY. Coleridge (*Biographia Literaria*) especially stressed, though he never fully explained, the difference. He called *imagination* the "shaping and modifying" power, FANCY the "aggregative and associative" power. The former "struggles to idealize and to unify," while the latter is merely "a mode of memory emancipated from the order of time and space." To illustrate the distinction Coleridge remarked that Milton had a highly imaginative mind, Cowley a very fanciful one. Leslie Stephen stated the distinction briefly, "FANCY deals with the superficial resemblances, and *imagination* with the deeper truths that underlie them."

While *imagination* is usually viewed as a "shaping" and ordering power, the function of which is to give art its special authority, the assumption is almost always present that the "new" creation shaped by the *imagination* is a new form of reality, not a FANTASY or a fanciful project. When Shakespeare writes

> As imagination bodies forth
> The forms of things unknown, the poet's pen
> Turns them to shapes and gives to airy nothing
> A local habitation and a name,

his reference is properly made to *imagination,* not to that power of inventing the novel and unreal by recombining the elements found in reality, which we commonly call FANCY and which expresses itself in FANTASY. See FANCY.

[References: J. W. Bray, *A History of English Critical Terms* (1898); R. L. Brett, *Fancy and Imagination* (1969); Denis Donoghue, *The Sovereign Ghost: Studies in Imagination* (1976); J. L. Lowes, *The Road to Xanadu: A Study in the Ways of the Imagination* (1927, rev. ed. 1955); I. A. Richards, *Coleridge on Imagination* (1960); Jean Paul Sartre, *Imagination: A Psychological Critique* (tr. 1962).]

Imagists: The name applied to a group of POETS prominent in England and America between 1909 and 1918. Their name came from the French title *Des Imagistes,* given to the first ANTHOLOGY of their work (1914); this, in turn, having been borrowed from a critical term that had been applied to some French precursors of the movement. The most conspicuous figures of the *imagist* movement were Ezra Pound, Hilda Doolittle ("H. D."), and F. S. Flint, who collectively formulated a set of principles as to treatment, DICTIONS, and RHYME. The *Imagist* IMAGE, according to Pound, presented "an intellectuall and emotional complex in an instant of time"—with the intellectual component borne by visual IMAGES, the emotional by auditory. According to Amy Lowell's *Tendencies in Modern American Poetry* (1917), the major objectives of the movement were: (1) to use the language of common speech but to employ always the exact word—not the nearly-exact; (2) to avoid all CLICHÉ expressions; (3) to create new RHYTHMS as the expressions of a new mood; (4) to allow absolute freedom in the choice of subject; (5) to present an IMAGE (that is, to be concrete, firm, definite in their pictures—harsh in outline); (6) to strive always for concentration, which, they were convinced, was the very essence of POETRY; (7) to suggest rather than to offer complete statements. Pound soon dismissed Lowell's writing and crusading as "Amygism," but her labors did help somewhat in conditioning the public to accept something new. As early as 1914, Pound moved from *Imagism* to VORTICISM, the more kinetic movement, and eventually let the coinage PHANOPOEIA supersede both IMAGE and *Imagism.*

[References: John T. Gage, *In the Arresting Eye: The Rhetoric of Imagism* (1981); Glenn Hughes, *Imagism and the Imagists* (1931); W. C. Pratt, *The Imagist Poem* (1963).]

Imitation: The concept of art as *imitation* has its origin with the CLASSICAL critics. Aristotle said at the beginning of his *Poetics* that all arts are modes of *imitation,* and he defines a TRAGEDY as an *imitation* of an ACTION of a certain sort. Aristotle seems here (and elsewhere) to be defending art against Plato's charge that it is twice removed from truth or reality. On the other hand, the Greek and Roman schools of RHETORIC used the *imitation* of literary models as an accepted form of composition. Both views of *imitation* have been persistently present in English literary history.

According to Aristotle, all the productive arts work by imitating, and what they particularly imitate is FORM. The Aristotelian concept of *imitation*—that art *imitates* NATURE—was pervasively present in English critical thought until the end of the eighteenth century. This *imitation of* NATURE came to be regarded as a realistic portrayal of life, a reproduction of natural objects and ACTIONS. Moreover, admiration of the success with which the greater CLASSIC writers had followed NATURE bolstered the rhetorical theory of following in their footsteps. CRITICS in the RENAISSANCE and the NEOCLASSIC PERIOD accepted *imitation* in this rhetorical sense of copying models in the various types of POETRY. They did not believe that *imitation* should replace genius, but an adherence to CLASSICAL models was considered a safe method of avoiding literary vices and attaining virtues. *Imitation* of this sort had several varieties: writing in the spirit of the masters and using merely their general principles; borrowing from the ancients with the necessity of accommodating the material to the poet's own age; the collection and use of special "beauties" in thought and expression from the works of the best poets; the exercise of PARAPHRASE and free TRANSLATION. *Imitation* as a copying of other writers was discussed and employed in all degrees of dependence, from the most inspired and dignified to the most servile.

In the ROMANTIC PERIOD, the MIMETIC THEORY OF ART was replaced by the EXPRESSIVE THEORY, and the meaning of Aristotle's term *imitation* underwent serious change as the concept of NATURE had been undergoing change. NATURE then became the creative principle of the universe, and Aristotelian *imitation* was considered to be "creating according to a true idea," and a work of art was "an idealized representation of human life—of character, emotion, action—under forms manifest to sense."

With the rise of REALISM and NATURALISM, a renewed emphasis on the accurate portrayal of the palpable actual returned, although the term *imitation* was not often used. Among contemporary critics there is some interest in the implications for the theory of *imitation* of the depth psychologies. See CRITICISM and CRITICISM, TYPES OF.

[References: S. H. Butcher, *Aristotle's Theory of Poetry and Fine Art*, 4th ed. (1911, reprinted 1951); R. S. Crane, ed., *Critics and Criticism* (1952); H. O. White, *Plagiarism and Imitation during the English Renaissance* (1935, reprinted 1965).]

Implied Author: A term applied, particularly by Wayne C. Booth, to the sense of a human presence presenting the materials of a literary work to the reader. The concept of the *implied author* is similar to Aristotle's concept of the ETHOS of a piece of persuasive ORATORY, in that the ETHOS is the IMAGE of the speaker projected by the speech as a whole (see ETHOS). Booth feels that an *implied author,* always present, is a created, idealized version of the real author; it is important, however, to discriminate fastidiously between the real author and the *implied author,* who remains always a creation, figment, or PERSONA, even when bearing the same name as the real author (a phenomenon that turns up in NOVELS by Somerset Maugham and Christopher Isherwood). See ETHOS, PERSONA.

[Reference: Wayne Booth, *The Rhetoric of Fiction*, 2nd ed. (1983).]

Implied Reader: A hypothetical reader of a text, defined by Wolfgang Iser as one who "embodies all those predispositions necessary for a literary work to exercise its effect—predispositions laid down, not by an empirical outside reality, but by the text itself. Consequently, the implied reader as a concept has his roots firmly planted in the structure of the text; he is a construct and in no way to be identified with any real reader." Iser concentrates on the implied reader of literature and especially on the *implied reader* of a NOVEL, in which determinable social norms are of great importance.

[References: Stanley Fish, *Surprised by Sin* (1967), and *Self-Consuming Artifacts* (1972); Wolfgang Iser, *The Act of Reading: A Theory of Aesthetic Response*, tr. 1978, and *The Implied Reader: Patterns of Communication in Prose Fiction from Bunyan to Beckett* (tr. 1974).]

Imprecation: A CURSE; an INVOCATION of evil; a MALEDICTION.

Impression: All the copies of a book printed at one time or without removing the type or plates from the press; a PRINTING. See EDITION.

Impressionism: A highly personal manner of writing in which the author presents CHARACTERS, SCENES, or MOODS as they appear to an individual temperament at a precise moment and from a particular vantage point rather than as they are presumed to be in actuality. The term is borrowed from painting. About the middle of the nineteenth century the French painters Manet, Monet, Degas, Renoir, and others revolted from the conventional academic conceptions of painting and held that it was more important to retain the impressions that an object makes on the artist than meticulously to present the appearance of that object by precise detail and careful, realistic finish. Their special concern was with the use of light on their canvases. They suggested the chief features of an object with a few strokes; they were more interested in ATMOSPHERE than in perspective or outline. "Instead of painting a tree," says Lewis Mumford, the impressionist "painted the effect of a tree." The movement had its counterpart in literature, writers accepting the same conviction that the personal attitudes and moods of the writer were legitimate elements in depicting CHARACTER or SETTING or ACTION. Briefly, the literary impressionist holds that the registration of such elements as these through the fleeting impression of a moment is more significant artistically than a photographic presentation of cold fact. The object of the impressionist, then, is to present material not as it is to the objective observer but as it is *seen* or *felt* to be by the impressionist or a CHARACTER in a single passing moment. The impressionistic writer employs highly selective details, the "brush strokes" of sense-data that can suggest impressions. In POETRY *impressionism* was an important aspect of the work of the IMAGISTS; in FICTION it is present in the works of writers like Joseph Conrad, Ford Madox Ford, Dorothy Richardson, and Virginia Woolf and in the "Camera Eye" sections of Dos Passos' *U.S.A. Impressionism* differs from EXPRESSIONISM significantly in avoiding conscious distortion and abstraction. See EXPRESSIONISM, IMAGISTS.

[References: Maria Elisabeth Kronegger, *Literary Impressionism* (1973); H. Peter Stowell, *Literary Impressionism: James and Chekhov* (1980).]

Impressionistic Criticism: A type of CRITICISM that attempts to communicate what the CRITIC subjectively sees and feels in the presence of a work of art. Anatole France called *impressionistic criticism* "the adventures of a sensitive soul among masterpieces." See CRITICISM, TYPES OF and CRITICISM.

Imprimatur: An official approval or license to print a work; usually the sign of approval of the Roman Catholic Church. The term is also used ironically to refer to the approval of an autocratic critic self-appointed as custodian of public morality or TASTE. *Imprimatur* literally means, "Let it be printed."

Incantation: A formulaic use of language, usually spoken or chanted, either to create intense emotional effects or to produce magical results. It is common in primitive literature, FOLKLORE, and FAIRY TALES. The witches' CHANTS in *Macbeth* are well-known examples, as is Ariel's SONG "Full fathom five" in *The Tempest.*

Incident: A single event or occurrence; the smallest unit of ACTION. An *incident* is usually connected to, or dependent on, something else that is larger and of which it is a subordinate part. When *incidents* do not merely constitute aimless activity but are arranged in some kind of logical pattern, they begin to be elements of PLOT. See PLOT.

Inciting Moment: The name used by Freytag for the event or force that sets in motion the RISING ACTION of a PLAY. It is also called the EXCITING FORCE. See FREYTAG'S PYRAMID, DRAMATIC STRUCTURE.

Incremental Repetition: A form of iteration frequently found in the BALLAD. This kind of REPETITION is not that of a REFRAIN but the repeating of phrases and LINES in such a way that their meaning is enhanced either by their appearing in changed contexts or by minor successive changes in the repeated portion of the BALLAD. A common form of *incremental repetition* occurs in the question and answer pattern in the BALLAD. These two STANZAS from "Child Waters" illustrate *incremental repetition:*

> There were four and twenty ladies
> Were playing at the ball,
> And Ellen, she was the fairest lady,
> Must bring his steed to the stall.
>
> There were four and twenty ladies
> Was a playing at the chess,
> And Ellen, she was the fairest lady,
> Must bring his horse to grass.

A complex instance of *incremental repetition* occurs in the "Nevermore" at the end of each STANZA of Poe's "The Raven," where the meaning of the word changes as the POEM progresses.

[Reference: Louise Pound, *Poetic Origins and the Ballad* (1921, reprinted 1962).]

Incunabulum: A term applied to any book printed in the last part of the fifteenth century (before 1501). Since the first printed books resembled in size, form, and appearance the medieval manuscript, which had been developed to a high degree of artistic perfection, *incunabula* are commonly large and ornate. As examples of early printing, *incunabula* are prized by modern collectors. From a historical and literary point of view, they are valuable as reflecting the intellectual and literary interests of the late fifteenth century. The number of existing *incunabula* is large, including about 360 printed in England. Among famous English *incunabula* are Caxton's edition of Chaucer's *Canterbury Tales* and *Le Morte Darthur* of Malory.

[References: C. F. Bühler, *The Fifteenth-Century Book* (1960); J. M. Lenhart, *Pre-Reformation Printed Books* (1935); Margaret B. Stillwell, *Incunabula and Americana* (1930, 2nd ed. 1961).]

Indeterminacy: The concept that the meaning or reference of a text is ultimately undecidable; sometimes applied to all human discourse, sometimes limited to certain realms bounded by semantic, psychological, or cultural constraints, and sometimes limited (as by Marjorie Perloff) to certain modern movements in the arts. The general notion supposes that no final or determinate appeal is possible outside a given system of SIGNS.

[References: Charles Altieri, *Act and Quality: A Theory of Literary Meaning and Humanistic Understanding* (1981); Geoffrey H. Hartman, *Saving the Text: Literature/Derrida/Philosophy* (1981); Marjorie Perloff, *The Poetics of Indeterminacy: Rimbaud to Cage* (1981).]

Index Expurgatorius: A list of passages that are to be expurgated from books that may be read by members of the Roman Catholic Church.

Index Librorum Prohibitorum: A list of prohibited books; a list of titles of works—most of them heretical—forbidden by church authority to be read by Roman Catholics, pending revision or deletion of some parts. Enumerations of forbidden books go back as far as the Muratorian Canon (about A.D. 170) and a list promulgated by Pope Innocent I in 405; the Gelasian Decree of 496 is sometimes mentioned as the first *Index Librorum Prohibitorum,* but it was 1559 before a list of forbidden books carried the name *"Index."* Subsequently there were many revisions, and Pope Leo XIII sponsored the issuance of a new *Index* (1900) that went through several editions, the last coming in 1948. A good deal of sentiment against the *Index* emerged during Vatican Council II, and in 1966 it was announced by Cardinal Ottaviani that there would be no further editions.

Indirect Satire: Whereas direct or FORMAL SATIRE is cast in the form of direct address, the satiric voice being the instrument by which ridicule is expressed, *indirect satire* is in NARRATIVE or dramatic form, and the CHARACTERS who speak and act are themselves the objects of the SATIRE in which they appear. See SATIRE.

Induction: An old word for *introduction.* This term was sometimes used in the sixteenth century to denote a framework introduction (see FRAMEWORK-STORY). Thus, Sackville's "Induction" to a portion of *The Mirror for Magistrates* tells how the POET was led by Sorrow into a region of Hell where dwelt the shades of the historical figures whose tragic lives are the subject of the *Mirror*. In the book proper each "shade" relates his own sad tale; the *induction* supplies the FRAMEWORK much as the famous "Prologue" supplies the FRAMEWORK for the stories making up Chaucer's *Canterbury Tales*. In *The Taming of the Shrew* Shakespeare employs an *induction* in which a drunken tinker is persuaded that he is a lord, for whose amusement is performed a play—*The Taming of the Shrew* itself.

Industrial Revolution: The social-political-economic struggle that characterized life in England for a hundred years or more, most intensely in the last quarter of the eighteenth and first quarter of the nineteenth centuries. Invention, scientific discovery, and changing economic, political, and social ideas and ideals all contributed to the furor during these years. By 1760 blast furnaces had begun to manufacture iron; the textile industry grew apace with the invention of the spinning jenny and the power loom (1785). The number of English looms increased in less than two decades from three thousand to one hundred thousand. James Watt made even greater strides possible through his perfection of the steam engine. Roads, canals, and railroads increased transportation facilities. Agriculture was all but deserted; by 1826 not a third of the former population was left on the farms. Hundreds of thousands of men wandered through the country, many dying, impoverished and diseased. The sweatshop was born; the master craftsman found his trade taken from him by the machine. Home work gave way to factory work. Industry and commerce flourished in cities, which grew rapidly. The villages were all but deserted. A middle-class capitalistic group developed almost overnight and progressed at the expense of men, women, and children, whom they overworked in their mills.

The writers of the period concerned themselves with these problems. Crabbe in such pieces as *The Village* and *The Borough* set forth pictures of the conditions; Charles Kingsley in such novels as *Yeast* and *Alton Locke* and Mrs. Gaskell in *Mary Barton, a Tale of Manchester Life* presented the struggles and unfairness of the times in FICTION. Dickens turned his attention to the relief of the poor. Ruskin and Carlyle sought to point the way to reform; Arnold in his *Essays* condemned a Philistine England that measured her greatness by her wealth and her numbers. Mill (*Principles of Political Economy*), Bentham (*Radical Reform*), Robert Owen (*New View of Society*), and Malthus (*Principles of Political Economy*) wrestled with the problems of the time from the point of view of the social sciences.

Influence: A term used in literary history for the impact that a writer, a work, or a school of writers has on an individual writer or work. Early in this century the tracing of *influence* (often called by the German word *Einfluss*) was a major activity of literary historians. Despite much good work, however, the *influence* tracing was often strained and far-fetched, and the method generally fell into disrepute. Today a very sophisticated approach to *influence* is being made by some of the most noted literary CRITICS. A revisionist approach, founded on a Freudian construction of certain TROPES, appears in Harold Bloom's *The Anxiety of Influence*. Bloom's thesis is that *influence* involves a misprision or misreading—sometimes quite remarkable—of a previous writer

as an unconscious strategy of creating room for a writer's present activity, so that every POEM is a misinterpretation of a hypothetical parent POEM. A related approach—less psychologistic and more typological and acoustic—is illustrated by John Hollander's *Vision and Resonance* and *The Figure of Echo.*
[Reference: Harold Bloom, *The Anxiety of Influence* (1973).]

Informal Essay: As distinguished from the FORMAL ESSAY, the *informal essay* is less obviously serious in purpose, usually shorter, freer of STRUCTURE, easier of STYLE, and is written to please and entertain rather than to instruct. See ESSAY.

Inkhornists: A group in the RENAISSANCE Period who favored the introduction of heavy Latin and Greek words into the standard English vocabulary. See PURIST and CRITICISM.

In medias res: A term from Horace, literally meaning "in the midst of things." It is applied to the literary technique of opening a STORY in the middle of the ACTION and then supplying information about the beginning of the ACTION through FLASHBACKS and other devices for EXPOSITION. The term *in medias res* is usually applied to the EPIC, where such an opening is one of the conventions.

In Memoriam Stanza: A QUATRAIN of IAMBIC TETRAMETER rhyming *abba.* A few earlier POETS, such as Ben Jonson, used such a STANZA occasionally, but it remained for Tennyson to invest the FORM with singular dignity and variety. As an added constraint in Tennyson's *In Memoriam,* all the RHYMES are MASCULINE, and all of the constituent "lyrics" have at least three STANZAS.

Inns of Court: The four voluntary, unchartered societies or legal guilds in London, which have the privilege of admitting persons to the bar. They take their names from the buildings they occupy—the Inner Temple, the Middle Temple, Lincoln's Inn, and Gray's Inn, buildings that they have occupied since the fourteenth century. Though the origin of these societies is lost in the medieval inns of law, it is clear that in late medieval times they became great law schools and so continued for centuries: today they are little more than lawyers' clubs, though they do exert considerable influence in guarding admissions to the bar. The *Inns of Court* were cultural institutions in the sixteenth and seventeenth centuries, with their libraries as well as their spirit of fellowship fostering literary interests. Regular DRAMA, as well as MASQUES and INTERLUDES, was nurtured by the *Inns.* Shakespeare's *Comedy of Errors* was acted before the fellows of Gray's Inn during the Christmas season of 1594. The *Inns,* like the universities, saw much playwriting and amateur acting on the part of "gentlemen" who would scorn connection with the early PUBLIC THEATERS. Many English authors have received their education, in whole or in part, in the *Inns of Court.* Chaucer may have belonged to one; Sir Thomas More was a Lincoln's Inn product; George Gascoigne and Francis Bacon were admitted to law practice from Gray's Inn; Thomas Shadwell and Nicholas Rowe were members of the Inner Temple. A vivid description of life in the *Inns* appears in Thackeray's *Pendennis.*
[Reference: A. Wigfall Green, *The Inns of Court and the Early English Drama* (1931, reprinted 1965).]

Innuendo: An insinuation or indirect suggestion, often with harmful or sinister CONNOTATION.

Inscape: A term used by Gerard Manley Hopkins to refer to the "individually-distinctive" inner structure or nature of a thing; hence, the essence of a natural object, which, being perceived through a moment of illumination—an EPIPHANY—reveals the unity of all creation. *Inscape* is the inward quality of objects and events, as they are perceived by the joined observation and introspection of a POET, who in turn embodies them in unique poetic FORMS. One of Hopkins's POEMS says, "Each mortal thing does one thing and the same"; it forcibly "selves"—a verb coined by Hopkins in a typical gesture to catch the unique *inscape* of the universal activity. See INSTRESS.

Instress: A term used by Gerard Manley Hopkins to refer to the force, ultimately divine, which creates the INSCAPE of an object or an event, and impresses that distinctive inner structure of the object on the mind of the beholder, who can perceive it and embody it in a work of art. See INSCAPE.

Intentional Fallacy: In contemporary CRITICISM, a term that describes the error of judging the meaning and the success of a work of art by the author's expressed or ostensible intention in producing it. The term was introduced by W. K. Wimsatt, Jr., and M. C. Beardsley (see *The Verbal Icon,* by Wimsatt) to insist that "the poem is not the critic's own and not the author's. . . . What is said about the poem [by the author] is subject to the same scrutiny as any statement in linguistics or in the general science of psychology or morals." The *intentional fallacy,* like the AFFECTIVE FALLACY, is an error particularly when viewed from an OBJECTIVE THEORY OF ART, for holders of the OBJECTIVE THEORY tend—at least in their extreme statements—to see the work of art as AUTOTELIC. The degree to which biographical facts, data regarding linguistic change, and knowledge of the social and intellectual climate in which the work was produced become relevant factors, along with the author's statement of intention, are matters of sharp disagreement among contemporary CRITICS. It should be noted that Wimsatt and Beardsley say, "The author must be admitted as a witness to the meaning of his work." It is merely that they would subject the author's testimony to rigorous scrutiny in the light of the work itself. Insofar as the artist is competent and articulate, and insofar as the work may be construed as the objective realization of some subjective state that we can recognize as common, no specific intention can be recovered or reconstructed from anything in a well-executed work of art, which will be, in effect, "nearly anonymous" (in John Crowe Ransom's phrase). See also AFFECTIVE FALLACY, AUTOTELIC, HISTORICAL CRITICISM, INTERTEXTUALITY.
  [Reference: W. K. Wimsatt and M. C. Beardsley, *The Verbal Icon* (1954).]

Interior Monologue: One of the techniques for presenting the STREAM OF CONSCIOUSNESS of a CHARACTER. It records the internal, emotional experience of the CHARACTER on any one level or on combinations of several levels of consciousness, reaching downward to the nonverbalized level where IMAGES must be used to represent sensations or emotions. It assumes the unrestricted and uncensored portrayal of the totality of interior experience on the level or levels being represented. It gives, therefore, the appearance of being illogical, associational, free of auctorial control. There are two distinct forms of *interior monologue:* direct, in which the author seems not to exist and the interior self of the CHARACTER is given directly, as though the reader were overhearing an articulation of the stream of thought and feeling flowing through the CHARACTER's mind; and indirect, in which the author serves as selector, presenter, guide, and commentator. The Molly Bloom section at the close of Joyce's *Ulysses* is the best-known example of direct *interior monologue* in English; the NOVELS of Virginia Woolf illustrate the indirect. It is generally agreed that Édouard Dujardin, in *Les Lauriers sont coupés* (1887), first used the *interior monologue* extensively. The term is often, although erroneously, used as a SYNONYM for STREAM OF CONSCIOUSNESS.

Some of Browning's POEMS may be taken as *interior monologues:* "Johannes Àgricola in Meditation" and "Soliloquy of the Spanish Cloister" are instances. Some of Eliot's poems—"The Love Song of J. Alfred Prufrock" and "Gerontion," for example—may be read in much the same way. See STREAM OF CONSCIOUSNESS, IMPRESSIONISM.

Interlaced Rhyme: CROSSED RHYME; that is, the rhyming of words in the middle of long-line COUPLETS, as well as of the end words of the LINES, thus breaking the COUPLET into four short lines that RHYME alternately. See CROSSED RHYME.

Interlocking Rhyme: A RHYME pattern in which one LINE in a rhyming unit carries forward the RHYME for the next unit. An example is TERZA RIMA, in which the middle line in each three-line unit establishes the RHYME for the first and third lines of the succeeding three-line unit. Robert Frost extended this sort of practice to the QUATRAIN in "Stopping by Woods on a Snowy Evening." See TERZA RIMA.

Interlude: A kind of DRAMA that developed in late fifteenth- and early sixteenth-century England and that played an important part in the secularization of the DRAMA and in the development of REALISTIC COMEDY. The word may mean a PLAY brief enough to be presented in the interval of a dramatic performance, entertainment, or feast (for example, Medwall's *Fulgens and Lucres*, 1497), or it may mean a PLAY or DIALOGUE between two persons. Some *interludes* imitate French FARCE and do not exhibit symbolic technique and didactic purpose, while others appear to have developed from the MORALITY PLAY, and still others from the Latin SCHOOL DRAMA: the two latter types are likely to be moralistic. Tucker Brooke, stressing its aristocratic character, says that the *interlude* was understood in Tudor times to mean a short PLAY exhibited by professionals at the meals of the great and on other occasions where, later, MASQUES would be fashionable. The essential qualities are brevity and WIT. Some writers regard such an episode as that of the sheep-stealing Mak in the Towneley *Second Shepherd's Play* as an *interlude.* The chief developers of the *interlude* were John Heywood and John Rastell, the first English dramatists, so far as known, to recognize that a PLAY might be justified by its ability to amuse. Heywood's *interludes* were produced in the 1520s and 1530s, the most famous being *The Four P's* (the Palmer, the Pardoner, the 'Pothecary, and the Pedlar, who engage in a sort of lying contest managed as a SATIRE against women) and *The Merry Play of John John the Husband, Tyb His Wife,* *and Sir John the Priest* (in which the priest and Tyb hoodwink the husband). Rastell's *interludes* include *The Nature of the Four Elements, The Field of the Cloth of Gold,* and *Gentilness and Nobility.* Homely details and realistic treatment are significant features of the *interludes,* which still followed the allegorical pattern of the MORALITY and yet represented the growth away from the abstract and toward the individual and particular.

[References: C. F. Tucker Brooke, *The Tudor Drama* (1911, reprinted 1964); E. K. Chambers, *The Mediaeval Stage,* vol. 2 (1903); A. W. Reed, *Early Tudor Drama* (1926, reprinted 1969).]

Internal Rhyme: RHYME that occurs at some place before the last syllables in a LINE of VERSE. In the opening line of Eliot's "Gerontion"—"Here I am, an old man in a dry month"—there is *internal rhyme* between "an" and "man" and between "I" and "dry." There are two instances of proximate *internal rhyme* in these lines by Dickinson:

> It dropped so low—in my Regard—
> I heard it hit the Ground . . .

See RHYME, LEONINE RHYME, CROSSED RHYME.

Interpretation, Four-fold Method: The levels employed in Biblical interpretation in the Middle Ages and the RENAISSANCE. In our time, a similar method has been advanced by Northrop Frye. See FOUR SENSES OF INTERPRETATION.

Intertextuality: The notion, derived from Saussurean LINGUISTICS, that a text, insofar as it can be construed as a system of SIGNS, refers only to itself (in what could be called a gesture of "intratextuality") or to other texts and not (in what could be called "extratextuality") to any reality outside the confines of itself or the general system of texts to which it may belong. In an extreme application of this notion, we can argue that no text exists in and of itself and that any text exists only as an entity among other texts. By much the same argument, we can say that no text depicts or represents any determinate reality outside itself, not even the BIOGRAPHY of the maker of the text or the immediate historical background. *Intertextuality* is observable more in certain works than in others, and perhaps more in POETRY than in PROSE. Eliot's *The Waste Land,* for example, makes a point of foregrounding self-reflexive elements of REPETITION and ANNOTATION as well as intertextual elements of QUOTATION, ALLUSION, ECHO, PARODY, and revision. Hawthorne's *The Scarlet Letter,* by its very title, presents itself as a comment on another text: the single color-coded letter that Hester Prynne is sentenced to wear.

Intrigue Comedy: A COMEDY in which the major interest is in PLOT complications resulting from scheming by a CHARACTER or characters. See COMEDY OF SITUATION.

Introduction: The opening sentences or paragraphs of a piece of writing. All literary compositions have been said to have three parts: beginning, middle, and end. On this basis the *introduction* is the beginning to the beginning. Sometimes the term is applied to an ESSAY printed at the beginning of a book—much like a PREFACE—to explain the author's chief ideas, purposes, hopes, and disillusions regarding the book. See INDUCTION, PROLEGOMENON, FOREWORD.

Intrusive Narrator: An OMNISCIENT NARRATOR who freely and frequently interrupts the NARRATIVE to explain, interpret, or qualify, sometimes in the form of ESSAYS. An *intrusive narrator* must be accepted as authoritative unless strong clues point to an ironic intention. Fielding in *Tom Jones,* Tolstoi in *War and Peace,* and George Eliot in *Adam Bede* (particularly Chapter 17) are good examples of the *intrusive narrator.* See POINT OF VIEW.
[Reference: Wayne Booth, *The Rhetoric of Fiction,* 2nd ed. (1983).]

Invective: Harsh, abusive language; vituperative writing. The *Letters* of Junius and the open letter written by Stevenson in defense of Father Damien have qualities of *invective,* as do many writings of Wyndham Lewis, H. L. Mencken, and Ezra Pound.

Invention: Originality in thought, STYLE, DICTION, IMAGERY, or PLOT. In this present-day sense the term implies creative power of an independent sort. But the use of the term by early English CRITICS often is colored by an older meaning and by the implications of the theory of IMITATION, and the student will do well to remember that RENAISSANCE and NEOCLASSIC CRITICS in their use of the term may have in mind the older idea of the "discovery" of literary material as something to be imitated or represented. In Latin RHETO-RIC *inventio* meant the "finding" of material and was applied, for example, to an orator's "working up" of his case before making a speech. According to the Aristotelian doctrine of IMITATION, authors did not create their materials "out of nothing"; they found them in NATURE. A CRITIC influenced by these CLASSICAL conceptions would not think of *invention* in its narrower, modern sense. Yet the idea of ORIGINALITY, of using "new" devices, and of avoiding the trite expression appears in the use of the term in England as early as RENAISSANCE times. As the term was used somewhat loosely for several centuries, it is not possible to give a single DEFINITION explaining all the passages in which the term appears in writings of the sixteenth, seventeenth, and eighteenth centuries. In the ROMANTIC PERIOD and since, *invention,* in the sense of the discovery or creation of an original or organizing principle, has been replaced by IMAGINATION.

Inversion: The placing of a sentence element out of its normal position either to gain EMPHASIS or to secure a so-called poetic effect. *Inversion* used with restraint and care is an effective rhetorical device but, used too frequently or grotesquely, will result in artificiality. Probably the most offensive common use of *inversion* is the placing of the adjective after the noun in such expressions as "home beautiful." Of the several varieties of *inversion,* the commonest are noun-adjective, object-verb, and adverb-auxiliary. The last sort is made possible by the peculiar structure of verb forms in Germanic languages, whereby a fairly neutral clause like "I have never seen such a mess" gains a measure of EMPHASIS in the inverted form "Never have I seen such a mess." Once in a while, as in "Jerk though he may be," even conjunctions can be dramatically relocated.

The device is often happily employed in POETRY. Where the writer of PROSE might say: "I saw a vision of a damsel with a dulcimer," Coleridge writes:

> A damsel with a dulcimer
> In a vision once I saw.

It can also be a very effective rhetorical device for securing variety as well as EMPHASIS IN PROSE.

Invocation: An address to a deity for aid. In CLASSICAL literature CONVENTION demanded an opening address to the MUSES, requesting their assistance in the writing. EPICS, particularly, were likely to begin in this way. Milton, in *Paradise Lost,* accepts the tradition, but instead of invoking one of the MUSES of POETRY, he addresses the

> Heavenly Muse, that, on the secret top
> Of Oreb, or of Sinai, didst inspire
> That shepherd who first taught the chosen seed
> In the beginning how the heavens and earth
> Rose out of Chaos: . . .

Ionic: A CLASSICAL FOOT with two long and two short syllables. It is used by Horace in his *Odes.* When it is occasionally attempted in English, stressed syllables are used for the long ones and unstressed for the short. This "greater" *Ionic* foot is rarer in English than the "lesser," which amount to a PYRRHIC followed by a SPONDEE. Something of the sort may turn up as a variation in a generally IAMBIC poem, as in Tennyson's LINE "On the bald street breaks the blank day." In SONGS, which permit some license in shortening and lengthening syllables, we may occasionally hear a "lesser" *Ionic* effect in lines like "In the evening by the moonlight."

Ipse Dixit: Any dogmatic statement. Literally the Latin means: "He himself has said." Hence, the term is used to characterize any edict or brief statement emphatically uttered but unsupported by proof.

Irish Literary Movement, Irish Literary Revival, Irish Renaissance: Variant terms for the movement that encouraged the production of Anglo-Irish literature. See CELTIC RENAISSANCE.

Irish Literature: The early literature of Ireland is greater in bulk, earlier in date, and more striking in character than any other preserved vernacular Western European literature. It has furnished a storehouse of literary materials for later writers, especially those of the early ROMANTIC PERIOD and of the CELTIC RENAISSANCE. It is possible, too, that it supplies a clue to the origins of ARTHURIAN LEGEND. The development of this extensive native literature, as well as the remarkable flourishing of Latin learning in Ireland in the early Middle Ages, is due in part to the fact that the Teutonic invasions, which destroyed Roman power in the fifth century, failed to reach Ireland, which became a refuge for European scholars and for several centuries the chief center of Christian culture in Western Europe. The Irish clerics, too, seem to have been unusually tolerant of native pagan culture and therefore aided in preserving a great mass of native, often primitive, legendary and literary materials of interest to the student of FOLKLORE and LINGUISTICS.

Although POETRY in Irish was written in very early times, definite metrical FORMS that employed ALLITERATION and RHYME having been developed as early as the seventh century, the bulk of early *Irish literature* is in PROSE. The early Irish EPICS are distinguished from most other early EPIC literature by their use of PROSE instead of VERSE (though the Irish PROSE EPICS frequently include poetic PARAPHRASES or commentaries—"rhetorics"—scattered throughout the text). The basic STORIES of the chief EPIC cycle reflect a state of culture prevailing about the time of Christ. Orally preserved from generation to generation for centuries, they seem to have been written down as early as the seventh and eighth centuries. These early copies of the old stories were largely destroyed and scattered as a result of the Norse invasion (eighth and ninth centuries), the stories being imperfectly recovered and again recorded in manuscripts by the patriotic antiquarians of the tenth and later centuries. Two large manuscripts of the twelfth century containing these retellings of ancient story are still in existence, the *Book of the Dun Cow* (before 1106) and the *Book of Leinster* (before 1160).

The early SAGA literature is divided into three great CYCLES: the "mythological," based on early Celtic MYTHS and historical LEGENDS concerning population groups or "invasions"; the Ulster Cycle, or "Red Branch," of which Cuchulain is the central heroic figure; and the Fenian Cycle, concerned with the exploits of Finn mac Cool and his illustrious companions. The Ulster Cycle was more aristocratic than the Fenian and is preserved in greater volume in the early manuscripts. The chief STORY is the *Táin bó Cualnge,* "The Cattle Raid of Cooley," the greatest of the early Irish EPICS. Other important stories of this cycle are *The Feast of Bricriu* (containing a beheading game like that in *Sir Gawain and the Green Knight*), *The Wooing of Etaine* (a fairy mistress STORY), and *The Exile of the Sons of Usnech* (the famous Deirdre STORY). The Fenian stories, perhaps later in origin than the Ulster tales, have shown greater vitality in oral tradition, many of them still being current among the Gaelic peasants of Ireland and Scotland. They were utilized by James Macpherson in the eighteenth century. See FORGERIES, LITERARY.

Early Irish professional POETS (*fili*) or storytellers were ranked partly by the extent of their repertory of TALES, the highest class being able to recite no less than 350 separate STORIES. These stories were divided into numerous classes or types, such as cattle raids, wooings, battles, deaths, elopements, feasts, exiles, destructions, slaughters, adventures, voyages, and visions.

In addition to the SAGA literature, there has been preserved (partly in Latin) a vast amount of historical, legal, and religious literature, the latter including a great many SAINTS' LIVES as well as HYMNS, martyrologies, and one of the earliest examples of medieval biographical writing, Adamnan's *Vita Sancti Columbae,* "The Life of Saint Columba" (before A.D. 700).

The traditional literary technique of the native Irish writers was much altered after the spread of English power and culture in Ireland in the seventeenth century, and the decline in the employment of the Irish language since that time has been accompanied by a lowering and lessening of literary activity. In modern times the versatile writer Brendan Behan was best known for PLAYS in English PROSE but could write respectable POEMS in the Irish language as well. For "revivals" of Gaelic literature and culture see CELTIC RENAISSANCE, CELTIC REVIVAL, GAELIC MOVEMENT.

[References: Myles Dillon, *Early Irish Literature* (1948); Robin Flower, *The Irish Tradition* (1947); Douglas Hyde, *A Literary History of Ireland* (1899); Patrick Rafroidi, *Irish Literature in English: The Romantic Period*, 2 vols. (1980).]

Irony: A broad term referring to the recognition of a reality different from appearance. Verbal *irony* is a FIGURE OF SPEECH in which the actual intent is expressed in words that carry the opposite meaning. *Irony* is likely to be confused with SARCASM, but it differs from SARCASM in that it is usually lighter, less harsh in its wording, though in effect probably more cutting because of its indirectness. Its presence is marked by a sort of grim HUMOR and "unemotional detachment" on the part of the writer, a coolness in expression at a time when the writer's emotions appear to be really heated. Characteristically it speaks words of praise to imply blame and words of blame to imply praise, though its inherent critical quality makes the first type much more common than the second. In a recent popular SONG, a farmer says to the wife who has abandoned him, "You picked a fine time to leave me, Lucille." At a certain depth of *irony*, saying what you do not mean gives way to being unable to say what you mean, as Mr. Prufrock's outburst, "It is impossible to say just what I mean!" (which, ironically, seems to be just what he means). The effectiveness of *irony* as a literary device is the impression it gives of restraint. The ironist writes with tongue in cheek; for this reason *irony* is more easily detected in speech than in writing, since the voice can, through its intonation, easily warn the listener of a double significance. One of the most famous ironic remarks in literature is Job's "No doubt but ye are the people, and wisdom shall die with you." Antony's insistence, in his oration over the dead Caesar, that "Brutus is an honorable man" bears a similar ironic imprint. Goldsmith, Jane Austen, and Thackeray, in one NOVEL or another, make frequent use of this form. Jonathan Swift is an archironist—his "Modest Proposal" for saving a starving Ireland, by suggesting that the Irish sell their babies to the English landlords to be eaten—is perhaps the most savagely sustained ironic writing in our literature. Alexander Pope used *irony* brilliantly in POETRY. The NOVELS of Thomas Hardy and Henry James are elaborate artistic expressions of the ironic spirit, for *irony* applies not only to statement but also to event, SITUATION, and STRUCTURE. In DRAMA, *irony* has a special meaning, referring to knowledge held by the audience but hidden from the CHARACTERS. TRAGIC IRONY is a form of DRAMATIC IRONY in which characters use words that mean one thing to them but have foreboding, different meaning to those who understand the situation better. In contemporary CRITICISM *irony* is used to describe a poet's "recognition of incongruities" and his or her controlled acceptance of them. Recent CRITICISM, prompted particularly by Northrop Frye's *Anatomy of Criticism*, has concentrated on many sorts of *irony* as the typical habit of the EIRON, who does not and cannot speak directly. Other CRITICS important in the ANALYSIS or *irony* are Wayne Booth and Harold Bloom. Among the devices by which *irony* is achieved are HYPERBOLE, UNDERSTATEMENT, and SARCASM. See DRAMATIC IRONY.

[References: Wayne Booth, *A Rhetoric of Irony* (1974); Northrop Frye, *Anatomy of Criticism* (1957); Norman Knox, *The Word Irony in Its Context, 1500–1755* (1961); G. G. Sedgewick, *Of Irony, Especially in Drama* (1948); F. McD. C. Turner, *The Element of Irony in English Literature* (1926).]

Irregular Ode: An ODE that does not follow either the pattern of STROPHE, ANTISTROPHE, and EPODE of the PINDARIC ODE or the REPETITION of STANZAS of the HORATIAN ODE but freely alters its stanzaic forms both in number and in length. It was introduced by Abraham Cowley in the seventeenth century. Wordsworth's *Ode on Intimations of Immortality* is a noted example. It is sometimes called the "pseudo-Pindaric ode." See ODE.

Issue: A distinct set of copies of an EDITION of a book. An *issue* is distinguishable from other copies or sets of copies of the EDITION by variations in the printed matter. A PRINTING may contain more than one *issue* if variations in the printed matter occur during the PRINTING.

Italian Sonnet: A SONNET divided into an OCTAVE rhyming *abbaabba* and a SESTET rhyming *cdecde*. That is the CLASSIC FORM, which asserts the avoidance of RHYME in COUPLETS in the SESTET and a limiting of the overall number of rhymes to five. Ideally, the sense of the LINES falls into groups different from the rhyme groups, thus: *ab-ba-ab-ba-cde-cde*, so that nowhere do we encounter a pat COUPLET. The least objectionable departures are the *abbaacca* OCTAVE and the *cdcdcd* SESTET. See SONNET.

J

Jacobean Age: That portion of the RENAISSANCE Period during the reign of James I (1603–1625), so-called from the Latin form of James, *Jacobus.* Early Jacobean literature was a rich flowering of ELIZABETHAN literature, while late Jacobean writing showed the attitudes characteristic of the CAROLINE AGE. During the *Jacobean Age* the breach between Puritan and Cavalier steadily widened, and there was a robust growth of REALISM in art and CYNICISM in thought. It is the greatest period for the English DRAMA; Shakespeare wrote his greatest TRAGEDIES and his TRAGI-COMEDIES; Jonson flourished, producing CLASSICAL TRAGEDY, REALISTIC COMEDY, and MASQUES; and Beaumont and Fletcher, Webster, Chapman, Middleton, and Massinger were at their peaks. In POETRY, Shakespeare published his *Sonnets,* Drayton his *Poems,* and Donne his METAPHYSICAL VERSE. In PROSE, it saw the publication of the King James TRANSLATION of the BIBLE, Bacon's major work, Donne's and Andrewes' sermons, Burton's *Anatomy of Melancholy,* the CHARACTER essays, and Dekker's realistic "NOVELS." See RENAISSANCE and *Outline of Literary History.*

Jargon: Confused speech, resulting particularly from the mingling of several languages or dialects. The term is also used to refer to any strange language that sounds uncouth to us; in this sense, outlandish speech. Sometimes *jargon* means simply nonsense or gibberish. *Jargon* also, like CANT, signifies the special language of a group or profession, as legal *jargon,* pedagogic *jargon,* thieves' *jargon.*

Jeremiad: A work that foretells destruction because of the evil of a group or a nation. It takes its name from the Hebrew prophet Jeremiah, who opens his prophecy with the Lord saying, "Out of the north an evil shall break forth upon all the inhabitants of the land . . . who have forsaken me, and have burned incense unto other gods, and worshiped the works of their own hands" (Jeremiah 1:14, 16). The term is also used for severe expressions of great grief and complaint, similar to Jeremiah's *Lamentations,* an expression of his deep sorrow over the capture of Jerusalem.

Jest Books: A name applied to collections of humorous, witty, or satirical ANECDOTES and jokes. *Jest books* had some vogue in England and Germany and other European countries in the sixteenth and succeeding centuries. The "jests" in these miscellanies owe something to the Latin *facetia,* the medieval FABLIAU and EXEMPLUM, the EPIGRAM, the PROVERB, and the ADAGE. They are usually short and often end with a "moral." Coarseness, ribaldry, REALISM, SATIRE, and CYNICISM often characterize the witty turns. The material in the *jest books* probably is similar in character to the stock-in-trade of the medieval MINSTRELS, the printing press making possible the dissemination of such matter in book form. Women, friars, cuckolds, Welshmen, courtiers, tradesmen, foreigners, military officers, doctors, students, travelers, and many other classes are butts of the WIT or victims of practical jokes. The earliest English *jest book* is *A Hundred Merry Tales* (*ca.* 1526). Another famous one was *The Gest of Skoggan* (*ca.* 1565), which illustrates a tendency of *jest books* to be "biographical" in making the jokes cluster about a single person. There were in the seventeenth and eighteenth centuries *jest books* on Ben Jonson. One famous court jester, Archie Armstrong, published his own *jest book, A Banquet of Jests and Merry Tales* (1630). It is divided into "Court Jests," "Camp Jests," "College Jests," "City Jests," and "Country Jests."

[Reference: W. C. Hazlitt, ed., *Shakespeare Jest-Books*, 3 vols. (1864).]

Jesuits: Members of the Society of Jesus, a Catholic religious order founded by Saint Ignatius Loyola in 1534. In contrast with the ascetic ideals of the medieval Catholic orders, the *Jesuits* were conceived as a band of disciplined spiritual soldiers who were expected to engage actively in affairs. The discipline was strict, the individual having no rights as such but vowing to serve God through the Society of Jesus. The members were bound by personal vows of poverty, chastity, and obedience. The head of the Order, called the "General," lives in Rome and is subject to the Pope. The *Jesuits* became famous as schoolmasters and made effective efforts to raise the educational as well as spiritual standards of the clergy. Their activities as missionaries are well known; the letters of *Jesuit* missionaries in America give important pictures of early life in the colonies. They were very active in New France. Although political activities were technically forbidden, the objectives of the Order actually led the *Jesuits* into political intrigue, and this fact has led to much criticism of the Order, which is often accused of duplicity and casuistry, a charge perpetuated unjustly in the use of "Jesuitical" as a derogatory adjective. English POETRY has been enriched by the poetic work of some *Jesuit* POETS, notably Robert Southwell (1561–1595), whose *Saint Peter's Complaint* and his more brilliant short POEMS such as 'The Burning Babe," anticipate both the seriousness of Milton and the CONCEITS of Donne, and another *Jesuit*, Gerard Manley Hopkins (1844–1889), whose *Poems,* posthumously published in 1918, demonstrated an intensity of feeling and a mastery of experimental poetic devices that have made him a potent figure in modern poetry. Nothing too crisp can be said about such matters, but it is at least probable that Hopkins's extraordinary rigorous training as a *Jesuit* contributed much to his linguistic and verbal sensitivity and to his philosophical breadth and subtlety.

Jeu d'esprit: A witty playing with words, a clever sally. Much of Thomas Hood's VERSE, for example, may be said to be marked by a happy *jeu d'esprit.* The term is also applied to brief, clever pieces of writing, such as Benjamin Franklin's "BAGATELLES."

Jewish-American Literature: A field of study that has emerged since about 1935 and concentrated on the work of Jewish writers living in America. Although some POETS (such as Karl Shapiro and Allen Ginsberg) have been studied in this setting, most of the critical attention has gone to playwrights (such as Arthur Miller) and, pre-eminently, to FICTION writers (such as J. D. Salinger, Norman Mailer, Saul Bellow, Mark Harris, Philip Roth, and Bernard Malamud—some of whom raise the question of what constitutes "Jewishness"). Studies have been made of linguistic, social, cultural, religious, political, and historical backgrounds; and some attention has been paid to the importance of certain continental precursors (Proust and Kafka, for example) and certain recurrent THEMES or problems (violence, generational strife, guilt, political loyalty).

Jig: A nonliterary farcical dramatic performance, the words being sung to the accompaniment of dancing. It was popular on the Elizabethan stage, often being used as an afterpiece. "He's for a *jig*, or a tale of bawdry," Hamlet says of Polonius. See DROLL.

[Reference: C. R. Baskervill, *The Elizabethan Jig* (1929, reprinted 1965).]

Jingle: A versicle, or short verse or sentence, set to catchy music and used to sell something. The heyday of the *jingle* was during the flourishing of radio, around 1930–1950. The effect of *jingle* in a different sense implying short LINES, percussive RHYMES, and unevolved RHYTHM, temporarily entertaining but eventually disagreeable, was found by Emerson in the POEMS of Poe and Tennyson.

Jongleur: A French term for a professional musical entertainer of medieval times, analogous to the Anglo-Saxon GLEEMAN and the later MINSTREL. Though primarily one who sang or recited the LYRICS, BALLADS, and STORIES of such original POETS as the TROUBADOUR and the TROUVÈRE, the *jongleur* sometimes composed and sometimes supplied nonmusical forms of entertainment, such as juggling and tumbling. The dissemination of literary forms and materials from nation to nation in the Middle Ages owes a good deal to the activities of the *jongleur* and the MINSTREL.

Journal: A form of autobiographical writing including a day-by-day account of events and a record of personal impressions. It is usually less intimate than a DIARY and more obviously chronological than an AUTOBIOGRAPHY. The term *journal* is also applied to any PERIODICAL publication that contains news or deals with matters of current interest in any particular sphere, as *The Journal of Southern History*. As a point of etiquette, some learned and literary periodicals prefer *journal* to MAGAZINE, the latter term being considered appropriate for organs less dignified and more miscellaneous.

Judicial Criticism: A kind of CRITICISM that, in contradistinction to IMPRESSIONISTIC CRITICISM, attempts by the rigorous application of general standards and objective criteria to analyze, classify, define, and evaluate works of art. See CRITICISM, TYPES OF.

Jungian Criticism: Literary CRITICISM based on the psychology of Carl Jung, a Swiss psychiatrist and the founder of analytical psychology. His postulate of two dimensions in the unconscious—the personal, consisting of repressed events in the individual's life, and the archetypal, which is a part of the collective unconscious—has been widely employed by CRITICS, particularly those interested in MYTH CRITICISM. See ARCHETYPE and MYTH.

[Reference: Bettina L. Knapp, *A Jungian Approach to Literature* (1984).]

Juvenalian Satire: A kind of direct or FORMAL SATIRE in which the satiric speaker, using a dignified STYLE, attacks vice and error with contempt and indignation. It is so called because in TONE and attitude it is like the SATIRES of Juvenal. Samuel Johnson's "The Vanity of Human Wishes" is a well-known English example. *Juvenalian satire* in its REALISM and its harshness is in strong contrast to HORATIAN SATIRE, the other principal type of FORMAL SATIRE. See SATIRE.

Juvenilia: Literary works produced in the author's youth and usually marked by immaturity. Dryden's POEM "Upon the Death of Lord Hastings," written when he was eighteen, Pope's *Pastorals,* written when he was sixteen, and Lord Byron's *Hours of Idleness,* written when he was eighteen, are examples, as is Poe's volume *Tamerlane and Other Poems,* published when he was eighteen.

K

Kabuki Plays: The most popular form of theatrical entertainment in Japan since the mid-seventeenth century. *Kabuki* is an eclectic theatrical form using STORIES, scenes, dances, and music, some of which are more than a thousand years old. It is a dance and musical theater, with elaborate stage settings. The actors are all men, some of whom are trained to impersonate women. They are skilled dancers and acrobats. The PLAYS themselves seem of dubious literary value, being primarily important as vehicles for SPECTACLE. They are of several kinds: EPIC plays, of the heroic period in Japanese history; "common-people's plays," tending toward naturalistic TRAGEDY; FARCES; and dance plays. All are marked by formalism and careful attention to theatricality. As Henry W. Wells has said, "The playwrights, if such they may be called, possessed an uncanny sense for the theatrical but a truly subversive view of dramatic literature." See NOH PLAYS.

Kailyard School: A name given to a group of Scottish writers whose work dealt idealistically with ordinary people in modern village life in Scotland. DIALECT was an important element in their writing. J. M. Barrie and "Ian Maclaren" are two of the best-known members of the school, which was popular toward the close of the nineteenth century. *Kailyard* is a Scottish term for a cabbage garden.

Kenning: A stereotyped figurative phrase used in OLD ENGLISH and other Germanic languages as a SYNONYM for a simple noun. *Kennings* are often picturesque metaphorical compounds. Specimen *kennings* from *Beowulf* are "the bent-necked wood," "the ringed prow," "the foamy-necked," "the sea-wood," and the "sea-farer," for *ship;* "the swan-road" and the whale-road" for the *sea;* the "leavings of the file" for the *sword;* the "twilight-spoiler" for the *dragon;* the "storm of swords" for *battle;* and the "peace-bringer among nations" for the *queen.*

Kenosis: Literally an emptying, an evacuation; theologically the deed or process by which Christ took on humble human form, surrendering divinity. In some of Harold Bloom's CRITICISM, *kenosis* is treated as a TROPE, presumably a turn from a high level to a lower.

Kind: A term widely used during the NEOCLASSIC PERIOD for GENRE or literary type. Implicit in the use of the term is the assumption that literary GENRES have an objective, absolute existence analogous to the *"kinds"* of the natural world and that they obey "the laws of *kind."* See GENRE.

Kit-Cat Club: A club generally believed to have existed in London between 1703 and 1733, founded by members of the Whig Party and dedicated in part to the ensuring of a Protestant succession to the throne. Among its members were Addison, Steele, Congreve, Vanbrugh, and Marlborough. It met at the "Cat and Fiddle" pastryshop, kept by Christopher Cat, from whom it is assumed to have taken its name. In the summer it met in a room with a very low ceiling at the home of the publisher Jacob Tonson. When Sir Godfrey Kneller painted the portraits of the members to hang in this room, he was forced to use small canvases, 36 by 28 inches, dimensions later called *kit-cat* size.

Knickerbocker Group: A name given to a group writing in and about New York during the first half of the nineteenth century. The name "Knicker-bocker" was made famous by Washington Irving in his *Knickerbocker's History of New York.* The heyday of the group was the first third of the century, although it was represented in the *Knickerbocker Magazine* (1833–1865); the remnants of the *Knickerbocker* school were pilloried in Poe's *The Literati of New York City.* Journalism, editorship, the frontier, POETRY, NOVELS, SONGS, and, in the case of Bryant at least, TRANSLATION from the CLASSICS, were the sorts of things that claimed the attention of these writers. The term "school" is, for them, a misnomer, since they consciously held few tenets in common and worked to no deliberate collective purpose. Their association was one of geography and chance rather than of close organization. At the turn of the nineteenth century, New York was forging ahead of Boston as a center of activity and of population, so that the city was becoming more important as a literary center. The more illustrious members of the school were: Washington Irving, James Fenimore Cooper, William Cullen Bryant, Joseph Rodman Drake, Fitz-Greene Halleck, John Howard Payne, Samuel Woodworth, and George P. Morris.

Koran: A Moslem collection of scriptural writings. The text is believed to have been revealed to Mohammed from time to time over a period of years and, after many changes and much editing, took shape in an official transcription after Mohammed's death (A.D. 632). The book is the sacred scripture of millions of followers and presents—in addition to matters of theology—moral teaching, liturgical directions, and advice on religious conduct and ceremonials. The speaker is usually God.

Künstlerroman: A form of the APPRENTICESHIP NOVEL in which the PROTAGONIST is an artist of some sort who struggles from childhood to maturity against an inhospitable environment and within himself toward an understanding of his creative mission. The most famous *Künstlerroman* in English is James Joyce's *A Portrait of the Artist as a Young Man.* See APPRENTICESHIP NOVEL.

L

Lai: A SONG or short NARRATIVE POEM. See LAY.

Lake Poets and **Lake School:** A name used to characterize Coleridge, Words-worth, and Southey—three POETS who at the beginning of the nineteenth century were living in the Lake District (Cumberland, Westmorland, and Lancashire). The pejorative label "lakers" is credited to the *Edinburgh Review,* which for several years adopted a very contemptuous attitude toward the poets. There was no "school" in the sense of the three all working for common objectives, but it is true that Coleridge and Wordsworth had certain convictions in common and on occasion worked together.

Lament: A POEM expressing some great grief, usually more intense and more personal than that expressed in a COMPLAINT. *Deor's Lament,* an early Anglo-Saxon POEM, for instance, presents the plaintive regret of the SCOP at his changed status after a rival had usurped his place in the esteem of a patron. The separate "tragedies" in such collections as the sixteenth-century *Mirror for Magistrates,* in which the ghosts of dead worthies tell the STORIES of their fall from fortune, were called *laments* in RENAISSANCE times, an example being Sackville's "Lament" for the Duke of Buckingham. See COMPLAINT.

Lampoon: Writing that ridicules and satirizes the CHARACTER or personal appearance of a person in a bitter, scurrilous manner. *Lampoons* were written in either VERSE or PROSE. Lampooning became a dangerous sport and fell into disuse with the development of the libel laws. See EPIGRAM.

Language Poets, The: A descriptive term—about as vague as any in the history of literary nomenclature and taxonomy—applied around 1980 to a group of younger American POETS whose work shows radical suspicion, skepticism, or CYNICISM about the efficacy of written language to record, register, represent, communicate, or express anything much beyond its own intramural apparatus.

Late Victorian Age, 1870–1901: The period between 1870 and the death of Queen Victoria saw the full flowering of the movement toward REALISM, which had begun as early as the 1830s but had been subordinated to the dominant ROMANTICISM of the first half of Victoria's reign. George Eliot and Thomas Hardy carried the realistic NOVEL to new heights. Spencer, Huxley, Newman, Arnold, and Morris, in the ESSAY, argued the meaning of the new science, the new religion, and the new society. The DRAMA, which had been sleeping for more than a century, awoke under the impact of Ibsen and the CELTIC RENAISSANCE. Stevenson, W. H. Hudson, and Kipling revived romantic FICTION. Oscar Wilde and the "decadents" wrote witty POETRY and DRAMA. Walter Pater advanced the doctrine of "ART FOR ART'S SAKE." The tendency to look with critical eyes on human beings, society, and God, to ask pragmatic questions, and to seek utilitarian answers—a tendency that had begun in the second quarter of the century—had become the dominant mode of thought and writing by the time that Queen Victoria died. See REALISTIC PERIOD IN ENGLISH LITERATURE, VICTORIAN, and *Outline of Literary History.*

Laureate: One honored by a crown of laurel; hence, one especially singled out because of distinctive achievement. The term has come to be most frequently used in the British post of POET LAUREATE. It is also applied to the recipient of other major honors, as a Nobel *laureate.* See POET LAUREATE.

Lay *(lai)*: A SONG or short NARRATIVE POEM. The word has been applied to several different poetic FORMS in French and English literature. The earliest existing French *lais* were composed in the twelfth century and were based on earlier SONGS or VERSE TALES sung by Breton minstrels on THEMES drawn from Celtic legend; hence the term "Breton *lay.*" Though some of the early French *lais* were LYRIC, most of them were NARRATIVE, like those of Marie de France, who wrote at the court of the English King Henry II about 1175. A few of her *lais* are related to ARTHURIAN LEGEND. The prevailing VERSE form of the early French *lais* was the eight-syllable LINE rhyming in COUPLETS. Later French *lais* developed more complicated forms.

The word *lay* was applied to English POEMS written in the fourteenth century in imitation of the Breton *lays.* Though a few of them followed the short COUPLET form, more use the popular TAIL-RHYME STANZA. Any short NARRATIVE POEM similar to the French *lai* might be called a "Breton *lay*" by the English POETS. Actually THEMES from various sources were employed, including CLASSICAL, Oriental, and Celtic. Some of the best-known English Breton *lays* are the *Lay of Launfal, Sir Orfeo, Sir Gowther,* and Chaucer's *Franklin's Tale.*

Since the sixteenth century, *lay* has been used by English writers as synonymous with SONG. In the early nineteenth century *lay* sometimes meant a short historical BALLAD, as Scott's *Lay of the Last Minstrel* and Macaulay's *Lays of Ancient Rome. Lais* as used by François Villon for the title of the POEMS now known as *Petit Testament* (1456) is a different word, corresponding to modern French *legs,* "bequest" or "legacy."

Legend: A NARRATIVE or TRADITION handed down from the past. A *legend* is distinguished from a MYTH in that the *legend* has more of historical truth and perhaps less of the supernatural. *Legends* often indicate the lore of a people and, in this way, serve as at least partial expressions of a racial or national spirit. Saints' *legends* are NARRATIVES of the lives of the early church heroes. *Legend* is also used for any brief explanatory comment or code accompanying paintings, charts, maps, or photographs.

Legitimate Theater: The presentation of regular PLAYS, depending entirely on acting, on a stage before an audience, using living actors. Today it distinguishes what are commonly called "stage plays" from FILMS, television, VAUDEVILLE, puppet shows, ballets, and MUSICAL COMEDY. The term derives from the PATENT THEATERS to which the presentation of DRAMA in the traditional sense was restricted from 1660 to 1843 in England.

Leitmotif: In art, an intentional and recurrent REPETITION of some word, phrase, situation, or idea. Such REPETITION tends to unify a work through its power to remind the reader of its earlier occurrences. The phrases "A stone, a leaf, an unfound door" and "Ghost, come back again" in Thomas Wolfe's *Look Homeward, Angel* are examples of the *leitmotif.* In a subtler way, "rain" in *A Farewell to Arms* functions as a *leitmotif.* See MOTIF.

Leonine Rhyme: A particular FORM of INTERNAL RHYME characterized by the rhyming of the last stressed syllable before the CAESURA with the last stressed syllable of the LINE. Ordinarily *Leonine rhyme* is restricted to PENTAMETERS and HEXAMETERS, but less rigidly the term is applied to VERSES such as the "Stabat Mater" of the Church. The expression is said to be derived from the name of a writer of the Middle Ages, Leoninus, canon of St. Victor in Paris, who wrote ELEGIAC lines containing this variety of INTERNAL RHYME. An example of *Leonine rhyme* is italicized in the following: "There's a whisper down the *field* where the year has shot her *yield"* (Kipling, "Envoy"). Also called INTERNAL RHYME. See RHYME.

Letterpress: Used to distinguish the reading matter, or the "text," of a book from the illustrative matter. This use of the term may have derived from the fact that, in the older processes of printing, the *letterpress* printed directly from type instead of from the plates, woodcuts, or blocks used for illustrations. The term is also employed to refer to the typography of a work or to printing in a general sense. Among book manufacturers, *letterpress* refers to the process of printing by direct contact of the sheet to the inked raised surfaces of type, cuts, or those kinds of plates that duplicate raised type. *Letterpress* is then used in distinction to offset, gravure, and images printed by such methods as Xerography or cathode-ray scanner-printing.

Letters: A general name sometimes given to literature (see BELLES-LETTRES). More specifically, it refers to notes and EPISTLES. A great body of informal literature is preserved through collections of actual *letters.* The correspondence of such figures as Lord Byron, Jane and Thomas Carlyle, Lord Chesterfield, Charles Dickens, Edward FitzGerald, William Hazlitt, Charles Lamb, Mary Wortley Montagu, Thomas Gray, Horace Walpole, Sydney Smith, Ezra Pound, and Robert Louis Stevenson—to mention a few of the notable letter writers—constitutes a pleasant byway in the realm of literature. *Letters,* in this sense, are distinguished from EPISTLES in that they present personal and natural relationships among friends, whereas EPISTLES are usually more formal documents prepared with a view to their being read by some public. Numerous modern POETS have written POEMS in the form of the *letter:* examples are Pound's "The River-Merchant's Wife: A Letter" and "Exile's Letter," Auden's long funny "Letter to Lord Byron," and later poems by Richard Hugo and Jim Harrison.

 Yet another sense has to do with the constituents of the alphabet, figuratively employed to mean "literal" (as in "letter of the law").

Lexicography: The art of making DICTIONARIES or LEXICONS. The most ancient DICTIONARY extant is said to be a Greek LEXICON called *Homeric Words,* prepared by Apollonius the Sophist in the reign of Augustus (27 B.C.–A.D. 14). The technique of making LEXICONS and DICTIONARIES developed slowly from the mere explanation of hard words by means of simpler ones in the same language, to the preparation of elaborate lists, alphabetically arranged, with derivations, pronunciations, spellings, and illustrative quotations, and meanings, either in the same or other languages. For English *lexicography,* see DICTIONARIES and ENGLISH.

Lexicon: A word list or wordbook; a vocabulary; one of the standard terms for DICTIONARY, although in the past it was usually applied only to dictionaries of Greek or Hebrew. See LEXICOGRAPHY.

Libretto: The text or book, containing the STORY, TALE, or PLOT of an OPERA or of any long musical composition—a cantata, for instance. It is the diminutive form of the Italian *libro,* a book.

Light Ending: In METRICS, a FEMININE ENDING.

Light Opera: A form of OPERA that lacks the dignity and seriousness of grand OPERA and usually stresses sentiment rather than passion. It is unlike COMIC OPERA in that spoken DIALOGUE is not commonly employed. An example is M. W. Balfe's *The Bohemian Girl* (1843).

Light Verse: Humorous, comic, witty POEMS, gay and bantering in tone, sportive in mood, and often sophisticated in subject and formal in treatment. There are many varieties of *light verse:* PARODY, LIMERICK, OCCASIONAL VERSE, EPIGRAMS, VERS DE SOCIÉTÉ, CLERIHEWS, NONSENSE VERSE. Grace and ease of expression, fancifulness and will to delight, charming but mordant WIT, and frequently some serious or satiric intent are characteristic of a kind of POETRY that has been practiced with grace and honor by Aristophanes, Shakespeare, Goethe, Milton, Jonson, the CAVALIER LYRICISTS, Swift, Pope, Dorothy Parker, Lewis Carroll, Edward Lear, W. S. Gilbert, T. S. Eliot, Phyllis McGinley, Christopher Morley, Helen Bevington, Ogden Nash, X. J. Kennedy, George Starbuck, John Updike, John Hollander, and Roy G. Blount, Jr. Writers of *light verse* often employ difficult and challenging FORMS, delighting in particular in the FRENCH FORMS.

Limerick: A form of LIGHT VERSE that follows a definite pattern: five anapestic LINES of which the first, second, and fifth, consisting of three FEET, rhyme; and the third and fourth lines, consisting of two feet, RHYME. Sometimes a *limerick* is written in four lines, but when so composed, its third line bears an INTERNAL RHYME and might easily be considered two lines. Some of Edward Lear's HOLOGRAPH-illustrated texts suggest that Lear thought of the FORM as two, three, or four lines—in some cases, his contributions are indistinguishable from COUPLETS or POULTER'S MEASURE with INTERNAL RHYME and anapestic RHYTHM. There seem to be associations among the *limerick,* POULTER'S MEASURE, and the SHORT MEASURE of the hymnals. (*Limericks* can be sung to the tune of the SHORT-MEASURE HYMN, "Blest Be the Tie That Binds.")

 Limericks have been written by the most distinguished modern POETS, including Robert Frost and W. H. Auden, as well as by hundreds of humble, anonymous vernacular writers whose output has been gathered in prodigious collections by Gershon Legman.

 The origin of the *limerick* is not definitely known. Though originally a kind of epigrammatic SONG, passed around orally, *limericks* increased the range of their subject matter to encompass every possible THEME, nothing being sacred to their HUMOR. They were chiefly concerned, however, with the manners, morals, and peculariaties of imaginary people. Their first recorded appearance in print was in 1820, when *Anecdotes and Adventures of Fifteen Young Ladies* and *The History of Sixteen Wonderful Old Women* were published, but they reached the peak of their vogue when Edward Lear published his *Book of Nonsense* in 1846.

Line: A fundamental conceptual unit, normally realized as a single spoken or written sequence of elements and possibly zoned by various sorts of punctuation, METER, RHYME, and other devices. Necessarily, PROSE is printed in conventional *lines,* but the *lines* are seldom distinguished by demarcation. A *line* of POETRY, also called a VERSE, conventionally equates a spatial measure with a temporal, but the two arrays need not be closely linked. Some POEMS, including the Old English poems in the Exeter Book, can be written out as PROSE; two paragraphs printed as ordinary prose in Fitzgerald's *This Side of Paradise* turn out, on inspection, to be SPENSERIAN STANZAS. As a rule, however, POEMS look like POEMS.

Linguistics: The scientific study of language. It is concerned with the description, comparison, or history of languages. *Linguistics* studies phonology (speech sounds), morphology (the history of word forms), semantics (the meaning of words), and syntax (the relationships among elementary components of larger units). Although once considered a division of PHILOLOGY, *linguistics* is today an independent and highly complex science. See PHILOLOGY.

Linguistics and Literary Criticism: This connection is as old as LINGUISTICS and CRITICISM themselves, but it reached one high point of importance in the nineteenth century (with the Grimms' philological examination of both LANGUAGE and FOLKLORE) and another after the Second World War when the techniques of STRUCTURAL LINGUISTICS were extended to individual texts and to literature as a whole. Any realm that can be understood in some way as a system of SIGNS can be studied as though it were a language, subject to the common linguistic rules of differentiation, closure, variation, transformation, and the weakness or absence of reference and signification outside the system of the language itself. See DECONSTRUCTION; PHILOLOGY; STRUCTURALISM.

[References: Leonard Bloomfield, *Language* (1933, reprinted 1965); Noam Chomsky, *Chomsky: Selected Readings* (1971); David Crystal, *Linguistics* (1971); Victoria Fromkin and Robert Rodman, *An Introduction to Language* (1983); Roman Jakobson, *Main Trends in the Science of Language* (1973); Winfred P. Lehmann, *Language: An Introduction* (1983); Ferdinand de Saussure, *Course in General Linguistics* (1916) (posthumous); Benjamin Lee Whorf, *Language, Thought, and Reality* (1956).]

Link Sonnet: An English SONNET in which the three QUATRAINS are linked by having the second RHYME of one QUATRAIN the first RHYME of the succeeding QUATRAIN. The Spenserian SONNET, rhyming *abab bcbc cdcd ee* is a *link sonnet.* See SONNET.

Linked Rhyme: Another name for FUSED RHYME.

Litany: A ritualistic form of supplication commonly used in the Catholic Church. A series of petitions often chanted by a choir in procession. The form is sometimes adopted by writers for poetic expression.

Literal: Accurate to the letter; without embellishment. Thus, in the first sense, the word is used, as in a "literal translation," to signify accuracy and thoroughness in presenting the exact meaning of the original—a TRANSLATION that more or less preserves the usual meaning of the text and allows no freedom of expression or imagination to the translator—quite different from PARAPHRASE. We have to say "more or less" because the ideal implicit in "word-for-word" TRANSLATION is unattainable, even at an elementary level. What is one word in Latin, say, may take many words to be translated into English; some common words in English, such as many prepositions and any article, simply do not exist in Latin. Most attempts to transfer the lexical units and syntactic arrangement of one language to another yield nonsense. In the second sense of "without embellishment," the term is frequently used to distinguish language that is matter of fact from language that is given to much use of FIGURES OF SPEECH. *Literal* language is the opposite of FIGURATIVE.

Literary Ballad: A BALLAD composed by an author, as opposed to the FOLK BALLAD. See ART BALLAD.

Literary Club, The (Doctor Johnson's Circle): A club formed in London in 1764 at the suggestion of Sir Joshua Reynolds, the famous painter, and with the cooperation of Dr. Samuel Johnson. Among the seven other charter members were Edmund Burke and Oliver Goldsmith. Famous men admitted to membership during Johnson's lifetime included Bishop Percy (ballad collector), David Garrick (actor), Edward Gibbon (historian), Adam Smith (economist), and James Boswell (Johnson's biographer). At first the members met at a weekly supper, and later at a fortnightly dinner during Parliament. At these meetings there was free and spirited discussion of books and writers, CLASSIC and contemporary, Johnson frequently dominating the conversation. Johnson became a sort of literary dictator, and the Club itself exercised a formidable power: whole EDITIONS of a book were sold off in one day by its sanction. Though commonly thought of only in connection with late eighteenth-century literature, the Club has continued in existence, its later membership including fifteen prime ministers and such authors as Scott, Macaulay, Hallam, and Tennyson.

Literary Epic: A long NARRATIVE POEM by a POET self-consciously employing the EPIC FORMULA. It is also called the ART EPIC. See ART EPIC, EPIC.

Litotes: A form of UNDERSTATEMENT in which a thing is affirmed by stating the negative of its opposite. To say "She was not unmindful" when one means that "She gave careful attention" is to employ *litotes*. Although a common device in ironic expression, *litotes* was also one of the characteristic FIGURES OF SPEECH of OLD ENGLISH POETRY. In Tennyson's "Ulysses," the heroic speaker resorts to *litotes* several times, with an effect of stoic restraint and (this is still the crafty warrior) subtlety: "little profits" for "profits not at all," "not least" for "great," "not to fail" for "succeed splendidly," and "not unbecoming" for "thoroughly appropriate."

Litterateur: A literary person, one who occupies himself or herself with the writing or CRITICISM or appreciation of literature. Although the term means one who is engaged in literary work or who has adopted literature as a profession, in practical usage it has—like "literatus"—a CONNOTATION of the DILETTANTE or of the "precious."

Little Magazine: A term used to designate literary JOURNALS of small circulation, limited capital, and usually quite short lives, dedicated to the fostering of AVANT-GARDE aesthetic ideas and to publishing experimental POETRY and PROSE. Notable early examples were *The Yellow Book* (1894–1897) and *The Savoy* (1896), which gave expression to the English revolt against Victorian ideas, ideals, and materialism. Early American *little magazines* were *The Lark* (1895–1897) and *The Chap-Book* (1894–1898), but the most influential of all such American journals has been *Poetry: A Magazine of Verse,* founded by Harriet Monroe in Chicago in 1912 and still in existence.

A heyday of the *little magazine* came between the First World War and the depression of the thirties. In England, in the United States, and particularly in Paris, a generation of artists in revolt against their culture and its standards found in the *little magazine* an outlet for their ideas. *The Little Review* (1914–1929), *The Seven Arts* (1916–1917), *The Fugitive* (1922–1925), *The Dial* (after its move to New York in 1916 and to its end in 1929), *Hound and Horn* (1927–1934), *Secession* (1922–1924), *transition* (1927–1938), *Broom* (1921–1924), and *The Double Dealer* (1921–1925) were among the best of hundreds of such publications.

In the depression young writers tended to desert AVANT-GARDE aesthetic positions for radical social postures, and the *little magazines* were in large measure casualties. After the Second World War, experimental writing and CRITICISM found an effective sounding board in university circles, and the equivalent of the *little magazine* was frequently a joint student-faculty production operating under a grant from the parent institution.

Beginning in the late 1960s, however, a new *little magazine* movement got vigorously underway, as a result partly of the UNDERGROUND PRESS partly of the antiestablishmentarian new AVANT-GARDE. Although most of these *little magazines* are too numerous to count and too new and untried to evaluate, there are several that have lasted long enough to achieve distinction; we can mention a series superintended by Robert Bly (*The Fifties, The Sixties, The Seventies*), Cid Corman's *Origin,* and—liveliest and most uncompromising of all—George Hitchcock's *Kayak,* which endured pluckily from the late 1960s to the middle 1980s.

Thousands of pages of bad experimental POETRY, FICTION, and CRITICISM have been published in the *little magazines,* but these deficits are more than offset by the fact that James Joyce, T. S. Eliot, Sherwood Anderson, Ernest Hemingway, William Faulkner, Wallace Stevens, Ezra Pound, Hart Crane, E. E. Cummings, Edmund Wilson, the New Critics, Gertrude Stein, Thornton Wilder, John Crowe Ransom, and Allen Tate, among many others, found in the pages of the *little magazines* their first sympathetic publication. Their present-day equivalents may now be publishing in today's *little magazines.*

[Reference: Elliott Anderson and Mary Kinzie, *The Little Magazine in America: A Documentary History* 1978).]

Little Theater Movement: A term applied to a succession of efforts to encourage the writing and production of significant PLAYS, as opposed to productions designed primarily for box-office success. The movement was originated by André Antoine in Paris in 1887 for the purpose of trying out certain dramatic experiments. There gathered about Antoine, himself a gifted actor, a group of young authors, whose plays he produced at the *Théâtre Libre* before a select audience. His attempts to advance the cause of good DRAMA included also the introduction of foreign plays by such writers as Tolstoi, Ibsen, Hauptmann, Björnson, Strindberg, and Turgenev. His experiment aided in the development of French dramatists and influenced the founding of two other French *little theaters:* Lugné-Poë's *Théâtre de l'Oeuvre* (1893) and Jacques Copeau's *Vieux Colombier* (1913). In Germany the *Frei Bühne* was established in 1899, followed by a rapid development of native talent: Hauptmann, Max Halbe, Otto Erich Hartleben, and others.

In England the movement began with the opening of the Independent Theatre (1891) under the management of Jacob Grein. Shaw, Jones, Pinero, Barrie, Galsworthy, and Barker were to some degree products of the movement. In Ireland the Irish Literary Theatre (1899) attempted to encourage Irish writers and the use of Irish THEMES, William Boyle, Lennox Robinson, J. M. Synge, Lady Gregory, and William Butler Yeats wrote for the Abbey players (see ABBEY THEATRE). The *little theater movement* began in America in 1906 and 1907 when three groups were organized in Chicago: the New Theatre, the Robertson Players, and the Hull House Theatre. In 1911–1912 came additional establishments: the Little Theatre of Maurice Browne (Chicago), Mrs. Lyman Gale's Toy Theatre (Boston), and the Festival Players of the Henry Street Settlement, the Provincetown Players, and the Washington Square Players (New York) whose members formed the Theatre Guild, which operated with spectacular success and by 1925 could build its own million-dollar playhouse. A splinter from the Guild formed the Group Theatre, which produced PLAYS by writers like Paul Green and Clifford Odets. Despite these professional successes, however, the *little theater movement* in America remained essentially local and amateur, spread over thousands of groups in towns and cities across the country. It sometimes had a strong university flavor, coming largely from the work of George P. Baker at Harvard and later at Yale and Frederich H. Koch at the University of North Carolina. The *little theater movement* established a flexible theater for serious writing and acting, brought the DRAMA to thousands who might never otherwise have seen it, and developed such talent as Eugene O'Neill, Paul Green, Philip Barry, Thornton Wilder, and R. E. Jones.

An outgrowth of the *little theater movement* came in 1936 with the establishment of the Federal Theatre Project, which annually employed over 13,000 theater workers and in its three years of existence produced more than 1200 plays. Its purpose was to supplement the commercial stage with serious and experimental DRAMA at low prices.

[References: Alexander Dean, *Little Theater Organization and Management* (1926); Constance d'Arcy Mackay, *The Little Theater in the United States* (1917).]

Liturgical Drama: A term sometimes applied to the early phase of MEDIEVAL religious DRAMA when the MYSTERY PLAYS were performed as part or extension of the liturgical service of the church. In their earliest form, in Latin, they were operatic in character, the LINES being chanted or sung rather than spoken. *Liturgical drama* is also sometimes used for the MYSTERY PLAYS developed from the liturgy. See MYSTERY PLAY, MEDIEVAL DRAMA.

Local Color Writing: Writing that exploits the speech, dress, mannerisms, habits of thought, and topography peculiar to a certain region. All FICTION has a LOCALE, but *local color writing* exists primarily for the portrayal of the people and life of a geographical SETTING. About 1880 this interest became dominant in American literature; what was called a "local color movement" developed. The various sectional divisions of America were "discovered." Bret Harte, Mark Twain, and Joaquin Miller wrote of the West; George Washington Cable, Lafcadio Hearn, Mary Noailles Murfree, and Joel Chandler Harris of the South; Sarah Orne Jewett and Mary E. Wilkins Freeman of New England.

  Local color writing was marked by the attempt at accurate DIALECT reporting, a tendency toward the use of eccentrics as CHARACTERS, and the use of sentimentalized pathos or whimsical HUMOR in plotting. A subdivision of REALISM, *local color writing* lacked the basic seriousness of true REALISM; by and large it was content to be entertainingly informative about the surface peculiarities of special regions. It emphasized VERISIMILITUDE of detail without being concerned often enough about truth to the larger aspects of life or human nature. Although local color NOVELS were written, the bulk of the work done in the movement was in the SKETCH and the SHORT STORY, aimed at the newly developing mass-circulation MAGAZINE audience. See REGIONALISM.

Locale: The physical SETTING of some ACTION. It denotes geographical and scenic qualities rather than the less tangible aspects of SETTING. *Locale* is the actual physical context of the action. See SETTING.

Locution: A term applied to a word or a group of words that constitutes a meaning group. It is also applied to a STYLE of verbal expression, particularly when it involves some peculiarity of IDIOM or manner.

Logaoedic: In CLASSICAL PROSODY a VERSE composed of ANAPESTS and IAMBS or DACTYLS and TROCHEES. The term is also used to designate any mixed METER.

Logical Positivism: A twentieth-century philosophical movement that places a primary emphasis on empirical sensory observation as the means of evaluating claims about matters of fact. It uses rigorous methods of logical analysis to clarify the meaning of statements. Among the major advocates of *logical positivism* are Rudolf Carnap and Ludwig Wittgenstein.

Logocentrism: A key term in DECONSTRUCTION; it argues that there is a persistent but morbid centering of *Logos* (meaning thought, truth, law, reason, logic, word, and the Word) in Western thought since Plato. Putting Logos at the center of discourse gives it an unquestioned status of priority and privilege—a maneuver sometimes extended to a privileging of the male order in the form of "phallogocentrism." Jonathan Culler, following Jacques Derrida, defines *logocentrism* as "the orientation of philosophy toward an order of meaning . . . conceived as existing in itself, as foundation." *Logocentrism* is the fundamental error of mistaking what is an arbitrary and artificial construct for a verifiable event.

[Reference: Jonathan Culler, *On Deconstruction* (1982).]

Logopoeia: A term coined by Ezra Pound to identify one of the ways in which POETRY charges language with meaning. MELOPOEIA has to do with the ear, PHANOPOEIA with the eye, and *logopoeia* with the mind and emotions—an exploitation of DENOTATION, CONNOTATION, roots, overtones, undertones, IRONY, AMBIGUITY, and so forth.

Lollards: The name applied to the followers of John Wycliffe, who inspired a popular religious reform movement in England late in the fourteenth century. Lollardism sprang from the clash of two ideals—that of worldly aims, upheld by the rulers of church and state, and that of self-sacrificing religion, separated from worldly interests, upheld by the humbler elements among the clergy and the laity. Although Wycliffe himself died in 1384 after sponsoring and aiding in the translation of parts of the BIBLE into English, the movement continued to gain strength. In 1395 the *Lollards* presented a petition to Parliament demanding reform in the church. It was not successful, but its terms stand as early expressions of the attitude that triumphed with the Reformation in the sixteenth century. It denounced the riches of the clergy, asked that war be declared unchristian, and expressed disbelief in such doctrines and practices as transubstantiation, image-worship, and pilgrimages. Though suppressed early in the fifteenth century, Lollardism lived on secretly and later flared up in time to furnish a strong native impetus to the Lutheran Reformation in England early in the sixteenth century. This survival of Lollardism helps explain the fact that the English Reformation movement in its early stages was a popular movement rather than a scholarly one. Some *Lollards* were burned as heretics. Early Lollardism is reflected in *Piers Plowman's Crede* (1394) (popular attitude). Chaucer's country parson, sympathetically described in the *Prologue* to the *Canterbury Tales,* was accused by the Host of being a "Loller." Lollardist attitudes find late expression in many of the PAMPHLETS of the Reformation controversy.

Long Measure: A STANZA consisting of four LINES of IAMBIC TETRAMETER and rhyming either *abcb* or *abab.* Compare with BALLAD STANZA, COMMOM MEASURE.

Loose Sentence: A sentence grammatically complete at some point (or points) before the end; the opposite of a PERIODIC SENTENCE. A complex *loose sentence* consists of an independent clause followed by a dependent clause. Most of the complex sentences we use are *loose* (the term implies no fault in structure), the PERIODIC SENTENCE being usually reserved for emphasis, drama, and variety. The constant use of the PERIODIC SENTENCE would impose too great a strain on the reader's attention. *Loose sentences* with too many dependent clauses become "stringy."

Lost Generation: A term applied to the American writers, born around 1900, who fought in the First World War and constituted a group reacting against certain tendencies of older writers in the 1920s. Although many of them spent much of their time in Paris, others lived and worked in New York, and some remained in the Middle West and the South. They were very active in the publication of LITTLE MAGAZINES. The term "Lost Generation" came from Gertrude Stein's remark to a mechanic (or vice versa) that "You are all a lost generation." Hemingway used it as one of the EPIGRAPHS of his NOVEL *The Sun Also Rises,* whose HERO, the emasculated Jake Barnes, is often considered the archetypal man of the generation. It was widely applied to such figures as F. Scott Fitzgerald, Hemingway, Hart Crane, Louis Bromfield, and Malcolm Cowley, as descriptive of the loss to them of traditional values as a result of the war and other large-scale social evils. Hemingway subsequently hinted that he had wanted his novel to counter the Stein epigraph, not confirm or illustrate it, but his disavowal seems disingenuous.

    [References: Malcolm Cowley, *Exile's Return* (1934, new ed. 1951, reprinted 1976), and *A Second Flowering: Works and Days of the Lost Generation* (1973).]

Low Comedy: The opposite of HIGH COMEDY, *low comedy* has been called "elemental comedy," in that it is lacking in seriousness of purpose or subtlety of manner and has little intellectual appeal. Some typical features of *low comedy* are: quarreling, fighting, noisy singing, boisterous conduct in general, boasting, BURLESQUE, trickery, buffoonery, clownishness, drunkenness, coarse jesting, wordplay, servants' chatter (when unrelated to the serious action), scolding, and shrewishness. In English dramatic history *low comedy* appears first as an incidental expansion of the ACTION, often originated by the actors themselves, who speak "more than is set down for them." Thus, in MEDIEVAL religious DRAMA Noah's wife exhibits stubbornness and has to be taken into the ark by force and under loud protest, or Pilate or Herod engage in uncalled-for ranting. In the MORALITY PLAYS the elements of *low comedy* became much more pronounced, with the antics of the Vice and other boisterous horseplay. In ELIZABETHAN DRAMA such elements persisted, in spite of their violation of DECORUM, because they were demanded by the public; but playwrights like Shakespeare frequently made them serve serious dramatic purposes (such as relief, marking passage of time, echoing main action). A few of the many examples of *low comedy* in Shakespeare are: the porter scene in *Macbeth,* Launcelot Gobbo and old Gobbo in *The Merchant of Venice,* the Audrey-William lovemaking scene in *As You Like It,* and the Trinculo-Stephano-Caliban scene in *The Tempest.* The famous Falstaff scenes in *King Henry the Fourth* are examples of how Shakespeare could lift *low comedy* into pure COMEDY by stressing the human and character elements and by infusing an intellectual content into what might otherwise be mere buffoonery. *Low comedy* is not a recognized special type of PLAY as is the COMEDY OF HUMOURS, for example, but may be found either alone or combined with various sorts of both COMEDY and TRAGEDY. See COMEDY, FARCE, VAUDEVILLE.

Luddites: English workmen of the late eighteenth and early nineteenth centuries who sabotaged textile machinery that they thought was taking away their jobs. The term connotes opposition to progress.

[Reference: Ola E. Winslow, *Low Comedy as a Structural Element in English Drama from the Beginning to 1642* (1926).]

Lyric: A brief subjective POEM strongly marked by IMAGINATION, melody, and emotion, and creating a single, unified impression. The early Greeks distinguished between *lyric* and choric POETRY by terming *lyric* that POETRY that was the expression of the emotion of a single singer accompanied by a lyre, and "choric" those VERSES that were the expression of a group and were sung by a CHORUS. This distinction has now disappeared, though the conception of the *lyric* as the individual and personal emotion of the POET still holds and is, perhaps, the chief basis for discriminating between the *lyric* and other poetic forms. No longer primarily designed to be sung to an accompaniment, the *lyric* nevertheless is essentially melodic, since the melody may be secured by a variety of RHYTHM patterns and may be expressed either in rhymed or unrhymed VERSES. Subjectivity, too, is an important element of a form that is the personal expression of personal emotion imaginatively phrased. It partakes, in certain high examples, of the quality of ecstasy. With a record of existence for thousands of years in every literature of the world, the *lyric* has naturally been different things to different people at different times. Strict definition is impossible.

The history of the *lyric* in English starts almost with the beginnings of our literature. In *Beowulf* certain passages have *lyric* qualities. *Deor's Lament* is essentially lyrical in purpose. Later the introduction of Latin HYMNS and the NORMAN CONQUEST brought in French and Italian elements. By about 1280 we have in "Sumer is icumen in" what would pass the strictest CRITIC today as a lyrical expression. By 1310 a manuscript collection of POEMS was made that, in addition to South European FORMS, presented some forty English *lyrics.* Before 1400 Chaucer had written a fair body of *lyrics,* particularly modeled on FRENCH FORMS. The TROUBADOUR of France so awakened interest in lyrical forms as to make them common to the various European literatures, and Petrarch gave currency to the SONNET. Thomas Wyatt and the Earl of Surrey in England popularized these Italian lyrical FORMS, particularly the SONNET, and by the time Tottel's *Miscellany* appeared (1557) the body of English *lyrics* was large and creditable. In ELIZABETHAN England the *lyric* burst into full bloom in the work of such poets as Sidney, Spenser, Daniel, and Shakespeare. SONGS, MADRIGALS, airs became numerous. Johnson and Herrick carried the tradition further. To seventeenth-century England Cowley introduced the IRREGULAR ODE (a *lyric* form), and later Dryden adopted the FORM. Milton was a great *lyric* POET. The romantic revival brought English literature some of its noblest POETRY in the ODES of Gray, Collins, Wordsworth, and Coleridge. Burns raised the *lyric* to new power. Coleridge and Wordsworth made it the vehicle of ROMANTICISM. Scott, Byron, Shelley, and Keats molded the FORM to new perfection. Bryant, Emerson, the Brownings, Arnold, Whittier, Longfellow, and Poe gave it expression in America. Victorian poets spoke through it frequently. Tennyson, the Rossettis, William Morris, Swinburne—England's greatest poets of the period—were also some of our greatest lyricists. And in twentieth-century England and America the *lyric*—in its various types—is still the most frequently used poetic expression.

The *lyric* is perhaps the most broadly inclusive of all the various types of VERSE. In a sense it could be argued to be not so much a FORM as a manner of writing. Subjectivity, IMAGINATION, melody, emotion—these qualities have been fairly persistently adhered to by the poets. But as the *lyric* spirit has flourished, the manner has been confined in various ways with the result that we have, within the *lyric* type, numerous subclassifications. HYMNS, SONNETS, SONGS, BALLADS, ODES, ELEGIES, VERS DE SOCIÉTÉ, the whole host of FRENCH FORMS, BALLADE, RONDEL, RONDEAU—all these are varieties of lyrical expression classified according to differing qualities of FORM, subject matter, and mood.

[References: Maurice Bowra, *Mediaeval Love-Song* (1961); C. Day Lewis, *The Lyric Impulse* (1965); John Drinkwater, *The Lyric* (1915); W. R. Johnson, *The Idea of Lyric* (1982); Jerome Mazzaro, *Transformations in the Renaissance Lyric* (1970); E. B. Reed, *English Lyric Poetry from Its Origins to the Present Time* (1912); Ernest Rhys, *Lyric Poetry* (1913); W. E. Rogers, *The Three Genres and the Interpretation of Lyric* (1983).]

Lyrical Drama: A term used for a dramatic POEM (see DRAMATIC POETRY) in which the form of DRAMA is used to express LYRIC themes (author's own emotions or ideas of life) instead of relying on a STORY as the basis of the action. Newman's "The Dream of Gerontius" is an example.

Lyrical Novel: A species of NOVEL in which conventional elements of objective NARRATION of ACTION are subordinated to the presentation of inner thoughts, feelings, and moods. According to Ralph Freedman, the *lyrical novel* transforms "the materials of fiction (such as characters, plots, or scenes) into patterns of imagery. . . . In this strangely alienated, yet somehow essential genre, the direct portrayal of awareness becomes the outer frontier where novel and poem meet."

[Reference: Ralph Freedman, *The Lyrical Novel: Studies in Hermann Hesse, Andre Gide, and Virginia Woolf* (1963).]

M

Mabinogion: A term applied to a collection of old Welsh tales translated by Lady Charlotte Guest from the *Red Book of Hergest,* a Welsh manuscript from the thirteenth or fourteenth century containing TALES composed centuries earlier. Only four of these tales, *Pwyll, Prince of Dyved; Branwen, Daughter of Llyr; Manawyddan, Son of Llyr;* and *Math, Son of Mathonwy* (the so-called four branches), are in the strictest sense of the word included in the term *mabinogion.* Although some modern authors follow Lady Charlotte Guest in explaining this word as meaning "a collection of tales for the young," later authorities explain *mabinogion* as the plural of *mabinogi,* "a collection of tales every young poet should know," a *mabinog* being a young literary apprentice receiving instruction from a qualified BARD. For a classification of the contents of the *Mabinogion* and for the possible relation of the tales to Arthurian ROMANCES, see WELSH LITERATURE.

Macaronic Verse: A type of VERSE that mingles two or more languages. More especially it refers to POEMS incorporating modern words (given Latin or Greek endings) with Latin or Greek. The origin of this often nonsensical sort of VERSE is credited to Tisi degli Odassi, who interspersed Latin with Italian in *Carmen Maccaronicum* (1488). A Benedictine monk, Teofilo Folengo (1491–1544), wrote a famous MOCK HEROIC called *Liber Macaronicus* (1520). Verse of the sort was soon written in France and other European countries; the best example in English is said to be the *Polemo-Middinia,* credited to William Drummond of Hawthornden. The following, by "E.C.B.," will be a self-explanatory example to anyone who knows his Latin (or his Mother Goose):

> Cane carmen SIXPENCE, pera plena rye,
> De multis atris avibus coctis in a pie:
> Simul hæc apert'est, cantat omnis grex,
> Nonne permirabile, quod vidit ille rex?
> Dimidium rex esus, misit ad reginam
> Quod reliquit illa, sending back catinum.
> Rex fuit in aerario, multo nummo tumens;
> In culina Domina, bread and mel consumens;
> Ancell' in horticulo, hanging out the clothes,
> Quum descendens cornix rapuit her nose.

Macaronic verse was not always NONSENSE VERSE; its intent was frequently that of serious SATIRE. The term is sometimes applied to any VERSE having two languages, such as William Dunbar's "Lament for the Makaris" (*ca.* 1508), which uses a Latin REFRAIN, *"Timor mortis conturbat me."* Serious use of a macaronic technique may be found in Eliot's *The Waste Land* and Pound's *Cantos.*

Machinery: In the NEOCLASSICAL PERIOD, the term *machinery* was applied, in Pope's words, "to signify that part which the deities, angels or demons are made to act in a poem." It was derived from the mechanical means used by Greek dramatists to introduce a god on the stage (see DEUS EX MACHINA). It was extended from this use in TRAGEDY to EPIC POETRY, where it refers to supernatural beings who participate in the ACTION. Thus, *machinery* is applied to the being introduced by the machine rather than the machine itself.

Macron: The name of the symbol (–) used to indicate a long syllable in QUANTITATIVE VERSE.

Madrigal: A short LYRIC, usually dealing with love or a PASTORAL theme and designed for—or at least suitable for—a musical SETTING. In the ELIZABETHAN PERIOD the term was used for a kind of SONG sung without accompaniment by five or six voices with intricate interweaving of words and melody. The Italian *madrigal* usually consisted of six to thirteen LINES based on three RHYMES. Today the term is used quite loosely. Shakespeare's "Take, O, take those lips away" from *Measure for Measure* is a *madrigal*.

Magazine: A term applied to any of several kinds of PERIODICAL miscellanies containing various kinds of material by several authors. In fastidious usage, *magazine* is reserved for the more informal sort of PERIODICAL, distinguished from JOURNAL.

Magnum Opus: A great work, a masterpiece. Formerly the term was used in all seriousness, but nowadays it often carries a suggestion of IRONY or SARCASM.

Malapropism: An inappropriateness of speech resulting from the use of one word for another, which has some similarity to it. The term is derived from a character, Mrs. Malaprop, in Sheridan's *The Rivals,* who was constantly giving vent to such expressions as the following: "as headstrong as an allegory on the banks of the Nile," "a progeny of learning," "illiterate him, I say, quite from your memory." The Nurse in *Romeo and Juliet* says "confidence" for "conference," and the *malapropism* prompts Benvolio to say, "She will indite [for "invite"] him to some supper." In *The Innocents Abroad* by Mark Twain a versifier (apparently based on Bloodgood Haviland Cutter) calls himself "the poet lariat." Instances can be found in Smollett and much DIALECT writing; the most notable modern instance is in the works of James Joyce.

Malediction: A CURSE. The opposite of benediction since it invokes evil rather than good. The famous "Cursed be he that moves my bones" used as an EPITAPH for Shakespeare is an example.

Manichaeism: An Oriental religion founded about A.D. 250 by a Persian, Mani (or Manes). *Manichaeism* sees God and Satan as coeval and engaged in an eternal struggle. The forces of light (good) do endless battle against the forces of darkness (evil). This cosmic struggle also takes place in all individuals. Our bodies, like all material substance, are evil and belong to Satan, but they are also infused with a modicum of godly light, and the struggle between the material (the body) and the godly (the light or spirit) continues as long as body and soul are united. The elect succeed in freeing the light from the evil of darkness. Through metempsychosis the unelect may progress upward toward election. Such beliefs led to a very ascetic way of life for the true believers. Mani borrowed from the Gnostics, various Oriental religions, including the Zoroastrian, and Christianity. His teachings were popular through the fifth century but since the sixth century have been considered a major source of heresy in most religions. See GNOSTICISM.

Mannerism: In the nomenclature of art history, a highly affected STYLE that was fashionable in the graphic arts around the turn of the sixteenth century, roughly contemporary with GONGORISM and MARINISM in literature. It resembles both in specializing in exaggeration, distortion, and eccentricity. In a looser sense, *Mannerism* is applied to any artwork in which manner eclipses matter.

Manners: When used in the sense of defining various literary GENRES, *manners* refers to prevailing modes of social conduct of a specific class at a definite period of time. It involves, in addition to the accepted rules of polite behavior for that class, its system of values and mores, as reflections of moral attitudes. See COMEDY OF MANNERS, NOVEL OF MANNERS.

Manuscript, Medieval: The art of manuscript-making was highly developed in the Middle Ages; the finer existing "illuminated" manuscripts and early printed books modeled on them show an artistry equal to that of the best examples of modern bookmaking. Since no mechanical means such as printing existed for multiplying copies, each manuscript required for its manufacture a prodigious amount of skilled labor. Parchment was first employed, the finest kind being vellum (made from calfskin), though paper was employed in the later Middle Ages. The actual writing was done chiefly in the monasteries, first by ordinary monks and later by professional scribes. The process of making a book included (1) the copying of the text by the scribe on separate sheets, (2) the inspection by the corrector, (3) the insertion of the capital letters, rubrics, and other colored decorative matter by the rubricator and illuminator, (4) the binding by a binder who arranged the sheets (usually by folding a group of four sheets once to make a "quire" of eight leaves, or sixteen pages) and completed the binding by the use of wooden boards, leather, and velvet. The result was a substantial "manuscript" in form much like a modern book of large size but far sturdier in construction. The illuminator did his work with great care. Favorite colors were gold, blue, and red—indeed, the origin of "rubric" is a Latin word for "red"—though green, purple, and yellow were frequently used. In spite of losses from fire, war, robbery, and neglect, thousands of *medieval manuscripts* are still in existence, carefully preserved in numerous public and private libraries. Early printed books (see INCUNABULUM) were modeled on the manuscript. In England, many *medieval manuscripts* are thought to have been destroyed as a result of the suppression of the monasteries during the Protestant Reformation.

[References: J. A. Herbert, *Illuminated Manuscripts*, 2nd ed. (1912); Falconer Madan, *Books in Manuscript* (1893, rev. ed. 1927, reprinted 1968); G. H. Putnam, *Books and Their Makers during the Middle Ages* (1896–97, reprinted 1962); B. L. Ullman, *Ancient Writing and Its Influence* (1932, reprinted 1969).]

Märchen: German FAIRY TALES. They may be simple FOLKTALES of the sort collected by Wilhelm and Jakob Grimm, known as *Volksmärchen,* or they may be short ALLEGORIES laid in a fantastic realm of the sort written in the nineteenth century by Goethe, Novalis, Tieck, and E. T. A. Hoffmann, known as the *Kunstmärchen* (art tales).

Marginalia: Notes and comments written in the margins of a book by a reader as commentaries on the text. In some cases such *marginalia* have value in reconstructing the reader's life and mind, as such *marginalia* by Herman Melville have, or make valuable critical comments, as *marginalia* of Coleridge's do. The term is also sometimes used to characterize brief critical OBITER DICTA, as in Edgar Allan Poe's *Marginalia.*

Marinism: An affected poetic STYLE practiced by the Italian POET Giambattista Marino (1569–1625) and his followers. It is the manifestation of a general tendency toward a strained, flamboyant, or shocking STYLE during the later phases of the RENAISSANCE, in some respects analogous to the BAROQUE in art. Marino expressed this aspect of his creed thus:

> Astonishment's the poet's aim and aid:
> Who cannot startle best had stick to trade.
> *(Fletcher's translation)*

A typical CONCEIT of Marino is his calling stars "blazing half-dimes of the celestial mint." Another aspect of *Marinism* was its "effeminate voluptuousness." Some English METAPHYSICAL poets were influenced by Marino: Lord Herbert of Cherbury, Thomas Stanley, Sir Edward Sherburne, and Richard Crashaw, See EUPHUISM, CONCEIT, GONGORISM, METAPHYSICAL VERSE, BAROQUE.

[Reference: J. B. Fletcher, *Literature of the Italian Renaissance* (1934, reprinted 1964).]

Marprelate Controversy: In the 1580s the Puritan opposition to the bishops of the established church in England, whose power was greatly strengthened by state support, expressed itself in outspoken PAMPHLETS. Some of the authors of these tracts were severely punished—one executed—and in 1585 the censoring of such publications was made more rigid by a provision limiting printing rights to London and the two universities. In defiance of these regulations the Puritan party began issuing, in 1588, a series of violent attacks on the episcopacy, printed surreptitiously and signed by the pen name "Martin Marprelate." The attacks were answered with corresponding scurrility by the conservatives, including Robert Greene, John Lyly, and Thomas Nash. The authorship of the Marprelate pamphlets has never been definitely established, but, whoever the author or authors, they and their opponents supplied interesting examples of spirited prose SATIRES. The controversy was suppressed by the death in prison of one alleged author and the execution in 1593 of two others.

Marxism: The social, economic, and political doctrines of Karl Marx, Friedrich Engels, and their disciples. *Marxism* assumes the independent reality of matter and its priority over mind (dialectical materialism). It teaches a theory of value based on labor, the economic determination of all social actions and institutions, the class struggle as the basic pattern in history, the inevitable seizure of power through the revolution of the proletariat, the dictatorship of that proletariat, and the ultimate establishment of a classless society. In one sense *Marxism* is an interpretation of history and a prophecy of an evolutionary process in which revolution is not necessary. In another sense, that taken by the Communists, *Marxism* is a revolutionary program. The principal Marxist doctrines were set forth in *The Communist Manifesto,* by Marx and Engels (1848), and *Das Kapital,* by Marx (1867). The impact of *Marxism* on historical theory has been pervasive, and in this sense it has permeated much twentieth-century thought, even that of the anti-Marxist. *Marxism* has had notable influence on FICTION, particularly that of radical sociological leanings, and on sociologically inclined literary CRITICISM. It was a strong influence on the writing done in America in the 1930s, and to some extent on English writing of the same period. It has, of course, been a dominant influence on Russian writing of all kinds. The leading Marxist CRITIC of our time was the Hungarian Georg Lukács.

Masculine Ending: A line of VERSE that ends on a stressed syllable, as any regular IAMBIC line does. Compare with FEMININE ENDING.

Masculine Rhyme: RHYME that falls on the stressed, concluding syllables of the RHYME words. *Masculine rhyme* accounts for a large majority of RHYMES in English. "Mount" and "fount" make a *masculine rhyme,* "mountain" and "fountain" a FEMININE.

Masked Comedy: A name applied to COMMEDIA DELL'ARTE because all the actors except the two playing the romantic lovers wore masks. See COMMEDIA DELL'ARTE.

Masque: In England as well as in other European countries there existed in medieval times (partly as survivals or adaptations of ancient pagan seasonal ceremonies) species of games or SPECTACLES characterized by a procession of masked figures. In these DISGUISINGS or MUMMINGS, which were usually of a popular or folk character, a procession of masquers would go through the streets, enter house after house, silently dance, play at dice with the citizens or with each other, and pass on. Adopted by the aristocracy, these games, modified by characteristics borrowed from civic pageants, chivalric customs, sword-dances, and the RELIGIOUS DRAMA, developed into elaborate SPECTACLES, which evolved into the entertainments known as *masques.* Because of this gradual evolution of the FORM and the scanty records, it is impossible to say when the *masque* actually came into existence. The famous EPIPHANY spectacle of 1512, given by and participated in by Henry VIII, is sometimes referred to as the first English *masque.*

The chief development of the *masque* came in the latter part of Elizabeth I's reign and, especially, in the reigns of James I and Charles I, and reached its climax under such poets as Daniel, Beaumont, Middleton, and Jonson. The greatest development was due to the poetic and dramatic genius of Jonson and Inigo Jones, famous court architect and deviser of stage MACHINERY. The "essential" *masque,* as distinguished from the "literary" *masque* (for example,

Milton's *Comus*), makes an appeal to the eye and the ear, with a succession of rapidly changing scenes and TABLEAUX crowded with beautiful figures. The gods of Olympus, the monsters of Tartarus, the HEROES of history, the ladies of ROMANCE, the fauns, the satyrs, the fairies, the witches were presented to the eye, while musical instruments charmed the ear.

Masques became increasingly expensive, almost unbelievable amounts being spent on costumes, scenery, and properties and for professional musicians, dancers, and actors. In the *masque* proper, which was the arrival and dancing of masked figures, the actors were amateurs drawn from the court society—princes and princesses, even queens and kings, taking part. With the development by Jonson of the ANTIMASQUE, the dramatic and literary qualities increased. Mythological and PASTORAL elements were emphasized, Jonson maintaining (against Daniel and Jones) that the *masque* should be based on some poetic idea and that the ACTION should be significant as well as spectacular, so that Milton's *Comus* (1634), one of the best known of all *masques*, represents a legitimate development of what was originally little but SPECTACLE. The *masque* commonly was a feature of some celebration, such as a wedding or coronation, served as a formal preliminary entertainment to a court ball, and was frequently employed at the entertainments in the INNS OF COURT. *Masques* exerted much influence on the POETRY and DRAMA of the RENAISSANCE. Spenser, for example, incorporates *masque*-like episodes in *The Faerie Queene* (e.g., the procession of the Seven Deadly Sins in book I, canto iv, and the *masque* of Cupid in III, xii). The effect on the popular DRAMA itself was probably great, since some dramatists wrote for both the court and the London stage. Peele's *Arraignment of Paris* is a PASTORAL play much like a *masque.* Many of Shakespeare's PLAYS show the influence; the betrothal *masque* in *The Tempest* is an example. *As You Like It* has been called a mere "series of tableaux and groupings," *masque*-like in the deficiency of serious action, in the prominence of music, and in the spectacular appearance of Hymen as a DEUS EX MACHINA at the end. The glorious era of the *masque* ended with the triumph of the Puritan Revolution (1642). See ANTIMASQUE.

[References: Angus Fletcher, *The Transcendental Masque: An Essay on Milton's Comus* (1971); A. Wigfall Green, *The Inns of Court and Early English Drama* (1936, reprinted 1965); Allardyce Nicoll, *Stuart Masques and the Renaissance Stage* (1938, reprinted 1963); Mary Sullivan, *Court Masques of James I* (1913); Sarah P. Sutherland, *Masques in Jacobean Tragedy* (1983); Enid Welsford, *The Court Masque* (1927, reprinted 1962).]

Matin: A morning SONG, as of birds. When used in the plural, *matins* refers to the first of the seven canonical hours in the Catholic Church at which prescribed prayers are sung.

Maxim: A short, concise statement, usually drawn from experience and inculcating some practical advice; an ADAGE. "When in doubt, win the trick," a saying of Hoyle's, is a *maxim* in bridge. See APHORISM, PROVERB.

Meaning: It is possible to distinguish four different aspects in the *meaning* of a statement. As given by I. A. Richards, they are (1) sense, the denotative "something" that the speaker or writer is trying to communicate; (2) feeling,

the attitude the speaker or writer has toward this sense; (3) TONE, the attitude
the speaker or writer has toward the audience; and (4) intention, the effect
the speaker or writer consciously or unconsciously intends to produce through
what is said or written, how he or she feels about it, and the attitude he or
she takes toward the audience. In another way, *meaning* can be seen as of
two kinds: DENOTATION and CONNOTATION. For a literary work there are
also four possible kinds of *meaning:* the literal, the allegorical, the tropological
or moral, and the anagogical or spiritual. See DENOTATION, CONNOTATION,
FOUR SENSES OF INTERPRETATION.

Measure: Frequently used as a SYNONYM for METER, *measure* is more strictly
either a metrical grouping, such as a FOOT or a VERSE, or a period of time.
In various musical theories of PROSODY a *measure* is usually the time sequence
beginning with an accented syllable and running to the next accented syllable.
In the PROSODY of HYMNS, *measure* refers to the FORM of the STANZA, as in
COMMON MEASURE and LONG MEASURE.

Medieval Drama: A general term used to include all FORMS of DRAMA in
the Middle Ages, though the religious DRAMA and its allied forms are usually
meant. The medieval religious DRAMA grew out of the liturgical services of
the church. As early as the tenth century, perhaps in northern France, TROPES
or musical elaborations of the church services, particularly of the Easter Mass,
developed into true DRAMA when the Latin lines telling the story of the Resurrection, instead of being sung antiphonally by the two parts of the choir, were
sung or spoken by priests who impersonated the two angels and the three
Marys in the scene at the tomb of Christ.

Such dramatic TROPES later became detached from the liturgical service,
and *medieval drama* was born. That such performances appeared early in
England is shown by the existence of the *Concordia Regularis* (*ca.* 975), a
complete set of instructions (stage directions) supplied to the Benedictine
monks by the Bishop of Winchester. The conscious dramatic intent is shown
in the first few LINES of the *Concordia:* "While the third lesson is being chanted,
let four brethren vest themselves. Let one of these, vested in an alb, enter
as though to take part in the service, and let him approach the sepulchre
without attracting attention and sit there quietly with a palm in his hands
. . . and let them all . . . stepping delicately as those who seek something,
approach the sepulchre" (Chambers' translation). Dramatic TROPES developed
around the Christmas and Easter services.

This use of the dramatic method for the purpose of making religious rites
and instruction vivid must have struck a responsive chord in the medieval
audience, and it was not long till further important developments, the stages
of which cannot now be exactly traced, took place. The performances were
transferred from the church to the outdoors; Latin gave way to native language;
and eventually the performances became secularized when the town authorities, utilizing the trade guilds as dramatic companies, took charge of the production of the PLAYS. Eventually great CYCLES of scriptural PLAYS developed in
which the whole plan of salvation was dramatically set forth (see MYSTERY
PLAY). Plays employing the same technique as the scriptural plays but based
on the lives of saints, especially miracles performed by saints including the

Virgin Mary (MIRACLE PLAYS, or SAINTS' PLAYS), also developed about A.D. 1100, though they seem not to have been numerous in England. Much later (*ca.* 1400) the MORALITY PLAY (dramatization of a moral ALLEGORY) became popular and with the somewhat similar play known as an INTERLUDE became an immediate precursor of ELIZABETHAN DRAMA. There was also a considerable body of FOLK DRAMA in the late Middle Ages, performed out of doors on such festival days as Hock Tuesday—Robin Hood PLAYS, sword-dance PLAYS, MUMMINGS, and DISGUISINGS. Perhaps also there were PLAYS based on MEDIEVAL ROMANCES.

The CYCLIC DRAMA (MYSTERY PLAYS) and the MORALITIES became so secularized as to bring on the disapproval of the church. The development of secular elements, especially the stressing of comic features such as the shrewish behavior of Noah's wife or the addition of comic scenes not demanded by the serious action, such as the sheep-stealing episode in the Towneley *Second Shepherd's Play*, led definitely toward Elizabethan COMEDY. Though it is difficult to analyze the full influence of *medieval drama* on later DRAMA, it is certain, as Felix E. Schelling remarks, that "it was in the ruins and debris of the miracle play and morality that Elizabethan Drama struck its deepest roots." For the method of performance of the medieval religious drama see MYSTERY PLAY. See DRAMA, MIRACLE PLAY, LITURGICAL DRAMA, TROPE, MORALITY PLAY, FOLK DRAMA, INTERLUDE.

[References: C. F. Tucker Brooke, *Tudor Drama* (1911, reprinted 1964); E. K. Chambers, *The Mediaeval Stage* (1903); Hardin Craig, *English Religious Drama of the Middle Ages* (1955); Allardyce Nicoll, *British Drama* (1925); A. W. Pollard, *English Miracle Plays*, 8th ed. (1927); H. C. Schweikert, ed., *Early English Plays* (1928); Arnold Williams, *The Drama of Medieval England* (1961); Karl Young, *The Drama of the Medieval Church* (1922).]

Medieval Romance: *Medieval romances* are tales of adventure in which knights, kings, or distressed ladies, acting under the impulse of love, religious faith, or the mere desire for adventure, are the chief figures. The *medieval romance* appears in Old French literature of the twelfth century as a FORM that supplants the older CHANSON DE GESTE, an EPIC FORM. The EPIC reflects an heroic age, whereas the *romance* reflects a chivalric; the EPIC has weight and solidity, whereas the *romance* exhibits mystery and FANTASY; the EPIC does not much stress rank or social distinctions, important in the *romance;* the tragic seriousness of the EPIC is not matched in the lighter-hearted *romance;* the heroic figures of the EPIC are more consistently conceived than the heroes of *romance;* where the EPIC HERO aims at high achievement, the HERO of *romance* is usually satisfied with more or less aimless adventure; the EPIC observes narrative UNITY, whereas the STRUCTURE of the *romance* is loose; love is usually absent or of minor interest in the EPIC, whereas it is supreme in the *romances;* EPIC fighting is serious and well motivated, whereas fighting in the *romances* is spontaneous; the EPIC uses the dramatic method of having the CHARACTERS speak for themselves, whereas the reader of a *romance* is kept conscious of a NARRATOR. The *romances* became extremely popular in Western Europe, occupying a place comparable with that of the NOVEL in modern literature. The earliest *romances* were in VERSE (hence the term METRICAL ROMANCES), but PROSE was also employed later. The materials for the early French *romances* were drawn chiefly from the Charlemagne material or CHANSONS DE GESTE ("Matter of France"), ancient history and literature ("Matter of Rome the Great"), and Celtic lore, especially Arthurian material ("Matter of Britain").

Romances were produced in English as early as the thirteenth century. They flourished in the fourteenth century and continued to be produced in the fifteenth and sixteenth centuries, though the disfavor that they met at the hands of Renaissance HUMANISTS caused them to lose standing, and RENAISSANCE versions as well as versions appearing in seventeenth- and eighteenth-century CHAPBOOKS are frequently degenerate forms, written to appeal chiefly to the middle and lower social classes. Middle English *romances* may be grouped on the basis of their subject matter. The "Matter of England" includes STORIES based on Germanic (including English) tradition and embraces *King Horn* (*ca.* 1275), *Richard Lionheart* (1350), *Beves of Hampton* (*ca.* 1300), *Havelock the Dane* (before 1300), *Guy of Warwick* (*ca.* 1300), and *Athelston* (*ca.* 1350). The "Matter of France" includes stories of Charlemagne and William of Orange, drawn from the CHANSONS DE GESTE. Important *romances* of the group are *Sir Ferumbras* (*ca.* 1375), *Otuel* (*ca.* 1300), *The Song of Roland* (fifteenth century), and *Huon of Bordeaux* (thirteenth century). The "Matter of Antiquity" includes various legends of Alexander the Great, legends of Thebes, and legends of Troy (including Chaucer's famous *Troilus and Criseyde*). The "Matter of Britain" includes the important Arthurian literature and is represented by such CLASSICS as the fourteenth-century METRICAL ROMANCE *Sir Gawain and the Green Knight* and the fifteenth-century PROSE *Le Morte Darthur* of Malory. The Arthurian *romances* developing around the legend of King Arthur (see ARTHURIAN LEGEND) had eventually developed into great CYCLES of stories in Old French literature, some of the heroes of which, such as Tristram and Lancelot, did not belong to the original legend of Arthur. They were greatly elaborated in the bulky thirteenth-century French PROSE *romances* ("VULGATE Romances"), which became sources for such English treatments of Arthurian themes as Malory's. A fifth group might include *romances* of miscellaneous origin, especially Oriental. Examples are *Amis and Amiloun* (before 1300), *Floris and Blanchefleur* (*ca.* 1250), *Sir Isumbras* (1350–1400), and *Ipomedon* (twelfth century).

The MIDDLE ENGLISH *romances* are largely in VERSE, a few alliterative, others in COUPLETS or stanzaic forms borrowed from France. In comparison with French *romances* they usually show inferior artistry, less attention to psychological treatment (as COURTLY-LOVE characteristics), less sophistication, more credulity and use of the GROTESQUE (like Richard's eating the lion's heart), and a higher moral tone.

Structurally, the *medieval romance* follows the loose pattern of the quest. Usually the PROTAGONIST sets out on a journey to accomplish some goal—rescue a maiden, meet a challenge, obey a kingly command, seek the HOLY GRAIL. On this journey, which forms the controlling outline of the PLOT, he encounters numerous adventures, many of them unrelated to his original quest except that they impede him or occur in a chronological sequence. Hence, except in the very best of these *romances*, the PLOTS are little better than threads on which the beads of EPISODES are strung in chronological rather than logical order. See ROMANCE, ARTHURIAN LEGEND, COURTLY LOVE, MIDDLE ENGLISH.

[References: Walter H. French and C. B. Hale, eds., *Middle English Metri-*

cal Romances (1930); Laura A. H. Loomis, *Medieval Romance in England* (1924, reprinted 1979); W. P. Ker, *Epic and Romance* (1896, reprinted 1957); George Saintsbury, *The Flourishing of Romance* (1897); John Stevens, *Medieval Romance: Themes and Approaches* (1973); A. B. Taylor, *An Introduction to Medieval Romance* (1930); Eugène Vinaver, *The Rise of Romance* (1971); J. E. Wells, *A Manual of the Writings in Middle English, 1050–1400* (1916, reprinted 1967).]

Medievalism: A spirit of sympathy for the Middle Ages along with a desire to preserve or revive certain qualities of medieval life. Traces can be found as early as Spenser and throughout the seventeenth and eighteenth centuries, with their more or less amateur interest in antiquities. It was nineteenth-century ROMANTICISM, however, that sponsored the most robust flourishing of *medievalism*, the development of which was aided by increasingly accurate and thorough scholarship in language, literature, and history, along with a growing respect for the Roman Catholic unity of pre-Reformation Europe. One or more elements of *medievalism* can be found in Keats, Tennyson, the Pre-Raphaelites, Ruskin, Poe, Newman, Hopkins, and such twentieth-century figures as E. A. Robinson, C. M. Doughty, T. E. Lawrence, J. R. R. Tolkien, C. S. Lewis, Charles Williams, and a host of writers of FANTASY and SCIENCE FICTION.

Meditative Poetry: A term applied to certain kinds of METAPHYSICAL POETRY of the sixteenth and seventeenth centuries that yoke a practice of religious meditation of that period with RENAISSANCE poetic techniques. "The Practical Methode of Meditation" (1614), by the Jesuit Edward Dawson, describes the religious practice, which was probably strongly indebted to Ignatius Loyola's *Spiritual Exercises.* The aim of such meditation was to employ all human faculties to apprehend the presence of God. Most *meditative poetry,* through its use of striking and often sensuous IMAGERY, its records of studying religious topics until they are understood and deeply felt, and its technique for dramatizing the self in intense meditative experiences, deals with memorable moments of self-knowledge and of union with some transcendent reality. Louis L. Martz, while acknowledging that a precise DEFINITION of *meditative poetry* is probably impossible, suggests that it is POETRY in which "the central meditative action consists of an interior drama, in which a man projects a self upon a mental stage, and there comes to understand that self in the light of a divine presence." Often such POEMS were written as part of the author's preparation for religious ceremonies, such as the American POET Edward Taylor's *Preparatory Meditations before my Approach to the Lord's Supper.* Among notable writers of *meditative poetry* were Robert Southwell (1561–1595), John Donne (1572–1631), George Herbert (1593–1633), Richard Crashaw (*ca.* 1612–1649), Henry Vaughan (1621–1692), and Thomas Traherne (1637–1674). The TRADITION may be said to continue through Tennyson's *In Memoriam* and into the twentieth century in Eliot's *Four Quartets.*

    [References: Louis Martz, (ed.) *The Meditative Poem: An Anthology of Seventeenth-Century Verse* (1963), and *The Poetry of Meditation* (1954, rev. ed. 1962).]

Meiosis: Intentional UNDERSTATEMENT for humorous or satiric effect and occasionally for EMPHASIS. See UNDERSTATEMENT, LITOTES, IRONY.

Melic Poetry: POETRY written to be accompanied by the music of the lyre or flute. It was to this POETRY that the Alexandrians applied the term LYRIC, which is the designation under which it is generally known. *Melic poetry* was written in a variety of METERS and STANZAS. It flourished in Greece between the seventh and the fifth centuries, B.C. Among its greatest POETS were Sappho, Anacreon, and Pindar.

Meliorism: A name applied to the belief that society has an innate tendency toward improvement and that that tendency can be furthered by conscious human effort. The belief was widely held in the late nineteenth century. Writers like George Eliot embraced it in the faith that by our frail and faulty efforts to aid the world, we move, though imperceptibly, toward a better world. At the conclusion of *Middlemarch* she expresses the idea very clearly: ". . . the growing good of the world is partly dependent on unhistoric acts; and that things are not so ill with you and me as they might have been, is half owing to the number who lived faithfully a hidden life, and rest in unvisited tombs." Thomas Hardy believed in what he called—maybe in jest—an evolutionary *meliorism,* although his optimism about its operation or its rate was much smaller than George Eliot's. In his "Apology" in *Late Lyrics and Earlier,* he says, "Whether the human and kindred animal races survive till exhaustion or destruction of the globe . . . pain to all upon it, tongued or dumb, shall be kept down to a minimum by loving-kindness, operating through scientific knowledge, and actuated by the modicum of free will conjecturally possessed by organic life when the necessitating forces . . . happen to be in equilibrium, which may or may not be often."

Melodrama: A PLAY based on a romantic PLOT and developed sensationally, with little regard for convincing MOTIVATION and with an excessive appeal to the emotions of the audience. The object is to keep the audience thrilled by the awakening anyhow of strong feelings of pity or horror or joy. POETIC JUSTICE is superficially secured, the CHARACTERS (who are either very good or very bad) being rewarded or punished according to their deeds. Though typically a *melodrama* has a happy ending, TRAGEDIES that use much of the same technique are sometimes referred to as a melodramatic. Likewise, by a further extension of the term, STORIES are sometimes said to be melodramatic.

The term literally means "a play with music," and at one time it was applied to the OPERA in a broad sense. *Melodrama* came into widespread use in England in the nineteenth century as a device to circumvent the Licensing Act, which restricted "legitimate" PLAYS to the PATENT THEATERS but which allowed musical entertainments in other theaters. The use of SONGS, recitative, and incidental music disguised the dramatic nature of popular stage pieces, and they came to be known as *melodramas.* The first English *melodrama* is believed to have been Thomas Holcroft's *A Tale of Mystery,* produced in 1802. These *melodramas* usually exhibited the deplorable characteristics already listed, and finally the term by extension was applied to these characteristics independent of the presence or absence of music.

[References: T. H. Dickinson, *The Contemporary Drama of England* (1920); Robert B. Heilman, *Tragedy and Melodrama* (1968).]

Melopoeia: A Greek term revived and given a new meaning by Ezra Pound, who used it to refer to the whole articulatory-acoustic-auditory range of PO-ETRY.

Memoirs: A form of autobiographical writing dealing usually with the recollections of those who have been a part of or have witnessed significant events. *Memoirs* differ from AUTOBIOGRAPHY proper in that they are usually concerned with personalities and actions other than those of the writer, whereas the AUTOBIOGRAPHY lays a heavier stress on the inner and private life of its subject. Since "autobiography" did not come into widespread use until well into the nineteenth century, some works that we call "autobiography" (such as Benjamin Franklin's) were called something else, usually *memoirs,* by their authors.

Menippean Satire: A form of SATIRE originally developed by the Greek cynic Menippus and transmitted by his disciples Lucian and Varro. Varro in turn influenced Petronius and Apuleius. *Menippean satire* deals more with mental attitudes than with fully realized CHARACTERS. It uses PLOT freely and loosely to present a view of the world in terms of sharply controlled intellectual patterns. In its shorter forms *Menippean satire* is a DIALOGUE or a COLLOQUY, with its interest in the conflict of ideas. In longer works the Menippean satirist piles up vast accumulations of fact and presents this erudition through some intellectual organizing principle. Robert Burton's *Anatomy of Melancholy* is an outstanding example of *Menippean satire.* Other works that may be so classified include *Gulliver's Travels,* by Swift; *Imaginary Conversations,* by Landor; Peacock's NOVELS; *Alice in Wonderland,* by Lewis Carroll; *Noctes Ambrosianae,* by Christopher North; *Tristram Shandy,* by Laurence Sterne; and the whaling material in *Moby-Dick,* by Melville. A recent work that is an almost perfect example of *Menippean satire* is *Giles Goatboy,* by John Barth. Thomas Pynchon's novels—*V., The Crying of Lot 49,* and *Gravity's Rainbow*— display many Menippean elements, including masses of fantastic learning and patches of VERSE mixed in with PROSE. Such works are sometimes referred to by the term ANATOMY rather than *Menippean satire.* The current usage of *Menippean satire* to define a GENRE was made popular by Northrop Frye in his *Anatomy of Criticism.*

Mesostich: An ACROSTIC in which the middle letters form a word. See ACROSTIC.

Meta-: A prefix often applied by contemporary literary CRITICS to various literary terms, forming such words as METACRITICISM and METAFICTION. The basic meaning of the prefix *meta-* is "beyond, above, of a higher logical type." When it is added to form a new noun from the name of a discipline or process, it designates a new but related discipline or process that deals logically and critically with the nature, structure, logic, or behavior of the original discipline or process. For example, "metatheory" is a theory that investigates, analyzes, or describes theory itself. Probably the most reasonable use of the prefix is in "metalinguistics," since one common function of language is to talk about language, as in " 'I' is a pronoun," in which treatment of the word as such changes its grammatical person from first to third. It is likely that any system of SIGNS comes equipped with a built-in mechanism of metasystemic metasigns, so to speak, which permit the establishment and clarification of contact, CODE, and rule. See METACRITICISM, METAFICTION.

Metacriticism: A process or method whose primary subject is the critical examination of the technical terms, basic premises, logical principles, or structure of CRITICISM itself. For example, if a writer asserts that *War and Peace* is a better NOVEL than *Nicholas Nickleby* and sets out to demonstrate why the statement is true, we get a work of CRITICISM. If another writer sets out to explore the bases on which the judgment that one novel is better than another can be made, we get a piece of *metacriticism.* The metacritic criticizes CRITICISM, and the metacritic's major efforts are devoted to the ANALYSIS of meaning and the logical appraisal of critical reasoning. The metacritic may emphasize methods of explication, the validity of description, theories of interpretation, DEFINITIONS of artistic qualities, the bases of evaluation, or forms of metalinguistics. In one sense then, *metacriticism* is simply a SYNONYM for THEORETICAL CRITICISM when it is distinguished from PRACTICAL CRITICISM. However, as it is currently used, it always implies an intellectual rigor and a logical concern with underlying principles. See META-, METAFICTION.

Metafiction: A work of FICTION, a major concern of which is the nature of FICTION itself or the process by which FICTION makes its statements. John Fowles's *The French Lieutenant's Woman* is a *metafiction,* as are many modern works, even as far back as Henry James, Joseph Conrad, and Marcel Proust. By now, virtually any serious fiction—that, say, of Samuel Beckett, J. D. Salinger, John Barth, Donald Barthelme, Kurt Vonnegut, Jr., and Norman Mailer—contains, as one of its structural and thematic dimensions, a testing of the process of FICTION itself. See META-, METACRITICISM.

Metalepsis: A complex FIGURE, also called TRANSUMPTION, dismissed by CLASSICAL and Renaissance CRITICS (Quintilian, Puttenham) as affected and farfetched but during the 1970s and 1980s given newly sympathetic attention by some sensitive critics (Angus Fletcher, Harold Bloom, John Hollander). Definitions vary and even diverge, but the point of *metalepsis* seems to be the adding of one TROPE or FIGURE to another, along with such extreme compression that the LITERAL sense of the statement is eclipsed or reduced to anomaly or nonsense.

The figure seems to crop up in rhetorical situations of maximal DRAMA and interest. We can say discursively, for example, that the sisters Helen and Clytemnestra had much to do with causing the Trojan War and certain events in its aftermath, such as the murder of Agamemnon. The many parts and steps of this complex process are transumed in the very powerful *metaleptic* figure in Marlowe's *Doctor Faustus:* "Was this the face that launched a thousand ships / And burnt the topless towers of Ilium?" In two LINES, Marlowe compounds a dozen FIGURES, including question, METONYMY, METAPHOR, HYPERBOLE, and PARADOX (fortified by an elementary reference to water and fire, a deletion of all human elements, and emphatic ALLITERATION and megaphonic IAMBS with very short syllables and very long ones).

Then, in Yeats's "Leda and the Swan," the same topic is enlarged to embrace the event that led to the birth of Helen and Clytemnestra: the rape

of Leda by Zeus in the form of a swan. Yeats's *metalepsis* here transumes
even more than does Marlowe's:

> A shudder in the loins engenders there
> The broken wall, the burning roof and tower
> And Agamemnon dead.

Now, the process of orgasm, conception, gestation, birth, and so forth that
leads by and by, after forty years or so, to the killing of Agamemnon by Clytemnestra is collapsed into a figure that reduces to a paradoxical "Shudder . . .
engenders . . . Agamemnon dead" instead of the logical "shudder . . . engenders . . . Clytemnestra" (who caused the death of Agamemnon).

Metaphor: An implied ANALOGY imaginatively identifying one object with
another and ascribing to the first object one or more of the qualities of the
second or investing the first with emotional or imaginative qualities associated
with the second. It is one of the TROPES; that is, one of the principal devices
by which poetic "turns" on the meaning of words are achieved. I. A. Richards's
distinction between the TENOR and the VEHICLE of a *metaphor* has been
widely accepted and is very useful. The TENOR is the idea being expressed
or the subject of the comparison; the VEHICLE is the IMAGE by which this
idea is conveyed or the subject communicated. When Shakespeare writes:

> That time of year thou mayst in me behold
> When yellow leaves, or none, or few, do hang
> Upon those boughs which shake against the cold,
> Bare ruined choirs where late the sweet birds sang.

the TENOR is old age, the VEHICLE is the season of late fall or early winter,
conveyed through a group of IMAGES unusually rich in implications. The TENOR
and VEHICLE taken together constitute the FIGURE OF SPEECH, the TROPE,
the "turn" in meaning that the *metaphor* conveys. The purposes for using
metaphors can vary widely. At one extreme, the VEHICLE may be merely a
means of decorating the TENOR; at the other extreme, the TENOR may be
merely an excuse for having the VEHICLE. ALLEGORY, for example, may be
thought of as an elaborate and consistently constructed extended *metaphor*
in which the TENOR is never expressed, although it is implied. In the simplest
kinds of *metaphors* there is an obvious direct resemblance objectively existing
between the TENOR and the VEHICLE, and in some *metaphors,* particularly
those that lend themselves to elaborate CONCEITS, the relation between TENOR
and VEHICLE is in the mind of the maker of the *metaphor,* rather than in
specific qualities of VEHICLE or TENOR. The first kind tends to be sensuous
and the second witty.

Aristotle praised the *metaphor* as "the greatest thing by far" for POETS—
a sentiment seconded by Ezra Pound, who endorsed Aristotle's calling apt
metaphor "the hallmark of genius"—and saw it as the product of their insight,
which permitted them to find the similarities in seemingly dissimilar things.
It ought to be noted that Aristotle's attention to the art of finding resemblances
resembles the lineaments of his doctrine of formal *mimesis;* art in a way is a
metaphor for NATURE. Modern CRITICISM follows Aristotle in placing a simi-

larly high premium on poets' abilities in the making of *metaphors*, and ANALYT-ICAL CRITICISM tends to find almost as much rich suggestiveness in the differences between the things compared as it does in the recognition of surprising but unsuspected similarities. Cleanth Brooks uses the term "functional *metaphor*" to describe the way in which the *metaphor* is able to have "referential" and "emotive" characteristics and to go beyond them and become a direct means in itself of representing a truth incommunicable by any other means. Clearly when a *metaphor* performs this function, it is behaving as a SYMBOL.

Metaphors may be simple, that is, may occur in the single isolated comparison, or a large *metaphor* may function as the CONTROLLING IMAGE of a whole work (see Edward Taylor's poem quoted in the article on CONTROLLING IMAGE), or a series of VEHICLES may all be associated with a single TENOR, as in Hamlet's "To be or not to be" SOLILOQUY. In this last kind of case, however, unless the IMAGES can harmoniously build the TENOR without impressing the reader with a sense of their incongruity, the possibility of a MIXED FIGURE is imminent.

The whole nature of our vocabulary is highly metaphorical. According to a fairly ingenuous notion of language, abstractions can be treated only in terms that are not abstract, presumably because the primitive mind cannot handle abstractions. But no evidence establishes the existence of any such limitations. To presume that any human being has to have a grasp of physical "pulling away" (*abs + trahere*) before being able to grasp an abstract "abstraction" is little more than bigotry. Even so, mentally negotiable systems of SIGNS do resemble metaphoric displacements and substitutions enough for Emerson to assert, "Every word was once a poem . . . . Language is fossil poetry." See IMAGE, TROPE, FIGURE OF SPEECH, CONTROLLING IMAGE, ALLEGORY, METAPHYSICAL CONCEIT.

[References: Christine Brooke-Rose, *A Grammar of Metaphor* (1958, reprinted 1970); Terence Hawkes, *Metaphor* (1972); L. C. Knights and Basil Cottle, eds., *Metaphor and Symbol* (1960); Paul Ricoeur, *The Rule of Metaphor* (tr. 1977); Sheldon Sacks, ed., *On Metaphor* (1979); Philip Wheelwright, *Metaphor and Reality* (1962, reprinted 1968).]

Metaphysical Conceit: A highly ingenious kind of CONCEIT widely used by the metaphysical poets, who explored all areas of knowledge to find in the startlingly esoteric or the shockingly commonplace telling and unusual ANALOGIES for their ideas. The use of such unusual CONCEITS as CONTROLLING IMAGES in their POEMS is a hallmark of the writers of METAPHYSICAL POETRY. The *metaphysical conceit* often exploits verbal logic to the point of the GROTESQUE, and it sometimes achieves such extravagant turns on meaning that it becomes absurd, as when Richard Crashaw writes of Mary Magdalene's eyes as

> Two walking baths; two weeping motions,
> Portable and compendious oceans.

But when a *metaphysical conceit* strikes from our minds the same spark of recognition that the POET experienced, so that it gives us a perception of a real but previously unsuspected similarity that is enlightening, it speaks to both our minds and our emotions with force, as in Donne's "The Flea" or his comparison of the union of himself with his lover in the figure of a draftsman's compass in "A Valediction Forbidding Mourning" or in Taylor's "Huswifery" (quoted in the article on CONTROLLING IMAGE). Something of the vigor and audacity of the *metaphysical conceit* can be seen in modern poems, such as that by Pound beginning "Your mind and you are our Sargasso Sea" and that by Frost beginning "She is as in a field a silken tent." See METAPHYSICAL POETRY, CONCEIT, CONTROLLING IMAGE, METAPHOR.

Metaphysical Poetry: Sometimes used in the broad sense of philosophical POETRY, VERSE dealing with metaphysics, POETRY "unified by a philosophical conception of the universe and of the role assigned to the human spirit in the great drama of existence" (H. J. C. Grierson). In this sense Lucretius and Dante wrote *metaphysical poetry.* Herbert Read sees it as the "emotional apprehension of thought," felt thought, to be contrasted with the LYRIC, and regards some of the poetry of Chapman and Wordsworth, as well as that of John Donne and his followers, as *metaphysical.*

Commonly, however, the term is used to designate the work of the seventeenth-century writers referred to as the "Metaphysical Poets." They formed a school in the sense of employing similar methods and of being actuated by a spirit of revolt against the romantic conventionalism of Elizabethan love poetry, in particular the PETRARCHAN CONCEIT. Their tendency toward psychological analysis of the emotions of love and religion, their penchant for the novel and the shocking, their use of the METAPHYSICAL CONCEIT, and the extremes to which they sometimes carried their techniques resulted frequently in obscurity, rough VERSE, and strained IMAGERY. These faults gave them a bad reputation in the NEOCLASSIC PERIOD. However, there has been a twentieth-century revival of interest in their work and admiration for their accomplishments. Consequently the reader will find the word *metaphysical* used in both a derogatory and a complimentary sense. In the tidal vicissitudes of fashion, Donne's reputation, very high indeed around 1912–1972, may now be ebbing somewhat as the Romantic counterattack forces our attention in other directions. The term *metaphysical* was applied to Donne in derogation of his excessive use of philosophy by Dryden in 1693, but its present use to designate a special poetic manner originated with Samuel Johnson's description of *metaphysical poetry* in his "Life of Cowley."

The characteristics of the best *metaphysical poetry* are logical elements in a technique intended to express honestly, if unconventionally, the poet's sense of the complexities and contradictions of life. The POETRY is intellectual, analytical, psychological, disillusioning, bold; absorbed in thoughts of death, physical love, religious devotion. The DICTION is simple compared with that of the ELIZABETHAN AGE or the NEOCLASSIC PERIOD and may echo the words and the CADENCES of common speech. The IMAGERY is drawn from the commonplace or the remote, actual life or erudite sources, the figure itself often being elaborated with self-conscious ingenuity. The FORM is frequently that of an ARGUMENT with the poet's lover, with God, or with himself. The metaphysical poets wrote of God and of theology, of the court and of the church, of love and of NATURE—often elaborately—but usually with a high regard for FORM and the more intricate subtleties of METER and RHYME. Yet the VERSE is often intentionally rough; Ben Jonson thought Donne "deserved hanging" for not observing ACCENT. The roughness may be explained in part by the dominance of thought over strict FORM, in part by the fact that ruggedness or irregularity matches a sense of the seriousness and perplexity of life, with the realistic method, with the spirit of revolt, and with the sense of an argument expressed in speech rather than SONG.

Whatever the reasons behind *metaphysical poetry*, CRITICS of the eighteenth and nineteenth centuries usually found the result unpleasing. Samuel Johnson called *metaphysical poetry* DISCORDIA CONCORS, inverting Horace's phrase *concordia discors*, "harmony in discord." DISCORDIA CONCORS described, he said, "a combination of dissimilar images or discovery of occult resemblances in things apparently unlike."

No exact list of metaphysical poets can be drawn up. Donne was the acknowledged leader. Crashaw and Cowley have been called the most typically *metaphysical*. Some were Protestant religious mystics, like Herbert, Vaughan, and Traherne; some Catholic, like Crashaw; some were CAVALIER LYRICISTS, like Carew and Lovelace; some were satirists, like Donne and Cleveland; one was an American clergyman, Edward Taylor. The new recognition that has come to the metaphysical poets has arisen from a realization of the seriousness of their art, an interest in their spirit of revolt, their REALISM, their intellectualism, and other affinities with modern engagements, as well as from the fact that they produced some fine poetry. T. S. Eliot, John Crowe Ransom, and Allen Tate are modern poets affected by the metaphysical influence. Among those even younger, the same influence may be detected in some of the work of Charles Tomlinson, Richard Wilbur, and W. D. Snodgrass.

If the results of the metaphysical manner are not always happy, if the unexpected details and surprising figures are not always integrated imaginatively and emotionally, it must be remembered that these POETS were attempting a more difficult task than confronts the complacent writer of conventional VERSE. Their failures appear most strikingly in their fantastic METAPHYSICAL CONCEITS. When they succeed—as they often do—their POETRY, arising out of their own sense of incongruity and confusion, is an effective "emotional apprehension of thought," hauntingly real to us in our perplexing world. See CONCEIT, METAPHYSICAL CONCEIT, CONTROLLING IMAGE, BAROQUE, MARINISM.

[References: T. S. Eliot, *Selected Essays*, 3rd ed. (1951); H. J. C. Grierson, *Metaphysical Lyrics and Poems of the Seventeenth Century* (1921, reprinted 1959); George Williamson, *The Donne Tradition* (1930, reprinted 1958).]

Metathesis: The interchange of position between sounds in a word. Many modern English words have undergone *metathesis;* an example is the word "curly," which in Chaucer was "crulle." When *metathesis* occurs between words, the result is a SPOONERISM. Usually such swapping yields nonsense, like "fattle carm."

Meter: The recurrence in POETRY of a rhythmic pattern, or the RHYTHM established by the regular or almost regular occurrence of similar units of sound pattern. In POETRY there are four basic kinds of rhythmic patterns: (1) QUANTITATIVE, in which the RHYTHM is established through units containing regular successions of long and short syllables; this is the CLASSICAL *meter;* (2) accentual, in which the occurrence of a syllable marked by STRESS or ACCENT determines the basic unit regardless of the number of unstressed or unaccented syllables surrounding the stressed syllable; OLD ENGLISH VERSIFI-

CATION employs this kind of *meter,* and so does SPRUNG RHYTHM; (3) syllabic, in which the number of syllables in a LINE is fixed, although the ACCENT varies; much Romance VERSIFICATION employs this *meter;* and (4) ACCENTUAL-SYLLABIC, in which both the number of syllables and the number of ACCENTS are fixed or nearly fixed; when the term *meter* is used in English, it usually refers to ACCENTUAL-SYLLABIC RHYTHM.

The rhythmic unit within the line is called a FOOT. In English ACCENTUAL-SYLLABIC VERSE, the standard feet are: IAMBIC (⌣ ⁄), TROCHAIC (⁄ ⌣), ANAPES-TIC (⌣ ⌣ ⁄), DACTYLLIC (⁄ ⌣ ⌣), SPONDAIC (⁄ ⁄), and PYRRHIC (⌣ ⌣), although others sometimes occur. The number of FEET in a line forms another means of describing the *meter.* The following are the standard English lines: MONOME-TER, one foot; DIMETER, two; TRIMETER, three; TETRAMETER, four; PENTAME-TER, five; HEXAMETER, six, also called the ALEXANDRINE; HEPTAMETER, seven, also called the "FOURTEENER" when the feet are IAMBIC. See ACCENT, SUBSTI-TUTION, CATALEXIS, OLD ENGLISH VERSIFICATION, QUANTITATIVE VERSE, FOOT, SCANSION.

Metonymy: A FIGURE OF SPEECH characterized by the substitution of a term naming an object closely associated with the word in mind for the word itself. In this way we commonly speak of the king as "the crown," an object closely associated with kingship thus being made to stand for "king." So, too, in the book of Genesis we read, "In the sweat of thy face shalt thou eat bread," a FIGURE OF SPEECH in which "sweat" represents that with which it is closely associated, "hard labor." Recent CRITICS, led by Roman Jakobson, have come to consider *metonymy,* which involves a continuous association from whole to part, radically different from METAPHOR, which involves a discontinuous ANALOGY between two wholes. According to Jakobson, neurological research into common forms of aphasia confirmed his hypothesis about the functions of speech and the structure of the brain, both of which involve a process of selecting and combining units according to rules of continuity and discontinu-ity, association and analogy, paradigm and syntax, all subsumable under catego-ries of *metonymy* and METAPHOR broadly conceived. The distinction promises important implications for the differences between PROSE and POETRY, say, or between two sorts of poetry. Frost's, for example, may be classified as radi-cally metonymic, so that his POEM called "New Hampshire" concerns the state of New Hampshire as a metonymic figure representing the whole United States of America. Eliot's, on the other hand, is radically metaphoric, so that *his* "New Hampshire" has virtually nothing to do with the state except as a local METAPHOR for the human soul. (This is merely a tentative suggestion.) See HYPALLAGE, SYNECDOCHE.

Metrical Accent: The ACCENT demanded by the RHYTHM pattern in POETRY. See ACCENT.

Metrical Romance: A romantic TALE in VERSE. The term is applied both to such medieval VERSE ROMANCES as *Sir Gawain and the Green Knight* and to the type of VERSE ROMANCES produced by Sir Walter Scott (*The Lady of the Lake, Marmion*) and Lord Byron (*The Bride of Abydos, The Giaour*). The latter kind reflects the tendencies of ROMANTICISM in its freedom of tech-nique and its preference for remote SETTINGS (the past in Scott, the Near East in Byron) as well as in its sentimental qualities. See MEDIEVAL ROMANCE.

Metrics: The systematic examination of the patterns of RHYTHM in POETRY and the formulation of principles describing their nature; another term for PROSODY.

Middle English: English as spoken and written in the period following the NORMAN CONQUEST and preceding the Modern English period beginning at the RENAISSANCE. The dates most commonly given are 1100 to 1500, though both are approximate, since the NORMAN CONQUEST came in 1066 and some writings earlier than 1500 (for example, Malory's *Le Morte Darthur*) may properly be called "Modern" English. For the qualities in the language that mark *Middle English,* see ENGLISH LANGUAGE.

Middle English Period: The period in English literature between the replacement of French by MIDDLE ENGLISH as the language of court and art and the early appearances of definitely modern English writings, roughly the period between 1350 and 1500. The Age of Chaucer (1350–1400) was marked by political and religious unrest, the Black Death (1348–1350), Wat Tyler's Rebellion (1381), and the rise of the LOLLARDS. The fifteenth century was badly torn by the Wars of the Roses. There was a steadily increasing nationalistic spirit in England, and at the same time early traces of HUMANISM were appearing.

The great CYCLES of MYSTERY PLAYS flourished. Toward the end of the period the MORALITY came into existence, and the last years of the fifteenth century saw the arrival of the INTERLUDE, while the FOLK DRAMA was popular among the common people. In PROSE it was the period of Wycliffe's sermons and his TRANSLATION of the BIBLE, of Mandeville's *Travels,* of the medieval CHRONICLES, of prose ROMANCES, and, supremely, of Malory's *Le Morte Darthur.* ROMANCES, both PROSE and metrical, continued to be popular, with *Sir Gawain and the Green Knight* as the finest example. The period between 1350 and 1400 was a rich poetic age: it saw the first major English POET, Chaucer, as well as POETRY like *The Pearl, The Vision of Piers Plowman,* and Gower's *Confessio Amantis.* There was a revival of ALLITERATIVE VERSE, although the ACCENTUAL-SYLLABIC METERS of Chaucer and his school eventually carried the day. The fifteenth century was a weak poetic age; its POETRY consisted chiefly of Chaucerian imitations, and only Hoccleve, Skelton, and James I of Scotland gave it any distinction. The popular BALLAD flourished. With the establishment of the Tudor Kings on the English throne in 1485, however, England once more had internal peace, possessed a flexible language very close to Modern English, and had a powerful dramatic tradition. The glories of the RENAISSANCE were almost ready to burgeon forth. See MIDDLE ENGLISH PERIOD in *Outline of Literary History.*

[References: C. S. Baldwin, *Three Medieval Centuries of Literature in England* (1932, reprinted 1968); E. K. Chambers, *English Literature at the Close of the Middle Ages* (1954); W. J. Courthope, *A History of English Poetry,* 6 vols. (1895–1910, reprinted 1962); J. J. Jusserand, *A Literary History of the English People,* vol. 1 (1895); George Kane, *Middle English Literature* (1951); W. P. Ker, *English Medieval Literature* (1912); W. W. Lawrence, *Medieval Story* (1916, 2nd ed. 1938, reprinted 1962); Henry Morley, *English Writers,* 11 vols. (1887–95); W. L. Renwick and H. Orton, *The Beginnings of English Literature to Skelton,* 3rd ed. (1966); W. H. Schofield, *English Literature from* the Norman Conquest to Chaucer (1906); P. G. Thomas, English Literature before Chaucer (1924); R. M. Wilson, Early Middle English Literature (1939); David M. Zesmer, Guide to English Literature from Beowulf through Chaucer and Medieval Drama (1961).]

Miles Gloriosus: The braggart soldier, a STOCK CHARACTER in COMEDY. The type appeared in Greek COMEDY as the ALAZON, was stressed by the Roman playwrights (Terence's Thraso in Eunuchus and Plautus's Miles Glorious), and adopted by RENAISSANCE dramatists. An early example is Ralph Roister Doister, the central figure in the PLAY named after him (the "first" English COMEDY). Examples in ELIZABETHAN DRAMA are Captain Bobadil in Jonson's Every Man in His Humour, Quintiliano in Chapman's May Day, and Shakespeare's Sir John Falstaff (King Henry the Fourth, 1, 2), Don Adriano de Armado (Love's Labour's Lost), Parolles (All's Well), and Ancient Pistol (King Henry the Fifth). Although the treatments differ in different examples, the miles gloriosus is likely to be cowardly, parasitical, bragging, and subject to being victimized easily by practical jokers. The aptly named Miles Standish is something of a miles gloriosus in Longfellow's Courtship POEM. Joan in Shaw's PLAY is a combination of two virtually antithetical and mutually exclusive types: miles gloriosus (she is a soldier and she even cusses, though unwittingly) and ingenue (she is a virgin and dies while still a teenager); she is also a bumpkin, a visionary, and a proper saint. George C. Scott's film portrayal of Patton was a lively study of the contradictions and complexities of a modern miles glorious.

Milieu: The political, social, intellectual, and cultural environment in which an author lives or a work is produced. Much literary history and CRITICISM in the nineteenth and early twentieth centuries made the author's milieu a major factor in literary interpretation. Hippolyte Taine, in his very influential Histoire de la litterature anglaise (1864), for example, made race, momentum, and milieu the essentials to literary interpretation.

Miltonic Sonnet: A variation made by Milton on the ITALIAN SONNET, in which the RHYME scheme is retained but the "turn" between the OCTAVE and the SESTET is eliminated. See SONNET.

Mime: A form of popular COMEDY developed by the ancients (fifth century B.C. in southern Italy). It portrayed the events of everyday life by means of dancing, imitative gestures, and witty DIALOGUE. It finally degenerated into sensual displays, and the performers sank to a low social level. The Christian Church frowned on the performances, and they were largely driven from the public stage. They were kept alive, however, by wandering entertainers. In England, the exhibitions seem to have consisted generally of low forms of buffoonery. The mime aided in preserving the comic spirit in DRAMA, its influence possibly being apparent in the medieval MYSTERY PLAY and the Renaissance INTERLUDE—perhaps also the Renaissance "DUMB SHOW" and through it the modern PANTOMIME. Many elements of modern VAUDEVILLE are in direct line of descent from the mime. The mime is not regarded as a true link between ancient classical drama and modern drama, except as it aided in keeping alive the acting profession in the DARK AGES. Samuel Beckett's Act Without Words is a modern counterpart of the mime PLAY.

[References: Joan Lawson, *Mime* (1957); Allardyce Nicoll, *Masks, Mimes, and Miracles* (1931, reprinted 1963).]

Mimesis: The Greek word for IMITATION, often used in CRITICISM to indicate Aristotle's theory of IMITATION.

[References: Erich Auerbach, *Mimesis: The Representation of Reality in Western Literature* (tr. 1953); Northrop Frye, *Anatomy of Criticism* (1957).]

Mimetic Theory of Art: A theory emphasizing the actuality imitated in the art work. See CRITICISM.

Minnesinger: "Singer of love," a medieval German LYRIC POET whose art was perhaps inspired by that of the TROUBADOUR. Though the German poets reflect the system known as COURTLY LOVE, their POETRY in general is more wholesome than that of the TROUBADOURS. They flourished in the twelfth and thirteenth centuries. Walther von der Volgelweide is regarded as the greatest of the class.

Minor Plot: A subordinate ACTION or COMPLICATION running through a work of FICTION or DRAMA. See SUBPLOT.

Minstrel: A musical entertainer or traveling POET of the later Middle Ages who carried on the tradition of the earlier GLEEMAN and JONGLEUR. *Ministrels* flourished especially in the late thirteenth and the fourteenth centuries and played a prominent part in the cultural life of the time. The typical *minstrel* may be thought of as a gifted wandering entertainer, skilled with the harp and tabor, singing SONGS, reciting ROMANCES, and carrying news from town to town, castle to castle, country to country, delighting all classes of society, from kings and knights to priests, burgesses, and laborers. Love LYRICS, BALLADS, LEGENDS, and ROMANCES were so composed and disseminated. They were at once the actors, journalists, POETS, and orchestras of their time. The *Lay of Havelok the Dane* is a good example of the "minstrel romance." Flourishing in Chaucer's day, minstrelsy declined in the fifteenth century and tended to disappear with the increase of literacy following the introduction of printing. In their enthusiasm for "primitive" or untutored poetic genius and for medievalism in general, the poets and novelists of the ROMANTIC PERIOD, such as Beattie and Scott, imparted an idealized meaning to *minstrel* as they did to BARD.

Minstrel Show: A form of VAUDEVILLE very popular in America in the last half of the nineteenth century and the early years of the twentieth. In the *minstrel show* white men with blackened faces—"in blackface"—impersonated stereotypical Negro characters in SONG and dance routines and in exchanges between a white "straight man" (compare with the satiric ADVERSARIUS) and the blackface characters who usually won in the battle of wits. The straight man was called "Mr. Interlocutor"; he exchanged repartee with the "end men," "Mr. Tambo," who played a tambourine, and "Mr. Bones," who played bone castinets. The blackface *minstrel show* had its beginning in 1830 when T. D. Rice began to "dance Jim Crow." Christy's Minstrels, which began in 1842 and later featured songs by Stephen Foster, developed the form of the *minstrel show,* which became immensely popular. In John

Berryman's *The Dream Songs* there is a character of sorts named Mr. Bones, who is partly a *minstrel-show* figure and partly the central character's skeleton.

Miracle Play: Although this term is used by many authorities on English DRAMA in a broad sense that includes the scriptural CYCLIC DRAMA (see MYSTERY PLAY), it is retricted by others to its early sense of a nonscriptural PLAY based on the legend of some saint or on a miracle performed by some saint or sacred object (such as the sacramental bread). However common *miracle plays* in this stricter sense may have been in medieval England, very few have been preserved. It is known that a play of St. Catherine, probably in Latin or ANGLO-NORMAN, was performed at Dunstable about A.D. 1100. At this time *miracle plays* on St. Nicholas were being produced in France. A play called *Dux Moraud* (thirteenth or fourteenth century), in English, which exists in a fragmentary form, may have been a *miracle play*, possibly one in which the Virgin Mary supplied the DEUS EX MACHINA. Other extant English plays that are either *miracle plays* or plays of very similar character are the *Play of the Sacrament* (late fifteenth century) and the *Conversion of St. Paul* and *Saint Mary Magdalene* (ca. 1500). See MYSTERY PLAY.

[References: C. F. Tucker Brooke, *Tudor Drama* (1911, reprinted 1964); G. R. Coffman, *A New Theory Concerning the Origin of the Miracle Play* (1914).]

Miscellany: A group of various and diverse items. In literature a *miscellany* is a book that collects compositions by several authors, usually dealing with a variety of topics. The first such *miscellany* in English was the collection of POEMS by Wyatt, Surrey, and others, published by Richard Tottel in 1557 as *Songs and Sonnets*, commonly known as *Tottel's Miscellany* (see COURTLY MAKERS). It set a fashion that resulted in the publication of nearly twenty poetical *miscellanies* within the next half-century, usually under highly figurative or alliterative titles and varying greatly in quality and kind of VERSE printed. Some are posthumous publications of COMMONPLACE BOOKS such as the *Paradise of Dainty Devices* of Richard Edwards (1576), a very popular collection of POEMS of a serious character. Some *miscellanies* have a specialized character, like the *Handful of Pleasant Delights* (1584), a collection of BALLADS. Some of the later ones, like *England's Parnassus* (1600), are collections not of complete poems but of poetical quotations. One, *The Passionate Pilgrim* (1599), was published as Shakespeare's and does contain some of Shakespeare's VERSE. Frequently the *miscellany* was made up of poems selected from other *miscellanies* or from manuscript sources. Much of the VERSE is anonymous, some is falsely ascribed, and some indicates authorship by initials not now understandable. Much uncertainty and some intentional mystification are connected with the parts played by collectors or editors. New poems were frequently printed along with old, and old ones sometimes appear in variant forms. The *miscellanies* are important as reflecting the great poetical activity of the time, particularly of the years preceding the appearance of Spenser, Sidney, and other major figures. They reflect, too, the metrical experiments of this earlier period. The poems in *A Gorgeous Gallery of Gallant Inventions* (1584), for example, make free use of ALLITERATION and employ a wide variety of metrical forms. Such poet-dramatists as Shakespeare borrowed LYRICS from the earlier *miscellanies* and lived to see their own VERSE appear in the later. Aside from *Tottel's*, particularly important *miscellanies* are *The Phoenix Nest*

(1593) and *England's Helicon* (1600). The former contains POEMS by Sidney, Spenser, Lodge, and others. The latter, the best of them all, is a storehouse of Elizabethan POETRY selected from many POETS, great and small.

The practice of publishing poetical *miscellanies* thus begun in the sixteenth century, of course, has continued to the present time. Arthur E. Case, in *Bibliography of English Poetical Miscellanies, 1521–1750,* lists several hundred titles of various sorts of poetical collections.

Mise en Scène: The stage setting of a PLAY, including the use of scenery and properties, and the general arrangement of the piece. Modern DRAMA relies far more on *mise en scène* for its effects than did earlier DRAMA. Indeed, the lack of scenery has been given as a partial explanation of the high literary quality of ELIZABETHAN DRAMA, the playwright being forced to rely on language for descriptive effects; while the increased dependence on scenery is said to be one of the reasons for the decreased attention to purely literary devices on the modern stage. By extension the term *mise en scène* is applied to the total surroundings of any event.

In FILM CRITICISM *mise en scène* refers to the entire part of the filmmaking process that takes place on the set, as opposed to effects produced by other means, such as MONTAGE. It includes direction, actors, costumes, setting, lighting—literally everything that goes to make a SCENE.

Mixed Figures: The mingling of one FIGURE OF SPEECH with another immediately following with which the first is incongruous. A notable example is the sentence of Castlereagh: "And now, sir, I must embark into the feature on which this question chiefly hinges." Here, obviously, the sentence begins with a nautical figure ("embark") but closes with a mechanical ("hinges"). The effect is grotesque. Lloyd George is reported to have said, "I smell a rat. I see it floating in the air. I shall nip it in the bud." Mixed IMAGERY, however, is sometimes deliberately used by writers with great effectiveness when the differing figures contribute cumulatively to a single referent, which is increasingly illuminated as they pile up. It is important, however, that the cumulative effect of the various IMAGES not be one of incongruity. See METALEPSIS, METAPHOR, TENOR, VEHICLE.

Mock Drama: A term applied to PLAYS one of whose purposes is to ridicule the customs, CONVENTIONS, and playwrights of the theater of their time. Henry Fielding, in *The Tragedy of Tragedies; or, The Life and Death of Tom Thumb the Great* (1731) held up to boisterous ridicule the CONVENTIONS of the HEROIC DRAMA, as the Duke of Buckingham's *The Rehearsal* (1671) had also done. Oscar Wilde, in *The Importance of Being Earnest* (1895), produced a PARODY of the WELL-MADE PLAY and the sentimental COMEDY popular in his time and mocked, as well, his fellow playwrights for their failure to acknowledge the hypocrisy and self-deception of their age.

Mock Epic or **Mock Heroic:**   Terms frequently used interchangeably to designate a literary FORM that burlesques the EPIC by treating a trivial subject in the "grand style" or uses the EPIC FORMULAS to make ridiculous a trivial subject by ludicrously overstating it. Usually the characteristics of the classical EPIC are employed, particularly the INVOCATION to a deity; the formal statement of THEME; the division into books and CANTOS; the grandiose speeches (challenges, defiances, boastings) of the HEROES; descriptions of warriors (especially their dress and equipment), battles, and games; the use of the EPIC or HOMERIC SIMILE; and the employment of supernatural machinery (gods directing or participating in the ACTION). When the mock POEM is much shorter than a true EPIC, some prefer to call it *mock heroic*, a term also applied to poems that mock ROMANCES rather than EPICS. In ordinary usage, however, the terms are interchangeable. Chaucer's *Nun's Priest's Tale* is partly *mock heroic* in character, as is Spenser's finely wrought *Muiopotmos*, "The Fate of the Butterfly," which imitates the opening of the *Aeneid* and employs elevated STYLE for trivial subject matter. Swift's *Battle of the Books* is an example of a cuttingly satirical *mock epic* in PROSE. Pope's *The Rape of the Lock* is perhaps the finest *mock heroic* poem in English, satirizing in polished VERSE the trivialities of polite society in the eighteenth century. The cutting of a lady's lock by a gallant is the central act of heroic behavior, a card game is described in military terms, and such airy spirits as the sylphs hover over the scene to aid their favorite heroine. A brilliantly executed *mock epic* has a manifold effect: to ridicule trivial or silly conduct; to mock the pretensions and absurdities of EPIC proper; to bestow an affectionate measure of elevation on low or foolish CHARACTERS; and to bestow a humanizing, deflating, or debunking measure of lowering on elevated characters.

[Reference: Richmond P. Bond, *English Burlesque Poetry, 1700–1750*, (1932, reprinted 1964).]

Mode: In literary CRITICISM a term applied to broad categories of treatment of material, such as ROMANCE, COMEDY, TRAGEDY, or SATIRE. In this usage *mode* is broader than GENRE. Northrop Frye sees ROMANCE, COMEDY, TRAGEDY, and IRONY as *modes* of increasing complexity.

Modern: A term applied to one of the main directions in writing in this century. For most of its history, *"modern"* has denoted or connoted something bad. In a general sense it means having to do with recent times and the present day, but we shall deal with it here in a narrow sense more or less synonymous with that of "modernist." It is not a chronological designation but one suggestive of a loosely defined congeries of characteristics. Much twentieth-century literature is not *"modern"* in the common sense of the term, as much that is contemporary is not. *Modern* refers to a group of characteristics, and not all of them appear in any one writer who merits the designation *modern*.

In a broad sense *modern* is applied to writing marked by a strong and conscious break with traditional forms and techniques of expression. It employs a distinctive kind of IMAGINATION, one that insists on having its general frame of reference within itself. It thus practices the solipsism of which Allen Tate accused the modern mind: it believes that we create the world in the act of perceiving it. *Modern* implies a historical discontinuity, a sense of alienation, loss, and despair. It not only rejects history but also rejects the society of whose fabrication history is a record. It rejects traditional values and assumptions, and it rejects equally the RHETORIC by which they were sanctioned and communicated. It elevates the individual and the inner being over the social human being and prefers the unconscious to the self-conscious. The psychologies of Freud and Jung have been seminal in the *modern* movement in literature (see FREUDIANISM and JUNGIAN CRITICISM). Its most interesting artistic strategies are its attempts to deal with the unconscious and the MYTHO-POEIC. In many respects it is a reaction against REALISM and NATURALISM and the scientific postulates on which they rest. Although by no means can all *modern* writers be termed philosophical existentialists, EXISTENTIALISM has created a schema within which much of the *modern* temper can see a reflection of its attitudes and assumptions (see EXISTENTIALISM). The *modern* revels in a dense and often unordered actuality as opposed to the practical and systematic, and in exploring that actuality as it exists in the mind of the writer it has been richly experimental with language, FORM, SYMBOL, and MYTH.

The *modern* has meant a decisive break with tradition in most of its manifestations, and what has been distinctively worthwhile in the literature of this century has come, in considerable part, from this *modern* temper. Merely to name some of the writers who belong in the *modern* tradition, although none of them partake of all of it, is to indicate the vitality, variety, and artistic success of *modern* writing: T. S. Eliot, Ezra Pound, Wallace Stevens, Ernest Hemingway, William Faulkner, W. B. Yeats, W. H. Auden, D. H. Lawrence, James Joyce, Henry Adams, André Gide, Marcel Proust, Albert Camus, Jean-Paul Sartre, Stéphane Mallarmé, Rainer Maria Rilke, Thomas Mann, Eugene O'Neill, Tennessee Williams, Arthur Rimbaud. And such a list could be continued for many pages.

[References: Carlos Baker, *The Echoing Green: Romanticism, Modernism, and the Phenomena of Transference in Poetry* (1984); Carol T. Christ, *Victorian and Modern Poetics* (1984); Peter Faulkner, *Modernism* (1977); Irving Howe, ed., *The Idea of the Modern in Literature and the Arts* (1967); Monroe K. Spears, *Dionysus and the City: Modernism in Twentieth-Century Poetry* (1970).]

Modernist Period in English Literature: The *Modernist Period* in England may be considered to begin with the First World War in 1914, to be marked by the strenuousness of that experience and by the flowering of talent and experiment that came during the boom of the twenties and that fell away during the ordeal of the economic depression in the 1930s. The catastrophic years of the Second World War, which made England an embattled fortress, profoundly and negatively marked everything British, and it was followed by a period of desperate uncertainty, a sadly diminished age. By 1965, which to all purposes marked an end to the *Modernist Period,* the uncertainty was giving way to anger and protest.

In the early years of the *Modernist Period,* the novelists of the EDWARDIAN AGE continued as major figures, with Galsworthy, Wells, Bennett, Forster, and Conrad dominating the scene, joined before the 'teens were over by Somerset Maugham. A new FICTION, centered in the experimental examination of the inner self, was coming into being in the works of writers like Dorothy Richardson and Virginia Woolf. It reached its peak in the publication in 1922 of James Joyce's *Ulysses,* a book perhaps as influential as any PROSE work by a British writer in this century. In highly differing ways D. H. Lawrence, Aldous Huxley, and Evelyn Waugh protested against the nature of modern society; and the maliciously witty NOVEL, as Huxley and Waugh wrote it in the twenties and thirties, was typical of the attitude of the age and is probably as truly representative of the English novel in the contemporary period as is the NOVEL exploring the private self through the STREAM OF CONSCIOUSNESS. In the thirties and forties, Joyce Cary and Graham Greene produced a more traditional FICTION of great effectiveness, and Henry Green made grim comedy of everyday life. Throughout the period English writers have practiced the SHORT STORY with distinction; notable examples being Katherine Mansfield and Somerset Maugham, working in the tradition of Chekhov.

The theater saw the social PLAYS of Galsworthy, Jones, and Pinero, the PLAY of ideas of Shaw, and the COMEDY OF MANNERS of Maugham—all well-established in the EDWARDIAN AGE—continue and be joined by Noel Coward's COMEDY, the proletarian DRAMA of Sean O'Casey, the serious VERSE plays of T. S. Eliot and Christopher Fry, and the high craftsmanship of Terence Rattigan.

Perhaps the greatest changes in literature, however, came in POETRY and CRITICISM. In 1914 Bridges was POET LAUREATE; he was succeeded in 1930 by John Masefield, who died in 1967. Wilfred Owen was one of the most powerful poetic voices of the early years of the contemporary period, but his career ended with an untimely death in the First World War. Through the period Yeats continued poetic creation, steadily modifying his style and subjects to his late form. At the time of his death in 1939 he probably shared with T. S. Eliot the distinction of being the most influential POET in the British Isles. Yet Eliot's *The Waste Land,* although its author was American, was the most important single poetic publication in England in the period. (One striking feature of *The Waste Land* is its specificity as to geography in the "City" part of London, along with its global scope, which includes even Australia and the South Pole while omitting—as if deliberately—virtually any reference to the United States.) In the work of Yeats and Eliot, of W. H. Auden, Edith Sitwell, and Gerard Manley Hopkins, whose POEMS were posthumously published in 1918, a new POETRY came emphatically into being. The death at thirty-nine of Dylan Thomas in 1953 silenced a powerful LYRIC voice, which had already produced fine POETRY and gave promise of doing even finer work. T. S. Eliot and I. A. Richards, along with T. E. Hulme, Wyndham Lewis, Herbert Read, F. R. Leavis, Cyril Connolly, William Empson, and others, created an informed, essentially anti-Romantic ANALYTICAL CRITICISM, centering its attention on the work of art itself.

Between 1914 and 1965, modernism (see MODERN) as a literary mode developed and gained a powerful ascendancy, and, disparate as many of the writers and movements of the period were, they seem, in hindsight, to have shared most of the fundamental assumptions about art, humanity, and life embraced in the term MODERN. But, however much the literary movement in the Modern Period seems to have a unified history, Great Britain was during the time in the process of national and cultural diminution, for England in the twentieth century has watched her political and military supremacy gradually dissipate, and since the Second World War she has found herself greatly reduced in the international scene and torn by internal economic and political troubles. Her writers during these turbulent and unhappy years turned inward for their subject matter and expressed bitter and often despairing cynicism. Her major literary figures in the *Modernist Period,* as they were in the EDWARDIAN AGE, were often non-English. Her chief POETS were Irish, American, and Welsh; her most influential novelists, Polish and Irish; her principal dramatists, Irish and American. See *Outline of Literary History*.

Modulation: In music a change in key in the course of a passage or between passages. IN POETRY a variation in the metrical pattern by the SUBSTITUTION of a FOOT that differs from the basic METER of the LINE or by the addition or deletion of unstressed syllables. Hardy's "The Voice" may be said to modulate from a largely DACTYLLIC rhythm in its first three STANZAS to a largely TROCHAIC rhythm in the fourth.

Monodrama: The term *monodrama* is used in three senses, all related to its basic meaning of a dramatic situation in which a single person speaks. At its simplest level a *monodrama* is a DRAMATIC MONOLOGUE. It is more often applied to a series of extended DRAMATIC MONOLOGUES in various METERS and STANZA FORMS that tell a connected story. The standard example is Tennyson's *Maud*, which the poet called a *monodrama.* The term is also applied to theatrical presentations that feature only one actor.

Monody: A DIRGE or LAMENT in which a single mourner expresses individual grief, for example, Arnold's *Thyrsis, A Monody.* See DIRGE, ELEGY, THRENODY.

Monograph: A rather indefinite term for a piece of scholary writing, usually on a relatively limited topic. *Monographs* may be published as separate volumes, alone or as part of a series, but their size normally falls between that of an ARTICLE and that of a full-length book.

Monologue: A composition, oral or written, presenting the discourse of one speaker only. By convention, a *monologue* is a speech that represents what someone would speak aloud in a situation with listeners, although they do not speak; the *monologue* therefore differs somewhat from the SOLILOQUY, which is a speech that represents what someone is thinking inwardly, without listeners. Any speech or NARRATIVE presented wholly by one person. Sometimes loosely used to signify merely any lengthy speech. See DRAMATIC MONOLOGUE, INTERIOR MONOLOGUE, MONODRAMA.

Monometer: A LINE of VERSE consisting of one FOOT. See SCANSION, METER.

Monorhyme: A POEM that uses only one RHYME. Even short examples are uncommon: Browning's "Home-Thoughts, from the Sea" is seven LINES, Frost's "The Hardship of Accounting" five. Longer examples are rarer yet: Browning's "Through the Metidja to Abd-el-Kadr" is a forty-line POEM on one RHYME sound, but, because of a recurring REFRAIN, there are only twenty-six different rhyme words; Hardy's "The Respectable Burgher," thirty-five lines on one rhyme sound with thirty-five different rhyme words, seems to have established a record.

Monostich: A POEM consisting of a single LINE. A recent instance is A. R. Ammons's "Coward."

Monostrophic: A term used by Milton to describe the FORM for the CHORUSES in *Samson Agonistes.* These choruses are continuous, each consisting of a single sustained STROPHE not subdivided into such quantitative parts as the traditional strophe, ANTISTROPHE, and EPODE.

Montage: A French term that means "mounting" or "editing." The Soviet FILM director Sergei Eisenstein believed that by juxtaposing contrasting shots properly it was possible to create a meaning different from that actually recorded in any of the shots, and he developed a method of rhythmic pacing of shots that became known as "Soviet *montage.*" In American filmmaking *montage,* sometimes called "dynamic cutting," refers to the deliberate and stylized rapid transition from shot to shot to produce a particular effect. *Montage* in the film is an expressionistic device, as opposed to the REALISM of MISE EN SCÈNE.

In twentieth-century experimental FICTION a similar device, borrowed from FILM, is used to establish a SCENE or an ATMOSPHERE by a series of brief pictures or impressions following one another quickly without apparent logical order. The "Newsreels" in Dos Passos' *U.S.A.* and the "choruses" in Mailer's *The Naked and the Dead* are examples of *montages.* The device is sometimes used in the INTERIOR MONOLOGUE.

Mood: A state of mind in which one feeling, emotion, or range of sensibility has ascendancy. In a literary work the *mood* is the emotional or emotional-intellectual attitude that the author takes toward the subject or THEME. It is relatively easy to distinguish between subject matter and *mood.* A group of POEMS on the subject of death may range from a *mood* of noble defiance in Donne's "Death, Be Not Proud," to PATHOS in Frost's "Out, Out—," to IRONY in Housman's "To an Athlete Dying Young," to morbidly joyous acceptance in Whitman's "When Lilacs Last in the Dooryard Bloom'd." Clearly the state of mind with which each author views the subject of death is different, and we would say, therefore, that the *moods* differ. The literary work should be a unified vehicle for the communication of this state of mind. As Willa Cather expressed it, "[T]he language, the stresses, the very structure of the sentences are imposed upon the writer by the special *mood* of the piece"—that is, the *mood* as expression of the author's attitude becomes a control over the techniques of literary expression.

To distinguish between *mood* and TONE is more difficult, and some CRITICS say it is impossible. Brooks and Warren, in *Understanding Poetry,* for instance, use TONE exclusively, assigning to it the qualities here presented as peculiar to *mood.* If a distinction is made between *mood* and TONE, it will be the fairly subtle one between *mood* as the emotional attitude of the author toward the subject and TONE the attitude of the author toward the audience. In cases where the author uses ostensible "authors" within the work, *mood* and TONE can be quite distinct, as in Washington Irving's use of Diedrich Knickerbocker. Byron, in canto III of *Don Juan,* has "a poet" (presumably Southey) write a POEM beginning "The isles of Greece, the isles of Greece!", which seems solemn, brave, and freedom-loving in *mood;* yet the TONE of Byron (not the *mood* of the imaginary "poet") is mocking and satiric. There are obviously a great variety of *moods* and no accepted system of naming or classifying them. In grammar and music, *mood* is the equivalent of "mode" and means a particular arrangement of parts (such as the indicative, subjunctive, and imperative *moods* of the verb.) See TONE.

Mora, Morae: Terms used to designate periods of duration in QUANTITATIVE VERSE, the *mora* being the duration of a short syllable and the *morae* being that of a long syllable. The symbol (⌣) that indicates a *mora* is called a BREVE, one (—) indicating a *morae* is called a MACRON.

Moral Criticism: Criticism that evaluates a work of art morally, judging it according to the ethical principles that, in a given critic's opinion, should govern human life. See CRITICISM, TYPES OF.

Morality or **Morality Play:** A kind of poetic DRAMA that developed in the late Middle Ages (probably late fourteenth century), distinguished from the religious DRAMA proper, such as the MYSTERY PLAY, by being a dramatized ALLEGORY in which the abstract virtues and vices (like Mercy, Conscience, Perseverance, and Shame) appear in personified form, the good and the bad usually struggling for the soul of a human being. The full-scope *morality* is one in which the THEME is the saving of a human soul, and the central figure represents humanity in general. The best-known example is *Everyman* (*ca.* 1500). The limited-scope *morality* deals with a single vice or moral problem or a situation applicable to a certain person. Thus, Skelton's *Magnificence*, possibly written as advice to Henry VII, has for its THEME the dangers of uncontrolled expenditures. Pedagogical, political, and theological themes became quite common. The later *morality* is superior dramatically because of its independence and greater concreteness and realism. *Morality plays* can be classified by content or purpose, as religious (*Everyman*), doctrinal (John Bale's *King Johan*), didactic-pedagogical (*Wyt and Science*), or political (*Magnificence*). By the sixteenth century some of the *morality plays* had admitted so much realistic and farcical material that they began to establish a tradition of English COMEDY and doubtless contributed much to the INTERLUDE. Such comic figures as the Vice and the Devil were especially well-developed and influenced later COMEDY. Though *morality* THEMES were widely employed in RENAISSANCE drama of the sixteenth century, the *morality plays* as such lost their popularity in ELIZABETHAN times.

    [References: C. F. Tucker Brooke, *Tudor Drama* (1911, reprinted 1964); E. K. Chambers, *The Mediaeval Stage* (1903); W. R. Mackenzie, *The English Moralities from the Point of View of Allegory* (1914, reprinted 1966).]

Mosaic: A term applied to HETEROMEROUS RHYME. *Mosaic* is also applied to compositions consisting of quotations from one or more authors. See CENTO.

Motif (Motive): A simple element that serves as a basis for expanded NARRATIVE; or, less strictly, a conventional situation, device, interest, or incident employed in FOLKLORE, FICTION, or DRAMA. The carrying off of a mortal queen by a fairy lover is a *motif* around which full STORIES were built in MEDIEVAL ROMANCE. In the BALLAD called *The Elfin Knight*, the "fairy music" *motif* appears when the sound of the knight's horn causes the maiden to fall in love with the unseen HERO. In music and art the term is used in various other senses, as for a recurring melodic phrase, a prevailing idea or design, or a subject for detailed sculptural treatment. In literature, recurrent IMAGES, words, objects, phrases, or actions that tend to unify the work are called *motives*. Nabokov's *Lolita*, for example, is saturated by a light-dark *motif* that is found in the names of the PROTAGONIST and ANTOGONIST (Humbert Humbert and Clare Quilty); patterns of day and night, blonde and brunette, summer and winter, north and south, white and black; and the game of chess. See LEITMO-TIF.

Motivation: The presentation of the reasons, justifications, and explanations for the ACTION of a CHARACTER in any work of FICTION, including DRAMA and FILM. *Motivation* results from a combination of the character's moral nature with the circumstances in which the CHARACTER is placed. These qualities and circumstances unite to produce the motives that determine what the CHARACTER does or fails to do, says or fails to say, and feels or fails to feel. When *motivation* is persuasively presented, the reader or viewer accepts the ACTION as convincing and true; when the *motivation* is inadequate, the ACTION may seem arbitrary, facile, or contrived. The FICTION of adventure, with its emphasis on thrilling and unusual EPISODES, often uses little psychological *motivation,* for its ACTION and CHARACTERS are frequently conventional. In more serious literature, great attention is paid to *motivation,* which is often developed with subtlety and depth.

Movement: A critical term denoting ACTION or incident. Thus, a PLAY is spoken of as having, or not having, *movement,* implying that the dramatic action is strong or weak, rapid or slow. The term is also used to indicate a new development in literary activity or interest, as the OXFORD MOVEMENT, the FREE-VERSE movement. Occasionally, in a work with a title drawn from music, like T. S. Eliot's *Four Quartets,* the sections are called *movements.*

"Muckrakers": A group of American writers who between 1902 and 1911 worked actively to expose the dishonest methods and unscrupulous motives operative in big business and in city, state, and national government. A group of MAGAZINES—*The Arena, Everybody's, McClure's,* the *Independent, Collier's,* and the *Cosmopolitan*—led the movement, publishing the writings of the leading *"muckrakers"*—Ida Tarbell, Lincoln Steffens, T. W. Lawson, Mark Sullivan, and Samuel H. Adams. Upton Sinclair's NOVEL *The Jungle* and some of the novels of Winston Churchill and D. G. Phillips are "muckraking" books. The term comes from a CHARACTER in Bunyan's *Pilgrim's Progress* who is so busy raking up muck that he does not see a celestial crown held over him. It was applied derogatorily to this group by Theodore Roosevelt.

Multiple Meanings: A term sometimes used by contemporary CRITICS as a substitute for AMBIGUITY when that word is used to designate the capacity of words to stimulate several quite different streams of thought, all of which make sense. See AMBIGUITY, PLURISIGNATION.

Mummery: A simple dramatic performance usually presented by players masked or disguised. A farcical presentation; a sort of PANTOMIME. See MASQUE.

"Mummings": Masked folk processions, dancing, and PLAYS. See MASQUE.

Muses: Nine goddesses represented as presiding over SONG, the various departments of literature, the liberal arts, and even science. They are generally considered to be the daughters of Zeus and Mnemosyne (memory). In literature, their traditional significance is that of inspiring and helping POETS. In various periods of CLASSICAL history, the *Muses* were given different names and attributes, but the conventionally accepted list and the area of interest ascribed to each are: Calliope (EPIC POETRY), Clio (history), Erato (LYRICS and love POETRY), Euterpe (music), Melpomene (TRAGEDY), Polyhymnia (sacred POETRY), Terpsichore (choral dance and SONG), Thalia (COMEDY), and Urania (astronomy).

Musical Comedy: A combination of music with comic DRAMA. Though much use is made of music, both vocal and orchestral, the DIALOGUE is spoken, not sung. The success of the FORM depends partly on the success of the SONGS and partly on the spectacular staging. Satirical kidding of current figures and interests is frequent. The comic effects are sometimes farcical (see FARCE). Closely related, especially in its earlier forms, to BURLESQUE and VAUDEVILLE, *musical comedy* developed in the early twentieth century in England and America into one of the most popular of all dramatic forms. Its heyday was during the decades between 1920 and 1950. Some, such as *Oklahoma!* and *South Pacific*, were more than simple COMEDIES with music, and later, when Stephen Sondheim flourished, the FORM took on quite a serious coloration.

Mystery Play: A medieval religious PLAY based on Biblical history; a scriptural play. *Mystery plays* originated in the liturgy of the Church and developed from LITURGICAL DRAMAS into the great CYCLIC PLAYS, performed outdoors and ultimately upon movable PAGEANTS. They were the most important forms of the MEDIEVAL DRAMA of Western Europe and flourished in England from the late Middle Ages until well into RENAISSANCE times. They seem to have developed around three nuclei, which presented the whole scheme of salvation: (1) Old Testament PLAYS dealing with such events as the Creation, the fallen angels, the fall of Adam and Eve, the death of Abel, and the sacrifice of Isaac, and the Prophet plays, which prepared for (2) the New Testament PLAYS dealing with the birth of Christ—the Annunciation, the birth, the visit of the wise men, the shepherds, and the visit to the temple; and (3) the Death and Resurrection PLAYS—entry into Jerusalem, the betrayal by Judas, trial and crucifixion, lamentation of Mary, sepulchre scenes, the resurrection, appearances to disciples, Pentecost, and sometimes the Day of Judgment. *Mystery plays* were often known as CORPUS CHRISTI PLAYS because of the habit of performing the plays on PAGEANTS connected with the Corpus Christi processional. The great CYCLES whose texts have been preserved to us are the York, Chester, Coventry, and Wakefield (or "Towneley"). They differ in length and in the list of PLAYS or SCENES included as well as in literary and dramatic value, the Towneley PLAYS being especially important in dramatic development.

After the PLAYS left the Church and became secularized, they were performed by trade guilds, sometimes on fixed stages or stations (the crowds moving from station to station), sometimes on movable PAGEANTS. A writer of the sixteenth century, Archdeacon Rogers, who witnessed a late production of the Chester cycle at Whitsuntide, has left this frequently quoted description:

> Every company had its pageant, or part, which pageants were a high scaffold with two rooms, a higher and a lower upon four wheels. In the lower they appareled themselves, and in the higher room they played, being all open on the top, that all beholders might hear and see them. The places

where they played them was in every street. They began first at the Abbey gates, and when the first pageant was played it was wheeled to the high cross before the mayor, and so to every street; and so every street had a pageant playing before them at one time, till all the pageants for the day appointed were played: and when one pageant was near ended, word was brought from street to street, that so they might come in place thereof exceeding orderly, and all the streets have their pageants afore them all at one time playing together; to see which players there was great resort, and also scaffolds and stages made in the streets in those places where they determined to play their pageants.

The word *mystery* was first applied to these plays by an eighteenth-century editor (Robert Dodsley, 1744), on the analogy of the French *mystère*, a scriptural play; medieval writers were more likely to refer to the plays as CORPUS CHRISTI PLAYS, "Whitsuntide PLAYS," "PAGEANTS," etc., and possibly as MIRACLE PLAYS, the term preferred for them by many modern authorities. Increasingly in recent years, it has been conjectured that *mystery* is related not only to Latin *mysterium* ("secret rite") but also to *ministerium* ("work," "occupation"), the latter sense pertaining to the guilds that were involved in the staging of the plays, so that *mystery play* may bascially mean *guild play*. (It is thought that the Latin *ministerium* in Vulgar Latin or Late Latin became shortened to *misterium*, which was confused or at least associated with *mysterium*, "secret rite"; *misterium* eventually yielded the French *métier*, "trade or occupation.") See MEDIEVAL DRAMA, MIRACLE PLAYS, LITURGICAL DRAMA, PAGEANT, DRAMA.

Mystery Story (or **Novel**): A term used to designate a work of PROSE fiction in which the element of mystery or terror plays a controlling part. It is applied to such various types of FICTION as the DETECTIVE STORY, the GOTHIC NOVEL, the STORY of strange or frightening adventure, the "suspense" novel, the TALE of espionage, the tale of crime, and the STORY in which the PROTAGONIST, usually a woman, is relentlessly pursued by some unknown but alarming menace. See DETECTIVE STORY, GOTHIC NOVEL.
[Reference: Howard Haycraft, ed., *The Art of the Mystery Story* (1946).]

Mysticism: The theory that a knowledge of God or immediate reality is attainable through the use of some human faculty that transcends intellect and does not use ordinary human perception or logical processes. *Mysticism* takes many different forms and does not yield itself readily to DEFINITION. Each mystical experience is unique and by its very nature ineffable; yet there seem to be characteristics common to all mystical experiences that make its definition, although difficult, possible. W. T. Stace finds in all mystical experiences five common characteristics: (1) a sense of objectivity or reality, (2) a sense of peace or blessedness, (3) a feeling of holiness, sacredness, or divinity, (4) a paradoxical quality, and (5) an ineffability. There are two broad types of *mysticism;* in one, God is seen as transcendent, outside the human soul, and union with Him is achieved through a series of steps or stages; in the other, God is immanent, dwelling within the soul and to be discovered by penetrating deeper into the inner self.

The terminology of *mysticism,* since it is forced to be figurative, is often difficult and obscure. A conventional statement of the Christian mystic's progress on the path to God is as follows: the soul undergoes a purification (the purgative way), which leads to a sense of illumination in the love of God (the illuminative way), and after a period the soul enters into a union with God (the unitive way), and progresses into a final ecstatic state of perfect knowledge of God (the spiritual marriage), during some period of which there comes a time of alienation and loss in which the soul cannot find God at all (the soul's dark night).

Aspects of *mysticism* and the mystical experience are common in English and American literature, although to call any single writer—with a few exceptions like Richard Rolle of Hampole and William Blake—a mystic is to invite a challenge. Clearly, however, there are mystical elements in the work of Crashaw, George Herbert, Bunyan, Cowper, Wordsworth, Coleridge, Shelley, Carlyle, the New England TRANSCENDENTALISTS, Whitman, I. B. Singer, and T. S. Eliot. To survey the works of so heterodox a group of writers is to realize that *mysticism* refers to a wide spectrum of experience and is a means of perceiving reality or absolute truth in many different forms and in many different patterns of religious belief. During the first half of the twentieth century, prevailing critical sentiments favored clarity and precision, and numerous influential writers—including Irving Babbitt, T. E. Hulme, Wyndham Lewis, and Ezra Pound—expressed doubt or suspicion when it came to the claims of *mysticism*. But there has been something of a reaction in the second half of the century, and many of the most important CRITICS—including Northrop Frye, Harold Bloom, Mircea Eliade, and Helen Vendler—have found ways of judging and appreciating the mystical dimensions in Blake, Emerson, Whitman, D. H. Lawrence, and Eliot.

[References: D. H. S. Nicholson and A. H. E. Lee, eds., *The Oxford Book of English Mystical Verse* (1917); Caroline F. E. Spurgeon, *Mysticism in English Literature* (1913); Evelyn Underhill, *The Essentials of Mysticism* (1920); Helen C. White, *The Metaphysical Poets: A Study of Religious Experience* (1936).]

Myth: An anonymous STORY or stories having roots in the primitive folk-beliefs of races or nations and presenting supernatural EPISODES as a means of interpreting natural events in an effort to make concrete and particular a special perception of human beings or a cosmic view. *Myth* is the absence of anomaly—at least from one perspective. From another, staked out by Émile Durkheim's school of sociology, *myth* represents a projection of social and cultural patterns upward onto a superhuman level that sanctions and stabilizes the secular ideology. *Myths* differ from LEGENDS by comprising less of historical background and more of the supernatural; they differ from the FABLE in that they are less concerned with moral didacticism and are the product of a racial group rather than the creation of an individual. Every country and literature has its mythology; the most familiar to English readers being the Greek, Roman, and Norse. But the mythology of all groups takes shape around certain common THEMES: they all attempt to explain creation, divinity, and religion; to probe the meaning of existence and death; to account for natural phenomena; and to chronicle the adventures of racial HEROES.

They also have a startlingly similar group of MOTIFS, CHARACTERS, and ACTIONS, as a number of students of *myth* and religion, particularly Sir James Frazer, Georges Dumézil, and Claude Lévi-Strauss, have pointed out. Although there was a time when *myth* was a virtual synonym for error, notably in the NEOCLASSIC PERIOD, the tendency today is to see *myths* as dramatic or NARRATIVE embodiments of a people's perception of the deepest truths. Various modern writers have insisted on the necessity of *myth* as a material with which the artist works, and in varying ways and degrees have appropriated the old *myths* or created new ones as necessary substances to give order and a frame of meaning to their personal perceptions and images; notable among such "myth-makers" have been Blake, Yeats, Pound, T. S. Eliot (particularly in *The Waste Land*), Joyce, Stevens, and Hart Crane.

Since the introduction of Jung's concept of the "racial unconscious" (see ARCHETYPE) and of Ernst Cassirer's theories of language and *myth*, contemporary CRITICS have found in the *myth* a useful device for examining literature. There is a type of IMAGINATION, Philip Wheelwright insists, that can properly be called "the Archetypal Imagination, which sees the particular object as embodying and adumbrating suggestions of universality." The possessors of such IMAGINATION arrange their works in archetypal patterns and present us with NARRATIVES that stir us as "something at once familiar and strange." They thus give concrete expression to something deep and primitive in us all. Thus, those critics—and they are many—who approach literature as *myth* see in it vestiges of primordial ritual and ceremony; the repository of racial memories; a structure of unconsciously held value systems; an expression of the general beliefs of a race, social class, or nation; or a unique embodiment of ideology. One significant difference should be noted, however; *myth* in its traditional sense is an anonymous, nonliterary, essentially religious formulation of the cosmic view of a people who approach its formulations not as representations of truth but as truth itself; *myth* in the sophisticated literary sense in which it is currently used is the intelligible and often self-conscious use of such primitive methods to express something deeply felt by the individual artist that will, it is hoped, prove to have universal responses. It has been suggested—by C. G. Jung among others—that sophisticated works of literary art, which may be shaped by a strong individual subjectivity, are of less use in the discovery of *myths* than rather vulgar, unsophisticated works like popular NOVELS and even comic strips. The MYTHOPOEIC poet attempts to return to the role of the prophet-seer, by creating a *myth* that strikes resonances in the minds of readers and speaks with something of the authority of the old *myths*. See ARCHETYPE, JUNGIAN CRITICISM, MYTHOPOEIC.

[References: Albert Cook, *Myth and Language* (1980); Mircea Eliade, *Myth and Reality* (tr. 1963); Northrop Frye, *Anatomy of Criticism* (1957); C. M. Gayley, ed., *Classic Myths in English Literature and in Art* (1904, rev. ed. 1911, reprinted 1974); William Righter, *Myth and Literature* (1975); K. K. Ruthven, *Myth* (1976).]

Mythic Criticism: Criticism that explores the nature and significance of the ARCHETYPES and archetypal patterns in a work of art. See MYTH; JUNGIAN CRITICISM; ARCHETYPE; CRITICISM, TYPES OF.

Mythopoeia: Myth-making, construed as either an individual function of a single artist or a collective spirit.

Mythopoetics: A term applied to CRITICISM that places an emphasis on MYTH and ARCHETYPE. See MYTH, ARCHETYPE, JUNGIAN CRITICISM.

N

Naive Narrator or Hero: An ingenuous CHARACTER who is the ostensible author (often the oral NARRATOR) of a NARRATIVE, the implications of which are much plainer to the reader than they are to the NARRATOR. The *naive narrator* can be a device for IRONY, either gentle or savage, or it can be a device for PATHOS, as it frequently is when a child narrates, with innocence, events with tragic or horrible implications. The *naive narrator* is used a great deal by Sherwood Anderson in SHORT STORIES like "I'm a Fool" and "The Egg"; Swift employs the device in "A Modest Proposal" with savage effectiveness; Mark Twain's *Adventures of Huckleberry Finn* and Ring Lardner's "Hair-Cut" are also well-known examples of the use of the *naive narrator.* William Faulkner made memorable use of various sorts of *naive narrator* in *The Sound and the Fury* and *As I Lay Dying.* A similar approach can be seen in J. D. Salinger's *The Catcher in the Rye* and Ken Kesey's *One Flew Over the Cuckoo's Nest.*

Narration: That one of the four types of composition (see ARGUMENTATION, DESCRIPTION, and EXPOSITION) the purpose of which is to recount an event or a series of events. *Narration* may exist, of course, entirely by itself, but it is most likely to incorporate considerable DESCRIPTION. There are two forms of *narration: simple narrative,* which is content to recite events and is largely chronological—as in a newspaper account of a fire; and NARRATIVE with PLOT, which is less often chronological and more often arranged according to a pre-conceived artistic principle determined by the nature of the PLOT and the type of STORY intended (see PLOT). The chief purpose of *narration* is to interest and entertain, though, of course, it may be used to instruct and inform. It is conventionally said that *narration* deals with time, DESCRIPTION with space.
[References: Wayne Booth, *The Rhetoric of Fiction,* 2nd ed. (1983); E. M. Forster, *Aspects of the Novel* (1927); Percy Lubbock, *The Craft of Fiction* (1921); Robert Scholes and Robert Kellogg, *The Nature of Narrative* (1966); Meir Sternberg, *Expositional Modes and Temporal Ordering in Fiction* (1978).]

Narrative: An account in PROSE or VERSE of an actual or fictional event or a sequence of such events; anything that is narrated. See NARRATION.

Narrative Essay: An INFORMAL ESSAY in NARRATIVE form—ANECDOTE, INCIDENT, or ALLEGORY. It differs from a SHORT STORY not only in its simpler STRUCTURE but especially in its ESSAY-like intent, the STORY being a means of developing an idea rather than being an end in itself. Addison's *Vision of Mirzah* is an example. See ESSAY.

Narrative Hook: A term applied to any device used at the opening of a work of FICTION to capture the interest of readers and lead them to continue reading. The *narrative hook* may be an exciting INCIDENT, an unusual statement, or a beginning IN MEDIAS RES.

Narrative Poem: A nondramatic POEM that tells a story or presents a narrative, whether simple or complex, long or short. EPICS, BALLADS, and METRICAL ROMANCES are among the many kinds of *narrative poems.*

Narratology: The sophisticated ANALYSIS of the relations among a STORY—conceived in simple terms—and all the other elements involved in the telling thereof. Some narratological questions include the possibility of a "straight" or neutral quasi-historical telling of a STORY; the presence and function of a NARRATOR with a PERSONA, voice, and STYLE; the importance of verb tense and pronoun person in establishing the connections among STORY, teller, and AUDIENCE; the different CODES and levels of discourse; the possible variations in amount of outward and inward knowledge involved in the act of NARRATION; and the relation between the real author, the IMPLIED AUTHOR, and the narrating voice or voices.

Narrator: In the broadest sense anyone who recounts a NARRATIVE, either in writing or orally. In FICTION the term is used in a more technical sense, as the ostensible author or teller of a STORY. In FICTION presented in the first person, the "I" who tells the story is the *narrator;* the *narrator* may be in any of various relations to the events described, ranging from being their center (the PROTAGONIST) through various degrees of minor importance (minor characters) to being merely a witness. In FICTION told from an OMNISCIENT-AUTHOR POINT OF VIEW, the author acts self-consciously as *narrator,* recounting the STORY and freely commenting on it. A *narrator* is always present, at least by implication, in any work of FICTION, except a STORY in which a SELF-EFFACING AUTHOR relates events with apparent OBJECTIVITY; yet even there the *narrator* exists in fact, although we and the author act as though the *narrator* did not. A *narrator* may be reliable or unreliable. If the *narrator* is reliable, the reader should accept without serious question the statements of fact and judgment that are made. If the *narrator* is unreliable, the reader should question or seek to qualify the statements of fact and judgment made. See NAIVE NARRATOR, UNRELIABLE NARRATOR, POINT OF VIEW, PANORAMIC METHOD.

Naturalism: A term sometimes applied to writing that demonstrates a deep interest in NATURE, such as Wordsworth and other Romantic writers had; and sometimes used to describe any form of extreme REALISM, although this usage is a very loose one. It should properly be reserved to designate a literary movement in the late nineteenth and early twentieth centuries in France, America, and England.

In its simplest sense *naturalism* is the application of the principles of scientific DETERMINISM to FICTION and DRAMA. It draws its name from its basic assumption that everything that is real exists in NATURE, conceived as the world of objects, actions, and forces that yield the secrets of their causation and their being to objective scientific inquiry. The naturalistic view of human beings is that of animals in the natural world, responding to environmental forces and internal stresses and drives, over none of which they have control and none of which they fully understand. It tends to differ from REALISM, not in its attempt to be accurate in the portrayal of its materials but in the selection and organization of those materials, selecting not the commonplace but the representative and so arranging the materials that the structure of the NOVEL or PLAY reveals the pattern of ideas—in this case, scientific theory—which forms the author's view of the nature of experience. In this sense *naturalism* shares with ROMANTICISM a belief that the actual is important not in itself but in what it can reveal about some larger reality; it differs sharply from ROMANTICISM, however, in finding that reality not in transcendent ideas or absolute ideals but in the scienfific laws perceptible through the action of individual instances. This distinction may be illustrated in this way. Given a block of wood and a force pushing on it, producing in it a certain acceleration: REALISM will tend to concentrate its attention on the accurate description of that particular block, that special force, and that definite acceleration: RO-MANTICISM will tend to see in the entire operation an illustration or symbol or suggestion of a philosophical truth and will so represent the block, the force, and the acceleration—often with complete fidelity to fact—that the idea or ideal that it bodies forth is the center of the interest; and *naturalism* will tend to see in the operation a clue or a key to the scientific law that undergirds it and to be interested in the relationship among the force, the block, and the produced acceleration, and will so represent the operation that Newton's second law of motion (even on occasion in its mathematical expression—$F = ma$) is demonstrated or proved by this representative instance of its universal occurrence in nature.

In this sense *naturalism* is the writer's response to the revolution in thought that modern science has produced. From Newton it gains a sense of mechanistic determinism; from Darwin (the greatest single force operative on it) it gains a sense of biological DETERMINISM and the inclusive METAPHOR of competitive jungle that it has used perhaps more often than any other; from Marx it gains a view of history as a battleground of vast economic and social forces; from Freud it gains a view of the determinism of the inner and subconscious self; from Taine it gains a view of literature as a product of inexorable deterministic forces; from Comte it gains a view of social and environmental determinism. In the most influential statement ever made of the theory of *naturalism*, Émile Zola's *Le roman expérimental*, the ideal of the naturalist is stated as the selection of truthful instances subjected to labora-tory conditions in a NOVEL, where the hypotheses of the author about the nature and operation of the forces that work on human beings can be put to the test. Zola's term *expérimental*, usually translated "experimental," is more properly understood as "empirical" or "experiential."

Although the fidelity to detail and the disavowal of the assumptions of the romanticists give *naturalism* clear affinities with REALISM, so that it is often confused in its origins with that movement, so that Balzac and Flaubert are credited with being naturalists, the Goncourt brothers and Zola are gener-ally recognized as having begun the naturalistic NOVEL and codified its theory. Strong elements of *naturalism* are to be seen in the work of George Eliot and Thomas Hardy, but American novelists have been generally more recep-tive to its theories than have the English. Frank Norris (1870–1902) wrote naturalistic novels in conscious imitation of Zola and made an American critical defense of the school, *The Responsibilities of the Novelist*, in which he saw that its real enemy was REALISM and not ROMANTICISM. Stephen Crane (1871–1900) used the devices of IMPRESSIONISM in producing naturalistic novels. Jack London (1876–1916) wrote naturalistic novels with Nietzschean "super-men" (and "superdogs") as PROTAGONISTS. But the greatest American natural-istic novelist—after Zola perhaps the greatest of all—was Theodore Dreiser (1871–1945), whose *An American Tragedy* is an archetypal American example. In the DRAMA Eugene O'Neill employed *naturalism* with distinction. James

T. Farrell, John O'Hara, and James Jones, among others, kept the school alive in America.

The works produced in this school have tended to emphasize either a biological determinism, with an emphasis on the animal nature of human beings, particularly their heredity, portraying them as animals engaged in the endless and brutal struggle for survival, or a socioeconomic determinism, portraying them as the victims of environmental forces and the products of social and economic factors behond their control or full understanding. Occasionally, as in the works of Thomas Hardy, human beings are seen as the victims of "destiny" or "fate." But, whichever of these views is taken, the naturalist strives to be honest and objective, even documentary, in the presentation of material; to be amoral in the view of the struggle in which human animals find themselves, neither condemning nor praising human beings for actions beyond their control; to be pessimistic about human capabilities—life, the naturalists seems to feel, is a vicious trap, a cruel game; to be frank and almost clinically direct in the portrayal of human beings as animals driven by fundamental urges—fear, hunger, and sex; to be deterministic in the portrayal of human actions, seeing them as explicable in cause-and-effect relationships; and to exercise a bias in the selection of CHARACTERS and ACTIONS, frequently choosing primitive CHARACTERS and simple, violent ACTIONS as best giving "experimental conditions." No single naturalistic work displays completely this catalog of qualities, but taken together they tend to define the directions and intentions of *naturalism*.

[References: Stopford A. Brooke, *Naturalism in English Poetry* (1920); Donald Pizer, *Realism and Naturalism in Nineteenth-Century American Literature* (1976), and *Twentieth-Century Literary Naturalism* (1982); Émile Zola, *Le roman expérimental* (tr. 1964 as *The Naturalist Novel*, ed. Maxwell Geismar).]

Naturalistic and Symbolistic Period in American Literature: The period between 1900 and 1930 in America was the age of the birth of contemporary attitudes and contemporary writing. It is sharply divided by the First World War, the part before the war being a time dominated by NATURALISM, and the part after being marked by a growing international awareness, a sensitivity to European literary models, and a steadily developing SYMBOLISM in POETRY and FICTION. There had been forerunners of naturalistic writing before 1900—several in Europe, as well as Stephen Crane and Edwin Arlington Robinson in America—but the period did not receive energetic definition or motivation until the turn of the century. (See FIN DE SIÈCLE, NATURALISM.) The first decade of the twentieth century saw the flourishing of the "muckraking" MAGAZINE exposé and the corresponding NOVEL. During this decade Henry James, living in England, probably carried American REALISM to its greatest height in *The Ambassadors, The Wings of the Dove,* and *The Golden Bowl;* Mark Twain, although still alive, was no longer producing works comparable to those of the 1880s, and his pessimism was growing more darkly marked; Howells, too, was still producing his NOVELS and his amiable critical ESSAYS but without the strength of his heyday. Frank Norris, Theodore Dreiser, and Jack London were producing crude but powerful examples of the naturalistic NOVEL. William Vaughn Moody was writing a socially conscious VERSE and extremely popular DRAMA; and Edwin Arlington Robinson had launched the career that was to flower into distinction and popularity in the second and third decades of the century.

The second decade saw the virtual birth of modern American POETRY, with the founding of *Poetry* magazine in Chicago in 1912 by Harriet Monroe, the emergence of the IMAGISTS, the beginning of the careers of Frost, Pound, Eliot, Stevens, and W. C. Williams. The realistic NOVEL continued in the works of Howells, Ellen Glasgow, Willa Cather, and Edith Wharton. As the decade ended, the plays of Eugene O'Neill gave promise of a theatrical revival to match the growing LITTLE THEATER MOVEMENT and the development of the FOLK DRAMA. Prior to the twentieth century American CRITICISM had been sporadic and uncertain, but the work of W. C. Brownell, James Huneker, and a group of young CRITICS demanding a "usable past"—among them, Randolph Bourne and Van Wyck Brooks—joined with the developing artistic concern of the AVANT-GARDE groups and the LITTLE MAGAZINES to produce an increasingly sensitive body of critical work as the second decade of the century drew toward a close.

The First World War produced a major dislocation of a number of talented young men, most of them born between 1895 and 1902, who became volunteer ambulance and ammunition truck drivers in the French and Italian armies, came early in contact with European culture, and emerged from the war disillusioned with American "idealism" and with the crassness of American culture. This postwar generation, considering itself self-consciously as a "LOST GENERATION," set about a repudiation of American culture in three ways: one group, largely from the East, went back to Europe and there published LITTLE MAGAZINES, waited upon Gertrude Stein, took part in DADAISM, and formulated a polished and *symbolistic* style—among them were F. Scott Fitzgerald, Ernest Hemingway, Edmund Wilson, E. E. Cummings, Malcolm Cowley, and Sherwood Anderson, and, on the English side of the channel, Ezra Pound and T. S. Eliot; another group, largely from the Middle West, came east and in Cambridge, New Haven, and Greenwich Village produced a literature that was realistic, satiric, and critical, aimed at the standardized mediocrity of the American village—among them were Ring Lardner and Sinclair Lewis; and another group, largely Southern, repudiated the meaningless mechanism of capitalistic America by looking backward to a past that had tradition and order—these were the POETS and critics who published the *Fugitive* in Nashville and were AGRARIANS, and others who contributed to magazines like the *Double Dealer* in New Orleans. Out of this last group came the modern Southern NOVEL and much of the NEW CRITICISM; the group included John Crowe Ransom, Allen Tate, Robert Penn Warren, Cleanth Brooks, and William Faulkner.

All of these groups—expatriates, revolters against the village, and seekers of a tradition of order—sought for art forms and critical standards different from those of the traditional American writer, and they found them in the methods of the French symbolists, in the work of Joyce and Proust, in the complex intellectual POETRY of the seventeenth century "Metaphysicals," and in the kind of experimentation that the LITTLE MAGAZINES fostered. By the end of the period a group of academic critics, the NEW HUMANISTS, were formulating a doctrine of life and art that repudiated the contemporary artist, and in the late fall of 1929 the collapse of the stock market, signaling the beginning of the Depression, marked an effective end to a period in which most of the seeds of contemporary American writing had been sown. See *Outline of Literary History.*

Nature: Few terms are so important to the student of literature—or so difficult—as this one. Since conformity with *nature*—the resort to *nature* as a norm or standard for judging artistic expression—long permeated critical thinking (the MIMETIC THEORY OF ART), some knowledge of the "normative" meanings of the term is necessary to the understanding of much CRITICISM and literature. Professor A. O. Lovejoy found as many as sixty different meanings for *"nature"* in its normative functions. Both neoclassicists and romanticists would "follow *Nature"*; but the former drew from the term ideas of order, regularity, and universality, both in "external" *nature* and in human *nature,* while the latter found in *nature* the justification for their enthusiasm for irregularity ("wildness") in external *nature* and for individualism in human *nature.* Other contradictory senses may be noted: the term *nature* might mean, on the one hand, human *nature* (typical human behavior) or, on the other hand, whatever is antithetical to human *nature* and human works—what has not been "spoiled" by human beings. In certain formulaic sets of antitheses, *nature* is opposed to nurture or to culture.

The neoclassic view of *nature* as implying universal aesthetic validity led to a reverence for "rules" drawn from long-continued acceptance by human beings, such acceptance being taken as an evidence of their basis in what is universal in human *nature.* The rules were based on proved models. Opposed to this was the romantic tendency to regard as "natural" the primitive, the unsophisticated, the uncultivated, the naive—a conception that justified the disregard of rules and precedents and the exaltation of the freedom of individual expression. Among some neoclassic writers the words "reason" and "nature" were closely allied in meaning, because both were related to the idea of "order" (John Dennis said that *nature* was order in the visible world, while reason was order in the invisible realm). The distinction between *nature* and WIT (in one of its senses) was not always clear, since both provided tests of excellence, though, properly, WIT was specific while *nature* was generic, thought of as an ultimate, as indicated in the familiar LINES from Pope's *Essay on Criticism:*

> True Wit is Nature to advantage dressed,
> What oft was thought, but ne'er so well expressed.

Nature in the sense of "external nature"—the objects of the natural world such as mountains, trees, rivers, flowers, and birds—has supplied a large part of the imaginative substance of literature, especially POETRY, from the earliest times. Some survey, therefore, of the attitudes toward external *nature* may be useful. POETS make the following different uses of external *nature:* (1) they express childlike delight in the open-air world; (2) they use *nature* as the BACKGROUND or SETTING to human action or emotion; (3) they see *nature* through historic coloring; (4) they make *nature* sympathize with their own feelings; (5) they dwell on the infinite side of *nature;* (6) they give description of *nature* for its own sake; (7) they interpret *nature* with imaginative sympathy; (8) they use *nature* as a symbol of the spirit.

The greatest attention to *nature* in English literature came in the ROMAN-TIC PERIOD, when the revolt against the conventionalities of neoclassic fashions led to much theorizing about the relation of human beings to external *nature* and the production of a vast amount of POETRY putting the new theories into practice. To be sure, earlier English literature had made much use of *nature*. The comparatively small amount of ANGLO-SAXON literature remaining reflects some love of *nature*, a power for picturesque description—as in the "Riddles" (see RIDDLE) and such POEMS as the *Wife's Complaint* and the *Husband's Message*—and especially a sense of mystery and awe in the presence of *nature*, as in *Beowulf*. The *nature* here seems to be partly a disagreeable and even hostile force—winters, oceans, beasts, long nights. Late medieval literature—Chaucer and the ROMANCES—was apt to present *nature* in idyllic, conventionalized forms, a pleasant garden or "bower" on a spring morning. In the RENAISSANCE there was sometimes a genuine, subjective response to natural surroundings, as in some of Surrey's poems, though often the treatment was conventional in character, as in the PASTORALS and the SONNETS. Shakespeare, of course, though no theorist like Wordsworth, shows a wide knowledge of *nature* and an unsurpassed faculty for drawing on subjects from *nature*, whether conventional or fresh, to give appropriate settings and to impart an air of reality to dramatic situations and human moods.

The eighteenth century brought the great conflict between NEOCLASSI-CISM and ROMANTICISM, and nowhere were the issues sharper between the two schools than in their treatment of external *nature*. In their zeal to follow "correct" models, to restrain enthusiasm, and to favor urban over rural life, the neoclassicists found little room for recording intimate observations of *nature*, though they did, of course, employ natural imagery, usually conventionalized, and use *nature* descriptions as SETTINGS and as a basis for philosophical reflections. For the wilder aspects of *nature* they expressed abhorrence. Winter was "the deformed wrong side of the year," while mountains were a positive blemish upon the landscape and the ocean was a dangerous, wearying waste of waters. The writers who adumbrated the coming change, such as Lady Winchilsea, John Dyer, James Thomson (especially *The Seasons*, 1726–1730), were giving voice to the new enthusiasm for *nature* while NEOCLASSICISM was at its height, and the movement grew with Gray, Collins, Cowper, and others till readers a little later were ready to respond to the values of the homelier aspects of *nature*—even mice and lice—as sung by Robert Burns.

With Wordsworth came a new complexity, as the POET seemed both closer to *nature* and alienated therefrom. Wordsworth often seems to be turning to *nature*—registered as "the earth" as opposed to "the world" of culture—in the hope of finding a realm comparable with his spiritual needs. In some POEMS Wordsworth seems to find what he is looking for; in others, however, he seems to discover that *nature* is "other" rather than "self." Coleridge, too, gave climactic expressions to the romantic enthusiasm for the wilder, disordered aspects of *nature* that the neoclassicists could not tolerate. Observe the sharp contrast between the following passages, the first from Pope, and the second from Coleridge:

> Here hills and vales, the woodland and its plain,
> Here earth and water seem to strive again;
> Not chaos-like together crushed and bruised,

> But, as the world, harmoniously confused:
> Where order in variety we see,
> And where, though all things differ, all agree.
> *(Windsor Forest)*

> But oh! that deep romantic chasm which slanted
> Down the green hill athwart a cedarn cover!
> A savage place! as holy and enchanted
> As e'er beneath a waning moon was haunted
> By woman wailing for her demon lover!
> *(Kubla Khun)*

The POETRY of the other major romantic POETS, Shelley, Keats, and Byron, is shot through with intimate, subjective presentations of *nature*, from the delicate and mysterious to the GROTESQUE and awesome. This attitude not only was reflected widely in American literature (Bryant, Longfellow, Lowell, Whittier, Emerson, Thoreau) but persisted in much of the VERSE of the Victorians, notably Tennyson.

The widespread acceptance of the Darwinian concepts of *nature* and of a natural struggle for existence has colored and modified the view of *nature*, and Wordsworth's gentle instructor in beauty can become "nature red in tooth and claw" in Tennyson's *In Memoriam*, although that is not his persistent attitude. With the development of NATURALISM a view of *nature* as a raw and primitive jungle where the struggle for survival relentlessly continues came into being, with *nature* viewed as a scientific fact, devoid of meaning in philosophical terms. However, in its calmer moments, it still can minister to the human spirit, as can be seen in Hemingway's "Big Two-Hearted River" or the fishing scenes in *The Sun Also Rises* or in Faulkner's "The Bear." *Nature* is for contemporary writers what it has always been for writers, not an objective fact, but the "world's body" through which they speak in concrete terms their perceptions of themselves and the world, and it is capable of having fluctuating meanings in the same author's work and at the same time of speaking with authority. Emerson's *nature*, in his essay *Nature*, exists for five uses: as commodity, beauty, language, discipline, and, finally, ideal symbol. These varying uses are found by one man writing from a pronounced point of view. The reader is, therefore, well warned that *nature*, like one of Humpty Dumpty's words in *Alice in Wonderland*, means exactly what its user intends it to mean, just that, and nothing more!

[References: Edmund Blunden, *Nature in English Literature* (1929); George Economou, *The Goddess Natura in Medieval Literature* (1972); Norman Foerster, *Nature in American Literature* (1923); Christopher Hussey, *The Picturesque* (1927, reprinted 1967); Myra Reynolds, *The Treatment of Nature in English Poetry between Pope and Wordsworth*, 2nd ed. (1909); J. C. Shairp, *On Poetic Interpretation of Nature* (1884).]

Near Rhyme: The REPETITION in accented syllables of the final consonant sound without the correspondence of the preceding vowel sound, which would make true RHYME, as in "grope" and "cup," "restored" and "word," "drunkard" and "conquered." Near rhyme of this sort is a kind of CONSONANCE. Complementarily, repetition of vowel sound without exact correspondence of succeeding consonants amounts to *near rhyme* that is a kind of ASSONANCE, as between "enough" and "love." Here, as with "face" and "ways," the consonant components tend to be the unvoiced and voiced forms of the same basic articulation—or, as with "dame" and "lane," identical articulation (voiced-nasal) of neighboring sounds. It is also called HALF RHYME, SLANT RHYME, and OBLIQUE RHYME.

Negative Capability: A celebrated phrase put forward in a letter (December 1817) by John Keats to account for "what quality went to form a Man of Achievement especially in Literature & which Shakespeare possessed so enormously—I mean *Negative Capability,* that is when man is capable of being in uncertainties, Mysteries, doubts, without any irritable reaching after fact & reason. . . ." As a counterexample, Keats mentioned Coleridge, who "would let go by a fine isolated verisimilitude caught from the Penetralium of mystery, from being incapable of remaining content with half knowledge." In some ways a TRANSFERRED EPITHET, this phrase sounds as though it may mean an absence or deficit of capability, but Keats clearly meant it to be a positive quality involving alertness, sympathy, and OBJECTIVITY.

[Reference: W. J. Bate, *Negative Capability: The Intuitive Approach in Keats* (1939, reprinted 1976).]

Nemesis: In Greek mythology, the goddess of retributive justice or vengeance. The term *nemesis* is applied to the divine retribution, when an evil act brings about its own punishment and a tragic POETIC JUSTICE prevails. The term is also applied to both an agent and an act of merited punishment. It thus often becomes synonymous with FATE, although at least a latent sense of justice is almost always associated with the term.

Neoclassic Period: The period in English literature between the return of the Stuarts to the English throne in 1660 and the full assertion of ROMANTICISM that came with the publication of *Lyrical Ballads* by Wordsworth and Coleridge in 1978. It falls into three relatively distinct segments: the RESTORATION AGE (1660–1700), the AUGUSTAN AGE (1700–1750), and the AGE OF JOHNSON (1750–1798).

In the RESTORATION AGE England underwent a strong reaction against the Puritanism of the COMMONWEALTH INTERREGNUM; its already strong interest in scientific investigation and philosophical thought increased; and NEOCLASSICISM, with particularly strong French influences, developed steadily. The HEROIC COUPLET became a major verse FORM; the ODE was a widely used poetic GENRE; and the poetic muse usually served didactic or satiric purposes. In PROSE, despite the tendency toward utilitarian goals, the "modern" STYLE was developing, notably in Dryden's work. In DRAMA the reopening of the theaters and the establishment of the PATENT THEATERS led to the development of the HEROIC DRAMA in COUPLETS and the COMEDY OF MANNERS in PROSE. Milton, Bunyan, and Dryden were the principal writers of the period, with *Paradise Lost* and *Pilgrim's Progress,* although atypical of the spirit of license and revolt dominant in the age, perhaps its major achievements in literature. Dryden's accomplishments, although none quite reached the individual heights of Milton or Bunyan, were signally fine and pointed forward toward the AUGUSTAN AGE. Otway, Wycherley, and Congreve enriched the stage, while the PROSE of Locke found its way into a permanent place in English thought.

In the AUGUSTAN AGE, NEOCLASSICISM found its highest English expression. The CLASSICAL ideals of taste, polish, "common sense," and reason (drawn from the ancients, from France, and from the RESTORATION AGE, and modified by current philosophical and scientific activities) were more important than emotion and IMAGINATION. DEISM was advancing steadily, and the same rule of reason resulted in a literature that was realistic, satirical, moral, correct, and affected strongly in its origins and its expressions by politics and intrigue. POETRY sparkled with the polished COUPLETS of Pope. It was concerned with truth, with the satiric, and the didactic. The MOCK EPIC and the verse ESSAY were common forms. In the work of James Thomson was to be found, in BLANK VERSE and the SPENSERIAN STANZA, a growing concern with NATURE and science; and in the "GRAVEYARD SCHOOL," a sentimental melancholy.

On the stage the HEROIC DRAMA was no more, being replaced by the DOMESTIC TRAGEDY of writers like Lillo and imitations of CLASSICAL TRAGEDY such as Addison's *Cato.* SENTIMENTAL COMEDY replaced the less "moral" COMEDY OF MANNERS, in such work as that of Cibber and Steele. The Licensing Act of 1737 imposed a stifling political censorship on the English theater.

It was a great age of PROSE. The essay PERIODICAL was adumbrated in JOURNALS like Defoe's *Review* and attained its epitome in *The Tatler* and *The Spectator*—journals that had a profound influence on English prose STYLE and were followed by a host of imitators. The audacious prose SATIRES of Swift were among the glories of the age. The prose FICTION of Defoe and the early NOVELS of Richardson, Fielding, and Smollett had all appeared before the mid-century mark.

The AGE OF JOHNSON was a period of transition that was still dominated by the critical energies and the prose vigor of a prodigious representative of the passing tradition, Dr. Samuel Johnson. The developing interest in human freedom, the impact of German ROMANTICISM, the widening range of intellectual interests and human sympathies, the developing appreciation of external NATURE and the country life, the evolving cult of the primitive—all joined with political events like the American and the French revolutions and religious occurrences like the rise of Methodism to establish the bedrock on which English ROMANTICISM was to rest.

In POETRY Gray, Cowper, Burns, and Crabbe flourished. An interest in folk literature and popular BALLADS developed. In the DRAMA Goldsmith and Sheridan returned laughter to the stage with the COMEDY OF MANNERS, although SENTIMENTAL COMEDY still flourished. Shakespeare—often in a laundered or distorted form—was immensely popular on the stage; and BURLESQUE, the PANTOMIME, and the MELODRAMA—forms that freed the DRAMA (although at a high price) from the sharp restrictions of the PATENT THEATERS—developed. In prose the NOVEL advanced steadily. Sterne and Mackenzie developed the NOVEL OF SENSIBILITY; Walpole, Mrs. Radcliffe, and Clara Reeves the GOTHIC NOVEL. By the end of the century Brooke and Godwin were producing novels of political and philosophical purpose.

In the AGE OF JOHNSON the greatest literary figures were Johnson himself, as POET, CRITIC, novelist, journalist, and lexicographer—a superlative embodiment of the ideals of the *Neoclassic Period*—and Robert Burns, as poet of the common people, the Scottish soil, and the Romantic soul—an adumbration of the coming ROMANTIC PERIOD. By 1798, Wordsworth, Coleridge, and Blake had already launched their careers; Johnson and Burns were dead; and Shelley,

Byron, and Keats had been born. See the *Outline of Literary History*, AUGUS-
TAN AGE, RESTORATION AGE, and the AGE OF JOHNSON.

Neoclassicism: The term applied to the CLASSICISM that dominated English
literature in the RESTORATION AGE and in the eighteenth century. It draws
its name from its finding in CLASSICAL literature and in contemporary French
neoclassical writings the models for its literary expressions and a group of
attitudes toward life and art. It was, at least in part, the result of the reaction
against the fires of enthusiasm that had blazed in the RENAISSANCE. On the
RENAISSANCE idea of the limitless human potentiality was imposed a view
of human beings as limited, dualistic, imperfect; on the intensity of human
responses were imposed a reverence for order and a delight in reason and
rules; on the burgeoning of IMAGINATION into new and strange worlds was
imposed a distrust of innovation and INVENTION: on expanding individualism
was imposed a view that saw human beings most significantly in their generic
qualities and group activities; on the enthusiasms of religious MYSTICISM was
imposed the restrained good sense of DEISM. From the French critics, from
Horace, Virgil, and other writers of CLASSICAL literature came the artistic
ideals of order, concentration, economy, utility, logic, restrained emotion, accuracy, "correctness," "good taste," and DECORUM. A sense of symmetry, a delight
in design, and a view of art as centered in humanity, with human beings as
its primary subject matter, and the belief that literature should be judged in
terms of its service to humanity (see PRAGMATIC THEORY OF ART) resulted
in the seeking of proportion, UNITY, harmony, and grace in literary expressions
that aimed to delight, instruct, and correct human beings, primarily as social
animals. It was that great age of the ESSAY, of the LETTER and EPISTLE, of
SATIRE, of moral instruction, of PARODY, and of BURLESQUE. The play of mind
upon life was regarded as more important than the play of feeling, with the
result that a polite, urbane, witty, intellectual art developed.

Neoclassic ideals had concrete effects on literature. POETIC DICTION and
IMAGERY tended to become conventional, with detail subordinated to design.
The appeal to the intellect rather than to the emotions resulted in a fondness
for WIT and the production of much SATIRE, in both PROSE and VERSE. The
irregular or unpleasant aspects of external NATURE, such as mountains, ocean,
winter, were less frequently utilized than the pleasanter phases as represented
in stars, flowers, or a formal garden. A tendency to REALISM marked the presentation of life with the generic qualities and common attributes and actions
of men and women being stressed. Literature exalted FORM—polish, clarity,
brilliance. It avoided the obscure or the mysterious. It valued the CLASSICAL
critical requirements of universality and DECORUM. It "imitated" (see IMITA-
TION) the CLASSICS and cultivated CLASSICAL literary FORMS and types, such
as SATIRE and the ODE. The earlier English authors whose works were produced
in a "less cultivated" age either were ignored or were admired more for their
genius than for their art. Didactic literature flourished. Though BLANK VERSE
and the SPENSERIAN STANZA were cultivated, rhymed COUPLETS were the
favorite form of VERSE. Although many of the attitudes and mannerisms of
the neoclassicists were swept aside by the great tide of ROMANTICISM, the
movement exerted a permanently wholesome effect in its clarifying and chas-
tening effect on English PROSE style and in establishing in English literature
the importance of certain classical graces, such as order, good form, unified

structure, clarity, conciseness, and restraint. (Not that such models as Horace were necessarily spotless exemplars of all these values, or that the eighteenth-century practitioners themselves were consistent models of decorum and sanity.) Poetic technique as developed by Pope, too, has become a permanent heritage. In the twentieth century there has been a strong noeclassical tendency in much of the best POETRY and CRITICISM, growing out of a reaction against ROMANTICISM and out of distrust of the potentialities of human beings, together with a new respect for the place of intellect in life and art. Writers like T. E. Hulme, T. S. Eliot, Ezra Pound, Wyndham Lewis, Irving Babbitt, Mark Van Doren, Edith Sitwell, Hugh Kenner, Louis Zukofsky, Guy Davenport, Richard Wilbur, W. H. Auden, and the New Critics are on many issues at one with *neoclassicism.*

[References: W. J. Courthope, *History of English Poetry,* 6 vols. (1895–1910, reprinted 1962); John Dennis, *The Age of Pope,* 11th ed. (1921); Oliver Elton, *A Survey of English Literature, 1730–1780,* 2 vols. (1928); E. Gosse, *A History of Eighteenth-Century Literature (1660–1780)* (1897); Leslie Stephen, *English Literature and Society in the Eighteenth Century* (1904, reprinted 1955).]

Neologism or Neology: A word newly introduced into a language, especially as a means of enhancing literary STYLE. There was much conscious use of *neologisms,* especially from Greek and Latin, in the RENAISSANCE, partly as a reult of a definite critical attitude toward the enrichment of the native English vocabulary. But the practice is not confined to any one period. Too often, authors employ *neologisms* in a failing effort to give their STYLE an atmosphere of freshness or erudition (see PEDANTRY), but the variety, flexibility, and resourcefulness of the modern English vocabulary are partly the cumulative result of the successful use of *neologisms.* A vast number of *neologisms,* of course, employed by individual authors or by stylistic "schools" (see EUPHUISM, GONGORISM), have not gained permanent foothold in the vocabulary. The current of English is constantly fed by a steady stream of new words, some of them eventually platitudinous (as the oversupply of "gate"-suffix scandals after "Watergate"), some entertaining (like "palimony" or Kenneth Tynan's invention to describe both bland and grandiose: "blandiose"). See COINED WORDS.

Neoplatonism: A system of belief that originated in Alexandria in the third century, composed of elements of PLATONISM mixed with Oriental beliefs and with some aspects of Christianity. Its leading representative was Plotinus. See PLATONISM.

New Comedy: Greek COMEDY of the fourth and third centuries, B.C. After the decline of Greece and the rise of Macedonia, the OLD COMEDY, of which Aristophanes was the greatest creator, was replaced by a COMEDY OF MANNERS, featuring STOCK CHARACTERS and conventional PLOTS. The LOCALE was usually a street, the CHARACTERS young lovers, courtesans, parsimonious elders, and scheming servants. The best writers of the *New Comedy* were Menander, Philemon, and Diphilus. The *New Comedy* had a powerful influence on the Roman COMEDIES of Plautus and Terence, and through them on much of the COMEDY written since. See COMEDY.

New Criticism: In a strict sense the term is applied to the CRITICISM written by John Crowe Ransom, Allen Tate, R. P. Blackmur, Robert Penn Warren, and Cleanth Brooks, and it is derived from Ransom's book *The New Criticism,* published in 1941, which discusses a movement in America in the 1930s that paralleled movements in England led by CRITICS like T. S. Eliot, I. A. Richards, and William Empson. Generally the term is applied, however, to the whole body of recent CRITICISM that concentrates on the work of art as an object in itself; finds in it a special kind of language opposed to—or at least different from—the languages of science or philosophy; and examines it through a process of close analysis. The New Critics constitute the school in contemporary criticism that most completely employs the OBJECTIVE THEORY OF ART. The movement has varied sources; among them are I. A. Richards's *The Principles of Literary Criticism* (1924), Laura (Riding) Jackson's criticism that appeared in the late 1920s, William Empson's *Seven Types of Ambiguity* (1930), the work of Remy de Gourmont, the anti-ROMANTICISM of T. E. Hulme, the French EXPLICATION DE TEXTE, the psychological theories of the ARCHETYPE, the concepts of order and tradition of the southern AGRARIANS, and the work of Ezra Pound and T. S. Eliot.

Not even the group to which the term can be applied in its strictest sense has formed a school subscribing to a fixed dogma; when to this group are added others like Yvor Winters and Kenneth Burke, it can be seen that the *New Criticism* is really a cluster of attitudes toward literature rather than an organized critical system. The primary concern of these critics has been to discover the intrinsic worth of literature, to demonstrate that worth to intelligent readers, and to defend that worth against the types of attack they believe to be inherent in contemporary thought. Indeed, the *New Criticism* is primarily a protest against certain conventional and traditional ways of viewing life and art. The New Critics are protesting against the mechanistic and positivistic nature of much of the modern world; and their protest is framed in terms of a cultural tradition, a religious order, and sometimes an aristocratic social system. They are protesting against a view of life and knowledge that rests on fact and inference from fact alone; and their protest takes the form of an insistence on literature as a valid form of knowledge and as a communicator not of the truths of other languages but of the truths incommunicable in other terms than those of the language of literature itself. They are protesting against ROMANTICISM with its doctrines of self-expression, its EXPRESSIVE THEORY OF ART, and its philosophy of perfectibility; and their protest takes the form of the OBJECTIVE THEORY OF ART, of the impersonal and "nearly anonymous" artist, and of neoclassic restraint. They are protesting against IMPRESSIONISM in criticism; and their protest takes the form of intense methodological concern and often of semantic analysis. They were originally protesting against the NEW HUMANISM of Babbitt and More; and their protest took the form of an insistence that the morality and value of a work of art are functions of its inner qualities and that literature cannot be evaluated in general terms or terms not directly related to the work itself. Their concern has been with the IMAGE, the SYMBOL, the MEANING, and only infrequently with GENRE, with PLOT, or with CHARACTER. This aspect of the *New Criticism* has led to attacks by critics interested in GENRE or FORM who assert that the New Critics reduce literature to a linguistic or symbolic monism that makes the significant discrimination among types impossible. In actual practice the *New Criticism* has most often been applied, and has worked best when applied, to the LYRIC; it has been less successful when applied to extended works of FICTION or DRAMA. See CRITICISM, TYPES OF; INTENTIONAL FALLACY; AFFECTIVE FALLACY; IMAGERY; EXPLICATION DE TEXTE; AUTOTELIC; ARCHETYPE; MYTH; OBJECTIVE THEORY OF ART.

[References: Cleanth Brooks, *The Well Wrought Urn* (1947); R. S. Crane, ed., *Critics and Criticism* (1952); Frank Lentricchia, *After the New Criticism* (1980); John Crowe Ransom, *The New Criticism* (1941).]

New Humanism, The: An American critical school in the first third of the twentieth century that emphasized the moral qualities of literature. See HUMANISM, THE NEW.

New Journalism, The: A species of writing that owes something to the example of H. L. Mencken, John Dos Passos, and Ernest Hemingway (especially his *Death in the Afternoon*) and even reaches back as far as Daniel Defoe for precursors. As it emerged after the Second World War, the *New Journalism* was founded on conventional journalistic or historical coverage of events or phenomena but gave up the traditional impersonality and invisibility of the journalist as such and offered instead a subjective STYLE and voice that openly admit the personal presence and involvement of a human witness. The most vocal and visible practitioners have been Tom Wolfe, Norman Mailer, S. Hunter Thompson, Joan Didion, Mark Harris, John McPhee, and Truman Capote. Many of these writers also work as producers of ordinary FICTION, and to their ostensibly journalistic chores they take along a number of imaginative devices—including INTERIOR MONOLOGUE, FLASHBACKS, shifts of focus from documentation to philosophy, and the invention of imaginary CHARACTERS.

New Novel: A term, literally from the French phrase *nouveau roman*, often applied to the contemporary ANTI-NOVEL. See ANTI-NOVEL.

New York School: A group of American POETS who flourished around 1950–1970, distinguished by urbanity, WIT, learning, spontaneity, and exuberance. Led by Frank O'Hara (1926–1966), these poets exploited certain interests and sympathies: the culture of France, modern painting (SURREALISM and abstract expressionism in particular), jazz, Hollywood movies, and city life.

Newgate: A prison of unsavory reputation in London, dating from the twelfth century to 1902, when it was demolished. Originally it was in the gate house of the principal west gate of the city. Until 1868 executions were held outside *Newgate* and attracted large crowds. The *Newgate Calendar* (begun 1773) was a biographical record of the most notorious criminals confined in the prison. NOVELS and TALES dealing with London crime and criminals are often referred to as *Newgate* NOVELS and TALES.

Nihil obstat: A Latin phrase meaning "nothing obstructs" and used in the Roman Catholic Church to grant permission to publish a book. See IMPRIMATUR.

Nine Worthies, The: Late medieval and early RENAISSANCE literature reflects the widespread tradition or classification of the HEROES known as the *"nine* *worthies."* Caxton lists them in his preface to Malory's *Le Morte Darthur* in the conventional three groups: Hector, Alexander, Julius Caesar (pre-Christian pagans); Joshua, David, Judas Maccabeus (pre-Christian Jews); Arthur, Charlemagne, Godfrey of Boulogne (Christians). They are impersonated in the BURLESQUE PLAY incorporated in Shakespeare's *Love's Labour's Lost.*

Nobel Prize: A large sum of money awarded anually to the person having produced during the year the most eminent piece of work in the field of idealistic literature. In actuality the recipient's total career seems to be more important than any single work. This award, granted through the Swedish Academy in Stockholm, was made possible by Alfred Bernhard Nobel (1833–1896), a Swedish chemist and engineer. Nobel willed the income from practically his entire estate for the establishment of such annual prizes and the endowment of research foundations, not only in the field of literature but also in physics, chemistry, and medicine or physiology, and for the promotion of world peace. Much later, a prize in "economic science" was added. The amount of each prize varies with the income from the main fund but is now well in excess of $100,000. Nationality does not enter into consideration at all in the awarding of the prizes, which was begun on December 10, 1901, the fifth anniversary of Nobel's death. A further stipulation of Nobel's will empowers the Swedish Academy, which awards the prize for literature, to withhold the grant for any one year; if no work during that year is judged worthy of the recognition, the amount of the prize reverts to the main fund. The Nobel laureates in literature are listed in the Appendix.
[Reference: S. M. Sinha, *Nobel Laureates of Literature, 1901–1973* (1975).]

Noble Savage: The idea that primitive human beings are naturally good and that whatever evil they develop is the product of the corrupting action of civilization and society. Montaigne, in his essay "Of Cannibals" (1580), stated the basic concept. Dryden, in his heroic PLAY *The Conquest of Granada* (1671), has a character say:

> I am as free as nature first made man,
> Ere the base laws of servitude began
> When wild in wood the noble savage ran.

Aphra Behn, in *Oroonoko: or, The Royal Slave* (1688), portrayed a *noble savage* in chains. But the greatest impulse toward the doctrine of a natural nobility came from Rousseau's *Émile* (1762): "Everything is well when it comes fresh from the hands of the Maker; everything degenerates in the hands of Man." The idea was used extensively by Chateaubriand, and it became a commonplace of ROMANTICISM. The continuing popularity of Tarzan (who is also the literally noble Lord Greystoke) is testimony to the durability of the idea. See PRIMITIVISM.

Nocturne: A poetic and often sentimental composition, expressing moods appropriate to evening or night time. A SERENADE; a SONG.

Noh (or Nō) Plays: The most important form of Japanese DRAMA, *noh* literally meaning "highly skilled or accomplished." The *noh plays* are harmonious combinations of dance, POETRY, music, MIME, and acting. Their origins are in early religious ceremony; they began as religious ritual and have so continued. There are 240 *noh plays* in the standard repertory, all of them written between 1300 and 1600. *Noh plays* were originally a part of the ritual of the Japanese feudal aristocracy, and they continue that tradition. They are short, one or two ACTS, and are usually presented at a religious festival in programs consisting of one each of the five types of *noh plays*: (1) a PLAY of praise to a god, adorned with dancing, (2) a play about a warrior HERO from the EPIC period in Japanese history, (3) a "female-wig" or "woman" play, in which a male actor impersonates a woman, (4) a play of great violence, sensationalism, and often of ghosts and supernatural beings, and (5) a solemn play of warlike dancing, which ends with a grateful recognition of the occasion of the festival. These plays aim at creating a serene and elegant contemplation of aesthetic beauty and a sense of religious sublimity. They are performed on stylized sets, with lavish, symbolic costuming. Elevated speech is in VERSE and common speech in PROSE. Their performance techniques, SETTINGS, costuming, and acting styles represent an unbroken tradition stretching back to the fourteenth century. They thus constitute the oldest continuous aesthetic tradition in the world. Among modern Western writers, W. B. Yeats and Ezra Pound exploited certain features of *Noh* DRAMA. See KABUKI PLAYS.

[References: Donald Keene, ed., *Twenty Plays of the Nō Theatre* (1970); Ezra Pound, ed., *Certain Noble Plays of Japan* (1916, reprinted 1971); L. C. Pronko, *Guide to Japanese Drama* (1973).]

Nom de plume (pen name): A name adopted by a writer for professional use or to disguise his or her true identity. For example, William Sydney Porter assumed the pen name "O. Henry"; and Amandine Aurore Lucie Dupin, Baroness Dudevant, almost unknown by her real name, was famous as the French novelist, George Sand. In certain traditions, notably the Japanese and the French, the pen name is more the rule than the exception. Some fastidious writers insist that pen names should always be cited in their full form with quotation marks; this practice applies especially to those like "Mark Twain" and "Sholem Aleichem" that are really phrases and not a first name plus a last name. See PSEUDONYM.

Nominalism: A philosophical doctrine first advanced by Roscellinus (twelfth century) and revived and popularized by William of Ockham (fourteenth century). It holds that abstract concepts, general terms, and universals have no objective referents but exist only as names. This doctrine, which leads toward materialism and empiricism in its insistence that only particular things exist, has been popular in the nineteenth and twentieth centuries.

Nonce Word: In earlier forms of a language a word for which there is a single recorded occurrence. There are a number of *nonce words* in Old English writing. In modern times a *nonce word* is one invented by an author for a particular usage or special meaning. James Joyce made *nonce words* one of the chief elements of his later STYLE.

Nonfiction Novel: A classification offered by Truman Capote for his *In Cold Blood,* in which a historical event (a multiple murder in Kansas) is described in a way that exploits some of the devices of FICTION, including a nonlinear time sequence and access to inner states of mind and feeling not commonly present in historical writing. Later used by Norman Mailer (in *Armies of the Night* and other books) and John McPhee (in *Levels of the Game* and *The Deltoid Pumpkin Seed*), the form is indebted to such earlier writers as "Isak Dinesen" (especially *Out of Africa*) and Ernest Hemingway (*Green Hills of Africa*). Mark Harris (*Drumlin Woodchuck: Saul Bellow*) has argued that there is no such thing as a PROSE POEM or a *nonfiction novel;* others have suggested that hyphenated forms of behavior, like the TV-movie and the prayer-breakfast, do justice to neither of their components.

Nonsense Verse: A variety of LIGHT VERSE entertaining because of its strong rhythmic quality and lack of logic or consecutive development of thought. In addition to the marked RHYTHM, *nonsense verse* is often characterized by the presence of coined nonsense words, NONCE WORDS ("frabjous day"), a mingling of words from various languages (MACARONIC VERSE), "tongue twisters," and a calling on the printer for freakish arrangement of type to portray Christmas trees, pipes, men falling downstairs—anything that occurs to the fancy of the versifier. LIMERICKS are a popular *nonsense verse* FORM. Edward Lear and Lewis Carroll have built large reputations through writing *nonsense verse.* Calling such things "nonsense" amount to either HYPERBOLE or a misnomer, since, strictly speaking, genuinely nonsensical writing is completely unintelligible.

Norman Conquest: The conquest of England by the Normans following the victory of William I in 1066 at the Battle of Senlac (Hastings). It affected English literature and the English language drastically by the introduction of Norman-French culture and by the introduction of the French language. It was followed by three centuries of social, political, and linguistic readjustment, out of which modern England was to come. See ANGLO-NORMAL (LANGUAGE), ANGLO-NORMAN PERIOD, ENGLISH LANGUAGE, MIDDLE ENGLISH, MIDDLE ENGLISH PERIOD.

Note: A markedly short piece of writing that makes a single point. The term is also used for an item of explanatory apparatus (such as Eliot's "Notes" to *The Waste Land*) or for pieces supposedly—and maybe by UNDERSTATEMENT—informal and incomplete, such as Eliot's *Notes towards the Definition of Culture,* Stevens's *Notes toward a Supreme Fiction,* and Baldwin's *Notes of a Native Son.*

Nouvelle: A SHORT NOVEL or NOVELETTE; a work of FICTION of intermediate length and complexity between the SHORT STORY and the NOVEL. Henry James used the French term *nouvelle* for SHORT NOVEL. See SHORT NOVEL.

Novel: *Novel* is used in its broadest sense to designate any extended fictional PROSE narrative. In practice, however, its use is customarily restricted to NARRATIVES in which the representation of CHARACTER occurs either in a static condition or in the process of development as the result of events or ACTIONS (see CHARACTERIZATION). Often the term implies that some organizing principle—PLOT, THEME, or idea—should be present in a NARRATIVE that is called a *novel.* Almost without exception, *novel* refers to a PROSE work, although

Chaucer's *Troilus and Criseyde* has been called a *novel.* The term *novel* is an English counterpart of the Italian NOVELLA, a short, compact, broadly realistic TALE popular in the medieval period and perhaps best represented by the TALES in the *Decameron.* In most European countries the word *roman* is used rather than *novel,* thus linking the *novel* with that body of legendary, imaginative, and poetic material associated with the older ROMANCE, of which, in one sense, the *novel* is a modern extension. The conflict between the imaginative and poetic recreation of experience implied in *roman* and the realistic representation of the soiled world of common people and actions implied in *novel* has been present in the FORM from its beginning, and it accounted for a distinction often made in the eighteenth and nineteenth centuries between the ROMANCE and the *novel,* in which the ROMANCE was the TALE of the long ago, the far away, or the imaginatively improbable; whereas the *novel* was bound by the facts of the actual world and the laws of probability.

All *novels* are representations in fictional NARRATIVE of life or experience, but the FORM is itself as protean as life and experience themselves. Serious FICTION deals with human beings in significant action. The world that appears to be a significant stage for such ACTION varies greatly from author to author. An author's world may be only within the lowest recesses of the human unconscious; it may be the haunted deck of a whaling ship; it may be the fixed social structure of an aristocratic society; it may be a vast city or a jungle in Africa; it may be the ideal structure of an Utopian dream. And human beings in their essential selves can be viewed in an equally variable series of guises. Basically what we are saying here is that the subject matter of the *novel* defies cataloging or analysis; it may range from the puckish recollections of *Tristram Shandy* to the complex and seemingly total actuality of *War and Peace.*

In shaping this various material to the formal demands of FICTION, novelists have displayed an equal variety. The *novel* may concentrate on CHARACTER, almost to the exclusion of INCIDENT or PLOT. It may amount to no more than a series of INCIDENTS strung together like beads on a string, as the PICARESQUE NOVEL tends to. It may be solidly plotted, with a STRUCTURE as firm and sure as that of a TRAGEDY (see DRAMATIC STRUCTURE). It may attempt to present the details of life with a scientist's detached and objective completeness, as in NATURALISM; or it may try by IMAGE and linguistic and syntactic modification to reproduce the unconscious flow of the emotions, as in the STREAM-OF-CONSCIOUSNESS NOVEL. It may be episodic, loose in structure, EPIC in proportion—what is called "panoramic"—or it may be as tightly knit as a WELL-MADE PLAY, bringing its material forward in dramatic orderliness—what is called "scenic."

But, however diffuse and various the *novel* is as a FORM, it has always submitted itself to the dual test of artistic success and imitative accuracy or truth. It has, therefore, proved to be a continuing problem to the CRITIC, while it has spoken with unique authority to the average reader of the past two and a half centuries. Its best definition is ultimately the history of what it has been.

The English *novel* is essentially an eighteenth-century product. However, without the richness of literary activity that preceded the eighteenth century, the *novel* could not have matured. The NARRATIVE interest developed in the stories of Charlemagne and Arthur, the various romatic CYCLES, the FABLI-

AUX; the descriptive values and appreciation of NATURE found in the PASTO-RALS; the historical interest of DIARIES and JOURNALS; the enthusiasm for CHARACTER portrayal developed in SKETCHES and BIOGRAPHIES; the use of SUSPENSE in TALES and MEDIEVAL ROMANCES—all these had to be familiar and understood before writers could evolve the *novel*, a FORM that draws certain elements from many preceding literary types.

But the matter is hardly so simple as this situation may suggest. CLASSICAL literature of Greece and Italy had its counterparts of the modern *novel*. In the second century B.C., Aristides wrote a series of tales of his home town, Miletus, a collection called *Milesiaka* but not extant today, though, as Edmund Gosse asserted, it may have been the beginning of the modern *novel*. Six centuries later Heliodorus, a Syrian, wrote *Aethiopica*—a love STORY at least somewhat true to life. *Daphnis and Chloë* (Greek), attributed to Longus of the third century, can be strictly called a *novel*. In Latin there were various contributory works, such as the *Golden Ass* of Apuleius, a translation from the Greek, and the *Satyricon* of Petronius, which presented the life and customs of the time of Nero.

The NOVELLA of Italy is one of the early literary forms to which the modern *novel* is indebted both for its NARRATIVE FORM and for its name. The appearance of *Cento Novelle Antiche* just before the opening of the fourteenth century gave great vogue to the NOVELLA form. These NOVELLE (or NOVELLAS) were stories of scandalous love, of chivalry, of mythology and morals, of the type best known to modern English readers through the STORIES of Boccaccio's *Decameron* (*ca.* 1348). Loose women, unscrupulous priests, rough peasants, and high-born nobles formed the central figures of most of these TALES. A few of the more famed collections of NOVELLE are: Sacchetti's *Trecente Novelle*, Fiorentino's *Il Pecorone*, Masuccio's *Novellino*, and Bandello's *Novelle*.

From Spain came at least two works that were major influences on the development of the *novel:* the *Lazarillo de Tormes* of 1554 and Cervantes' *Don Quixote* of 1605 (see PICARESQUE NOVEL).

France, like Italy, produced NOVELLE. About 1450 came the *Quinze Joies de Mariage* (anonymous) in the Italian manner. Antoine de La Sale's *Cent Nouvelles Nouvelles* and Bonaventure Despériers' *Nouvelles Récréations* carried on this interest. In 1535 appeared the *Gargantua* of Rabelais, which, while not a *novel*, neverthesess has sustained NARRATIVE interest. Honoré d'Urfé's *Astrée* (1610) has more definitely the qualities we demand in a *novel* today, and by the middle of the seventeenth century Mlle de Scudéry (1607–1701) was writing ROMANCES that might pass muster in the twentieth century. The romantic qualities of Scudéry called forth a realistic reaction by Scarron, who wrote *Roman Comique*. Some literary historians assign to Marguerite Pioche de la Vergne the honor of having created the first full-blown French *novels* in her *Princesse de Montpensier* (1662) and *Princesse de Clèves* (1678). Other French works important in the development of the *novel* were: La Fontaine's *Psyché* (1669), Fénelon's *Télémaque* (1669), Le Sage's *Gil Blas* (1715, Books I–II), Marivaux's *Marianne* (1731), and Prévost's *Manon Lescaut* (1731).

English writers of the eighteenth century had as a background the experience of continental Europe. The CLASSICAL literature of Greece and Rome, the CYCLES OF ROMANCE, PASTORAL literature, the PICARESQUE TALE of adventure, the interest in human character portrayed through the ANA—all these elements and others held in solution the material that was eventually to crystallize into the English *novel*. In addition to these beginnings from Europe, the English novelists had native parallels of their own—the Arthurian materials, the *Euphues* of Lyly (1579), the *Arcadia* of Sir Philip Sidney (1580–1581), the NARRATIVE interest in Lodge's *Rosalynde* (1590), the PICARESQUE element in Nash's *The Unfortunate Traveler* (1594), the NARRATIVE CHRONICLE of Aphra Behn's *Oroonoko* (1688), the extended NARRATIVE of moral significance in John Bunyan's *Pilgrim's Progress* (1678–1684), and the CHARACTER element present in the *Spectator* papers of Addison and Steele. Defoe, in *Robinson Crusoe* (1719) and *Moll Flanders* (1722), using very loose NARRATIVE structures, and Swift, in *Gulliver's Travels* (1726), using satiric ALLEGORY, had brought VERISIMILITUDE to the chronicling of human life, two component parts of the later *novel* FORM.

With these NARRATIVE qualities already rooted in various types of English and European writing, the ground was fertile, tilled, and seeded when Samuel Richardson, in 1740, issued his *Pamela; or, Virtue Rewarded*, the first English book that practically all CRITICS and historians are willing to call a fully realized *novel*. Richardson's three *novels*, *Pamela*, *Clarissa Harlow* (1747–1748), and *Sir Charles Grandison* (1753) are chiefly in the EPISTOLARY form.

After Richardson's success with *Pamela*, other significant *novels* came rapidly. Henry Fielding started his *Joseph Andrews* (1742) as a SATIRE on *Pamela*—Joseph is supposedly Pamela's brother, whose problem with his employer is the mirror image of hers—but before going far he forgot his ironical intent and told a vigorous story of his own. In 1748 Smollett published *Roderick Random;* in 1749 came Fielding's greatest novel, *Tom Jones,* important for its development of PLOT and its realistic interpretation of English life; in 1751 both Smollett and Fielding repeated, the first with *Peregrine Pickle* and the second with *Amelia.* Defoe, Richardson, Fielding, and Smollett stand at the source of the English *novel*. The succeeding years brought other *novels* and novelists, but the first real impetus to long FICTION was given by them. Sterne wrote *Tristram Shandy* (1760–1767), a work that broke, even so early, the narrative FORM of the *novel* and, applying Locke's psychological theories, undertook the exploration of the inner self. Horace Walpole made much of GOTHIC mysteries in his *Castle of Otranto* (1764). Two years later Oliver Goldsmith published the *Vicar of Wakefield.* Then came such works as Fanny Burney's NOVEL OF MANNERS, *Evelina* (1778), and Ann Radcliffe's GOTHIC *novel, Mysteries of Udolpho* (1794).

The nineteenth century saw the flowering of the English *novel* as an instrument portraying a middle-class society. Jane Austen produced NOVELS OF MANNERS, and Scott created the HISTORICAL NOVEL and carried it to a high point in the first quarter of the century. The great Victorian novelists—Dickens, Thackeray, and Trollope—created vast fictional worlds loaded with an abundance of social types and ACTIONS and arranged in complex and intricate melodramatic PLOTS. In Thomas Hardy and George Eliot the last half of the century found writers who, in differing degrees, applied some of the tenets of NATURALISM to the *novel.*

In the twentieth century the English *novel* has probed more and more deeply into the human mind. Virginia Woolf, Dorothy Richardson, and James Joyce, writing STREAM-OF-CONSCIOUSNESS NOVELS, have greatly expanded and deepened the subject matter of the *novel* and modified the techniques of FICTION so that this new subject matter may be dealt with. This century has been marked, too, by a growing concern over critical and technical issues in FICTION.

For fifty years after Richardson published *Pamela,* no *novels* were written in America, although *Pamela* appeared in an American edition within two years of its English publication. The first *novel* written by an American and published in America, *The Power of Sympathy,* a moralistic TALE of seduction, by William Hill Brown, did not appear until 1789. With Charles Brockden Brown, America produced her first important novelist. Brown, who wrote chiefly in the GOTHIC manner, was the author of four readable TALES: *Wieland* (*1798*), *Arthur Mervyn* (1799), *Ormond* (1799), and *Edgar Huntley* (1799), as well as others less well known. Some twenty years later James Fenimore Cooper published *The Spy* (1821), *The Pioneers* (1823), and *The Pilot* (1823). In addition to *The Pioneers,* his Leatherstocking Series included *The Deerslayer* (1841), *The Last of the Mohicans* (1826), *The Pathfinder* (1840), and *The Prairie* (1827). By 1850, when Hawthrone's *The Scarlet Letter* appeared, the American *novel* had come into its full powers, a fact made abundantly clear by the publication in 1851 of Herman Melville's *Moby-Dick.* In the last half of the nineteenth century, REALISM, articulated as a theory by William Dean Howells and well-exemplified in his work and made the basis of a highly self-conscious art by Henry James, dominated the American *novel.* This control gave way in the early years of the twentieth century to the NATURALISM of Norris and Dreiser. After the First World War, a group of talented young novelists introduced a number of ideas drawn from the French REALISTS and symbolists into American FICTION and produced a new, vital, but essentially romantic *novel* with strong naturalistic overtones. Foremost among them were F. Scott Fitzgerald, Ernest Hemingway, and William Faulkner. Today the American *novel* is a varied form practiced with self-conscious skill by a number of novelists and read by large audiences more earnestly than any other serious literary form. John Updike's work is both serious and popular; Thomas Pynchon (b. 1937), who seems to be a sort of logarithm of Hawthorne, Poe, and Melville, has written three *novels* of prodigious scope and great brillance, and he has enjoyed a measure of commercial success at the same time.

Attempts to classify the *novel* usually come to grief, however helpful they may be, for the terms are by no means mutually exclusive. In this *Handbook* special forms of the *novel* are discussed in separate entries, broadly classified by subject matter. They are DETECTIVE NOVEL, PSYCHOLOGICAL NOVEL, SOCIOLOGICAL NOVEL, SENTIMENTAL NOVEL, PROPAGANDA NOVEL, HISTORICAL NOVEL, NOVEL OF MANNERS, NOVEL OF CHARACTER, NOVEL OF INCIDENT, NOVEL OF THE SOIL, REGIONAL NOVEL, PICARESQUE NOVEL, GOTHIC NOVEL, APPRENTICESHIP NOVEL, STREAM-OF-CONSCIOUSNESS NOVEL, PROBLEM NOVEL, EPISTOLARY NOVEL, KÜNSTLERROMAN. The principal modes in which novelists write are the general modes of their ages; such modes are the products of STYLE, literary CONVENTION, and the author's attitude toward life. They are defined in this *Handbook* under general terms such as REALISM, ROMANTICISM, IMPRESSIONISM, EXPRESSIONISM, NATURALISM, NEOCLASSICISM.

[References: E. A. Baker, *History of the English Novel,* 10 vols. (1924–1939, reprinted 1950); R. M. Lovett and H. S. Hughes, *History of the Novel in England* (1932); Edwin Muir, *The Structure of the Novel* (1928, new ed.

1957, reprinted 1963); Lionel Stevenson, *History of the English Novel: Volume XI: Yesterday and After* (1967).]

Novel of Character: A NOVEL that places its major emphasis on the representation and development of CHARACTER rather than on exciting EPISODE, as in the NOVEL OF INCIDENT, or on unity of PLOT or STRUCTURE. See NOVEL, CHARACTERIZATION.

Novel of Incident: A term applied to NOVELS in which action in more or less unrelated EPISODES dominates and PLOT and CHARACTER are subordinate. In this type of NOVEL the STRUCTURE is loose; emphasis is on thrilling incident rather than on CHARACTERIZATION or sustained SUSPENSE. If one may call Defoe's *Robinson Crusoe* a NOVEL, then it may be used to illustrate the *novel of incident.* Here the EPISODES of the shipwreck, the meeting with Friday, the clash with visiting natives, and other incidents follow each other chronologically, but they are more or less independent of one another. Dumas' *Three Musketeers* is also a *novel of incident,* though here the PLOT is more developed than in Defoe's story.

Novel of Manners: A NOVEL in which the dominant forces are the social customs, manners, conventions, and habits of a definite social class at a particular time and place. In the true *novel of manners* the mores of a specific group, defined and described in detail and with great accuracy, become powerful controls over characters. The *novel of manners* is often, although by no means always, satiric; it is always realistic in manner, however. The HISTORICAL NOVEL is sometimes called the *"novel of manners* laid in the past." The NOVELS of Jane Austen, Edith Wharton, and John P. Marquand are *novels of manners.* See NOVEL, MANNERS.

Novel of Sensibility: A NOVEL in which the characters have a heightened and highly emotional response to events, ACTIONS, and sentiments, all of which can produce in the reader a similar heightened emotional response. Sterne's *Tristram Shandy* is a major example, and Mackenzie's *Man of Feeling* unconsciously carries the idea of intensity of character response beyond the limits of reason. See SENTIMENTAL NOVEL.

Novel of the Soil: A special kind of REGIONALISM in the NOVEL, in which the lives of people struggling for existence in remote rural sections are starkly portrayed. Examples are Ellen Glasgow's *Barren Ground,* O. E. Rölvaag's *Giants in the Earth,* and Elizabeth Madox Roberts's *Time of Man.* It should be emphasized that the term *novel of the soil* refers primarily to matter rather than to manner; however, the term is usually restricted to portrayals of country life in the manner of REALISM or NATURALISM.

Novelette: A work of prose FICTION of intermediate length, longer than a SHORT STORY and shorter than a NOVEL. Since, however, there is little agreement on maximum length for any of these types, the distinction that in general the *novellette* displays the customarily compact structure of the SHORT STORY with the greater development of CHARACTER, THEME, and ACTION of the NOVEL may be useful. Melville's *Billy Budd,* Stevenson's *Dr. Jekyll and Mr.*

Hyde, Henry James's *The Turn of the Screw,* and Conrad's *Heart of Darkness* are examples. See SHORT NOVEL.

Novelization: The conversion of a FILM or a television PLAY into NOVEL form in order to capitalize on its popularity or notoriety.

Novella: A TALE or SHORT STORY. The term is particularly applied to the early TALES of Italian and French writers—such as the *Decameron* of Boccaccio and the *Heptameron* of Marguerite of Valois. The form is of special interest to students of English literature for two reasons: (1) many of these early *novelle* were used by English writers as sources for their own work, and (2) it was from this form that the term *novel* developed. The *novelle* were among the significant formative influences on the English NOVEL. (See NOVEL.) *Novella* is also a term borrowed from the German and applied to the kind of SHORT NOVELS that developed in Germany in the nineteenth century.

Numbers: A term, now just about obsolete, meaning "measured language" or regular VERSE in general. Pope, confessing to have been a POET virtually since infancy, says, "I lisped in numbers." Longfellow's "A Psalm of Life" begins, "Tell me not, in mournful numbers. . . ."

Nursery Rhyme: Brief VERSES, often anonymous and traditional, with heavy RHYTHM and frequent, heavy RHYME, written for young children. The first important collection of *nursery rhymes* in English was made in the eighteenth century by "Mother Goose," whose actual identity has long been a matter of dispute. *Nursery rhymes* include SONGS, "counting-out" games, NARRATIVES, NONSENSE VERSE, and RHYMES that seem to have links with English political history.

O

Obiter dicta: Things said "by the way"; incidental remarks: opposed to statements based on calculated, deliberate judgment. Though legal in origin, the term is sometimes used in literary association, as in speaking of one author's *obiter dicta* being weightier and wiser than another's serious, labored expressions.

Objective Correlative: A term used by T. S. Eliot to describe a pattern of objects, actions, or events, or a situation that can serve effectively to awaken in the reader an emotional response without being a direct statement of that subjective emotion. It is an impersonal or objective means of communicating feeling. Eliot calls the *objective correlative* "the only way of expressing emotion in the form of art" and defines it as "a set of objects, a situation, a chain of events which shall be the formula of that *particular* emotion, such that when the external facts, which must terminate in sensory experience, are given, the emotion is immediately evoked." Eliot's argument—to the effect that *Hamlet* is an "artistic failure"—is that Shakespeare's TRAGEDY lacks an adequate *objective correlative* for Hamlet's state of mind. The term has had wide currency in this sense among contemporary CRITICS. It was used by Washington Allston in a lecture on art as early as 1850 to describe the process by which the external world produces pleasurable emotion, but Eliot gave it new meaning and made of it a new term. See NEGATIVE CAPABILITY, AESTHETIC DISTANCE.

Objective Theory of Art: A critical term applied by M. H. Abrams to the view that holds the literary work to be most significant as an object in itself, independent of the facts of its composition, the actuality it imitates, its author's stated intention, or the effect it produces on its audience. See CRITICISM, AUTOTELIC, NEW CRITICISM.

Objectivism: A term used by a various philosophies and ideologies to stress the reality or value of the objective or phenomenal world, the need for some sort of objectivity, or the importance of the status of an artwork as a physical, somatic object. This rather vague term has been appropriated by writers as divergent as William Carlos Williams, Louis Zukofsky, and Ayn Rand.

Objectivity: A quality in a literary work of impersonality, of freedom from the expression of personal sentiments, attitudes, or emotions by the author. In much contemporary CRITICISM *objectivity* is a desirable quality in art. See AESTHETIC DISTANCE, OBJECTIVE CORRELATIVE, NEGATIVE CAPABILITY.

Obligatory Scene: An EPISODE in a PLAY the circumstances of which are so strongly foreseen by the audience in the development of the PLOT that the playwright is obliged to write the *scene*. It is characteristic of the WELL-MADE PLAY. *Obligatory scene* is the English equivalent of the French term SCÈNE À FAIRE.

Oblique Rhyme: Approximate but not true RHYME; *oblique rhyme* is another term for NEAR RHYME, HALF RHYME, and SLANT RHYME. See RHYME, NEAR RHYME.

Occasional Verse: POETRY written for some social, historical, or personal occasion. Although the term can include VERS DE SOCIÉTÉ, it usually designates writing of more serious and more dignified purpose. POETS LAUREATE are called on to produce *occasional verse* in the discharge of their responsibilities. Love POEMS of a highly personal nature and addressed to a specific person are sometimes called *occasional.* Among notable examples of *occasional verse* are Spenser's "Epithalamion," celebrating his marriage; Dryden's "Astraea Redux," celebrating the return to the throne of Charles II; Marvell's "Horatian Ode upon Cromwell's Return from Ireland"; Milton's "Lycidas," on the death of Edward King; and Whitman's "When Lilacs Last in the Dooryard Bloom'd," commemorating the death of Lincoln. Many POEMS of our own age, including Yeats's "September 1913" and "Easter 1916" and Auden's "September 1, 1939," seem to begin as *occasional* works but transcend the anecdotal limits of an occasion and become profoundly serious.

Octameter: A LINE of VERSE of eight FEET. *Octameter* is difficult and very rare in English VERSE. These lines from Tennyson's "Locksley Hall" illustrate HEADLESS IAMBIC *octameter:*

> In the spring a fuller crimson comes upon the robin's breast;
> In the spring the wanton lapwing gets himself another crest.

Octastich: A group of eight LINES of VERSE.

Octave: An eight-line STANZA. The chief use of the term, however, is to denote the first eight-VERSE division of the ITALIAN SONNET as separate from the last six-VERSE division, the SESTET. In this sense it is a SYNONYM for OCTET. In the strict SONNET usage the *octave* rhymes *abbaabba* and serves to state a position later applied or resolved in the SESTET, and comes to such a complete close at the end of the eighth LINE as to be marked by a full stop. An *octave* is also an eight-line, unrhymed individual POEM in IAMBIC PENTAMETER.

Octavo: A BOOK SIZE designating a book whose SIGNATURE results from sheets folded to eight leaves or sixteen pages. See BOOK SIZES.

Octet: A group of eight LINES of VERSE; an OCTASTICH. Frequently used as a SYNONYM for OCTAVE, the first eight lines of an ITALIAN SONNET.

Octosyllabic Verse: Strictly speaking, simple POETRY in LINES of eight syllables; however, the term is customarily applied to TETRAMETER VERSE in IAMBIC or TROCHAIC feet. It is used in a great variety of stanzaic FORMS, including LONG MEASURE and the *In Memoriam* STANZA, but it most frequently appears in the octosyllabic COUPLET. It lends itself to what Byron called a "fatal facility."

Ode: A single, unified strain of exalted lyrical VERSE, directed to a single purpose, and dealing with one THEME. The term connotes certain qualities of both manner and FORM. In manner the *ode* is an elaborate LYRIC, expressed in language dignified, sincere, and imaginative and intellectual in tone. In FORM the *ode* is more complicated than most of the LYRIC types. One useful distinction of FORM is the division into STROPHES: the STROPHE, ANTISTROPHE, and EPODE. Originally a Greek FORM used in dramatic POETRY, the *ode* was choral. Accompanied by music, the CHORUS of singers moved up one side during the STROPHE, down the other during the ANTISTROPHE, and stood in place during the EPODE. In a general way this movement emphasized the rise and fall of emotional power. In English POETRY there are three types of *odes:* the PINDARIC (regular), the HORATIAN or homostrophic, and the IRREGU-LAR. The PINDARIC is characterized by the three-STROPHE division: the STROPHE and the ANTISTROPHE alike in form, the EPODE different. The METER and LINE-length may vary within any one STROPHE of the *ode,* but when the movement is repeated, the metrical scheme for corresponding divisions should be similar though accompanied by new RHYMES. It is not essential that STROPHE, ANTISTROPHE, and EPODE alternate regularly, since the EPODE may be used at the end or inconsistently between the STROPHE and the ANTI-STROPHE (Collins's "Ode to Liberty"). The second type of *ode,* the HORATIAN or homostrophic, consists of only one STANZA type, and that type may be almost infinitely varied within its pattern (Coleridge's "Ode to France"). The third type of *ode,* the IRREGULAR, is credited to Cowley, who seems to have thought he was writing PINDARIC ODES. As with the second type, freedom within the STROPHE is characteristic. But here the STROPHES are rules unto themselves, and all claim to STANZA pattern may be discarded. The length of the LINES may vary, the number of lines per STROPHE may fluctuate widely, the RHYME pattern need not be carried over from STANZA to STANZA, and the metrical movement will quicken and slacken with the MOOD of the poet and the emotional intensity. Much more flexible than the two other types considered, the IRREGULAR ODE affords greatest freedom of expression and, consequently, greatest license. In English POETRY these three types are well represented in the following: Gray's "The Bard," an example of the strict PINDARIC ODE; Collins's "Ode to Evening," an example of the HORATIAN ODE; and Wordsworth's "Ode on Intimations of Immorality," an example of the IRREGULAR ODE. For his *odes,* Keats devised a number of regular or irregular STANZAS, the basic being ten IAMBIC LINES mostly in PENTAMETER with a RHYME SCHEME combining the HEROIC QUATRAIN (or first QUATRAIN of an ENGLISH SONNET) and the SESTET of an ITALIAN SONNET: *ababcdecde.* In contemporary POETRY the public nature, solemn DICTION, and stately grav-ity of the *ode* have on occasion been effectively used for ironic overtones, as in Allen Tate's "Ode to the Confederate Dead."

[References: John Heath-Stubbs, *The Ode* (1969); Carol Maddison, *Apollo and the Nine: A History of the Ode* (1960); Robert Shafer, *The English Ode to 1660* (1918); George N. Shuster, *The English Ode from Milton to Keats* (1940, reprinted 1964).]

Oedipus Complex: In psychoanalysis a libidinal feeling that develops in a child, especially a male child, between the ages of three and six, for the parent of the opposite sex. This attachment is generally accompanied by hostility to the parent of the child's own sex. The *Oedipus complex* is usually repressed. In instances when it persists, it can wreak emotional havoc. The *Oedipus* *complex* is named for Oedipus, a Theban HERO of ancient LEGEND and of Greek TRAGEDY, who unwittingly slew his father and married his mother. See ELECTRA COMPLEX, with which it is in contrast, and FREUDIANISM.

[References: André Green, *The Tragic Effect: The Oedipus Complex in Tragedy* (tr. 1979); Ernest Jones, *The Oedipus-Complex as an Explanation of Hamlet's Mystery: A Study in Motive* (1910).]

Old Comedy: Greek COMEDY of the fifth century B.C. performed at festivals of Dionysus. *Old Comedy* was a blend of religious ceremony, SATIRE, WIT, and buffoonery. It was farcical and bawdy, and it contained much social SATIRE, laughing harshly at most religious, political, military, and intellectual institutions and issues of its day, and containing LAMPOONS of individuals. It used STOCK CHARACTERS: the ALAZON, the EIRON, the sly dissembler, the entertaining clown, and the FOIL. It used a CHORUS costumed as animals. The greatest writer of the *Old Comedy* was Aristophanes. Probably the most energetic modern counterpart is Eliot's fragmentary *Sweeney Agonistes*, subtitled *An Aristophanic Melodrama*.

Old English (Language): That form of language spoken in the British Isles between the ANGLO-SAXON invasions in the fifth century and the NORMAN CONQUEST in the eleventh; a Germanic dialect. See ENGLISH LANGUAGE.

Old English Period: The period in English history and literature between the invasion of England by the Teutonic tribes of Angles, Saxons, and Jutes, beginning about 428, and the establishment of the Norman rule of England around 1100, following the triumphant Conquest of England by the Norman French under William the Conqueror. Saxon monarchies were established in Sussex, Wessex, and Essex in the fifth and sixth centuries; Anglian monarchies in Northumbria, East Anglia, and Mercia in the sixth and seventh centuries. Christianity was introduced early and gradually won out over the pagan culture. It was an age of intertribal conflict and, in the ninth century, of struggles with the invading Danes. The greatest of the rulers of the period was Alfred, who, in the ninth century, effected a unification of the Teutonic groups. Still, even after a thousand years, Alfred remains the only English ruler to be styled "The Great."

Learning and culture flourished in the monasteries, with Whitby the cradle of English POETRY in the North and Winchester of English PROSE in the South. Although much writing throughout the period was in Latin, Christian monks began writing in the vernacular that we call OLD ENGLISH about 700. In the earliest part of the period the POETRY, written in accentual METER and linked by ALLITERATION (see OLD ENGLISH VERSIFICATION), was centered on the life of the Germanic tribes and was basically pagan, although Christian elements were incorporated early. The best of the POEMS that have survived are the great EPIC *Beowulf* (*ca.* 700), "The Seafarer," "Widsith," and "Deor's Lament." Early POETRY of a more emphatically Christian nature included Caedmon's "Song"; Biblical PARAPHRASES such as *Genesis, Exodus, Daniel, Judith;* religious NARRATIVES such as the *Crist, Elene, Andreas;* and the allegorical *Phoenix* (a translation from Latin). Literature first flourished in Northumbria, but in the reign of Alfred the Great (871–899) West Saxon became the literary DIALECT. Under Alfred, much Latin literature was translated into English PROSE, such as Pope Gregory's *Pastoral Care,* Boethius's *Consolation of Philosophy,* and Bede's *Ecclesiastical History;* and the *Anglo-Saxon Chronicle* was revised and expanded. A second PROSE revival took place in the HOMILIES of Aelfric and Wulfstan (tenth and eleventh centuries), works noted for their richness of STYLE, reflecting Latin models. Late examples of Anglo-Saxon VERSE are the "Battle of Maldon" and the "Battle of Brunanburgh," heroic POEMS. The NORMAN CONQUEST (1066) put an end to serious literary work in the OLD ENGLISH LANGUAGE. See OLD ENGLISH (LANGUAGE), OLD ENGLISH VERSIFICATION, ENGLISH LANGUAGE, and *Outline of Literary History.*

[References: S. A. Brooke, *English Literature from the Beginning to the Norman Conquest* (1898, reprinted 1921); Stanley B. Greenfield, *A Critical History of Old English Literature* (1965); J. J. Jusserand, *A Literary History of the English People* (1895); F. M. Stenton, *Anglo-Saxon England,* 3rd ed. (1971); P. G. Thomas, *English Literature before Chaucer* (1924); E. E. Wardale, *Chapters in Old English Literature* (1935); C. L. Wrenn, *A Study of Old English Literature* (1966); David M. Zesmer, *Guide to English Literature from Beowulf through Chaucer and Medieval Drama* (1961).]

Old English Versification: The metrical system employed by English POETS in the period before 1100. It is essentially an accentual system (see METER), consisting of equal numbers of accented syllables to the LINE and varying numbers of unaccented syllables. The normal Old English line fell into two HEMISTICHS, each having two accented syllables and with the HEMISTICHS separated by a heavy CAESURA. The ACCENTS are grammatical; that is, they fall on syllables that would normally carry stress in that particular construction. The HEMISTICHS are bound by ALLITERATION, one or both the accented syllables of the first alliterating with the first accented syllable of the second or much more rarely with the second accented syllable. Variant lines were: the rare "short line," which contains only two stressed syllables and no CAESURA, the stressed syllables being bound by ALLITERATION; and the HYPERMETRICAL line in which three or more stressed syllables may appear in each HEMISTICH. To go beyond such a schematic outline is to enter an area of great scholarly uncertainty and controversy. Some modern poets have attempted to use the measure: Ezra Pound in his "Canto I" ("Bore sheep aboard her and our bodies also") rather loosely; W. H. Auden throughout his long poem *The Age of Anxiety* much more strictly; and Richard Wilbur and W. S. Merwin occasionally.

[References: A. J. Bliss, *The Metre of Beowulf* (1958); John C. Pope, *The Rhythm of Beowulf* (1942); Eduard Sievers, *An Old English Grammar,* 3rd ed. (tr. 1903.]

Omar Khayyam **Stanza:**   See RUBÁIYÁT STANZA.

Omnibus: A volume made up of selected works, usually be one author but sometimes by several authors on one subject. The works are usually reprinted from earlier volumes.

Omniscient Point of View: A term used to describe the POINT OF VIEW in a work of FICTION in which the narrator is capable of knowing, seeing, and telling whatever he or she wishes. It is characterized by freedom in shifting from the exterior world to the inner selves of a number of CHARACTERS and by a freedom in movement in both time and place; but to an even greater extent it is characterized by the freedom of the narrator to comment on the meaning of actions. See POINT OF VIEW.

One-Act Play: A form of DRAMA that has attracted attention since about 1890. Before that date *one-act plays* had been used chiefly on VAUDEVILLE programs and as CURTAIN RAISERS in the LEGITIMATE THEATER. Special attention to the *one-act play* came with the LITTLE THEATER MOVEMENT and the practice of staging a group of such short PLAYS for a single evening's entertainment. The fact that the FORM was adopted by playwrights of high ability (J. M. Barrie, A. W. Pinero, Gerhart Hauptmann, G. B. Shaw) furthered its development. A widening circle of authors has produced *one-act plays* in the twentieth century, in both England and America, including John Masefield, Lord Dunsany, Lady Gregory, J. M. Synge, John Galsworthy, A. A. Milne, Betty Smith, Eugene O'Neill, Paul Green, Thornton Wilder, Noel Coward, Tennessee Williams, Arthur Miller, and Edward Albee. The technique of the *one-act play* is highly flexible, the most important demand being for unity of EFFECT, with consequent vigor of DIALOGUE, stressing of CHARACTER, and economy of NARRATIVE materials. Its relation to the longer DRAMA has been likened to that of the SHORT STORY to the NOVEL.

[References: Helen Louise Cohen, ed., *One-Act Plays by Modern Authors*, 2nd ed. (1934); Percival Wilde, *The Craftsmanship of the One-Act Play* (1923).]

Onomatopoeia: The use of words that by their sound suggest their meaning. Some onomatopoeic words are "hiss," "buzz," "whirr," "sizzle." However, *onomatopoeia* in the hands of a POET becomes a much more subtle device than simply the use of such words when, in an effort to suit sound to sense, the poet creates VERSES that themselves carry their meaning in their sounds. A notable example appears in *The Princess* by Tennyson:

> The moan of doves in immemorial elms,
> And murmuring of innumerable bees.

The RHYTHM of the LINES, the succession of sounds, and the effect of RHYMES all contribute to the effect by which the POEM as a pattern of sounds echoes the sense that its words denote. Such devices fall into several subdivisions. The "Gr-r-r" in Browning's "Soliloquy of the Spanish Cloister" comes close to being a direct transcription of noise and is not actually a word. Some *onomatopoeic* forms represent a sound, like "coo," while others, like "cuckoo," refer to the thing that makes the sound. Some forms are not recognizably mimetic or echoic and must be classified as merely formulaic or conventional *onomatopoeia*. No dog ever uttered a sound resembling "bow-wow," and yet we use that word to mean both the sound and the creature. By a sort of sentimental or associative bonding, most people seem to feel that words somehow "sound like" what they mean or connote. But "soft," say, with its three unvoiced consonants, is hardly a soft sound, and "hard," with no unvoiced consonants, is hardly hard. Mallarmé complained that the French word for "day" (*jour*) sounded dark, while "night" (*nuit*) sounded bright. "Big" is a relatively small syllable, "small" relatively big. One needs, therefore, to exercise a good deal of caution in the search for relations between sound and sense. The great

Swiss linguist Saussure argued convincingly that there is no such relation, even in exclamations or *onomatopoeia,* except according to conventions that are completely arbitrary and, as he said, "unmotivated." It remains possible for *onomatopoeia* to retain or suggest the *form* of a sound without really echoing its *substance.* A dog, for instance, may not say "bow-wow," but whatever it does say rhymes, as do "bow" and "wow." The cuckoo may not say "cuckoo," but whatever it does say is repetitive and reduplicative, as is "cuckoo." Although now discredited by fastidious linguists, the old sentimental-associative case was well argued by Pope in *An Essay on Criticism:*

> 'Tis not enough no harshness gives offense,
> The sound must seem an echo to the sense:
> Soft is the strain when Zephyr gently blows,
> And the smooth stream in smoother numbers flows:
> But when the loud surges lash the sounding shore,
> The hoarse, rough verse should like the torrent roar:
> When Ajax strives some rock's vast weight to throw,
> The line too labors, and the words move slow.

"Murmuring of innumerable bees" (Tennyson's *The Princess*) has often been advanced as an example of apt *onomatopoeia,* but John Crowe Ransom responded that sound and sense are mutually irrelevant, that Tennyson's LINE means what it means because of the discursive significance of the words and that one could change the whole meaning or sense of the line without changing the sound very much at all: "murdering of innumerable beeves." The sentiment favoring answerable or significant *onomatopoeia* remains robust, however, and it has been observed by recent existenialist-phenomenological critics and by others, as well, that POETRY percussively directs our attention to sound as such, with all its powers and mysteries, and the heart of many sophisticated POEMS seems situated in a region of *onomatopoeia* made significiant—as, say, Eliot's *The Waste Land* ends with a fable of interpreting a single onomatopoeic Sanskrit syllable: "DA."

Open Couplet: A COUPLET in which the second LINE is not complete but depends on the first line of the succeeding COUPLET for completion. Browning uses the *open couplet* in "My Last Duchess" with such virtuosity that many readers fail to notice the presence of RHYME:

> That's my last Duchess painted on the wall,
> Looking as if she were alive. I call
> That piece a wonder, now. . . .

Consider also the beginning of Browning's "Rudel to the Lady of Tripoli":

> I know a Mount, the gracious Sun perceives
> First, when he visits, last, too, when he leaves
> The world; and, vainly favored, it repays
> The day-long glory of his steadfast gaze
> By no change of its large calm form of snow.

Opera: Though the primary interest in *opera* is musical, it is a dramatic FORM that has exerted influence on English stage history. Only its connection with English DRAMA will be discussed here. *Opera* is musical DRAMA in the sense that the DIALOGUE instead of being spoken is sung, to the accompaniment of instrumental music, now always an orchestra. A PLAY in which incidental music is stressed may be called "operatic," but is not true *opera* if the DIALOGUE is spoken. Greek DRAMA contained DIALOGUE sung to the accompaniment of the lyre or flute and is therefore a precursor, in fact somewhat of a model, for modern *opera*, which developed in Italy about 1600 as a result of amateur efforts to recapture the quality of the musical effects of Greek TRAGEDY by means of musical recitation instrumentally accompanied. The form was at first a MONODY, as in Jacopo Peri's *Euridice* (1600), the first public production in the new style. From these beginnings the important form now known as grand *opera* developed. Italian *opera* reached England soon after 1700, but before this date certain definite advances in the direction of *opera* had taken place on the English stage. To some degree an outgrowth of the Renaissance MASQUE, Sir William D'Avenant's *Siege of Rhodes* (1656) is a precursor of the English *opera*, since it was a musical entertainment, written in RHYME and designed to be sung in recitative and aria. The attention to scenery as well as the SONGS and orchestral accompaniment were suggestive of later English *opera*. During the RESTORATION AGE operatic versions of some of Shakespeare's PLAYS (*The Tempest, Macbeth*) were called "dramatic *operas*," but the DIALOGUE was spoken, not sung. About 1689 Henry Purcell and Nahum Tate brought out *Dido and Aeneas*, in which the DIALOGUE was in recitative. Early in the eighteenth century Italian *operas* were "translated" and sung by English singers, among them *Arsinoë, Queen of Cypress* (Drury Lane, 1706) and *Camilla* (1706). Later "bilingual" *operas* appeared, in which Italian singers sang part of the DIALOGUE in Italian while English singers sang the rest in English. The first completely Italian *opera* sung in Italian in England was *Almahide* (1710), which established the success of the FORM in England. About this time George Frederick Handel came to England. He produced *Rinaldo* in 1711 and exerted a powerful influence for many years thereafter. From the first, efforts to employ Italian singers and *opera* met with disfavor, as evidenced by Addison's SATIRE and by John Gay's famous BURLESQUE *opera*, *The Beggar's Opera* (1728). The success of *opera* and various forms of BUR-LESQUE *opera* at this time probably had much to do with the tendency toward lyrical and spectacular elements on the English stage, which the presence of the PATENT THEATERS encouraged in the eighteenth and nineteenth centuries. For later literature in English, the *operas* of Mozart and Wagner proved to be most influential, particularly for George Bernard Shaw, who wrote a book on Wagner and appropriated certain operatic devices and effects in *Man and Superman* and other plays; and for W. H. Auden, who wrote TRANSLATIONS and also an occasional *libretto*. See BALLAD-OPERA, COMIC OPERA.

Opéra bouffe: A French term for a very light form of COMIC OPERA developed from VAUDEVILLE music and said to be the ancestor of the COMIC OPERAS of Gilbert and Sullivan.

Operetta: A COMIC OPERA, with music, SONGS, and spectacular effects but with the DIALOGUE spoken. See COMIC OPERA, OPERA.

Opsis: Aristotle's term for the *spectacle* as an element in DRAMA—the least important, coming sixth in order after *mythos, ethos, dianioa, lexis,* and *melos.*

Nowadays the term is used for both spectacle as what an audience sees and the visual or graphic aspect of what a reader sees on a page. Relatively unimportant except in POETRY.

Oral Transmission: The transmission of material from person to person and from generation to generation by word of mouth and memory. Materials such as the FOLK EPIC, the BALLAD, FOLKLORE, PROVERBS, and many SONGS that originated among illiterate or semiliterate people were presented to their audiences by recitation and singing and transmitted by memory rather than in written form. Such materials use many formulaic expressions, pronounced CADENCES, and other devices to aid memory. Materials preserved through *oral transmission* have usually undergone many changes and often exist in several versions.

[References: A. B. Lord, *The Singer of Tales* (1960, reprinted 1968); Walter J. Ong, *Orality and Literacy: The Technologizing of the Word* (1982).]

Oration: A formal speech intended to inspire to some action. Carefully prepared and delivered in an impassioned manner, the *oration* carries its greatest power in its emotional appeal. Although a major cultural interest in CLASSICAL days and even up to a few decades ago, the *oration* has lost its popular appeal and is now heard but rarely in legislative halls, the courtroom, the church. The CLASSICAL *oration* has seven parts: (1) the entrance, or EXORDIUM, to catch the audience's attention; (2) the NARRATION, to set forth the facts; (3) the EXPOSITION or DEFINITION, to define terms and open issues to be proved; (4) the proposition, to clarify the points at issue and state exactly what is to be proved; (5) the confirmation, to set forth the arguments for and against and to advance proof; (6) the confutation or refutation, to refute the opponent's arguments; and (7) the conclusion or EPILOGUE, to sum up the arguments and stir the audience.

Organic Form: A concept of FORM in which the structure of a literary work is said to grow from its conception in the thought, feeling, and personality of the writer, rather than being arbitrarily shaped through mechanical force in a preconceived mold. In the theory of *organic form* the work grows like a living organism, its parts inseparable and indivisible, the whole greater than the sum of its parts. The concept of *organic form* was advanced by Coleridge, most vigorously in his defense of Shakespeare against the charge of formlessness. The casting aside of the established and preconceived FORMS as mechanical in favor of the concept of organic growth was not, Coleridge felt, a surrender to lawlessness or anti-intellectualism. Rather it was the acceptance of the reign of law pervasive in living nature. In the growth of a tree, Coleridge saw "a law which all the parts obey," and this law was an "essential principle" of trees. He said: "No work of true genius dare want its appropriate form; neither indeed is there any danger of this. As it must not, so neither can it, be lawless! For it is even this that constitutes its genius—the power of acting creatively under laws of its own origination. The true ground of the mistake [about Shakespeare's formlessness] lies in the confounding mechanical regularity with organic form. The form is mechanic, when on any given material we impress a predetermined form, not necessarily arising out of the properties of the material;—as when to a mass of wet clay we give whatever shape we wish it to retain when hardened. The organic form, on the other hand, is innate; it shapes, as it develops, itself from within, and the fulness of its development is one and the same with the perfection of its outward form. Such as the life is, such is the form." And he defines Shakespeare as "himself a nature humanized, a genial understanding directing self-consciously a power and an implicit wisdom deeper even than consciousness." This concept of the nature of the creative act and the created work of art has been pervasive for the past 150 years. The SYMBOL most frequently used for such a literary work has been that of a plant, as having a *form* and a growth uniquely true to its individual nature. Cleanth Brooks's statement that "The parts of a poem are related as are the parts of a growing plant" is a representative example. As R. G. Collingwood argued, something produced by a mechanical, technical operation can be analyzed according to principles of form and matter, end and means, cause and effect; such artifacts can be mass-produced, and their modular parts or components may be detached and interchanged. None of this applies to art proper, because it is not mechanical but vital and organic.

Originality: The use of new subject matter, FORMS, or STYLES rather than the traditional or conventional. At various periods in literary history the value placed on *originality* has fluctuated greatly. Poe described the conscientious writer as "keeping originality *always* in view." See INVENTION.

Ossianic Controversy: The controversy surrounding a famous English literary deception in the eighteenth century. See FORGERIES, LITERARY.

Ottava rima: A STANZA pattern consisting of eight IAMBIC PENTAMETER (or HENDECASYLLABIC) lines rhyming *abababcc*. Boccaccio is credited with originating this pattern, which was much used by Tasso and Ariosto. Some of the English POETS making important use of *ottava rima* are Wyatt (the earliest in English), Spenser, Milton, Keats, Byron, Longfellow, Browning, and Yeats (notably in fifteen of his greatest later POEMS). The COUPLET of the STANZA, like that at the end of a SHAKESPEAREAN SONNET, is often used for a pithy summary, a reversal, a sudden concentration of information, or (as in the example from Byron) surprise and deflation. The following STANZA is from Byron's *Don Juan:*

> But words are things, and a small drop of ink
>   Falling like dew, upon a thought, produces
> That which makes thousands, perhaps millions, think;
>   'Tis strange, the shortest letter which man uses
> Instead of speech, may form a lasting link
>   Of ages; to what straits old Time reduces
> Frail man, when paper—even a rag like this,
> Survives himself, his tomb, and all that's his!

Outride: A term Gerard Manley Hopkins applied to a SLACK SYLLABLE— that is, an unstressed syllable—added to a FOOT. An *outride* does not change the basic SCANSION of a LINE, for, in Hopkins's system, only the stressed syllables determine the SCANSION. There may be as many as three *outrides* attached to a FOOT—that is, following a stressed syllable.

Oxford Movement: Also known as the "Tractarian Movement" and the "An-glo-Catholic Revival." During the first third of the nineteenth century the English Church had become lax in urging the ancient doctrines, in enforcing discipline, in carrying out ritual, and in keeping up the church edifices. In 1833 a movement for reform got under way at Oxford following a sermon on "national apostasy" by John Keble. The leader was John Henry Newman, who wrote the first of the ninety papers (*Tracts for the Times*, 1833–1841) in which the ideas of the group were advocated. Other leaders were R. H. Froude, Isaac Williams, Hugh James Rose (Cambridge), and E. B. Pusey. The reformers aimed primarily at combating liberalism and skepticism and restor-ing to the Church and to church worship the dignity, beauty, purity, and zeal of earlier times. They hoped also to protect the Church from the encroach-ment of the State, as threatened by the Whig Reform Bill of 1832 and other measures aimed at reducing the revenues of the Church and curbing its author-ity.

To provide a solid foundation for their reforms, the sponsors of the move-ment undertook to prove the divine origin of the Church and the historical continuity connecting the early Church with the Church of England. This led them to an espousal of doctrines regarded by some as Roman Catholic, and after the publication of Newman's final tract in 1841 a storm of criticism arose, as a result of which Newman lost his position at Oxford, became a layman, and finally (1845) joined the Roman Catholic Church, eventually to become Cardinal. When Charles Kingsley attacked his sincerity, Newman re-plied with the famous *Apologia pro Vita Sua* (1864), a full statement of his spiritual and mental history, the candor, beauty, and force of which won for him high regard. Though some of Newman's followers also became Roman Catholics, the main movement, led now by Pusey, continued, through in its later stages it became less controversial and theoretical and more practical, furthering the establishment of guilds, the improvement of church music, the revival of the ritual, and the building and beautifying of church buildings. The movement attracted the attention of various literary men, with Carlyle heaping disdain on it and Arnold attacking it. Also, the sponsors of the move-ment wrote a number of PROPAGANDA NOVELS, like Newman's *Loss and Gain* and Charlotte M. Yonge's *The Heir of Redclyffe*. The Episcopal Church in the United States reflects much of the reform doctrine of the Tractarians.

[Reference: R. W. Church, *The Oxford Movement* (1891, reprinted 1970).]

Oxford Reformers: A term applied to a group of humanist scholars whose associations began at Oxford University in the early RENAISSANCE, particularly the three friends John Colet, Sir Thomas More, and the Dutch scholar Erasmus. Though Erasmus, who had come to Oxford to study Greek and who spent part of his life in England, was the most famous member of the group and More the best loved, Colet seems to have been the real leader. The group was interested in effecting certain reforms in Church and State based on hu-manist ideas. Moral training and reform were to be accomplished through rational rather than emotional processes. Reason should dominate. Humanity should be uplifted through education and the improvement of individual char-acter. The Church should be reformed from within by purging it of corrupt practices and by improving the moral and educational standards of the clergy. The group advocated the historical method in the study of the BIBLE, opposed medieval SCHOLASTICISM and asceticism, and advocated education as a means of improving religion, private character, and political institutions. More recorded his dream of a perfect human society and government in his *Utopia* (1516); Colet when dean of St. Paul's founded with his own funds the St. Paul's school for boys, where new methods of instruction were developed and sons of the common folk might be admitted; Erasmus outlined his ideals of State in his *Education of a Christian Prince*. Keenly interested in purging the Church of the evils that Luther a few years later rebelled against, the *Oxford Reformers* were unwilling to follow either Luther or Henry VIII in breaking with Rome, and died good Catholics, though disappointed idealists.

[Reference: Frederic Seebohm, *The Oxford Reformers,* 3rd ed. (1887, reprinted 1913).]

Oxymoron: A self-contradictory combination of words or smaller verbal units; usually noun-noun, adjective-adjective, adjective-noun, adverb-adverb, or adverb-verb. *"Oxymoron"* itself is an *oxymoron,* from the Greek meaning "sharp-dull." Others are "bittersweet," "jumbo shrimp," "pianoforte," and "chiaroscuro." The Latin MAXIM *Festina lente* ("Hurry slowly") is an *oxymoron.* The second half of George Herbert's "Bitter-Sweet" seems to be an exercise in religious PARADOX and *oxymoron:*

> I will complain, yet praise;
> I will bewail, approve;
> And all my sour-sweet days
> I will lament and love.

An exaggerated employment of *oxymoron* is seen in Romeo's speech early in *Romeo and Juliet:*

> Why, then, O brawling love! O loving hate!
> O anything, of nothing first create!
> O heavy lightness! serious vanity!
> Misshapen chaos of well-seeming forms!
> Feather of lead, bright smoke, cold fire, sick health!
> Still-waking sleep, that is not what it is!

P

Paean: A SONG of praise or joy. Originally the term was restricted to ODES sung by a Greek CHORUS in honor of Apollo; later the term was broadened to include praise sung to other deities. The word has come now to mean simply any SONG of joy. Homer indicates, too, that *paeans* were frequently sung on military occasions: before an attack, after a victory, when a fleet set sail.

Paeon: In METRICS a FOOT consisting of one long or stressed syllable and three short or unstressed syllables. *Paeons* are named in terms of which one of the four syllables is long or stressed, a "first *paeon*" being ╱ ◡ ◡ ◡ , a "second" ◡ ╱ ◡ ◡, a "third" ◡ ◡ ╱ ◡ , and a "fourth" ◡ ◡ ◡ ╱. Although not common in English VERSE, this essentially classic FOOT does occasionally appear, notably in the POETRY of Gerard Manley Hopkins.

Pageant: Used in three senses: (1) a scaffold or stage on which DRAMAS were performed in the Middle Ages; (2) PLAYS performed on such stages; (3) modern dramatic SPECTACLES designed to celebrate some historical event, often of local interest. The medieval *pageant,* constructed on wheels for processional use, as in celebrating Corpus Christi day, was designed for use by a particular guild for the production of a particular PLAY and usually reflected this special purpose. Thus, the *pageant* of the fisherman, designed to present the PLAY of Noah, would be constructed and painted to represent the Ark. For a contemporary description of the medieval *pageant* and its use, see MYSTERY PLAY.

Though the modern *pageant* is an outgrowth of a very ancient tradition, which includes primitive religious festivals and Roman "triumphs," its recent development in England and especially in America makes it essentially a twentieth-century FORM. It is usually understood to mean an outdoor exhibition consisting of several SCENES presented with recitation (PROLOGUES, etc.), usually with DIALOGUE, with historically appropriate costumes, often with musical features, the whole being designed to commemorate some event that appeals to the emotional loyalties of the populace. Sometimes the *pageant* is a processional, with a series of "floats," uniformed marchers, and mounted officials, though it is sometimes presented in an outdoor theater of some sort, such as an athletic stadium. In America *pageants,* with actors, dramatic SCENES, dances, and SONGS have become widespread for the celebration of historical events of special local interest. *The Lost Colony,* by the playwright Paul Green, which has run for the summer months every year since 1937, at Manteo, North Carolina, the scene of much of its action, is the best known of these historical *pageants.*

Palilogy (or Palillogy): The deliberate REPETITION of words or phrases for EMPHASIS, as in Lincoln's "Gettysburg Address": "that government of the people, by the people, for the people, shall not perish from the earth."

Palimpsest: A writing surface, whether of vellum, papyrus, or other material, that has been used twice or more for manuscript purposes. Before the invention of paper, the scarcity of writing material made such substances very valuable, and the vellum surfaces were often scraped or rubbed or the papyrus surfaces washed. With material so used a second time it frequently happened that the earlier script either was not completely erased or that, with age, it showed through the new. In this way many documents of very early periods have been preserved for posterity. In one instance, a Syriac text of St. Chrysostom of perhaps the tenth century was found to be superimposed on a sixth-century grammatical work in Latin, which again had covered some fifth-century Latin records. Modern chemical methods and the use of special lighting make it possible today to recover many of the original texts. Since almost any piece of language has been used already over and over again, both Ezra Pound and Hilda Doolittle ("H. D.") have used *palimpsest* metaphorically to suggest the many layers and tissues of meaning in any text.

Palindrome: A word, sentence, or VERSE that reads the same both from left to right and from right to left, such as the word "civic" or the statement falsely attributed to Napoleon, "Able was I ere I saw Elba." "Et tu, Brute" is almost a *palindrome*. A near-palindromic mirror-image pattern of consonants occurs in Dickinson's LINE "His notice sudden is." It would seem that on the acoustic or graphic level, *palindrome* is a species of CHIASMUS. See ANAGRAM.

Palinode: A piece of writing recanting or retracting a previous writing, particularly such a recanting, in VERSE form, of an earlier ODE.

Pamphlet: A short ESSAY or treatise, usually on a current topic, issued as a separate publication. A *pamphlet* has fewer pages than a book, is always unbound, and may or may not have paper covers. Most *pamphlets* are polemical tracts of only transitory value.

Panegyric: A formal written or oral composition lauding a person for an achievement; a EULOGY. In Roman literature *panegyrics* were usually presented in praise of a living person, thing, or achievement. In Greek literature they were often reserved for praise of the dead. This was a popular form of ORATORY among fulsome speakers who praised living emperors. Two famous *panegyrics* are those of Gorgias, the *Olympiacus,* in praise of those who established the festivals, and that of Pliny the Younger delivered when he became consul, a speech praising Trajan. The term is now often used with a derogatory CONNOTATION. See ENCOMIUM.

Panoramic Method: In the CRITICISM of FICTION, a term applied to that POINT OF VIEW in which an author presents material by NARRATIVE EXPOSITION rather than in SCENES, giving ACTIONS and conversations in summary rather than in detail. In FILM CRITICISM, it refers to SCENES photographed at some distance or by moving the camera over a series of connected distant objects. It is similar to DEEP FOCUS or COMPOSITION IN DEPTH. See SCENES (OF A DRAMA), POINT OF VIEW, COMPOSITION IN DEPTH.

Pantheism: A philosophic-religious attitude that finds the spirit of God manifest in all things and holds that whereas all things speak the glory of God it is equally true that the glory of God is made up of all things. Finite objects are at once both God and the manifestation of God. The term is impossible to define exactly, since it is so personal a conviction as to be differently interpreted by different philosophers; but for its literary significance it is clearly enough described as an ardent faith in NATURE as both the revelation of deity and deity itself. The word was first used in 1705 by the deist John Toland who called himself a pantheist (from *pan* meaning "all" and *theos* meaning "deity"). The pantheistic attitude, however, is much older than the eighteenth century, since it pervades the early thought of Egypt and India, was common in Greece long before the time of Christ, was taken up by the Neoplatonists of the Middle Ages, and has played an important part in Christian and Hebraic doctrine. Spinoza is, from the philosophic point of view, the greatest exponent of *pantheism*, as Goethe is the great POET of the idea. In literature *pantheism* finds frequent expression. Wordsworth in England and Emerson in America may be selected from many as giving typical expression to the pantheistic conception. The following LINES from Wordsworth's *Lines Composed a Few Miles above Tintern Abbey* express the idea clearly:

> . . . a sense sublime
> Of something far more deeply interfused,
> Whose dwelling is the light of setting suns,
> And the round ocean and the living air
> And the blue sky, and in the mind of man;
> A motion and a spirit, that impels
> All thinking things, all objects of all thought,
> And rolls through all things.

Pantomime: In its broad sense the term means silent acting; the form of dramatic activity in which silent motion, gesture, facial expression, and costume are relied on to express emotional states or NARRATIVE situations. Ritual dances of primitive and not-so-primitive society are pantomimic. Partly pantomimic was the Roman MIME and completely so the English DUMB SHOW. In English stage history, *pantomime* usually means the spectacular dramatic form that flourished from the early years of the eighteenth century. Though "*pantomime* proper" (no speaking) is said to have been introduced by a dancing master in 1702 at the Drury Lane Theatre, the usual form of *pantomime*, as sponsored at Lincoln's Inn Fields theater by John Rich some years later, was more varied. There was usually a serious legendary STORY told through dancing and SONGS. In these STORIES moved the figures of the COMMEDIA DELL' ARTE, burlesquing in silent movement the action of the TALE. A background of the most spectacular description, the lavish use of "machinery," and many changes of SCENE made the *pantomime* visually exciting. The *pantomime* flourished throughout the eighteenth century and until near the close of the nineteenth century. English *pantomimes* (sometimes with a girl as the "leading boy," and including dance, SONG, and SLAPSTICK) have been common in this century and are often built around such traditional THEMES as Humpty-Dumpty, Dick Whittington and his cat, and Cinderella. In FILM, particularly in the days of silent motion pictures, *pantomime* acting was a major way of storytelling. Charlie Chaplin and Buster Keaton were notable *pantomime* actors; something of the art has persisted into the "age of sound," as, say, in some of Red Skelton's television routines.

[References: Allardyce Nicoll, *A History of Early Eighteenth-Century Drama, 1700–1750* (1925); A. E. Wilson, *King Panto: The Story of Pantomime* (1935).]

Pantoum: The *pantoum* may consist of an indefinite number of four-line STANZAS, but in any case the second and fourth LINES of one STANZA must reappear as the first and third VERSES of the following STANZA. The STANZAS are QUATRAINS rhyming *abab*. In the final STANZA the first and third lines of the first STANZA recur in reverse order, the POEM thus ending with the same line with which it began. Usually considered as one of the sophisticated FRENCH FORMS, the *pantoum* was actually taken over from the Malaysian by Victor Hugo and other French POETS.

Parabasis: In Greek OLD COMEDY a long address to the audience by the CHORUS speaking for the author. It usually consisted of witty remarks on contemporary affairs, frequently with overt personal references. It was not directly related to the PLOT of the COMEDY itself. See OLD COMEDY.

Parable: An illustrative STORY answering a question or pointing a moral or lesson. A true *parable,* however, is much more than an ANECDOTE since, implicitly at least, it parallels, detail for detail, the situation that calls forth the *parable* for illustration. A *parable* is, in this sense, an ALLEGORY. In Christian countries the most famous *parables* are those told by Christ, the best known of which is that of the Prodigal Son.

Paradox: A phrase or statement that while seemingly contradictory or absurd may actually be well-founded or true. *Paradox* is a rhetorical device used to attract attention, to secure emphasis. As we approach the conceptual limits of discourse—as commonly happens in philosophy and theology—language seems to rely increasingly on *paradox*. Incarnation, Immaculate Conception, Virgin Birth, and the Holy Trinity all involve some elements of *paradox,* as do many of St. Paul's utterances, particularly in 2 Corinthians ("For when I am weak, then I am strong"). *Paradox* teases and challenges the mind and tests the limits of language; it can be a potent device. Richard Bentley's statement that there are "none so credulous as infidels" is an illustration. *Paradox* is a common element in epigrammatic writing, as the work of G. K. Chesterton or Oscar Wilde shows. The presence of *paradox* in POETRY has become a serious concern of some of the New Critics, notably Cleanth Brooks, who sees *paradox* as a fundamental element of poetic language. In Brooks's celebrated formulation, the language of science necessarily relies on the principles of noncontradiction, leaving a countervailing principle of contradiction, registered somehow as a *paradox,* to be the necessary language of POETRY.
[Reference: Cleanth Brooks, *The Well Wrought Urn* (1947).]

Paragoge: The addition of an extra and unneeded letter, syllable, or sound at the end of a word, as in "dearie" for "dear." Such extra syllables are frequently added for the sake of the METER in NURSERY RHYMES and BALLADS, as in these LINES from "The Baffled Knight":

> Quoth he, "Shall you and I, lady,
> Among the grass lie down a?
> And I will have a special care
> Of rumpling of your gown a."

Paragoge still turns up once in a while in the vernacular, as in the locutions spelled "drownded" and "oncet" (for "drowned" and "once").

Parallelism: Such arrangement of parts of a sentence, sentences, paragraphs, and larger units of composition that one element of equal importance with another is similarly developed and phrased. The principle of *parallelism* dictates that coordinate ideas should have coordinate presentation. Within a sentence, for instance, where several elements of equal importance are to be expressed, if one element is cast in a relative clause the others should be expressed in relative clauses. Conversely, of course, the principle of *parallelism* demands that unequal elements should *not* be expressed in similar constructions. Practiced writers are not likely to attempt, for example, the comparison of positive and negative statements, of inverted and uninverted constructions, of dependent and independent clauses. And, for an example of simple *parallelism,* the sentence immediately preceding may serve. Some departures from *parallelism* may qualify as "SLEIGHT OF 'AND,'" but most are just signs of carelessness, as when someone says, "I don't like to fish or swimming." But a deliberate violation of *parallelism* can be highly dramatic. Consider the COUPLET in Housman's "Hell Gate" in which coordinating conjunctions (POLYSYNDETON) create the expectation of a parallel group of active verbs but abruptly end with a linking verb:

> Then the sentry turned his head,
> Looked, and knew me, and was Ned.

Parallelism is characteristic of Oriental poetry, being notably present in the Psalms, as in:

> The Heavens declare the glory of God;
> And the firmament sheweth his handywork.

It is also characteristic of the SONGS and CHANTS of the American Indians. *Parallelism* seems to be the controlling principle of the POETRY of Walt Whitman. It shapes the following POEM of his on almost every level from that of the word to that of the central idea:

> A noiseless patient spider,
> I mark'd where on a little promontory it stood isolated,
> Mark'd how to explore the vacant vast surrounding,
> It launch'd forth filament, filament, filament out of itself.
> Ever unreeling them, ever tirelessly speeding them.
>
> And you O my soul where you stand,
> Surrounded, detached, in measureless oceans of space,
> Ceaselessly musing, venturing, throwing, seeking the spheres to
>   connect them,

Till the bridge you will need be form'd, till the ductile anchor hold,
Till the gossamer thread you fling catch somewhere, O my soul.

Paraphrase: A restatement of an idea in such a way as to retain the meaning while changing the DICTION and FORM. A *paraphrase* is often an amplification of the original for the purpose of clarity, though the term is also used for any rather general restatement of an expression or passage. Thus, one might speak of a *paraphrase* from the French meaning a loose statement of the idea rather than an exact TRANSLATION, or of a *paraphrase* of a POEM indicating a PROSE explanation of a difficult passage of VERSE. In some contemporary CRITICISM the paraphrasing of works of literary art is frowned on, and the followers of the NEW CRITICISM condemn what they call the "heresy of the *paraphrase*," a term suggesting their stand that the essential nature of a POEM is incommunicable in terms other than its own. Allen Tate states it succinctly when he says, "We know the particular poem, not what it says that we can restate."

Parataxis: An arrangement of sentences, clauses, phrases, or words in coordinate rather than subordinate constructions, often without connectives, as in Julius Caesar's "Veni, vidi, vici" (I came, I saw, I conquered), or with coordinate conjunctions, as in Hemingway's or Whitman's extensive use of "and" as a connective. Thus, POLYSYNDETON (especially in the form "and . . . and . . . and . . .") often accompanies *parataxis*. As a rule *parataxis* is found more in speech than in writing and more in juvenile or uncultivated utterance than in mature or sophisticated. See HYPOTAXIS.

Parenthesis: An explanatory remark thrown into the body of a statement and frequently separated from it by parentheses ( ). However, any comment that is an interruption of the immediate subject is spoken of as a *parenthesis*, whether it be a word, phrase, clause, sentence, or paragraph. Commas and dashes are substituted for the *parenthesis* marks when the interruption is not so abrupt as to demand the ( ). Brackets [ ] are used for parenthetical material more remote from the subject of the sentence than *parentheses* will control and also to enclose material injected or interpolated by some editorial hand. Modern novelists, interested in accurately reporting the fluid and unstable nature of thought and feeling, frequently employ *parentheses*, although often without formal punctuation. Joyce and Faulkner are noted examples. Others, anxious to qualify and define precise shades of meaning find the extensive use of parenthetical material helpful, as does Henry James. J. D. Salinger's later FICTION makes ample and varied use of the device; in a stroke of typographical wit, Buddy Glass, the NARRATOR of "Seymour: An Introduction," concludes a very long sentence addressed to the reader, "I privately say to you, old friend (unto you, really, I'm afraid), please accept from me this unpretentious bouquet of very early-blooming parentheses: (((( ))))."

Parnassians: A group of nineteenth-century French POETS, so called from their journal *Parnasse contemporain* (1866–1876). Influenced by Gautier's doctrine of ART FOR ART'S SAKE, they were in reaction against the prevailing ROMANTICISM of the first half of the century. The *Parnassians* wrote impersonal POETRY with great objective clarity and precision of detail. They had a strong preoccupation with FORM and reintroduced the FRENCH FIXED FORMS. Their leader was Leconte de Lisle; among the other *Parnassians* were Sully-Prudhomme, Albert Glatigny, François Coppée, and Théodore de Banville. In the 1870s they influenced some English poets, including Swinburne, Dobson, Gosse, and Lang, particularly in the use of the FRENCH FIXED FORMS. The influence continued in some of the poetry of Ezra Pound and T. S. Eliot, particulary in their poems in QUATRAINS around 1915–1920.

Parnassus: The name of a mountain in Greece famed as the haunt of Apollo and the MUSES. The word has also been used as a title for a collection or ANTHOLOGY of POEMS or poetical extracts, such as *England's Parnassus* (1600).

Parodos: In ancient Greek DRAMA the ODES sung by the CHORUS when they first enter.

Parody: A composition burlesquing or imitating another, usually serious, piece of work. It is designed to ridicule in humorous fashion, or to criticize by brilliant treatment, an original piece of work or its author. When the *parody* is directed against an author or the author's style, it is likely to fall simply into barbed witticisms, often venting personal antagonisms of the parodist against the parodied. When the subject matter of the original composition is parodied, however, it may prove to be a valuable indirect criticism or it may even imply a flattering tribute to the original writer. Often a *parody* is more powerful in its influence on affairs of current importance—politics, for instance—than an original composition. The *parody* is in literature what the CARICATURE and the cartoon are in art. Known to have been used as a potent means of SATIRE and ridicule even as far back as Aristophanes, *parody* has made a definite place for itself in literature and has become a popular type of literary composition. *Parody* makes fun of some familiar STYLE, typically by keeping the STYLE more or less constant while markedly lowering or debasing the subject. Thus Dickinson's:

> The Soul selects her own Society—
> Then—shuts the Door—

has been parodied:

> The Soul selects her own Sorority—
> Then—shuts the Dorm—

(Note that the craft of *parody* prizes minimal tampering.) The opposite strategy—keeping a subject more or less constant while lowering or debasing STYLE—generates BURLESQUE or TRAVESTY. See BURLESQUE.
   [References: Dwight Macdonald, ed., *Parodies* (1960); Carolyn Wells, ed., *A Parody Anthology* (1904.)]

Paronomasia: An old term for a PUN or play on words.

Pasquinade: A SATIRE or LAMPOON hung up in a public place. The term is derived from Pasquilla or Pasquino, the name given to a mutilated statue exhumed in Rome in 1501, which was saluted on St. Mark's Day by having satirical VERSES in Latin hung on it. Such VERSES were called *pasquinades*, and the term was later extended to any LAMPOON displayed in a public place.

Passion Play: A DRAMA that portrays a portion of the life of a god. The plays in the MYSTERY PLAY CYCLES that dealt with the life of Christ were *Passion Plays*. The term is now customarily restricted to PLAYS dealing with the last days, trial, crucifixion, and resurrection of Christ. ("Passion" here means "suffering.") Such a *Passion Play* has been presented every tenth year at Oberammergau, in Upper Bavaria, since the 1630s.

Pastiche: A French word for a PARODY or literary imitation. Perhaps for humorous or satirical purposes, perhaps as a mere literary exercise or JEU D'ESPIRIT, perhaps in all seriousness (as in some CLOSET DRAMAS), a writer imitates the STYLE or technique of some recognized writer or work. Amy Lowell's *A Critical Fable* (1922) might be called a *pastiche*, since it is written in the manner of James Russell Lowell's *A Fable for Critics*. In art a picture is called a *pastiche* when it manages to catch something of a master's peculiar style. In music *pastiche* is applied to a medley or assembly of various pieces into a single work. The term is also applied to literary patchworks formed by piecing together extracts from various works by one or several authors. See CENTO, PARODY.

Pastoral: A POEM treating of shepherds and rustic life, after the Latin word for shepherd, *pastor*. The *pastoral* began in the third century B.C. when the Sicilian POET Theocritus included poetic sketches of rural life in his *Idylls*. The Greek *pastorals* existed in three forms: the DIALOGUE or singing-match, usually between two shepherds, often called the ECLOGUE because of the number of singing-matches in Virgil's "Selections"; the MONOLOGUE, often the PLAINT of a lovesick or forlorn lover or a POEM praising some personage; and the ELEGY or LAMENT for a dead friend. The *pastoral* early became a highly conventionalized form of POETRY, the POET (Virgil is an example) writing of friends and acquaintances as though they were poetic shepherds moving through rural scenes. The FORM is artificial and unnatural—the "shepherds" of the *pastoral* often speaking in courtly language and appearing in dress more appropriate to the drawing room than to rocky hills and swampy meadows. Between 1550 and 1750 many such conventionalized *pastorals* were written in England. In modern use the term often means any poem of rural people and setting (Louis Untermeyer, for instance, called Robert Frost a *"pastoral"* poet). Since this classification is based on subject matter and manner rather than on FORM, we often use the term in association with other poetic types; we thus have *pastoral* LYRICS, ELEGIES, DRAMAS, or even *pastoral* EPICS. Milton's *Lycidas*, Shelley's *Adonais*, and Arnold's *Thyrsis* are examples of English *pastorals*, as is Spenser's *The Shepheardes Calender*. Although the term can be construed broadly enough to include, say, Whitman's "When Lilacs Last in the Dooryard Bloom'd," its application is usually limited to poems that somehow adhere to the literal sense of *"pastoral"* and include "shepherds," however farfetched. Often, in Judeo-Christian environments, the *pastoral* will include some recollection of the imagery of the Psalms and other parts of the BIBLE.

Many twentieth-century critics employ a highly sophisticated concept of the *pastoral* advanced by William Empson. In this specialized usage the *pastoral* is considered a device for literary INVERSION, a means of "putting the complex into the simple"—of expressing complex ideas through simple personages, for example. In Empson's ingenious and rather audacious scheme, *pastoral* is opposed to HEROIC. Empson, using his specialized definition, finds *pastoral* elements in such widely differing works as the proletarian NOVEL (whose HERO undergoes an INVERSION of function) and *Alice in Wonderland.* See IDYLL, BUCOLIC, ECLOGUE, PASTORAL DRAMA, PASTORAL ELEGY.

[References: William Empson, *Some Versions of Pastoral* (1935); W. W. Greg, *English Pastoral Poetry and Pastoral Drama* (1906); Frank Kermode, *English Pastoral Poetry* (1952); Harold E. Toliver, *Pastoral Forms and Attitudes* (1971).]

Pastoral Drama: The PASTORAL conventions so popular at times in POETRY (as the ECLOGUE) and in the PASTORAL ROMANCE are reflected also in a form of DRAMA occasionally cultivated by English dramatists. Whether the *pastoral drama* originated in simple dramatic ECLOGUES or is more closely related to such fifteenth-century mythological PLAYS as Politian's *Orfeo,* it is certain that the type developed in Italy in the sixteenth century and was affected by the PASTORAL ROMANCE. Tasso's *Aminta* and Guarini's *Il Pastor Fido* (1590) were models for English RENAISSANCE pastoral PLAYS by Samuel Daniel, John Fletcher, and Ben Jonson. The best is Fletcher's *The Faithful Shepherdess* (acted 1608–1609). Some of Shakespeare's ROMANTIC COMEDIES, such as *As You Like It,* were affected by the PASTORAL influences and are sometimes called PASTORAL plays. The eighteenth-century stage saw some translations and imitations of Italian *pastoral drama,* and pastoral CONVENTIONS were utilized along with the mythological in the more spectacular forms of dramatic activity that flourished in the eighteenth and nineteenth centuries.

[Reference: Jeanette Marks, *English Pastoral Drama* (1908).]

Pastoral Elegy: A POEM employing conventional PASTORAL IMAGERY, written in dignified, serious language, and taking as its THEME the expression of grief at the loss of a friend or important person. The FORM represents a combining of the pastoral ECLOGUE and the ELEGY. The conventional divisions, as evidenced in Milton's *Lycidas,* are: the invocation of the MUSE, an expression of the grief felt in the loss of a friend, a procession of mourners, a DIGRESSION (on the church), and, finally, a consolation in which the POET submits to the inevitable and declares that everything has turned out for the best, usually through a strengthened belief in immortality. Other CONVENTIONS often present include: appearance of the POET as shepherd, praise of the dead "shepherd," the PATHETIC FALLACY, flower symbolism, invective against death, reversal of the ordinary processes of NATURE as a result of the death, bewilderment caused by grief, declaration of belief in some form of immortality, use of a REFRAIN and of the RHETORICAL QUESTION. Moschus's LAMENT for Bion (second century B.C.), the November ECLOGUE of Spenser's *The Shepheardes Calender,* and Shelley's *Adonais* are examples of the form. In many such elegies, "Shepherd" becomes a conventional code word for "poet," and those for whom Milton, Shelley, and Arnold wrote their elegies were poets (King, Keats, and Clough). Accordingly, almost any poet's ELEGY for another poet—such as W. H. Auden's for W. B. Yeats—will display some PASTORAL elements. See ECLOGUE, ELEGY, PASTORAL.

[Reference: Thomas Perrin Harrison, Jr., ed., *The Pastoral Elegy: An Anthology* (1939).]

Pastoral Romance: A PROSE NARRATIVE, usually long and complicated in PLOT, in which the characters bear PASTORAL names and in which PASTORAL conventions dominate. It often contains interspersed SONGS. Though the Greek *Daphnis and Chloë* of Longus (third century) is classed as a *pastoral romance,* the form was reborn in the RENAISSANCE with Boccaccio's *Ameto* (1342). Montemayor's *Diana Enamorada* (*ca.* 1559) is an important Spanish *pastoral romance.* Typical English examples are Sir Philip Sidney's *Arcadia* (1580–1581) and Thomas Lodge's *Rosalynde* (1590), which was the source of Shakespeare's *As You Like It.* See ECLOGUE, PASTORAL, and PASTORAL DRAMA.

Pastourelle: A medieval type of DIALOGUE POEM in which a shepherdess is wooed by a man of higher social rank. In the Latin *pastoralia* a scholar does the courting; in the French and English, a POET. The body of the POEM is the DIALOGUE in which the case is argued. Sometimes the suit is successful, but often a father or brother happens along and ends the wooing. In the English forms the POET asks permission to accompany the maid to the fields; she refuses and threatens to call her mother. The *pastourelle* possibly developed from popular wooing-games and wooing-SONGS, though one of Theocritus's IDYLLS (no. 27) is much like the medieval *pastourelle.* The form seems to have influenced the PASTORAL dialogue-LYRICS of the Elizabethans and may have figured in the development of early romantic DRAMA in England. Robert Frost's "The Subverted Flower" may be read as a shocking, realistic inversion of the lineaments of the *pastourelle.*

Patent Theaters: The removal of the ban against theatrical performances in England in 1660 resulted in much rival activity among groups seeking to operate playhouses. Sir William D'Avenant and Thomas Killigrew secured from Charles II a "patent" granting them the privilege of censorship of PLAYS and the right to organize two companies and erect two theaters that should have a monopoly. Though opposed by the jealous master of the revels, Sir Henry Herbert, and by some of the independent managers, D'Avenant and Killigrew succeeded in enforcing their rights. D'Avenant's company, the "Duke of York's Company," occupied in 1661 a new theater in Lincoln's Inn Fields and later one at Dorset Garden. Killigrew's company, the "King's Company," erected the Theatre Royal, the first of a famous succession of houses on this spot, all known as Drury Lane, since 1663. The theaters used by these two favored companies are known as *"patent" theaters.* The companies united in 1682, but in 1695 Betterton led a rebellious group of actors to a second theater in Lincoln's Inn Fields. After a generation of confusion, Parliament passed a licensing act in 1737, reaffirming the patent rights and establishing the monopoly of Drury Lane and Covent Garden (erected 1732). Despite strenuous efforts of rival managers to encroach on the privileges of the patentees, this act remained in force until 1843, when it was repealed and the patents revoked. Among the managers of Drury Lane after Killigrew are Cibber, Garrick, and Sheridan; of Covent Garden, John Rich, the elder Colman, and John P. Kemble. See PRIVATE THEATERS.

[Reference: Allardyce Nicoll, *History of Restoration Drama, 1660–1700,* 2nd ed. (1928).]

Pathetic Fallacy: A phrase (maybe exemplifying the TRANSFERRED EPITHET and involving, in any event, a rare sense of "pathetic") coined by Ruskin to denote the tendency to credit NATURE with the emotions of human beings. In a larger sense the *pathetic fallacy* is any false emotionalism resulting in a too impassioned description of nature. It is the carrying over to inanimate objects of the moods and passions of a human being. This crediting of nature with human qualities is a device often used by POETS. A frequently occurring expression of the IMAGINATION, it becomes a fault when it is overdone to the point of absurdity, in which case it approaches the CONCEIT. The following passage from Ruskin (*Modern Painters*, vol. 3, part IV, chap. xii) discusses the *pathetic fallacy:*

> They rowed her in across the rolling foam—
> The cruel, crawling foam.

> The foam is not cruel, neither does it crawl. The state of mind which attributes to it these characters of a living creature is one in which the reason is unhinged by grief. All violent feelings have the same effect. They produce in us a falseness in all our impressions of external things, which I would generally characterize as the "pathetic fallacy."

It should be noted that the fallacy may be in the mind of a CHARACTER who is upset or "unhinged," so that an author who shows such a state of mind in a CHARACTER is not guilty of fallacious logic or technique. Indeed, no one can get through a day without saying something like "happy birthday" that could be classified as a *pathetic fallacy* on the grounds that a day is incapable of feeling happiness, sadness, or whatever.

Pathos: From the Greek root for suffering or deep feeling, *pathos* is the quality in art and literature that stimulates pity, tenderness, or sorrow in the reader or viewer. Although in its strict meaning it is closely associated with the pity that TRAGEDY is supposed to evoke, in common usage it describes an acquiescent or relatively helpless suffering or the sorrow occasioned by unmerited grief, as opposed to the stoic grandeur and awful justice of the TRAGIC HERO. In this distinction, Hamlet is a tragic figure and Ophelia a pathetic one; Lear's fate is tragic, Cordelia's pathetic. See BATHOS.

Pattern Poem: Another name for CARMEN FIGURATUM or FIGURE POEM.

Pedantry: A display of learning for its own sake. The term is often used in critical reproach when an author's STYLE is marked by a superfluity of quotations, foreign phrases, ALLUSIONS, and such. Holofernes in Shakespeare's *Love's Labour's Lost* can hardly open his lips without giving expression to *pedantry:*

> Most barbarous intimation! yet a kind of insinuation, as it were, *in via,*
> in way, of explication; *facere,* as it were, replication, or, rather, *ostentare,* to
> show, as it were, his inclination,—after his undressed, unpolished, uneducated,
> unpruned, untrained, or rather, unlettered, or, ratherest, unconfirmed fash-
> ion—to insert again my *haud credo* for a deer.

Pegasus: The winged horse of Grecian FABLE said to have sprung from Medusa's body at her death. *Pegasus* is associated with the inspiration of POETRY (though in modern times in a somewhat jocular vein) because, by one blow of his hoof, he is supposed to have caused Hippocrene, the inspiring fountain of the MUSES, to flow from Mount Helicon. Poets have sometimes invoked the inspiring aid of *Pegasus* instead of the MUSES.

Pelagianism: A theological doctrine asserting the original innocence of human beings and their capacity to achieve moral and spiritual power through their own unaided efforts. Although it was attacked by St. Augustine and officially declared a heresy early in the fifth century, unofficial items of Pelagian thought—and particularly the denial of original sin—have persisted through to the present. Randall Jarrell found the sentiment in the POETRY of William Carlos Williams; in *After Strange Gods: A Primer of Modern Heresy,* T. S. Eliot found fault with both D. H. Lawrence and Ezra Pound because of their failure to accept the orthodox (anti-Pelagian) position on original sin. Walt Whitman, who seems to have denied that any such thing as sin or evil ever existed, can be seen as an adherent of *Pelagianism.* See CALVINISM, AUGUS-TINIANISM.

Penny Dreadful: A cheaply produced paperbound NOVEL or NOVELETTE of mystery, adventure, or violence in the late nineteenth and early twentieth centuries in England; a British equivalent of the American DIME NOVEL.

Pentameter: A LINE of VERSE consisting of five FEET. Serious VERSE in English since the time of Chaucer—EPIC, DRAMA, MEDITATIVE, NARRATIVE—and many conventional forms—TERZA RIMA, HEROIC QUATRAIN, RHYME ROYAL, OTTAVA RIMA, the SPENSERIAN STANZA, and the SONNET—have made *pentameter* the staple measure. See SCANSION.

Pentastich: A POEM or a STANZA of five LINES; a QUINTET; A CINQUAIN.

Period of the Confessional Self in American Literature, 1960–: The 1960s marked a time of uncertainty, revolt, and cynicism in America and a strong turning inward of many American writers. The most important event of the decade was American involvement in the war in Vietnam and Cambodia, a conflict that steadily increased in intensity from a few military advisers to a vast American expeditionary force. The most unpopular war in the history of the United States, it ignited a massive revolt of the young against war and against many aspects of the "establishment." Higher education was marked by widespread student revolt and by sporadic violence. Many individuals sought to withdraw from any public social contract during this time by joining Eastern religions, retreating to agrarian communes, and sometimes by using narcotics. The dominant philosophy was EXISTENTIALISM, the fundamental ethical positions highly individual, and the public stance of the nation Epicurean bordering on hedonistic. Adding to the disillusionment of the nation was the gradual uncovering of the Watergate scandal in Washington, a disclosure that drove Richard Nixon to resign the Presidency in 1974. American withdrawal from Vietnam, an apparent slackening of the "cold war," and a renewal of communication with China substantially reduced intensity of feeling about foreign policy, but in the 1970s severe energy shortages and major environmental problems continued to raise serious questions about technology. The struggle for the civil rights of minorities in the 1960s was a rallying point for many, but by the 1970s that struggle appeared to be well on the way to being won.

The result of these varying forces was a tendency for the writers of imaginative literature to find their chief values in the self rather than in society and to see the proper realm of art to be introspection and confession rather than the creation of imaginary worlds. The rebellion of the late sixties found political expression in new LITTLE MAGAZINES, a remarkable freedom of language, and the gesture as public act. The POETRY of many of the older poets tended toward strict forms and academic tidiness. A younger group, including Anne Sexton, Sylvia Plath, and a number of black poets, practiced an intensely personal poetry of a marked confessional quality. They were joined by older writers such as Theodore Roethke, John Berryman, and most notably Robert Lowell. The novelists of the sixties who gave the greatest promise of substantial work were William Styron, Saul Bellow, Bernard Malamud, John Updike, and Norman Mailer. Novelists such as John Barth and Thomas Pynchon produced works of great experimental ingenuity. The Southern writers who had dominated the 1930s, 1940s, and 1950s were largely dead or silent, and a group of Jewish writers—Bellow, Malamud, Philip Roth, and Mailer—came closest to being their successors as a group. Edward Albee, writing a skillful kind of absurdist DRAMA, joined with Tennessee Williams to dominate the American stage, as television made increasing inroads on both FILM and legitimate DRAMA. CRITICISM, under the influence of European theoreticians, such as the structuralists, the deconstructionists, and the phenomenologists, seemed increasingly to regard literary expression as a complex linguistic strategy.

At the middle of the 1980s, American writers appeared to be committed to a private, largely asocial exploration of the self, toward experiments in form, and toward an intensely romantic concept of POETRY and FICTION. The emergence of a generation of writers born after 1940 and even after 1950—including the CRITICS Edward Mendelson and Jonathan Culler and the POETS James Tate, Louise Glück, Alan Williamson, Robert Morgan, Everette Maddox, Kathleen Norris, and Albert Goldbarth—promised a continuation of varied and vigorous accomplishment in American literature. See *Outline of Literary History*.

Period of Modernism and Consolidation in American Literature 1930–1960: The year 1930 marked a decided turning point in American social and cultural history as well as the beginning of the period in literary history that lasted to 1960. In October 1929 the stockmarket crash heralded the end of the prosperous twenties, and by the end of 1930 the impact of the depression was being felt throughout American life and thought. As the depression intensified, the social and economic revolution called the New Deal occurred, and a steadily increasing concern with social or sociological issues occupied the serious writer. Shortly after the depression began, the expatriate group that had in Paris made a religion of art came back to America and joined the radical movements that earned the thirties the name of "The Red Decade."

Hemingway's career had been launched in the twenties, and his work in the thirties added little to his stature; but Faulkner was to produce in the first half of the decade the largest single body of his best work. Dos Passos wrote his trilogy, *U.S.A.;* and James T. Farrell, Thomas Wolfe, and John Steinbeck acquired fame and did their best work. A radical social point of view was present in most of these writers, a critical approach to American institutions. In the meantime, the poets who had in the twenties produced the *Fugitive* magazine in Nashville reacted strongly against the radical political thought and the sociological literary orientations of their world; they expressed their politico-economic reaction through the principles of AGRARIANISM and their rejection of sociological concerns in the artist through the formulation of the NEW CRITICISM. Edwin Arlington Robinson, Robert Frost, T. S. Eliot, Edna St. Vincent Millay, and Carl Sandburg continued their dominant position in poetry, and E. E. Cummings, Robinson Jeffers, Archibald Macleish, and William Carlos Williams raised newer strong poetic voices. Maxwell Anderson, Eugene O'Neill, Clifford Odets, and Thornton Wilder dominated the stage. Gertrude Stein cannot be tidily classified, but her influence was certainly felt in American DRAMA, FICTION, POETRY, CRITICISM, OPERA, AUTOBIOGRAPHY, and even FOLKLORE.

The signing of the Russo-German pact in 1939 and the coming of the Second World War put an effective end to the radicalism of the thirties. The war and its aftermath resulted in an age of conformity and conservatism, bolstered by a burgeoning economy. American life, thought, and writing in the forties and the fifties were marked by a tendency to conformity, to traditionalism, and to reverence for artistic form and restraint; while, at the same time, the period was marked by informality in social conduct and freedom of subject matter in art.

The postwar DRAMA revealed the strong new talents of Arthur Miller and Tennessee Williams, while Thornton Wilder was doing his most mature work and Eugene O'Neill was at the end of his career dramatizing with powerful effectiveness the tragic lineaments of his own experience. Both POETRY and CRITICISM tended to retreat to the critical quarterlies, where each operated with a high level of technical skill but without great distinction or vitality. The major figures in the NOVEL were still Hemingway and Faulkner, both of whom received the NOBEL PRIZE, although neither was producing work of the quality of what they had done in the twenties and thirties. Of the newer novelists, Robert Penn Warren showed skill, seriousness, and virtuosity, and John P. Marquand carried the satirical NOVEL OF MANNERS to a high level of accomplishment. Despite a small output (one short NOVEL and scarcely more than a dozen STORIES, some fairly long), J. D. Salinger became one of the best and most important American FICTION writers. To the vernacular humor of Ring Lardner's writing, Salinger added the grace, sophistication, and depth of Fitzgerald's along with elements of Jewish and Oriental culture, the symbolist POETRY of Rilke and Eliot, and the idiom of show business. Ralph Ellison's *Invisible Man* made high art of the black man's situation. In James Jones, Norman Mailer, and a group of other young neonaturalists, a strong, frank, and rather unkempt kind of fiction appeared. But the remark that, perhaps, best characterizes the literature of America from the Second World War to 1960 is that most of its major works and its major literary events were produced by writers whose careers had been firmly established in the twenties and the thirties and who had done their best work then. The chaos of a hot war and the constraint of a cold one conspired to produce a literature either of conformity or of confusion. See *Outline of Literary History*.

Periodic Sentence: A sentence not grammatically complete before its end; the opposite of a LOOSE SENTENCE. The characteristic of a *periodic sentence* is that its construction is such as constantly to throw the mind forward to the idea that will complete the meaning. The *periodic sentence* is effective when it is designed to arouse interest and curiosity, to hold an idea in suspense before its final revelation is made. Periodicity is accomplished by the use of parallel phrases or clauses at the opening, by the use of dependent clauses preceding the independent clause, and by the use of such correlatives as *neither . . . nor, not only . . . but also,* and *both . . . and.* The first STANZA of Longfellow's "Snowflakes" is a maximally *periodic sentence,* beginning with a succession of adverbial phrases and not grammatically complete until the very last word, which is the subject:

> Out of the bosom of the Air,
>> Out of the cloud-folds of her garments shaken,
> Over the woodlands brown and bare,
>> Over the harvest-fields forsaken,
>>> Silent, and soft, and slow,
>>> Descends the snow.

Periodical: A term applied to any publication that appears at regular intervals; it includes such publications as JOURNALS, MAGAZINES, and REVIEWS but customarily not newspapers. See MAGAZINE.

Periodical Essay: A term applied to an ESSAY written for publication as the principal or only item in an issue of a PERIODICAL. The most notable *periodical essays* were written for *The Tatler* and *The Spectator,* but the form was very popular throughout most of the eighteenth century. See ESSAY.

Periods of English and American Literary History: See ENGLISH LITERATURE, AMERICAN LITERATURE, and *Outline of Literary History.*

Peripety: The REVERSAL of fortune for a PROTAGONIST—possibly either a fall as in a TRAGEDY or a success as in a COMEDY. See DRAMATIC STRUCTURE.

Periphrasis: An indirect, abstract, roundabout method of stating ideas; the application to writing or speech of the old conviction that "the longest way 'round is the shortest way home." Used with restraint and with deliberate intent, *periphrasis* may be a successful rhetorical device, but the danger is that it will be overdone and will result in mere Polonius-like verbosity. Some people, anxious to seem cultivated, never say they want a drink; they are "desirous of obtaining a beverage" or some such. Fowler cites as an objectionable use of *periphrasis* (for "No news is good news") the periphrastic circumlocution, "The absence of intelligence is an indication of satisfactory developments." Authors frequently use the form to secure humorous effects; for example, Shenstone refers to pins as "the cure of rents and separations dire, and chasms enormous." In T. S. Eliot's "East Coker," after a lyric passage, the poet comments, "That was a way of putting it—not very satisfactory: / A periphrastic study in a worn-out poetical fashion." See ANTOMASIA.

Peroration: The conclusion of an ORATION or discourse in which the discussion is summed up and the speaker fortifies the argument by an appeal to the emotions of the audience; a recapitulation of the major points of any speech.

Persiflage: Light, inconsequential chatter, written or spoken; gay, satirical banter; a trifling, flippant manner of dealing with something.

Persistence of Vision: The physiological phenomenon that makes motion pictures possible. An image is retained on the retina of the eye for a very brief time after the object creating the image has disappeared. When another image only slightly changed is seen before the first image fades, the illusion of motion is created. Because of the *persistence of vision*, a FILM, which consists of a series of individual photographs of objects in successive states of motion, when projected rapidly and sequentially on a screen, creates the illusion of motion. The term *persistence of vision* is applied to this physiological phenomenon, which Ingmar Bergman has called a "defect." See PHI PHENOMENON.

Persona: Literally a mask. The term is widely used in the CRITICISM of FICTION to refer to a "second self" created by the author and through whom the NARRATIVE is told. The *persona* may be a NARRATOR; such a *persona* exists in Huck Finn, and the debate about the freedom that the use of Huck Finn gave Mark Twain as a mask through whom he could speak things he dared not utter in his own person is instructive about the function of the *persona* as teller and as mask. The *persona* can be not a CHARACTER in the STORY but "an implied author"; that is, a voice not directly the author's but created by the author and through which the author speaks. All FICTION is in some sense a STORY told by someone; all self-consciously artistic FICTION is told by someone created by the author and who serves, therefore, as a mask, a *persona*. The term is also used in literary BIOGRAPHY to describe the public self that some writers presented to the world and behind which they worked. In this sense "Papa Hemingway" was a *persona* behind which Ernest Hemingway hid. *Persona* takes on special coloration in Jungian psychology; and there is always the sense in which everybody presents a more or less prepared "mask" or face to the world. See NARRATOR.

Personal Essay: A kind of INFORMAL ESSAY, with an intimate STYLE, some autobiographical content or interest, and an urbane conversational manner. See ESSAY.

Personification: A FIGURE that endows animals, ideas, abstractions, and inanimate objects with human form, character, or sensibilities; the representing of imaginary creatures or things as having human personalities, intelligence, and emotions; also an impersonation in DRAMA of one CHARACTER or person, whether real or fictitious, by another person. Keats's *personification* of the Grecian urn as the

> Sylvan historian, who canst thus express
> A flowery tale more sweetly than our rhyme . . .

is an obvious *personification,* as are his earlier references to the urn as an "unravished bride of quietness" and as a "foster child of silence and slow time." *Personification* as a FIGURE OF SPEECH is also called PROSOPOPOEIA. See ALLEGORY.

Personism: A term coined by Frank O'Hara (1926–1966) for his own sort of POETRY. He seems to have been serious but in no way solemn, and he did not offer a logical DEFINITION of the term. To judge from his strongest POEMS as examples of *personism,* however, one could say that the emphasis is on persons and personalities and the informal communications within and between them—shapely, elegant, spontaneous, sophisticated, urbane. O'Hara, for whom "the Enemy," according to Marjorie Perloff, was "the Great Insight or the Mythic-Symbolic Analogue," ridiculed philosophy, abstraction, emotional "identification" in the place of living "recognition," and what conventionally passes for a kind of aesthetically posed "personality or intimacy." "The poem," according to O'Hara's description of *personism,* "is at last between two persons instead of two pages."

Persuasion: That one of the major types of composition whose purpose is to convince of the wisdom of a certain line of action. *Persuasion* is really a phase of ARGUMENTATION and resembles it in its purpose to establish the truth or falsity of a proposition but is distinct in that it is calculated to arouse to some action. (In general use, this distinction is all but meaningless and the terms are often used interchangeably.) *Persuasion* may draw on the other types of composition—ARGUMENTATION, DESCRIPTION, EXPOSITION, and NARRATION—for support and incorporates within itself elements of each. The most common form of *persuasion* is the ORATION. See ETHOS.

Petrarchan Conceit: The kind of CONCEIT used by the Italian POET Petrarch in his love SONNETS and widely imitated or ridiculed by RENAISSANCE English sonneteers. It rests on elaborate and exaggerated comparisons expressing in extravagant terms the beauty, cruelty, and charm of the beloved and the suffering and despair of the forlorn lover. Hyperbolic analogies to ships at sea, marble tombs, wars, and alarums are used; OXYMORON is common. Shakespeare in "Sonnet 130," which begins,

> My mistress' eyes are nothing like the sun;
> Coral is far more red than her lips' red:
> If snow be white, why then her breasts are dun;
> If hairs be wires, black wires grow on her head,

satirizes the Petrarchan conventions while giving a reasonably accurate catalog of some of the more common.

Petrarchan Sonnet: The ITALIAN SONNET, with OCTAVE rhyming *abbaabba* and SESTET usually rhyming in various patterns, the most interesting being *cdecde* and *cdcdcd* (just so the pat COUPLET is avoided and the number of RHYME sounds is five or fewer); called *Petrarchan* after Petrarch, its most successful producer.

Phanopoeia: A word that Ezra Pound began using after *"imagism"* was vitiated by misuse and turned by Amy Lowell into "Amygism." *Phanopoeia,* like Aristotle's *opsis,* has to do with the power of language to cast visual images onto the mind or imagination. One of its roots also appears in *epiphany,* an outward and visible showing-forth of an inward and invisible meaning.

Phenomenology: *Phenomenology* is a philosophical system that has proved to be the effective basis for a contemporary school of CRITICISM. *Phenomenology* is a method that inspects the data of consciousness without presuppositions about epistemology or ontology. (Epistemology is the theory of the nature of knowledge, ontology that of the nature of being.) To the phenomenologist any object, although it has existence in time and space, achieves meaning or intelligibility only through the active use of a consciousness in which the object registers. Hence, *phenomenology* finds reality not in a noumenal realm—in cause or material being—but in the psychical realm of awareness, to which it applies exhaustive ANALYSIS and DESCRIPTION. Edmund Husserl, the founder of *phenomenology*, saw it as a psychology that distinctly separated the physical from the psychical and concentrated its attention on the psychical. To accomplish the analysis of the object as it registers in the consciousness, the phenomenologist suspends all presuppositions, inferences, or judgments about the object outside the consciousness.

Phenomenology as such has scarcely mattered in the creation of literature, unless one considers the sentence from Husserl's *Ideas*—"The natural wakeful life of our Ego is a perceiving"—that turns up in Eliot's fragmentary "Triumphal March." When phenomenological philosophy is applied to literary CRITICISM, the result is a form of EXISTENTIAL CRITICISM, such as that practiced by the GENEVA SCHOOL. Phenomenological CRITICISM sees the work of art as aesthetic object, existing only in the consciousness of the perceiver; an aesthetic object does not have existence in a material universe of temporal and spatial coordinates but only in the coordinates of pure consciousness. Phenomenological CRITICS, of whom Gaston Bachelard, Roman Ingarden, Mikel Dufrenne, and Georges Poulet are chief, tend to see IMAGINATION as essentially free of perception and thus an expression of freedom. They tend to have little interest in the ontology of the aesthetic object—a major concern of the NEW CRITICISM—and instead to value highly the affective aspects of works of art. They tend to see the experience of reading as an aesthetic meditation or intuitive communication between the aesthetic object and the reader. Frequently the phenomenological CRITIC examines the corpus of an author's work to seek out the intentions behind the creation of the autonomous aesthetic objects. In this sense, phenomenological CRITICISM, when applied to FILM, becomes like the AUTEUR THEORY. Phenomenological CRITICISM is thus, in the simplest sense, the description of the way in which the consciousness becomes aware of a work of art. See GENEVA SCHOOL, EXISTENTIALISM.

[References: Gaston Bachelard, *The Poetics of Reverie* (tr. 1969); Robert Detweiler, *Story, Sign, and Self: Phenomenology and Structuralism as Literary Critical Methods* (1978); Hans-Georg Gadamer, *Philosophic Hermeneutics* (tr. 1976); Vernon W. Gras, ed., *European Literary Theory and Practice: From Existential Phenomenology to Structuralism* (1973); Robert R. Magliola, *Phenomenology and Literature: An Introduction* (1977); José Ortega y Gasset, *Phenomenology and Art* (tr. 1975).]

Phi Phenomenon (or Effect): The psychological perception of motion resulting from PERSISTENCE OF VISION, called the *phi phenomenon* by the GESTALT psychologists. The *phi phenomenon* is the psychological basis of FILM. See PERSISTENCE OF VISION.

Philippic: Any speech or HARANGUE bitterly invective in character; a discourse filled with denunciations and accusations. The term comes from the twelve orations of Demosthenes berating Philip II of Macedon as an enemy of Greece.

Philistinism: The worship of material and mechanical prosperity and the disregard of culture, beauty, and spirt. The term was made popular by Matthew Arnold's use of it in "Sweetness and Light," the first chapter of *Culture and Anarchy.* Arnold wrote:

> If it were not for this purging effect wrought upon our minds by culture, the whole world, the future as well as the present, would inevitably belong to the Philistines. The people who believe most that our greatness and welfare are proved by our being very rich, and who most give their lives and thoughts to becoming rich, are just the very people whom we call Philistines. Culture says: "Consider these people, then, their way of life, their habits, their manners, the very tones of their voices; look at them attentively; observe the literature they read, the things which give them pleasure, the words which come forth out of their mouths, the thoughts which make the furniture of their minds; would any amount of wealth be worth having with the condition that one was to become just like these people by having it?"

Philology: In its general sense *philology* means the scientific study of both language and literature. Thus, there are philological clubs and journals devoted to linguistic and literary research. *Philology* was at one time used in a narrower sense to mean the scientific and historical study of language. Today, however, the systematic study of language by scientific principles is usually called LINGUISTICS, with *philology* confined to language study whose end is literary.

Phoneme: In LINGUISTICS the smallest potentially significant unit of articulated sound in a language.

Picaresque Novel: A CHRONICLE, usually autobiographical, presenting the life story of a rascal of low degree engaged in menial tasks and making his living more through his wits than his industry. Episodic in nature, the *picaresque novel* is, in the usual sense of the term, structureless. The *picaro*, or central figure, through the nature of his various pranks and predicaments and by virtue of his associations with people of varying degree, affords the author an opportunity for SATIRE on the social classes. Romantic in the sense of being an ADVENTURE STORY, the *picaresque novel* nevertheless is strongly marked by realistic methods in its faithfulness to petty detail, its frankness of expression, and its presentation of incidents from low life.

From earliest times the rogue has been a favorite CHARACTER presentation. As far back as the *Satyricon*, Petronius at the court of Nero recognized the possibilities of the type. In the Middle Ages the FABLES continued the manner, though they transferred roguery from people to animals. Reynard is a typical *picaroon*. He lives by his wits; gets into trouble and out of it, but always interests the reader. It was not until the sixteenth century that this rogue literature crystallized into a definite type. A NOVEL called *La Vida de Lazarillo de Tormes y de sus fortunas y adversidades*, probably dating from 1554, was one of the most-read books of the century. Cervantes took up the manner in *Don Quixote*. Soon French imitators sprang up. Of French PICA-RESQUE NOVELS Le Sage's *Gil Blas* (1715) was the most popular. So definitely was the type fixed as a Spanish FORM that the French writers—Le Sage among them—gave their CHARACTERS Spanish names and placed their EPISODES in Spain.

The English adopted the picaresque manner. In 1594 appeared *The Unfortunate Traveller: or, The Life of Jack Wilton* by Thomas Nash—the first important *picaresque novel* in the language. With Daniel Defoe in the eighteenth century the type became important in English literature. His *Moll Flanders* presents the life record of a female picaroon. Fielding in *Jonathan Wild* and Smollett in *Ferdinand, Count Fathom* lent dignity to the type.

Seven chief qualities distinguish the *picaresque novel*. (1) It chronicles a part or the whole of the life of a rogue. It is likely to be done in the first person—as AUTOBIOGRAPHY—but not necessarily. (2) The chief figure is drawn from a low social level, is of "loose" character, according to conventional standards, and, if employed at all, does some menial work. (3) The NOVEL presents little PLOT—just a series of EPISODES only slightly connected. (4) There is little character interest. Progress and development of character do not take place. The central figure starts as a *picaro* and ends as a *picaro*, manifesting the same qualities throughout. When change occurs, as it sometimes does, it is external, brought about by the *picaro's* falling heir to a fortune or by marrying money. Internal character development seldom occurs in the *picaresque novel*. (5) The method is realistic. While the story may be romantic in itself, it is presented with a plainness of language, a freedom in vocabulary, and a vividness of detail such as only the realist is permitted. (6) SATIRE is prominent. Thrown with people from every class and often from different parts of the world, the *picaro* serves them intimately in one lowly capacity or another and learns all their foibles and frailties. The *picaresque novel* may in this way be made to satirize social castes, national types, or racial peculiarities. (7) The HERO of the *picaresque novel* usually stops just short of being an actual criminal. The line between crime and petty rascality is a hazy one, but somehow the *picaro* always manages to draw it. Carefree, amoral perhaps, the *picaro* avoids actual crime and turns from one peccadillo to disappear down the road in search of another.

The *picaresque novel* shares with the MEDIEVAL ROMANCE loose STRUCTURE, emphasis on INCIDENT, sequential as opposed to consequential ACTION, and the journey PLOT. It differs from the ROMANCE in presenting not an idealized but a realistic and usually satiric view of human beings and society.

[References: Robert Alter, *Rogue's Progress: Studies in the Picaresque Novel* (1964); F. W. Chandler, *The Literature of Roguery* (1907, reprinted 1958); A. A. Parker, *Literature and the Delinquent: A Study of the Picaresque Novel* (1947).]

Picturesque: A word applied to certain kinds of writing by ANALOGY to a type of painting that grew out of the effort to find a middle ground between the SUBLIME and the beautiful as defined by Edmund Burke's very influential ESSAY "Of the Sublime and the Beautiful" (1756). The *picturesque* was a regulative principle that allowed the painter to organize NATURE into what Pope called a "wild civility" rather than a series of SUBLIME elements. William Gilpin codified the *picturesque* in his series of illustrated tours in the 1790s and established a group of CONVENTIONS for nineteenth-century painters. Among its features were irregularity of line, roughness and ruggedness of texture, contrasts of light and shadow, and intricacy. Typical objects in a *picturesque* painting were fractured rocks, blighted or twisted trees, winding streams, and ruins. The *picturesque* painter usually sought a prospect view for landscapes. American painters of the Hudson River School were noted for their use of the *picturesque*. It was also widely used in the DESCRIPTION of landscapes in FICTION. James Fenimore Cooper's and Washington Irving's use of the *picturesque* method in their writing has been frequently noted. See SUBLIME.

[Reference: Christopher Hussey, *The Picturesque: Studies in a Point of View* (1927, reprinted 1967).]

Pièce bien faite: A type of French DRAMA popular in the nineteenth century. See WELL-MADE PLAY, the English equivalent term.

Pindaric Ode: The regular ODE, characterized by a division into units containing three parts—the STROPHE and ANTISTROPHE, alike in form, and the EPODE, different from the other two. See ODE.

Pirated Edition: An unauthorized EDITION of a work, usually stolen from one country and produced for sale in another. It represents an infringement of COPYRIGHT through illegal publication. The term is most often applied to the period before the establishment of modern international COPYRIGHT conventions, when the use without permission or payment of literary works copyrighted in another nation was a common practice. However, in recent years Taiwanese and Russian publishers have reprinted works both in the original language and in translation without permission of or payment to the copyright owners, a clear type of piracy. See COPYRIGHT.

Pitch: A potentially significant quality of articulated sound, determined by relative frequency, intensity, and volume; its importance varies from language to language and, in some, forms an element of PROSODY.

Plagiarism: Literary theft. A writer who steals the detailed PLOT of some obscure, forgotten story and uses it as new in a story of his or her own is a plagiarist. *Plagiarism* is more noticeable when it involves a stealing of language than when substance only is borrowed. From flagrant exhibitions of stealing both thought and language, *plagiarism* shades off into such less serious actions as unconscious borrowing, borrowing of minor elements, and mere IMITATION. In fact, the critical doctrine of IMITATION, as understood in RENAISSANCE times, often led to what would nowadays be called *plagiarism*. Thus, Spenser's free borrowings from other romantic EPICS in composing his *Faerie Queene* were by him regarded as virtues, since he was "following" a predecessor in the same type of writing. A modern dramatist could not with impunity borrow PLOTS from other DRAMAS and from old STORIES in the way Shakespeare did. With *plagiarism* compare LITERARY FORGERIES, its converse, where authors pretend that another has written what has actually been written by the authors themselves.

Although the basic concept of *plagiarism* is clear—that it is the use as one's own of material originated by others—the actual practice involves many shades and gradations. It is difficult to prove the borrowing of an idea and easy to demonstrate the stealing of a passage. Hence, as a legal term, *plagiarism* has very sharp limits and is considered to be a clearly demonstrable use of material plainly taken from another without credit. One may accommodate quotation, reference, ALLUSION, ECHO, imitation, derivation, revision, PARODY, PASTICHE, and even larceny, but many of these devices of transmission and tribute were considered *plagiarism* by Poe, and he made its detection and punishment a stock-in-trade of his REVIEWS. Most of the time he was right, or at least on the right track, but once in a while he went too far. See GHOST WRITER.

Plain Style: The simplest of the three CLASSICAL types of STYLE; the others are the high and the middle. *Plain style* is free, natural, untrammeled by contrived CADENCES. Its fundamental characteristic is an artful simplicity. At various periods *plain style* has been considered highly desirable; it was, for example, much prized by the American Puritan preachers. *Plain style*, sometimes called "low style," is one of the DEMOTIC STYLES.

Plainsong: A term derived from the Latin phrase *cantus plānus,* even or level singing. *Plainsong* resulted from the singing or chanting of nonmetrical materials. It has the free RHYTHM of ordinary speech. After the sixth century, it was known as the Gregorian chant.

Plaint: VERSE expressing grief or tribulation; a chant of lamentation; a LAMENT; an expression of sorrow. See COMPLAINT.

Planh: Provençal equivalent of "plaint," used by Ezra Pound in the title of a TRANSLATION.

Platonic Criticism: A term used by contemporary CRITICS to describe a type of CRITICISM that finds the values of a work of art in its extrinsic rather than its intrinsic qualities, in its usefulness for ulterior nonartistic purposes. The term is used in opposition to ARISTOTELIAN CRITICISM, which finds the value of a work within the work itself. See ARISTOTELIAN CRITICISM; CRITICISM, TYPES OF.

Platonism: The idealistic philosophical doctrines of Plato, because of their concern with the aspirations of the human spirit, their tendency to exalt mind over matter, their grappling with the great problems of the universe and of human beings' relation to the cosmic forces, and their highly imaginative elements, have appealed strongly to certain English authors, particularly the PO-ETS of the RENAISSANCE and of the ROMANTIC PERIOD. Plato himself declined to "codify" his philosophical views and perhaps altered them much during his own life. He left expressions of them in his great *Dialogues,* in which various Greeks (such as Socrates, Alcibiades, and Aristophanes) discuss philosophical problems, particularly those involving the universe and our relation to it, the nature of love and beauty, the constitution of the human soul, the relation of beauty to virtue. Unlike Aristotelian philosophy, which tends to be systematic, formal, scientific, logical, and critical, occupying itself chiefly with the visible universe, the natural world, and secular humanity, *Platonism* is flexible and interested in the unseen world. Plato founded his famous "Academy" in 380 B.C., where for a third of a century he taught students attracted from far and near (including Aristotle himself). Later followers now known as "neo-Platonists" modified Plato's teachings. It is difficult to distinguish the purely Platonic elements from elements added by later Platonists. Among the "neo-Platonists" were two groups of special importance: (1) The Alexandrian school; this group, especially Plotinus (third century), stressed the mystical elements and amalgamated them with many ideas drawn from other sources. Their NEOPLATONISM was in fact a sort of religion, which, though itself supplanted by Christianity, supplied medieval Christian thinkers (including Boethius and St. Augustine) with many ideas. (2) The NEOPLATONISTS of the Italian RENAISSANCE; under the leadership of Marsilio Ficino (1433–1499), who led the Platonic Academy at Florence and who translated and explained Plato, a highly complex and mystical system developed, one of the aims of which was the fusing of Platonic philosophy and Christian doctrine. This particular kind of NEOPLATONISM kindled the imagination of such RENAISSANCE poets as Sidney and Spenser.

Important Platonic doctrines found in English literature include: (1) The doctrine of ideas (or "forms"). True reality is found not in the mutable realm of sense but in the higher, spiritual realm of the ideal and the universal. Here exist the "ideas" or images or patterns of which material objects are but transitory symbols or expressions. As Yeats put it: "Plato thought nature but a spume that plays/Upon a ghostly paradigm of things. . . ." (2) The doctrine of recollection. This implies the preexistence and immortality of the soul, which passes through a series of incarnations. Most of what the soul has seen and learned in "heaven" it forgets when imprisoned in the body of clay, but it has some power of "recalling" ideas and images; hence human knowledge. (3) The doctrine of love. There are two kinds of love and beauty, a lower and a higher. The soul or lover of beauty in its quest for perfect beauty ascends gradually from the sensual, through a process of idealization, to the spiritual and thereby develops all the virtues both of thought and of action. Beauty and virtue become identified.

An interesting exposition of the NEOPLATONIC doctrines of love may be read in the fourth book of Castiglione's *The Book of the Courtier.* Representative English POEMS embodying Platonic ideas include: Spenser's "Hymn in Honor of Beauty," Shelley's "Hymn to Intellectual Beauty," and Wordsworth's "Ode on Intimations of Immortality from Recollections of Early Childhood."

[References: J. S. Harrison, *Platonism in English Poetry of the Sixteenth and Seventeenth Centuries* (1903, reprinted 1965); W. R. Inge, *The Platonic Tradition in English Religious Thought* (1926); P. E. More, *The Religion of Plato* (1921); A. E. Taylor, *Platonism and Its Influence* (1924, reprinted 1963); Edgar Wind, *Pagan Mysteries in the Renaissance,* 2nd ed. (1968).]

Play: A literary composition of any length, ordinarily written to be performed by actors who impersonate the CHARACTERS, speak the DIALOGUE, and enact the appropriate ACTIONS. A *play* usually, but not always, assumes that this enactment will be on a stage before an audience.

Pléiade: A term originally applied to an ancient group of seven authors (named after the constellation of the Pleiades) and to several later groups, the most important of which was the group of critics and poets that flourished in France in the second half of the sixteenth century. The leading figures were Ronsard, Du Bellay, and (later) Desportes. The poetic manifesto of the "school" is Du Bellay's *Défense et Illustration de la Langue Francaise* (1549). It shows an interest in developing a new vernacular literature following the types cultivated by CLASSICAL writers. The popular and the medieval were to be avoided, except that certain medieval courtly pieces were to be rewritten. The native language was to be enriched by coining words, by borrowing from the Greek and Latin, and by restoring to use lost native words, so that a literary language might be produced that would make possible the creation of a new French literature comparable with classical literature. The high function of the POET and of POETRY was stressed. The influence of the group was constructive and important for Elizabethan poets, notably Spenser, and the more or less mythical AREOPAGUS has been regarded as an English counterpart of the *Pléiade*, since Sidney and his group were engaged in the effort to refine the English language and to found a new national literature based on humanistic ideals.

Pleonasm: The superfluous use of words. *Pleonasm* may consist of needless repetition or of the addition of unnecessary words in an effort to express an idea completely. For example, in the sentence, "He walked the entire distance to the station on foot," "the entire distance" and "on foot" are pleonastic. Although *pleonasm* is a violation of fastidious usage, it is employed occasionally to add EMPHASIS, and in such instances its use may legitimate. Many common locutions qualify as *pleonasm:* "focal point" for "focus," "third-down situation" for "third down," "is supportive of" for "support," and so forth. See TAUTOLOGY.

Ploce: In classical RHETORIC, a kind of REPETITION whereby different forms and senses of a word are "woven" through an utterance, as in Blake's ". . . And mark in every face I meet/Marks of weakness, marks of woe": the first "mark" is a verb; the second and third are nouns. Also found in "cognate objects," such as "say your say," "mail the mail," and "nail the nail"; or "cognate subjects," such as "The small rain down can rain."

Plot: Although an indispensable part of all FICTION and DRAMA, whether in PROSE or VERSE, *plot* is a concept about which there has been much disagreement. Aristotle, who assigns it the chief place of honor in writing and calls it "the first principle, and, as it were, the soul of a TRAGEDY," formulated, in his *Poetics*, a very precise definition, which has been the basis for most discussions of *plot*. He called it "the imitation of an action" and also "the arrangement of the incidents." The action imitated should be "a whole"—that is, it should have a beginning, "that which does not itself follow anything by causal necessity, but after which something naturally is or comes to be"; a middle, "that which follows something as some other thing follows it"; and an end, "that which itself follows some other thing, either by necessity, or as a rule, but has nothing following it." A *plot*, Aristotle maintained, should have UNITY: it should "imitate one action and that a whole, the structural union of the parts being such that, if any one of them is displaced or removed, the whole will be disjointed and disturbed." He disliked episodic *plots*, "in which the acts succeed one another without probable or necessary sequence." His test for a sound *plot* was "whether any given event is a case of *propter hoc* or *post hoc.*" (*"Propter hoc"* means "on account of this," "post hoc" merely "after this." Since effects come after causes and also on account of them, it can be hard to figure out whether a given sequence is logical as well as chronological.) Thus, causality was a fundamental quality of a *plot* for Aristotle. The writer, he believed, "should first sketch the general outline [of the plot], and then fill in the episodes and amplify in detail." He seems to mean that the *plot,* a general idea of a MOVEMENT, is realized by "episodizing"—that is, by creating INCIDENTS to flesh it out.

E. M. Forster made a helpful distinction between STORY and *plot.* A STORY is "a narrative of events in their time-sequence. A *plot* is also a narrative of events, the emphasis falling on causality." A STORY arouses only curiosity; a *plot* demands intelligence and memory. Thus, plotting is the process of converting STORY into *plot,* of changing a chronological arrangement of incidents into a causal and inevitable arrangement. (A viewer will automatically supply linkage in an effort to connect things and make sense of them.) This functioning of some kind of intelligent overview of ACTION, which establishes principles of selection and relationship among EPISODES, makes a *plot.* Clearly there must be more than one episode, and equally clearly the relation among the episodes must be close. Out of the welter of experience, a selection of episodes is made that in itself constitutes a "whole" action.

Many CRITICS, particularly in the nineteenth and twentieth centuries, have quarreled with Aristotle's assigning *plot* the chief place in a dramatic composition, and have insisted that CHARACTER and CHARACTERIZATION are more important, the *plot* being merely a mechanical means by which a STRUCTURE designed to display CHARACTERS is arranged. In some schemes CRITICS speak of a *plot* of ACTION (*mythos*) in Aristotle's sense but also a *plot* of CHARACTER (*ethos*) and a *plot* of thought (*dianoia*), all involving potentially maximal change. The Neo-Aristotelian critics, largely at the University of Chicago, have attempted to extend the meaning of *plot* to make it a function of a number of elements in the work of art. Ronald S. Crane says, "The form of a given plot is a function of the particular correlation among . . . three variables which the completed work is calculated to establish, consistently and progressively, in our minds." These variables are "(1) the general estimate we are induced to form . . . of the moral character and deserts of the hero . . . (2) the judgments we are led similarly to make about the nature of the events that actually befall the hero . . . as having either painful or pleasurable consequences for him . . . permanently or temporarily; and (3) the opinions we are made to entertain concerning the degree and kind of his responsibility for what happens to him." In such a definition, although much has been added to the simple idea of a STRUCTURE of incidents, the basic view of *plot* as some large and controlling frame is still present. In the presentation of a work there will be a "lighting *plot*" and other *plots* involving scenery and costumes. We can even contemplate grammatical and acoustic *plots* and *plots* of SYMBOL and IMAGE.

The minimal definition of plot is "pattern." Only slightly less simple is "pattern of events." EPISODES do not in themselves make a *plot;* the *plot* lies in relations among episodes. Hence, we may formulate a definition like this: *Plot* is an intellectual formulation about the relations among the incidents of a DRAMA or a NARRATIVE, and it is, therefore, a guiding principle for the author and an ordering control for the reader. For the author it is the chief principle for selection and arrangement; for the reader it is something perceived as STRUCTURE and UNITY. To define *plot* as an intellectual formulation is not, however, to define it as abstract idea or philosophic concept. Such a generality may help in shaping the formulation, but that formulation is of incidents—CHARACTERS and ACTIONS—and how they relate. An ALLEGORY has *plot* not because it makes an abstract statement, but because it constructs that statement from INCIDENTS involving PERSONIFICATIONS and ACTIONS that embody a THEME.

Since the *plot* consists of CHARACTERS performing actions in incidents that comprise a "single, whole, and complete" ACTION, this relation involves conflict between opposing forces (see CONFLICT for a detailed statement of the types of such struggle available to the writer). Without conflict, without opposition, *plot* does not exist. We must have a Claudius flouting a Hamlet, an Iago making an Othello jealous, if we are to have *plot*. These forces may be physical (or external), or they may be spiritual (or internal); but they must in any case afford an opposition. This opposition knits one INCIDENT to another and dictates the causal pattern that develops the struggle. This struggle between the forces, moreover, comes to a head in some one incident—the CRISIS—that forms the turning point of the STORY and usually marks the moment of greatest SUSPENSE. In this climactic EPISODE the RISING ACTION comes to a termination and the FALLING ACTION begins; and as a result of this incident some DÉNOUEMENT or CATASTROPHE is bound to follow.

Plot is, in this sense, an artificial rather than a natural ordering of events. Its function is to simplify life by imposing order thereon. It would be possible, though most tedious, to recite *all* incidents, *all* events, *all* thoughts passing through the minds of one or more CHARACTERS during a period of, say, a week. The demands of *plot* stipulate that the author *select* from this welter of events and reflection those items that have a certain UNITY, that point to a certain end, and have a common relation represent not more than two or three threads of interest and activity. *Plot* brings order out of life; it selects only one or two emotions out of a dozen, one or two conflicts out of hundreds, only two or three people out of thousands, and a half-dozen EPISODES from possible millions. In this sense it focuses and clarifies life.

And, at least in most modern writing, it focuses with one principal idea in mind—CHARACTER. The most effective incidents are those springing naturally from the given characters, the most effective *plot* presents such struggle as would engage these given characters, and the most effective emotion for the *plot* to present is that inherent in the quality of the given characters. The function of *plot*, from this point of view, is to translate CHARACTER into ACTION.

The use of a DEUS EX MACHINA to solve a COMPLICATION is now generally condemned as a weakness, since it is generally conceded that *plot* action should spring from the innate quality of the CHARACTERS participant in the action. But *fate*, since it may be interpreted as working through CHARACTER, is, with the development of the realistic method, still very popular. It is important in any concept of *plot* to keep fate in mind as a major controlling principle. See DRAMATIC STRUCTURE, CHARACTERIZATION, CONFLICT.

[Reference: R. S. Crane, ed., *Critics and Criticism* (1952).]

Plurisignation: A term sometimes used by contemporary CRITICS to describe the kind of AMBIGUITY that results from the capacity of words to stimulate several different streams of thought. Richard Wilbur's *The Beautiful Changes*, for example, has a double signification set up by the possibility of reading it as both a noun plus a verb and an adjective plus a noun. See AMBIGUITY, MULTIPLE MEANINGS.

Poem: It is generally agreed that a *poem* is a cultural artifact of some sort; beyond that vapid claim, however, there is no agreement. A *poem* may not be in words at all, and a *poem* can exist without being written down. Even so, it is commonly accepted that most *poems* are literary compositions typically characterized by IMAGINATION, emotion, significant meaning, sense impressions, and concrete language that invites attention to its own physical features (such as sound and appearance on the page). Most *poems* have an orderly arrangement of parts subsumed under some principle of UNITY, and they seem to have been composed with the dominant purpose of giving aesthetic or emotional pleasure. *Poem*, notoriously, means different things to different people at different times. See POETRY.

Poesie or **Poesy:** A variant and SYNONYM of POETRY, current until about 1650 but thereafter picking up CONNOTATIONS of ARCHAISM, preciousness, affectation, and folly.

Poet: In the strictest sense, anyone who writes POETRY, a maker of VERSES. However, the term *poet,* in its original meaning of "maker," is applied to certain qualities held in unusual degree by a writer without reference to the particular type of composition; these qualities include great imaginative power, flexible and effective expressiveness, a special sensitivity to experience, a skill in compressed expression, and a sense of appropriateness, grace, and energy in the use of language. By further extension, the term is sometimes used for an artist in other fields than writing whose work has the qualities of IMAGINATION, spontaneity, and lyricism, as in a phrase like "a *poet* of the violin." (In some languages—German and Japanese, for instance—the standard word for *poet* is reserved for special honorific uses. In Japan, you may say, "I am a writer [*shi-jin*]," but to say, "I am a poet [*hai-jin*]" is bad manners.)

Poet Laureate: In medieval universities there arose the custom of crowning with laurel a student who was admitted to an academic degree, such as the bachelor of arts. (The "laurel" root word is still evident in "baccalaureate.") Later the phrase *poet laureate* was used as a special degree conferred by a university in recognition of skill in Latin grammar and VERSIFICATION. There also existed in the late Middle Ages the custom of bestowing a crown of laurel on a poet for distinctive work, Petrarch being so honored in 1341. Independent of these customs and usages was the ancient practice of kings and chieftains, in cultivated and barbarous nations alike, of maintaining "court poets," persons attached to the prince's household and kept around for the purpose of celebrating the virtues of the royal family or singing the praises of military exploits. Court poets of this type included the SCOP among ANGLO-SAXON peoples, the SKALD among the Scandinavian, the FILIDH among the Irish, and the higher ranks of BARDS among the Welsh.

The modern office of *Poet Laureate* in England resulted from the application of the academic term *poet laureate* to the traditional court poet. It was established in the seventeenth century, though there were interesting anticipations earlier. Henri d'Avranches, for example, was an official *versificator regis* for Henry III. At the courts of Henry VII and Henry VIII, an academic *poet laureate* named Bernardus Andreas of Toulouse was officially recognized as a *Poet Laureate,* wrote Latin ODES for his masters, and received a pension. The tradition was not carried on after this poet's death. The first officially appointed *Poet Laureate* was John Dryden, though Skelton, Spenser, Daniel, Drayton, Ben Jonson, and William D'Avenant are often included in the list, the latter two with strong justification. Jonson received a pension and a grant of wine, and was an official writer of MASQUES for James I and Charles I; his contemporaries called him "the *Poet Laureate.*" After Jonson's death in 1637, D'Avenant was hailed as Jonson's successor and at the RESTORATION (1660) was informally recognized as Jonson's successor as *Poet Laureate,* though he seems not to have received any official designation during his lifetime. On D'Avenant's death, however, Dryden received (1670) an official appointment to the office; thus, Dryden was the first whose official appointment is recorded. After the Revolution Dryden was displaced, and in 1689 Thomas Shadwell was appointed *Poet Laureate.* Successive laureates were: Nahum Tate (1692–1715), Nicholas Rowe (1715–1718), Laurence Eusden (1718–1730), Colley Cibber (1730–1757), William Whitehead (1757–1785), Thomas Warton (1785–1790), Henry James Pye (1790–1813), Robert Southey (1813–1843), William Wordsworth (1843–1850), Alfred Tennyson (1850–1892), Alfred Austin (1896–1913), Robert Bridges (1913–1930), John Masefield (1930–1967), Cecil Day Lewis (1968–1972), Sir John Betjeman (1973–1984), Ted Hughes (1984–   ).

The early, primary duty of the laureate was to render professional service to the royal family and the court. The practice of composing ODES in celebration of royal birthdays, the New Year, and other occasions developed in the seventeenth century and became obligatory on the laureate in the eighteenth century. Each year such an ODE was sung at a formal court reception held to wish the monarch a happy New Year. This custom lapsed during the illness of George III and was abolished in Southey's time. Sometimes the laureate has served as a "poet-defender" of the monarch in personal and political as well as national disputes (for example, Dryden). Later the more appropriate custom of expecting a POEM in times of national stress or strong patriotic feeling developed, though since Southey the writing of VERSE for special occasions has not been obligatory. Two of the best-known "laureate" poems are Tennyson's "Ode" written to be sung at the funeral of the Duke of Wellington and his "Charge of the Light Brigade."

The perfunctory character of the laureate's duties often prevented the appointment of the best living poets, though since Wordsworth's time the appointment has with occasional exception been regarded as a recognition of poetic distinction. Gray, Scott, and Samuel Rogers declined appointments as *Poet Laureate.*

[References: E. K. Broadus, *The Laureateship* (1921); Kenneth Hopkins, *The Poet Laureate* (rev. ed. 1974).]

Poetaster: A writer of incompetent or inferior VERSE; a pretended POET. The term is always derogatory both of the writer and of the writer's work.

Poète Maudit: The doomed or damned POET; a figure coming out of France in the second half of the nineteenth century. Typically brilliant, moody, morbid, consumptive, alcoholic, self-destructive, sometimes even self-destroyed: once a serious term (for the likes of Poe and Baudelaire) but now a CLICHÉ and a caricature.

Poetic Diction: Words chosen for a supposedly inherent poetic quality. At one time POETS and CRITICS in England sought a special language for POETRY different from the language of common speech. Some dictionaries label entries "poetical" if the item (such as "yestreen" for "yesterday evening") is thought to exist only in POETRY. Spenser sought in ARCHAISMS, for example, the materials out of which to fashion a DICTION properly poetic; the POETS of the AUGUSTAN AGE subjected poetic language to the test of DECORUM and evolved a special vocabulary for POETRY. The Romantic poets, led by Wordsworth, denied the essential difference between the proper language of POETRY and that of PROSE or everyday speech. The tendency in our own time is to allow the POET the widest possible vocabulary range and to use a consciously *poetic diction* only for ironic effect. Amateurs may think they are writing POETRY if they distort their normal diction and say "upon," "beneath," and "about" instead of "on," "under," and "around." They are wrong. As Elder Olson has argued, the only genuinely *poetic diction* is appropriate DICTION.

Poetic Drama: A term properly restricted to poetic PLAYS written to be acted. It is thus distinguished from DRAMATIC POETRY and CLOSET DRAMA, although some writers treat *poetic drama* as synonymous with DRAMATIC POETRY, and some use *poetic drama* to designate CLOSET DRAMA.

Poetic Justice: Loosely, that ideal judgment that rewards virtue and punishes vice among the CHARACTERS of a NARRATIVE. (The term was first used by Thomas Rymer 300 years ago.)

Aristotle announced that "the mere spectacle of a virtuous man brought from prosperity to adversity moves neither pity nor fear; it merely shocks us." Suffering as an end in itself is intolerable dramatically. Hamlet dead with poison, Desdemona smothered, Juliet dead—all these placed before us on the stage unmotivated, unexplained, constitute not TRAGEDY but sheer pain. Such SCENES would be exhibitions of fate over which the CHARACTERS had no control and for which they were not responsible; they would be mere accidents and have no claim to *poetic justice.* But, in a higher, more dramatic sense, *poetic justice* may be said to have been attained, since, in the way in which Shakespeare wrote the PLAYS, the actions moved logically, thoughtfully, consistently to some such CATASTROPHES as those that awaited these three tragic characters. *Poetic justice,* then, in this higher sense, is something greater than the mere rewarding of virtue and the punishing of vice; it is the logical and motivated outcome of the given conditions and terms of the tragic plan as presented in the earlier ACTS of the DRAMA even though, from a worldly sense, virtue meets with disaster and vice seems temporarily rewarded. With CATASTROPHES less severe than those that visited Hamlet and Desdemona, TRAGEDY would be in danger of becoming COMEDY; DRAMA, in its purest sense, would disappear. For the reader of poetic TRAGEDY, the beauty of sorrow, the CATHARSIS that comes with the spectacle of the mysteries of life, are greater values than the knowledge that Claudius had perhaps been exiled and Iago hanged, or that Hamlet had been married to Ophelia and Othello had lived to look on Desdemona's wrinkled cheek. In its modern sense, then, *poetic justice* may be considered as fulfilled when the outcome, however dangerous to virtue, however it may reward vice, is the logical and necessary result of the action and principles of the major CHARACTERS as they have been presented by the dramatist. It should be noted that such an outcome as that described here presupposes a universe in which the author sees order and organizing principles. In the absence of such principles in the author's world view, even this *poetic justice* as the motivated and logical outcome of the given conditions and terms of the NARRATIVE is impossible, as witness Kafka's *The Trial.* In common parlance we use *"poetic justice"* to describe an apt symmetry of fortune, as when a hangman is hanged.

Poetic License: The privilege, sometimes claimed by poets, of departing from normal order, DICTION, RHYME, or pronunciation in order that their VERSE may meet the requirements of their metrical pattern. The idea of a certain measure of *license* goes back at least as far as Quintilian, and the Elizabethan CRITIC George Gascoigne granted that some distortions and deviations may be justified *"per licentiam Poeticam";* in the seventeenth century Dryden described such *license* as the liberty taken by all POETS in all ages to liberate their work from the strictness and severity of PROSE.

The best poets, however, rarely resort to *poetic license,* since they take care to avoid such distortions. Readers of POETRY should not be too hasty in setting down as *license* some such irregularity as the use of an archaic word or the departure from normal word order—which may have been deliberately planned by the POET to establish a desired poetic effect. If one applies the strict demands of PROSE to POETRY, of course, many poetic expressions will consist of *poetic license.* The decision is largely relative. PROSE, for instance, would state boldly: "Kubla Khan decreed that a stately palace be built in Xanadu." Coleridge, however, has it that:

> In Xanadu did Kubla Khan
> A stately pleasure-dome decree. . . .

The Coleridge form includes (1) INVERSION of order (since "in Xanadu" precedes the subject and predicate and the parts of the verb ("did . . . decree") are arranged to flank the subject ("Kubla Khan") and the object ("pleasure-dome"), (2) the expletive use of "did" for the simple past tense "decreed," and (3) a coined expression, "pleasure-dome," for "palace" or "pavilion." Yet all that is distorted is the normal PROSE form; as POETRY the LINES are completely acceptable. The poet uses *license* as a poet only when it is necessary to distort DICTION or grammar for the sake of form. Few POETS need to take advantage of such license, though, which has devolved to mean a license to be stupid or silly.

Poetical Miscellanies: Collections of lyric POETRY made during the RENAISSANCE. See MISCELLANIES, POETICAL.

Poetics: A system or body of theory concerning the nature of POETRY; the principles and rules of poetic composition. The term is used in two forms, *poetic* and *poetics,* with *poetics* the more common, both referring to the body of principles promulgated or exemplified by a poet or critic. The CLASSIC example, of course, is Aristotle's *Poetics,* and the first paragraph of that work indicates that it is Aristotle's purpose to treat of "poetry in itself and of its various kinds, noting the essential quality of each; to inquire into the structure of the plot as requisite to a good poem; into the number and nature of the parts of which a poem is composed; and similarly into whatever else falls within the same inquiry." The term is often used today as equivalent to "aesthetic principles" governing the nature of any literary form. Thus, critics sometimes speak of a "*poetics* of FICTION." In a large sense, justified by its supposed etymology, a *poetics* is the science of any activity that produces a product, whether a set of SONNETS or a set of dentures.

Poetry: A term applied to the many forms in which human beings have given rhythmic expression to their most imaginative and intense perceptions of the world, themselves, and the relation of the two. No literary historian presumes to point out the beginnings of *poetry,* though the first conscious literary expression probably took the form of primitive VERSE. Evidence comes from early tribal ceremonials; races without written literature employ poetic and rhythmic forms in their tribal ceremonies. The first *poetry* presumably was associated with music and the dance. When a people experienced any great event, a war, a migration, a flood, it seemed fitting to chronicle and preserve these episodes in dance and song.

Poetry deals with *emotions* as they are aroused by some scene, experience, attachment. It is often rich in sentiment and passion. *Poetry* is imaginative, a quality Shakespeare described in *A Midsummer Night's Dream:*

> As imagination bodies forth
> The forms of things unknown, the poet's pen
> Turns them to shapes and gives to airy nothing
> A local habitation and a name.
> Such tricks hath strong imagination,
> That, if it would but apprehend some joy,
> It comprehends some bringer of that joy.

Poetry has *significance;* it adds to our store of knowledge or experience. This is what Matthew Arnold meant when he wrote of it as a "criticism of life"; what Watts-Dunton meant when he called it an "artistic expression of the human mind." The existence of an idea, a significance, a meaning, an attitude, or a feeling distinguishes *poetry* from DOGGEREL. However, the fact that *poetry* is concerned with meaning does not make it didactic. Great DIDACTIC POETRY exists, but it is not great because it is didactic.

Another key to the content of *poetry* can be found in *beauty.* All poets will agree to this element although by no means will all agree as to what is beautiful. But beauty, of some sort or degree, must be present. If it is a new, strange beauty of some familiar object, so much the better. The POET, like the artist and the musician, differs from most other people because of a sensitivity to beauty, along with some capacity for objectively registering that sense. "Poetry," says Shelley, "turns all things to loveliness; it exalts the beauty of that which is most beautiful, and it adds beauty to that which is most deformed . . . strips the veil of familiarity from the world, and lays bare the naked and sleeping beauty, which is the spirit of its forms," an idea that Dylan Thomas expresses as the "movement from overclothed blindness to a naked vision." (This function of refreshing the senses by stripping away habits of familiarity has been the particular focus of FORMALISM.)

The first characteristic of *poetry*, from the standpoint of FORM, is the presence of RHYTHM. True, good PROSE has a more or less conscious RHYTHM, but the RHYTHM of *poetry* is marked by a degree of regularity far surpassing that of PROSE (see PROSE RHYTHM). In fact, one of the chief rewards of reading *poetry* is the satisfaction that comes from finding "variety in uniformity," a shifting of RHYTHMS that, nevertheless, constantly return to the basic pattern (see RHYTHM and METER). The ear recognizes the existence of recurring AC-CENTS at stated intervals and recognizes, too, variations from these RHYTHM patterns. Whatever the pattern, IAMBIC PENTAMETER, DACTYLLIC DIMETER, or any of the many possible combinations in any of the other rhythmic systems (see METER), there is, even in FREE VERSE, a recurrence more regular than in PROSE. Frequently RHYME affords an obvious difference by which one may distinguish *poetry* from PROSE. Another key is *arrangement, order*. The demands of the VERSE pattern—the combinations of RHYTHM and RHYME—often exact a "poetic" arrangement of the phrases and clauses. INVERSION is rather more justified in *poetry* than in PROSE; SYNCOPE is more common. The poet is granted a license (though modern poets hesitate to avail themselves thereof) in sequence and syntax that is denied the PROSE writer. Since most *poetry* is relatively short, it is likely to be characterized by compactness of thought and expression, and intense UNITY, and some careful arrangement in climactic order. A vital element of great *poetry* is its *concreteness*. *Poetry* insists on the specific, the concrete, and the bodily. The point may be made more obvious by citing Shakespeare:

> Our revels now are ended. These our actors,
> As I foretold you, were all spirits, and
> Are melted into air, into thin air:
> And, like the baseless fabric of this vision,
> The cloud-capp'd towers, the gorgeous palaces,
> The solemn temples, the great globe itself,
> Yea, all which it inherit, shall dissolve,
> And, like this insubstantial pageant faded,
> Leave not a rack behind. We are such stuff
> As dreams are made on; and our little life
> Is rounded with a sleep.

Here almost every LINE presents a concrete IMAGE. The lines are alive with specific language. In a passage on the IMAGINATION Shakespeare has written imaginatively. PROSE would express the idea simply and bluntly; it might, indeed, be content with the first five words of the passage.

The language of *poetry* may differ still further from that of PROSE. To Milton the language of *poetry* was "simple, sensuous, and impassioned." Since the function of *poetry* is to present IMAGES concretely, it is the responsibility of the poet to select language that succeeds in making those IMAGES concrete. The specific word, rich in connotative value and carrying implications of sound, color, and action—these are the special stock of the genuine POET. Modern *poetry* tends to dispense with the special vocabulary that was once thought of as the language of *poetry* (see POETIC DICTION). The language of the poet is rich in the FIGURE OF SPEECH, in METONOMY, SYNECDOCHE, and METAPHOR. No such device, however, necessarily distinguishes the language of *poetry* from any other language. *Poetry* is not fundamentally a kind of language or a kind of use of language. With *poetry*, the chief, the ultimate purpose is *to please*. The various senses of sight, sound, and color may be appealed to, the various emotions of love, fear, and appreciation of beauty may be called forth, but, whatever the immediate appeal, the ultimate effect of *poetry* is the giving of pleasure.

The art of poetic composition has undergone a long process of change. From its general, racial, collective interest it has become intensely individualistic; from the ceremonial recounting of tribal and group movements it has become the vehicle for DRAMA, history, and personal emotion. It is, however, still common today to classify *poetry* into three great type-divisions: the EPIC, the DRAMATIC, and the LYRIC. These three types are, in turn, broken into further classifications. Numerous set patterns such as the SONNET, the ODE, the ELEGY have evolved. Further subdivisions have been made on the basis of MOOD and purpose, such as the PASTORAL and DIDACTIC *poetry*. Most of these types and manners are discussed in their own entries in this *Handbook*.

[References: R. M. Alden, (ed.) *English Verse* (1903), and *Introduction to Poetry* (1909); Francis B. Gummere, *The Beginnings of Poetry* (1901); René Wellek and Austin Warren, *Theory of Literature*, 3rd ed. (1956).]

Point of Attack: A term, usually limited to DRAMA although applicable to all FICTION, that designates the moment in the work at which the main action of the PLOT begins. *Point of attack* may, but does not necessarily, coincide with the actual beginning of the STORY being told. It can come just before the CATASTROPHE, with the antecedent events and situations being presented through various kinds of EXPOSITION as the PLOT advances to its inevitable conclusion.

Point of View: A term used in the ANALYSIS and CRITICISM of FICTION to describe the way in which the reader is presented with the materials of the STORY or, regarded from another angle, the vantage point from which the author presents the ACTIONS of the STORY. If the author serves as a seemingly all-knowing maker, not restricted to time, place, or character, and free to move and to comment at will, the *point of view* is usually called OMNISCIENT. (This use is somewhat exaggerated, since "OMNISCIENT" means "all-knowing.") At the other extreme, a CHARACTER within the STORY—major, minor, or marginal—may tell the story as he or she experienced, saw, heard, and understood it. Such a character is usually called a first-person NARRATOR; if the character does not comprehend the implications of what he or she is telling, the character is called a NAIVE NARRATOR. The author may tell the story in the third person and yet present it as it is seen and understood by a single character—major, minor, or marginal—restricting information to what that character sees, hears, feels, and thinks; such a *point of view* is said to be limited to one character. The author may employ such a *point of view* and restrict the presentation to the interior responses of the *point of view* character, resulting in the INTERIOR MONOLOGUE. The author may present material by a process of narrative EXPOSITION, in which actions and conversations are presented in summary rather than in detail; such a method is usually called PANORAMIC. On the other hand, the author may present actions and conversations in detail, as they occur, and more or less objectively—without authorial comment; such a method is usually called SCENIC. If the SCENIC METHOD is carried to the point where the author never speaks in his or her own person and does not ostensibly intrude into the scenes presented, the author is said to be SELF-EFFACING. In extended works of FICTION authors frequently employ several of these methods. The concern with *point of view* in current CRITICISM and the experimentation with *point of view* by many current novelists are both very great. Since the flourishing of Joseph Conrad and Henry James, both of whom wrote technique-centered prefaces, *point of view* has often been considered the technical aspect of FICTION that leads the critic most readily into the problems and the meanings of a NOVEL or a SHORT STORY. Since about the middle of the nineteenth century, a particular sort of NOVEL, defined by its artistic management of *point of view*, has become a favorite: a charismatic but mysterious HERO (Heathcliff, Ahab, Holmes, Kurtz, Gatsby, Leverkühn, McMurphy, Seymour Glass, and so forth) is presented by a bureaucratic but attractive NARRATOR (Lockwood, Ishmael, Watson, Marlow, Carraway, Zeitblom, Bromden, Buddy Glass, and so forth). See NARRATOR and PANORAMIC METHOD.

[Reference: Wayne Booth, *The Rhetoric of Fiction*, 2nd ed. (1983).]

Point of View Shot: In a FILM a shot that shows a SCENE as viewed by a CHARACTER. The TECHNIQUE is also called SUBJECTIVE CAMERA.

Polemic: A vigorously argumentative work, setting forth its author's attitudes on a highly controversial subject, usually on religion, social issues, economics, or politics. John Milton's *Areopagitica* is the best-known English example. *The American Crisis*, by Thomas Paine, is a series of American *polemics.*

Political Novel: A NOVEL that deals directly with significant aspects of political life and in which those aspects are essential ingredients of the work and not merely background material or secondary concerns. Works like Henry Adams's *Democracy*, Joyce Cary's *Chester Nimmo* trilogy, C. P. Snow's *Strangers and Brothers* series, and John Dos Passos' *District of Columbia* trilogy are *political novels.*

Polyhyphenation: The use of more than a usual number of hyphens. The simple-seeming hyphen is oddly versatile: it can make one word out of two or more, and two or more out of one. An example of *polyhyphenation* is the COINAGE "dapple-dawn-drawn" in Hopkins's "The Windover."

Polyptoton: The REPETITION in close proximity of words that have the same roots. *Polyptoton* may involve the use of the same word but in a different grammatical case; more commonly there is a basic difference in the words, although they share common roots. Shakespeare gives three examples in two LINES of *Troilus and Cressida* (I, i):

> The Greeks are strong and skilful in their strength,
> Fierce to their skill, and to their fierceness valiant.

Polyptoton is present in "strong-strength," "skilful-skill," and "fierce-fierceness." See PLOCE.

Polysyndeton: A form of PARATAXIS in which sentences, clauses, phrases, or words in coordinate constructions are linked by coordinate conjunctions. Milton's Satan, for example:

> . . . pursues his way,
> And swims, or sinks, or wades, or creeps, or flies.

The opposite of *polysyndeton* is ASYNDETON. See PARATAXIS.

Popular Ballad: A traditional BALLAD of unknown authorship and transmitted orally. See BALLAD.

Popular Culture: The phenomenon of what people really but unofficially do and say to amuse and cultivate themselves; also the academic study thereof. Presumably, once it becomes the subject of objective classification and analysis, a piece of slang or music loses much of its vitality. Even so, *popular culture* has emerged since about 1960 as a serious and legitimate precinct of aesthetic and anthropological study. (For instance, one can perceive the persistence and metamorphosis of certain figures or MOTIVES from Shakespeare's *The Tempest* in the television series "Fantasy Island" and elsewhere.) In many respects *popular culture* is similar to FOLKLORE.

Pornography: Writing designed specifically to arouse sexual lust, either normal or perverted. To such a definition is usually added: "and without major serious or aesthetic intention." Clearly the issue is highly subjective and varies greatly from individual to individual, and it varies even more from one age or nation to another. *Pornography* is of two principal kinds: that dealing with the physical aspects of what passes in a given culture as "normal" love, called "erotica"; and that dealing with abnormal or deviant sexual practices, called "exotica," of which the works of the Marquis de Sade are major examples. There have been pornographic elements in the literatures of every age and every language; for example, Aristophanes's *Lysistrata*, the *Satyricon* of Petronius, or Boccaccio's *Decameron;* but the first masterpiece of English *pornography* was John Cleland's *Memoirs of a Woman of Pleasure; or, the Life of Fanny Hill* (1749). The nineteenth and twentieth centuries have seen many ostensibly pornographic books and magazines, some of which, though initially banned, have come to be recognized as literary masterpieces. Notable among such works are James Joyce's *Ulysses* (1922), D. H. Lawrence's *Lady Chatterley's Lover* (1928), Henry Miller's *Tropic of Cancer* (1934) and *Tropic of Capricorn* (1939), and Nabokov's *Lolita* (1955). In addition to being a moral and aesthetic issue for the individual, *pornography* is also a legal issue for the state. The most important of the American legal decisions was made by Judge John Woolsey in 1933, which lifted the ban on *Ulysses.* It rested on a view of the book as a whole, on the author's intention, and on the reaction of a normal reader. One workable definition of *pornography* is: that which deals explicitly with sex in a way that society at that time judges to be prurient in intention, without major redeeming elements, and commercially or morbidly motivated. Recently, some have tried to discriminate between so-called hard-core and soft-core *pornography*, the former having no art or redeeming purpose whatever; but the distinction seems to have little critical and no legal validity. We seem doomed to have to cope with inconsistent standards inconsistently applied: one set of rules (loose) for BOOKS, another (middling) for FILM, yet another (strict) for radio and television.

Portmanteau Words: Words concocted by accident or for deliberate effect by telescoping two words into one, as the making of "squarson" (attributed to Bishop Wilberforce) from "squire" and "parson," "smog" from "smoke" and "fog," "motel" from "motor car" and "hotel," "brunch" from "breakfast" and "lunch," and "meld" from "melt" and "weld." More recent examples are Paul Harvey's "palimony" and "Reagonomics" and Kenneth Tynan's "blandiose." *"Portmanteau words"* was a name given by Lewis Carroll to this type of fabrication, which he used in *Through the Looking Glass.* An example occurs in his famous "Jabberwocky" POEM where, for instance, he made "slithy" of "lithe" and "slimy." In his "Preface" to *The Hunting of the Snark* Carroll explained the system by which such words were made: "For instance, take the two words 'fuming' and 'furious.' Make up your mind that you will say both words, but leave it unsettled which you will say first. Now open your mouth and speak. If your thoughts incline ever so little towards 'fuming' you will say 'fuming-furious'; if they turn by even a hair's breadth toward 'furious,' you will say 'furious-fuming'; but if you have that rarest of gifts, a perfectly balanced mind, you will say 'frumious.' " James Joyce in *Ulysses* and particularly in *Finnegans Wake* employs many *portmanteau words.*

Positivism: A philosophy that denies validity to speculation or metaphysical questions, maintaining that the proper goal of knowledge is the description and not the explanation of experienced phenomena. Although its history stretches back as far as Berkeley and Hume, the doctrine, as it was developed in the nineteenth century, was formulated by Auguste Comte, who coined the term *positivism.* In the twentieth century *positivism* has developed into LOGICAL POSITIVISM, a form of scientific empiricism, that introduced the methods of mathematics and experimental science into philosophy. It regards philosophy, as the nineteenth-century positivists had, as analytical rather than speculative, as an activity not a theory. LOGICAL POSITIVISM developed in Vienna in the first quarter of the twentieth century. The leader in its articulation was Wittgenstein, who defined the object of *positivism* to be the logical clarification of thought. *Positivism* has permeated much of twentieth-century hought, and, although its influence on literature and CRITICISM is indirect, it has been widely pervasive and powerful. Given the great differences among Berkeley, Hume, Comte, and Wittgenstein, it is virtually impossible to apply the term *"positivism"* with anything like useful precision. See LOGICAL POSITIVISM.

[References: R. L. Hawkins, *Positivism in the United States (1853–1861)* (1938); Walter M. Simon, *European Positivism in the Nineteenth Century* (1963).]

Post-Modern: Early in the century the Roman Catholic church condemned a good many doctrines and practices, ancient *and* modern, under the capacious umbrella of "modernism," and right away, as early as 1914, in spite of the strong appearance of nonsense in the term, theologians began speaking of "Post-Modernism" by careless analogy with "Post-Impressionism" and other such concoctions. *"Post-modern"* has been applied to much contemporary writing, particularly with reference to the use of experimental forms. The fundamental philosophical assumptions of modernism, its tendency toward historical discontinuity, alienation, asocial individualism, solipsism, and EXISTENTIALISM (see MODERN) continue to permeate contemporary writing, perhaps in a heightened sense. But the tendencies of the modernist to construct intricate FORMS, to interweave SYMBOLS elaborately, to create works of art that, however much they oppose some established present order, create within themselves an ordered universe, have given way since the 1960s to a denial of order, to the presentation of highly fragmented universes in the created world of art, and to critical theories that are forms of PHENOMENOLOGY. Myth has given way to experiencing aesthetic surfaces. Traditional FORMS, such as the NOVEL, have given way to denials of those forms, such as the ANTI-NOVEL. The typical PROTAGONIST has become not a HERO but an ANTI-HERO. Writers like Robbe-Grillet, Pynchon, Barthelme, and Pinter are called *post-modern* in that they carry modernist assumptions about the world into the very realm of art itself.

[References: Donald Allen and George F. Butterick, eds., *The Postmoderns: The New American Poetry Revised* (1982); Ihab Hassan, *The Dismemberment of Orpheus: Toward a Postmodern Literature,* 2nd ed. (1982); Jean François Lyotard, *The Postmodern Condition* (tr. 1984); Jerome Mazzaro, *Postmodern American Poetry* (1980); Martin Pops, *Home Remedies* (1984); Manfred Putz and Peter Freese, eds., *Postmodernism in American Literature: A Critical Anthology* (1984).]

Post-Modernist Period in English Literature (1965–): Little changed during the 1960s in the national life of England; what had been characteristic in the 1950s continued and was accentuated. The Empire continued to shrink to an island kingdom. Struggles in Ireland between Catholics and Protestants intensified and demanded more and more of the attention of the English. Inflation continued to function as a great equalizer of classes. Extensive strikes often almost paralyzed the country. A kind of spiritual malaise seemed to envelop many of the English people, a malaise sharply defined by Margaret Drabble in her novel *The Ice Age* (1977).

In literature it was a time of continuance and completion. Graham Greene, Kingsley Amis, and Lawrence Durrell continued to produce work typical of their younger days. Doris Lessing completed the *Children of Violence* series of NOVELS. C. P. Snow brought his ambitious *Strangers and Brothers* series to a conclusion, and Anthony Powell completed his series *A Dance to the Music of Time.* The most challenging new novelistic talents were John Fowles and Margaret Drabble, both serious although very different experimenters in form. The death of Cecil Day Lewis in 1972 vacated the poet laureateship, which was filled by Sir John Betjeman. When Betjeman died in 1984, Ted Hughes took his place. Of the newer playwrights, John Osborne, Harold Pinter, and Tom Stoppard showed the most vitality and talent.

As England entered the last quarter of the twentieth century, it seemed to be groping for position and definition in a diminished world, both of social and political reality and of art. See *Outline of Literary History.*

Posy (Posie): Sometimes used in the sense of "a collection of flowers" to indicate an ANTHOLOGY. The term also signifies a motto, usually in VERSE, inscribed on a ring. When the "mouse-trap" PLAY begins and the PROLOGUE has been spoken, Hamlet asks Ophelia: "Is this a prologue, or the posy of a ring?"

Potboiler: A SLANG term given to a book or an article written solely for the income derived from it. It is writing that will "keep the author's pot boiling" and thus supply sustenance, it is hoped, for work more worthy.

Poulter's Measure: A metrical pattern, now rarely used, consisting of a COUPLET composed of a first LINE in IAMBIC HEXAMETER and a second line in IAMBIC HEPTAMETER. It seems to be an adaptation of SHORT MEASURE, a QUATRAIN of TRIMETER, TRIMETER, TETRAMETER, TRIMETER rhyming *abab* (as in the hymn "Blest Be the Tie That Binds"). *Poulter's measure* reduces the four lines to two and eliminates one of the RHYMES. The term is said to have originated from a custom of the London poulters of giving customers twelve eggs in their first dozen and fourteen in the second (presumably, like a "baker's dozen" of thirteen, to make up for breakage). Wyatt and Surrey, Sidney, Nicholas Grimald, Barnabe Googe, and Arthur Brooke are some of the poets who have used this form. The opening lines of Brooke's *Romeus and Juliet* afford an example of *poulter's measure:*

> There is beyond the Alps, a town of ancient fame,
> Whose bright renown yet shineth clear, Verona men it name;
> Built in a happy time, built on a fertile soil,
> Maintained by the heavenly fates, and by the townish toil.

After enjoying something of a vogue around 1575, when it was one of the most popular verse FORMS in England, *poulter's measure* faded out, although faint lineaments may survive in SHORT MEASURE (especially if it rhymes *abcd*) and even in the LIMERICK, which has the same basic METER although a different RHYTHM and RHYME SCHEME.

Practical Criticism: CRITICISM in which the CRITIC'S principles of art and aesthetic beliefs are applied to specific works of art; often called "applied criticism," the term is used in opposition to THEORETICAL CRITICISM, in which general principles and broad tenets are sought. See CRITICISM, TYPES OF.

Pragmatic Theory of Art: A theory of art, according to M. H. Abrams, in which the CRITIC'S major interest is in the effect that the art object produces in its audience. See CRITICISM.

Pragmatism: A term, first used by C. S. Peirce in 1878, describing a philosophical doctrine that determines value and meaning through the test of consequences or utility. (Eventually, believing that the force of his original coinage had been drained by overuse and misuse, Peirce took to saying "pragmaticism" instead.) Its principal exponents have been William James and John Dewey, through whose work and influence it has made itself pervasively felt in America. The pragmatist insists that no questions are significant unless the results of answering them in one way rather than another have practical consequences. In William James's words: "The 'whole meaning' of a conception expresses itself in practical consequences, consequences either in the shape of conduct to be recommended, or in that of experience to be expected, if the conception be true." John Dewey and his followers emphasized the implications of *pragmatism* on logical processes, insisting that logical thinking must be subordinate to practical life and that thought aims not at abstract truth but at satisfying some practical end that life demands. The world of the pragmatists is pluralistic, attentive to context, relativistic in its beliefs about truth and value systems, devoid of metaphysical concerns except as they have practical consequences. On the other hand, it places a high premium on conduct and ethical concerns. In literature *pragmatism* found its most vigorous expression in the REALISM that developed in America after 1870. (Henry James, who was a friend of Peirce's when both were young, once drolly claimed to have been "unconsciously pragmatizing" all along.)

Preamble: An introductory portion of a written document. In formal sets of "resolutions" there is usually a *preamble* setting forth the occasion for the resolutions. This *preamble* is introduced by one or more statements beginning with "Whereas" and is followed by the resolutions proper, each article of which is introduced by the word "Therefore."

Preciosity: A critical term sometimes applied to writing that is consciously "pretty," labored or affected in STYLE, fastidious in DICTION, overrefined in manner. See DANDYISM.

Précis: An ABSTRACT or EPITOME of the essential facts or statements of a work, retaining the order of the original.

Predestination: The belief that God or fate has foreordained all things. See CALVINISM and FATALISM.

Preface: A short introductory statement printed at the beginning of a book or article—and separate from it—in which the author states the purpose of the work, makes necessary acknowledgments of assistance, points out difficulties and uncertainties in connection with the writing of the book, and, in general, informs the reader of such facts as the author thinks pertinent. Some writers, notably Dryden, Shaw, and Henry James, have written *prefaces* that are really extended ESSAYS.

Prelude: A short POEM, introductory in character, prefixed to a long poem or to a section of a long poem. Lowell's *The Vision of Sir Launfal* contains *preludes* of the latter sort. Rarely, as in the case of Wordsworth's famous *Prelude*, a poem so entitled may itself be lengthy, although Wordsworth's *Prelude* was written as an introduction to a much longer but incomplete work. (*The Prelude* is the title given to the POEM by Wordsworth's wife after his death.) Some so-called *preludes*, such as some early poems by Eliot and Aiken, are not *preludes* to anything, strictly speaking, but may capture something of the spirit of similarly nonprelusive *preludes* in the music of Chopin and Debussy.

Pre-Raphaelitism: The Pre-Raphaelite movement began with the establishment in 1848 of the Pre-Raphaelite brotherhood by Dante Gabriel Rossetti, Holman Hunt, John Everett Millais, and others as a protest against the conventional methods of painting then prevalent. The Pre-Raphaelites wished to regain the spirit of simple devotion and adherence to NATURE that they found in Italian religious art before Raphael. (Although Raphael's particular responsibility for any radical change is unclear—the point seems to be rather to suggest a time, before 1500 or so, rather than a practice.) Ruskin asserted that *Pre-Raphaelitism* had but one principle, that of absolute uncompromising truth in all that it did, truth attained by elaborating everything, down to the most minute detail, from NATURE and from nature only. This meant the rejection of all CONVENTIONS designed to heighten effects artificially. Several of the group were both painters and POETS, and the effect of the cult was felt in English literature. Rossetti's "Blessed Damozel," printed in 1850 in one of the four issues of *The Germ,* the organ of the group, is a NARRATIVE POEM with pictorial qualities. Characteristics of Pre-Raphaelite POETRY are: pictorial elements, SYMBOLISM, sensuousness, a tendency to metrical experimentation, attention to minute detail, and an interest in the medieval and the supernatural. Certain critics, who deemed sensuousness the dominant characteristic of their poetry, called the Pre- Raphaelites the "FLESHLY SCHOOL." The chief literary products of the movement were Rossetti's translation of Dante, SONNETS, and BALLAD-like VERSE; Christina Rossetti's LYRICS; and the poems of William Morris, such as "The Earthly Paradise" and "The Defense of Guinevere." Morris's practical application of medieval craftsmanship to business effected a change in taste in home decoration.

[References: P. H. Bate, *The English Pre-Raphaelite Painters* (1901); W. E. Fredeman, *Pre-Raphaelitism: A Bibliocritical Study* (1965); Lionel Stevenson, *The Pre-Raphaelite Poets* (1972).]

Primitivism: The doctrine that supposedly primitive peoples, because they had remained closer to NATURE and had been less subject to the influences of society, were nobler and more nearly perfect than civilized peoples. The idea flourished in eighteenth-century England and France and was an important element in the creed of the "sentimentalists" of the ROMANTIC MOVEMENT. Though it is impossible to trace all the steps in the development of the primitivistic doctrine, a few may be suggested. The rationalistic philosopher, the third Earl of Shaftesbury (*fl. ca.* 1710), in his effort to show that God had revealed himself completely in NATURE—and that NATURE was therefore perfect—reasoned that primitive peoples were close to God and therefore essentially moral. Human beings are by nature prone to do good: their evil comes from self-imposed limitations of their freedom. Romantic accounts of savage peoples by writers of travel literature added impetus to the movement, as did the fanciful researches into an origin of language by such men as Lord Monboddo (*The Origin and Progress of Language,* 1773–1792), and the effort of various scholars to find the reason for Homer's greatness in his assumed primitive surroundings. The movement was given great impetus from France by the writings of Rousseau, particularly his belief that human beings were potentially perfect and that their faults were due to the vicious effect of conventional society, which tended progressively to restrict freedom and lessen moral goodness.

One aspect of *primitivism* significant in English literature was its doctrine that the best POETRY should be natural or instinctive, which resulted in a search for a perfect "untutored" POET. Among the many savages brought by the primitivists to England in their search for the perfect natural human being, the enthusiasts searched for evidence of poetic genius. The "inspired peasant" was sought for, too, among the unlettered population of Great Britain, and many were feted by high society till their fame wore out: Henry Jones, the poetical bricklayer; Stephen Duck, the "thresher-poet"; James Woodhouse, the poetical shoemaker, and Ann Yearsley, the poetical milk-woman of Bristol, who signed her poems "Lactilla" and was sponsored by the BLUESTOCKINGS. Gray's *The Bard* (1757) and James Beattie's *The Minstrel* (1771–1774) reflect such a doctrine of primitive genius. For a time the forged "Ossian" poems of James Macpherson (see LITERARY FORGERIES) seemed an answer to the romantic prayer for the discovery in Britain of a primitive EPIC poem. When Robert Burns appeared, the search for the peasant poet seemed over, and the Scottish bard was received with enthusiasm.

All England did not go primitivistic. The movement was attacked by such conservatives as Doctor Johnson and Edmund Burke. The "NOBLE SAVAGE" idea produced the idealized American Indian, as in Cooper's NOVELS, and American life was exploited as ideal because it was primitive, as in Crèvecoeur's *Letters from an American Farmer* and Gilbert Imlay's novel of pioneer life, *The Emigrants.* Elements of *primitivism,* related to the idea of natural goodness, appear throughout American writing in the nineteenth century.

A common and useful distinction is made between CULTURAL PRIMITIVISM and CHRONOLOGICAL PRIMITIVISM, CULTURAL being used for the *primitivism* that prefers the natural to the man-made, the uninhibited to the controlled, the simple and primitive to that on which people have worked, NATURE to art; and CHRONOLOGICAL being used for the *primitivism* that looks backward to a "Golden Age" and sees our present sad state as the product of what culture and society have done to them. If this distinction is made—and it should be recognized that the terms are not mutually exclusive—it becomes apparent that many of the political doctrines of the American founding fathers were influenced by CHRONOLOGICAL PRIMITIVISM, while CULTURAL PRIMITIV-ISM has been a powerful, although silent, force in American REALISM. Any number of nineteenth-century intellectual movements—the Grimms' FOLK-LORE and PHILOLOGY, Darwin's developmental-historical biology, Freud's psychoanalysis (stimulated in part by Darwin's *The Descent of Man*), medievalism, scientific ethnography and anthropology—contributed to the flourishing of manifestations of PRIMITIVISM in the arts, from Longfellow's *The Song of Hiawatha* to Wagner's OPERAS. Frazer's monumental *The Golden Bough* stimulated interest in MYTH and FOLKLORE, so that what seemed to be experimental, sophisticated art in the vanguard of human enterprise turned out to receive a sanction of antiquity and primordiality from the pervasive spirit of *primitivism.* Many influential artists born during the 1880s—Pablo Picasso, James Joyce, Igor Stravinsky, D. H. Lawrence, T. S. Eliot—moved forward technically while (and by) moving backward culturally. Few movements or general sentiments can match the decisive importance of *primitivism* in twentieth-century art and thought.

[References: H. N. Fairchild, *The Noble Savage* (1928, reprinted 1961); A. O. Lovejoy, *Essays in the History of Ideas* (1944); C. B. Tinker, *Nature's*

Simple Plan (1922, reprinted 1964); Lois Whitney, *Primitivism and the Idea of Progress* (1934, reprinted 1965).]

Printing: A *printing* is the copies of a book or other publication printed at the same time; interchangeable with IMPRESSION. See EDITION.

Printing, Introduction into American Colonies: Although the Spaniards had brought printing presses to Mexico and elsewhere much earlier, the real beginning of printing in America dates from 1639, when, according to Governor Winthrop's *Diary,* a printing house was begun by Stephen Daye. Actually Daye was the printer, not the proprietor. The first document printed was *The Freeman's Oath,* the next an ALMANAC, and the third the famous *Bay Psalm Book* (1640), the earliest surviving American book. William Bradford was printing in Philadelphia as early as 1683. Later he moved to New York and became the government printer. The introduction of printing into Virginia was opposed by Governor Berkeley, and a printing establishment was suppressed in 1682, though printing was reintroduced not long thereafter.

Printing, Introduction into England: The circumstances of the invention and development of printing in Western Europe (the Chinese and Japanese had practiced a simple form of printing centuries before) are so obscure that it is impossible to assign the invention to any country, person, or exact date. Although there seems to have been some sort of forerunner of the printed book in Holland, it is fairly certain that the most important development of the art took place in Mainz, Germany, during the 1440s and 1450s. The earliest existing book that can be dated is an "Indulgence" (Mainz, 1454); the most famous existing early book is the so-called Gutenberg Bible (Mainz, 1456). On the authority of fifteenth-century writers, John Gutenberg of Mainz is commonly given credit for the invention.

From Mainz the art spread to Italy, France, Holland, and other countries, reaching England in 1476, when William Caxton set up his famous press at Westminster. Caxton had learned printing on the Continent, and at Bruges, probably in 1475, had brought out the first book printed in English, the *Recuyell of the Historyes of Troye.* The first printed books in England were probably PAMPHLETS, some of them in Latin, but the first dated English book printed in England was Caxton's *Dicts or Sayings of the Philosophers* (1477). Before his death Caxton had printed about a hundred separate books. He did much to direct the public taste in reading. He specialized in TRANSLATIONS, POETRY, and ROMANCES, two of his most important books being his edition of Chaucer's *Canterbury Tales* (1483) and his publication of Malory's *Le Morte Darthur* (1485). Other early presses in England include one at Oxford (1478) and one at St. Albans (1479), both devoted chiefly to learned works. Caxton himself was succeeded by his assistant, Wynkyn de Worde, a printer without literary talent but important because he published, during his long career, about 800 books, some of them of literary interest. An important contemporary printer was Richard Pynson (*fl.* 1490–1530).

[References: H. G. Aldis, *The Printed Book,* 3rd ed. (1951); W. Blades, *The Biography and Typography of William Caxton* (1877, reprinted 1971); T. L. de Vinne, *The Invention of Printing* (1876, reprinted 1969); D. C. Murtrie, *The Invention of Printing: A Bibliography* (1962); J. C. Oswald, *History of*

Printing (1928); H. R. Plomer, *A Short History of English Printing,* 2nd ed. (1915); C. J. Sawyer, *English Books, 1475–1900* (1927).]

Private Theaters: The term *private theater* came along about 1596, when the Blackfriars theater was so described by its sponsors, who were seeking privileges not granted to the PUBLIC THEATERS. The *private theaters,* though they charged a higher admission fee and attracted in general a higher class of spectators than did their "public" rivals, were open to all classes. They differed from the PUBLIC THEATERS in being indoor institutions, artificially lighted, smaller, and typically rectangular. In origin, they were connected with companies of child actors and continued to be used chiefly, but not exclusively, by such companies. These companies performed at various times at the Blackfriars, St. Paul's, the Inns of Court, and the Court. Shakespeare's company in the early seventeenth century controlled both the Blackfriars, the chief *private theater,* and the Globe, the chief PUBLIC THEATER. The *private theaters,* being indoor institutions of a somewhat aristocratic character, gained importance in the seventeenth century, when the Court was fostering elaborate exhibitions (see MASQUE) and encouraging DRAMA with spectacular features, and it is from them rather than from the PUBLIC THEATERS that the playhouses of the RESTORATION and later times directly descended. See PUBLIC THEATERS.

Problem Novel: The type of PROSE FICTION that derives its chief interest from working out, through CHARACTERS and INCIDENTS, some central problem. In a loose sense almost every NOVEL or PLOT presents a problem, since the opposition of forces making for PLOT and CONFLICT also should arouse some interest in the reader as to "how this is to turn out." However, the term is usually more restricted. It is sometimes carelessly applied to those novels written for deliberate purpose, a thesis, which are better called PROPAGANDA NOVELS, since they present a brief for or against one class of people, one type of living, one activity of civilization. Since human character is the subject matter surest to interest readers and since humankind is constantly confronted by the problems of life and conduct, it follows that the *problem novel*—when it is thought of as a STORY *with* a purpose rather than *for* a purpose—is fairly common. The REALISTIC NOVEL, centered as it is in social SETTING, has often employed social issues as the cruxes of its PLOTS. This matter of illustrating a problem by showing people confronted thereby is at the core of the *problem novel.* See PROPAGANDA NOVEL.

Problem Play: Like the PROBLEM NOVEL, its ANALOGUE in nondramatic FICTION, this term is used both in a broad sense to cover all serious DRAMA in which problems of human life are presented as such, for example, Shakespeare's *King Lear,* and in a more specialized sense to designate the modern "drama of ideas," as exemplified in the PLAYS of Ibsen, Shaw, Galsworthy, and many others. It is most commonly used in the latter sense, and here it means the representation in dramatic form of a general social problem or issue, shown as it is confronted by the PROTAGONIST. Any PLAY can be construed as a *problem play,* but none deserves the name unless the problem as such upstages and eclipses all other elements.

[References: Ramsden Balmforth, *The Problem-Play and Its Influence on Modern Thought* (1928); T. H. Dickinson, *An Outline of Contemporary Drama*

(1927, reprinted 1969); W. W. Lawrence, *Shakespeare's Problem Comedies* (1931, reprinted 1969).]

Proem: A brief introduction; a PREFACE or PREAMBLE.

Profile: An ESSAY that combines a biographical sketch and a character study of a contemporary figure. The type of ESSAY and the term *profile* come from the *New Yorker* magazine, which has been publishing such sketches and has called them *"Profiles"* for many years.

Progress: The belief that some human history shows some pattern of improvement is called "the idea of *progress.*" In some cases this idea is almost made into a system under which *progress*—that is, the improvement of human and social conditions—is inevitable with the passage of time. In its naive statements it can be a childishly optimistic doctrine. When held by serious and thoughtful people, as it often has been, the idea of *progress* is a strong antidote to the doctrine of CHRONOLOGICAL PRIMITIVISM. It has been said that American ROMANTICISM in the nineteenth century rested on the doctrine of natural goodness (CULTURAL PRIMITIVISM) and the idea of *progress.* See PRIMITIVISM.

Projective Verse: A kind of FREE VERSE, which regards METER and FORM as artificial, and in which the poet "projects" a voice primarily through the content and the propulsive quality of breathing, which alone determines the LINE. *Projective verse* is also called "breath verse" because of this primary role of breathing in determining the line structure. The projectivists passionately deny that FORM creates meaning and are actively in revolt against all formalist doctrines, including those of the New Critics. Charles Olson was the chief theoretician of the projectivists. Since Robert Duncan and Robert Creeley, along with Olson, were teaching at Black Mountain College when they developed the concept of *projective verse,* the movement is also sometimes called "The BLACK MOUNTAIN SCHOOL." The influence of "projectivism" reached back to William Carlos Williams and forward to a large number of POETS born after 1920, including Denise Levertov, Ed Dorn, and Imamu Amiri Baraka.

[References: Paul Christensen, *Charles Olson: Call Him Ishmael* (1979); Charles Olson, *Projective Verse* (1959); Sherman Paul, *Olson's Push* (1978).]

Prolegomenon: A formal FOREWORD or PREFACE. The heading *prolegomena* (the plural form) may be given to the introductory section of a book containing observations. Occasionally a whole book will be called *"prolegomenon"* or (the plural) *"prolegomena,"* suggesting a sustained study or set of studies somehow preliminary to further work, as in Jane Harrison's *Prolegomena to the Study of Greek Religion.*

Prolepsis: An anticipating; the type of ANACHRONISM in which an event is pictured as taking place before it could have done so, the treating of a future event as if past. Rhetorically, the word may be applied to a preliminary statement or summary that is to be followed by a detailed treatment. In ARGUMENTATION *prolepsis* may mean the device of anticipating and answering an opponent's argument before the opponent has an opportunity to introduce it, thus detracting from its effectiveness if later employed. In *The White Goddess* Robert Graves applies *prolepsis* to trances in which one is given a glimpse of the future.

Prologue: A PREFACE or INTRODUCTION most frequently associated with DRAMA and especially common in England in the PLAYS of the RESTORATION and the eighteenth century. In the plays of ancient Greece a speaker announced, before the beginning of the play proper, such salient facts as the audience should know to understand the PLAY itself. In Latin DRAMA the same custom prevailed, Plautus having left some of the most sophisticated *prologues* in dramatic literature. European dramatists in France and England followed the CLASSICAL tradition, from the time of the MIRACLE and MYSTERY PLAYS (which may be said to have used *prologues* of a "moral" nature) well into modern times. *Prologues* were frequently written by the author of a PLAY and delivered by one of the chief actors; in the eighteenth century, however, it was common practice for writers of established reputations, such as Pope, Doctor Johnson, and Garrick, to write *prologues* for plays by their friends and acquaintances. Sometimes, as in the play within the play in *Hamlet,* the actor who spoke the *prologue* was himself called "the *prologue.*" The first part of Shakespeare's *King Henry the Fourth* opens with an explanatory speech, not formally a *prologue,* which serves the function of a real *prologue.* Part two of the same play opens with a *prologue* called an INDUCTION. See INDUCTION and EPILOGUE.

Prolusion: One of many words meaning a piece of writing preliminary to the main body of a work; also a preliminary exercise, as in those of Milton's called "Oratorical Performances (Prolusions)" (or *Prolusiones*).

Propaganda Novel: A NOVEL dealing with a special social, political, economic, or moral issue or problem and strongly advocating a doctrinaire solution. If the propagandistic purpose dominates the work so as to dwarf or eclipse all other elements, such as PLOT and CHARACTER, then the NOVEL belongs to the realm of the DIDACTIC and probably cannot be understood or appreciated for its own sake as a work of art. It may be good propaganda and bad literature at the same time. See PROBLEM NOVEL.

Proparalepsis: The addition of a syllable to the end of a word, as in "dampen" from "damp."

Propriety: In the general sense, conformity to accepted standards of taste or conduct. The term is used in literary CRITICISM in the special sense of correspondence to the demands of the situation within the particular work of art, as in DRAMATIC PROPRIETY.

Proscenium: The term now designates that part of the stage in a modern theater that lies between the orchestra and the curtain. In the ancient theater the *proscenium* extended from the orchestra to the background, and the term is sometimes used, even nowadays, merely as a SYNONYM for the stage itself. The arch over the front of the stage from which the CURTAIN hangs and which, together with the CURTAIN, separates the stage from the audience is called the *proscenium* arch. In a BOX SET it forms the FOURTH WALL of the stage-as-room.

Prose: In its broadest sense the term is applied to all forms of written or spoken expression not having a regular rhythmic pattern (see METER). *Prose* is most often meant to designate a conscious, cultivated writing, not merely a bringing together of vocabularies, a listing of ideas, or a catalog of objects. And, while *prose* is like VERSE in that good *prose* has a RHYTHM, it is unlike VERSE in that this RHYTHM is not to be scanned by normal metrical schemes or marked by such devices of reiteration as FREE VERSE exploits. But a clear line between *prose* and POETRY is difficult to draw. Some of the qualities of *prose* are: (1) it is without sustained rhythmic regularity; (2) it has some logical, grammatical order, and its ideas are connectedly stated rather than merely listed; (3) it is characterized by STYLE, though the style will vary from writer to writer; (4) it will achieve variety of expression through DICTION and through sentence structure.

Prose in all literatures has developed more slowly than VERSE. English *prose* is usually said to find its beginnings in the work of Alfred, whose *Handbook* (887) is sometimes cited as the earliest specimen of finished English *prose*. Other names significant in the development of English *prose* are Thomas Usk, John Wycliffe, Malory, Caxton, Roger Ascham, Holinshed, Lyly, Ralegh, Donne, Jeremy Taylor, Milton, Dryden, Addison, Mark Twain, and Hemingway. For many centuries English *prose* had to compete with Latin for recognition, and for many more years Latin forms and syntax shaped its STYLE. The single book that did most to mold present English *prose* style was the King James version of the BIBLE.

[References: Robert Adolphe, *The Rise of Modern Prose Style* (1968); G. P. Krapp, *Modern English* (1909, reprinted 1966), and *The Rise of English Literary Prose* (1915, reprinted 1963); George Williamson, *The Senecan Amble: A Study in Prose Form from Bacon to Collier* (1951).]

Prose Poem: A POEM printed as PROSE, with a justified right margin. Largely a modern phenomenon, the *prose poem* can be found in the works of Baudelaire, Rimbaud, and Valéry in France and, derivatively, in Eliot's "Hysteria" (around 1915). Despite some doubts about the possibility of such a hyphenated transgeneric form, the *prose poem* has persisted; John Ashbery's *Three Poems* is a whole book consisting of three long pieces of PROSE. The point seems to be that a writing in prose, even the most prosaic, is a POEM if the author says so. Mark Harris has argued, polemically if not rationally, that neither the *prose poem* nor the "nonfiction novel" really exists.

Prose Poetry: A form of PROSE with marked (although preferably not too regular) CADENCE and frequently with extensive use of FIGURATIVE LANGUAGE and IMAGERY. If *prose poetry* is to be distinguished from polyphonic prose, the distinction is that polyphonic prose is usually reserved for a kind of writing with marked VERSE characteristics in PROSE form, whereas *prose poetry* is predominantly prose but borrows enriching characteristics from the RHYTHMS and IMAGERY of POETRY. See PROSE RHYTHM.

Prose Rhythm: The recurrence of STRESS and EMPHASIS at regular or, much more usually, irregular intervals, affording to some PROSE a pleasurable rise and fall of MOVEMENT. *Prose rhythm* is distinguished from the rhythm of verse in that it never for long falls into a recognizable pattern, for if it does it becomes VERSE rather than PROSE. RHYTHM in PROSE is essentially an aspect of STYLE. The greater freedom of *prose rhythm,* as compared with the RHYTHM of VERSE, springs from its wider choice in the placing of STRESS. There is no necessity to force a LINE to a certain rhythmic or metrical pattern. The normal ACCENT of words first determines the rhythmic EMPHASIS. But this is augmented by the secondary ACCENTS (in such words as ob"-ser-va'-tion and el"-e-men'-ta-ry) and increased again by the tendency of the reader to emphasize certain words importantly placed or rendered significant because of their meaning. (See RHETORICAL ACCENT and ACCENT.) Attempts have been made from time to time to evolve a system of SCANSION for PROSE, but none has proved satisfactory. As far as various kinds of lexical and acoustic RHYTHM are concerned, the rhythm of PROSE is essentially indistinguishable from that of POETRY. Indeed, there are passages in the prose of Dickens, Melville, and Hemingway that can be scanned as more or less regular VERSE. Distinguishable *prose rhythm* probably occurs only at the levels of syntax and concept.

Prosody: The theory and principles of VERSIFICATION, particularly as they refer to RHYTHM, ACCENT, and STANZA. See METER, SCANSION, VERSIFICATION.

Prosopopoeia: A term sometimes used for PERSONIFICATION.

Protagonist: The chief CHARACTER in a PLAY, STORY, or FILM. The word *protagonist* was originally applied to the "first" actor in early Greek DRAMA. The actor was added to the CHORUS and was its leader; hence, the continuing meaning of *protagonist* as the "first" or chief player in a DRAMA. In Greek DRAMA an AGON is a contest. The *protagonist,* the chief CHARACTER, and the ANTAGONIST, the second most important character, are the contenders in the AGON. The *protagonist* is the leading figure both in terms of importance in the PLAY and in terms of ability to enlist our interest and sympathy, whether the cause is heroic or ignoble. The term *protagonist* is used in a similar sense for the leading CHARACTER in any work of FICTION. In Shakespeare's *Hamlet,* Hamlet is himself the *protagonist,* as his fortunes are the chief interest of the play. King Claudius and Laertes are his ANTAGONISTS. The sentence "The protagonists of Christopher Marlowe's tragedies are usually the super-personality type" illustrates a usual use of the word. *Protagonist* is sometimes used in the looser sense of champion or chief advocate of a cause or movement, as when Bryan is called the *protagonist* of the free-silver movement in 1896.

Protasis: The term applied by CLASSICAL critics to the introductory ACT or the EXPOSITION of a DRAMA. See DRAMATIC STRUCTURE.

Prothalamion: From the Greek, literally meaning "before the bridal chamber." The term was coined by Edmund Spenser as the title of a POEM celebrating the double weddings of Lady Elizabeth and Lady Katherine Somerset. Spenser concocted the term by analogy with EPITHALAMION.

Prothesis: The addition of a letter or a syllable at the beginning of a word for EMPHASIS or effect or to meet metrical needs, as in Keats's LINE, "The owl for all his feathers was a-cold."

Prototype: A first form or original instance of a thing; a model, paradigm, or pattern for later forms or examples. Thus, the PERIODICAL ESSAY of the eighteenth century as written by Addison or Steele may be called the *prototype* of the FAMILIAR ESSAY as written by Lamb or Stevenson, the later FORM being developed from the earlier. Or the "Vice" of the MORALITY PLAYS may be regarded as the *prototype* of the clown of ELIZABETHAN DRAMA.

Proverb: A sentence or phrase briefly and memorably expressing some recognized truth or shrewd observation about practical life; originally preserved by oral tradition, though it may be transmitted in written literature as well. As far as FORM goes, *proverbs* may owe their appeal to the use of a METAPHOR ("Still waters run deep"); ANTITHESIS ("Man proposes, God disposes"); a play on words ("Forewarned, forearmed"); RHYME ("A friend in need is a friend indeed"); or ALLITERATION or PARALLELISM. Some are epigrammatic. Since the true *proverb* is old, its language is sometimes archaic. Words, meanings, idioms, or grammatical constructions not now common may be used. A misunderstanding of the original meaning may result. Thus, in "Time and tide wait for no man" *tide* is probably the old word for "season." In "The exception proves the rule," the "proves" ought to retain its old meaning of "tests" or "challenges"; exceptions do not establish rules, certainly, except in a *proverb* that has achieved currency. The range of interest of the *proverb* is wide: the weather, remedies for illness, legal shifts, superstitions, agriculture, efficiency in practical life, SATIRE on other races or on rival regions. *Proverbs* pass freely from language to language.
[Reference: Archer Taylor, *The Proverb* (1931, reprinted 1962).]

Provincialism: A word, phrase, manner of expression, or attitude peculiar to a special region and not commonly used outside that region; therefore, not fashionable or sophisticated. The term is applied not only to language but to customs, dress, and other characteristics of a special region. Derived from French usage, *provincialism* covers quite a range of meanings—parochialism, rusticity, rawness, uncouthness, bad manners, backwardness, and cultural myopia.

Pruning Poem: A POEM in which succeeding RHYME words have initial sounds or letters pared away. The FORM is rare, but a notable example is George Herbert's "Paradise," a POEM in TRIPLETS in which RHYME words are created by paring the preceding RHYME word, as in:

> What open force, or hidden *charm*
> Can blast my fruit, or bring me *harm*
> While the inclosure is thine *arm?*

Psalm: A lyrical composition of praise. Most frequently the term is applied to the sacred and devout LYRICS in the Book of Psalms ascribed to David. The contemporary American POET W. S. Merwin has written some distinguished POEMS call *psalms.*

Pseudonym: A fictitious name sometimes assumed by writers and others. See NOM DE PLUME, PUTATIVE AUTHOR, ALLONYM.

Pseudo-Shakespearean Plays: Plays attributed to Shakespeare at one time or another but now not accepted as his by the best authorities. Some non-Shakespearean PLAYS, such as *Locrine,* were printed during Shakespeare's lifetime with his initials or name on the title page; others, such as *The Birth of Merlin,* were so printed after Shakespeare's death. Another group, including *Mucedorus,* consists of plays labeled as Shakespeare's in the copies of them found in the library of Charles II. Many others, including *Sir Thomas More* (the manuscript copy of which is thought by some experts to be partly in Shakespeare's handwriting) and *Arden of Feversham,* have been assigned to Shakespeare by editors, booksellers, or critics chiefly on the basis of literary or technical qualities. A collection of *pseudo-Shakespearean plays* has been printed by Tucker Brooke in his *Shakespeare Apocrypha.* Some of the plays dubiously assigned to Shakespeare, such as *Cardenio,* have not survived.

Psychic Distance: The necessary DISTANCE between a work of art and a member of its audience. The reader or viewer needs, aestheticians say, to maintain a separation between his or her personal needs and feelings and the situation and emotion represented in a work of art, so that the work—DRAMA, POEM, NOVEL, FILM, painting, sculpture—may be viewed objectively and not in terms of the individual situations or feelings of the reader or viewer. See DISTANCE.

Psychoanalytical Criticism: The emphasis in literary CRITICISM on the values of SYMBOLS and language that, often unconsciously, explain meanings or unconscious intention. The term is also often applied to the examination of the motives and actions of CHARACTERS in a work of FICTION or a DRAMA, as in Ernest Jones's study *Hamlet and Oedipus.* Most *psychoanalytical criticism* employs the doctrines of Sigmund Freud. See FREUDIANISM.

Psychological Novel: PROSE FICTION that places unusual emphasis on interior CHARACTERIZATION and on the motives, circumstances, and internal ACTION that spring from, and develop, external ACTION. The *psychological novel,* not content to state what happens, goes on to explain the *why* of this action. In this type of writing CHARACTERIZATION is more than usually important. In one sense the psychological story is as old as the first DRAMA, TALE, or BALLAD, which accounted for external action by recounting the qualities of the CHARACTER of the PROTAGONIST. Chaucer's *Troilus and Criseyde* is a *psychological novel* in VERSE. *Hamlet* is a psychological DRAMA: but so are most of Shakespeare's better PLAYS. The *psychological novel* is, as one CRITIC has said, an interpretation of "the invisible life." The term was first importantly applied to a group of novelists in the middle of the nineteenth century, of whom Mrs. Gaskell, George Eliot, and George Meredith were the chief. Mrs. Gaskell stated that "all deeds however hidden and long passed by have their external consequences"—thus giving expression to an attitude long realized and felt if not always deliberately expressed. Thackeray and Dickens, too, were interested enough in motives and mental states to be classified, in a looser sense, with the forerunners of the *psychological novel.* Hardy and Conrad were also interested in the picturing of interior motive and psychological effect. Henry James, with his intense concern for the psychological life of his characters and with his development of a novelistic technique that centered itself in the representation of the effect produced in the inner self by external events, may be said to have created the modern *psychological novel*. In the twentieth century, with the advance of scientific psychology, the term has come into popular use. FREUDIANISM particularly gave impetus to the type. The modern *psychological novel* may at one extreme record the inner experience of CHARACTERS as reported by an author, as James tends to do, or at the other extreme utilize the INTERIOR MONOLOGUE to articulate the nonverbalized and subconscious life of a CHARACTER, as in some of the work of James Joyce and William Faulkner. See NOVEL, STREAM-OF-CONSCIOUSNESS NOVEL, INTERIOR MONOLOGUE.

Public Theaters: The English playhouse developed in the ELIZABETHAN AGE in response to the increased interest in the DRAMA. In earlier times PLAYS had been produced on PAGEANTS and in such indoor rooms as guild halls and the halls of great houses, schools, INNS OF COURT, and inn-yards, which were square or rectangular courts enclosed by the inner porches or balconies of the inn building. At one end would be erected a temporary stage connected with rooms of the inn. The spectators might stand in the open court ("groundlings") or get seats on the surrounding balconies. Meantime the need for a place for bear- or bull-baiting spectacles and acrobatic performances had been met in the development of a sort of ring or amphitheater. Out of the physical features of the inn-yard (surrounding galleries or boxes, open central space or pit, stage extending into pit) and the bear garden (circular form of building), the plan of the first *public theater* was evolved. The front stage was open to the sky, the rear stage covered by a ceiling. Above this ceiling was a room for the machinery needed in lowering persons and objects to the stage below, or raising them from it. There was an "inner" stage at the rear, provided with a CURTAIN and connected with a balcony above, also curtained. The rear stage was used chiefly for special SETTINGS such as a forest or bedroom, while the bare outer stage was used for street scenes, battles, and the like. The scenery and the costumes of the actors were largely conventional and symbolic, though certainly very realistic at times.

The first *public theater* in London was the Theatre, built in 1576 by James Burbage in Shoreditch. It was followed in 1577 by the Curtain in the same neighborhood. About ten years later Henslowe built the Rose on the Bankside, and in this locality appeared also the Swan (1594). In 1599 the Theatre was torn down and re-erected on the Bankside as the Globe, the most important of the *public theaters.* The Globe was used and controlled by the company to which Shakespeare belonged. Henslowe built the Fortune in 1600, the Red Bull appeared soon after in St. John's Street, and the Hope in 1614 near the Rose and the new Globe. For distinction between "public" and "private" theaters, see PRIVATE THEATERS.

[References: J. Q. Adams, *Shakespearean Playhouses* (1917); A. H. Thorndike, *Shakespeare's Theater* (1916).]

Pulitzer Prizes: Annual prizes for journalism, literature, and music, awarded annually since 1917 by the School of Journalism and the Board of Trustees of Columbia University. The prizes are supported by a bequest from Joseph Pulitzer. An Advisory Board of the Pulitzer Prizes selects work published or produced in the United States during the preceding year and recommends recipients to the Board of Trustees, who make the awards. Eight prizes are awarded for various kinds of meritorious service rendered by newspapers. One prize is awarded for a musical composition. Six awards are given in literature: for the most distinguished NOVEL, preferably dealing with American life; for the American PLAY best showing the power and educational value of the theater; for the finest book on American history; for the best BIOGRAPHY or AUTOBIOGRAPHY, teaching patriotic and unselfish services to people; for the most distinguished volume of VERSE; and for the best book of general nonfiction not fitting into any of these categories. There has been much debate over the recipients of the awards in literature and DRAMA. Since FICTION enjoys a larger audience than does DRAMA or POETRY, the award for a NOVEL seems to inflame passions more than the other awards have usually done. A listing of the *Pulitzer Prizes* in FICTION, POETRY, and DRAMA is given in the Appendix.

Pulp Magazines: MAGAZINES printed on rough pulp paper, cheaply produced, with lurid illustrations and gaudy covers, and filled with melodramatic TALES of love, crime, and the West. Popular in the first half of the twentieth century, particularly in the 1920s and 1930s, the *pulp magazines* were the successors to the DIME NOVELS.

Pun: A play on words based on the similarity of sound between two words with different meanings. An example is Thomas Hood's: "They went and told the sexton and the sexton tolled the bell." The *pun* is a humble thing, and many find it trifling or irritating. Even so, *puns* are found in the most sublime scriptures (as in the names "Isaac" and "Peter" in the BIBLE) and throughout Shakespeare's works (drawing the contempt of CRITICS as diverse as Samuel Johnson and Thomas Wolfe). From its earlier low or marginal status, the *pun* has steadily risen in dignity, to the point of being a main structural principle of Joyce's *Ulysses* and *Finnegans Wake*. Most *puns* are exotic, parochial, and short-lived; some, however, such as those involving "son" and "sun" and "I" and "eye," are important staples of English literature. See EQUIVOQUE.

Pure Poetry: A term applied to POETRY supposedly free from conceptualized statement, instructive content, or moral preachment; or those portions of a POEM remaining after such materials as can be paraphrased adequately in PROSE are removed. The term was first used by Baudelaire in an ESSAY on Edgar Allan Poe. For many critics Poe's theory and practice of POETRY are archetypically pure; as George Moore said of Poe's POEMS when including them in an anthology of *pure poetry*, they "are almost free from thought." Wallace Stevens is often cited as a modern poet who practiced an art close to that of *pure poetry*. Moore classified as "pure" such POEMS as are "born of admiration of the only permanent world, the world of things." Moore's rather quaint ANTHOLOGY came out in 1924; twenty years later, Robert Penn Warren published his ESSAY "Pure and Impure Poetry," a subtler argument than Moore's and a case that has become the CLASSIC summary of modern thinking on a difficult subject.
  [References: George Moore, ed., *Anthology of Pure Poetry* (1924); Robert Penn Warren, *Selected Essays* (1958).]

Purist: One who habitually stresses, or overstresses, correctness or "purity" in language, particularly in minor or fine points of grammar, DICTION, pronunciation, and rhetorical STYLE. The term is commonly used in a spirit of deprecation or mild reproach, but it must be remembered that it is difficult to draw the line between the *purist* and the person who takes a commendable interest in achieving decent accuracy and precision.

A related though different use of the word is its application to a person who feels that the "purity" of a language can be preserved by the exclusion of foreign words and of words not used by the best stylists. Thus, the so-called CICERONIANS of the RENAISSANCE, a group of Latin stylists who would not use any Latin word that could not be found in Cicero's writings, have been called *purists*, as have the English scholars of the sixteenth century and later who insisted on a "pure" English diction "unmixed and unmangled with borrowing of other tongues." The famous schoolmasters Sir John Cheke and Roger Ascham and the rhetorician Thomas Wilson were leaders in this movement. In the main they were not absolute *purists*, however, since they recognized that English might legitimately be enriched by the use of some foreign words; and they opposed strongly the pedantic tendency of the time that threatened to make literary English a mere Latin *patois*. The struggle between these *purists* and their INKHORNIST opponents is sometimes referred to as the "purist-improver" controversy.

Later movements toward purism included: the unsuccessful effort in the seventeenth century to establish (on the model of the French Academy) a British Academy to regulate language; eighteenth-century efforts at standardization through the establishment of some definite linguistic authority (opposed by Doctor Johnson); and efforts to stress the ANGLO-SAXON elements in the vocabulary and to check the importation of foreign words (noteworthy is Edna St. Vincent Millay's attempt to write a long POEM, *The King's Henchman*, employing only words of ANGLO-SAXON derivation). In both PROSE and POETRY Charles M. Doughty strove to regain a measure of what he regarded as "purity" of DICTION, and the results are still readable. There has been a Society for Pure English well into our own day; and a number of important writers—Morris, Hardy, Hopkins, and Bridges, for example—have been involved in a *purist* sentiment of "linguistic nationalism" of much the same sort that prompted Beethoven to abandon for a while the alien "piano" and adopt in its stead the good Germanic "Hammerklavier." Some of the effects of this sentiment have to be called salubrious—as in Hopkins's preference for the potent native "windhover" over the colorless "kestrel"; but Modern English is so mixed and has long been so hospitable to so-called loan-words that the effort to replace "omnibus" with "folkwain," say, or to place spelling on a "rational" basis (one of George Bernard Shaw's hobbyhorses) seems utterly vain. Another species of *purist* emphasizes "purity" of DICTION on the basis of fidelity to historical roots (saying, for instance, "oblivious *of*" instead of "oblivious *to*"), and it may be conceded that that effort has more respectable results in clarity and economy than the *purist's* longing for a "native" vocabulary.

[Reference: G. P. Krapp, *Modern English* (1909, reprinted 1966).]

Puritanism: A religious-political movement that developed in England about the middle of the sixteenth century and later spread its influence into the New England colonies in America. While it died politically with the return of Charles II to London in 1660, *Puritanism* left its impress and many of its attitudes on the habits and thought of the people, especially those of America today. As a term, *Puritan* was, in Elizabeth's reign, applied in derision to those who wished to "purify" the Church of England. The spirit behind *Puritanism* was an outgrowth of CALVINISM that had spread from Geneva and Scotland to England.

In principle the Puritans objected to certain forms of the Established Church. They objected, for instance, to the wearing of the surplice and to government by the prelates, and they demanded the right to partake of the communion in a sitting posture. Their Millenary Petition (1603) requested a reform of the church courts, a doing away with "superstitious" customs, a discarding of the use of APOCRYPHAL books of the BIBLE, a serious observance of the Sabbath, and various ecclesiastical reforms. While at first *Puritanism* in England was not directly affiliated with Presbyterianism, it later on allied itself, largely for political reasons, very definitely with that movement. Thomas Cartwright, the first important spokesperson of *Puritanism*, most emphatically hated the Church of England.

The conception of the Puritans popularly held today, however, is unfair to the general temper of the early sponsors of the movement. These early English Puritans were not long-faced reformers, teetotalers, or haters of art and music. They were often patrons of art and lovers of music, fencing, and dancing. They were intelligent, disciplined, plainly dressed citizens who held to simplicity and to democratic principles. But under the persecution of Charles and the double-dealing of Laud they were harried into bitterness.

Puritanism was a logical aftermath of the RENAISSANCE, the REFORMATION, the establishment of the Church of England, and the growth of Presbyterianism. Through all of these great movements one sees emerging the right of the individual to political and religious independence. The reading of the BIBLE had become general. The Catholic Church had lost its pristine power in England, but there were still thousands of Catholics who wanted their old power restored. The people were always suspicious that their rulers, a James I or a Charles I, might swing back to the faith of Spain and Italy. Political power for the commoners lay with Presbyterianism, a religious movement based on the political control of presbyters drawn from the people. Catholicism and even the Church of England were far too reminiscent of autocracy and of divine right to rule. Whitgift and Laud wished to stamp out *Puritanism;* James I had promised that if necessary he would "harry the Puritans out of the land." Charles I and Laud fought popular rights and suppressed Parliament. From 1642 to 1646 there raged civil war, from which rose to power a new Puritan leader, Oliver Cromwell. In 1649 Charles was beheaded. The Puritan Commonwealth was established, to end when, on May 25, 1660, Charles II landed at Dover.

Some of the "Brownists," a group of Puritans who had earlier left England for seclusion in Holland, came to America in the *Mayflower*. They wished to set up a new theocracy in which the Puritan ideas of religion and government were to go hand in hand. "I shall call that my country where I may most glorify God and enjoy the presence of my dearest friends," said young Winthrop. In one year as many as three thousand rebels left England for the Colonies; in ten years there were twenty thousand English in America. Many of these newcomers were people of education, intelligence, family position, and culture. Those who settled in and around Massachusetts were bent on forming a new government, a theocracy, with God and Christ at the head, and with their own chosen rulers to interpret God's will for them. What now seems, as we look back at it, a movement toward conservatism, a threat against freedom of speech, art, and individualism, was at that time essentially a radical movement with leanings that have even been characterized as communistic.

In America a dozen or more writers attained positions in literature largely because they happened to stand at the source of the stream. Such theologians as John Cotton, Thomas Hooker, John Eliot, Cotton Mather; such historians as William Bradford, John Winthrop, Thomas Hutchinson, and Samuel Sewall; and such POETS as Nathaniel Ward, Anne Bradstreet, Michael Wigglesworth, and Edward Taylor derive importance from their work and their historical position. *The Bay Psalm Book* (1640) became almost the book of a people.

With the Scotch-Irish settlements of the Middle Atlantic and Southern colonies came another and a stronger strain of *Puritanism*, that of the Scotch Presbyterians. And as the restless and the discontented, North and South, moved westward into the beckoning frontier they carried with them the BIBLE, a simple and fundamentally Puritan faith, and the stern impulse to independence and freedom. Across the pages of American literature *Puritanism* is written large. It may almost be considered the ethical mode of American thought. As an extreme form of the Protestant sensibility, *Puritanism* exaggerated those Protestant traits—especially industry and frugality—which, according to Max Weber and other analysts of social history, contributed to the rise of capitalism. See CALVINISM.

[References: Sacvan Bercovitch, *The American Jeremiad* (1978), (ed.) *The American Puritan Imagination* (1974), and *The Puritan Origins of the American Self* (1975); William Haller, *The Rise of Puritanism* (1938); M. M. Knappen, *Tudor Puritanism* (1939, reprinted 1963); Alan Simpson, *Puritanism in Old and New England* (1955); Page Smith, *As a City upon a Hill* (1966); G. M. Trevelyan, *England under the Stuarts,* 16th ed. (1933).]

"Purple Patch": A piece of "fine writing." Now and then authors in a strongly emotional passage will give free play to most of the stylistic tricks in their bag. They will write PROSE intensely colorful, more than usually rhythmic, marked by an involved PARALLELISM, full of IMAGERY and FIGURES OF SPEECH, characterized by a POETIC DICTION. When there is an unusual piling up of these devices in such a way as to evidence a self-conscious literary effort, the section is spoken of as a *purple patch*—a colorful passage standing out from the writing around it. (The expression comes from Horace, for whom purple dye was much rarer—hence more conspicuous—than it is for us.) Although frequently used in a nonevaluative, descriptive sense, the term is more often employed in a derogatory sense, to suggest overstraining.

Puseyism: The later OXFORD MOVEMENT, particularly at the time of the debates over ritualism in the Church of England; so-called for one of the leaders, Edward B. Pusey. See OXFORD MOVEMENT and ERASTIANISM.

Putative Author: The fictional author of a work, supposedly written by someone other than its actual author. Lemuel Gulliver is the *putative author* of his *Travels,* not Jonathan Swift; Tristram Shandy is the *putative author* of his *Life and Opinions,* not Laurence Sterne. When an author uses a NOM

DE PLUME, it merely hides actual identity behind an assumed name, but the author using a *putative author* creates a CHARACTER who writes the book. Washington Irving merely hid his name when he signed the *Sketch Book* as "Geoffrey Crayon," but he created a *putative author* who wrote and signed Diedrich Knickerbocker's *History of New York*. See POINT OF VIEW, NARRA-TOR, and PERSONA.

Pyrrhic: A FOOT of two unaccented syllables (⌣ ⌣); the opposite of SPONDEE (⁄ ⁄). The *pyrrhic* is unusual in English VERSIFICATION and is not accepted as a FOOT at all by some prosodists since it contains no accented syllable. As an occasional phenomenon, the *pyrrhic* FOOT is unavoidable in English, with its large population of unstressed syllables and combinations of slight preposi-tions and articles; but it is virtually inconceivable that a whole POEM could be written in the FOOT.

Quadrivium: In the medieval university curriculum, the four subjects leading to the M.A. degree: arithmetic, music, geometry, and astronomy. See SEVEN LIBERAL ARTS.

Quantitative Verse: VERSE whose basic RHYTHM is determined by QUANTITY, that is, duration of sound in utterance. CLASSICAL poetry was *quantitative*, as English POETRY has been qualitative or ACCENTUAL-SYLLABIC. However, a number of English POETS have experimented with *quantitative verse* forms, among them Campion, Sidney, Spenser, Coleridge, Tennyson, Longfellow, and Lanier. Special (and quite elastic) rules have been devised for the calculation of long and short syllables in a language distinguished by the extreme variability of its syllables and its preference for accent over length. A few of the CLASSICAL *quantitative* forms occasionally are used in English, among them ALCAICS, CHORIAMBICS, ELEGIACS, HENDECASYLLABICS, SAPPHICS. See METER, QUANTITY.

Quantity: In classical PROSODY, *quantity*, the fundamental rhythmic unit, is the relative length of time required to utter a syllable. In Greek and Latin VERSIFICATION a syllable was considered long if it contained a long vowel or a short vowel followed by two consonants; otherwise, it was considered short, except for a few vowels and syllables that varied in duration between these limits and were called common. A long syllable was roughly the equivalent of two short syllables in duration, or a long syllable may be thought of as equivalent to a quarter note in music and a short syllable to an eighth. While duration is unquestionably a quality in English VERSIFICATION, the distinguishing and determining rhythmic pattern of English is ACCENTUAL-SYLLABIC, so that the RHYTHMS that a skillful poet gains from the control of *quantity* or duration are subsidiary or complementary to the fundamental rhythms of regularly recurring ACCENT. See METER, ACCENT, ACCENTUAL-SYLLABIC VERSE, STRESS.

Quarterly Review: A British Tory critical JOURNAL founded in 1809. See EDINBURGH REVIEW.

Quarto: A BOOK SIZE designating a book whose SIGNATURES result from sheets folded to four leaves or eight pages. See BOOK SIZES.

Quaternion: A literary work with a set or sets of fours forming a basic part of its STRUCTURE. *Quaternion* usually implies several interlocking sets of fours. Floyd Stovall, for example, calls "The Bells," by Poe, a *quaternion* because it consists of four parts, describes four bells, made of four metals, and represents four stages in a man's life. Eliot's *Four Quartets*, the title of which suggests a double *quaternion*, has four main sections based, none too programatically, on the four elements along with the seasons and directions. Whether any quadratic or fourfold work—*Paradise Regained*, Blake's "London," or *Finnegans Wake*, say—ought to be called a *quaternion* depends on whether the quantitative structure is markedly foregrounded.

Quatorzain: A STANZA or POEM of fourteen LINES. The term, however, is no longer specifically applied to the SONNET (though of course the SONNET is a fourteen-line FORM) but is usually reserved for fourteen-line POEMS not conforming to one or another of the SONNET patterns.

Quatrain: A STANZA of four LINES. In its narrow meaning the term is restricted to a complete POEM consisting of four lines only, but in its broader sense it signifies any one of many four-LINE STANZA forms. The possible RHYME SCHEMES vary from an unrhymed *quatrain* to almost any arrangement of one-RHYME, two-RHYME, or three-RHYME lines. Perhaps the most common form is the *abab* sequence; other popular rhyme patterns are *aabb; abba; aaba; abcb*. Robert Frost's unique POEM "In a Disused Graveyard" consists of four *quatrains*, in IAMBIC TETRAMETER, each in a different RHYME SCHEME: *abba, aaaa, aabb, abab*—quite a *tour de force*.

Question: The grammatical form of asking; interrogation. Whether the answer is known beforehand or not, the *question* seems to be an inherently interesting and exciting form of utterance. It is a peculiarly powerful way of ending a POEM, such as Keats's "Ode to a Nightingale" and many of Yeats's POEMS. See RHETORICAL QUESTION.

Quibble: A PUN or play on words, or especially a verbal device for evading the point at issue, as when debaters engage in *quibbles* over the interpretation of a term.

Quintain or Quintet: Any STANZA consisting of five LINES.

Quip: A retort or sarcastic jest; hence any witty saying, especially a PUN or QUIBBLE.

R

Raisonneur: A CHARACTER in a DRAMA who is the level-headed, calm personification of reason and logical action. This character is usually not closely connected to the central action and is in the PLAY for any of three reasons: (1) to serve as a standard against which the actions of other CHARACTERS may be measured, (2) to articulate the questions in the audience's mind, as the CHORUS did in Greek DRAMA, and (3) to utter judgments on the characters and their actions, thus serving as an author-SURROGATE. The *raisonneur,* a very common character in the WELL-MADE PLAY of the nineteenth century, plays a role somewhat like that of the CONFIDANT in a NOVEL.

Ratiocination: A systematic process of reasoning that proceeds from the examination of data to the formulation of conclusions. The term was given literary significance by Poe, who wrote several tales that he called "ratiocinative," among them "The Murders in the Rue Morgue," "The Gold Bug," "The Purloined Letter," "The Mystery of Marie Rogêt," and "Thou Art the Man." The introductory paragraphs of "The Murders in the Rue Morgue" manifest Poe's high respect for the type of mind that works so. In general, then, *ratiocination,* as a literary or critical term, signifies a type of writing that solves, through the application of logical processes, some sort of enigma. It was once commonly applied to the DETECTIVE STORY.

Rationalism: This term embraces related "systems" of thought (philosophical, scientific, religious) that rest on the authority of reason rather than sense-perceptions, revelation, or traditional authority. In England the rationalist attitude, especially in the eighteenth century, profoundly affected religion and literature. The early humanists (see OXFORD REFORMERS) had insisted on the control of reason, but their teachings had little effect on prevailing religious thought until reinforced by the scientific thinking of the seventeenth century (Newton), although as early as 1624 Lord Herbert of Cherbury had drawn up certain general principles that he thought all existing religious factions could accept. By the end of the century the theologians were generally agreed that the most vital religious doctrines were deducible from reason or NATURE. The more conservative ("supernatural rationalists") insisted on the importance of revelation in addition, while the more radical "deists" (see DEISM) rejected revelation. The former group included Newton himself and the great philosopher John Locke. The "natural religion" arising from *rationalism* stressed reason as a guide and good conduct as an effect. Its three propositions were: (1) there is an omnipotent God, (2) he demands virtuous living in obedience to his will, and (3) there is a future life where the good will be rewarded and the wicked punished. This creed was accepted by both radicals and conservatives. The stressing of reason made *rationalism* an ally of NEOCLASSICISM, while the stressing of the potential power and good in human nature, as was done by Shaftesbury, led toward ROMANTICISM. For some of the effects of *rationalism* on literature, see DEISM, PRIMITIVISM, ROMANTICISM, SENTIMENTALISM, NEOCLASSICISM, HUMANISM. See also CALVINISM, PURITANISM, and MYSTICISM for opposing attitudes.

[References: Alfred W. Benn, *A History of English Rationalism in the Nineteenth Century* (1906, reprinted 1962); W. E. H. Lecky, *History of the Rise and Influence of the Spirit of Rationalism in Europe* (1865, reprinted 1955); J. H. Randall, *The Making of the Modern Mind* (rev. ed. 1940, reprinted 1976); Leslie Stephen, *History of Thought in the Eighteenth Century*, 3rd ed. (1902, reprinted 1962).]

Rationalize: A verb used to indicate a rather specious form of *ex parte* reasoning. An author is said "to *rationalize*" when, once having accepted a position or a belief, through some prejudice or intuitive process, the author tries to justify the stand by some process of the mind. That is, writing is said to *rationalize* when the author reasons insincerely and with intellectual sophistry to justify a position prompted by emotions rather than by reason. A different sense of the word means "to put into rational form."

Reader Response Criticism: A recent manifestation of the PRAGMATIC THEORY: not necessarily vitiated by subjective IMPRESSIONISM, this kind of CRITICISM suggests that a piece of writing scarcely exists except as a text designed to be read; indeed, scarcely exists until somebody reads it. As a critical procedure, the READER-RESPONSE approach does not so much analyze a reader's responding apparatus as scrutinize those features of the text that arouse, shape, and guide a reader's reading. A work that generates and then discharges, seemingly in itself, the terms of its own understanding has been called "self-consuming" by Stanley Fish. From the usual charges of excessive relativism, subjectivism, and IMPRESSIONISM, *reader response criticism* escapes by recourse to a concept of a hypothetical reader different from any "real" reader—a hypothetical construct of norms and expectations that can be derived or projected or extrapolated from the work and that may even be said to inhere in the work. This hypothetical reader becomes, in effect, a part of the FICTION itself. Wolfgang Iser has analyzed many types: contemporary, fictitious, hypothetical, ideal, implied, intended, and informed readers, along with Michael Riffaterre's "superreader." (See IMPLIED READER.) Once such a reader is situated in a text, then the immediate drawbacks of the AFFECTIVE FALLACY can be at least forestalled if not avoided completely. The debate continues. See AFFECTIVE STYLISTICS.

[References: Wayne Booth, *Critical Understanding: The Powers and Limits of Pluralism* (1979); Wolfgang Iser, *The Act of Reading: A Theory of Aesthetic Response* (tr. 1978), and *The Implied Reader: Patterns of Communication in Prose Fiction from Bunyan to Beckett* (tr. 1974).]

Realism: *Realism* is, in the broadest sense, simply fidelity to actuality in its representation in literature; a term loosely synonymous with VERISIMILITUDE; and in this sense it has been a significant element in almost every school of writing in human history. In order to give it more precise definition, however, one needs to limit it to the movement that arose in the nineteenth century, at least partially in reaction against ROMANTICISM, which was centered in the NOVEL and dominant in France, England, and America from roughly mid-century to the closing decade, when it was replaced by NATURALISM. In this latter sense *realism* defines a literary method, a philosophical and political attitude, and a particular range of subject matter. Along one axis *realism* opposes idealism; along another it opposes NOMINALISM. Confusingly, the latter kind of *realism*, asserting that only ideas are "real," seems idealistic; while NOMINALISM, asserting that ideas are only names, would seem to be what most people probably mean by "realistic." The point to be made here is that *realism*, like NATURE, is a most complex and difficult term, which must be used with the greatest of care.

Realism has been defined as "the truthful treatment of material" by one of its most vigorous advocates, William Dean Howells, but the statement means little until the realists' concept of truth and their selection of materials are designated. Generally, realists are believers in PRAGMATISM, and the truth they seek to find and express is a relativistic or pluralistic truth, associated with discernible consequences and verifiable by experience. Generally, too, realists are believers in democracy, and the materials they elect to describe are the common, the average, the everyday. Furthermore, *realism* can be thought of as the ultimate of middle-class art, and it finds its subjects in bourgeois life and manners. Where romanticists transcend the immediate to find the ideal, and naturalists plumb the actual or superficial to find the scientific laws that control its actions, realists center their attention to a remarkable degree on the immediate, the here and now, the specific action, and the verifiable consequence. (See NATURALISM for a further discussion of the distinctions among these three terms.)

Realists espouse what is essentially a MIMETIC THEORY OF ART, centering their attention in the thing imitated and asking for something close to a one-to-one correspondence between the representation and the subject. They usually have, however, a powerful interest in the audience to whom their work is addressed, feeling it to be their obligation to deal with it with absolute truthfulness. Furthermore, realists are unusually interested in the effect of their work on the audience and its life (in this respect they tend toward a PRAGMATIC THEORY OF ART); George Eliot, in chapter XVII of *Adam Bede* (a CLASSIC statement of the intention of the realist), expresses her desire that her pictures of common life and average experience should knit more tightly the bonds of human sympathy among her readers. Howells, concerned with his audience of young ladies, felt so strongly the obligation not to do them moral injury that he shut the doors of his own works to most of the parts of life connected with passion and sex.

Realists eschew the traditional patterns of the NOVEL. In part the rise of *realism* came as a protest against the supposed falseness and sentimentality of romantic FICTION. Life, they felt, lacked symmetry and PLOT; FICTION truthfully reflecting life should, therefore, avoid symmetry and PLOT. Simple, clear, direct PROSE was the desirable vehicle, and objectivity on the part of the novelist the proper attitude. The central issues of life tend to be ethical—that is, issues of conduct. FICTION should therefore concern itself with such issues and—since selection is a necessary part of any art—select with a view to presenting these issues accurately as they affect us in actual situations. Furthermore, the democratic attitudes of realists tended to make them value the individual very highly and to praise CHARACTERIZATION as the center of the NOVEL. Hence, they had a great concern for the effect of ACTION on CHARACTER and a tendency to explore the psychology of the actors in their STORIES. In Henry James, perhaps the greatest of the realists, this tendency to explore the inner selves of characters confronted with complex ethical choices earned for him not only the title of "father of the PSYCHOLOGICAL NOVEL" but also that of "biographer of fine consciences."

The surface details, the common actions, and the minor catastrophes of a middle-class society constituted the chief subject matter of the movement. Most of the realists avoided situations with tragic or cataclysmic implications. Their TONE was often comic, frequently satiric, seldom grim or somber. Their general attitude was broadly optimistic, though James is a great exception.

Although aspects of *realism* appeared almost with the beginnings of the English NOVEL, for they are certainly present in Defoe, Richardson, Fielding, Smollett, Austen, Trollope, Thackeray, and Dickens, the realistic movement found its effective origins in France with Balzac, in England with George Eliot, and in America with Howells and Mark Twain. Writers like Arnold Bennett, John Galsworthy, and H. G. Wells in England, and Henry James, Edith Wharton, Ellen Glasgow, Sinclair Lewis, John O'Hara, John P. Marquand, and Louis Auchincloss in America kept and are keeping the realistic tradition alive in the contemporary NOVEL. (The concept of "social *realism*" or "socialist *realism*" that was once a staple of Marxist criticism seems to have receded, although *realism* itself remains important in the work of such Marxist thinkers as Georg Lukács.)

It should be emphasized that no single realistic NOVEL exemplifies all the characteristics that are listed in this article. In general, though, the realistic NOVEL tends toward the directions here indicated. What has happened to *realism* in the past century or so seems to be a reflection of changes in what we generally consider "real." Our science has come to concentrate on phenomena so remote or minute, and our philosophy and psychology on forces so mysterious and obscure, that we may be returning to an earlier state of belief that, in effect, what is real cannot be seen. See NATURALISM, ROMANTICISM.

[References: Erich Auerbach, *Mimesis: The Representation of Reality in Western Literature* (tr. 1953); George J. Becker, *Documents of Modern Literary Realism* (1963); Harry Levin, *The Gates of Horn: A Study of Five French Realists* (1963); G. Lukács, *Studies in European Realism* (tr. 1964); Donald Pizer, *Realism and Naturalism in Nineteenth-Century American Fiction* (1960); R. Stang, *The Theory of the Novel in England, 1850–1870* (1961); Ian Watt, *The Rise of the Novel* (1957); René Wellek, *Concepts of Criticism* (1963).]

Realist Theory: In FILM CRITICISM a theory that sees the primary value of FILM in its ability to record the literal world around it. In contrast to FORMATIVE THEORY, which emphasizes artistic aspects of FILM, the *realist theory* advocates close correspondence between FILM and the literal world. See FORMATIVE THEORY.

Realistic Comedy: Any COMEDY employing the methods of REALISM but particularly the COMEDY developed by Jonson, Chapman, Middleton, and other Elizabethan and Jacobean dramatists. It is opposed to ROMANTIC COMEDY; in fact, it appeared more or less as a protest against the romantic comedy of the Elizabethans. It reflects the general reaction in the late 1590s against Elizabethan ROMANTICISM and extravagance as well as an effort to produce an English COMEDY after the manner of CLASSICAL comedy. This *realistic comedy* deals with London life, is strongly satirical and sometimes cynical in TONE, is interested in both individuals and character types, and rests on observation of contemporary life. The appeal is intellectual and the tone coarse. This COMEDY is sometimes treated as COMEDY OF MANNERS, various subclasses being distinguishable in Jacobean PLAYS. It became especially popular in the reign of James I. The COMEDY OF HUMOURS was a special form representing the first stage of the development of important *realistic comedy.* Jonson's *The Alchemist* and Middleton's *A Trick to Catch the Old One* are typical Jacobean *realistic comedies.* Though in the main Shakespeare represents the tradition of ROMANTIC COMEDY, some of his plays, including the comic SUBPLOT of the *King Henry the Fourth* plays, are realistic in technique. The RESTORATION COMEDY OF MANNERS, though chiefly a new growth, owes something to this earlier form, and one RESTORATION dramatist (Shadwell) actually wrote COMEDY of the Jonsonian type.

Realistic Novel: A type of NOVEL that places a strong emphasis on the truthful representation of the actual in FICTION. See REALISM.

Realistic Period in American Literature, 1865–1900:   In the period between the end of the Civil War and the turn of the twentieth century, modern America was born and grew to a lusty although not always happy or attractive adolescence. The Civil War had been, at least in part, a struggle between agrarian democracy and industrial-capitalist democracy, and the result of the Northern victory was the triumphant emergence of industralism. This industrialism was to yield mechanical and material advances, but it was also to bring difficulties in the form of severe labor disputes, economic depression, and strikes that erupted in violence; its capitalistic aspect was to produce a group of powerful and ruthless moneyed men who have gone down in history as the "robber barons"; its application to politics, particularly in the rapidly developing great cities, was to produce "bossism" and a form of political corruption known by Lincoln Steffens's phrase, "the shame of cities." The impact of invention and industrial development was tremendous. The greatest advances were made in communications: the Atlantic cable was laid in 1866; the transcontinental railroad was completed in 1869; the telephone was invented in 1876; and the automobile with the internal-combustion engine was being manufactured by the 1890s. By the last two decades of the century many thoughtful people had begun to march under various banners declaring that somewhere and somehow the promise of the American dream had been lost—they often said "betrayed"—and that drastic changes needed to be made in order to recapture it. The Populist Party, the Grange, Henry George's "single tax," and the socialism of the American intellectual were all reflections of a disillusionment never before so widespread.

Intellectually, too, average Americans were living in a new world, although they did not always realize it. The impact of Darwin, Marx, Comte, Spencer, and others advancing a scientific view sharply at variance with the older religious view was cutting from beneath thoughtful Americans—even while they vehemently denied it—their old certainty about perfectibility and about the inevitability of progress. The passing of the physical frontier around 1890 removed from their society a natural safety valve that had acted to protect them against the malcontents and the restless in their world; now they must absorb them and adjust to the fact of their presence; no longer could they seek virgin land. The rapid growth of education and the rise of the mass-circulation MAGAZINE, paying its way by advertising, created an enormous audience for authors, and the passage in 1891 of the International Copyright Act protected foreign authors from piracy in America and by the same token protected the native literary product from being undercut by PIRATED EDITIONS of foreign works.

In POETRY the field appeared to be held by a group of sweetly singing but sentimental imitators of the English Romantics—Stedman, Stoddard, Hovey, Aldrich—but, in fact, three new and authentic poetic voices were raised in the period: Walt Whitman's in his democratic chant cast in experimental rhythmic POETRY; Sidney Lanier's in his moral statements couched in experimental musical poetry; and Emily Dickinson's in her profound GNOMIC utterances cast in variations on traditional FORMS. Toward the close of the century Stephen Crane used a haunting but strident voice in sparse experimental VERSE that was close to that of the IMAGISTS of the twentieth century, and Edwin Arlington Robinson published his first volume in an orthodox style but in a somber TONE of stoic IRONY. A word may be added here to suggest the popularity of the versifier James Whitcomb Riley. No one goes to extremes nowadays in claiming profundity or complexity for Riley's verse, but it was wholesomely patriotic and charming, and it had not only warmth but also a marked degree of technical finish and originality (Riley wrote the first American VILLANELLE). His influence on Ezra Pound's idea of American speech can be traced, and something ought to be recorded in praise of the POET whose "Little Orphant Annie" inspired a comic strip of prodigious longevity, an important Broadway musical comedy, and the Raggedy Ann doll.

On the stage the older melodramatic habits held, and the "star system" subordinating PLAY and players to a "name" actor continued to fill the American theater with SPECTACLE but little meaning. American DRAMA saw little that was new and felt only slight impacts of the new European PROBLEM PLAYS before the end of the century. James A. Herne's *Margaret Fleming* demonstrated a realistic promise that was largely unrealized. *Uncle Tom's Cabin* and *Rip Van Winkle* continued to dominate the American boards.

In FICTION, however, the new turbulence and the growing skepticism and disillusionment found an effective voice. The developing mass audience was served by LOCAL-COLOR WRITING, which filled the popular MAGAZINES, and by the HISTORICAL NOVEL, which had a great upsurge of popularity as the century drew toward a close. But in the work of Mark Twain, William Dean Howells, and Henry James, the greatest contributions of the age were made. In the works of these and of lesser writers—largely from the Middle West—REALISM was formulated as a literary doctrine and practiced as an art form that came to dominate the American literary scene. William James's PRAGMATISM not only expressed the mood of the *Realistic Period* but also shaped its literary expression, an expression that became increasingly critical of American life as the century drew toward its end.

By the 1890s a cynical application of Darwinism to social structures, together with an acceptance of Nietzsche's doctrine of the superman and of Émile Zola's concept of the experimental NOVEL, resulted in a NATURALISM markedly different from anything America had previously known. The publication of Theodore Dreiser's *Sister Carrie* in 1900 told, perhaps more clearly than any historical document could have done, that a new America had grown from the travail of the post-Civil War period. See REALISM, *Outline of Literary History*.

Realistic Period in English Literature, 1870–1914: In the latter portion of the reign of Queen Victoria and during the reign of Edward VII, the reaction to ROMANTICISM, a reaction with its beginnings fairly early in Victoria's reign, reached its peak in full-fledged REALISM, and by the beginning of the First World War had itself begun to come under attack. This fact brings into question the customary division of the literature of England in the nineteenth century, a division in which ROMANTICISM is considered to dominate until 1832, after which time VICTORIAN literature holds sway until the end of the century. The early portion of Victoria's reign saw a continuance and a gradual weakening of ROMANTICISM (see EARLY VICTORIAN AGE); whereas the LATE VICTORIAN AGE witnessed the arrival of a literary movement that was to reach its fruition and pass into the early years of its decline in the EDWARDIAN AGE.

The last three decades of the nineteenth century saw the great parliamentary contests between Gladstone and Disraeli, the rise of the concept of British imperialism, and a growth in British sophistication and cosmopolitanism. Intellectually, serious English men and women began to feel the impact of the scientific revolution that distinguished nineteenth-century thought. Newton's mechanics, Darwin's evolution, Marx's view of history, Comte's view of society, Taine's view of literature—each in its way chipped away at the complacency and the optimism that had characterized the early years of the Victorian rule. Foreign writers began to be widely read—Zola, Balzac, Flaubert, Maupassant, Sudermann, Ibsen, Tolstoi, Chekhov, Turgenev, Whitman. By the turn of the century a reaction to Victorian life and to complacent earnestness was being expressed, notably in the work of DECADENTS like Oscar Wilde, Ernest Dowson, and Aubrey Beardsley. A full-fledged revolt against Victorian mores and standards marked the early years of the twentieth century. Politically, the protest of writers like Carlyle and Ruskin gave way to a full embracing of Fabian socialism in writers like William Morris and George Bernard Shaw. The imperial adventure of the Boer War (1899–1902) was hailed by many as a proper extension of the empire, and at the same time it raised grave doubts.

In POETRY the voices of the great Victorians, Tennyson and Browning, were still heard, but a new poetry, interested in FRENCH FORMS and lacking in "moral earnestness," was present in Swinburne and the DECADENTS. Hardy, Kipling, Yeats, and Bridges were to do distinguished work before the beginning of the First World War.

In DRAMA the French stage and Ibsen combined to offer examples of REALISM. The LITTLE THEATER MOVEMENT got under way in England in the 1890s, about the same time that the CELTIC RENAISSANCE was enlivening the Irish stage. The PROBLEM PLAY established itself as a serious and respectable form in the works of A. W. Pinero, H. A. Jones, and John Galsworthy. In the last decades of the century Wilde's wit and the LIGHT OPERAS of Gilbert and Sullivan brightened the English theater, while the comedy and philosophy of G. B. Shaw's PLAYS enlightened most of the period. Under the impact of REALISM the British stage abandoned Shakespeare for a life of its own.

In the serious ESSAY Arnold, Huxley, Spencer, and Pater explored a variety of topics with earnestness and force, but it was in the NOVEL that the age found its profoundest expression. A few writers like Kipling and Stevenson continued a romantic vein, but George Eliot, Thomas Hardy, George Meredith, George Gissing, Joseph Conrad, John Galsworthy, Arnold Bennett, H. G. Wells, and Samuel Butler established a realistic mode for the NOVEL strong enough to make it the point against which the SYMBOLISTS of the next age launched their attacks. See REALISM, EDWARDIAN AGE, LATE VICTORIAN AGE, and *Outline of Literary History*.

Recantation: A PALINODE, a formal repudiation of something done or written earlier. *The Canterbury Tales* ends with a *recantation* of Chaucer's "enditynges of worldly vanitees . . . and many a song and many a lecherous lay. . . ." After his "A Hymn to the Name and Honour of the Admirable St. Theresa," Richard Crashaw placed a sort of *recantation* called "An Apology for the Foregoing Hymn, as having been writ when the Author was yet among the Protestants."

Recension: A copy of a text that incorporates the most plausible readings taken by critical editing from several sources. The word means "survey," so that a *recension* is a critical text established through a survey of all surviving sources. It has been most often applied to texts of materials existing in manuscript sources, such as Biblical texts. In this sense *The New English Bible* may be called a *recension*.

Recessive Accent: When the METRICAL ACCENT—demanded by the rhythmical pattern of a POEM—forces the STRESS to fall on the first syllable of a word normally accented on the second syllable, it is called *recessive accent*, as in this LINE from *Love's Labour's Lost*:

The extreme parts of time extremely forms.

In current speech a normally iambic word like "entire" may become a TROCHEE, for some speakers if not all, in a phrase like "the entire world."

Recognition Plot (or Scene): A *recognition plot* is one in which the principal REVERSAL or PERIPETY results from someone's acquisition of knowledge previously withheld (either by the CHARACTERS in the PLAY or STORY or by the author in constructing the PLOT) but which, now known, results in a decisive change. In *Oedipus Rex*, considered by Aristotle the finest example of a *recognition plot*, the King, seeking to discover and banish the one whose crime has brought on the national calamity, at last discovers that he himself has killed his father and married his mother. In James's *The Ambassadors* Lambert Strether discovers the true nature of the liaison between Chad and Madame de Vionnet, with the result that his whole course of action is changed. A *recognition plot* may result in either TRAGEDY or COMEDY. A DETECTIVE STORY, for instance, is sometimes said to have a *recognition plot* used as an end in itself, in that the entire purpose of the PLOT is to have the PROTAGONIST (the detective) come into knowledge ("whodunit") not possessed at the beginning of the story. The SCENE in a DRAMA, a NOVEL, or a SHORT STORY in which the recognition occurs is called a *recognition scene*. See DRAMATIC STRUCTURE; ANAGNORISIS.

Redaction: A revision or editing of a MANUSCRIPT. The purpose of *redaction* is to appropriately express writing phrased inappropriately or stated in a wrong form. Sometimes, too, the term implies simply a DIGEST of a longer piece of work or a new version or EDITION of an older piece of writing. Malory's *Le Morte Darthur* is a *redaction* of many of the Arthurian stories.

Redondilla: A Spanish MEASURE, usually in OCTOSYLLABIC COUPLETS or QUATRAINS with various RHYME SCHEMES; used in Ezra Pound's early "Redondillas."

Reductio ad absurdum: A "reducing to absurdity" to show the falsity of an ARGUMENT or position. As a method of argument or PERSUASION, this is a process that carries to its extreme, but logical conclusion, some general statement. One might say, for instance, that the more sleep one gets the healthier one is, and then, by the logical *reductio ad absurdum* process, someone would be sure to point out that, on such a premise, one who has sleeping sickness and sleeps for months on end is really in the best of health. This term is also used to refer to a type of reductive-deductive SYLLOGISM:

> *Major premise:* Either A or B is true.
> *Minor premise:* A is not true.
> *Conclusion:* B is true.

The particular *reductio* here comes in the minor premise, where one alternative is reduced to falseness or "absurdity."

Redundant: Characterized by superfluous words. As a critical term *redundant* is applied to a literary STYLE marked by verbiage, an excess of REPETITION, or PLEONASM. (See PLEONASM, TAUTOLOGY.) The use of repetition and pleonasm may, on occasion, be justified for EMPHASIS, but redundancy differs from these devices in that it is usually applied to the superfluous, the unjustified REPETITION that springs from carelessness or ignorance. Polonius is shown to be a doddering old man through the redundancies of his expression:

> Madam, I swear I use no art at all.
> That he is mad, 'tis true; 'tis true 'tis pity;
> And pity 'tis 'tis true; a foolish figure;
> But farewell it, for I will use no art.
> Mad let us grant him, then; and now remains
> That we find out the cause of this effect,
> Or rather say, the cause of this defect,
> For this effect defective comes by cause;
> Thus it remains and the remainder thus.

A COUPLET in Pope's "The Rape of the Lock" exploits the comic possibilities of multiple *redundancy:*

> Or alum styptics with contracting power
> Shrink his thin essence like a riveled flower—

in which "alum" or "styptics" would suffice and "with contracting power" is completely unnecessary, since that is what "alum" connotes and "styptics" denotes anyway.

Reform Bill of 1832:   This important liberal enactment of the English Parliament was proposed in 1830 and passed in 1832 with the support of King
William IV and the Whig Party under Earl Grey over the strong opposition
of Wellington. The measure denied Parliamentary representation to 56 "rotten" boroughs, provided representation for 156 new communities, and extended the voting power to include large numbers of the middle classes hith-
erto denied the ballot; it did not, however, give the franchise to the laborers.
It was the beginning of a series of reform measures that followed during the
next decade, including the suppression of slavery in the British colonies (1833),
the curbing of commercial monopoly, a lessening of pauperism, a liberalization
of the marriage laws, and great expansion and extension of public educational
facilities. These events stimulated the idealism of many of the authors of the
time, some of whom were active agitators for reform, and affected profoundly
the spirit of literature in the VICTORIAN period. Carlyle and Ruskin in their
lectures and ESSAYS; Dickens, Disraeli, Mrs. Gaskell, Kingsley, and George
Eliot in their NOVELS; and Hood, Tennyson, and Mrs. Browning in their POEMS
reflect the new aspirations aroused by these humanitarian movements and
the subsequent efforts for further reforms in social, political, and educational
realism.The Reform Bill of 1867, passed by the Conservatives under pressures
from the Liberals, further extended the franchise. By this stage, however,
many observers became skeptical. To these reforms toward "completed Democracy," Carlyle responded with the polemical *Shooting Niagara: And After?*
Democratic representation was carried still further by the Reform Bill of 1884,
extending suffrage to nearly all men. In 1918 suffrage was extended to all
men and to women over thirty, and in 1928 to all persons over twenty-one.
See CHARTISM, INDUSTRIAL REVOLUTION.

Refrain: A group of words forming a phrase or sentence and consisting of
one or more LINES repeated at intervals in a POEM, usually at the end of a
STANZA. *Refrains* are of various types. First and most regular is the use of
the same line at the close of each STANZA (as is common in the BALLAD).
Another, less regular form is that in which the *refrain* line (or lines) recurs
somewhat erratically throughout the STANZA—sometimes in one place, sometimes in another. Again a *refrain* may be used with a slight variation in wording
at each recurrence, though here it approaches the REPETEND. Still another
variety of the *refrain* is the use of some rather meaningless phrase that, by
its mere repetition at the close of STANZAS presenting different ideas and
moods, seems to take on a different significance on each appearance—as in
Poe's "Nevermore" and William Morris's "Two red roses across the moon."
In this century, apart from popular SONGS and FOLKLORE, the *refrain* appears
in some of the POEMS of W. B. Yeats.

Regionalism: Fidelity in literature to a particular geographical section; the
accurate representation of its habits, speech, manners, history, FOLKLORE, or
beliefs. A test of *regionalism* is that the ACTION and personages of a work
called regional cannot be moved, without major loss or distortion, to any other
geographical setting. Thomas Hardy, in his portrayal of life in Wessex, wrote
regional NOVELS. The LOCAL COLOR WRITING in America in the last third of
the nineteenth century was a form of *regionalism.* Arnold Bennett's NOVELS
of the Five Towns are markedly regional, as is Margaret Drabble's treatment

of the same region. The literature of the recent American South has been regional in large part.

In this century a concept of *regionalism* much more complex and philosophically deeper than that of its nineteenth-century counterpart has developed, partly as the result of the work of cultural anthropologists and sociologists (notably Howard W. Odum), and has expressed itself in literature through the conscious seeking out, in the local and the particular, of those aspects of character and destiny common to all people in all ages and places. In this respect the work of Willa Cather, Ellen Glasgow, William Faulkner, and Robert Penn Warren has great distinction. See LOCAL COLOR WRITING.

Reification: The treatment of abstractions as concrete things. The representation of ideas as though they had concrete form. "Truth is a deep well," "Love is a many splendored thing," "Thoughts sink into the sea of forgetfulness"— each of these statements represents *reification*. MARXISM has given *reification* an additional meaning that has to do with the translation of abstract concepts into the form of material things; such a transformation includes the reduction of people and ideas into marketable commodities.

Relativism: A belief or sentiment, opposed to absolutism. *Relativism* denies the existence or validity of principles and standards that are everlasting, ubiquitous, changeless, and ABSOLUTE. A contextual *relativism* would claim that the meaning of some such symbol as whiteness is relative to its immediate context—Melville's *Moby-Dick* or Frost's "Design," for example—and cannot be referred to some ABSOLUTE extrinsic standard. Similarly, cultural *relativism* would claim that any artifact or convention has meaning only in a way *relative* to its immediate cultural context. Looking at color symbolism again, for example, we can notice that brides wear white in some societies, while, in others, white is worn only by widows; or, say, the same yellow that Americans sentimentally associate with cowardice connotes courage in many parts of Asia. A kind of critical-historical *relativism* can even claim that literature as an institution has no permanent role or significance but fluctuates—in function, structure, status, and so forth—from place to place and time to time.

Relief Scene: A SCENE in a TRAGEDY, usually as a part of the FALLING ACTION, whose purpose is to provide emotional relaxation for the audience. There is also a sense of *"relief"* that means simple "contrast" without relaxation—quite the contrary. See DRAMATIC STRUCTURE.

Religious Drama: A term applied to the DRAMA of the Middle Ages, when its relation to the church and to religious subject matter was very great. See MEDIEVAL DRAMA, MYSTERY PLAY, MIRACLE PLAY, MORALITY PLAY.

Relique: An old spelling for "relic," something surviving. The most famous use of the term is in the title of Bishop Percy's collection of old ballads: *Reliques of Ancient English Poetry* (1765).

Renaissance: This word, meaning "rebirth," is commonly applied to the movement or period marking the transition from the medieval to the modern world in Western Europe. Special students of the movement are inclined to trace the impulse back to the earlier *Renaissance* of the twelfth and thirteenth centuries and to date the full realization or effects of *Renaissance* forces as late as the eighteenth century. In the usual sense of the word, however, *Renaissance* suggests especially the fourteenth, fifteenth, sixteenth, and early seventeenth centuries, the dates differing for different countries (the English *Renaissance*, for example, being a full century behind the Italian *Renaissance* in its flowering). The break from medievalism was gradual, some *Renaissance* attitudes going back into the heart of the medieval period and some medieval traits persisting well into or even through the *Renaissance*. Yet the fact that a break *was* effected is the essential thing about the *Renaissance*, and the change when completed was so profound that "medieval" on the one hand and *Renaissance* or "modern" on the other imply a sharp contrast.

It is best to regard the *Renaissance* as the result of a new emphasis on, and a new combination of, tendencies and attitudes already existing, stimulated by a series of historical events. It resulted from new forces arising within the old order, with attempts to effect some kind of adjustment between traditional allegiances and modern demands. So it was an age of compromise, a chief aspect of which was a noble but difficult and confusing endeavor to harmonize a newly interpreted Christian tradition with an ardently admired and in part a newly discovered tradition of pagan CLASSICAL culture.

The new humanistic learning (see HUMANISM) that resulted from the rediscovery of CLASSICAL literature is frequently taken as the beginning of the *Renaissance* on its conscious, intellectual side, since it was to the treasures of classical culture and to the authority of classical writers that the people of the *Renaissance* turned for inspiration. Here the break with medievalism was inescapable. In medieval society people's interests as individuals were subordinated to their function as elements in a social unit (see FEUDALISM); in medieval theology people's relations to the world about them were largely reduced to a problem of adapting or avoiding the circumstances of earthly life in an effort to prepare their souls for a future life. But *Renaissance* people had caught from their glimpses of CLASSICAL culture a vision of human life quite at odds with these attitudes. The Hellenistic spirit (see HEBRAISM) had taught them that human beings, far from being groveling worms, were glorious creatures capable of individual development in the direction of perfection, set in a world it was theirs not to despise but to interrogate, explore, and enjoy.

The individualism implied in this view of life exerted a strong influence on English *Renaissance* life and literature, as did many other facts and forces, such as: the Protestant Reformation, itself in part an aspect of the *Renaissance* in Germany; the introduction of printing (see PRINTING, INTRODUCTION INTO ENGLAND), leading to a commercial market for literature; the great economic and political changes leading to the rise of democracy, the spirit of nationalism, an ambitious commercialism, and opportunities for individuals to rise above their birth economically and politically; the revitalized university life; the courtly encouragement of literature; the new geography (discovery of America); the new astronomy (Copernicus, Galileo); and the growing "new science," which made human beings and NATURE the results of natural and demonstrable law rather than a mysterious group of entities subject to occult powers.

The period in English literature generally called the *Renaissance* is usually considered to have begun a little before 1500 and to have lasted until the COMMONWEALTH INTERREGNUM. It consisted of the EARLY TUDOR AGE (*ca.*

1500–1557), the ELIZABETHAN (1558–1603), the JACOBEAN (1603–1625), and the CAROLINE (1625–1642). In the early period English authors felt the impact of CLASSICAL learning and of foreign literatures, together with the sudden, although painful, release from the authority of the church. The new world lying to the west was transforming England into a trading nation no longer at the periphery of the world but at its very crossroads. During the reign of Elizabeth, England reached status as a world power; its DRAMA and its POETRY attained great heights in the work of writers like Spenser, Sidney, and Shakespeare. By the time that James came to the throne, a reaction was beginning to set in, expressed through a growing cynicism, a CLASSICAL dissatisfaction with the extravagance and unbounded enthusiasm of the sixteenth century, a tendency toward melancholy and DECADENCE. At the same time, as though in reaction to this reaction, there was a flourishing of BAROQUE elements in literature. As the conflict of Puritan and Cavalier grew in intensity, these elements grew also. And by the time Charles lost his head, the PURITANISM that was itself a major outgrowth of the intense individualism of the *Renaissance* had spelled an end to most of its literary greatness. Yet Cromwell had as Latin Secretary the last of the great English *Renaissance* figures, John Milton, who was to produce his greatest work in the hostile world of the NEOCLASSICAL RESTORATION. For details about the *Renaissance* in England, see EARLY TUDOR AGE, ELIZABETHAN AGE, JACOBEAN AGE, CAROLINE AGE, HUMANISM, ELIZABETHAN DRAMA, and *Outline of Literary History*.

[References: J. M. Berdan, *Early Tudor Poetry* (1920); W. J. Courthope, *A History of English Poetry*, 6 vols. (1895–1910, reprinted 1962); Lewis Einstein, *The Italian Renaissance in England* (1902), and *Tudor Ideals* (1921, reprinted 1962); J. J. Jusserand, *A Literary History of the English People* (1895); Henry Morley, *English Writers*, 11 vols. (1887–1895); F. E. Schelling, *English Literature in the Lifetime of Shakespeare* (1910); T. Seccombe and J. W. Allen, *The Age of Shakespeare*, 2 vols. (1914).]

Rendering: A term made popular by Henry James to describe the complex presentation of an ACTION rather than the flat reporting of it; the use of the SCENIC METHOD as opposed to EXPOSITION or summary; a direct representation of details, IMAGES, ACTIONS, and speech. See SCENIC METHOD.

Repartee: A "comeback"; a quick, ingenious response or rejoinder; a retort aptly twisted; conversation made up of brilliant witticisms; loosely, any clever reply; also anyone's facility and aptness in such ready WIT. The term is borrowed from fencing terminology. Sydney Smith, Charles Lamb, and Oscar Wilde are important figures in literature who are famous for their command of *repartee*. An instance of *repartee* may be cited from an Oxford account of the meeting of "Beau" Nash and John Wesley. According to this tradition the two met on a narrow pavement. Nash was brusque. "I never make way for a fool," he said insolently. "Don't you? I always do," responded Wesley, stepping to one side.

Repetend: A poetical device marked by a REPETITION or partial repetition of a word, phrase, or clause more or less frequently throughout a STANZA or POEM. *Repetend* differs from REFRAIN in that the refrain usually appears at predetermined places within the poem, whereas the chief poetic merit of the *repetend* is the element of pleasant surprise it is supposed to bring to the reader through its refreshingly irregular appearance. A further difference from the REFRAIN lies in the fact that the *repetend* only partially repeats, whereas the refrain usually repeats in its entirety a whole LINE or combination of lines. Both Coleridge and Poe make frequent use of the *repetend*. In this example from Poe's "Ulalume" the *repetends* are italicized:

> The skies *they were* ashen *and* sober:
> *The leaves they were* crisped *and sere*—
> *The leaves they were* withering *and sere;*
> *It was* night in the lonesome October
> Of my most immemorial year;
> *It was* hard *by the* dim lake *of Auber,*
> *In the* misty mid region *of Weir*—
> *It was* down *by the* dank tarn *of Auber,*
> *In the* ghoul-haunted woodland *of Weir.*

Repetition: A rhetorical device reiterating a word or phrase, or rewording the same idea, to secure EMPHASIS. *Repetition* used carelessly (see TAUTOLOGY, PLEONASM) is unpleasantly noticeable. Employed by deliberate design, it adds force and clarity to a statement. Particularly effective in PERSUASION, *repetition* is a favorite form with orators. The use in VERSE of the REPETEND or REFRAIN makes *repetition* more obvious than is usual in PROSE. One of the most notable examples is, of course, Poe's "The Bells." *Repetition* as a stylistic and poetic device gives pleasure by arousing, by satisfying, or by producing surprise by failing to satisfy a sense of expectancy. In the broadest sense *repetition* is present in RHYME of all kinds, in METER, and in STANZA forms. It appears to be an inescapable element of POETRY. Whitman, for example, who eschews *repetition* in the form of RHYME, METER, or STANZA, employs it widely in his elaborate verbal and grammatical PARALLELISM. FIGURES that use *repetition* and that are defined in this *Handbook* are: ALLITERATION, ANADIPLOSIS, ANAPHORA, ANASTROPHE, ANTIMETABOLE, ANTISTROPHE, ASSONANCE, EPANALEPSIS, EPANAPHORA, EPISTROPHE, PLOCE, POLYPTOTON, POLYSYNDETON, and SYMPLOCE. See REFRAIN, REPETEND, PLEONASM.

Requiem: A CHANT embodying a prayer for the repose of the dead; a DIRGE; a solemn mass beginning as in *Requiem aeternam dona eis, Domine* ("Give eternal rest to them, O Lord"). The following LINES are an example from Matthew Arnold's *Requiescat:*

> Strew on her roses, roses
> And never a spray of yew!
> In quiet she reposes;
> Ah, would that I did too!

In our time the word has been broadened to mean almost anything sad: Faulkner's *Requiem for a Nun,* Serling's *Requiem for a Heavyweight,* Corso's "Spontaneous Requiem for the American Indian," for example.

Resolution: The events following the CLIMAX in a PLOT. See FALLING ACTION, for which it is a SYNONYM, and PLOT and DRAMATIC STRUCTURE.

Resolved Stress: A term used interchangeably with HOVERING STRESS and DISTRIBUTED STRESS.

Rest: A pause or silence that, as in music, is counted as a prosodic element. In some of Shakespeare's "short" LINES, the situation suggests that a dramatic silence may fill out the PENTAMETER, as when Seyton reports, "The Queen, my lord, is dead" [*rest* for four syllables] and Macbeth says, "She should have died hereafter" [*rest* for three syllables]. Since the printing of Shakespeare's PLAYS cannot be trusted, we may consider a later example. In a preliminary draft of a POEM, Gerard Manley Hopkins wrote a characteristic line of IAMBIC PENTAMETER with a feminine ending: "Keeps grace, and that keeps all his goings graces." In revising, Hopkins added a colon after "grace" and eliminated the "and": "Keeps grace: that keeps all his goings graces" [*rest* of one syllable before "that"].

Restoration Age: The restoration of the Stuarts in the person of Charles II in 1660 has given a name to a period of literary history embracing the latter part of the seventeenth century. The fashionable literature of the time reflects the reaction against PURITANISM, the receptiveness to French influence, and the dominance of the CLASSICAL point of view in CRITICISM and original compositions. The revival of the DRAMA, under new influences and theories, is an especially interesting feature of the *Restoration Age*. The COMEDY OF MANNERS was developed by such writers as Etheredge, Wycherly, and Congreve; the HEROIC DRAMA by such as Dryden, Howard, and Otway. Dryden was the greatest POET of the whole period although no one equaled Milton, whose greatest works came in the 1660s and 1670s. John Locke, Sir William Temple, and Samuel Pepys were, in their differing ways, the major PROSE writers after John Bunyan. See NEOCLASSIC PERIOD and *Outline of Literary History*.

[References: R. Garnett, *The Age of Dryden* (1895, reprinted 1922); Edmund Gosse, *A History of Eighteenth-Century Literature, 1660–1780* (1897, reprinted 1911); Allardyce Nicoll, *History of Restoration Drama, 1660–1700*, 2nd ed. (1928).]

Revenge Tragedy: A form of TRAGEDY made popular on the Elizabethan stage by Thomas Kyd, whose *Spanish Tragedy* is an early example of the type. It is largely SENECAN in its inspiration and technique. The THEME is the revenge of a father for a son or vice versa, the revenge being directed by the ghost of the murdered man, as in *Hamlet*. Other traits often found in the *revenge tragedies* include the hesitation of the HERO, the use of either real or pretended insanity, suicide, intrigue, an able scheming villain, philosophic SOLILOQUIES, and the sensational use of horrors (murders on the stage, exhibition of dead bodies, etc.). Examples of the type are Shakespeare's *Titus Andronicus*, Marston's *Antonio's Revenge*, Shakespeare's *Hamlet*, *Hoffman* (author not certain but attributed to Henry Chettle), and Tourneur's *Atheist's Tragedy*. In the management of the dynamics of revenge, we encounter (1) the offense, which can be maximized by the multiplication of injuries and the adding of insult; (2) the ANTAGONIST, most effectively some really formidable (but still vulnerable) person or force; (3) clarification of strategy and marshaling of resources; (4) a series of delays, obstacles, diversions, mistakes, reservations, and so forth—anything to retard the momentum; (5) some unforeseen development that almost thwarts the scheme, but not quite; and finally (6) the showdown, with the revenge carried out in some answerable style. See SENECAN TRAGEDY, TRAGEDY OF BLOOD.

Reversal: The change in fortune for a PROTAGONIST; the PERIPETY. See PERIPETY, DRAMATIC STRUCTURE.

Review: A notice of a current book or PLAY, published in a PERIODICAL. It is important to distinguish between a *review* and other sorts of serious CRITICISM. The *review* announces a work, describes its subject, discusses its method and its technical qualities, and examines its merit; its function is to give readers an accurate idea of the book under consideration, in order that they may decide whether they wish to read it or not. The CRITIC, on the other hand, usually writes about works of some established standing and not brand new, judging them by critical standards either consciously formulated or implied in the critical article. The boundary line between the two forms is very uncertain in actual practice, however. For example, Poe's *review* of Hawthorne's *Twice-Told Tales* fits almost perfectly the description given here and yet is one of the major critical documents in American literary history. On the other hand, the critical quarterlies often carry pieces that are ostensibly CRITICISM and yet remain at the core merely journalistic *reviews*.

Review is also used in the titles of PERIODICALS to indicate the presence in the journal both of critical ARTICLES and of articles on current affairs; for example, the *North American Review,* the *Saturday Review,* the *Edinburgh Review,* the *Sewanee Review.* At one time it was said by the fastidious that periodicals called *reviews* were for CRITICISM, those called JOURNALS were for scholarship; but such distinctions have faded. See CRITICISM, TYPES OF.

Revolutionary Age in American Literature, 1765–1790: In the period between the Stamp Act in 1765 and the formation of the Federal Government in 1789, American writers were, by and large, engaged in nonbelletristic pursuits. POETRY was largely NEOCLASSICAL, with the influence of Pope dominating, although strains of early ROMANTICISM, notably those associated with the GRAVEYARD SCHOOL and with a renewed appreciation of wild NATURE, were felt. Trumbull, Freneau, Hopkinson, Dwight, and Barlow sang a patriotic strain in varied FORMS, often BURLESQUE and satiric. The first PLAY written by an American and acted in America, Godfrey's *The Prince of Parthia,* was performed in 1767, and the stage grew to be an increasing influence on American art outside of New England. In Philadelphia and New York it was particularly important, and after 1773 it was a significant aspect of Southern life through the theater at Charleston. Much of the PROSE writing of the age was polemical, like that of Thomas Paine, Samuel Adams, and Hamilton and Madison (*The Federalist* papers). The first American NOVEL, *The Power of Sympathy* by William Hill Brown, was published in 1789. But the two major PROSE writers of the period were Franklin, with his memoirs (later called his *Autobiography*), and Jefferson, whose Declaration of Independence has certainly proved to be one of the most influential pieces of writing in human history. See REVOLUTIONARY AND EARLY NATIONAL PERIOD IN AMERICAN LITERATURE and *Outline of Literary History.*

Revolutionary and Early National Period in American Literature, 1765–1830: The period in American history between the Stamp Act and the triumph of the "second revolution" represented by the ascendancy of Jacksonian democracy was the time of the establishment of the new nation. A time of beginnings, it saw the first strong reaction to British rule in the response to the Stamp Act in 1765, the First Continental Congress in 1774, the beginnings of armed rebellion in 1775, the Declaration of Independence in 1776, the surrender of Cornwallis in 1781, the Constitutional Convention in 1787, the establishment of a Federal Government in 1789, the founding of the Library of Congress in 1800, and in 1812–1814 a second successful war with England. In 1820 the Missouri Compromise, following by twelve years the abolition of the importing of slaves, established a pattern of political compromise over the issue of slavery; in 1823 America asserted its dominance in the New World through the Monroe Doctrine. In 1829 Andrew Jackson, the seventh president, brought backwoods egalitarianism into triumph over the conservative Federalism that had dominated for a while the early life of the country.

It was a time of literary beginnings as well. There are two relatively distinct ages, that of the Revolution, 1765–1790, and that of the Federalists, 1790–1830. During this time the faint and imitative voices of the Revolutionary POETS—Brackenridge, Freneau, and Hopkinson—and the HARTFORD WITS gave way before the calm strength of Bryant's VERSES. By 1827 Poe had published *Tamerlane*. In 1767 Thomas Godfrey's *Prince of Parthia*, the first American PLAY to be acted, was performed, and American playwriting was established, although it was to be highly imitative of English DRAMA and largely lacking in literary value throughout the period. In 1789 the first American NOVEL, *The Power of Sympathy* by William Hill Brown, was published. Charles Brockden Brown, the first American novelist of marked ability, flourished briefly between 1798 and 1801; his *Wieland* (1798) was a distinguished piece of American GOTHIC. Before 1830 the career of James Fenimore Cooper, America's first major novelist, was well launched; his first significant novel, *The Spy*, appeared in 1821, and the first of the "Leatherstocking Tales" in 1823. Washington Irving, writing with urbane wit and Addisonian grace, became the first truly successful American PROSE writer, gaining international fame, particularly for his *Knickerbocker's History* (1809) and his *Sketch Book* (1820). The first major American MAGAZINE that was to have a long history, the *North American Review*, was established in 1815.

In 1830 America was a young nation, fully established, rawboned, robust, and self-confident, but possessed of a great internal problem, slavery, which was just beginning to put the Federal Union to a serious test. Those who were to produce the important literary works of the nation's first major artistic period had already been born, and many were already at work. See FEDERALIST AGE IN AMERICAN LITERATURE, REVOLUTIONARY AGE IN AMERICAN LITERATURE, and *Outline of Literary History*.

Revue: A light musical entertainment without connected PLOT and consisting of a variety of SONGS, dances, CHORUSES, and SKITS. Satiric comment on contemporary personalities and events is a characteristic element as is the effort to impress by a spectacular display in SETTING, scenery, and costume.

Rhapsody: A selection from EPIC POETRY sung by a rhapsodist—that is, a wandering MINSTREL or court POET of ancient Greece. Originally the rhapsodist got his name from the "stitching together" of the work of various POETS with the rhapsodist's own POETRY, but by 500 B.C. the term *rhapsodist* was applied to professional reciters of EPIC POETRY, principally the *Iliad* and *Odyssey*. The term has come to be applied to highly emotional utterance, in either PROSE or VERSE, marked by great intensity and limited rational organization. It has also been occasionally applied to a literary MISCELLANY or a disconnected series of works. Since Eliot's "Rhapsody on Windy Night" is hardly rhapsodic in any usual sense, the title may be taken as IRONIC.

Rhetoric: The art of PERSUASION. It incorporates principles and theories having to do with the presentation of facts and ideas in clear, persuasive, and attractive language. *Rhetoric* as an art has had a long career in the curricula of ancient and modern schools. The founder of *rhetoric* is believed to have been Corax of Syracuse, who in the fifth century B.C. stipulated fundamental principles for public argument and laid down five divisions for a speech: PROEM, NARRATIVE, ARGUMENT, remarks, and PERORATION or conclusion. Aristotle wrote a *rhetoric* about 320 B.C.; Quintilian's *Institutio Oratoria* (about A.D. 90) served as the background for study in the more modern days of Oxford and Cambridge; Longinus wrote an *Art of Rhetoric* (about A.D. 260), and Aphthonius (about A.D. 380) gave the subject a code and organization that have persisted. To the ancients the aim of *rhetoric* was to make ORATORY effective. According to the Aristotelian conception *rhetoric* was a manner of effectively organizing material for the presentation of truth, for an appeal to the intellect through speech; and it was distinct from POETICS, a manner of composition presenting ideas emotionally and imaginatively. At one time the sophists and others so exalted *rhetoric* that it threatened to become little more than a system of public discussion whereby, rightly or wrongly, by fair means or foul, a point was carried. It was, as Isocrates once noted, "the art of making great matters small, and small things great." This tendency has given to modern ears the suggestion of oratorical emptiness that we often associate with the word "rhetorical." Along with grammar and logic, *rhetoric* made up the TRIVIUM of medieval academic study. Some later CLASSICAL students of *rhetoric*, following Aristotle's lead, subdivided *rhetoric* into the "deliberative" (having to do with debate and deliberation of public action), the "forensic" (from "forum"—having to do with legal decisions of guilt and innocence), and the "epideictic" (having to do with formal praise). During the Middle Ages *rhetoric* was continued as a serious study through this place in the TRIVIUM, and intricate rhetorical systems kept alive an interest in the forms of expression.

In England the RENAISSANCE brought little that was new to *rhetoric*, though such books as Sir Thomas Wilson's *The Arte of Rhetorique* (1553) and George (or Richard) Puttenham's *Arte of English Poesie* (1589) did much to popularize the best practice of the CLASSICAL writers on the subject. In modern education *rhetoric* continues as a phase of study in courses in composition and persists in debating and oratorical contests. In CRITICISM the study of the devices of PERSUASION has again become important. (See RHETORICAL CRITICISM.) The great number of rhetorical terms included in this *Handbook* shows, perhaps as clearly as any other testimony, the basic importance of rhetorical principles in their relation to literature.

Rhetorical Accent: The ACCENT resulting from the placement of STRESS as determined by the meaning or intention of the sentence; used in METRICS in opposition to METRICAL ACCENT, in which only the prosodic pattern of the LINE determines the placement of STRESS. Although articles and prepositions are normally unaccented, special circumstances may dictate a departure: "She's laughing *at* you, not *with* you." "Are you *the* Otis Sistrunk?" See ACCENT.

Rhetorical Criticism: A kind of CRITICISM that emphasizes communication between author and reader. *Rhetorical criticism* analyzes the elements employed in a literary work to impose on the reader the author's view of the meaning, both denotative and connotative, of the work. RHETORIC is the art of PERSUASION; *rhetorical criticism* examines the devices that the author of POETRY or NARRATIVE uses to persuade the reader to make the "proper" interpretation, in the broadest sense, of the work. See HERMENEUTICS; READER RESPONSE CRITICISM.

Rhetorical Question: A question propounded for its rhetorical effect and not requiring a reply or intended to induce a reply. The *rhetorical question* is most used in PERSUASION and in ORATORY, the principle supporting the use of the *rhetorical question* being that since its answer is obvious and usually the only one possible, a deeper impression will be made on the hearer by raising the question than by the speaker's making a direct statement. The too frequent use of this device imparts a tone of artificiality and insincerity to discourse. Pope's LINES from "The Rape of the Lock" illustrate the use of *rhetorical questions* for MOCK HEROIC effect:

> Was it for this you took such constant care
> The bodkin, comb, and essence to prepare?
> For this your locks in paper durance bound?
> For this with tort'ring irons wreath'd around?
> For this with fillets strain'd your tender head,
> And bravely bore the double loads of lead?
> Gods! shall the ravisher display your hair,
> While the fops envy, and the ladies stare!

Note that most *rhetorical questions* generate strongly negative answers. We may once in a while register an emphatic "yes" by asking a *rhetorical question:* "Is the Pope a Catholic?" Usually, however, when we ask "Who knows?" and "Who cares?" with a special intonation, we mean "Nobody knows" and "Nobody cares." Often, the negative element is built into the question: "Aren't we all patriots?" Many of W. B. Yeats's POEMS contain questions. Not all are *rhetorical:* those at the end of "The Second Coming" and "Leda and the Swan" are not. On the other hand, his "No Second Troy" consists of nothing but *rhetorical questions.*

Rhopalic: A sequence that "thickens" as it moves toward its end. In *rhopalic* VERSE each word is a syllable longer than the preceding one, as in this LINE from a prayer by Ausonius:

> Spes dues æternæ stationis conciliator.

The term is sometimes applied to a STANZA in which each line is a FOOT longer than the preceding, as in Crashaw's "Wishes To His (Supposed) Mistress":

Who ere shee bee,
That not impossible shee
That shall command my heart and mee. . . .

Rhyme: Close similarity or identity of terminal sound between accented syllables occupying corresponding positions in two or more LINES of VERSE. The
correspondence of sound is based on the *vowels and succeeding consonants*
of the accented syllables, which must, for a true *rhyme*, be preceded by different consonants. That is, "fan" and "ran" constitute true *rhymes* because the
vowel and succeeding consonant sounds ("an") are the same but the preceding
consonant sounds are different. *Rhyme*, in that it is based on this correspondence of sounds, is related to ASSONANCE and ALLITERATION, but it is unlike
them in construction and in being commonly used at stipulated intervals,
whereas ASSONANCE and ALLITERATION are likely to range with relative freedom through various positions.

Rhyme is more than a mere ornament or device of VERSIFICATION, for
it performs valuable functions. The ear of the reader recognizes a sound already
echoing in the consciousness, and the accord the two similar sounds set up
is likely to bring the reader a sensuous gratification. The recurrence of *rhyme*
at regular intervals helps to establish the FORM of the STANZA. *Rhyme* serves
to unify and distinguish divisions of the POEM, since it is likely that the *rhyme*
sounds followed in one STANZA—the Spenserian for instance—will be changed
when the next stanza is started, although the RHYME SCHEME remains the
same. This principle gives unity to one stanza and marks it off as separate
from the next, affording a sense of movement to the POEM as a whole. The
fact that these qualities, as well as others, reside in *rhyme* will be granted
when we recall how commonly FOLKLORE and the play of children—to take
only two of many instances—resort to *rhyme* to make memorizing easy.

The types of *rhyme* are classified according to two schemes: (1) the position
of the rhymed syllables in the LINE, and (2) the number of syllables involved.

On the basis of position, we have: (1) END RHYME, much the most common
type, which occurs at the end of the LINE; (2) INTERNAL RHYME (sometimes
called LEONINE RHYME), which occurs at some place after the beginning and
before the closing syllables of the LINE; (3) BEGINNING RHYME, which occurs
in the first syllable (or syllables). On the basis of the number of syllables presenting similarity of sound, we have: (1) MASCULINE RHYME, where the correspondence of sound is restricted to the final accented syllable as in "fan" and
"ran." This type of *rhyme* is generally more forcible, more vigorous than
those following: (2) FEMININE RHYME, where the rhyming stressed syllable is
followed by an undifferentiated unstressed syllable exactly matching another
such unstressed syllable in the other *rhyme* words (note that FEMININE RHYME,
as between "fountain" and "mountain," differs considerably from the so-called
COMPOUND RHYME, as between "childhood" and "wildwood," in which there
is *rhyme* between both pairs of components) (DOUBLE RHYME is another name
for FEMININE RHYME); (3) TRIPLE RHYME, where the rhyming stressed syllable
is followed by two undifferentiated unstressed syllables, as in "glorious" and
"victorious." Triple rhyme has been used for serious work—such as Thomas
Hood's "Bridge of Sighs" and Thomas Hardy's "The Voice"—but usually it is
reserved for humorous, satirical VERSE, for the sort of use Byron made of it
in his satiric poems and Ogden Nash in his comic verse.

While most poets have occasionally used poor *rhymes* or have violated consciously one or another of the rhyming customs, certain conventions about *rhyme* persist. These are: (1) A true *rhyme* is based on the correspondence of sound in *accented* syllables as opposed to unaccented syllables. "Stating" and "mating" thus make a true *rhyme,* and for the same reason, "rating" and "forming" make an imperfect *rhyme* since the correspondence is between unaccented syllables. If there is unequal accent on rhyming syllables, as between "afraid" and "decade," the *rhyme* is sometimes called "ironic" because of its subtlety and slight DISSONANCE; this kind of *rhyme* occurs often in Pound's *Hugh Selwyn Mauberley* and in much of Laura Riding's POETRY. (2) For a true *rhyme* all syllables *following* the accented syllable must be identical; "fascinate" and "deracinating" would not be true *rhyme,* because of the difference between the last syllables. (3) The REPETITION of the same vowel sounds in different *rhymes* that occur near each other should ordinarily be avoided. For instance, "stone" and "bone" are good *rhymes* as are "home" and "tome," but a QUATRAIN composed of those four *rhymes* would usually be considered poor because of the repetition of the same vowel sound throughout followed by nasalized consonants. (4) There should not be too great a separation between *rhyme* sounds, since such separation will result in a loss of effect. A *rhyme* occurring in the first LINE and the sixth line, for instance, places a strain on the reader's attention. Such strain can be useful in achieving certain unifying effects. In Eliot's largely unrhymed "Gerontion," two passages ten lines apart end "Titians" and "ambitions," with a touch of surprise and refreshment. The *rhyme* between "gates" and "straits," almost seventy lines apart in the same POEM, may add a bit to a MOTIF of narrow or blocked passages, since the rhyming words have similar meanings. (5) It is permissible, when not done too frequently, for a *rhyme* to fall on an unaccented syllable. If a word of three or more syllables with a dactylic ending is placed in a rhyming position, then, by an old CONVENTION, the second unstressed syllable is given a courtesy "promotion" to accented status with some alteration of vowel quality and quantity. "Liberty," say, is normally a DACTYL—a stressed syllable followed by two unstressed—but, if the word is put into a rhyming position (as in "My country, 'tis of these, / Sweet land of liberty"), then the third syllable is promoted, lengthened, and modified as to vowel quality. Note that the normal rhyme word "thee" precedes the promoted word, to guide the ear. (Marvell and Blake so promote "eternity"and "symmetry" that they *rhyme* with "lie" and "eye.") If the promoted rhyme word precedes the normal (as in the *rhyme* between "rarity" and "me" at the end of Browning's "My Last Duchess"), then the effect is slightly unusual and adds emphasis to the second rhyme word. Promotion can also yield an IDENTICAL RHYME, which does not constitute true *rhyme* (as when Shakespeare in a SONNET puts "memory" and "masonry" in a rhyming position). "Full" *rhyme* occurs between stressed syllables with more or less equal accent; "ironic" *rhyme* between stressed syllables with detectably unequal accent ("good" and "childhood," say); "promotion" when conventional "courtesy" stress is given to the last syllable of a DACTYL; the very rare attempt to squeeze a *rhyme* out of inflexibly unstressed syllables (as between "water" and "number") has no name but could be called "puny." One could continue such nomenclature to the point of saying "puny IDENTICAL" (as in "water" and "sister"), but enough is enough. (6) Syllables that are spelled differently but have the same pronunciation (such as "rite" and "right") (called IDENTICAL RHYME or RIME RICHE) do not make acceptable *rhymes*.

What constitutes a *rhyme* changes as pronunciation changes, and sometimes between nations or sections of nations. In the eighteenth century "join" was pronounced as though it were spelled "jine" and made a true *rhyme* with "divine." Allen Tate once observed that some *rhymes* of his that were true with his southern pronunciation were considered SLANT RHYMES in New England.

Rhyme and the importance it enjoys in modern VERSIFICATION are comparatively modern developments. Ancient Greek and Latin POETRY was not rhymed; our earliest English VERSE (*Beowulf* is an example) was not based on *rhyme*. Historians of PROSODY sometimes credit the development of *rhyme* to ceremonials within the Catholic Church and suggest that the priests made use of *rhyme* as a device to aid the worshipers in their singing and memorizing of the ritualistic procedure. *Dies Irae* is an example of one of the earliest rhymed SONGS of the Church. Since even so-called Late Latin remained a markedly synthetic and suffixal language, loading the end of virtually every noun, verb, and adjective with one or more weakly accented syllables of inflection, most of these church SONGS were either unrhymed (as is "Adeste Fideles" in Latin and in the English TRANSLATION) or else rhymed on syllables once or twice removed from the ends of words (that is, FEMININE or TRIPLE RHYME). It seems that *rhyme* as a common feature of POETRY does not and maybe cannot emerge until a language can furnish a large number of usable words that have a stressed syllable at or very near the end—until, that is, a synthetic-suffixal language loosens up in the direction of becoming analytic-prefixal.

Among contemporary poets a tendency to use imperfect *rhymes*, substituting ASSONANCE, CONSONANCE, and DISSONANCE for true *rhymes*, is widespread; and most present-day POETS take interesting liberties with the traditional "rules" for *rhyme* cited in this article. Among the names given such variations are SLANT RHYME, NEAR RHYME, OBLIQUE RHYME, off-rhyme, para-rhyme. See ASSONANCE, CONSONANCE, DISSONANCE.

[References: R. M. Alden, *Introduction to Poetry* (1909); H. Lanz, *The Physical Basis of Rime* (1931); C. F. Richardson, *A Study in English Rhyme* (1909); George Saintsbury, *Historical Manual of English Prosody* (1910); W. K. Wimsatt, *The Verbal Icon* (1954).]

Rhyme Royal: A seven-line IAMBIC PENTAMETER STANZA rhyming *ababbcc*, sometimes with an ALEXANDRINE (HEXAMETER) seventh LINE. The name has been said to derive from its employment by the Scottish King James I; but since Chaucer and other predecessors of James had used *rhyme royal* extensively, it must be attributed to James, if at all, as an honor in recognition of the fact that a king wrote VERSE rather than that he originated the pattern. Chaucer used *rhyme royal* in the *Parlement of Foules*, the *Man of Law's Tale*, the *Clerk's Tale*, and *Troilus and Criseyde*, and found the form adapted to his best descriptive, NARRATIVE, and reflective manners. Some other POETS who have written in *rhyme royal* are Lydgate, Hoccleve, Dunbar, Skelton, Wyatt, Shakespeare, Wordsworth, Morris, and W. H. Auden. John Masefield wrote both *The Widow in the Bye Street* and *Dauber* in *rhyme royal*. The last stanza of Shakespeare's *Rape of Lucrece* is a good example:

When they had sworn to this advised doom,
They did conclude to bear dead Lucrece thence;
To show her bleeding body thorough Rome,
And so to publish Tarquin's foul offence:
Which being done with speedy diligence,
  The Romans plausibly did give consent
  To Tarquin's everlasting banishment.

An idea of the pleasingly various tonalities available in *rhyme royal* can be had by comparing Auden's *Letter to Lord Byron* and "The Shield of Achilles" (in part) with Wordsworth's "Resolution and Independence."

Rhyme Scheme: The pattern, or sequence, in which the RHYME sounds occur in a STANZA or POEM. *Rhyme schemes,* for the purpose of analysis, are usually presented by the assignment of the same letter of the alphabet to each similar sound in a stanza. Thus, the pattern of the SPENSERIAN STANZA is *ababbcbcc.* An example of another RHYME pattern is the STANZA:

The time I've lost in wooing,	*a*
In watching and pursuing	*a*
The light that lies	*b*
In woman's eyes,	*b*
Has been my heart's undoing,	*a*
Tho' wisdom oft has sought me,	*c*
I scorned the lore she brought me,	*c*
My only books	*d*
Were woman's looks,	*d*
And folly's all they've taught me.	*c*

                     —Thomas Moore

Here *wooing, pursuing, undoing* all have the same RHYME and are arbitrarily marked with the symbol *a; lies, eyes* are alike and assigned the symbol *b; sought me, brought me, taught me* are all alike and given the symbol *c; books* and *looks* are alike and are set down as symbol *d*. Thus, the *rhyme scheme* of the stanza is *aabbaccddc.* Sometimes italics, capital letters, or "prime" marks are used to indicate REPETITIONS. See RONDEL.

Rhythm: The passage of regular or approximately equivalent time intervals between definite events or the recurrence of specific sounds or kinds of sounds or the recurrence of stressed and unstressed syllables. Human beings have a seemingly basic need for such regularity of recurrence, or for the effect produced by it, as laboratory experiments in psychology have demonstrated and as one can see for oneself by watching a crew of workers digging or hammering or by listening to CHANTEYS and work SONGS.

    In both PROSE and POETRY the presence of rhythmic patterns lends both pleasure and heightened emotional response to the listener or reader, for it establishes a pattern of expectations and rewards the listener or reader with the pleasure of a series of fulfillments or gratifications of expectation. In POETRY three different elements may function in a pattern of seemingly regular temporal occurrence: QUANTITY, ACCENT, and number of syllables (see METER). In English poetry the rhythmic pattern is most often established by a combination of ACCENT and number of syllables. This pattern of a fairly regular number of syllables with a relatively fixed sequence of stressed and unstressed syllables lends itself to certain kinds of basic rhythmic analysis in English VERSIFICATION. The *rhythm* may be "marching" or DUPLE—that is, involve one stressed and one unstressed syllable, as in IAMBS and TROCHEES. Or it may be "dancing" or TRIPLE—that is, involve one stressed and two unstressed syllables, as in DACTYLS and ANAPESTS. It may be RISING—that is, beginning with unstressed and ending with stressed syllables, as in IAMBS and ANAPESTS; or FALLING— that is, beginning with stressed and ending with unstressed syllables, as in TROCHEES and DACTYLS. Other kinds of *rhythm* than these are possible (and even common) in English verse, as witness SPRUNG RHYTHM and FREE VERSE, as well as the *rhythm* in OLD ENGLISH VERSIFICATION or in Walt Whitman's poetry.

In PROSE, despite the absence of the formal regularity of pattern here described for VERSE, CADENCE is usually present and in impassioned prose it often establishes the definite patterns of rhythmic recurrence. See PROSE RHYTHMS, QUANTITY, ACCENT, METER, SCANSION.

[Reference: Susanne K. Langer, *Problems of Art* (1957).]

Riddle: The modern *riddle* has its more dignified ancestor in the *riddles* of medieval literature. Based on Latin prototypes, *riddles* became an important "type" of the vernacular literatures of Western Europe, including Old English. The *riddles* of Aldhelm (seventh century), though written in Latin, are English in tone, and the Exeter Book (eleventh century) contains an interesting collection of nearly a hundred *riddles* in Old English. They are of unknown authorship (formerly ascribed to Cynewulf). The interpretation of the *riddles* is sometimes obvious, sometimes obscure; but the descriptive power of the POETRY is often high, and the IMAGERY is fresh and picturesque. The new moon is a young Viking sailing the skies; the falcon wears the bloom of trees on her breast; the swan is a wandering spirit wearing a "noiseless robe." The swan, the falcon, the helmet, the horn, the hen, the onion, beer, the BIBLE manuscript, the storm-spirit, and many other objects connected with war, seamanship, NATURE, religion, and everyday life describe themselves by descriptive EPITHET, characteristic act, apt METAPHOR, and end with a "Tell me what I'm called." These *riddles* contain some of the best existing evidence of the use of external nature in the period and have been termed the most secular of all existing Old English literature. *Riddles* persist among serious POETS: see Dickinson's "A Narrow Fellow" and Frost's "Three Guesses."

[References: Paull F. Baum, *Anglo-Saxon Riddles of the Exeter Book* (1963); Archer Taylor, *English Riddles from Oral Tradition* (1951).]

Rime Couée: A TAIL RHYME STANZA, one in which two LINES, usually in TETRAMETER, are followed by a short line, usually in TRIMETER, two successive short lines rhyming—as, for example, *aabccb*, where the *a* and *c* lines are TETRAMETER and the *b* TRIMETER. SEE TAIL RHYME STANZA.

Rime Riche: Rhyming words with identical sounds but different meanings, as "stair" and "stare" or "well" (adjective) and "well" (noun). See IDENTICAL RHYME.

Rising Action: The part of a dramatic PLOT that has to do with the COMPLICATION of the ACTION. It begins with the EXCITING FORCE, gains in interest and power as the opposing groups come into CONFLICT (the HERO usually being in the ascendancy), and proceeds to the CLIMAX or turning point. See DRAMATIC STRUCTURE.

Rising Rhythm: In METRICS a FOOT in which the last syllable is accented; thus, in English either the IAMB or the ANAPEST. Coleridge illustrates *rising rhythm* in these lines:

> ˊ ˘ ˊ ˘ ˊ ˘ ˊ
> Iambics march from short to long.

> ˘ ˘ ˊ ˘ ˘ ˊ ˘ ˘ ˊ ˘ ˘ ˊ
> With a leap and a bound the swift Anapests throng.

Rocking Rhythm: In METRICS a FOOT in which a stressed syllable falls between two unstressed syllables, an AMPHIBRACH. *Rocking rhythm* is illustrated in this LINE from Swinburne:

> ˘ ˊ ˘ ˘ ˊ ˘ ˘ ˊ ˘ ˘
> The search, and | the sought, and | the seeker, | —the

> ˊ ˘ ˘ ˊ ˘ ˘ ˊ ˘
> soul and | the body | that is.

Rococo: In the history of European architecture the *Rococo* Period follows the BAROQUE and precedes the NEOCLASSIC, embracing in time most of the eighteenth century. The style arose in France, flourished on the Continent, but made little headway in England. It was marked by a wealth of decorative detail suggestive of grace, intimacy, playfulness. The fashion spread to furniture. It avoided the grandiose, the serious, the "logical" effects. Since the style was often regarded in England as a decadent phase of the RENAISSANCE or BAROQUE styles, the term *rococo* has frequently been employed in a derogatory sense to suggest the overdecorative or "impudently audacious" and is not infrequently confused with the BAROQUE (also unfavorably interpreted). In its older sense Swinburne uses the term as the title of one of his love lyrics—one in which the lover implores his three-day mistress not to forget their ardent but brief love. A more discriminating reference to the earlier meaning is found in Professor Friedrich Brie's phrase the *rococo* EPIC, as applied to such pieces as Pope's "Rape of the Lock" and Gay's "Fan," in which the small luxuries of life, particularly of fashionable women, are prominent sources of interest. See BAROQUE.

[References: Helmut Hatzfeld, *The Rococo: Eroticism, Wit, and Elegance in European Literature* (1972); George Hitchcock, *The Rococo Eye* (1970).]

Rodomontade: Ostentatious bragging or blustering. Falstaff's famous description of his bold fight with the highwaymen is an example of *rodomontade*, as is his boastful, "There live not three good men unhanged in England, and one of them is fat and grows old. . . ." So called after the braggart Moorish king Rodomonte in Ariosto's *Orlando Furioso*. See MILES GLORIOSUS.

Roman à Clef: A NOVEL in which actual persons and events are presented under the guise of FICTION. (Like the "Schlüssel" in SCHLÜSSELROMAN, the "clef" here means "key," in the sense of a program of true identities.) Notable examples of the GENRE have been Madeleine de Scudéry's *Clélie*, Thomas

Love Peacock's *Nightmare Abbey*, Hawthorne's *The Blithedale Romance*, Somerset Maugham's *Cakes and Ale*, Aldous Huxley's *Point Counter Point*, and Ernest Hemingway's *The Sun Also Rises*.

Romance: A word first used for Old French as a language derived from Latin or "Roman" to distinguish it from Latin itself, a meaning that has now been extended so that the languages proximately derived from Latin are called *Romance* languages. Later the term *romance* was applied to any work written in French, and as STORIES of knights and their chivalric deeds were a dominant FORM of Old French literature, the word *romance* was applied to such stories. The first Old French *romances* were translated from Latin, and this fact may have helped to fix the name *romance* on them. For a further account of these early *romances*, see MEDIEVAL ROMANCE. In RENAISSANCE criticism ROMANTIC EPICS, such as *The Faerie Queene*, were called *romances*.

The term *romance* has had special meanings as a kind of FICTION since the early years of the NOVEL. In his PREFACE to *Incognita* (1692) William Congreve made a distinction between NOVEL and *romance* as works of long fiction, and in 1785 Clara Reeve in *The Progress of Romance* declared, "The Novel is a picture of real life and manners, and of the times in which it was written. The Romance in lofty and elevated language, describes what has never happened nor is likely to." This distinction has resulted in two distinct uses of *romance* in reference to modern fictional FORMS. In common usage, it refers to works with extravagant CHARACTERS, remote and exotic places, highly exciting and heroic events, passionate love, or mysterious or supernatural experiences. In another and more sophisticated sense, *romance* refers to works relatively free of the more restrictive aspects of realistic VERISIMILITUDE and expressive of profound, transcendent, or idealistic truths. As Hawthorne expressed it in the "Preface" to *The House of the Seven Gables*, the *romance* "sins unpardonably, so far as it may swerve aside from the truth of the human heart"; yet it has, he insisted, "a right to present that truth under circumstances, to a great extent, of the writer's own choosing or creation." In America particularly, the *romance* has proved to be a serious, flexible, and successful medium for the exploration of philosophical ideas and attitudes, ranging through such differing works as Hawthorne's *The Scarlet Letter*, Melville's *Moby-Dick*, Fitzgerald's *The Great Gatsby*, Faulkner's *Absalom, Absalom!*, and Warren's *World Enough and Time*. According to Northrop Frye's very useful scheme of modes (*Anatomy of Criticism*), *romance* occupies the zone between MYTH and MIMESIS; in this special application *romance* has to do with CHARACTERS whose powers exceed those of normal human beings but fall short of those of gods. See MEDIEVAL ROMANCE, METRICAL ROMANCE, ARTHURIAN LEGEND, ROMANTICISM, ROMANTIC NOVEL.

[References: Northrop Frye, *Anatomy of Criticism* (1957); E. C. Pettet, *Shakespeare and the Romance Tradition* (1949).]

Romanesque: A term sometimes used to characterize writing that is fanciful or fabulous. It is more rarely used simply to denote the presence of a ROMANCE quality in a work.

Romantic Comedy: A COMEDY in which serious love is the chief concern and source of interest, especially the type of COMEDY developed on the early

Elizabethan stage by such writers as Robert Greene and Shakespeare. Greene's *James the Fourth* represents the *romantic comedy* as Shakespeare found it and is supposed to have influenced Shakespeare in his *Two Gentlemen of Verona*. A few years later Shakespeare perfected the type in such PLAYS as *The Merchant of Venice* and *As You Like It*. Characteristics commonly found include: love as chief motive; much out-of-door ACTION; an idealized HEROINE (who usually masks as a man); love subjected to great difficulties; POETIC JUSTICE often violated; balancing of characters; easy reconciliations; happy ending. Shakespeare's last group of plays, the TRAGICOMEDIES or "serene romances" (such as *Winter's Tale* and *Cymbeline*), are in some sense a modification of the earlier *romantic comedy*.

[Reference: Peter G. Phialas, *Shakespeare's Romantic Comedies* (1966).]

Romantic Criticism: A term sometimes used for the body of critical ideas that developed late in the eighteenth and early in the nineteenth centuries as a part of the triumph of ROMANTICISM over NEOCLASSICISM. It accompanied and to some extent guided the revolt against the CLASSICAL attitudes of the eighteenth century, and it was inspired in part by the necessity of "answering" conservative CRITICS such as Francis Jeffrey, Sydney Smith, and William Gifford. The "artificial" character of Pope's poetic IMAGERY was attacked by W. L. Bowles, who in turn was "answered" by Lord Byron and others. New theories about the genius of Shakespeare were espoused by Coleridge and others: instead of being regarded as a "wild, irregular genius," who succeeded in spite of his violation of the "laws" of dramatic composition, his art was studied on the assumption that it succeeded because it followed laws of its own organism, which were more authentic than artificial "formal" rules. (See ORGANIC FORM.) This view harmonized with the new ideas of IMAGINATION. The *romantic criticism* of Shakespeare thus led to the view that Shakespeare, like NATURE, was infallible. "If we do not understand him, it is our fault or the fault of copyists or typographers" (Coleridge). Much extravagant "Bardolatry" followed. Another aspect of *romantic criticism* was Wordsworth's theory of POETRY as calling for simple THEMES drawn from humble life expressed in the language of ordinary life—a sharp reaction from the conventions of NEOCLASSIC poetry. In general the romantic CRITIC saw art as an expression of the artist (the EXPRESSIVE THEORY OF ART), valued it as a living organism, and sought its highest expressions among simple people, primitive cultures, and aspects of the world unsullied by artifice or by commerce with human society. See PRIMITIVISM; CULTURAL PRIMITIVISM; ROMANTICISM; CRITICISM, TYPES OF; and ORGANIC FORM.

Romantic Epic: A type of long NARRATIVE POEM developed by Italian RENAISSANCE poets (late fifteenth and sixteenth centuries) by combining the materials and something of the method of the MEDIEVAL ROMANCE with the manner and technique of the classical EPIC. Such POETS as Pulci, Boiardo, and Ariosto produced *romantic epics* that were like MEDIEVAL ROMANCES in stressing the love element, in their complicated and loose STRUCTURE, in the multiplicity of CHARACTERS and EPISODES, and in freedom of VERSE FORM. Yet they were like the Virgilian EPIC in their use of a formal INVOCATION, statement of THEME, set speeches, formal descriptions, use of epic SIMILES, supernatural MACHINERY, and division into books. Later Tasso (*Jerusalem De-*

livered, 1581) infused a strong TONE of moral instruction and religious propaganda into the type. The method of ALLEGORY was also employed in the Italian *romantic epics.* The literary CRITICS of the time were divided in their attitudes toward the new type of EPIC, the conservatives strongly opposing it because of its departure from CLASSICAL standards. The form proved generally popular with readers, however, and when Edmund Spenser came to write his ambitious English epic, he actually modeled his POEM largely on the *romantic epics* of Ariosto (*Orlando Furioso,* 1516) and Tasso. Thus, *The Faerie Queene,* EPIC in its high patriotic purpose and in much of its technique, romantic in its chivalric atmosphere and Arthurian SETTING, became, by following the general method of Ariosto and Tasso, the great example in English literature of a *romantic epic.*

Romantic Novel: A type of NOVEL marked by strong interest in ACTION and presenting EPISODES often based on love, adventure, and combat. The term *"romantic"* owes its origin to the early type of STORY embraced by the ROMANCE of medieval times, but with the march of time other elements have been added. The FABLIAU and the NOVELLA, particularly, have contributed qualities. A romance, in its modern meaning, signifies that type of NOVEL more concerned with action than with CHARACTER; more properly fictional than legendary since it is woven so largely from the IMAGINATION of the author; read more as a means of escape from existence than of familiarity with the actualities of life. The writers of modern ROMANCE are too numerous to mention: Sir Walter Scott's name may be allowed to represent the long list of romancers in English and American literature. In another sense *romantic novel* is used interchangeably with ROMANCE, as a form relatively free of the demands of the actual and thus able to reflect imaginative truth. See ROMANCE.

Romantic Period in American Literature, 1830–1865: The period between the "second revolution" of the Jacksonian Era and the close of the Civil War in America saw the testing of the American nation and its development by ordeal. It was an age of great westward expansion, of the increasing gravity of the slavery question, of an intensification of the spirit of embattled sectionalism in the South, of a powerful impulse to reform in the North. Its culminating act was the trial by arms of the opposing views of the two sections in a civil war, whose conclusion certified the fact of a united nation dedicated to the concepts of industry and capitalism and philosophically committed to the doctrine of egalitarianism. In a sense it may be said that the three decades following the inauguration of Andrew Jackson as president in 1829 put to the test his views of democracy and saw emerge from the test a secure union committed to essentially Jacksonian principles.

In literature it was America's first great creative period, a full flowering of the romantic impulse on American soil. Surviving from the FEDERALIST AGE were its three major literary figures: Bryant, Irving, and Cooper. Emerging as new writers of strength and creative power were the novelists Hawthorne, Simms, Melville, and Harriet Beecher Stowe; the POETS Poe, Whittier, Holmes, Longfellow, Lowell, and Whitman; the essayists Thoreau, Emerson, and Holmes; the CRITICS Poe, Lowell, and Simms. The South, moving toward a concept of Southern independence, advanced three distinguished PERIODICALS, the

Southern Review, the *Southern Literary Messenger,* and the *Southern Quarterly Review.* In the North the *Knickerbocker Magazine* and the *Democratic Review* joined the continuing arbiter of Northern taste, the *North American Review,* and then were followed by *Harper's Magazine* (1850) and the *Atlantic Monthly* (1857). Between 1830 and 1855 the GIFT BOOKS and ANNUALS proved to be remunerative markets for ESSAYS and TALES.

The POETRY of the period was predominantly romantic in spirit and form. Moral qualities were significantly present in the VERSE of Emerson, Bryant, Longfellow, Whittier, Holmes, Lowell, and Thoreau. The sectional issues were debated in POETRY by Whittier and Lowell speaking for abolition, and Timrod, Hayne, and Simms speaking for the South. Poe formulated his theory of POETRY and in some fifty LYRICS practiced a symbolist VERSE that was to be, despite the charge of triviality by such contemporaries as Emerson, the strongest single poetic influence emerging from pre-Civil War America, particularly in its impact on European POETRY. Lowell wrote satiric VERSE in DIALECT. Whitman, beginning with the 1855 edition of *Leaves of Grass,* was the ultimate expression in America of a POETRY organic in FORM and romantic in spirit, united to a concept of democracy that was pervasively egalitarian.

In the ESSAY and on the lecture platform the New England transcendentalists—Emerson, Thoreau, Margaret Fuller, and Alcott—carried the literary expression of philosophic and religious ideas to a high level. In critical ESSAYS Lowell wrote with distinction, Simms with skill, and Poe with genius. Until 1850 the NOVEL continued to follow the path of Scott, with Cooper and Simms as its major producers. In the 1850s, however, emerged the powerful symbolic NOVELS of Hawthorne and Melville and the effective PROPAGANDA NOVEL of Harriet Beecher Stowe. Poe, Hawthorne, and Simms practiced the writing of SHORT STORIES throughout the period, taking up where Irving had left off in the development of the form. Humorous writing by A. B. Longstreet, George W. Harris, Artemus Ward, Josh Billings, and the early Mark Twain was establishing a basis for a realistic literature in the vernacular, but it failed in this period to receive the critical attention that was to come its way later.

In the DRAMA the "star" system, the imitation of English "SPECTACLE" DRAMA, and ROMANTIC TRAGEDY modeled on Shakespeare were dominant. Although N. P. Willis and R. M. Bird were successful dramatists, only George Henry Boker, with his *Francesca da Rimini,* displayed any distinctive literary talent in the theater. *Uncle Tom's Cabin* and *Rip Van Winkle* began stage careers that were to be phenomenally successful.

At the end of the Civil War a new nation had been born in the ordeal of war, and it was to demand and receive a new literature less idealistic and more practical, less exalted and more earthy, less consciously artistic and more honest than that produced in the age when the American dream had glowed with greatest intensity and American writers had made a great literary period by capturing on their pages the enthusiasm and the optimism of that dream. See *Outline of Literary History.*

Romantic Period in English Literature, 1798–1870: In the period between the publication of *Lyrical Ballads* (1798) and the death of Dickens, English literature was dominated by the spirit of ROMANTICISM. One common way of designating literary periods in English history is to call the AGE OF THE ROMANTIC MOVEMENT (1798–1832) the *Romantic Period* and to lump together the time between the death of Scott in 1832 and the end of the century as the VICTORIAN AGE, since Queen Victoria reigned through much of it. However, the romantic impulse, which flowered with such spectacular force in 1798, remained the dominant literary impulse well into the 1860s; hence the divisions employed in this *Handbook*. (See REALISTIC PERIOD IN ENGLISH LITERATURE.)

The *Romantic Period* came into being during the Napoleonic Wars and flourished during the painful economic dislocations that were their aftermath. It saw union with Ireland; it witnessed the suffering attendant on the INDUSTRIAL REVOLUTION; it was torn by CHARTISM and the great debates centering on the REFORM BILL; it developed a sensitive humanitarianism out of witnessing the suffering of the masses; it both espoused and despised the doctrine of UTILITARIANISM. An industrial England was being born in pain and suffering. The throes of developing democracy, the ugliness of the sudden growth of cities, the prevalence of human pain, the blatant presence of the "profit motive"—all helped to characterize what was in many respects "the best of times . . . the worst of times."

In the first half of the period a philosophical ROMANTICISM based on value in the individual, on the romantic view of NATURE, and on an organic concept of art dominated the English literary mind. There was some skepticism and CYNICISM, expressed in the form of abusive PARODY and SATIRE, but optimism was the spirit of the times, although it was often an optimism closely associated with the impulse to revolt and with radical political reform. In the second half of the period, the EARLY VICTORIAN AGE, the impact of the INDUSTRIAL REVOLUTION was more deeply felt and the implications of the new science on philosophy and religious belief began to be obvious. The romantic philosophy still held, and the spirit of ROMANTICISM permeated literature and much of life; but it found itself seriously in conflict with much of the world around it, and out of that conflict came a literature of doubt and questioning. If, for example, the attitudes of Coleridge and Shelley are compared with those of Carlyle—all three clearly romantics—the extent to which the ROMANTICISM of the earlier period was being qualified by the conditions of industrial England and was being used to test those conditions becomes clearer.

In POETRY the *Romantic Period* was a golden age, rich with the sonorous voices of Wordsworth, Coleridge, Shelley, Keats, Byron, Tennyson, Arnold, and the Pre-Raphaelites, and enlivened by the harsher tones of Browning. It was a great age for the NOVEL, producing Godwin, Scott, Austen, the Brontës, Thackeray, Dickens, Trollope, and the early George Eliot. A period of serious critical and social debate in PROSE, it produced Carlyle, Ruskin, Macaulay, Arnold, Pater, and Newman. In the INFORMAL ESSAY it produced Lamb, Hazlitt, Hunt, and De Quincey. Only in the DRAMA, bound by the PATENT THEATERS and a blind idolatry of Shakespeare and hampered by the "star" system, did the *Romantic Period* fail to produce work of true distinction; it was virtually the weakest period in the English stage since Elizabeth I ascended the throne.

For the literary history of the period, see AGE OF THE ROMANTIC MOVEMENT, EARLY VICTORIAN AGE, and *Outline of Literary History*. See also ROMANTICISM.

Romantic Tragedy: Nonclassical TRAGEDY. The term is used for such modern tragedy as does not conform to the traditions or aims of CLASSICAL TRAGEDY.

It differs from the latter in its greater freedom of technique, its wider scope of THEME and treatment, its greater emphasis on CHARACTER (as compared with emphasis on PLOT), its looser STRUCTURE, its freer employment of IMAGINATION, its greater variety of STYLE, and its readiness to admit humorous and even GROTESQUE elements. ELIZABETHAN tragedy is largely romantic, for example, Shakespeare's. See CLASSICAL TRAGEDY, TRAGEDY, CRITICISM.

Romanticism: A MOVEMENT of the eighteenth and nineteenth centuries that marked the reaction in literature, philosophy, art, religion, and politics from the NEOCLASSICISM and formal orthodoxy of the preceding period. *Romanticism* arose so gradually and exhibited so many phases that a satisfactory definition is not possible. The aspect most stressed in France is reflected in Victor Hugo's phrase "liberalism in literature," meaning especially the freeing of the artist and writer from the restraints and rules of the classicists and suggesting that phase of individualism marked by the encouragement of revolutionary political ideas. The POET Heine noted the chief aspect of German *romanticism* in calling it the revival of medievalism in art, letters, and life. A late nineteenth-century English CRITIC, Walter Pater, thought the addition of strangeness to beauty (the neoclassicists having insisted on order in beauty) constituted the romantic temper. An American transcendentalist, Dr. F. H. Hedge, thought the essence of *romanticism* was aspiration, having its origin in wonder and mystery. An interesting schematic explanation calls *romanticism* the predominance of IMAGINATION over reason and formal rules (CLASSICISM) and over the sense of fact or the actual (REALISM), a formula that recalls Hazlitt's statement (1816) that the CLASSIC beauty of a Greek temple resided chiefly in its actual form and its obvious CONNOTATIONS, while the "romantic" beauty of a GOTHIC building or ruin arose from associated ideas that the IMAGINATION was stimulated to conjure up. The term is used in many senses, a recent favorite being that which sees in the romantic mood a psychological desire to escape from unpleasant realities.

Perhaps more useful to the student than definitions will be a list of romantic characteristics or earmarks, though *romanticism* was not a clearly conceived system. Among the aspects of the romantic movement in England may be listed: SENSIBILITY; PRIMITIVISM; love of NATURE; sympathetic interest in the past, especially the medieval (see GOTHIC); MYSTICISM; individualism; ROMANTIC CRITICISM; and a reaction against whatever characterized NEOCLASSICISM. Among the specific characteristics embraced by these general attitudes are: the abandonment of the HEROIC COUPLET in favor of BLANK VERSE, the SONNET, the SPENSERIAN STANZA, and many experimental VERSE FORMS; the dropping of the conventional POETIC DICTION in favor of fresher language and bolder figures; the idealization of rural life (Goldsmith); enthusiasm for the wild, irregular, or GROTESQUE in NATURE and art; unrestrained IMAGINATION; enthusiasm for the uncivilized or "natural"; interest in human rights (Burns, Byron); sympathy with animal life (Cowper); sentimental melancholy (Gray); emotional psychology in FICTION (Richardson); collection and imitation of popular BALLADS (Percy, Scott); interest in ancient Celtic and Scandinavian mythology and literature (see CELTIC REVIVAL); renewed interest in Spenser, Shakespeare, and Milton. Typical literary FORMS of the romantic writers include the LYRIC, especially the love lyric, the reflective lyric, the nature lyric (see NATURE), and the lyric of morbid melancholy (see GRAVEYARD SCHOOL);

the SENTIMENTAL NOVEL; the METRICAL ROMANCE; the SENTIMENTAL COM-
EDY; the BALLAD; the PROBLEM NOVEL; the HISTORICAL NOVEL; the GOTHIC
ROMANCE; the SONNET; and the CRITICAL ESSAY (see ROMANTIC CRITICISM).

Although the romantic movement in English literature had its beginnings
or anticipations in the earlier eighteenth century (Shaftesbury, Thomson, Dyer,
Lady Winchilsea), it was not until the middle of the century that its characteris-
tics became prominent and self-conscious (Blair, Akenside, Joseph and Thomas
Warton, Gray, Richardson, Sterne, Walpole, Goldsmith, and somewhat later
Cowper, Burns, and Blake), while its complete triumph was reserved for the
early years of the nineteenth century (Wordsworth, Coleridge, Scott, Southey,
Byron, Shelley, Keats, Jane Austen, Mary Shelley). A little later in the nine-
teenth century came the great ROMANTIC PERIOD IN AMERICAN LITERATURE
(Bryant, Emerson, Lowell, Thoreau, Whittier, Hawthorne, Melville, Poe, Whit-
man, Dickinson, Holmes).

The last third of the nineteenth century witnessed the substitution of a
soberer mood than prevailed earlier in the century, and, although the late
nineteenth century and the early twentieth century, in both England and
America, have been marked by a sharp reaction against the romantic, especially
the sentimental, spirit in literature, it is to be remembered that much late
VICTORIAN literature was romantic and that the vitality of *romanticism* is
evidenced by the great volume of romantic writing being produced in the
twentieth century.

By way of caution it may be said that such descriptions of *romanticism*
as this one probably overstress the distinction between *romanticism* and CLAS-
SICISM or NEOCLASSICISM and cannot hope to resolve the confusion over what
"romantic" means which, Professor A. O. Lovejoy asserts, has "for a century
been the scandal" of literary history and CRITICISM. As early as 1824 an effort
to discover what the authorities meant by the term proved disappointing,
and the succeeding century-and-a-half has increased the number of divergent,
often contradictory, senses in which the term is employed. Some writers, like
Professor Walter Raleigh and Sir Arthur Quiller-Couch, have even urged the
desirability of abandoning the terms "romantic" and "classic," pointing out
that their use adds to the critical confusion and tends to distort the facts of
literary history and divert attention away from the natural processes of literary
composition. Several have noted that Homer's *Odyssey*, for example, is cited
by some as the very essence of the romantic, by others as a true exemplar
of CLASSICISM. Professor Lovejoy, noting that the "romantic" movement has
meant different things in different countries and that even in a single country
"romantic" is often used in conflicting senses, proposes that the term be employed in the plural only, as a recognition of the various *romanticisms*. Even
if the term "romantic" were always employed in the same sense and its characteristics could be safely and comprehensively enumerated, it would still be
true that one could not use a single characteristic, like the love of wild scenery
or the use of BLANK VERSE, as a "key" for classifying as romantic any single
POEM or poet.

Yet, viewed in philosophical terms, *romanticism* does have a fairly definite
meaning for the student of literature. The term designates a literary and philosophical theory that tends to see the individual at the very center of all life
and experience, and it places the individual, therefore, at the center of art,
making literature most valuable as an expression of unique feelings and particu-

lar attitudes (the EXPRESSIVE THEORY OF ART) and valuing its accuracy in portraying the individual's experiences, however fragmentary and incomplete, more than it values its adherence to completeness, UNITY, or the demands of GENRE. It places a high premium on the creative function of the IMAGINA-TION, seeing art as a formulation of intuitive imaginative perceptions that tend to speak a nobler truth than that of fact, logic, or the here and now. Although *romanticism* tends at times to regard NATURE as alien, hostile, and intractible to interpretation, it more often sees in nature a revelation of Truth, the "living garment of God," and often, pantheistically, a sensate portion of deity itself, and certainly a more suitable subject for true art than those aspects of the world sullied by artifice (CULTURAL PRIMITIVISM). It differs significantly from the literary movements that were to follow it, REALISM and NATURALISM, in the locus of its values. Some manifestations of *romanticism* are marked by the presence—in concept, SETTING, STYLE, or IMAGERY—of the exotic, the farfetched, the imaginary, the arcane, and the occult; but the main *romantic* tendency is to employ the commonplace, the natural, the simple as its materials. It seeks to find the Absolute, the Ideal, by transcending the actual, whereas REALISM finds its values in the actual and NATURALISM in the scientific laws that undergird the actual (see NATURALISM).

Ultimately, it must be admitted that the continuing conflict of ideas and attitudes that occurred in the eighteenth century and saw the triumph of *romanticism* over CLASSICISM, however much exaggerated in standard literary histories, did go a very long way toward the establishment of our modern democratic world, and, where REALISM and NATURALISM are significantly different from *romanticism*, they are closer to it than to the CLASSICISM with which it broke. Wherever faith in the individual and in freedom from rules, systems, or even from RATIONALISM appears, there, one aspect of *romanticism* speaks. Contradictory as its attributes are and however true Professor Lovejoy's assertion that it should be spoken of always in the plural, *romanticisms* shape the controlling attitudes of the democratic world. See NATURALISM, REALISM, NEOCLASSICISM, CLASSICISM, PRIMITIVISM, GOTHIC, ROMANTIC CRITICISM, RO-MANTIC PERIOD IN ENGLISH LITERATURE, ROMANTIC PERIOD IN AMERICAN LITERATURE.

[References: M. H. Abrams, *The Mirror and the Lamp* (1953); Irving Babbitt, *Rousseau and Romanticism* (1919, reprinted 1947); H. A. Beers, *A History of English Romanticism* (1926); Ernest Bernbaum, *Guide through the Romantic Movement* (1915, reprinted 1958); Harold Bloom, ed., *Romanticism and Consciousness; Essays in Criticism* (1970); Douglas Bush, *Mythology and the Romantic Tradition in English Poetry*, 1937; W. J. Courthope, *A History of English Poetry*, 6 vols. (1895–1910), reprinted 1962; Oliver Elton, *Survey of English Literature, 1730–1780*, 2 vols. (1928), and *Survey of English Literature, 1780–1830*, 2 vols. (1912); Northrop Frye, ed., *Romanticism Reconsidered* (1963); J. B. Halstead, *Romanticism*, 1969; C. H. Herford, *The Age of Wordsworth* (1897, reprinted 1916); T. E. Hulme, *Speculations*, ed. Herbert Read (1924, reprinted 1954); Frank Kermode, *The Romantic Image* (1957); A. O. Lovejoy, *Essays in the History of Ideas* (1944); T. S. Omond, *The Romantic Triumph* (1909, reprinted 1923); W. L. Phelps, *The Beginnings of the Romantic Movement* (1893); Logan Pearsall Smith, *Words and Idioms*, 5th ed. (1943); C. E. Vaughan, *The Romantic Revolt* (1907); René Wellek, *Concepts of Criticism* (1963).]

Romany: The language of the gypsies. It is a DIALECT form of the Indian branch of the Indo-Iranian languages, blended with many words and phrases from various European languages and spoken in many dialects. A gypsy; or a descriptive way of designating anything pertaining to the gypsies. *Romany* ways and manners have been much written about by George Borrow.

Rondeau: A set French VERSE pattern, artificial but very popular with many English POETS. Generally used for light and fanciful expression. The *rondeau* pattern consists characteristically of fifteen LINES, the ninth and fifteenth being short lines—a REFRAIN. Only two RHYMES (exclusive of the refrain) are allowed, the RHYME SCHEME running *aabba aabc aabbac.* The *c*-RHYME here represents the REFRAIN, a group of words, usually the first half of the line, selected from the opening VERSE. The form divides itself into three STANZAS with the refrain at the end of the second and third stanzas. The VERSES most frequently consist of eight syllables. There is also a form of the *rondeau* consisting of twelve lines, ten using two RHYMES plus REFRAINS, rhyming *abba abc abbac.* Another, known as the *rondeau redoublé,* consists of six QUATRAINS rhyming *abab,* with the first four lines forming in succession the last LINES of the second, third, fourth, and fifth quatrains.

Rondel: A French VERSE form, a variant of the RONDEAU, to which it is related historically. It consists of fourteen or thirteen LINES (depending on whether the two-line REFRAIN is kept at the close or simply one line). The RHYME SCHEME most usual is *ab* baabab abba*ab* (the italicized RHYMES here representing LINES used as a REFRAIN and repeated in their entirety). As in the other FRENCH FORMS, repetition of RHYME words is not allowed. The *rondel* differs from the RONDEAU in two chief respects: the number of lines and the use of complete (rather than partial) lines for the REFRAIN. Chaucer sometimes used the *rondel* as a STANZA and not as a POEM in itself; in his examples unity is achieved by the use of recurring lines or RHYME sounds.

Round: A SONG for at least three voices, in which each singer begins a line or a phrase behind the preceding one but repeats what the preceding one is singing. Sometimes called a CATCH.

Round Character: A term used by E. M. Forster to designate a CHARACTER drawn with sufficient complexity to be able to surprise the reader without losing credibility. A *round character,* Forster says, "has the incalculability of life about it." See CHARACTERIZATION, FLAT CHARACTER.

Roundel: A variation of the French RONDEAU pattern, generally attributed to Swinburne, who wrote "A Century of Roundels" and gave the FORM its popularity. The *roundel* is characterized by its eleven-line form and the presence, in the fourth and eleventh LINES, of a REFRAIN taken, as in the RONDEAU, from the first part of the first line. The RHYME SCHEME (using *c* to indicate the refrain) is *abacbababac. Roundel* is also the Chaucerian spelling for RONDEL.

Roundelay: A modification of the RONDEL, a French LYRIC VERSE FORM. The *roundelay* is a simple POEM or SONG of about fourteen lines in which part of one LINE frequently recurs as a REFRAIN. The term may also mean the musical SETTING of a RONDEAU so that it may be sung or chanted as an accompaniment for a folk dance.

Roundheads:　During the English Civil War the members of the Puritan or Parliamentarian party. See CAVALIER LYRICISTS.

Rubáiyát:　The plural of the Arabic word for QUATRAIN; hence a collection of four-line STANZAS. The best-known use of the word in English is in Edward FitzGerald's TRANSLATION of *The Rubáiyát of Omar Khayyám.*

Rubáiyát Stanza:　The STANZA that FitzGerald used for his TRANSLATION of *The Rubáiyát of Omar Khayyám:* a QUATRAIN of IAMBIC PENTAMETER lines rhyming *aaba.*

Rubric:　From the Latin for "red." A title, description, direction, or other element independent but explanatory of the text. The term derives from the fact that the directions for religious services in liturgical books were printed in red to distinguish them from the text proper.

Rune:　A character in a sort of alphabet developed about the second or third century by the Germanic tribes in Europe. A *boc* (modern "book") was a runic tablet of beech wood. Later, *runes* were carved on stones, drinking horns, weapons, and ornaments. In very early times *rune* developed the special meaning of a character, sign, or written formula with magical power. *Runes* were used for charms, healing formulas, and incantations. The Norse god Odin is said to have been driven to insanity by the power of a *rune* sent to him by a certain maiden who was declining his love. Likewise, a *rune* came to mean any secret means of communication. Thus, the ANGLO-SAXON poet Cyne-wulf signed some of his POEMS by placing in runic characters in these poems a sequence of words the first letters of which spelled his name. Runic writing was very common in Anglo-Saxon England until gradually crowded out by the Latin alphabet used by the Christian missionaries. *Rune* may also mean a Finnish poem and (less accurately) an old Scandinavian poem. Emerson even used the word in the sense of "any song, poem, or verse."

Run-on Lines:　The carrying over of sense and grammatic structure from one line to a succeeding one for completion. The opposite of END-STOPPED LINES. See ENJAMBEMENT.

S

Saga: In its strictest sense, applied to Icelandic or other Scandinavian STORIES of the medieval period recording the legendary and historical accounts of heroic adventure, especially of members of certain important families. The earlier Icelandic *sagas*, like the early Irish EPICS and ROMANCES, were in PROSE. There were also "mythological" *sagas*. The term came to be used for a historical LEGEND developed by ORAL TRANSMISSION till it was popularly accepted as true—a FORM lying between authentic history and intentional FICTION. The meaning is not confined to Scandinavian pieces, and the commonest meaning now for SAGA is a NARRATIVE having the characteristics of the Icelandic *sagas;* hence any traditional TALE of heroic achievement or extraordinary or marvelous adventure. The best example of the true *saga* is that of Grettir the Strong, suggestive of the story of Beowulf. Others are included in the famous *Heimskringla*, from which Longfellow drew material for his *Saga of King Olaf*. John Galsworthy has used the term in the title of his story of the Forsytes, a series of NOVELS called *The Forsyte Saga*.

[References: Theodore M. Andersson, *The Icelandic Family Saga* (1967); Carol J. Clover, *The Medieval Saga* (1982); W. A. Craigie, *The Icelandic Sagas* (1913); M. I. Steblin-Kamenskij, *The Saga Mind* (tr. 1973).]

Saints' Lives: Highly eulogistic accounts of the miraculous experiences of the saints; a kind of religious ROMANCE extremely popular in the medieval world. Chaucer's "Man of Law's Tale" in *The Canterbury Tales* is typical in everything except its literary excellence. See BIOGRAPHY, HAGIOGRAPHY.

[References: G. H. Gerould, *Saints' Legends* (1916); Charles Williams Jones, *Saints' Lives and Chronicles in Early England* (1947).]

Saint's Play: A medieval PLAY based on the LEGEND of some saint. See MIRACLE PLAY.

Sapphic: A stanzaic pattern deriving its name from the Greek POET Sappho, who wrote love LYRICS of great beauty about 600 B.C. The pattern consists of three LINES of eleven syllables each (ᴗ | ᴗ | ᴗᴗ | ᴗ | ᴗ) called HENDECASYLLABICS and a fourth of five syllables (ᴗᴗ | ᴗ). The pattern has been frequently tried in English, but the demand for three SPONDEES in each STANZA results too often in distortion. Swinburne and Ezra Pound are generally conceded to have been the most successful modern writers of *sapphics*. The following stanza is by Swinburne:

Then to | me so | lying a | wake a | vision

Came with | out sleep | over the | seas and | touched me,

Softly | touched mine | eyelids and | lips; and | I too,

Full of the | vision.

Sarcasm: A form of verbal IRONY in which, under the guise of praise, a caustic and bitter expression of strong and personal disapproval is given. *Sarcasm* is personal, jeering, intended to hurt. See IRONY.

Satanic School: A phrase used by Southey in the "Preface" to his *Vision of Judgment* (1821) to designate the members of the literary group made up of Byron, Shelley, Hunt, and their associates, whose irregular lives and radical ideas—defiantly flaunted in their writings—suggested the term. They were not infrequently contrasted with the "pious" group of the LAKE SCHOOL— Wordsworth, Coleridge, and Southey. By a natural extension in the use of the term, writers of more recent times who have attacked conventional moral standards sometimes have been spoken of as belonging to the *Satanic School* of literature.

Satanism: The worship of Satan, probably a survival of heathen fertility cults. In the twelfth century it gained strength through a secret rebellion against the Church. At its center is the Black Mass, an ugly and blasphemous PARODY of the Christian Mass, with a nude woman on the altar with the Host sometimes being the ashes and blood of murdered children. It was revived during the reign of Louis XIV in France and was again revived in the 1890s, when it attracted some literary attention. Interest in *Satanism*, or at least its literary expression, seems to be increasing. It is closely connected with witchcraft.

Satire: A literary manner that blends a critical attitude with HUMOR and WIT for the purpose of improving human institutions or humanity. True satirists are conscious of the frailty of human institutions and attempt through laughter not so much to tear them down as to inspire a remodeling. If CRITICS simply abuse, they are writing INVECTIVE; if they are personal and splenetic, they are writing SARCASM; if they are sad and morose over the state of society, they are writing IRONY or a JEREMIAD. As a rule modern *satire* spares the individual and follows Addison's self-imposed rule: to "pass over a single foe to charge whole armies." Most often, *satire* deals less with great sinners and criminals than with the general run of fools, knaves, ninnies, oafs, codgers, and frauds. Indeed, a good deal of enduring *satire* has to do with literature and the literary life itself.

    Satire existed in the literature of Greece and Rome. Aristophanes, Juvenal, Horace, Martial, and Petronius are indicative of that rich satiric vein. Through the Middle Ages *satire* persisted in the FABLIAU and BEAST EPIC. In Spain the PICARESQUE NOVEL developed a strong element of *satire;* in France Molière and Le Sage handled the manner deftly, and somewhat later Voltaire established himself as an arch-satirist. In England, from the time of Gascoigne (*Steel Glass,* 1576) and Lodge (*Fig for Momus,* 1595), writers condemned the vices and follies of the age in VERSE and PROSE (Hall, Nash, Donne, Jonson). By the time of Charles I, however, interest in *satire* had declined, only to revive with the struggle between Cavaliers and Puritans. At the hands of Dryden the HEROIC COUPLET, already the favorite FORM with most English satirists, developed into the finest satiric VERSE form. The eighteenth century in England became a period of *satire;* POETRY, DRAMA, ESSAYS, CRITICISM, all took on the satirical manner at the hands of such writers as Dryden, Swift,

Addison, Steele, Pope, and Fielding. In the nineteenth century Byron and Thackeray were fine satirists.

Early American *satire* naturally followed English in STYLE. Before the Revolution, American *satire* dealt chiefly with the political struggle. Of the HARTFORD WITS Trumbull produced *M'Fingal*, a Hudibrastic *satire* on Tories. Hopkinson amusingly attacked the British in his "Battle of the Kegs" (1778). Freneau (*The British Prison Ship*) wrote the strongest Revolutionary *satire*. Shortly after the Revolution, the *Anarchiad* (VERSE), by Trumbull, Barlow, Humphreys, and Hopkins, and *Modern Chivalry* (FICTION), by Brackenridge, attacked domestic political difficulties and the crudities of our frontier. Irving's good-humored *satire* in *The Sketch Book* and *Knickerbocker's History*, Holmes's SOCIETY VERSE, Lowell's DIALECT poems (*Biglow Papers*), and Mark Twain's PROSE represent the general trend of American *satire* up to the twentieth century.

In the twentieth century English writers like G. B. Shaw, Noel Coward, Evelyn Waugh, and Aldous Huxley have maintained the satiric spirit in the face of the gravity of NATURALISM and the earnestness of SYMBOLISM. In America Eugene O'Neill (on occasion), Edith Wharton, Sinclair Lewis, George Kaufman and Moss Hart, John P. Marquand, and Joseph Heller have commented critically on human beings and their institutions.

Satire is of two major types: FORMAL (or direct) SATIRE, in which the satiric voice speaks, usually in the first person, either directly to the reader or to a character in the *satire*, called the ADVERSARIUS; and INDIRECT SATIRE, in which the *satire* is expressed through a NARRATIVE and the CHARACTERS or groups who are the butt are ridiculed not by what is said about them but by what they themselves say and do. Much of great literary *satire* is indirect; one of the principal forms of INDIRECT SATIRE is the MENIPPEAN.

FORMAL SATIRE is fundamentally of two types, named for its distinguished CLASSICAL practitioners: *Horatian satire* is gentle, urbane, smiling; it aims to correct by gentle and broadly sympathetic laughter; *Juvenalian satire* is biting, bitter, angry; it points with contempt and moral indignation to the corruption and evil of human beings and institutions. Addison is a *Horatian* satirist, Swift a *Juvenalian*.

For centuries the word *satire*, which literally means "a dish filled with mixed fruits," was reserved for long POEMS, such as the pseudo-Homeric *Battle of the Frogs and Mice*, the poems of Juvenal and Horace, Langland's *The Vision of Piers Plowman*, Chaucer's "Nun's Priest's Tale," Butler's *Hudibras*, Pope's "The Rape of the Lock," Lowell's *A Fable for Critics*. Almost from its origins, however, the DRAMA has been suited to the satiric spirit, and from Aristophanes to Shaw and Noel Coward, it has commented with penetrating IRONY on human foibles. There was a notable concentration of its attention on Horatian *satire* in the COMEDY OF MANNERS of the RESTORATION AGE. But it has been in the fictional NARRATIVE, particularly the NOVEL, that *satire* has found its chief vehicle in the modern world. Cervantes, Rabelais, Voltaire, Swift, Fielding, Jane Austen, Thackeray, Mark Twain, Edith Wharton, Sinclair Lewis, Aldous Huxley, Evelyn Waugh, John P. Marquand, Joseph Heller, Thomas Pynchon, all have made extended fictional NARRATIVES the vehicles for a wide-ranging and powerfully effective satiric treatment of human beings and their institutions.

In England since 1841 *Punch* has maintained a high level of comic *satire*.

In America the *New Yorker* has demonstrated since 1925 the continuing appeal of sophisticated Horatian *satire*. The motion pictures, the plastic and graphic arts, and the newspaper comic strip and political cartoon have all been instruments of telling, satiric comment on human affairs.

For satiric methods, see IRONY, BURLESQUE, PARODY, SARCASM, INVECTIVE, INNUENDO, FORMAL SATIRE, INDIRECT SATIRE, MENIPPEAN SATIRE.

[References: R. M. Alden, *The Rise of Formal Satire in England* (1899, reprinted 1962); R. C. Elliott, *The Power of Satire: Magic, Ritual, Art* (1960); John Heath-Stubbs, *The Verse Satire* (1969); Alvin Kernan, *The Cankered Muse: Satire of the English Renaissance* (1959); Ronald Paulson, *Satire and the Novel in Eighteenth-Century England* (1967); John Peter, *Complaint and Satire in Early English Literature* (1956); James Sutherland, *English Satire*, 1958; David Worcester, *The Art of Satire* (1940).]

Saturday Club: A club of literary and scientific people in and around Cambridge and Boston in the mid-nineteenth century who came together chiefly for social intercourse and good conversation, at irregular intervals. There were no bylaws. Some of the more famous members were: Emerson, Longfellow, Agassiz, Prescott, Whittier, and Holmes; among the frequent visitors were Hawthorne, Motley, and Sumner. Holmes paid tribute to the organization in VERSE (*At the Saturday Club*), and Dr. E. W. Emerson wrote an official history of the club.

Satyr Play: The fourth and final PLAY in the bill of TRAGEDIES in Greek DRAMA: so called because the CHORUS was made up of horse-tailed goat-men called satyrs. The *satyr play* was intended to bring comic relief after the three TRAGEDIES that preceded it. It had the STRUCTURE of a TRAGEDY and subject matter from serious mythology but was grotesquely comic in manner. Euripides' *Cyclops* is the only surviving *satyr play*. It has been conjectured that Euripides' *Alcestis* may belong to the type, and a few lineaments survive in that play's modern avatar, Eliot's *The Cocktail Party*. Thornton Wilder wrote a modern *satyr play*.

Saussurean Linguistics: A most productive and influential body of thought derived from or stimulated by the work of the Swiss linguist Ferdinand de Saussure (1857–1913). Saussure tried to put LINGUISTICS on a scientific footing by emphasizing the priority of the abstract underlying system of language (*la langue*) over particular mutable manifestations thereof in actual speech (*la parole*), along with the priority of timeless or simultaneous phenomena considered synchronically over historical or successive phenomena considered diachronically. He defined the linguistic SIGN as a combination of a "signifier" and a "signified" and insisted that the essential nature of the sign is an arbitrary and conventional relation that does not reach out, back, or down to any substance, entity, or absolute outside language. Saussure's emphasis on synchronic systems—instead of diachronic "organisms" somehow evolving continuously—has had far-reaching effects in linguistic and literary study, not to mention anthropology, psychiatry, and historiography. Since signifier and signified are radically discontinuous, and since the system of language is similarly discontinuous from any world conceived of as its environment, a staggering range of concepts have to be modified. We are enjoined to take care in thinking about etymology, say, as important; "noon" and "November," say, both contain an element that historically means "nine," but noon is not the ninth hour and November is not the ninth month: these signs are arbitrary and can function perfectly as long as the community of speakers can agree on the meaning of "noon" and "November." (In his thinking about arbitrariness and discontinuousness, Saussure admitted a debt to the earlier American linguist William Dwight Whitney and to the school of German "Neogrammarians"; he could almost as well have seen a kinship with Stéphane Mallarmé.) Because of Saussure, CRITICS have had to revise their ideas of everything from ONOMATOPOEIA to MIMESIS and expression. More recently, the Saussurean concept of language as a system of differences without positive terms has been centrally important in both STRUCTURALISM and DECONSTRUCTION.

[References: Jonathan Culler, *Ferdinand de Saussure*, 1976, *On Deconstruction: Theory and Criticism after Structuralism*, 1982, and *Structuralist Poetics: Structuralism, Linguistics, and the Study of Literature*, 1975; Ferdinand de Saussure, *Course in General Linguistics*, tr. 1959.]

Scald: Variant spelling for SKALD, an early Scandinavian POET. See SKALD.

Scansion: A system for describing more or less conventional poetic RHYTHMS by dividing the LINES into FEET, indicating the locations of binomial ACCENTS, and counting the syllables. Three methods for the *scansion* of English VERSE exist: the traditional graphic one; the musical, employing musical notations; and the acoustic, developed by linguists using complex machines. However, only the traditional graphic one is readily comprehensible without much specialized knowledge.

The graphic method is a written means of indicating the mechanical elements by which the POET has established the rhythmical effects. The METER, once the scanning has been performed, is named according to the number of FEET employed in a LINE. In English VERSE the major feet, explained elsewhere, are IAMB ($\smile$ $\prime$), TROCHEE ($\prime$ $\smile$), ANAPEST ($\smile$ $\smile$ $\prime$), DACTYL ($\prime$ $\smile$ $\smile$), SPONDEE ($\prime\prime$), and PYRRHIC ($\smile$ $\smile$). A verse of one foot (of any type) is called MONOMETER; two, DIMETER; three, TRIMETER; four, TETRAMETER; five, PENTAMETER; six, HEXAMETER; seven, HEPTAMETER; eight, OCTAMETER. Thus, a verse consisting of two trochaic feet is called TROCHAIC DIMETER; of five iambic, IAMBIC PENTAMETER; of six dactylic, DACTYLIC HEXAMETER; and so on.

The *scansion* of this STANZA from Keats's *The Eve of St. Agnes* shows (when the lines are treated mechanically and the accents emphasized in reading) the following ACCENTS and divisions into FEET:

And still | she slept | an az | ure-lid | ded sleep |

In blanch | ed lin | en, smooth | and lav | endered, |

While he | from forth | the clos | et brought | a heap |

Of can | died ap | ple, quince, | and plum, | and gourd; |

With jel | lies sooth | er than | the cream | y curd, |

˘　　　´　　˘　　　　´　　　　　´　　　˘　　　´　　　˘　　　´
And lu | cent syr | ops, tinct | with cin | namon; |

´　　　˘　　˘　　　´　　˘　　´　　　˘　　　´　　˘　　´
Manna | and dates, | in ar | gosy | transferred |

˘　　　´　　˘　　　´　　˘　　´　　˘　　´　　　˘　　´
From Fez; | and spic | ed dain | ties, ev | ery one |

˘　　　´　　˘　　´　　˘　　´　　˘　　´　　˘　　´
From silk | en Sam | ar cand | to ce | dared Leb | a non. |

Such a mechanical marking of ACCENTS and division into FEET discloses that the RHYTHM of the STANZA is predominantly composed of one unaccented syllable followed by an accented, called an IAMBIC FOOT, as explained previously. Next we discover that characteristically there are five of these FEET to the line; such a line is called PENTAMETER. We are now, as the result of our scanning, prepared to state that the RHYTHM and METER of *The Eve of St. Agnes* can be summed up as IAMBIC PENTAMETER. As our example STANZA is scanned, there are only two obvious exceptions to this pattern: (1) the first FOOT of the seventh LINE consists of an accented syllable preceding an unaccented (and is thus a TROCHEE) and (2) the ninth LINE consists of six FEET instead of five (and is thus a HEXAMETER or an ALEXANDRINE). (One further possible exception is suggested by uncertainty as to the scanning of "argosy," which in normal pronunciation is a DACTYL; the final syllable may, however, receive some "courtesy" stress of the sort called "promotion"; see RHYME.) So, finally, we have found that our STANZA consists of eight IAMBIC PENTAMETER LINES with a ninth that is an ALEXANDRINE—a pattern called the SPENSERIAN STANZA. *Scansion* is often considered to include the RHYME SCHEME as well as the VERSE analysis. In that case we would say of the preceding STANZA that it rhymes *ababbcbcc*. Since, however, the RHYME SCHEME in the case of the SPENSERIAN STANZA is always the same, it would be redundant to say that Keats's LINES make up a SPENSERIAN STANZA rhyming *ababbcbcc*.

It should be noted that this binary mechanical system of *scansion*, which is almost universally employed in the analysis of English POETRY, was borrowed from classical QUANTITATIVE VERSE and does not always fit readily on the English ACCENTUAL-SYLLABIC rhythmic pattern. It cannot be applied easily to SPRUNG RHYTHM or to FREE VERSE. An additional caveat is in order: the failure of a LINE or a STANZA of English poetry to fit readily into a regular *scansion* pattern does not necessarily indicate ineptness on the part of the POET; it may indicate that the POEM is constructed on rhythmic patterns that do not readily lend themselves to such mechanical analysis. The art of RHYTHM in any poem shows as much in apt departure from patterning as in apt adherence. See METER, ACCENT, RHYTHM, ELISION, ANACRUSIS, TRUNCATION, CATALEXIS, STRESS, SECONDARY STRESS.

[References: Paul Fussell, *Poetic Meter and Poetic Form* (rev. ed. 1979); John Hollander, *Rhyme's Reason* (1981); George Saintsbury, *Manual of English Prosody* (1930).]

Scazon: Another name for the CHOLIAMB; sometimes CHOLIAMB is limited to the deliberate reversal of an iamb. This rare and delicate effect occurs at the end of a LINE when a TROCHEE or DACTYL takes the place of the IAMB or ANAPEST that the ear has been conditioned to expect. It can be refreshing, surprising, and even shocking. Consider the line "that the wind came out of the cloud, chilling" in Poe's "Annabel Lee," wherein the TROCHAIC "chilling" supplants the RISING RHYTHM established by the rest of the POEM. Line 186 of Tennyson's "Lucretius" shows the same effect, with a DACTYL supplanting an IAMB at the end: "Strikes through the wood, sets all the tops quivering." There is a dramatic reversal at the end of one of the LINES in Wallace Stevens's "Sunday Morning": "Elations when the forest blooms; gusty." Robert Frost wrote a few such lines, and the contemporary American POET John Frederick Nims has accomplished a virtually unique *doubling* of the reversal in the last two FEET of the first line of his "Love Poem": "My clumsiest dear, whose hands shipwreck vases."

Scenario: A skeleton outline of a DRAMA, which gives the sequence of ACTIONS making up the PLOT and the successive appearances of the principal CHARACTERS. The plot of a DRAMA is itself sometimes called the *scenario*. The form of a PLAY written as the basis of a FILM is also called a *scenario*.

Scène à faire: A SCENE in a PLAY so thoroughly prepared for that the author is obliged to write it. See OBLIGATORY SCENE, which is the English equivalent.

Scenes (of a Drama):   The division of an ACT of a DRAMA into *scenes* is somewhat less systematic than the division of the PLAY itself into acts, for there is incomplete agreement about what constitutes a *scene*. Sometimes the entrances and exits of important personages determine the beginning and ending of *scenes,* as in French DRAMA. In some plays a *scene* is a logical unit in the development of the ACTION. Many English dramatists regard the clearing of the STAGE as the sign of a change of *scene*. Some authorities, however, think that not all stage-clearings or entrances and exits really indicate a new *scene*. Thus, Sir Edmund Chambers (*Elizabethan Stage*) uses *scene* as "a continuous section of action in an unchanged locality." Theoretically, a well-managed *scene* should have a STRUCTURE comparable to that of a PLAY itself, with the five logical parts (see DRAMATIC STRUCTURE). The plays of Shakespeare, of course, do not conform to this requirement, though some of the *scenes* can be analyzed successfully on this basis, and we must remember that our present-day divisions into *scenes* of these plays were not made by Shakespeare himself. The most important principle in *scene*-construction, perhaps, is that of climactic arrangement. *Scenes* have been loosely classified on such varying principles as length, structural function, internal technique, external background. Thus, there may be long *scenes* and short *scenes,* transitional *scenes,* expository *scenes,* development *scenes,* climactic *scenes,* relief *scenes,* messenger *scenes,* MONOLOGUE *scenes,* DIALOGUE *scenes,* ensemble *scenes,* forest *scenes,* battle *scenes,* balcony *scenes,* street *scenes,* garden or orchard *scenes,* court *scenes,* banquet-hall *scenes,* and chamber *scenes*. In some PLAYS not nominally divided into ACTS, the main parts or sections may be called *scenes* (as in O'Neill's *The Hairy Ape* and *The Emperor Jones*), a practice that suggests, perhaps, that the dramatic ACTION or activity implicit in "act" is subordinate to the static or symbolic display suggested by the neutral *scene*.

Scenic Method: In the NOVEL that can be called dramatic, that is, presenting its actions as they are imagined to occur rather than summarizing them in

NARRATIVE EXPOSITION, there is a tendency for the author to construct the story in a sequence of self-explanatory scenes, similar in many respects to those of the DRAMA. This tendency in novels using the SELF-EFFACING AUTHOR is sufficiently marked to result in the dramatic technique of the NOVEL being called the *scenic method.* The construction of a typical chapter of a Henry James novel illustrates the *scenic method:* such a chapter (it may be selected almost at random from *The Portrait of a Lady*) will usually open with a detailed description of SETTING and of the interior state of the CHARACTER through whom the action is being presented (Isabel Archer, say); then, when everything has been well prepared for, the ACTION and conversation are presented directly and in great detail, the ACTION rising to a CLIMAX on which the CURTAIN figuratively falls at the abrupt ending of the chapter. See SCENES (OF A DRAMA), RENDERING, POINT OF VIEW.

Schema: A fancy word for "outline," applied nowadays to the elaborate SCHE-MATA (Greek plural) that Joyce gave out to diagram the design of *Ulysses.*

Scheme: In RHETORIC an unusual arrangement or rearrangement of words in which the literal sense of the words is not modified by the arrangement. It is thus a pattern of words in which sound rather than sense is changed. Hence, it is a RHETORICAL FIGURE OF SPEECH. See TROPE.

Schlüsselroman: German for a "NOVEL with a key." See the more frequent term *roman à clef.*

Scholasticism: The name is said to have come from the title *doctor scholasticus* applied to a teacher in the religious "schools" established in the ninth and tenth centuries. Although such doctors were supposed to teach all of the SEVEN ARTS, they became chiefly professors of logic. As developed a century or so later, *scholasticism* became a complicated system that relied on logical methods in an effort to reconcile the tenets of Christianity with the demands of reason. Using logical methods derived from Aristotle, *scholasticism* undertook the solution of a number of philosophical and theological problems: the relations to one another of the persons of the Trinity, the nature and attributes of God, and the relation of the finite to the infinite.

Scholastic reasoning as applied by different thinkers led to diverging views. The "first era" of *scholasticism* (twelfth century) marked the break from the freer reasoning of the earlier ("patristic") theologians and includes Abelard, Bernard of Clairvaux, and Anselm, "father of *scholasticism.*" The second era (thirteenth century) was the flourishing period, marked by the dominance of Aristotelian influence, and includes the two great Schoolmen Thomas Aquinas and Duns Scotus, heads of opposing groups known as "Thomists" and "Scotists." The third era (especially fifteenth century) marked the decline of *scholasticism,* when it became largely occupied with trivialities. This lost vitality made it an easy victim of the intellectualism of the RENAISSANCE, and *scholasticism* lost its dominance by the early sixteenth century. Indeed, the great Erasmus, typical of Renaissance HUMANISTS, at first an adherent of the scholastic method, is said to have been persuaded to forsake it by the English scholar John Colet. *Scholasticism* employed the deductive method of reasoning, and its overthrow prepared the way for the inductive method, advocated by Francis Bacon, which has led to the achievements of modern science. The positive effect of scholastic thinking on all medieval literature and thinking was incalculable in extent, and its insistence on rigid, accurate reasoning has had a wholesome effect on succeeding thought and writing.

[References: George P. Fisher, *History of Christian Doctrine* (1908); Étienne Gilson, *The Spirit of Thomism* (1964); Jacques Maritain, *Art and Scholasticism* (tr. 1930, reprinted 1962); Erwin Panofsky, *Gothic Architecture and Scholasticism* (1951); H. O. Taylor, *The Medieval Mind*, 4th ed. (1925, reprinted 1959).]

School of Donne: Another name for the metaphysical poets. In the Preface to *For Lancelot Andrewes* (1928), T. S. Eliot announced that he had in preparation three small books, including one to be called *The School of Donne.* No such book ever appeared, but in 1961 A. Alvarez, with Eliot's permission, used the title for his own study of the METAPHYSICALS.

School of Night: A group of Elizabethan dramatists, POETS, and scholars, with, perhaps, some of the nobility. Its leader was Sir Walter Ralegh, and its members included Christopher Marlowe, George Chapman, and the mathematician Thomas Herriot. They studied the natural sciences, philosophy, and religion, and were suspected of being atheists. Shakespeare seems to condemn them in *Love's Labour's Lost* in the lines:

> . . . Black is the badge of hell,
> The hue of dungeons and the School of Night.

[References: Arthur Acheson, *Shakespeare and the Rival Poet* (1903); Muriel C. Bradbrook, *The School of Night: A Study in the Literary Relationships of Raleigh* (1936).]

School of Spenser: A name given to a group of seventeenth-century POETS who showed the influence of Edmund Spenser. The chief poets of the school were Giles and Phineas Fletcher, William Browne, George Wither, William Drummond of Hawthornden, Sir John Davies, and the Scottish Sir William Alexander. The school is marked by such characteristics as sensuousness, melody, PERSONIFICATIONS, pictorial quality, interest in NARRATIVE, medievalism (especially in use of ALLEGORY), ARCHAISMS, modified or genuine SPENSERIAN STANZA, pastoralism, moral earnestness. The art and outlook of the school led in the direction of Milton, whom they influenced. They thus form a link between Spenser and Milton, the two great Puritan poets of the English RENAISSANCE.

School Plays: One of the most important traditions contributing to the development of ELIZABETHAN DRAMA was the practice of writing and performing PLAYS at schools. Little is known of the history, extent, or character of dramatic activities in universities before the RENAISSANCE, though there is some evidence that student PLAYS existed throughout the late Middle Ages. Records of *school plays* from the fifteenth century possibly refer to such medieval forms as DISGUISINGS (see MASQUE). The interest in Latin DRAMA aroused by the Italian RENAISSANCE (Petrarch wrote a Terentian comedy about 1331) led to TRANSLATIONS and imitations of Plautus and Terence in other countries, such as Germany and Holland (where *school plays* in the "Prodigal Son" FORMULA flourished), and eventually England (early sixteenth century). Boys in grammar schools (St. Paul's, Eton) acted both CLASSICAL and original plays in the 1520s. By 1560 both Latin and English PLAYS were produced at Eton, and in Spenser's time (1560s) Richard Mulcaster's boys at the Merchant Taylors' School performed plays annually before the queen. Nicholas Udall's *Ralph Roister Doister*, probably written before 1553 for performance by the boys of Westminster School, is regarded as the first regular English COMEDY.

However important the production of PLAYS in the grammar schools may have been, of greater significance in the development of the DRAMA was the practice, common in the sixteenth century, of writing and performing plays at the universities. Plays by Terence were acted by undergraduates in Cambridge as early as 1510. In 1546 at Trinity College, Cambridge, refusal of a student to take part in a PLAY was punishable by expulsion. Though the primary purpose of the plays was educational, entertainment for its own sake was more and more recognized, and the use of English became more and more common. When Queen Elizabeth visited Cambridge in 1564 and Oxford in 1566, she was entertained with a series of PLAYS of various types, foreshadowing later FORMS on the Elizabethan stage. The earliest extant university play in English is *Gammer Gurton's Needle* (written *ca.* 1560). Some university pieces were connected with later Elizabethan plays, such as Thomas Legge's SENECAN TRAGEDY on Richard III, which may have contributed features to Shakespeare's PLAY. The plays were usually performed at night in the college hall before a restricted audience. The actors were costumed.

The UNIVERSITY WITS left the universities at a time when academic PLAYS were flourishing and went to London to play important roles during the formative period of ELIZABETHAN DRAMA. In the main the academic DRAMA transmitted to the professional drama the CLASSICAL forms represented by Seneca in TRAGEDY and by Plautus and Terence in COMEDY, though Italian sources were also employed.

Schoolmen: Medieval philosophers who followed the method of SCHOLASTICISM in their "disputations." Called "hair-splitters" by Francis Bacon. See SCHOLASTICISM.

Science Fiction: A form of FANTASY in which scientific facts, assumptions, or hypotheses form the basis, by logical extrapolation, of adventures in the future, on other planets, in other dimensions in time or space, or under new variants of scientific law. Conceivably, if the element of time (either past or future) is conspicuously important, then some SCIENCE FICTION may qualify as HISTORICAL FICTION. The first edition of this *Handbook* (1936), by the way, does not mention *science fiction;* in the half-century since then, however, the MODE or GENRE has spread in popularity, gained in seriousness and dignity, and come up in the world, both in writing and in FILM, boosted, probably, by impressive advances in science and engineering and by quantum improvements in special effects. *Science fiction* has been honored by a number of influential CRITICS, such as J. O. Bailey, Kingsley Amis, and Susan Sontag. Many distinguished writers, including Ray Bradbury, Kurt Vonnegut, Jr., Calder Willingham, Doris Lessing, Davis Grubb, and Thomas Pynchon, have either written *science fiction* outright or employed many of its devices and CONVENTIONS in works not belonging to the GENRE. Many readers—and many critics and scholars as well—have come to appreciate *science fiction* in itself and in its potential relations to FANTASY, UTOPIA, FOLKLORE, and medievalism. See FANTASY.

[References: Kingsley Amis, *New Maps of Hell: A Survey of Science Fiction* (1960); J. O. Bailey, *Pioneers through Space and Time: Trends and Patterns in Scientific and Utopian Fiction* (1947, reprinted 1972); H. Bruce Franklin, *Future Perfect: American Science Fiction of the Nineteenth Century* (1966, rev. ed. 1978); Ursula K. Le Guin, *The Language of the Night: Essays on Fantasy and Science Fiction* (1979); Walter E. Meyers, *Aliens and Linguists: Language Study and Science Fiction* (1980); Darko Suvin, *Metamorphoses of Science Fiction: On the Poetics and History of a Literary Genre* (1979); Colin Wilson, *Science Fiction as Existentialism* (1978).]

Scop: A sort of ANGLO-SAXON court POET. Though the *scop* probably traveled around from court to court like the GLEEMAN, he occupied a position of importance and permanence in the king's retinue comparable to that of the Welsh BARD (see WELSH LITERATURE) and the Irish FILIDH (see IRISH LITERATURE). He was a composer as well as a reciter, and his THEMES were drawn chiefly from the heroic TRADITIONS of the early Germanic peoples, though later he employed Biblical themes, and he no doubt was expected to eulogize the family that employed him. He has been called a precursor of the modern POET LAUREATE.

Scottish Chaucerians: POETS of fifteenth- and sixteenth-century Scotland who wrote in imitation of Chaucer's STYLE and FORMS. They included Robert Henryson (*The Testament of Cresseid*), William Dunbar (*Thrissil and the Rois, Goldyn Targe*), Gavin Douglas, translator of the *Aeneid*, and James I (*The Kingis Quair*).

Scottish Literature: The main stream of the literature of Scotland is rightly regarded as a part of English literary history. The fact of political independence in early times and the use of the Scots language or Scottish DIALECT of English by many writers, however, warrants special notice of *Scottish literature*. John Barbour's *Bruce* (1375), a sort of Scottish national EPIC (in twenty books), is often taken as the beginning of *Scottish literature*. In the fifteenth and sixteenth centuries there flourished a school of SCOTTISH CHAUCERIANS. Somewhat later appeared Sir David Lyndsay's *Satire of the Three Estates*, an ambitious MORALITY play said to have been acted in 1540. Early Scotland is noted, too, for her popular BALLADS, some of which probably belong to the fifteenth and sixteenth centuries, though most of the existing ones seem to have been composed a century or more later. The controversial PROSE, on religious and historical or political topics, of the famous John Knox (sixteenth century) encouraged the use of English by Scottish writers. Among the POETS Alexander Montgomerie (*ca.* 1545–*ca.* 1610) is sometimes called the last of the native Scottish "makers." By the seventeenth century the Scots DIALECT as a literary vehicle was rare.

A migration of Scottish professional and business people to London in the seventeenth and eighteenth centuries makes a separation of Scottish and

English literature increasingly difficult. In POETRY the works of James Thomson (*The Seasons*) and Robert Blair (*The Grave*) are noteworthy in English literary history, as are such PROSE pieces as Adam Smith's *Wealth of Nations* and David Hume's *Enquiry Concerning Human Understanding.* At the very end of the century appeared Robert Burns, whose use of native DIALECT (following a tradition set by Allan Ramsay and others) found an immediate response in the literary circles of Edinburgh.

Though much conscious feeling for native TRADITION appears in some nineteenth-century Scottish writers (like Sir Walter Scott) and though the native DIALECTS have been employed by such writers of regional literature as J. M. Barrie (see KAILYARD SCHOOL), in general literary writers of Scottish birth (for example, Carlyle, Stevenson) have been regarded, since 1800, as "English." One notable achievement in English literary history was the establishment in Scotland in the early nineteenth century of literary and critical MAGAZINES, among them the *Edinburgh Review* (1802). The best-known modern Scottish writer has been C. M. Grieve ("Hugh MacDiarmid").

[References: Alan Bold, *Modern Scottish Literature* (1983); T. F. Henderson, *Scottish Vernacular Literature,* 3rd ed. (1910); Maurice Lindsay, *History of Scottish Literature* (1977); Agnes M. Mackenzie, *An Historical Survey of Scottish Literature to 1714* (1933); J. H. Millar, *Literary History of Scotland* (1903); Trevor Royle, *The Macmillan Companion to Scottish Literature* (1983).]

Scriblerus Club: A club of writers organized in London in 1714 by Jonathan Swift with the object of satirizing literary incompetence. Among its members were Pope, Arbuthnot, Bolingbroke, Gay, and Congreve. It expressed its opinions of the false taste of the age, particularly in learning, through the satiric fragment, *The Memoirs of the Extraordinary Life, Works, and Discoveries of Martinus Scriblerus,* written in large part by Dr. Arbuthnot.

Scriptural Drama: PLAYS based on the Old and New Testaments, produced first by churches and then by town guilds in the Middle Ages. See MYSTERY PLAY.

Secondary Stress: A STRESS put on a syllable that is medial in weight (or force) between a full (primary) STRESS and an unstressed syllable. It usually occurs in polysyllabic words but is sometimes the result of the CADENCE and sense of the LINE. In the word elementary the third syllable carries a STRESS, indicated by the mark ˏ, lighter than that on the first syllable. However, in the SCANSION of English VERSE, the rhythmic pattern is formed of stressed and unstressed syllables, and those with *secondary stress* are conventionally resolved into one or the other. In actual practice, however, *secondary stress* creates effective variations within basically regular lines. See DIPODY.

Self-effacing Author: When, in the NOVEL or the SHORT STORY, OBJECTIVITY is so used in the narrative POINT OF VIEW that the author ostensibly ceases to exist and seems to become merely an impersonal and nonevaluating medium through whom the ACTIONS and actors of the story are seen, the author is said to be *self-effacing.* The *self-effacing author* is a typical device in the SCENIC METHOD. See NARRATOR, POINT OF VIEW, OBJECTIVITY, SCENIC METHOD.

Semantics or Semasiology: Most generally, the study of meaning and meanings; sometimes limited to linguistic meaning (see LINGUISTICS); and sometimes used to discriminate between surface and substance, as when someone says, "There is merely a *semantic* difference among 'automobile,' 'car,' 'auto,' and 'motor car.' "

Semiotics: The study of the systems of rules and conventions that enable social and cultural phenomena, considered as SIGNS, to have meaning. Hence, in literary CRITICISM, *semiotics* is the analysis of literature in terms of its use of language as dependent on and influenced by literary conventions and modes of discourse.

If there is a causal relationship between form and meaning, as in "That wound was made by a bullet," the form is called an index and the relationship between form and meaning can be studied by an appropriate branch of science and not by *semiotics*. If the relationship is one of natural resemblance, as in "This photograph is of John Banks," the form is called an icon, to be analyzed by philosophical theories of representation and not by *semiotics*. If there is a so-called motivated relationship between the object and its respondent, as between the Cross and a believing Christian, or if the relationship between form and meaning is the "unmotivated" or arbitrary product of convention, the form is a sign and can be analyzed by *semiotics*.

When *semiotics* is used in literary CRITICISM, it deals not with the simple relation between object or sign and meaning or significance, but with literary CONVENTIONS, such as those of PROSODY or GENRE or received interpretations of literary devices at particular times. It studies how these conventions create meanings unique to such literary expression. If a PROSE statement is converted into VERSE, although it may still literally say the same thing, its meaning undergoes change through the effect on it of the conventions of VERSIFICATION used in making the conversion; *semiotics* would attempt to concentrate on those conventions. In practice, *semiotics* often appears to emphasize the extent to which works of art are about the making of works of art. With an increase in anxious skepticism and linguistic sophistication, a reader may grow morbidly aware of the limitations of any system of SIGNS, so that a work of art may be dismissed, ignored, or attacked as a mere FICTION with no relevance. MODERN writing in particular seems to have become "self-conscious" of its precarious, contingent situation about which both reader and writer entertain doubts. Joseph Conrad, for example, often seems not to be telling a STORY directly but rather to be telling a STORY about telling a STORY (so doing the thing, as Henry James observed, that it takes the most doing); Tennessee Williams seems, in the *The Glass Menagerie,* not to be presenting a PLAY directly but rather to be dramatizing one process by which a playwright arrives at the position of being able to write a play. But, paradoxically, the very presence of an uncertain author-SURROGATE such as Conrad's Marlow or Williams's Tom Wingfield seems to disarm our skepticism so that we may regard the work as REALISTIC after all. In scrutinizing these devices, we may be helped and encouraged by *semiotics*.

[References: Jonathan Culler, *The Pursuit of Signs—Semiotics, Literature, Deconstruction* (1981); Julia Kristeva, *Revolution in Poetic Language* (tr. 1984); Robert Scholes, *Semiotics and Interpretation* (1982); Wendy Steiner, ed., *The Sign in Music and Literature* (1981).]

Senecan Style: The anti-Ciceronian STYLE of the late sixteenth and seventeenth centuries. It is curt, abrupt, and uneven, giving the effect of unadorned factual statement. Its chief characteristic is the so-called exploded period, a series of independent statements set down in simple sentences or clauses and tied together, if at all, by coordinating conjunctions. It tends to be jagged and excited or to flow in unevaluated directness. It is sometimes called ATTIC. See CICERONIAN STYLE.

[Reference: George Williamson, *The Senecan Amble: A Study in Prose Form from Bacon to Collier* (1951).]

Senecan Tragedy: The nine Latin TRAGEDIES attributed to the Stoic philosopher Seneca (first century). They were modeled largely on the Greek TRAGEDIES of Euripides (but written to be recited rather than acted) and exerted a great influence on RENAISSANCE playwrights, who thought them intended for actual performance. In general the PLAYS are marked by: (1) conventional five-ACT division (a formal design that we seem to owe to Seneca); (2) the use of a CHORUS (for comment rather than participation in the ACTION) and such STOCK CHARACTERS as a ghost, a cruel tyrant, the faithful male servant, and the female CONFIDANTE; (3) the presentation of much of the ACTION (especially the horrors) through long NARRATIVE reports recited by messengers as a substitute for stage action; (4) the employment of sensational THEMES drawn from Greek mythology, involving much use of "blood and lust" material connected with unnatural crimes, such as adultery, incest, infanticide, and often motivated by revenge and leading to retribution; (5) a highly rhetorical STYLE marked by HYPERBOLE, detailed DESCRIPTIONS, exaggerated comparisons, APHORISMS, EPIGRAMS, and the sharp line-for-line DIALOGUE known as STICHOMYTHIA; (6) lack of careful CHARACTER delineation but much use of introspection and SOLILOQUY.

Renaissance HUMANISM stimulated interest in the *Senecan tragedies,* and they were translated and imitated in early SCHOOL and court DRAMA in Italy, France, and England. The first English TRAGEDY, Sackville and Norton's *Gorboduc* (acted 1562), was an IMITATION of Seneca, as were such later INNS-OF-COURT plays as *Jocasta* (acted 1566), *Tancred and Gismund* (acted 1568), and *The Misfortunes of Arthur* (1588), some of which were influenced by Italian Senecan plays rather than by the Latin PLAYS themselves. After 1588 two groups of English *Senecan tragedies* are to be distinguished. The Countess of Pembroke and playwrights under her influence produced "true" Senecan PLAYS modeled on the French *Senecan tragedies* of Robert Garnier. In this group are Kyd's TRANSLATION of Garnier's *Cornélie,* Daniel's *The Tragedy of Cleopatra* and his *Philotas* (1605), and Fulke Grenville's original plays based on Senecan models, for example, *Mustapha.*

The second and far more important group begins with the PLAYS produced by Marlowe and Kyd for the popular stage. These plays combined native English tragic TRADITION with a modified Senecan technique and led directly toward the typical ELIZABETHAN TRAGEDY. Kyd's *Spanish Tragedy,* for example, though reflecting such Senecan traits as sensationalism, bombastic rhetoric, and the use of the CHORUS and the ghost, departed from the Senecan method in that it placed the murders and horrors on the stage, in response to popular Elizabethan taste and in defiance of Horace's dictum that good taste demanded the leaving of such matters for off-stage action. The fashion so inaugurated led to a long line of ELIZABETHAN TRAGEDIES, the greatest of which is Shakespeare's *Hamlet*. The importance of the Latin Senecan plays in the evolution of English TRAGEDY is very great. They called attention to DRAMA not only as an EXPOSITION of events or as an ALLEGORY of life but also as a field for the study of human emotion. Their RHETORIC aroused interest in the drama as literature and POETRY, and their reflective STYLE encouraged an effort to elevate TRAGEDY into the realm of philosophy. Two of T. S. Eliot's most important ESSAYS are "Seneca in Elizabethan Translation" and "Shakespeare and the Stoicism of Seneca" (both 1927). Grover Smith and Hugh Kenner are among the CRITICS who have pointed out the importance of Seneca (directly from the Latin or indirectly through the Elizabethans) in Eliot's POETRY and DRAMA. See REVENGE TRAGEDY, TRAGEDY OF BLOOD.

[References: H. B. Charlton, *The Senecan Tradition in Renaissance Tragedy* (1946); J. W. Cunliffe, *Influence of Seneca on Elizabethan Tragedy* (1893, reprinted 1907); T. S. Eliot, *Selected Essays*, 3rd ed. (1951, reprinted 1972); F. L. Lucas, *Seneca and Elizabethan Tragedy* (1922); F. J. Miller, tr., *The Tragedies of Seneca* (1917, reprinted 1953); A. H. Thorndike, *Tragedy* (1908, reprinted 1965).]

Sensibility: A term used to indicate emotionalism as opposed to RATIONALISM; a reliance on the feelings as guides to truth and conduct as opposed to reason and law as regulations in both human and metaphysical relations. It is connected with such eighteenth-century attitudes as PRIMITIVISM, SENTIMENTALISM, the nature movement (see NATURE), and other aspects of ROMANTICISM. Joseph Warton in *The Enthusiast* (1744) reflects many of the attitudes of the School of Sensibility in that he expressed a distrust of cities, formal gardens, conventional society, business, law-courts, and AUGUSTAN STYLE, while he asserted a love of the simple life, solitude, mountains, stormy seas, NOBLE SAVAGES, untutored POETS, and TRAGEDIES of terror. The high value that the eighteenth century put on *sensibility* was a reaction against the STOICISM of the seventeenth century and the theories advanced by Hobbes and others that human beings were motivated primarily by self-interest. Benevolence, resting on the ability to sympathize to a marked degree with the joys and the sorrows of one's fellows, was asserted by many, notably the Earl of Shaftesbury, as an innate human characteristic. From this position to the idea of the virtue of the sympathetic tear was a short distance soon traveled. This extreme *sensibility* expressed itself in SENTIMENTAL COMEDY and in the SENTIMENTAL NOVEL.

In the twentieth century the term *sensibility* is used in a radically different sense, to designate the innate sensitivity of the POET (and the reader) to sensory experience, out of which the poet fashions his or her art. It is most common in the phrase "DISSOCIATION OF SENSIBILITY," by which T. S. Eliot designates the disunion of feeling and thought that presumably occurred in English POETRY with Dryden and Milton. See METAPHYSICAL POETRY, SENTIMENTALISM, SENTIMENTAL COMEDY, SENTIMENTAL NOVEL, DISSOCIATION OF SENSIBILITY.

[References: E. Bernbaum, *The Drama of Sensibility* (1915, reprinted 1958), and *Guide through the Romantic Movement*, 2nd ed. (1949).]

Sensual and Sensuous: *Sensuous* is a critical term characterizing writing that plays fully on the various senses of the reader. The term is not to be confused with *sensual,* which is now generally used in an unfavorable sense and implies writing that is fleshly or carnal, in which the author displays the voluptuous. *Sensuous,* then, denotes writing that makes a restrained use of the various senses; *sensual* denotes writing that approaches unrestrained abandonment to one sense—the passion of physical love. Through the careful use of pictures and IMAGES that appeal to the senses, such as Keats makes in *The Eve of St. Agnes,* writing may be said to be made *sensuous,* a quality that Milton stipulated as characterizing good POETRY in his famous estimate of poetry as "simple, sensuous, and passionate." The writing of Ernest Hemingway, with its use of physical IMAGES and its attempt to "rub the fact on the exposed nerve end," is markedly *sensuous,* although it is only occasionally *sensual.* In a quite different style, Thomas Wolfe's writing, evoking sharp sensory response, is also *sensuous.*

Sentence: A rhetorical term formerly in use in the sense of APOTHEGM or MAXIM (Latin *sententia*), usually applied to quoted "wise sayings." In old writings, too, the student may come on the use of *sentence* for *sense, gist,* or *theme,* as when Chanticleer in Chaucer's *Nun's Priest's Tale* tells Pertelot (trickily) that the *sentence* of the Latin phrase is such and such. Chaucer describes the speech of his taciturn Clerk as "short and quyk and ful of hy sentence" (the last four words echoed five centuries later by J. Alfred Prufrock). In modern grammatical usage *sentence* is restricted to a group of words having a subject and a predicate and expressing a complete thought.

Sententia: A Latin term for a short, pithy statement of general truth. See APHORISM, MAXIM, SENTENCE.

Sentimental Comedy: Just as the COMEDY OF MANNERS reflected in its immorality the reaction of the RESTORATION from the severity of the Puritan code of the Commonwealth period, so the COMEDY that displaced it, known as *sentimental comedy,* or "reformed comedy," sprang up in the early years of the eighteenth century in response to a growing reaction against the TONE of Restoration PLAYS. Signs of this reaction appeared soon after the dethronement of James II (1688) and found influential expression in Jeremy Collier's famous *Short View of the Immorality and Profaneness of the English Stage* (1698), which charged that plays as a whole "rewarded debauchery," "ridiculed virtue and learning," and were "disserviceable to probity and religion." Although Colley Cibber's *Love's Last Shift* (1696) shows transitional anticipations of the new reformed COMEDY, Richard Steele is generally regarded as the founder of the type. His *The Funeral* (1701), *The Lying Lover* (1703), and *The Tender Husband* (1705) reflect the development of the form, while his *The Conscious Lovers* (1722) is the CLASSIC example of the fully developed type.

Because of the violence of its reaction, *sentimental comedy* became very weak dramatically, lacking humor, reality, spice, and lightness of touch. The CHARACTERS were either so good or so bad that they became mere CARICATURES, and PLOTS were violently handled so that virtue would triumph. The dramatists resorted shamelessly to sentimental emotion in their effort to interest and move the spectators. The HERO in *The Conscious Lovers* ("conscious" in the sense of "conscientious") is perfectly moral; he has no bad habits; he is indifferent to "sordid lucre"; he is good to inferiors from principle, even thanking servants for paid services; he is guided by a sense of honor and is superior to all ordinary passions. His conversations with the HEROINE Indiana, whom he loves but who agrees with him that he must marry Lucinda to please his parents, are veritable TRAVESTIES of the art of lovemaking. Where the COMEDY OF MANNERS of the preceding age had sacrificed moral TONE in its effort to amuse, the *sentimental comedy* sacrificed dramatic reality in its effort to instruct through an appeal to the heart. The domestic trials of middle-class couples are usually portrayed: their "private woes" are exhibited with much emotional stress intended to arouse the spectator's pity and suspense in advance of the approaching melodramatic happy ending.

This COMEDY held the boards on the English stage for more than a half century. Hugh Kelly's *False Delicacy* (1768), first acted shortly before the appearance of Goldsmith's *Good Natured Man* (brought out in protest against *sentimental comedies*), and Richard Cumberland's *The West Indian* (1771) illustrate the complete development of the type. Though weakened by the attacks and dramatic creations of Goldsmith and Sheridan, who revived in a somewhat chastened FORM the old COMEDY OF MANNERS, plays of the sentimental type lived on till after the middle of the nineteenth century, though no longer dominant. The DOMESTIC TRAGEDY of a sentimental sort developed by Nicholas Rowe (1674–1718) and George Lillo (1693–1739) shows many of the same characteristics as the COMEDY with which it coexisted. Both forms are based on the same fundamentals as those of MELODRAMA.

[References: E. Bernbaum, *The Drama of Sensibility* (1915, reprinted 1958); Allardyce Nicoll, *History of Early Eighteenth-Century Drama, 1700–1750* (1925).]

Sentimental Novel: The SENTIMENTALISM of the eighteenth century was reflected not only in the SENTIMENTAL COMEDY and the DOMESTIC TRAGEDY but in the early NOVELS as well. Richardson's *Pamela, or Virtue Rewarded* (1740) was the beginning of the vogue; and although the rival REALISTIC NOVEL sprang up in protest (for example, Fielding's *Tom Jones*), the *sentimental novel* (also called NOVEL OF SENSIBILITY) continued to be popular for many years. One of the best of the type is Goldsmith's *The Vicar of Wakefield* (1766), and one of the most extravagant is Henry Mackenzie's *Man of Feeling* (1771). Laurence Sterne's *Tristram Shandy* (1760–1767) is another example of the type. See NOVEL, SENTIMENTALISM.

Sentimentalism: The term is used in two senses important in the study of literature: (1) an overindulgence in emotion, especially the conscious effort to induce emotion in order to analyze or enjoy it; also the failure to restrain or evaluate emotion through the exercise of the judgment; (2) an optimistic overemphasis of the goodness of humanity (SENSIBILITY), representing in part a reaction against orthodox Calvinistic theology, which regarded human nature as depraved. It is connected with the development of PRIMITIVISM. In the first sense given above *sentimentalism* is found in MELODRAMA, in the fainting HEROINES of sentimental FICTION, in the melancholic VERSE of the GRAVEYARD SCHOOL, in humanitarian literature, and in such modern phenomena as FILM and legal and political oratory. In the second sense it appears in SENTIMENTAL COMEDY, sentimental FICTION, and primitivistic POETRY. Both types of *sentimentalism* figured largely in the literature of the romantic movement. Writers reflecting eighteenth-century *sentimentalism* include Richard Steele (*The Conscious Lovers*); Joseph Warton (*The Enthusiast*); William Collins and Thomas Gray in their poetry; Laurence Sterne (*A Sentimental Journey*); Oliver Goldsmith (*The Deserted Village*); and Henry Mackenzie (*The Man of Feeling*). The neoclassicists themselves, though opposed fundamentally to *sentimentalism,* sometimes exhibit it, as when Addison avers that he resorts to Westminster Abbey for the purpose of enjoying the emotions called up by the sombre surroundings. In its broadest sense *sentimentalism* may be said to result whenever a reader or an audience is asked to experience an emotional response in excess of that merited by the occasion or one that has not been adequately prepared for. See SENSIBILITY.

[References: L. I. Bredvold, *The Natural History of Sensibility* (1962); James E. Cox, *The Rise of Sentimental Comedy* (1926, reprinted 1976); Arthur Sherbo, *English Sentimental Drama* (1957).]

Sentimentality: The effort to induce an emotional response disproportionate to the situation, and thus to substitute heightened and generally unthinking feeling for normal ethical and intellectual judgment. It is a particularly pernicious form of anti-intellectualism. See SENTIMENTALISM.

Septenary: A seven-stress VERSE often employed in medieval and RENAISSANCE poetry. See FOURTEENERS.

Septet: A STANZA of seven LINES. One of the few FORMS of the *septet* in English POETRY is the RHYME ROYAL.

Septuagint: A Greek version of the Old Testament begun in the third century before Christ. It is still in use in the Greek Church and is the version from which New Testament writers quote. It takes its name (meaning "Seventy") from an old but discredited story that was prepared by seventy or seventy-two Jewish scholars at the request of Ptolemy Philadelphus (309–246 B.C.).

Sequel: A literary work that continues the CHARACTERS and ACTIONS from a preceding work. A *sequel* may in fact be written before rather than after the work whose NARRATIVE it follows; whether a work is a *sequel* to another depends on the chronology of the ACTION in the works and not on the order of their being written. For example, Cooper's *The Last of the Mohicans,* written in 1826, is technically the *sequel* to *The Deerslayer,* not written until 1841.

Serenade: A sentimental composition, written as though intended to be sung out of doors at night under a lady's window and in praise of a loved one. Bayard Taylor's "Bedouin Song," the last STANZA of which is quoted, is a *serenade* that once was very popular:

> My steps are nightly driven,
>   By the fever in my breast,
> To hear from thy lattice breathed
>   The word that shall give me rest.

Open the door of thy heart,
And open thy chamber door,
And my kisses shall teach thy lips
The love that shall fade no more
Till the sun grows cold,
And the stars are old,
And the leaves of the Judgment Book unfold!

Serial: The publication of a work—usually of PROSE FICTION—in periodical installments. *Serial* publication was the rule around the middle of the nineteenth century, with NOVELS published month-by-month in MAGAZINES before being issued in book form. In some cases the work was finished before serialization began, but many writers, including Dickens, composed their installments (ordinarily of a few chapters) as the *serial* was being published. The conditions of *serial* publication often have a discernible effect on the shape of the eventual novel, since it was the habit—still persisting in television and film *serials*—to end an installment at a moment of suspense or surprise (a "cliffhanger"). Some newspapers and MAGAZINES continue the practice, and Norman Mailer experimented with *serial* composition and publication of his NOVEL *An American Dream,* but there has been a great falling off from the heyday of *serial* writing.

Series: Generally, items arranged in a row with some sort of coherence. According to Sally M. Gall and M. L. Rosenthal, a "linked SERIES" of POEMS presents more of design than a mere collection or MISCELLANY but less than a fully sustained "sequence." *Series* is also used for a group of works centering on a single CHARACTER or set in a single place or time, as when we speak of Lucy Maud Montgomery's "Anne of Green Gables Series" or, more familiarly, "Anne Series."

Serpentine Verse: A LINE of POETRY that begins and ends with the same word.

Sesquipedalian: Literally "a foot and a half"; used to designate a STYLE that is unduly and pretentiously polysyllabic. The word itself illustrates its usage.

Sestet: The second, six-line division of an ITALIAN SONNET. Following the eight-line division (see OCTAVE), the *sestet* usually makes specific a general statement that has been presented in the OCTAVE or indicates the personal emotion of the author in a situation that the OCTAVE has developed. The most authentic RHYME SCHEME is the *cdecde* (following the *abbaabba* of the OCTAVE), and the next best is *cdcdcd* or any other that (1) avoids the pat and pouncing rhymed COUPLET and (2) uses not more than a total of five RHYMES for the SONNET as a whole. Strictly speaking, any six-line POEM or STANZA is a *sestet.*

Sestina: One of the most difficult and complex of the various FRENCH FORMS. The *sestina* is a POEM consisting of six six-line STANZAS and a three-line ENVOY. It makes no use of the REFRAIN. This form is usually unrhymed, the effect of RHYME being taken over by a fixed pattern of end-words. These end-words in each STANZA must be the same, though arranged in a different sequence each time. If we take 1–2–3–4–5–6 to represent the end-words of the first STANZA, then the first LINE of the second STANZA must end with 6 (the last end-word used in the preceding STANZA), the second with 1, the third with 5, the fourth with 2, the fifth with 4, the sixth with 3—and so to the next STANZA. The order of the first three STANZAS, for instance, would be: 1–2–3–4–5–6; 6–1–5–2–4–3; 3–6–4–1–2–5. The conclusion, or ENVOY, of three lines must use as end-words 5–3–1, these being the final end-words, in the same sequence, of the sixth STANZA. But the POET must exercise even greater ingenuity than all this, since buried in each line of the ENVOY must appear the other three end-words, 2–4–6. Thus, so highly artificial a pattern affords a FORM that, for most poets, can never prove anything more than a poetic exercise. Yet it has been practiced with success in English by Sidney, Swinburne, Kipling, Auden, Nims, Ashbery, and Merrill. (A variant, with RHYMES instead of REPETITIONS, is used in Eliot's "The Dry Salvages.") The strictest construction of the rule requires complete and unvarying repetition of end-words, but some license is granted in the use of identicals. In James Merrill's very clever "Tomorrows," for instance, the original set of end-words consists of "one," "two," "three," "four," "five," and "six," in that order. Later lines end with "won" and "someone"; "to," "Timbuctoo," *tu*," "into," and "too"; "for," "fore," and "before"; "belief I've"; "Sikhs" and "classics."

[Reference: J. F. Nims, *A Local Habitation: Essays on Poetry,* 1985.]

Setting: The physical, and sometimes spiritual, BACKGROUND against which the action of a NARRATIVE (NOVEL, DRAMA, SHORT STORY, POEM) takes place. The elements making up a *setting* are: (1) the actual geographical location, its topography, scenery, and such physical arrangements as the location of the windows and doors in a room; (2) the occupations and daily manner of living of the CHARACTERS; (3) the time or period in which the ACTION takes place, for example, epoch in history or season of the year; (4) the general environment of the characters, for example, religious, mental, moral, social, and emotional conditions through which the people in the NARRATIVE move. From one point of view most FICTION can be broken up into four elements: *setting*, INCIDENT (or PLOT), CHARACTERIZATION, and EFFECT. When *setting* dominates, or when a piece of FICTION is written largely to present the manners and customs of a locality, the writing is often called LOCAL COLOR WRITING or REGIONALISM. The term is also often applied to the stage *setting* of a PLAY. See MISE EN SCÈNE.

Seven Cardinal Virtues: In medieval theology the *seven cardinal virtues* were faith, hope, and love (drawn from Biblical teaching) and prudence, justice, fortitude, and temperance (adapted from the four cardinal virtues of the Greeks and called the natural virtues).

Seven Deadly Sins: The seven cardinal sins, which, according to medieval theology, entailed spiritual death and could be atoned for only by perfect penitence: pride, envy, wrath, sloth, avarice, gluttony, and lust. Dante treats all seven as arising from imperfect love—pride, envy, and wrath resulting from perverted love; sloth from defective love; avarice, gluttony, and lust from excessive love. Pride was the most heinous of the sins because it led to treachery and disloyalty, as in the case of Satan. Innumerable didactic and theological works on the *seven deadly sins* appeared in the Middle Ages, and thousands of sermons were based on them. The conception of the *seven deadly sins* was so widespread that it permeated the literature of medieval and RENAISSANCE times, its influence not only appearing in the ideas implicit in many literary works but often controlling the very structure, as in the "visions" built around a framework of the seven sins. A few examples of the idea in English literature are: Chaucer's "Parson's Tale" in the *Canterbury Tales;* Langland's *The Vision of Piers the Plowman,* Gower's *Confessio Amantis,* and Spenser's *The Faerie Queene* (book 1, canto iv).

Seven Liberal Arts: The seven subjects studied in the medieval university. The three studies pursued during the four-year course leading to the A.B. degree were known as the TRIVIUM. They were grammar (Latin), logic, and RHETORIC (especially public speaking). The four branches followed in the three-year course leading to the M.A. degree were arithmetic, music, geometry, and astronomy. These were called the QUADRIVIUM.

Shakespeare, Early Editions of: About half of Shakespeare's PLAYS were printed separately during his lifetime in QUARTO *editions,* presumably without the author's consent in most cases. Shakespeare was a shareholder in the company that acted his plays, and companies owning acting rights often objected to efforts to sell their plays to the public in printed form while the PLAYS were in their current repertoire. Though there may have been an imperfect effort in 1619, three years after the dramatist's death, to get together a collection of Shakespeare's plays (involving the false dating of certain QUARTOS), the first *edition* is the famous First Folio (1623) prepared by Shakespeare's friends, the actors John Heminge and Henry Condell. For several reasons the texts of the PLAYS in the First Folio vary greatly in accuracy. Some of them follow QUARTO texts closely, others vary in both length and readings, and there are a good many mistakes—for example, the printing of one word for another word similar in sound or spelling—so that in many passages we cannot be sure what Shakespeare wrote. There is also reason for thinking that the FOLIO both omits plays that Shakespeare wrote, at least in part (as *Pericles*), and includes some that he possibly had little to do with (see PSEUDO-SHAKESPEAREAN PLAYS). This situation has created a series of problems that have greatly concerned later editors and critics eager to find out as nearly as possible just what Shakespeare wrote. The Second Folio appeared in 1632 and a third in 1663, the third being reissued in 1664 with *Pericles* and six "spurious" plays added. The fourth FOLIO was printed in 1685. These late folios were only slightly edited.

The first real editor of Shakespeare was Nicholas Rowe, POET LAUREATE. In his editions (1709 and 1714) Rowe made some corrections in the text, modernized the punctuation and spelling, supplied lists of CHARACTERS, made ACT and SCENE divisions for most of the PLAYS (this had been partly done in the FOLIOS), and added stage directions. In 1725 Alexander Pope undertook to make an "authoritative" *edition.* In fact, however, he did much mischievous tampering with Rowe's text. He "corrected" the METER, emended (by guess largely) difficult passages, placed "degrading" passages at the foot of the page, and placed marks of approval on what he thought to be fine passages. He omitted the seven plays not in the First Folio. Pope's work was followed by a careful edition by Lewis Theobald (1733), who had before exposed some of Pope's mistakes and made some ingenious *emendations.* In retaliation Pope made Theobald the chief dunce in the revised *edition* of his *Dunciad.* In 1744 Sir Thomas Hanmer printed an elegant *edition,* which followed Pope. William Warburton's *edition* (1747) was of little value, but in 1765 appeared the famous *edition* of Samuel Johnson, whose "Preface" and notes have high critical value.

Edward Capell (1768) made the first serious effort to prepare a scientific text based on all the early *editions,* including QUARTOS. In 1773 appeared the Johnson-Steevens VARIORUM EDITION; this reappeared in 1785 with revisions by Isaac Reed. In 1790 was printed an *edition* by the important scholar Edward Malone, whose still more extensive "third variorum" *edition,* published after Malone's death by James Boswell (the younger), came in 1821. Many *editions* have appeared after 1800. Most of the PLAYS have been edited separately in the *New Variorum Shakespeare* (beginning in 1871), by Henry Howard Furness (father and son), which undertakes to give a complete ABSTRACT of all earlier efforts to establish a text and of all important *Shakespearean* CRITICISM.

[References: T. R. Lounsbury, *The Text of Shakespeare* (1906); Allardyce Nicoll, *The Editors of Shakespeare from the First Folio to Malone* (1924).]

Shakespearean Sonnet: The ENGLISH SONNET, consisting of three QUATRAINS rhyming *abab cdcd efef* and a COUPLET rhyming *gg.* It is called the *Shakespearean sonnet* because Shakespeare was its most distinguished practitioner. See SONNET.

Shanty: A sailor's working SONG. See CHANTEY.

Shaped Verse: A POEM so constructed that its printed version takes a form that suggests its subject matter. See CARMEN FIGURATUM.

Short Couplet: An octasyllabic COUPLET; TWO lines of either IAMBIC TETRAMETER or TROCHAIC TETRAMETER that rhyme.

Short Measure (or Meter): A STANZA widely used for HYMNS, consisting of four VERSES, rhyming either *abab* or *abcb.* It usually has the first, second, and fourth lines in IAMBIC TRIMETER and the third in IAMBIC TETRAMETER. "Blessed Be the Tie That Binds" is perhaps the best-known HYMN in *short measure.* It has been observed that a single basic metrical pattern runs through *short measure,* POULTER'S MEASURE, the LIMERICK, and certain NURSERY RHYMES (such as "Hickory Dickory Dock").

Short Novel: A work of FICTION of an intermediate length between the SHORT STORY and the NOVEL, generally considered to be between 15,000 and 50,000 words. It is more often defined, however, in terms of a group of characteristics relative to the short story and the novel. Where the SHORT STORY is usually content to reveal a CHARACTER through an ACTION, to be what Joyce called an EPIPHANY, the *short novel* is concerned with character development. Where the NOVEL in its concern with character development employs a broad canvas, a number of characters, and frequently a broad time span, the *short* *novel* concentrates on a limited cast of characters, a relatively short time span, and one connected chain of events. Thus, it is an artistic attempt to combine the compression of the SHORT STORY with the CHARACTER development of the NOVEL. However, such definitions are relative. No one has ever formulated a wholly satisfactory definition of the *short novel,* but it has had a distinctive history. Henry James, who did distinguished work in the form, called it "our ideal, the beautiful and blest *nouvelle.*" Other writers who have found it an attractive form in which to work include: Thomas Mann, Laurence Sterne, Tolstoi, Kafka, Camus, Gide, Moravia, Melville, Conrad, Edith Wharton, Wolfe, Steinbeck, Faulkner, Virginia Woolf, Willa Cather, Thornton Wilder, Fitzgerald, and John O'Hara. See NOVEL, SHORT STORY, NOUVELLE, NOVELETTE.

Short-Short Story: A brief SHORT STORY, usually between 500 and 2,000 words, with a "twist" or surprise ending. Its best-known practitioner was O. Henry.

Short Story: STORIES, in one form or another, have existed throughout history. Egyptian papyri, dating from 3000 to 4000 B.C., reveal how the sons of Cheops regaled their father with NARRATIVE. Some three hundred years before the birth of Christ, we had such Old Testament stories as those of Jonah and of Ruth. Christ spoke in PARABLES. A hair-raising werewolf STORY is embedded in Petronius's *Satyricon.* The Greeks and Romans left us EPISODES and INCIDENTS in their early CLASSICS. In the Middle Ages the impulse to storytelling manifested itself in FABLES and EPICS about beasts and in the MEDIEVAL ROMANCE. In England, about 1250, some two hundred well-known TALES were collected in the *Gesta Romanorum.* In the middle of the fourteenth century Boccaccio assembled a hundred tales in a book called *The Decameron.* In the same century Chaucer wrote his framework collection, *The Canterbury Tales.* In the fifteenth century Malory, in *Le Morte Darthur,* gathered a series of long NARRATIVES recounting the exploits of ancient knighthood. In the eighteenth century came the NOVEL, growing out of the PICARESQUE NOVEL of the sixteenth and seventeenth centuries, both continuing tributes to the human love of NARRATIVE and both factors in the development of a formal kind of storytelling. The eighteenth century also saw the development of the INFORMAL ESSAY, which frequently derived some of its interest from such EPISODES and SKETCHES as Addison uses in the "Sir Roger de Coverley papers" or in "The Vision of Mirzah." In the nineteenth century came Sir Walter Scott, Washington Irving, Nathaniel Hawthorne, Edgar Allan Poe, Mérimée and Balzac, Gautier and Musset, Maupassant, Chekhov, and E. T. A. Hoffman. With these writers the *short story* as a distinct literary GENRE came into being.

In view of this long development it seems foolish to name one person as the founder of the *short story* or to credit one nation with its development. A FORM that comes to us from the ancient past and was known in both the Orient and the Occident, that drew its first breath from oral TRADITION and has existed as a portion of much of human literary expression in all ages, can ultimately be said to have no origin more specific than the inherent creative spirit of human beings satisfying their desire to tell and to hear stories. Yet in the nineteenth century a group of writers did consciously formulate the *short story* as an art form, notable among them being Hawthorne and Poe in America, Mérimée and Balzac in France, and Hoffman in Germany. This development flowered with such speed and force in America that the modern *short story* is often called an American art FORM, with only minor exaggeration.

In the middle nineteenth century, under the impulse of Poe's persuasive statement in his 1842 review of Hawthorne's *Twice-Told Tales*, CRITICS formulated a definite STRUCTURE and technique for the *short story*. To this was added around the end of the century the tightly constructed "surprise-ending story" of O. Henry, and the *short story* came to be thought of as corresponding to a FORMULA, a pattern that was repeated in endless retellings of its limited variations in the popular *short story*. Around the turn of the century, however, the impact of REALISM and the advent of NATURALISM joined with the example of Chekhov's SLICE OF LIFE stories to force open the formula for the serious writer, and such masters of the form as Somerset Maugham and Katherine Mansfield in England and Sherwood Anderson, F. Scott Fitzgerald, and Ernest Hemingway in America began producing *short stories* of great integrity that reflected the complex formlessness of life itself.

A practical definition of the *short story* must be broad enough to include the "surprise-ending" STORY of Maupassant and O. Henry; the TALE of unified effect of Poe, the SLICE OF LIFE story of Chekhov, Katherine Mansfield, and Sherwood Anderson; and the symbolic and mythic STORIES that are popular in the LITTLE MAGAZINES today. At the same time, within the breadth that such a statement must have, there should be distinguishing characteristics that set off the *short story* from other prose FICTION forms.

A *short story* is a relatively brief fictional NARRATIVE in PROSE. It may range in length from the SHORT-SHORT STORY of 500 words up to the "long-short story" of 12,000 to 15,000 words. It may be distinguished from the SKETCH and the TALE in that it has a definite formal development, a firmness in construction; however, it finds its UNITY in many things other than PLOT—although it often finds it there—in effect, in THEME, in CHARACTER, in TONE, in MOOD, even, on occasion, in STYLE. It may be distinguished from the NOVEL in that it tends to reveal character through a series of ACTIONS or ordeals, the purpose of the story being accomplished when the reader comes to know what the true nature of a CHARACTER (or sometimes a SITUATION) is (James Joyce called a *short story* an EPIPHANY because of this quality of "revelation"); the NOVEL tends, on the other hand, to show CHARACTER developing as a result of actions and under the impact of events. This generalization, like every generalization about the *short story* and the NOVEL, grossly overstates its case; yet in a broad sense it does define a basic difference between the two GENRES.

However natural and formless the *short story* may sometimes give the impression of being, however much it may appear to be the simple setting down of an overheard oral NARRATION, as in Ring Lardner's or Somerset Maugham's stories, or the unadorned report of an action, as in Hemingway's or John O'Hara's, a distinguishing characteristic of the GENRE is that it is consciously *made,* that it reveals itself, on careful analysis, to be the result of conscious craftsmanship and artistic skill. Furthermore, however slight the *short story* may appear, it consists of more than a mere record of an INCIDENT or an ANECDOTE. It has a beginning, a middle, and an end; it possesses at least the rudiments of PLOT, with the conscious STRUCTURE that plot implies.

To be more specific as to FORM about so protean a GENRE would be to invite error. Although it differs from DRAMA, even from the ONE-ACT PLAY, in not being prepared for dramatic presentation but for reading, and from the NOVEL in the attitude it takes toward CHARACTERIZATION, the comments on the nature of DRAMATIC STRUCTURE, of TRAGEDY, of the NOVEL, of CHARACTERIZATION, and of PLOT made elsewhere in this *Handbook* apply to the *short story.*

[References: Henry Seidel Canby, *The Short Story in English* (1909, reprinted 1926); Eugene Current-Garcia and Walton R. Patrick, *What Is the Short Story?* (1961); Sean O'Faolain, *The Short Story* (1948, reprinted 1964); Fred Lewis Pattee, *The Development of the American Short Story* (1923, reprinted 1966); Blanche Colton Williams, *A Handbook on Story Writing* (1917), and *Short Story Writing* (1930).]

Showing Versus Telling: An empirical concept, unsophisticated but still useful, that emphasizes the superiority of dramatization, demonstration, enactment, and embodiment over the mere telling of a STORY. In *To Have and Have Not,* for example, Hemingway could have told us something rather abstract—"Shots were fired"—but he chose instead to make us see and hear: "The first thing a pane of glass went and the bullet smashed into a row of bottles on the show-case wall to the right. I heard the gun going and, bop, bop, bop, there were bottles smashing all along the wall."

Sigmatism: The marked use of the sibilant ("hissing") sorts of sound represented alphabetically by the letters *s, z, sh, zh,* and so forth. Too great profusion of such *sibilant* sounds constitutes a fault that good writers avoid. On the other hand, for certain effects they have been much used in POETRY. Poe, in the "Valley of Unrest," has twenty-seven LINES each with its sibilants, the whole somehow planned to give an effect of unease:

> Now ea*ch* vi*s*itor *sh*all confe*ss*
> The *s*ad valley'*s* re*s*tle*ss*ne*ss*.
> Nothing there *is* motion*less*—
> Nothing *s*ave the air*s* that brood
> Over the magic *s*olitude.

Tennyson tried to avoid the too frequent use of sibilants and is credited with calling his efforts to rid his VERSE of them "kicking the geese out of the boat."

Sign: A radically important problem in SEMIOTICS and SAUSSUREAN LINGUISTICS with a great deal of influence on CRITICISM. The ideal "linguistic *sign,*" according to Saussure, is made up of two elements, a signifier (such as a sound-image) and a signified (such as a mental concept), and the relation between the two is arbitrary, conventional, and "unmotivated"—that is, no property of the signifier, as substance or entity, qualifies it to be a signifier. In certain systems of thought, a pure *sign* or SYMBOL is arbitrary and variable from context to context; the letter "H" means certain things in English and something else in the Greek alphabet (*eta:* the long *e*) and something else in the Russian alphabet (*n*). A *sign* called an ICON is said to resemble the signified, as a portrait resembles its subject or a blueprint resembles the layout of a building. A *sign* called an index or symptom is a part of what it signifies or is closely associated with it, as a high temperature may be a symptom or *sign* of a disease. Systems of *signs* can also be perceived in chains: a high temperature is a *sign* of fever, fever a *sign* of illness, illness a *sign* of exposure to contagion, contagion a *sign* of unwholesome living conditions, and so forth. METAPHOR and METONYMY have been classified as two sorts of signifying operation—the former by resemblance, the latter by participation; both are obviously important for literature. ALLEGORY, likewise, is a process of serial signification, in which words signify a journey, say, and the journey signifies life (as when we call a birthday a "milestone").

[Reference: Jonathan Culler, *The Pursuit of Signs: Semiotics, Literature, Deconstruction* (1981).]

Signature (in printing): A letter or figure placed at the foot of the first page of each GATHERING or section of a book, such a gathering consisting of the pages resulting from a sheet folded to page size and cut; hence, the term *signature* is also applied to the GATHERING itself or to the sheet after it is folded and ready to be gathered. In early printing the *signature* was often placed on the first, third, fifth, and seventh pages of an OCTAVO GATHERING (sixteen pages). See BOOK SIZE.

Silver-Fork School: A name applied in derision to a group of nineteenth-century English novelists who placed a great emphasis on gentility and matters of etiquette. Among the members of the *Silver-Fork School* were Frances Trollope, Theodore Hook, Lady Blessington, Lady Caroline Lamb, and Benjamin Disraeli.

Simile: A FIGURE OF SPEECH in which a similarity between two objects is directly expressed, as in Milton's "A dungeon horrible, on all sides round, / As one great furnace flamed. . . ." Here the comparison between the dungeon (Hell) and the great furnace is directly expressed in the *as,* which labels the comparison a *simile.* Most *similies* are introduced by *as* or *like* or even by such a word as "compare," "liken," or "resemble." In the preceding illustration the similarity between Hell (the dungeon) and the furnace is based on the great heat of the two. A *simile* is generally the comparison of two things essentially unlike, on the basis of a resemblance in one aspect. It is, however, no *simile* to say, "My house is like your house," although, of course, comparison does exist. Another way of expressing it is to say that in a *simile* both TENOR and VEHICLE are clearly expressed and are joined by some indicator of resemblance such as "like" or "as." See METAPHOR, EPIC SIMILE, ANALOGY.

Situation: A term used in the discussion of PLOT to denote (1) a given group of circumstances in which a CHARACTER or characters find themselves or (2) the given conditions under which a STORY opens before the ACTION of the PLOT proper actually begins. Thus, to use *Hamlet* for illustration, the question might be asked, in the first sense, what the proper line of action was for Hamlet when he found himself in the *situation* brought about by the fact that Laertes had challenged him to a duel. In the second, and more technical, sense the *situation* consists of those events that had taken place before the PLAY opened: the murder of Hamlet's father, the incestuous acts of his mother, the general down-at-the-heel condition of the state. In its primary relation to PLOT, then, the *situation* is the group of circumstances in which the CHARACTER or characters find themselves at the beginning of the dramatic action.

Situation Comedy (Sitcom):   A term used in television and elsewhere to refer to a general sort of COMEDY, normally in a continuing SERIES, involving scrapes, jams, and mild predicaments besetting a group of STOCK CHARACTERS.

Skald (Scald):   An ancient Scandinavian POET, especially of the Viking period, corresponding roughly to the Anglo-Saxon SCOP. (The word *skald* may be related to *scold*.)

Skeltonic Verse ("Skeltonics" or "Skeltoniads"):   A rollicking form of VERSE employed by the English POET John Skelton (*ca.* 1460–1529) consisting of short LINES rhymed in groups of varying length, intentionally designed to give the effects of unconventionality and lack of dignity. Skelton felt such VERSE to be a fitting vehicle for his "poetry of revolt." *Skeltonic verse* is, especially for a modern reader, closely akin to DOGGEREL. Something of its spirit and characteristics, though not its full variety, may be found in the following brief passage from *The Tunnynge of Elynoure Rummynge:*

> But to make up my tale,
> She brueth noppy ale,
> And maketh thereof sale
> To travellers, to tinkers,
> To sweaters, to swinkers,
> And all good ale-drinkers,
> That will nothing spare
> But dryncke till they stare
> And bring themselves bare,
> With now away the mare
> And let us slay Care,
> As wise as an hare.

Much of Skelton's POETRY is satirical, and Skelton himself was at odds with the humanists of his day. In his desire to shock, to be novel, and to write in a verse FORM that was as defiant as his SATIRE, he plays with this peculiar VERSE in a fashion that was apparently intentionally irritating to his more formal and orthodox contemporaries. *Skeltonic verse* has its analogues in French and in Italian; it derives from a form of medieval Latin verse associated with the unruly side of university life, which was particularly distasteful to Skelton's humanistic, learned contemporaries. *Skeltonic verse* is also called TUMBLING VERSE.

[References: J. M. Berdan, *Early Tudor Poetry* (1920); Stanley Fish, *John Skelton's Poetry* (1965); William Nelson, *John Skelton, Laureate* (1939).]

Sketch: A brief composition simply constructed and usually most unified in that it presents a single SCENE, a single CHARACTER, a single INCIDENT. It lacks developed PLOT or very great CHARACTERIZATION. Originally used in the sense of an artist's *sketch* as preliminary groundwork for more developed work, it is now often employed for a finished product of simple proportions, as a CHARACTER *sketch*, a VAUDEVILLE *sketch*, a descriptive *sketch*. See SHORT STORY.

Skit: A short dramatic SKETCH or a brief, self-contained comic or BURLESQUE SCENE, usually presented as a part of a REVUE or on a television or radio program.

Slack Syllable: In METRICS an unstressed syllable.

Slang: A vernacular speech, not accepted as suitable for formal usage, though much used in conversation and colloquial expression. The purpose behind the origin of all *slang* is that of stating an idea vividly and freshly, though sometimes the expressions themselves are not always obvious enough to reveal how this purpose is accomplished. The aptness of *slang* is usually based on its HUMOR, its exaggeration, its ONOMATOPOEIC effect, or on a combination of these qualities. Frequently, too, SLANG develops as a shortcut, an abbreviated form of expression. There are, as well, the special terms used in professions or trades, in sports, in localities, among groups possessing any common interest, and in the underworld.

Collections of *slang* date from the sixteenth century, but there are plenty of instances to show that *slang* expressions developed much earlier. François Villon, for instance, introduced much rogue's *argot* in his VERSES of the fifteenth century. *Slang* terms ultimately pass in one of three directions: (1) they die out and are lost unless their vividness is such that (2) they continue as *slang* over a long period, in which case (3) they frequently become accepted as good usage. "Skidoo" in the sense of "go away" is an instance of the first; "guy" meaning "a man" is an instance of the second; and "banter" in the sense of "ridicule" is an example of the third. The thoroughly respectable English "salary" may have come from Roman soldiers' *slang* meaning "salt-money" or "just salt" (much as current *slang* calls money "dough" or "bread"). See JARGON.

[References: H. L. Mencken, *The American Language,* 3 vols. and *Supplements* (1919–1948); Eric Partridge, *A Dictionary of Slang and Unconventional English,* 8th ed. (1985), and *Slang, Today and Yesterday,* 4th ed. (1970).]

Slant Rhyme: Approximate or NEAR RHYME; usually the substitution of ASSO-NANCE or CONSONANCE for true RHYME. Although *slant rhyme* is a common device in contemporary POETRY, readers should always be certain that they are dealing with something intended to be an imperfect RHYME rather than a mere change in pronunciation with the passage of time or change from one region to another before they assign the term *slant rhyme. Slant rhyme* is also called NEAR RHYME, OBLIQUE RHYME, off-rhyme, and pararhyme. See RHYME.

Slapstick: Low COMEDY involving physical action, practical jokes, and such actions as pie-throwing and pratfalls. The name is taken from a paddle consisting of two flat pieces of wood so attached to a handle (and maybe spring-loaded) that it makes a loud sound when a painless blow is struck with it.

Slave Narratives: In the period between 1830 and 1860, as a part of the abolition movement in America, a number of autobiographical accounts of slavery by escaped slaves were published. They are known as *slave narratives.* The best of them was *A Narrative of the Life of Frederick Douglass: An American Slave* (1845).

Sleight of "and":   A general term that indicates those TROPES—such as HEN-DIADYS, SYLLEPSIS, and ZEUGMA—that turn on use of "and" or some other coordinating conjunction.

Slice of Life: A term used to describe the unselective and nonevaluative presentation of a segment of life in its unordered totality, which was considered one of the objectives of the naturalists. *Slice of life* is the English translation of the French *tranche de vie*, which was applied to the work of Zola and the French naturalists.

Slick Magazine: A MAGAZINE printed on coated—"slick"—paper, illustrated lavishly, and carrying extensive advertising. The term was applied in the 1920s, 1930s, and 1940s to general circulation MAGAZINES with broad popular appeal, such as the *Saturday Evening Post* and the *American Magazine.* Although the name is taken from the kind of paper on which the MAGAZINE is printed, its use is restricted to general-purpose, mass-circulation publications. Many MAGAZINES printed on coated paper but addressed to specialized audiences are anything but *slick magazines,* as the *New Yorker, House Beautiful,* and the *National Geographic* illustrate.

Society Verse: Light, sophisticated VERSE. See VERS DE SOCIÉTÉ, OCCASIONAL VERSE, and LIGHT VERSE.

Sociological Novel: A form of the PROBLEM NOVEL that centers its principal attention on the nature, function, and effect of the society in which the CHARACTERS live and on the social forces playing on them. Usually the *sociological novel* presents a thesis and argues for it as a resolution to a social problem, but it is by no means always a PROPAGANDA NOVEL. The serious examination of social issues became an important element of FICTION with the INDUSTRIAL REVOLUTION, which concentrated on the condition of laborers and their families and resulted in such NOVELS as Dickens's *Hard Times,* Kingsley's *Yeast,* and Gaskell's *Mary Barton.* George Eliot in *Middlemarch* subjected an entire provincial town to sociological examination. American novelists have often had a serious interest in social issues. Stowe's *Uncle Tom's Cabin* explored the conditions and the social status of the Negro, a THEME that was to prove of enduring interest as a social problem through such works as G. W. Cable's *The Grandissimes* and the NOVELS of Richard Wright and Ralph Ellison. The MUCKRAKERS at the turn of the century produced a number of *sociological novels,* the most successful being Upton Sinclair's *The Jungle.* John Steinbeck, John Dos Passos, Erskine Caldwell, and James T. Farrell have all written NOVELS whose central issues were sociological in implication. See PROBLEM NOVEL.

Sock: The low-heeled slipper conventionally worn by the comic actor on the ancient stage, hence (figuratively) COMEDY itself. See BUSKIN.

Socratic: The *"Socratic* method" in argument or explanation is the use of the question-and-answer formula employed by Socrates in Plato's *Dialogues.* Socrates would feign ignorance of the subject under discussion and then proceed to develop his point by the question-and-answer device. The method of assuming ignorance for the sake of taking advantage of an opponent in debate is known as *"Socratic* IRONY." This pretense of ignorance on the part of Socrates, who was really regarded as the most intelligent of the group, was referred to as his IRONY by his companions.

Solecism: A violation of grammatical structure or IDIOM in speech or writing. "He don't" and "between you and I" are *solecisms.* Loosely any error in

DICTION, grammar, or propriety is called a *solecism.* Strictly interpreted, however, the term *solecism* is reserved for errors in grammar and idiom and is distinguished from "impropriety," which is employed to indicate the false use of one part of speech for another (as "to dialogue" and "parenting" for "to converse" and "being a parent"), and from BARBARISM, which is used to indicate words coined from analogies falsely made with other words in good standing (as "preventative" for "preventive"). A scrupulous writer needs to be on guard against most instances of *solecism,* impropriety, and BARBARISM since—among other drawbacks—they may have undesired or unforeseen rhetorical effects. Even so, language must change to stay alive, and some practices classified as wrong today have not always been so (Chaucer, for example, freely indulged in "double negatives"); practices now classified as wrong (the use of "loan" as a verb, for example) may gain in acceptance. Besides, a resourceful writer may use a *solecism* with fine effect. Gerard Manley Hopkins, for example, uses an objective pronoun in a position calling for the nominative, as in "what I do is me" and "My taste was me." This *solecism* has at least three effects: surprise; colloquial ease (for, indeed, most speakers of English have long said things like "It's me"); and transformation of a colorless linking intransitive verb into such a dynamic transitive verb that the concept of "being" takes on drama, action, energy, and life.

Soliloquy: A speech of a CHARACTER in a PLAY or other composition delivered while the speaker is alone (*solus*) and calculated to inform the audience or reader of what is passing in the character's mind or to give information concerning other participants in the action. Hamlet's famous *soliloquy,* "To be, or not to be," is an obvious example. Browning's "Soliloquy of the Spanish Cloister" is indeed a *soliloquy;* "Porphyria's Lover" and "Johannes Argicola in Meditation" may be *soliloquies,* although the titles make no explicit statement. See also ASIDE, MONOLOGUE.

Solution: A term sometimes employed in place of CATASTROPHE or DÉNOUEMENT to indicate the outcome of a piece of FICTION. It is used in the sense that a *solution* is presented for the COMPLICATION that was developed in the PLOT. See PLOT, DRAMATIC STRUCTURE.

Song: A LYRIC POEM adapted to musical expression. *Song* LYRICS are usually short, simple, sensuous, emotional—perhaps the most spontaneous lyric FORM. Since people have always sought emotional outlet through *songs,* either communal or individual, the record of the form extends back into the dim past. *Songs* have been of every type and subject; no satisfactory classification for the various types can be devised. There have been, for instance, a variety of working *songs,* dance *songs,* love *songs,* war *songs,* play *songs,* drinking *songs,* and *songs* for festivals, church gatherings, and political meetings, as well as a host of others. Perhaps the period in English literature richest in *songs* was the ELIZABETHAN, when Shakespeare gave us such *song* POEMS as "Who is Sylvia?" and Jonson, "Drink to Me Only with Thine Eyes." The so-called popular *song* is ubiquitous and influential nowadays. "*Song*" has, furthermore, long been applied to works that cannot really be sung in the usual sense: Longfellow's *Song of Hiawatha* and Whitman's *Song of Myself* are not literally singable, nor are Eliot's "The Love-Song of J. Alfred Prufrock" and the POEMS called "dream songs" that Eliot and John Berryman wrote.

Sonnet: A LYRIC POEM almost invariably of fourteen LINES and following one of several set RHYME SCHEMES. CRITICS of the *sonnet* have recognized various FORMS, but only two types need be discussed if the reader will understand that each of them has undergone various modifications. The two basic *sonnet* types are the ITALIAN or PETRARCHAN and the ENGLISH or SHAKESPEAREAN. The Italian form is distinguished by its division into the OCTAVE and the SESTET: the octave consisting of eight lines rhyming *abbaabba* and the sestet consisting of six lines rhyming *cdecde, cdcdcd,* or *cdedce.* The OCTAVE presents a NARRATIVE, states a proposition, or raises a question; the SESTET drives home the narrative by making an abstract comment, applies the proposition, or solves the problem. English POETS have varied these requirements greatly. The OCTAVE and SESTET division is not always kept; the RHYME SCHEME is often varied, but within the limitation that no Italian *sonnet* properly allows more than five RHYMES. IAMBIC PENTAMETER is usually the METER, but certain POETS have experimented with HEXAMETER and other METERS.

In the ENGLISH or SHAKESPEAREAN *sonnet,* instead of the OCTAVE and SESTET, four divisions are used: three QUATRAINS (each with a RHYME SCHEME of its own, usually rhyming alternate lines) and a rhymed concluding COUPLET. The typical rhyme scheme for the ENGLISH SONNET is *abab cdcd efef gg.* The COUPLET at the end is often a commentary on the preceding QUATRAINS and is an epigrammatic close. The SPENSERIAN SONNET combines the ITALIAN and the Shakespearean forms, using three QUATRAINS and a COUPLET but having linking RHYMES among the QUATRAINS, thus *abab bcbc cdcd ee.* (Note how the RHYME SCHEME resembles that of the SPENSERIAN STANZA.) The Spenserian *sonnet* is very rare; among modern POETS of any distinction, Richard Wilbur is virtually alone in using the form (see his "Praise in Summer").

Certain qualities are common to the *sonnet* as a FORM. Its definite restrictions make it a challenge to the artistry of the poet and call for all the technical skill at the poet's command. The more or less fixed RHYME patterns afford a pleasant effect on the ear of the reader and can create musical effects. The rigidity of the FORM precludes a too great economy or too great prodigality of words. EMPHASIS is placed on exactness and perfection of expression. The brevity of the form favors concentrated expression of idea or passion.

The *sonnet* as a FORM developed in Italy probably in the thirteenth century. Petrarch, in the fourteenth century, raised it to its greatest Italian perfection and gave it, for English readers at least, his name. The form was introduced into England by Thomas Wyatt, who translated PETRARCHAN SONNETS and left over thirty of his own compositions in English. Surrey, an associate, shares with Wyatt the credit for introducing the form to England and is important as an early modifier of the ITALIAN SONNET. Gradually the Italian *sonnet* pattern was changed, and since Shakespeare attained fame for the greatest POEMS of this modified type, his name has often been given to the English form. Among the most famous sonneteers in England have been Sidney, Shakespeare, Milton, Wordsworth, Keats, D. G. Rossetti, and Meredith. Longfellow, Jones Very, E. A. Robinson, Frederick Goddard Tuckerman, Robert Frost, and E. E. Cummings are generally credited with writing some of the best *sonnets* in America. With the interest in this poetic FORM, certain POETS following the example of Petrarch have written a series of *sonnets* linked to one another and dealing with a single, although sometimes generalized, subject. Such series are called SONNET SEQUENCES. Some of the most famous SONNET SEQUENCES in English literature are Shakespeare's *Sonnets,* Sidney's *Astrophil and Stella,* Spenser's *Amoretti,* Rossetti's *House of Life,* Elizabeth Barrett Browning's *Sonnets from the Portuguese,* and Meredith's *Modern Love.* William Ellery Leonard, Elinor Wylie, Edna St. Vincent Millay, John Berryman, Allen Tate, and W. H. Auden have done distinguished work in the SONNET SEQUENCE in this century. The psychiatrist-poet Merrill Moore is said to have written 10,000 *sonnets.* In the last decade of his life, Robert Lowell wrote scores of fourteen-line poems that, without rhyming or adhering to any very strict pattern of RHYTHM and METER, manage to preserve the appearance of *sonnets,* along with something of the spirit, passion, and personal focus of the *sonnet.*

[References: J. W. Lever, *The Elizabethan Love Sonnet* (1956); Hallett Smith, *Elizabethan Poetry* (1952); C. Tomlinson, *The Sonnet, Its Origin, Structure, and Place in Poetry* (1874, reprinted, 1970).]

Sonnet Cycle or **Sequence:** A connected group of SONNETS. See SONNET.

"Sons of Ben": POETS of the reign of Charles I who were admirers and imitators of the LYRIC POETRY of Ben Jonson; they are more commonly called the "TRIBE of BEN."

Sound-Over: In filmmaking the technique by which DIALOGUE or other sound begun at the end of one SCENE is completed at the beginning of the next, often by the same person or object but sometimes by a different person or object. It is thus a sound bridge between scenes. The term should not be confused with VOICE-OVER.

Source: The person, manuscript, or book from which information is derived. If such a person, manuscript, or book represents a direct and immediate acquaintance with the information—a person with firsthand experience, a book that is itself the subject of the discussion, a manuscript written at the time or on the scene—the *source* is called a "primary" *source.* If the person, book, or manuscript represents an indirect acquaintance with the information—the person recounting experience at second or third hand, the book being about the book under discussion, the manuscript being a copy or a summary of primary material—the *source* is called a "secondary" *source.* The term *source* is also used to designate the origin of literary works, philosophical ideas, or artistic forms. In this sense Lodge's *Rosalynde* is a *source* for Shakespeare's *As You Like It,* since the dramatist took his PLOT in part from the prose IDYLL. At one time, up to about 1930, much academic scholarship was devoted to *Quellenforschung:* research into *sources* and ANALOGUES, with heavy emphasis on FOLKLORE and PHILOLOGY. J. L. Lowes' study of Coleridge, *The Road to Xanadu,* remains a classic of *source*-study. Grover Smith's *T. S. Eliot's Poetry and Plays: A Study in Sources and Meaning* has been a valued companion for nearly three decades. Some of the less-inspired labors in such research have been dismissed as "*source*-hunting" and even caricatured as the activity of "carrion-eaters." Although the NEW CRITICISM and other schools of thought have drawn attention away from extrinsic genealogy, the study of *sources* remains an important area of scholarship and CRITICISM.

Spasmodic School: A phrase applied by W. E. Aytoun in 1854 to a group of English POETS who wrote in the 1840s and 1850s. Their VERSE (influenced by Shelley and Byron) reflected discontent and unrest, while their style was marked by jerkiness and forced or strained EMPHASIS. In his POEM "America" (1855) Sydney Dobell in addressing "Columbia" refers to the typical early English progenitor of Americans as "thy satchelled ancestor." Belonging to the group were Dobell, Alexander Smith, P. J. Bailey, George Gilfillan, and others. The general *spasmodic* tendency is said also to appear in the early verse of Robert Browning and Elizabeth Barrett Browning, and in Tennyson's *Maud.* Some members of the BEAT GENERATION have been characterized as "Neo-Spasmodics."

Spatial Form: A term applied by Joseph Frank to forms of twentieth-century writing in which the author attempts by various means to suspend or abolish the customary temporal STRUCTURE of POETRY or NARRATIVE and to substitute virtual space for time as the controlling dimension. Joyce's *Ulysses* and T. S. Eliot's *The Waste Land* are examples of *spatial form* in this sense.

[Reference: Joseph Frank, *The Widening Gyre: Crisis and Mastery in Modern Literature* (1963).]

Spectacle: A SCENE, ACTION, or event that is large, lavish in detail, unusual, or striking, and usually employed as much for its own spectacular EFFECT as for its role in the work. During the nineteenth century, under the influences of the large PATENT THEATERS and the star system, the DRAMA relied to an unusual extent on *spectacle. Spectacle* often occurs in the NOVEL; the huge ball on the eve of Waterloo in Thackeray's *Vanity Fair* is an example. *Spectacle* is frequent in FILM, its greatest exponent and exploiter probably being the director Cecil B. DeMille.

Speculum: (Latin, "mirror"), an important figure in medieval and RENAISSANCE literature, representing reflection and portraiture for the sake of MIMESIS and also for purposes of instruction. The idea is found in titles (*Mirror for Magistrates,* mid-sixteenth-century) and in METAPHORS, as when Ophelia says that Hamlet has been "The glass of fashion and the mould of form" (meaning a model) or when, soon after, Hamlet tells the players that the purpose of their art is "to hold, as 'twere, the mirror up to nature."

Speech Act Theory: A recent development in the philosophy of language according to which we can divide utterances into the "constative" (that have to do with describing some state of affairs and can be judged as true or false) and the "performative" (that, in the act of being uttered, perform what they utter or say and are not subject to judgment as to truth or falsity, as when one says "I promise" and performs the *speech act* of promising simultaneously). The theory also divides speech acts into the "locutionary" (the act of uttering), the "illocutionary" (the act of carrying out some performative function, such as warning), and the "perlocutionary" (the act of achieving some ulterior rhetorical purpose, such as persuading). So far, the theory has been useful in clearing up some philosophical problems in the study of language but has not yet been extensively applied to problems of literature.

[References: J. L. Austin, *How to Do Things with Words* (1975); John Searle, *Speech Acts: An Essay in the Philosophy of Language* (1969).]

Spell: A kind of charm, formula, or INCANTATION designed or believed to influence the behavior of a person or thing.

Spenserian Sonnet: A SONNET of the ENGLISH type in that it has three QUA-
TRAINS and a COUPLET but is modified in the direction of the ITALIAN SONNET
by having the QUATRAINS joined by the use of linking RHYMES. The RHYME-
SCHEME is *abab bcbc cdcd ee.* It was used by Spenser in his SONNET SEQUENCE,
Amoretti. Virtually the only competent instance in the modern age is Richard
Wilbur's "Praise in Summer." See SONNET.

Spenserian Stanza: A stanzaic pattern consisting of nine VERSES, the first
eight being IAMBIC PENTAMETER and the ninth an IAMBIC HEXAMETER. The
RHYME SCHEME is *ababbcbcc.* (See SCANSION.) The FORM derives its name
from Edmund Spenser, who created the pattern for *The Faerie Queene,* from
which the first STANZA of canto I is cited as an example:

> A Gentle Knight was pricking on the plaine,
> Y-cladd in mightie armes and silver shielde,
> Wherein old dints of deepe wounds did remaine,
> The cruell markes of many' a bloudy fielde;
> Yet armes till that time did he never wield:
> His angry steede did chide his foming bitt,
> As much disdayning to the curbe to yield:
> Full jolly knight he seemed, and faire did sitt,
> As one for knightly giusts and fierce encounters fitt.

This stanzaic FORM is notable for three qualities: (1) the method of "tying-
in" the three RHYMES promotes unity of effect and tightness of thought; the
unity is somewhat relieved by the shifting variety of RHYME (two *a,* four *b,*
three *c*) with the sense so distributed that PENTAMETER COUPLETS containing
a complete thought are avoided; (2) the ALEXANDRINE at the close adds dignity
to the sweep of the FORM; and (3) at the same time, it affords an opportunity
for summary and epigrammatic expression. (C. S. Lewis has suggested that
the fifth line of the *Spenserian stanza* is crucial because it completes the
first *couplet,* acoustically if not grammatically). Other POETS than Spenser
have made notable use of the form. Burns used the *Spenserian stanza* in
The Cotter's Saturday Night, Shelley in *The Revolt of Islam* and in *Adonais;*
Keats used it in *The Eve of St. Agnes,* and Byron in *Childe Harold.* A part
of Tennyson's "The Lotos-Eaters" is written in the *Spenserian stanza.* In our
century, however, the STANZA has fallen into disuse; except for two STANZAS
printed as paragraphs of PROSE in Fitzgerald's *This Side of Paradise,* it is
hard to find twentieth-century examples of any distinction.

Spondee: A FOOT composed of two accented syllables (´´). The ideally perfect
form is rare in English VERSE, since most of our polysyllabic words carry a
primary ACCENT. *Spondees* in our POETRY are usually composed of two monosyllabic words as *all joy!* Poe in writing of the subject found only three or
four instances (one of which was *football*) in English where real *spondees*
occurred in a single word. Untermeyer finds a longer list (really compounds
composed of monosyllabic words) and cites *heartbreak, childhood, bright-eyed,
bookcase, wineglass,* and *Mayday.* In Milton's LINE:

> Silence, ye troubled waves, and thou deep, peace!

"deep, peace" is a perfect spondaic FOOT. Despite the paucity of perfect *spondees*, English contains thousands of usable approximations involving pairs of syllables with some degree of STRESS. The *spondee*, like its converse, the PYRRHIC, cannot seriously be used as the only FOOT in a POEM or even in a LINE, but most poets have been able to vary predominantly IAMBIC poetry with *spondees* and other feet for substitution. Here are two lines with *spondees* and other feet but no iambs, even though the lines come from IAMBIC poems:

Hot sun, | cool fire, | tempered with | sweet air

(Peele)

On the | bald street | breaks the | blank day

(Tennyson)

Spoonerism: An accidental interchange of sounds, usually the initial ones, in two or more words, such as *bl*ushing *cr*ow for *cr*ushing *bl*ow or well-*b*oiled icicle for well-oiled *b*icycle. The term owes its name to Dr. W. A. Spooner, of New College, Oxford, who was inordinately guilty of such transpositions. Research suggests that Spooner's affliction (or gift) has been vastly exaggerated, but the FOLKLORE has been abundant and amusing. He is supposed to have told a lazy student, "You've hissed all your mystery lectures and tasted two whole worms."

Sprung Rhythm: A term coined by Gerard Manley Hopkins for RHYTHM based on the number of stressed syllables in a LINE without regard to the number of unstressed syllables. Put another way, *sprung rhythm* may be said to designate the METER of a VERSE that contains FEET of varying numbers of syllables, with the first syllable accented in each case. The feet possible are the monosyllabic (a single stressed syllable), the TROCHEE, the DACTYL, and the first PAEON: ´ | ´ ˘ | ´ ˘ ˘ | ´ ˘ ˘ ˘. The obvious result of a LINE composed of combinations of such varying FEET is extreme metrical irregularity. The SCANSION of such POETRY is, as W. B. Yeats noted, difficult because "it may not be certain at first glance where the stress falls." The following lines from Hopkins's "The Starlight Night" indicate both the effect of *sprung rhythm* and the difficulty of scanning it:

Look at the | stars! | look | up at the | skies!

O | look at all the | fire- | folk | sitting in the | air!

The | bright | borough, the | circle | citadels | there! |

Down in | dim woods the | diamond | delves! the | elves'-eyes!

(Note that a FOOT may continue to the beginning of the next line.) These opening lines of a SONNET are pretty clearly PENTAMETER but of an indeterminable type of foot.

Hopkins said that he used *sprung rhythm* because "it is nearest to the rhythm of prose, that is the native and natural rhythm of speech," and he cited as earlier users the author of *Piers Plowman*, the CHORUS in Milton's *Samson Agonistes*, and old NURSERY RHYMES. Both "One, two" and "Buckle your shoe" have two stresses, but the first contains only two syllables; the second contains four. See PROSE RHYTHM, ACCENT, METER, OLD ENGLISH VERSIFICATION.

Stanza: A recurrent grouping of two or more LINES of a POEM in terms of length, metrical form, and, often, RHYME SCHEME. However, the division into *stanzas* is sometimes made according to *thought* as well as form, in which case the *stanza* is a unit not unlike a paragraph of PROSE. STROPHE is another term used for *stanza*, but one should avoid VERSE in this sense, since VERSE has so many other meanings. Some of the more common stanzaic FORMS are COUPLET, TERCET, QUATRAIN, RHYME ROYAL, OTTAVA RIMA, and the SPENSE-RIAN STANZA, all of which are discussed in their proper places.

State: Just as an EDITION (all the copies made from a setting of type) may comprise more than one IMPRESSION or PRINTING (all the copies made at one given time), an IMPRESSION may comprise more than one state (all the copies in exactly the same condition, with no accidental or deliberate changes).

Static Character: A CHARACTER in a NOVEL, a SHORT STORY, or a DRAMA who changes little if at all in the progress of the ACTION. Things happen to *static characters* without modifying their interior selves; the pattern of action reveals characters as they are without showing them in the process of development. See CHARACTERIZATION.

Stave: A STANZA, particularly of a POEM intended to be sung.

Stereotype: The metal duplication of a printing surface, cast from a mold made of the surface, usually by wet paper pulp. A *stereotype* plate enables the original surface to be exactly duplicated many times. By extension, *stereotype* has come to mean anything that repeats or duplicates something else without variation; hence something that lacks individualizing characteristics. The term is applied to commonly held and oversimplified mental pictures or judgments of a person, a race, an issue, a kind of art, etc. Note that *stereotype*, like CLICHÉ and "rubber-stamp" (meaning perfunctory or bureaucratic treatment), comes from the idiom of printing.
[Reference: Marshall McLuhan, *From Cliché to Archetype* (1970).]

-stich: A stem meaning "line," as in HEMISTICH, a half LINE, or in DISTICH, a COUPLET.

Stichomythia: A form of REPARTEE developed in CLASSICAL DRAMA and often employed by Elizabethan writers, especially in PLAYS that imitated the SENE-CAN TRAGEDIES. It is a sort of line-for-line "verbal fencing match" in which the principals in the DIALOGUE retort sharply to each other in lines that echo and vary the opponent's words and FIGURES OF SPEECH. ANTITHESIS is freely used. The thought is often sententious. A few LINES quoted from Hamlet's interview with his mother in the SCENE where Polonius is killed will serve as an instance of *stichomythia:*

> *Hamlet:* Now, mother, what's the matter?
> *Queen:* Hamlet, thou hast thy father much offended.
> *Hamlet:* Mother, you have my father much offended.
> *Queen:* Come, come, you answer with an idle tongue.
> *Hamlet:* Go, go, you question with a wicked tongue.

A more sustained example is found in the interview between King Richard and the Queen in *Richard III* (IV, iv, 343 ff.).

Stock Characters: Conventional CHARACTER types belonging by custom to given FORMS of literature. Thus, a boisterous CHARACTER known as the Vice came to be expected in a MORALITY PLAY. The Elizabethan REVENGE TRAGEDY commonly employed, among other *stock characters,* a high-thinking vengeance-seeking HERO (Hamlet), the ghost of a murdered father or son, and a scheming murderer-villain (Claudius). In Elizabethan dramatic TRADITION in general, one may expect such stock figures as a disguised romantic HEROINE (Portia), a melancholy man (Jaques), a loquacious old counsellor (Polonius), a female servant-CONFIDANTE (Nerissa), a court fool (Feste), a witty clownish servant (Launcelot Gobbo). In fairy tales the cruel stepmother and prince charming are examples. In the SENTIMENTAL NOVEL one expects a fainting HEROINE. Every type of FICTION—NOVELS, ROMANCES, DETECTIVE TALES, FILMS, the various kinds of COMEDIES and TRAGEDIES, METRICAL ROMANCES—tends to develop *stock characters* whose conventional nature readers do well to recognize so that they can distinguish between the individual, personal characteristics of a given CHARACTER and the conventional traits drawn from the TRADITION of the STOCK CHARACTER represented. A feature of MODERN art is its tendency to take *stock characters* from the past, move them from the periphery to the center of attention, and reveal and explore new complexities. Shaw's St. Joan begins as a standard INGENUE, for example. Eliot's "Gerontion" is a *gerontion*—the word itself is the name of a favorite *stock character* of Greek (and later) COMEDY: the geezer, codger, "little old man." See further under various types of literature, such as COMEDY OF HUMOURS, PICARESQUE NOVEL.

Stock Response: The traditional, conventional response to literature or art; poor artists and writers, like the preparers of advertising copy, call for *stock responses* by the use of STOCK CHARACTERS, STOCK SITUATIONS, and traditional SYMBOLS and standardized attitudes, such as the flag, mother love, peace, nature, the organic, and the "holistic." Such materials supposedly have a "built-in" response for the unsophisticated and almost as much for the sophisticated—since sophistication itself is one of the ideals that call forth a *stock response.* Serious artists and writers, however, attempt to provide solid grounds for the desired responses within the work itself.

Stock Situation: A SITUATION recurring frequently in a literary FORM, whether it be a general PLOT situation, such as boy-meets-girl or rags-to-riches, or a recurrent detail, such as mixed identity or birthmarks that betray kinship.

Note, however, that certain fundamental SITUATIONS, such as the search for a father, death and rebirth, the Oedipus attachment, and the loss of Paradise are more nearly archetypal patterns than *stock situations,* since they seem to echo recurrent human views of life and its meaning. See ARCHETYPE.

Stoicism: The philosophical doctrine of the Stoics, a group of Greek philosophers, founded by Zeno late in the fourth century B.C. *Stoicism* exalts the ideals of virtue, endurance, and self-sufficiency. Virtue consists in living in conformity to the laws of NATURE; "to live consistently with nature" was one of the Stoics' most common admonitions. Endurance lies in the recognition that what is experienced is experienced by necessity and therefore must be endured. Self-sufficiency resides in extreme self-control, which holds in restraint all feelings, whether pleasurable or painful. *Stoicism* was the most attractive of the Greek philosophies to the Roman world, and its great influence in English literature comes through three Roman writers: Cicero, Epictetus, and Marcus Aurelius. There is also a strain of *Stoicism* in Seneca. There have been notable instances of the use of Stoic philosophy in English literature from "The Knight's Tale" in *The Canterbury Tales* to Addison's TRAGEDY, *Cato*—perhaps the most complete statement of the Stoic position in our language—to Ernest Hemingway's ideal of courage, defined as "grace under pressure."

[Reference: Duane J. MacMillan, ed., *The Stoic Strain in American Literature* (1979).]

Storm and Stress: An eighteenth-century German literary MOVEMENT. See STURM UND DRANG.

Story: In its broadest sense any account, written, oral, or in the mind, true or imaginary, of ACTIONS in a time sequence; any NARRATIVE of events in a sequential arrangement. The one merit of *story,* as *story,* is its ability to make us want to know what happened next; other merits may be gained through what is done to *story* and not through *story* alone. In this broad sense it is time, and time only, that is the determinant of selection—this happened, and then this, and then this, and now what?—other and higher concerns do not enter *story* as *story.*

Story is thus the basis of all literary GENRES that are NARRATIVE or DRAMATIC, for in each of them *story* is the collection of things that happen in the work. It is thus a common element (E. M. Forster would insist the only common element) among NOVELS, ROMANCES, SHORT STORIES, DRAMAS, FILMS, EPIC POEMS, NARRATIVE POEMS, ALLEGORIES, PARABLES, SKETCHES, and all other FORMS with any basis in a sequence of events. *Story* may be regarded as the raw material for all these FORMS, and they differ significantly in how and why they use *story* in the shaping of the work. *Story,* in this sense, is not PLOT but is an ingredient of plot. Plot takes a *story,* selects its materials in terms not of time but of causality; gives it a beginning, a middle, and an end; and makes it serve to elucidate or develop CHARACTER, embody a THEME, express an idea, incite to an ACTION, or express an abstract concept. See PLOT.

Straight Man: In a MINSTREL SHOW or other situation in which comic or satiric DIALOGUE occurs, the *straight man* is the CHARACTER or person who asks the seemingly serious questions or makes the grave comment that serves as the trigger for the comic or satiric answer or retort. He often plays the same role as that of the ADVERSARIUS in FORMAL SATIRE.

Stream of Consciousness: The total range of awareness and emotive-mental response of an individual, from the lowest pre-speech level to the highest fully articulated level of rational thought. The assumption is that in the mind of an individual at a given moment a *stream of consciousness* (the phrase originated in this sense with William James) is a mixture of all the levels of awareness, an unending flow of sensations, thoughts, memories, associations, and reflections; if the exact content of the mind ("consciousness") is to be described at any moment, then these varied, disjointed, and illogical elements must find expression in a flow of words, images, and ideas similar to the unorganized flow of the mind. However, since consciousness is neither a stream nor a thing given to verbal articulation, the *stream-of-consciousness* technique has become as artificial and convention-bound as any other literary technique, although it may give the impression or illusion of preserving a lifelike resemblance to real consciousness. Joyce's approximation involved the removal of customary signals, such as quotation marks, hyphens in compounds, and chapter numbers and titles. By moving the written text closer to the realm of speech, which is normally unpunctuated, Joyce gave the impression, in effect, of moving his discourse from the outer world of the reading eye to the inner world of the listening ear.

[References: Dorrit Cohn, *Transparent Minds: Narrative Modes for Presenting Consciousness in Fiction* (1978); Melvin Friedman, *Stream of Consciousness: A Study in Literary Method* (1955); Robert Humphrey, *Stream of Consciousness in the Modern Novel* (1954).]

Stream-of-Consciousness Novel: The type of PSYCHOLOGICAL NOVEL taking as its subject matter the uninterrupted, uneven, and endless flow of the STREAM OF CONSCIOUSNESS of one or more of its characters. The *stream-of-consciousness novel* uses varied techniques to represent this consciousness adequately. In general, most PSYCHOLOGICAL NOVELS report the flow of conscious and ordered intelligence, as in Henry James, or the flow of memory activated by association, as in Marcel Proust; but the *stream-of-consciousness novel* tends to concentrate its attention chiefly on the pre-speech, nonverbalized level, where the IMAGE must express the unarticulated response and where the logic of grammar belongs to another world. However differing the techniques employed, the writers of the *stream-of-consciousness novel* seem to share certain common assumptions: (1) that the significant existence of human beings is to be found in their mental-emotional processes and not in the outside world, (2) that this mental-emotional life is disjointed and illogical, and (3) that a pattern of free psychological association rather than of logical relation determines the shifting sequence of thought and feeling.

Attempts to concentrate the subject matter of FICTION on the inner consciousness are not new by any means. The earliest impressive example seems to be Laurence Sterne's *Tristram Shandy* (1759–1767), with its motto from

Epictetus: "It is not actions, but opinions about actions, which disturb men," and with its application of Locke's psychological theories of association and duration to the functioning of the human mind. Yet Sterne, although he freed the sequence of thought from the rigors of logical organization, did not get beneath the speech level in his portrait of Tristram's consciousness. Henry James, in his PSYCHOLOGICAL NOVELS, too, remained on a consciously articulated level. In a major sense the present-day *stream-of-consciousness novel* is a product of Freudian psychology with its structure of subliminal psychological levels, although it first appeared in *Les lauriers sont coupés*, by Edouard Dujardin, 1888, where the INTERIOR MONOLOGUE was used for the first time in the modern sense. Other important users of the INTERIOR MONOLOGUE to create reports on the *stream-of-consciousness* have been Dorothy Richardson, Virginia Woolf, James Joyce, and William Faulkner. The tendency today is to see the *stream-of-consciousness* subject matter and the INTERIOR MONOLOGUE technique as tools to be used in the presentation of complex CHARACTER, but not as the exclusive subjects or methods of whole NOVELS. See PSYCHOLOGICAL NOVEL, INTERIOR MONOLOGUE, STREAM OF CONSCIOUSNESS.

Stress: The vocal EMPHASIS given a syllable in the SCANSION of VERSE. There is debate by prosodists as to whether *stress* is the equivalent of ACCENT or whether *stress* should be used for metrical EMPHASIS and accent be reserved for emphasis that is determined by the meaning of the sentence (see RHETORICAL ACCENT). There is no agreement among prosodists on this matter, and in this *Handbook stress* and ACCENT have both been used for the articulatory vocal EMPHASIS placed on a syllable. See ACCENT, FOOT, METER, ARSIS, ICTUS, SCANSION, RECESSIVE ACCENT.

Strong Curtain: A dramatically powerful conclusion to an ACT or a PLAY. See CURTAIN.

Strophe: A STANZA. In the PINDARIC ODE (see ODE) the *strophe* signifies particularly the first stanza, and every subsequent third stanza—that is, the fourth, seventh, and so forth. To avoid fuzziness, some writers limit STANZA to regular, recurrent, and usually rhymed quantitative subdivisions of a POEM, leaving *strophe* to cover the irregular and unrhymed subdivisions.

Structuralism: A primarily French movement in contemporary thought utilizing the methods of structural linguistics and structural anthropology. Where linguists, such as Ferdinand de Saussure, study the underlying system of language rather than concrete speech events and where anthropologists, such as Claude Lévi-Strauss, try to explain cultural phenomena in terms of the underlying formal systems of which they are manifestations, structuralist literary CRITICS, such as Roland Barthes, seek not explication of unique texts but an account of the modes of literary discourse and their operation. The line separating such study of the STRUCTURES and CONVENTIONS of literature from SEMIOTICS, the study of SIGNS, is thin and frequently crossed. What is really "structural" about Saussure's linguistic science is its insistence on the decisive importance of structures and relations, along with the insignificance of substances as such. No matter what we may superstitiously or sentimentally feel, a given articulatory-acoustic entity or substance, such as the usual sound of *k* or *n*, say, has absolutely no inherent meaning by itself. It acquires meaning only as part of a complex set of structural relations. Neither the dot nor the dash in Morse code has any absolutely defined duration or inherent meaning. A beginner's transmitted dot may be longer than an expert's dash. All that matters—as far as the meaning of SIGNS is concerned—is the structural relation *between* dot and dash. How short is the dot? Shorter than the dash. How long is the dash? Longer than the dot. Such procedures can be applied likewise to any other system of arbitrary and conventional signs. (These systems are said to comprise such units as graphemes, PHONEMES, lexemes, sememes, mythologems, and so forth.)

There are two basic types of *structuralism*. One concentrates its study on the patterns formed by linguistic elements in the work and examines these patterns to find which ones unify the text and throw certain elements in relief. The other and more common type, one with very close affinities to SEMIOTICS, sees literary CONVENTIONS and FORMS as constituting a system of CODES that contribute to and convey meaning. The special interest here is on the organization and function of distinctively literary elements, on how meaning is conveyed rather than what meaning is conveyed, on how a literary device or even GENRE functions rather than how it imitates an external reality or expresses an internal feeling. *Structuralism* has been employed most frequently in the analysis of PROSE FICTION, but there is a growing body of work applying structuralist principles to POETRY.

Although primarily a European and particularly a French movement reaching its first flowering in the 1960s, *structuralism* represented at one time a growing interest among American CRITICS. As a revolt against literary history and biographical CRITICISM, it is a return to the text, but unlike the NEW CRITICISM it seeks to see the text in terms of a methodological model. See SEMIOTICS, PHENOMENOLOGY.

[References: Jonathan Culler, *Structuralist Poetics* (1975); Jacques Ehrmann, ed., *Structuralism* (1970); Terence Hawkes, *Structuralism and Semiotics* (1977); Michael Lane, ed., *Structuralism* (1970); Jean Piaget, *Structuralism* (tr. 1970); Robert Scholes, *Structuralism in Literature: An Introduction* (1974); John Sturrock, ed., *Structuralism and Since: From Lévi-Strauss to Derrida* (1979).]

Structure: The planned framework of a piece of literature. Though such external matters as kind of language used (French or English, PROSE or VERSE, or kind of VERSE, or type of sentence) are sometimes referred to as "structural" features, the term usually is applied to the general plan or outline. Thus, the scheme of topics (as revealed in a topical outline) determines the *structure* of a FORMAL ESSAY. The logical division of the ACTION of a DRAMA (see DRAMATIC STRUCTURE) and also the mechanical division into ACTS and SCENES are matters of *structure*. In a NARRATIVE the PLOT itself is the structural element. Groups of STORIES may be set in a larger structural plan (see FRAMEWORK STORY) such as the pilgrimage in Chaucer's *Canterbury Tales*. The *structure* of an ITALIAN SONNET suggests first its division into OCTAVE and SESTET, and more minutely the internal plan of each of these two parts. A PINDARIC ODE follows a special structural plan that determines not only the development of the THEME but the sequence of stanzaic forms. Often authors advertise their *structure* as a means of securing clarity (as in some college textbooks), while at other times their artistic purpose leads them to conceal the *structure* (as in NARRATIVES) or subordinate it altogether (as in some INFORMAL ESSAYS). In the NOVEL, the SHORT STORY, and the DRAMA, the *structure* is generally regarded today as the most reliable as well as the most revealing key to the meaning of the work. In the contemporary CRITICISM of POETRY, too, *structure* is used to define not only verse FORM and formal arrangement but also the sequence of IMAGES and IDEAS that unite to convey the meaning of the POEM. The elementary basis of *structure* seems to be binary or binomial, a matter of contrastive relations that are differential, without positive or absolute terms. A perfected work of good art is a conspicuous example of foregrounded *structure* with many levels and sorts of organization (graphic, acoustic, grammatical, semantic, thematic, and so forth). A shapely work of art has both an endoskeleton and an exoskeleton: inward and outward *structures*. An entity inside a work of art generates its meaning and power inside the well-marked limits of the work. Hamlet, for example, means whatever he means inside the PLAY as a complex function of many binary relations (with Horatio, Laertes, Ophelia, Claudius, Gertrude, and so forth). Outside the play, as a portrait of a legendary Danish prince named Amlotha or as a self-portrait of Shakespeare or as an incarnation of an ill-resolved Oedipal fixation, Hamlet has no determinate meaning because those relations lack both *structure* and substance. Compare with STRUCTURALISM.

Sturm und Drang (**Storm and Stress**):   A literary MOVEMENT in Germany during the last quarter of the eighteenth century. The movement derives its name from the title of a DRAMA, *Sturm und Drang* (1776) by Klinger, although Goethe's *Götz von Berlichingen* was probably the most significant literary production of the group. Goethe's NOVEL *The Sorrows of Young Werther* reflects the *Sturm und Drang* attitude, as does Schiller's *Die Räuber* (1781). The real founder and pioneer of the movement was Herder (1744–1803). Other leaders were Lenz, Klinger, and Friedrich Müller. The DRAMA was much used as a medium of expression, and the dramatists were greatly influenced by Shakespeare and his freedom from CLASSICAL standards. The *Sturm und Drang* MOVEMENT was a revolt from classical CONVENTIONS and the tenets of French CLASSICISM. The writing was imbued with a strong nationalistic and folk element; was characterized by fervor and enthusiasm, a restlessness of spirit, the portrayal of great passion, and a reliance on emotional experiences and spiritual struggles; and was intensely personal.

Style: The arrangement of words in a manner best expressing the individuality of the author and the idea and intent in the author's mind. The best *style*, for any given purpose, is that which most nearly approximates a perfect adaptation of one's language to one's ideas. *Style* is a combination of two elements: the idea to be expressed and the individuality of the author. It is, as J. R. Lowell said, "the establishment of a perfect mutual understanding between the worker and his material." From this point of view it is impossible to change the DICTION or to alter the phrasing of a statement and thus to say exactly the same thing; for what the reader receives from a statement is not alone what is said, but also certain CONNOTATIONS that affect the reader's consciousness. And from this it follows that, just as no two personalities are alike, no two *styles* are exactly alike.

There are, in fact, many *styles*. Critics are fond of categories and fix a label to a Milton, a Pope, or a Hemingway; give a name to a *style* and call it ornamental, forceful, poetic, or whatnot, in the conviction perhaps that they have described the *style* of a writer when all they have done has been to place the writer in a group with others who have written ornate or forceful or poetic PROSE. A mere recital of some of these categories may, however, be suggestive of the infinite range of manners the word *style* covers. We speak, for instance, of journalistic, scientific, or literary *styles;* we call the manners of other writers ABSTRACT or concrete, rhythmic or pedestrian, sincere or artificial, dignified or comic, original or imitative, dull or vivid, as though each of these were somehow a final category of its own. But, if we are actually to estimate a *style*, we need more delicate tests than these; we need terms so scrupulous in their sensitiveness as ultimately to distinguish the work of each writer from that of all other writers, since, as has been said, in the last analysis no two *styles* are exactly comparable.

A study of *styles* for the purpose of analysis will include, in addition to the infinity of personal detail suggested above, such general qualities as: DICTION, sentence structure and variety, IMAGERY, RHYTHM, REPETITION, COHERENCE, EMPHASIS, and arrangement of ideas. There is a growing interest in the study of *style* and language in FICTION. See PHENOMENOLOGY, SEMIOTICS, STRUCTURALISM.

[References: M. W. Croll, *Style, Rhetoric, and Rhythm,* ed. J. Max Patrick et al. (1966); D. C. Freeman, ed., *Linguistics and Literary Style* (1970); Northrop Frye, *The Well-Tempered Critic* (1963); Graham Hough, *Style and Stylistics* (1969); F. L. Lucas, *Style* (1955); J. Middleton Murry, *The Problem of Style* (1922, reprinted 1960); Herbert Read, *English Prose Style* (1928, reprinted 1952); Leo Spitzer, *Linguistics and Literary History* (1948).]

Stylistics: The study of STYLE in literature. It concentrates on the choices available to a writer, chiefly: VOCABULARY (familiar or not, plain or fancy, and so forth); SYNTAX (HYPOTAXIS versus PARATAXIS, LOOSE versus PERIODIC, and so forth); level and texture of DICTION; acoustic and graphic effects.

Subjective: A term frequently used in CRITICISM to denote writing that is expressive in an intensely personal manner of the inward convictions, beliefs, dreams, or ideals of the author. *Subjective* writing is opposed to objective, which is impersonal, concrete, and concerned largely with NARRATIVE, analysis, or the DESCRIPTION of externalities. One might, for instance, speak of the *subjective* element in Shakespeare's SONNETS and the objective qualities of *The Rape of Lucrece;* the first tells of Shakespeare's reflective spirit; the second retells an old Roman story.

Another way of seeing the distinction between *subjective* and objective is to associate *subjective* with the seer of an object or the reporter of it and objective with the object seen or reported. If the emphasis is on the response of the reporter, the work is *subjective;* if it is on the object reported, the work is objective. It should be noted that *subjective* may be used in two distinct senses, just as the PERSONA has two possible distinct connections with the author. *Subjective,* in one sense, may refer to the presence in the work of events and emotions that are autobiographical (the PERSONA speaks the author's personal responses, as the character Eugene Gant speaks Thomas Wolfe's). In the other sense, *subjective* may refer to the recounting of an emotional response by a PERSONA who is a dramatically realized CHARACTER, assumed to be feeling emotions peculiar to the dramatic situation and not necessarily those of the author, as the NARRATOR Ishmael speaks dramatically rather than autobiographically in Melville's *Moby-Dick.* By present-day critical standards the first kind of subjectivity is suspect, the second admirable. See OBJECTIVITY, NEGATIVE CAPABILITY, OBJECTIVE CORRELATIVE, AESTHETIC DISTANCE.

Subjective Camera: In a FILM, camera work that shoots a SCENE from the point of view of a CHARACTER; also called POINT OF VIEW SHOT.

Sublime: Characterized by nobility and grandeur, impressive, exalted, raised above ordinary human qualities—these were asserted to be the essential qualities of great art in the aesthetic treatise *On the Sublime* by "Longinus" (A.D. 50) "Longinus" regarded the *sublime* as a thing of spirit, a spark leaping from writer to reader, rather than a product of technique. He lists five sources of the *sublime,* the first two of which—great thoughts and noble feelings—are gifts of NATURE, and the last three of which—lofty FIGURES OF SPEECH, DICTION, and arrangement—are products of art.

Edmund Burke in 1756 wrote *A Philosophical Inquiry into the Origin of our Ideas of the Sublime and the Beautiful.* Kant followed Burke's line of thinking, in his *Critique of Judgment* (1790), which links beauty with the finite and the *sublime* with the infinite. Burke's doctrine of the *sublime* was powerfully influential on eighteenth- and nineteenth-century writers. He believed that a painful idea creates a sublime passion and thus concentrates the mind on that single facet of experience and produces a momentary suspension of rational activity, uncertainty, and self-consciousness. If the pain producing this effect is imaginary rather than real, a great aesthetic object is achieved. Thus, great mountains, storms at sea, ruined abbeys, crumbling castles, and charnel houses are appropriate subjects to produce the *sublime.* Burke's theory of the *sublime* underlies the POETRY of the "GRAVEYARD SCHOOL" and the GOTHIC NOVEL. Edgar Allan Poe's theory that the death of a beautiful woman is the most poetic of subjects is an instance of the theory. Among contemporary CRITICS, Elder Olson seems the most sympathetic to Longinus. Olson has carefully analyzed *On the Sublime* and even reconstructed some of its missing parts. A good deal of Olson's MONOGRAPH on the POETRY of Dylan Thomas amounts to an application of Longinian CRITICISM to a challenging body of modern POETRY. Note, by the way, that *Peri Hypsous,* or *Hupsous,* the title given to Longinus's treatise, is burlesqued in Pope's *Peri Bathous: Or, Martinus Scriblerus, His Treatise on the Art of Sinking on Poetry.* See PICTURESQUE.

[References: Harold Bloom, *Poetry and Repression: Revisionism from Blake to Stevens* (1976); W. J. Hipple, *The Beautiful, the Sublime, and the Picturesque in Eighteenth-Century British Aesthetic Theory* (1957); Samuel Holt Monk, *The Sublime: A Study of Critical Theories in XVIII-Century England* (1935, reprinted 1960).]

Subplot: A subordinate or minor COMPLICATION running through a piece of FICTION. This secondary PLOT interest, if skillfully handled, has a direct relation to the main plot, contributing to it in interest and in complication and struggle. (See PLOT.) Some writers have carried the intricacies and surprises of PLOT relations so far as to create not only one but sometimes three, four, or more *subplots.* The characteristic difference, it has been observed, between the FICTION of France, Italy—the Romance countries in general—and the FICTION of the Anglo-Saxons is that the Romance authors are generally satisifed with simple, unified PLOT relations, whereas northern writers are more given to an intricate series of *subplots* supporting and complicating the major PLOT. There are said to be seventy-five CHARACTERS in Dickens's *Our Mutual Friend* and sixty in Thackeray's *Vanity Fair.* When so many people are introduced into a work of FICTION, it is obvious that their relationship to the chief characters of the main PLOT must shade off into very subordinate *subplots.* As an instance of *subplot* in Shakespeare may be cited from *Hamlet* the Laertes-Hamlet struggle (as subordinate to the Claudius-Hamlet major PLOT). It may be observed that writers use *subplots* of at least two different degrees: first, those directly related to, and giving impetus and action to, the main plot; and second, those more or less extraneous to the chief PLOT interest and on hand frankly as a secondary story to give zest and EMPHASIS, or relief, to the main PLOT.

Substitution: In PROSODY a term used to describe the use of one kind of FOOT in place of the one normally demanded by the METER of a VERSE, as a TROCHEE for an IAMB or a DACTYL or ANAPEST for a trochee or iamb. Once a rhythmic pattern is established or realized, the need for variety and surprise dictates plentiful *substitution,* particularly in the early part of a LINE. The IAMB, much the commonest foot in English, is the one most often displaced by *substitution,* usually by a TROCHEE, SPONDEE, PYRRHIC, or ANAPEST. When an iambic line has a so-called FEMININE ENDING, we could say that an AMPHI-BRACH has been substituted for the final iamb. Since a whole POEM using the spondee or pyrrhic is virtually impossible, those FEET almost always function as *substitutions.* Here, tentatively scanned, are two opening lines from POEMS more or less in BLANK VERSE, although, because of thoroughgoing *substitution,* the prevailing form is obscured:

Mary | sat mus|ing on | the lamp-|flame at | the table

(Frost)

Here I | am, an | old man | in a | dry month

(Eliot)

See **COMPENSATION.**

Subtitle: A secondary title, usually an elaboration or explanation of the TITLE proper. *Subtitles* have been fairly common in literature since the RENAIS-SANCE, and from time to time they seem to enjoy quite a vogue. For some centuries "or" was used to indicate *subtitles,* along with an unregulated sprinkling of periods, colons, semicolons, and commas. If a standard FORMAT could be settled on, its punctuation would probably follow the model of Goldsmith's "An Essay on the Theatre; or, a Comparison Between Laughing and Sentimental Comedy" or Aphra Behn's "The Dumb Virgin; or, the Force of Imagination"; but variations are plentiful. *Twelfth Night, or What You Will* seems to be the only Shakespearean PLAY equipped with a full *subtitle,* although *All Is True* is sometimes given as the *subtitle* (or alternate or alternative TITLE) of *The Famous History of the Life of King Henry the Eighth.* Since the seventeenth century, what might be called the "formal" *subtitle,* specifying the FORM of the work, has been popular. In 1667 Milton published *Paradise Lost. A Poem Written in Ten Books* and then, in 1674, *Paradise Lost. A Poem in Twelve Books.* Occasionally we encounter multiple *subtitles;* one of Dryden's works is called "Alexander's Feast; or the Power of Musique. An Ode, in Honour of St. Cecilia's Day." Successive versions or EDITIONS of a work may undergo changes of TITLE and *subtitle;* Fielding's *Tom Thumb: A Tragedy* (1730) appeared later in a revised FORM with the title *The Tragedy of Tragedies; or the Life and Death of Tom Thumb the Great* (and two further *subtitles*) (1731). Thackeray gave *Vanity Fair* two different *subtitles:* first *Pen and Pencil Sketches of English Society,* then later *A Novel Without a Hero.* In our age the "or" has all but vanished (Nabokov's *Ada, or Ardor* being one droll exception), and "formal" *subtitles* for imaginative works have been waning somewhat, although we ought to pay attention to provocative suggestions in such works as Chekhov's *The Cherry Orchard: A Comedy in Four Acts* or Fitzgerald's *The Last Tycoon: A Western.* Even as imaginative writers were disembarking from the *subtitle* bandwagon, however, scholars were crowding on. From about 1930 many perfunctory works of scholarship and CRITICISM adopted a formulaic sort of title that soon devolved into CLICHÉ: typically a dramatic adjective (such as "broken" or "angry") and a more or less concrete noun (such as "weapon"), or else two vivid nouns ("wound" and "bow," say), and then, after a portentous colon, a thoroughly bland explanatory *subtitle.* Caricaturists enjoyed a field day, concocting titles like *The Wing and the Prayer: Optical Allusions in the Poetry of George Herbert.* See TITLE.

Surrealism: A MOVEMENT in art and literature emphasizing the expression of the IMAGINATION as realized in dreams and presented without conscious control. It developed in France under the leadership of André Breton, whose *Manifeste du surréalisme* appeared in 1924. *Surrealism* is often regarded as an outgrowth of DADA, although it has discernible roots reaching back to Baudelaire and Rimbaud, and it demonstrates the marked influence of Freud. As a literary MOVEMENT it has flourished most robustly in Spain, France, and Latin America. As a MOVEMENT in modern art it has had many followers, among them Dali, Miró, Duchamp, and Max Ernst. What seems genuinely "super-real" or "surreal" about *surrealism,* whether in graphic or literary art, is its habit of lucidly juxtaposing scarcely compatible tokens of potentially symbolic concrete objects (so that music, which does not represent the concrete, cannot be *surrealistic*). Literary *surrealism* finally reached the United States after the Second World War and became an important feature in the work of Robert Lowell and many younger POETS: Philip Lamantia, John Ashberry, Frank O'Hara, Kenneth Koch, Michael Benedikt, Robert Bly, James Wright, James Tate, Kathleen Norris, Charles Simic, and others. To a lesser extent, some surrealist features are found in recent American FICTION, from Nathanael West's *The Dream Life of Balso Snell* to Bob Dylan's *Tarantula.* See DADA.

[References: Savone Alexandrian, *Surrealist Art* (1970); Ferdinand Alguié,

The Philosophy of Surrealism (1969); C. W. E. Bigsby, *Dada and Surrealism* (1972); J. H. Matthews, *An Introduction to Surrealism* (1965); Maurice Nadeau, *The History of Surrealism* (tr. 1968); Patrick Waldberg, *Surrealism* (1965).]

Surrogate: A person or a thing that is substituted for, or speaks for, another. In FICTION, if an author creates a CHARACTER—such as the RAISONNEUR of the WELL-MADE PLAY—who embodies the ideals of the author or who utters speeches expressive of the author's opinions and judgments, such a CHARACTER is said to be an author-SURROGATE.

Suspense: The poised anticipation of the reader or audience as to the outcome of the events of a SHORT STORY, a NOVEL, or a DRAMA, particularly as these events affect a CHARACTER in the work for whom the reader or audience has formed a sympathetic attachment. *Suspense* is a major device for the securing and maintaining of interest in all FORMS of FICTION. It may be either of two major types: in one, the outcome is uncertain and the *suspense* resides in the question of who or what or how; in the other, the outcome is inevitable from the events that have gone before (see DRAMATIC IRONY) and the *suspense* resides in the audience's frightened anticipation, in the question of when. It has been argued that, on a verbal level, the function of AMBIGUITY is to create *suspense*, which is also a possible effect of RHYME.

Suspension of Disbelief: The willingness to withhold questions about the truth, accuracy, or probability of CHARACTERS or ACTIONS in a literary work. This willingness to suspend doubt makes possible the reader's temporary acceptance of the vicarious participation in an author's imaginative world. The phrase *suspension of disbelief* comes from Coleridge's *Biographia Literaria*, which describes "that willing suspension of disbelief for the moment, which constitutes poetic faith." See BELIEF, THE PROBLEM OF.

"Sweetness and Light": A phrase given great popularity by Matthew Arnold, who used it as the TITLE of the first chapter of *Culture and Anarchy* (1869). Arnold borrowed it from Swift's *The Battle of the Books,* where Swift, in recounting the APOLOGUE of the Spider and the Bee, summarized the argument relating to the superiority of ancient over modern authors (see ANCIENTS AND MODERNS, QUARREL OF) in these words: "Instead of dirt and poison we have rather chosen to fill our hives with honey and wax, thus furnishing mankind with the two noblest of things, which are sweetness and light." These two "noblest of things," as Arnold uses the term, are *beauty* and *intelligence*— and it is to these two qualities that "sweetness and light" refer.

Syllabic Verse: VERSE in which the measure of the LINE is determined by the number of syllables in the line regardless of STRESS. The naming of lines in *syllabic verse* is by the use of numerical prefixes added to *syllabic,* as *monosyllabic* for one syllable, *trisyllabic* for three, *decasyllabic* for ten, HEN-DECASYLLABIC for eleven, and so forth. In English—and in the Germanic, Slavic, and Celtic languages in general—the syllable is a highly variable phenomenon, ranging from a single simple unstressed neutral vowel of short duration (as at the end of "comma") all the way to amalgams of as many as six or seven sounds (as in "traipsed" and "strengths"); accordingly, the syllable as such makes an unstable and presumably uninteresting unit for MEASURE. The situation is different in Chinese, Japanese, and many Romance languages, which tend towards marked uniformity of syllable (a simple consonant followed by a simple vowel, say) along with a leveling of STRESS. If your language abounds in such words as *ditalini* and *sayonara*, then the syllable, being relatively uniform and stable, becomes a viable unit for MEASURE, as indeed it has been in Italian and Japanese. (See HAIKU, RHOPALIC.)

Syllabus: An outline or ABSTRACT containing the major heads of a book, a course of lectures, an ARGUMENT, or program of study. A DIGEST of the chief "points" of a larger work. *Syllabus* (the offspring of an uncouth misreading of a Latin text) does not differ significantly (except as an elegant substitution) from *outline* or *schedule,* the preferable terms.

Syllepsis: A grammatically correct construction in which one word is placed in the same grammatical relationship to two words but in quite different senses, as *stain* is linked in different senses to *honor* and *brocade* in Pope's LINE, "Or stain her honor, or her new brocade." Most instances of *syllepsis* involve a word that can take an object and can have both a concrete and an abstract meaning, or else a literal and a metaphorical meaning. The two kinds of words that fit this category are prepositions and transitive verbs. *Syllepsis* occurs when one of these object-taking words takes two or more objects that are on different levels. "Stain," say, is a transitive verb capable of taking both a concrete object ("brocade") and an ABSTRACT ("Honor"). By putting "honor" first and "brocade" second, Pope adds ANTICLIMAX to *syllepsis*, since the step from abstract to concrete is downward. See SLEIGHT OF "AND"; ZEUGMA.

Syllogism: A formula for presenting an argument logically. The *syllogism* affords a method of demonstrating the logic of an argument through analysis. In its simplest form, it consists of three divisions: a major premise; a minor premise, and a conclusion.

> *Major premise:* All public libraries should serve the people.
> *Minor premise:* This is a public library.
> *Conclusion:* Therefore, this library should serve the people.

There are, it is to be noticed, three terms as well as three divisions to the *syllogism.* In the major premise "should serve the people" is the "major term"; in the minor premise "this (library)" is the "minor term"; and the term appearing in both the major and the minor premise, "public library," is called the "middle term." This kind of deductive or categorical *syllogism* always take the form of three statements: a certain class has a certain quality; a given entity belongs to that class; that entity has that quality. Accordingly, the minor premise and the conclusion share a subject, and the major premise and the conclusion share a predicate. Note, as well, that the REDUCTIO AD ABSURDUM is another kind of *syllogism.*

Symbol: On the literal level, a *symbol* is something that is itself and yet stands for or suggests or means something else; as the letters *a p p l e* form a word that stands for a particular objective reality; or as a flag is a piece of colored cloth that stands for a nation. All language is symbolic in this sense, and many of the objects that we commonly use in daily life are also.

In a literary sense a *symbol* is a TROPE that combines a literal and sensuous quality with an abstract or suggestive aspect. However, in CRITICISM it is necessary to distinguish *symbol* from IMAGE, ALLEGORY, and METAPHOR. If we consider an image to have a concrete referent in the objective world and to function as image when it powerfully evokes that referent, then a *symbol* is like an image in doing the same thing but different from it in going beyond the evoking of the objective referent by making that referent suggest to the reader or audience a meaning beyond itself; in other words, a *symbol* is an IMAGE that evokes an objective, concrete reality and has that reality suggest another level of meaning. However, the *symbol* does not "stand for" the meaning; it evokes an object that suggests the meaning. As Coleridge said, "It partakes of the reality which it renders intelligible." *Symbol* differs from ALLEGORY in that in allegory the objective referent evoked is without value until it is translated into the fixed meaning that it has in its own particular structure of ideas (see ALLEGORY), whereas a *symbol* includes permanent objective value, independent of the meanings that it may suggest. It differs from METAPHOR in that a metaphor evokes an object in order to illustrate an idea or demonstrate a quality, whereas a *symbol* embodies the idea or the quality. As W. M. Urban said, "The metaphor becomes a symbol when by means of it we embody an ideal content not otherwise expressible."

Literary *symbols* are of two broad types: one includes those embodying universal suggestions of meaning, as flowing water suggests time and eternity, a voyage suggests life. Such *symbols* are used widely (and sometimes unconsciously) in the world's literature. The other type of *symbol* secures its suggestiveness not from qualities inherent in itself but from the way in which it is used in a given work. Thus, in *Moby-Dick* the voyage, the land, the ocean are objects pregnant with meanings that seem almost independent of Melville's use of them in his story; on the other hand, the white whale is invested with meaning—and differing meanings for different crew members—through the handling of materials in the NOVEL. The very title of *The Scarlet Letter* points to a double *symbol:* a color-coded letter of the alphabet; the work eventually develops into a testing and critique of *symbols,* and the meanings of "A" multiply. Thomas Pynchon's *V.* continues much the same line of testing an alphabetical symbol. Similarly, in Hemingway's *A Farewell to Arms,* rain, which is a mildly annoying meteorological phenomenon in the opening chapter, is converted into a *symbol* of death through the uses to which it is put in the book. The meaning of practically any general *symbol* is thus a function of its cultural or aesthetic environment. See ALLEGORY, IMAGE, IMAGERY, METAPHOR, SIMILE, TROPE.

[References: Ernst Cassirer, *The Philosophy of Symbolic Forms,* 3 vols. (tr. 1953–1957), and *Symbol, Myth, and Culture* (1979).]

Symbolism: In its broad sense *symbolism* is the use of one object to represent or suggest another; or, in literature, the use of SYMBOLS in writing, particularly the serious and extensive use of such SYMBOLS. Recently the word has taken on a pejorative connotation of mere rhetoric without reality, surface SYMBOL without substance, speciousness and tokenism, all smoke and no fire, all hat and no cattle.

In America in the middle of the nineteenth century, *symbolism* of the sort typical of ROMANTICISM was the dominant literary mode. In this symbolist MOVEMENT the details of the natural world and the actions of people were used to suggest philosophical ideas and THEMES. Romantic *symbolism* was the fundamental practice of the Transcendentalists (see TRANSCENDENTAL-ISM). Emerson, the chief exponent of the MOVEMENT, declared that "Particular natural facts are symbols of particular spiritual facts" and that "Nature is the symbol of spirit," and Henry David Thoreau made life itself a symbolic action in *Walden.* The symbolic method was present in the POETRY of these two and also in that of Walt Whitman. *Symbolism* was a distinctive feature of the NOVELS of Hawthorne—notably *The Scarlet Letter* and *The Marble Faun*—and of Melville, whose *Moby-Dick* is probably the most original work of symbolic art in American literature.

Symbolism is also the name given to a literary MOVEMENT that originated in France in the last half of the nineteenth century, strongly influenced British writing around the turn of the century, and has been a dominant force in much British and American POETRY in the twentieth century. This *symbolism* represents one of the romantic reactions to REALISM. It sees the immediate, unique, and personal emotional response as the proper subject of art, and its full expression as the ultimate aim of art. Since the emotions experienced by a POET in a given moment are unique to that person and that moment and are finally both fleeting and incommunicable, the poet is reduced to the use of a complex and highly private kind of symbolization in an effort to give expression to an evanescent and ineffable feeling. The result is a kind of writing consisting of what Edmund Wilson has called "a medley of metaphor" in which SYMBOLS lacking apparent logical relation are put together in a pattern, one of whose characteristics is an indefiniteness as great as the indefiniteness of the experience itself and another of whose characteristics is the conscious effort to use words for their evocative musical effect, without very much attention to precise meaning. As Baudelaire, one of the principal forerunners of the movement, said, human beings live in a "forest of symbols," which results from the fact that the materiality and individuality of the physical world dissolve into the "dark and confused unity" of the unseen world. In this process SYNAESTHESIA takes place. Baudelaire and the later symbolists, particularly Mallarmé and Valéry, were greatly influenced by the theory and poetic practice of Edgar Allan Poe. Other important French writers in the movement were Rimbaud, Verlaine, Laforgue, Remy de Gourmont, and Claudel, as well as Maeterlinck in the DRAMA and Huysmans in the NOVEL. The Irish writers of this century, particularly Yeats in POETRY, Synge in the DRAMA, and Joyce in the NOVEL, have been notably responsive to the movement. In Germany, Rilke and Stefan George functioned as symbolist poets. In America, the IMAGIST poets reflected the movement, as did Eugene O'Neill in the drama. Through its pervasive influence on T. S. Eliot, *symbolism* has affected much of the best British and American POETRY in our time. One of the most evocative passages of *symbolist* poetry is that beginning "Garlic and sapphires in the mud" in Eliot's "Burnt Norton." See SYMBOL.

[References: Maurice Bowra, *The Heritage of Symbolism* (1943); C. K.

Ogden and I. A. Richards, *The Meaning of Meaning: A Study of the Influence of Language upon Thought and of the Science of Symbolism*, 8th ed. (1956); Arthur Symons, *The Symbolist Movement in Literature* (1899, reprinted 1958); Philip Wheelwright, *The Burning Fountain: A Study in the Language of Symbolism* (1954); Edmund Wilson, *Axel's Castle* (1931).]

Symploce: A FIGURE OF SPEECH combining ANAPHORA and EPISTROPHE, resulting in REPETITION of a word or a phrase at the beginning of successive clauses, along with the repetition of another or the same word or phrase at the end of these successive clauses, as in this example from Sidney's *Arcadia:* "Such was as then the estate of this Duke, as it was no time by direct means to seek her, and such was the estate of his captive will, as he could delay no time in seeking her."

Symposium: A Greek word meaning "a drinking together" or banquet. As such convivial meetings were characterized by free conversation, the word later came to mean discussion by different persons of a single topic, or a collection of speeches or ESSAYS on a given subject. One of Plato's best-known DIALOGUES is *The Symposium,* and later literary uses of the word are much under its influence.

Synaesthesia: The concurrent response of two or more of the senses to the stimulation of one. The term is applied in literature to the description of one kind of sensation in terms of another—that is, the description of sounds in terms of colors, as a "blue note," of sound in terms of taste, as "how sweet the sound," of colors in terms of temperature, as a "cool green." Poe employed *synaesthesia* often; Baudelaire gave it wide currency through his practice and particularly his SONNET, *"Correspondances."* Rimbaud, in a famous sonnet, more or less systematically assigned colors to the commonest French vowels. *Synaesthesia* is one of the most distinctive characteristics of the POETRY of the symbolist movement. Dame Edith Sitwell employed it as a major device.

Syncopation: A term used in music to describe the effect produced by a temporary displacing or shifting of the regular metrical accent, or beat. In PROSODY it is used to describe the effect produced by SUBSTITUTION and also the effect produced when the METRICAL ACCENT and the RHETORICAL ACCENT differ sufficiently in a VERSE to create the effect of two different metrical patterns existing concurrently in the LINE. In another sense *syncopation* occurs in POETRY when a STRESS is forced out of its normal place in a metrical line by the omission of an expected syllable or the inclusion of more unstressed syllables than the metrical pattern demands. Gerard Manley Hopkins classified the first two FEET of his line "Generations have trod, have trod, have trod" as *syncopation;* a more familiar source of *syncopation* is popular music, with syncopated DIPODIC lines like "January, February, June or July."

Syncope: A cutting short of words through the omission of a letter or a syllable. *Syncope* is distinguished from ELISION in that it is usually confined to the omission of elements (usually vowels) inside a word, whereas ELISION usually runs two words together by the omission of a final or initial letter. *Ev'ry* for *every* is an example of *syncope.* The greatest use for this omission of sounds is in VERSE where a desired metrical effect is sought. The "juvescence" in Eliot's "Gerontion" represents a *syncope* of "juvenescence." However, *syncope* has taken place frequently in English simply to shorten words, as *pacificist* has become *pacifist*. *Syncope* sometimes results when the addition of a suffix creates repetition or reduplication, which some speakers, according to a sentiment built in to Indo-European languages. "Inimitable" and "educable" may so come about, as may "poulter," "fruiter," and "windhover," and as "narcissism" is becoming "narcism." Many Latin words have undergone *syncope* when passing into other languages, especially if an intervocalic consonant ("between vowels") is involved, as in *magister*, which becomes, variously, "master," "maître," "maestro," "Meister," and so forth.

Synecdoche: A TROPE in which a part signifies the whole or the whole signifies the part. In order to be clear, a good *synecdoche* must be based on an *important* part of the whole and not a minor part and, usually, the part selected to stand for the whole must be one directly associated with the subject under discussion. Thus, under the first restriction we say "threads" and "wheels" for "clothes" and "car," and under the second we speak of infantry on the march as *foot* rather than as *hands* just as we use *hands* rather than *foot* for people who are at work at manual labor. See METONYMY.

Synonyms: Words in the same language with the same or similar meanings. Rarely in English are two words exact *synonyms*, although it may happen that in a single sentence any one of two or three words may serve the desired purpose. Conventional usage has given most of our words certain associations and CONNOTATIONS, certain idiomatic connections, which make impossible a free substituting of one for another. As one commentator has pointed out, "alter" and "change" seem synonymous, but "He changed his pants" differs markedly from "He altered his pants"; similarly, "brief" and "short" seem to be *synonyms* until one confronts the difference between "I'll be there shortly" and "I'll be there briefly." The presence of Romance words in English has proved a rich source of *synonyms*, offering a choice between forms; for example, the Romance *assist* for the English *help*.

Synopsis: A summary, a résumé of the main points of a composition or ARGUMENT so made as to show the relation of each part to the whole; an ABSTRACT. A *synopsis* is usually more connected than an outline, since it is likely to be given in complete sentences.

Syzygy: In classical PROSODY, a term used to designate two coupled FEET serving as a unit. As used by Sidney Lanier and later prosodists, it refers to the use of consonant sounds at the end of one word and at the beginning of another that can be spoken together easily and harmoniously. Both Poe and Lanier were greatly concerned with *syzygy*. More broadly, *syzygy* means the articulation or "yoking together" of terminal and initial consonants, whether euphonious or cacophonous. In this LINE of Thomas Hardy's, for example, notice the relatively difficult *syzygy* in the passage from one word to the next:

The land's sharp features seemed to be . . . .

T

Tableau: An INTERLUDE during a SCENE of a PLAY in which the actors freeze in position and then resume ACTION as before or hold their positions until the CURTAIN falls. In the nineteenth century many plays ended their ACTS with *tableaux,* and frequently a play ended with a *tableau.* For the costumed representation of well-known scenes, pictures, or personages, the term *tableau vivant* (living picture) was used. Such *tableaux* are often presented in PAGEANTS or on floats. The identification of the figure represented in a *tableau vivant* was once a social game; an instance is described in *The House of Mirth* by Edith Wharton.

Tail-Rhyme Romance: A term applied to METRICAL ROMANCES employing the TAIL-RHYME STANZA, especially the large group, including *Amis and Amiloun, Athelston, Horn Childe* (and some twenty others), which employed a TAIL-RHYME STANZA of twelve LINES made up of four groups or parts, each with a short "tail" line, such as aa*b* aa*b* cc*b* dd*b.* There existed a "school" of minstrels writing *tail-rhyme romances* in East Anglia in the fourteenth century.

Tail-Rhyme Stanza: A STANZA containing, among longer LINES, two or more short lines that RHYME with each other and serve as "tails" to the divisions of the STANZA. The FORM developed in medieval times and is known in French as RIME COUÉE. Chaucer's "Rime of Sir Thopas" in *The Canterbury Tales* is written in *tail-rhyme stanza.*

Tale: A relatively simple NARRATIVE in PROSE or VERSE. Formerly no very real distinction was made between the *tale* and the SHORT STORY; the two terms were used interchangeably. *Tale,* however, has always been a more general term than SHORT STORY, since the latter has been reserved for fictional NARRATIVE having a conscious structure and the former has been loosely used to denote any short narrative, either true or fictitious. Some TITLES of full-length NOVELS seem to suggest UNDERSTATEMENT—for example, *A Tale of Two Cities.*

Tall Tale: A kind of humorous TALE common on the American frontier, which uses realistic detail, a literal manner, and common speech to recount extravagantly impossible happenings, usually resulting from the superhuman abilities of a CHARACTER. The TALES about Mike Fink and Davy Crockett are typical frontier *tall tales.* The German *Adventures of Baron Munchausen* is, perhaps, the best-known literary use of the *tall tale.*

Tanka: A type of Japanese POETRY similar to the HAIKU. It consists of thirty-one syllables, arranged in five LINES, each of seven syllables, except the first and third, which are each of five. (Note that the HAIKU—and *senryu* as well—seems to amount to the first three lines and first seventeen syllables of the *tanka.*) See HAIKU.

Taste: A term used in CRITICISM to designate the basis for the personal accep- tance or rejection of a work of art as producing pleasure or pain in its reader, hearer, or viewer. Perhaps no critical term remains, despite all efforts at analy- sis, more purely subjective than does *taste.* However, as it is commonly used, it has two distinct meanings: it may refer to the mere condition of liking or disliking an object, in which case it may be deplored but not debated ("There is no accounting for taste," "Each to his own taste," *"De gustibus non est disputandum"*); on the other hand, it may refer to the ability to discern the beautiful and to appreciate it, in which case *taste* is capable of being educated and is subject to examination in terms of its operating principles. T. S. Eliot had such a view of *taste* when he saw one of the functions of CRITICISM to be "the correction of taste," and so had Addison when he said that *taste* "dis- cerns the Beauties of an Author with Pleasure, and the Imperfections with Dislike." *Taste* in the first sense is used to describe a purely impressionistic response, as in the criticism of Croce; in the second sense it designates a kind of aesthetic judgment, as it does with Eliot. In the latter case, *taste* be- comes a sense of what is harmonious, appropriate, or beautiful, a kind of critical tact, and as such it designates a desirable quality.

[Reference: H. A. Needham, *Taste and Criticism in the Eighteenth Century* (1952).]

Tautology: The use of superfluous, repetitious words. *Tautology* differs from the kinds of REPETITION used for clarity, EMPHASIS, or effect, in that it repeats the idea without adding force or clarity. "Devoid," say, means "completely empty," so that "wholly devoid" is a *tautology* and "completely, totally, wholly, and entirely devoid" even worse.

Technique: The sum of working methods or special skills. *Technique* may be applied very broadly, as when one says, "The symbolic journey is a major *technique* in Joyce's *Ulysses,*" or very narrowly to refer to the minutiae of method, or in an intermediate sense, as in STREAM OF CONSCIOUSNESS *tech- nique.* In all cases, however, *technique* refers to *how* something was done rather than to *what* was done. *Technique,* FORM, STYLE, and "manner" overlap somewhat, with *technique* connoting the literal, mechanical, or procedural parts of execution.

Telestich: An ACROSTIC in which the final letters form a word. See ACROSTIC.

Tenor and **Vehicle:** Terms used by I. A. Richards for the two essential ele- ments of a METAPHOR. The *tenor* is the discourse or subject that the *vehicle* illustrates or illuminates; or, stated another way, the *vehicle* is the FIGURE that carries the weight of the comparison, while the *tenor* is the subject to which the *vehicle* refers. According to Richards's definition, a METAPHOR al- ways involves these two ideas. If it is impossible to distinguish them, we are dealing with a literal statement; if we can distinguish them, even slightly, we are dealing with a metaphoric expression. Hamlet's question, "What should such fellows as I do crawling between earth and heaven?" is metaphoric. While Hamlet may literally crawl, there is, as Richards points out, "an unmistak- able reference to other things that crawl . . . and this reference is the vehicle as Hamlet . . . is the tenor." See METAPHOR.

[Reference: I. A. Richards, *The Philosophy of Rhetoric* (1936).]

Tension: A term introduced into contemporary CRITICISM by Allen Tate, by which he means the integral UNITY that results from the successful resolution of the conflicts of abstraction and concreteness, of general and particular, of DENOTATION and CONNOTATION. The term results from removing the prefixes from two terms in logic: *intension,* which refers to the abstract attributes of objects that can properly be named by a word; and *extension,* which refers to the specific object named by the word. Good POETRY, Tate asserts, is the "full, organized body of all the extension and intension that we can find in it." This concept was widely used by the New Critics, particularly in their examination of POETRY as a pattern of PARADOX or as a form of IRONY. See CONCRETE UNIVERSAL.

Tercet: A STANZA of three lines, a TRIPLET, in which each LINE ends with the same RHYME. The term is also used to denote either of the two three-line groups forming the SESTET of the ITALIAN SONNET. A *tercet* of the type first mentioned is quoted from Herrick:

> Whenas in silks my Julia goes,
> Then, then, methinks, how sweetly flows
> That liquefaction of her clothes.

The term is also applied to the TERZA RIMA STANZA.

Terminal Rhyme: RHYME that occurs at the ends of LINES. The commonest form of RHYME in English POETRY.

Terza rima: A three-line STANZA, supposedly devised by Dante, of which the RHYME SCHEME is *aba, bcb, cdc, ded,* and so forth. In other words one RHYME sound is used for the first and third lines of each STANZA, and a new RHYME introduced for the second line, this new rhyme, in turn, being used for the first and third lines of the subsequent STANZA. A given set of such STANZAS can close with some variation—a COUPLET or QUATRAIN, say—that will avoid leaving "loose ends" among the RHYMES. Usually the METER is IAMBIC PENTAMETER. The opening of Shelley's *Ode to the West Wind,* which is written in *terza rima,* illustrates it:

O wild West Wind, thou breath of Autumn's being,	*a*
Thou, from whose unseen presence the leaves dead	*b*
Are driven, like ghosts from an enchanter fleeing	*a*
Yellow, and black, and pale, and hectic red.	*b*
Pestilence-stricken multitudes: O thou,	*c*
Who chariotest to their dark wintry bed	*b*

The *terza rima* has been popular with English POETS, being used by Wyatt, Milton, Shelley, Byron, Yeats, Eliot, Ransom, and Auden. The RHYME SCHEME but not the usual METER was used by Hardy, and the principle of interlocking stanza-to-stanza RHYME appears in Frost's "Stopping by Woods on a Snowy Evening." Shelley, John Fredrick Nims, and Robert Morgan have written fourteen-line POEMS in *terza rima,* a form sometimes called "*terza rima* SONNET";

Frost's "Acquainted with the Night" is a *terza rima* sonnet with a return to the *a*-rhyme and a repeated LINE at the end, so that the effects of *terza rima* and the sonnet are abetted by those of the RONDEL.

Testament: As a literary form the term has two distinct meanings. It may be a literary "last will and testament" or a piece of literature that "bears witness to" or "makes a convenant with" in the Biblical sense. The former sort of *testament* originated with the Romans of the decadent period and was developed by the French in the late medieval and early RENAISSANCE periods. It was especially popular in the fifteenth century and was often characterized by HUMOR, ribaldry, and SATIRE, as in the half-serious, half-ribald *Grand Testament* and *Petit Testament* of François Villon, perhaps the greatest examples of this type. In the popular literature of the first half of the sixteenth century in England, there were many wills and *testaments* of the humorous and satiric sort, such as *Jyl of Breyntford's Testament, Colin Blowbol's Testament,* and Humphrey Powell's popular *Wyll of the Devil* (around 1550). Some literary *testaments*, however, were more serious; for example, the *Testament of Cresseid* by Robert Henryson (1430–1506), a continuation of Chaucer's *Troilus and Criseyde,* picturing Cressida as thoroughly degraded in character and suffering from leprosy. In her proverty-stricken last days she bequeaths her scant belongings to her fellow sufferers. Another serious *testament* is the love COMPLAINT, "The Testament of the Hawthorne" in *Tottel's Miscellany* (1557).

The second type of *testament,* that which "bears witness to," was also developed in the late medieval period. Its best representative in English is perhaps *The Testament of Love* by Thomas Usk (?), written about 1384. This is a long PROSE treatise in which Divine Love appears in a role similar to that of Philosophy in Boethius's *Consolation of Philosophy.* A modern representative is Robert Bridges' *The Testament of Beauty* (1929).

Tetralogy: Four works, usually DRAMAS or NOVELS, that constitute a group. Thus, Shakespeare's CHRONICLE PLAYS *Richard II, Henry IV,* Parts One and Two, and *Henry V* constitute a *tetralogy.* Greek DRAMA was presented in *tetralogies,* consisting of three TRAGEDIES followed by a SATYR PLAY. Lawrence Durrell's *Alexandria Quartet* is a modern *tetralogy.*

Tetrameter: A LINE consisting of four FEET. See SCANSION.

Textual Criticism: A scholarly activity that attempts by all available means to establish the authoritative text of a work. According to Fredson Bowers, the four basic functions of the textual CRITIC are (1) to analyze the characteristics of an extant manuscript, (2) to recover the characteristics of the lost manuscript that served as copy for a printed text, (3) to study the transmission of a printed text, and (4) to present an established and edited text to the public. Some critics, espousing the idea that there are no texts but only relations among texts, look down on *textual criticism* as a jejune and unaesthetic kind of science or engineering. Contrariwise, other CRITICS put *textual criticism* ahead of all other species, since, without a reliable text, no critic has anything definite to criticize. More than one critic has had the embarrassing experience of making a big intellectual deal out of what *textual criticism* has shown to be a misprint. See CRITICISM, TYPES OF.

Texture: A term applied to the elements remaining in a literary work after a PARAPHRASE of its ARGUMENT has been made. Among such elements are details of SITUATION, METAPHOR, METER, IMAGERY, TONE COLOR, RHYME—in fact, all elements that are not considered part of the STRUCTURE of the work. The separation of *texture* and STRUCTURE is a strategy employed by John Crowe Ransom and some others among the New Critics.

Theater in the Round: The presentation of PLAYS on a stage surrounded by the audience. See ARENA STAGE.

Theater of Cruelty: DRAMA that subordinates words to action, gesture, and sound in an effort to overwhelm the spectators and liberate their instinctual preoccupations with crime, cruelty, and eroticism. See CRUELTY, THEATER OF.

Theater of the Absurd: An AVANT-GARDE kind of DRAMA that represents the absurdity of the human condition by abandoning rational devices and realistic FORM. See ABSURD, THEATER OF THE.

Theme: A central or dominating idea in a work. In nonfiction PROSE it may be thought of as the general topic of discussion, the subject of the discourse, the THESIS. In POETRY, FICTION, and DRAMA it is the abstract concept that is made concrete through its representation in person, ACTION, and IMAGE in the work. No proper *theme* is simply a subject or an activity. Both *theme* and THESIS imply a subject and a predicate—not just vice in general, say, but some such proposition as "Vice seems more interesting than virtue but turns out to be destructive."

Theoretical Criticism: A kind of CRITICISM that attempts to arrive at the general principles of art and to formulate inclusive and enduring aesthetic and critical tenets. Anglo-American CRITICISM has been predominantly practical, a matter of detail more than design; but the CHICAGO CRITICS, on their own and in a running debate with several New Critics, returned criticism to a theoretical basis around 1950. Thereafter, *theoretical criticism* gained in scope and influence, stimulated by the example of French intellectual fashions. See CRITICISM, TYPES OF.

Thesis: An attitude or position on a problem taken by a writer or speaker with the purpose of proving or supporting it. The term is also used for the paper written to support the *thesis*. That is, *thesis* is used both for the problem to be established and for the ESSAY that, presumably, establishes it. In academic circles the word has the special meaning of a paper expounding some special problem and written as a requirement for a degree. (See DISSERTATION.) *Thesis*, as a term in PROSODY, was used by the Greeks to refer to stressed syllables; however, later Latin usage applied ARSIS to the stressed and *thesis* to the unstressed syllables. The terms are rarely used today, but when they are, the later Latin usage is almost always intended. See ARSIS, ACCENT.

Thesis Novel: A NOVEL that deals with some social, economic, political, or religious problem in such a way that it suggests a THESIS, usually in the form of a solution to the problem. Among the types of NOVELS that are called *thesis novels* are SOCIOLOGICAL NOVELS, POLITICAL NOVELS, PROBLEM NOVELS, and PROPAGANDA NOVELS. The French *"roman à thèse"* is sometimes used instead of *thesis novel.*

Thesis Play: A DRAMA that presents a social problem and proposes a solution; sometimes known by the French *"pièce à thèse."* See PROBLEM PLAY, for which *thesis play* is a corresponding term.

Threnody: A SONG of death, a DIRGE, a lamentation.

Title: The chief distinguishing name attached to any written production. Although modern *titles* are usually brief, an older practice produced *titles* that sometimes filled a closely printed page. For bibliographical purposes the entire *title* page, including the author's name and the publication facts, is considered the *title,* and when it is copied, the actual typography and lineation are usually indicated. In most cases we use the *title* that the author gave the work. With some works, however, convention has evolved a *title* different from what the author may have called the work. Horace's EPISTLE to his friends the Pisos on the art of POETRY is called his *Ars Poetica* or *De Arte Poetica.* Benjamin Franklin died some decades before "autobiography" achieved much currency in English usage, but we conventionally use *Autobiography* as the *title* of the MEMOIRS he wrote on and off in his later years. See SUBTITLE.

Tmesis: Literally a "cutting." A fairly rare verbal FIGURE whereby a word is cut into two parts between which other verbal matter—one word or more—is inserted. American vernacular usage offers the example of "a whole nother thing," in which, by *tmesis,* the word "another" is split into "a" and "nother" with "whole" inserted between. "Enough" and "whatsoever" have received similar treatment. Gerard Manley Hopkins converted "brimful in a flash" into "brim, in a flash, full"; Pound uses "consti-damn-tution" in *The Cantos. Tmesis* is a rare and rather violent figure and should probably be avoided in ordinary discourse. It has been argued that the English infinitive, although conventionally written as two words, is essentially one word, as the infinitive is a single verbal unit in virtually every other language; so that the so-called split infinitive amounts to *tmesis.*

Tone (Tone Color): *Tone* has been used in CRITICISM, following I. A. Richards's example, as a term designating the attitudes toward the subject and toward the audience implied in a literary work. In such a usage a work may have a *tone* that is formal, informal, intimate, solemn, sombre, playful, serious, ironic, condescending, or any of many other possible attitudes. Clearly, *tone* in this sense contributes in a major way to the effect and the effectiveness of a literary work.

In another sense *tone* is used to designate the MOOD of the work itself and the various devices that create that mood. In this sense *tone* results from combinations and variations of such things as METER, RHYME, ALLITERATION, ASSONANCE, CONSONANCE, DICTION, SENTENCE STRUCTURE, REPETITION, IMAGERY, SYMBOLISM, and so forth.

Tone or *tone color* is sometimes used to designate a musical quality in language that Sidney Lanier discussed in *The Science of English Verse*, which asserts that the sounds of words have qualities equivalent to timbre in music. "When the ear exactly coordinates a series of sound's with primary reference to their tone-color, the result is a conception of (in music, flute-tone as distinct from violin-tone, and the like; in verse, rhyme as opposed to rhyme, vowel varied with vowel, phonetic syzygy, and the like), in general . . . tone-color."

Topographical Poetry: A GENRE established in English POETRY by John Denham's *Cooper's Hill* (1642), *topographical poetry* is VERSE in which, according to Samuel Johnson's definition, "the fundamental subject is some particular landscape." It was immensely popular in the seventeenth and eighteenth centuries. Among its practitioners were Thomson, Dyer, and Crabbe. During its ascendancy CRITICS recognized nine categories of *topographical poetry*, such as hills, towns, rivers, caves, and buildings.

Topos: Literally a place, surviving in "common place." In CLASSICAL RHETORIC, *topos* was a rhetorical commonplace in terms of either STRUCTURE or the *loci communes* (literary commonplaces or CONVENTIONS), or both. E. R. Curtius used the rhetorical term to apply to frequently used literary situations or subjects in the Middle Ages, such as POETS decrying their inability to do justice to their subject, the illustration of a disordered world by having fish in trees or servants ruling masters, the description of ideal gardens, the CARPE DIEM idea, and many others. In modern CRITICISM the more frequently used term is MOTIF.

Touchstone: A term used metaphorically as a critical standard by Matthew Arnold in "The Study of Poetry." A *touchstone* is literally a hard black stone once used to test the quality of gold or silver by comparing the streak left on the stone by one of these metals with that made by a standard alloy of the metal. *Touchstones* for Arnold were "lines and expressions of the great masters," which the critic should hold always in mind and apply" as a touchstone to other poetry." They form, he believed, an infallible way of "detecting the presence or absence of high poetic quality . . . in all other poetry which we may place beside them." Most of Arnold's *touchstones* met his expressed standard that great POETRY should have "high seriousness."
[Reference: J. S. Eells, *The Touchstones of Matthew Arnold* (1955).]

Tour de force: Actually any feat of strength and virtuosity. *Tour de force* is used in literary CRITICISM to refer to works or passages that make outstanding demonstrations of skill. Although some works so called have great literary merit, such as Joyce's *Ulysses*, James's *The Turn of the Screw*, and Faulkner's *The Sound and the Fury*, *tour de force* more often implies technical virtuosity than literary strength.

Tract: A PAMPHLET, usually an argumentative document on some religious or political topic, often distributed free for propaganda purposes. For a classic example of the use of the term, see OXFORD MOVEMENT.

Tractarianism: The religious attitudes and principles of the founders of the OXFORD MOVEMENT, as set forth in the ninety *Tracts for the Times* (1833–1841). See OXFORD MOVEMENT.

Tradition: A body of beliefs, customs, sayings, or skills handed down from age to age or from generation to generation. Thus, BALLADS and folk literature in general as well as superstitions and popular proverbs are passed on by oral *tradition*. (See ORAL TRANSMISSION.) A set idea may be called a *tradition*, like the idea prevailing throughout the Middle Ages that Homer's account of the Trojan War was to be discredited in favor of certain forged accounts claiming to be written by participants in the war. The *tradition* of PASTORAL literature means the underlying conceptions and technique of pastoral litera-ture carried down, with modifications, from Theocritus (third century B.C.) to Pope. A traditional element in literature suggests something inherited from the past rather than something of the author's own invention. In another sense *tradition* may be thought of as the inheritance from the past of a body of literary CONVENTIONS that are still alive in the present, as opposed to conven-tions of the past that died with their peculiar age and circumstance.

[References: J. V. Cunningham, *Tradition and Poetic Structure* (1960); Harold Rosenberg, *The Tradition of the New* (1959); Arthur Waugh, *Tradition and Change: Studies in Contemporary Literature* (1919).]

Traditional Ballad: A term sometimes applied to the FOLK BALLAD. See BAL-LAD, FOLK BALLAD.

Tragedy: A term with many meanings and applications. In DRAMA it refers to a particular kind of PLAY, the definition of which was established by Aristotle in his *Poetics*. In NARRATIVE, particularly in the Middle Ages, it refers to a body of work recounting the fall of persons of high degree. In POETRY and FICTION, especially the NOVEL, it refers to the effort of the work to exemplify what has been called "the tragic sense of life"; that is, the sense that human beings are inevitably doomed, through their own failures or errors or even the action of their virtues, or through the nature of fate, destiny, or the human condition to suffer, fail, and die, and that the measure of a person's life is to be taken by how he or she faces that inevitable failure. In whatever FORM the tragic impulse takes its expression, it celebrates courage and dignity in the face of defeat and attempts to portray the grandeur of the human spirit.

In DRAMA a *tragedy* is a PLAY, in VERSE or PROSE, that recounts an impor-tant and causally related series of events in the life of a person of significance, such events culminating in an unhappy CATASTROPHE, the whole treated with great dignity and seriousness. According to Aristotle, who gave in the *Poetics* a normative DEFINITION of TRAGEDY, illustrated by the Greek PLAYS, with Sophocles' *Oedipus Rex* as the best example, the purpose of a *tragedy* is to arouse pity and fear and thus to produce in the audience a CATHARSIS of these emotions. Given this purpose, Aristotle says that fear and pity may be aroused by SPECTACLE or by the STRUCTURE and INCIDENTS of the PLAY. The latter method is, he insists, the better; hence, PLOT is "the soul of a trag-edy." Such a plot must involve a PROTAGONIST who is better than ordinary people, and this virtuous person must be brought from happiness to misery. Such a DEFINITION is broad enough to admit almost any DRAMA that is serious and that ends with an unhappy CATASTROPHE, if the protagonist has signifi-cance or importance. But its various formulations have been interpreted from time to time in terms of various attitudes and CONVENTIONS. The question of what constitutes significance for the tragic HERO is answered in each age by its concept of significance. In a period of monarchy Shakespeare's PROTAGO-NISTS were rulers; in other ages they have been and will be other kinds of persons. In a democratic nation, founded on an egalitarian concept, a tragic hero can be the archetypal common citizen—a worker, a police officer, a gangster, a New England farmer, a slave. But to qualify as a tragic PROTAGONIST, the HERO or HEROINE, whatever constitutes the criteria of significance of the age, must be a person of high character and must face his or her destiny with courage and nobility of spirit. From time to time the basis of UNITY in *tragedy* has been debated. With the CLASSICAL writers of the RENAISSANCE and in the NEOCLASSIC PERIOD, the "unities" were observed with rigor. Yet ages that find unity in aspects of DRAMA other than its TECHNIQUE may wed the serious and the comic, may take liberties with time and place, may use multiple plots, and still achieve a unified effect as the nonclassic RENAISSANCE writers did. CLASSICAL TRAGEDY and ROMANTIC TRAGEDY both emphasize the significance of a choice made by the PROTAGONIST but dictated by the protagonist's HAMARTIA (but see HAMARTIA for the great breadth of the concept). To insist, however, that *tragedy* be confined to this particular view of the universe is to limit it in unacceptable ways. Clearly, as the STRUCTURE of Aristotle's DEFINITION indicates, the central purpose of *tragedy* is so to deal with fear and pity that a CATHARSIS of them is produced in the audience; the other elements are all means toward that end; and, as customs, religions, beliefs, and social structures change, those elements also change, while the tragic purpose remains as a goal. In the nineteenth century, for example, both Hegel and Nietzsche, in greatly differing ways, evolved definitions of *tragedy* for their philosophical stances. With some *tragedies,* such as that of *Antigone,* we can gain a good deal of insight from Hegel's notion that *tragedy* comes from the dynamic conflict between two almost equally powerful laws or other principles of conduct. Clearly *tragedy* defies specific definition, each age producing works that speak in the conventions and beliefs of that age the enduring sense that human beings have of the tragic nature of their existence and of the grandeur of the human spirit in facing it.

In the Middle Ages the term *tragedy* did not refer to a DRAMA but to any NARRATIVE recounting how a person of high rank, through ill fortune or vice or error, fell from high estate to low. The *tragedies* recounted in Chaucer's "Monk's Tale," in Lydgate's *Fall of Princes,* and in the RENAISSANCE collection *The Mirror for Magistrates* are of this sort. In the sixteenth century the influence of CLASSICAL TRAGEDY, particularly of SENECAN TRAGEDY, combined with notable elements of the MEDIEVAL DRAMA to produce English *tragedy.* In 1559 came the first TRANSLATION of a Senecan tragedy, and in 1562 Sackville and Norton's *Gorboduc,* "the first regular English *tragedy,*" was acted. The genius for the stage that characterized the ELIZABETHAN AGE worked on this FORM to produce the greatest flowering in the DRAMA that England has known. Yet the *tragedy* that emerged was not the CLASSICAL TRAGEDY of Aristotle's definition, despite the efforts of writers like Ben Jonson to school it into being so, but PLAYS of a heterogeneous character known as ROMANTIC TRAGEDY—plays that tended to ignore the UNITIES, followed medieval tradition in mixing sadness and mirth, and strove at any cost—including SUBPLOTS and comic RELIEF SCENES—to satisfy the spectators with vigorous ACTION and gripping SPECTACLE. Shakespeare worked in the forms of the REVENGE TRAGEDY, the DOMESTIC TRAGEDY, and the CHRONICLE PLAY.

The seventeenth century saw the ELIZABETHAN *tragedy* continued with a growing emphasis on violence and shock during its first half, to be replaced with the HEROIC DRAMA, with its stylized conflict of love and honor, during its second half. Milton's *Samson Agonistes* is a bold experiment involving the use of Hellenic manner for Hebraic matter to yield the lineaments of classic *tragedy*. The eighteenth century saw the development of a DRAMA around middle-class figures, known as DOMESTIC TRAGEDY, which was serious in intent but superficial in importance. With the emergence of Ibsen in the late nineteenth century came the concept of middle-class *tragedy* growing out of social problems and issues. In the twentieth century middle-class and laboring-class CHARACTERS are often portrayed in their circumstances as the victims of social, hereditary, and environmental forces. When, as often happens, they receive their fate with a self-pitying whimper, they can hardly be said to have tragic dimensions. But when, as also happens in much modern serious DRAMA, they face their destiny, however evil and unmerited, with courage and dignity, they are probably as truly tragic, *mutatis mutandis*, as Oedipus was to Sophocles' Athenians or Hamlet to Shakespeare's Londoners.

If a generalization can be made about so protean a subject, it is probably that *tragedy* treats human beings in terms of their godlike potential, of their transcendent ideals, of the part of themselves that is in rebellion against not only the implacable universe but the frailty of their own flesh and will. In this sense *tragedy* as the record of human strivings and aspirations is in contrast to COMEDY, which is the amusing spectacle of people's limitations and frailties. See DRAMATIC STRUCTURE, CATHARSIS, DRAMA, COMEDY, HAMARTIA.

[References: A. C. Bradley, *Shakespearean Tragedy* (1904); L. B. Campbell, *Shakespeare's Tragic Heroes, Slaves of Passion* (1930, reprinted 1968); Lane Cooper, *Aristotle on the Art of Poetry* (1913); W. M. Dixon, *Tragedy*, 3rd ed. (1929); Bonamy Dobrée, *Restoration Tragedy, 1660–1720* (1924, reprinted 1963); C. C. Green, *The Neo-Classic Theory of Tragedy* (1934, reprinted 1966); Dorothea Krook, *Elements of Tragedy* (1969); F. L. Lucas, *Tragedy in Relation to Aristotle's Poetics* (1927, reprinted 1957); Allardyce Nicoll, *The Theory of Drama* (1931); George Steiner, *The Death of Tragedy* (1961); A. H. Thorndike, *Tragedy* (1908, reprinted 1965); C. E. Vaughan, *Types of Tragic Drama* (1908).]

Tragedy of Blood: An intensified FORM of the REVENGE TRAGEDY popular on the Elizabethan stage. It works out the THEME of revenge and retribution (borrowed from Seneca) through murder, assassination, mutilation, and carnage. The horrors that in the Latin Senecan PLAYS had been merely described were placed on the stage to satisfy the craving for morbid excitement displayed by an Elizabethan audience brought up on bear-baiting SPECTACLES and public executions (hangings, mutilations, burnings). Besides including such revenge plays as Kyd's *Spanish Tragedy* and Shakespeare's *Titus Andronicus* and *Hamlet*, the *tragedy of blood* led to such later "horror" TRAGEDIES as Webster's *The Duchess of Malfi* and *The White Devil*. Thomas Pynchon's NOVEL *The Crying of Lot 49* contains a TRAVESTY of this sort of tragedy. See REVENGE TRAGEDY, SENECAN TRAGEDY.

Tragic Flaw: The theory that there is a flaw, error, or defect in the tragic HERO that is the cause of his or her downfall. The theory has been revised or refuted by CRITICISM that considers the supposed "flaw" as an integral and even defining part of the hero's CHARACTER. Oedipus's thirst for knowledge and Antigone's devotion to duty are hardly "flaws"; rather, these qualities are at the heart of the heroes' CHARACTER. It may be better to consider this element as more of an inconsistency or contradiction, a sort of APORIA in character that opens the way for undeserved tragic consequences. See HAMARTIA, for which *tragic flaw* is often loosely used as a synonym.

Tragic Irony: That form of DRAMATIC IRONY in which a CHARACTER in a TRAGEDY uses words that mean one thing to the speaker and another to those better acquainted with the real situation, especially when the character is about to become a victim of fate. Othello's ALLUSION to the VILLAIN who is about to deceive him as "honest Iago" is an example.

Tragicomedy: A PLAY that employs a PLOT suitable to TRAGEDY but ends happily, like a COMEDY. The ACTION, serious in THEME and subject matter and sometimes in TONE also, seems to be leading to a tragic CATASTROPHE until an unexpected turn in events, often in the form of a DEUS EX MACHINA, brings about the happy DÉNOUEMENT. In this sense Shakespeare's *The Merchant of Venice* is a *tragicomedy*, though it is also a ROMANTIC COMEDY. If the "trick" about the shedding of blood were omitted and Shylock allowed to "have his bond," the play might easily be made into a TRAGEDY; conversely, Shakespeare's *King Lear,* a pure tragedy, was made into a COMEDY by Nahum Tate for the RESTORATION stage. In English dramatic history the term *tragicomedy* is usually employed to designate the particular kind of PLAY developed by Beaumont and Fletcher about 1610, a type of which *Philaster* is typical. Fletcher's own definition may be quoted: "A tragicomedy is not so called in respect of mirth and killing, but in respect it wants deaths, which is enough to make it no tragedy, yet brings some near it, which is enough to make it no comedy, which must be a representation of familiar people, with such kind of trouble as no life be question'd; so that a god is as lawful in this [*tragicomedy*] as in a tragedy, and mean people as in a comedy" (from "To the Reader," *The Faithful Shepherdess*). Some of the characteristics are: improbable PLOT; unnatural SITUATIONS; actors of high social class, usually of the nobility; love as the central interest, pure love and gross love often being contrasted; highly complicated PLOT; rapid ACTION; contrast of deep villainy and exalted virtue; saving of HERO and HEROINE in the nick of time; penitent VILLAIN (as Iachimo in *Cymbeline*); disguises; surprises; jealousy; treachery; intrigue; enveloping action of war or rebellion. Shakespeare's *Cymbeline* and *The Winter's Tale* are examples of the GENRE. Fletcher's *The Faithful Shepherdess* is a PASTORAL *tragicomedy*. Later seventeenth-century *tragicomedies* are Killigrew's *The Prisoner,* D'Avenant's *Fair Favorite,* Shadwell's *Royal Shepherdess,* and Dryden's *Secret Love* and *Love Triumphant.* Such PLAYS as these tended to approach the HEROIC DRAMA. The type practically disappeared in the early eighteenth century, although a number of its characteristics reappear in the MELODRAMA of the nineteenth and twentieth centuries.

[References: Marvin Herrick, *Tragicomedy: Its Origin and Development in Italy, France, and England* (1955); Allardyce Nicoll, *The Theory of Drama* (1931); F. H. Ristine, *English Tragicomedy* (1910); F. E. Schelling, *Elizabethan Drama,* 2 vols. (1908, reprinted 1959).]

Transcendental Club: An informal organization of leading transcendentalists living in or near Boston. After their first meeting in 1836 at the home of George Ripley, they met occasionally at Ralph Waldo Emerson's home in Concord and elsewhere for seven or eight years, calling themselves "The Symposium" and the "HEDGE CLUB." Their chief interests were new developments in theology, philosophy, and literature; they came together to discuss the "new thought" of the day. The movement was closely associated with the growth of the Unitarian spirit in New England. The leading members of the Club were Emerson, Convers Francis, Frederick Henry Hedge, Amos Bronson Alcott, Ripley, Margaret Fuller, Nathaniel Hawthorne, Henry D. Thoreau, and William Ellery Channing. See TRANSCENDENTALISM.

Transcendentalism: A reliance on the intuition and the conscience, a form of idealism; a philosophical ROMANTICISM reaching America a generation or two after it developed in Europe. *Transcendentalism,* though based on doctrines of ancient and modern European philosophers (particularly Kant) and sponsored in America chiefly by Emerson after he had absorbed it from Carlyle, Coleridge, Goethe, and others, took on special significance in the United States, where it so largely dominated the New England authors as to become a literary movement as well as a philosophic conception. The movement gained its impetus in America in part from meetings of a small group that came together to discuss the "new thought" of the time. While holding different opinions about many things, the group seemed in general harmony in their conviction that within the nature of human beings there was something that transcended human experience—an intuitive and personal revelation. (See TRANSCENDENTAL CLUB.) As the movement developed, it informally sponsored two important activities: the publication of THE DIAL (1840–1844) and BROOK FARM.

Some of the various doctrines that have somehow been accepted as "transcendental" may be restated here. Transcendentalists believed in living close to nature (Thoreau) and taught the dignity of manual labor (Thoreau). They strongly felt the need of intellectual companionships and interests (BROOK FARM) and placed great emphasis on the importance of spiritual living. Every person's relation to God was a personal matter to be established directly by the individual (UNITARIANISM) rather than through the intermediation of the ritualistic church. They held firmly that human beings were divine in their own right, an opinion opposed to the doctrines held by the Puritan Calvinists in New England, and they urged strongly the essential divinity of human beings and one great brotherhood. Self-trust and self-reliance were to be practiced at all times, since to trust self was really to trust the voice of God speaking intuitively within us (Emerson). The transcendentalists felt called on to resist the "vulgar prosperity of the barbarian," believed firmly in democracy, and insisted on an intense individualism. Some extremists went so far as to evolve a system of dietetics and to rule out coffee, wine, and tobacco—all on the basis that the body was the temple of the soul and that for the tenant's sake it was well to keep the dwelling undefiled. Most of the transcendentalists were by nature reformers, though Emerson—the most vocal interpreter of the group—refused to go so far in this direction as, for instance, Bronson Alcott. Emerson's position is that it is each person's responsibility to be "a brave and upright man, who must find or cut a straight path to everything excellent in the earth, and not only go honorably himself, but make it easier for all who follow him to go in honor and with benefit." In this way most of the reforms were attempts to awaken and regenerate the human spirit rather than to prescribe particular and concrete movements. The transcendentalists were, for instance, among the early advocates of the enfranchisement of women.

Ultimately, despite these practical manifestations, *transcendentalism* was an epistemology—a way of knowing—and the ultimate characteristic that tied together the frequently contradictory attitudes of the loosely formed group was the belief that human beings can intuitively transcend the limits of the senses and of logic and directly receive higher truths and greater knowledge denied to more mundane methods of knowing.

The documents that most definitely give literary expression to general transcendentalist views are Emerson's *Nature* (1836) and Thoreau's *Walden* (1854).

[References: Paul F. Boller, Jr., *American Transcendentalism, 1830–1860: An Intellectual Inquiry* (1974); O. B. Frothingham, *Transcendentalism in New England* (1876, reprinted 1959); Perry Miller, ed., *The Transcendentalists: An Anthology* (1950); Lindsay Swift, *Brook Farm* (1900, reprinted 1961).]

Transferred Epithet: An adjective used to limit a noun that it really does not logically modify. Examples abound in ordinary discourse ("foreign policy" is *domestic* policy, and the "foreign minister" and "foreign office" are not at all foreign) and in literature, especially in POETRY (Carew's "A Rapture" mentions "Petrarch's learned arms"—an obvious transference). See EPITHET.

Translation: The rendering of a work, originally in one language, into another. At one extreme of *translation* stands the literal rendering of the work into the other language, "word for word," without concern for the primary differences in IDIOM and IMAGERY between the two languages. "Word-for-word" is something of a misnomer, since what is one word in one language may amount to a half-dozen in another or may have no counterpart at all. *Translation* cannot take place consistently at the level of the syllable or the word. Even common elements like number, gender, tense, mood, and aspect cannot be translated on a one-for-one basis. At the other extreme is the ADAPTATION of the work into the other language, an attempt to comprehend and communicate the spirit and meaning of the work by adapting it to the conventions and idioms of the language into which it is being rendered. Each translator must strike some kind of balance between these extremes—which Croce called "faithful ugliness or faithless beauty." Some *translations* have great literary merit in themselves; notably, the King James Version of the Holy BIBLE, Amyot's Plutarch, Schlegel's Shakespeare, Baudelaire's Poe, and Putnam's Cervantes. Chaucer was a notable translator, as were many later writers: Wyatt, Surrey, Golding, Sir Thomas North, Hobbes, Pope, Longfellow, Bayard Taylor, A. E. Housman, Pound, Auden, J. F. Nims, Robert Bly, W. S. Merwin, Richard Howard, Michael Alexander—to name but a few.

[References: William Arrowsmith and Roger Shattuck, eds., *The Craft and Context of Translation* (1961); Walter Benjamin, *Illuminations* (tr. 1970); R. A. Brower, ed., *On Translation* (1966); C. H. Conley, *The First English Translators of the Classics* (1927); F. O. Matthiessen, *Translation: An Elizabethan Art* (1931); E. Nida, *Toward a Science of Translating* (1964).]

Transumption: Another name for METALEPSIS.

Travesty: Writing that by its incongruity of STYLE or treatment ridicules a subject inherently noble or dignified. The derivation of the word—the same as that of "transvestite"—suggests presenting a subject in a dress intended for another type of subject. *Travesty* may be thought of as the opposite of the MOCK EPIC, since the latter treats a frivolous subject seriously and the *travesty* usually presents a serious subject frivolously. *Don Quixote* is a *travesty* on the MEDIEVAL ROMANCE. In general, PARODY ridicules a STYLE by lowering the subject; *travesty*, BURLESQUE, and CARICATURE ridicule a subject by lowering the style. See BURLESQUE.

"Tribe of Ben": A contemporary nickname for the young POETS and dramatists of the seventeenth century who acknowledged "rare Ben Jonson" as their master. Their chief was Robert Herrick, and the group included the CAVALIER LYRICISTS and others of the younger Jacobean writers. Jonson influenced his followers in the direction of classical polish and sense of FORM, imitation of CLASSICAL writers and literary types (as the ODE, the EPIGRAM, the SATIRE), and classical ideas of CRITICISM. The attitude represented a revolt from the PURITANISM and Italian ROMANTICISM represented in Spenser. The poets strove to make the LYRIC graceful and in general followed the creed: "Live merrily and write good verses." They were also called the "SONS OF BEN."

Tribrach: A metrical FOOT of three short or unstressed syllables. It rarely occurs in English VERSE, and many prosodists regard an English FOOT without a stressed syllable as impossible. In any event a whole POEM with no foot but the *tribrach* is virtually inconceivable. The foot may occur as in a SUBSTITUTION for a DACTYL, ANAPEST, AMPHIBRACH, or AMPHIMACER. There may be a *tribrach* or two in Hardy's "The Voice," in which the predominant FOOT is the dactyl:

⏑ ⏑ ⏑ / ⏑ ⏑ ⏑ / ⏑ ⏑ ⏑ / ⏑ ⏑ ⏑
Or is it | only the | breeze, in its | listlessness . . .

Trilogy: A literary composition in three substantial parts, each of which is in itself a complete unit. Shakespeare's *King Henry VI* is an example. A *trilogy* usually is written against a large background, which may be historical, philosophical, or social in its interests. O'Neill's *Mourning Becomes Electra* is a dramatic *trilogy;* Faulkner's *The Hamlet, The Town,* and *The Mansion* are called "The Snopes Trilogy."

Trimeter: A LINE of three FEET. See SCANSION.

Triolet: One of the simpler French VERSE forms. (See FRENCH FORMS.) It consists of eight LINES, the first two being repeated as the last two lines and the first recurring also as the fourth line. There are only two RHYMES, and their arrangement is: *ab aa abab.* (Italics indicate whole lines that are repeated.) Skillful POETS have given meanings to the REFRAIN lines that are different from the meanings that they carried at the opening of the POEM, as in this example by Austin Dobson:

> Rose kissed me today,
>   Will she kiss me tomorrow?
> Let it be as it may,
> Rose kissed me today.
> But the pleasure gives way
>   To a savor of sorrow;—
> Rose kissed me today,—
>   *Will* she kiss me tomorrow?

A serious *triolet* is very hard to write, but Hardy produced one.

Triple Meter: In METRICS a LINE consisting of FEET of three syllables; that is, of ANAPESTS, DACTYLS, AMPHIBRACHS, or AMPHIMACERS.

Triple Rhyme: RHYME in which the rhyming stressed syllable is followed by two unstressed, undifferentiated syllables, as in "meticulous" and "ridiculous." See RHYME.

Triplet: A sequence of three rhyming LINES, sometimes introduced as a variation in the HEROIC COUPLET. With heroic couplets, the *triplet* may be indicated by marginal braces; the third line may be HEXAMETER. See TERCET.

Tristich: A STANZA of three LINES. See TERCET, TRIPLET.

Trite Expression: A CLICHÉ.

Trivium: The three studies leading to the bachelor's degree in the medieval universities: grammar, logic, and RHETORIC. See SEVEN LIBERAL ARTS.

Trochee: A FOOT consisting of an accented and an unaccented syllable, as in the word *happy*. Trochaics are generally unpopular with POETS for sustained writing, since they soon degenerate into rocking-horse RHYTHM, a fact that makes them popular with children. On the other hand, for short SONGS and lyrics the *trochee* has been popular. Long rhymed trochaic POEMS are extremely rare, since all the RHYMES would have to be FEMININE, and such rhymes are relatively few and can be monotonous. Long unrhymed trochaic poems are less rare than the rhymed. Longfellow's *Song of Hiawatha* is in unrhymed trochaic TETRAMETER. (This POEM and Longfellow's *Evangeline* and *The Courtship of Miles Standish*—both in DACTYLIC HEXAMETERS—are virtually unique in being long works in a regular unrhymed MEASURE that is *not* BLANK VERSE). Browning's "One Word More" is a 200-line POEM in unrhymed trochaic PENTAMETER.

Trope: In RHETORIC a *trope* is a FIGURE OF SPEECH involving a "turn" or change of sense—the use of a word in a sense other than the literal; in this sense figures of comparison (see METAPHOR, SIMILE) as well as ironical expressions are *tropes* or FIGURES OF SPEECH. Until recently, *tropes* occupied a subordinate place in literary studies. When the NEW CRITICISM began to regard POETRY as a special kind of use of language, however, certain *tropes*—IRONY and PARADOX in particular—began to enjoy an unprecedented measure of prestige. Beginning around 1970, Harold Bloom attempted to align (1) certain *tropes* in a certain order, (2) the parts of a typical post-Enlightenment "strong" POEM, and (3) certain Freudian "defense mechanisms." Along with Angus Fletcher and John Hollander, Bloom has joined Kenneth Burke in giving "tropology" a new meaning and a new viability much exceeding its early function as a branch of Biblical studies.

Another use of the word is important to students of the origin of MEDIEVAL DRAMA. As early as the eighth or ninth centuries, certain musical additions to the Gregorian ANTIPHONS in the liturgy of the Catholic Church were permitted as pleasurable elaborations of the service. At first they were merely prolongations of the melody on a vowel sound, giving rise to *jubila,* the manuscript notation for a *jubilum* being known as a *neuma,* which looked somewhat like shorthand notes. Later, words were added to old *jubila* and new compositions of both words and music added, the texts of which were called *tropes.* These *tropes,* or "amplifications of the liturgical texts," were sometimes in PROSE, sometimes VERSE; sometimes purely musical, sometimes requiring DIALOGUE, presented antiphonally by the two parts of the choir. From this dialogue form of the *trope* developed the LITURGICAL DRAMA. See MEDIEVAL DRAMA.

[References: Harold Bloom, *A Map of Misreading* (1975); Kenneth Burke, *A Grammar of Motives* (1945); Francis Fergusson, *Trope and Allegory: Themes Common to Dante and Shakespeare* (1977); Hayden White, *Tropics of Discourse* (1978).]

Troubadour: A name given to the aristocratic LYRIC poets of Provence (southern France) in the twelfth and thirteenth centuries. The name is derived from a word meaning "to find," suggesting that the *troubadour* was regarded as an inventor and experimenter in poetic technique. *Troubadours* were essentially lyric POETS, occupied with THEMES of love and chivalry. The conventional themes arose from the social conditions, the *troubadour* usually addressing his VERSE to a married lady, whose patronage he courted. *Troubadour* POETRY figured importantly in the development of COURTLY LOVE and influenced the TROUVÈRE of northern France. The earliest *troubadour* of record is William, Count of Poitiers (1071–1127), other famous *troubadours* being Bernard de Ventadour, Arnaut de Mareuil, Bertran de Born, and Arnaut Daniel. Some of the FORMS invented by the *troubadours* are: the CANSO (love song), *ballada* (dance song), *tenson* (dialogue), PASTOURELLE (pastoral wooing song), and ALBA (dawn song). Much use was made of RHYME, and varied stanzaic forms were developed, including the SESTINA used later by Dante and others. The SONNET form probably developed from *troubadour* stanzaic inventions. The POETRY was intended to be sung, sometimes by the *troubadour* himself, sometimes by an assistant or apprentice or professional entertainer, such as the JONGLEUR. Influence of the *troubadours* reaches in our time to Ezra Pound's POETRY and, through Pound, to T. S. Eliot's as well.

[Reference: H. J. Chaytor, *The Troubadours* (1912, reprinted 1970).]

Trouvère: A term applied to a group or school of POETS who flourished in northern France in the twelfth and thirteenth centuries. The *trouvères,* much influenced by the art of the TROUBADOURS of southern France, concerned themselves largely with LYRICS of love, though they produced also CHANSONS DE GESTE and CHIVALRIC ROMANCES. To one of them, the famous Chrétien de Troyes (twelfth century), we owe some of the earliest and best of the Arthurian romances. See ARTHURIAN LEGEND.

Truncation: In METRICS the omission of a syllable or syllables at the beginning or end of a LINE. See CATALEXSIS.

Tudor: The royal house that ruled England from 1485 to 1603. Henry VII (1485–1509), Henry VIII (1509–1547), Edward VI (1547–1553), Mary (1553–1558), and Elizabeth (1558–1603).

Tumbling Verse: A rough, heavily stressed POETRY. See SKELTONIC VERSE, for which it is another name.

Type: A group of persons or things having certain characteristics in common that distinguish them as being members of a definite group or class. In literary CRITICISM the term *type* has two distinct usages. In one it refers to a literary GENRE, a KIND, with definable distinguishing characteristics. In the other it is applied to a CHARACTER who is a representative of a class or kind of person. Henry James uses it in this sense in "The Art of Fiction" when he says, "She had got her direct personal impression, and she turned out her *type*. She knew what youth was, and what Protestantism; she also had the advantage of having seen what it was to be French, so that she converted these ideas into a concrete image and produced a reality [of French Protestant youth]." A *type* CHARACTER in this sense differs markedly from a STOCK CHARACTER. The *type* character need not have any qualities borrowed from literary TRADITIONS and may be sharply individualized; a *type* character is one that embodies a substantial number of significant distinguishing characteristics of a group or class. Such a CHARACTER becomes almost a kind of SYNECDOCHE, a representative of the whole of which he or she is a part. A STOCK CHARACTER, on the other hand, is a STEREOTYPE, a character modeled on other and frequently used characters, but often is representative of no actual group but simply of similar STOCK CHARACTERS. F. Scott Fitzgerald once remarked that, if you set out to create an individual, you may create a *type*, but, if you set out to create a *type*, you will create nothing. In creating the individual Jay Gatsby, Fitzgerald certainly seems to have created an abiding *type* as well. *Type* is also sometimes used as a SYNONYM for SYMBOL, particularly in the religious sense of standing for something that is to come, as in the statement, "The Old Testament sacrificial lamb was a *type* of Christ." This latter sense is the usual meaning of the province of "typology." John Hollander's *Types of Shape*—the title and the book alike—illustrates at least four meanings of *type*.

U

Ubi sunt Formula: A CONVENTION much used in VERSE, especially in the
FRENCH FORMS, rhetorically asking "where are" (*ubi sunt*) these things, and
these, and these, the poetic impression on the reader being largely effected
by the EMPHASIS the FORMULA places on the transitory qualities of life. The
most famous example in English is probably Dante Gabriel Rossetti's "The
Ballade of Dead Ladies," a poetic TRANSLATION of François Villon's BALLADE:

> But where are the snows of yester-year?

(Villon's "où sont" is the exact counterpart of "ubi sunt.") Some variant of
"ubi sunt" appears in Wordsworth ("Where is it now, the glory and the
dream?"), Keats ("Where are the songs of spring?"), and Lamb ("Where are
they gone, the old familiar faces?"). In Justin H. McCarthy's poem "I Wonder
in What Isle of Bliss," successive STANZAS close with "Where are the Gods
of Yesterday?" "Where are the Dreams of Yesterday?" "Where are the Girls
of Yesterday?" "Where are the Snows of Yesterday?" In Edmund Gosse's "The
Ballad of Dead Cities," the three STANZAS begin with "Where are the Cities
of the plain?" "Where now is Karnak, that great fane . . . ?" "And where is
white Shushan, again . . . ?" Each of the STANZAS in this poem closes with
"Where are the cities of old time?" The FORMULA, especially as transmitted
through Villon's BALLADE, has touched the modern literary imagination powerfully and productively. Edgar Lee Masters's "The Will" asks, "Where are Elmer,
Herman, Bert, Tom and Charley . . . ?" The formula may almost be said to
haunt not only POETRY but DRAMA (Tennessee Williams's *The Glass Menagerie*)
and FICTION (Heller's *Catch-22*) as well. These examples illustrate the tendency
to place the *ubi sunt* query in the opening line of a STANZA or to use it as a
REFRAIN or REPETEND.

Ultima Thule: The farthest possible place. Used often in the sense of a remote
goal, an ideal and mysterious country. To the ancients *Thule* was one of the
northern lands of Europe, most likely one of the Shetland Islands, although
Iceland and Norway have been suggested. From the Latin reference to the
region as the *ultima* (farthest) *Thule,* the expression has taken on literary
significance, conspicuous in Poe's "Dreamland" (in which "ultimate dim Thule"
is a repeated phrase) and Longfellow's late "Ultima Thule."

Unanimism: A sentiment and movement associated with "Jules Romains"
in the first quarter of the twentieth century; emphasizing the collective spirit
(unanimity) in society and even in language. The movement owed something
of its impetus to Walt Whitman, and it interested Ezra Pound in his youth.

Underground Press: The mid-1960s saw the beginning of a large number
of *underground* publications by numerous groups, some of them clandestine
but many associated with universities. Many of these publications were newspapers, but a number were MAGAZINES publishing ESSAYS, POETRY, and FICTION,
usually of an experimental, AVANT-GARDE, or politically radical sort. The term

underground is now applied to any AVANT-GARDE art that is privately produced and concerned with artistic or social experiment. There are *underground* films, *underground* art, as well as the *underground press.* Much of
the work produced by the *underground press* is in the form of LITTLE MAGA-
ZINES, of which there are now thousands with very limited—and in most cases
very local—circulation. See LITTLE MAGAZINES.

Understatement: A common FIGURE OF SPEECH in which the literal sense
of what is said falls detectably short of (or "under") the magnitude of what
is being talked about. When someone says "pretty fair" but means "splendid,"
that is clear *understatement. Understatement* is particularly noticeable in Old
Germanic literature. See LITOTES.

Unintrusive Narrator: When a NARRATOR merely describes or reports AC-
TIONS in dramatic scenes, without commentary or personal judgment, the
work is being presented through an *unintrusive narrator.* No NARRATOR narrates with complete, dispassionate objectivity; every selection of detail and
treatment represents a subjective decision. Even so, a narrator who does not
indulge in editorial comments, ASIDES, exclamations, addresses to the CHARAC-
TERS or the "dear reader," and so forth, may seem relatively *unintrusive.*
See NARRATOR, SELF-EFFACING AUTHOR, SCENIC METHOD.

Unitarianism: The creed of a sect coming into importance in America about
1820; it discarded the earlier faith in the existence of a Trinity and retained
belief in the unity of God, accepting Christ as divine in the same sense that
a human being is but not as a member of a divine Trinity. In its more evolved
form, this new *Unitarianism* stood for "the fatherhood of God, the brotherhood
of man, the leadership of Jesus, salvation by character, and the progress of
mankind onward and upward forever." The members joined with the Univer-
salists in 1961 to form the Unitarian Universalist Association.

Unities: The principles of DRAMATIC STRUCTURE involving *action, time,* and
place. The most important *unity* and the only one enjoined by Aristotle is
that of ACTION. He called a TRAGEDY "an imitation of an action that is complete,
and whole, and of a certain magnitude"; a whole should have beginning, middle, and end, with the parts related in a clear causal pattern. Inevitability
and concentration result from adherence to the *unity of action.* This *unity,*
Aristotle warned, was not necessarily obtained simply by making one person
the subject. Later CRITICS declared that a SUBPLOT tends to destroy the *unity*
of any serious PLAY and that tragic and comic elements should not be mixed.
Thus, the legitimacy of TRAGICOMEDY was for a long time a matter of dispute;
Sidney opposed it and Johnson vindicated it.
     The *unity of time* was developed from Aristotle's simple and undogmatic
statement concerning tragic usage: "Tragedy endeavors, as far as possible,
to confine itself to a single revolution of the sun, or but slightly to exceed
this limit." Italian CRITICS of the sixteenth century formulated the doctrine
that the action should be limited to one day; many French and English critics
of the seventeenth and eighteenth centuries accepted this *unity,* and many
dramatists used it. There were different interpretations of the *unity of time*—
some favored the natural cycle of twenty-four hours, others the artificial day

of twelve hours, and others the several hours that correspond to the actual time of theatrical representation. Seldom does the "represented time" amount to less than the actual elapsed time. A three-hour play will usually represent an *action* longer than three hours, sometimes by many years.

The *unity of place*, limiting the ACTION to one place, was the last to emerge and was not mentioned by Aristotle. It logically followed the requirement of limiting the action to a particular time; as the RENAISSANCE critics of Italy developed their theories of VERISIMILITUDE, of making the action of a PLAY approximate that of stage representation, the *unity of place* completed the trilogy. Some CRITICS were content to have the action confined merely to the same town or city. The *unity of place* was closely allied to that of time in the theory and practice of neoclassic writers.

The dramatic *unities* have had a long and extremely complicated history. For more than two centuries in England the three *unities* were denounced and defended and (as in Dryden's *Essay of Dramatic Poesy*) debated. When NEOCLASSICISM gave way to ROMANTICISM, they lost much of their importance.

Many great English PLAYS violate all three *unities*. *Unity of action*, however, is commonly recognized as an important requirement in serious DRAMA, and Shakespeare's greatest TRAGEDIES, such as *Hamlet* and *Othello*, show the effects of such *unity*. In two plays, the *Comedy of Errors* and *The Tempest*, Shakespeare observed all three of the *unities*. The theory of the *unities* has been a matter of concern more to CRITICS than to dramatists. Yet the concentration and strength that result from efforts at attaining *unity of action, time, and place* may be regarded as dramatic virtues.

Modern dramatists are less interested in traditional FORMULA than in the *unity of impression*, the singleness of emotional EFFECT, which is related to the *unity of action*. Moreover, in recent years effective experiments with the minor *unities of time and place* have been made in stage plays and FILMS. In a PLAY (later a film) called *The Rope*, the elapsed time exactly matched the represented time. See CRITICISM and UNITY.

Unity: The concept that a literary work shall have in it some organizing principle to which all its parts are related so that, viewed in the light of that principle, the work is an organic whole. A work with *unity* is cohesive in its parts, complete, self-contained, and integrated; it possesses oneness. The concept of *unity* in the DRAMA has often been mechanically applied (see UNITIES). In other literary forms it is often considered to reside in a unified ACTION or PLOT, or in CHARACTERIZATION. A work may, however, be unified by FORM, by intent, by THEME, by SYMBOLISM—in fact, by any means that can so integrate and organize its elements that they have a necessary relationship to one another and an essential relation to the whole of which they are parts. For many CRITICS and thinkers, *unity* of some sort has been among the highest ideals. Irving Babbitt opposed what he regarded as romantic confusion to CLASSICAL unity of spirit and effort. Henry Adams opposed twentieth-century multiplicity to thirteenth-century *unity*. Both W. B. Yeats and T. S. Eliot saw disunity and chaos as afflictions of the modern age and expressed a longing for a predissociation world, which they located in ancient Rome, medieval Byzantium, or RENAISSANCE Italy and England. Among critics, Poe expounded uncompromising *unity* of EFFECT, and the CHICAGO CRITICS—pre-eminently R. S. Crane and Austin M. Wright—have concentrated on principles of *unity*.

Universality: A critical term frequently employed to indicate the presence in a piece of writing of an appeal to all readers of all time. When writing presents the great human emotions common to all peoples of all civilizations— jealousy, love, pride, courage, and so forth—in literary FORM and through CHARACTERS and ACTIONS that remain meaningful to other ages, it may be said to have *universality*. Of all qualities that make for *universality* in litera- ture, the successful portrayal of human CHARACTER is the most important, but only slightly more so than fidelity to the unchanging physical facts of the natural world. See CONCRETE UNIVERSAL.

University Plays: PLAYS produced by undergraduates at Oxford and Cam- bridge during the ELIZABETHAN AGE. See SCHOOL PLAYS.

University Wits: A name used for certain young University people who came to London in the late 1580s and undertook careers as professional writers. They played an important part in the development of the great literature, especially the DRAMA, that characterized the latter part of Elizabeth's reign. The most important was Christopher Marlowe. Others were Robert Greene, George Peele, Thomas Lodge, Thomas Nash, and Thomas Kyd. Some authori- ties include John Lyly, though Lyly was older and perhaps not personally associated with the others. They lived irregular lives, Greene and Marlowe being particularly known as Bohemians. Their literary work, while uneven in quality, much of it being hack work, was varied and influential. They were largely instrumental in freeing TRAGEDY from the artificial restrictions imposed by CLASSICAL authority, and their cultivation of BLANK VERSE, especially the "mighty line" of Marlowe, paved the way for Shakespeare's masterful use of this FORM. They devised or developed types of PLAYS later perfected by Shake- speare: the REVENGE TRAGEDY or TRAGEDY OF BLOOD (Kyd), the TRAGEDY built around a great personality (Marlowe), the ROMANTIC COMEDY (Greene and Peele), the CHRONICLE PLAY (Marlowe and others), and the COURT COM- EDY (Lyly). Lodge and Greene cultivated the PASTORAL ROMANCE, and Nash wrote the first PICARESQUE NOVEL in English. The group was especially active between 1585 and 1595.

Unreliable Narrator: A NARRATOR or viewpoint CHARACTER who may be in error in his or her understanding or report of things and who thus leaves readers without the guides essential for making judgments about the character and the ACTIONS with any confidence that their conclusions are those intended by the author. The *unreliable narrator* is most frequently found in works by a SELF-EFFACING AUTHOR. For example, Lambert Strether, the viewpoint CHARACTER in Henry James's *The Ambassadors,* is often wrong in his conclu- sions about things, but we must await the outcome of events in order to find out when he is. In James's *The Turn of the Screw* the debate over what actually happens in the STORY is really over the reliability of the Governess's NARRA- TIVE. Huck Finn, in Mark Twain's *Adventures of Huckleberry Finn,* is often uncomprehending about the situations he describes, as most NAIVE NARRATORS are; hence, he is *unreliable.* Immature NARRATORS—such as Huckleberry Finn, Quentin Compson in *The Sound and the Fury,* and Holden Caulfield in *The Catcher in the Rye*—may be unreliable on account of their lack of sophistica- tion. Others—such as Benjy in *The Sound and the Fury* and Humbert in

Lolita—suffer some retardation or derangement that impedes or precludes reliability. See NARRATOR, NAIVE NARRATOR.

Utilitarianism: A theory of ethics formulated in England in the eighteenth century by Jeremy Bentham, who believed that the test of ethical concerns was their usefulness to society and who defined utility as "the greatest happiness for the greatest number." The theory was advanced and modified in the nineteenth century by James Mill and his son John Stuart Mill, both of whom wanted to define "happiness" in qualitative rather than quantitative terms, whereas Bentham had equated it with pleasure. It is a significant MOVEMENT in nineteenth-century thought not only because of the excellence with which John Stuart Mill expounded it but also because it was a central issue for a number of writers, among them Carlyle and Dickens, both of whom attacked the system. It is sometimes called "Benthamism."
    [References: Alfred C. Lyall, *Studies in Literature and History* (1915); Leslie Stephen, *The English Utilitarians* (1900, reprinted 1968).]

Utopia: A form of FICTION describing an imaginary ideal world. The term comes from Sir Thomas More's work *Utopia,* written in Latin in 1516, describing a perfect political state. The word *Utopia* is a PUN on the Greek words "outopia," meaning "no place" and "eutopia," meaning "good place." The earliest Utopian work was Plato's *Republic.* Many Utopian FICTIONS have been produced since More's, including Campanella's *Civitas Solis* (1623), Bacon's *New Atlantis* (1627), Harrington's *Oceana* (1656), Samuel Butler's *Erewhon* (1872), Bellamy's *Looking Backward* (1888), William Morris's *News from Nowhere* (1891), and H. G. Wells's *A Modern Utopia* (1905). DYSTOPIA, meaning "bad place," is the term applied to unpleasant imaginary places, such as those in Aldous Huxley's *Brave New World,* and George Orwell's *1984.*
    [References: Joyce O. Hertzler, *The History of Utopian Thought* (1923); Mark Holloway, *Heavens on Earth: Utopian Communities in America, 1680–1880,* 2nd ed. (1966); Lewis Mumford, *The Story of the Utopias,* rev. ed. (1966).]

V

Vade mecum: An article that one keeps constantly on hand. By association the term has come to mean any book much used, as a *handbook,* a *thesaurus.* The phrase means "go with me."

Vapours: A word commonly used in eighteenth-century literature to account for the eccentric action of people. *Vapours* were exhalations, presumably given off by the stomach or other organs of the body, that rose to the head causing depression, melancholy, hysteria, and so forth. In 1541 Sir Thomas Elyot wrote that "of humours some are more grosse and cold, some are subtyl and hot and are called vapours." HEROINES of eighteenth-century FICTION were particularly subject to attacks of this malady. Young, in 1728, gave us these lines:

> Sometimes, thro' pride the sexes change their airs;
> My lord has vapours, and my lady swears.

See HUMOURS.

Variorum Edition: An EDITION of an author's work presenting complete variant readings of the possible texts and full notes of critical comments and interpretation. The term is an abbreviation of the Latin *cum notis variorum* ("with notes of various persons"). In English literature the most conspicuous successes in this type of editing are the "New Variorum Shakespeare" edited by Furness and the "Variorum Spenser." edited by Edwin Greenlaw. Lately, *variorum editions* have tended to present various readings rather than commentary by various CRITICS.

Varronian Satire: A form of INDIRECT SATIRE, named for the Roman writer Varro. The more common names are MENIPPEAN SATIRE and ANATOMY.

Vatic: From the earliest times it was believed that some POETS or BARDS were divinely inspired and were thus seers who spoke prophetic truth; such poets were called *vates,* of which Sybil was the most famous. Hence, the term *vatic* in reference to a POET or a POEM means that it is regarded as divinely inspired, prophetic, or oracular. Smart, Blake, Whitman, Ginsberg, and Snyder have been called *vatic* poets.

Vaudeville: An entertainment consisting of successive performances of unrelated SONGS, dances, dramatic SKETCHES, acrobatic feats, juggling, PANTOMIME, puppet shows, animal acts, and varied stunts. The word is derived from *Vau-de-Vire,* a village in Normandy, where a famous composer of lively, satirical songs lived in the eighteenth century. From these SONGS, modified later by PANTOMIME, developed the variety shows known as *vaudeville.* The elements of *vaudeville* are old (see LOW COMEDY, BURLESQUE, FARCE), but the modern *vaudeville* show developed in the eighteenth and nineteenth centuries. Under the direction of John Rich these shows became very popular in eighteenth-century England, continued so through the nineteenth century and for about the first half of the twentieth. The name *vaudeville* seems to have become finally attached to the variety show as a result of its development in America, especially in the early years of the twentieth century, when *vaudeville* actors were organized into "circuits" by B. F. Keith and others and when elaborate theaters were devoted to their use. The popularity of *vaudeville* decreased after the advent of the talking moving pictures, radio, and television.

Vehicle: The immediate subject, as opposed to the ultimate or ulterior intentional subject of a METAPHOR. The *vehicle* "carries" the meaning of the TENOR. If you call an easy job "a piece of cake," the piece of cake is the *vehicle* and the easiness of the job is the TENOR. See TENOR.

Venus and Adonis Stanza: Six LINES of IAMBIC PENTAMETER rhyming *ababcc*, named from its use in Shakespeare's POEM.

Verbum Infans Formula: A conventional paradoxical *topos*, meaning "the unspeaking word," applied to the infant (*infans*, "not speaking") Christ, who incarnates the Word (*verbum*). The formula, which comes from patristic sources, was used by Lancelot Andrewes in combination with two other paradoxical COMMONPLACES; *Tonans Vagiens* ("thundering-mewling") and *Immensum Parvulum* ("measureless-diminutive"). The PARADOX recurs in many of T. S. Eliot's POEMS, as both "Word without a word" and "Word within a word, unable to speak a word."

Verisimilitude: The semblance of truth. The term has been used in CRITICISM to indicate the degree to which a writer faithfully creates the appearance or semblance of the truth. In his *Life of Swift*, Scott writes: "Swift possessed the art of verisimilitude." The word was a favorite with Poe, who used it in the sense of presenting details, howsoever far-fetched, in such a way as to give them the *semblance* of truth. In "The Facts in the Case of M. Valdemar," for instance, Poe gives way to the wildest kind of romancing, but the items are so marshaled as to sweep the reader into at least a momentary acceptance, and the story may, therefore, be said to respect Poe's own demands for *verisimilitude*. A popular example of *verisimilitude* to support an amazing story is Daniel Defoe's "True Relation of the Apparition of One Mrs. Veal" (1706). *Verisimilitude* normally means that a work possesses certain qualities conventionally identified as lifelike.

Vers de société: Brief lyrical VERSE written in a genial, sportive mood and sophisticated in both subject and treatment. Sometimes called LIGHT VERSE. Its characteristics are polish, *savoir faire*, grace, and ease of expression. It usually presents aspects of conventional social relationships. Locker-Lampson in a much-quoted introduction to his collection of *vers de société*, *Lyra Elegantiarum*, states: "Occasional verse should be short, graceful, refined, and fanciful, not seldom distinguished by chastened sentiment, and often playful. The tone should not be pitched high; it should be terse and idiomatic, and rather in the conversational key. The rhythm should be crisp and sparkling, the rhyme frequent and never forced, while the entire poem should be marked by tasteful moderation, high finish and completeness." Though gaining in favor in recent centuries, such VERSE was popular in CLASSICAL literature. The seventeenth and eighteenth centuries in England saw a high development of the type. In the nineteenth century *vers de société* was practiced by Fitz-Greene Halleck and N. P. Willis in the United States and by C. S. Calverley and W. M. Praed in Britain. See LIGHT VERSE, OCCASIONAL VERSE.

[References: Frederick Locker-Lampson, *Lyra Elegantiarum* (1867, rev. ed. 1891); Carolyn Wells, *A Vers de Société Anthology* (1907, reprinted 1976).]

Vers libre: A nineteenth-century French poetic movement to free POETRY from strict rules of VERSIFICATION resulted in cadenced and rhythmic POETRY called *vers libre.* The term, which literally means *free verse,* has been used as a SYNONYM for FREE VERSE in English. Since language and every other cultural institution are governed by rules of selection and combination, the "freedom" of *vers libre* is relative and may even be illusory. T. S. Eliot is supposed to have said that "no *vers* is *libre* for the man who wants to do a good job."

Verse: Used in two senses: (1) as a unit of POETRY, in which case it has the same significance as STANZA or LINE; and (2) as a name given generally to metrical composition. In the second sense *verse* is simply a generic term applied to rhythmical and, most frequently, metrical and rhymed composition, in which case it implies little as to the merit of the composition, the term POETRY or POEM being reserved for *verse* of high merit. An inherent suggestion that *verse* is of a lower order than POETRY lies in the fact that *verse* is used in association with such terms as *society verse* and *occasional verse,* which, it is generally conceded, are rarely applied to great POETRY. The use of *verse* to indicate a STANZA, while common, is not justified.

Verse Paragraph: A nonstanzaic, continuous VERSE form, in which the lines are grouped not through a regular, recurring pattern but in unequal blocks of thought, meaning, logic, or content. The beginning of a *verse paragraph* may be indicated by indentation, as in PROSE. The verse FORM for POETRY written in *paragraphs* rather than STANZAS is usually either BLANK VERSE or FREE VERSE. Milton's *Paradise Lost* is in BLANK VERSE *paragraphs;* much of Whitman's *Leaves of Grass* is in FREE VERSE *paragraphs.* Dryden, Pope, Johnson, Goldsmith, and other virtuosi of the HEROIC COUPLET routinely wrote in *verse paragraphs* of various lengths.

Versification: The art and practice of writing VERSE. Like PROSODY the term is inclusive, generally connoting all the mechanical elements going to make up poetic composition: ACCENT, RHYTHM, METER, RHYME, STANZA form, DICTION, and such aids as ASSONANCE, ONOMATOPOEIA, and ALLITERATION. In a narrower sense *versification* signifies simply the structural FORM of a POEM as revealed by SCANSION. The word is also applied to the transformation of PROSE into VERSE. Some passages of Shakespeare's *Antony and Cleopatra,* for example, amount to little more than a *versification* of the prose in North's TRANSLATION of Plutarch.

Vice: A STOCK CHARACTER in the MORALITY PLAY, a tempter both sinister and comic. Most historians of the DRAMA see the *Vice* as a predecessor of the cynical VILLAIN and also of certain Elizabethan comic CHARACTERS. Shakespeare's Falstaff has many of the qualities of the *Vice.* See MORALITY PLAY.

Victorian: A term used (1) to designate broadly the literature written during the reign of Queen Victoria (1837–1901) or its characteristics; and (2) more narrowly, to suggest a certain complacency or hypocrisy or squeamishness more or less justly assumed to be traceable to or similar to prevailing Victorian attitudes. A certain prudery and squeamishness led to egregious exaggeration in costume, furnishings, architecture, and industrial design. Pride in the growing power of England, optimism born of the new science, the dominance of Puritan ideals tenaciously held by the rising middle class, and the example of a royal court scrupulous in its adherence to high standards of "decency" and respectability combined to produce a spirit of moral earnestness linked with self-satisfaction, all of which was protested against at the time and in the generations to follow as hypocritical, false, complacent, narrow, solemn, and mean. The cautious manner in which "mid-Victorian" writers in particular were prone to treat such matters as profanity and sex has been especially responsible for the use of *"Victorian"* or *"mid-Victorian"* to indicate false modesty, empty respectability, or callous complacency. Though justified in part, this use of *Victorian* rests in some degree on exaggeration and at best fails to consider the fact that even in the heart of the *Victorian* period a very large part of the literature either did not exhibit such traits or set itself flatly in protest against them. Many-sided and complex, *Victorian* literature reflects both romantically and realistically the great changes that were going on in life and thought. The religious and philosophical doubts and hopes raised by the new science, the social problems arising from the new industrial conditions, the conscious resort of literary men and women to foreign sources of inspiration, and the rise of a new middle-class audience and new media of publication (the MAGAZINES) are among the forces that colored literature during Victoria's reign. Since there are marked differences between the literature of the early years of Victoria's reign and that of the later years, this *Handbook* treats the early years as a part of the ROMANTIC PERIOD and the later years as a part of the REALISTIC PERIOD. See EARLY VICTORIAN AGE, LATE VICTORIAN AGE, ROMANTIC PERIOD IN ENGLISH LITERATURE, REALISTIC PERIOD IN ENGLISH LITERATURE, and *Outline of Literary History.*

[References: W. C. Brownell, *Victorian Prose Masters* (1901); G. K. Chesterton, *The Victorian Age in Literature* (1913, reprinted 1963); Oliver Elton, *A Survey of English Literature, 1830–1880,* 2 vols. (1920, reprinted 1955); W. H. Hudson, *A Short History of English Literature in the Nineteenth Century* (1918); D. C. Somervell, *English Thought in the Nineteenth Century* (1929).]

Vignette: A SKETCH, ESSAY, or brief NARRATIVE characterized by precision and delicacy. The term is borrowed from that used for unbordered but delicate decorative designs for a book, and it implies writing with comparable grace and economy. It may be a separate whole or a portion of a larger work. The term is also applied to very brief SHORT-SHORT STORIES, less than five hundred words in length.

Villain: An evil CHARACTER, guilty of, or at the least thoroughly capable of, serious crimes; he or she acts in opposition to the HERO. The *villain* is the ANTAGONIST in a DRAMA.

Villanelle: A fixed nineteen-line FORM, originally French, employing only two RHYMES and repeating two of the LINES according to a set pattern. Line

1 is repeated as lines 6, 12, and 18; line 3 as lines 9, 15, and 19. The first and third lines return as a rhymed COUPLET at the end. The scheme of RHYMES (or REPETITIONS) is *aba aba aba aba abaa.* The *villanelle* first appeared in English VERSE in the second half of the nineteenth century, originally for fairly lighthearted POEMS. (The earliest American *villanelle* was written by James Whitcomb Riley.) The obsessive repetition that can represent ecstatic affection also works for static preoccupation, as in serious *villanelles* by E. A. Robinson and William Empson. The finest *villanelle* in any language— and one of the greatest modern POEMS in any FORM—is Dylan Thomas's "Do Not Go Gentle into That Good Night."

Virgin Play: A medieval nonscriptural PLAY based on SAINTS' LIVES, in which the Virgin Mary takes an active role in performing miracles. See MIRACLE PLAY.

Virgule: A slanting or an upright line used in PROSODY to mark off metrical FEET, as in the following example from Shelley:

The sun | is warm, | the sky | is clear,

The waves | are dan | cing fast | and bright.

Since the Second World War, the *virgule,* sponsored by Ezra Pound and Charles Olson, has joined the fashionable punctuation of POEMS. With the legalistic "and/or" (unnecessary, since "or" means "and/or"), the *virgule* has come to supplant the hyphen.

Voice-Over: In FILM the use of a NARRATOR'S or commentator's words when the speaker is not seen by the viewer. The *voice-over* may be a NARRATIVE bridge between SCENES, a statement of facts needed by the viewer, or a comment on the CHARACTERS and ACTIONS in the scene. In special cases the *voice-over* may be in the voice of the character represented in the scene but not a part of the action in the SCENE. In Olivier's *Hamlet,* for example, we hear Olivier in a *voice-over* speaking the words of SOLILOQUIES while we see his motionless, pensive face on the screen. Compare with SOUND-OVER.

Volta: The turn in thought—from question to answer, problem to solution— that occurs at the beginning of the SESTET in the ITALIAN SONNET. The *volta* sometimes occurs in the SHAKESPEAREAN SONNET between the twelfth and the thirteenth lines. The *volta* is routinely marked at the beginning of LINE 9 (Italian) or 13 (Shakespearean) by "but," "yet," or "and yet." The design of Hardy's "Hap" is perspicuous:

Line 1: "If . . ."
Line 5: "Then . . ."
Line 9: "But not so . . ."

The distinctive characteristic of the MILTONIC SONNET is the absence of the *volta* in a fixed position, although the FORM is Italian in RHYME SCHEME.

Vorticism: Earlier, a term applied to the binomial epistemology of Descartes. A movement in modern POETRY related to the manifestation of certain abstract developments and methods in painting and sculpture. *Vorticism* originated in 1914 with Wyndham Lewis's effort to oppose Romantic and vitalist theories with a kind of verbal and visual art based on SPATIAL FORM, clarity, definite outline, and mechanical dynamism. Ezra Pound used the vorticist idea in POETRY as an extension of IMAGISM, which seemed constrained to work only in short works or limited passages and to lack force. In *vorticism* abstraction frees the artist or POET from the IMITATION of NATURE, and the vortex is energy changed by the poet or artist into FORM, this form being paradoxically both still and moving. Aside from the work of Pound, *vorticism* had limited influence. The practice of *vorticism* in the graphic arts can best be seen in Lewis's paintings and Henri Gaudier-Brzeska's sculpture.

[References: Timothy Materer, *Vortex: Pound, Eliot, and Lewis* (1979); William C. Wees, *Vorticism and the English Avant-Garde* (1972).]

Vulgate: The word comes from Latin *vulgus,* "crowd," and means "common" or "commonly used." Note two chief uses: (1) the *Vulgate* BIBLE is the Latin version made by Saint Jerome in the fourth century and is the authorized Bible of the Catholic Church; (2) the "*Vulgate* ROMANCES" are the versions of various CYCLES of ARTHURIAN romance written in Old French PROSE (common or colloquial speech) in the thirteenth century and were the most widely used FORMS of these STORIES, forming the basis of Malory's *Le Morte Darthur* and other later treatments. See ARTHURIAN LEGEND.

W

War of the Theaters: A complicated series of quarrels among certain Elizabethan dramatists (1598–1602). Ben Jonson and John Marston were the chief opponents, though many other dramatists, including Dekker certainly and Shakespeare possibly, were concerned. Among the causes of the quarrel were the personal and professional jealousies among some of the playwrights and the keen competition among the rival theaters and their companies of players. Particularly important was the struggle for supremacy between the stock companies of professionals (see PUBLIC THEATERS) and the companies of boy actors, the "Children of the Chapel"—acting at the Blackfriars—and the "Children of Paul's." The child actors were becoming very popular and were threatening to supersede the "common stages," as Shakespeare termed his fellows and himself in his allusion to the situation in *Hamlet* (II, ii). The details of the affair have not been completely recovered by modern students. Some of the PLAYS concerned are: Jonson's *Every Man in his Humour* (1598), Marston's *Histriomastix* (1599) and *Jack Drum's Entertainment* (1600), Dekker and others' *Patient Grissel* (1600), Jonson's *Cynthia's Revels* (1600), and Dekker's *Satiromastix* (1601). Shakespeare's connection with the quarrel is inferred from the statement in the university play *The Return from Parnassus* (1601–1602) that Shakespeare had bested Jonson and from the theory that *Troilus and Cressida* reflects the "war." See SCHOOL PLAYS.

[References: Alfred Harbage, *Shakespeare and the Rival Traditions* (1952); R. B. Sharpe, *The Real War of the Theaters* (1925); R. A. Small, *The Stage-Quarrel Between Ben Jonson and the So-Called Poetaster* (1899).]

Wardour-Street English: A style strongly marked by ARCHAISMS; an insincere, artificial expression. Wardour Street, in London, houses many antique dealers selling genuine and imitation antiques. *Wardour-Street English* is a term coined on the ANALOGY of imitation ARCHAISMS in writing and imitation antiques in furniture. It was, for instance, applied to William Morris's translation of the *Odyssey.* Such writing persists in commerce and journalism with "ye olde," "yclept," "Shoppe," and so forth. Ezra Pound, late in life, dismissed his youthful POETRY as *"Wardour-Street."*

Weak Ending: A syllable at the end of a LINE, with METRICAL ACCENT somewhat in excess of normal or rhetorical ACCENT. These lines from Shakespeare's *Antony and Cleopatra* illustrate *weak ending,* in that "shall" as an auxiliary would not normally be stressed and yet is placed where the METER calls for STRESS:

> Your scutcheons and your signs of conquest shall
> Hang in what place you please.

In this passage from *The Tempest,* "that" and "with" make for *weak endings* (usually, as here, a matter of articles, prepositions, and conjunctions):

Some food we had, and some fresh water, that
A noble Neapolitan, Gonzalo,
Out of his charity, who being then appointed
Master of this design, did give us, with
Rich garments, linens, stuffs, and necessaries,
Which since have steaded much. So, of his gentleness,
Knowing I loved my books, he furnished me
From mine own library with volumes that
I prize above my dukedom.

Well-Made Novel: A NOVEL with a tightly constructed PLOT, a freedom from extraneous INCIDENTS or SUBPLOTS, a clear MOTIVATION for the ACTIONS of its CHARACTERS, and a sense of economy and inevitability in its development. In a *well-made novel* all the necessary parts of the STORY are in a strict causal relation to one another. Despite the fact that such requirements sound mechanical, great NOVELS have been produced that are justifiably called *well-made.* Jane Austen was remarkably successful with the *well-made novel,* and Hawthorne's *The Scarlet Letter* and Emily Brontë's *Wuthering Heights* display a clarity and symmetry of design that qualify them as *well-made.* The qualities of the *well-made novel,* however, more frequently appear in the SHORT NOVEL than in the full-length NOVEL.

Well-Made Play: A term applied to PROBLEM PLAYS, COMEDIES OF MANNERS, and FARCES in the nineteenth century, particularly in France, where the equivalent term was PIÈCE BIEN FAITE, but also in England and America. The term describes the tight, logical construction of these PLAYS, with their apparent inevitability. They usually contained these CONVENTIONS in their STRUCTURE: (1) a PLOT based on a withheld secret that, being revealed at the CLIMAX, produces a favorable REVERSAL for the HERO; (2) a steadily mounting SUSPENSE depending on rising ACTION, exactly timed entrances, mistaken identity, withholding of information from CHARACTERS, misplaced letters and documents, and a battle of wits between HERO and VILLAIN; (3) a CLIMAX culminating in an OBLIGATORY SCENE (SCÈNE À FAIRE) in which the withheld secret is revealed and the REVERSAL of the hero's fortunes achieved; and (4) a logical DÉNOUEMENT. Often this pattern was followed in each of the ACTS as well as in the total PLAY. The chief creator of the *well-made play* was the French dramatist Eugène Scribe; after Scribe the best of the *well-made plays* were by Victorien Sardou. Much French DRAMA of the nineteenth century was influenced by Scribe and Sardou, and their plays were translated and performed with great success in England and America. The popular British playwrights Bulwer-Lytton, Tom Taylor, and T. W. Robertson wrote *well-made plays,* and Henrik Ibsen directed more than twenty Scribe plays in Norway before he launched his own powerfully influential DRAMAS, which incorporate in their STRUCTURE some of the tightly knit characteristics of the *well-made play.*

Welsh Literature: Though records are scanty, it is probable that there was much literary activity in Wales in the early Middle Ages (sixth to ninth centuries). In eastern and central Wales there developed the *englyn,* a form of epigrammatic VERSE possibly derived from Latin literature. The northern district produced the most famous of early Welsh POETS, Taliessin and Aneurin (sixth century?) who sang of early Welsh warriors, including HEROES traditionally associated with King Arthur. This literature is probably related to the Irish. The Western CYCLE deals with very early material, such as MYTHS of the gods. Chiefly from this Western literature come the best-known STORIES of early Welsh authorship, those now collected in the famous MABINOGION. The TALES were probably collected and written down in the eleventh and twelfth centuries, though the manuscripts of the Mabinogion date from a few centuries later. The stories in the Mabinogion fall into five classes. The first is the Mabinogion proper, or the "four branches." It includes four STORIES (the written versions of spoken TALES belonging to the repertory of the lower orders of Welsh BARDS) that preserve primitive tradition: *Pwyll Prince of Dyved, Branwen daughter of Llyr, Manawyddan son of Llyr,* and *Math son of Mathonwy.* The second group includes two TALES based on legendary British historical tradition: *Dream of Macsen Wledig* and *Llud and Llefelys.* The third class, old Arthurian FOLKTALES current in southwest Wales retold by eleventh- or twelfth-century writers with some admixture of other matter, partly Irish, is represented by *Culhwh and Olwen.* This story, of great interest to students of Arthurian ROMANCE, may reflect a very early stage of the development of Arthurian stories, before magic and grotesqueness had been displaced by chivalric manners. The fourth class consists of Arthurian stories paralleled in courtly French versions of the twelfth century (some and perhaps all based partly on the French versions): *Peredur, Gereint, The Lady of the Fountain* (or *Owein*). The fifth class (sophisticated literary TALES) is represented by *The Dream of Rhonabwy.*

Under Gruffydd ab Cynan (1054–1137) there was a renaissance of Welsh POETRY with courtly patronage—the bardic system was now flourishing. These court POETS followed a traditional TECHNIQUE, employing ancient CONVENTIONS and archaic words to such an extent that a contemporary could hardly understand the VERSE. With the English conquest (1282) the old POETRY declined, and in the fourteenth and fifteenth centuries, known as a "golden age," under the leadership of the poet Dafydd ap Gwilym, a contemporary of Chaucer, modern Welsh poetry had its earliest beginnings. The language actually spoken was employed, and love and NATURE were exploited as poetic THEMES. Under the TUDORS the aggressive English influence depressed native Welsh POETRY, though the BARDS remained active till the middle of the seventeenth century. A new school of POETS utilizing native folk materials arose, and in the eighteenth century came the CLASSICAL revival under the influence of the English AUGUSTANS. Poetry in the nineteenth century was largely religious.

The development of PROSE in Wales, as in England, in the sixteenth and seventeenth centuries was fostered by the availability of the printing press and by the vogue of controversial writings, especially those connected with the religious movements of early Protestant times. In the late eighteenth and early nineteenth centuries the liberal movement in politics stimulated further activity in PROSE, and thereafter *Welsh literature,* both prose and poetry, has been inclined to follow general European movements, as has CRITICISM. Coincident with other phases of the CELTIC RENAISSANCE there was a distinct revival of literary activity in the late nineteenth and early twentieth centuries. Although few modern poets of the first rank are speakers of the Welsh language, several have exploited Welsh devices (such as the CYNGHANEDD throughout

Gerard Manley Hopkins's work). Dylan Thomas wrote in English, but a Welsh contour comes through his bardic or VATIC PERSONA and in the gorgeous resonance and complexity of his POETRY.

[References: Thomas Parry, *A History of Welsh Literature* (1955); Gwyn Williams, *An Introduction to Welsh Poetry* (1953); Ifor Williams, *The Beginnings of Welsh Poetry* (1972).]

Westerns: SHORT STORIES and NOVELS laid in the western United States and dealing with the adventurous lives of frontier men and women, Indian fighters, scouts, lumberjacks, loggers, railroad laborers, and cowboys. Western material has been a major source for American ROMANCE since early in the nineteenth century. Cooper's *The Prairie* (1827) has many of the characteristics of the *Western*. *Westerns* were staple fare in the DIME NOVELS and the PULP MAGAZINES, and through these popular mass media *Westerns* passed into the consciousness of the American public. *Westerns* are usually written to a very simple FORMULA, in which the HERO, with gun and horse, defends justice against the threat of the VILLAIN. Within that formula the CHARACTERS are conventionalized and the actions so stylized that they often seem like movements in an intricate dance. A few novelists, like Owen Wister (*The Virginian*, 1902) and Walter van Tilburg Clark (*The Ox-Bow Incident*, 1940), have produced FICTION of substantial literary worth using these materials, but most *Westerns* have been written by prolific writers such as Zane Grey, Max Brand, Ernest Haycox, W. M. Raine, C. E. Mulford, B. M. Bower, and Louis L'Amour. The *Western* became a stock PLOT for low-budget FILMS, and since the advent of television, these STEREOTYPE stories have been among the most common fictional fare of the average American. If out of the American experience there has come a representative action that has the characteristics of a MYTH and expresses in PLOT and CHARACTER the average American's view of the cosmos, it appears to be the *Western*. F. Scott Fitzgerald's unfinished *The Last Tycoon* is a "Hollywood NOVEL," but it is subtitled "A Western"—a reminder that the NARRATOR of *The Great Gatsby* reflects that he, Gatsby, Tom, Daisy, and Jordan are all "Westerners" of some sort; it is significant that he and Gatsby live in West Egg. The finest contemporary Western writing is to be found in the stories of Norman Maclean (who is also one of the CHICAGO CRITICS).

Whimsical: A general term characterizing writing that is fanciful, odd, eccentric. Whimsy, in a sense now obsolete, was used as "a whimsy in the head, or in the blood," implying a sort of vertigo. *Whimsical* writing, then, is writing inspired by a fantastic or fanciful mood. Lamb's ESSAYS are often *whimsical* in this sense.

Widow: In printing, a short line ending a paragraph and appearing at the top of a page or a column. It looks "abandoned" and alone, and printers (including Updike's Rabbit) try to avoid them.

Wisdom Literature: Literature in which routine aesthetic values—PLOT, CHARACTER, and so forth—are subordinate to the direct formulaic expression of moral wisdom and truth. Clearest in scripture like the Book of Proverbs and the *Bhagavad-Gita* but also present in some form in the writing of Samuel Johnson and D. H. Lawrence.

Wit and Humor: Although neither of these words originally was concerned with the laughable, both now find their chief uses in this connection. At present the distinction between the two terms, though generally recognized to exist, is difficult to draw, although there have been numerous attempts at DEFINI-TION. One great "wit" in fact made a witticism out of his observation that any person who attempted to distinguish between *wit* and *humor* thereby demonstrated that he himself possessed neither *wit* (in the sense of superior mental powers) nor *humor* (which implies a sense of proportion and self-evaluation that would show him the difficulty of attempting a cold analysis of so fugitive a thing as *humor*).

Humor is the American spelling of HUMOUR, originally a physiological term that, because of its psychological implications, came to carry the meaning of "eccentric": from this meaning developed the modern implications of the term. *Wit,* meaning originally knowledge, came in the late Middle Ages to signify "intellect," "the seat of consciousness," the "inner" senses as contrasted with the five "outer" senses. The serious side of *"wit"* persists in words like "witless," "halfwit," "dimwit," and "unwitting." In RENAISSANCE times, though used in various senses, *wit* usually meant "wisdom" or "mental activity." An important critical use developed in the seventeenth century when the term, as applied for example to the metaphysical poets (see METAPHYSICAL VERSE), meant "fancy," in the sense of inspiration, ORIGINALITY, or creative IMAGINA-TION—the literary virtues particularly prized at the time. With the coming of NEOCLASSICISM, however, the term took on new meanings to reflect new critical attitudes, and for a hundred years many philosophers (including Hobbes, Locke, and Hume) and CRITICS (including Dryden, Addison, Pope, and Johnson) wrestled with efforts to define *wit.* Hobbes asserted that FANCY without judgment or reason could not constitute *wit,* though judgment without fancy could. Pope used the word in both of the contrasting senses of fancy and judgment. Dryden had called *wit* "propriety of thought and words," and Locke thought of it as an agreeable and prompt assemblage of ideas, an ability to see comparisons (similar to Aristotle's placing of a premium on the aptness of a poet's METAPHORS). Hume stressed the idea that *wit* is what pleases ("good taste" being the criterion). Amid the confusing variety of eighteenth-century uses of the word, this notion of *wit* as a social grace that gives pleasure led to its comparison with *humor,* and before 1800 both words came to be associated with the laughable, though the older, serious meaning of *wit* did not die out, as the earlier meanings of *humor* (both the medical meaning of one of the four liquids of the human body and the derived meaning of "individual disposition" or "eccentricity") had done. A modern *wit* (the usage is an instance of SYNECDOCHE) is distinguished by quickness and brightness, especially in the use of language.

It is for the most part agreed that *wit* is primarily intellectual, the perception of similarities in seemingly dissimilar things—the "swift play and flash of mind"—and is expressed in skillful phraseology, plays on words, surprising contrasts, PARADOXES, EPIGRAMS, comparisons, and so forth, while *humor* implies a sympathetic recognition of human values and deals with the foibles and incongruities of human nature, good-naturedly exhibited. A few quotations from writers who have made serious attempts to distinguish between the two terms may help to clarify the conceptions. *Humor* "deals with incongruities of character and circumstance, as Wit does in those of arbitrary ideas" (Hunt).

"Wit is intensive or incisive, while humor is expansive. Wit is rapid, humor is slow. Wit is sharp, humor is gentle. . . . Wit is subjective while humor is objective. . . . Wit is art, humor is nature" (Carolyn Wells). "Wit apart from Humor, generally speaking, is but an element for professors to sport with. In combination with Humor it runs into the richest utility, and helps to humanize the world" (Hunt). "Humor always laughs, however earnestly it feels, and sometimes chuckles; but it never sniggers" (Saintsbury).

Falstaff in Shakespeare's *King Henry the Fourth*, Part I, is an example of a subtle interweaving of *wit* and *humor.* The verbal fencing, the punning, and particularly the sophistical maneuvering whereby Falstaff invariably extricates himself from difficult situations with an apparent saving of face, rest on his *wit.* Between boast and complaint, Falstaff says, "I am not only witty in myself, but the cause that wit is in other men." On the other hand, the easy recognition on the part of the reader not only that Falstaff is bluffing and is cutting a highly ludicrous figure but also that the old rascal is inwardly laughing at himself, that he sees clearly the incongruities of his situation and behavior and knows that his lies will be recognized as such by the Prince, is an element of *humor.* See HUMOURS, COMEDY, SATIRE.

[References: Louis Cazamanian, *The Development of English Humor* (1930, reprinted 1965); G. K. Chesterton, *Alarms and Discursions* (1910); Max Eastman, *The Sense of Humor* (1921); William Empson, *The Structure of Complex Words* (1951); C. S. Lewis, *Studies in Words* (1961); D. J. Milburn, *The Age of Wit: 1650–1750* (1966); Samuel S. Seward, *The Paradox of the Ludicrous* (1930); Carolyn Wells, *An Outline of Humor* (1923); George Williamson, *The Proper Wit of Poetry* (1961).]

Women as Actors: Although they appeared on the Italian and French stages during the RENAISSANCE, women were not countenanced on the professional stage in England, where boys were specially trained to act women's parts. Some CRITICS have conjectured that Shakespeare, Webster, and other playwrights of the age gave some of their women CHARACTERS—Cordelia, Cleopatra, Juliet, The Duchess of Malfi—an extra dimension of personality and brilliance in compensation for the obvious limitations on the boy actors. There were sporadic cases of the appearance of women on the stage in England, as in the case of the French actresses in London in 1629, but they were unfavorably received. The part of Ianthe in D'Avenant's *Siege of Rhodes* (1656) was played by Mrs. Coleman, and the tradition of English actresses is usually dated from this event. However, this piece was more musical and spectacular than dramatic, and Mrs. Coleman's appearance may have been regarded as justified by the custom of having women (not professional actresses) take parts in MASQUES. With the sudden revival of dramatic activity in 1660, actresses became a permanent feature of the English stage. The influence of the French theater and the lack of a supply of trained boy actors were perhaps chiefly responsible. Boy actors were by no means unknown in feminine roles on the RESTORATION stage, however. Some women who early gained fame as actresses were: Mrs. Barry, Mrs. Betterton, Mrs. Bracegirdle (seventeenth century); and Mrs. Susannah Cibber, Mrs. Oldfield, Mrs. Prichard, and Mrs. Siddons (eighteenth century).

Word Accent: The normal or accepted placement of STRESS on the syllables of a word. See ACCENT, RHETORICAL ACCENT.

Wrenched Accent: An alteration in the customary pronunciation of a word—
that is, a shift in WORD ACCENT—to accommodate the demands of METRICAL
ACCENT in a LINE of VERSE. "Utah," say, is a TROCHEE, but these lines by
Robert Frost impose a RHYME pattern that transforms the word into an IAMB
rather humorously exaggerated:

> Something I saw or thought I saw
> In the desert at midnight in Utah . . .

See ACCENT.

Y

Yellow Journalism: Newspapers and MAGAZINES specializing in scandal and sensation. *Yellow journalism* has flourished robustly all through the twentieth century. (The best explanation of the curious nomenclature here has to do with the notorious *New York World*, in which the "Yellow Kid" cartoon appeared.)

Young Man from the Provinces: A phrase used by Lionel Trilling to describe a kind of NOVEL popular since the eighteenth century, which deals with the experiences of a young provincial in a great city. The last third of Fielding's *Tom Jones* is the story of such a provincial in London, as is Fanny Burney's *Evelina*. Other examples are Stendhal's *The Red and the Black,* Balzac's *Lost Illusions,* Dickens's *Great Expectations,* Flaubert's *Sentimental Education,* Fitzgerald's *The Great Gatsby,* and Thomas Wolfe's *Of Time and the River.* With a twist—the corrupting forces of the city move to the outermost provinces and corrupt a pure savage—the same pattern appears in Aldous Huxley's *Brave New World.*

Z

Zeugma: A term used in several ways, all involving a sort of "yoking": (1) as a SYNONYM of SYLLEPSIS: when an object-taking word (preposition or transitive verb) has two or more objects on different levels, such as concrete and abstract, as in Goldsmith's witty sentence, "I had fancied you were gone down to cultivate matrimony and your estate in the country," wherein figurative and literal senses of the transitive "cultivate" are yoked together by "and"; (2) when two different words that sound exactly alike are yoked together, as in "He bolted the door and his dinner," wherein "bolted" is actually two different concrete verbs; (3) a grammatical irregularity that arises when a conjunction yokes together forms that cannot all be reconciled with other material in the sentence, as in "Either you or he was responsible," wherein the "you" cannot be reconciled with the verb "was." See SLEIGHT OF "AND"; SYLLEPSIS.

Zoom Shot: In filmmaking the shot resulting from the use of a camera lens with an adjustable focal length, so that the viewer appears to move rapidly closer to or farther from an object.

Outline of
Literary History:
English and American

In the following outline English and American literary history has been divided into relatively arbitrary *periods,* and historical subdivisions within these periods are called *ages.* Treatments of these units are given in the *Handbook,* where brief essays on the *periods* and shorter comment on the *ages* appear among the alphabetic listings.

Beginning with the year 1607 American items appear in a separate column.

Titles are often abbreviated or modernized to forms commonly encountered by the student. Translated titles appear in quotation marks in the early periods.

Dates of printed books are ordinarily the dates of first publication. Dates for works written before the era of printing are dates of composition, often approximate.

The following abbreviations and symbols are used:

?	questionable date or statement of fact
*	non-English item
w	written
a	acted
ca.	*circa,* around, about: dating is approximate
fl.	flourishing, or flourished
et. seq.	and following
Lat.	Latin
A.S.	Anglo-Saxon
MS	manuscript
estab.	established

? B.C.–A.D. 428 Celtic and Roman Britain

? B.C.–A.D. 82	Celtic Britain
55, 54 B.C.	Julius Caesar invades Britain.
A.D. 43–410	Roman-Celtic period in Britain: government Roman, population largely Celtic. No literature extant.
43	Invasion of Claudius.
ca. 85	Roman power established in Britain.
98	*Tacitus, *Germania* (Lat.): early account of Teutonic ancestors of English.
313	*Christianity established at Rome by Constantine.
410	*Rome sacked by Alaric.
	Roman legions leave Britain.

428–1100 Old English (Anglo-Saxon) Period

ca. 428	Germanic tribes begin invasion of Britain
449	Traditional date (from Gildas and Bede) for Germanic invasion of Britain under Hengist and Horsa.

ca. 450–*ca.* 700	Probable period of composition of Old English poems reflecting Continental life: *Beowulf,* epic; *Waldhere,* fragmentary epic of Theodoric saga; *Finnsburg,* fragmentary, related to *Beowulf* background; *Widsith,* lyric, adventures of a wandering poet; *Deor's Lament,* lyric account of poet's troubles; *The Wanderer,* reflective poem on cruelty of fate; *The Seafarer,* reflective, descriptive lyric on sailor's lot in life; *The Wife's Complaint, The Husband's Message:* love poems notable for romantic treatment of nature; *Charms,* miscellaneous incantations reflecting early superstitions, ceremonies, and remedies; formulistic.
ca. 500–*ca.* 700	*Christian culture flourishes in Ireland after being almost obliterated on Continent by Teutonic invasion; activity of Irish missionaries in Scotland, Iceland, France, Germany, Switzerland, and Italy aids in rechristianizing Western Europe.
ca. 524	*Böethius, "Consolation of Philosophy" (Lat.); translated into English, successively, by King Alfred, Chaucer, and Queen Elizabeth.
563	St. Columba (Irish Monk) establishes monastery at Iona, thus preparing for spread of Celtic Christianity in Scotland and northern England.
597	Saint Augustine (the missionary) places Roman Christianity on firm basis in southern England.
600–700	Establishment of powerful Anglo-Saxon kingdoms.
ca. 600–*ca.* 800	*Irish saga literature assumes written form.
ca. 633	*The Koran; texts recorded; canonical version, 651–52.
640?–709	Aldhelm: famous scholar of Canterbury school—Latin works survive; English poems (probably ballads) lost.
664	Synod of Whitby: triumph of Roman over Celtic Christianity in Britain.
ca. 670	Caedmon, *Hymns,* etc.: first English poet known by name.
ca. 690	Adamnan, *Life of St. Columba* (Lat.): first biography in Britain.
ca. 700	"School of Caedmon" *fl.:* Genesis, Exodus, Daniel—Biblical paraphrases; Judith, apocryphal.
	Beowulf composed in present form: great A.S. epic.
731	Bede (Baeda) the Venerable, "Ecclesiastical History" (Lat.): first history of English people.

750

ca. 750–*ca.* 800	Flourishing period of Christian poetry in Northumbria (preserved in later West Saxon versions).
	Cynewulf and his "school": *Crist,* narrative; *Elene, Juliana, Fates of the Apostles, Andreas,* saints' legends. *The Phoenix,* myth interpreted as Christian allegory.
787	First Danish invasion.
ca. 800	Nennius (a Welshman), "History of the Britons" (Lat): first mention of Arthur.

850

ca. 850	Danish conquest of England.
871–899	Reign of Alfred the Great. Alfred's translations of Pope Gregory's *Pastoral Care,* Böethius, Orosius, Bede; *Anglo-Saxon Chronicle* revised and continued to 892; West Saxon *Martyrology;* sermons; saints' lives.

ca. 875–900	*Probable beginnings of medieval drama. Dramatization of liturgy. First known text an Easter trope, *Queen Quaeritis,* from Swiss monastery of St. Gall.
878	Peace of Wedmore; partial Danish evacuation.
893	Asser, *Life of Alfred the Great:* "first life-record of a layman."
901–1066	Later Old English Period. *Chronicle* continued; poetry, sermons, Biblical translations and paraphrases, saints' lives, lyrics.
ca. 937	*Battle of Brunanburh:* heroic poem.
ca. 950	*Junius* MS written: contains "School of Caedmon" poems.
950–1000	Monastic revival under Dunstan, Aethelwold, and Aelfric.
971	*Blickling Homilies:* colloquial tendencies.
ca. 975	St. Aethelwold's *Regularis Concordia:* earliest evidence of dramatic activity in England.
979–1016	Second period of Danish invasions.
ca. 991	*Battle of Maldon:* heroic poem.

1000

1000–1200	Transition period, English to Norman French. Decline of A.S. heroic verse; reduced literary activity in English.
ca. 1000	A.S. *Gospels* written. Aelfric, *Sermons.*
	Beowulf MS written.
ca. 1000–1025	The *Exeter Book:* A.S. MS containing Cynewulf poems.
ca. 1000–1100	*Vercelli Book:* A.S. MS containing *Andreas,* etc.
	*Probable period of full development of Christmas and Easter cycles of plays in Western Europe.
1017–1042	Danish kings (Canute to Hardicanute).
1042–1066	Saxon kings restored (Edward the Confessor to Harold II).
1066	Battle of Senlac (Hastings). Norman Conquest.
1066–1154	Norman kings (William I to Stephen).
1086	*Domesday Book:* important English census.
1087–1100	William II: centralization of kingdom.
1096–1099	The First Crusade.

1100–1350 Anglo-Norman Period

1100–1200	*French literature dominating Western Europe.
1100–1135	Reign of Henry I ("Beauclerc").
ca. 1100–1250	*Icelandic sagas written: *Grettirsaga, Volsungsaga,* etc.
ca. 1100	"Play of St. Catherine" (*a.* at Dunstable): first recorded "miracle" or saint's play in England.
	*Earlier tales in Welsh *Mabinogion* (*w*).
	*Great period of French poetry begins. *Chanson de Roland:* French epic.
ca. 1124	Eadmer, *Life of Anselm:* human element in biography.
ca. 1125	Henry of Huntingdon and William of Malmesbury: chronicles.
ca. 1125–1300	Latin chronicles *fl.*

1135–1154	Reign of Stephen.
ca. 1136	Geoffrey of Monmouth, "History of the Kings of Britain" (Lat. chronicle). First elaborate account of Arthurian court.

1150

1154	End of entries in *A.S. Chronicle* (Peterborough).
1154–1399	Plantagenet kings (Henry II to Richard II).
1154–1189	Reign of Henry II: his court a center of literature and learning—historians, philosophers, theologians, poets.
ca. 1170	*Poema Morale.*
ca. 1185–1190	*Giraldus Cambrensis, "Itinerary": description of Wales.
1189–1199	Reign of Richard I ("The Lion-hearted").
ca. 1190	Nigel Wireker, *Speculum stultorum* (Lat.), "The Fool's Looking-glass."
1199–1216	Reign of John.

1200

ca. 1200	Walter Map *fl.:* court satirist.
	Orm, *Ormulum:* scriptural poem.
ca. 1200–1225	*The Vulgate Romances (expansion of Arthurian romance material in French prose).
ca. 1200–1250	*King Horn, Beves of Hamptom* (earliest form): English metrical romances using English themes.
ca. 1205	Layamon, *Brut.*
1215	*Magna Charta.*
1216–1272	Reign of Henry III.
ca. 1225	*St. Thomas Aquinas born. Died 1274.
ca. 1230, ca. 1270	*Roman de la Rose* by Guillaume de Lorris and Jean de Meun.

1250

ca. 1250	Nicholas of Guilford, *The Owl and the Nightingale.* The "Cuckoo Song" (*Sumer is Icumen in*).
ca. 1250	*Gesta Romanorum.*
ca. 1250–1300	*Sir Tristem, Floris and Blanchefleur* (romances).
1258	Henry III uses English as well as French in proclamation.
1265	*Dante born. Died 1321.
1272–1307	Reign of Edward I.
ca. 1294	*Dante, *Vita Nuova.*

1300

1300–1400	English displaces French in speech of upper classes and in schools and law pleadings. Mystery plays now in hands of guilds: more actors, more spectators, outdoor stages, comic elements, "cyclic" development (York plays probably oldest existing cycle).
ca. 1300	*Marco Polo, "Travels."
	Cursor Mundi.
ca. 1300–1350	*Guy of Warwick, Havelok the Dane, Richard Lionheart, Amis and Amiloun:* romances.

ca. 1307–1321	*Dante's *Divina Commedia.*
1304	*Petrarch born. Died 1374.
1307–1327	Reign of Edward II.
1311	Feast of Corpus Christi, established in 1264, was made operative, leading to popularization of cyclic plays at this summer festival and perhaps to use of movable stages or "pageants."
1313	*Boccaccio born. Died 1375.
1314	Battle of Bannockburn.
1327–1377	Reign of Edward III.
1328(?)	Chester cycle of plays composed.
1337–1453	The Hundred Years' War.
ca. 1340	Geoffrey Chaucer born. Died 1400.
	The Prick of Conscience.
1342	*Boccaccio, *Ameto:* "first pastoral romance."
1346	Battle of Crécy.
1348–1350	The Black Death in England.

1350–1500 Middle English Period

1350–1400	*Sir Eglamour, Morte Arthure, Sir Gawayne and the Green Knight, Athelston, William of Palerne, Sir Ferumbras, Sir Isumbras,* and other romances.
ca. 1350	*Petrarch, eclogues (Lat.), printed 1504. "Sonnets to Laura" partly written.
	*Boccaccio, *Decameron.*
1356(?)	"Sir John Mandeville," *Voyage and Travels.*
ca. 1360	*The Pearl.*
1362	English language used in court pleadings and in opening Parliament.
ca. 1362 *et seq.*	*Piers Plowman.*
ca. 1370	Chaucer, *The Book of the Duchess.*
ca. 1375	Barbour, *Bruce.*
	"Paternoster" and "Creed" plays (*a*): forerunners of morality plays.
1377–1399	Richard II.
ca. 1379	Chaucer, *House of Fame.*
ca. 1380	Wycliffe and others, translation of Bible into English.
1381	Wat Tyler's rebellion.
ca. 1383	Chaucer, *Troilus and Criseyde.*
ca. 1385	English replaces French as language of the schools.
	Chaucer, *Legend of Good Women.*
ca. 1387	Chaucer, "Prologue" to *Canterbury Tales* (tales themselves written, some earlier, some later).
ca. 1388	Usk, *The Testament of Love.*
ca. 1390	Gower, *Confessio Amantis.*
1399–1461	House of Lancaster (Henry IV to Henry VI).

1399–1413	Reign of Henry IV.
1400	Death of Chaucer.

1400

1400–1450	Later romances in prose and verse.
1400	*Froissart, *Chronicles.*
1400–1425	Wakefield cycle of plays (MS, *ca.* 1450).
	The Pride of Life (fragmentary): earliest extant morality play.
ca. 1405	*Castle of Perseverance;* first complete morality play.
ca. 1412	Hoccleve, *The Regiment of Princes* (*w*).
1413–1422	Reign of Henry V.
1415	Battle of Agincourt.
ca. 1415	Lydgate, *Troy Book.*
1422–1461	Reign of Henry VI.
1422–1509	The *Paston Letters:* family correspondence reflecting social conditions.
ca. 1425	Humanists active under patronage of Humphrey, Duke of Gloucester: Lydgate, Pecock, etc.
1440	Galfridus Grammaticus, *Promptorium Parvulorum:* English-Latin word-list, beginning of English lexicography.

1450

1450	Jack Cade's rebellion.
ca. 1450	"Tiptoft" School of humanists active.
	*Gutenberg press: beginning of modern printing.
	Beginning of Lowland Scotch as northern literary dialect.
ca. 1450–1525	Scottish poets of Chaucerian school: Henryson, Dunbar, Douglas, and probably King James I of Scotland.
1453	*Fall of Constantinople: end of Eastern Empire.
1455–1485	Wars of the Roses: depressing effect on literary activity.
1456	*The Gutenberg Bible.
ca. 1460	John Skelton born. Died 1529.
1461–1485	House of York (Edward IV to Richard III).
1461–1483	Reign of Edward IV.
1469	Sir Thomas Malory completes composition of *Le Morte Darthur* (pub. 1485).
ca. 1474	Caxton prints (at Bruges) the *Recuyell of the Histories of Troy:* first book printed in English.
ca. 1477	Caxton's press set up at Westminster: first printing press in England. *Dictes and Sayings of the Philosophers,* the first dated book (1477) printed in England.
1478	Sir Thomas More born. Died 1535.
1483	Reign of Edward V.
1483–1485	Reign of Richard III.
1485	Caxton publishes Malory's *Le Morte Darthur.*

1485–1603	House of Tudor (Henry VII to Elizabeth).
1485–1509	Reign of Henry VII.
1490–1520	"Oxford Reformers" (Linacre, Grocyn, Colet, Erasmus, More) active.
1491	Greek taught at Oxford.
1492	*Discovery of America by Columbus.
ca. 1497	Medwall, *Fulgens and Lucres* (a).
1499	Erasmus in England.

1500–1660 The Renaissance

1500–1557 Early Tudor Age

ca. 1500	*Everyman.*
1500–1550	Romances: *Valentine and Orson,* Lord Berners' *Arthur of Little Britain, Huon of Bordeaux,* etc.
1503 (?)	Sir Thomas Wyatt born. Died 1542.
ca. 1508	Skelton, *Philip Sparrow.*
1509–1547	Reign of Henry VIII.
1509	Barclay, *Ship of Fools.*
	Hawes, *Pastime of Pleasure.*
	*Erasmus, "The Praise of Folly" (Lat.) (w), social satire.
1510	Acting of Terence's comedies becomes an established practice at Oxford and Cambridge.
1515	Roger Ascham born. Died 1568.
1516	More, *Utopia* (Lat.).
ca. 1516	*Ariosto, *Orlando Furioso.*
	Skelton, *Magnificence.*
1517	*Luther posts his theses in Wittenberg; leads to Protestant Revolution, 1520 *et seq.*
ca. 1517	Henry Howard, Earl of Surrey born. Died 1547.
1519	Rastell, *The Four Elements:* first published interlude. Advocates adequacy of English for literary purposes.
	*Cortez conquers Mexico.
ca. 1520	Skelton's poetical satires (*Colin Clout, Why Come Ye Not to Court,* etc.).
1520–1530	Latin plays acted in grammar schools.
1523	Lord Berners' trans. of Froissart's *Chronicles.*

1525

1525	Tyndale, *New Testament:* printed at Worms; first printed English translation of any part of Bible.
1528	*Castiglione, *The Courtier.*
1529	Simon Fish, *Supplication for the Beggars.*
	Fall of Wolsey.
ca. 1530	The "New Poetry" movement under way.

ca. 1530–1540	Heywood's "Interludes": realistic farce.
1531	Elyot, *The Boke Named the Governour.*
1532	*Machiavelli, *The Prince* (*w* 1513).
	*Rabelais, *Pantagruel.*
1533	Separation of English church from Rome.
	John Leland made "King's Antiquary."
1534	Act of Supremacy: Henry VIII head of Church of England.
1535	Execution of More.
	Coverdale's first complete English Bible.
1536	Execution of Tyndale.
	*Calvin, *Institutes of Christian Religion* (Lat.).
1538	Sir Thomas Elyot, *Dictionarie.*
1539	English Bible (the "Great Bible") published.
1540	Lyndsay, *Satyre of the Three Estaits.*
1542	Death of Wyatt.
	Hall's *Chronicle.*
1542 (?)	George Gascoigne born. Died 1577.
1545	Ascham, *Toxophilus.*
	*Council of Trent.
1547	Execution of Surrey.
1547–1553	Reign of Edward VI.
1549–1552	*Book of Common Prayer.*

1550

ca. 1552	Edmund Spenser born. Died 1599.
	Sir Walter Ralegh born. Died 1618.
	Udall, *Ralph Roister Doister* (*w*): first "regular" English comedy.
1553	Wilson, *Arte of Rhetorique.*
1553–1558	Reign of Mary.
1554	Sir Philip Sidney born. Died 1586.
ca. 1555	Roper, *Life of Sir Thomas More* (*w*).
	Cavendish, *Life of Cardinal Wolsey* (*w*).
1557	*Songs and Sonnets* ("Tottel's Miscellany"), containing Surrey's trans. of two books of the *Aeneid* in blank verse.
	North's trans. of Guevara's *Dial of Princes.*
	Stationer's Company incorporated.

	1558–1603 Elizabethan Age
1558–1603	Reign of Elizabeth.
1558	John Knox, *First Blast of the Trumpet against the Monstrous Regiment of Women.*
1558–1575	Translations numerous; classics often translated into English through French versions. Much interest in lyrics.

1559	Elizabethan Prayer-book.
	The Mirror for Magistrates.
	*Amyot, Plutarch's *Lives* translated into French: basis of North's English version of Plutarch.
	*Minturno, *De Poeta:* Italian critical work.
1559 (?)	George Chapman born. Died 1634.
ca. 1560	*Gammer Gurton's Needle* (*w*).
1561	Hoby's translation of Castiglione's *The Courtier.*
	Francis Bacon born. Died 1626.
	*Scaliger, *Poetics:* Italian critical work.
1562	Sackville and Norton, *Gorboduc* (*a*): first English tragedy.
	Samuel Daniel born. Died 1619.
1563	Foxe, *Book of Martyrs* (Lat. original, 1559).
	Sackville's "Induction" (to portion of *Mirror for Magistrates*).
	Michael Drayton born. Died 1631.
ca. 1563	Sir Humphrey Gilbert, *Queen Elizabeth's Academy.*
1564	Preston, *Cambises* (*a*).
1564	Christopher Marlowe born. Died 1593.
	William Shakespeare born. Died 1616.
	*Galileo born. Died 1642.
1565–1567	Golding's translation of Ovid's *Metamorphoses.*
1566	Gascoigne's *Supposes* (*a*) and *Jocasta* (*a*).
1566–1567	Painter, *Palace of Pleasure.*
1567	Turberville, *Epitaphs, Epigrams, Songes, and Sonets.*
1570	Ascham, *Schoolmaster.*
ca. 1573	John Donne born. Died 1631.
	Ben Jonson born. Died 1637.

1575

1575	Gascoigne, *The Posies:* poems with first English treatise on versification appended.
	Mystery plays still being acted at Chester.
1576	*Paradise of Dainty Devices.*
	The Theatre (first London playhouse) built.
	Gascoigne, *The Steel Glass.*
	George Pettie, *A Petite Palace of Pettie his Pleasure.*
1576–1580	Spenser's early poetry (*w*).
1577	Holinshed, *Chronicles.*
	A Gorgeous Gallery of Gallant Inventions: poetical miscellany.
1577–1580	Drake circumnavigates globe.
1579	Lyly, *Euphues, the Anatomy of Wit.*
	Spenser, *The Shepheardes Calendar* (pub. anonymously).
	Gosson, *School of Abuse:* attack on poetry and the stage.

	North, trans. of Plutarch's *Lives.*
	John Fletcher born. Died 1625.
1580	*Montaigne, *Essays:* beginning of modern "personal" essay.
1580–1600	Elizabethan "novels" popular: Lyly, Greene, Lodge, Sidney, Nash, Deloney. Pastoral poetry popular.
ca. 1581	Peele, *Arraignment of Paris* (*a*).
	Sidney, *Defence of Poesie* (*w*) (pub. 1595).
1582	Stanyhurst, trans. of Virgil's *Aeneid* (i–iv) in quantitative verse.
1582–1600	Hakluyt publishes various collections of "voyages"—Renaissance and medieval, notably *Principal Navigations* (1st ed. 1589).
1583	P. Stubbs, *Anatomie of Abuses.*
ca. 1583	Lyly, *Alexander and Campaspe* (*a*).
1584	Scot, *Discovery of Witchcraft.*
	Handful of Pleasant Delights: ballad miscellany.
1585–1586	Ralegh fails in effort to colonize Virginia.
1586	Kyd, *The Spanish Tragedy* (*a*).
	Warner, *Albion's England.*
	Camden, *Britannia* (Lat.).
	Death of Sidney.
1586 (?)	Shakespeare comes to London.
1587	Marlowe, *Tamburlaine* (*a*).
	Execution of Mary Queen of Scots.
1588	Defeat of Spanish Armada.
ca. 1588	Marlowe, *Doctor Faustus* (*a*).
1588–1589	"Martin Marprelate" papers.
1589	Greene, *Menaphon.*
	Puttenham (?), *The Arte of English Poesie.*

1590

1590	Lodge, *Rosalynde.*
	Sidney, *Arcadia* (*w ca.* 1581).
	Spenser, *Faerie Queene,* Books I–III.
ca. 1590	Greene (?), *James IV* (*a*).
	Shakespeare begins career as playwright, with *The Comedy of Errors.*
1591	Spenser, *Complaints:* includes *Mother Hubberd's Tale.*
	Harrington, trans. of Ariosto's *Orlando Furioso.*
	Sidney, *Astrophel and Stella.*
	Robert Herrick born. Died 1674.
1591–1596	Sonnet cycles: Sidney, Daniel, Drayton, Lodge, Spenser, and others.
1592–1593	Shakespeare, *Richard III* (*a*).

1593	Shakespeare, *Venus and Adonis.*
	Phoenix Nest: poetical miscellany.
	Death of Marlowe.
	Izaak Walton born. Died 1683.
	George Herbert born. Died 1633.
1594	Hooker, *Ecclesiastical Polity,* Books I–IV.
	Shakespeare, *Rape of Lucrece.*
	Nash, *The Unfortunate Traveler:* picaresque romance.
1595	Spenser, *Amoretti; Epithalamion.*
	Sidney, *Defence of Poesie* (*w ca.* 1581).
	Daniel, *Civil Wars.*
	Lodge, *A Fig for Momus.*
	Donne's poetry circulating in manuscript.
1595	Shakespeare, *Midsummer Night's Dream* (*a*).
1596	Ralegh, *Discovery of Guiana* (*w*) (pub. 1606).
	Shakespeare, *Romeo and Juliet* (*a*).
	Spenser, *Faerie Queene,* Books IV–VI.
1597	Shakespeare, *Merchant of Venice* (*a*).
	Drayton, *Heroical Epistles.*
	Bacon, *Essays* (1st ed.).
	Hall, *Virgidemiarum,* Vol. I.
	King James (of Scotland), *Demonology:* answers Scot and defends reality of witchcraft.
1597–1600	Shakespeare's Falstaff plays (*a*): *Henry IV,* 1, 2; *Henry V; Merry Wives of Windsor.*
1598	Shakespeare, *Julius Caesar* (*a*).
	Meres, *Palladis Tamia,* "Wit's Treasury."
	Ben Jonson begins career as playwright—*Everyman in His Humour* (*a*).
	Chapman, translation of *Iliad* (seven books in fourteeners).
ca. 1598	Deloney, *The Gentle Craft.*
1598–1600	Shakespeare's "joyous comedies": *Much Ado about Nothing; As You Like It; Twelfth Night.*
1599	*The Passionate Pilgrim:* miscellany containing some of Shakespeare's poems.
	Globe theater built: used by Shakespeare's company.
	Death of Spenser.

1600

1600	*England's Helicon:* poetical miscellany.
1601	Shakespeare, *Hamlet* (*a*).
1602	Campion, *Observations in the Art of English Poesie.*
	Founding of the Bodleian Library (Oxford).
ca. 1602	Daniel, *Defence of Ryme.*

1602–1604	Shakespeare, the "bitter comedies": *Troilus and Cressida, All's Well That Ends Well, Measure for Measure* (a).

1603–1625 Jacobean Age

1603–1688	The Stuarts.
1603–1625	Reign of James I: union of English and Scottish crowns.
1603	T. Heywood, *A Woman Killed with Kindness* (a).
	Jonson, *Sejanus* (a).
	Florio, translation of Montaigne.
1604	Shakespeare, *Othello* (a).
1605	Bacon, *Advancement of Learning*.
	Gunpowder Plot.
	*Cervantes, *Don Quixote*, Part I.
	Sir Thomas Browne born. Died 1682.
	Shakespeare, *Macbeth* (a), *King Lear* (a).
1606	Jonson, *Volpone* (a).
	Sir William D'Avenant borne. Died 1668.

ENGLISH

AMERICAN

1607–1765 Colonial Period

	ENGLISH	AMERICAN
1607	Shakespeare, *Antony and Cleopatra* (a).	Settlement at Jamestown, Virginia.
	Beaumont and Fletcher, *Knight of the Burning Pestle* (a).	
1608	John Milton born. Died 1674.	Capt. John Smith, *True Relation:* early experiences in Virginia.
	Joseph Hall, *Characters of Virtues and Vices*.	
1609	Shakespeare, *Sonnets* (w earlier).	Champlain discovers Lake Champlain.
	Beaumont and Fletcher, *Philaster* (a).	Henry Hudson explores Hudson River.
	Dekker, *Gull's Hornbook*.	

1610

	ENGLISH	AMERICAN
1609–1611	Shakespeare, tragicomedies: *Cymberline, Winter's Tale, Tempest* (a).	
1610	Jonson, *Alchemist* (a).	Strachey, *True Repertory*.
1611	King James translation of the Bible.	
ca. 1611	Shakespeare returns to Stratford.	

	ENGLISH	AMERICAN
1612	Bacon, *Essays* (2nd ed.).	Capt. John Smith, *A Map of Virginia*.
	Donne, First and Second *Anniversaries*.	
	Samuel Butler born. Died 1680.	Anne Bradstreet born (in England). Died 1672.
1613	*Purchas His Pilgrimage:* travel literature.	
	Wither, *Abuses Stript and Whipt*.	
1614	Overbury, *Characters*.	
	Ralegh, *History of the World*.	
	Webster, *Duchess of Malfi* (*a*).	
1614–1616	Chapman, Odyssey translated.	
1615	Harrington, *Epigrams*.	
1616	Deaths of Shakespeare and *Cervantes.	Capt. John Smith, *A Description of New England*.
1618	Ralegh executed.	
	Harvey discovers circulation of the blood.	
	Abraham Cowley born. Died 1667.	
1619	Drayton, *Collected Poems*.	First American legislative assembly, at Jamestown.
	Death of Daniel.	Negro slavery introduced into Virginia.

1620

	ENGLISH	AMERICAN
1620	Bacon, *Novum Organum* (Lat.).	Pilgrims land at Plymouth. *Mayflower Compact* (*w*).
1621	Burton, *Anatomy of Melancholy*.	
1622	Donne, *Sermon on Judges xx.* 15 (other sermons published in 1623, 1624, 1625, 1626, 1627, and later.)	George Sandys completes translation of Ovid's *Metamorphoses*.
		Mourts' *Relation* by Bradford and others: journal.
1623	First Folio edition of Shakespeare's plays.	
1624		Capt. John Smith, *General History of Virginia*.
		Edward Winslow, *Good News out of New England*.

ENGLISH   AMERICAN
1625–1649 Caroline Age

1625

	ENGLISH	AMERICAN
1625–1649	Reign of Charles I.	
1625	Bacon, *Essays,* final edition.	Morrell, *Nova Anglia.*
1626	Death of Bacon.	Minuit founds New Amsterdam.
1627	Bacon, *New Atlantis* (Lat.): fragmentary "utopia."	Thomas Morton sets up Maypole at Merrymount: reflects opposition to Puritans.
	Drayton, *Battle of Agincourt.*	
1628	John Bunyan born. Died 1688.	
1629	Ford, *The Broken Heart* (*a*).	
	Milton, *Ode on the Morning of Christ's Nativity* (*w*).	

1630

1630	Milton, *On Shakespeare* (*w*).	Massachusetts Bay Colony established at Salem.
1630–1647		Bradford, *History of the Plymouth Plantation* (*w*).
1630–1649		Winthrop, *History of New England* (*w*).
1631	Deaths of Drayton and Donne.	
	John Dryden born. Died 1700.	
1632	Second Folio edition of Shakespeare.	Thomas Hooker, *The Soul's Preparation.*
1633	Herbert, *The Temple.* Donne, *Poems* (first collected edition).	
	Phineas Fletcher, *The Purple Island.*	
1633 (?)	Milton's *L'Allegro* and *Il Penseroso* written.	
	Samuel Pepys born. Died 1703.	
1634	Milton, *Comus* (*a*).	Maryland settled by English.
	D'Avenant, *The Temple of Love:* French Platonic love.	Connecticut Valley settled.
	Death of George Chapman.	
1635	Quarles, *Emblems.*	
1636	*Corneille, *The Cid.*	Roger Williams founds Providence, all sects tolerated.
		Harvard College founded.

	ENGLISH	AMERICAN
1637	Death of Jonson.	Pequót War.
	*Descartes, *Discours sur la Méthode*.	Thomas Morton, *New English Canaan*.
1638	Milton, *Lycidas*.	
1639		First printing press in America set up at Cambridge.
		Increase Mather born. Died 1723.

1640

	ENGLISH	AMERICAN
1640	Jonson, *Timber, or Discoveries Made upon Men and Matter*.	*Bay Psalm Book:* first book printed in America.
	Izaak Walton, *Life of Donne*.	
1641	Aphra Behn born. Died 1689.	Shepard, *The Sincere Convert*.
1642	Fuller, *Holy State*.	
	Denham, *Cooper's Hill*.	
	Sir Thomas Browne, *Religio Medici*.	
	Sir Isaac Newton born. Died 1727.	
	Civil War. Theaters closed.	
1644	Milton, *Areopagitica*.	Roger Williams, *Bloody Tenent of Persecution*.
	Milton, *Tractate on Education* and divorce pamphlets.	Roger Williams visits Milton; teaches him Dutch.
1645	Howell, *Familiar Letters*.	
	Waller, *Poems*.	
	Founding of Philosophical Society.	
ca. 1645		Edward Taylor born. Died 1729. *Poems,* posthumously pub. 1939.
1646	Vaughan, *Poems*.	
1647		Nathaniel Ward, *Simple Cobbler of Aggawam*.
1648	Herrick, *Hesperides*.	
	1649–1660 Commonwealth Interregnum	
1649	Execution of Charles I.	
	Lovelace, *Lucasta*.	

1650

	ENGLISH	AMERICAN
1650	D'Avenant, *Gondibert*.	Anne Bradstreet, *The Tenth Muse, Lately Sprung up in America*.
	Taylor, *Holy Living*.	

	ENGLISH	AMERICAN
ca. 1650	Many French romances and novels translated into English.	
1650–1728		Flourishing of the "Mather Dynasty."
1651	Milton, *Defence of the English People* (Lat.).	*Cambridge Platform* passed by General Court.
	Hobbes, *Leviathan*.	
1652	"Quaker" Movement culminating.	
1653	Walton, *The Compleat Angler*.	
1654	Boyle, *Parthenissa*.	Capt. Edward Jonson, *Wonder-Working Providence*.
1656	Cowley, *Poems, Davideis, Pindaric Odes*.	Hammond, *Leah and Rachel, or The Two Fruitful Sisters, Virginia and Maryland*.
	D'Avenant, *Siege of Rhodes* (*a*).	
		Quakers arrive in Massachusetts.
1658	Dryden, *Stanzas on the Death of Cromwell*.	
1659		John Eliot, *The Christian Commonwealth*.

1660–1798 Neo-Classical Period

1660–1700 Restoration Age

	ENGLISH	AMERICAN
1660–1714	Stuarts restored (Charles II to Anne).	
1660–1685	Reign of Charles II.	
1660	Dryden, *Astraea Redux:* welcomes Charles II.	
ca. 1660	Daniel Defoe born. Died 1731.	
1660–1669	Pepys's *Diary* (*w*) (pub. 1825).	
1660–1700		Verse elegies popular.
1661	Anne Finch, Countess of Winchilsea, born. Died 1720.	
1662	Fuller, *Worthies of England*.	Wigglesworth, *Day of Doom*.
	The Royal Society founded as reorganization of the Philosophical Society.	"Half-Way Covenant": lowers requirements for church membership in Massachusetts.
1663	Butler, *Hudibras*, Part I.	Eliot translates Bible into Indian language.

	ENGLISH	AMERICAN
	Drury Lane Theatre (first called Theatre Royal) built.	Cotton Mather born. Died 1728.
1664	Dryden and Howard, *The Indian Queen* (a).	
1665	Dryden, *The Indian Emperor.*	Baptist Church established in Boston.
	Head, *The English Rogue.*	
1666	Bunyan, *Grace Abounding.*	George Alsop, *A Character of the Province of Maryland.*
1667	Jonathan Swift born. Died 1745.	
1667	Sprat, *History of the Royal Society.*	
	Milton, *Paradise Lost.*	
1668	Sprat, *Life of Cowley:* starts tradition of "discreet" biography.	
	Dryden, *Essay of Dramatic Poesy.*	

1670

1670	Dryden, *Conquest of Granada* (a).	Denton, *Brief Description of New York.*
	Dryden made Poet Laureate.	Mason, *Pequót War* (w) (pub. 1736).
1671	Milton, *Paradise Regained* and *Samson Agonistes.*	Eliot, *Progress of the Gospel Among the Indians in New England.*
	Villiers (Buckingham) and others, *The Rehearsal* (a).	
1672	Joseph Addison born. Died 1719.	Eliot, *The Logick Primer:* "for the use of praying Indians."
	Sir Richard Steele born. Died 1729.	
1673		Increase Mather, *Woe to Drunkards.*
1674	Wycherley, *The Plain-Dealer* (a).	
	Death of Milton and Herrick.	
1674–1729		Samuel Sewall, *Diary* (w).
1676	Etheredge, *The Man of Mode.*	
1677		Urian Oakes, *Elegy on Thomas Shepard.*
1678	Bunyan, *Pilgrim's Progress,* Part I.	
	Dryden, *All for Love.*	
	Popish Plot.	

ENGLISH | AMERICAN

1680

	ENGLISH	AMERICAN
1680		*The Burwell Papers* (*w*).
1681	Dryden, *Absalom and Achitophel.*	
1682	Otway, *Venice Preserved.*	Penn settles Pennsylvania.
	Dryden, *MacFlecknoe.*	La Salle explores Mississippi.
		Mary Rowlandson, *Narrative of the Captivity* (*w*): life among the Indians.
1683		Increase Mather, *Discourse Concerning Comets.*
1684		Increase Mather, *Illustrious Providences.*
1685		Cotton Mather, *Memorable Providences.*
1685–1688	Reign of James II.	
1687	Sir Isaac Newton, *Principia* (Lat.).	Church of England worship established in Boston.
	Dryden, *The Hind and the Panther.*	
1688	The "Bloodless Revolution."	
	Death of Bunyan.	
	Alexander Pope born. Died 1744.	
	Aphra Behn, *Oroonoko.*	
1689–1702	Reign of William and Mary.	
1689	Lady Mary Wortley Montagu born. Died 1762.	
	Samuel Richardson born. Died 1761.	

1690

	ENGLISH	AMERICAN
1690	Locke, *Essay Concerning the Human Understanding.*	
1691	Dunton, *Athenian Gazette.*	(or earlier) *New England Primer.*
1692	Sir William Temple, *Essays.*	Salem witchcraft executions.
1693		Cotton Mather, *Wonders of the Invisible World.*
1694	Wotton, *Reflections upon Ancient and Modern Learning.*	
1695	Congreve, *Love for Love.*	
1696	Toland, *Christianity not Mysterious.*	
1697	Dryden, *Alexander's Feast.*	

	ENGLISH	AMERICAN
1698	Jeremy Collier, *Short View of the Immorality and Profaneness of the English stage.*	
1699		Jonathan Dickinson, *God's Protecting Providence.*

1700–1750 Augustan Age

	ENGLISH	AMERICAN
1700	Death of Dryden.	Samuel Sewall, *The Selling of Joseph.*
1701	Steele, *The Christian Hero; The Funeral.*	Cotton Mather, *Death Made Easy and Happy.*
		Yale University founded.
1702	*The Daily Courant:* first daily newspaper.	Cotton Mather, *Magnalia Christi Americana.*
	Defoe, *The Shortest Way with the Dissenters.*	Increase Mather, *Ichabod.*
1702–1714	Reign of Anne.	
1703	John Wesley (founder of Methodist Church) born. Died 1791.	Jonathan Edwards born. Died 1758.
	Rowe, *The Fair Penitent.*	
1704	Swift, *Battle of the Books (w ca. 1697); Tale of a Tub.*	First American newspaper, *Boston News Letter.*
		Sarah K. Knight, *Journal of a Journey (w).*
1704–1713	Defoe, *The Review.*	
1705	Steele, *The Tender Husband.*	Anon., *Questions and Proposals.*
1706		Benjamin Franklin born. Died 1790.
1707	Henry Fielding born. Died 1754.	
1708		Ebenezer Cook, *Sot-Weed Factor.*
1709	Pope, *Pastorals.*	
	Rowe's edition of Shakespeare.	
	Samuel Johnson born. Died 1784.	
1709–1711	Steele (and Addison), *The Tatler.*	

1710

	ENGLISH	AMERICAN
1710	Berkeley, *Principles of Human Knowledge.*	Cotton Mather, *Essays To Do Good.*
	First complete performance of Italian opera in England (*Almahide*).	John Wise, *The Churches' Quarrel Espoused.*

	ENGLISH	AMERICAN
	Handel comes to England.	
1710–1713	Swift, *Journal to Stella* (*w*).	
1711	Pope, *Essay on Criticism.*	
	Shaftesbury, *Characteristics of Men.*	
1711–1712	Addison, Steele, etc. *The Spectator.*	
1712, 1714	Pope, "Rape of the Lock."	
1713	Pope, *Windsor Forest.*	Increase Mather, *A Plain Discourse Showing Who Shall and Who Shall Not Enter Heaven.*
	Addison, *Cato.*	
1714–1901	House of Hanover (George I to Victoria).	
1714–1727	George I.	
1714	Mandeville, *Fable of the Bees.*	
	Spectator revived.	
1715	Pope, trans. *Iliad*, i–iv.	
	Jacobite Revolt.	
1716	Thomas Gray born. Died 1771.	
1717	Horace Walpole born. Died 1797.	William Southeby, *An Anti-Slavery Tract.*
	David Garrick born. Died 1779.	
1719	Watts, *Psalms and Hymns.*	Establishment of *Boston Gazette* and the *American Weekly Mercury* (Phila.).
	Defoe, *Robinson Crusoe.*	
	Death of Addison.	

1720

1720	"South Sea Bubble."	Wadsworth, *The Lord's Day Proved To Be the Christian Sabbath.*
		James Franklin establishes the *New England Courant.*
1722	Defoe, *Journal of the Plague Year; Moll Flanders.*	Benjamin Franklin, *Silence Dogood* papers.
	Steele, *The Conscious Lovers* (*a*).	
	Parnell, *Night-Piece on Death.*	
1723		Death of Increase Mather.
1724	Swift, *Drapier's Letters.*	
	Ramsay, *The Evergreen:* collection of old Scotch poetry.	

	ENGLISH	AMERICAN
1725	Pope's edition of Shakespeare.	Josiah Dwight, *Essay to Silence the Outcry . . . Against Regular Singing.* *New York Gazette* estab.
1725–1775		Nathaniel Ames, *Astronomical Diary and Almanac.*
1726	Thomson, *Winter.* Swift, *Gulliver's Travels.* Dyer, *Grongar Hill.*	
1727		Byles, *Poem on Death of King George I.*
1727–1760	George II.	
1728	Pope, *Dunciad.* Gay, *Beggar's Opera.* Oliver Goldsmith born. Died 1774.	First newspaper in Maryland estab. Death of Cotton Mather.
1729	Swift, *A Modest Proposal* Death of Steele. Edmund Burke born. Died 1797.	Byrd, *History of the Dividing Line* (w). Death of Edward Taylor.

1730

1730	Methodist Society at Oxford. Tindal, *Christianity as Old as the Creation.*	Seccomb, *Father Abbey's Will.* Printing press set up in Charleston, South Carolina.
1731	*Gentleman's Magazine* estab. Lillo, *The London Merchant.* Death of Defoe. William Cowper born. Died 1800.	
1732	Covent Garden Theatre built.	Byles, *Sermon on the Vileness of the Body.*
1732–1757		Franklin, *Poor Richard's Almanac.*
1733	Pope, *Essay on Man.* Theobald's edition of Shakespeare.	William Byrd, *Journal of Journey to the Land of Eden* (North Carolina) (w). Georgia settled by Oglethorpe. J. P. Zenger begins publication of *New York Weekly Journal* Edwards conducts his first great revival meetings at Northampton.
1735	Pope, *Epistle to Dr. Arbuthnot.*	John and Charles Wesley visit America.

	ENGLISH	AMERICAN
1735		Zenger found not guilty in libel suit over *Journal;* first important "freedom of the press" suit.
1736	Joseph Butler, *The Analogy of Religion.*	First newspaper in Virginia.
1737	Edward Gibbon born. Died 1794.	
	Theatre Licensing Act.	
1737–1742	Shenstone, *Schoolmistress.*	
1738	Johnson, *London.*	
	Wesley, *Psalms and Hymns.*	
	Bolingbroke, *Letters on the Study of History.*	Whitefield's first preaching tour in America.

1740

1740	Cibber, *Apology for the Life of Colley Cibber.*	
	Richardson, *Pamela.*	
1740–1745		The "Great Awakening" (religious revival).
1741		Edwards, *Sinners in the Hands of an Angry God.*
1742	Fielding, *Joseph Andrews.*	
	Young, *Night Thoughts.*	
1742–1744	Roger North, *Lives of the Norths.*	
1743	Blair, *The Grave.*	Thomas Jefferson born. Died 1826.
1744	Joseph Warton, *The Enthusiast.*	
	Johnson, *Life of Richard Savage.*	
	Death of Pope.	
1745	Death of Swift.	
	Jacobite Rebellion.	
1747	Collins, *Odes.*	Stith, *First Discovery and Settlement of Virginia.*
1748	Thomson, *Castle of Indolence.*	
	Richardson, *Clarissa Harlowe.*	
	Smollett, *Roderick Random.*	
	Hume, *Inquiry Concerning Human Understanding.*	

	ENGLISH	AMERICAN
1749	Fielding, *Tom Jones.*	University of Pennsylvania founded.
	Johnson, *The Vanity of Human Wishes.*	

1750–1798 Age of Johnson

	ENGLISH	AMERICAN
1750–1752	Johnson, *The Rambler:* periodical essays.	
1751	Gray, "Elegy Written in a Country Churchyard."	Bartram, *Observations on American Plants.*
		Franklin, *Experiments and Observations in Electricity.*
1752	Gregorian Calendar adopted.	Philip Freneau born. Died 1832.
1753	British Museum founded.	
1754	T. Warton, *Observations on the Fairy Queen of Spenser.*	Edwards, *Freedom of the Will.*
1755	Johnson, *Dictionary.*	
1755–1772		Woolman, *Journal (w)* (pub. 1774).
1756	J. Warton, *Essay on Pope.*	
	Home, *Douglas.*	
1757	Gray, *The Bard* and *The Progress of Poesy.*	Witherspoon, *Serious Inquiry into the Nature and Effects of the Stage.*
	William Blake born. Died 1827.	Edwards, *The Great Christian Doctrine of Original Sin Defended.*
		Death of Edwards.
1758–1760	Johnson, The "Idler" papers.	
1759	Johnson, *Rasselas.*	Winthrop, *Lectures on the Comets.*
	Annual Register established.	
	Robert Burns born. Died 1796.	

1760

	ENGLISH	AMERICAN
1760–1820	George III.	
1760	Macpherson publishes his Ossianic *Fragments.*	
1760–1761	Goldsmith, *Letters from a Citizen of the World.*	
1760–1767	Sterne, *Tristram Shandy.*	
1761	Churchill, *The Rosciad.*	Otis, Speeches.
1762	Macpherson, *Fingal.*	Printing press set up in Georgia.
	Leland, *Longsword.*	
1764	Walpole, *Castle of Otranto.*	Otis, *Rights of British Colonies.*

	ENGLISH	AMERICAN
	Literary Club established in London (Samuel Johnson and others).	
1764–1770	The Chatterton poems (w) (pub. 1777).	

1765–1830 Revolutionary and Early National Period

1765–1790 Revolutionary Age

	ENGLISH	AMERICAN
1765	Percy, *Reliques of Ancient English Poetry.*	The Stamp Act.
	Invention of steam engine by Watt.	
1766	Goldsmith, *The Vicar of Wakefield.*	Franklin, *Examination before the House of Commons.*
1766–1770	Brooke, *The Fool of Quality.*	
1767		Godfrey, *Prince of Parthia* (a): tragedy, first American play to be acted.
1767–1768		Dickinson, *Letters of a Farmer in Pennsylvania.*
1768	Kelly, *False Delicacy* (a). Goldsmith, *Good-Natured Man* (a).	
	Gray, *Poems.*	
	Sterne, *Sentimental Journey.*	
	Spinning machine invented.	
1769		Samuel Adams (and others), *Appeal to the World.*
1769–1772	*Letters of Junius.*	

1770

	ENGLISH	AMERICAN
1770	Goldsmith, *Deserted Village.*	
	Burke, *Thoughts on the Present Discontent.*	
	William Wordsworth born. Died 1850.	
1771, 1784, and later		Franklin, *Autobiography* (w).
1771	Beattie, *The Minstrel,* Book I.	Charles Brockden Brown born. Died 1810.
	Smollett, *Expedition of Humphrey Clinker.*	
	Sir Walter Scott born. Died 1832.	

	ENGLISH	AMERICAN
1772	Samuel Taylor Coleridge born. Died. 1834.	Trumbull, *Progress of Dullness*, Part I.
		Freneau, *Rising Glories of America*.
1773	Goldsmith, *She Stoops To Conquer*.	Phillis Wheatley (Peters), *Poems:* poetry written by a young slave girl.
	Steevens's edition of Shakespeare.	
	Lord Monboddo, *Origin and Progress of Language*.	First theater in Charleston, South Carolina.
1774	T. Warton, *History of English Poetry*, Vol. I.	Jefferson, *Summary View of Rights of British America*.
	Chesterfield, *Letters to His Son*.	Rush, *Natural History of Medicine Among Indians of North America*.
	Death of Goldsmith.	
	Robert Southey born. Died 1843.	First Continental Congress.
1775–1783	War with American colonies.	Revolutionary War.
1775	Sheridan, *The Rivals*.	Trumbull, *M'Fingal*, Canto I.
	Burke, *Speech on Conciliation*.	Mrs. Warren, *The Group*.
	Mason, *Memoirs of the Life and Writings of Thomas Gray*.	Battles of Lexington and Bunker Hill.
	Charles Lamb born. Died 1834.	
	Walter Savage Landor born. Died 1864.	
	Jane Austen born. Died 1817.	
1776	Gibbon, *Decline and Fall of the Roman Empire*.	Paine, *Common Sense*.
	Adam Smith, *Wealth of Nations*.	Brackenridge, *Battle of Bunkers Hill*.
		Jefferson, Declaration of Independence.
1776–1783		Thomas Paine, *The Crisis*.
1777	Sheridan, *School for Scandal* (*a*).	*Articles of Confederation*.
	Burke, *Letter to the Sheriffs of Bristol*.	Surrender of Burgoyne.
1778	Frances Burney, *Evelina*.	Franklin, *Ephemera*.
	William Hazlitt born. Died 1830.	Freneau, *American Independence*.
1778		Carver, *Travels*.

	ENGLISH	AMERICAN
		Hopkinson, *Battle of the Kegs.*
1779	Johnson, *Lives of the Poets.*	Odell, *The Conflagration.*
	Rev. John Newton and William Cowper, *Olney Hymns.*	Ethan Allen, *Narrative of the Captivity.*
	Hume, *Natural History of Religion.*	Paul Jones's naval victories.

1780

	ENGLISH	AMERICAN
1781	Macklin, *Man of the World.*	Surrender of Cornwallis at Yorktown.
		Articles of Confederation ratified.
1782	Cowper, *Table Talk.*	Crèvecoeur, *Letters from an American Farmer.*
		Paine, *Letter to the Abbé Raynal.*
1783	Crabbe, *The Village.*	Washington Irving born. Died 1859.
	Blair, *Rhetoric.*	
	Ritson, *Collection of English Songs.*	England acknowledges American independence.
1783–1785		Noah Webster, *Grammatical Institute of the English Language* (speller, grammar, reader).
1784	Death of Samuel Johnson.	Franklin, *Information for Those Who Would Remove to America.*
	Leigh Hunt born. Died 1859.	
1785	Cowper, *The Task.*	Dwight, *Conquest of Canaan:* epic.
	Thomas De Quincey born. Died 1859.	
1786	Burns, *Poems.*	Freneau, *Poems.*
	Beckford, *Vathek.*	
1786–1787		Trumbull and others, *The Anarchiad.*
1787–1788		Hamilton (and others), *The Federalist.*
1787		Barlow, *Vision of Columbus:* epic.
		Tyler, *The Contrast* (*a*): first American comedy acted by professionals.
		Constitutional Convention.
1788	George Gordon, Lord Byron, born. Died 1824.	Markoe, *The Times.*
		Constitution ratified by eleven states.
1789	Blake, *Songs of Innocence.*	William Hill Brown, *The Power of Sympathy:* first American novel.
	Bowles, *Fourteen Sonnets.*	

	ENGLISH	AMERICAN
	*French Revolution begins.	James Fenimore Cooper born. Died 1851.
		Federal government established.
		1790–1830 Federalist Age
1790	Burke, *Reflections on the Revolution in France.*	Death of Franklin.
	Malone's edition of Shakespeare.	
1791	Boswell, *Life of Johnson.*	William Bartram, *Travels Through North and South Carolina.*
	Erasmus Darwin, *The Botanic Garden.*	
	Mrs. Susanna Rowson, *Charlotte Temple.*	
1791–1792		Paine, *Rights of Man.*
1792	Wollstonecraft, *Rights of Woman.*	
	Percy Bysshe Shelley born. Died 1822.	
1792–1815		Brackenridge, *Modern Chivalry.*
1793	Wordsworth, *Descriptive Sketches.*	Barlow, *Hasty Pudding* (w).
	Godwin, *Political Justice.*	Imlay, *Emigrants.*
	War with France.	
1794	Blake, *Songs of Experience.*	Dwight, *Greenfield Hill.*
	Radcliffe, *Mysteries of Udolpho.*	Dunlap, *Leicester: "The Fatal Legacy"* (a).
	Godwin, *Caleb Williams.*	William Cullen Bryant born. Died 1878.
1794–1796		Paine, *Age of Reason.*
1795	John Keats born. Died 1821.	Murray, *English Grammar.*
	Thomas Carlyle born. Died 1881.	
1796	Coleridge, *The Watchman.*	Washington, *Farewell Address.*
	Southey, *Joan of Arc.*	Dennie, *Lay Preacher.*
	Colman, *Iron Chest* (a).	
	Lewis, *The Monk.*	
	Death of Burns.	
1797	Wordsworth, *The Borderers* (w) (pub. 1842).	Tyler, *Algerian Captive.*
1797–1798	*The Anti-Jacobin.*	

ENGLISH	AMERICAN

1798–1870 Romantic Period

1798–1832 Age of the Romantic Movement

	ENGLISH	AMERICAN
1798	Wordsworth and Coleridge, *Lyrical Ballads.* Landor, *Gebir.* Malthus, *Essay on Population.*	C. B. Brown, *Alcuin: a Dialogue on the Rights of Women; Wieland.*
1799	Campbell, *Pleasures of Hope.*	Brown, *Ormond; Arthur Mervyn,* Part I; *Edgar Huntly.*

1800

	ENGLISH	AMERICAN
1800	Coleridge, trans. of Schiller's *Wallenstein.* Maria Edgeworth, *Castle Rackrent.* Wordsworth and Coleridge, *Lyrical Ballads,* 2d ed., with famous *Preface.* Thomas Babington Macaulay born. Died 1859.	Weems, *Life of Washington.* Brown, *Arthur Mervyn,* Part II. Library of Congress founded.
1801	Southey, *Thalaba.* John Henry Newman born. Died 1890.	Brown, *Clara Howard, Jane Talbot.*
1802	Scott, *Minstrelsy of the Scottish Border.* *Edinburgh Review* founded.	
1803	Jane Porter, *Thaddeus of Warsaw.* Bulwer-Lytton born. Died 1873.	Wirt, *Letters of a British Spy.* Louisiana Purchase. Ralph Waldo Emerson born. Died 1882.
1804	Benjamin Disraeli, Earl of Beaconsfield, born. Died 1881.	J. Q. Adams, *Letters.* Nathaniel Hawthorne born. Died 1864.
1805	Wordsworth, *Prelude* (*w*) (pub. 1850). Scott, *Lay of the Last Minstrel.*	
1806	Elizabeth Barrett (Browning) born. Died 1861. John Stuart Mill born. Died 1873.	Noah Webster, *Compendious Dictionary of the English Language.* William Gilmore Simms born. Died 1870.

	ENGLISH	AMERICAN
1807	Byron, *Hours of Idleness*.	Barlow, *Columbiad*.
	C. and M. Lamb, *Tales from Shakespeare*.	Irving and Paulding, *Salma-gundi Papers*.
	Abolition of slave trade.	John Greenleaf Whittier born. Died 1892.
		Henry Wadsworth Longfellow born. Died 1882.
1808	Hunt, *The Examiner*.	Bryant, *The Embargo*.
	Scott, *Marmion*.	
	Lamb, *Specimens of English Dramatic Poets*.	
1809	Byron, *English Bards and Scotch Reviewers*.	Irving, *Knickerbocker's History*.
	Charles Darwin born. Died 1882.	Edgar Allan Poe born. Died 1849.
	Alfred, Lord Tennyson born. Died 1892.	Oliver Wendell Holmes born. Died 1894.
	William E. Gladstone born. Died 1898.	Abraham Lincoln born. Died 1865.
	First issue of *Quarterly Review*.	

1810

	ENGLISH	AMERICAN
1810	Scott, *Lady of the Lake*.	
	Porter, *Scottish Chiefs*.	
	Crabbe, *The Borough*.	
	Southey, *Curse of Kehama*.	
	Elizabeth Cleghorn Gaskell born. Died 1896	
1811	Austen, *Sense and Sensibility*.	Harriet Beecher Stowe born. Died 1896.
	William Makepeace Thackeray born. Died 1863.	
1812–1815		War with England.
1812	Byron, *Childe Harold*, Cantos I, II.	
	Charles Dickens born. Died 1870.	
	Robert Browning born. Died 1889.	
1813	Byron, *Bride of Abydos*.	Allston, *Sylphs of the Seasons*.
	Shelley, *Queen Mab*.	
	Austen, *Pride and Prejudice*.	
	Southey made Poet Laureate.	

	ENGLISH	AMERICAN
1814	Scott, *Waverley:* begins vogue of historical novel. Wordsworth, *Excursion.*	
1815	Scott, *Guy Mannering.* Battle of Waterloo. Anthony Trollope born. Died 1882.	Freneau, *Poems on American Affairs.* *North American Review* estab.
1816	Coleridge, *Christabel* (*w* 1797–98 and 1800). Byron, *Prisoner of Chillon.* Shelley, *Alastor.* Peacock, *Headlong Hall.*	Pickering, *Vocabulary of Americanisms.*
1817	Mary Shelley, *Frankenstein.* Byron, *Manfred.* Coleridge, *Biographia Literaria.* Keats, *Poems.* *Blackwood's Magazine* estab.	Bryant, *Thanatopsis* (*w* 1811). Henry David Thoreau born. Died 1862.
1818	Keats, *Endymion.* Scott, *Heart of Midlothian.* Shelley, *Revolt of Islam.* Austen, *Northanger Abbey* (*w ca.* 1800).	Payne, *Brutus* (*a* London).
1819	Byron, *Don Juan*, I, II. Shelley, *The Cenci:* tragedy. Mary Ann Evans ("George Eliot") born. Died 1880. John Ruskin born. Died 1900. Charles Kingsley born. Died 1875.	Halleck, *Fanny.* Drake, *The Culprit Fay* (*w*). James Russell Lowell born. Died 1891. Herman Melville born. Died 1891. Walt Whitman born. Died 1892.
1820–1830	George IV.	
1820	Scott, *Ivanhoe.* Shelley, *Prometheus Unbound.* Keats, *Lamia . . . and other Poems.* Maturin, *Melmoth the Wanderer.* Herbert Spencer born. Died 1903.	Missouri Compromise. Irving, *Sketch Book.*
1820–1823	Lamb, *Essays of Elia.* Scott, *Kenilworth.*	Bryant, *Poems.* Cooper, *The Spy.*
1821	Southey, *Vision of Judgment.* Shelley, *Adonais.*	

	ENGLISH	AMERICAN
	De Quincey, *Confessions of an English Opium-Eater.*	
	Byron, *Cain.*	
	Death of Keats.	
1822	Byron, *Vision of Judgment.*	Irving, *Bracebridge Hall.*
	Matthew Arnold born. Died 1888.	
	Death of Shelley.	
1823	Scott, *Quentin Durward.*	Cooper, *Pioneers:* first of Leatherstocking series.
	Carlyle, *Life of Schiller.*	Francis Parkman born. Died 1893.
1824	Landor, *Imaginary Conversations,* Vol. I.	Irving, *Tales of a Traveler.*
	Death of Byron.	E. Everett, *Progress of Literature in America.*
1825	Macaulay, *Essay on Milton.*	Halleck, *Marco Bozzaris.*
	Hazlitt, *Spirit of the Age.*	Italian opera introduced into America.
	Thomas Henry Huxley born. Died 1895.	
1826	Scott, *Woodstock.*	Cooper, *Last of the Mohicans.*
	Disraeli, *Vivian Gray.*	Payne, *Richelieu* (a).
		The Atlantic Souvenir: annual "gift book."
1827		Cooper, *The Prairie.*
		Poe, *Tamerlane.*
		Willis, *Sketches:* poems.
1827–1838		Audubon, *Birds of America.*
1828	Catholic Emancipation Act.	Hawthorne, *Fanshawe.*
	Dante Gabriel Rossetti born. Died 1882.	Irving, *Columbus.*
		Webster, *An American Dictionary.*
	George Meredith born. Died 1909.	Hall, *Letters from the West.*
1828–1830	Taylor, *Historic Survey of German Poetry.*	
1829	Jerrold, *Black-ey'd Susan.*	Irving, *Conquest of Granada.*
		Henry D. Timrod born. Died 1867.

1830–1865   Romantic Period

1830–1837	William IV.	
1830	Tennyson, *Poems Chiefly Lyrical.*	Holmes, *Old Ironsides.*
		Seba Smith starts the "Jack Downing Letters."

	ENGLISH	AMERICAN
	Moore, *Letters and Journals of Lord Byron.*	
		Godey's Lady's Book founded.
	Scott, *Letters on Demonology and Witchcraft.*	
		Emily Dickinson born. Died 1886.
	Christina Rossetti born. Died 1894.	
1830–1833	Lyell, *Principles of Geology.*	
	Scott, *Castle Dangerous.*	Poe, *Poems.*
1831	Disraeli, *The Young Duke.*	Whittier, *Legends of New England.*
		Garrison founds the *Liberator.*
		William T. Porter founds *Spirit of the Times.*
		New England Anti-Slavery Society founded.

1832–1870 Victorian Age

	ENGLISH	AMERICAN
1832	Reform Bill.	Poe: five tales appear in *Philadelphia Saturday Courier.*
	C. L. Dodgson ("Lewis Carroll") born. Died 1898.	
	Death of Scott and *Goethe.	Bryant, *Poems* (2d ed.).
		Simms, *Atalantis.*
		Irving, *The Alhambra.*
		Dunlap, *History of the American Theatre.*
1833	Lamb, *Last Essays of Elia.*	Longfellow, *Outre-Mer* (first numbers).
	Browning, *Pauline.*	
	Newman, *Tracts for the Times* (begun).	Poe, *Manuscript Found in a Bottle.*
1833	Surtees, *Jorrocks' Jaunts and Jollities.*	
1833–1834	Carlyle, *Sartor Resartus.*	
1833–1841	The Oxford Movement (Tractarians).	
1834	Bulwer-Lytton, *Last Days of Pompeii.*	Bancroft, *History of the United States,* Vol. I.
	William Morris born. Died 1896.	Crockett, *Autobiography.*
		Southern Literary Messenger estab.
	Death of Coleridge and Lamb.	
1835	Browning, *Paracelsus.*	Simms, *The Partisan; The Yemassee.*
	Samuel Butler born. Died 1902.	
	Alfred Austin born. Died 1913.	

	ENGLISH	AMERICAN
		Longstreet, *Georgia Scenes.*
		S. L. Clemens ("Mark Twain") born. Died 1910.
1836	Dickens, *Pickwick Papers.*	Emerson, *Nature.*
	Marryat, *Mr. Midshipman Easy.*	Holmes, *Poems.*
		Irving, *Astoria.*
1837–1901	Victoria.	
1837	Dickens, *Oliver Twist.*	Hawthorne, *Twice-Told Tales.*
	Browning, *Strafford.*	Whittier, *Poems.*
	Carlyle, *French Revolution.*	Emerson, *The American Scholar.*
	Lockhart, *Life of Scott.*	
	Algernon Charles Swinburne born. Died 1909.	William Dean Howells born. Died 1920.
1838	Ocean steamships connect England and United States.	Morse demonstrates telegraph apparatus before President Van Buren.
1838–1849	The Chartist Movement for extending the franchise.	
1839	Bulwer-Lytton, *Cardinal Richelieu.*	Longfellow, *Hyperion; Voices of the Night.*
	Carlyle, *Chartism.*	
	Walter Pater born. Died 1894.	

1840

	ENGLISH	AMERICAN
1840	Browning, *Sordello.*	Cooper, *Pathfinder.*
	Dickens, *Old Curiosity Shop.*	Dana, *Two Years Before the Mast.*
	Thomas Hardy born. Died 1928.	Poe, *Tales of the Grotesque and Arabesque.*
1840		Brook Farm estab.
		The Dial estab. (discontinued 1844).
1841	Browning, *Pippa Passes.*	Cooper, *The Deerslayer.*
	Carlyle, *Heroes and Hero-Worship.*	Emerson, *Essays.*
	Macaulay, *Warren Hastings.*	Longfellow, *Ballads and Other Poems.*
	Boucicault, *London Assurance (a).*	T. B. Thorpe, "The Big Bear of Arkansas."
1842	Browning, *Dramatic Lyrics.*	Longfellow, *Poems on Slavery.*
	Tennyson, *Poems.*	Griswold, *Poets and Poetry of America.*
	Dickens, *American Notes.*	Sidney Lanier born. Died 1881.
	Macaulay, *Lays of Ancient Rome.*	
	Newman, *Essay on Miracles.*	

	ENGLISH	AMERICAN
1843	Carlyle, *Past and Present.*	Prescott, *Conquest of Mexico.*
	Dickens, *Christmas Carol.*	
	Ruskin, *Modern Painters,* Vol. I.	Whittier, *Lays of My Home and Other Poems.*
	Wordsworth made Poet Laureate.	Henry James born. Died 1916.
	Repeal of Licensing Act of 1737: end of monopoly of the "patent" theaters in London.	
1844	Thackeray, *Barry Lyndon.*	Emerson, *Essays: Second Series.*
	Elizabeth Barrett (Browning), *Poems.*	
	Disraeli, *Coningsby*	
	Robert Bridges born. Died 1930.	
	Gerard Manley Hopkins born. Died 1889.	
1845	Dickens, *Cricket on the Hearth.*	Poe, *The Raven.*
	Repeal of Corn Laws.	Margaret Fuller (Ossoli), *Woman in the Nineteenth Century.*
		Johnson J. Hooper, *Some Adventures of Simon Suggs.*
1846	Brontë sisters, *Poems.*	Hawthorne, *Mosses from an Old Manse.*
		Holmes, *Poems.*
		Melville, *Typee.*
1847	E. Brontë, *Wuthering Heights.*	Emerson, *Poems.*
	C. Brontë, *Jane Eyre.*	Longfellow, *Evangeline.*
	Tennyson, *The Princess.*	Prescott, *Conquest of Peru.*
1847	Hunt, *Men, Women, and Books.*	Agassiz, *Introduction to Natural History.*
		Melville, *Omoo.*
1847–1848	Thackeray, *Vanity Fair.*	
1848	Mill, *Political Economy.*	Lowell, *A Fable for Critics; Biglow Papers.*
	Macaulay, *History of England,* Vols. I, II.	Bartlett, *Dictionary of Americanisms.*
	Pre-Raphaelite Brotherhood founded by Rossetti.	
1849	Ruskin, *Seven Lamps of Architecture.*	Whittier, *Voices of Freedom.*
		Parkman, *Oregon Trail.*

ENGLISH	AMERICAN
Bulwer-Lytton, *The Caxtons.*	Thoreau, *Week on the Concord and Merrimac Rivers.*
	Melville, *Mardi.*
	Death of Poe.

1849–1850 — Dickens, *David Copperfield.*

1850

1850

ENGLISH	AMERICAN
E. B. Browning, *Sonnets from the Portuguese.*	Emerson, *Representative Men.*
Thackeray, *Pendennis.*	Hawthorne, *Scarlet Letter.*
Tennyson, *In Memoriam.*	Irving, *Mahomet.*
Hunt, *Autobiography; Table Talk.*	Whittier, *Songs of Labor.*
Kingsley, *Alton Locke.*	Poe, *Poetic Principle.*
Death of Wordsworth.	*Harper's Magazine* established.
Tennyson made Poet Laureate.	
Robert Louis Stevenson born. Died 1894.	

1851

Ruskin, *Stones of Venice.*	Hawthorne, *House of the Seven Gables.*
Borrow, *Lavengro.*	Melville, *Moby-Dick.*
	Kate Chopin born. Died 1904.

1852

Thackeray, *Henry Esmond.*	Hawthorne, *Blithedale Romance.*
Tennyson, *Ode on the Death of the Duke of Wellington.*	Harriet Beecher Stowe, *Uncle Tom's Cabin.*
Lady Augusta Gregory born. Died 1932.	

1853

Thackeray, *English Humorists.*	
Dickens, *Bleak House.*	
Mrs. Gaskell, *Cranford.*	
Kingsley, *Hypatia.*	
Arnold, *Poems.*	
C. Brontë, *Villette.*	

1854

Dickens, *Hard Times.*	Thoreau, *Walden.*
The Crimean War.	

1855

Browning, *Men and Women.*	Whitman, *Leaves of Grass.*
Tennyson, *Maud.*	Longfellow, *Hiawatha.*
Thackeray, *The Newcomes.*	
Trollope, *The Warden.*	
Kingsley, *Westward Ho.*	

	ENGLISH	AMERICAN
		Irving, *Life of Washington* (begun, completed 1859).
		Hayne, *Poems.*
		Boker, *Francesca da Rimini.*
1856	E. B. Browning, *Aurora Leigh.*	Emerson, *English Traits.*
	Oscar Wilde born. Died 1900.	Motley, *Rise of the Dutch Republic.*
	George Bernard Shaw born. Died 1950.	
1857	Trollope, *Barchester Towers.*	Child, ed., *English and Scottish Popular Ballads.*
	Dickens, *Little Dorrit.*	*Atlantic Monthly* estab.
	Joseph Conrad born. Died 1924.	Dred Scott decision.
1858	George Eliot, *Scenes of Clerical Life.*	Holmes, *Autocrat of the Breakfast Table.*
	Morris, *Defence of Guinevere.*	Longfellow, *Courtship of Miles Standish.*
1859	Tennyson, *Idylls of the King.*	Margaret Fuller (Ossoli), *Life Without and Life Within.*
	Dickens, *Tale of Two Cities.*	Joseph Jefferson, *Rip Van Winkle* (a).
	Thackeray, *The Virginians.*	
	George Eliot, *Adam Bede.*	
	Meredith, *Ordeal of Richard Feverel.*	
	FitzGerald, trans. *Rubáiyát of Omar Khayyám.*	
	Darwin, *Origin of Species.*	
	John Stuart Mill, *On Liberty.*	
	Deaths of Macaulay, Hunt, De Quincey.	
	Alfred E. Housman born. Died 1936.	
	Arthur Conan Doyle born. Died 1930.	
	Francis Thompson born. Died 1907.	

1860

1860	George Eliot, *Mill on the Floss.*	Emerson, *Conduct of Life.*
	"Owen Meredith," *Lucile.*	Hawthorne, *Marble Faun.*
	Collins, *Woman in White.*	Timrod, *Poems.*
	James Barrie born. Died 1937.	Marsh, *Lectures on the English Language.*
1860–1863	Thackeray, *Roundabout Papers.*	Homes, *Elsie Venner.*
		Lincoln becomes President.

ENGLISH	AMERICAN
George Eliot, *Silas Marner.*	Outbreak of Civil War.
Reade, *The Cloister and the Hearth.*	
Arnold, *On Translating Homer; Thyrsis.*	

	ENGLISH	AMERICAN
1862	Ruskin, *Unto This Last.*	Browne, *Artemus Ward: His Book.*
	Spencer, *First Principles.*	
	Meredith, *Modern Love.*	Battle of Shiloh; *Monitor* and *Merrimac.*
1863	George Eliot, *Romola.*	Longfellow, *Tales of a Wayside Inn.*
	Huxley, *Man's Place in Nature.*	Louisa M. Alcott, *Hospital Sketches.*
	Kingsley, *Water Babies.*	
	Death of Thackeray.	Lincoln, Gettysburg Address.
1864	Browning, *Dramatis Personae.*	Thoreau, *The Maine Woods.*
	Tennyson, *Enoch Arden.*	Lowell, *Fireside Travels.*
	Newman, *Apologia pro Vita Sua.*	Bryant, *Thirty Poems.*
	*Taine, *History of English Literature.*	Whittier, *In War Times.*
1865	Arnold, *Essays in Criticism.*	Thoreau, *Cape Cod.*
	Ruskin, *Sesame and Lilies.*	Lowell, *Commemoration Ode.*
	Lewis Carroll, *Alice's Adventures in Wonderland.*	Whitman, *Drum Taps.*
	Robertson, *Caste.*	Whittier, *National Lyrics.*
	Swinburne, *Atalanta in Calydon.*	End of Civil War.
	Dickens, *Our Mutual Friend.*	
	Rudyard Kipling born. Died 1936.	
	William Butler Yeats born. Died 1939.	

1865–1900 Realistic Period

	ENGLISH	AMERICAN
1866	Swinburne, *Poems and Ballads.*	Shaw, *Josh Billings: His Sayings.*
	Ruskin, *Crown of Wild Olive.*	Whittier, *Snow-Bound.*
	Kingsley, *Hereward the Wake.*	Howells, *Venetian Life.*
	H. G. Wells born. Died 1946.	Atlantic cable completed.

	ENGLISH	AMERICAN
1867	Bagehot, *English Constitution*. Darwin, *Animals and Plants Under Domestication*. *Karl Marx, *Das Kapital*. Arnold Bennett born. Died 1931. John Galsworthy born. Died 1933.	Mark Twain, *The Celebrated Jumping Frog of Calaveras County*. George W. Harris, *Sut Lovingood's Yarns*. Holmes, *Guardian Angel*. Lanier, *Tiger Lilies*. Longfellow, translation of Dante. Lowell, *Biglow Papers* (2d series).
1868	Collins, *The Moonstone*. Morris, *Earthly Paradise*, Vols. I, II.	Alcott, *Little Women*. Hawthorne, *American Notebooks*.
1869	Trollope, *Phineas Finn*. Blackmore, *Lorna Doone*. Ruskin, *Queen of the Air*. Arnold, *Culture and Anarchy*. Browning, *The Ring and the Book*. Suez Canal opened.	Mark Twain, *The Innocents Abroad*. Whittier, *Among the Hills*. Transcontinental railroad completed. Edwin Arlington Robinson born. Died 1935. William Vaughn Moody born. Died 1910.

1870–1914 Realistic Period

1870–1901 Late Victorian Age

	ENGLISH	AMERICAN
1870	Rossetti, *Poems*. Huxley, *Lay Sermons*. Death of Dickens.	Lowell, *Among My Books* (1st series). Harte, *Luck of Roaring Camp*. Bryant, translation of *Iliad*.
1871	Darwin, *Descent of Man*. John Millington Synge born. Died 1909.	Eggleston, *Hoosier Schoolmaster*. Whitman, *Democratic Vistas*. Howells, *Their Wedding Journey*. Theodore Dreiser born. Died 1945.
1871		Bryant, translation of *Odyssey*.
1872	Butler, *Erewhon*. Hardy, *Under the Greenwood Tree*. George Eliot, *Middlemarch*.	Mark Twain, *Roughing It*.

	ENGLISH	AMERICAN
1873	Arnold, *Literature and Dogma.* Pater, *Studies in the Renaissance.* Newman, *The Idea of a University.*	Aldrich, *Marjorie Daw.*
1874	Hardy, *Far from the Madding Crowd.* John Stuart Mill, *Autobiography.*	Robert Frost born. Died 1963. Amy Lowell born. Died 1925. Gertrude Stein born. Died 1946.
1875	Arnold, *God and the Bible.*	Howells, *A Foregone Conclusion.*
1876	George Eliot, *Daniel Deronda.* Morris, *Sigurd the Volsung.* Tennyson, *Queen Mary* (a). Trevelyan, *Life of Macaulay.*	Mark Twain, *Tom Sawyer.* Henry James, *Roderick Hudson.* Invention of telephone.
1877		James, *The American.* Lanier, *Poems.*
1878	Stevenson, *An Inland Voyage.* Hardy, *Return of the Native.*	
1879	Meredith, *The Egoist.* Spencer, *Data of Ethics*, Part I of *Principles of Ethics.* Browning, *Dramatic Idylls* (1st series). Bagehot, *Literary Studies.* *Ibsen, *The Doll's House.*	Howells, *The Lady of the Aroostook.* Cable, *Old Creole Days.* Henry George, *Progress and Poverty.* James, *Daisy Miller.* Wallace Stevens born. Died 1955.

1880

1880	Gissing, *Workers in the Dawn.*	Longfellow, *Ultima Thule.* Harris, *Uncle Remus.* Cable, *The Grandissimes.* Lanier, *Science of English Verse.*
1881	Stevenson, *Virginibus Puerisque.* Rossetti, *Ballads and Sonnets.* Swinburne, *Mary Stuart.* Death of Carlyle.	James, *The Portrait of a Lady; Washington Square.* Cable, *Madame Delphine.*

	ENGLISH	AMERICAN
1882	Swinburne, *Tristram of Lyonesse.*	Mark Twain, *The Prince and the Pauper.*
	Stevenson, *Familiar Studies, New Arabian Nights.*	Howells, *A Modern Instance.*
	Froude, *Life of Carlyle.*	Whitman, *Specimen Days.*
	Deaths of Darwin, Rossetti, Trollope.	
	James Joyce born. Died 1941.	
1883	Schreiner, *The Story of an African Farm.*	Mark Twain, *Life on the Mississippi.*
	Stevenson, *Treasure Island.*	Howe, *Story of a Country Town.*
		William Carlos Williams born. Died 1963.
1884	Tennyson, *Becket.*	Mark Twain, *Huckleberry Finn.*
	Jones, *Saints and Sinners* (a).	Jewett, *A Country Doctor.*
		"Charles Egbert Craddock," *In the Tennessee Mountains.*
1885	Hudson, *The Purple Land.*	Howells, *Rise of Silas Lapham.*
	Gilbert and Sullivan, *The Mikado* (a).	Ezra Pound born. Died 1972.
	Meredith, *Diana of the Crossways.*	
	Ruskin, *Praeterita.*	
	Pater, *Marius the Epicurean.*	
	Karen Blixen ("Isak Dinesen") born. Died 1962.	
	D. H. Lawrence born. Died 1930.	
1886	Hardy, *Mayor of Casterbridge.*	Howells, *Indian Summer.*
	Stevenson, *Doctor Jekyll and Mr. Hyde; Kidnapped.*	James, *The Bostonians; Princess Casamassima.*
	Tennyson, *Locksley Hall Sixty Years After.*	Hilda Doolittle ("H. D.") born. Died 1961.
	Kipling, *Departmental Ditties.*	
1887	Lang, *Myth, Ritual, and Religion.*	Page, *In Ole Virginia.*
	Edith Sitwell born. Died 1964.	Freeman, *A Humble Romance.*
		Marianne Moore born. Died 1972.
1888	Kipling, *Plain Tales from the Hills.*	James, *Partial Portraits; Aspern Papers.*
	Ward, *Robert Elsmere.*	Bellamy, *Looking Backward.*
	Death of Arnold.	Howard, *Shenandoah* (a).

	ENGLISH	AMERICAN
	Katherine Mansfield born. Died 1923.	T. S. Eliot born. Died 1965.
		Eugene O'Neill born. Died 1953.
		John Crowe Ransom born. Died 1974.
1889	Browning, *Asolando.*	Mark Twain, *A Connecticut Yankee at King Arthur's Court.*
	Stevenson, *Master of Ballantrae.*	
	Pater, *Appreciations.*	
1889	Barrie, *A Window in Thrums.*	
	Death of Browning.	

1890

1890	Watson, *Wordsworth's Grave.*	Dickinson, *Poems.*
	Bridges, *Shorter Poems.*	James, *Tragic Muse.*
		William James, *Principles of Psychology.*
1891	Hardy, *Tess of the D'Urbervilles.*	Garland, *Main-Travelled Roads.*
	Doyle, *Adventures of Sherlock Holmes.*	Bierce, *Tales of Soldiers and Civilians.*
	Kipling, *The Light that Failed.*	Freeman, *A New England Nun.*
	Barrie, *The Little Minister.*	Howells, *Criticism and Fiction.*
	Gissing, *New Grub Street.*	
	Independent Theater opens: start of "Little Theater" movement in England.	International Copyright Act: protecting rights of foreign authors and publishers.
1892	Kipling, *Barrack-Room Ballads.*	Page, *The Old South.*
	Zangwill, *Children of the Ghetto.*	Howard, *Aristocracy (a).*
		Djuna Barnes born. Died 1982.
	Wilde, *Lady Windermere's Fan (a).*	
	Death of Tennyson.	
1893	Thompson, *Poems.*	James, *The Real Thing and Other Tales.*
	Shaw, *Mrs. Warren's Profession (w,* acted 1902).	Crane, *Maggie: A Girl of the Streets.*
	Pinero, *The Second Mrs. Tanqueray (a).*	
1894	Yeats, *Land of Heart's Desire.*	Howells, *A Traveler from Altruria.*

	ENGLISH	AMERICAN
	Moore, *Esther Waters.*	Hearn, *Glimpses of Unfamiliar Japan.*
	Kipling, *Jungle Book.*	
	Death of Stevenson.	Mark Twain, *Pudd'nhead Wilson.*
	Jean Rhys born. Died 1979.	
1895	Wilde, *The Importance of Being Earnest* (a).	Crane, *The Red Badge of Courage.*
	Wells, *The Time Machine.*	
	Conrad, *Almayer's Folly.*	
	Kipling, *The Brushwood Boy.*	
1896	Housman, *A Shropshire Lad.*	Robinson, *The Torrent and the Night Before.*
	Barrie, *Sentimental Tommy.*	
	Hardy, *Jude the Obscure.*	Jewett, *Country of the Pointed Firs.*
	Alfred Austin made Poet Laureate.	Frederic, *The Damnation of Theron Ware.*
		F. Scott Fitzgerald born. Died 1940.
1897	Conrad, *The Nigger of the "Narcissus."*	Allen, *The Choir Invisible.*
		James, *What Maise Knew; Spoils of Poynton.*
	Kipling, *Captains Courageous.*	William Faulkner born. Died 1962.
1898	Hardy, *Wessex Poems.*	Page, *Red Rock.*
	Shaw, *Plays Pleasant and Unpleasant.*	Dunne, *Mr. Dooley in Peace and War.*
	Wilde, *Ballad of Reading Gaol.*	
	Moore, *Evelyn Innes.*	
	Wells, *The War of the Worlds.*	
1899	Irish Literary Theatre founded in Dublin.	Churchill, *Richard Carvel.*
		Crane, *War Is Kind.*
		James, *The Awkward Age.*
		Markham, *The Man with the Hoe.*
		Ade, *Fables in Slang.*
		Hart Crane born. Died 1933.
		Ernest Hemingway born. Died 1961.

1900–1930 Naturalistic and Symbolistic Period

1900	Conrad, *Lord Jim.*	Bacheller, *Eben Holden.*
	Hudson, *Nature in Downland.*	Dreiser, *Sister Carrie.*

	ENGLISH	AMERICAN
	*Edmond Rostand, *L'Aiglon.*	Bacheller, *Eben Holden.*
	Death of Ruskin.	Dreiser, *Sister Carrie.*
		Dunne, *Mr. Dooley's Philosophy.*
		Tarkington, *Monsieur Beaucaire.*
1901	Barrie, *Quality Street.*	Moody, *Poems.*
	Kipling, *Kim.*	Norris, *The Octopus.*
	Binyon, *Odes.*	Washington, *Up From Slavery.*
	Death of Victoria.	James, *The Sacred Fount.*
		Laura (Riding) Jackson born.

1901–1914 Edwardian Age

1901–1910	Reign of Edward VII.	
1902	Bennett, *Anna of the Five Towns.*	Glasgow, *The Battle-Ground.*
	Conrad, *Youth.*	James, *The Wings of the Dove.*
	Masefield, *Saltwater Ballads.*	Wister, *The Virginian.*
		Death of Bret Harte.
1902	Yeats, *Cathleen ni Houlihan.*	
	Death of Samuel Butler.	
1903	Conrad, *Typhoon and Other Stories.*	James, *The Ambassadors.*
	Butler, *The Way of All Flesh.*	London, *The Call of the Wild.*
	Kipling, *The Five Nations.*	Norris, *The Pit.*
	Shaw, *Man and Superman.*	
1904	Barrie, *Peter Pan.*	Churchill, *The Crossing.*
	Conrad, *Nostromo.*	O. Henry, *Cabbages and Kings.*
	Hardy, *The Dynasts* (first part).	James, *The Golden Bowl.*
	Hudson, *Green Mansions.*	London, *The Sea-Wolf.*
	Kipling, *Traffics and Discoveries.*	Moody, *The Fire-Bringer.*
	Synge, *Riders to the Sea.*	Steffens, *The Shame of Cities.*
1905		Wharton, *The House of Mirth.*
1906	Conrad, *Mirror of the Sea.*	O. Henry, *The Four Million.*
	Kipling, *Puck of Pook's Hill.*	Sinclair, *The Jungle.*
	Watson, *Collected Poems.*	Beginning of "Little Theater" movement in America.
1907	Russell ("A. E."), *Deirdre.*	Fitch, *The Truth.*
	Synge, *The Playboy of the Western World.*	Adams, *The Education of Henry Adams.*
	Yeats, *Discoveries.*	William James, *Pragmatism.*

	ENGLISH	AMERICAN
	W. H. Auden born. Died 1973.	
1908	Barrie, *What Every Woman Knows.*	O. Henry, *The Voice of the City.*
	Bennett, *The Old Wives' Tale.*	Theodore Roethke born. Died 1963.
	Wells, New Worlds for Old.	
1909	Galsworthy, *Plays.*	London, *Martin Eden.*
	Kipling, *Actions and Reactions.*	Moody, *The Great Divide.*
		Pound, *Personae.*
	Pinero, *Mid-Channel.*	Reese, *A Wayside Lute.*
	Wells, *Ann Veronica; Tono-Bungay.*	Stein, *Three Lives.*
	Deaths of Meredith and Swinburne.	

1910

1910–1936	Reign of George V.	
1910	Bennett, *Clayhanger.*	Robinson, *The Town Down the River.*
	Lord Dunsany, *A Dreamer's Tales.*	Sheldon, *The Nigger.*
	Galsworthy, *Justice.*	Deaths of William Vaughn Moody, Mark Twain.
	Kipling, *Rewards and Fairies.*	
	Noyes, *Collected Poems.*	
1911	Beerbohm, *Zuleika Dobson.*	Belasco, *The Return of Peter Grimm.*
	Bennett, *Hilda Lessways.*	Dreiser, *Jennie Gerhardt.*
	Masefield, *The Everlasting Mercy.*	Wharton, *Ethan Frome.*
		Elizabeth Bishop born. Died 1979.
1912	Bridges, *Poetical Works.*	Dreiser, *The Financier.*
	Galsworthy, *The Pigeon.*	*Poetry: A Magazine of Verse* founded.
	Monro (ed.), *Georgian Poetry.*	Millay, *Renascence.*
	Shaw, *Pygmalion.*	
	Stephens, *The Crock of Gold.*	
	Tomlinson, *The Sea and the Jungle.*	
1913	D. H. Lawrence, *Sons and Lovers.*	Cather, *O Pioneers!*
	Masefield, *Dauber.*	Glasgow, *Virginia.*
	Death of Alfred Austin.	Lindsay, *General William Booth Enters into Heaven.*
	Robert Bridges made Poet Laureate.	Frost, *A Boy's Will.*

ENGLISH	AMERICAN

1914–1965 Modernist Period

1914–1940 Georgian Age

	ENGLISH	AMERICAN
1914–1918	First World War.	
1914	Sinclair, *The Three Sisters.*	Frost, *North of Boston.*
	Dylan Thomas born. Died 1953.	Lindsay, *The Congo.*
		Amy Lowell, *Sword Blades and Poppy Seeds.*
		Stein, *Tender Buttons.*
1915	Conrad, *Victory.*	Brooks, *America's Coming of Age.*
	Brooke, *Collected Poems.*	
	Galsworthy, *The Freelands.*	Cabell, *The Rivet in Grandfather's Neck.*
	Maugham, *Of Human Bondage.*	Masters, *Spoon River Anthology.*
	D. Richardson, *Pointed Roofs.*	Saul Bellow born.
1916	W. H. Davies, *Collected Poems.*	Frost, *Mountain Interval.*
	Lord Dunsany, *Tales of Wonder.*	Amy Lowell, *Men, Women, and Ghosts.*
		Robinson, *Man Against the Sky.*
	Joyce, *Portrait of the Artist as a Young Man.*	Sandburg, *Chicago Poems.*
	Moore, *The Brook Kerith.*	Mark Twain, *The Mysterious Stranger.*
	Wells, *Mr. Britling Sees It Through.*	Deaths of Henry James, Jack London.
1917	Douglas, *South Wind.*	United States enters war.
	Shaw, *Heartbreak House.*	Garland, *A Son of the Middle Border.*
	Hodgson, *Poems.*	Eliot, *Prufrock.*
	Barrie, *Dear Brutus.*	Pound, First *Cantos* (magazine publication).
		Robert Lowell born. Died 1977.
1918	D. H. Lawrence, *New Poems.*	Cather, *My Antonia.*
	Hopkins, *Poems* (first published).	Sandburg, *Cornhuskers.*
		O'Neill, *Moon of the Caribees.*
	Strachey, *Eminent Victorians.*	Theatre Guild established.
1919	Conrad, *The Arrow of Gold.*	S. Anderson, *Winesburg, Ohio.*
	Maugham, *The Moon and Sixpence.*	Cabell, *Jurgen.*
	Hardy, *Collected Poems.*	Amy Lowell, *Pictures of the Floating World.*
	Masefield, *Reynard the Fox.*	J. D. Salinger born.

	ENGLISH	AMERICAN
	1920	
1920	De la Mare, *Collected Poems.*	Eliot, *Poems 1920.*
	Mansfield, *Bliss.*	Fitzgerald, *This Side of Paradise.*
	Wells, *The Outline of History.*	Lewis, *Main Street.*
		Millay, *A Few Figs from Thistles.*
		O'Neill, *Beyond the Horizon: The Emperor Jones.*
		Robinson, *Lancelot.*
		Wharton, *The Age of Innocence.*
1921	De la Mare, *Memoirs of a Midget.*	S. Anderson, *The Triumph of the Egg.*
	Strachey, *Queen Victoria.*	Dos Passos, *Three Soldiers.*
	Huxley, *Crome Yellow.*	O'Neill, *Anna Christie.*
	D. H. Lawrence, *Women in Love.*	Tarkington, *Alice Adams.*
	Moore, *Héloise and Abelard.*	Wylie, *Nets to Catch the Wind.*
		Richard Wilbur born.
1922	Galsworthy, *The Forsyte Saga* (1906–1922).	Cummings, *The Enormous Room.*
	Housman, *Last Poems.*	Eliot, *The Waste Land.*
	Joyce, *Ulysses.*	Lewis, *Babbitt.*
	Mansfield, *The Garden Party.*	O'Neill, *The Hairy Ape.*
	Woolf, *Jacob's Room.*	
	Philip Larkin born.	
1923	Coppard, *The Black Dog.*	Cather, *A Lost Lady.*
	Hardy, *Collected Poems.*	Frost, *New Hampshire.*
	Huxley, *Antic Hay.*	Rice, *The Adding Machine.*
	D. H. Lawrence, *Studies in Classic American Literature.*	Santayana, *Poems.*
	Shaw, *Saint Joan.*	Stevens, *Harmonium.*
		Williams, *Spring and All.*
		Denise Levertov born (in England).
1924	Ford, *Some Do Not.*	M. Anderson (with L. Stalling), *What Price Glory.*
	Forster, *A Passage to India.*	Hemingway, *in our time.*
	Masefield, *Sard Harker.*	Jeffers, *Tamar and Other Poems.*
	Death of Conrad.	Melville, *Billy Budd* (first published).
		Ransom, *Chills and Fever.*

	ENGLISH	AMERICAN
1925	Galsworthy, *Caravan.* Woolf, *Mrs. Dalloway.* *Gide, *The Counterfeiters.* *Kafka, *The Trial.* Nobel Prize awarded to Shaw.	Cather, *The Professor's House.* Cummings, *XLI Poems.* Dos Passos, *Manhattan Transfer.* Dreiser, *An American Tragedy.* Fitzgerald, *The Great Gatsby.* Glasgow, *Barren Ground.* Lewis, *Arrowsmith.* O'Neill, *Desire Under the Elms.* Death of Amy Lowell.
1926	Kipling, *Debits and Credits.* D. H. Lawrence, *The Plumed Serpent.* T. E. Lawrence, *The Seven Pillars of Wisdom.* Stephens, *Collected Poems.*	Glasgow, *The Romantic Comedians.* Hemingway, *The Sun Also Rises.* O'Neill, *The Great God Brown.* Roberts, *The Time of Man.* A. R. Ammons born. James Merrill born. Robert Creeley born. Allen Ginsberg born. Frank O'Hara born. Died 1966. Robert Bly born.
1927	Chesterton, *Collected Poems.* T. E. Lawrence, *Revolt in the Desert.* Tomlinson, *Gallions Reach.* Woolf, *To the Lighthouse.*	Cather, *Death Comes for the Archbishop.* Jeffers, *The Women at Point Sur.* O'Neill, *Marco Millions.* Robinson, *Tristram.* Wilder, *The Bridge of San Luis Rey.* John Ashbery born. W. S. Merwin born. James Wright born. Died 1980.
1928	Huxley, *Point Counter Point.* D. H. Lawrence, *Lady Chatterley's Lover.* Death of Thomas Hardy.	Benét, *John Brown's Body.* Frost, *West-Running Brook.* MacLeish, *The Hamlet of A. MacLeish.*

ENGLISH

AMERICAN

Laura (Riding) Jackson, *Contemporaries and Snobs; Anarchism Is Not Enough.*

Tate, *Mr. Pope and Other Poems.*

1929

Aldington, *Death of a Hero.*

Bridges, *The Testament of Beauty.*

Galsworthy, *A Modern Comedy.*

Graves, *Goodbye to All That.*

Woolf, *A Room of One's Own.*

Connelly, *Green Pastures.*

Faulkner, *The Sound and the Fury.*

Glasgow, *They Stooped to Folly.*

Hemingway, *A Farewell to Arms.*

Lewis, *Dodsworth.*

Wolfe, *Look Homeward Angel.*

Richard Howard born.

John Hollander born.

Adrienne Rich born.

1930–1960 Period of Conformity and Criticism

1930

Maugham, *Cakes and Ale.*

Coward, *Private Lives.*

Edith Sitwell, *Collected Poems.*

Waugh, *Vile Bodies.*

Death of Bridges.

Masefield made Poet Laureate.

Ted Hughes born.

Eliot, *Ash Wednesday.*

M. Anderson, *Elizabeth the Queen.*

H. Crane, *The Bridge.*

Dos Passos, *The 42nd Parallel.*

Porter, *Flowering Judas.*

Lewis awarded the Nobel Prize.

Gary Snyder born.

1931

Binyon, *Collected Poems.*

Galsworthy, *Maid in Waiting.*

Woolf, *The Waves.*

Cather, *Shadows on the Rock.*

Faulkner, *Sanctuary.*

O'Neill, *Mourning Becomes Electra.*

1932

Auden, *The Orators.*

Huxley, *Brave New World.*

Shaw, *Pen Portraits.*

Nobel Prize awarded Galsworthy.

Geoffrey Hill born.

Caldwell, *Tobacco Road.*

Farrell, *Young Lonigan.*

Faulkner, *Light in August.*

Dos Passos, *1919.*

Glasgow, *The Sheltered Life.*

MacLeish, *Conquistador.*

Sylvia Plath born. Died 1963.

	ENGLISH	AMERICAN
1933	Auden, *Dance of Death.* Spender, *Poems.* Woolf, *Flush, a Biography.* Yeats, *Collected Poems.*	Caldwell, *God's Little Acre.* Cozzens, *The Last Adam.* MacLeish, *Frescoes for Mr. Rockefeller's City.* Stein, *The Autobiography of Alice B. Toklas.* Death of Hart Crane.
1934	Graves, *I, Claudius.* Swinnerton, *Elizabeth.* Waugh, *A Handful of Dust.*	Farrell, *The Young Manhood of Studs Lonigan.* Fitzgerald, *Tender Is the Night.* O'Hara, *Appointment in Samarra.*
1935	C. Day Lewis, *A Time to Dance.* MacNeice, *Poems.* Spender, *The Destructive Element.*	M. Anderson, *Winterset.* Eliot, *Murder in the Cathedral.* Farrell, *Judgment Day* (completes the "Studs Lonigan Trilogy"). Stevens, *Ideas of Order.* Wolfe, *Of Time and the River.*
1936	Auden, *Look, Stranger.* Housman, *More Poems.* Huxley, *Eyeless in Gaza.* Thomas, *25 Poems.* Edward VIII, 1936.	Frost, *A Further Range.* Faulkner, *Absalom, Absalom!* Dos Passos, *The Big Money* (completes the "U.S.A. Trilogy"). Mitchell, *Gone with the Wind.* Sandburg, *The People, Yes.* O'Neill awarded the Nobel Prize.
1936–1952 1937	George VI Maugham, *Theatre.* Woolf, *The Years.*	Marquand, *The Late George Apley.* Millay, *Conversations at Midnight.* Steinbeck, *Of Mice and Men; The Red Pony.* Stevens, *The Man with the Blue Guitar.* Thomas Pynchon born.
1938	Graves, *Collected Poems.* Hughes, *In Hazard.*	Hemingway, *The Fifth Column and the First Forty-Nine Stories.* Wilder, *Our Town.*

ENGLISH	AMERICAN
Richardson, *Pilgrimage* (12-novel sequence completed).	Pearl Buck awarded the Nobel Prize.
C. Day Lewis, *Overtures to Death.*	Death of Wolfe.

1939–1945 Second World War

1939

Joyce, *Finnegans Wake.*	Taylor, *Poetical Works* (first published).
C. Day Lewis, *A Hope for Poetry.*	Porter, *Pale Horse, Pale Rider.*
Thomas, *The World I Breathe.*	Steinbeck, *The Grapes of Wrath.*
Death of Yeats.	Wolfe, *The Web and the Rock.*

1940–1965 Diminishing Age

1940

Auden, *Selected Poems.*	Faulkner, *The Hamlet.*
Snow, *Strangers and Brothers* (begun; completed in 11 novels, 1970).	Hemingway, *For Whom the Bell Tolls.*
Yeats, *Last Poems and Plays.*	Pound, *Cantos LII-LXXI.*
	Wolfe, *You Can't Go Home Again.*
	Wright, *Native Son.*
	Death of Fitzgerald.

1941

Baker, *Selected Poems.*	Attack on Pearl Harbor; the United States declares war on Japan.
Cary, *Herself Surprised.*	
De la Mare, *Bells and Grass.*	Fitzgerald, *The Last Tycoon.*
Huxley, *Grey Eminence.*	Glasgow, *In This Our Life.*
Spender, *Ruins and Visions.*	Jeffers, *Be Angry at the Sun.*
Deaths of Joyce, Virginia Woolf, Walpole.	Welty, *A Curtain of Green.*

1942

Cary, *To Be a Pilgrim.*	Cozzens, *The Just and the Unjust.*
Coward, *Blithe Spirit.*	
Waugh, *Put Out More Flags.*	Faulkner, *Go Down, Moses.*
	Jarrell, *Blood for a Stranger.*
	Wilder, *Skin of Our Teeth.*

1943

Coward, *This Happy Breed.*	Dos Passos, *Number One.*
H. Green, *Caught.*	Eliot, *Four Quartets.*
	Warren, *At Heavens' Gate; Selected Poems.*

	ENGLISH	AMERICAN
1944	Barker, *Eros in Dogma*.	R. Lowell, *Land of Unlikeness*.
	Cary, *The Horse's Mouth*.	
	Connolly, *The Unquiet Grave*.	Porter, *The Leaning Tower*.
		Shapiro, *V-Letter*.
	Huxley, *Time Must Have a Stop*.	Robert Morgan born.
1945	Connolly, *The Condemned Playground*.	Frost, *A Masque of Reason*.
	H. Green, *Loving*.	Jarrell, *Little Friend, Little Friend*.
	Isherwood, *Prater Violet*.	Ransom, *Selected Poems*.
	C. Day Lewis, *Short is the Time*.	T. Williams, *The Glass Menagerie*.
	Waugh, *Brideshead Revisited*.	Wright, *Black Boy*.
1946	H. Green, *Back*.	Jeffers, *Medea*.
	Orwell, *Animal Farm*.	O'Neill, *The Iceman Cometh*.
	Spender, *European Witness*.	Warren, *All the King's Men*.
	Thomas, *Deaths and Entrances*.	Welty, *Delta Wedding*.
		W. C. Williams, *Paterson, I*.
		Death of Gertrude Stein.
1947	Auden, *The Age of Anxiety*.	Dreiser, *The Stoic*.
	Barker, *Love Poems*.	Frost, *A Masque of Mercy*.
	Spender, *Poems of Dedication*.	Stevens, *Transport to Summer*.
		T. Williams, *A Streetcar Named Desire*.
		Cleanth Brooks, *The Well Wrought Urn*.
1948	Fry, *The Lady's Not for Burning*.	Cozzens, *Guard of Honor*.
	H. Green, *Concluding*.	Faulkner, *Intruder in the Dust*.
	G. Greene, *The Heart of the Matter*.	Jarrell, *Losses*.
	Huxley, *Ape and Essence*.	Mailer, *The Naked and the Dead*.
	Waugh, *The Loved One*.	Pound, *Pisan Cantos*.
1949	Cary, *A Fearful Joy*.	Dos Passos, *The Grand Design* (completes "District of Columbia Trilogy").
	Orwell, *Nineteen Eighty-Four*.	
	Spender, *The Edge of Being*.	Marquand, *Point of No Return*.
		Miller, *Death of a Salesman*.
		Welty, *The Golden Apples*.

1950

1950	Auden, *The Enchafèd Flood*.	Cummings, *XAIPE: Seventy-One Poems*
	Barker, *The Dead Seagull*.	

	ENGLISH	AMERICAN
	De la Mare, *Inward Companion.*	Eliot, *The Cocktail Party.*
	H. Green, *Nothing.*	Hemingway, *Across the River and Into the Trees.*
	Thomas, *Twenty-six Poems.*	Stevens, *Auroras of Autumn.*
	Death of Shaw.	Faulkner awarded the Nobel Prize for 1949.
1951	Auden, *Nones.*	Faulkner, *Requiem for a Nun.*
	Fry, *A Sleep of Prisoners.*	Jarrell, *Seven-League Crutches.*
	G. Greene, *The End of the Affair.*	Jones, *From Here to Eternity.*
	Spender, *World Within World.*	R. Lowell, *Mills of the Kavanaughs.*
	Beckett, *Molloy.*	Salinger, *Catcher in the Rye.*
		Death of Sinclair Lewis.
1952	Betjeman, *First and Last Loves.*	Davis, *Winds of Morning.*
	Beckett, *Waiting for Godot.*	Hemingway, *The Old Man and the Sea.*
	Cary, *Prisoner of Grace.*	Steinbeck, *East of Eden.*
	H. Green, *Dying.*	
	Thomas, *In Country Sleep.*	
	Elizabeth II, 1952–.	
1953	Cary, *Except the Lord.*	Roethke, *The Waking.*
	Waugh, *Love Among the Ruins.*	Warren, *Brother to Dragons.*
	Churchill awarded the Nobel Prize.	T. Williams, *Camino Real.*
		Death of O'Neill.
	Death of Thomas.	
1954	Barker, *A Vision of Beasts and Gods.*	Eliot, *The Confidential Clerk.*
	Betjeman, *A Few Late Chrysanthemums.*	Faulkner, *A Fable.*
	MacNeice, *Autumn Sequel.*	Jeffers, *Hungerfield and Other Poems.*
	Thomas, *Under Milk Wood.*	Hemingway awarded the Nobel Prize.
	Amis, *Lucky Jim.*	
1955	Auden, *The Shield of Achilles.*	E. Bishop, *North and South—A Cold Spring.*
	Cary, *Not Honour More.*	T. Williams, *Cat on a Hot Tin Roof.*
	Thomas, *Adventures in the Skin Trade.*	Death of Wallace Stevens.
		Pound, *Section: Rock Drill.*
1956	O'Casey, *Mirror in My House.*	Ginsberg, *Howl.*

	ENGLISH	AMERICAN
	Osborne, *Look Back in Anger.*	O'Neill, *A Long Day's Journey into Night.* Wilbur, *Things of This World.*
1957	Edith Sitwell, *Collected Poems.* Hartley, *The Hireling.* Joyce, *Letters.* Osborne, *The Entertainer.* Waugh, *The Ordeal of Gilbert Pinford.*	Agee, *A Death in the Family.* Cozzens, *By Love Possessed.* Faulkner, *The Town.* O'Neill, *A Touch of the Poet.* Warren, *Promises.*
1958	Beckett, *Endgame.* C. Day Lewis, *Pegasus and Other Poems.* White, *The Once and Future King.*	Cummings, *95 Poems.* MacLeish, *J. B.* Pound, *Pavannes and Divagations.* W. T. Scott, *The Dark Sister.*
1959	Cary, *The Captive and the Free.* Golding, *Free Fall.* Sacheverell Sitwell, *Journey to the Ends of Time,* Vol. I.	Eliot, *The Elder Statesman.* Faulkner, *The Mansion.* R. Lowell, *Life Studies.* Snodgrass, *Heart's Needle.*

1960– Period of the Confessional Self

	ENGLISH	AMERICAN
1960	Durrell, *Alexandria Quartet* (completed). Powell, *Casanova's Chinese Restaurant.* Redgrove, *The Collector.*	Hellman, *Toys in the Attic.* Jarrell, *The Woman at the Washington Zoo.* Pound, *Thrones.* O'Connor, *The Violent Bear It Away.*
1961	Hughes, *The Fox in the Attic.* MacNeice, *Solstices.* Murdock, *A Severed Head.* Osborne, *Luther.* Wain, *Weep Before God.*	Dos Passos, *Midcentury.* Heller, *Catch-22.* Salinger, *Franny and Zooey.* Steinbeck, *The Winter of Our Discontent.* Wilbur, *Advice to a Prophet.* Death of Hemingway.
1962	Graves, *New Poems 1962.* C. Day Lewis, *The Gate.* Powell, *The Kindly Ones.* Edith Sitwell, *The Outcasts.* Ustinov, *Photo Finish.*	Albee, *Who's Afraid of Virginia Woolf?* Ashbery, *The Tennis Court Oath.* Bly, *Silence in the Snowy Fields.* Faulkner, *The Reivers.*

	ENGLISH	AMERICAN
		Frost, *In the Clearing.*
		Koch, *Thank You and Other Poems.*
		W. C. Williams, *Pictures from Brueghel.*
		Porter, *Ship of Fools.*
		T. Williams, *The Night of the Iguana.*
		Deaths of Cummings, Faulkner, Jeffers.
		Steinbeck awarded the Nobel Prize.
1963	Fowles, *The Collector.*	Cummings, *73 Poems.*
	G. Greene, *A Sense of Reality.*	Ginsberg, *Reality Sandwiches.*
	MacBeth, *The Broken Places.*	Jeffers, *The Beginning and the End.*
		Merwin, *The Moving Target.*
		Pynchon, *V.*
		Salinger, *Raise High the Roof Beam, Carpenters.*
		Simpson, *At the End of the Open Road.*
		Wright, *The Branch Will Not Break.*
		Deaths of Frost, Roethke, W. C. Williams.
1964	Larkin, *The Whitsun Weddings.*	Ammons, *Expressions of Sea Level.*
	Powell, *The Valley of Bones.*	Bellow, *Herzog.*
	Thomas, *The Bread of Truth.*	Berryman, *77 Dream Songs.*
		Hemingway, *A Moveable Feast.*
		Frank O'Hara, *Lunch Poems.*
		O'Neill, *More Stately Mansions.*
		Roethke, *The Far Field.*
		R. Lowell, *For the Union Dead.*
		Shapiro, *The Bourgeois Poet.*

1965– Post-Modernist Period

	ENGLISH	AMERICAN
1965	C. Day Lewis, *The Room.*	Albee, *Tiny Alice.*
	Walcott, *The Castaway.*	Ammons, *Corsons Inlet; Tape for the Turn of the Year.*

	ENGLISH	AMERICAN
		Dickey, *Buckdancer's Choice.*
		Mailer, *American Dream.*
1965	Waugh, *Sword of Honor.*	O'Connor, *Everything That Rises Must Converge.*
		Death of T. S. Eliot.
1966	Fowles, *The Magus.*	Albee, *A Delicate Balance.*
	G. Greene, *The Comedians.*	Barth, *Giles Goat-Boy.*
	MacNeice, *One for the Grave.*	Malamud, *The Fixer.*
		Plath, *Ariel.*
	West, *The Birds Fall Down.*	Pynchon, *The Crying of Lot 49.*
		Death of Frank O'Hara.
1967	Isherwood, *A Meeting by the River.*	Ashbery, *Rivers and Mountains.*
	MacDiarmid, *A Lap of Honour.*	Bly, *The Light Around the Body.*
	A. Wilson, *No Laughing Matter.*	Merwin, *The Lice.*
		Moore, *Complete Poems.*
	Death of John Masefield.	Potok, *The Chosen.*
		Styron, *Confessions of Nat Turner.*
		Tate, *The Lost Pilot.*
		Wilder, *The Eighth Day.*
1968	Amis, *I Want It Now.*	Beagle, *The Last Unicorn.*
	Barker, *Collected Poems, 1930–1965.*	G. Brooks, *In the Mecca.*
	Burgess, *Enderby.*	Sackler, *The Great White Hope.*
	Durrell, *Tunc.*	Snyder, *The Back Country.*
	Murdoch, *The Nice and the Good.*	Wright, *Shall We Gather at the River.*
		Death of John Steinbeck.
1969	Fowles, *The French Lieutenant's Woman.*	Berryman, *The Dream Songs.*
	Lessing, *Children of Violence* (series completed).	Cheever, *Bullet Park.*
		Connell, *Mr. Bridge.*
	Heaney, *Door Into the Dark.*	Hollander, *Types of Shape.*
		Howard, *Untitled Subjects.*
		R. Lowell, *Notebook 1967–1968.*
		Pound, *Drafts and Fragments of Cantos CX to CXVII.*
		Roth, *Portnoy's Complaint.*

	ENGLISH	AMERICAN
		1970

<table>
<tr><td>1970</td><td>Hughes, Crow.
Braine, Stay with Me Till Morning.
Ian Hamilton, The Visit.
Death of E. M. Forster.</td><td>Ashbery, The Double Dream of Spring.
Hemingway, Islands in the Stream.
Bellow, Mr. Sammler's Planet.
Merwin, The Carrier of Ladders.
Synder, Regarding Wave.
Van Duyn, To See, To Take.
Welty, Losing Battles.
Deaths of Dos Passos and O'Hara.</td></tr>
<tr><td>1971</td><td>Forster, Maurice.
Compton-Burnett, The First and the Last.
G. Greene, A Sort of Life.
Hill, Mercian Hymns.</td><td>Warren, Meet Me in the Green Glen.
Hawkes, The Blood Oranges.
Jesus Christ, Superstar.
Updike, Rabbit Redux.
Wright, Collected Poems.</td></tr>
<tr><td>1972</td><td>Auden, Epistle to a Godson.
Drabble, The Needle's Eye.
Lessing, The Story of a Non-Marrying Man.</td><td>Ammons, Collected Poems: 1951–1971.
Berryman, Delusions, Etc.
Gardner, The Sunlight Dialogues.
Laura (Riding) Jackson, The Telling.
Schuyler, The Crystal Lithium.
Welty, The Optimist's Daughter.
Death of Pound.</td></tr>
<tr><td>1973</td><td>Enright, The Terrible Shears.
G. Greene, The Honorary Consul.
Murdoch, The Black Prince.
Thwaite, Inscriptions.
Death of Auden.</td><td>Ginsberg, The Fall of America.
Lowell, The Dolphin.
Pynchon, Gravity's Rainbow.
Wilder, Theophilus North.</td></tr>
<tr><td>1974</td><td>Auden, Thank You, Fog.
Durrell, Monsieur.
Fowles, The Ebony Tower.
Larkin, High Windows.</td><td>Ammons, Sphere.
Baldwin, If Beale Street Could Talk.
Heller, Something Happened.
Kinnell, The Avenue Bearing the Initial of Christ Into the New World.</td></tr>
</table>

	ENGLISH	AMERICAN
1975	Heaney, *North.*	Ashbery, *Self-Portrait in a Convex Mirror.*
	Jhabvala, *Heat and Dust.*	
	Lessing, *Memoirs of a Survivor.*	Bellow, *Humboldt's Gift.*
		Doctorow, *Ragtime.*
	Powell, *Hearing Secret Harmonies* (completes *A Dance to the Music of Time,* begun 1951).	Gaddis, *JR.*
1976	Amis, *The Alteration.*	Guest, *Ordinary People.*
	Hughes, *A Season of Songs.*	Haley, *Roots.*
	Waugh, *Diaries.*	Sexton, *45 Mercy Street.*
	White, *A Fringe of Leaves.*	Vonnegut, *Slapstick.*
1977	Fowles, *Daniel Martin.*	Cheever, *Falconer.*
	McCullough, *The Thorn Birds.*	Didion, *A Book of Common Prayer.*
	Tolkien, *The Silmarillion.*	R. Lowell, *Day by Day.*
	Drabble, *The Ice Age.*	Stegner, *The Spectator Bird.*
		Warren, *A Place to Come to.*
		Death of Lowell.
1978	Greene, *Human Factor.*	Harper, *Images of Kin.*
	White, *Book of Merlyn.*	Irving, *The World According to Garp.*
		Morrison, *Song of Solomon.*
		Updike, *The Coup.*
1979	Burgess, *Abba Abba.*	Heller, *Good as Gold.*
	Hill, *Tenebrae.*	Hill, *Hanta Yo.*
	Lewis, *Naples '44.*	O'Connor, *The Habit of Being: Letters.*
	Wain, *The Pardoner's Tale.*	

1980

	ENGLISH	AMERICAN
1980	Golding, *Rites of Passage.*	Fussel, *Abroad.*
	Hughes, *Moortown.*	Howard, *Misgivings.*
	Rhys, *Smile, Please.*	Merrill, *Scripts for the Pageant.*
		Schuyler, *The Morning of the Poem.*
		Toole, *A Confederacy of Dunces.*
1981	James, *Charles Charming's Challenges.*	Ammons, *A Coast of Trees.*
	Lessing, *The Sirian Experiments.*	Barthelme, *Sixty Stories.*
		Betts, *Heading West.*
	Murdoch, *Nuns and Soldiers.*	Plath, *Collected Poems.*
	Osborne, *A Better Class of Person.*	

	ENGLISH	AMERICAN
		Price, *The Source of Light.*
		Updike, *Rabbit Is Rich.*
1982	Coward, *Diaries.*	Barth, *Sabbatical.*
	Durrell, *Constance.*	Bellow, *The Dean's December.*
	Fowles, *Mantissa.*	Harrison, *Selected and New Poems.*
	Sillitoe, *Her Victory.*	Kinnell, *Selected Poems.*
		Nims, *Selected Poems; The Kiss: A Jambalaya.*
		Starbuck, *The Argot Merchant Disaster.*
		Wright, *This Journey.*
1983	Beckett, *Worstward Ho.*	Ammons, *Lake Effect Country.*
	Burgess, *The End of the World News.*	Clampitt, *The Kingfisher.*
	Coward, *Collected Stories.*	Creeley, *Collected Poems.*
		Garrett, *The Succession.*
		Goldbarth, *Original Light.*
		Knott, *Becos.*
		Mailer, *Ancient Evenings.*
		McMurtry, *The Desert Rose.*
		Merrill, *The Changing Light at Sandover.*
		Oliver, *American Primitive.*
1984	Connolly, *Selected Essays.*	Adams, *Superior Women.*
	Powell, *O, How the Wheel Becomes It!*	Burroughs, *The Place of Dead Roads.*
		Heller, *God Knows.*
		Howard, *Lining Up.*
		Kizer, *Yin.*
		Matthews, *A Happy Childhood.*
		Pynchon, *Slow Learner.*
		Wurlitzer, *Slow Fade.*

Appendices

Nobel Prizes for Literature

1901	René F. A. Sully-Prudhomme (1839–1907), French
1902	Theodor Mommsen (1817–1903), German
1903	Björnstjerne Björnson (1832–1910), Norwegian
1904	Frédéric Mistral (1830–1914), French
	José Echegaray (1832–1916), Spanish
1905	Henryk Sienkiewicz (1846–1916), Polish
1906	Giosuè Carducci (1835–1907), Italian
1907	Rudyard Kipling (1856–1936), British
1908	Rudolf C. Eucken (1846–1926), German
1909	Selma Lagerlöf (1858–1940), Swedish
1910	Paul J. L. Heyse (1830–1914), German
1911	Maurice Maeterlinck (1862–1949), Belgian
1912	Gerhart Hauptmann (1862–1946), German
1913	Rabindranath Tagore (1861–1941), Indian
1914	No award
1915	Romain Rolland (1866–1944), French
1916	Verner von Heidenstam (1859–1940), Swedish
1917	Karl A. Gjellerup (1857–1919), Danish
	Henrik Pontoppidan (1857–1943), Danish
1918	No award
1919	Carl F. G. Spitteler (1845–1924), Swiss
1920	Knut Hamsun (1859–1952), Norwegian
1921	Anatole France (1844–1924), French
1922	Jacinto Benavente y Martinez (1866–1954), Spanish
1923	William Butler Yeats (1865–1939), Irish
1924	Ladislaus S. Reymont (1868–1925), Polish
1925	George Bernard Shaw (1856–1950), British (b. Ireland)
1926	Grazia Deledda (1875–1936), Italian
1927	Henri Bergson (1859–1941), French
1928	Sigrid Undset (1882–1949), Norwegian (b. Denmark)
1929	Thomas Mann (1875–1955), German
1930	Sinclair Lewis (1885–1951), American
1931	Erik A. Karlfeldt (1864–1931), Swedish (awarded posthumously)
1932	John Galsworthy (1867–1933), English
1933	Ivan A. Bunin (1870–1953), French (b. Russia)
1934	Luigi Pirandello (1867–1936), Italian
1935	No award
1936	Eugene O'Neill (1888–1953), American
1937	Roger Martin du Gard (1881–1958), French
1938	Pearl S. Buck (1892–1973), American
1939	Frans E. Sillanpää (1888–1964), Finnish

1940   No award

1941   No award

1942   No award

1943   No award

1944   Johannes V. Jensen (1873–1950), Danish

1945   Gabriela Mistral (1889–1957), Chilean

1946   Hermann Hesse (1877–1962), Swiss (*b.* Germany)

1947   André Gide (1869–1951), French

1948   T. S. Eliot (1888–1965), British (*b.* United States)

1949   William Faulkner (1897–1962), American

1950   Bertrand A. W. Russell (1872–1970), British

1951   Pär F. Lagerkvist (1891–1974), Swedish

1952   François Mauriac (1885–1970), French

1953   Sir Winston Churchill (1874–1965), British

1954   Ernest Hemingway (1899–1961), American

1955   Halldór K. Laxness (1902–   ), Icelandic

1956   Juan Ramón Jiménez (1881–1958), Spanish

1957   Albert Camus (1913–1960), French

1958   Boris L. Pasternak (1890–1960), Russian (prize declined)

1959   Salvatore Quasimodo (1901–1968), Italian

1960   Saint-John Perse (1887–1975), French

1961   Ivo Andríc (1892–1975), Yugoslav

1962   John Steinbeck (1902–1968), American

1963   George Seferis (1900–1971), Greek

1964   Jean-Paul Sartre (1905–1980), French (award declined)

1965   Mikhail A. Sholokov (1905–1984), Russian

1966   Samuel J. Agnon (1888–1970), Israeli (*b.* Poland)
        Nelly Sachs (1891–1970), Swedish (*b.* Germany)

1967   Miguel Angel Asturias (1899–1974), Guatemalan

1968   Yasunari Kawabata (1899–1972), Japanese

1969   Samuel Beckett (1906–   ), Anglo-French (*b.* Ireland)

1970   Alexander I. Solzhenitsyn (1919–   ), Russian

1971   Pablo Neruda (1904–1973), Chilean

1972   Heinrich Böll (1917–   ), German

1973   Patrick White (1912–   ), Australian

1974   Eyvind Johnson (1900–1976), Swedish
        Harry Edmund Martinson (1904–1978), Swedish

1975   Eugenio Montale (1896–1981), Italian

1976   Saul Bellow (1915–   ), American

1977   Vicente Aleixandre (1898–1984), Spanish

1978   Isaac Bashevis Singer (1904–   ), American (*b.* Poland)

1979   Odysseus Elytis (1911–   ), Greek

1980   Czeslaw Milosz (1911–   ), Polish-American
1981   Elias Canetti (1905–   ), Bulgarian
1982   Gabriel García Marquez (1928–   ), Colombian
1983   William Golding (1911–   ), British
1984   Jaroslav Seifert (1901–   ), Czech
1985   Claude Simon (1913–   ), French

Pulitzer Prizes for Fiction

1917   No award

1918   *His Family,* by Ernest Poole

1919   *The Magnificent Ambersons,* by Booth Tarkington

1920   No award

1921   *The Age of Innocence,* by Edith Wharton

1922   *Alice Adams,* by Booth Tarkington

1923   *One of Ours,* by Willa Cather

1924   *The Able McLaughlins,* by Margaret Wilson

1925   *So Big,* by Edna Ferber

1926   *Arrowsmith,* by Sinclair Lewis (prize declined)

1927   *Early Autumn,* by Louis Bromfield

1928   *The Bridge of San Luis Rey,* by Thornton Wilder

1929   *Scarlet Sister Mary,* by Julia Peterkin

1930   *Laughing Boy,* by Oliver LaFarge

1931   *Years of Grace,* by Margaret Ayer Barnes

1932   *The Good Earth,* by Pearl S. Buck

1933   *The Store,* by T. S. Stribling

1934   *Lamb in His Bosom,* by Caroline Miller

1935   *Now in November,* by Josephine Winslow Johnson

1936   *Honey in the Horn,* by Harold L. Davis

1937   *Gone with the Wind,* by Margaret Mitchell

1938   *The Late George Apley,* by John Phillips Marquand

1939   *The Yearling,* by Marjorie Kinnan Rawlings

1940   *The Grapes of Wrath,* by John Steinbeck

1941   No award

1942   *In This Our Life,* by Ellen Glasgow

1943   *Dragon's Teeth,* by Upton Sinclair

1944   *Journey in the Dark,* by Martin Flavin

1945   *A Bell for Adano,* by John Hersey

1946   No award

1947   *All the King's Men,* by Robert Penn Warren

1948   *Tales of the South Pacific,* by James A. Michener

1949   *Guard of Honor,* by James Gould Cozzens

1950   *The Way West,* by A. B. Guthrie, Jr.

1951   *The Town,* by Conrad Richter

1952   *The Caine Mutiny,* by Herman Wouk

1953   *The Old Man and the Sea,* by Ernest Hemingway

1954   No award

1955   *A Fable,* by William Faulkner

1956   *Andersonville,* by MacKinlay Kantor

1957   No award

1958   *A Death in the Family,* by James Agee

1959   *The Travels of Jaimie McPheeters,* by Robert Lewis Taylor

1960   *Advise and Consent,* by Allen Drury

1961   *To Kill a Mockingbird,* by Harper Lee

1962   *The Edge of Sadness,* by Edwin O'Connor

1963   *The Reivers,* by William Faulkner

1964   No award

1965   *The Keepers of the House,* by Shirley Ann Grau

1966   *Collected Short Stories,* by Katherine Anne Porter

1967   *The Fixer,* by Bernard Malamud

1968   *The Confessions of Nat Turner,* by William Styron

1969   *House Made of Dawn,* by M. Scott Momaday

1970   *Collected Stories,* by Jean Stafford

1971   No award

1972   *Angle of Repose,* by Wallace Stegner

1973   *The Optimist's Daughter,* by Eudora Welty

1974   No award

1975   *The Killer Angels,* by Michael Shaara

1976   *Humboldt's Gift,* by Saul Bellow

1977   No award

1978   *Elbow Room,* by James Alan McPherson

1979   *The Stories,* by John Cheever

1980   *The Executioner's Song,* by Norman Mailer

1981   *A Confederacy of Dunces,* by John Kennedy Toole

1982   *Rabbit Is Rich,* by John Updike

1983   *The Color Purple,* by Alice Walker

1984   *Ironweed,* by William Kennedy

1985   *Foreign Affairs,* by Alison Lurie

Pulitzer Prizes for Poetry

Previous to the establishment of this prize in 1922, the following awards had been made from gifts provided by the Poetry Society:

1918   *Love Song,* by Sara Teasdale

1919   *Old Road to Paradise,* by Margaret Widdemer

1919   *Corn Huskers,* by Carl Sandburg

The Pulitzer Poetry Prizes follow:

1922   *Collected Poems,* by Edwin Arlington Robinson

1923   *The Ballad of the Harp-Weaver; A Few Figs From Thistles;* eight sonnets in *American Poetry, 1922, A Miscellany;* by Edna St. Vincent Millay

1924   *New Hampshire: A Poem with Notes and Grace Notes,* by Robert Frost

1925   *The Man Who Died Twice,* by Edwin Arlington Robinson

1926   *What's O'Clock,* by Amy Lowell

1927   *Fiddler's Farewell,* by Leonora Speyer

1928   *Tristram,* by Edwin Arlington Robinson

1929   *John Brown's Body,* by Stephen Vincent Benét

1930   *Selected Poems,* by Conrad Aiken

1931   *Collected Poems,* by Robert Frost

1932   *The Flowering Stone,* by George Dillon

1933   *Conquistador,* by Archibald MacLeish

1934   *Collected Verse,* by Robert Hillyer

1935   *Bright Ambush,* by Audrey Wurdemann

1936   *Strange Holiness,* by Robert P. Tristram Coffin

1937   *A Further Range,* by Robert Frost

1938   *Cold Morning Sky,* by Marya Zaturenska

1939   *Selected Poems,* by John Gould Fletcher

1940   *Collected Poems,* by Mark Van Doren

1941   *Sunderland Capture,* by Leonard Bacon

1942   *The Dust Which is God,* by William Rose Benét

1943   *A Witness Tree,* by Robert Frost

1944   *Western Star,* by Stephen Vincent Benét

1945   *V-Letter and Other Poems,* by Karl Shapiro

1946   No award

1947   *Lord Weary's Castle,* by Robert Lowell

1948   *The Age of Anxiety,* by W. H. Auden

1949   *Terror and Decorum,* by Peter Viereck

1950   *Annie Allen,* by Gwendolyn Brooks

1951   *Complete Poems,* by Carl Sandburg

1952   *Collected Poems,* by Marianne Moore

1953   *Collected Poems 1917–1952,* by Archibald MacLeish

1954   *The Waking,* by Theodore Roethke

1955   *Collected Poems,* by Wallace Stevens

1956   *Poems—North & South,* by Elizabeth Bishop

1957   *Things of This World,* by Richard Wilbur

1958   *Promises: Poems 1954–1956,* by Robert Penn Warren

1959   *Selected Poems 1928–1958,* by Stanley Kunitz

1960   *Heart's Needle,* by W. D. Snodgrass

1961   *Times Three: Selected Verse from Three Decades,* by Phyllis McGinley

1962   *Poems,* by Alan Dugan

1963   *Pictures from Brueghel,* by William Carlos Williams

1964   *At the End of the Open Road,* by Louis Simpson

1965   *77 Dream Songs,* by John Berryman

1966   *Selected Poems,* by Richard Eberhart

1967   *Live or Die,* by Anne Sexton

1968   *The Hard Hours,* by Anthony Hecht

1969   *Of Being Numerous,* by George Oppen

1970   *Untitled Subjects,* by Richard Howard

1971   *The Carrier of Ladders,* by W. S. Merwin

1972   *Collected Poems,* by James Wright

1973   *Up Country,* by Maxine Winokur Kumin

1974   *The Dolphin,* by Robert Lowell

1975   *Turtle Island,* by Gary Snyder

1976   *Self-Portrait in a Convex Mirror,* by John Ashbery

1977   *Divine Comedies: Poems,* by James Merrill

1978   *The Collected Poems,* by Howard Nemerov

1979   *Now and Then: Poems 1976–1978,* by Robert Penn Warren

1980   *Selected Poems,* by Donald Justice

1981   *The Morning of the Poem,* by James Schuyler

1982   *Collected Poems,* by Sylvia Plath

1983   *Selected Poems,* by Galway Kinnell

1984   *American Primitive,* by Mary Oliver

1985   *Yin,* by Carolyn Kizer

Pulitzer Prizes for Drama

1917   No award

1918   *Why Marry?* by Jesse Lynch Williams

1919   No award

1920   *Beyond the Horizon,* by Eugene O'Neill

1921   *Miss Lulu Bett,* by Zona Gale

1922   *Anna Christie,* by Eugene O'Neill

1923   *Icebound,* by Owen Davis

1924   *Hell-Bent fer Heaven,* by Hatcher Hughes

1925   *They Knew What They Wanted,* by Sidney Howard

1926   *Craig's Wife,* by George Kelly

1927   *In Abraham's Bosom,* by Paul Green

1928   *Strange Interlude,* by Eugene O'Neill

1929   *Street Scene,* by Elmer L. Rice

1930   *The Green Pastures,* by Marc Connelly

1931   *Alison's House,* by Susan Glaspell

1932   *Of Thee I Sing,* by George S. Kaufman, Morrie Ryskind, and Ira Gershwin (with music by George Gershwin)

1933   *Both Your Houses,* by Maxwell Anderson

1934   *Men in White,* by Sidney Kingsley

1935   *The Old Maid,* by Zoë Akins

1936   *Idiot's Delight,* by Robert E. Sherwood

1937   *You Can't Take It with You,* by Moss Hart and George S. Kaufman

1938   *Our Town,* by Thornton Wilder

1939   *Abe Lincoln in Illinois,* by Robert E. Sherwood

1940   *The Time of Your Life,* by William Saroyan (declined)

1941   *There Shall Be No Night,* by Robert E. Sherwood

1942   No award

1943   *The Skin of Our Teeth,* by Thornton Wilder

1944   No award

1945   *Harvey,* by Mary Chase

1946   *State of the Union,* by Russel Crouse and Howard Lindsay

1947   No award

1948   *A Streetcar Named Desire,* by Tennessee Williams

1949   *Death of a Salesman,* by Arthur Miller

1950   *South Pacific,* by Richard Rodgers, Oscar Hammerstein II, and Joshua Logan

1951   No award

1952   *The Shrike,* by Joseph Kramm

1953   *Picnic,* by William Inge

1954   *The Teahouse of the August Moon,* by John Patrick

1955   *Cat on a Hot Tin Roof,* by Tennessee Williams

1956   *The Diary of Anne Frank,* by Albert Hackett and Frances Goodrich

1957   *Long Day's Journey into Night,* by Eugene O'Neill

1958   *Look Homeward, Angel,* by Ketti Frings

1959   *J. B.,* by Archibald MacLeish

1960   *Fiorello!,* book by Jerome Weidman and George Abbott, music by Jerry Bock, and lyrics by Sheldon Harnick

1961   *All the Way Home,* by Tad Mosel

1962   *How to Succeed in Business Without Really Trying,* by Frank Loesser and Abe Burrows

1963   No award

1964   No award

1965   *The Subject Was Roses,* by Frank D. Gilroy

1966   No award

1967   *A Delicate Balance,* by Edward Albee

1968   No award

1969   *The Great White Hope,* by Howard Sackler

1970   *No Place To Be Somebody,* by Charles Gordone

1971   *The Effect of Gamma Rays on Man-in-the-Moon Marigolds,* by Paul Zindel

1972   No Award

1973   *The Championship Season,* by Jason Miller

1974   No Award

1975   *Seascape,* by Edward Albee

1976   *A Chorus Line,* by James Kirkwood and Nicholas Dante

1977   *The Shadow Box,* by Michael Cristofer

1978   *The Gin Game,* by Donald L. Coburn

1979   *Buried Child,* by Sam Shepard

1980   *Talley's Folly,* by Lanford Wilson

1981   *Crimes of the Heart,* by Beth Henley

1982   *A Soldier's Play,* by Charles Fuller

1983   *'Night, Mother,* by Marsha Norman

1984   *Glengarry Glen Ross,* by David Mamet

1985   *Sunday in the Park with George,* by Stephen Sondheim and James Lapine

Index of Proper Names

Manning, Robert, of Brunne Chronicle.

Mansfield, Katherine Modernist Period (English); Short Story.

Mantuan (or Mantuanus), Johannes Baptista Spaguolo Eclogue.

Map, Walter Anglo-Norman Period; Goliardic Verses.

Marchetti, Giovanni *Canzone.*

Marckwardt, Albert A. American Language.

Marcus Aurelius Antoninus Stoicism.

Marguerite of Valois *Novella.*

Marie de France Lay.

Marino, Giambattista Marinism.

Maritain, Jacques Existentialism; Scholasticism.

Marivaux, Pierre Carlet de Chamblain de Novel.

Marks, Jeanette Pastoral Drama.

Marlborough, John Churchill, 1st Duke of Kit-Cat Club.

Marlowe, Christopher Baconian Theory; Blank Verse; Chronicle Play; Elizabethan Age; Iamb; Metalepsis; School of Night; Senecan Tragedy; University Wits.

Marot, Jean *Chant Royal.*

Marquand, J. P. Brahmins; Epistolary Novel; Flashback; Horatian Satire; Novel of Manners; Period of Criticism and Conformity (American); Realism; Satire.

Marsh, E. H. Georgian.

Marsh, Ngaio Detective Story.

Marston, John Dumb Show; Revenge Tragedy; War of the Theaters.

Martial (Marcus Valerius Martialis) Decadence; Epigram; Satire.

Martin of Tours, Bishop Christianity, Established in England.

"Martin Marprelate" Marprelate Controversy.

Martyn, Edward Celtic Renaissance.

Martz, Louis Meditative Poetry.

Marvell, Andrew Balance; Caesura; *Carpe Diem;* Commonwealth Interregnum; Dissociation of Sensibility; Horatian Ode; Occasional Verse; Rhyme.

Marx Brothers Farce-Comedy.

Marx, Karl Dialectic; Hegelianism; Marxism; Naturalism; Realistic Period (American); Realistic Period (English).

Mary I Tudor.

Masefield, John Domestic Tragedy; Drama; Edwardian Age; Georgian; Modernist Period (English); One-Act Play; Poet Laureate; Rhyme Royal.

Mason, William Biography.

Massinger, Philip Comedy; Jacobean Age.

Masters, Edgar Lee *Ubi Sunt* Formula.

Masuccio Salernitano Novel.

Materer, Timothy Vorticism.

Mather, Cotton Awakening, Great; Essay; Puritanism.

Mather, Increase Awakening, Great.

Mathews, M. M. American Language.

Matthews, Brander Closet Drama; Drama; Historical Novel.

Matthews, J. H. Surrealism.

Matthews, William Arthurian Legend.

Matthiessen, F. O. Documentary Novel; Translation.

Maugham, (William) Somerset Apprenticeship Novel; Comedy of Manners; Cynicism; Drama; Flashback; Georgian Age; Implied Author; Modernist Period (English); *Roman à Clef;* Short Story.

Maupassant, Guy de *Conte;* Realistic Period (English); Short Story.

Mayhew, Henry Burletta.

Maynadier, G. H. Arthurian Legend.

Mazzara, Jerome Lyric; Post-Modern.

McCarthy, Justin H. *Ubi Sunt* Formula.

McDavid, Raven I. American Language.

McDiarmid, Hugh (pseudonym of Christopher Murray Grieve) Scottish Literature.

McGinley, Phyllis Light Verse.

McKay, Claude Afro-American Literature; Harlem Renaissance.

McKeon, Richard Chicago Critics; Criticism.

McKerrow, R. B. Bibliography.

McKnight, G. H. English Language.

McLuhan, Marshall Stereotype.

McMurtry, Larry Frontier Literature.

McNeill, John Thomas Calvinism.

McPhee, John Essay; New Journalism; Nonfiction Novel.

Medwall, Henry Interlude.

Mehl, Dieter Dumb Show.

dus) Decadence; Panegyric.
Plomer, H. R. Printing.
Plutarch Anecdote; Criticism; Hagiography; Translation.
Poe, Edgar Allan Acrostic; Aestheticism; Anastrophe; Annuals; Apocalyptic; Arabesque; Assonance; Catalexis; Coined Words; Criticism; Dandyism; Description; Effect; Essay; Exordium; Federalist Age; Freudianism; Gothic Novel; Grotesque; Incremental Repetition; Jingle; Juvenilia; Knickerbocker Group; Marginalia; Medievalism; Novel; Plagiarism; *Poète Maudit;* Pure Poetry; Quaternion; Ratiocination; Refrain; Repetend; Review; Revolutionary and Early National Period (American); Romantic Period (American); Romanticism; Scazon; Short Story; Sigmatism; Spondee; Sublime; Symbolism; Synaesthesia; Translation; *Ultima Thule;* Unity; Verisimilitude.
Politian (Angelo Poliziano, pseudonym of Agnolo Ambrogini) Pastoral Drama.
Pollard, A. W. Bad Quartos; Bible, English Translations of; Medieval Drama.
Ponsonby, Arthur Diary.
Pope, Alexander Adversarius; Age of Johnson; Alexandrine; Anticlimax; Antithesis; Augustan; Bathos; Blues; Chiasmus; Classicism; Closed Couplet; Convention; Criticism; Criticism, Types of; Decorum; Didactic Poetry; Distich; End-stopped Lines; Enlightenment; Epigram;

Epistle; Epitaph; Essay; Great Chain of Being; Grub Street; Hartford Wits; Heroic Couplet; Horatian Satire; Humanism; Irony; Juvenilia; Light Verse; Machinery; Mock Epic; Nature; Numbers; Onomatopoeia; Prologue; Redundant; Rhetorical Question; Rococo; Satire; Scriblerus Club; Shakespeare, Early Editions of; Style; Sublime; Syllepsis; Tradition; Translation; Verse Paragraph; Wit and Humor.
Pope, John C. Old English Versification.
Pops, Martin Post-Modern.
Poulet, Georges Geneva School; Phenomenology.
Pound, Ezra Alliteration; Anagram; Assonance; Basic English; Blank Verse; Cadence; Canto; Catalog; Classicism; Collaboration; Collage; Complaint; Conceit; Confession; Criticism; Envoy; Epic; Expatriate; Eye Rhyme; Free Verse; Gallicism; Haiku; Imagists; Invective; Letters; Little Magazine; Logopoeia; Melopoeia; Metaphor; Metaphysical Conceit; Modern; Mysticism; Myth; Naturalistic and Symbolistic Period (American); Neoclassicism; New Criticism; Noh Plays; Old English Versification; Palimpsest; Parnassians; Pelagianism; Phanopoeia; Planh; Realistic Period (American); *Redondilla;* Rhyme; Sapphic; Tmesis; Translation; Troubadour; Unanimism; Virgule; Vorticism; Wardour-Street English.

Pound, Louise Incremental Repetition.
Powell, Anthony Diminishing Age; Post-Modernist Period (English).
Powell, Humphrey Testament.
Praed, Winthrop Mackworth Georgian; *Vers de Société.*
Pratt, W. C. Imagists.
Prescott, William Hickling Saturday Club.
Prévost D'Exiles, Antoine François (Abbe Prévost) Novel.
Pritchard, Hannah Mary Women as Actors.
Procopius Anecdote.
Pronko, L. C. Noh Plays.
Propp, Vladimir Formalism, Russian.
Proust, Marcel Jewish-American Literature; Metafiction; Modern; Naturalistic and Symbolistic Period (American); Stream-of-Consciousness Novel.
Pryor, Richard Farce-Comedy.
Ptolemy Philadelphus Septuagint.
Pulci, Luigi Romantic Epic.
Pulitzer, Joseph Pulitzer Prizes.
Purcell, Henry Opera.
Purvey, John Bible, English Translations of.
Pusey, Edward Bouverie Erastianism; Oxford Movement; Puseyism.
Putnam, G. H. Manuscript, Medieval.
Putnam, Samuel Translation.
Puttenham, George (or Richard) Decorum; Metalepsis; Rhetoric.
Putz, Manfred Post-Modern.
Pye, Henry James Poet Laureate.